"This handbook is an essential resource for researchers. Its broadly accessible, insightful essays cover a range of topics from different disciplines and about different nations, and it demonstrates the importance of conspiracy theories in contemporary politics and society."

*Mark Fenster, Levin College of Law at University of Florida, USA*

"This wide-ranging collection brings together many different strands of scholarship on conspiracy theories. Sociologists, political theorists, historians, psychologists, and philosophers provide new and compelling ways to examine who believes in these theories, why they believe them, and what we can do about them. An essential exploration of one of the defining features of our age."

*Kathryn Olmsted, University of California, USA*

# ROUTLEDGE HANDBOOK OF CONSPIRACY THEORIES

Taking a global and interdisciplinary approach, the *Routledge Handbook of Conspiracy Theories* provides a comprehensive overview of conspiracy theories as an important social, cultural and political phenomenon in contemporary life.

This handbook provides the most complete analysis of the phenomenon to date. It analyses conspiracy theories from a variety of perspectives, using both qualitative and quantitative methods. It maps out the key debates, and includes chapters on the historical origins of conspiracy theories, as well as their political significance in a broad range of countries and regions. Other chapters consider the psychology and the sociology of conspiracy beliefs, in addition to their changing cultural forms, functions and modes of transmission. This handbook examines where conspiracy theories come from, who believes in them and what their consequences are.

This book presents an important resource for students and scholars from a range of disciplines interested in the societal and political impact of conspiracy theories, including Area Studies, Anthropology, History, Media and Cultural Studies, Political Science, Psychology and Sociology.

**Michael Butter** is professor of American Studies at the University of Tübingen, Germany. He is the author of *Plots, Designs, and Schemes: American Conspiracy Theories from the Puritans to the Present* (2014) and *The Nature of Conspiracy Theories* (2020).

**Peter Knight** is professor of American Studies at the University of Manchester, UK. He is the author of *Conspiracy Culture* (2000), *The Kennedy Assassination* (2007) and *Reading the Market* (2016) and editor of *Conspiracy Nation* (2002) and *Conspiracy Theories in American History: An Encyclopedia* (2004).

Together they directed the COST Action COMPACT [Comparative Analysis of Conspiracy Theories].

# Conspiracy Theories
**Series Editors:**
**Michael Butter**
*University of Tübingen*
**and**
**Peter Knight**
*University of Manchester*

Conspiracy theories have a long history and exist in all modern societies. However, their visibility and significance are increasing today. Conspiracy theories can no longer be simply dismissed as the product of a pathological mind-set located on the political margins.

This series provides a nuanced and scholarly approach to this most contentious of subjects. It draws on a range of disciplinary perspectives, including political science, sociology, history, media and cultural studies, area studies and behavioural sciences. Issues covered include the psychology of conspiracy theories, changes in conspiratorial thinking over time, the role of the Internet, regional and political variations, and the social and political impact of conspiracy theories.

The series will include edited collections, single-authored monographs and short-form books.

**Impossible Knowledge**
Conspiracy Theories, Power, and Truth
*Todor Hristov Dechev*

**The Stigmatization of Conspiracy Theory since the 1950s**
"A Plot to Make us Look Foolish"
*Katharina Thalmann*

**Conspiracy Theories in Turkey**
Conspiracy Nation
*Doğan Gürpınar*

**Routledge Handbook of Conspiracy Theories**
*Edited by Michael Butter and Peter Knight*

# ROUTLEDGE HANDBOOK OF CONSPIRACY THEORIES

*Edited by Michael Butter and Peter Knight*

Routledge
Taylor & Francis Group
LONDON AND NEW YORK

First published 2020 by Routledge

2 Park Square, Milton Park, Abingdon, Oxon OX14 4RN
605 Third Avenue, New York, NY 10017

*Routledge is an imprint of the Taylor & Francis Group, an informa business*

First issued in paperback 2021

Copyright © 2020 selection and editorial matter, Michael Butter and Peter Knight; individual chapters, the contributors

The right of Michael Butter and Peter Knight to be identified as the authors of the editorial matter, and of the authors for their individual chapters, has been asserted in accordance with sections 77 and 78 of the Copyright, Designs and Patents Act 1988.

All rights reserved. No part of this book may be reprinted or reproduced or utilised in any form or by any electronic, mechanical, or other means, now known or hereafter invented, including photocopying and recording, or in any information storage or retrieval system, without permission in writing from the publishers.

Notice:
Product or corporate names may be trademarks or registered trademarks, and are used only for identification and explanation without intent to infringe.

Publisher's Note

The publisher has gone to great lengths to ensure the quality of this reprint but points out that some imperfections in the original copies may be apparent.

*British Library Cataloguing-in-Publication Data*
A catalogue record for this book is available from the British Library

*Library of Congress Cataloging-in-Publication Data*
Names: Butter, Michael, editor.
Title: Routledge handbook of conspiracy theories / edited by Michael Butter and Peter Knight.
Description: Abingdon, Oxon ; New York, NY : Routledge, 2020. | Includes bibliographical references and index. |
Identifiers: LCCN 2019049150 | ISBN 9780815361749 (hbk) | ISBN 9781138321229 (pbk) | ISBN 9780429452734 (ebk)
Subjects: LCSH: Conspiracy theories. | Conspiracy.
Classification: LCC HV6275 .R685 2020 | DDC 001.9–dc23
LC record available at https://lccn.loc.gov/2019049150

ISBN: 978-0-8153-6174-9 (hbk)
ISBN: 978-1-03-217398-6 (pbk)
DOI: 10.4324/9780429452734

Typeset in Bembo
by Wearset, Boldon, Tyne and Wear

Printed in the United Kingdom
by Henry Ling Limited

# CONTENTS

*List of contributors* xii
*Acknowledgements* xx

    General introduction 1

## SECTION 1
## Definitions and approaches 9

    Introduction 11
    *Todor Hristov, Andrew McKenzie-McHarg and Alejandro Romero-Reche*

1 Conceptual history and conspiracy theory 16
   *Andrew McKenzie-McHarg*

2 Conspiracy theory in historical, cultural and literary studies 28
   *Michael Butter and Peter Knight*

3 Semiotic approaches to conspiracy theories 43
   *Massimo Leone, Mari-Liis Madisson and Andreas Ventsel*

4 Philosophy and conspiracy theories 56
   *Juha Räikkä and Juho Ritola*

5 Psychoanalysis, critical theory and conspiracy theory 67
   *Nebojša Blanuša and Todor Hristov*

6 Conspiracy theory as occult cosmology in anthropology 81
   *Annika Rabo*

| | |
|---|---|
| 7 Sociology, social theory and conspiracy theory<br>*Türkay Salim Nefes and Alejandro Romero-Reche* | 94 |
| 8 Conspiracy theories in political science and political theory<br>*Julien Giry and Pranvera Tika* | 108 |
| 9 Social psychology of conspiracy theories<br>*Olivier Klein and Kenzo Nera* | 121 |
| 10 Social network analysis, social big data and conspiracy theories<br>*Estrella Gualda Caballero* | 135 |

## SECTION 2
## Psychological factors — **149**

| | |
|---|---|
| Introduction<br>*Jan-Willem van Prooijen, Karen M. Douglas, Aleksandra Cichocka and Michał Bilewicz* | 151 |
| 1 Personality traits, cognitive styles and worldviews associated with beliefs in conspiracy theories<br>*Anthony Lantian, Mike Wood and Biljana Gjoneska* | 155 |
| 2 Social-cognitive processes underlying belief in conspiracy theories<br>*Jan-Willem van Prooijen, Olivier Klein and Jasna Milošević Đorđević* | 168 |
| 3 Motivations, emotions and belief in conspiracy theories<br>*Karen M. Douglas, Aleksandra Cichocka and Robbie M. Sutton* | 181 |
| 4 Conspiracy beliefs as psycho-political reactions to perceived power<br>*Roland Imhoff and Pia Lamberty* | 192 |
| 5 How conspiracy theories spread<br>*Adrian Bangerter, Pascal Wagner-Egger and Sylvain Delouvée* | 206 |
| 6 Conspiracy theories and intergroup relations<br>*Mikey Biddlestone, Aleksandra Cichocka, Iris Žeželj and Michał Bilewicz* | 219 |
| 7 Consequences of conspiracy theories<br>*Daniel Jolley, Silvia Mari and Karen M. Douglas* | 231 |
| 8 Countering conspiracy theories and misinformation<br>*Péter Krekó* | 242 |

## SECTION 3
## Society and politics — 257

Introduction — 259
*Eiríkur Bergmann, Asbjørn Dyrendal, Jaron Harambam and Hulda Thórisdóttir*

1 Who are the conspiracy theorists? Demographics and conspiracy theories — 263
*Steven M. Smallpage, Hugo Drochon, Joseph E. Uscinski and Casey Klofstad*

2 Conspiracy theory entrepreneurs, movements and individuals — 278
*Jaron Harambam*

3 Conspiracy theories and gender and sexuality — 292
*Annika Thiem*

4 Conspiracy theories, political ideology and political behaviour — 304
*Hulda Thórisdóttir, Silvia Mari and André Krouwel*

5 Functions and uses of conspiracy theories in authoritarian regimes — 317
*Julien Giry and Doğan Gürpınar*

6 Conspiracy theory and populism — 330
*Eiríkur Bergmann and Michael Butter*

7 Radicalisation and conspiracy theories — 344
*Benjamin Lee*

8 Antisemitism and conspiracism — 357
*Kjetil Braut Simonsen*

9 Conspiracy theory and religion — 371
*Asbjørn Dyrendal*

## SECTION 4
## Media and transmission — 385

Introduction — 387
*Stef Aupers, Dana Crăciun and Andreas Önnerfors*

1 Rumours, urban legends and the verbal transmission of conspiracy theories — 391
*Anastasiya Astapova*

2 Conspiracy theorising and the history of media in the eighteenth century — 401
*Andrew McKenzie-McHarg and Claus Oberhauser*

3  Genres of conspiracy in nineteenth-century British writing  415
   Ben Carver

4  Conspiracy in American narrative  427
   Timothy Melley

5  Conspiracy theories and visual culture  441
   Ute Caumanns and Andreas Önnerfors

6  Conspiracy theories in films and television shows  457
   Michael Butter

7  Decoding mass media/encoding conspiracy theory  469
   Stef Aupers

8  The Internet and the spread of conspiracy content  483
   Simona Stano

9  Networked disinformation and the lifecycle of online conspiracy theories  497
   Hugo Leal

10 Conspiracy theories and fake news  512
   Kiril Avramov, Vasily Gatov and Ilya Yablokov

## SECTION 5
## Histories and regions  525

Introduction  527
Ilya Yablokov, Pascal Girard, Nebojša Blanuša and Annika Rabo

1  Conspiracy theories in the Roman Empire  531
   Victoria Emma Pagán

2  Conspiracy theories in the Middle Ages and the early modern period  542
   Cornel Zwierlein

3  Freemasons, Illuminati and Jews: Conspiracy theories and the French Revolution  555
   Claus Oberhauser

4  Conspiracy theories in Europe during the twentieth century  569
   Pascal Girard

## Contents

5. Conspiracy theories in Putin's Russia: The case of the 'New World Order'    582
   *Ilya Yablokov*

6. Conspiracy theories in and about the Balkans    596
   *Nebojša Blanuša*

7. Conspiracy theories in Turkey    610
   *Doğan Gürpınar and Türkay Salim Nefes*

8. Conspiracy theories in the Middle East    624
   *Matthew Gray*

9. Conspiracy theories in Southeast Asia    638
   *Viren Swami, Hanoor Syahirah Zahari and David Barron*

10. Conspiracy theories in American history    648
    *Michael Butter*

11. Populism and conspiracy theory in Latin America: A case study of Venezuela    660
    *Rosanne Hooper*

*Index*    674

# CONTRIBUTORS

**Anastasiya Astapova** is a research fellow in Folklore in the University of Tartu. She defended two PhDs and published over 30 peer-reviewed works on migration, nationalism and humour. She is co-editor of the book *Conspiracy Theories in Eastern Europe: Trends and Tropes* (Routledge, forthcoming).

**Stef Aupers** is a cultural sociologist and works as professor of Media Culture at the Institute for Media Studies, department of Communication Sciences, Leuven University. He has published widely on media culture, online game culture and conspiracy culture in international, peer-reviewed journals.

**Kiril Avramov** is a post-doctoral research fellow of the Intelligence Studies Project (I.S.P.) at the University of Texas, Austin. Dr Avramov's main research interests are information warfare, psychological operations and mass cognitive hacking, as well as the 'weaponisation of information' and its respective application and effects on decision-making processes.

**Adrian Bangerter** is professor of Work Psychology at the University of Neuchâtel. His areas of research are social interactions at work, especially personnel selection; multimodal coordination in joint actions; and social transmission of beliefs, including the role of media in public understanding of science and the spread of conspiracy theories.

**David Barron** is a reader and deputy director at the Centre for Psychological Medicine at Perdana University. His work is primarily focused on the measurement and outcomes of schizotypy, particularly in different cultural settings.

**Eiríkur Bergmann** is professor of Politics at Bifrost University, Iceland. He writes mainly on nationalism, populism, European integration, Icelandic politics and participatory democracy. He is also a novelist.

**Mikey Biddlestone** is an associate lecturer and PhD student in Political Psychology at the University of Kent. He investigates the social identity motivations and group processes involved in conspiracy beliefs. Notable topics of interest include motivations, values and intergroup stereotypes. He has contributed to the 2019 interim report on the 2011 riots in South London.

**Michał Bilewicz** is a professor at the Faculty of Psychology, University of Warsaw and a director of the Center for Research on Prejudice at the same institution. He is interested in social psychology of intergroup relations, dehumanisation and infrahumanisation processes, contact hypothesis and prejudice reduction, as well as linguistic aspects of discrimination.

**Nebojša Blanuša** is associate professor of Political Psychology at the University of Zagreb. His main research interests are the symptoms of the political unconscious and cultural trauma. He wrote the book *Conspiracy Theories and Croatian Political Reality 1980–2007* (Zagreb: Plejada, 2011; in Croatian) and co-edited the volume *EU, Europe Unfinished: Mediating Europe and the Balkans in a Time of Crisis* (Rowman & Littlefield, 2016).

**Michael Butter** is professor of American Studies at the University of Tübingen. He is the author of *Plots Designs, and Schemes: American Conspiracy Theories from the Puritans to the Present* (de Gruyter, 2014) and *The Nature of Conspiracy Theories* (Polity, 2020). Together with Peter Knight, he directed the C.O.S.T. Action C.O.M.P.A.C.T. [Comparative Analysis of Conspiracy Theories].

**Ben Carver** teaches Anglophone Literature and Culture at Aarhus University, Denmark. He is the author of *Alternate Histories and Nineteenth-Century Literature* (Palgrave, 2017) and is currently working on a project on the relation of detail to suspicion. Other interests include invasion fiction, the circulation of money in novels and the literature imagination of progress.

**Ute Caumanns** is a lecturer in the Department of History and Cultures in Eastern Europe at the Heinrich-Heine-Universität Düsseldorf, Germany. She teaches modern and contemporary Central-East European history. Her current research interests lie in visual and oral representations of conspiracy theories, especially in media aspects of Stalinist show trials.

**Aleksandra Cichocka** is a senior lecturer in Political Psychology at the University of Kent. Her research interests include intergroup relations, political ideologies and political engagement. She examines the intergroup dimensions of conspiracy theories and the ways self- and group-evaluations are associated with conspiracy beliefs. She co-edited *The Psychology of Conspiracy* (Routledge, 2015).

**Dana Crăciun** is a senior lecturer in the Department of Modern Languages and Literatures at the University of Timișoara. She teaches courses in Literary Studies, Creative Writing and Translation Studies. Her research interests include contemporary literature and theory, conspiracy narratives, and the theory and practice of translation.

**Sylvain Delouvée** is associate professor (H.D.R.) in Social Psychology in Rennes 2 University. His research topics are focused on collective beliefs and social thought. He is particularly interested in behaviours and conduct known as irrational through conspiracy theories and rumours, collective memory and social representations, collective fears and social identity.

**Karen M. Douglas** is professor of Social Psychology at the University of Kent. Her research focuses on why people believe in conspiracy theories, and what the consequences of these beliefs are for individuals, groups and society.

**Hugo Drochon** is assistant professor in Political Theory at the University of Nottingham and author of *Nietzsche's Great Politics* (Princeton U.P., 2016). He has compiled three European and U.S. conspiracy theory surveys. Preliminary findings have appeared in Joseph Uscinski's *Conspiracy Theories and the People Who Believe Them* (O.U.P., 2019).

**Asbjørn Dyrendal** is a professor at the Department of Philosophy and Religious Studies, Norwegian University of Science and Technology. His research centres on contemporary religion, mostly new religious movements, and conspiracy culture. Among his recent books are *The Invention of Satanism* (Brill, 2016), *Handbook of Conspiracy Theory and Contemporary Religion* (Brill, 2018) and *Hva er konspirasjonsteorier* (Universitetsforlaget, 2019).

**Vasily Gatov** is a Russian media researcher and author with more than 28 years of professional experience in domestic and international media such as on the Chernobyl nuclear disaster, the 1991 failed coup'd'état, Boris Yeltsin's presidency and the first Chechen war (1994–1997). He later served as an executive and strategist for several Russian media companies.

**Pascal Girard** is Associate Research Fellow in Political History at the CRULH, University of Lorraine, Nancy-Metz (France). The subject of his PhD was conspiracies in France and Italy from 1944 to 1958. He is particularly interested in conspiracy theories and political violence and the dynamics at work between these two phenomena.

**Julien Giry** is a French political scientist and sociologist, and currently a research fellow at the University of Rennes. Since 2009, he has worked on conspiracy theories and far-right activism. He has published more than 20 articles and regularly appears in the media.

**Biljana Gjoneska** is a research associate at the Macedonian Academy of Sciences and Arts. She is interested in the neurophysiological and behavioral correlates of ideological division and group distinction, which may be at the core of conspiratorial beliefs. She has published in *Computational Intelligence and Neuroscience* (2009) and *Lancet* (2012).

**Matthew Gray** is a professor in the School of International Liberal Studies, Waseda University, Tokyo, Japan. He is the author of *Conspiracy Theories in the Middle East: Sources and Politics* (Routledge, 2010) and various other works on Middle Eastern politics.

**Estrella Gualda Caballero** is professor of Sociology at the Universidad de Huelva, Spain, where she is the Director of the Social Studies and Social Intervention Research Centre. She is President of the Andalusian Sociological Association and is currently working on social networks and social big data in connection to conspiracy theories.

**Doğan Gürpınar** is an associate professor at İ.T.Ü. He has published three books in English: *Ottoman Imperial Diplomacy* (I.B. Tauris, 2013), *Ottoman/Turkish Visions of the Nation: 1860–1950* (Palgrave Macmillan, 2013) and *Conspiracy Nation: Conspiracy Theories in Turkey* (Routledge, 2019). He has published articles on Turkish intellectual history, Turkish nationalism and historiography.

**Jaron Harambam** is an interdisciplinary qualitative sociologist working on conspiracy theories in today's technologically mediated information ecosystem. His PhD is from Erasmus University, Rotterdam. He held a postdoctoral research position (University of Amsterdam), and is now a

Marie Sklodowska-Curie Individual Fellowship holder (Leuven University). His monograph on conspiracy culture is forthcoming with Routledge.

**Todor Hristov** teaches Literary Theory, Critical Theory and Biopolitics at the University of Sofia. His research on late capitalist governmentality and pragmatics of conspiracy theories is published in several journals and a short book, *Impossible Knowledge: Conspiracy Theories, Power and Truth* (Routledge, 2019).

**Roland Imhoff** received his PhD from the University of Bonn, Germany in 2010. He is currently Professor for Social and Legal Psychology at the Johannes Gutenberg University, Mainz, Germany. In his research, he bridges basic works on social cognition, issues of political psychology, sexology and intergroup relations. He has three fabulous children.

**Daniel Jolley** is a senior lecturer in Social Psychology at Staffordshire University. He is particularly interested in using experimental methods to examine the social consequences of exposure to conspiracy theories and test tools to alleviate the negative impact of conspiracy theories.

**Olivier Klein** teaches Social Psychology at the University Libre de Bruxelles, Belgium, where he heads the centre for social and cultural psychology. He is co-chief editor of the *International Review of Social Psychology*. Besides conspiracy theories, his research interests include intergroup relations, gender, food psychology and research methods.

**Casey Klofstad** is an associate professor of Political Science at the University of Miami. He studies how psychology, society and biology influence human decision-making.

**Peter Knight** is professor of American Studies at the University of Manchester. He is the author of *Conspiracy Culture* (Routledge, 2000), *The Kennedy Assassination* (Edinburgh U.P., 2007) and *Reading the Market* (Johns Hopkins U.P., 2016), and editor of *Conspiracy Nation* (New York U.P., 2002) and *Conspiracy Theories in American History: An Encyclopedia* (A.B.C.-Clio, 2004). Together with Michael Butter, he directed the C.O.S.T. Action C.O.M.P.A.C.T. [Comparative Analysis of Conspiracy Theories].

**Péter Krekó** is a social psychologist and political scientist. He is a senior lecturer at the Social Psychology Department, E.L.T.E. University, Budapest, Hungary and a non-resident associate fellow at Johns Hopkins University S.A.I.S. Bologna Institute of Policy Research. During 2016–2017, he worked as a Fulbright Visiting Professor at Indiana University.

**André Krouwel** is an associate professor of Political Science and Political Communication at the Vrije Universiteit, Amsterdam. His research focuses on political parties, party systems, populism, voting behaviour, public opinion, extremism, belief in conspiracies, online polling, Big N data and Vote Advice Applications.

**Pia Lamberty** is a social psychologist and working on her PhD at the Johannes Gutenberg University, Mainz. In her research, she focuses mainly on the psychological aspects of conspiracy theories and their impact on society.

**Anthony Lantian** is an associate professor at the Université Paris Nanterre. His research interests lie in the origins, functional roles and social consequences of beliefs that people hold about the world, such as belief in conspiracy theories or belief in free will.

*Contributors*

**Hugo Leal** is a research associate at the Centre for Research in the Arts, Social Sciences and Humanities (C.R.A.S.S.H.), University of Cambridge. He was a postdoctoral fellow in the Internet branch of the project 'Conspiracy & Democracy' and is currently a methods fellow at Cambridge Digital Humanities (C.D.H.).

**Benjamin Lee** is a senior research associate at the Centre for Research and Evidence on Security Threats (C.R.E.S.T.), Lancaster University. His research work has focused on the use of digital tools by the far-right and he has published work in journals including *Democracy and Security*, *Behavioral Science of Terrorism and Political Aggression* and *Studies in Conflict and Terrorism*.

**Massimo Leone** is professor of Semiotics, Cultural Semiotics and Visual Semiotics at the Department of Philosophy and Educational Sciences, University of Turin, Italy and Permanent Part-Time Visiting Full Professor of Semiotics in the Department of Chinese Language and Literature, University of Shanghai, China. He is a 2018 E.R.C. Consolidator Grant recipient.

**Mari-Liis Madisson** is a research fellow at the Department of Semiotics at the University of Tartu and a post-doctoral researcher at Queen's University Belfast. Her research interests lie in cultural semiotics, political semiotics, international relations and media studies. Her work has been recently published in *Problems of Post-Communism*, *Semiotica and Folklore* and the *Electronic Journal of Folklore*.

**Silvia Mari** is an associate professor at the University of Milano-Bicocca. Her research interests cover attitudes and conspiracy beliefs in different behavioural domains, including intergroup relationships, political psychology and the social media context.

**Andrew McKenzie-McHarg** is currently a Frances Yates long-term fellow at the Warburg Institute of the University of London, where he is working on a project examining forms of secrecy in eighteenth-century secret societies. He was formerly a member of the Leverhulme-funded Conspiracy and Democracy Project at the University of Cambridge.

**Timothy Melley** is professor of English and Director of the Humanities Centre at Miami University. He is the author of *The Covert Sphere: Secrecy, Fiction, and the National Security State* (Cornell, 2012), *Empire of Conspiracy: The Culture of Paranoia in Postwar America* (Cornell, 2000) and over 30 essays and stories.

**Jasna Milošević Đorđević** teaches Social Psychology at the Faculty of Media and Communication, Serbia and is Vice Dean for Science. As a research associate in the Institute for Political Studies and consultant in Ipsos Serbia, she leads numerous projects. She is interested in science scepticism, conspiracy theories, gender and collective action.

**Türkay Salim Nefes** is a William Golding Junior research fellow at Brasenose College, University of Oxford. He is the author of *Online Anti-Semitism in Turkey* (Palgrave, 2015) and various articles in journals such as the *British Journal of Sociology* and *International Sociology*.

**Kenzo Nera** is pursuing a doctorate in Social Psychology at the Université Libre de Bruxelles, Belgium. He works on the collective underpinnings of conspiracy theories.

**Rosanne Hooper** completed her B.A. in American and Latin American Studies and M.A. in Languages and Cultures at the University of Manchester. She focused on the role of conspiracy theories in political discourse and her Master's thesis explored this theme in Venezuela. She is now a solicitor specialising in financial services regulation in the City of London.

**Claus Oberhauser** is professor of History Didactics at the Pedagogical University of Tyrol and principal investigator at the University of Innsbruck of a project about secret service and diplomatic activities in the eighteenth and nineteenth centuries. He works on historical conspiracy theories and how to deal with conspiracy theories in schools.

**Andreas Önnerfors** is an associate professor in the History of Sciences and Ideas at the University of Gothenburg, Sweden. He teaches intellectual history and political theory across various faculties. His research concerns both the cultural history of the eighteenth century, in particular Freemasonry, and contemporary right-wing rhetoric and radicalisation.

**Victoria Emma Pagán** is professor of Classics at the University of Florida. She is the author of *Conspiracy Narratives in Roman History* (2004) and *Conspiracy Theory in Latin Literature* (2012). She edited *A Companion to Tacitus* (2012) and her most recent book is *Tacitus* (2017).

**Annika Rabo** is emeritus professor of Social Anthropology, Stockholm University, Sweden. Since the late 1970s, she has conducted fieldwork, mainly in the Middle East, focusing on various topics. Her main research interest is on state-citizen relations and on systems of classification.

**Juha Räikkä** is a professor of Practical Philosophy at the University of Turku, Finland. His research interests include topics such as justice, privacy, forgiveness, remorse, self-deception, just war theory, equality, burden of proof and conspiracy theories.

**Juho Ritola** is a lecturer in Argumentation Theory at the University of Turku, Finland, where he received his PhD in 2004. He has worked in universities in Finland, Estonia and the Netherlands. His main research interest lies in the philosophical questions of argument and inference. He has published on fallacies, the notion of critical thinking and deliberative democracy.

**Alejandro Romero-Reche** teaches Contemporary Social Theory and Electoral Sociology at the University of Granada. His research in the sociologies of humour and knowledge has been published in several journals and in the book *El humor en la sociología postmoderna* (*Humour in Postmodern Sociology*) (Fundamentos, 2010).

**Kjetil Braut Simonsen** received his PhD in History from the University of Oslo (2016). His main research interests are antisemitism, National Socialism and the history of occupation. He currently works as a researcher for the Jewish Museum in Oslo.

**Steven M. Smallpage** is assistant professor of Political Science at Stetson University, DeLand, Florida. His research interests are in experimental political psychology, American political culture and development, and the history of normative political philosophy.

**Simona Stano** is a Marie Curie Fellow and works as Post-Doctoral Researcher at the University of Turin, Italy and Visiting Researcher at New York University, U.S.A. She deals mainly with food and cultural semiotics and communication studies and has published several papers, edited journals and monographs.

*Contributors*

**Robbie M. Sutton** is a professor of Social Psychology at the University of Kent. As well as conspiracy theories, he studies how people reason about intentions, morality, causality and justice.

**Viren Swami** is professor of Social Psychology at Anglia Ruskin University and Director of the Centre for Psychological Medicine at Perdana University. His research focuses on cross-cultural issues related to body image specifically and social identity generally, and he is the author of *Attraction Explained* (Routledge, 2015).

**Annika Thiem** is a PhD candidate and research fellow in the American Studies Department at the University of Tübingen.

**Hulda Thórisdóttir** is an associate professor at the University of Iceland. Her broad interest is political ideology, its structure, causes and consequences. She has written on the role of fear in ideology, psychology of the 2008 economic crisis, political polarisation and voter turnout.

**Pranvera Tika** is a PhD candidate and a research fellow at the Centre of Political Research at Panteion University, Athens. Her main research interests focus on processes of democratisation of the Balkan countries, populist radical right parties in Europe, Holocaust remembrance, antisemitism and aggressive nationalism.

**Joseph E. Uscinski** is associate professor of Political Science at University of Miami, Coral Gables, F.L. He studies conspiracy theories, public opinion and mass media. He is co-author of *American Conspiracy Theories* (O.U.P., 2014) and editor of *Conspiracy Theories & the People Who Believe Them* (O.U.P., 2019).

**Jan-Willem van Prooijen** is associate professor at the Department of Experimental and Applied Psychology, V.U. Amsterdam and senior researcher at the N.S.C.R. His research focuses on the psychological aspects of belief in conspiracy theories. Furthermore, he has ongoing research on various related topics including ideological extremism and unethical behavior.

**Andreas Ventsel** is senior researcher of Semiotics at the University of Tartu. His research topics are political semiotics, information warfare and strategic communication. His work has been recently published in *Sign Systems Studies*, *Theory, Culture & Society* and *Semiotica*.

**Pascal Wagner-Egger** is lecturer in Social Psychology in the Psychology Department of the University of Fribourg. His research interests are the study of beliefs, social representations and reasoning.

**Mike Wood** is a lecturer in the Psychology Department at the University of Winchester. His research concerns how conspiracy theory beliefs fit into broader worldviews or ideologies, as well as how conspiracy theories are spread, discussed and understood through online social environments.

**Ilya Yablokov** received his doctoral degree from the University of Manchester (2014). His research interests include conspiracy theories, nation building and politics in post-Soviet Russia, the history of post-Soviet journalism and international broadcasting. His book *Fortress Russia:*

*Conspiracy Theories in the Post-Soviet World* (Polity, 2018) deals with anti-Western conspiracy theories in Russia post-1991.

**Hanoor Syahirah Zahari** is a research administrator at the Centre for Psychological Medicine at Perdana University. She has an educational background in biomedical science and public health. Her research interests include public health education and community engagement.

**Iris Žeželj** is an associate professor of Social Psychology at the University of Belgrade, Serbia, interested in intergroup relations and motivated cognition, specifically biases in memory and group-perception. She studies ethnic/sexual discrimination, collective memory, anti-scientific attitudes, political and health-related conspiracy theories, using a variety of methods – from lab-experiments to cross-cultural surveys.

**Cornel Zwierlein** is currently Heisenberg-Fellow of the German Research Foundation attached to the University of Bamberg. Prior to this he was a PhD student at L.M.U. Munich, a junior professor at Bochum and a Henkel/Marie Curie Research Fellow at Harvard, Cambridge (C.R.A.S.S.H.) and M.W.K. Erfurt. His most recent book is *Imperial Unknowns: The French and the British in the Mediterranean, 1650–1750* (Cambridge University Press, 2016).

# ACKNOWLEDGEMENTS

This project results from the C.O.S.T. Action (European Cooperation in Science and Technology) project C.O.M.P.A.C.T. (Comparative Analysis of Conspiracy Theories), whose generous funding enabled us to establish a network of scholars in Europe and beyond working on this interdisciplinary topic (www.conspiracytheories.eu). The editors would like to thank Craig Fowlie, Rebecca McPhee and Jessica Holmes at Routledge for supporting this handbook and the accompanying book series on conspiracy theories, and Nicole Abbott, Ashleigh Phillips and Paul Martin for seeing the volume through to publication. We are also grateful to the research students who have acted as grant managers at the University of Tübingen (Annika Brunck, Marina Lieb, Marina Pingler, Janine Schwarz and Annika Thiem), as well as to Lindsay Porter and the assistants at Tübingen (Alexandra Dempe, Mona Fischer, Hannah Herrera, Sophia Kummler and Müzeyen Tasdelen) for their tireless work on editing the manuscript. Finally, we would like to extend our thanks to all the members of the C.O.M.P.A.C.T. network, especially those involved in hosting the meetings and organising the project, and those who generously acted as section editors for the handbook. What happened in Bilderberg, stays in Bilderberg.

# GENERAL INTRODUCTION

*Michael Butter and Peter Knight*

In April 2005, 22-year-old American Dylan Avery released *Loose Change*, a film about the terrorist attacks of 11 September 2001. He had put the documentary together on his laptop, drawing mainly on material available online. The film was distributed, often for free, on DVD and available for watching and downloading online, first via Google Video, later on YouTube. *Loose Change: Second Edition* was released as early as December 2005, then *Loose Change: Final Cut* about two years later, followed by *An American Coup*, a further update, in September 2009. The films were so successful that *Vanity Fair* called them the 'first Internet blockbuster' (Sales 2006). And while the original version cost only a couple of thousand dollars to make, the final one was professionally produced for more than a million. For each new film, Avery deleted some scenes and material, and added new ones in their stead (partly in reaction to copyright infringement lawsuits). The films' argument thus changed considerably over time. They started from the premise that there were anomalies in the official account that needed explaining. At first, Avery suggested that the planes that had hit the World Trade Center had been remotely controlled, and later he suggested that the Twin Towers were brought down by controlled demolition. All versions, however, make the same central claim: the 9/11 attacks were not committed by Islamist terrorists led by Osama bin Laden, but were orchestrated in secret by the U.S. government in order to infringe on civil liberties at home and wage wars in Afghanistan and Iraq, seemingly with the aim of securing access to oil.

The *Loose Change* films articulate what is commonly called a conspiracy theory. According to historian Geoffrey Cubitt (1989: 13), conspiracy theories are a way of making sense of current events and the grand sweep of history that is characterised by intentionalism, dualism and occultism. They assume that everything has been planned and nothing happens by coincidence; they divide the world strictly into the evil conspirators and the innocent victims of their plot; and they claim that the conspiracy works in secret and does not reveal itself even after it has reached its goals. Political scientist Michael Barkun (2013: 3–4) highlights similar characteristics in his influential definition of conspiracy theories: nothing happens by accident; nothing is as it seems; and everything is connected.

Conspiracy theories are widespread. Recent polls, for example, show that a majority of people believe in at least one conspiracy theory. From Bond to Bourne, conspiracy narratives have been a prominent feature of Hollywood cinema. The imagination of secret plots has also been a significant concern of literary and popular fiction, from Shakespearean drama to the postmodern metafictions of Thomas Pynchon. President Trump's path to the White House was kick-started by his promotion of the Birther conspiracy theory that alleged that President Obama was not born in the U.S.A., and he appeared on the Alex Jones show, an online conspiracy channel with a following in the millions. In May 2019, the F.B.I., for example, issued an internal intelligence bulletin warning that domestic terrorism (of the kind that led to the El Paso shooting in August 2019) was often underpinned by a particular form of white supremacist conspiracism. Conspiracy theories that circulate globally online such as the Great Replacement conspiracy theory, which claims that there is a plan to replace the Christian populations of Western countries with Muslim immigrants, seem to constitute a particularly 'sticky' form of fake news (Lewandowsky, van der Linden, Cook 2018), even if the evidence is not yet clear whether the Internet has in fact led to a proliferation of conspiracy theories, or merely made them more highly visible and easily available. In many countries, the leaders of populist parties and movements frequently draw on conspiracy tropes, and their followers appear to be particularly receptive to them. Conspiracism (a worldview in which conspiracies are seen as central to the unfolding of history; Mintz 1985) plays a significant role in many political contexts around the world, from the disinformation factories of Russia that churn out fake news stories, to the use of conspiracist narratives in the inter-ethnic conflict between the Dayaks and Madurese in Borneo, and from the pronouncements of President Chávez in Venezuela, to the popular rumour in the Middle East that the U.S.A. orchestrated the 2011 Arab uprisings.

However, conspiracy theories are not identical with fake news. For one thing, not all fake news claims that a sinister plot is afoot. Moreover, the producers of fake news know that they are spreading lies. They do so intentionally to create confusion, mobilise their audience or smear opponents. By contrast, the majority of those who articulate conspiracy theories genuinely believe in what they are saying (or, at the very least, in an era of relentless scepticism, they don't fully disbelieve the theory, suspecting that it might be true or might as well be true: cf. Knight 2000: 47–8). They are convinced that they are helping to reveal the truth. But there also those who spread conspiracy theories that they do not necessarily believe in themselves to make money or to achieve certain political goals. U.S. radio host Alex Jones, who has built a multi-million-dollar business based on conspiracy theories, would be an example of the former; Viktor Orban, prime minister of Hungary since 2010, would be an example of the latter, as he regularly uses the Great Replacement conspiracy theory to mobilise Hungarians against refugees and the E.U.

Far from being mere trivia, conspiracy theories have played a significant role in history and they continue to matter in the present, not least with the current rise of populism in many countries. At times they can have serious consequences, prompting some people to commit extremist violence (e.g. 28-year-old Australian Brenton Harrison Tarrant, who, motivated by the Great Replacement conspiracy theory, killed 50 people and injured as many at Al Noor Mosque and Linwood Islamic Centre in Christchurch, New Zealand, when he opened fire on the Muslim congregation gathered there for Friday prayers on 15 March 2019) and others to disengage from politics. Research has demonstrated, for example, that people are less likely to take active steps to reduce their carbon footprint if they become convinced that the notion of climate change is a hoax (Douglas, Jolley 2014). Conspiracy theories can also help bolster a sense of individual or group identity, for better or worse. Yet, they can also provide a harmless and vicarious pleasure to many who are attracted to their status as 'alternative' narratives known only to an enlightened few, while the ignorant 'sheeple' believe the orthodox version of events.

The *Loose Change* films, for example, consciously set themselves in opposition to the official version of events, a characteristic that some accounts consider to be another defining feature of conspiracy theories (e.g. Bratich 2008; Räikkä 2018). However, as a number of studies have shown, conspiracy theories can also constitute the official version endorsed by the authorities. Outside the West, for example in Russia or parts of the Arab world, conspiracy theories are still regularly put forward by government officials and mainstream media (Gray 2010; Yablokov 2018). Instead of grassroots dissent against the status quo (a film school reject living in a small town in upstate New York, putting a film together for loose change on his laptop that accused his own government of lying), conspiracy theories can just as often be deployed by political elites to suppress opposition and to rally support for the regime. Moreover, even in Europe and the U.S.A., conspiracy theories in the past were likewise not confined to the fringes but were an accepted – and even sophisticated – form of knowledge articulated by ordinary people as well as elites (Roisman 2006; Campbell *et al.* 2007; Butter 2014). Consequently, conspiracy theories have not always targeted elites, as they currently tend to in the West. For most of the past, conspiracy theories on both sides of the Atlantic accused enemies from outside, from below or a combination of the two, of plotting against the state and those in power. Blaming those already in power only became the dominant mode of conspiracy theorising in the West during the twentieth century (Campion-Vincent 2005).

In the U.S.A. as well as in Europe, this shift occurred hand in hand with a transition from what Barkun calls 'event' and 'systemic' conspiracy theories to 'superconspiracy' theories (2013: 6). On this schema, the first versions of *Loose Change*, for example, constitute event conspiracy theories because they focus almost exclusively on the 9/11 attacks. The final version, *An American Coup*, counts as a systemic conspiracy theory because it integrates the attacks into the larger narrative of a plot by a specific group – in this case, the U.S. government. Since then, the 9/11 attacks have been inscribed into a number of superconspiracy theories, that is, theories that claim that several groups of powerful conspirators are secretly in cahoots. Some 9/11 conspiracy theories, for instance, claim that the attacks were part of a much larger plot to control the course of history by a superconspiracy involving not only the U.S. government, but also the Jews, the Illuminati and even alien lizard people, all part of a vast, secret plan called the New World Order.

Most commentators, both journalists and academics, tend to take a common-sense approach to defining conspiracy theory that follows Justice Potter Stewart's much cited definition of pornography in the *Jacobellis v. Ohio* obscenity trial of 1964 ('I know it when I see it'). However, conspiracy theories have a complex history, and they continue to evolve in unexpected ways in the present. Although the *Loose Change* films would seem to constitute an exemplary case study of a conspiracy theory, we need to consider to what extent the features they exhibit – the historical origins of the claims they make, the social and psychological background of their creator, the medium in which they are disseminated, their rhetorical and visual forms, the political role they play and the effects they have on their audiences – are universal, and to what extent they are specific to the particular context in which they were produced. In Avery's case, that was a mixture of anti-Bush activism, coupled with a residual legacy of early-Internet-era cyberlibertarianism fuelled by the mantra that all information wants to be free, along with the emergence of a hacktivist aesthetic that found creative potential in recombining existing samples of film, music or facts. Although most conspiracy theories share certain psychological, structural and functional qualities, their particular combination and resonance can vary greatly according to context.

Defining what counts as a conspiracy theory is thus not as straightforward as the definitions by Cubitt and Barkun we drew on above might imply. After all, the term 'conspiracy theory' is anything but neutral in everyday discourse. Often, the label is used in a pejorative sense; it seems to provide a diagnosis of a flawed and delegitimised way of thinking, the aim of which is often simply to end discussion. The term can serve as an insult, implying that one does not need to take seriously the claims made by an interlocutor, because they are outlandish and absurd, perhaps even wrong by definition (cf. Pipes 1997). Some of the early research on conspiracy theories (and still much journalistic commentary) tends to treat conspiracy theories as merely a curiosity at best, and a sign of fringe, delusional thinking at worst. However, as this handbook makes clear, more recently, scholars have moved away from associating those who believe in conspiracy theories simply with paranoia or other mental problems. This is partly in the light of the scholarship that has shown the prominence of conspiracy thinking among the intellectual and political elites both in previous centuries and in particular regimes in the present; partly as a result of research in social psychology and political science that has gathered evidence that belief in conspiracy theories is widespread among the general population (in the West, at least); but also as a consequence of studies that have shown the close affiliation between conspiracy theories and other more 'respectable' ways of making sense of historical causality – the idea that, akin to conspiracy theories, critical research in the humanities and social sciences is often motivated by a 'hermeneutic of suspicion' (Ricoeur 1970 [1965]), a desire to reveal the underlying causal factors hidden beneath the deceptive surface appearance (cf. Boltanski 2014).

The second reason that conspiracy theories are hard to define is that conspiracies do actually happen. We are thus not dealing with a way of thinking that is inherently flawed, even if many examples seem far-fetched and unwarranted. Given the long history of secret machinations, both by and against the established order, it is therefore not *prima facie* unreasonable in particular circumstances for people to develop a theory that current events might be the result of a conspiracy behind the scenes. However, most commentators want to make a distinction between believing in an individual conspiracy and believing that conspiracy provides the ultimate explanation for 'what is really going on'. (To complicate matters further, what counts as a 'conspiracy' itself has a long and fraught history, part philosophical and part legal: where do you draw the boundary between complicity, collusion and conspiracy?) An important question, then, is the relationship between the imagination and the reality of conspiracy. For example, are conspiracy theories about the U.S. government more prominent in the twentieth century precisely because we have learnt more about its clandestine and illegal activities (Olmsted 2009)?

The third reason determining what counts as a conspiracy theory is far from straightforward and is that the very term 'conspiracy theory' is a comparatively recent coinage that only entered popular usage to any significant degree in the 1970s. Given that what we now recognise and call 'conspiracy theory' is evident in the historical record as far back as classical antiquity (and some scholars, drawing on evolutionary psychology, have even posited that the phenomenon is evident in all human societies: cf. van Prooijen and van Vugt 2018), we need to consider why it has only recently become a recognisable and useful concept. Scholarly engagement with what later became known as conspiracy theories began in the middle decades of the twentieth century, largely motivated by a desire to understand and to challenge what they theorised as the 'mass hysteria' of totalitarian movements (cf. Thalmann 2019). 'Conspiracy theory' as both an object of knowledge and matter for public concern thus has a complex history, meaning that we can never simply take the phenomenon for granted as a natural and immutable category.

Research into conspiracy theories has only really started to gain momentum in the past two decades. After the first wave of studies from the middle decades of the twentieth century that were rooted in the psycho-historical analysis of mass movements, cultural studies scholars revisited the topic in the 1990s and 2000s. They investigated the varied cultural manifestations of conspiracy theories (primarily in the U.S.A.), and analysed the political uses to which they are put – sometimes surprising and creative, but often reactionary. Since then, social psychologists and political scientists have turned their gaze on conspiracism, conducting experiments and surveys in order to learn more about the underpinning mental dispositions and demographic traits of conspiracy theorists. It is clear, then, that conspiracy theories are a complex phenomenon, requiring a multi-perspectival approach to fully understand them. The bibliography of research on conspiracy theories is by now extensive, and includes studies of an increasing number of regions, historical periods and political traditions, some of which draw on scholarship in a variety of languages. Given the rapid development of this field of enquiry and the current proliferation of studies in a wide range of disciplines, it has become quite difficult for scholars to gain an overview of what different approaches have found out about conspiracy theories, where they disagree and where research is currently heading.

It is the intention of this handbook to offer just such an orientation. This volume is the major outcome of the COST (European Cooperation in Science and Technology) Action 'Comparative Analysis of Conspiracy Theories' [COMPACT], which ran from 2016 to 2020. By the time the handbook went into print, the network comprised more than 150 scholars from more than 40 countries and more than a dozen disciplines. The goal of the project was to synthesise research done on conspiracy theories across disciplines and language boundaries, and to open up new research venues for interdisciplinary work. The handbook provides this synthesis; it is by far the most comprehensive account of conspiracy theory research currently available with regard to both the topics that it covers and the disciplines that have contributed to it. Many of the individual chapters were co-written by scholars from different disciplines and/or different countries, precisely in order to promote a comparative analysis. They address the central questions that are raised by the phenomenon of conspiracy theories: What is a conspiracy theory? Who believes in conspiracy theories and why? Have there always been conspiracy theories? How do conspiracy theories spread? Are conspiracy theories dangerous and, if so, what should we do about them?

The handbook is arranged in five sections: 'Definitions and approaches', 'Psychological factors', 'Society and politics', 'Media and transmission' and 'Histories and regions'. The first section opens with a chapter on the history of the term 'conspiracy theory' because the phenomenon it describes is old, but the term itself is fairly young and anything but neutral, no matter how hard scholars try to shed the derision and ridicule that characterises the term's use in everyday discourse. The other contributions to the section survey the research done in a variety of disciplines. They discuss how and from what premises different disciplines define and approach conspiracy theories, what questions they ask and which methods they employ to answer them. With regard to the *Loose Change* films, for instance, philosophers might investigate if the arguments the films put forward are epistemologically plausible or not, if, in other words, the films articulate a warranted conspiracy theory, which could turn out to be true, or an unwarranted one, which is logically impossible. Semioticians, by contrast, usually do not concern themselves with questions of truth. They would be interested, however, in the filmic transmission of the conspiracist ideas, in how different systems of signs – animations, footage of the attacks, interviews, voice-over narration, etc. – are combined to get a specific meaning across. Scholars of cultural studies might also be interested in this question, but they might also focus on those among the film's audience who believe its claims and the effects of their interpellation as conspiracy theorists for identity. A sociologist – to give one final example – might investigate how the success of the *Loose Change* films as counternarratives that challenge the official version of events is related to a deep-seated crisis of traditional epistemic authorities in the U.S.A. in particular and the Western world in general.

The second section, 'Psychological factors', presents the research done in social psychology, currently the most vibrant of the disciplines that contribute to conspiracy theory studies. Social psychologists employ quantitative methods to find out why some people believe in conspiracy theories and others do not, and what effects this might have. For example, a social psychologist might use a questionnaire to investigate what sets those who find the claims of the *Loose Change* films convincing emotionally and/or cognitively apart from those who do not. But social psychology is also interested in the relation between environmental factors such as social status or education and the belief in specific conspiracy theories or what is often referred to as conspiracy mentality more generally. Moreover, social psychology is also concerned with the consequences of belief in conspiracy theories. In the case of 9/11 conspiracy theories, the distrust of elites might lead to a refusal to participate in elections or a turn to populists who exploit the distrust. But psychologists have also shown that belief in conspiracy theories about vaccines or global warming leads to a refusal to vaccinate oneself or one's children, or an unwillingness to reduce one's carbon dioxide footprint. Finally, since social psychology tends to highlight the dangers of belief in conspiracy theories more than other disciplines, it has also most thoroughly investigated the questions whether and how such theories should and can be debunked.

The interest in environmental factors connects research in social psychology with the third section, which focuses on 'Society and politics'. In this section, the interdisciplinary nature of conspiracy theory research comes to the fore particularly clearly, as the section is concerned with topics that are studied in a broad variety of disciplines. The chapters in this section discuss the social, cultural and political factors that fuel conspiracy theorising and the effects of conspiracy theories on society and politics. For example, why is it usually men who produce conspiracy videos like the *Loose Change* films and occupy the leading positions in communities such as the 9/11 Truth Movement? Are conspiracy theories a remedy for an experienced crisis of masculinity and is that the reason why mostly men put their conspiracist narratives out there, or are there patriarchal structures of oppression at work in conspiracist counter-publics as well so that men automatically gather more attention and are taken more seriously? These are questions that are asked by gender studies and cultural studies as much as by political science, the discipline represented in this section that has most in common with social psychology because it also employs quantitative methods. But questions about demographic and ideological factors that drive belief in 9/11 conspiracy theories in particular and conspiracy theories more generally might also be asked by sociologists or anthropologists who might employ qualitative methods such as participant observation. And, while the *Loose Change* films do not resort to antisemitic tropes, other 9/11 conspiracy narratives do and are therefore of interest to scholars working on that issue. Closely related is the question after the connection between conspiracy theories and radicalisation and what such radicalisation can lead to.

The fourth section, 'Media and transmission', shifts the focus from content to form and from causes and consequences to circulation and distribution. The success of the *Loose Change* films, for example, would have been impossible before the advent of the digital age and the Internet in particular. The possibilities of digital filmmaking allowed Dylan Avery to put his film together at such low costs, and the Internet provided him with the material he sampled. It also enabled him, as an at-that-point completely unknown filmmaker, to reach a global audience. Obviously, then, the Internet has greatly accelerated the circulation of conspiracy theories, but how exactly has it influenced the rhetoric and structure of such theories? How do conspiracy theories circulate as rumours, and how have other media revolutions – for example, the advent of print in the fifteenth century or the emergence of magazine cultures in the eighteenth centuries – shaped conspiracy theorising? And what is the relationship between the allegedly factual accusations that we find in sermons, pamphlets and documentaries and openly fictional renderings of conspiracy scenarios in novels or movies? The chapters in section four, mostly written by scholars from media and literary studies, address these and related questions.

The final section, 'Histories and regions', adopts a more explicitly comparative approach, to consider how conspiracy theories fulfil different functions in variety of historical moments and regional contexts. Whereas research in psychology and political science often aims to reach generalisable conclusions from specific data, the chapters in this section are concerned with mapping out in detail the political role that conspiracism plays in particular histories and regimes, and the varying cultural forms that these conspiracy theories take. What are the similarities and differences between the conspiracy theories developed in the *Loose Change* films about the plane crashes of 9/11 and, for example, conspiracy theories in Indonesia about the disappearance of flight MH370? What functional role do pro-government, anti-Western conspiracy theories play in deflecting attention away from home-made political and economic failings in Muslim-majority societies in Southeast Asia, and how do they compare to the anti-government conspiracy theories that circulate in the West? How do these forms of conspiracism draw on existing historical accounts of victimisation by the West, and to what extent do these kinds of story defend or challenge the status quo? To what extent are conspiracy theories employed by political elites to justify authoritarian rule and the suppression of dissent? While the underlying psychological mechanisms and rhetorical forms of conspiracy theories might be universal, the historical traditions they draw on and the specific uses to which they are put in local contexts can vary widely. The case studies in this section can thus shed light back on some of the generalised conclusions summarised in the earlier sections of the handbook. Although the chapters in this section map out what we know so far about the complex genealogy of conspiracy culture and some of its contemporary manifestations, it is clear that there is still much research needed, especially in non-Western contexts.

The 48 chapters in this handbook present the current state of the art on each topic, providing a guide to current scholarship along with original research findings. Although much of the research converges on some broad conclusions, there is also still considerable debate between the positions set out in the individual chapters (Butter, Knight 2019). The first section, in particular, is therefore designed to make clear what is at stake in taking different methodological approaches, and where the residual points of tension lie. Although this volume represents a comprehensive overview of current research, these chapters also map out what we still don't know and suggest avenues for future research.

## References

Barkun, M. (2013) *A culture of conspiracy: apocalyptic visions in contemporary America*, 2nd ed., Berkeley, CA: University of California Press. Comparative Studies in Religion and Society 15.

Boltanski, L. (2014) *Mysteries and conspiracies: detective stories, spy novels and the making of modern societies*, trans. C. Porter, Malden, MA: Polity Press.

Bratich, J.Z. (2008) *Conspiracy panics: political rationality and popular culture*, Albany, NY: State University of New York Press.

Butter, M. (2014) *Plots, designs, and schemes: American conspiracy theories from the puritans to the present*, Berlin/Boston: de Gruyter, Linguae & Litterae 33.

Butter, M. and Knight, P. (2019) 'The history of conspiracy theory research: a review and commentary', in J.E. Uscinski (ed.) *Conspiracy theories and the people who believe them*, New York: Oxford University Press, pp. 33–46.

Campbell, P.R., Kaiser, T.E. and Linton, M. (eds.) (2007) *Conspiracy in the French Revolution*, Manchester: Manchester University Press.

Campion-Vincent, V. (2005) 'From evil others to evil elites: a dominant pattern in conspiracy theories today', in G.A. Fine, V. Campion-Vincent and C. Heath (eds.) *Rumor mills: the social impact of rumor and legend*, Piscataway: Aldine Transaction.

Cubitt, G. (1989) 'Conspiracy Myths and Conspiracy Theories', *Journal of the Anthropological Society of Oxford*, 20(1): 12–26.

Douglas, K.M. and Jolley, D. (2014) 'The social consequences of conspiracism: exposure to conspiracy theories decreases intentions to engage in politics and to reduce one's carbon footprint', *British Journal of Psychology*, 105(1): 35–56.

Gray, M. (2010) *Conspiracy theories in the Arab world: sources and politics*, London/New York: Routledge.

Knight, P. (2000) *Conspiracy culture: from the Kennedy assassination to 'The X-Files'*, London/New York: Routledge.

Lewandowsky, S., van der Linden, S. and Cook, J. (2018) 'Can we inoculate against fake news? *CREST Security Review*, Spring: 10–1.

Mintz, F.P. (1985) *The liberty lobby and the American right: race, conspiracy, and culture*, Westport, CT: Greenwood Press. Contributions in Political Science 121.

Olmsted, K. (2009) *Real enemies: conspiracy theories and American democracy, World War I to 9/11*, New York, NY: Oxford University Press.

Pipes, D. (1997) *Conspiracy: how the paranoid style flourishes and where it comes from*, New York/London: Free Press.

Räikkä, J. (2018) 'Conspiracies and conspiracy theories: an introduction', *Argumenta*, 3(2): 205–16.

Ricoeur, P. (1970 [1965]) *Freud and philosophy: an essay on interpretation*, trans. D. Savage, New Haven: Yale University Press.

Roisman, J. (2006) *The rhetoric of conspiracy in ancient Athens*, Berkeley, CA: University of California Press.

Sales, N.J. (2006) 'Click here for conspiracy', *Vanity Fair*, 10 October. Available at: www.vanityfair.com/news/2006/08/loosechange200608. [Accessed 10 September 2019.]

Thalmann, K. (2019) *The stigmatization of conspiracy theory since the 1950s: 'A Plot to Make us Look Foolish'*, London: Routledge.

Van Prooijen, J.-W. and van Vugt, M. (2018) 'Conspiracy theories: evolved functions and psychological mechanisms', *Perspectives on Psychological Science*, 13(6): 770–88.

Yablokov, I. (2018) *Fortress Russia: conspiracy theories in the Post-Soviet world*, Malden, MA: Polity Press.

# SECTION 1

# Definitions and approaches

# 1.0
# INTRODUCTION

*Todor Hristov, Andrew McKenzie-McHarg and
Alejandro Romero-Reche*

A glance at the contents of this first section of this handbook will make one thing immediately apparent to the reader: Many disciplines have something to say about conspiracy theory. This observation only seems unremarkable until one is challenged to name another phenomenon whose elucidation can draw upon such disparate research endeavours. Anthropological fieldwork in tribal societies can shed light on conspiracy theory, but this is also true of the data-crunching algorithms applied to digital media by social network analysis. Tests carried out by social psychologists on human subjects can be similarly illuminating, while the deep reading of post-modern novels offered by literary scholars also warrants attention. What other object of study can claim to be a point of convergence for so many researchers coming from so many disciplines? If nothing else, the cursory glance at the chapter headings in this section will suggest to the reader that there are few other phenomena that can hold a candle to conspiracy theory in this respect.

The next remarkable point, not so obvious from the chapter headings themselves but clear from a perusal of their contents, is that this research is all of relatively recent origin. Throughout the twentieth century, scholars occasionally asked questions and pursued lines of inquiry that in retrospect can be assimilated into the prehistory of research on this phenomenon (Thalmann 2019). And yet it was only in the 1990s, and more particularly under the auspices of cultural studies, that research into conspiracy theories established itself as an ongoing concern. The mysterious workings of the *Zeitgeist* were in play here; Fenster (1999), Knight (2000) and Melley (2000) assure us that they all alighted upon the theme of conspiracy theory independently of each other. With the appearance of their works in close succession at the end of the previous millennium, the field of research spluttered into life. Since then it has been picking up momentum and drawing more researchers from different fields into its orbit. Today, new work is being produced at such a rate that, even for an academic who is committed to research on this topic, it has become a challenge in its own right to keep up.

So why did it take so long? If a historical perspective can identify the presence of conspiracy theories at far earlier stages of the historical record, why was it only in the twentieth century that people started to notice the existence of a generic phenomenon? And why was it only at the end of that century that people started to engage in a sustained conversation about them? And, finally, why was it only in the first decades of this new century that a burgeoning research field began to manifest itself in the form of a flurry of publications and grants awarded to projects devoted to this topic?

The answer has at least in part to do with the conflicted nature of our relationship to conspiracy theories. On the one hand, they are an object of study like any other phenomenon that engages the attention of social scientists and scholars in the humanities. On the other hand, conspiracy theory is a competitor of sorts. In parallel to academic research, it also is equipped to observe political events, cultural trends and economic forces. Likewise, to account for these observations, it fashions and submits explanations, often in accordance with a logic that can seem unnervingly similar to that of accredited scholarship and that at times generates discussion about a common 'hermeneutics of suspicion'. The result is a situation in which explanations seeking the imprimatur of legitimate academic research are compelled to distance themselves from conspiracy theory. This naturally results in a negative default setting, evident already in the pejorative connotations associated with the concept 'conspiracy theory' and its morphological variations ('conspiracy theories', 'conspiracy theorist', etc.).

A description of this situation can be refined by enlisting the notion of boundary-work outlined in the well-known essay by the sociologist of science Thomas Gieryn (1983) and elaborating upon his conception of scientific activity by adding a complementary notion of object-work. Boundary-work, according to Gieryn, entailed the deployment of a historically and situationally variable ideology of science to justify the preferential treatment of one form of investigatory and interpretative activity over another. Consequently, this kind of work justifies its recognition of certain kinds of research and certain kinds of explanation as *bona fide* science by denying this recognition to other kinds of 'non-scientific' research and explanation. Yet scientists do not just do boundary-work. To denote the other kind of work they conduct, once they have secured research funds and built up institutional infrastructure by dint of boundary-work, one might speak of 'object-work'. It comprises of activities such as observation, experimentation, description and theorisation. This pairing of object-work and boundary-work captures (some of) the complexities of intellectual inquiry into conspiracy theory: dealing with conspiracy theory requires researchers to multi-task by engaging simultaneously, or at least in short alteration, in both object-work and boundary-work. Juggling these dual demands is not an easy task. It requires us, for example, to approach conspiracy theories in a spirit of open-minded neutrality, just as other researchers approach their objects of study, while insisting at the same time that conspiracy theories are not to be taken seriously or seen as legitimate alternatives to our own explanations; after all, boundary-work is never neutral.

Different disciplines manage these dual demands in different ways. Because conspiracy theories often submit alternative explanations for sociological phenomena, sociologists are, for example, subjected to the demands of boundary-work to a greater degree than, say, psychologists, whose explanations do not generally stand in such a competitive relationship to those of conspiracy theory – though, even here, conspiracy theory can offer itself as a mode of explanation to account for certain kinds of mental impairment and trauma for which psychologists devise distinct explanations (Showalter 1997). In this first section of the handbook, we gather together contributions from a multitude of disciplines that have, each in their own way, embraced the dual challenge of object-work and boundary-work on conspiracy theories. The contributors describe the specific understanding of conspiracy theory developed by their discipline, the methods their discipline has developed and the track record it has to show in terms of research activity and output.

The section opens with two chapters that lay some of the essential foundations for the contemporary study of conspiracy theory: the chapter by McKenzie-McHarg (1.1) outlines the genealogy of the concept 'conspiracy theory' and uncovers the origins of the ambivalence it tends to elicit, while the chapter by Butter and Knight (1.2) summarises the field-defining work carried out in cultural, literary and historical studies, has provided key insights informing the recent surge in scholarly research on conspiracy theory.

After a chapter by Leone, Madisson and Ventsel (1.3), which focuses on the semiotics of conspiracy theory as systems for the production of meaning, two chapters follow that tack between the contrasting approaches of analytical and continental philosophy: Räikkä and Ritola (1.4) examine philosophical debates on the definition, epistemic justification and ethical status of conspiracy theory, while, by focusing on psychoanalysis and critical theory, Blanuša and Hristov (1.5) delve into the pathologisation of conspiracism, the role that desire plays in conspiracist thinking and the interpretation of conspiracy theory as a symptom of late capitalism.

The next chapters explore the approaches developed by three classical social sciences. Rabo (1.6) focuses on the cultural dimension of conspiracy theory and explains how anthropological research methods (particularly participant observation) can be used in its study. The chapter by Nefes and Romero-Reche (1.7) on sociology and social theory discusses how conspiracy theory is associated with modernity and the processes it sets in motion (rationalisation and secularisation, emergence of the nation-state, etc.). The chapter by Giry and Tika (1.8) highlights the political dimension of conspiracy theory, focusing on its relations to political institutions and actors.

The final two chapters look forward. The chapter by Klein and Nera (1.9) succinctly outlines the history and methods of research conducted by social psychologists on conspiracy theory and thus functions as a bridge to section 2 of this handbook. The chapter by Gualda Caballero (1.10) explores the possibilities afforded by social media analysis for large-scale research on the dissemination of conspiracy theories.

This brief overview of this section's contents prompts two general comments. First, while relatively comprehensive, the range of contributions is not exhaustive. Although we have aimed to solicit contributions from as many fields as possible, gaps remain, leaving us to speculate about what chapters from those disciplines absent from this section might have hypothetically added to the conversation. Thus, it will be noticed that there is no chapter written by economists. Is there an economics of conspiracy theorising? And, if so, in what sense? Claire Birchall's essay about 'the commodification of conspiracy theory' (2002) would represent one possible point of departure in initiating object-work in this direction. And it would certainly seem that economists might have something to say about the aspect of boundary-work. After all, the experiences of depression, inflation, displacement, lay-offs and economic hardship in general have long been grist to the mill of conspiracy theorising. It would be interesting to consider the practices of demarcation with which economists seek to ensure that their explanations are not confused or conflated with those submitted by conspiracy theorists.

And, as one further example, what about gender studies? The seminal contributions of Fenster, Knight and Melley identified rich material and submitted stimulating analysis, amply demonstrating the relevance of this perspective. Thus, Knight examined the efforts of American feminists to draw upon conspiracy theory and at the same time disavow it in accounting for the disappointments and disillusionment experienced by the feminist cause. In doing so, he detailed the ambivalences of boundary-work as performed in popular, non-academic feminist writings. More recently, an essay by Birte Christ (2014) offered an example of the insights to be derived from the particular kind of object-work that gender studies was uniquely positioned to perform – and supplemented this analysis with the added bonus of suggestive reflection on why research into conspiracy theory is marked by a conspicuous male bias (of which the team of sub-editors for this section of the handbook must, somewhat sheepishly, admit itself as a further exhibit).

The second comment pertains to the order of the contributions. The section begins with a contribution on conceptual history, based on the notion that any inquiry should clarify the concepts and terms it employs at the outset. The order of the rest of the chapters is not based on a simple chronology of how different academic disciplines came to address the issue of conspiracy theories, because much of the work emerged more or less simultaneously and was often interdisciplinary in outlook. Instead, the chapters are arranged thematically, suggesting the links – but also the tensions – between the differing approaches.

This absence of a rigid ordering principle in this opening section has a wider significance. Today, we no longer have a *trivium* (logic, grammar, rhetoric) that grounds a *quadrivium* (arithmetic, geometry, astronomy and music), both of which are then encyclopaedically rounded by a universalistic conception of stable knowledge. We are similarly no longer beholden to a scheme of cognitive faculties, made up of memory, reason and imagination, just as we have also abandoned the notion of a hierarchy of academic faculties whose order can potentially be called into question by a 'conflict of the faculties'. Of course, the demise of such overarching epistemic taxonomies and architectures occasioned its own bouts of conspiracy theorising, which tended to implicate Enlightenment *philosophes* as the culprits guilty of subversion. Yet, leaving aside these flights of conspiracist fantasy, the service rendered in the past by these taxonomies and architectures is instructive: They regulated the relationship between the disciplines. Now that this regulative function is left unattended, the question about these relationships poses itself with an unprecedented urgency and generates calls for interdisciplinarity. Suddenly, we are forced to consider how autonomous disciplines should not only regard external reality but the other neighbouring disciplines with which they share building space on university campuses and with which they compete for student enrolments, funds, grants and public recognition, but from which they can also potentially learn and be inspired and stimulated. Gieryn has suggested that disciplines also engage in boundary-work vis-à-vis neighbouring disciplines – indeed, disciplines *are* disciplines because they have the 'discipline' to remain loyal to their own distinct perspectives – and yet this boundary-work would seemingly occur according to slightly different rules than those that apply to non-scientific knowledge (such as conspiracy theory). The call for interdisciplinarity might equate to a demand to re-evaluate these rules. Be that as it may, the first section of the handbook does not itself perform the (hard) work of interdisciplinarity but, by gathering its individual contributions and placing them in close proximity, creates conditions conducive to its occurrence. Subsequent sections of this handbook will then rise to the challenge of this work.

A second service of traditional epistemic taxonomies lay in their assurance that the field of knowledge was limited and, with sufficient diligence and adequate resources, could be mastered. That is no longer the case, and even a sub-field such as that devoted to the phenomenon of conspiracy theory demonstrates how our knowledge has become dynamic and ever-expanding. If, as noted above, that now makes it hard to keep up, the following chapters and this handbook in general might be thought to merely exacerbate the problem: yet more reading material to process! The aim of this section, however, is to provide vantage points from which to survey this rapidly expanding field of inquiry, and a map of how different disciplines make sense of conspiracy theories.

## References

Birchall, C. (2002) 'The commodification of conspiracy theory', in P. Knight (ed.) *Conspiracy nation: the politics of paranoia in postwar America*, New York: New York University Press, pp. 233–53.

Christ, B. (2014) '"What kind of man are you?": the gendered foundations of U.S. conspiracism and of recent conspiracy theory scholarship', in M. Butter and M. Reinkowski (eds.) *Conspiracy theories in the United States and the Middle East*. Berlin/Boston: de Gruyter, pp. 311–32.

Fenster, M. (1999) *Conspiracy theories: secrecy and power in American culture*, Minneapolis: University of Minnesota Press.

Gieryn, T. (1983) 'Boundary-work and the demarcation of science from non-science: strains and interests in professional ideologies of scientists', *American Sociological Review*, 48(6): 781–95.

Knight, P. (2000) *Conspiracy culture: from Kennedy to the X-Files*, London: Routledge.
Melley, T. (2000) *Empire of conspiracy: the culture of paranoia in postwar America*, Ithaca: Cornell University Press.
Showalter, E. (1997) *Hystories: hysterical epidemics and modern culture*, London: Picador.
Thalmann, K. (2019) *The stigmatization of conspiracy theory since the 1950s:'A Plot to Make us Look Foolish'*, London: Routledge.

# 1.1
# CONCEPTUAL HISTORY AND CONSPIRACY THEORY

*Andrew McKenzie-McHarg*

### Introduction

One of the striking features of the scholarship devoted to conspiracy theories is an acutely felt need to define the object of study. The study of other objects, by contrast, does not appear to labour under the same onus. Students of literature are not burdened to the same degree with the duty of defining, say, what an autobiography is, anthropologists can describe their experiences in the field without feeling compelled to submit a definition of shamanism and political scientists can discuss declining membership in trade unions without feeling the same pressure to first determine what constitutes the essence of such an organisation. As impressionistic as this observation might be, it can nevertheless serve as a springboard for some reflections about what intellectual commitments we are actually making by prefacing our inquiry into conspiracy theories with the search for a definition. What alternative avenues of inquiry we foreclosing - perhaps inadvertently or unconsciously - as a result of treating the object of study in this manner?

In this first contribution to the first section of this handbook, the aim is to examine one particular approach that exhibits a more qualified attitude to definitions. This is the approach known as conceptual history. In his *Genealogy of Morality*, Friedrich Nietzsche made a quotable aside: 'only something which has no history can be defined' (Nietzsche 2007: 53). Nietzsche's succinct rebuttal of the ahistorical metaphysics that often implicitly underpins attempts at definition has served on more than one occasion as a reference point for practitioners of conceptual history (see, for example, Koselleck 2004: 85). Distilled down into its starkest implications, it would seemingly confront us with two options: either admit the historical variability of conspiracy theory as a phenomenon and relinquish thereby the desire to define it, or insist upon its definability and deny that the phenomenon exhibits any variability in the course of history.

In fact, there are good reasons to regard the search for definitions with a degree of scepticism even without appealing to historical variability. The demand for a definition is often a reaction to what is felt to be a vagueness that inheres to *conspiracy theory* as a concept. It is, however, worth considering to what degree this vagueness is 'baked in' to the concept from the very start and therefore might not necessarily represent some conceptual flaw to be rectified through the work of definition (*locus classicus* for this consideration: Gallie 1956). A further source of unease derives from an awareness that the concept of *conspiracy theory* hardly qualifies as neutral. Instead, it is attended by an entourage of negative connotations that help it to achieve one of its primary functions, namely: to disqualify what are deemed to be unorthodox and aberrant accounts of social and political reality. Richard Hofstadter was particularly unabashed in ascribing such a negative function to his own synonymous coinage, *the paranoid style*. As he wrote in his famous essay, 'the term "paranoid style" is pejorative, *and it is meant to be*' (Hofstadter 1996 [1965]: 5 [my italics]). *Conspiracy theory* and its derivates (in particular: *conspiracy theorist*) have a similar 'illocutionary' profile. This is evident not least from the habit of disavowing any general association with the phenomenon, as exemplified by the leading clause 'I am not a conspiracy theorist but…', which then prefaces what in most cases can be described as a conspiracy theory (Knight 2001: 17; Harambam 2017: 181–3; McKenzie-McHarg, Fredheim 2017: 162–3).

One work that has squarely faced both the vagueness inhering to the concept of *conspiracy theory* and its usage as a term of derision and disqualification is Jack Bratich's *Conspiracy Panics* (2008). According to Bratich, the vagueness is built into the concept because of the flexibility that it then is able to offer liberal regimes in their efforts to draw the line between legitimate and illegitimate forms of discourse. Bratich thus adopts a meta-position that accounts for both those features that have unsettled many researchers invested in a study of conspiracy theories that aspires to be both precise and value-neutral. And, yet, these valuable insights have been developed in a manner that is largely devoid of a historical dimension and that indeed suggests that conspiracy theories do not even really exist until the concept used to label them as such has emerged (Butter 2014: 289). It is here that conceptual history can provide a remedy by cultivating a sensitivity to the concept not only as it operates to safeguard the rationality of regimes of liberalism, but also as it varies over time.

## Conceptual history as a methodology

Bratich's line of argument, implies that conspiracy theories, if they exist at all, only do so from the moment at which the term has emerged to designate them as such. This position represents one extreme in a range of answers to the question about when conspiracy theories themselves first emerge in the historical record. The uncertainty that besets scholars in trying to formulate definitions of conspiracy theories thus finds its pendant among historians in the diverging opinions about the specific time and place at which the historical record unambiguously bears witness to their presence in social and political discourse. Located at the opposite end of the spectrum from Bratich are those scholars who regard conspiracy theorising as an anthropological constant. Thus, in an early article that aimed to sketch a first map of the phenomenon, the historian Dieter Groh (1987) characterised conspiracy theorising as a universal activity not specific to any time and place. An essentially equivalent position with regard to the temporal range of this phenomenon has been put forward in the recent volume *Am Anfang war die Verschwörungstheorie [In the Beginning was the Conspiracy Theory]* (Raab et al. 2017). In this book's first chapter, the authors claim that a proclivity for conspiracy theorising emerged as humans transited from nomadic forms of existence to sedentary lives; settlements that humans began to inhabit engendered a more acute spatial awareness of boundaries drawn between those on the inside and those on the outside, and this development fostered the earliest forms of conspiracy theorising.

In the absence of written sources, such an argument remains speculative. Some historians are, however, adamant that the documentary record of both ancient Athens and ancient Rome attests to the presence of conspiracy theories within the political culture of these societies (Pagán 2004; Roisman 2006; Pagán 2008). Conspiracy theories are also thought to have left their imprint on certain episodes of medieval history, especially the accusations of collusion levelled at Jews, Muslims and lepers in southern France in 1320 and 1321 (Barber 1981; Ginzburg 2004 and, for a different reading of these episodes, Nirenberg 1996). Such observations have not hindered German historian Cornel Zwierlein from suggesting that the first genuine conspiracy theories actually emerged in the early modern period as an infrastructure for the exchange of information, most visible in the northern Italian city-states, encouraged new forms of political calculation and prognostication (Zwierlein 2013). Michael Butter, by contrast, sees conspiracy theories 'as a product of the Enlightenment'; 'They first emerged during the seventeenth century and assumed the form we associate with them today in the second half of the eighteenth century' (Butter 2014: 11), a position that directly contradicts the one adopted by Groh, who maintained that 'the emergence and spread of conspiracy theories was obviously not greatly influenced by the universal-historical caesura whose core period extended from 1750 to 1850' (Groh 1987: 11). At the same time, Butter felt confident in having demonstrated that 'conspiracy theories exist independently of the designation "conspiracy theory"' (Butter 2014: 289) – an assertion that obviously is at odds with the position staked out by Bratich, whose understanding of conspiracy theories as part of the tool kit employed by liberal forms of governance in policing the boundaries of acceptable discourse implies a dependence upon an availability of the explicit term.

Thus, there is a spectrum of possible answers about the time and place of the emergence of conspiracy theory as a phenomenon, and this spectrum obviously implies divergent answers about what a conspiracy theory is. Within this spectrum, the emergence of the concept itself might, however, represent a development whose analysis has the potential to illuminate the nature of the phenomenon in question. For, if historians and social scientists have difficulties in reaching a consensus about when the first *bona fide* conspiracy theories appear in the historical record, it should be easier to reach agreement about when the concept begins to emerge. This is because the concept is linked to words and expressions with an undeniable presence in the historical documents.

Framing the inquiry in this manner leads to the following conclusion: in a period extending roughly from 1870 to 1970, *conspiracy theory* enters the conceptual vocabulary of society. Expressing this result in a slightly different manner, it is possible to say that society first began to 'observe' conspiracy theories within this period. Obviously, this finding does not preclude the possibility that conspiracy theories existed before 1870 (*pace* Bratich). In fact, it raises an intriguing line of inquiry, expressed in the form of the following question: if we can specify the conditions that between 1870 and 1970 induced this generalised awareness of conspiracy theories, can we work back from this insight to arrive at a more refined appreciation of what conspiracy theories are? This appreciation need not lead to an infallible or unobjectionable definition that enlightens us about the essence of a conspiracy theory. What might instead be achieved is something akin to an x-ray image of the concept that helps us better understand the structure of that segment of reality to which the concept applies.

Conceptual history as a distinctive approach within historiography came into its own in the second half of the twentieth century as a sense of linguistic change imposed itself on society at large. Of course, people had previously been aware of linguistic variation, whether it applied to the differences between languages and dialects or between the registers of the same language (high/low, upper-class/lower-class, etc.). The drastic transformation of societies in the twentieth century now alerted people to diachronic variation, i.e. to shifts in the meaning of words, observable within their own lifetimes. Thus, cultural historian Raymond Williams relates in the introduction to his own contribution to this field *Keywords: A Vocabulary of Culture and Society* the sense of bewilderment he shared with a fellow student at Cambridge upon returning to the university after active service during the Second World War: 'the fact is, they just don't speak the same language' (Williams 1983: 11). Williams's sense of linguistic disorientation centred at first on the concept of *culture*, but it soon spread to other significant points on the conceptual map: *class, art, industry, democracy*. The experience sharpened the awareness that the meaning of such concepts had always been in flux.

Among historians as that subset of people most directly involved in the attempt to make sense of the past, an awareness of semantic changes took the form of apprehensions about the old bugbear of their profession, namely anachronism ('the worst of all sins, the sin that cannot be forgiven' [Febvre 1982 : 5]). Historians came to realise that one can only truly come to terms *with* the past on the terms *of* the past, i.e. by appreciating how the older usage and meaning of terms might differ from the usage and meaning familiar to us in the present. Thus, anachronism is not simply a case of objects that later narratives erroneously insert into historical contexts in which they did not exist, as, for example, famously happens when Shakespeare allows Cassius to note, while conspiring with Brutus against Caesar, that 'The clock hath stricken three' (Shakespeare Act 2, Scene 1). More subtle anachronisms distort the view of the past when it is forgotten that the present exists not only at a temporal distance to the past but also at a linguistic and conceptual one. Conceptual history built on the intuition that, rather than further obscuring the past, this linguistic and conceptual displacement could, if studied systematically and with the appropriate methods, actually illuminate history.

In the endeavour to transform this awareness of the historicity of language into a method and then into a research programme, conceptual history could draw upon resources that had been recently made available by linguists and philosophers of language (Saussure, Wittgenstein, Heidegger, etc.). In this regard, conceptual history numbers among the beneficiaries of the 'linguistic turn'. Precisely for this reason, it sets itself apart from an older history of ideas that was more vulnerable to the anachronisms entailed by a notion of ideas that are imagined hovering semi-platonically above a discourse. The conceptual historian is, by contrast, aware that a linguistic dimension inheres to concepts in a way that is not necessarily so true of ideas. This linguistic dimension anchors a concept within a social, political and historical context.

And yet while participation in the linguistic turn is relatively uncontentious, debate has opened up on a number of fronts. The first debate concerns the concept itself – or, one might say, the concept of the *concept*. Concepts are obviously not the things themselves to which they refer nor are they simply the words or terms that achieve this act of reference. Various proposals have been put forward in an effort to clarify this relationship (see, for example, Weitz 1977; Busse 1987), yet this article will desist from any attempt to adjudicate in this regard, other than to affirm the good sense in drawing a three-way distinction: 1. thing/phenomenon; 2. word/term; 3. concept. It will be observed by orthographic differentiation: plain text refers to the thing itself, discussion of the word or the term is marked by quotation marks, while the concept itself is indicated by the use of italics. In due course, the reasons for distinguishing between 'conspiracy theory' as a term and *conspiracy theory* as a concept will become apparent.

If the preceding discussion pertains to the concept itself and how it is 'built' internally, a second debate has been set in motion by the concern that the concept might not be the appropriate unit of analysis in exploring the linguistic dimension of the historical record. These doubts culminate in the apprehension that a focus on the singular concept artificially isolates it from the semantic field in which it is embedded; such isolation is thought to incur the risk of a relapse into an older form of the history of ideas. Clearly one way to offset this apprehension is to emphasise how the concept is indeed related to the semantic field. In this regard one might decide to follow the historian J.G.A. Pocock, who has identified specific 'languages' as distinct sets of rhetorical rules and conventions specific to a particular political tradition or ideology. Or, alternatively, one could turn to Michel Foucault and his notion of discourse as a combination of language and practices that embodies a set of power relations and is generative of a certain type of knowledge.

Even if both Pocock and Foucault might prefer to treat 'languages' or discourses themselves as the unit and object of analysis rather than specific concepts, there is then an even grander question concerning how language in general relates to the non-linguistic environment and how, more specifically, historical actors figure within it: are they sites of agency that exist outside the text or is this a spectral illusion to be deconstructed via the means of discourse analysis? A range of positions can be found on these issues among the innovators of historical methodology in the second half of the twentieth century, whether they come from the direction of Foucault's discourse analysis, the contextualist readings of early modern political philosophy put forward by the Cambridge School or from Reinhart Koselleck as the *primus inter pares* presiding over the expansive lexicon tracing the semantic shifts in European political and social concepts (with a particular focus on German), the eight-volume *Geschichtliche Grundbegriffe* (GG). Although the mutual awareness between these lines of inquiry was only slight and their interaction only sporadic, it is not difficult to identify a common sensibility to linguistic change that, even if insufficient for the purpose of subsuming these endeavours under the heading of one project, nevertheless justifies the view that sees them as all part of the same broader intellectual movement.

The fact that these undertakings have reached a state of completion or appear to have run their course has raised the question about the future prospects of conceptual history. Proponents of this approach are currently grappling with both challenges and opportunities. If conceptual history advanced due to the tailwind generated by the linguistic turn, other turns – visual, material – have since opened up new perspectives onto the past; one challenge is to relate these lines of inquiry to conceptual history. (See, for preliminary explorations of the link to the visual turn, some of the contributions in Hampsher-Monk *et al.* 1998). A further challenge is to globalise the application of conceptual history, to thereby extend is application to cultures beyond the Western hemisphere and to consider what kind of light it can shed upon cultural transfer, specifically by asking how concepts are translated from one language to another (see, for an initiative in this direction, Pernau and Sachsenmaier 2016). Admittedly, the preliminary research to be sketched in this entry to the handbook is liable to dash any hopes that the conceptual history of *conspiracy theory* will contribute to the broader project of 'provincializing Europe' or more broadly the Western hemisphere (Chakrabarty 2000). Insofar as the story is a global one, it seems to be one of how the concept, after having been fashioned within a transatlantic context, has then been exported to other parts of the world – a pattern that might reflect the actual dissemination of the phenomenon of conspiracy theory itself (Butter 2018: 140–1).

In confronting these challenges, conceptual history can profit from the exciting opportunity presented to it in the form of big data and the digital humanities (see, for a bold attempt to innovate new methods on this basis in excavating the conceptual history of human rights, de Bolla 2013). If the breadth of sources drawn upon by earlier conceptual historians was impressive, particularly as demonstrated by many articles in the GG, it is nevertheless clear that the limitations of time, energy and access to sources skewed these efforts in the direction of studies focusing on the more rarefied heights of intellectual debate as preserved in books and journals. New databases make it possible for historians to tap into other levels of discourse where old concepts have been reshaped and new ones forged (Müller 2014). This development opens up avenues that are especially relevant for conspiracy theory studies, given that conspiracy theories have tended to find a home outside academic discourse.

Thus, Joseph Uscinski and Joseph Parent have drawn upon the letters to the editors sent to the *New York Times* and the *Chicago Tribune* as one source of empirical data for the longitudinal analysis they carry out in their book *American Conspiracy Theories* (2014). As another example with a more specifically conceptual focus, my colleague Rolf Fredheim and I recently authored a study that drew upon *Hansard* (i.e. the records of the debates in the British parliament) as a unique source of reported speech in examining how the absorption of *conspiracy theory* into the conceptual vocabulary employed within parliament was correlated with a decline in the level of accusations of conspiracy voiced in its chambers. This decline occurred in part (one would presume) because members of parliament have become keen to avoid exposure to the charge that they are peddling conspiracy theories (McKenzie-McHarg, Fredheim 2017). The article is thus an attempt to take the measure of the illocutionary profile of *conspiracy theory* as that aspect of the concept that deprives it of its neutrality and therefore engenders doubt in some minds about its legitimate place in the context of the social sciences and historical research.

Even if conceptual history rises to these challenges and takes advantage of these opportunities, there is no reason to suppose that its status will change. It is, and always has been, essentially a *Hilfswissenschaft*, an 'auxiliary science' that does not presume to put forward a comprehensive model of what historical research should be but instead offers itself as a supplementary and complementary source of clarification and insight into certain aspects of the past. *Conspiracy theory* as a concept provides a cogent demonstration of its potential in this regard. Thus, the decision to examine *conspiracy theory* is motivated by the expectation that this approach will guide and inspire further research into conspiracy theory as a real-world phenomenon.

## The merger of *conspiracy* and *theory*

An obvious point of departure in exploring the conceptual history of *conspiracy theory* is to take note of the fact that it is a compound concept. As a result, purely on a lexical level the concept encourages us to break it down into its constituent parts (i.e. *conspiracy* and *theory*) and to consider what each part contributes to the characterisation of the phenomenon in question. Adopting this approach, it would seem that *conspiracy theory* achieves the feat of uniting a concept of a political provenance, namely *conspiracy*, with a concept exhibiting primarily a scientific pedigree, namely *theory*. It is advisable to exercise caution here as it would be naïve to assume that the conceptual breakdown into *conspiracy* and *theory* corresponds to a useful or tenable analytical decomposition of the phenomenon itself. And yet undoubtedly our understanding of conspiracy theories will profit from a more thorough appreciation first of the historical changes experienced individually by the concepts *conspiracy* and *theory*, and second of the circumstances that brought about the conjoinment of these concepts roughly from 1870 onwards. High expectations in this regard are justified because the current state of affairs in the research literature is not satisfactory. When accounts of conspiracy theory acknowledge the noteworthiness of the concept, there is an almost obligatory compulsion to point out the etymological derivation of *conspiracy* from the Latin verb *conspirare* (to breathe [*spirare*] together [*con-*]), just as there is an almost inevitable tendency to ignore *theory*, presumably on the grounds that the status and function of this part of the concept are more self-evident and self-explanatory.

A first step in remedying this situation might be taken by turning to the *GG* for some insight into the history of the political component of the concept in question, namely *conspiracy* (or, in German, *Verschwörung*). However, disappointment awaits in this regard. When it comes to conspiracy (*Verschwörung*, *Konspiration*, etc.), the *GG* is not overly forthcoming and the relevant comments are, for the most part, limited to a subsection of the article on revolution and rebellion (Bulst *et al.* 1984: 674–81). Nevertheless, for the purpose of outlining a conceptual history of *conspiracy theory*, it is possible to make heuristic use of the general theoretical comments with which Koselleck introduces this expansive project of post-war, West-German historiography (1972). This is particularly true if Koselleck's comments are supplemented by the initiative recently taken by the younger historian Christian Geulen to extend the *GG* project into more modern times (Geulen 2010). In this manner, we can achieve a first approximation in understanding the fusion of *conspiracy* and *theory*.

According to Koselleck, in the period spanning the century from 1750 to 1850 – a period that, with a focus on conditions in the German-speaking lands, he called the *Sattelzeit* – an older conceptual vocabulary, attuned to the hierarchical distinctions of the old order, was reconfigured in order to answer the needs of a new social and political reality whose normative framework had been most dramatically articulated in the ideals of the French Revolution. In attempting to disaggregate the general trends involved in this fundamental reconfiguration of the conceptual architecture of European political discourse, Kosellek identified the following forces for the *Sattelzeit* (1750–1850): Democratisation/temporalisation/ideologisation/politicisation.

It might be asked whether, once a concept such as *freedom* had traversed the 'saddle' of the *Sattelzeit* by divesting itself of the connotations of aristocratic privilege and by acquiring new associations linking it to the affordances of modern citizenship, it found its place within a new stable conceptual architecture. Geulen (2010) has argued that, in fact, the shifts in conceptual meaning continued apace after the *Sattelzeit*. In conscious emulation of the framework put forward by Koselleck, he has likewise proposed a quadripartite schema, made up of the following forces that dominated conceptual change in the period that he has simply designated as 'modernity' (1850–ca.1970) and that succeeded the *Sattelzeit*: Scientisation/spatialisation/popularisation/volatilisation or disintegration.

Without making excessive commitments to the two analytical breakdowns of semantic change as proposed successively by Koselleck and Geulen, one trend from each schema seems relevant in modelling the process by which *conspiracy* and then *theory* were nudged into positions that allowed them to dock into each other and thus create the modern concept of *conspiracy theory*.

We can begin with democratisation. If *democracy* has been recognised to be an 'appraisive' concept (Gallie 1956: 184) in the manner in which it prescribes norms to be observed by politicians and policy-makers operating within a democratic liberal state, democratisation, by constrast, a broader category. Its purpose is to neutrally register how certain opportunities, activities, courses of action and interpretations of the meaning of that action, all of which were once the exclusive preserve of an elite group, were subsequently extended to the generality (even though restrictions based on gender, age, religious affiliation or ethnicity might continue to apply). An example is provided by the concept of *interest*. As historian J.A.W. Gunn has pointed out, while originally kings and princes 'had spoken mysteriously of their interests', the concept was democratised in the course of the seventeenth century, leading to a new conception of human behaviour underscored by the recognition that 'all men had such interests' (Gunn 1968: 556). In other words, interest as 'the guide for princes might be, and in fact was, the same as that for all human beings' (Gunn 1968: 557).

The exposure of the concept of *conspiracy* to a similar process of democratisation is suggested by the observation, made by Machiavelli in his *Discorsi* at the beginning of the sixteenth century, that 'all conspiracies have been made by men of standing (*uomini grandi*) or else by men in immediate attendance on a prince, for other people, unless they be sheer lunatics, cannot form a conspiracy' (Machiavelli 2003: 402). This observation can be contrasted with the statements of Lucien de la Hodde, an agent infiltrating the milieu of nineteenth-century French republican secret societies in which republican ideals and copious wine created a heady mix: 'recruiting went on exclusively among the very lowest classes of society, where, it is well known, a conspiracy is not retarded by being prosecuted with glass in hand' (de la Hodde 1856: 219). Clearly, conspiracy was no longer an activity confined to the court of the prince. By the nineteenth century, the concept and the form of action it designated had slipped its original moorings and had now lodged itself in a shadowy, proletarian *demi-monde* populated by figures whose humble background would have precluded their forebears from any involvement in politics in general and conspiracies in particular.

In fact, in the course of the eighteenth century, a causal link was forged that tied the concept of *conspiracy* to the concept of *revolution* and that the expansive works of Augustin Barruel, John Robison and Johann August Starck consummated with their common claim that the French Revolution had been set in motion by a conspiracy of philosophers, Freemasons and Illuminati (Oberhauser 2013). By the middle of the nineteenth century, it was natural for de la Hodde to see in revolution the *modus operandi* of 'secret associations, whose designs are not only a change of persons but an overthrow of society' (de la Hodde 1856: 219). In this manner, conspiracy was no longer regarded as a merely episodic convulsion set off by a 'power grab' in the world of politics. Rather, it had become the hidden cause of profound political and social change. It was this process of democratisation that primed *conspiracy* for its use in the concept *conspiracy theory*.

But what were the circumstances that compelled later observers to then see such explanations invoking conspiracy through the conceptual prism provided by *theory*? In fact, *theory* only began to offer itself as the semantic 'handle' with which to denote such explanations in the second period for which Geulen has proposed his own schema as a successor to Koselleck's. It makes sense to pay close attention to the specific process denoted as scientisation in attempting to make sense of how and why *theory* advanced to the term fulfilling this function within the framework of what is now known as *conspiracy theory*. Scientisation denotes the process by which scientific standards, norms and models were imitated and emulated in areas of society that were previously legitimised by tradition or other sources of authority. Closer scrutiny reveals that the process of scientisation induced a pairing of *conspiracy* and *theory* within two distinct discourses: (i) the first was associated with the prosecution of crime and its forensic investigation, (ii) the second arose in the twentieth century in the form of the social sciences.

(i) *Criminal Forensics*: Some of the idiosyncrasies of the first discourse can be now uncovered by using databases that have digitised masses of American newspapers and made them searchable for specific words and phrases. In this manner, it has proved possible to locate occurrences of the term 'conspiracy theory' that predate the twentieth century in which it was originally supposed that the term first arose. (See the entry dating 'conspiracy theory' to the year 1909 in Ayto 1999: 18.) Indeed, from the 1870s onwards, the term 'conspiracy theory' appears in reports on criminal and also civil cases in American newspapers. In a recently published article (McKenzie-McHarg 2019), I have argued that these occurrences of the term are to be understood against the backdrop of (i) an adoption of scientific methods in the forensic investigation of crimes and (ii) an effort on the part of journalists to be more objective (and therefore more 'scientific') in reporting on crime. Thus, in the 1870s, we see 'conspiracy theory' emerge as simply one compound term among others constructed according to the same template (crime X + theory) whenever discussion in newspapers turns to the tentative explanations that are provisionally put forward and subjected to the forms of methodological testing that were being developed within the framework of criminal forensics. In surveying the newspaper articles penned by journalists responsible for reporting on ongoing investigations and trials, it is also possible to find references to the 'murder theory', the 'abduction theory', the 'blackmail theory' and the like.

One factor conducive to the appearance of the 'conspiracy theory' in this context had to do with the status of conspiracy as a crime in Anglo-American common law. Yet the charge of conspiracy could also find traction in cases involving civil law, as is evident from the flurry of occurrences of 'conspiracy theory' as a term generated by the scandal that ensnared the famous preacher Henry Ward Beecher in accusations of adultery in the early 1870s. The highly publicised trial that absorbed so much of the attention of the newspaper-reading public from early

1875 onwards was brought by Beecher's erstwhile friend Theodore Tilton, with whose wife Beecher was alleged to have had illicit relations. The criminal, forensic dimension of a 'conspiracy theory' was more prominent when, in 1881, the term 'conspiracy theory' was deployed to denote speculation about the assassination of President Garfield, who, after being shot in July 1881, finally succumbed to his injury in September of that year.

A number of features of the term 'conspiracy theory' as it appears in this discourse deserve particular attention. First among these is its status as a term, rather than a concept. As it appears in these contexts, there is no evidence suggesting that 'conspiracy theory' formed part of a conceptual vocabulary, understood as a semantic memory bank from which concepts can be retrieved on successive occasions. Rather, the specific combination of words was generated each time anew by the specific needs of each specific case. A sure sign of the term's purely denotative status is the fact that one never finds talk of 'conspiracy theories' (i.e. 'conspiracy theory' in the plural). Within the discourse of criminal forensics there is thus no awareness of conspiracy theory as a generic phenomenon whose existence embraces a bewildering array of specific manifestations (allegations of Judeao-Masonic responsibility for revolutions or military defeat, reports of alien abduction, claims that the moon landing was faked, etc.) and which therefore might call forth use of the corresponding concept to categorise its particular instantiations. Instead of a process of memory retrieval that applies for (generic) concepts, 'conspiracy theory' as a term is not retrieved but rather conjured into existence each time on the basis of processes that for their part entail deeper-lying shifts in the conceptual vocabulary, particularly as they pertain to the concept *theory*.

The fact that, whenever the term 'conspiracy theory' appears within the discourse of criminal forensics, it is produced anew and not retrieved, carries with it a further, noteworthy implication: In this context, 'conspiracy theory' is completely bereft of those connotations, negative or otherwise, that attend to the generic concept and are a source of unease for some researchers who would prefer to use a more neutral, less obviously biased term. To a certain degree, this wish is sustained by a muted awareness of this discourse (even if it is registered only as a possibility and not as a historical reality) in which 'conspiracy theory' does indeed have a neutral meaning, denoting without any prejudice those explanations that entertain the conjecture of multiple perpetrators of a crime working together 'in cahoots'. This neutral – and naïve – usage of the term 'conspiracy theory' received a new lease of life first in the wake of the traumatic spate of assassinations that rocked American politics in the 1960s and then following the Watergate scandal. One of the first books to contain the term of interest in the title, *Government by Gunplay: Assassination Conspiracy Theories from Dallas to Today* (1976), collected a number of essays authored by members or associates of a citizens' initiative known as the Assassination Information Bureau that dedicated itself to informing the public about the seedy underbelly of American politics. As befitted such a mission, the term 'conspiracy theory' appeared in the title as an entirely neutral designation for those explanations of an assassination that, rather than positing a lone assassin, posited instead a multiplicity of actors who had colluded in planning the act of violence. And yet the plural form indicates how the tumult of American politics in these years had given rise to an awareness of a generic phenomenon. This development set the term 'conspiracy theory' within the discourse of criminal forensics on a collision course with the concept *conspiracy theory* as it had emerged in a distinct discourse associated with the social sciences.

(ii) *Social Science*: *Conspiracy theory* was not simply a concept within the social science discourse but a negatively connoted one. The negative connotations reflected fundamental reservations about conspiracy as the model for explaining not so much individual crimes (such as assassinations) but broader social trends or large-scale political events (such as revolutions). *Conspiracy* in this tradition did not point to a specific crime but instead adumbrated an over-arching narrative or an encompassing framework of subversion – with the implication that the meaning of specific events would first reveal itself once these events were placed in the broader context created by this subversion. The fact that *conspiracy* was in itself inadequate to the task of reaching these heights of abstraction becomes apparent in view of the need initially felt to append to *conspiracy theory* some general entity. Thus, we find talk of the *conspiracy theory of society* (Popper 1950), *of history* (Neumann 1957), *of events* and *of politics* (Bell 1960, 1963; see also, for the latter option, Baum 1960, and, for an astute analysis of the intellectual engagement with conspiracy theories during these decades, Thalmann 2019).

It suffices here to point to one precursor of this conceptual usage of *conspiracy theory*, first because it predates the previously cited sources but, unlike them, has thus far gone unnoticed, and second because it nevertheless exemplifies much of the logic of this particular tradition. Born in 1903 in San Bernardino, California, the political scientist Marshall Edward Dimock led an unobtrusive yet productive life in which periods of tenure at various American universities alternated with stints of public service. His primary interests were in the study of effective administration and in determining and adjudicating upon the responsibilities entailed by governing a modern, industrialised society. In 1937, he published *Modern Politics and Administration: A Study of the Creative State*. This work was an attempt to bring theories of public administration up to speed with developments that, particularly in the wake of the New Deal, had seen state action extend well beyond the traditional remit of protecting the population from external enemies and preserving the inner peace. Several theories, partly descriptive and partly normative in nature, competed in describing what the function of the modern state was or should be. One of them Dimock denoted as 'the "conspiracy theory" of government'. As a first observation, Dimock's coinage registers a development that assigned to the state authorities the role of the perpetrators of a conspiracy. These authorities were therefore no longer regarded as merely the conspiracy's target, as corresponded to the traditional understanding of the concept. This inversion of the traditional scheme reflects the real-world trend that induced increasing numbers of Americans throughout the twentieth century to identify the state (or the government) as the point of origin of subversion, as noted and described first and foremost by historian Kathryn S. Olmsted (2009).

Dimock was aware that, in speaking of 'the "conspiracy theory" of government' in 1937, he was putting forward a neologism – his formulation was at this point in time 'not customarily employed in political science' – yet, at the same time, he was adamant that this formulation 'best describes a position *that needs to be identified*' (Dimock 1937: 50 [my italics]). He went on to note that:

> Anyone who assumes that social relations are governed almost solely by careful calculation and design, the laying of plans against others, may be said to subscribe to the conspiracy theory. It is a simple explanation of political behaviour, and there is considerable substance in it; but there is great danger in trying to read too much into it.
>
> *(Dimock 1937: 50)*

The important point was that Dimock's conspiracy theory was a generic object, a recurrent pattern of thought that did not measure up to the more sociologically and psychologically sophisticated theories with which it competed and which, according to Dimock, could be legitimately dismissed on these grounds. Unlike the singular conspiracy theories to emerge from the forensic tradition, there were therefore a priori reasons for dismissing the conspiracy theories that came into view as distinct 'epistemic objects' against the backdrop of the modern social sciences. And yet at the same time, a note of equivocation reverberated through Dimock's argument. As the above quotation indicates, he was ready to concede that the conspiracy theory was not without 'considerable substance'. Formulating robust refutations of the conspiracy theory of government, of society, of history, of politics and of events would continue to present a challenge to social scientists and historians. The challenge would intensify once the unwieldy abstraction (government, society, history, etc.) was dropped (as already occurs in the passage from Dimock's 1937 book reproduced above). As a consequence, one was left with a polyvalent term in which the difference between the term as produced by the discourse of forensics on the one hand and the concept as generated by the discourse of social science on the other was elided.

The end result was a concept troubled by the inadequacy of the dismissal of conspiracy theories as practised by the discourse of social science, given that conspiracies really did occur (as the discourse of forensics knew full well). The source of much of the ambivalence that we feel towards conspiracy theories becomes thus comprehensible when we use conceptual history to reconstruct the genealogy of the corresponding concept. It lays bare a 'conflicted' concept that has absorbed two distinct semantics, corresponding to two distinct attitudes towards conspiracy theory. In one semantic, 'conspiracy theory' was a neutral term employed to do 'object-work' in the field of criminal forensics; in the other, *conspiracy theory* was a negatively connoted concept that performed 'boundary-work' in the social sciences. (For the distinction between 'object-work' and 'boundary-work', see the introduction to this section). This insight has admittedly not brought us any closer to a definition – and certainly not to one that satisfies the strict criteria that philosophers since Aristotle have specified as preconditions for grasping the essence of a phenomenon. It has, however, hopefully sharpened our appreciation for conspiracy theory as a historically variable, epistemically complex phenomenon.

## References

Ayto, J. (1999) *Twentieth century words: the story of the new words in the English language over the last hundred years*, Oxford: Oxford University Press.
Barber, M. (1981) 'Lepers, Jews and Moslems: the plot to overthrow Christendom in 1321', *History*, 66(216): 1–17.
Baum, W.C. (1960) *The conspiracy theory of politics of the radical right in the United States*, thesis, State University of Iowa.
Bell, D. (1960) *The end of ideology: on the exhaustion of political ideas in the fifties*, Glencoe, Ill.: Free Press.
Bell, D. (ed.) (1963) *The radical right*, New York: Doubleday & Co.
Blumenthal, S. and Yazijian, H. (1976) *Government by gunplay: assassination conspiracy theories from Dallas to today*, New York: Signet.
De Bolla, P. (2013) *The architecture of concepts: the historical formation of human rights*, New York: Fordham University Press.
Bratich, J.Z. (2008) *Conspiracy panics: political rationality and popular culture*, Albany: State University of New York Press.
Bulst, N., Fisch, J., Koselleck, R. and Meier, C. (1984) 'Revolution, Rebellion, Aufruhr, Bürgerkrieg', in O. Brunner, W. Conze and R. Koselleck (eds.) *Geschichtliche Grundbegriffe: Historisches Lexikon zur politisch-sozialen Sprache in Deutschland*, vol. 5, Stuttgart: Klett-Cotta.
Busse, D. (1987) *Historische Semantik: Analyse eines Programms*, Stuttgart: Klett-Cotta.
Butter, M. (2014) *Plots, designs, and schemes: American conspiracy theories from the puritans to the present*, Berlin/Boston: de Gruyter.
Butter, M. (2018) *‚Nichts ist, wie es scheint': über Verschwörungstheorien*, Berlin: Suhrkamp.
Chakrabarty, D. (2000) *Provincializing Europe: postcolonial thought and historical difference*, Princeton: Princeton University Press.
Dimock, M.E. (1937) *Modern politics and administration: a study of the creative state*, New York: American Book Company.
Febvre, L. (1982) *The problem of unbelief in the sixteenth century: the religion of Rabelais*, trans. B. Gottlieb, London: Harvard University Press.
Gallie, W.B. (1956) 'Essentially contested concepts', *Proceedings of the Aristotelian Society*, 56(1): 167–98.

Geulen, C. (2010) 'Plädoyer für eine Geschichte der Grundbegriffe des 20. Jahrhunderts', *Zeithistorische Forschungen/Studies in Contemporary History*, vol. 7, pp. 79–97.

Ginzburg, C. (2004) *Ecstasies: deciphering the witches Sabbath*, Chicago: University of Chicago Press.

Groh, D. (1987) 'The temptation of conspiracy theory: or why do bad things happen to good people?', in C.F. Graumann and S. Moscovici (eds.) *Changing Conceptions of Conspiracy*, New York: Springer.

Gunn, J.A.W. (1968) '"Interest will not lie": a seventeenth-century political maxim', *Journal of the History of Ideas*, 29(4): 551–64.

Hampsher-Monk, I., Tilmans, K. and Van Vree F. (eds.) (1998) *History of concepts: comparative perspectives*, Amsterdam: Amsterdam University Press.

Harambam, J. (2017) *'The truth is out there': conspiracy culture in an age of epistemic instability*, unpublished thesis, Erasmus University Rotterdam.

de la Hodde, L. (1856) *History of secret societies and of the republican party of France from 1830 to 1848*, trans. J.W. Phelps, Philadelphia: J.B. Lippincott and Co.

Hofstadter, R. (1996 [1965]) *The paranoid style in American politics and other essays*, reprint, Cambridge: Harvard University Press.

Knight, P. (2001) 'Making sense of conspiracy theories', in P. Knight, *Conspiracy theories in American history: an encyclopedia*, Santa Barbara: ABC Clio, pp. 15–25.

Koselleck, R. (1972) 'Einleitung', in O. Brunner, W. Conze and R. Koselleck (eds.) *Geschichtliche Grundbegriffe: historisches Lexikon zur politisch-sozialen Sprache in Deutschland*, vol. 1, Stuttgart: Klett-Cotta.

Koselleck, R. (2004) *Futures past: on the semantics of historical times*, New York: Columbia University Press.

Machiavelli, N. (1517) *The discourses*, reprint, London: Penguin, 2003.

McKenzie-McHarg, A. (2019) 'Conspiracy theory: the nineteenth-century prehistory of a twentieth-century concept', in J. Uscinski (ed.) *Conspiracy theories and the people who believe them*, Oxford University Press: New York, pp. 62–81.

McKenzie-McHarg, A. and Fredheim, R. (2017) 'Cock-ups and slapdowns: a quantitative analysis of conspiracy rhetoric in the British Parliament 1916–2015', *Historical Methods: A Journal of Quantitative and Interdisciplinary History*, 50(3): 156–69.

Müller, J.-W. (2014) 'On conceptual history', in D. McMahon and S. Moyn (eds.) *Rethinking modern European intellectual history*, Oxford: Oxford University Press, pp. 74–93.

Neumann, F. (1957) 'Anxiety and politics', in F. Neumann and H. Marcuse (eds.) *The democratic and the authoritarian state: essays in political and legal theory*, New York: The Free Press.

Nietzsche, F. (1887) *On the genealogy of morality*, ed. by Ansell-Pearson, K., trans. by Diethe, C., reprint, Cambridge: Cambridge University Press, 2007.

Nirenberg, D. (1996) *Communities of violence: persecution of minorities in the middle ages*, Princeton: Princeton University Press.

Oberhauser, C. (2013) *Die verschwörungstheoretische Trias: Barruel – Robison – Starck*, Innsbruck: Studien Verlag.

Olmsted, K.S. (2009) *Real enemies: conspiracy theories and American democracy, World War I to 9/11*, Oxford: Oxford University Press.

Pagán, V.E. (2004) *Conspiracy narratives in Roman history*, Austin: University of Texas Press.

Pagán, V.E. (2008) 'Toward a model of conspiracy theory for ancient Rome', *New German Critique*, 103: 27–49.

Pernau, M. and Sachsenmaier, D. (eds.) (2016) *Global conceptual history: a reader*, London: Bloomsbury.

Popper, K. (1950) *The open society and its enemies*, Princeton: Princeton University Press.

Raab, M., Carbon, C.-C. and Muth, C. (2017) *Am Anfang war die Verschwörungstheorie*, Berlin: Springer Verlag.

Roisman, J. (2006) *The rhetoric of conspiracy in ancient Athens*, Berkeley: University of California Press.

Shakespeare, W. (1981) *Julius Caesar*, London: Penguin Classics.

Thalmann, K. (2019) *The stigmatization of conspiracy theory since the 1950s: 'A plot to make us look foolish'*, London: Routledge.

Uscinski, J.E. and Parent, J.M. (2014) *American conspiracy theories*, New York: Oxford University Press.

Weitz, M. (1977) *The opening mind: a philosophical study of humanistic concepts*, Chicago: University of Chicago Press.

Williams, R. (1983) *Keywords: a vocabulary of culture and society*, rev. edn, New York: Oxford University Press.

Zwierlein, C. (2013) 'Security politics and conspiracy theories in the emerging European state system (15th/16th C.)', *Historical Social Research*, 38(1): 65–95.

# 1.2
# CONSPIRACY THEORY IN HISTORICAL, CULTURAL AND LITERARY STUDIES

*Michael Butter and Peter Knight*

## Introduction

Are conspiracy theories a universal part of human nature, an anthropological constant that is hard-wired into our psychology through our shared evolution as a species? Or are conspiracy theories particular ways of making sense of causality and motive, that have their own particular history and dynamic, varying over time and between different cultures and political regimes? Historical, cultural and literary studies start from the assumption that the latter view is more significant than the former in explaining the popularity of conspiracy thinking. For these disciplines, the meaning, style and consequences of believing that nothing happens by accident, nothing is as it seems and everything is connected are historically and culturally conditioned. Scholars in these disciplines have focused on a variety of elements in their analysis of conspiracy theories: The narrative structures, dynamics, images and metaphors of particular texts; the continuities and recombinations of familiar tropes over time and across cultures; the changing modes of transmission; the social and political context in which conspiracy theories are produced and consumed; and the psychic investment in the forms of interpretation encouraged by conspiracy theories.

This chapter discusses how historical, cultural and literary studies have analysed conspiracy theories. It summarises the key contributions in each field and assesses their strengths and weaknesses. The first section traces the shift from conspiracist interpretations as the norm in the nineteenth century, to their becoming characterised as a flawed approach by the middle of the twentieth century. A more concerted focus on the dangers of conspiracism as a significant aspect of European and American political history came with attempts from a psychohistorical perspective to explain the rise of mass political movements. The second section shows how cultural studies scholars around the turn of the millennium challenged the psychopathologising interpretation of the 'paranoid style' of American politics, instead viewing conspiracy theories as increasingly justified, creative and potentially radical challenges to the status quo. The third section explains how literary scholars have examined the connection between conspiracy plots and narrative plots in literature and film, with a focus on post-war American culture at first, but more recently taking in other historical periods and national traditions. Finally, we consider the discomfiting parallels between the interpretive manoeuvres of conspiracy theory and ideological critique itself, before going on to suggest avenues for future research.

## Historical studies

Conspiracy theories may not be an anthropological given but, as several of the contributions to section 5 of this handbook highlight, they are a phenomenon with a long historical tradition (see, for example, Chapters 5.1, 5.2 and 5.10). By contrast, the historiographic engagement with conspiracy theories only began in the twentieth century; earlier historians did not analyse conspiracy theories and their impact on history, but articulated conspiracist interpretations of history themselves. For example, in books that from today's perspective would be classified as contemporary history, Augustin Barruel, John Robison and Johann August Starck promoted a conspiracist understanding of the French Revolution in the first decade of the nineteenth century, blaming the Illuminati and the Freemasons for orchestrating the event (see Chapter 5.3). In similar fashion, the idea that a group of powerful slaveholders – the so-called Slave Power – was controlling the American government and secretly manipulating events to introduce slavery everywhere in the country not only was the founding ideology of the Republican Party (Butter 2014: 198), but it remained the dominant explanation for the outbreak of the Civil War among historians such as Horace Greeley and Henry Wilson until the early twentieth century (Richards 2000: 16).

The longevity of the conspiracist take on history among professional historians is not surprising, as recent studies have shown how normal it was to believe in conspiracy theories in Europe and North America far into the twentieth century (Klausnitzer 2007; Butter 2014). In fact, the status of conspiracy theory as a legitimate form of knowledge only began to be challenged from the 1940s onwards. Sociologists such as Karl Popper, who also coined the modern meaning of the term 'conspiracy theory' in the second volume of *The Open Society and Its Enemies* (1950), criticised conspiracy theories for overestimating intentional action and underestimating structural causes and unintended effects. At the same time, writing in the aftermath of the Holocaust, another group of scholars, most notably Theodor Adorno, began to stress the dangers of conspiracy theories and tried to understand which personality types tended to articulate them and why the masses were drawn to authoritarian leader figures (Thalmann 2019; see also Chapter 5.10 in this volume). These two traditions finally merged in Richard Hofstadter's seminal essay 'The Paranoid Style in American Politics' (1964) in which Hofstadter pathologised belief in conspiracy theories as a form of paranoia and claimed, wrongly, that while conspiracy theories had a long history in the U.S.A., they had always 'been the preferred style only of *minority* movements' (1964: 7 [italics in the original]).

Hofstadter was, however, not the first historian to critically engage with conspiracy theories in the past. As early as 1909, French historian Augustin Cochin challenged the conspiracist historiography of the French Revolution and spoke of 'la thèse du complot' that informed many accounts of this event (1909). A few years later, Vernon Stauffer (1918) examined the New England Illuminati scare of the 1790s (which led to the passing of the Alien and Sedition Acts), without assuming that there was an actual Illuminati plot against the U.S.A. Unlike Cochin, Stauffer did not attempt at all to label or theorise the phenomenon – a particularly powerful instance of conspiracy theorising. This distinguishes him from Charles Beard, who coined the phrase 'Devil Theory of War' in 1936 to criticise conspiracist explanations of the origins of the First World War. Finally, while Hofstadter was developing his ideas about conspiracy theory, Bernard Bailyn was working on a revisionist history of the American Revolution. In the introduction to his edition of pamphlets (1965) and a subsequent monograph (1967), he demonstrated that 'the fear of a comprehensive conspiracy against liberty […] lay at the heart of the Revolutionary movement' (1965: x).

While Bailyn's book was highly acclaimed and recalibrated the historiography of the Revolutionary period, parts of its reception testify to the harm done by Hofstadter's stigmatising conceptualisation of conspiracy theory as paranoid and a minority phenomenon to research in the history of conspiracy theories. Linking Bailyn's analysis to Hofstadter's powerful theorisation, a number of historians began to cast Washington, Jefferson and other important figures of the period as paranoid. 'Were the American Revolutionaries mentally disturbed?' begins a seminal essay by Gordon Wood (1982), a student of Bailyn's, in which he takes on such psychohistorical studies and demonstrates in great detail why it was perfectly rational to believe in conspiracy theories in the eighteenth century. However, even Wood refrained from challenging Hofstadter's general argument. In closing, he suggested that conspiracy theorising was a rational way of worldmaking up to the end of the eighteenth century and became quickly irrational after the turn to the nineteenth century, and thus swiftly moved from the centre to the margins of society.

This was unfortunate because Hofstadter's conceptualisation of conspiracy theory as a paranoid minority phenomenon impeded historical research for decades. It left historians with two problematic choices. On the one hand, they could embrace the framing of conspiracy theorising as pathological, but this often led them to underestimate the importance of these theories, or made them dismiss the anxieties that fuelled them far too quickly. In *The Slave Power Conspiracy and the Paranoid Style* (1969), for example, David Brion Davis approached the topic on the basis of Hofstadter's 'paranoid style' and thus, unsurprisingly, arrived at the conclusion that northern allegations had little foundation in truth and were indicators of collective delusion. Also drawing on Hofstadter, Daniel Pipes (1996) blamed the popularity of conspiracy theories in the Arab world on the alleged irrationality of this ethnicity, thus avoiding a discussion of the historical injustices that drove them, and, in a subsequent study (1997), associated the alleged rise of conspiracy theories in the Western world with a decline in rationality.

On the other hand, historians could reject the Hofstadterian framework if they were aware that they were not studying a fringe issue driven by insanity, but this decision left them without any theorisation. Hugh Brogan (1986), for example, wrote of perceived 'plots', detected 'conspiracies' and collective 'paranoia' on nearly every other page in his discussion of the antebellum period in *The Penguin History of the United States of America*. He never mentioned Hofstadter and clearly did not consider what he describes as an irrational minority phenomenon, but, since he had no concept of conspiracy theory, his discussion of the topic is not as precise as it could be. The same holds true for a study that significantly revises Davis's work on the alleged Slave Power plot, Leonard L. Richards's *The Slave Power: The Free North and Southern Domination 1780–1860* (2000). Richards argues convincingly that northerners exaggerated southern unity and plotting, but he also acknowledges that they had much cause to complain since the slave states enjoyed an undue influence on the federal level. As with Brogan, however, the lack of a theory of conspiracy theory prevents him from pushing his interpretations further.

European historians engaged even less with manifestations of conspiracy across the ages than their American counterparts from the 1960s to the turn of the century, but there were some notable exceptions. Johannes Rogalla von Bierberstein (1976) wrote a comprehensive history of conspiracy theories in Germany from the eighteenth century to the Second World War in which he highlights how widespread and influential these suspicions were. He thus partly paved the way for a group of German historians whose explorations of historical conspiracy theories were published in two edited volumes (Caumanns, Niendorf 2001; Reinalter 2002). The most influential article in these collections is Pfahl-Traughber's contribution (2002), which develops a theory of conspiracy theory that avoids the pitfalls of the Hofstadterian 'paranoid style'. The same goes for Geoffrey Cubitt's definition (1989), upon which we drew in the introduction to this volume. Cubitt later demonstrated the productivity of his take on conspiracy theories in an analysis of conspiracy theories about the Jesuits in nineteenth-century France (1993).

In the past 20 years, the body of historical research has grown exponentially. Two factors appear to be responsible for this development. First, as discussed below, around the turn of the millennium, cultural studies scholars challenged the psychopathologising interpretation of the 'paranoid style' of American politics, providing theorisations of the phenomenon that allowed historians to approach the issue more neutrally. Matthew Gray (2010), for example, drew on the studies by Fenster (1999), Knight (2000) and Melley (2000) to revise Pipes's (1996) pathologisation of Arab conspiracy theories. Second, the plethora of conspiracy theories generated by the terrorist attacks of 11 September 2001 and the new visibility of such theories through the rise of the Internet led some scholars to explore the past for similar manifestations. Accordingly, in the past two decades, there have been studies of conspiracy theories in, for example, classical antiquity (Pagán 2004; Roisman 2006), the early modern period (Coward, Swann 2004; Zwierlein 2013), revolutionary France (Tackett 2000; Linton et al. 2010), nineteenth-century Europe (Klausnitzer 2007; Oberhauser 2013), post-war Italy (Girard 2008; Hof 2013) or twentieth-century U.S.A. (Olmsted 2009; Konda 2019). These studies do not pathologise conspiracy theories, but, instead, highlight how popular and influential they were in the periods they focus on.

The latest development in the historiographic engagement with conspiracy theories are diachronic studies that trace the shifting status of conspiracy theories across a longer period of time, or self-reflexively trace the development of the concept of conspiracy theory. Butter (2014) argues that conspiracy theories were more popular and influential in the U.S.A. before the middle of the twentieth century because they were then considered orthodox knowledge. He ascribes their visibility in the past decades (which has led other scholars to conclude that they have gained in popularity) to their relegation to heterodox knowledge, which has turned them into a widely discussed problem. Thalmann (2019) has traced this process of stigmatisation in great detail, providing a history of the discourse on conspiracy theory in which Hofstadter figures as the endpoint of the delegitimisation of this form of knowledge and not, as in earlier accounts, as its beginning. McKenzie-McHarg (2019; see also Chapter 1.1 in this volume) has traced the origins of the term 'conspiracy theory' to the second half of the nineteenth century and investigated its shifts in meaning and increasingly negative connotations up to Hofstadter.

## Cultural studies

In the field of cultural studies, too, Hofstadter's notion of the paranoid style set the template for many subsequent studies of conspiracy theories on what they regarded as the unscientific, irrational and extremist aspects of conspiracism (Robins, Post 1997; Barkun 2003). However, around the turn of the millennium, a number of scholars began to challenge the assumptions behind the orthodox position (e.g. Dean 1998; Fenster 1999; Melley 2000; Knight 2000; Birchall 2006; Bratich 2008). Mainly rooted in the discipline of cultural studies, these scholars started from the assumption that the task is not to condemn popular manifestations of conspiracy theory, but to understand their appeal and assess their cultural significance. The aim of these revisionist studies was to make sense of why conspiracist narratives have become so attractive, both for individual believers and cultural forms such as postmodern novels and Hollywood thrillers.

The cultural studies approach thus explicitly rejects the pathologising tendency in much of the work that had followed in the footsteps of Hofstadter. In Rogin's terms (1987), these studies opposed the 'symbolist' focus on the idiosyncratic psychology of conspiracy theorists and instead adopted a 'realist' approach to the all-too-real social and political conditions and vested political interests that made such conspiracy narratives plausible. The focus of analysis was therefore less individual psychopathology than the collective narratives that communities used to make sense of their worlds. In the post-war U.S.A., conspiracy theories thus constitute 'logical responses to technological and social change' (Melley 2000: 14), marked by increasing globalisation, corporatisation and media saturation. For other scholars (Olmsted 2009), seeing the world in terms of vast military-industrial-government conspiracies is an understandable response to the rise of the national security state (see Chapter 4.4 in this volume), with the many well documented examples of official conspiracies, from MK-ULTRA (the CIA's illegal mind control programme) to the Iran-Contra affair. During the Cold War, the imagination on the part of the authorities of enemies everywhere – at times genuinely fearful, at others cynically exploiting popular suspicion to legitimise the pursuit of otherwise unpalatable policies – fed into the creation of an official culture of secrecy and conspiring, which in turn fuelled an all-too-understandable public distrust of the authorities (Melley 2012).

Likewise, cultural studies scholars have argued that the prominence of conspiracy theories in African-American communities and cultural forms such as hip hop is not a sign of inherent 'racial paranoia', as various right-wing commentators alleged (D'Souza 1995: 487). Instead, the circulation of conspiracy rumours is a justifiable reaction to a long history of abuse (sometimes through negligence, or institutional racism, but at others quite deliberate). Washington (2006), for example, documents the long history of dubious science, therapeutic neglect and outright abusive treatment of African Americans by the mainstream American medical community, with the Tuskegee syphilis trials as merely one example in a long litany of scandals. For Washington (as for Turner 1993; Fiske 1994; Knight 2000), explaining the salience of conspiracy theories in terms of the psychological lack of trust on the part of individual believers ignores the warranted untrustworthiness of medical institutions and practices.

According to the cultural studies approach, then, conspiracy theory offers 'an odd sort of comfort in an uncertain age: it makes sense of the inexplicable, accounting for complex events in a clear, if frightening way' (Melley 2000: 8). In short, conspiracism 'provides an everyday epistemological quick-fix to often intractably complex problems' (Knight 2000: 8). Many of these studies draw on and extend the analysis of Fredric Jameson, who noted that

> conspiracy theories are the poor person's cognitive mapping in the postmodern age; it is a degraded figure of the total logic of late capital, a desperate attempt to represent the latter's system, whose failure is marked by its slippage into sheer theme and content.
>
> *(1988: 356)*

For Jameson, the obsession with conspiracies in popular film, television and fiction is a symptom of our contemporary inability to see how everything fits together, socially, politically and economically. Conspiracy theories satisfy the popular desire to see how everything is connected, but they mistakenly focus on imagined plots involving shadowy conspirators and high-tech surveillance. Jameson in effect reads conspiracy theory not as a mere symptom of a delusional mind-set, but as an *allegory*, at the level of form rather than content, of the complex social and economic changes of globalisation that cannot be understood in any straightforward way. Jameson's observations are thus in tune with the cultural studies axiom that popular culture is not merely a side-show but is in itself a site of political contestation.

Like other cultural studies scholars, Jameson starts from the assumption that we need to take the world as we find it. Rather than wishing for a more perfect form of cognitive mapping, we need to see the imaginative potential in 'degraded' popular forms like conspiracy theories. The cultural studies approach thus goes even further in its challenge of the Hofstadter paradigm that tended to present the 'paranoid style' of politics as 'epistemologically, psychologically and morally suspect' (Harambam 2017: 11). Conspiracy thinking is not merely an inevitable reaction to postmodernity, but at times it is a *creative* response. Far from being a dangerous threat to democracy, conspiracy theories on this line of thinking 'can in fact play the role of a productive challenge to an existing order – albeit one that excessively simplifies complex political and historical events' (Fenster 2008 [1999]: 90). In literal terms, conspiracy theories might not be strictly accurate, but they are one of the few popular attempts to address problems of power and secrecy in modern society. Conspiracism, far from being 'a label dismissively attached to the lunatic fringe', may instead be 'an appropriate vehicle for political contestation' (Dean 1998: 8) For Dean, even seemingly bizarre conspiracy theories such as alien abduction narratives can serve potentially progressive political ends because their very weirdness challenges 'consensus reality' that all too often serves the vested interests of the elite.

Other cultural studies scholars focus less on the meaning and function of particular conspiracy theories, than on the conditions of knowledge that create and sustain conspiracy theory as a distinct category. Bratich (2008), for example, argues that the very term 'conspiracy theory' is not neutral: It is often pejorative, used by elites to mark out particular beliefs as beyond the pale of rational political discourse. This means that certain 'extreme' (in the sense of non-mainstream) forms of political dissent can be delegitimised through what seems like an objective psychological diagnosis. Instead of explaining why ordinary people believe in conspiracy theories, Bratich insists that we need to consider why the spectre of popular conspiracism occasions panic among the elite, and how conspiracy theorists increasingly and self-consciously resist the stigmatisation of their worldview (Harambam, Aupers 2015). Birchall (2006) likewise explores how conspiracy theories can call into question the very boundary between the reasonable and the irrational, the official and the subjugated, given that any attempt to demarcate certain kinds of knowledge as legitimate is only ever a fiction. This is because there is no ultimate ground of justification that sets aside one way of knowing the world as intrinsically legitimate or true. Birchall suggests that the distinction between official and subjugated forms of knowledge is eroding in the present largely because of the influence of the Internet. Like other cultural studies scholars, she emphasises the playful and creative ways people engage with heterodox forms of knowledge.

Cultural studies thus provides a robust challenge to the Hofstadterian approach to conspiracy theories. However, there are more similarities with Hofstadter than might appear at first sight. We need to recognise that cultural studies has much in common with Hofstadter's focus on the psychological, cultural and symbolic aspects of American politics (Fenster 1999). In contrast to the familiar emphasis in political science on the material realities of partisanship and vested political interests, Hofstadter was concerned with the psychic investment that individuals and groups might have in imagining themselves to be under imminent threat from enemies, both internal and external. His discussion, after all, is concerned with the paranoid *style* of American politics, and he is attuned to both the rhetoric and psycho-social dynamic of conspiracy narratives that are, on his account, often motivated by a sense of status anxiety and sexual repression ('Anti-Catholicism has always been the pornography of the Puritan', Hofstadter observed [1964: 21]; see also Fraser 2018). Much work in cultural studies has likewise focused on the particular tropes, images and narratives deployed in conspiracy theories, as well as their specific emotional appeal that is embedded in their varying cultural forms. Why do so many conspiracy tales, for example, employ a narrative style that is marked out by a sense of endless rush towards uncovering the conspiracy, yet at the same time also endlessly defer the final revelation? Why are some examples of contemporary conspiracy culture driven more by a sense of 'insecure paranoia' than the more usual, and paradoxically comforting, sense of 'secure paranoia', as it seems that we can no longer clearly tell the difference between Them and Us (Knight 2000: 175–7)?

As productive as the revisionist accounts emerging from cultural studies have been, there are also some troubling implications of trying to understand conspiracy theories – charitably – on their own terms. First of all, they have tended to focus almost without thinking on the U.S.A. and are not always clear whether the conclusions they reach about the nature of American conspiracism apply to other cultures. (Hofstadter, for example, hedged his bets by stating that he listed only American examples of the paranoid style only because he happened to be an Americanist.) Indeed, there is often an implicit American exceptionalism at the heart of cultural studies research on conspiracy theories, since it starts from the assumption that the 'paranoid style' is distinctively or uniquely American and then searches for explanations (Pasley 2000). This is not necessarily a problem in itself: Melley, for example, provides a very plausible account why American culture especially (though not necessarily exclusively) is beset by anxieties about the erosion of a sense of masculine agency in the face of post-war corporate bureaucratisation (see Chapter 4.4 in this volume), in the context of a longer American obsession with sovereign individuality. Butter (2014) has added historical depth to this argument and identifies factors that made conspiracy theories particularly prominent in the U.S.A. in the eighteenth and nineteenth centuries. However, the large number of studies that have come out in the past few years that show how widespread conspiracy theories have been everywhere in Europe for centuries has strongly challenged this argument. Accordingly, Butter (2020) now rejects any notion of American exceptionalism when it comes to conspiracy theories.

Second, many of the studies cited above have been most interested in conspiracy culture from a particular historical period (the 1960s to the present). Again, it can mean that the more general conclusions reached in fact apply only to a distinctive – and possibly unrepresentative – phase. As discussed above, conspiracy theories have not always been a form of subjugated knowledge, but this has been the primary focus of research emerging from cultural studies. Moreover, the research has tended to concentrate on a particular kind of conspiracy theory text that revolves around questions of epistemology, doubt and trust. The prime example would be *The X-Files*, the hit television show from the 1990s, in which both the detective figures through whom the show is focalised (the F.B.I. agents Scully and Mulder) and the audience are confronted with the seemingly endless impossibility of knowing anything for certain. In effect, cultural studies scholars tend to latch onto those examples of conspiracy culture that encode – often self-reflexively – some of the central issues in discussions of poststructuralism and postmodernity. Although fascinating, these kinds of texts might well not be representative of the wider culture of conspiracy, both geographically and historically, but may be typical only of a specific moment in history (see Chapter 4.6). For example, the kinds of conspiracy texts under scrutiny in earlier cultural studies accounts are often as much a self-reflexive diagnosis of the dangers and attractions of popular conspiracism as they are an unwitting symptom. This is in large part because the focus has often been more on fictional texts (novels and films) than non-fictional ones, and usually highly sophisticated ones at that (e.g. the novels of Don DeLillo or the films of David Cronenberg). Moreover, although cultural studies is concerned with the relationship between producer, text and consumer, rarely have studies of conspiracy theories considered in detail how audiences engage with them. In addition, the choice of example is often skewed to those that most obviously lend themselves to an interpretation that emphasises the creative, countercultural potential.

Third, there is also a tendency to see all conspiracy culture as a coping mechanism in the face of the same broad sociological factors (globalisation, mass media, technology, etc.). While these interpretations might be justified in some cases, they can lack specificity. In this way they can end up oddly similar to the sweeping psycho-cultural diagnosis found in the Hofstadterian focus on the political pathology of paranoia; and it might even be argued that there is something pathological – paranoid even – in the insistence that ultimately everything is always about the impossibly vast and shadowy forces of capitalism. What is more, in their at least occasional disregard for nuance and differentiation, these accounts can also be said to mirror conspiracy theories that blame the CIA, the U.S. administration or the E.U. without acknowledging the diverging agendas of these institutions over time and the different personalities and agendas of their representatives.

Finally, in its desire to tune into the playful, creative, insightful and potentially progressive forms of conspiracism, the cultural studies approach at times can end up downplaying or ignoring the nonsensical and harmful kinds. In the afterword to his study, Fenster (1999) discusses the work of Fiske (1994), who advocated taking an agnostic stance when confronted with the seemingly bizarre claims he had heard on a black community radio station about H.I.V./A.I.D.S. being engineered in a U.S. government lab to inflict genocide on African Americans. In Fiske's account, these kinds of claims are rooted in a long history and continuing present of mistreatment, and, as forms of grassroots counterknowledge, conspiracy theories embody a potentially radical challenge to the status quo. In contrast, Fenster argues more cautiously that conspiracy theories are neither inherently reactionary nor inherently radical (as some writers had begun to suggest in the heady countercultural political atmosphere of the early 1970s). Instead, they can be articulated to political projects both good and bad, although Fenster ultimately concludes that they are indeed more often than not associated with reactionary political causes, as in the case of Timothy McVeigh, the white supremacist who blew up the Oklahoma City federal building in 1994.

## Literary studies

In addition to the general issues raised by the revisionist take of cultural studies, literary criticism has been interested in three aspects of conspiracy theories in particular. First, the tools of narratology have been brought to bear on the style, function and content of conspiracy theories. Second, literary critics have focused on the fascination with ideas of conspiracy in specific historical periods (e.g. post-war U.S. literature), genres (e.g. the popular thriller) and authors (e.g. Charles Brockden Brown). Although American literature is the primary focus, scholars have begun to investigate other literary traditions. And, third, there are suggestive parallels between conspiracist modes of interpretation and the work of ideological critique itself.

Conspiracism appears in both factual and fictional narratives (and some of the latter have focused on how conspiracy theories can lead to an erosion of a clear distinction between the two). Conspiracy theories have not been limited to a particular genre, but instead have appeared in a wide variety of different modes, including sermons, political speeches, pamphlets, history books, essays, radio addresses, congressional debates and confessional tales by renegades in earlier periods, and, more recently, in literary and popular novels, films, television shows, video documentaries, articles that circulate on the Internet and in lengthy tomes dense with footnotes. In American culture, prior to the twentieth century, most conspiracy narratives tended to be promoted in factual genres.

Although both factual and fictional versions share many qualities, it is important to distinguish between discursive and dramatising narratives. Discursive texts 'expose an alleged conspiracy by gathering and presenting evidence that is supposed to convince readers that a dangerous conspiracy exists', whereas fictional texts dramatise their conspiracy scenarios and usually provide an imaginative point of connection (Butter 2014: 25–7). In the U.S. context, discursive narratives usually follow well-trodden paths, but dramatising narratives have evolved significantly over time. Boltanski (2014), for example, argues that detective and conspiracy fiction emerges in the late nineteenth century in reaction to the rise of the modern bureaucratic state and its structural logic of secrecy and panoptic knowledge. Instead of merely representing the supposed conspiracy and its on-going cover-up, modern fictional conspiracy theory texts tend to encourage their readers to identify with an individual character, usually a lone, heroic detective figure. 'Reading for the plot' (Brooks 1984) in conspiracy fiction therefore often involves dual narrative impulses. On the one hand, we follow the story of the ordinary citizen or the maverick outsider forwards in time as s/he discovers that everything is not as it seems and begins chasing down the clues. On the other, that detective surrogate pieces together the narrative of how the conspiracy has developed, a story that often works its way backwards in time to find the ultimate origin of the evil plot. With its narrative focus on detective work, amid conditions of radical uncertainty, conspiracy fiction – especially in its late twentieth-century incarnation – often thematises questions of knowledge: What counts as proof? Who can you trust? Are appearances deceptive? Am I paranoid, or are 'They' making me think that I'm paranoid? This latter question, for example, represents the infinite regress of scepticism encountered by Oedipa Maas, the housewife-turned-detective protagonist in Thomas Pynchon's postmodernist conspiracy novella, *The Crying of Lot 49* (1966). In contrast, a television drama like *House of Cards* eschews a narrative framing device of detection, and instead focuses obsessively on the 'reality' of the insider conspiracy (on the shift from epistemological to ontological forms of conspiracy culture, see Jones and Soderlund 2017).

Literary criticism has thus begun to develop accounts of the typical narrative features of both discursive and dramatising conspiracy theories. Fenster (1999), for example, identifies three elements that are common to conspiracy narratives: Their 'narrative speed' and 'velocity' (high-paced action that zips around the world at an increasing pace); the importance of 'narrative pivots' (the moment when the protagonist begins to connect the dots); and the restoration of agency (either with the publication of the factual account, or, in fictional versions, the imaginary defeat of the conspiracy by the hero). Or, we might instead point to the centrality of the 'republican jeremiad' (Butter 2014: 32–67) in American conspiracy narratives, the conviction that unveiling and combatting an evil conspiracy will restore the U.S.A. to its divine mission. Although some combinations of these aspects are visible in many conspiracy narratives (most notably in Hollywood thrillers), they are not universal – especially so in factual forms of conspiracism from before the twentieth century, and in other cultures.

The theme of conspiracy – and its associated problems of epistemology, agency and causality – are central concerns in some of the most prominent post-war American writers, including Kathy Acker, William S. Burroughs, Don DeLillo, Philip K. Dick, William Gibson, Joseph Heller, Diane Johnson, Ken Kesey, Norman Mailer, Thomas Pynchon and Ishmael Reed. What distinguishes this writing is that it is reflective about the problem of 'paranoia' (in the sense of a mode of interpreting the world), even to the extent of self-consciously using that diagnostic terminology as it explores the creative and countercultural possibilities of conspiracy theory (see Chapter 4.4). Critics such as Tanner (1971), Melley (2000), Knight (2000), O'Donnell (2000) and Coale (2005) have considered how

> there is an abiding dream in American literature that an unpatterned, unconditioned life is possible, in which your movements and your stillnesses, choices and repudiations are all your own; and that there is also an abiding American dread that someone else is patterning your life, that there are all sorts of invisible plots afoot to rob you of your autonomy of thought and action, that conditioning is ubiquitous.
>
> *(Tanner 1971: 15)*

Earlier periods of American literature, although as rich in conspiracy theories as postmodernity, have received less scholarly attention, but there are some notable exceptions. Levine (1989) demonstrates the pervasiveness of the most important conspiracy theories of the early republican and antebellum periods through the works of Charles Brockden Brown, James Fenimore Cooper, Nathaniel Hawthorne and Herman Melville, and explicitly challenges Hofstadter's conceptualisation of conspiracy theory as paranoia from the fringes. The same holds true for Butter (2014), whose readings of Hawthorne, Melville and George Lippard show how nineteenth-century texts often affirm popular conspiracy theories while simultaneously challenging their assumptions as well. A slightly different take on the topic informs an important essay by White. Clearly influenced by the studies by Fenster, Knight and Melley, he argues that eighteenth-century conspiracy theories constituted a reasonable response to the challenges 'to late colonial modernity, offering a model of structural analysis from within' (2002: 26). His attempt to link the literature of earlier centuries to that of the present is continued by Wisnicki (2008), who discusses both British Victorian and American postmodernist fiction, arguing that there is a development from conspiracy narratives that dramatise plots to conspiracy theory narratives that self-reflexively ponder the possible existence of such plots.

Wisnicki's study stands out because it discusses more than one period and assumes an explicitly transnational approach. In general, articulation of conspiracy (theory) in European literature remains under-researched. Work published so far focuses on single texts or periods and hardly ever traces diachronic developments or considers the multiple entanglements of different national literatures. The genre that has arguably been best researched is the German *Geheimbundroman* or secret society novel (Voges 1987; Robert 2013), while the Victorian age is the period whose conspiracy literature has been most fully explored (Pionke 2004; Wisnicki 2008). Carver (2017) has built on these studies and, with special emphasis on invasion narratives, extends their focus into the early twentieth century. The two most ambitious studies of the European literary imagination of conspiracy are Klausnitzer (2007) and Ziolkowski (2013). Klausnitzer not only discusses literary works by Goethe, Schiller and Tieck. His book is also a thorough analysis of the intellectual discourses and media transformations of the *Sattelzeit*, which made conspiracy theories, as he argues, widespread and normal. Ziolkowski offers a far more sweeping account that traces fictional representations of secret societies and conspiracies from antiquity to the present.

Literary studies has also been interested in the self-reflexive meditations on paranoia in postmodernist texts because of the parallels between critical and conspiratorial modes of reading. In essays on Pynchon's *Gravity's Rainbow* and Umberto Eco's *Foucault's Pendulum*, McHale (1992) develops an argument about what he terms 'meta-paranoia'. Modernist texts invite paranoid readings, he argues, because they encourage readers to discover secret analogies between events, hidden significances, concealed allusions and so on. After 'the New Critical institutionalization of Modernism', he continues, 'paranoid reading comes to be taken for granted, assumed to be *the* appropriate norm of reading' (McHale 1992: 61–86, 87–114, 165–87). What is the reader then to make of '*post*modernist texts', McHale wonders, 'which assume and anticipate paranoid reading-habits on the part of their readers', with their representation and thematisation of paranoid reading in the form of conspiracy theories? McHale advocates the idea of meta-paranoia, which would involve 'some form of paranoiacally sceptical reading *of* those paranoid structures' that make up a book like *Gravity's Rainbow*.

In contrast, theorists such as Sedgwick (2003), Best and Marcus (2009) and Felski (2015) have argued that we need to move away from 'paranoid' modes of reading. Ricoeur (1970) influentially identified the 'hermeneutics of suspicion' as the driving force behind the tradition of critique that begins with Marx, Nietzsche and Freud in the nineteenth century, who (respectively) sought to reveal the hidden economic, moral and psychological forces that govern human behaviour and the unfolding of history. This tradition of critique starts from the assumption that 'a text's truest meaning lies in what it does not say, describes textual surfaces as superfluous, and seeks to unmask hidden meanings' (Best, Marcus 2009: 3). Suspicion is thus 'a distinctively modern style of interpretation that circumvents obvious or self-evident meanings in order to draw out less visible and less flattering truths' (Ricoeur 1970: 356). In contrast, Sedgwick (2003), thinking in part of the rise of blatant right-wing violence and the erosion of civil liberties legitimised through the scaremongering tactics of the War on Terror in the early 2000s, argued that 'paranoid' reading is not necessary. 'In a world where no one need be delusional to find evidence of systematic oppression', Sedgwick warns, 'to theorize out of anything but a paranoid critical stance has come to seem naïve or complaisant' (2003: 125–6). The idea is that we no longer need a rarified form of ideological detective work to uncover abuses of power that scarcely have to conceal themselves.

Likewise, Latour (2004) suggests that politically progressive forms of critique have run out of steam because populist conspiracy theories have adopted the language of unmasking hidden realities for their own – frequently reactionary and right-wing – purposes. Left-leaning laments for the death of critique in effect are based on a historical argument (not entirely accurate, as we have seen) that conspiracism is now (once again) firmly associated with right-wing demagoguery rather than the countercultural radicalism of figures like Burroughs and Pynchon. For Ngai (2009), both critique and conspiracy theory (as instantiated in the political thriller) are problematic because they rely on a distinct and outmoded form of masculine interpretation. In works of ideological critique such as Jameson's, she argues, 'the male conspiracy theorist seems to have become an exemplary model for the late twentieth-century theorist in general, and conspiracy theory a viable synecdoche for "theory" itself' (2009: 299).

There have been various suggestions for what should take the place of 'paranoid' reading. Where Sedgwick (2003) called broadly for a return to more 'reparative' modes of reading (that could nevertheless still serve progressive political ends), Best and Marcus (2009) advocate for 'surface reading' that pays attention to the aesthetic forms and materiality of the text, and the affect it produces in readers. These versions of 'postcritique' (Felski 2015) do not entirely reject the tradition of critique, but they do call into question the sometimes uncomfortably close affinities between literary criticism and conspiracy theory. As Freud put it in his musings about the similarities between the work of the scientist-analyst and the paranoid: 'the delusions of patients appear to me to be the equivalents of the constructions which we build up in the course of analytic treatment' (1937: 268).

## Conclusion

The research on conspiracy theories in historical, cultural and literary studies puts a spotlight on difference. Whereas other disciplines that contribute to conspiracy theory studies hold that similar – if not strictly identical – psychological and social factors drive belief in conspiracy theories everywhere and in all times, the studies discussed in this chapter show that conspiracy theories can assume many different forms, and their functions, knowledge status and plausibility can differ widely. However, the picture they paint is still very incomplete. This is most obvious in historiography where a far more sustained engagement with conspiracy theories is direly needed. There are still many countries and periods that have not been researched at all with regard to conspiracy theories, while others remain largely unresearched. We know basically nothing about the history of conspiracy theories outside of Europe and North America. There are, for example, no studies about Asia before the contact with the European powers or about the Arab world in past centuries. Thus, one of the most fundamental questions of conspiracy theories studies remains unresolved: Are conspiracy theories an anthropological given, or did they emerge in Europe at a certain point in the past and were then 'exported' to the rest of the world (Zwierlein 2013)?

Literary and especially cultural studies need to overcome their predominant focus on the U.S.A. Such a shift of perspective might finally do away with the remnants of American exceptionalism that still linger in conspiracy theory research. Moreover, increased attention to the literary and filmic engagements with plots and schemes in Europe and beyond might in turn pave the way for a truly transnational and comparative turn in the engagement with conspiracy theory. Books such as Griffin's monograph (2004) on anti-Catholic conspiracy theories in both England and the U.S.A. should be the rule and not an exception.

Finally, cultural and literary studies should not only consider 'interesting' – that is, complex and self-reflexive – treatments of conspiracy theory. Potboilers and B-movies also possess specific aesthetics that are worthy of scholarly attention. In that vein, research should also be more attentive to the impact of fictional representations of conspiracy on both allegedly factual accounts and the consumers of such fictions. While it is common knowledge that one of the most notorious conspiracy text of all times, The Protocols of the Elders of Zion, is a forgery, it is less well-known that the text is in large parts a plagiarism of a nineteenth-century German novel (Hagemeister, Horn 2012). Moreover, scholars cannot entirely rule out the possibility that the Protocols was originally intended as a satire of anti-Jesuit conspiracy theories, and thus clearly as fiction (Gregory 2012). Similarly, much of what can be found in conspiracy theories about the Illuminati on the Internet today can be traced back to Robert Shea and Robert Anton Wilson's Illuminatus! Trilogy, a satirical treatment of conspiracy theories (Porter 2005). Finally, even conspiracy texts that circulate as fictional can have real consequences. Timothy McVeigh, for instance, the Oklahoma bomber, was heavily influenced by the conspiracist novel The Turner Diaries. Thus, the role of fiction in driving belief in conspiracy theories and, at times, violent actions would be another fruitful avenue for future research.

## References

Bailyn, B. (ed.) (1965) *Pamphlets of the American Revolution, 1750–1776*, Cambridge, MA: Harvard University Press.
Bailyn, B. (1967) *The ideological origins of the American Revolution*, Cambridge: Belknap Press of Harvard University Press.
Barkun, M. (2003) *A culture of conspiracy: apocalyptic visions in contemporary America*, Berkeley, CA: University of California Press.
Beard, C.A. (1936) *The devil theory of war*, New York: Vanguard Press.
Best, S. and Marcus S. (2009) 'Surface reading: an introduction', *Representations* 108(1): 1–21.
Birchall, C. (2006) *Knowledge goes pop: from conspiracy theory to gossip*, New York: Berg.
Boltanski, L. (2014) *Mysteries and conspiracies: detective stories, spy novels and the making of modern societies*, Cambridge: Polity Press.
Bratich, J.Z. (2008) *Conspiracy panics: political rationality and popular culture*, Albany, NY: State of New York University Press.
Brogan, H. (1986) *The Penguin history of the United States of America*, London: Penguin.
Brooks, P. (1984) *Reading for the plot: design and intention in narrative*, Cambridge: Harvard University Press.
Butter, M. (2014) *Plots, designs, and schemes: American conspiracy theories from the Puritans to the present*, Berlin/Boston: de Gruyter.
Butter, M. (2020) *The nature of conspiracy theories*, London: Polity.
Carver, B. (2017) *Alternate histories and nineteenth-century literature*, Palgrave Studies in Nineteenth-Century Writing and Literature, Basingstoke, UK: Palgrave Macmillan.
Caumanns, U. and Niendorf, M. (ed.) (2001) *Verschwörungstheorien: anthropologische Konstanten – historische Varianten*, Einzelveröffentlichung des Deutschen Historischen Instituts Warschau 6, Osnabrück: fibre.
Coale, S.C. (2005) *Paradigms of paranoia: the culture of conspiracy in contemporary American fiction*, Tuscaloosa, AL: University of Alabama Press.
Cochin, A. (1909) *La crise de l'histoire révolutionnaire: Taine et M. Aulard*, Paris: Honoré Champion.

Coward, B. and Swann, J. (ed.) (2004) *Conspiracies and conspiracy theory in early modern Europe: from the Waldensians to the French Revolution*, Farnham, UK: Ashgate.
Cubitt, G. (1989) 'Conspiracy myths and conspiracy theories', *Journal of the Anthropological Society of Oxford*, 20(1): 12–26.
Cubitt, G. (1993) *The Jesuit myth: conspiracy theory and politics in nineteenth-century France*, Oxford, UK: Clarendon Press.
D'Souza, D. (1995) *The end of racism: principles for a multiracial society*, New York: The Free Press.
Davis, D.B. (1969) *The slave power conspiracy and the paranoid style*, Walter Lynwood Fleming Lectures in Southern History, Baton Rouge, LA: Louisiana State University Press.
Dean, J. (1998) *Aliens in America: conspiracy cultures from outerspace to cyberspace*, Ithaca, NY: Cornell University Press.
Felski, R. (2015) *The limits of critique*, Chicago: University of Chicago Press.
Fenster, M. (1999) *Conspiracy theories: secrecy and power in American culture*, rev. and upd. edn, 2008, Minneapolis, MN: University of Minnesota Press.
Fiske, J. (1994) 'Blackstream knowledge: genocide', in J. Fiske (ed.) *Media matters: everyday culture and political change*, Minneapolis: University of Minnesota Press, pp. 191–216.
Fraser, G. (2018) 'Conspiracy, pornography, democracy: the recurrent aesthetics of the American Illuminati', *Journal of American Studies*, November: 1–22.
Freud, S. (1937) 'Constructions in analysis', in J. Strachey (ed. and trans.) *Vol. 23 of the standard edition of the complete psychological works of Sigmund Freud*, London: Hogarth, pp. 1953–74.
Girard, P. (2008) 'Conspiracies and visions of conspiracies in France and Italy after the Second World War', *European Review of History*, 15(6): 749–65.
Gray, M. (2010) *Conspiracy theories in the Arab world*, New York: Routledge.
Gregory, S. (2012) 'Die Fabrik der Fiktionen: Verschwörungsproduktionen um 1800', in E. Horn and M. Hagemeister (eds.) *Die Fiktion von der jüdischen Weltverschwörung: zu Text und Kontext der 'Protokolle der Weisen von Zion'*, Göttingen: Wallstein, pp. 51–75.
Griffin, S.M. (2004) *Anti-catholicism and nineteenth-century fiction*, Cambridge: Cambridge University Press.
Hagemeister, M. and Horn, E. (eds.) (2012) *Die Fiktion von der jüdischen Weltverschwörung; zu Text und Kontext der 'Protokolle der Weisen von Zion'*, Göttingen: Wallenstein.
Harambam, J. (2017) *'The Truth Is Out There': conspiracy culture in an age of epistemic instability*, unpublished PhD thesis, Erasmus University Rotterdam.
Harambam, J. and Aupers, S. (2015) 'Contesting epistemic authority: conspiracy theories on the boundary of science', *Public Understanding of Science*, 24(4): 466–80.
Hof, T. (2013) 'The Moro Affair – left-wing terrorism and conspiracy in Italy in the late 1970s', *Historical Social Research/Historische Sozialforschung*, 38(1/143): 232–56.
Hofstadter, R. (1964) *The paranoid style in American politics, and other essays*, Cambridge, MA: Harvard University Press.
Jameson, F. (1988) 'Cognitive mapping', in C. Nelson and L. Grossberg (eds.) *Marxism and the Interpretation of Culture*, Basingstoke: Macmillan, pp. 347–58.
Jones, P. and Soderlund, G. (2017) 'The conspiratorial mode in American television: politics, public relations, and journalism in *House of Cards* and *Scandal*', *American Quarterly*, 69(4): 833–56.
Klausnitzer, R. (2007) *Poesie und Konspiration: Beziehungssinn und Zeichenökonomie von Verschwörungsszenarien in Publizistik, Literatur und Wissenschaft 1750–1850*, Spectrum Literaturwissenschaft 13, Berlin/Boston: de Gruyter.
Knight, P. (2000) *Conspiracy culture: from the Kennedy Assassination to 'The X-Files'*, London: Routledge.
Konda, T.M. (2019) *Conspiracies of conspiracies: how delusions have overrun America*, Chicago: University of Chicago Press.
Latour, B. (2004) 'Why has critique run out of steam? From matters of fact to matters of concern', *Critical Inquiry*, 30: 225–48.
Levine, R.S. (1989) *Conspiracy and romance: studies in Brockden Brown, Cooper, Hawthorne and Melville*, Cambridge Studies in American Literature and Culture 33, Cambridge: Cambridge University Press.
Linton, M., Kaiser, T.E. and Campbell, P.R. (eds.) (2010) *Conspiracy in the French Revolution*, Manchester: Manchester University Press.
McHale, B. (1992) *Constructing postmodernism*, London: Routledge.
McKenzie-McHarg, A. (2019) 'Conspiracy theory: the nineteenth-century prehistory of a twentieth-century concept', in J. Uscinski (ed.) *Conspiracy theories and the people who believe them*, New York, NY: Oxford University Press, pp. 62–81.

Melley, T. (2000) *Empire of conspiracy: the culture of paranoia in postwar America*, Ithaca, NY: Cornell University Press.
Melley, T. (2012) *The covert sphere: secrecy, fiction, and the national security state*, Ithaca: Cornell University Press.
Ngai, S. (2009) *Ugly feelings*, Cambridge, MA: Harvard University Press.
O'Donnell, P. (2000) *Latent destinies: cultural paranoia and contemporary US narrative*, Durham, NC: Duke University Press.
Oberhauser, C. (2013) *Die Verschwörungstheoretische Trias: Barruel-Robison-Starck*, Innsbruck/Vienna: Studienverlag.
Olmsted, K.S. (2009) *Real enemies: conspiracy theories and American democracy, World War I to 9/11*, Oxford: Oxford University Press.
Pagán, V.E. (2004) *Conspiracy narratives in Roman history*, Austin: University of Texas Press.
Pasley, J.L. (2000) 'Conspiracy theory and American exceptionalism from the Revolution to Roswell', *'Sometimes an Art': a symposium in celebration of Bernard Bailyn's fifty years of teaching and beyond*, Harvard University, New Haven, 13 May. Available at: http://pasleybrothers.com/conspiracy/CT_and_American_Exceptionalism_web_version.htm. [Accessed 17 September 2019.]
Pfahl-Traughber, A. (2002) '"Bausteine" zu einer Theorie über "Verschwörungstheorien": Definitionen, Erscheinungsformen, Funktionen und Ursachen', in H. Reinalter (ed.) *Verschwörungstheorien: Theorie – Geschichte – Wirkung*, Innsbruck: StudienVerlag, pp. 30–44.
Pionke, A.D. (2004) *Plots of opportunity: representing conspiracy in Victorian England*, Columbus, OH: Ohio State University Press.
Pipes, D. (1996) *The hidden hand: Middle East fears of conspiracy*, New York: St. Martin's Press.
Pipes, D. (1997) *Conspiracy: how the paranoid style flourishes and where it comes from*, New York: Free Press.
Popper, K. (1950) *The open society and its enemies*, Princeton: Princeton University Press.
Porter, L. (2005) *Who are the Illuminati?*, Collins & Brow: London: Collins & Brown.
Pynchon, T. (1966) *The crying of lot 49*, New York: Bantam.
Reinalter, H. (ed.) (2002) *Verschwörungstheorien: Theorie – Geschichte – Wirkung*, Quellen und Darstellungen zur europäischen Freimaurerei 3, Innsbruck: StudienVerlag.
Richards, L.L. (2000) *The slave power: the free north and southern domination 1780–1860*, Baton Rouge, LA: Louisiana State University Press.
Ricoeur, P. (1970) *Freud and philosophy: an essay on interpretation*, New Haven: Yale UP.
Robert, J. (2013) '"Ein Aggregat von Bruchstücken": Schillers Fragmente als *fermenta cognitionis*', in J. Robert (ed.) *'Ein Aggregat von Bruchstücken': Fragment und Fragmentarismus im Werk Friedrich Schillers*, Würzburg: Königshausen & Neumann.
Robins, R.S. and Post, J.M. (1997) *Political paranoia*, New Haven, CT: Yale University Press.
Rogalla von Bierberstein, J. (1976) *Die These von der Verschwörung 1776–1945: Philosophen, Freimaurer, Juden, Liberale und Sozialisten als Verschwörer gegen die Sozialordnung*, Frankfurt am Main: Lang.
Rogin, M.P. (1987) *Ronald Reagan, the movie and other episodes in political demonology*, Berkeley, CA: University of California Press.
Roisman, J. (2006) *The rhetoric of conspiracy in ancient Athens*, Berkeley, CA: University of California Press.
Sedgwick, E.K. (2003) 'Paranoid reading and reparative reading, or, you're so paranoid, you probably think this essay is about you', in E.K. Sedgwick (ed.) *Touching feeling: affect, pedagogy, performativity*, Durham: Duke University Press.
Stauffer, V. (1918) *New England and the Bavarian Illuminati*, New York, NY: Columbia University Press.
Tackett, T. (2000) 'Conspiracy obsession in a time of revolution: French elites and the origins of the terror, 1789–1792', *American Historical Review*, 105(3): 691–713.
Tanner, T. (1971) *City of words: American fiction 1950–1970*, London: Jonathan Cape.
Thalmann, K. (2019) *The stigmatization of conspiracy theory since the 1950s: 'A Plot to Make Us Look Foolish'*, London: Routledge.
Turner, P. (1993) *I heard it through the grapevine: rumor in African-American experience*, Berkeley, CA: University of California Press.
Voges, M. (1987) *Aufklärung und Geheimnis: Untersuchungen zur Vermittlung von Literatur- und Sozialgeschichte am Beispiel der Aneignung des Geheimbundmaterials im Roman des späten 18. Jahrhunderts*, Tübingen: Niemeyer.
Washington, H. (2006) *Medical apartheid: the dark history of medical experimentation on black Americans from colonial times to the present*, New York: Doubleday.
White, E. (2002) 'The Value of Conspiracy Theory', *American Literary History*, 14(1): 1–31.

Wisnicki, A.S. (2008) *Conspiracy, revolution, and terrorism from Victorian fiction to the modern novel*, Literary Criticism and Cultural Theory, London/New York: Routledge.

Wood, G.S. (1982) 'Conspiracy and the paranoid style: causality and deceit in the eighteenth century', *The William and Mary Quarterly*, 39(3): 402–41.

Ziolkowski, T. (2013) *Lure of the Arcane: the literature of cult and conspiracy*, Baltimore, MD: Johns Hopkins University Press.

Zwierlein, C. (2013) 'Security politics and conspiracy theories in the emerging European state system (15th/16th c.)', *Historical Social Research/Historische Sozialforschung*, 38(1/143): 66–95.

## 1.3

# SEMIOTIC APPROACHES TO CONSPIRACY THEORIES[1]

*Massimo Leone, Mari-Liis Madisson and Andreas Ventsel*

### Introduction

Especially after Donald Trump's presidential campaign and the Brexit referendum, public awareness of the power of viral conspiracy theories and their relationship to misinformation and fake news has risen significantly. It is thus appropriate to recall a definition of semiotics by Umberto Eco:

> semiotics is in principle the discipline studying everything which can be used in order to lie. If something cannot be used to tell a lie, conversely it cannot be used to tell the truth: it cannot in fact be used 'to tell' at all.
>
> *(Eco 1976: 7)*

Indeed, acknowledging the fundamental conventionality of sign processes and the accompanying possibility of lying and error are part of the core principles of the semiotic approach. Thus, a prominent purpose of semiotics is to analyse the success and failure of communication.

Semiotics developed into an independent discipline in the 1950s. Its research objects are the sign, sign relation and sign process. Although the notion of sign was already dealt with in antiquity (with the Stoics; Saint Augustine), the Middle Ages and early modernity (i.e. the problem of universals in scholasticism; John Locke), developments in structural linguistics, information theory, cybernetics and logic in the early twentieth century became the conditions for the emergence of semiotics as a discipline. Traditionally, semiotics is divided into two main currents, which are characterised by their fundamental difference in conceptualising the sign: The semiotics of Charles Sanders Peirce and Charles W. Morris on the one hand, and the semiology of Ferdinand de Saussure on the other. This division reflects, to a certain extent, the disciplines most important to the development of semiotics and is further supported by the fact that Saussure's approach was popular in Europe (especially in France), while Peirce's was popular in the U.S.A.

Peirce represents a philosophically and logically informed approach, one that understands the sign as triadic and emphasises the importance of the sign process. He conceptualises the sign as a relation between the representamen (for example, the word 'conspiracy'), the object or reference (the general meaning of the word 'conspiracy' that is necessary for the communicability of the sign) and the interpretant or the meaning evoked in the interpreter (the concrete meaning of the word 'conspiracy' depends on whether the latter's existence is presupposed or not). These relations are modified in the actual process of semiosis: The interpretation of the receiver becomes, for a second receiver, a sign that in turn evokes an interpretant, etc. The purpose of semiotics is to analyse, first, the relations forming the sign process and, second, the problems emerging from interpreting the three aspects of the sign.

Saussurean semiology conceptualises the sign as an intrasystemic arbitrary correlate between the signifier (for example, the word 'conspiracy') and the signified (conspiracy as an idea or mental concept). The concrete meaning of the sign emerges from the systemic relations to other signs and to the rules of association of signs. The meaning of the word 'conspiracy' depends on how it relates to other words in the same system, i.e. on the word's value within the system.

Although the two traditions differ in their understanding of the sign, they share a common purpose – to study not so much the perceived phenomenon itself but its meaning. In view of the fact that conspiracy theories are inherently semiotic phenomena (as they are always mediated via signs), it is surprising that relatively few studies concentrate on the semiotic explanation of conspiracy theories. Meaning-making in conspiracy theories is largely based on the search for secret signs of conspiracy and on demonstrating the significance of these signs. From the semiotic perspective, conspiracy theory is defined as a representation that explains a series of events by postulating a conspiracy as its cause; that is, the events are seen as 'the result of a group of people acting in secret to a nefarious end' (Birchall 2006: 216–7). In the preface of the special issue of semiotic journal *Lexia* dedicated to conspiracy theories (23–4, 2016), Massimo Leone argues that:

> If the work of semioticians on conspiracy theories has a purpose whatsoever, it is not that of indicating, from a supposedly superior vantage point, who is right and who is wrong, who is conspiring and who is not, who is creating a fake conspiracy theory and who is unveiling a dangerous social secret. The purpose of semiotics is, rather, that of indicating the discursive conditions that encourage the proliferation of such conspiratorial or anti–conspiratorial thinking, and simultaneously also the more difficult purpose of suggesting how to reframe conflict in a different discursive framework, one that does not simply create rhetorical conflict but casts the basis for social action.
> 
> *(Leone 2016: 15)*

Generally speaking, the main focus of semiotics consists in explaining sign-based models that people construct for mapping reality; in most cases, they tend to be simplifying (Madisson 2016a). Thus, the semiotic approach can neither determine whether a conspiracy exists nor evaluate the adequacy and validity of a conspiracy theory. It does not appraise either whether conspiracy theories are a beneficial or a harmful cultural phenomenon; it rather concentrates on the specific processes of meaning-making that are related to conspiracy theories.

The semiotic point of view differentiates between three interrelated levels in analysing conspiracy theories. The first relates to modelling through a specific filter of interpretation that presupposes the existence of a conspiracy. Analysing this level enables us to ascertain the mechanisms of conspiracist semiosis. The second level concentrates on conspiracy theories as verbal and/or visual representations – conspiracy theories are analysed as a text with its own specific boundaries. This second level is also closely related to specific audiences and to communicational situations to which the representations of conspiracies are targeted. Receivers here construct certain meta-level interpretations, or, in other words, interpretations of a conspiracy theory. The third level concentrates on analysing the identity construction and self-description of publics that are affected by conspiracy theories.

The present chapter concentrates on these three levels: First, we describe the main characteristics of conspiracist semiosis; second, we deal with the semiotic study of representations of conspiracies; and, third, we question how semiotics could be useful in elucidating mechanisms of identity construction in the context of conspiracy theories. At the end of this section, we briefly outline some directions for future research.

## Main characteristics of conspiracist semiosis

The conditions under which contemporary conspiracist thinking proliferates are complex. The major disruptions of the labour market and massive unemployment caused by economic crises, the unprecedented reconfiguration of social and communicative relations though the rapid evolution of digital media and the consequent shifting of political models cause a myriad of ideological contrapositions that feed, in their turn, the various levels and meta-levels of conspiracist thought.

It can thus be said that one of the main causes for the currency of conspiracy theories is the fear and confusion accompanying contemporary socio-cultural upheavals. In contemporary society, fear has become one of the most effective mobilising emotions (Bauman 2006; Castells 2009) and the media-fuelled proliferation of irrational fears is a powerful force undermining the capacity to critically assess the social world. The Tartu-Moscow school of cultural semiotics conceptualises the semiotic construction of conspiracy theories in relation to fear. Doing so, it elaborates both a semiotic approach to conspiracy theory and a semiotics of fear.

From the semiotic point of view, fear does not result from an actual horrifying event/object but from the fact that some elements of reality are interpreted as fearful omens and warning signs. Juri Lotman stresses that fear is not always triggered by danger, but, on the contrary, fear often pre-emptively triggers danger. The object of fear, indeed, is socially constructed through the semiotic codes that a collectivity adopts for modelling itself and the world (Lotman 1998). The dynamic of fear, thus, is inherently semiotic. The time lapse between the immediate experience of the object of fear and the interpretation of it allows meaning-making processes to intensify (M. Lotman 2009: 210).

Conspiracy theories are central epiphenomena of this kind of meaning-making in the context of an atmosphere of fear (M. Lotman 2009: 211). Conspiracy theories function as meaning-making templates, originating from cultural memory. They are instrumental in construing the danger of a certain tendency or event and in connecting it with historical scars as well as with horrific future scenarios.

The semiotic process that explains the emergence of fear and conspiracy theories is that of communion. The language of fear – and, consequently, the logic of conspiracy theories – is based upon communion in two forms. First, there is the penetrating contact, upon which the interacting subjects/objects enter into each other. As a result of this process, one party becomes branded with the traces of the other. Communion via penetrating contact thus functions according to the metonymic logic of contiguity – it suffices simply that one is present near the source of evil in order to be affected by it. The second form of communion is based on similarity – the more similar the objects, the more they are perceived to be connected. According to M. Lotman, then, conspiracy theories are characterised by both the metonymic logic of penetrating contact and the metaphoric logic based on similarity (2009: 1239).

When dealing with conspiracy theories, it is important to note that the opacity of reference plays a much larger role in cultural phobias than in individual ones. Reference is often very intense – while we cannot put our finger on why something is dangerous, we are nevertheless certain that it must be destroyed. Although the signs of natural languages are provided with strong reference by the sign's concrete meaning, the logic of fear is exactly the opposite. The most general and vague fears actively search for potential referents; individuals who are obsessed with conspiracies will no doubt find them, for example, in the visual representations of Coca-Cola, but also in geometrical shapes of any kind (M. Lotman 2009: 1244).

This type of semiosis, which is based on analogies unintelligible to outsiders, is explicated by Umberto Eco (1990) through the concepts of paranoid interpretation and hermetic semiosis. In this type of semiosis, every time that a new analogy is discovered, it brings about, in turn, a new analogy, and so on and so forth ad infinitum. The loose criterion of similarity established in hermetic semiosis gives rise to the assumption that the function of a sign consists in signifying a hidden meaning (Eco 1990: 163–6). Hence one important principle of hermetic semiosis: When two things are similar, the former is a sign of the latter and vice versa (Eco 1990: 164).

For example, conspiracy theorists tend to disagree with the media coverage of various shocking events for they, the conspiracy theorists, believe that journalists are using such events as a smoke screen to distract public attention and keep it occupied with 'pseudo-topics' while conspirators perform their evil deeds undisturbed. Nevertheless, that does not mean that conspiracy theorists are not interested in media. On the contrary, they often work through numerous visual and verbal narratives, enabling them to prove that there are paradoxes and contradictions in the official versions of events, because conspiracy theorists sometimes presume that the conspirators make mistakes and leave compromising traces that prove the existence of the conspiracy itself. Thus, they carefully examine media content in order to find interpretative keys that disclose hidden meanings.

Mark Fenster also points out that a conspiracy theorist sees even trivial everyday events as signs of manipulation by conspiring forces. Fenster outlines that conspiracy theories function as 'a form of hyperactive semiosis in which history and politics serve as reservoirs of signs that demand (over)interpretation, and that signify, for the interpreter, far more than their conventional meaning' (Fenster 2008: 95). Fenster, however, also underlines that such interpretative practices may be paradoxical but are not pathologically paranoiac, for they reflect their specific social and political conditions (Fenster 2008: 101).

Eco's theory of interpretation is also the point of departure of Massimo Leone's long essay 'Double Debunking: Modern Divination and the End of Semiotics' (2015), which compares present-day conspiracist thought with ancient divination and underlines the role of semiotics in providing a framework of reasonableness for both the debunking of unsubstantiated persuasion and the parallel debunking of conspiracy theories. In another article, 'Fundamentalism, Anomie, Conspiracy: Umberto Eco's Semiotics against Interpretive Irrationality' (2017), the same author claims that the issue of determining the role and effect of conspiracy theories in society comes down to the need of differentiating between critical and conspiracy theories, between deconstructive and conspiracy hermeneutics. Nevertheless, Leone contends, such distinction cannot be made in terms of contents; it must be made in terms of argumentative patterns. Conspiracy theories do not show their nature in what they say, but in how they say it, in the specific rhetoric that they adopt in order to communicate an aura of secrecy, create a symbolic elite, and reproduce the separation between insiders and outsiders. Here, according to Leone (2017), lies the main role of semiotics: Singling out the rhetorical and argumentative lines though which conspiracy theories are created and maintained in the social imaginary.

Building on this, Leone (2018a) has started to develop a semiotic reading of the traditional philosophical and social concept of 'common sense', arguing that conspiracy theories are disruptive of this important framework of public discourse. That which is usually called 'common sense' is nothing but the complex deposit of implicit cognitive, pragmatic and emotional rules through which the members of a society interact with each other and, simultaneously, affirm their belonging to the group. This sense is called 'common' both because it is current – meaning that it permeates the daily life of the group in all its manifestations – and because it is shared: It is something that belongs to the community as a whole and something through which, at the same time, the members of the community can belong. Proliferation of conspiracist discourse in a society creates micro-areas of shared meaning that are impermeable and in conflict with each other, and give rise, thus, to a fragile mismatching between a political community and its semiosphere of shared conversation. A key contribution of semiotics in this domain, then, is to provide insights on the formation of reasonable interpretations, as opposed to the unreasonable ones of conspiracy theories. Leone (2018b) inquires about the difference between interpreting in natural sciences and interpreting in the humanities. Despite evident and known divergences, humanities, too, can rank their interpretations and aspire to guide the interpretations of society. Three alternative methods can be used to test interpretive hypotheses, depending on whether the author's, the reader's or the text's meaningful intentionality is primarily investigated. The third method is superior to the first two since it leads to the creation of a common meta-discursive space for inter-subjective exchange about meaning. Although adopting an appropriate methodology is essential in textual analysis, that which is even more important is supporting the creation of a community of interpreters that, sharing the same method, engage in the constructive comparison and ranking of interpretive moves. The patient construction of this community of reasonable interpreters is the best antidote to divisive and conflictive conspiracy theories.

## Code-text as a unifying mechanism of conspiracist semiosis

Along the same line, Mari-Liis Madisson's work conceptualises conspiracy theories as a specific way of semiotic modelling, mostly relying on the theoretical frameworks of the Tartu-Moscow school of cultural semiotics and on Umberto Eco's ideas. A central aim of Madisson's works consists in demonstrating that conspiracy theories are dominated by mythological modelling, which plays an essential role in how they produce homomorphic resemblance. Mythological modelling, otherwise prevalent in pre-literary, oral cultures, gains ground in contemporary times under the conditions of social stress and fear (Lotman 1988a). According to Juri Lotman and Boris Uspenskij, mythological modelling is characterised by its focus on the sacral order, contained in a trans-cultural meta-text. This meta-text functions as a universal precedent, an invariant from which all the variants that comprise the world as perceived by mythological consciousness are derived (Lotman, Uspenskij 1978: 211). The authors indicate that clear examples of those meta-texts cannot be found in contemporary culture, for they were characteristic of archaic communities where they, along with rituals, formed a basis of the belief-system of archaic communities (Lotman, Uspenskii 1975: 24). Mythological modelling transforms the perception of present events to the extent that the interpreter can recognise, behind them, the original forms of the meta-text that has its source in cultural memory. Mythological modelling of contemporary conspiracy theories is not so intense and clear-cut as the one in archaic communities, but it still organises a specific kind of meaning-making that does not perceive events as a coincidence of tragic contingencies, but instead as motivated by one and the same original cause: Evil.

The model of mythological semiosis makes it possible to analyse how conspiracy theoretical meaning-making mixes together ideologies from disparate political movements, ideologies that are often contradictory. Les Back has developed the concept of 'liquid ideologies' in order to explain how extreme right-wing movements tend to use generally accepted discourses for the purpose of legitimising their own ethno-centric media practices (Back 2002). Although radical right-wing groups express certain continuity with Fascism and Nazism, they are today no longer strictly defined by these historical ideologies. This is due, on the one hand, to the negative general attitude towards Nazism in the post-Second World War period and, on the other, to the transformation of the space of communication and its mechanisms, since online communication is not organised so much from top to bottom, but is horizontal, a characteristic that makes it difficult to consciously control the development of ideologies. Madisson (2014, 2016a) explains this type of logic of connecting discrete elements by conceptualising conspiracy in terms of the code text that functions as a syntagmatically constructed totality, an organised structure of signs that is not expressed indirectly, but is realised as variants in the lower-level texts in the hierarchy of culture (Lotman 1988b: 35). The concept of code text enables us to explicate those situations of meaning-making that cannot be conceptualised according to the analogy mechanism proposed by Eco.

Non-mythological or descriptive types of modelling also play a significant role in conspiracy theories. Conspirers are usually interpreted as an extremely organised group, divided into intricate sub-systems. For example, a study on Facebook Estonian extreme right-wing content demonstrates that people often refer to a widespread systematic conspiracy bringing together cultural Marxists (this label applies to almost all left-wing or liberal public figures), L.G.B.T.Q. activists, Islamists, mainstream political forces and dominant media. The study shows that the coordinated malicious deeds of presumed conspirators are seen as associated with the low birth-rate of white Europeans, facilitating the migrant crisis and terrorism, the 'Islamization' of Europe and the eradication of nation-states (Kasekamp *et al.* 2018: 8). Social events are interpreted in light of overly deterministic models of causation (see Madisson 2014: 296–8).

The co-functioning of mythological and non-mythological types of modelling can be captured through the concept of code-text (Madisson 2016a: 33). The code-text functions as an informational centre that gives a unified meaning to essentially different text-elements, which are initially independent (e.g. minority groups, terrorism, low birth-rates) but are all identified as similar – as a means of intentional damage, manipulated by conspirators. For an external observer, code-text may be both ambivalent and polyvalent, to be divided into a paradigm of equivalent yet different meanings, or again into a system of antonymic oppositions, but for the members of the culture 'the code-text is nevertheless monolithic, compact and unambiguous […] organizing their memories and defining the limits to the possible variations of the text' (Lotman 1988b: 36).

## Conspiracy theories as representations

Semiotics enables the systematic study of interpretations of conspiracies expressed in concrete media – or, in other words, the study of representations – for example, in a written narrative or an audio-visual text. The levels of conspiracist semiosis and representation of conspiracy are, of course, closely related to each other (the former is usually the precondition for the emergence of the latter). It is, however, useful to distinguish them analytically because the latter is characterised by its textual and concrete existence, by a higher level of organisation and by its specific position in the communicative context. This is also the reason why representations of conspiracy are more amenable to research using the methods of textual analysis. In addition, this aspect enables one to explicate cases where the person spreading conspiracy theories is not directly engaged in an active interpretation of a secret plot, but instead has other purposes in propagating those theories, for example, creating an aesthetic experience, persuasion, disinformation, etc. To summarise, the chapter thus far has dealt with the topic of discovering conspiracies and with the logic of connection between elements of conspiracy; the rest of the chapter will focus on the representation of conspiracies, the construction of conspiracy theories and with conspiracy theories as a specific type of text.

From the semiotic perspective, it is noteworthy that, although a conspiracy theory can appear in different contexts and be transmitted via various channels, it nevertheless remains recognisable as a conspiracy theory – as a text sustaining specific connections. The range of media through which conspiracy theories are transmitted is extremely broad: Speech, the printed word, pictorial means of expression (drawings, diagrams, photos), videos and contemporary interactive and hybrid textual compositions combining all of the above. In addition, conspiracy theories are produced in various discourses, from the dominant to the peripheral.

One of the purposes of a semiotic study of conspiracy theories is to explicate the invariant relations or mechanisms of meaning-making that are common to all representations of conspiracy theories. Theoretical tools from cultural semiotics provide an opportunity to systematise disparate studies in various disciplines into a coherent theory of the signifying logic of conspiracy theories. One of these tools is, for example, the opposition of discrete and iconic/continuous modelling (in Lotman's theory, the latter is synonymous with mythological modelling). To generalise, conspiracy theory as a textual type can be classified as narrative (see Birchall 2006; Fenster 2008; Butter 2014), for it depicts actors involved in and events connected to the conspiracy, and for the principal signifying relations in conspiracy theories are those of temporality and causality (in other words, discrete modelling). It is, however, important to note that the causality outlined in conspiracy narratives is characterised by its subordination to the evil will of the conspirators, who are often depicted as being supernaturally powerful (Knight 2002; Campion-Vincent 2007; Madisson 2014, 2017). Representing the past or future damage done by the conspiracies, conspiracy theories sketch analogies (the principal signifying relation of iconic-continuous modelling) to the natural malevolence of secret societies.

As is often the case with theoretical models, mapping conspiracy theory as a textual type can lead to over-simplification and, thus, does not enable one to grasp the detailed nature of both the form and the content of conspiracy theories. This type of study, however, explicates the basic relations at work in conspiracy theories and helps researchers in deciding whether certain concrete representations could and should be regarded as conspiracy theories. As a development to this theory, conspiracy theories could be articulated into typologies mapping the variance of conspiracy theories or the representation of their basic elements (conspirators, nature of the conspiracy, victims of the conspiracy, secondary events related to the conspiracy) on the scale of discrete-non-discrete modelling. Considering conspiracy theory as a textual type could likewise answer the question of the minimal expression of conspiracies or, in other words, attempt to explicate which short textual forms (e.g. tweets, memes, status updates) can be considered conspiracy theories.

In addition to mapping the invariant characteristics of conspiracy theories, semiotics provides us with multi-faceted tools to analyse how the representations of conspiracies are constructed. For instance, frameworks of literary semiotics and narratology (Eco 1979; Genette 1980; Greimas 1983) enable us to explicate the principles of constructing concrete fictional conspiracy narratives (e.g. novels and films), the relations between plot and story, the devices for creating narrative tension and culmination, the motives underpinning the text, the narrator's position in relation to the narrative, textual milieu and tonality, etc. Semiotics regards non-fictional conspiracy narratives commonly as cases of historical (see Fenster 2008: 123) or everyday narratives (e.g. documentaries, news stories, vernacular explanations for events). Thus, the framework of classic semiotic discourse analysis (Eco 1976; Greimas, Courtès 1976; Barthes 1981; 1986) can be used to analyse the position of conspiracy events in historical-geographical and socio-cultural systems, the attribution of agency, the narrator's relation to the narrative, widespread textual tropes, the types of argumentation, ideological sub-texts, etc.

These cases where representations of conspiracy from different genres and textual spheres intermingle and form a specific explanatory whole (see Boym 1999; Cobley 2004; Ponzio 2016) are of special interest to semiotic research. For instance, non-fictional conspiracy narratives sometimes rely on influential fictional conspiracies, e.g. Don DeLillo's *Libra* or Dan Brown's *The Da Vinci Code*. These fictions are inexhaustible sources of analogies and sometimes even function as allegedly prophetic works dealing with real historical events. There have also been cases where novelists weave references to conspiracy theories similar to historical narratives into their works; for example, Umberto Eco's *The Prague Cemetery* clearly refers to the *Protocols of the Elders of Zion* and to theories about the Illuminati. Constructing these kinds of intertextual conspiracy representations has become especially important in the context of the signifying possibilities of hypermedia (adding hyperlinks, simple copying of textual fragments) and of the reference-heavy textual construction norms of participatory culture.

With online media and means of digital expression becoming central to conspiracy narratives, the function of visual and multimodal elements in representations of conspiracy needs to be interrogated. On the one hand, semiotics studies which visual tropes and symbols are used to illustrate conspiracies (for example, the pyramid, the octopus, the puppet master and the marionette are among the most widespread) (Ballinger 2011). On the other hand, the frameworks of semiotics (see Barthes 1977; Kress, van Leeuwen 1996; 2001) explain how conspiracy theories amplify their core ideas via visual modes of expression (e.g. underlining, foregrounding, usage of diagrams and graphs) and, doing this, inject them with emotional valence (see Caumanns 2016; Kimminich 2016; Turco 2016).

Representations of conspiracy are always constructed in view of concrete addressees and communication situations, which is why it is important to analyse how these representations relate to the larger socio-communicative context. The following section deals with the construction of identities via conspiracy theories or, more precisely, with the self-descriptions and auto-communication of conspiracy theorists.

## Conspiracy theories as a mechanism of identity creation

In the Saussurean tradition of semiotics, identity studies are an important field of research. Identity construction is closely connected to sign values. Conspiracy theorists tend to rely on a polarised logic of identification that is dominated by positing an antithetical opposition between 'us' and 'them'. The 'antithetical' model of culture (anti-culture) can be seen as a type of identity creation relegated to the 'inner' point of view of cultures that, imposing a strict principle of normativity (correctness) to their systems of expression, regard deviations in the plane of expression as disruptive of the order of meaning, rather than meaningless. From the point of view of one's own culture, anti-culture is understood as a sign-system that is dangerous to culture (Ventsel 2016a: 315; Ventsel 2016b). When an antithetic *enemy* is created, it is often constructed as a symmetrical copy of *one's own* structures with a minus sign or a mirror projection (Lotman, Uspenskij 1984). Mirror projection is often preceded by plain projection: First, 'our' problems are attributed to 'them'; second, the mirror-projective antithesis is created: 'their' problems are contrasted with the zero marker or absence of problems in 'our' structure (Lepik, 2008: 72). Such a semiotic opposition has a specific function in the constitution of a conspiracy theory as a semiotic unit. It is the dominant component that guarantees the integrity of the structure, 'focuses, rules, determines, and transforms the remaining ones' (Jakobson 1971: 82). These kinds of core structures are often rigidly organised. The villains imagined by conspiracy theorists, be they the NWO, Bilderbergers, the Jews, etc., are all understood as something that needs to be detected and eradicated from the social structure. In many cases, agents/social structures are demonised as evil, as the antithetic enemy of a constructed 'us' (Ventsel 2016a: 325). That is illustrated by the series of polarisations that characterise 'us' and 'them' (enemies): Lightness–darkness, nationalism–cosmopolitanism, prosperity of culture–cultural disaster, honesty–corruption, etc. (ibid., 315–6). Both the concrete articulations of and the degrees of belief in identities construed on the basis of such antithetic oppositions vary in each specific case, but the core opposition is characteristic of different conspiracy theories – as such, the opposition can be understood as making it possible to mark down the boundaries of a new community.

From the semiotic perspective, however, the cases in which conspiracy theories attempt to construct an internal, hidden enemy are perhaps more important. Here it is appropriate to return briefly to the semiotics of fear. Mihhail Lotman stresses, in connection with the atmosphere of fear, that the most intense fear is not directed towards the evidently 'other' but towards the other that presents itself as familiar, as one's own. Although those who are labelled as internal enemies often do not have much in common among themselves – for example, they are radicals from entirely opposing extremes, belong to different social groups, represent different nationalities, etc. – they are nevertheless described with similar or even identical semiotic models and signs. As a result, in socio-cultural environments there exists a semantic invariant for the figure of the enemy that is attributed to specific referents only in concrete situations (M. Lotman 2009).

As regards the causes for this semiotic mechanism, according to Mihhail Lotman, the referent of the sign becomes changeable: 1) when a given semantic set (for example, the Jews) resonates with the deep mechanisms of a given culture, so that the set can be recognised according to the invariant of the archetypal enemy; and 2) when a given culture expresses the need for an enemy, for the place of the referent cannot remain empty (2009: 1228). The search for such an enemy intensifies during social crises; the enemies of contemporary Russia, for instance, (be they the 'Chechen terrorist', the 'Georgian nationalist', the 'Estonian fascist' or the 'American imperialist') are all suspiciously sketched in a similar way – from the semiotic perspective, they all have the complexion of a specifically Russian fear. It can be concluded, thus, that it is not such or such specific event that gives rise to fear; fear, instead, emerges while searching for its own justifications, according to cultural mechanisms that codify the reality of fear in their own likeness (M. Lotman 2009: 1231).

## Autocommunication and self-description of conspiracy theorists

The above section pointed out the ways in which the elements of the opposition 'us' versus 'them' condition each other semiotically. A possibility to study identity construction in depth would consist in focusing on the addresser, that is, on the conspiracy theorists and their self-description. But on what kind of logic is this self-communication built?

Madisson and Ventsel have studied conspiracy theories that circulate on Estonian extreme-right websites. Conspiracy theories function as a basic rhetorical tool for rationalising the extreme right-wing worldview for both the believers and other interpreters. Conspiracy theories allow extreme right-wing authors to translate their feelings of intolerance, fear, anger and moral superiority from the level of personal conviction into more tangible and explicit language that can also be shared with others (Madisson 2016b; Madisson, Ventsel 2016a; 2018). Madisson and Ventsel (2016b), moreover, suggest that conspiracy theories are a significant component of extreme-right echo-chamber communication, which reproduces subcultural stereotypes and is generally self-referential in nature.

The cultural semiotic concept of auto-communication enables us to explicate which semiotic mechanisms sustain the closed communication of the believers in conspiracy theories. In auto-communicative meaning-making, the culture (i.e. the abstract 'me') is trying to increase its internal information, to improve its quality and to transform itself (Torop 2008: 729). Information is selected auto-communicatively and is predominantly open to associations that the potential addressee already knows (Madisson, Ventsel 2016a). Members of extreme right-wing communities who believe in particular conspiracy theories do not tend to be receptive or exposed to fundamentally different lines of thought. This semantic shift becomes possible only if a new code is added and, through that code, the previously known information is given new meaning. For example, the online discourse of Estonian extreme rightists ('Islamic migrants' are a threat to white Estonians, and part of a bigger E.U. plan to undermine the independence of the Estonian Republic) can be interpreted according to an economic code ('migrants are threatening the sustainability of the country because they "steal" jobs and encumber economic growth'), a social code ('providing social benefits to foreigners jeopardises the social welfare of Estonians') or a cultural code ('they wear burkas and aggressively spread their religion, which is dangerous for Estonian culture'). If a new code is added, the auto-communicative framework of associations that organises various extreme interpretations is confirmed once again. It widens and deepens the cluster of reasons for which the national spirit and the white race can be presented as being under serious threat (Madisson, Ventsel 2016a, 2016b). The extreme-right (auto) communication is an ongoing process of interpretation, but the semantics of the message is predetermined by a limited number of stereotypes and does not allow exchange of new information.

One central characteristic of this kind of conspiracy theorist's meaning-making is the tendency to identify with the normative text as opposed to an aggregate of rules according to which texts are created. In meaning-making that is oriented towards texts, the self views itself as a sum of precedents, cases of usages and texts (Lotman 2010: 61), while the normative ('the correct') is equated with the existence of that semiotic unity. In the case of the self-description of Estonian extreme-right bloggers, these normative texts can be concrete historical texts, e.g. the Constitution of the Republic of Estonia. The other widespread type of text is framed by the collective memory-texts of the community, including the general *text of victimhood*, which in the Estonian context is often associated with the 700-year history of serfdom, with the Soviet deportations and with the Soviet occupation (Madisson, Ventsel 2016a).

## Conclusion and future directions

There are relatively few studies that explicitly tackle semiotic aspects of conspiracy theories. But the research topic enjoys a growing popularity within the international community of semioticians, who are alert to how, in the so-called 'post-truth era', conspiracist rhetoric and the hermeneutics of suspicion are in the ascendancy in discourses that unfold in both traditional and social media. For example, *Lexia*, the international journal of semiotics, recently devoted a hefty issue (23/24) to the topic, seeking to cast a fresh look at conspiracy thought and conspiracy theories by combining semiotics and other qualitative methods.

Analyses included therein, demonstrate, for instance that there is an unbridgeable divide between those who believe that the importance of vaccines is artificially inflated by pharmaceutical companies and those who label such views as 'conspiracy theories' that can damage democracy through their rhetorical sleight-of-hand (a position that in itself sometimes characterises the attack on democracy as something akin to a conspiracy). Nevertheless, the gap between the two positions is less a matter of logic than semiotics. Even if one side or the other can be scientifically proven to be right or wrong, it is unlikely to heal the rift. People do not disagree and fight with each other because they believe in diverging conspiracy theories; instead, it is arguable that people who believe in discrepant conspiracy theories do so because they *want* to disagree, to give vent to the tensions that underpin society and that fail to find other channels for expression.

Future semiotic research on conspiracy theories might focus on their capacity to influence worldviews; such research should entail interdisciplinary collaboration. Contemporary communication is performed at an increasingly fast pace and is dominated by affective reactions to current events – a tendency enabled by the prevalence of emotionally and visually oriented messages. The information overload in social media communication has increased the relevance of focusers or filters of attention that can bring attention to a certain topic or event (Tufekci 2013: 856). People are more willing to share content that is perceived as novel, intriguing and somewhat mysterious or obscure. The affective aspect is intensified by fake news, conspiracy theories and so on, whose intriguing and sensational nature enables them to enact the attention-grabbing effect, increasing traffic to certain sites by creating a certain agenda. From a semiotic perspective, affect is an inseparable component of discourse and, thus, can be analysed by using Peirce's categories to explicate the interrelations between the emotional (affective) and the argumentative (discursive) aspects of meaning-making in conspiracy theories and its function as attention grabber.

Future studies should explain how some conspiracy theorists exploit the characteristics of particular interpretative communities and how their storytelling practices create a fertile ground for user-generated content supporting their agenda. Semiotics enables the analysis of the relationship between conspiracy theories and audiences and their meta-interpretations; in this context, several authors have dealt with the problem of constructing the audience. Eco (1979) has developed the concept of the model reader; Juri Lotman (1982) has coined the concept of the image of audience. Both authors show how the text constructs its own audience, and both provide concrete analytical tools for studying this phenomenon. Integrating them into academic studies on conspiracy theories would lead to a semiotic approach to strategic conspiracy theories. Future research should also explicate how different media support each other in particular representations of conspiracy, what are the dominant types of meaning-making and what kind of identification processes are related with particular strategic conspiracy narratives.

## Note

1 This work was supported by the research grants PRG314 'Semiotic fitting as a mechanism of biocultural diversity: instability and sustainability in novel environments' and PUTJD804 'Semiotic perspective on the analysis of strategic conspiracy narratives'; for the last revision, one of the authors, Massimo Leone, benefited from a Senior Fellowship of the Polish Institute of Advanced Studies.

## References

Back, L. (2002) 'When hate speaks the language of love', paper presented at Social Movement Studies Conference, London School of Economics, April.
Ballinger, D. (2011) *Conspiratoria – The Internet and the logic of conspiracy theory*, unpublished thesis, University of Waikato, Hamilton, New Zealand.
Barthes, R. (1977) *Image-music-text*, London: Fontana.
Barthes, R. (1981) 'The discourse of history', *Comparative Criticism*, 3(1): 7–20.
Barthes, R. (1986) *The rustle of language*, New York: Farrar, Straus and Giroux.
Bauman, Z. (2006) *Liquid fear*, Cambridge: Polity Press.
Birchall, C. (2006) *Knowledge goes pop*, Oxford, New York: Berg.
Boym, S. (1999) 'Conspiracy theories and literary ethics: Umberto Eco, Danilo Kiš and the protocols of Zion', *Comparative literature*, 51(2): 97–122.
Butter, M. (2014) *Plots, designs, and schemes: American conspiracy theories from the Puritans to the present*, Berlin/Boston: de Gruyter.

Campion-Vincent, V. (2007) 'From evil others to evil elites: a dominant pattern in conspiracy theories today', in G.A. Fine, V. Campion-Vincent, C. Heath (eds.) *Rumor mills: the social impact of rumor and legend*, New Jersey/New Brunswick: Transaction Publishers, pp. 103–22.

Castells, M. (2009) *Communication power*, Oxford: Oxford University Press.

Caumanns, U. (2016) 'Performing and communicating conspiracy theories: Stalinist show trials in eastern Europe during the Cold War', *Lexia*, 23–4: 269–88.

Cobley, P. (2004) 'The semiotics of paranoia: the thriller, abduction and the self', *Semiotica: Journal of the International Association for Semiotic Studies*, pp. 148, 317–35.

Eco, U. (1976) *A Theory of semiotics*, Bloomington: Indiana University Press.

Eco, U. (1979) *The Role of the Reader: Explorations in the Semiotics of Texts*. Advances in Semiotics. Bloomington: Indiana University Press.

Eco, U. (1990) *Interpretation and overinterpretation*, Cambridge: World, History, Texts Tanner Lectures.

Fenster, M. (2008) *Conspiracy theories: secrecy and power in American culture*, Florida: University of Florida.

Genette, G. (1980) *Narrative discourse*, Ithaca, NY: Cornell University Press.

Greimas, A. (1983) *Structural semantics: an attempt at method*, Lincoln, Nebraska: University of Nebraska Press.

Greimas, A. and Courtès, J. (1976) 'The cognitive dimension of narrative discourse', *New Literary History*, 7(3): 433–47.

Jakobson, R. (1971) 'The dominant', in L. Matejka and K. Pomorska (eds.) *Readings in Russian poetics: formalist and structuralist views*, Cambridge: MIT Press, pp. 82–7.

Kasekamp, A., Madisson, M. and Wierenga, L.J. (2018) 'Discursive opportunities for the Estonian populist radical right in a digital society', *Problems of Post-Communism*, 66(1): 1–12.

Kimminich, E. (2016) 'About grounding, courting and truthifying: conspiratorial fragments and patterns of social construction of reality in rhetoric, media and images', *Lexia*, 23(24): 35–54.

Knight, P. (2002) *Conspiracy Nation: the politics of paranoia in postwar America*, NY: New York University Press.

Kress, G. and van Leeuwen, T. (1996) *Reading images: the grammar of visual design*, London: Routledge.

Kress, G. and van Leeuwen, T. (2001) *Multimodal discourse: the modes and media of contemporary communication*, London: Arnold.

Leone, M. (2015) 'Double debunking: modern divination and the end of semiotics', *Chinese Semiotic Studies*, 11(4), 433–77.

Leone, M. (2016) 'Preface', in 'Complotto/Conspiracy', *Lexia*, 23–4: 2–16.

Leone, M. (2017) 'Fundamentalism, anomie, conspiracy: Umberto Eco's semiotics against interpretive irrationality' in T. Thellefsen (ed.) *Umberto Eco in his own words*, Berlin/Boston: de Gruyter, pp. 221–9.

Leone, M. (2018a) 'Rationality and reasonableness in textual interpretation', in A. Olteanu, A. Stables and D. Borțun (eds.) *Meanings & Co.: the interdisciplinarity of communication, semiotics and multimodality*, Dordrecht: Springer, pp. 53–70.

Leone, M. (2018b) 'The semiotics of common sense: patterns of meaning-sharing in the semiosphere', *Semiotica*, 226(1): 225–41.

Lepik, P. (2008) *Universals in the context of Juri Lotman's semiotics*. Tartu: Tartu University Press.

Lotman, J. (1982) 'The text and the structure of its audience', *New Literary History: a Journal of Theory and Interpretation*, 14(1): 81–7.

Lotman, J. (1988a) 'Технический прогресс как культурологическая проблема. [Progress of technology as problem of culturology]', Труды по знаковым системам *Vol. 22:* Зеркало: Семиотика зеркальности, pp. 97–116.

Lotman, J. (1988b) 'Text within a text', *Soviet Psychology*, 26(3): 32–51.

Lotman, J. (1998) 'Охота за ведьмами. Семиотика страха. [Witch-hunt: semiotics of fear]', *Sign Systems Studies*, 26: 61–80.

Lotman, J. (2010) 'Kultuuri õpetamise' probleem kui tüpoloogiline karakteristik. [The problem of teaching a culture as its typological characteristics]', in S. Salupere (ed.) *Kultuuritüpoloogiast*, Tartu: Tartu University Press, pp. 60–80.

Lotman, J. and Uspenskii, B. (1975) 'Myth – name – culture', *Soviet Studies in Literature*, 11(2–3): 17–46.

Lotman, J. and Uspenskij, B. (1978) 'On the semiotic mechanism of culture', *New Literary History*, 9(2): 211–32.

Lotman J. and Uspenskij B. (1984) 'The role of dual models in the dynamics of Russian culture (up to the end of the eighteenth century)', in M. Jurij, J. Lotman and B. Uspenskij, *The Semiotics of Russian Culture*, Ann Arbor: University of Michigan, pp. 3–35.

Lotman, M. (2009) 'Hirmusemootika ja vene kultuuri tüpoloogia [Semiotics of fear and typology of Russian culture] I–VI', *Akadeemia*, 1: 191–215; 2: 429–55; 3: 631–47; 5: 1035–64; 6: 1217–48.

Madisson, M. (2014) 'The semiotic logic of signification of conspiracy theories', *Semiotica: Journal of the International Association for Semiotic Studies*, 202: 273–300.

Madisson, M. (2016a) *The Semiotic construction of identities in hypermedia environments: the analysis of online communication of the Estonian extreme right*, Tartu: Tartu University Press.

Madisson, M. (2016b) 'NWO conspiracy theory: a key frame in online communication of Estonian extreme right', *Lexia*, 23(24): 117–36.

Madisson, M. (2017) 'Representation of the Snowden scandal in Estonian media: the construction of threats and fear', *Folklore: Electronic Journal of Folklore*, 69: 145–68.

Madisson, M. and Ventsel, A. (2016a) '"Freedom of speech" in the self-descriptions of the Estonian extreme right groupuscules', *National Identities*, 18(2): 89–104.

Madisson, M. and Ventsel, A. (2016b) 'Autocommunicative meaning-making in online-communication of Estonian extreme right', *Sign Systems Studies*, 44(3): 326–54.

Madisson, M. and Ventsel, A. (2018) 'Groupuscular identity-creation in online communication of Estonian extreme right', *Semiotica: Journal of the International Association for Semiotic Studies*, 222: 25–46.

Ponzio, J. (2016) 'Upsetting national events and conspiracy narratives in contemporary Italian literature', *Lexia*, 23(24): 345–66.

Torop, P. (2008) 'Multimeedialisus', *Keel ja Kirjandus*, 8(9): 721–34.

Tufekci, Z. (2013) '"Not this one": Social movements, the attention economy, and microcelebrity networked activism', *American Behavioral Scientist*, 57(7): 848–70.

Turco, F. (2016) '"It's all the President's fault". Tricks, conspiracies, and corruption in the American TV series set at the white house: homeland and scandal', *Lexia*, 23–4: 427–42.

Ventsel, A. (2016a) 'Political potentiality of conspiracy theories', *Lexia*, 23–4: 309–26.

Ventsel, A. (2016b) 'Rhetorical transformation in Estonian political discourse during World War II', *Semiotica: Journal of the International Association for Semiotic Studies*, 208: 103–32.

# 1.4
# PHILOSOPHY AND CONSPIRACY THEORIES

*Juha Räikkä and Juho Ritola*

## Introduction

Philosophers have always been interested in conspiracies, but the philosophical debate on conspiracy theories is a pretty recent phenomenon. Karl Popper (1950) wrote about the 'conspiracy theory of society', but his discussion concerned issues of intentional explanations in general rather than conspiracy theories proper. In this chapter, we will review the philosophical debate and distinguish between four questions that philosophers have considered. The questions we have in mind are (1) the conceptual question of what the appropriate definition of the term 'conspiracy theory' is; (2) the epistemic question about the rationality and justification of conspiratorial beliefs; (3) the moral question of the ethical status of conspiracy theorising; and (4) the practical question of how decision-makers should deal with conspiracy theories. Obviously, the questions are closely connected to one another. Whether conspiracy theories are, generally speaking, plausible or implausible explanations depends on what is meant by the concept. The ethical status of conspiracy theorising in turn depends partly on the plausibility of conspiracy theories. Finally, whether we should fight *against* the spreading of conspiracy theories surely depends, at least to some extent, on the ethical status of the theories. Therefore, by defining the key concept suitably, one can try to settle most of the questions in the debate – not an unusual situation in philosophy.

The aim of this chapter is to explain how philosophy could help studying conspiracy theories. The best way to explain this is to review critically the recent debates in philosophy of conspiracy theories. We will concentrate mainly on approaches that represent 'analytical' philosophy rather than 'continental' philosophy.

## The question of the definition

Examples of conspiracy theories include claims that deal with issues such as the death of Princess Diana, the origin of A.I.D.S. and the truth of 9/11. The concept of conspiracy theory is commonly used in a pejorative sense. According to common understanding, there is something suspect in being a supporter of a conspiracy theory. People may even blame someone whose view of the world resembles that of a conspiracy theorist (Dentith 2017). This suggests that, in ordinary language, people make a distinction between conspiracy theories and other explanations that refer to conspiracies. The latter are conceived as unproblematic. For example, the attempt to murder Emperor Nero and the 1953 Iranian coup d'état are usually explained by referring to conspiracies, but people do not think that there is something strange in this appeal to a specific form of political action. They find ordinary historical explanations that refer to conspiracies appropriate. Similarly, in many cases, they find political explanations that refer to conspiracies as appropriate. For instance, the Volkswagen emission scandal is usually explained by referring to a conspiracy and a gross deception, yet people do not think that there must be a better explanation than the one that involves the concept of conspiracy. Normal adults usually know that conspiracies happen and that there is no more exoticism in conspiracies than there is, say, in corruption.[1]

Philosophers disagree about whether conspiracy theories should be distinguished from ordinary social explanations that refer to conspiracies. Some philosophers have defended the idea that they should (Keeley 1999: 116; Coady 2003: 206; Levy 2007: 187; Räikkä 2018). In their view, conspiracy theories are explanations that refer to conspiracies or plots, and are *not supported* by the appropriate epistemic authorities, such as mainstream media, investigative journalists, various state authorities and agencies, the scientific community and professional historians. This understanding of the concept reflects the common language intuition that conspiracy theories are 'unofficial', and that they are not supported by the received view. The understanding is consistent with the fact that some top politicians seem to defend conspiracy theories. To say that conspiracy theories are 'unofficial' is to say only that they are not supported by the epistemic authorities, not that political authorities could not support them.

However, some philosophers have suggested that *all* the explanations that refer to conspiracies should be called 'conspiracy theories' (Pigden 2007: 230; Dentith 2016a: 587; Basham 2018). Conventional terminology should be *revised*. It is not altogether clear what is the motivation behind the revisionist move, but there are two important arguments here. First, anyone who would like it to be true that 'Many conspiracy theories are justified' can make their wish come true by defining the concept of 'conspiracy theory' so that ordinary conspiracy explanations are counted as conspiracy theories. Second, the stigmatisation of conspiracy theories may influence the journalists' and others' willingness to evaluate those theories fairly, that is, by concentrating on evidence presented. By refusing to use the concept of conspiracy theory in a pejorative sense we can, perhaps, increase the possibility that *all* the explanations that refer to conspiracies get an appropriate treatment, and not only those explanations that are supported by the epistemic authorities (cf. Coady 2012: 122). It has been argued that:

> We should not use the terms 'conspiracy theory', 'conspiracy theorist' or any of the language associated with these terms. Each time we do so, we are implying, even if we do not mean to, that there is something wrong with believing, wanting to investigate, or giving any credence at all, to the possibility that powerful people (and especially governments or government agencies of Western countries) are engaged in secretive or deceptive behaviour.
>
> *(Coady 2018)*

Obviously, an explanation of a political event should not be rejected only by claiming that it is 'merely a conspiracy theory' (Dentith 2016a: 582). Arguably, conspiracy theories are rejected on irrational grounds every now and then, for instance, on grounds that their conclusions are unpleasant (Räikkä, Basham 2018).

Ideally, however, conspiracy theories would get fair treatment even if we do not reject the distinction between conspiracy theories and ordinary conspiracy explanations. Furthermore, it is unclear whether philosophers' decision to revise language would solve the problem (i.e. if there is one). Therefore, the grounds for the revisionist move fail to convince.

## The epistemic status of conspiracy theories

It is often argued that, historically speaking, governments and business enterprises have frequently engaged in 'morally dodgy' conspiracies and that, therefore, it is not foolish to think that they do so, and foolish to think that they do not do so (Pigden 2006: 165; Dentith 2016a: 585; Basham 2018). However, for one reason or another, conspiracy theorists have not been successful in revealing conspiracies. Overwhelming evidence from history gives us a fairly clear idea of who has revealed conspiracies; usually they are revealed by historians, social scientists, research institutions, state agencies or investigative journalists. The role of leakers, who are either members of the plots or people who are otherwise close to the conspirators and know enough, have always been crucial. They have helped journalists and others. Therefore, the implication of the fact that we know of many conspiracies is that the conventional epistemic authorities seem able to reveal conspiracies and confirm their existence, not that conspiracy theories have managed to renew our understanding of the causes of social phenomena. If conspiracy theorists have any role in revealing conspiracies, it is that they provide others with a motivation to study further some political or economic issues.[2]

Are conspiracy theories, generally speaking, implausible – given that they challenge the views supported by the epistemic authorities (cf. Harris 2018)? One could argue that, as a group, conspiracy theories are neither plausible nor implausible, and that some conspiracy theories are plausible while others are not (Dentith 2016b: 29). It is implausible to claim that 'Nobody Died at Sandy Hook' school shooting tragedy (Fetzer, Palecek 2015), but this does not show that all the other conspiracy theories are implausible as well. However, there is a fundamental problem with the claim that we cannot estimate conspiracy theories in general terms: It is not true. Although it is obvious that conspiracy theories should be evaluated on a case-by-case basis (Räikkä 2018), it still makes sense to ask whether they are, in the main, plausible or implausible (cf. Byford 2011: 18). 'Generalism' (that allows us to make a general judgment about the plausibility of conspiracy theories) is completely consistent with 'particularism' (that encourages us to evaluate individual theories on the basis of evidence). The answer to the question of whether conspiracy theories are, generally speaking, implausible depends on our view about the trustworthiness of institutions that we normally use in the acquisition of our beliefs. That is, the question of whether conspiracy theories are implausible turns into the question of whether mainstream media, investigative journalists, various state authorities and agencies, the scientific community and professional historians are, in the main, trustworthy. As far as we accept that, generally speaking, fact-gathering institutions work tolerably well, we must conclude that every conspiracy theory is *prima facie* implausible and that the burden of proof rests on the side of the conspiracy theorists.

The question of whether the ordinary epistemic authorities are, generally speaking, trustworthy is far too large to be considered here, but three points are important. First, our reliance upon the expertise of others is very extensive and almost automatic (Adler 1995: 136; Fricker 2006: 225; Lehrer 2006: 145; Lackey 2011: 71). Although the epistemic authorities work imperfectly and make mistakes, they are still the main social institutions that we use in the acquisition of our beliefs. This is why they are 'epistemic authorities' in the first place. In badly corrupted countries, people find it completely irrelevant what major newspapers and national or local authorities say about this and that (Uslaner 1999) but, in democratic countries, the trustworthiness of media, scientific community and state agencies is a default stance in the formation of beliefs. If we are not justified in acquiring our beliefs in the way we do, then most of our beliefs are unjustified.

Second, critical and rational people often suspect the information provided by the epistemic authorities, but the suspicion is usually based on beliefs that are supported by the other views of the same authorities – and not, say, by the views of miracle-mongers. In general, we *know* about the failures of epistemic authorities because they have produced information that helps us to notice the failures, perhaps with the help given by 'citizen scientists'. A list of the failures of the epistemic authorities tends to support the claim that they work tolerably well, not the conclusion that they are untrustworthy.

Third, the supporters of conspiracy theories often think that 'it is possible that we live in a society that *merely* looks open' (Dentith 2018). However, those who claim that media, research institutes and so on can be untrustworthy and insincere seem to trust in them when they reveal conspiracies. In *these cases*, the epistemic authorities are considered perfectly trustworthy. This sort of selective trust need not be problematic, but surely a person who finds mainstream media, state agencies and so on *generally untrustworthy* should doubt them also when they reveal conspiracies. A person who seriously claims that all the 'official' experts who deny the existence of a conspiracy can be liars (see Dentith 2018) should probably add that all the 'official' experts who *confirm* the existence of a conspiracy can be liars as well. Perhaps the CIA's secret mind control programme MKUltra never happened? After all, we know about it only because we are told about it and have passively adopted mainstream news, without starting our own research on the issue.

It is sometimes argued that some conspiratorial scenarios 'are too "toxic" for our usual institutions of public information to disseminate to the public' (Basham 2018: 73) and that the epistemic authorities 'might be interested in downplaying the evidence' when the news concerns 'toxic truths' (Dentith 2018). These are interesting claims but, historically speaking, the 'usual institutions of public information' have been able and willing to publish news that must have seemed very 'toxic' at the time. Mainstream media, investigative journalists and historians have written about political corruption, targeted killings, questionable military programmes and reported on outrageous frauds and insolent deceptions committed by people in high and honourable positions. The *Washington Post* (which is certainly not the most radical newspaper in the world) revealed the Watergate conspiracy. Nothing seems to be too 'toxic'. It is true, however, that, in some cases, conspiracies get publicity surprisingly slowly even if they are revealed. For instance, the NSA spying system (the Echelon system) was originally leaked in 1972 and then discussed again on many occasions, but got more publicity only in 2013, after Edward Snowden's revelations (Jansen, Martin 2015: 665). Whether the delay was due to the 'toxicity' of the issue is unclear. Another interesting example is doping in sport, and in particular cycling (the Lance Armstrong case). There were rumours for many, many years, but they only developed into a scandal at a particular point.

Critics of conspiracy theories think that conspiratorial beliefs not only conflict with the received views but are also problematic in other ways. Conspiracy theorists are said to be inconsistent (Wood *et al.* 2012: 772), use only a 'sharply limited number of (relevant) informational sources' (Sunstein, Vermeule 2009: 204) and, in general, suffer from *epistemic vices*. According to critics, a conspiracy theorist is 'gullible, dogmatic, closed-minded, cynical, prejudiced, and so on' (Cassam 2016: 164). Furthermore, in many critics' view, conspiracy theories are irrefutable, and an acceptance of a conspiracy theory leads to the situation in which a conspiracy theorist must make 'claims of larger and larger conspiracies' – at least when the evidence for a theory fails to obtain and the believer wants to hold onto the view (Keeley 1999: 126). These kinds of claims, however, sound unfair. Although conspiracy theories seem, generally speaking, implausible, this does not imply that they must always include contradictory claims, or anything like that. (It is not inconsistent to think that Osama bin Laden may have died much before his 'official' dying day and that he may be alive (cf. Hagen 2018). A politically aware person who thinks that both theories are 'live' options is not irrational, although some critics of conspiracy theories have suggested that one should not believe in 'contradictory conspiracy theories' (Wood et al. 2012) or anything similar.)

Some conspiracy theories are fairly fine-grained, and the 'Everyone is involved!' move is quite rare. It would be misguided to think that all conspiracy theories must be false (Basham 2001, 2003, 2006; Hagen 2018). Epistemic authorities make mistakes and scientific misconduct is not uncommon. Perhaps a conspiracy theorist will one day reveal a conspiracy that is not revealed by the epistemic authorities; maybe it will be one in which an epistemic authority (such as a state agency) is involved. A person's general trust in the media, government agencies and the court of law is consistent with the view that some of them have a mistaken view (or have lied) about a particular issue (Clarke 2002: 141; Coady 2003: 203).

## The ethics of conspiracy theories

Conspiracy theorising is a form of human action and is thus an appropriate object of ethical evaluation. It is useful to distinguish between the ethical evaluation of conspiracy theorising in general and the ethical evaluation of individual theories. Possibly, conspiracy theorising is, ethically speaking, an undesirable phenomenon, but, still, certain individual conspiracy theories are morally unproblematic. It is also useful to distinguish between the ethical evaluation of developing and publishing conspiracy theories and the ethical evaluation of their inadvertent dissemination (say, by forwarding e-mails or website links). Possibly, active conspiracy theorising (by developing and publishing theories) has a different ethical status from the passive and inadvertent dissemination of conspiracy theories.

Those who find conspiracy theorising ethically approvable have argued that people not only have a moral right to develop and disseminate whatever conspiratorial thoughts they might have but also that conspiracy theories can be societally important and helpful in many ways. In particular, it has been argued that conspiracy theorists challenge 'us to improve our social explanations' (Clarke 2002: 148); that the theories can teach us to be critical and conscious citizens; and that the prevalence of conspiracy theories 'helps to maintain openness in society' (Clarke 2002: 148). According to defenders of conspiracy theorising, critics of conspiracy theories 'could be accused of being (no doubt inadvertently) enemies of the open society, because they discourage an activity that is essential to its survival, conspiracy theorizing' (Coady 2006: 170). Critics of conspiracy theories have provided conspirators 'with an intellectually respectable smokescreen behind which they can conceal their conspirational machinations' (Pigden 1995: 4). 'History shows there is a significant probability of political tyranny's development in any society which is not attentive to what its politicians are doing' (Basham, Dentith 2016: 13). The idea in most apologies of conspiracy theorising is that mainstream media and investigative journalists (who get help from leakers) are unable to satisfactorily fulfil their function as watchdogs. Conspiracy theorists are indispensable for supplementing their work or taking it on themselves.

Many philosophers and social scientists have criticised conspiracy theorising. It is frequently argued that conspiracy theories can produce and have produced socially undesirable consequences. When a conspiracy theory gets publicity, some people usually start to believe in it and that, in turn, can influence their behaviour (Sunstein 2014: 32; Douglas, Sutton 2015). The list of potentially, or actually, harmful conspiracy theories includes the ones that deal with vaccination or the extent of anthropogenic climate change. Some of the negative consequences have been rather serious. Violent programmes against the Jews have often been fuelled by murky conspiracy theories (Swami 2012). Campaigns against vaccination have probably caused deaths in some countries. Of course, not all conspiracy theories are immediately dangerous. Claims such as 'Shakespeare was somebody else' and 'The moon landing was faked' are conspiracy theories (as they go against official narratives and refer to conspiracies), but are probably rather harmless, considered as individual theories.

Possibly, the main problem of conspiracy theories is that, considered together as a whole, they cast a massive shadow over the institutions that have epistemic functions in our lives and lessen general trust in 'the behavior and motivations of other people and the social institutions they constitute' (Keeley 1999: 126). In totalitarian societies where general trust is low, for example, people are unable to make rational long-term plans and reasonable personal investments. Lessening epistemic trust is ethically questionable, given that there are no grounds for a general suspicion (as there are in totalitarian societies).[3] Conspiracy theories can therefore be seen as morally problematic and, possibly, as *more problematic* than other forms of sowing confusion and doubt. As opposed to science denialism or creationism, for instance, conspiracy theories tend to involve libels and false accusations that surely raise moral questions. Quite often, conspiracy theorists not only place people in a false light in the public eye but do so for their own ideological or personal benefit (Räikkä 2014: 81). We could say that, by conspiracy theorising, a bad thing is realised in a particularly bad way, that is, through libels and accusations against innocent people. Some conspiracy theories, for instance the above-mentioned theory that 'Nobody Died at Sandy Hook', show no concern for the feelings of the family members of the victims of the tragedy (Fetzer, Palecek 2015).

Suppose that conspiracy theories are morally problematic, say, because they bring us closer to the dystopia of a society where the trustworthiness of the fact-gathering institutions and the information they provide is not the default stance. Does it follow that conspiracy theorists are therefore morally blameworthy and responsible for a moral fault? Not necessarily. It can be argued that 'we should refrain from being excessively moralistic' since, in the case of a conspiracy theorist, 'we should also be willing to admit the possibility that he can't help himself' (Cassam 2016: 169). Conspiracy theorists can be non-culpably ignorant, and possibly they cannot control their vices (Cassam 2016). This argument, however, is unconvincing. If a person who develops and publishes conspiracy theories does not know what they are doing – that they spread claims that go against common knowledge as true claims – they certainly *should know* it. Similarly, in the case of disseminators, they should realise what they are doing, even if their intentions may be harmless (say, a worry about the safety of certain vaccines). Perhaps the ordinary dissemination of (very odd) conspiracy theories should be compared to littering. Litterbugs may appreciate a clean environment but refuse to do their own share to maintain a clean environment. Although a single litterbug's contribution can be small and harmless in their own eyes, the overall effect may be quite unpleasant. Both the ordinary disseminators of (very odd) conspiracy theories and litterbugs are responsible for their conduct, as they *should realise* what they are doing (Räikkä 2020). Whether the conspiracy theorists are collectively responsible for their conduct is an open question, but a case can be made that they are (Räikkä 2020).

Defenders of conspiracy theories sometimes claim that conspiracy theorists are just asking questions and that the point of the conspiracy theory is to highlight the fact that, in the public sphere, very few determine the beliefs of almost everyone else – that 'public knowledge' of many issues is conservative, biased and aims to silence critical voices. Raising questions and demanding fair public debate, in turn, cannot be wrong (Husting, Orr 2007). This argument, however, confuses conspiracism to what can be called critical agnosticism. First, conspiracy theorists are *not* merely 'asking questions'. On the contrary, they offer alternative answers – as opposed to agnostics. Second, conspiracy theorists are *not* primarily interested in the structural features of civic debate and its problems (that are real, no doubt). On the contrary, they are participating in the debate, often with a vociferously loud voice. For instance, instead of the official side trying to silence conspiracy theorists, in the discussion concerning vaccines it sometimes seems as if the conspiracy theorists are aiming to silence the official side.

## The fight against conspiracy theories

How to deal with conspiracy theories? This problem will also be addressed by various chapters in other sections of this handbook, but let us consider what philosophers have said about it. Those philosophers who find conspiracy theorising an important and desirable social activity encourage people to develop, disseminate and evaluate conspiracy theories open-mindedly. They warn people that they should not dismiss possible explanations of important political events simply on the grounds that the explanations are labelled conspiracy theories (Dentith 2017; Basham 2017). Those philosophers who are less optimistic about the constructive implications and desirability of conspiracy theories disagree how to deal with them, in particular, how *the state* should deal with them. Three approaches have been suggested: (1) prohibition; (2) direct fight; and (3) indirect actions.

1. *Prohibition.* The denial of 'historical truths' is illegal in some countries and many legal systems prohibit any denial of the Holocaust. It has been suggested that prohibitions should be extended to concern some other conspiracy theories, namely those that are plainly false and have a high probability of increasing seriously harmful behaviour. An example would be a conspiracy theory that includes the denial of anthropogenic climate change (cf. Lewandowsky et al. 2013; Lavik 2016). This suggestion is understandable in the sense that prohibitions would probably have some desirable social effects and the intentional misleading of people would decrease. However, according to critics, the idea of extending prohibitions to apply to certain conspiracy theories is problematic for various reasons. First of all, it is not clear which conspiracy theories should be classified as 'plainly false' and which as only 'implausible'. When conspiracies are revealed, the news is often very surprising. (Think of the Volkswagen emission scandal, for instance.) Many conspiracy theories probably look 'plainly false', although they are merely unlikely to be justified, as they contradict the view of relevant epistemic authorities (Räikkä 2018). Another thing is that prohibitions would limit people's freedom of speech on rather strange grounds.[4] It is one thing to limit freedom of speech in order to protect certain vulnerable groups from hate speech, as well as the libels and actions that they may cause, and another thing to restrict speech on the grounds that presenting certain views in public may have harmful social or environmental consequences – although presenting the views does not directly harm or threaten anyone. (In general, if a person behaves in a certain irresponsible way because they believe in a conspiracy theory, the person responsible for the behaviour is not primarily the conspiracy theorist as the originator of the conspiracy theory, but the person him-/herself.)

2. *Direct fight.* It has been suggested that the state should actively fight against false conspiracy theories – without prohibiting the dissemination of them. One option is

> cognitive infiltration of extremist groups, whereby government agents or their allies (acting virtually or in real space, and either openly or anonymously) will undermine the crippled epistemology of believers by planting doubts about the theories and stylized facts that circulate within such groups, thereby introducing beneficial cognitive diversity.
>
> *(Sunstein, Vermeule 2009: 219; Sunstein 2014: 22–32)*

This suggestion would avoid the problems related to restrictions on free speech. However, in critics' view, the suggestion has difficulties of its own. The idea that state agencies should engage in a conspiracy against groups that promote conspiracy theories would warrant the claim that there *are* conspiracies operated by the state (Hagen 2010: 154; 2011: 17). More importantly, to recommend cognitive infiltration is to 'recommend policies which could never be successful in a truly open society, and which, to the extent that they are successful, would make our society less open' (Coady 2018: 291). Such policy would be 'inconsistent with the values of liberal democracy' (Coady 2018).[5] Notice also that the idea of cognitive infiltration is based on the assumption that conspiracy theorists work typically in groups and do not listen to alternative explanations. Both empirical assumptions are questionable, if not obviously false.

*3. Indirect actions.* The state can be indirectly active concerning conspiracy theories and other forms of sowing doubt and confusion among people. The state authorities can try to ensure that the views of scientific communities get enough publicity, and that people have sufficient skills to interpret the media. The authorities could certainly have an important role in educating people in critical thinking and argumentation. (For instance, people should be told that, when a journalist interviews both a medical expert and a conspiracy theorist, it does not mean that both views are equally likely to be justified – although they are treated in this manner by the journalist.) Furthermore, the state can ensure that truly diverse views are published and receive publicity in civic debate, so that there would be less need for specific conspiracy theory forums. It is difficult to say to what extent certain explanations are dismissed in public discussion simply on the grounds that they refer to an alleged conspiracy (rather than on the grounds that the conspiracy allegations are presented by sources that are generally considered untrustworthy). In any case, such dismissals should not happen, and the state can certainly enhance diversity, say, by supporting newspapers that cannot survive without financial backing. The indirect actions by the state should not be a problem to the supporters of conspiracy theories. After all, the supporters' aim is to further critical democratic discussion, and the state's indirect actions would promote just that.

## Conclusion

In comparison to discussions in social psychology and political science, for instance, the reception of conspiracy theories has been rather positive among philosophers. A central contention within this reception has been that one is not warranted in rejecting a particular political explanation only on the grounds that it has been labelled as a conspiracy theory.

Unfortunately, the philosophical discussion on conspiracy theories has suffered from unnecessary antagonism and needlessly belligerent argumentation. For one reason or another, the willingness to understand the opposite side and the readiness to try to find the most sensible interpretation of the opponents' arguments have been in short supply. We fear that it is not an exaggeration to say that some philosophers have forgotten the principle of charity in their contributions to the debate, although truth-lovers (if that is what a philosopher can claim to be) should respect the principle. One explanation for the strong language is that many issues related to the epistemology and ethics of conspiracies have a political dimension. Possibly there are also other incentives not to find an agreement.

In addition to the conceptual questions about the definitions of 'conspiracy' and 'conspiracy theory', an essential disagreement among philosophers seems to concern the question of how well the 'fact-gathering institutions' work in ordinary democratic countries. Those who have defended conspiracy theories are not optimistic about the present state of the ordinary epistemic authorities, while others assume that they are likely to reveal conspiracies, sooner or later, if there is something to reveal. However, the question of how well the media, research institutes, state agencies, investigative journalists and historians do their job is largely empirical, and surely there are considerable differences between countries and time periods. This suggests that, in the final analysis, philosophers may have relatively little to give to the 'theory of conspiracy theories'. Although the epistemic question of when and why we are justified in using testimony as a basis of our beliefs is certainly a deep philosophical problem, examining the present state of existing knowledge-producing institutions in different countries is not primarily a philosophical project.

## Notes

1 In some cases, it may be difficult to say whether an explanation refers to a 'conspiracy' rather than to some other sort of confidential cooperation. However, secret cooperative activities whose aims and nature conflict with the so-called positive morality (that reflects our de facto moral commitments) or with specific *prima facie* duties are usually called 'conspiracies', especially if the members of the cooperation have a certain position, and if the goal of their activities differs from the goal they are authorised to pursue. Children may have morally questionable secret plans to influence events by secret means, but these incidents are seldom called conspiracies. Small children are not considered to be in a position to conspire. Secret military operations may be morally rotten, but as far as they have authorised goals, they are not usually called conspiracies. The members of an 'official' administrative meeting behind closed doors may secretly agree on issues they should not and start to pursue goals they should avoid. When this happens, the participants can rightfully be accused of conspiracy, as they have unauthorised goals now. Conspiracies involve secret cooperation, but that does not mean that the conspirators must meet secretly, so that outsiders do not know that they meet in the first place (see Räikkä 2018: 213).
2 It is not impossible that a member of an epistemic authority (say, a biologist or a climate scientist) earns a reputation for being a 'conspiracy theorist'. This can happen when an expert suggests that there is a conspiracy, say, concerning genetically modified food, but does not get much support for her claims from the other relevant experts. Obviously, epistemic authorities do not form a unitary body, but are rather composed of heterogeneous bodies that may conflict. Of course, this does *not* imply that we cannot normally say who belongs to 'epistemic authorities' and who does not.
3 In contemporary democracies, trust in government is seldom strong. Although the E.U. has established itself as a major political entity, it can still be considered an emerging governmental body, which so far has not achieved full democratic legitimacy. According to *Special Eurobarometer 461* from the year 2017, for example, while citizens' trust in the E.U. shows signs of increase, still less than half of the respondents (47%) are inclined to trust the E.U. The corresponding percentage is even smaller at the level of its member states: Only 40% of the respondents tend to trust their national government. Not more than 52% of the respondents say they are inclined to trust justice and their national legal system. Obviously, the deficits of trust merit concern. Citizens who are overly distrusting of their government – whether national or international – are unlikely to be willing to adhere to its rules, to engage in cooperative projects presupposing its mediation, or even to have interest in sustaining it. Indeed, research suggests that what have been called high-trust societies have stronger economies, higher levels of wellbeing and stronger social networks than so-called low-trust societies, and that distrust in government lowers tax morale and increases corruption, for instance (see e.g. Uslaner 2018; Catala 2015; Melo-Martín and Intemann 2018).
4 A person may say (and even think) that they support a conspiracy theory just because they would like to protest against the official system and social elites that govern public space. By 'supporting' a conspiracy theory, a person is able to manifest their distrust in the system, although they may not have any view of the plausibility of the theory they say they support. Surely, people should have a right to these kinds of manifestations. However, this raises the question of how to struggle against such 'supporting attitudes' if a person who has them does not really *believe* that a theory they support is *true*. Their support is *non-doxastic* in nature.
5 Coady (2018) writes that Sunstein's and Vermeule's position is based on

> an equivocation over the meaning of the term 'conspiracy theory'. This equivocation reflects a widespread assumption that conspiracy theories tend to be false, unjustified and harmful,

and that, as a result, we can speak as if all conspiracy theories are objectionable in each of these three ways.

Coady argues that 'this assumption is itself false, unjustified, and harmful' and that 'because people often conspire, we often have good reason to believe that people are conspiring, and there is often a significant public benefit in exposing their conspiracies'. Coady compares 'conspiracy theories to scientific theories' and argues that

> just as most of us regard bad scientific theories (i.e. false, unjustified and harmful ones) as an acceptable price to pay for good scientific theories, we should regard bad conspiracy theories as an acceptable price to pay for good conspiracy theories.

# References

Adler, J. (1995) *Belief's own ethics*, London: The MIT Press.
Basham, L. (2001) 'Living with the conspiracy', *The Philosophical Forum*, 32(3): 265–80.
Basham, L. (2003) 'Malevolent global conspiracy', *Journal of Social Philosophy*, 34(1): 91–103.
Basham, L. (2006) 'Afterthoughts on conspiracy theory: resilience and ubiquity, in D. Coady, (ed.) *Conspiracy Theories: the philosophical debate*, Hampshire: Ashgate, pp. 133–7.
Basham, L. (2017) 'Pathologizing open societies: a reply to the *Le Monde* social scientists', *Social Epistemology Review and Reply Collective*, 6(2): 59–68.
Basham, L. (2018) 'Joining to conspiracy', *Argumenta*, 3(2): 271–90.
Basham, L. and Dentith, M. (2016) 'Social science's conspiracy-theory panic: now they want to cure everyone', *Social Epistemology Review and Reply Collective*, 5(10): 12–9.
Byford, J. (2011) *Conspiracy theories: a critical introduction*, London: Palgrave Macmillan.
Cassam, Q. (2016) 'Vice epistemology', *The Monist*, 99(2): 169–80.
Catala, A. (2015) 'Democracy, trust, and epistemic justice', *The Monist*, 98(4): 424–40.
Clarke, S. (2002) 'Conspiracy theories and conspiracy theorizing', *Philosophy of the Social Sciences*, 32(2): 131–50.
Coady, D. (2003) 'Conspiracy theories and official stories', *International Journal of Applied Philosophy*, 17(2): 197–209.
Coady, D. (2006) 'The pragmatic rejection of conspiracy theories', in D. Coady (ed.) *Conspiracy Theories: the philosophical debate*, Hampshire: Ashgate, pp. 167–70.
Coady, D. (2012) *What to believe now: applying epistemology to contemporary issues*, Singapore: Wiley-Blackwell.
Coady, D. (2018) 'Cass Sunstein and Adrian Vermeule on conspiracy theories', *Argumenta*, 3(2): 291–302.
Dentith, M. (2016a) 'When inferring to a conspiracy might be the best explanation', *Social Epistemology*, 30(5–6): 572–91.
Dentith, M. (2016b) 'In defence of particularism: a reply to stokes', *Social Epistemology Review and Reply Collective*, 5(12): 27–33.
Dentith, M. (2017) 'Conspiracy theories on the basis of evidence', *Synthese*, 196(6): 2243–61.
Dentith, M. (2018) 'Expertise and conspiracy theories', *Social Epistemology*, 32(3): 196–208.
Douglas, K. and Sutton, R. (2015) 'Climate change: why the conspiracy theories are dangerous', *Bulletin of the Atomic Scientists*, 71(2): 98–106.
Fetzer, J. and Palecek, M. (2015) *Nobody died at Sandy Hook: it was a FEMA drill to promote gun control*, USA: Moon Rock Books.
Fricker, E. (2006) 'Testimony and epistemic autonomy', in J. Lackey and E. Sosa (eds.) *The Epistemology of Testimony*, Oxford: Clarendon Press, pp. 225–50.
Hagen, K. (2010) 'Is infiltration of "extremist groups" justified?', *International Journal of Applied Philosophy*, 24(2): 153–68.
Hagen, K. (2011) 'Conspiracy theories and stylized facts', *The Journal for Peace and Justice Studies*, 21(2): 3–22.
Hagen, K. (2018) 'Conspiracy theorists and monological belief systems', *Argumenta*, 3(2): 303–26.
Harris, K. (2018) 'What's epistemically wrong with conspiracy theorising?', *Royal Institute of Philosophy Supplement*, vol. 84, pp. 235–57.
Husting, G. and Orr, M. (2007) 'Dangerous machinery: "conspiracy theorist" as a transpersonal strategy of exclusion', *Symbolic Interaction*, 30(2): 127–50.

Jansen, S. and Martin, B. (2015) 'The Streisand effect and censorship backfire', *International Journal of Communication*, 9(1): 656–71.
Keeley, B. (1999) 'Of conspiracy theories', *The Journal of Philosophy*, 96(3): 109–26.
Lackey, J. (2011) 'Acquiring knowledge from others', in A.I. Goldman and D. Whitcomb (eds.) *Social Epistemology: Essential Readings*, Oxford: Oxford University Press, pp. 71–91.
Lavik, T. (2016) 'Climate change denial, freedom of speech and global justice', *Etikk i praksis. Nordic Journal of Applied Ethics*, 10(2): 75–90.
Lehrer, K. (2006) 'Testimony and trustworthiness', in J. Lackey and E. Sosa (eds.) *The Epistemology of Testimony*, Oxford: Clarendon Press, pp. 145–59.
Levy, N. (2007) 'Radically socialized knowledge and conspiracy theories', *Episteme: A Journal of Social Epistemology*, 4(2): 181–92.
Lewandowsky, S., Oberauer, K. and Gignac, G.E. (2013) 'NASA faked the moon landing – therefore, (climate) science is a hoax: an anatomy of the motivated rejection of science', *Psychological Science*, 24(5): 622–33.
Melo-Martín, I. and Intemann, K. (2018) *The fight against doubt: how to bridge the gap between scientists and the public*, Oxford: Oxford University Press.
Pigden, C. (1995) 'Popper revisited, or what is wrong with conspiracy theories?', *Philosophy of the Social Sciences*, 25(1): 3–34.
Pigden, C. (2006) 'Complots of mischief', in D. Coady (ed.) *Conspiracy Theories: The Philosophical Debate*, Hampshire: Ashgate, pp. 139–66.
Pigden, C. (2007) 'Conspiracy theories and the conventional wisdom', *Episteme*, 4(2): 219–32.
Popper, K. (1950) *The open society and its enemies*, Princeton: Princeton University Press.
Räikkä, J. (2014) *Social justice in practice*, Heidelberg: Springer.
Räikkä, J. (2018) 'Conspiracies and conspiracy theories: an introduction', *Argumenta*, 3(2): 205–16.
Räikkä, J. (2020) 'Conspiracy theories and collective responsibility', in S. Bazargan-Forward and D. Tollefsen (eds.) *Routledge Handbook on Collective Responsibility*. Forthcoming.
Räikkä, J. and Basham, L. (2018) 'Conspiracy theory phobia', in J. Uscinski (ed.) *Conspiracy Theories and People Who Believe Them*, New York: Oxford University Press, pp. 178–86.
Sunstein, C. (2014) *Conspiracy theories and other dangerous ideas*, New York: Simon & Schuster.
Sunstein, C. and Vermeule, A. (2009) 'Conspiracy theories: causes and cures', *The Journal of Political Philosophy*, 17(2): 202–27.
Swami, V. (2012) 'Social psychological origins of conspiracy theories: the case of the Jewish conspiracy theory in Malaysia', *Frontiers in Psychology*, vol. 3, p. 280.
Uslaner, E. (1999) 'Democracy and social capital', in E. Warren (ed.) *Democracy and Trust*, Cambridge: Cambridge University Press, pp. 121–50.
Uslaner, E. (ed.) (2018) *Oxford Handbook of Social and Political Trust*, New York: Oxford University Press.
Wood, M., Douglas, K. and Sutton, R. (2012) 'Dead and alive: beliefs in contradictory conspiracy theories', *Social Psychological & Personality Science*, vol. 3, pp. 767–73.

# 1.5
# PSYCHOANALYSIS, CRITICAL THEORY AND CONSPIRACY THEORY

*Nebojša Blanuša and Todor Hristov*

### Introduction: Beyond realist and symbolist approaches

Conspiracism is not a set of rational political positions that can be easily explained by examining their ideological content. Nor can it be entirely accounted for by analysing the vested interests it serves, or the countercultural energies it sometimes channels. Conspiracy theorists are driven not only by beliefs but also by desire. Conventional approaches to the phenomenon of conspiracism rarely take desire into account, and in effect they often inadvertently pathologise conspiracy theories as merely the products of delusional thinking. But psychoanalysis and critical theory provide concepts that can help explain why conspiracist narratives came to be so popular.

Although narratives about conspiracies have a long history, the concept of conspiracy theory emerged in large part out of the conceptualisation of conspiracist ideas as a pathology (see Chapter 1.1). The pathologisation of conspiracy theories invites intervention by administrative, medical and security authorities, which are ill-equipped to distinguish conspiratorial thinking from criticism and distrust. They can thus easily end up targeting legitimate distrust of authorities as abnormal or dysfunctional behaviour.

Psychoanalysis and critical theory provide concepts that can explain how conspiracy theories provoke desire, and at the same time allow critical analysis of their pathologisation. The chapter summarises the psychoanalytic accounts of conspiracist desire. The first section sets out the historical origins of the concept of paranoia, and the political consequences of this conceptualisation. The second section focuses in particular on the authors who applied the psychopathological idea of conspiracy to social theory. The next two sections discuss writers who try to dissociate conspiracy delusions from common conspiracy theories. Finally, the chapter maps out another aspect of psychoanalytic concepts relevant to the study of conspiratorial desire, namely the theory of fantasy developed by Jacques Lacan, which, along with its reinterpretation by Slavoj Žižek, aimed at explaining the unconventional idea of reality ('the real') entertained by conspiracy theorists.

We can get a sense of what is at stake in psychoanalytic approaches to conspiracy theory by considering the example of the American political scientist Michael Rogin. In the 1960s and 1970s, Rogin established his reputation as a historian of McCarthyism. In contrast to earlier interpretations that had viewed either the anti-communist senator or his followers as delusional, Rogin instead focused attention on the political and material vested interests of elite factions in the Republican party. Rogin's 'realist' account of the rise of anti-communism formed part of a wider challenge to the 'symbolist' approach of historians such as Richard Hofstadter, who had focused on McCarthyism as another episode in a long tradition of American countersubversive demonology, marked out by anxieties, unconscious frustrations, intolerance and anti-democratic potential. In contrast to the symbolist focus on the cultural and psychological dimensions of politics, the realist approach aimed to shed light on the cynical manipulation of popular fears for all-too-real political gain. Symbolists tended to focus on oppositional, fringe and mass movements, whereas realists argued that countersubversive demonology had long been at the heart of U.S. politics.

However, later in his career, Rogin (1987) revisited the realist versus symbolist debate. He was now willing to acknowledge the strengths and weaknesses of each position, but he also insisted that there still remained something that neither theory could explain: The unconscious fantasies that motivated even the most exploitative forms of political thought. Rogin turned to the psychoanalytic thought of Melanie Klein to try to develop a theory of conspiracist demonology that bridged the gap between realist and symbolist approaches. Rogin observes that conspiratorial demonisation often works by imitating the imagined subversions it attacks (Rogin 1987: 284). He claims that fantasies about the pre-Oedipal mother are a source of leaders' demonology (Rogin 1987: 293). In a liberal society, which insists 'on the independence of men, each from the other and from cultural, traditional, and communal attachments' (Rogin 1987: 135), as well as from 'fantasized feminine engulfment' from early childhood (Rogin 1987: 293), conspiracist politicians express anxiety about boundary breakdown and invasive, devouring exterminatory enemies. Their answer to such threats is to hang onto patriarchal order and satisfy their desires for merging by identifying themselves with the imagined unified nation as the replacement of mother, as well as to express violence against those who are considered outside the liberal realm (Rogin 1987: 293). In short, for Rogin, psychoanalytical theory came to provide an explanatory framework for the powerful unconscious appeal of conspiracist rhetoric in American politics.

## The pathologisation of conspiracy theory

We can trace the origins of the pathologisation of conspiracy theories in the discipline of psychiatry as it emerged in the nineteenth and twentieth centuries. There are three key steps:

1. Although psychiatrists still conceived of madness as the opposite of reason, they discovered a series of intermediary phenomena (Foucault 2006: 339–41, 136–9).
2. These intermediary phenomena formed a distinct field, the abnormal, covering irrational or dysfunctional behaviours that were not mad or criminal in themselves, but in which one could discern the seed of a coming madness or a future crime (Foucault 2003a: 42).
3. The abnormal behaviours that posed risks to society were articulated as targets of interventions by the state, the police, the court and, most importantly, by the clinic functioning as a relay that linked governmentality with knowledge, and psychiatric knowledge with power (Foucault 2003a: 55–6).

The long history of the pathologisation of conspiracy thinking begins with the identification of intellectual monomania by one of the founding figures of modern French psychiatry, Jean-Étienne Dominique Esquirol (1838), defined as reasoning formally indistinguishable from normal thinking, but dislodged from the social role or the rational self-interest of the subject which brought forth a partial delirium or delusion (Esquirol 1945 [1838]: 320). In the middle of the nineteenth century, the influential German psychiatrist Wilhelm Griesinger redefined delusions as the principal mechanism of the perversions of thought, and explained them as attempts to develop causal explanations of counterfactual ideas that deviate from reality not in their contents but in their intensity, characterised by uncommon or untypical exaggeration, exuberance or affect (Griesinger 1854: 70, 305–6). Building on that, Griesinger extended the concept of delusion beyond hallucinations to ideas that we now associate with conspiracy thinking, such as the sense of living among spies posing as ordinary members of society, being surrounded by plots, feeling persecuted by the Freemasons, etc. (Griesinger 1854: 71, 213). In consequence, conspiracist thinking was firmly located in the field of abnormal behaviours. Such pathologisation was a multi-layered practice that could not be reduced to stigmatisation or exclusion because it involved the problematisation of individual or social behaviours as risks that any responsible government should control in order to defend society (Foucault 2003b: 256–7).

The pathologisation of conspiratorial ideas triggered further institutional and conceptual developments in the second half of the nineteenth century, that later came together in the new diagnosis of 'paranoia'. Conspiratorial ideas were dissociated from the general concept of insanity still used by Griesinger and redefined as a symptom of a separate type of abnormal behaviour, 'delirium of persecution' (Lasègue, Falret 2008). It came to be associated with further symptoms, most importantly 'delirium of protest', which consisted in attempts to evade guilt by shifting the responsibility for one's situation onto others (Mendel 1884; Kraepelin 1907: 425–6, 432–3), and 'delirium of interpretation', which consisted in reasoning that started from general facts and distorted them so as to give them a personal, usually idiosyncratic meaning (Sérieux, Capgrass 2008: 448). The subjects whose behaviour could be described as delirium of persecution, protest or interpretation came to be increasingly dissociated from the mad, as the clinical experience invited the conclusion that their condition rarely deteriorated into complete insanity, and they could live normal, even successful, lives. The subjects susceptible to conspiracism were associated with a particular type of risk, the risk of sudden crises: Since delirium of interpretation, persecution or protest were indistinguishable from normal reasoning, they were socially invisible until they blew up into moral perversity, irrational acts of violence or until they violently disrupted the life of the normal families of the afflicted (Kahlbaum 1863).

At the turn of the century, the abnormal behaviours demarcated by such deliriums and characterised by the risk of social disruption were integrated in the concept of paranoia developed by the German psychiatrist Emil Kraepelin (1907: 425–6). The concept functioned as a relay that associated delusions with causes, grades of intensity and probable developments. Kraepelin distinguished between general paranoia and paranoid dementia, with the first being a stable system of delusions that did not afflict fully the behaviour of the subject, depended on hereditary predispositions and promised an only relatively unfavourable future. In contrast with general paranoia, paranoid dementia (integrated in the concept of dementia praecox, that later came to be identified as schizophrenia) lacked a stable system of delusions, afflicted completely the behaviour of the subject, indicated a metabolic rather than hereditary causality and promised a bleak future of rapid deterioration into insanity (Kraepelin 1907: 425–6).

Kraepelin's concept of paranoia operated differently from the older psychiatric concepts. Nineteenth-century psychiatrists still conceived of conspiratorial thinking as a symptom of disease whose cause was hidden in the depth of the subject as a lesion in the brain (Esquirol 1945 [1838]), as uncured melancholia (Griesinger 1854) or as neurological or psychological trauma (Mendel 1884). In contrast, Kraepelin's concept was flat. It promised to the psychiatrists that, instead of delving in the depths of abnormal subjectivity, instead of deciphering the difficult hieroglyphics of individual symptoms, they could diagnose abnormal behaviours by inscribing them in a table of differential features. Because of that, Kraepelin's concept outlived the specific context of nineteenth-century psychiatry in which it emerged. In the second half of the twentieth century, under the influence of the canonical *Diagnostic and Statistical Manuals* of the American Psychological Association, it was adjusted to the analytical techniques that shape knowledge production in the present-day social sciences, and it became a cornerstone in the type of psychiatry that achieved dominance in the second half of the twentieth century and that treats the abnormal subjects by medication rather than by interpretation (Foucault 2006: 342–4).

## Psychoanalytic accounts of paranoia in social theory

In contrast to the psychiatric definition, the psychoanalytic concept of paranoia had a more ambiguous relationship to the pathologisation of conspiratorial thinking. Freud generally accepted Kraepelin's classification of mental disorders, but criticised his aetiology (Dalzell 2011: 115–29). Freud's theory of paranoia was developed in his analysis of Daniel Paul Schreber's memoirs (Freud, Strachey 1976: 1974), where he tried to differentiate paranoia from dementia praecox. For Freud, both disorders are the consequences of psychological regression to the early stages of ego-development. Paranoia is less severe because it regresses from choosing another as an object of love only to the intermediary stage of narcissism, expressing itself in delusions, while dementia praecox is a complete abandonment of object-love and a return to infantile auto-eroticism (Freud, Strachey 1976: 2442). Furthermore, the main defence mechanism of paranoia is projection, while dementia praecox employs a hallucinatory (hysterical) mechanism (Freud, Strachey 1976). Freud's understanding of paranoia emphasised three constitutive elements: Suppressed homosexuality, projection and displacement of aggression onto the other.

With its focus on the mechanism of projection (i.e. external forces are blamed for internal problems), Freud's theory has been influential in the analysis of conspiracy thinking, most obviously in the work of Hofstadter. A curious detail is that Freud considered paranoia as the most rational mental illness with an uncomfortable similarity to science and philosophy (Melley 2000: 6; Parker 2001: 191). Yet, many authors continue to use this psychiatric concept for socio-political explanations (Boltanski 2014: 175), making it a powerful weapon for denigration, stigmatisation and social exclusion of those who are using and/or producing conspiracy theories.

Several prominent authors in the social sciences have made this association even stronger. The first was the American political scientist Harold Lasswell (1930), who directly relied on psychoanalysis to explore political phenomena and developed the general theory of the political personality. This is expressed in his famous formula of political man (Lasswell 1930: 75): $p \} d \} r = P$, where the 'private motives (p) are displaced (d) onto public objects, and then rationalised (r) in terms of the public interest, producing "political man"(P)'. This rationalisation is more thorough for those persons who are highly involved in politics; especially for the leadership type he calls agitators, marked by narcissistic and strong power-centred personalities who are prone to exaggerated mistrust of opponents, are contentious, hostile, hateful and exhibit anti-democratic behaviour. This psychological make-up, which expresses itself in specific identity symbols, rituals, styles of politics and 'pseudo-rational' propaganda, was adopted by later scholars, who added to Lasswell's depictions a rather pessimistic and derogatory tone to conspiracism and agitation (Thalmann 2019: 33–4).

Lasswell's model of political man considers politics as a compensatory activity and political actors as subjects whose original motives mostly remain repressed in the unconscious. Moreover, psychological displacement implies that private motives, goals and emotions are too problematic to be directly exposed in a society. Finally, it focuses on personal frustrations and defence mechanisms as the main instigators of political action (Šiber 1998: 22) expressing itself through projection, repressed libido and latent homosexuality, already mentioned as the main mechanisms of paranoia. As such, Lasswell's approach was predisposed to consider conspiracy theories a psychopathological phenomenon.

In a similar vein, the Frankfurt School, the birthplace of critical theory, tried to rework psychoanalytic concepts to make them applicable to seemingly irrational social phenomena characteristic of late capitalism (Hristov 2019: 27–8). Perhaps the most influential reconfiguration of paranoia is the concept of the paranoid personality developed by one of the leading thinkers of the school, Theodor Adorno. He believed that the mechanism of conspiracy theories is comparable to the mechanism of advertising. From a capitalist perspective, selling fascism is not substantially different from selling soft drinks (Adorno 1975: 45). In order to capture the abstract dimension of such mechanisms that is indifferent to their particular contents, Adorno conceptualised them as rhetorical devices. However, to make sense of the power of such devices, Adorno had to explain how they tapped into the desire of the public. Perhaps conspiracy entrepreneurs rationally exploit the unconscious desires of the audience, but if the audience unconsciously desires conspiracies, does that mean that its members suffer from a delusion of persecution; and why do others seem to be immune to such mass delusions, even though they are part of the same mass society? Adorno tried to answer such questions by positing a psychological type vulnerable to conspiracy theories. It is modelled after Lasswell's concept of political subjectivity as a projection onto public objects of private, often unconscious, motives rationalised as public interests whose intensity depends on the extent of the involvement in politics (Lasswell 1930: 75; Šiber 1998: 22).

As an example, let us take M1229, a student enrolled in the study of authoritarian psychological dispositions that Adorno joined in the late 1940s. M1229 listened to mildly conspiracist radio shows, and she believed that 'the Jews would be running the country before long' (Adorno 1975: 292). Was she unconsciously longing for violence? Certainly not: She knew that Jews differed among themselves and she believed in education that brought people from different origins or ethnicities together by helping them know each other and learn from each other that they were essentially the same, essentially human. Then why did she project her hatred on Jews and communists, and why did she extend it to African Americans? The interviewer noticed that M1229 was 'tight all over' (Adorno 1975: 293), and the very signifiers of the imaginary enemies produced in her unbearable tension. If we build on Adorno's discussions of similar cases, we can hypothesise that the tension was caused by the feeling that she was an alien in her social milieu. Because of that, M1229 experienced her social life as a series of frustrations caused by the tyrannical social order, and in trying to repair the loneliness of her insular experience she resorted to stereotypes that articulated her fantasy of a social group bound by love, despite the uneasiness that undermined her sense of belonging, and caused her to project aggression on other groups (Adorno et al. 1967 [1950]: 765; Adorno 1975: 325).

The concept of paranoid personality was introduced in DSM-I (1952: 34) and retained in the next editions of the canonical manual. It was also developed in a broader sense in the writings of a number of political scientists, sociologists and historians who began to tackle the topic of conspiracism from the late 1940s to the 1970s. According to Thalmann (2019: 28), such conceptualisations of conspiracy theories influenced by psychoanalysis were developed in three phases: As a reaction to the rise of totalitarian regimes (1930s–1950s), during the Red Scare (1950s) and, later, as a way to delegitimise political extremism (1960s–1970s), including by authors such as Lowenthal and Guterman (1949), Neumann (1957), Shils (1956), Rovere (1956), Bell (1955; 1963), Hofstadter (1955; 1996 [1965]), Bunzel (1967), Lipset and Raab (1970), etc. (see Chapter 5.10 in this volume). While Freud explains delusions of persecution as defence mechanisms against destructive desires, for Adorno and his followers conspiracy theories function as defence mechanisms against frustration caused by the social order. Adorno explains the appeal of conspiracy theories by the fact that they promise a relief from the frustrations of economic calamities such as the Great Depression. Conspiracy theorists seduce their audience because they relieve its frustrations and assuage its feeling of powerlessness. They do so by allowing their audience to make sense of a crisis of the social order that seems incomprehensible as natural disaster and irreversible as fate. But, at the same time, conspiracists foreclose any understanding of the causes of the crisis, any critique of the social order, any claim to power or any attempt to repair the situation and relieve the suffering. Conspiracism, by this line of thinking, is an opium that makes exploitation bearable.

Adorno's analysis of conspiracy thinking as a symptom of the general sense of powerlessness in the face of the complexities of a highly organised and institutionalised society, which frustrates the individual and triggers projective fantasies (Heins 2011: 69–70), was developed by several other critical theorists associated with the Frankfurt School, who tried to combine Marx and Freud in order to explain the underlying mechanisms of late capitalist societies. Leo Lowenthal and Norbert Guterman (1949) and Franz Neumann (1957) considered conspiracy theories an expression of modern mass society's problems. In his seminal work 'Anxiety and Politics', Neumann claims that the social order is competitive, and if a social group starts to lose its status and is unable to understand the causes of its decline, the anxiety characteristic of any competition can intensify into persecutory anxiety (Neumann 1957: 290–3). The cause of persecutory anxiety, however, cannot be reduced to pathological or dysfunctional beliefs because it is grounded in psychological alienation on the one hand, and in social and political alienation on the other. Psychological alienation is a consequence of the social repression of libidinous drives (an idea known as the 'repressive hypothesis'), manifested as an alienation of the ego from the libido. Social and political alienation is produced by monotonous, stultifying jobs and by the values of bourgeois society, which makes the middle class particularly prone to identification with authoritarian political leaders, regression to a horde mentality and behaviour, and loss of the ego. Life under ruthlessly competitive capitalism increases the fear of status degradation and the susceptibility to paranoid ideas exemplified by the conspiracy theories that authoritarian leaders tend to promote. These affective tendencies gradually disable citizens from independent thinking and active civic participation and foster political alienation or a rejection of the whole political system, leading to political apathy. This paves the way for authoritarian movements that despise rules and institutionalise fear (Blanuša 2011a: 96–7).

## Symptomatic readings

A great deal of the persuasive power of conspiracy theories lies in their capacity to present themselves as narratives that reveal some important truth. They engage in a 'symptomatic' reading of reality (i.e. a reading of reality on the look-out for symptoms) in which it is assumed that, under the influence of the undeclared (hidden) interest, there is a gap between the 'official', public meaning of some interpretation and its 'actual' intention (Žižek 1995: 10). This kind of storytelling exploits human curiosity and the desire for mystery in our disenchanted (post)modern lives.

In contrast to the psychopathologising approach to the phenomenon of conspiracy theories, other writers have tried to read the conspiracy theories themselves as distorted symptoms – not of individual psychology, but of society as a whole. The Marxist literary and cultural critic Frederic Jameson has provided the most influential interpretation of the fascination with conspiracy in contemporary entertainment culture. He argues that conspiracy theories in postmodern culture function as 'cognitive mapping' of the unrepresentable totality of the volatile and complex social order of late capitalism, albeit misleading and counterproductive (Jameson 1988: 356). Heavily leaning on the work of Jacques Lacan, Jameson claims that the desire for cognitive mapping in conspiracist texts, 'whatever other messages it emits or imply, may also be taken to constitute an unconscious, collective effort at trying to figure out where we are and what landscapes and forces confront us' (Jameson 1995: 3). Conspiracy novels and films represent the totality of the social order, either in the mode of a melancholic fantasy that everything is lost because everyone is controlled by the secret machine of power, or in the mode of a fervent fantasy that an event – a crisis or a revolution – could make anything possible. Conspiracist narratives tend to oscillate between the two modes (Jameson 2009: 593–603). Following the rhythm of that oscillation, Hollywood thrillers often represent a crisis unleashing the labyrinthine structures of shadowy power and omnipotent surveillance technologies as a distorted allegory of the sublime complexity of multinational neoliberal capitalism.

## Lacanian accounts of conspiracist desire

Symptomatic readings of conspiracy theories focus on their function as representations of social reality, but their social function does not explain the particular objects the conspiracist desire latches onto. Let us take for example the best-selling novel *When It Was Dark* (1903) by Guy Thorne, an obscure but prolific British writer from the first half of the twentieth century. It tells the story of a conspiracy to kill God. A Jewish communist millionaire, out of jealousy of the progress of Christian civilisation, bribes a brilliant and corrupt archaeologist to plant evidence that Joseph of Arimathea staged the resurrection. A symptomatic reading, perhaps, would see in this the banal spectre of antisemitism. If so, why did Thorne's Antichrist story captivate such a large readership? From a psychoanalytic perspective, the discursive figure of the Jewish millionaire is overdetermined by a particular form of knowledge that Jacques Lacan called paranoid (Lacan 2002: 90). One of the founding figures of post-structuralism, famous for his idea that the unconscious is structured as a language and for his opposition against biological interpretations of psychoanalysis, Lacan claims that one learns to choose the objects of one's desire by identifying with others. The object of one's desire is originally what is desired by the other; it is a reflection of the other's desire, and in that sense, desire is originally a form of jealousy. At this early point of the development of the ego, the knowledge about the other's desire is imaginary in its form. Yet, without it, the subject would be unable to develop beyond the identification with the mother and form a social ego capable of counterbalancing the enchantment and rivalry with others (Lacan 2002: 79). Furthermore, without the imaginary misrecognition of absolute knowledge and mastery ascribed to the other by primordial jealousy, the subject would be unable to rework paranoid knowledge into symbolic knowledge of the truth about her unconscious desire (Evans 1996: 95).

Thorne's Jewish communist millionaire, who is trying to steal from Christians the object of their enjoyment, can be interpreted as an inverted and overvalued projection of this paranoid knowledge. However, as God is debunked, the social order starts to crumble, Muslims stop recognising the hegemony of Christianity, the Balkans are engulfed in a religious war, losers start to rebel against the successful, market activity grinds to a halt, women suffer sexual abuse on a daily basis and, worst of all, Britain loses India. True believers pray for salvation, and it is given to them by a suspicious priest, who discloses the conspiracy with the help of the archaeologist's mistress and another Jewish millionaire who has converted to Christianity. In the end, God is resurrected, together with the social order.

The conspiracy-minded priest is driven by a desire to know the truth (Fenster 2008: 100). But the truth about the conspiracy hides a deeper truth about religion, and an even deeper truth about the priest himself – that he should be the one who has saved the Saviour. Yet, that private truth is unthinkable in any conventional sense, because claiming to be the saviour of the Saviour would amount to sacrilege: It can be represented only as a latent thought condensed in the manifest content of a story, only as far as it is substituted by a plot. So the object of the priest's desire, the truth, has been contaminated with the impossibility of its explicit representation (Lacan, 1988: 221; Fenster 2008: 103). Nevertheless, this conspiracist fantasy circulated beyond the realm of literature. The Bishop of London, for example, claimed in a sermon that the novel revealed the truth that the social order would disintegrate without religion (Cockburn 2002). The sermon became news that attracted the attention of Freud, who in turn discussed the novel as a counterfactual truth about how the social order underwritten by religion could disintegrate (Freud, Strachey 1976: 3792).

If the object of conspiracist desire is an impossible truth, conspiracy theorists can sustain their desire only by displacing it onto endless further details (Fenster 2008: 105). The suspicious priest in the novel, for example, tormented by his impossible desire to resurrect God after science supposedly confirmed His death, begins by noting an odd remark made by the Antichrist millionaire almost as a slip of the tongue, then another odd phrase by the archaeologist, then an odd story by a woman repenting her sinful life, then an envelope, a ticket, a hotel address, a repaid debt. This chain of insignificant details, however, only becomes meaningful if it is read as a symptom of his desire for revelation that can never be fulfilled. No matter how long this metonymic chain of details is, it never comes close to the impossible object of the priest's desire. It sustains the conspiracist desire only by deferring the realisation of its impossibility (Lacan 1981: 228–9; Fenster 2008: 105).

Fenster (2008: 95) argues that this excessive interpretive practice in an age of postmodernist scepticism 'manifests a popular desire to reconstruct the master narrative' of modern history and politics, or the final order of power behind all discovered conspiracies that always lies elsewhere. Although opposed to the pathologisation of conspiracy theories, Fenster claims that such a form of interpretive practice negatively influences civic participation by displacing citizens' desire for an active role in politics with a self-paralysing signifying regime which exhausts itself in 'an obsessive desire for information' (Fenster 2008: 96). The interpretive practice is paradoxical because it requires incessant creative digging of information and making connections between them, variable motives, actions, meanings, plots and references to the past, but the insights and conclusions are invariably the same – a grand conspiracy, whose discovery is a potentially endless task.

In this sense, conspiracy theorists are motivated by

> a kind of manic will to seek rather than to know ... akin to the Lacanian notion of desire which requires that its ultimate fulfilment be continually deferred ... and demand of this desire is not simply to expose the secret.
>
> *(Fenster 2008: 103)*

On the surface, such demand is orientated toward public recognition and resolution of the crisis provoked by conspiracy. If that happens, the day is saved, the enemy defeated, social order restored. However, such a possible resolution leads ironically to dissatisfaction of desire because the case is closed and the object of desire, the search for the hidden truth, is lost. According to Fenster, here lies the trap for conspiracy theorists. As they fetishise the continual search for evidence, they continue to apply the same framework to heterogeneous events and processes:

> There is always another conspiracy to track, and the new political and social order that replaces conspiracy would by definition constitute a new relation of power, which

would by definition require the deepest of suspicions. The 'Clinton Death List' grows, or changes name, or changes shape to include new, different events and figures. There is always another Clinton, just as, both before and after Bill, there is always another Bush.

(Fenster 2008: 105)

Moreover, in searching the truth that is constantly sliding away, conspiracism as an interpretative practice produces enormous chains of signifiers, each accompanied by affects and respective behaviours. In that process, it 'digests', transforms and recombines non-conspiratorial elements around the master signifier of 'conspiracy' (Fenster 2008: 111).

## Conspiracy theory and fantasy

If the object of conspiracist desire is impossible, if it cannot be satisfied, how can it produce the powerful affect that Marc Fenster calls 'conspiracy rush' (Fenster 2008: 110–11)? We can explain that if we take into account the function of fantasy in conspiracist desire.

In order to do that, however, we need to take into account the difference between desire, need and demand (Lacan 2002: 689–72). According to Lacan, desire emerges out of need, but the satisfaction of many human needs depends on others. So, to be satisfied, the need has to be communicated to the others, and therefore it has to be articulated by signifiers.

Signifiers make sense, however, only because they are inscribed in a symbolic order, just like words have meaning because they belong to a language. Yet, the symbolic order is not the subject of need, or, in other words, it is other to the subject of the need. Of course, the symbolic order is not a particular other, it is an abstract other like the language or the law, hence Lacanians call it the (big) Other. Now, since the articulation of need as demand depends on the Other, any demand is characterised by otherness that differentiates it from the need experienced by the subject, and it is precisely that difference between demand and need that opens up the proper dimension of desire (Lacan 2002: 689).

As we have said, the symbolic order is abstract, just like language is abstract in comparison with particular phrases. So, when the subject tries to communicate her or his demand to others, the symbolic order adds an abstract dimension, detached from particular objects. In that abstract dimension, any demand is essentially a demand for love that can be articulated as a question addressed to the Other: 'What do you want?' (Lacan 2002: 690).

That question is impossible to answer, however, for at least two reasons. First, the question 'What do you want?' can be answered only by the Other. But the Other is not an individual, it is the symbolic order in general, and the symbolic order is silent in itself, just like language cannot speak itself. Therefore, the question about the Other's desire is irredeemably open. It leads to a void, no matter how the particular others would respond to the demand, and since that question is the very ground of desire, desire is grounded on a void.

From a Lacanian perspective, this is the paradox of any desire: It is not causeless or objectless, but the object that causes it is the lacking answer of the question what does the Other want (Lacan 2002: 693). This inescapable paradox is precisely the second reason why the question about the desire of the Other is unanswerable. Because, if the Other were driven by desire, the object-cause of the Other's desire would also be lacking. But the Other to which any demand for love is addressed is not a particular other, the Other is the symbolic order itself, and the symbolic order cannot have a lack, just like language cannot lack one of its words. If the Other lacked something, it would be incoherent and it could not function as symbolic order.

Yet, although the question 'What do you want?' is impossible to answer, it is equally impossible not to answer it. Because abandoning it as an empty question would empty out the very ground of desire, and that would lead to the most severe form of poverty that Lacan called subjective destitution – the poverty of having nothing to desire (Lacan 1967: 6).

Lacan claimed that, in order to avoid subjective destitution, to sustain one's desire and to solve the double impossibility of the question about the desire of the Other, we develop fantasies, i.e. imaginary scenarios that stage the object-cause of our desire in order to answer what the Other wants. In that sense, conspiracy theories are fantasies, even if they turn out to be warranted, because fantasy is defined by its function as a support for desire rather than by its contents (Glynos 2001: 202).

## Lacan and the normalisation of paranoia

Conspiracy theories have an even deeper root than fantasy in the constitution of the subject. For Lacan, the precondition of all human knowledge is the 'paranoiac alienation of the ego' (Lacan 1953: 12), which occurs during the mirror-stage, sometime between the age of six to 18 months and represents the first step of self-recognition in the infant's life. At this stage, the nascent human subject transforms itself through the identification with an idealised picture (imago) of its own body.

For Lacan, this is one of the fundamental preconditions for the normal functioning of the human subject. An infant needs to develop an illusory image and sense of its own subjective unity, autonomy and mastery. Otherwise, it will stay in a fragmented psychological condition that leads to psychosis. The final moment of the mirror-stage is when an infant identifies itself with familiar human beings and objects and learns about the similarities and differences of the others and their desires, which will become its own desires through the process of internalisation. Those others are simultaneously like and unlike the infant, and the infant's perception of their behaviour toward herself or himself as a singular being establishes the first ego-boundaries as well as a primordial narcissism. As that imaginary knowledge about the others functions in an absolutist, either/or way by alternating between bipolar oppositions of recognition and misrecognition, this produces an ambivalence in the infant's identification – an oscillation between bliss/enchantment, in case of recognition, and hostile intrusions/social rivalry with others, in case of misrecognition by them. Such a relationship is constantly characterised by the libidinal tension between, on one hand, the constant pursuit of an illusory unity of the ego through identification with others who are never the same as it is, and, on the other hand, the persecutory anxiety and the aggressiveness towards the other when the identification fails. If we take that libidinal tension into account, then aggressiveness stems from the narcissism (Lacan 2002: 95) of the infant who still does not speak. Imaginary identification never attains the goal of stable identity and always lures away the infant from herself or himself to others, in other words to alienation. Through life, the subject preserves this striving toward illusory unity that is necessary for the sense of human agency and everyday functioning, but it is never fully attainable and sensed as threatened whenever someone else is perceived as desiring the opposite.

By introducing the necessary alienation of the ego, Lacan normalises paranoia as a phenomenon and makes it a part of everyday psychosocial functioning, or 'the most general structure of human knowledge, which constitutes the ego and objects as having the attributes of permanence, identity, and substance' (Lacan 2002: 90). However, the subject needs to enter into the world of language and social norms – or the symbolic order – to be able to articulate the perceived threats. Nevertheless, according to Lacan, the personifying logic of the imaginary knowledge, developed as a form of necessary delusion in the early dyadic relationships with other people and objects, does not disappear after the entrance in the symbolic order. The subject continues to apply it to the more complex social world of groups, institutions and wider entities.

However, the symbolic order, for Lacan, opens up the possibility of symbolic knowledge as a way out of paranoiac thinking. While imaginary knowledge is expressing paranoiac anxiety over stable things based on identity and being, symbolic knowledge is more nuanced: It loosens one's need to resolve the world into a set of fixed things and curtails ego's narcissistic tendency to rigidity and projection (Paradis 2007: 185). Symbolic knowledge opens up a way out in the psychoanalytic process whose goal is to lead one to the truth about one's unconscious paranoid desire (Evans 1996: 95), which involves insight into and distancing from the subject's own projections. Despite that possibility, the symbolic order cannot prevent conspiratorial interpretations. This is especially so when its power or meaning is questioned, e.g. in the case of crisis, instability, traumatic events or larger social change. One of the most influential contemporary critical theorists who used Lacanian concepts in order to explain a wide range of social or cultural phenomena, Slavoj Žižek (1997), has claimed that this is precisely what happened in the wake of postmodernism, and that one of the symptoms of the depleted power of the Other is the proliferation of conspiracy theories. From that perspective, conspiracy theories can be explained as an attempt to compensate for the impotence of the Other by positing an Other of the Other, or in other words, by imagining that behind the curtain of the apparent social order exists true reality ruled by a conspiracy of malevolent and powerful actors responsible for the societal troubles. According to Žižek, the possibility of conspiracist interpretation is triggered by a traumatic event that disrupts the symbolic order and opens up another order called 'the Real'. The Real in the Lacanian sense is not what we are used to calling reality, because reality is supposedly meaningful, and since its meaning is guaranteed by the social and language norms, it belongs to the symbolic order. The Real is rather the order of jouissance – of enjoyment so intense that it is impossible to bear, let alone to articulate (Lacan associated it with the death drive, i.e. the instincts striving to reduce the tension in the organism to zero, and therefore to destroy life). Since conspiracy theories are rooted in the Real, they start as an experience of breakdown of the fantasies answering the constitutive question of any desire, 'What does the Other want?'. In order to avoid subjective destitution, to protect her or his desire, the subject tries to answer that question by a fantasy about a threat (Žižek 1989: 128). For Lacanian psychoanalysis, such fantasies are the pre-ideological core of ideology. At the same time, the fantasy about a threat functions as a framework that coordinates desire or, in other words, as 'the formal matrix, on which are grafted various ideological formations' (Žižek 1995: 21).

The threat is generally represented as an image of the enemy related to the stereotypes of a given society, and it derives its meaning from a concrete historical-political process that is turned into a narrative. Thus, the core of conspiracy theory is the image of a group of enemies or some enemy of the community. What is the function of such an image? It provides the means by which people try to repair the real trauma through the imaginary and the symbolic order. Usually, the hostile others are conceived as powerful political figures and their allies – corrupt elites, shadowy organisations, institutions or other nations perceived as antagonists allegedly conspiring to achieve some immoral, unlawful or harmful goal. Here, conspiracy theories derive their impulse from the experience of the Real in the 'other', or in other words – from the unfathomable gap of the radical otherness of the Real. Facing this alien, traumatic core as an inert, inaccessible and enigmatic attribute of the other raises the questions: 'Why is our society not functioning?', 'Why are our people suffering?' or 'Who is to be blamed for this?'. According to Lacanian theory, the ultimate question we unconsciously pose in that situation is 'Who is stealing our enjoyment?'.

The general function of conspiracy theories is thus identificational: Defining the enemy in order to define oneself as its mirror image and therefore to anchor the signifiers that identify one's own group, community or society. This dimension of conspiracy theories involves a number of moral distinctions or asymmetrical binaries that ultimately claim to differentiate good from evil. Finally, conspiracy theories have a wider symptomatic function. As emotionally charged explanations, they articulate deeper political cleavages running through the political field by means of interpreting previous traumatic events and processes as encounters with supposed enemies. Conspiracy theory as a symptomatic reading of political reality, a sort of 'behindology' (from the Italian, *dietrologia* – cf. Bratich 2008: 15) reveals the stereotypical images of the hostile others and the objects of enjoyment threatened by them. Regardless of whether the conspiracy theories are warranted or unwarranted, they can function as unconscious mechanisms for citizens' political behaviour (Blanuša 2011b: 311).

## Conclusion

The origins of the pathologisation of conspiratorial thinking are deeply influenced by the psychiatric and psychoanalytic concepts of paranoia. This chapter attempted to sketch their genealogy, together with the application of psychoanalytic accounts by prominent critical social scientists who used them mostly in order to explain totalitarian and extremist threats to democracy during the twentieth century. Later, the Lacanian approach made a significant turn in the psychoanalytic understanding of conspiracy theories. Instead of treating paranoia as an aberration, this approach put it at the heart of human thinking and explained the role of the incessant chains of objects of desire and fantasies in conspiracist cognitive mapping, conceived of as a way to cope with the complexity of the postmodern world shaped by increasingly impersonal regulatory mechanisms. In that way, Lacanian psychoanalysis enables a more nuanced exploration of the function of conspiratorial imagination in the social struggles over meaning, as well as of its political consequences. Although many researchers in cultural studies, sociology or anthropology claim that conspiracy theories could have emancipatory potential, from the perspective of Lacanian psychoanalysis, they are the last ruse of power trying to mask its impotence by representing itself as a mask of an omnipotent clandestine Other (Žižek 2006: 219). Therefore, the proliferation of conspiracy theories is a symptom not of a growing threat to the social order, but of its impotence, just as New Age beliefs are a symptom of the declining power of organised religion, or alternative medicine is a symptom of the declining power of science.

## References

Adorno, T. (1975) *Soziologische Schriften*, vol. 2, Frankfurt: Suhrkamp.
Adorno, T., Frenkel-Brunswik, E., Levinson, D.J. and Sanford, R.N. (1967 [1950]) *The authoritarian personality*, reprint, New York: Wiley.
Bell, D. (ed.) (1955) *The new American right*, New York: Criterion.
Bell, D. (ed.) (1963) *The radical right*, New York: Doubleday.
Blanuša, N. (2011a) 'Depathologized conspiracy theories and cynical reason: discursive positions and phantasmatic structures', *Politička misao*, 48(1): 94–107.
Blanuša, N. (2011b) *Conspiracy theories and Croatian political reality*, Zagreb: Plejada.
Boltanski, L. (2014) *Mysteries and conspiracies: detective stories, spy novels and the making of modern societies*, Cambridge: Polity Press.
Bratich, J.Z. (2008) *Conspiracy panic: political rationality and popular culture*, Albany: State University of New York Press.
Bunzel, J.H. (1967) *Anti-politics in America: reflections on the anti-political temper and its distortions of the democratic process*, New York: Knopf.

Cockburn, C. (2002) 'The horror of it all', *Counterpunch*, 23 March. Available at: www.counterpunch.org/2002/03/23/the-horror-of-it-all/. [Accessed 15 August 2019.]

Dalzell, T. (2011) *Freud's Schreber between psychiatry and psychoanalysis: on subjective disposition to psychosis*, London: Karnac.

DSM-I (1952) *Diagnostic and statistical manual of mental disorders*, 1st edn, Washington: American Psychiatric Association.

Esquirol, E. (1945 [1838]) *Mental maladies: a treatise on insanity*, reprint, London: Lea and Blanchard.

Evans, D. (1996) *An introductory dictionary of Lacanian psychoanalysis*, London: Routledge.

Fenster, M. (2008) *Conspiracy theories: secrecy and power in American culture*, rev. and upd. edn, London: University of Minnesota Press.

Foucault, M. (2003a) *Abnormal: lectures at the Collège de France 1974–75*, London: Palgrave.

Foucault, M. (2003b) *'Society Must Be Defended': lectures at the Collège de France 1975–76*, London: Palgrave.

Foucault, M. (2006) *Psychiatric power: lectures at the collège de France 1973–74*, London: Palgrave.

Freud, S. and Strachey, J. (1976) *The complete psychological works of Sigmund Freud*, New York: W.W. Norton & Company.

Glynos, J. (2001) 'The grip of ideology: a Lacanian approach to the theory of ideology', *Journal of Political Ideologies*, 6(2): 191–214.

Griesinger, W. (1854) *Mental pathology and therapeutics*, London: New Sydenham Society.

Heins, V. (2011) *Beyond friend and foe: the politics of critical theory*, Leiden: Brill.

Hofstadter, R. (1955) 'The pseudo-conservative revolt', in D. Bell (ed.) *The new American right*, New York: Criterion Books, pp. 33–55.

Hofstadter, R. (1996 [1965]) *The paranoid style in American politics and other essays*, reprint, Cambridge: Harvard University Press.

Hristov, T. (2019) *Impossible knowledge: conspiracy theories, power, and truth*, London: Routledge.

Jameson, F. (1988) 'Cognitive mapping', in C. Nelson and L. Grossberg (eds.) *Marxism and the interpretation of culture*, Champaign: Illinois UP, pp. 347–60.

Jameson, F. (1995) *The geopolitical aesthetic*, Bloomington: Indiana University Press.

Jameson, F. (2009) *Valences of the dialectic*, London: Verso.

Kahlbaum, K. (1863) *Die Gruppierung derpPsychischen Krankheiten und die Einteilungen der Seelenstörungen*, Danzig: Kafemann.

Kraepelin, E. (1907) *Clinical psychiatry*, London: Macmillan.

Lacan, J. (1953) 'Some reflections on the ego', *International Journal of Psycho-Analysis*, 34(1): 11–7.

Lacan, J. (1967) 'Proposition on 9 October 1967 on the Psychoanalyst of the School', *The Irish Circle of the Lacanian Orientation*, trans. R. Grigg. Available at: http://iclo-nls.org/wp-content/uploads/Pdf/Propositionof9October1967.pdf. [Accessed 19 August 2018.]

Lacan, J. (1981) *The seminar of Jacques Lacan: book 3: the psychoses 1956–1957*, New York: Norton.

Lacan, J. (1988) *The seminar: book I: Freud's papers on technique, 1953–54*, New York: Norton.

Lacan, J. (2002) *Écrits*, London: Norton.

Lasègue, C. and Falret, J. (2008) 'Shared delusion', in F.-R. Cousin, J. Garrabé and D. Morozov (eds.) *Anthology of French language psychiatric texts*, New York: John Wiley & Sons, pp. 199–212.

Lasswell, H. (1930) *Psychopathology and politics*, Chicago: University of Chicago Press.

Lipset, S.M. and Raab, E. (1970) *The politics of unreason: right-wing extremism in America, 1790–1970*, New York: Harper and Row.

Lowenthal, L. and Guterman, N. (1949) *Prophets of deceit: a study of the techniques of the American agitator*, New York: Harper.

Melley, T. (2000) *Empire of conspiracy: the culture of paranoia in postwar America*, London: Cornell University Press.

Mendel, E. (1884) *Text-book of psychiatry: a psychological study of insanity for preactitioners and students*, reprint, trans. W. Krauss (ed.), Philadelphia: Davis & Co, 1907.

Neumann, F. (1957) *The democratic and the authoritarian state: essays in political and legal theory*, Glencoe: Free Press.

Paradis, K. (2007) *Sex, paranoia, and modern masculinity*, Albany: SUNY Press.

Parker, M. (2001) 'Human science as conspiracy theory', *The Sociological Review*, 48(52): 191–207.

Rogin, M. (1987) *'Ronald Reagan,' the movie: and other episodes in political demonology*, London: University of California Press.

Rovere, R.H. (1956) 'The easy chair: the conspirators', *The Harper's Monthly*, September: 12–21.

Sérieux, P. and Capgras, J. (2008) 'The reasoning insanities: delusion of interpretation', in F.-R. Cousin, J. Garrabé and D. Morozov (eds.) *Anthology of French Language Psychiatric Texts*, New York: John Wiley & Sons, pp. 447–57.

Shils, E. (1956) *The torment of secrecy: the background and consequences of American security politics*, Glencoe, Ill.: The Free Press.

Šiber, I. (1998) *Osnove političke psihologije*, Zagreb: Politička kultura.

Thalmann, K. (2019) *The stigmatization of conspiracy theories since the 1950s: 'A Plot To Make Us Look Foolish'*, London: Routledge.

Thorne, G. (1903) *When it was dark: The story of a great conspiracy*, London: G.P. Putnam's Sons.

Žižek, S. (1989) *The sublime object of ideology*, reprint, London: Verso, 2008.

Žižek, S. (1995) *Mapping ideology*, London: Verso.

Žižek, S. (1997) 'The big other does not exist', *Journal of European Psychoanalysis*. Available at: www.psychomedia.it/jep/number5/zizek.htm. [Accessed 28 November 2016.]

Žižek, S. (2006) *Interrogating the real*, London: Continuum.

# 1.6
# CONSPIRACY THEORY AS OCCULT COSMOLOGY IN ANTHROPOLOGY

*Annika Rabo*

### Introduction: Disciplinary foundations

Modern social and cultural anthropology – hereafter simply anthropology – developed in the historical context of colonialism as a study of non-Western people. Participant observation became the essential fieldwork technique, in large part due to the influence of Bronislaw Malinowski. He worked on the Trobriand Islands during the First World War and published many works that are still read and appreciated. To immerse oneself in the lives of people in a – for the anthropologist – strange place for a long period of time became the ideal guiding research. Fieldwork that extended over a long period of time was conducive to a holistic understanding of the society under scrutiny. What was, for example, conventionally classified as economy and politics or religion, kinship and rituals, should not be studied in isolation, but instead as interconnected and forming a social and cultural whole. By immersing oneself – by observing and participating – in the daily lives of the people, the researcher aims to understand *the natives' point of view*. This, so called, emic perspective (Malinowski 1922: 1–25) is in contrast to an etic, or outsider's perspective. Early anthropologists underlined that it was important to study what people said they were doing, and at the same time study what they actually were doing. Often there was a gap between the two, pointing to particularly interesting areas to understand and analyse. From the beginning, anthropologists also emphasised that nothing human is strange, and that all phenomena, all beliefs and all relations are interesting, and worthy of research and analysis.

Developed more than 100 years ago, these methodological ideals were rooted in anthropological fieldwork in small-scale societies, where relations were generally based on the possibility to have face-to-face relations and where the anthropologist could follow the flow of everyday life. Since then, anthropology has developed enormously as an academic discipline. Anthropologists have critically scrutinised the role of the discipline in different colonial projects, and the, often, naïve assumptions of cultural and social homogeneity in, so called, small-scale societies. Today, fieldwork is conducted all over the world, and anthropologists also come from all over the world, enriching the discipline.

Anthropologists have, furthermore, moved from research in settings where personal, or face-to-face, relations form the basis of social life, to research also in highly complex contexts with a myriad of impersonal social relations. Contemporary anthropologists carry out fieldwork in, for example, NGOs, the E.U., nuclear plants, tea plantations, refugee camps, investment banks and courts of law. Some anthropologists physically follow informants – interlocutors – from one site to another, while others work through the Internet. Some work with many informants while others base their research on a few. Some utilise audiovisual aids, while others still mainly use paper and pen. However, the historical roots of anthropology based on immersion, personal engagement, holism and emphasis on the context of human behaviour and action still guide those who practice the discipline inside, and outside, of academia. For anthropologists, hence, conspiracy theories must be understood in the light of other social and cultural phenomena. Until today, anthropologists have seldom focused mainly on conspiracy theory or related phenomena. These topics have rather emerged while doing fieldwork, and thus been analysed as part of society as a whole. An exception is Jaron Harambam (2017), who researched various arenas of conspiracy culture in the Netherlands. But, as conspiracy theory takes on increased public interest, and urgent concern, we can expect more research focusing on this, and related, phenomena.

The classical genre for anthropological texts has been ethnographies, detailed accounts of, for example, a particular group of people, a village, an urban quarter or an organisation. Such monographs, with what Clifford Geertz (1973) called *thick description*, have been essential for the development of anthropology as a comparative and cross-cultural discipline. Detailed ethnographies become the common empirical and analytical pool on which others can build. Anthropologists frequently turn to research of colleagues and reinterpret or reanalyse material of others, or simply use this material to compare with their own. In some of the works discussed below, the researcher has also been engaged in a particular field for a very long time, reassessing their empirical material. Anthropologists are thus constantly in dialogue with ethnographic material from situations, places or times, which might be far removed from that of the current analysis.

Participant observation, and the immersing of oneself in a field, has been a particular anthropological contribution to many other social and human science disciplines. Anthropologists are, of course, in turn, influenced by developments in other disciplines. Sociology, ethnology and anthropology have in many ways common historical roots and common ancestors. Sociology developed as the science of Western societies in the modern industrial era, ethnology as the discipline capturing the European peasant societies at the verge of their disappearance and anthropology as the study of non-Western societies. Today, such boundaries are no longer equally relevant, and sociologists, ethnologists and anthropologists can be found in similar locations, studying similar phenomena. There is also considerable exchange and overlap between research in anthropology and religious studies, gender studies, cultural studies and media studies. (See, for example, Chapters 3.2, 3.9, 4.1 and 4.7.) In the formative stage of anthropology, cross-cultural comparison was seen as a tool to develop laws about human societies and human behaviour. Today, anthropologists – like other social and cultural scientists – have given up on trying to – even wanting to – formulate universal models. The aim of research is rather to understand the contingency of meaning-making, both that of the interlocutors and that of anthropology.

## The problem of definitions

Debates over terminology frequently erupt in anthropology. How should, for example, *witchcraft* be defined? Is witchcraft the same as *sorcery*? Is *witch-doctor* a concept that obscures more than clarifies? Should the *occult* be closely tied to ideas of *evil*? Should anthropologists use local concepts only, rather than translate them into the languages we frequently use in academic texts? Such questions have no definite answer, but contribute to reflections on important issues in the practice of anthropology. Peter Geschiere, for example, notes that the English *witchcraft* – or the French equivalent *sorcellerie* – has been taken up as a common concept in many parts of the world (2013: xviii).

Generally speaking, anthropological research on conspiracy theory has developed in tandem with research on witchcraft, sorcery and evil forces. It can be summarised in two, often interrelated, lines of inquiry. In the first, anthropologists underline that occult cosmologies – perceptions of the reality of secret and hidden dimensions behind the running of the universe – are phenomena found also in the contemporary world, including the generic West, rather than phenomena human beings have left behind by reaching some stage of economic, social, and cultural development. Occult cosmologies, many argue, even seem to proliferate in the contemporary world and often appear as conspiracy theories. In the second line of inquiry, anthropologists focus on belief systems, on theories of being, and knowledge, among the groups of people we study. In both these lines of inquiry, anthropologists are interested in the ways interpersonal, as well as impersonal, relations are shaped and perceived among our interlocutors. As will be discussed later on, there are also anthropologists who underline that we should abandon the concern with belief and meaning-making of our interlocutors. They argue that, instead, we should analyse their doubts, gaps and inconsistencies in discourses, and in practical action.

## Witchcraft as ordinary *and* extraordinary

The starting point for much anthropological discussions on occult cosmologies is E.E Evans-Pritchard's extremely influential text on witchcraft. In 1926, as a graduate student in anthropology, he conducted fieldwork among the Azande in the southern part of Sudan. Witchcraft was not a topic he had meant to study, but since this was what the Azande were interested in, even obsessed by, and incessantly talked about, it became the focus of his monograph *Witchcraft, Oracles and Magic* (1937). Evans-Pritchard undertook his work on the Azande at a time when ideas of the primitive and irrational non-Westerners were firmly in place. To counteract such ideas, he stressed the rationality of Azande behaviour. Witchcraft accusations, and combating witchcraft with the help of witch-doctors, helped to contain conflicts and to maintain the overall stability of social relations. Such functionalist explanation constituted the dominant theoretical paradigm in, especially British, anthropology into the 1960s. In *Customs and Conflict in Africa*, a book published in 1956, based on BBC lectures for a general audience, Max Gluckman writes how witchcraft beliefs are a reasonable answer to explain misfortune. Witchcraft has its own logic.

The Azande, according to Evans-Pritchard, did not believe in coincidence and instead explained misfortunes, accidents and death by witchcraft. He explained, at great length, that the Azande did not deny that accidents happen. But witchcraft was the answer to the question of why a person was afflicted by misfortune, accidents, illness or death at a specific time, and in a specific place. This reasoning – connecting the dots so to speak and denying the possibility of coincidence – is quite similar to beliefs in conspiracies, as noted by many anthropologists. However, unlike conspirators who scheme in secret and are fully aware of their involvement in conspiratorial activity, witches among the Azande were humans who typically were not aware of being witches. Instead, they were identified by magical means, or with the help of oracles. Witches were responsible for their acts but could not really be blamed, and through various kinds of rituals the witch could repent and be forgiven. Among the Azande, according to Evans-Pritchard, accusations of witchcraft were not randomly distributed. Women did not accuse men, and men did not accuse men of higher status. A witch was typically a person with whom the afflicted (or dead) had personal relations, and he or she was a member of the local community.

Evans-Pritchard notes that some of the more respected members of the community were identified as witches. According to him, the Azande were quite preoccupied with the occurrence of witchcraft and spent time and effort on oracles to find out who bewitched them, or to avoid being bewitched. But they were angry with, rather than afraid of, witchcraft.

A very different situation to that of the Azande is described by Jeanne Favret-Saada in *Deadly Words: Witchcraft in the Bocage* (1980). She started fieldwork in a rural area in western France in the early 1970s. Evans-Pritchard did not have witchcraft in mind when he started his fieldwork, but was compelled to study it, since the Azande were constantly talking about it. Favret-Saada, on the contrary, who was very interested in the topic, had enormous difficulties in approaching the subject, because it was publicly seen as superstition. She writes, comparing Azandeland to the Bocage, that in the former bewitched persons act as part of an accepted idiom, while in the latter they shut themselves off from social life. When afflicted by misfortune, like broken machinery or a sick cow, they do seek the advice of a mechanic or a veterinarian. But these specialists only cure the symptoms. To get to the root cause, they need the help of an un-witcher, in secret (Favret-Saada 1980, 1989). In the Bocage, witchcraft is centred on words that wage a war, and ultimately intend to kill the victim.

The Bocage, as described by Favret-Saada, is a peripheral part of France, far away from the philosophical debates among intellectuals in Paris. But, villagers were still part of a world where the impact of both the Catholic Church and secular education intersected. Priests, teachers, doctors and other experts teach not only villagers in the Bocage, but people all over the world, that witches and beliefs in conspiracies and evil powers have no role – should have no role – in the modern enlightened world. Yet, such beliefs persist or make their appearance in many places. Among the Azande and in the Bocage, the anthropologists make no reference to the link between accusations of witchcraft and conspiracies. In the cases below, however, such a link was commonly made.

## Fear of satanic cults in the U.K. and elsewhere

In the late 1980s, allegations appeared in the U.K. that a great many children were being abused, and even murdered, as part of witchcraft, or of satanic cults. Some towns in the Midlands seemed to be particularly stricken, and social services took a number of children from their parents to rescue them from the clutches of these cults. No evidence for these satanic cults was ever produced, yet the accusations persisted for quite some time. Jean La Fontaine spent years looking into these allegations; interviewing social workers, police, victims, scrutinising official reports, court records and mass media. In *Speak of the Devil* (1998), she traces the development of this scare and puts it into a larger social and political context. She also uses anthropological research into witchcraft and witch hunts in other parts of the world, as well as analyses of the history of witchcraft accusation in early modern Europe. La Fontaine, Evans-Pritchard, Favret-Saada and other anthropologists are concerned with witchcraft in the contemporary world. Their research is, however, indebted to the long and rich tradition in history and ethnology studying witchcraft in the West in the medieval and early modern period (see Walker 1998 for useful references).

La Fontaine traces three phases in these allegations. In the first phase, the influence of discourses originating in the U.S.A. was very clear. Accusations of devil worship and satanic cults started among Pentecostal and charismatic preachers in the U.S.A. Religious activists and self-styled experts began to claim that children were in great danger by such cults. These ideas then spread to the U.K., not least because preachers and activists could speak directly to audiences on both sides of the Atlantic. The U.S. influence waned in the second phase when particular cases of satanic cults involving children were exposed, especially by social workers. They claimed to have collected testimonials from children pointing to the occurrence of rape, ritual murder and even cannibalism. A scrutiny of these testimonials revealed that they were never made by the children themselves, but instead constructed by adults, typically by social workers or therapists.

In this phase, the media was important in spreading sensational allegations and accusations, as well as in spreading doubt and counter-claims. Some social workers were adamant in their campaign to, as they claimed, protect children. Those opposing the reality of these cults were reproached for not taking the problem seriously. There was also a gendered aspect where female social workers accused male police officers of not looking into the charges. Sometimes the police, and other sceptics, were thought to cover-up and conspire to protect important men in high places, who were accused of participating in these vile acts. None of the accusations could be substantiated, and no perpetrator ever was brought to court. This, however, only added to those convinced of cover-ups and conspiracies. In the third phase, it was instead adult victims – survivors – of satanic cults who came to the fore, typically through the support of therapists. Here, they remembered and recounted what they had been exposed to as children when they had been part of satanic cults. Again, developments in the U.S.A. foreshadowed that in the U.K. La Fontaine sees the development, the peak and the fading of these allegations as akin to witch-finding movements. She also underlines that the national and local contexts are very important to understand how this satanic scare could gain momentum.

Another context of a satanism scare is provided by Nicky Falkof. She uses press material between the early 1980s to the early 1990s, the decade before the fall of the South African apartheid regime, to analyse how satanism appeared 'within the white imaginary' (Falkof 2019: 134). In this imaginary, Evangelical Christianity played an important role in depicting a religious war between God and the devil. In the cases discussed by La Fontaine above, adult survivors of a cult claimed to have been abused. Here, instead, the victims claimed to have been possessed. Interestingly, this satanism scare mirrored apartheid's ideology of keeping whites and blacks separate. The scare involved whites only and existed in parallel to, but apart from, black occult forces.

The social context in Falkof's research is the fear among whites at the end of apartheid. La Fontaine brings up the fears and anxiety over changing family dynamics that were rife in both the U.S.A. and the U.K. before the start of the scare. In the U.S.A., the children/victims came from well-off families and accusations were directed against non-family members. In the U.K., on the other hand, children came from deprived families and family members were typically those accused. La Fontaine also places the emergence of the satanic cult scare in the context of growing class differences, and in a situation when politicians frequently accused their opponents of cover-ups and conspiracies. At the time, links between high police officers, the Freemasons, and secret deals and conspiracies, were also common media narratives in the U.K. There are also clear parallels between these stories and historical European antisemitic conspiracy theories in which Jews are depicted as molesters of innocent Christian children (see Chapter 3.8).

Many of the themes discussed by La Fontaine – children versus adults, women versus men, the dangerous family and the dangers to the family, the enrichment of some and the impoverishment of others, cover-ups versus uncovering, courts and legislation, the role of mass media and new religious movements, as well as how ideas and tropes travel across space – reoccur in much of the research discussed below.

## The ambivalence of close relations

When Peter Geschiere did his first fieldwork in southeast Cameroon in the early 1970s, he, like Evans-Pritchard four decades earlier, had no intention of studying witchcraft. Rather, he was interested in modern development issues in a post-colonial state in Africa. But, like Evans-Pritchard's depiction of the Azande, witchcraft was a local idiom he could not ignore. In *The Modernity of Witchcraft* (1997), he discusses preoccupations with the presence of evil forces and the perception that witches and witchcraft have increased. Why did not modernity do away with them? In the following decades, Geschiere kept returning to this issue, and to the difficult question of how to analyse occult cosmologies without depicting his interlocutors as the exotic, superstitious and irrational Others. In *Witchcraft, Intimacy, and Trust: Africa in Comparison* (2013), he reassesses his own material by contrasting and comparing it, in time and space, to the cases of other researchers.

Analyses of contemporary and historical witchcraft underline that accusations are typically made against people who are close to the afflicted. Among the Azande, close kin were typically suspect; in the Bocage, it was the neighbours; and in the British case discussed, parents or other close family members were thought to subject children to satanic abuse. The danger of intimacy – kinship relations and relations in the family – and its connection to witchcraft, is a central theme also for Geschiere. He uses Freud's concept of the uncanny – *Unheimlich* – as a point of entry to understand why people who are close to you can also be people you fear. In Freud's analysis, the uncanny is closely related to *Heimlich*; the homely and the secret. There is a constant risk that the homely and familiar turn into the uncanny. Geschiere discusses how modernity, urbanisation and transnational migration in the post-colonial period has not decreased the importance of family and kinship links. On the contrary, these relations are grafted onto new social elements. This, he cautions, should not be understood in terms of 'African culture' but rather as a product of a particular history. The colonial period wreaked havoc in Cameroon, as in most other places in the world, and expectations were great that independence would usher in a new and better era. These expectations have remained unfulfilled, and family and kin – the *Heimlich* – has developed an elasticity 'to bridge ever deeper inequalities and ever greater distances', making relations 'stretched to a breaking point' (Geschiere 2013: xxviii). This ever-increasing gap between demands for help and support, and the possibility or willingness to act on them, leads to increasing accusations of witchcraft.

## From secret to public accusations

A dramatic change over the last decades is that talk of witchcraft has become open and public. Witchcraft accusations used to be secretive and were seldom made against persons outside the local community. The management of witchcraft – un-witching – was also typically locally grounded. Now, family members and kin live in many places and local witches have migrated too, even to Europe. Those better off fear the demands and the witchcraft of the less fortunate, who in turn may suspect that the better off have used occult means to enrich themselves. The worst accusation used to be that witches were cannibals who ate their victims. But, now, they turn people into zombies who work for them, making the witches ever richer and politically powerful.

But, accusations and fears also go beyond family and kindred. Mass media have played, and continue to play, a large role in the 'uncovering' of evil forces. Not only newspapers, radio and television spread news of witchcraft, but in films produced for a mass audience witches and occult forces were (and still are) a popular topic. Geschiere also discusses the role of the Christian revivalist movements, epitomised by Pentecostalism, in the affirmation of evil forces. Just as in La Fontaine's case, Pentecostalism has played a major role in establishing the reality of the devil. In the vocabulary of charismatic Protestantism, 'witchcraft is part of a cosmic battle between God and the devil' (Geschiere 2013: 182–3). In the minds of his interlocutors, this battle is, however, typically located in the intimacy of the family. Cases of witchcraft also make it to the courts. In the early post-independence period, courts were loath to take up such accusations. These were seen as traditional superstitions and not to be part of modern legislation. Now, because witchcraft is so publicly debated, it has to be taken seriously also by the courts. This, in turn, feeds into ideas of the prevalence and strength of witchcraft.

A claim can be made that conspiracy theory is the impersonal equivalent of witchcraft. But the issue is more complex and ambiguous. Contemporary conspiracy accusations seldom involve family members or neighbours, that is people with whom one has intimate or face-to-face relations. Instead, such accusations are often made against named and known others, such as political figures and economically successful individuals, but they are also typically directed at vaguely defined groups of people far away. In his analysis, Geschiere connects the tension between *Heimlich-Unheimlich* of the family and kin, to the increasing intimacy also in the public sphere. In this way, witchcraft and conspiracy theory can be linked in an analytically fruitful manner. That is, close and personal relations – entailing both positive and negative intimacy – have changed into impersonal bonds, and concomitantly public and more distant relations are expressed in increasingly intimate ways. Witchcraft accusations and conspiracy theories feed into each other at this entangled intersection.

## Occult cosmologies and globalisation

Many researchers focusing on witchcraft and conspiracy theories discuss the impact of modernity, globalisation and political upheaval. In such critical narratives, capitalism is closely associated with evil forces. Jean Comaroff and John Comaroff, for example, characterise the late twentieth century as an age of *futilarianism* where the promises of late capitalism are coupled with postmodern pessimism (1999: 279). In this age, there is a widespread allure that money can be made from nothing, coupled with a widespread fear that those who have made money, have done so by occult means. Comaroff and Comaroff delve into empirical material from South Africa, and analyse the gap between the enormous economic and political expectations in the post-apartheid period, and the reality of new inequalities. This gap has given rise to an occult economy characterised by 'pursuit of new magical means for otherwise unattainable ends' (1999: 284). In Comaroff's and Comaroff's material, accusations of evil deeds are directed against the rich and the powerful, but they note that persons hunted, maimed or killed as witches are typically old and defenceless (1999: 287). Like Geschiere, they underline that ideas of witchcraft, sorcery and conspiracies are not new, although they recognise that the manner in which they are voiced in public, and find their way into mass media and courts, as novel. The close connection between money, commodities, and evil – even the devil – is of course found in many cosmologies and ideologies (see e.g. Taussig 1977).

Zombies, ghosts, evil spirits and the work of the devil seem to have proliferated in many parts of the world. In the introduction to an edited volume, Harry C. West and Todd Sanders (2003) draw attention to the paradoxical connection between transparency and conspiracy. Since the late 1990s, *transparency* has become an international buzzword in the world of development and governance. At the same time, however, the world has become opaquer, leading to increased conspiracy thinking on the part of many people. In case studies from Indonesia, Korea, Nigeria, post-soviet Central Asia and the U.S.A., the authors analyse how their interlocutors grapple with increasing, and large-scale, economic and political inequalities, as well as with personal misfortune. Occult cosmologies and beliefs in conspiracies can provide answers to such dilemmas. In analysis of material from Timor-Leste, Judith Bovensiepen (2016), for example, underlines that visions of prosperity and visions of conspiracy are two sides of the same coin.

Middle-aged and elderly people in a small town in Georgia articulated their experiences of deprivation in the post-Soviet period, according to Katrine Gotfredsen (2016), by implicating the political leaders in national and international conspiracies. In such accounts, clarity and opacity are simultaneously present. The workings of the powerful are hidden, yet it is clear 'what is *really* going on' (2016: 43). Opacity represents the conspiracy, and clarity represents the conspiracy theory.

It is not difficult to find a link between capitalism, neo-liberal governance and the occurrence and even strength of belief in witchcraft and conspiracies. But, as underlined by Heike Behrend, it is important to 'pay close attention to witchcraft in specific social and historical settings' (2007: 43) rather than assume that it is a simple response to current economic and political developments. Her own case concerns increased instances of A.I.D.S.-related deaths from the late 1990s in western Uganda, and how these were blamed on the nefarious activities of witches. Since the 1950s, anthropologists have noticed a link between outbreaks of epidemics and witch-crazes. In the case discussed by Behrend, information campaigns have been successful in medicalising A.I.D.S. People accept that the disease is spread by sexual contact with an infected person. But this explanation is 'perfectly compatible with witchcraft accusations' (2007: 46), since witchcraft provides an answer as to why a *particular person* is infected or dies. Behrend also discusses local perceptions that the A.I.D.S. epidemic is caused by the West, in an attempt to reduce or even destroy the African population. She also analyses how lay organisations of the Catholic Church in western Uganda took up witch-hunts in which cannibals and witches were identified and given a chance to be healed and cleansed (2007: 52). It was these activities that made many people comprehend the enormity of evil in their midst. Paradoxically, the witch-hunt reinforced the belief in, as well as the power of, witches and evil occult powers.

The link between A.I.D.S. and witchcraft has been noted in much research in Sub-Saharan Africa where the disease has reached catastrophic proportions. However, according to Niehaus and Jonsson (2005: 181), in a village in the east of South Africa, people thought that deaths were *either* due to A.I.D.S. *or* to witchcraft. But, while relatives of the deceased claimed that witchcraft caused the death, in an effort to avert the shame related to the disease, outsiders would say that A.I.D.S. was the true cause. They also recorded great gender differences in how H.I.V./A.I.D.S. was talked about. Women 'were committed to biomedical explanations' (Niehaus, Jonsson 2005: 187) and blamed the spread of the disease on oppressive and unfaithful men because of their personal experiences. Men, instead, typically linked the disease to conspiracies outside the local community.

## Female and male idioms and explanations

In much of the material discussed above, conspiracy theories and ideas of witchcraft and sorcery co-exist, intermingle and even seem to reinforce each other. Similar themes and tropes may appear in both conspiracy theories and in witchcraft accusations. In other parts of the world, however, they seem more like parallel systems of belief or explanation. In the Mediterranean region, a masculine idiom of conspiracy is related to national or international politics where every event, no matter how trivial, is seen as planned by powerful and secretive conspirers (Rabo 2014: 222). Masculine talk of conspiracies involves public powerful figures, who are typically men, with whom one mainly has impersonal relationships. In parallel, there is a female idiom in which misfortunes for both women and men are expressed through ideas of sorcery, the evil eye and witchcraft. Such an analysis has, for example, been undertaken by Eva Evers-Rosander (1991). She started fieldwork in the middle of the 1970s, focusing on women and identity in the north of Morocco, in a region close to the Spanish enclaves of Ceuta and Melilla.

Women took it upon themselves to manage and both internalise and externalise problematic, and conflict ridden, interpersonal relations in the local patriarchal community. Both women and men can be afflicted by various representations of evil. But talking about the afflictions and their causes is a female genre, where women come to evaluate other women's behaviour. Through such talk, they reaffirm a gender ideology where women can be blamed for the misconduct, or misfortune, of men.

The importance of gender and age in who is either accused or afflicted by sorcery, witchcraft and conspiracy has been shown in much of the research discussed above. Among the Azande, for example, women never accused men of being witches. Children were the main victims in the accusation of satanic cults analysed by La Fontaine, and women were central in trying to protect them, and also accused men in authority of cover-ups and conspiracies. Adults who remembered childhood participation in satanic cults, where sexual abuse played a major part, were often supported by female therapists. In the U.S.A., most who see themselves as abducted by extra-terrestrials are women. Preoccupation with sex, sexuality and gendered identities is found everywhere, but it is expressed in a variety of ways. In the conservative Russian Parent's Movement, studied by Tova Höjdestrand (2017), for example, both foreign and domestic liberal schemers are perceived to deliberately pervert 'natural' sexuality in order to undermine healthy and traditional family relations.

## The U.S.A. and the transfer of conspiracy theories

The uncanny makes its appearance, not only in Peter Geschiere's work, but also in Susan Lepselter's ethnography of 'vernacular American poetics' (2016: 1). She follows the often ephemeral, muted and incoherent narratives of U.F.O.s, abductions, cover-ups and conspiracies as expressed by her interlocutors. Lepselter uses *apophenia* – the experience that unrelated objects or phenomena are connected – not to underline faulty perception in a person (as done in mainstream cognitive psychology), but instead to point to an ability to start to discern the unseen, to make sense of things seemingly senseless. She undertakes a concrete journey in the U.S.A., stopping in places particularly charged with meaning for those who can, or strive, *to connect the dots*, such as in Rachel, Nevada, located close to a large military complex. In such places, her interlocutors share narratives and memories in which the homely and familiar and the uncanny are mixed and mingled. She notes that abductions by extra-terrestrials and contact with the unseen are simultaneously loathed and embraced.

It is little surprising that millenarian movements and apocalyptic cults resurfaced at the turn of the twentieth century. In response, research focusing on such phenomena also emerged. Kathleen Steward and Susan Harding (1999) draw attention to the co-production of research on, and occurrence of, apocalyptic ideas. Christopher Roth writes about the intersections between the study of extra-terrestrials and unidentified flying objects on the one hand and academic social science on the other. In doing so, he points to the preoccupation with race, and that classification of race is found in both ufology and early anthropology. He also underlines that the Internet has 'facilitated a convergence between ufological and conspiracy-theory discourses that is now nearly total' (2005: 57). Debbora Battaglia (2005) situates the American concern with E.T. cultures in a context of economic and political insecurity, but also in a context of hope for a better future. Possible worlds out there in space might, after all, have the solutions to the problems that plague us on earth and here and now. The context for Lepselter is the ambivalence with which Americans view the state. Her interlocutors tap into the American trope of freedom: Freedom from the state, freedom to roam and to fulfil one's own dreams.

Another apocalyptic narrative emerging in the U.S.A. towards the end of the twentieth century was that of chemtrails. Since then, it has appeared in many parts of the world. In Greece, for example, it gained momentum after the economic crisis in 2009. Alexandra Bakalaki has followed this narrative through online forums, interviews with activists and discussions with Greeks from all walks of life. She frames the narrative in terms of a cosmological discourse where 'multiple relations between different scales of geography, power, and time,' is established (Bakalaki 2016: 13). In Greece, she notes, people are not only attacked through economic and political weapons, but also from the air, by planes. The chemtrail narrative, in which all organisms on earth are threatened, can be understood as part of broader concerns of human existence in the contemporary world. What makes it unique, she claims, 'is the depth of its pessimism' (Bakalaki 2016: 20).

Anthropologists, like other researchers studying the U.S.A., are clearly in dialogue with Richard Hofstadter's study (1964) *The Paranoid Style in American Politics*. George Marcus, for example, introduces the edited volume *Paranoia within Reason* by noting that 'a paranoid understanding of a social field … is both detectable and manifest in different ways' (Marcus 1999: 2). It is, for example, important to realise that the Cold War era thrived on, and developed, paranoid 'social thought and action' (Marcus 1999: 2). More recently, Ulf Hannerz has analysed U.S. politics as entertainment, which may find manifestations in conspiracy theory. He writes that 'the suspicion that things are not what they seem to be, or are made out to be, continues to find new expressions' (2017: 114). Hannerz calls the U.S.A. a *theatre state*, connecting his observations to Clifford Geertz' analysis of Bali's political history. Theatre politics entail not only a public front stage, but also the secret back stage. Subversive readings of everything connected to politics has been noted by anthropologists and others working in especially countries with totalitarian regimes. The entertainment aspect and theatrical performativity of conspiracy theories or conspiracy talk can be found also in other parts of the world (Rabo 2014: 223).

## Conspiracy theory and social theory

In much of the research discussed above – in much social science research in general – sorcery, witchcraft and conspiracy theory is understood as one particular way to handle and explain misfortune on the part of people lacking power and influence. But, powerful people are equally involved in using, spreading and constructing discourses of witchcraft and conspiracies. Critique against the emphasis on the sense-making aspects of conspiracy theories – a lingering functionalism – is raised by Mathijs Pelkmans and Rhys Machold. They argue that we also need to interrogate 'the links between power and truth' (Pelkmans, Machold 2011: 68). There is, thus, a need to be cautious when explaining witchcraft and conspiracy mainly as a response to illness, adversity or increased inequalities.

Anthropologists, like other researchers in the social sciences and humanities, have also found parallels between conspiracy theories and social theory. George Marcus reminds us that a paranoid style of thought is 'close to the surface' (1999: 3) in game theory and the so-called prisoner's dilemma, commonly used in political science. Martin Parker argues that 'contemporary theories of conspiracy share a narrative structure with much of human science generally' (2000: 191). The resemblance between conspiracy theories and sociological theories is also analysed by Stef Aupers and Jaron Harambam. They draw attention to the deep concern of social scientists to draw boundaries between their own theories and forms of knowledge, which can be labelled 'inferior, irrational' (2019: 58). Many elements in contemporary conspiracy theories such as chemtrails, extra-terrestrials or the attack on the Twin Towers in 2001 involve scientific material. In his study of the Dutch conspiracy milieu, Jaron Harambam (2017) found that his interlocutors were deeply sceptical of mainstream scientific claims about such phenomena. But, at the same time, they were actively seeking, or producing, their own claims by leaning on, or developing, alternative sources of knowledge, believed to represent better science. Ufology, for example, mirrors the practices of established academic science (Roth 2005). There are great conflicts over claims of truth in, what Harambam terms, our age of epistemic instability. Yet, rather paradoxically, many propagating, what is commonly called, conspiracy theories, claim that true knowledge is possible. *The truth is out there*, in a popular and popularised phrase.

## Clarity, opacity, belief and doubt

A common theme in the research discussed, as has already been stated, is the tension between what can be seen and that which is under the surface. People seek clarity but, instead, encounter opacity. Signs are searched and interpreted. Even hidden urban infrastructure – pipes and electricity lines – may become a site for divination, for finding clarity and answers to the stress of city life (Trovalla, Trovalla 2015). In the realm of witchcraft, evil cosmologies or in encounters with the uncanny, we may find un-witchers, therapists or support groups, working to find the hidden causes of an individual's suffering or misfortune, as discussed above. In the realm of conspiracy theory, there are experts who devote their life to explaining the unseen connections. There are also similarities between the anthropologist, the un-witcher and the conspiracy expert. The researcher takes note of the observable and then draws conclusions of what *really* is going on, and of what it all *really* means, or at least, gives plausible or insightful interpretations.

Participant observation generally entails intense and often personal, and sometimes stressful, relations with interlocutors. Working in an environment of witchcraft, sorcery and conspiracy accusations involves both ethical and epistemological dilemmas for the fieldworker. To representatives of churches and organisations for whom the devil and evil forces or scheming conspirators are very real, the anthropological stance of suspended disbelief can be very provocative (see Geschiere 2013). Decades ago, there were debates among anthropologists about the need to analytically distance oneself from the field and refrain from *going native*. E.E. Evans-Pritchard, for example, underlines that witches do not exist. But, he also explains that he found it very practical to follow the Azande habit of keeping and consulting oracles to see if ill will, or witchcraft, was afoot. Paul Stoller, on the other hand, not only studied witchcraft as a dispassionate observer, but, rather, between 1976 and 1984, enrolled as an apprentice among Songhay sorcerers in Niger. This had terrifying consequences when he was caught in power struggles between different sorcerers (Stoller, Olkes 1987). For Jeanne Favret-Saada, who did fieldwork in rural France in the 1970s, witchcraft was a highly secret affair among those afflicted, as discussed. But, being caught in its web became a powerful and frightening way for her to understand the forces and emotions at play.

An important shift in anthropology is the move away from *belief* to *doubt* when analysing religion, cosmologies and conspiracy theories. Mathijs Pelkmans argues that 'doubt connects belief and disbelief, action and inaction' and it 'is always on the move' (2013: 15). The anthropology of doubt, mistrust and un-belief reflects developments within the academic discipline where we are less and less certain of most issues. But it also reflects the complexity of social life in many places where, when listening carefully, anthropologists discern that people may claim to believe, to have found the truth, but simultaneously express doubt.

'I have never seen a cannibal witch. The closest I have ever come to seeing one was in June 1992.' These are the opening lines of Nils Bubandt's book (2014: ix) on witchcraft and doubt on a small Indonesian island. Instead of seeing the witch, he rather heard it scratching on the roof of his hut. Bubandt, like Stoller and Favret-Saada, discusses not only how their interlocutors fear witchcraft and sorcery, but how also he became afflicted by this emotion. Bubandt's fieldwork on this small island stretches across almost two years over a period of two decades. Like Favret-Saada, he is critical of the stress on belief and meaning among anthropologists and others when analysing witchcraft. For Favret-Saada, belief and disbelief in witchcraft cannot be separated, but are instead intertwined (see Kyriakides 2016) and, although cannibal witches are feared, doubt is the prevailing mode of thought among the islanders Bubandt lived with. Witchcraft accusations and witchcraft hunts in Europe, he argues, did not disappear through the spread of doubt and scepticism. On the contrary, such modes of thinking ushered in witch crazes. As has been discussed, fighting witchcraft makes the reality of witches credible. In the same vein, denying conspiracies reaffirms their reality and importance in the minds of – for lack of better and more sensitive vocabulary – conspiracy theorists.

## Conclusion

Anthropological research on occult cosmologies including conspiracy theories is, as discussed, wide-ranging and moves from an analysis of intimate relations to relations connected to political power and the global economy. A basic tenet in anthropology is that all people are united by a common humanity, but how we organise our societies and our life worlds differ. And these are the differences that interest us. Illness, adversity and misfortune are always present in the lives of human beings everywhere. They must be handled, explained and solved in ways that are socially and culturally meaningful. When analysing such heterogeneous and complex phenomena as conspiracy theory and occult cosmologies, it is important to contextualise their particular manifestations. Anthropological research points to the enormous versatility and adaptability of these phenomena, and to the possible connections between them. Thus, they are, paraphrasing the famous anthropologist Claude Levi-Strauss, good to think with because they point to fundamental concerns for humanity.

## References

Aupers, S. and Harambam, J. (2019) 'Rational enchantments. Conspiracy theory between secular scepticism and spiritual salvation', in A. Dyrendal, D. Robertson and E. Asprem (eds.) *Handbook of Conspiracy Theory and Contemporary Religion*, Leiden: Brill, pp. 48–69.
Bakalaki, A. (2016) 'Chemtrails, crisis, and loss in an interconnected world', *Visual Anthropology Review*, 32(1): 12–23.
Battaglia, D. (2005) 'Insider's voices in outerspaces', in D. Battaglia (ed.) *E.T. culture: anthropology in outerspaces*, Durham: Duke University Press, pp. 1–37.
Behrend, H. (2007) 'The rise of occult powers, AIDS and the Roman Catholic Church in Western Uganda', *Journal of religion in Africa*, 37(1): 41–58.
Bovensiepen, J. (2016) 'Visions of prosperity and conspiracy in Timor-Leste', *Focaal –Journal of Global and Historical Anthropology*, 75: 75–88.
Bubandt, N. (2014) *The empty seashell: witchcraft and doubt on an Indonesian island*, Ithaca: Cornell University Press.
Comaroff, J. and Comaroff, J. (1999) 'Occult economies and the violence of abstraction: notes from the South African postcolony', *American Ethnologist*, 26(2): 279–303.
Evans-Pritchard, E. (1937) *Witchcraft, oracles and magic among the Azande*, abridged version, Oxford: Clarendon Press, 1976.
Evers-Rosander, E. (1991) *Women in a borderland: managing Muslim identity where Morocco meets Spain*, Stockholm: Stockholm Studies in Social Anthropology.
Falkof, N. (2019) 'The satanism scare in apartheid South Africa', in A. Dyrendal, D. Robertson and E. Asprem (eds.) *Handbook of Conspiracy Theory and Contemporary Religion*, Leiden: Brill, pp. 133–51.
Favret-Saada, J. (1980) *Deadly words: witchcraft in the Bocage*, Cambridge: Cambridge University Press.

Favret-Saada, J. (1989) 'Unbewitching as therapy', *American Ethnologist*, 16(1): 40–56.
Geertz, C. (1973) *The interpretation of cultures*, New York: Basic Books.
Geschiere, P. (1997) *The modernity of witchcraft: politics and the occult in postcolonial Africa*, Charlottesville: University Press of Virginia.
Geschiere, P. (2013) *Witchcraft, intimacy and trust: Africa in comparison*, Chicago: Chicago University Press.
Gluckman, M. (1956) *Custom and conflict in Africa*, Oxford: Blackwell.
Gotfredsen Bendtsen, K. (2016) 'Enemies of the people: theorizing dispossession and mirroring conspiracy in the Republic of Georgia', *Focaal. Journal of Global and Historical Anthropology*, 74: 42–53.
Hannerz, U. (2017) 'American theater state: reflections on political culture', in V. Dominguez and J. Habib (eds.) *American observed: on an international anthropology of the United States*, New York: Berghahn, pp. 103–19.
Harambam, J. (2017) *'The truth is out there': Conspiracy culture in an age of epistemic instability*, Rotterdam: Erasmus University.
Hofstadter, R. (1964) *The paranoid style in American politics, and other essays*, New Haven: Harvard University Press.
Höjdestrand, T. (2017) 'Nationalism and civicness in contemporary Russia: grassroots mobilization in defense of traditional family values', in K. Fábián and E. Korolczuk (eds.) *Rebellious Parents: parental movements in Central-Eastern Europe and Russia*, Bloomington: Indiana University Press, pp. 31–60.
Kyriakides, T. (2016) 'Jeanne Favret-Saada's minimal ontology: belief and disbelief of mystical forces, perilous conditions, and the opacity of being', *Religion and Society – Advances in Research*, 7: 68–82.
La Fontaine, J. (1998) *Speak of the devil: tales of satanic abuse in contemporary England*, Cambridge: Cambridge University Press.
Lepselter, S. (2016) *The resonance of unseen things: poetics, power, captivity, and UFOs in the American uncanny*, Ann Arbor: University of Michigan Press.
Malinowski, B. (1922) *Argonauts of the western Pacific*, London: Routledge and Keegan Paul.
Marcus, G. (1999) 'Introduction: the paranoid style now', in G. Marcus (ed.) *Paranoia within reason: a casebook on conspiracy as explanation*, Chicago: The University of Chicago Press, pp. 1–11.
Niehaus, I. and Jonsson, G. (2005) 'Dr. Wouter Basson, Americans, and the wild beasts: men's conspiracy theories of HIV/AIDS in the south African Lowveld', *Medical Anthropology*, 24(2): 179–208.
Parker, M. (2000) 'Human science as conspiracy theory', *The Sociological Review*, 48(2): 191–207.
Pelkmans, M. (2013) 'Outline for an ethnography of doubt', in M. Pelkmans (ed.) *Ethnographies of doubt: faith and uncertainty in contemporary societies*, London: I.B. Tauris, pp. 1–42.
Pelkmans, M. and Machold, R. (2011) 'Conspiracy theories and their truth trajectories', *Focaal. Journal of Global and Historical Anthropology*, 59: 66–80.
Rabo, A. (2014) '"It has all been planned": talking about us and powerful others in contemporary Syria', in M. Butter and M. Reinkowski (eds.) *Conspiracy Theories in the United States and the Middle East*, Berlin/Boston: de Gruyter, pp. 212–27.
Roth, C. (2005) 'Ufology as anthropology: race, extraterrestrials, and the occult', in D. Battaglia (ed.) *E.T. Culture: anthropology in outerspaces*, Durham: Duke University Press, pp. 38–93.
Stewart, K. and Harding, S. (1999) 'Bad endings: American apocalypsis', *Annual Review of Anthropology*, 28: 285–310.
Stoller, P. and Olkes, C. (1987) *In sorcery's shadow*, Chicago: The University of Chicago Press.
Taussig, M. (1977) 'The genesis of capitalism amongst a South American peasantry: devil's labor and the baptism of money', *Comparative Studies in Society and History*, 19(2): 130–55.
Trovalla, E. and Trovalla, U. (2015) 'Infrastructure as a divination tool: whispers from the grids in a Nigerian city', *City*, 19(2–3): 332–43.
Walker, G. (1998) 'Witchcraft and history', *Women's History Review*, 7(3): 425–32.
West, H. and Sanders, T. (2003) 'Power revealed and power concealed in the new world order', in H. West and T. Sanders (eds.) *Transparency and conspiracy: ethnographies of suspicion in the new world order*, Durham: Duke University Press, pp. 1–37.

# 1.7
# SOCIOLOGY, SOCIAL THEORY AND CONSPIRACY THEORY

*Türkay Salim Nefes and Alejandro Romero-Reche*

### Introduction

Social thought, concerned with the workings of community, society and the body politic, is, arguably, as old as philosophy. Sociology, on the other hand, is much younger: Traditionally regarded as an offspring of modernity, in its first formulations it was designed to produce scientific knowledge about social reality in general, and the great social transformations of its time in particular, essentially by applying the same methods as the natural sciences. Scientific sociology, as conceived by founding fathers such as Comte or Durkheim, was not expected to speculate about social reality, it was supposed to ascertain how it worked: Empirical research, guided by theory, would unveil the hidden laws of society just as Newton had discovered the laws of physics.

Conspiracy theories are probably as old as social theory, even if the label under which we file them is relatively new. However, several authors (e.g. Bronner 2013; Byford 2015) argue that today's conspiracy theories are distinguished by a prevalence of 'beliefs in fantastic conspiracies with a planetary reach', which feed 'the confusion and uncertainty that seem to characterize contemporary society' (Campion-Vincent 2005: 7–8).

It is only to be expected that sociology, as a modern science, should be interested in modern (and postmodern) conspiracy theories, even more so when conspiracy theories often are 'social theories' (that is, theories about society) that provide rival explanations of social reality. Furthermore, sociology and conspiracy theories are, according to Boltanski (2012), deeply intertwined with one another and with the social and political processes that shape modern society. From its most empirically oriented approaches, as a science of public opinion, to the most abstract theorising, sociology needs to understand and, if possible, explain how conspiracy theories are spread, how people use them to make sense of the world and what social effects might be derived from belief in them.

This chapter examines how sociology and social theory have addressed conspiracy theories. The first sections consider how conspiracy theories have been understood as either alternative sociological theories or misguided social science, and show how sociology tends to conceptualise conspiracy theory, summarising a number of strategies deployed by sociologists and some critiques of their problematic nature. The next section addresses some of the essential methodological questions that any research strategy must respond to, briefly discussing the limitations and advantages of possible answers to such questions and providing a few examples. The chapter details the main theoretical perspectives that have been proposed when trying to understand the popularity and global appeal of conspiracy theories; unsurprisingly, modernity and its processes loom prominently over the field. The last sections outline some of the most relevant approaches for empirical research in the sociology of conspiracy theories and offer a few thoughts on where its future developments may be headed.

## Social reality as a conspiracy

Conspiracy theories are relevant to sociology and social theory, not only because they are socially and politically relevant, but also because they raise questions about sociology itself and how we should proceed in the quest for knowledge on social reality. Popper's notion of 'the conspiracy theory of society' was explicitly formulated as a model of what the social sciences should not do: Explain social reality as the successful outcome of intentional (secret) actions by powerful groups (2002 [1963]). Instead, he argued, social sciences should focus on the unintentional consequences of intentional actions: Conspiracy theorists 'assume that we can explain practically everything in society by asking who wanted it, whereas the real task of the social sciences is to explain those things that nobody wants' (Popper 2002: 167). In his defence of methodological individualism, Popper questions the scientific soundness in invoking collective 'entities' in explanations of social reality. Boltanski (2012) has called this challenge 'Popper's curse' and reads many of the methodological turns in contemporary social theory as attempts to defeat it.

Other social theorists have subscribed to this vision of conspiracy theories as misguided sociology, often distorted by 'radical' or 'critical' ideologies. Boudon, echoing Popper, states that 'Marxism has given a *learned* appearance and, therefore, legitimacy, to an eternal explicative scheme: *conspiracy theory*' (2004: 41). Taguieff (2013: 81–2) points out that sociologist Pierre Bourdieu entertained the notion of an 'invisible world government' in one of his latter books (*Contre-feux 2*, 2001), and offers it as an example of a 'sociology of unveiling', institutionalised in France by Bourdieu himself, which he regards as an updated version of Marxist 'unmasking' and, therefore, sharing its conspiracist undertones. Ho and Jin (2011), who examined in further detail the Taguieff-Bourdieu controversy, believe that methodological individualism is not an effective antidote to conspiracy theorising in sociology, since in their view it postulates a transparent and rationalised society that does not exist either.

Precisely from a Marxist perspective, Fredric Jameson, who famously deemed conspiracy 'the poor person's cognitive mapping in the postmodern age' (1988: 356), located the seedbed of conspiracy theorising in the shift from the discourse of social science ('a discourse without subject') to ideology ('how you map your relation as an individual subject to the social and economic organization of global capitalism'). Conspiracy is 'a narrative structure capable of reuniting the minimal basic components' when 'fantasizing an economic system on the scale of the globe itself': 'a potentially infinite network, along with a plausible explanation of its invisibility' (Jameson 1992: 9).

Conspiracy theorising has been sometimes regarded as a sort of popular or 'lay' sociology (Waters 1997; Boltanski 2012), which seems to provide the satisfactory, comprehensive explanations that scientific sociology cannot, even less when notions of contingency and indeterminacy make its findings tentative at best. If we can regard sociology (or specific sociologies) as conspiracy theorising, and conspiracy theorising as (a sort of) sociology, it is likely that they influence or even feed each other (Romero-Reche 2018). Sociology hones ideas for conspiracy theories: 'radical claims about social control, developed in the social sciences, are nowadays popularized by conspiracy theorists' (Aupers 2012: 29). Sociologists are conspiracy entrepreneurs themselves, for they help disseminate the conspiracy theories that they criticise (Campion-Vincent 2015). Social scientists create and popularise critical thinking tools that are later used against them by conspiracy theorists (Latour 2004).

As Ho and Jin put it:

> [It] is impossible to totally dissociate sociological theory from conspiracy theory. Would it not be conceivable that sociology feeds the imaginary of conspiracy and is fed back by it? Such is, in fact, the question that conspiracy theory raises: any condemnation of it leads to its acknowledgment.
>
> *(2011: 148)*

Sociologists respond to these accusations by arguing that empirical social science is far removed from conspiracy theorising, at the very least to the extent that its claims are methodically tested, rather than assumed as confirmed by cherry-picking or downright fabricating the most convenient proofs.

## Sociological definitions of conspiracy theory

Conspiracy theories can be regarded as sets of ideas and beliefs. However private and deeply personal these may be, ideas and beliefs have a social dimension that is essential to any sociological conception of conspiracy theories. Sociology's own theoretical and methodological traditions, and the discipline's focus on contemporary societies, which does not exclude historical approaches, shape how it conceptualises the notion of conspiracy theory and the way it is operationalised in sociological research.

As other chapters in this section attest, defining the term 'conspiracy theory' is not an easy undertaking. Any definition must be precise enough to distinguish conspiracy theories from other kinds of beliefs and ideas, but not so specific as to exclude important aspects of the phenomenon. Many of the problems in a definition of 'conspiracy theory' stem from the very notion of 'conspiracy': A detailed discussion of such problems, from a social theory standpoint, can be found in Boltanski (2012: 282–7), who points out that all the defining features that are normally used – secrecy, coordination, intention or illegality among others – can be easily challenged.

Given the normative connotations of the term 'conspiracy theory', sociology faces an additional problem when it comes to its usage, let alone its definition: For a discipline that historically prided itself in being value-free, taking a notion as value-charged as 'conspiracy theory' ('the intellectual equivalent of four-letter words', as Chomsky stated in an oft-quoted interview; Chomsky 2004) should imply certain theoretical challenges.

Faced with these challenges, sociologists have adopted four main strategies. One of the most frequent has been to simply avoid the formulation of any definition and to take it for granted, with or without its normative connotations. Even if the category is not clearly outlined, an author who adopts this approach assumes a sort of implicit consensus: Much like Supreme Court Justice Potter Stewart knew pornography when he saw it, readers are expected to recognise conspiracy theories without recourse to a specific profile already sketched by the author. Examples of this can be found in Bronner (2015) or Renard (2015), among others.

A second strategy is ostensive definition: The author does not explicitly define what is meant by conspiracy theory, but points to popular examples that most readers are supposed to agree upon. This is a common opener for papers and books on conspiracy theories: A list of well-known cases that provide a general idea of the kind of beliefs that the text will be analysing. For instance, in his early work on the relationship between conspiracy theories and fundamentalist ideologies, Nefes (2011) does not formulate a working definition of conspiracy theory, but instead uses *The Protocols of the Elders of Zion* as a representative case.

A third strategy is explicit definition, either accepting its normative connotations, or trying to exclude them from a neutral perspective. For instance, according to Campion-Vincent (2005: 9), conspiracy theories 'either refer to fantasy conspiracies, which do not exist, or deform the presentation of real conspiracies, usually enlarging them beyond reason. Conspiracies have to do with actions, conspiracy theories with *perceptions*'. Following Barkun (2003), she reiterates the three 'rules' of the conspiracy theorist: 'EVERYTHING IS CONNECTED' (in capitals), 'nothing happens by chance' and 'things are not what they seem to be' (Campion-Vincent 2005: 11–12), a set of axioms that has been later used by other sociologists, such as Bronner (2013: 12), in their own conceptualisation.

An example of the value-free position can be found in Harambam, who defines conspiracy theories as 'explanations of social phenomena involving the secret actions of some people trying to bring about a certain desired outcome' (2017: 4), and deliberately states that 'we should write about conspiracy theories in ways that leave normative judgments to the reader and not weave them into our texts' (Harambam 2017: 25).

A fourth strategy is the creation of a new term, including some or most of the phenomena covered by the previous label, but excluding the implicit value judgments that it carried. Hence 'conspiracism', 'conspiracy narratives' or 'conspiratorial distrust', which

> contrary to the colloquial understanding of conspiracy theory, is not necessarily false and in many cases, we are not in position to tell whether it is true or not. Therefore, no one can say that, by definition, it is an unwarranted accusation without merit.
> (Czech 2018: 667)

Each strategy has its strengths and weaknesses. Relying at least on a working definition of conspiracy theory (third strategy) seems to be a necessity in order to validate theoretical perspectives and methodological approaches as well as empirical findings. It is probably an essential step towards universal conclusions and international comparisons. Using a different term to dodge the pejorative connotations of conspiracy theory (fourth strategy) may prove useful, but it also might create conceptual confusion. Indeed, one reason to study conspiracy theory is to directly examine the value of negative views and possibly to challenge them.

The first and second strategies provide a de facto definition which, if explicitly stated, would echo Berger and Luckmann's (1966) approach to knowledge: If the sociology of knowledge should study anything that is deemed 'knowledge' in a given society, regardless of its validity or the criteria used to establish it, the sociology of conspiracy theory seems to study anything that is deemed a conspiracy theory in a given society.

However elusive such an approach may be, it points to another crucial problem, both for theoretical and empirical perspectives: How the value-charged notion of conspiracy theory is socially constructed, and how specific theories fall on the inner or outer side of its border (or somewhere in the fuzzy in-between zone where 'legitimate' and 'illegitimate' forms of knowledge overlap). As Harambam warns: 'A good sociological understanding of conspiracy culture can [...] not stay insensitive to the definitional practices construing conspiracy theories as deviant forms of knowledge' (2017: 21).

One of the most influential sociological examinations of the usage of the labels 'conspiracy theory' and 'conspiracy theorist' as tools for the exclusion of deviant ideas is Husting and Orr's

2007 article 'Dangerous Machinery'. Analysing discourses from print news and academic texts, the authors show how the terms are used to avoid discussing specific statements or claims, or evaluating them on their merits, by questioning those who propose them. This, in their view, is a predictable development in a public arena dominated by anxiety and fear, where 'new interactional mechanisms' emerge 'to shield authority and legitimacy from challenge or accountability in a society characterised by political, economic and cultural inequalities' (Husting, Orr 2017: 130). Hence, critics are discredited and excluded from public discussion, and uncomfortable and relevant questions about motive, corruption and power are circumvented. In addition to classic approaches (Hofstadter 1964; Pipes 1997) that pathologised conspiracy theories, Husting and Orr also examine how more nuanced analyses (Fenster 1999; Melley 2002, 2008; Knight 2002) contribute to a 'reification' of the label rather than to a reconsideration: 'suggestions of individual delusion sneak in sideways, and the power of the phrase to go meta remains unchallenged by those who seek to trouble facile uses of the label' (Husting, Orr 2007: 143). In response to such discursive attacks, those excluded develop defensive strategies, like the pre-emptive use of disclaimers: 'I'm not a conspiracy theorist, but …'.

## Methodological questions

Our understanding of the nature of conspiracy theories as social phenomena, and certainly our definition, will necessarily influence our epistemological assumptions. Depending on our understanding of what is meant by conspiracy theories, we will have different ideas regarding what we could know about them, and how we could acquire such knowledge.

In order to design a methodological approach, any sociological research on conspiracy theories is usually forced to address, whether implicitly or explicitly, the following questions:

1. *Normative or value-free approach?* Some sociologists open their reports on conspiracy theories by revealing their misgivings about or even their active opposition to the phenomenon they are studying, pointing to the damages it can inflict on democracy or public health (e. g. Bronner 2013: 16–8). Others, as has already been mentioned, defend a neutral position. Harambam insists that sociologists 'should not need to *take sides*, we should not say what is true or just, but we ought to make sure that the best available truth – whatever we define as *best* – will prevail' (2017: 273).

2. *How should the micro and macro dimensions be balanced?* Since both approaches are not mutually exclusive but, rather, enrich and complement each other, researchers need to consider to what extent they will focus on individual believers, on large-scale processes and/ or on the wide variety of social institutions that lie between both extremes. Close examinations of the personal *Erlebnis* of conspiracy theorists, collecting data on their feelings of anxiety and insecurity, usually need to connect such experiences with the wider social context and the processes that shape it.

While most of the academic studies on conspiracy theories have focused on the micro-level of the communication of individuals (e.g. Uscinski, Parent 2014; Uscinski et al. 2016), a minority in the field shed light on the macro-level significance of these accounts. For example, Nefes (2013, 2018) analyse the communication of these accounts among political parties in Turkey; McKenzie-McHarg and Fredheim (2017) explore conspiracy accounts in the British parliamentary debates between 1916 and 2015.

3. *Should the points of view of conspiracy theorists be taken account of?* And, specifically, *what role does rationality play in conspiracy theories?* Even some authors who eloquently take a stand against conspiracy theories, characterising them as incorrect, harmful ideas, assume that their adherents have reasons to believe in them, and that such reasons are essential to a sociological explanation (Boudon 2004; Bronner 2013, 2015; Renard 2015). Either conspiracy theories make sense, or

believers make sense of them: In their circumstances, it is *reasonable* to create, propagate and/or believe in conspiracy theories (Billig 1988; Bratich 2008). This basic assumption can lead to explicit Weberian *verstehende* approaches (Aupers 2012; Harambam 2017; Cicchelli, Octobre 2018) or to rational and social choice theory (Nefes 2015a, 2015b, 2017; Atkinson, Dewitt 2018). A structuralist view might under-examine reasons and meanings at an individual level, maybe endorsing the hypodermic needle theory of media influence, but at the risk of considering individuals as, in the celebrated term of ethnomethodologist Harold Garfinkel, 'cultural dopes'.

4. *Is culture enough to explain the prevalence of conspiracy theories or do we need independent variables?* Conspiracy theories are a cultural phenomenon. Sociology, often betraying a Marxian heritage, usually treats cultural products and processes as epiphenomena for other 'prime movers' in social life: Economic, political or social structure variables that explain the history of ideas. Alternatively, cultural sociology acknowledges the relative autonomy of culture, and examines the interplay of conspiracy theories with other cultural phenomena; unsurprisingly, this approach shares methodological strategies and theoretical tenets with social anthropology and cultural studies (see Chapters 1.2 and 1.6), and is influenced by the latter's recent prominence. For instance, Harambam and Aupers (2017) explore conspiracy culture in the Netherlands via an ethnographic fieldwork and note that conspiracy theories do not constitute a monolithic culture, but a network of groups of people coming from different worldviews, beliefs and practices.

5. *Are all conspiracy theories basically similar or are they diverse, beyond a handful of essential defining features?* Even admitting that all conspiracy theories are not re-iterations of a single basic theory, the diversity of variations acknowledged range from extremely narrow to extremely wide. If variations are minimal, researchers hardly need to bother with the contents and dynamics of specific theories; acknowledging a greater diversity calls for a more in-depth approach both to the specificity of each theory and that of the cultural, social and political circumstances in which it is created and diffused.

Nefes (2014) presented the similarities and variations of conspiratorial accounts while analysing online communication about the attempted assassination of Taiwanese President Chen Shui-bian in 2004 before a general election. The findings showed that people proposed different versions of conspiracy theories strictly in line with their political interests. Until he won the election, the president's supporters accused the opposing party of plotting his assassination; his opponents denied the claims of a conspiracy until losing the election, and then argued that the president had plotted a fake assassination attempt. This shows that, while defining principles of conspiratorial accounts, such as seeing secret plots behind important events, remain the same, conspiracy rhetoric is flexible enough to include opposing arguments.

6. *How must quantitative and qualitative methods be combined?* Qualitative methods allow for exploratory, nuanced approaches and produce more detailed descriptions of social milieus and dynamics in conspiracy theorising (Kay 2011). Group discussion, for instance, enables a recreation of reasoning processes in face-to-face interactions. Quantitative methods tend to be more practical when it comes to establishing comparisons between populations and social groups (Simmons, Parsons 2005) and estimating numbers of believers. Nevertheless, such methods might oversimplify the complexity of the phenomenon and underestimate the number of believers in stigmatised theories (since such believers may not be as willing to admit their belief to a pollster as they would to a friend or someone they had identified as sharing the same belief).

Nefes (2017) juxtaposes qualitative and quantitative content analysis in his paper on the impacts of the Turkish government's conspiratorial framing of the Gezi Park protests in 2013. While the quantitative analysis helps to test the main argument about whether there is a statistically significant relationship between political orientations of the users and their perceptions of conspiracy theories, the qualitative analysis affords an in-depth view of how the online users reject or accept these accounts. Thus, the quantitative approach could be used to understand overall trends, while qualitative methods could help to test the validity of the quantitative findings as well as provide in-depth analysis.

## Modernity as a conspiracy: Theorising conspiracy theories

This section examines how social theory has understood conspiracy theory within the framework of modernity and its variations, and the wide social processes that are associated with them. These are, first, the processes of rationalisation, secularisation and disenchantment of the world, which erode traditional worldviews and beliefs and replace them with the tentative methods of science and the abstract formality of bureaucracy, and obviously cannot provide ultimate answers or meaning to social reality. Second, there is the development of information technology and, with it, the spread of a growing consciousness of the contingency of social institutions and ideas, and also, in postmodern terms, the end of grand narratives and the prevalence of representations over reality. Third, there is the emergence of the nation-state as the political embodiment of a unified society, and its dilution in the globalisation process.

Assuming that conspiracy theories, in line with a broad definition, have a long history, sociologists have looked for shifts and transformations in particular aspects in order to analyse their development and to characterise the specificity of conspiracy theorising in (post/late/reflexive/liquid) modernity. These features include (Campion-Vincent 2005) the nature and the social standing of the conspirators (from foreign 'others' – see Donskis 1998 – to internal enemies and our own social institutions – see Aupers 2012); the scope of the conspiracy (ranging from specific goals pursued by a small group to world domination through a global plot); or the presence of conspiracy theories in public discourse. This last includes the standing of conspiracy theories within society, either in separate groups or in society as a whole, and their 'resonance', as Uscinski and Parent (2014: 131) define it, that is to say 'how natural, useful or acceptable an idea appears to society'.

The credibility of conspiracy theories increases when trust in official epistemic authorities decreases (Renard 2015). In other words, a lack of trust in official explanations creates a cultural environment in which alternate takes on reality, including conspiracy theories, can flourish. This happens when we suspect that the official version promotes the particular interests of those propagating it (Uscinski et al. 2016), or when partisan distrust, intrinsic to the democratic system, develops into conspiracy politics that validate the beliefs in conspiracy theories held by some voters (Moore 2018).

While not always explicitly addressing conspiracy theories, social theorists have long discussed the processes in modernity that produced a culture of suspicion (Remmling 1969; Carroll 1977). In their analysis of modernity and its ailments, many of the usual suspects identified by later theorists were lined up: Fear, anxiety, insecurity, individualism and loneliness. In this perspective, modern society was fragmenting into distrusting factions, each developing its own cultural products and questioning those of the others:

> The emergence of separate thought-styles with their corresponding universes of discourse has two consequences: each of these universes develops a *paranoidal* response to all the others [...] the process of meaningful communication between these mutually distrustful universes comes to a virtual standstill. Eventually all objective and factually grounded inquiry into the content of out-group utterances is replaced by the suspicious query: What are the ulterior motives behind the outside point of view?
> 
> *(Remmling 1969: 7–8; emphasis added)*

The default response, when we are faced with any proposition put forth by the other side, ranges from passive suspicion to active debunking. The academic expression of this 'modern mentality' is represented by disciplines such as the sociology of knowledge or the critique of ideologies (Remmling 1969; Latour 2004). The popular expression is found among cultural products such as detective or spy fiction, as well as in conspiracy theories.

Since Popper's seminal definition of the 'conspiracy theory of society', conspiracy theorising has been understood by social theorists as an undesired (and undesirable) by-product of one or another processes that constitute modernity. The first of these, identified by Popper himself, is secularisation. While it is 'held by very many rationalists' (Popper 2002: 165), the conspiracy theory of society 'in its modern form […] is the typical result of the secularization of religious superstitions' (Popper 2002: 459). Such a mode of thinking 'comes from abandoning God and then asking: 'Who is in his place?'' (Popper 2002: 166). If our ancestors believed that events in their social reality were caused by the will, or the actions, of the gods, conspiracy theorists believe that events in ours are caused by the will and subsequent actions of powerful, secret cabals that pull the strings behind the scenes: Someone, whether human or divine, must be responsible.

In Popper's conception, conspiracy theorising is a survival of earlier times, a mode of inference that has changed its external shape while maintaining the same basic structure. But, as he noted, holding a supernatural entity responsible has not the same social consequences as blaming a real group of people: The scapegoating of specific minorities, then, would be in such instances a consequence of the secularisation of this traditional model of causal explanation.

Popper's influential contribution to the analysis of modern conspiracy culture is complemented by the lesser-known concept of the 'conspiracy theory of ignorance': The notion that our ignorance is deliberately caused by some conspiring power that not only obscures the truth but infuses us with reluctance to its knowledge (Popper 2002: 4). While the conspiracy theory of society explains why things happen, the conspiracy theory of ignorance explains why we do not know why things happen: Someone (journalists working for the capitalist press, the clergy, etc.) does not want us to know, and is actively conspiring to keep the truth from us. This theory, Popper argues, is 'the almost inevitable consequence of the optimistic belief that truth, and therefore goodness, must prevail if only truth is given a fair chance' (Popper 2002: 10). But, this 'false epistemology' was also 'the major inspiration of an intellectual and moral revolution without parallel in history' (Popper 2002: 10). If the conspiracy theory of ignorance is a mistake, it is, Popper admits, a fruitful mistake. Conspiracy theories are not just side-effects of modernity but may have played a part in bringing modernity forth. If the accusation of 'priestly deception' is, in Popper's view, a prime example of the conspiracy theory of ignorance, its prominent role in the Enlightenment, and hence in the coming of modernity, must be conceded (see Lancaster, McKenzie-McHarg 2018).

The process of secularisation is closely related to the processes of disenchantment of the world (i.e. the gradual extinction of 'magic' in the social world) and of rationalisation. The two latter processes are also invoked by social theorists in their explanation of conspiracy theories (Ho, Jin 2011; Josset 2015). Aupers insists that 'notwithstanding its scientific ambitions and (often) atheist pretentions, conspiracy culture, too, is a response to existential insecurity in a disenchanted world' (2012: 30). Sense is made of a meaningless world by means of theories that re-establish meaning, even if it is a terrifying meaning: Things do happen for a reason, and life is not just a disorderly succession of random events. There is more to existence than the clockwork functioning of the social machinery, of impersonal systems and rational-legal iron cages, indifferent to human needs.

In Niklas Luhmann's terms, it is a matter of reducing complexity (Renard 2015). Once we have lost our trust in experts, scholars, teachers, media, politicians and politics, we need something else in its place, since 'distrust is not the opposite of trust: Individuals cannot psychologically exist in a permanent situation of unrest and anxiety. Distrusting individuals must also resort to complexity-reducing strategies' (Renard 2015: 108).

In a sense, the survival of conspiracy theories disprove trust in the rationalisation process itself: Modernity has not brought with it the demise of unfounded belief and the victory of (scientific) knowledge (Bronner 2013). They both exist side by side in an uneasy imbalance, which explains why some sociologists analyse conspiracy theories as a specific case within their broader theories on knowledge, belief and ideology (Boudon 1986, 1990).

More information, in the absence of traditional schemata of interpretation, means more noise (Cicchelli, Octobre 2018) or, potentially, more fear (Husting, Orr 2007). The development of information technology and free-speech principles in liberal democracies begat the liberalisation of the cognitive market (being 'the fictitious space where products informing our worldview are diffused' [Bronner 2013: 23]): faced with an overabundance of data, individuals 'can easily be tempted into constructing a representation of the world which is comfortable rather than true' (Bronner 2013: 33). Adopting a rational strategy, we pick the theories that entail an affordable cognitive cost.

The end of grand narratives and the prevalence of representations over reality, two of the recurring themes in postmodern social theory, call for new, 'outsider' meta-narratives displacing the teleological myth of progress (scientific or otherwise), the re-signification of symbols (Josset 2015) and the fictionalisation of social reality, which we fashion using familiar, exciting templates from popular fiction (Cicchelli, Octobre 2018). Those who reject the postmodern diagnosis may still have embraced the notion of contingency, ever-present in the writings of the main social theorists of the late twentieth century (from Luhmann to Bauman), and therefore understand conspiracy theorising as a return to necessity and destiny in history.

The emergence of the nation-state, with its stabilising pretentions over social reality, is another modern process that fosters, in its tensions and discontinuities, conspiracy theorising, both about conspiracies attacking the state from the outside and about the state as the façade of a conspiracy, concealing those who actually rule (Boltanski 2012). In social sciences, methodological nationalism equates society with the nation-state, but this identification is questioned by the very development of social theory, revealing that social reality is not monolithic.

Globalisation further disintegrates what Beck called 'the container theory of society', the myth of self-enclosed, self-sufficient and self-explaining national units. It is a fact that life-changing decisions, affecting millions of people, are made beyond the borders of the nation-state and above the political representatives directly elected by those affected; global financial earthquakes are also better understood as the result of a deliberate design than as the outcome of gross risk miscalculation and system failures in an interdependent world economy (Rosset 2012; Josset 2015).

## Empirical research

Within the general field of the discipline, sociology of conspiracy theory has one foot planted on sociology of knowledge and the other on sociology of public opinion. These two adjacent areas were identified by Robert K. Merton (1957: 439) as the 'European species' (knowledge) and the 'American species' (public opinion and mass communication) of the same line of inquiry, since both were devoted to 'the interplay between ideas and social structure'.

Merton examined several key differences between the two traditions, in terms of conceptualisation, research topics and methods. Regarding their object, he wrote:

> If the American version is primarily concerned with public opinion, with mass beliefs, with what has come to be called 'popular culture', the European version centers on

more esoteric doctrines, on those complex systems of knowledge which become reshaped and often distorted in their subsequent passage into popular culture.

(Merton 1957: 441)

The conspiracy theory, as an object, belongs to both categories, moving back and forth between esoteric doctrines and popular culture. It is for that reason that sociologists researching conspiracy theories seem to cull methods and approaches from very diverse disciplines, ranging from the history of ideas (a close relative of the sociology of knowledge) to communication studies (a neighbouring field to the sociology of public opinion).

Thus, sociological research on conspiracy theories can be categorised in terms of existing, often overlapping, approaches to both sociological traditions, which will be summarised below as general research questions, with a few examples of specific studies in the literature:

1. *What are the social causes of false ideas?* Historically, sociology of knowledge originated from sociology of prejudice and error and has never lost interest in the topic ('post-truth' is another contemporary notion that brings the sociologies of knowledge and public opinion together). Sociologists researching conspiracy theories have often tried to elucidate the social factors that contribute to the emergence of wrongful beliefs about conspiracies and make them credible. A recent example would be Bronner's (2015) study on the *Charlie Hebdo* conspiracy theories, which he argues were facilitated by the liberalisation of the cognitive market and the propagation of what he calls 'cognitive demagoguery'.

This approach is based upon the methodological discussion on the distinction between legitimate and illegitimate knowledge. For instance, Bale (2007) advanced a set of criteria for distinguishing true conspiratorial politics from 'bogus conspiracy theories', while Buenting and Taylor (2010) identified a specific type of evidence ('fortuitous data') that makes conspiracy theorising rationally adequate, as exemplified by the Watergate scandal.

2. *What kinds of relations exist between ideas and between different sets of ideas?* Ideological analysis is tasked with answering this question. The focus here is on the internal structure of conspiracy theories and their association with cognate ideological constructions. Billig (1988) examined how antisemitic conspiracy theories could be combined with pro-Zionist stances in the National Front. Torrens (2015) explained how theories about a world conspiracy against the Muslims worked as meta-narratives for Islamist Jihadism, in an endless feedback loop.

3. *What is the impact of conspiracy theories on social and political processes?* Ideas have consequences, intended or unintended. Propaganda and mass communication produce effects, even if not as mechanically as the propagandists would hope. Popper (2002) claimed that conspiracy theories, while invalid as explanations of social reality, were sociologically relevant when those who held them reached political power, since their political decisions were guided by such belief and tended to enact counter-conspiracies (Hitler and the Holocaust being the foremost example). This is one of the longest-running branches of scholarship on conspiracy theories, from Hofstadter's (1966) and Lipset and Raab's (1970) analyses of conspiracy theorising in the American right wing.

On the deliberate use of conspiracy theories to elicit an intended outcome, Taïeb (2010) examined how the conspiracy theory about the H1N1 vaccination campaign in France was used as a means of politicisation, and Billig (1988) documented the use of antisemitic conspiracy theories in the power struggle between competing factions in the National Front.

4. *Are conspiracy theories socially 'useful' in any way?* Or, to put it in more precise technical terms: *Are conspiracy theories fulfilling social functions?* Rather than focusing on their truth or lack of it, functional analysis explores how conspiracy theories work within specific social structures and how they contribute, if at all, to the operation of particular groups or society as a whole.

Most studies in this line of research have analysed the cognitive and sense-making functions of conspiracy theories, but such functions can be connected to others like social cohesion or identity construction. For instance, Gosa (2011) examined how conspiracy theories in hip-hop culture address race and class disadvantages, providing explanations for them while strengthening the cultural identity of the disadvantaged.

5. *What social groups believe in which conspiracy theories, and what roles are played by different agents in their diffusion?* This is the problem that Schutz (1976) denominated 'the social distribution of knowledge', and which in his view was the only sensible line of inquiry for sociology of knowledge. There are abundant studies on the social distribution of conspiracy theories: For example, Simmons and Parsons (2005) investigated whether African-American elites could play a role, as some commentators assumed, in dispelling beliefs in conspiracy theories among the larger African-American community, and found out that they would not, since they held essentially the same conspiracy beliefs.

6. *What social factors influence where the line separating 'legitimate' from 'illegitimate' knowledge is drawn?* As opposed to the sociology of error mentioned above, this is the sociology of 'anything that is deemed knowledge'. This line of research is fuelled by contemporary social epistemology (see Chapter 1.4) and the work of philosophers like Pigden (1995), who criticises Popper's pejorative conception of conspiracy theory. The best-known example in this vein is the work of Husting and Orr (2007).

## Conclusion: Future research in the sociology of conspiracy theory

Future research in sociology could choose to fill various gaps in the scholarship. Methodologically, only a few studies make use of mixed methods in the academic literature on conspiracy theories (e.g. Nefes 2017). Future research could transcend the boundaries between qualitative and quantitative methods in the literature, which could help to generate a more thorough understanding on the sociological significance of conspiracy theories. In addition, there are new research methods, such as qualitative experiments, which call 'on an experimental design by randomly distributing a sample into two or more conditions in which participants are exposed to different stimuli' (Robinson, Mendelson 2012: 336). Qualitative experiments have not yet been used, and they could help us to understand the influence of partisanship on the perception of conspiracy theories. One approach might be to inquire about interpretations of conspiracy rhetoric and political views, following which the subject is given a prime, such as a newspaper quotation from a favourite or opponent political party that contradicts their opinion. Then, researchers could invite respondents to reflect on the quote and re-consider their approach on conspiracy theories.

Theoretically, conspiracy theory scholarship, while somehow replicating a variety of approaches in the sociology of knowledge, still does not contain a comprehensive and systematic perspective from that discipline. The sociology of knowledge explores the social foundations of ideas and beliefs (Merton 1957; Mannheim 1997) and could help to analyse the social origins of conspiracy thinking in different contexts. In parallel, thematically, most of the research is based on the developed world and Western societies. Sociological research might shed light into other contexts of conspiracy theorising, where different dynamics could be in play. Furthermore, new theoretical conceptions of modernity, influenced by post-colonialism (Bhambra 2007), standpoint epistemology and other developments in the philosophy of the social sciences, are likely to suggest novel approaches to the modern incarnations of the conspiracy theory.

Last but not least, the scholarship on conspiracy theories has two tendencies with regards to their socio-political significance, namely classical and modern approaches (Nefes 2012). As hinted in Hofstadter's (1966) 'paranoid style' description, the former sees conspiracy theories as irrational accounts that fail to understand the nature of events and as a political pathology of marginal groups (e.g. Goertzel 1994; Pipes 1997). In contrast, the modern perspective views conspiracy theories as a rational attempt to understand social reality (e.g. Knight 2000; Birchall 2006). The classical and modern approaches do not provide all-round perspectives, as while the former negates these accounts as 'political paranoia', the cultural perspective might not adequately emphasise their harmful impacts (Fenster 1999). In that regard, future sociological work could go beyond this division by both accounting for the paranoid and rational aspects of conspiratorial accounts.

# References

Atkinson, M.D. and Dewitt, D. (2018) 'The politics of disruption: social choice theory and conspiracy theory politics', in J.E. Uscinski (ed.) *Conspiracy theories and the people who believe them*, New York: Oxford University Press.
Aupers, S. (2012) '"Trust no one": modernization, paranoia and conspiracy culture', *European Journal of Communication*, 27(1): 22–34.
Bale, J.M. (2007) 'Political paranoia v. political realism: on distinguishing between bogus "conspiracy theories" and genuine conspiratorial politics', *Patterns of Prejudice*, 41(1): 45–60.
Barkun, M. (2003) *A culture of conspiracy: apocalyptic visions in contemporary America*, Berkeley: University of California Press.
Berger, P. and Luckmann, T. (1966) *The social construction of reality: a treatise in the sociology of knowledge*, New York: Anchor Books.
Bhambra, G.K. (2007) *Rethinking modernity: postcolonialism and the sociological imagination*, New York: Palgrave Macmillan.
Billig, M. (1988) 'Rhetoric of the conspiracy theory: arguments in National Front propaganda', *Patterns of Prejudice*, 22(2): 23–34.
Birchall, C. (2006) *Knowledge goes pop: from conspiracy theory to gossip*, Oxford: Berg.
Boltanski, L. (2012) *Énigmes et complots: une enquête à propos d'enquêtes*, Paris: Gallimard.
Boudon, R. (1986) *L'Idéologie ou l'origine des idées reçues*, Paris: Fayard.
Boudon, R. (1990) *L'art de se persuader des idées douteuses, fragile ou fausses*, Paris: Fayard.
Boudon, R. (2004) *Pourquoi les intellectuels n'aiment pas le liberalism*, Paris: Odile Jacob.
Bourdieu, P. (2001) *Contre-feux 2*, Paris: Raisons D'agir.
Bratich, J.Z. (2008) *Conspiracy panics: political rationality and popular culture*, Albany: State University of New York Press.
Bronner, G. (2013) *La démocratie des crédules*, Paris: PUF.
Bronner, G. (2015) 'Pourquoi les théories du complot se portent-elles si bien? L'exemple de Charlie Hebdo', *Diogène*, 249–50: 9–20.
Buenting, J. and Taylor, J. (2010) 'Conspiracy theories and fortuitous data', *Philosophy of the Social Sciences*, 40(4): 567–78.
Byford, J. (2015) *Conspiracy theories: a critical introduction*, New York: Palgrave Macmillan.
Campion-Vincent, V. (2005) *La société paranoïaque: théories du complot, menaces et incertitudes*, Paris: Payot.
Campion-Vincent, V. (2015) 'Note sur les entrepreneurs en complots', *Diogène*, 249–50: 99–106.
Carroll, J. (1977) *Puritan, paranoid, remissive: a sociology of modern culture*, London: Routledge and Kegan Paul.
Chomsky, N. (2004) 'On historical amnesia, foreign policy and Iraq', *American Amnesia*, 17 February. Available at: https://chomsky.info/20040217/. [Accessed 9 June 2019.]
Cicchelli, V. and Octobre, S. (2018) 'Fictionnalisation des attentats et théorie du complot chez les adolescents', *Quaderni*, 95(1): 53–64.
Czech, F. (2018) 'Conspiracy theories are not only for election losers: anti-system parties and conspiratorial distrust in Poland', *Polish Political Science Yearbook*, 47(4): 663–75.
Donskis, L. (1998) 'The conspiracy theory, demonization of the other', *Innovation: The European Journal of Social Research*, 11(3): 349–60.
Fenster, M. (1999) *Conspiracy theories*, Minneapolis: University of Minnesota Press.
Goertzel, T. (1994) 'Belief in conspiracy theories', *Political Psychology*, 15: 733–44.

Gosa, T. (2011) 'Counterknowledge, racial paranoia, and the cultic milieu: decoding hip hop conspiracy theory', *Poetics*, 39(3): 187–204.

Harambam, J. (2017) *"The truth is out there": conspiracy culture in an age of epistemic instability*, Erasmus University Rotterdam.

Harambam, J. and Aupers, S. (2017) '"I am not a conspiracy theorist": relational identifications in the Dutch conspiracy milieu', *Cultural Sociology*, 11(1): 113–29.

Ho, P. and Jin, C. (2011) 'La théorie du complot comme un simulacre de sciences sociales?', *Sociétés*, 112: 147–61.

Hofstadter, R. (1964) *The paranoid style in American politics and other essays*, Cambridge: Harvard University Press.

Husting, G. and Orr, M. (2007) 'Dangerous machinery: "conspiracy theorist" as a transpersonal strategy of exclusion', *Symbolic Interaction*, 30(2): 127–50.

Jameson, F. (1988) 'Cognitive Mapping', in C. Nelson and L. Grossberg (eds.) *Marxism and the interpretation of culture*, London: Macmillan.

Jameson, F. (1992) *The geopolitical aesthetic: cinema and space in the world system*, London: BFI & Indiana University Press.

Josset, R. (2015) *Complosphère: l'esprit conspirationniste à l'ère des reseaux*, Paris: Lemieux.

Kay, J. (2011) *Among the truthers: a journey through America's growing conspiracist underground*, New York: Harper-Collins.

Knight, P. (2000) *Conspiracy culture: from the Kennedy assassination to the X-files*, London: Routledge.

Knight, P. (ed.) (2002) *Conspiracy nation: the politics of paranoia in postwar America*, New York: New York University Press.

Lancaster, J.T. and McKenzie-McHarg, A. (2018) 'Priestcraft. Early modern variations on the theme of sacerdotal imposture', *Intellectual History Review*, 28(1): 1–6.

Latour, B. (2004) 'Why has critique run out of steam? From matters of fact to matters of concern', *Critical Inquiry*, 30(2): 225–48.

Lipset, S.M. and Raab, E. (1970) *The Politics of Unreason: Right-Wing Extremism in America 1790–1977*, reprint, Chicago: The University of Chicago Press, 1978.

Mannheim, K. (1997) *Ideology and Utopia*, London: Routledge.

McKenzie-McHarg, A. and Fredheim, R. (2017) 'Cock-ups and slap-downs: a quantitative analysis of conspiracy rhetoric in the British parliament 1916–2015', *Historical Methods: A Journal of Quantitative and Interdisciplinary History*, 50(3): 156–69.

Melley, T. (2002) 'Agency panic and the culture of conspiracy', in P. Knight (ed.) *Conspiracy nation: the politics of paranoia in postwar America*, New York: New York University Press.

Melley, T. (2008) 'Brainwashed! Conspiracy theory and ideology in the postwar United States', *New German Critique*, 103: 145–64.

Merton, R.K. (1957) *Social theory and social structure*, Glencoe: The Free Press.

Moore, A. (2018) 'On the democratic problem of conspiracy politics', in J.E. Uscinski (ed.) *Conspiracy theories and the people who believe them*, New York: Oxford University Press.

Nefes, S.T. (2011) 'Conspiracy theories as conduits of fundamentalist knowledge', in U. Martensson, U. Bailey, P. Ringrose and A. Dyrendal (eds.) *Fundamentalism in the modern world vol. 1: fundamentalism, politics and history: the state, globalization and political ideologies*, London: I.B. Tauris, pp. 219–39.

Nefes, S.T. (2012) 'The history of the social constructions of Dönmes (converts)', *Journal of Historical Sociology*, 25(3): 413–39.

Nefes, S.T. (2013) '"Political parties" perceptions and uses of anti-Semitic conspiracy theories in Turkey', *The Sociological Review*, 61(2): 247–64.

Nefes, S.T. (2014) 'Rationale of conspiracy theorizing: who shot the president Chen Shui-bian?', *Rationality and Society*, 26(3): 373–94.

Nefes, S.T. (2015a) *Online Anti-Semitism in Turkey*, New York: Palgrave Macmillan.

Nefes, S.T. (2015b) 'Scrutinizing impacts of conspiracy theories on readers' political views: a rational choice perspective on anti-Semitic rhetoric in Turkey', *British Journal of Sociology*, 66(3): 557–75.

Nefes, S.T. (2017) 'The impacts of the Turkish government's conspiratorial framing about the Gezi Park Protests', *Social Movement Studies*, 16(5): 610–22.

Nefes, S.T. (2018) 'The conspiratorial style in Turkish politics: discussing the deep state in the parliament', in J. Uscinski (ed.) *Conspiracy theories and the people who believe them*, New York: Oxford University Press, pp. 385–95.

Pigden, C. (1995) 'Popper revisited, or what is wrong with conspiracy theories?', *Philosophy of the Social Sciences*, 25(1): 3–34.

Pipes, D. (1997) *Conspiracy: how the paranoid style flourishes and where it comes from*, New York: The Free Press.

Popper, K. (2002) *Conjectures and refutations: the growth of scientific knowledge*, reprint, New York: Routledge & Kegan Paul.

Remmling, G. (1969) *Road to suspicion: a study of modern mentality and the sociology of knowledge*, New York: Appleton-Century-Crofts.

Renard, J.-B. (2015) 'Les causes de l'adhésion aux théories du complot', *Diogène*, 249–50: 107–19.

Robinson, S. and Mendelson, A. (2012) 'A qualitative experiment: research on mediated meaning construction using a hybrid approach', *Journal of Mixed Methods Research*, 6(4): 332–47.

Romero-Reche, A. (2018) 'The conspiracy theory of ignorance in the classical sociology of knowledge', *Critique & Humanism*, 49: 357–68.

Rosset, Arnaud (2012) 'Théories du complot ou théories globales: tracé d'une frontière épistémologique', *Raison publique*, 16: 43–53.

Schutz, A. (1976) 'The well-informed citizen', in A. Broedersen (ed.) *Collected papers II*, Dordrecht: Springer, pp. 120–34.

Simmons, W. and Parsons, S. (2005) 'Beliefs in conspiracy theories among African Americans: a comparison of elites and masses', *Social Science Quarterly*, 86(3): 582–98.

Taguieff, P.-A. (2013) *Court traité de complotologie*, Paris: Mille et Une Nuits.

Taïeb, E. (2010) 'Logiques politiques du conspirationnisme', *Sociologie et sociétés*, 42(2): 265–89.

Torrens, X. (2015) 'Teoría de la conspiración como metanarrativa del islamismo yihadista', in J.A. Mellón (ed.) *Islamismo Yihadista: Radicalización y Contrarradicalización*, Valencia: Tirant lo Blanch.

Uscinski, J.E., Klofstad, C. and Atkinson, M.D. (2016) 'What drives conspiratorial beliefs? The role of informational cues and predispositions', *Political Research Quarterly*, 69(1): 57–71.

Uscinski, J.E. and Parent, J.M. (2014). *American Conspiracy Theories*, Oxford: Oxford University Press.

Waters, A. (1997) 'Conspiracy theories as ethnosociologies: explanation and intention in African American political culture', *Journal of Black Studies*, 28(1): 112–25.

# 1.8
# CONSPIRACY THEORIES IN POLITICAL SCIENCE AND POLITICAL THEORY

*Julien Giry and Pranvera Tika*

### Introduction

Although, today, the study of conspiracy theories is widely acknowledged and firmly established within the disciplines of political science and political theory, it is worth remembering that it is a relatively recent topic of research within the field. If Hofstadter's seminal work *The Paranoid Style in American Politics, and Other Essays* (1964) is usually mentioned as the first significant contribution, it is fair to say that, since antiquity (see Chapter 5.1), conspiracies, both real and imagined, have been a subject for analysis, with political philosophers and political actors over the centuries, like the ancient Roman Suetonius or Machiavelli during the Renaissance, addressing the issue. Later, in the nineteenth century, the French philosopher Guizot (1845) seems to be the first to distinguish, in pure political terms and taking into consideration the social context in which they occur, the real conspiracies to topple governments, the 'pseudo-conspiracies' forged by rulers to strengthen their power and silence their opponents, and the purely imagined conspiracy. Guizot also clearly warned against the temptation to believe in 'conspiracy theories' even though this expression does not appear as such: 'the number and frequency of conspiracies demonstrate the poor state of the society and the government misbehaviour' but it is nonetheless dangerous to 'seek or only see conspiracy where there is none' (132).

Despite these earlier contributions, it was after the Second World War that conspiracy theories really became a topic for political science and theory in tandem with its gradual development, institutionalisation and differentiation from other disciplines (Parish, Parker 2001). In Europe, in the 1940s, Popper introduced the expression 'conspiracy theory of society' to designate a defective social phenomenon. According to the Austrian philosopher, conspiracy theories are:

> The view that an explanation of a social phenomenon consists in the discovery of the men or groups who are interested in the occurrence of this phenomenon (sometimes it is a hidden interest which has to be revealed) and who have planned and conspired to bring it about.
>
> *(1945: 94)*

In the U.S.A., historians like Hofstadter (1955, 1964) or Davis (1971) are seen as the pioneers of conspiracy theory studies as designated by the 'paranoid style' in politics, i.e. 'a heated exaggeration, suspiciousness and conspiratorial fantasy … a feeling of persecution … systematized in grandiose theories of conspiracy … the spokesman of the paranoid style finds it directed against a nation, a culture (or) a way of life' (Hofstadter 1964: 3–5). However, since the 1980s, U.S. and European scholars have followed separate paths in their development of conspiracy-theory research.

In the French-speaking world, historians of ideas like Poliakov (1980), Giradet (1986) or Taguieff (1992) addressed the issue of conspiracy theories that had been neglected since the end of the Second World War and the fall of the Vichy regime, during which antisemitism and anti-Masonism stood as official policies. It is only since the beginning of the twenty-first century that conspiracy theories have established themselves as a legitimate subject in French academia (Taguieff 2005; Jamin 2009; Taïeb 2010; Giry 2014).

Elsewhere in the world, research on conspiracy theories since the 1990s considered the fall of authoritarian communist regimes in the post-Soviet space (Ortmann, Heathershaw 2012; Panczová, Janeček 2015; Yablokov 2018); Middle Eastern countries (Ashraf 1992; Gray 2010; Butter, Reinkowski 2014; see also Chapter 5.8 in this volume) and South/Latin America (Pérez Hernáiz 2009; Taragoni 2018; see also Chapter 5.11 in this volume).

In brief, from the end of the Second World War to today, many political scientists throughout the world have embraced the issue of conspiracy theories and contributed to the institutionalisation and the internationalisation of a pluralistic academic field animated by intensive methodologic debates, intellectual controversies and theoretical discussions, which this chapter aims to summarise. First, we will consider elements of political science historical development, and then we will present the main topics and issues addressed by scholars and the different kind of methods they use to study conspiracy theories. We will synthesise the most relevant findings, which will lead us to attempt to give a definition of conspiracy theories that finds a consensus in the field of political science. Finally, we will try to open up some perspectives for stimulating future research.

## Political science and its context: A brief introduction

Although its origins are widely recognised to lie in the philosophical debates on politics since the time of ancient Greece, political science as a structured discipline engaged in empirical research only began to emerge at the end of nineteenth century. There followed a period of rather modest gains during the interwar period, followed by a gradual development towards acquiring more 'genuine professional characteristics' (Almond 1996: 50) to ensure academic independence and a more systematic way of researching within the field. Indeed, throughout its academic establishment process, political science faced three structural obstacles: Institutional, intellectual and cultural (Baudouin 2017). Despite the foundation of the American Political Science Association in 1903, political science faced an institutional obstacle, due to politics being divided over different disciplines, with a blurring of lines between, say, history, law, philosophy, etc. Because of this, it was difficult to develop and establish a 'science of politics' as a genuine academic discipline with its own department, methods, subjects, etc. This lack of consensus among scholars on the scope, purpose and central arguments of the emerging discipline created in turn intellectual and cultural obstacles, hindering the creation of a dynamic scholarly community able to legitimate the discipline.

Nonetheless, after the end of the Second World War, the International Political Science Association was established in 1949 under the auspices of UNESCO and the development of political science was expressed in the form of the delimitation of its own domain of scientific inquiry (Lipset 1950, 1969; Crick 1959), i.e. the allocation and transfer of power in decision making, the roles and systems of governance, including governments and international organisations, political thoughts and behaviours, or social movements. Hence, under the influence of behaviourists, political science developed several lines of argument. First, it sought to differentiate itself from political philosophy and speculation about the best system of government by excluding from its domain moral estimations, to focus instead on the collection and analysis of empirical data. Second, it distanced itself from public law by focusing the research on real processes rather than formal-legal ones. Third, it distinguished itself from history, where an analysis of empirical data was aimed more at generalisations, by focusing on knowledge of a specific reality in space and time.

To summarise, political science today can be defined as the 'the study or the research with the methodology of empirical sciences on different aspects of the political reality for explaining it as totally as possible' (Della Porta 2008: 12). More generally speaking, political science is considered the academic discipline that studies formal and informal, conscious and unconscious, visible and invisible relations of power, authority and domination amongst individual and/or collective actors of all kinds. Political science is then divided into several sub-disciplines such as (social) history of ideas, political sociology, public policies, public institutions, government studies, comparative politics or international relations.

## Topics and methodologies: How political scientists deal with conspiracy theories

If issues of power and its relationship with conspiracy beliefs constitute a theoretical issue for political science, and even though studies on right-wing extremism in American history constitutes one of the first contributions on conspiracy theories in political science (Lipset, Raab 1970; Thurlow 1978; James 2000; Quinn 2000), the period after the election of Barack Obama – a time particularly rich in conspiratorial claims (Barkun 2013; Fine 2015) – constituted a further point in the development of empirical inquiries in political science about conspiracy theories (Uscinski 2018). Indeed, if some investigations in conspiracy theories have flourished before the beginning of the 2010s, most of them adopted theoretical rather than empirical perspectives. Thus, due to their persistence and wide dissemination across a broad political spectrum, the study of conspiracy theories is now considered a mainstream topic. If pioneering research had originally adopted Hofstadter's conceptualisation in terms of 'paranoid style' (Davis 1971; Pipes 1997; Melley 2000; Taguieff 2013), theoretical approaches (Thurlow 1978; Fenster 1999; Goldberg 2001; Jamin 2009; Byford 2011; Barkun 2013; Giry 2015a) are well-established today. However, other research initiatives have recently renewed methodological perspectives. While social psychology–inspired quantitative methods based on polls, questionnaires or Internet data about conspiratorial items are now dominant (Bronner 2013; Uscinski, Parent 2014; Frampton et al. 2016), qualitative methods dealing with interviews and empirical observations are finding increasing application (Giry 2015b, 2018b; Harambam, Aupers 2016; France, Motta 2017).

In addition, studies that address the reasons for supporting conspiracy beliefs have become a predominant theoretical mantra halfway between political science and social psychology. At the global level, scientific contributions commonly interrogate the relationship between (mis) information (Sunstein, Vermeule 2009; Bronner 2013), extremisms or ideologies in democratic regimes (Bronner 2009; van Prooijen et al. 2015), partisanship (Berinsky 2011; Nyhan 2012; Uscinski, Parent 2014) and conspiracy theories. Furthermore, at the individual level, researchers investigate the social determinants that make people prone to believe in conspiracy theories. They question the links between beliefs in conspiracy theories and social needs, such as the maintenance of a positive image of the self or the in-group (Cichocka et al. 2016; Giry 2017b), social status or positions (Crocker et al. 1999), income level (Uscinski, Parent 2014), understanding and trust in politics (Uscinski, Parent 2014; Miller *et al.* 2016), prejudices against others (Campion-Vincent 2005; Imhoff, Bruder 2014) or – political – alienation (Abalakina-Paap *et al.* 1999). Researchers also focus on the consequences of conspiratorial beliefs, both for individuals and for society (see Chapter 2.7). They investigate the effect of exposure to conspiracy theories in terms of institutional trust (Einstein, Glick 2014) and participation in politics (Jolley, Douglas 2013).

It is no surprise, then, that political science investigations concentrate on the understanding of conspiracy beliefs in relation to politics. That is to say, conspiracy beliefs are considered an outcome deriving from the institutions and expectations associated with contemporary democracies. As Moore notices, 'they bear directly on central themes in democratic theory, from the public sphere and public deliberation, to partisanship and polarisation, to theories of elite power and influence' (2017: 8–9).

## Main findings and debates: What political scientists know and dispute about conspiracy theories

Taking these investigations and concerns as a point of departure, it is now possible to present the main findings in this discipline. In brief, it appears that conspiracy theories are not a marginal phenomenon and their presence extends throughout the entire political spectrum and up and down the social ladder (Goertzel 1994). No ideology, no party, no social class, no gender, in short, no one, is immune to beliefs in conspiracy theories by virtue of inherent nature or acquired education. Oliver and Wood argue that 'predispositions are widely distributed across the population and vary by a wide variety of political and psychological variables. These predispositions are not a uniform expression of any one demographic or psychological characteristics' (2014: 961). That is to say, there is a wide range of social actors who are involved in conspiracy theories at different levels or intensity. We will first present them as ideal-types. Then, we will explore whether there is any potential correlation between some social properties and beliefs in conspiracies or whether some social actors are more prone than others to believe in conspiracy theories.

Conspiracy theories concern at least five categories of actors. Some are characterised as conspiracist leaders, i.e. professional conspiracy theorists or political entrepreneurs in conspiracy theories (Giry 2014; see also Chapter 3.2 in this volume). Generally well-educated, they produce and publically endorse, even sometimes before the courts, conspiratorial claims and narratives as a worldview. On the basis of either conviction or (economic) opportunism, they offer structured alternative explanations to tragic events in terms of large-scale conspiracy or sophisticated plot. Among this category are Alex Jones, an American radio personality who hosts the website Infowars; Lyndon LaRouche, the former leader of a cult organisation who ran eight times for the U.S. presidency (Giry 2015b, 2018a); Louis Farrakhan, the leader of Nation of Islam, a black supremacist organisation; or Alain Soral, a French self-proclaimed national-socialist activist. Distinct from such leaders, is a second category, 'citizen sleuths' (Olmsted 2011). Like fictional detectives (Boltanski 2012), they are ordinary people who progressively come to promote a conspiracy theory focused on a specific event (the assassination of President John F. Kennedy, the 9/11 attacks, the Charlie Hebdo massacre, etc.). Step by step, they come to devote their lives to investigating the case. Some of them, like Edward Epstein and other prominent 'Warrenologists' (Penn Jones, Lilian Castellano or Sylvia Meagher), or the 9/11 'Jersey Girls' (Kristen Breitweiser, Patty Casazza, Lorie Van Auken and Mindy Kleinberg – four widows who pressed the American administration to commission investigations on the 9/11 attacks), for example, manage to gain visibility in the public sphere, and even sometimes to professionalise. Notice that, if conspiracist leaders are nearly always male, there are many women amongst the citizen sleuths. Like many social fields, it seems that conspiracism, too, has a glass ceiling (Giry 2018b). In the third category is the vast number of people who, mostly using pseudonyms, nicknames or avatars, post, relay or spread conspiratorial videos, content, speeches or comments on the Internet. They are more opinion *dealers* than *leaders* because they do not properly initiate conspiracy narratives. Fourth, there are countless mere believers, viewers or consumers of conspiracy theories, mostly through Internet videos. Finally, it is necessary to mention the 'debunkers' (Jane, Fleming 2014) i.e. individual or collective social actors (Dunbar, Reagan 2011), websites like HoaxBuster, Snopes, Debunkin911 or ConspiracyWatch (Giry 2014), short (web) television programmes (*Le Complot* on the French network *Canal +*, YouTube videos, etc.) or educational material (On_te_manipule.fr in France or America.gov/conspiracy_theories in the U.S.A.) engaged in the deconstruction, denunciation or even mockery of conspiracy theories.

Many political scientists agree that conspiracy theories are a political myth (Girardet 1986; Giry 2015a), a global vision of the world that can espouse different kinds of ideologies even though they have, in democratic countries at least, affinities with government distrust (Moore 2017), extremism (Bronner 2009; Bartlett, Miller 2010), populism (Bergmann 2018; see also Chapter 3.6 in this volume) and far-right activism (Hofstadter 1964; Sunstein, Vermeule 2009; Appelrouth 2017). More generally speaking, in terms of affiliation, political scientists have found that people are more likely to believe in conspiracy theories when they feel involved, when they tend to exonerate them or the group they belong to (Waters 1997; Russell *et al.* 2011; Frampton *et al.* 2016) and when they implicate their political opponents (Oliver, Wood 2014; Uscinski, Parent 2014). Hence, conservative or right-wing social actors are more likely to believe in conspiracy theories that implicate liberal actors or the left, and vice-versa. Moreover, Usinscki and Parent argue that 'conspiracy theories are for losers' (2014: 130; see also Crocker *et al.* 1999), i.e. the political camp that loses the election is more likely to endorse conspiratorial views than the winning side. Consequently, it seems that conspiracy theories are a misleading form of politicisation. To some extent, conspiracy narratives constitute ethnosociologies – 'theories that ordinary people or laymen use to explain social phenomena' (Waters 1997: 114; see also Jameson 1981) – and theories of power that try to give and make sense of harmful social phenomena (unemployment, drug addictions, epidemics, etc.) or political dysfunctions (misrepresentation of certain social groups, power confiscation, etc.). Going further, Uscinski considers that, in democratic regimes, conspiracy theories are 'necessary for the healthy functioning of society' because they act like 'defense lawyer(s)'

> They are opposing counsel in the war of political ideas, where the establishment is the prosecution, and they challenge prevailing wisdom.... Fundamentally conspiracy theories are about the views of the strong versus the weak, the pros versus the amateurs, and the experts versus the novices.
>
> *(2018: 238)*

The link between education level and conspiracy theories is widely disputed. Some researchers argue that actors with some cultural capital and political resources are more likely to believe conspiracy theories than those with less education (Simmons, Parsons 2005; Frampton *et al.* 2016). Other studies suggest that those with fewer academic qualifications are more prone to believe conspiracy theories (Stempel *et al.* 2007; Uscinski, Parent 2014; Ifop 2018). In accordance with Waters (1997), Renard (2015) assumes that beliefs in conspiracy theories follow an inverted 'U-shaped' curve, with those with high-school degrees or little higher education more supportive of conspiracy theories than others. Contrary to common assumptions, however, conspiracism does not seem to be an expression of political ignorance (Nyhan 2012) and people 'who endorse conspiracy theories are not less informed about basic political facts than average citizens' (Oliver, Wood 2014: 964). In contrast to preconceived notions prevalent in the media (Locke 2009; Giry 2017a), conspiracy theory believers are not solely paranoid kooks or cranks, naive young people with little education and/or individuals from lower classes raised in economically deprived areas.

Indeed, if recent studies have shown that teenagers or young people are more likely to support conspiracy theories than older people, it is still not clear, regarding longitudinal approaches (Appelton 2000) or sociological hypothesis (Boltanski 2012), if this testifies to an age effect – conspiracy theories have always been more appealing to the young –, a generation effect – the current young generation is particularly receptive to conspiracy theories – or something in-between.

Similar to the age issue, the question of affinities between ethnocultural minorities and conspiracy theories is highly debated. Whereas some psycho-sociological studies suggest that racial minorities are more likely to believe in conspiracy theories (van Prooijen *et al.* 2018), political scientists argue that there is no correlation (Frampton *et al.* 2016). However, researchers agree that racial or religious minorities are more likely to believe in conspiracy theories that make specific sense or appeal to their communities (e.g. conspiracy theories about A.I.D.S. for African Americans or conspiracy theories about purported Zionist control over Islamist terrorism for European Muslims) (Ross *et al.* 2006; Russell *et al.* 2011; Frampton *et al.* 2016). To summarise, Knight concludes that:

> Conspiracy theories are a popular explanation of the workings of power, responsibility, and causality in the unfolding of events. They have appealed to both the Left and the Right, both the uneducated and intellectuals, and have been told both by and about those at the very heart of power. Sometimes they take the form of racist scapegoating, and at others counterattacks on the powerful. They have offered alternative explanations of a vast range of topics, from the economic to the religious, and the political to the cultural. They are sometimes without foundation and at others beyond doubt.
>
> *(2003: xi)*

This diversity of aspects compels us to consider the issue of defining conspiracy theories.

## Definitions and labels: Conspiracy theories according to political scientists

Despite the different approaches, methodologies and findings, it is nonetheless possible to reach a consensus on the key features that characterise conspiracy theories as a political science subject (Giry 2015a). But, let us first remind ourselves of some seminal definitions: Fenster considers that conspiracy theories express 'the conviction that a secret, omnipotent individual or group covertly controls the political and social order or some part thereof circulates solely on the margins of society' (1999: 1). This corresponds closely to Taïeb, who believes that

> we can identify the conspiratorial thinking when it is postulated that the course of history and its striking events are uniformly caused by the secret action of a small group of people keen to achieve a project of population control and domination.
>
> *(2010: 267)*

Following those definitions, Uscinski and Parent consider conspiracy theories as 'an explanation of historical ongoing, or future events that cites as a main causal factor a small group of powerful persons, the conspirators, acting in secret for their own benefit against the common good' (2014: 32), while Sunstein and Vermeule describe 'an effort to explain some event or practice by reference to the machinations of powerful people, who attempt to conceal their role (at least until their aims are accomplished)' (2009: 205). Moreover, Goldberg says that:

> The script has become familiar: Individuals and groups, acting in secret, move and shape recent ... history. Driven by a lust for power and wealth, they practice deceit, subterfuge, and even assassination, sometimes brazenly executed. Nothing is random or the matter of coincidence. Institutional process, miscalculation, and chance bend to the conspirators' single-minded will
>
> *(2001: ix)*

In sum,

> conspiracy theory, in accordance with academic literature, is a text that falsely accuses a group of individuals of orchestrating a plot that has harmed or will harm society ... and that simplifies the complex workings of society by creating causal relationships between tangentially related evidence.
>
> *(Hall 2006: 207)*

We propose to build on these definitions to create one as consensual as possible from a political science point of view. We, therefore, consider that conspiracy theories can be characterised by a couple of common patterns or key features. First, conspiracy theories are a worldview based on the fear of 'could-be-true' (Uscinski 2018: 327) but 'not yet proven' (Olmsted 2009: 3), impossible/unable to prove or fantasied conspiracies. Of course, this is not to say that genuine conspiracies – commonly defined as the illegal and secret action of a small group of people to do something bad or harmful to other people or to take over the power – do not exist. Thus, in accordance with the paradoxical formula 'conspiracies *do* exist, but the Conspiracy does not' (Goldschläger, Lemaire 2005: 7), we suggest that 'a conspiracy theorist is not someone who simply accepts the truth of some specific conspiracies. Rather, a conspiracy theorist is someone with a certain general methodological approach and set of priorities' (Albert, Shalom 2002). Acknowledging that everyone is prone to endorse one conspiracy theory, if a conspiracy theorist is someone who believes in a single conspiracy theory, we are either all conspiracy theorists ... or there is none. In that respect, conspiracy theories are not the fear, the denunciation or the belief in certain purported conspiracies but a hegemonic and systemic political worldview in which the idea or the hypothesis of a conspiracy is omnipresent – or at least, overspread – but never questioned. It is a theory of power, of its practices and representations in which plots, pacts, secrecy and concealment play a decisive and central part. Consistent with Simmel's pioneering investigations (1906), secrecy takes on three complementary forms: The (so-called) secret itself, the socialisation of the (so-called) secret within a (so-called) secret/discrete group/society, and the (so-called) secret activities of this (so-called) secret/discrete group/society. In the case of conspiracy theories, the issue of secrecy interacts with those three levels. Indeed, conspiracy theories aim to reveal to the public the purported conspiracy of silence, the dissimulation of the conspiracy or the cover-up operated by powerful actors. They deal with the purported harmful activities or manipulations orchestrated by secret (Illuminati, shape-shifting reptilians, etc.) or discrete (Jesuits, Freemasons, etc.) groups, minorities (Jews, communists, etc.), powerful elites (governments, bankers, media tycoons, etc.) or committees (Council on Foreign Relations, Trilateral Commission, Bilderberg group, etc.) to take power, strengthen their positions and/or harm the people (Campion-Vincent 2005). Consequently, conspiracy theories are based on a simplistic dualism in which 'us', the ordinary and innocent vast majority of people, are endlessly threatened by an evil 'them' motivated by the quest of absolute economic and political power. In this dualistic vision, the conspirators are not only the enemies of the people but also genuine *outsiders*.

Furthermore, according to these definitions, it seems that conspiracy theories ignore notions such as randomness, contingency, misfortune, fatality, coincidence or simply fate. On the contrary, those who believe in conspiracy theories imagine themselves to be rational and logical, for they assume that nothing happens accidentally, nothing is as it seems and everything is connected into a large-scale plot orchestrated by evil forces. Necessary causal connections and determinism are key motivations for supporting conspiracy theories. Hence, remarkable events (Kennedy's assassination, the 9/11 attacks, etc.) or catastrophes (epidemics, economic crises, etc.) necessarily originate from malevolent intention, cruelty or evil agency. 'Official versions' are mere smoke screens created by the conspirators to hide the 'true truth' from the people. Consequently, conspiratorial thinking proceeds from a paradox that leads to a victim and accusatory pseudo-form of criticism. Despite the hypercritical claim that nothing – no institutions, no experts, no officials, etc., – can be trusted, conspiracy theories are meanwhile trapped into an infra-critical position in which the hypothesis of a conspiracy led by omnipotent evil enemies against innocent peoples is never questioned (Giry 2017a).

Resulting from those definitions, key features and characterisations, it is imperative to recall that conspiracy theories, with the exception of stigma reversal strategies (Goffman 1963),[1] constitute a heteronomous label given by researchers, government officials, journalists or anti-conspiracy-theory militants that produces many effects of disqualification in different social fields (Taïeb 2010). From this perspective, Barkun (2013) rightfully presents conspiracy theories as fringe and stigmatised knowledge in opposition with mainstream representations and learnings. Therefore, because conspiracy theories constitute a real, but conceptually delimited, social and political phenomenon, we recommend that researchers make prudent use of this disqualification label and not to apply it to each and every form of social criticism directed towards established institutions or neoliberalism, whatever our personal beliefs and preferences. Conversely, a legitimate, even radical, form of social criticism must be on guard against the temptation of conspiratorial thinking (Corcuff 2009). Indeed, there are two difficulties that must be avoided in the study and appraisal of conspiracy theories from a political science point of view (Giry 2017a), which are, in fact, two sides of the same coin. On the one hand is a tendency to overextend the scope and use of the 'conspiracy theory' label intentionally to disqualify[2] a wide range of fringe political or social behaviours, beliefs or speeches criticising, for instance, the E.U., governments, big companies or the media. This tendency is often observed in the 'paranoid' approaches of conspiracy theories (Giry 2018c) – see for instance Taguieff (2013: 149–52) – and with some dominant social actors or 'anti-conspiracist' militants. On the other hand, we face a kind of denialism that tends to consider the 'conspiracy theory' label simply as a concept forged on purpose by the dominants to automatically disqualify left-wing and anti-capitalist movements.

In sum, conspiracy theory as a political-science and political-theory label arouses epidemiologic problematics very similar to populism (Berlin 1965) and antisemitism. If the existence of those phenomena is no longer under debate for most academics, the discussions and even controversies are now about their uses, scopes and appraisals.

## Further perspectives: What political scientists could/should do about conspiracy theories

If conspiracy theories or conspiracism is a relatively new field of investigation for political scientists, there is very little doubt that this subject is rapidly becoming a mainstream issue. First limited to the American case study, recent stimulating studies consider new domains, methods and geographic areas. Let us briefly introduce some of them.

First, Moore (2017: 10) is right to notice that political science should develop comparative and comprehensive approaches of conspiracy theories in post-colonial states, transitional democracies, authoritarian regimes (see Chapter 3.5) and, more generally speaking, in countries with restricted public spheres and liberties. Even though there is promising research emerging for the cases of Russia (François, Schmitt 2015; Haluzík 2015; Hagemeister 2018; Yablokov 2018), Eastern European countries (Heathershaw 2012; Ortmann, Heathershaw 2012; Panczová, Janeček 2015), the Arab Muslim world (Gray 2010; De Poli 2018; see also Chapter 5.8 in this volume), Iran (Ashraf 1992), Turkey (Baer 2013; Nefes 2013; Yazmaci 2014) and South/Latin America (Pérez Hernáiz 2009; Taragoni 2018; see also Chapter 5.11 in this volume), it seems that earlier political scientists do not have enough data to provide robust conclusions about the conspiracy-theory phenomenon in those areas or to draw relevant comparisons with the better-known American case. Again, it seems to be too early to affirm or deny any specificities or common features.

Another necessary development is to investigate on a large scale the role played by conspiracy theories in contemporary violent radicalisation processes in Europe and North America (Frampton *et al.* 2016; Cicchelli, Octobre 2018; Giry *et al.* 2018; Steiner, Önnerfors 2018; see Chapter 3.7 in this volume). Against the backdrop of a revival of Islamist terrorism, relevant data is urgently needed, particularly with regard to studying conspiracy theories amongst Muslim minorities in Europe (van Prooijen *et al.* 2018). It is also pressing to lead investigations on emerging anti-Islamic conspiracy theories like the so-called 'Eurabia' or 'Great Replacement', which until now are little studied by scholars (Zúquete 2008). In view of changing demographic dynamics and the development of Islamophobia throughout the West, it should be a crucial field for political scientists in the coming years.

Third, political science has until now provided very little empirical qualitative research on specific organised groups of conspiracy theorists. To our knowledge, fieldwork and interviews with Truthers have been conducted by France and Motta (2017), Giry (2015b, 2018a) has studied the LaRouche movement since 2010, and Harambam and Aupers have investigated the Dutch conspiracist milieu (2016), yet the research in political science is widely focused on individual adhesion to conspiracy theories or views from the top dealing with conspiracist leaders. Hence, we recommend developing ground-up and grassroots perspectives dealing with ordinary people engaged in structured conspiratorial organisations or movements.

Last, if conspiracy theories in popular culture have been the focus of research for cultural studies since at least the beginning of the 2000s (Bale, Bennion-Nixon 2000; Knight 2000; Melley 2000; Coale 2005; Arnold 2008), political scientists could fruitfully provide new perspectives, examining the process of reception as it takes place among consumers of conspiracy theories. It has been hypothesised that cultural objects like conspiratorial films, television series or books participate in or contribute to a culture of conspiracy or conspiratorial socialisation, but no empirical study has conclusively demonstrated these effects. The Internet, and the role it plays in the dissemination of conspiracy theories, needs also decisive and specific attention from scholars in the coming years (Uscinski *et al.* 2018). This is a big issue and political science, along with communication science, should take a leading role in examining how the Internet and social media promote conspiracy theories in the context of both democratic and non-democratic forms of political culture.

## Notes

1 Goffman considers stigma reversal strategies as the claim and re-appropriation operated by some social actors of slanderous or disqualification labels.
2 McKenzie-McHarg and Fredheim (2017) noticed that, in more codified and polite circles, the British parliament in the case they studied, the expression 'cock-ups' had progressively replaced 'conspiracy theories' to disqualify government failures in terms of incompetency rather than evil intents.

## References

Abalakina-Paap, M., Stephan, W.G., Craig, T. and Gregory, W.T. (1999) 'Beliefs in conspiracies', *Political Psychology*, 20(3): 637–47.
Albert, M. and Shalom, S. (2002) 'Conspiracies or institutions? 9–11 and beyond', *Z Magazine*, 1 July.
Almond, G. (1996) 'Political science: the history of the discipline', in R. Goodin and H. Klingemann (eds.) *A new handbook of political science*, Oxford: Oxford University Press.
Appelrouth, S. (2017) 'The paranoid style revisited: pseudo-conservatism in the 21st century', *Journal of Historical Sociology*, 30(2): 342–68.
Appelton, S. (2000) 'Trends: assassinations', *Public Opinion Quarterly*, 64(4): 495–522.
Arnold, G.B. (2008) *Conspiracy theory in film, television and politics*, Westport: Praeger Publishers.
Ashraf, A. (1992) 'Conspiracy theories', *Encyclopaedia Iranica*, 6(2): 138–47.
Baer, M. (2013) 'An enemy old and new: the Dönme, anti-semitism, and conspiracy theories in the Ottoman empire and the Turkish republic', *Jewish Quarterly Review*, 103(4): 523–55.
Bale, D. and Bennion-Nixon, L.J. (2000) 'The popular culture of conspiracy/the conspiracy of popular culture', *The Sociological Review*, 48(2): 133–52.
Barkun, M. (2013) *A culture of conspiracy: apocalyptic vision in contemporary America*, Berkeley: University of California Press.
Bartlett, J. and Miller, C. (2010) *The power of unreason: conspiracy theories, extremism and counter-terrorism*, London: Demos.
Baudouin, J. (2017) *Introduction à la science politique*, Paris: Dalloz.
Bergmann, E. (2018) *Conspiracy & populism: the politics of misinformation*, New York: Springer International.
Berinsky, A. (2011) *Rumors, truth, and reality: a study of political misinformation*, paper presented at Annual Meeting of the Midwest Political Science Association in Chicago.
Berlin, I. (1965) 'J.G. Herder', *Encounter*, 25(1–2): 42–51.
Boltanski, L. (2012) *Enigmes et complots. Une enquête à propos d'enquêtes*, Paris: Gallimard.
Bronner, G. (2009) *La Pensée extrême. Comment des hommes ordinaires deviennent des fanatiques*, Paris: Denöel.
Bronner, G. (2013) *La démocratie des crédules*, Paris: PUF.
Butter, M. and Reinkowski, M. (eds.) (2014) *Conspiracy theories in the United States and the Middle East: a comparative approach*, Berlin: De Gruyter.
Byford, J. (2011) *Conspiracy theories: a critical introduction*, Basingstoke: Palgrave Macmillan.
Campion-Vincent, V. (2005) 'From evil others to evil elites: a dominant pattern in conspiracy theories today', in G.A. Fine, V. Campion-Vincent and C. Heath (eds.) *Rumor mills: the social impact of rumor and legend*, Piscataway: Aldine Transaction.
Cicchelli, V. and Octobre, S. (2018) 'Théories du complot et radicalité informationnelle', in O. Galland, A. Muxel (eds.) *La tentation radicale. Enquête auprès des lycéens*, Paris: Puf.
Cichocka, A., Marchlewska, M., Golec de Zavala, A. and Olechowski M. (2016) 'They will not control us': in-group positivity and belief in intergroup conspiracies', *British Journal of Psychology*, 107(3): 556–76.
Coale, S.C. (2005) *Paradigms of paranoia: the culture of conspiracy in contemporary American fiction*, Tuscaloosa: University Alabama Press.
Corcuff, P. (2009) "'Le complot' ou les mésaventures tragi-comiques de 'la critique'", *Mediapart*, 19 June.
Crick, B. (1959) *The American science of politics: its origins and conditions*, Berkeley: University of California Press.

Crocker, J., Luhtanen, R., Broadnax, S. and Blaine, B.E. (1999) 'Belief in U.S. government conspiracies against blacks among black and white college students: powerlessness or system blame?', *Personality and Social Psychology Bulletin*, 25(8): 941–5.

Davis, D.B. (ed.) (1971) *The fear of conspiracy: images on un-American subversion from the revolution to present*, London: Cornell University Press.

De Poli, B. (2018) 'Anti-Jewish and anti-Zionist conspiracism in the Arab world: historical and political roots' in A. Dyrendal, D.G. Robertson and E. Asperm (eds.) *Handbook of conspiracy theory and contemporary religion*, Leyde: Brill.

Della Porta, D. (2008) *Introduzione alla scienza politica*, Bologna: il Mulino.

Dunbar, D. and Reagan, B. (eds.) (2011) *Debunking 9/11 myths: why conspiracy theories can't stand up to the facts: an in-depth investigation by popular mechanics*, New York: Hearst Communications.

Einstein, K.L. and Glick, D.M. (2014) 'Do I think BLS Data are BS? The consequences of conspiracy theories', *Political Behavior*, 37(3): 679–701.

Fenster, M. (1999) *Conspiracy theories: secrecy and power in American culture*, Minneapolis: University of Minneapolis.

Fine, G.A. (2015) 'Barack Obama and uncertain knowledge', *Diogène*, 249–50: 190–202.

Frampton, M., Goodhart, D. and Mamhood, K. (2016) 'Unsettled belonging: a survey of Britain's Muslim communities', paper published by *Policy Exchange*. Available at: https://policyexchange.org.uk/wp-content/uploads/2016/12/PEXJ5037_Muslim_Communities_FINAL.pdf. [Accessed 22 August 2019.]

France, P. and Motta, A. (2017) 'En un combat douteux. Militantisme en ligne, 'complotisme' et disqualification médiatique: le cas de l'association ReOpen911', *Quaderni*, 94: 13–26.

François, S. and Schmitt, O. (2015) 'Le conspirationnisme dans la Russie contemporaine', *Diogène*, 249–50: 120–9.

Girardet, R. (1986) *Mythes et mythologies politiques*, Paris: Seuil.

Giry, J. (2014) *Le conspirationnisme dans la culture politique et populaire aux Etats-Unis. Une approche sociopolitique des théories du complot*, unpublished thesis, University of Rennes 1.

Giry, J. (2015a) 'Le conspirationnisme. Archéologie et morphologie d'un mythe politique', *Diogène*, 249–50: 40–50.

Giry, J. (2015b) 'Le mouvement LaRouche à l'international. Impact du territoire et stratégies politiques d'implantation à l'échelle nationale et locale. Approche comparée France États-Unis', *Politeïa*, 28: 433–52.

Giry, J. (2017a) 'Etudier les théories du complot en sciences sociales: enjeux et usages', *Quaderni*, 94: 5–11.

Giry, J. (2017b) 'A specific social function of rumors and conspiracy theories: strengthening community's ties in trouble times. A multilevel analysis', *Slovak Ethnology*, 65(2): 187–202.

Giry, J. (2018a) 'Quand la radicalité en vient à questionner la rationalité (en) politique. Lyndon LaRouche, une étude de cas', in S. François (ed.) *Un XXIe siècle irrationnel? Analyses pluridisciplinaires des pensées 'alternatives'*, Paris: Éditions du CNRS.

Giry, J. (2018b) 'Devenir complotiste: trajectoires de radicalisation et de professionnalisation de deux groupes de citoyen(ne)s enquêteur(rice)s', *Critique & Humanism*, 49: 429–49.

Giry, J. (2018c) 'Archéologie et usages du 'style paranoïaque'. Une épistémologie critique', *Critica Masonica*, 12: 75–92.

Giry, J., Taïeb, E. and Tournay, V. (2018) 'Les radicalisations. Culture et post-modernité', *Quaderni*, 95: 5–12.

Goertzel, T. (1994) 'Beliefs in conspiracy theories', *Political Psychology*, 15(4): 731–42.

Goffman, E. (1963) *Stigma: notes on the management of spoiled identity*, Upper Saddle River: Prentice Hall.

Goldberg, R.A. (2001) *Enemies within: the culture of conspiracy in modern America*, New Haven: Yale University Press.

Goldschläger, A. and Lemaire, J.-C. (2005) *Le complot judéo-maçonnique*, Brussels: Labor.

Gray, M. (2010) *Conspiracy theories in the Arab world: sources and politics*, London: Routledge.

Guizot, F. (1845) *Des conspirations et de la justice politiques*, Paris: Editeurs des fastes de la gloire.

Hagemeister, M. (2018) 'The third Rome against the third temple: apocalypticism and conspiracism in post-Soviet Russia' in A. Dyrendal, D.G. Robertson and E. Asperm (eds.) *Handbook of conspiracy theory and contemporary religion*, Leyde: Brill.

Hall, J.A. (2006) 'Aligning darkness with conspiracy theory: the discursive effect of African American interest in Gary Webb's 'Dark Alliance'', *The Howard Journal of Communication*, 17(3): 205–22.

Haluzík, R. (2015) "Qui y a-t-il derrière tout ça?' Révolutions et théories du complot en Europe de l'Est', *Diogène*, 249–50: 130–49.

Harambam, J. and Aupers S. (2016) '"I am not a conspiracy theorist": relational identifications in the Dutch conspiracy milieu', *Cultural Sociology*, 11(1): 113–29.

Heathershaw, J. (2012) 'Of national fathers and Russian elder brothers: conspiracy theories and political ideas in post-Soviet Central Asia', *The Russian Review*, 71: 610–29.

Hofstadter, R. (1955) *The age of reform*, New York: Vintage Book.

Hofstadter, R. (1964) *The paranoid style in American politics, and other essays*, New York: Knopf.

Ifop (2018) *Enquête sur le complotisme*, ConspiracyWatch and Foundation Jean Jaurès. Available at: https://jean-jaures.org/sites/default/files/redac/commun/productions/2018/0108/115158_-_rapport_02.01.2017.pdf. [Accessed: 22 August 2019.]

Imhoff, R. and Bruder, M. (2014) 'Speaking (un-)truth to power: conspiracy mentality as a generalised political attitude', *European Journal of Personality*, 28: 25–43.

James, N. (2000) 'Militias, the patriot movement, and the internet: the ideology of conspiracism', *The Sociological Review*, 48(2): 63–92.

Jameson, F. (1981) *The political unconscious: narrative as a socially symbolic act*, Ithaca: Cornell University Press.

Jamin, J. (2009) *L'imaginaire du complot. Discours d'extrême droite en France et aux États-Unis*, Amsterdam: Amsterdam University Press.

Jane, E.A. and Fleming, C. (2014) *Modern conspiracy: the importance of being paranoid*, London: Bloomsbury Academic.

Jolley, D. and Douglas, K.M. (2013) 'The social consequences of conspiracism: exposure to conspiracy theories decreases intentions to engage in politics and to reduce one's carbon footprint', *The British Journal of Psychology*, 105: 35–56.

Knight, P. (2000) *Conspiracy culture: from Kennedy to the X-Files*, London: Routledge.

Knight, P. (2003) 'Preface', in P. Knight (ed.) *Conspiracy theories in American history: an Encyclopaedia*, Santa Barbara: ABC-Clio.

Lipset, M.S. (1950) *Political man: the social bases of politics*, New York: Doubleday.

Lipset, M.S. (1969) *Politics and the social sciences*, Oxford: Oxford University Press.

Lipset, M.S. and Raab, E. (1970) *The politics of unreason: right-wing extremism in America, 1790–1970*, Chicago: University of Chicago Press.

Locke S. (2009) 'Conspiracy culture, blame culture, and rationalization', *The Sociological Review*, 57(4): 567–85.

Machiavelli, N. (1531) *Discourses on Livy*, reprint, trans. Harvey Mansfield, Chicago: The University of Chicago Press, 1996.

McKenzie-McHarg, A. and Fredheim, R. (2017) 'Cock-ups and slap-downs: a quantitative analysis of conspiracy rhetoric in the British parliament 1916–2015', *Historical Methods: A Journal of Quantitative and Interdisciplinary History*, 50(3): 156–69.

Melley, T. (2000) *Empire of conspiracy: the culture of paranoia in postwar America*, Ithaca: Cornell University Press.

Miller, J.M., Saunders, K.L. and Farhart, C.E. (2016) 'Conspiracy endorsement as motivated reasoning: the moderating roles of political knowledge and trust', *American Journal of Political Science*, 60(4): 824–44.

Moore, A. (2017) 'Conspiracies, conspiracy theories and democracy', *Political Studies Review*, 16(1): 2–12.

Nefes, T.S. (2013) 'Political parties' perceptions and uses of anti-semitic conspiracy theories in Turkey', *The Sociological Review*, 61(2): 247–64.

Nyhan, B. (2012) 'Political knowledge does not guard against belief in conspiracy theories', *You Gov: Model Politics*. Available at: https://today.yougov.com/topics/politics/articles-reports/2012/11/05/political-knowledge-does-not-guard-against-belief. [Accessed 22 August 2019.]

Oliver, J.E. and Wood, T.J. (2014) 'Conspiracy theories and the paranoid style(s) of mass opinion', *American Journal of Political Science*, 58(4): 952–66.

Olmsted, K.S. (2009) *Real enemies: conspiracy and American democracy, World War I to 9/11*, New York: Oxford University Press.

Olmsted, K.S. (2011) 'The truth is out there: citizen sleuths from the Kennedy assassination to the 9/11 truth movement', *Diplomatic History*, 35(4): 671–93.

Ortmann, S. and Heathershaw, J. (2012) 'Conspiracy theories in the post-Soviet space', *The Russian Review*, 71: 551–64.

Panczová, Z. and Janeček, P. (2015) 'Théories du complot et rumeurs en Slovaquie et Tchéquie', *Diogène*, 249–50: 150–97.

Parish, J. and Parker, M. (2001) *The age of anxiety: conspiracy theory and the human sciences*, Hoboken: Wiley-Blackwell.
Pérez Hernáiz, H.A. (2009) 'Teorías de la Conspiración. Entre la Magia, el Siento Común y la Ciencia', *Revista de Ciencias Sociales*, 2: 1–17.
Pipes, D. (1997) *Conspiracy: how the paranoid style flourishes and where it comes from*, London: Touchstone.
Poliakov, L. (1980) *La Causalité diabolique, t. 1: Essai sur l'origine des persécutions*, Paris: Calmann-Lévy.
Popper, K. (1945) *The open society and its enemies*, vol. 2, London: Routledge.
Quinn, A. (2000) '*Tout est lié*: the front national and media conspiracy theories', *The Sociological Review*, 48(2): 112–32.
Renard, J.B. (2015) 'Qu'est-ce que le conspirationnisme?', *Diplomatie Magazine*, 73: 38–42.
Ross, M.W., Essien, E.J. and Torres, I. (2006) 'Conspiracy beliefs about the origin of AIDS in four racial/ethnic groups', *Journal of Acquired Immune Deficiency Syndrome*, 41(3): 342–4.
Russell, S.L., Katz, R.V., Wang, M.Q., Lee, R., Green, B.L., Kressin, N.R. and Claudio C. (2011) 'Belief in AIDS origin conspiracy theory and willingness to participate in biomedical research studies: findings in Whites, Blacks, and Hispanics in seven cities across two surveys', *HIV Clinical Trials*, 12(1): 37–47.
Simmel, G. (1906) 'The sociology of secrecy and of secret societies', *American Journal of Sociology*, 11(4): 441–98.
Simmons, W. and Parsons, S. (2005) 'Beliefs in conspiracy among African Americans: a comparison of elites and masses', *Social Science Quarterly*, 86(3): 582–98.
Steiner, K. and Önnerfors, A. (2018) (eds.) *Expressions of radicalization – global politics, processes and practices*, London: Palgrave.
Stempel, C., Hargrove, T. and Stempel, G.H. (2007) 'Media use, social structure and belief in 9/11 conspiracy theories', *Journalism and Mass Communication Quarterly*, 84(2): 353–73.
Suetonius (121 B.C.), *The Twelve Caesars*, trans. Robert Graves (1957) Harmondsworth: Penguin.
Sunstein, C.R. and Vermeule, A. (2009) 'Symposium on conspiracy theories: conspiracy theories: causes and cures', *Journal of Political Philosophy*, 17(2): 202–27.
Taguieff, P.-A. (1992) *Les protocoles des sages de sion. Faux et usages d'un faux*, Paris: Berg International.
Taguieff, P.-A. (2005) *La foire aux Illuminés. Ésotérisme, théories du complot, extrémisme*, Paris: Mille et une nuits.
Taguieff, P.-A. (2013) *Court traité de complotologie*, Paris: Mille et une nuits.
Taïeb, E. (2010) 'Logiques politiques du conspirationnisme', *Sociologie et société*, 42(2): 265–89.
Taragoni, F. (2018) *Le peuple et le caudillo: la question populiste en Amérique Latine contemporaine*, Rennes: PUR.
Thurlow, R.C. (1978) 'The powers of darkness: conspiracy belief and political strategy', *Patterns of Prejudice*, 12(6): 1–12, 23.
Uscinski, J. (2018) 'The study of conspiracy theories', *Argumenta*, 6 (3–2), 233–45.
Uscinski, J. and Parent, J. (2014) *American conspiracy theories*, Oxford: Oxford University Press.
Uscinki, J., DeWitt, D. and Atkinson, M.D. (2018) 'A web of conspiracy? Internet and conspiracy theory' in A. Dyrendal, D.G. Robertson and E. Asperm (eds.) *Handbook of conspiracy theory and contemporary religion*, Leyde: Brill.
Van Prooijen, J.-W., Krouwel, A.P.M. and Pollet, T.V. (2015) 'Political extremism predicts belief in conspiracy theories', *Social Psychological and Personality Science*, 6(5): 570–8.
Van Prooijen, J.-W., Staman, J. and Krouwel, A.P.M. (2018) 'Increased conspiracy beliefs among ethnic and Muslim minorities', *Applied Cognitive Psychology*, 32(5): 661–7.
Waters, A.M. (1997) 'Conspiracy theories as ethnosociologies: explanation and intention in African American political culture', *Journal of Black Studies*, 28(1): 112–25.
Yablokov, I. (2018) *Fortress Russia: conspiracy theories in post-Soviet Russia*, Cambridge: Polity Press.
Yazmaci, U. (2014) 'La démocratisation à l'épreuve des théories du complot: l'expérience de l'AKP en Turquie', paper presented at the 23rd Congress of the International Political Science Association in Montréal. Available at: www.academia.edu/7560937/La_d%C3%A9mocratisation_%C3%A0_l_%C3%A9preuve_des_th%C3%A9ories_du_complot_l_exp%C3%A9rience_de_l_AKP_en_Turquie. [Accessed: 22 August 2019.]
Zúquete, J.P. (2008) 'The European extreme-right and Islam: new directions?', *Journal of Political Ideologies*, 13(3): 321–44.

# 1.9
# SOCIAL PSYCHOLOGY OF CONSPIRACY THEORIES

*Olivier Klein and Kenzo Nera*

## Introduction

Consider these claims: Conspiracy theories serve as a means to respond to people's need for uniqueness (Lantian *et al.* 2017). Political extremism predicts belief in conspiracy theories (van Prooijen *et al.* 2015). When attending to visual scenes, conspiracy theorists are prone to 'tunnel vision', focusing their attention on details as opposed to the 'global picture' (van Elk 2015). These are examples of broad conclusions paraphrased from recent social psychological publications exploring conspiracy theories. How confident can one be in such claims? What justifies them? This chapter aims to answer these questions.

We define conspiracy theories as beliefs about a group of actors who join together in secret agreement to achieve a hidden goal that is perceived as unlawful or malevolent (Zonis, Joseph 1994: 448–9). Note that, in this psychological definition, conspiracy theories are seen as beliefs held by individuals (they need not be shared) and need not be false. A consequence of this broad definition is that, rather than focusing on specific conspiracy theories, social psychology mostly aims at capturing their common features.

In the past few years, social psychological research on conspiracy theories has grown exponentially. For non-specialists interested in conspiracy theories, this wealth of studies can seem intimidating. The chapters in section 2 of this volume, or accessible summaries of the literature (e.g. van Prooijen 2018), provide a suitable overview of the scholarship, but they do not unpack the epistemological principles guiding research on the topic. For scholars versed in the humanities or social sciences, the kinds of questions that preoccupy social psychologists and the standards on which they evaluate evidence may not be evident. For a historian interested in conspiracy theories in ancient Rome or for an anthropologist studying conspiracies in a fringe political community, to give but two examples, the broad statements social psychologists are accustomed to, especially when they are transformed into news headlines, may either raise eyebrows or be taken at face value, without the critical eye they would accord to research emanating from their own domain. Both attitudes impede interdisciplinary dialogue. The purpose of this chapter is to help navigate the literature with a better insight into the way social (and political) psychologists approach this subject matter. Ultimately, this may help foster more fruitful interdisciplinary exchanges on this topic, allowing a richer understanding of beliefs in conspiracy theories. A secondary purpose of this chapter is to help the reader appraise the relevance of social psychological research in the real world, beyond the laboratory. But, before discussing conspiracy theories, it is important to understand what social psychology is.

## Characterising social psychology

Social psychology is a field of psychology that dates to the beginning of the twentieth century. It investigates how cognitions, judgments and behaviours are influenced by others. It does so generally (although not exclusively) through quantitative methods. Social psychologists seek to understand general phenomena (e.g. obedience to authority, conformism, prejudice and so on). This usually means constructing a causal model of such phenomena grounded in a larger theory. Typically, this will imply identifying contextual factors that 'cause' the psychological phenomenon under investigation. The impact of these factors will usually be channelled by intermediary variables (named mediators) that are thought to 'explain' the effect of the contextual factor on the phenomenon of interest. For example, the effect of a political crisis (contextual factor) on belief in conspiracy theories may be channelled through uncertainty (mediator). In order to test models of such phenomena, social psychologists gather empirical data (e.g. through randomised experiments or surveys), often in carefully controlled settings, and draw inference on the validity of these models using statistical analyses. Social psychology is a diverse field that includes sub-areas or approaches that span a spectrum ranging from neuroscience to sociology.

The cognitive approach (social cognition) aims at examining the information processing mechanisms people use to appraise the world that surrounds them. An example of the social cognitive approach of conspiracy theories can be found in research examining the relation between conspiracy belief and pattern perception (Dieguez *et al.* 2015; see also Chapter 2.2 in this volume). In contrast to the cognitive approach, the motivational perspective seeks to understand the needs and motivations associated with the social phenomenon that is being studied. For example, conspiracy beliefs may respond to a feeling of uncertainty (van Prooijen, Jostmann 2013).

Another important distinction in social psychology involves the opposition between individual-level and group-level approaches of social phenomena. In the study of conspiracy theories, individual-level approaches seek to understand how individual psychological processes influence adhesion to those beliefs (as in the example cited). Collective approaches are more interested in how membership of specific groups impinge on such processes and/or the roles conspiracy theories may play at a group level. Although conspiracy theories are shared beliefs that are strongly associated with membership of specific groups, comparatively little research has adopted this angle. An example of this approach (Crocker *et al.* 1999) shows that the greater endorsement of conspiracy theories by African Americans, compared to European Americans, was driven by a motivation to blame the 'system' (for being discriminatory and prejudiced) as opposed to a sense of powerlessness.

Finally, note that social psychology is preoccupied with the general processes governing social behaviour. The study of conspiracy theories does not escape this rule. Hence, they are not perceived as 'pathological' forms of belief, that only a minority of individuals may adhere to. By contrast, they are viewed as the outcome of normal societal and psychological processes that may impact any individual regardless of his or her psychological makeup.

## History of research on conspiracy theories in social psychology

While conspiracy theories are a very ancient phenomenon (van Prooijen, Douglas 2017), psychological scholarship on this topic, with a few isolated exceptions, is a relatively recent affair, dating back to the 1970s. An early investigation of conspiracy theorising was provided by McCauley and Jacques (1979), when the memory of the assassination of John F. Kennedy and the associated conspiracy theories were still fresh. These authors sought to examine the 'proportionality bias', i.e. the idea that people seek large causes for large effects. Using an experimental approach, they showed that people were more likely to explain a gunshot at the U.S. president as driven by a conspiracy if the shot succeeded in killing him than if it failed: Whereas a missed shot tolerates a lone shooter as an explanation, only large-scale conspiracies can result in a 'hit'.

After this initial study, no notable empirical paper was published in the 1980s. The main contribution to the literature was an edited book by Graumann and Moscovici (1987). Among other notable contributions, this volume contains a seminal chapter by Serge Moscovici (1987), who, building on a historical analysis of conspiracy theories, posited the existence of a 'conspiracy mentality', which he views as the core of a social representation of society opposing two classes: The evil conspiring 'others' and the virtuous, normal, lawful 'us'. This chapter, richly grounded in historical, philosophical and sociological scholarship, anticipates many of the issues later studied and embraces a 'collective' perspective of conspiracy theories. Moscovici views them as a way of preserving the identity of the group in the face of minorities, whose very existence is threatened by them. Importantly, he emphasises the 'normal' aspects of conspiracy theorising, which he views as a 'matrix of collective thought in our epoch' (Moscovici 1987: 168).

It is in the 1990s that a programme of empirical research on conspiracy theories really started. Notably, Goertzel (1994) reports a survey of New Jersey respondents on belief in ten different conspiracy theories. Such belief was investigated by presenting a conspiracy (e.g. 'the AIDS virus was created deliberately in a government laboratory') and asking participants to evaluate the statement on a scale ranging from one ('certainly false') to five ('certainly true'). Using a common psychometric index, Cronbach's alpha, Goertzel found that judgments on these ten items were strongly intercorrelated. In other words, it appeared that people who espouse one conspiracy theory tend to espouse others, to the point that belief in conspiracy theories seemed to reflect one single underlying dimension. To account for this finding, which will prove to be the 'most consistent finding on the psychology of conspiracy theories' according to Sutton and Douglas (2014: 255), Goertzel introduced the notion of 'monological belief systems', i.e. belief systems closed on themselves, in which each conspiracy belief reinforces others, buttressing a general assumption that the world is orchestrated by sinister forces (for a critical account of this view, see Sutton and Douglas 2014). Abalakina-Paap *et al.* (1999) produced another landmark study, ushering in a field of research on the relationship between belief in conspiracy theories and different personality traits (or other individual differences) such as authoritarianism, self-esteem, etc.

In the 2000s, the number of publications on the topic increased further. One of the most influential papers of this period was produced by Karen Douglas and Robbie Sutton (2008), who showed that people were poor at estimating the influence of exposure to conspiracy beliefs on their own judgment. Specifically, they underestimated their own 'permeability' to conspiracy theories while expecting that others would be much more vulnerable (known as the 'third-person effect'). Another important paper of this period was Wagner-Egger and Bangerter's 'La vérité est ailleurs' ('The truth is out there') (2007). Besides those targeting minorities (on which Moscovici focused his interest), these scholars identified another category of conspiracy theories, targeting dominant, majority groups (known as 'system' conspiracy theories). They showed that fear predicts the former whereas irrationality specifically predicts endorsement of system-related conspiracy theories. The interest for conspiracy theories really surged in the 2010s. Douglas and Sutton and their (former) students (Daniel Jolley, Robert Brotherton, Mike Wood) spearheaded this tendency. Other scholars, such as Jan-Willem van Prooijen, Roland Imhoff, Viren Swami and Michal Bilewicz, emerged as well, putting conspiracy theories at the centre of social psychology. The wealth of publications dating from this period is too voluminous to be covered in this chapter. Rather, we shall consider the assumptions on which social psychological knowledge on conspiracy theories (as much of the rest of the field) has been conducted. In order to do so, we shall delve into a specific study in detail.

## Theoretical modelling in social psychology: An example

The study was conducted by Jolley and Douglas (2014b: Study 1) and is typical of the way experimental psychologists formulate and test a theory. These authors suggest that exposure to conspiracy theories reduces civic engagement. Why? Because, when people are exposed to conspiracy theories, they feel more powerless and doubt the effectiveness of their actions on behalf of the collective. So, in this model, three theoretical constructs are postulated:

1. Exposure to conspiracy theories, i.e. the postulated causal factor, or independent variable;
2. Civic disengagement, i.e. the construct affected by the causal factor, or dependent variable;
3. Feelings of powerlessness, i.e. the mechanism through which the independent variable influences the dependent variable, or the mediator.

Let us consider some of the assumptions underlying such an approach. Note that these apply to most empirical papers in social psychology. Jolley and Douglas are interested in general processes that should operate regardless of the content of the conspiracy theory being considered. The model is expected to hold for a wide variety of conspiracy theories. The same holds with respect to the outcome: Civic engagement. Exposure to conspiracy theories should influence a variety of instances (or 'operationalisations' in technical parlance) of political engagement, such as voting, participating in a political campaign, etc.

This assumption of generalisability is not self-evident: One could imagine for example that two narratives fitting the definition of conspiracy theories may have different effects on political engagement and/or that exposure to some conspiracy theories may exacerbate some forms of political engagement (e.g. voting) while making others less likely (e.g. marching on behalf of a specific party). The issue is usually addressed by examining how the respondents' answers to items supposed to measure a single, more generic construct, are intercorrelated. In the study, they used a scale measuring seven instances of civic engagement (e.g. donate money to a party, vote during the next elections, etc.). The seven items yielded a good internal consistency; in other words, they were strongly intercorrelated, suggesting that the items could be considered as measuring a single construct, i.e. civic engagement.

A further assumption of this approach is that the psychological entities under consideration are measurable, i.e. that they can be transformed into numbers on a meaningful scale. While social psychology has used many measurement techniques, the most common one in the field of conspiracy theories is the use of rating scales. For example, in the present study, belief in conspiracy theories was measured by asking people to express how likely they found 12 statements of the type 'The British government was involved in the death of Princess Diana' from 1 ('extremely unlikely') to 7 ('extremely likely'). Their average rating was treated as an index of their belief in conspiracy theories. It may seem peculiar to view such a scale as continuous, but psychometricians have argued that this is warranted when the distribution of the underlying construct follows a normal (i.e. 'bell-shaped') distribution in the population of interest (e.g. all British citizens). When the distribution observed in the sample of people actually participating in the study is compatible with this theoretical distribution, psychologists tend to treat response scales of this type as continuous (for a critical discussion of this assumption, see Liddell and Kruschke 2018). A direct implication of this approach is that an individual's score on a given scale is not per se informative of anything, but is rather to be put in perspective with a sample that enables comparison between participants.

In experimental social psychology, an additional assumption is that manipulating the causal variable should produce effects on the outcome if the model is correct. Practically, this involves finding a sample of people for whom the model is expected to hold (which is, generally, all 'normal' adults, unless otherwise specified) and then assigning each participant in the study to an experimental condition on a purely random basis. Since experiments are conducted in a controlled environment, researchers can make sure that the causal variable is the only parameter that varies between conditions. Therefore, if the expected outcome is observed, it can be attributed to the causal factor.

The researcher then uses statistical tests to calculate the probability of the observed data under the assumption that the 'null hypothesis' is true. In the case of a group comparison, the 'null hypothesis' is the assumption that there are actually no differences between the groups, and that the observed differences are merely the consequence of random sampling variations. If the observed differences between the experimental and control conditions are more extreme than could be reasonably explained by chance under the assumption that the null hypothesis is true, the model is considered to be supported by the data.

Conventionally, the hypothesised model is considered to be supported to the extent that the difference between groups is less than 5 per cent likely to be produced by chance under the null hypothesis. This probability is named the '$p$-value' (typically written $p$.), and it is considered 'significant' if it is lower than 0.05. In effect, this means that mistakenly attributing a difference produced by chance to the hypothesised causal factor will occur 5 per cent of the time (for an introduction to inference testing, see Perezgonzalez 2015).

Jolley and Douglas tested their model with 168 British students. Their experimental manipulation involved inviting them to read an article that supposedly promoted the existence of government-sponsored conspiracy theories. Half of the participants read an article advocating that the U.K. government was involved in conspiracies (around, among other events associated with popular conspiracy theories, the death of Princess Diana), while the other read an article defending the opposite view.

Participants' belief in government-led conspiracy theories, their feelings of powerlessness and their political engagement were then measured using appropriate rating scales. For all variables, participants' answers to the items were averaged into scores used in the statistical analyses.

As expected, participants exposed to the 'pro-conspiracy' article obtained lower scores on the political engagement scale than those exposed to the 'anti-conspiracy text'. The difference between these two means (2.67 and 3.20 respectively) was statistically significant ($p=0.005$) using the appropriate test. The reported p-value means that there were five chances out of 1000 to observe this result if there were actually no 'real' differences between the groups.

The authors also relied on a more complex statistical method (mediation) to establish that, indeed, this difference was explained by the effect of exposure to the text on feelings of powerlessness.

## Interpreting findings

How confident should we be in the support of such data for the theoretical model that is being postulated? The p-value is of interest, as it indicates whether the results could have been produced by chance. What it does not tell us, however, is how strong the effect is: in the case of group a comparison, how large is the difference between the groups? Hence, effect size is distinct from statistical significance, and should always be reported in a social psychology paper. The p-value is, indeed, very sensitive to sample size, such that a very small effect can be significant when the sample size is very large.

In the present case, the effect size is $d=0.46$, which is considered (almost) 'medium' according to the conventions set out by Cohen (1988). This is roughly the mean effect size found in all research published in social psychology (Richard et al. 2003). To provide a rough idea of what this means, look at Figure 1.9.1, which represents the theoretical distribution of the score in the 'conspiracy group' (solid line) and the 'control' group (dotted line) assuming a $d$ of 0.46 and the observed means. As can be seen from this graph, the two graphs overlap to a large extent.

From an applied perspective, one is often more interested in the strength of the effects than in whether they are significant or not. Yet, the social psychological literature has placed much more emphasis on significance than on effect size. In the case of Jolley and Douglas's study, the observed effect size is not considered 'large' by Cohen's standards. However, considering that the manipulation was relatively mild (reading an article), this can be considered a relatively meaningful effect. Going back to McCauley and Jacques's reasoning: A strong effect is more meaningful when the cause is small than when the cause is large.

## Correlations

We have examined an example of experimental study on conspiracy theories. However, the most frequent statistical method used by social and political psychologists to study conspiracy theories are correlation and regression, methods developed in the nineteenth and early twentieth century by Francis Galton and Karl Pearson. A correlation coefficient (noted $r$) is an indicator of

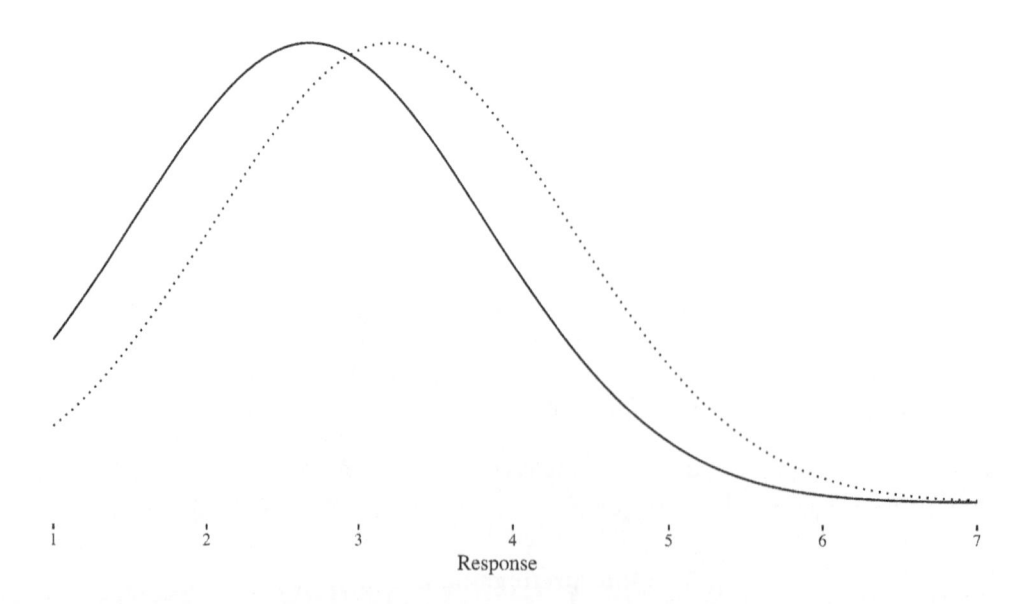

*Figure 1.9.1* Theoretical distribution of the score of political engagement in the 'conspiracy group' (solid line) and the 'control' group (dotted line).

the association between two variables. It can vary between −1 (when the two variables are completely negatively associated) and 1 (when the two variables are completely positively associated). A correlation coefficient of 0 means that there is no association. However, in practice, such 'perfect' correlations are never found, and we can only observe that some variables tend to be more or less associated, positively or negatively, with others.

Let us imagine that, among a sample of 300 people, you measure the motive to appear rational and the endorsement of a conspiracy theory, both on a multi-items scale. You can plot the scores of the former on an X-axis and the scores of the latter on a Y-axis such that each dot on the graph represents a participant in the sample. Figure 1.9.2 represents imaginary data exemplifying this situation.

In the present case, a positive correlation coefficient will be indicated by the observation that the 'cloud' of data seems to be directed upwards such that higher values on one dimension are associated with higher values on the other dimensions (a negative correlation will be indicated by a 'downwards'-oriented cloud). If the correlation is perfect (which never happens in psychology), all points will be aligned on a line (here the black line in Figure 1.9.2). In this figure, the correlation coefficient equals −0.38. Typically, social psychologists will interpret such findings as suggesting that variable 1 is (negatively) associated with variable 2, for example that a motive to appear rational is associated with a weaker endorsement of a conspiracy theory.

It is, however, important to be cautious when interpreting between-subject correlation coefficients: While a positive correlation coefficient certainly shows that people who score high on X tend to score high on Y, it does not demonstrate unequivocally that a general psychological process associating X and Y is present. That X and Y are correlated may be the outcome of a

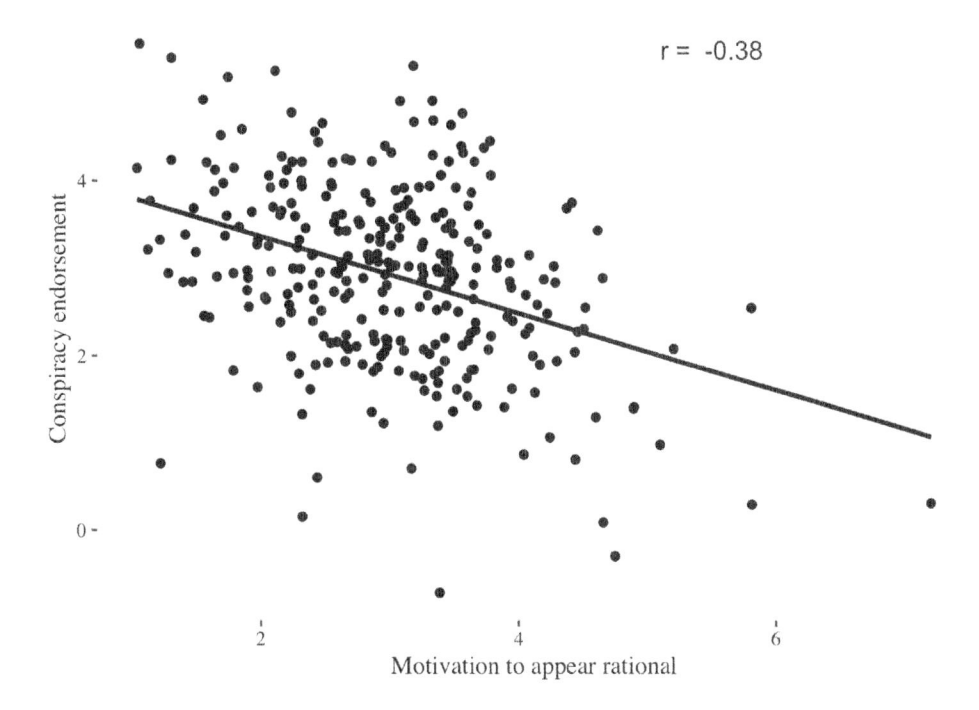

*Figure 1.9.2* Correlation between wanting to appear rational and the endorsement of a conspiracy theory.

third variable, e.g. both showing motivation to appear rational and disregard towards conspiracy theories could be explained by respondents' motives to respond in socially desirable ways, since conspiracy theories are stigmatised (Lantian et al. 2018).

Linear regression is another common method, which is roughly equivalent to correlation. However, it differs in two ways: First, one variable is identified as the 'predictor' (i.e. the postulated causal factor) and the other as the 'outcome'. The method is meant to predict the value of the latter based on the former. Second, this method allows us to include several potential predictors in the model, and hence allows measuring the effect of one predictor while controlling for others.

## Study designs

Conspiracy theories are studied in several ways. A wealth of research seeks to examine the relation between endorsement of conspiracy theories and a variety of traits or attitudes that vary between individuals using the correlational approach just described (for a review and meta-analysis, see Goreis and Voracek 2019). These include personality traits (e.g. paranoia: Imhoff and Lamberty 2018), political attitudes (e.g. van Prooijen et al. 2015), endorsement of other beliefs such as the paranormal (e.g. Drinkwater et al. 2012) or demographic characteristics such as socioeconomic status, education (e.g. van Prooijen 2017) or ethnicity (e.g. Davis et al. 2018).

A second category of studies seeks to examine whether people who believe in conspiracy theories are, more than others, prone to a variety of cognitive biases such as the conjunction fallacy, i.e. the tendency to view the conjunction of two events as more likely than each event separately (Brotherton, French 2014); the proportionality bias, i.e. the tendency to consider that large causes should have large effects (McCauley, Jacques 1979); the tendency to overestimate one's capacity to explain phenomena (Vitriol, Marsh 2018) or the tendency to see intentionality in inanimate objects (Douglas et al. 2016; see also Chapter 2.4 in this volume).

Note that, while interesting, the design of these studies does not allow us to establish the causal direction of these relations. This is because such studies are purely correlational. If there is a correlation between the two variables, this could be:

- Due to the bias causing the conspiracy belief: For example, people who tend to see intentionality where there is apparently none may come to endorse conspiracy theories;
- Due to the conspiracy belief causing the bias: People who endorse the conspiracy belief may develop a propensity to see intentionality where there is none;
- Due to a third, unmeasured factor (e.g. intelligence) causing both the conspiracy belief and the bias.

Longitudinal designs, in which the variable of interests are measured on several occasions, would be better equipped to tackle such causal relations. Indeed, as a cause is necessary anterior to its effect, such an approach allows us to establish causality more convincingly. Nonetheless, such designs are rarely used in research on conspiracy theories. (For an exception, see Golec de Zavala and Federico 2018.)

The most compelling demonstration of causality is provided by experimental designs in which observations are randomly assigned to a treatment. If the outcome varies above what would be expected by chance alone, this suggests that the treatment was indeed effective. A considerable amount of research on conspiracy theories relies on such designs. Aside from studies in which conspiracy theories are used as exposure material, as in the study by Jolley and Douglas (2014b) discussed previously, a common approach involves scenario studies in which people are presented with a fictitious event and asked to estimate the likelihood that a conspiracy produced it (e.g. van Prooijen, Jostmann 2013, study 2). In the present case, belief in conspiracy theories is measured as the outcome variable. Relying on a fictitious setting has several advantages: People's belief in pre-existing conspiracy theories may be unlikely to be affected by relatively subtle experimental manipulations. Second, the story can be easily adapted to incorporate the the manipulation (e.g., an instance of political corruption in Van Prooijen, Jostmann, 2013), which would be much more difficult using existing theories. Naturally, the drawback of this choice is that the endorsement of this fictitious theory carries little meaning and personal implications for participants.

## Main scales used to measure belief in conspiracy theories

There are many ways to measure endorsement of conspiracy theories. A common approach involves evaluating beliefs in specific conspiracy theories that are relevant given the social context of the study. For example, in a study conducted in Hungary, studies by Marchlewska, Cichocka and Kossowska (2018) probed people's beliefs regarding the cause of the 2010 plane crash that killed the former Polish president Lech Kaczynski, among many other victims.

Another option involves measuring belief in some of the most globally notorious conspiracy theories. This is the approach taken by Swami et al. (2017) in the 'Belief in conspiracy theories inventory', a 15-item scale that measures belief in 15 different theories such as 'US agencies intentionally created the A.I.D.S. epidemic and administered it to Black participants' or 'The Apollo moon landings never happened and were staged in a Hollywood film studio'. The approach, here, seems to be to evaluate belief in the 'top fifteen' conspiracy theories. Other authors have sought to measure endorsement of conspiracy theories through statements that do not involve contextually specific theories. A prominent example of this approach is the Generic Conspiracy Belief Scale of Brotherton, French and Pickering (2013). The statements are so general that they could refer to many possible conspiracies and contexts (e.g. 'The government uses people as patsies to hide its involvement in criminal activity' or 'A lot of important information is deliberately concealed from the public out of self-interest'). Bruder et al.'s work (2013) offers another avenue for circumventing the context-specificity of measures of endorsement of conspiracy theories. They evaluate an individual trait that they term 'conspiracy mentality' (based on Moscovici 1987). This trait is thought to reflect a general propensity to subscribe to 'theories blaming a conspiracy of ill-intending individuals' (Bruder et al. 2013: 2). They rely on items such as 'I think that many important things happen in the world which the public is never informed about' or 'There are secret organizations that greatly influence political decisions'.

In the same vein, Lantian, Muller, Nurra and Douglas (2016) developed a one-item measure of conspiracy beliefs, which provides a highly economical way of evaluating this dimension. After an introductory text mentioning the 'debates' over various social and political events (the 9/11 attacks, the death of Princess Diana, the J.F.K. assassination), participants have to indicate their agreement with the following statement: 'I think that the official version of the events given by the authorities very often hides the truth'. For a comparison of the psychometric properties of the main scales considered here, readers may consult Swami et al. (2017).

## The contributions of social psychology to the understanding of conspiracy theories

After this brief review of how social psychology appraises social phenomena in general and conspiracy theories more specifically, we would like to reflect briefly on how the field contributes to the understanding of conspiracy theories.

The most direct, obvious contribution is that social psychology has explored many of the antecedents and consequences of beliefs in conspiracy theories, on a multiplicity of levels (for reviews, see Douglas et al. 2016; van Prooijen, Douglas 2018.) The accumulated research has painted an increasingly rich and nuanced picture of the phenomenon. Since this knowledge relies on the assumption that conspiracy theories are underpinned by a generic belief system, we wish to discuss this assumption in the remaining paragraphs and address a recurring criticism.

As has been stated, the most robust finding in the social psychology research on this topic is that people who find a specific conspiracy theory likely to be true strongly tend to find others also likely to be true, even when they are seemingly unrelated. In statistical terms, beliefs in conspiracy theories as measured in social psychology surveys are strongly and positively intercorrelated, to the point that they can be considered to reflect a single construct.

Such internal consistency, however, should not be overinterpreted. For example, philosophers such as Hagen (2017) or Basham (2017) have harshly criticised the tendency among social psychologists to identify as 'solid belief' what is actually only an assessment of plausibility. While this criticism is to some extent legitimate, it would be erroneous to discard the field's contribution to the understanding of conspiracy theories on this basis.

Indeed, while social psychologists should acknowledge the substantial gap between firmly believing in a conspiracy theory and finding a conspiracy theory plausible, it is both a truism and a scientific fact that a belief is more easily espoused when it fits the pre-existing belief system of the individual (e.g. Bronner 2003). On the other hand, individuals may be more willing to scrutinise information when it is incongruent with their pre-existing belief system (Gilead et al. 2018; Lord et al. 1979). Hence, while those who score high on conspiracy mentality scales may not necessarily be hardcore conspiracy theorists and should not be considered as such, they will be more easily convinced by arguments in favour of a conspiracy theory.

Another contribution of social psychology to the understanding of conspiracy theories pertains to its methodological standards. Conspiracy theories are a complex social phenomenon with blurry boundaries. Philosophers have argued that there is no clear criterion that allows us to distinguish warranted accusations of conspiracy from unwarranted conspiracy theories (e.g. Keeley 1999). Studying conspiracy theories is even harder, considering that, in practice, labelling a belief a 'conspiracy theory' amounts to disqualifying the possibility that it may be valid at all (e.g. Husting, Orr 2007). On the other hand, conspiracy theories are intimately associated with political extremism and populist discourses (e.g. Silva et al. 2017). Researchers on this topic therefore face an intractable conundrum: On the one hand, their research may be weaponised to delegitimise political alternatives; on the other hand, they examine a social phenomenon that, in many instances, represents an actual danger for contemporary democracies. Given such ideological stakes, keeping a rigorous scientific line of reasoning is a challenge.

While the social psychological literature is far from being exempt of ideological biases (e.g. Duarte et al. 2015), the methodological standards in social psychology, and especially their latest developments following the replication crisis of the early 2010s (i.e. the realisation that, in social psychology, as in other sciences, seemingly established findings were not replicable) offer tools to reduce the extent to which conclusions may be contaminated by the researcher's ideological background. The aforementioned methodology may appear rigid or even artificial for outsiders. However, it provides a substantial advantage: If rigorously applied, it can minimise the researchers' propensity to privilege data that validate their initial intuition (often rooted in ideological considerations), over information that may contradict it. In cognitive psychology, such propensity is referred to as 'confirmation bias' (Wason 1960; Nickerson 1998).

Since the replication crisis, many authors have emphasised the necessity to address methodological flaws in social psychological research (e.g. Świątkowski, Dompnier 2017). Rigor and transparency are increasingly valued over innovative results. The best illustration of this evolution may be the development of what is called 'registered research reports': In many journals, articles can be now submitted for publication before data collection. If the research question is considered worthy of publication, and the method considered robust enough by the editor and reviewers, those articles may be accepted for publication in principle, pending respect of the methodology. It would be naive to believe that this raised concern for methodological rigor will ultimately lead to the elimination of confirmation bias in social psychology, but these recent developments indubitably constitute a leap in the discipline's scientific maturity.

## Limitations

In its current state of development, social psychological research on conspiracy theories has several limitations. A first limitation relates to sampling. There has been a move in psychology towards relying on larger sample sizes as they are necessary for providing statistically conclusive findings. Accessing such samples often means relying on convenience samples (e.g. college students) or community samples, who are not particularly versed in conspiracy theories. This also means that endorsement of such theories is often relatively low. For example, in the study by Swami et al. (2010), the mean score of a community sample of 817 British respondents' score on the BCTI (Belief in Conspiracy Theories Inventory) was 3.31 (whereas the scale range is from 1 to 9). Generally, such absolute levels of disagreement with conspiracy accounts do not trouble researchers too much. Indeed, social psychologists are interested in the processes associated with believing in conspiracy theories rather than in people's absolute level of endorsement. Whether average belief in a sample is low or high does not really matter to the extent that the effects the researcher is interested in (i.e. correlations with other variables or differences between experimental conditions) can be ascertained.

Yet, such examples suggest that research on conspiracy theories often focuses more on rejection of such theories than on actual endorsement or adhesion to them. Factors driving extreme endorsement of conspiracy theories may not be simply the polar opposite of those that drive forceful rejection of them. For example, the desire to appear rational may drive both endorsement of conspiracy theories and rejection of conspiracy theories. If the range is restricted to people who reject conspiracy theories, this should translate into a negative relationship between the desire to appear rational and endorsement of conspiracy theories. However, having access to the full sample (which is fictitious here) would reveal that the trend reverses when considering people who are moderate-to-strong believers: They, also, want to appear rational. Researchers should be careful not to draw conclusions about the endorsement of conspiracy theories that may only apply to their rejection. For this reason, reliance on highly diverse samples, but also on samples composed of actual conspiracy believers, is much desired in future research.

In addition, as with much psychological research (Henrich et al. 2010), most of the samples studied are Western, with a predominance of American, British, German and Dutch samples due to the nationality of the researchers, although there is also research conducted in Eastern Europe (e.g. Orosz et al. 2016; Marchlewska et al. 2018). Beyond this geographical horizon, there is a lack of published studies in English. For example, we could find only one study on conspiracy theories in Africa (Nattrass 2013). This means that cross-cultural comparisons are lacking (for an exception including Middle Eastern samples, see Bruder et al. 2013). Most importantly, given that conspiracy theories are intimately associated with a specific political context, the fact that the literature mostly showcases work conducted in Western liberal democracies is a significant limitation.

Other limitations derive from the fact that research on conspiracy theories relies almost exclusively on rating scales. Such scales have many advantages: Precision in assessing the construct of interest through careful wording, ease of administration to large samples, standardisation across respondents and straightforward quantification. However, they suffer from several drawbacks. For example, rather than measuring individuals' actual endorsement of conspiracy theories, such scales may measure how plausible individuals find conspiracy theories. Furthermore, we know very little about the relationship between conspiracy endorsement and actual behaviour. For example, while endorsement of anti-vaccine conspiracies is negatively associated with self-reported vaccination intentions (Jolley, Douglas 2014a), this may reflect a consistency bias (i.e. people wanting to make their responses seem consistent, regardless of their actual behaviour). While more costly, objective indicators of actual behaviour would be welcome and a more reliable indicator of the real-life consequences of belief in conspiracy theories.

Furthermore, due to the almost exclusive use of this survey format, we actually know very little about the formation of conspiracy theories. Most of the available research relies on people's endorsement of either existing conspiracy theories or of theories that were crafted by the researchers. We know comparatively little about how people elaborate and construct such theories, be it intra-individually or through interactions with other group members. In this regard, greater reliance on qualitative material would be welcome.

An additional limitation of such research is that it relies greatly on intra-individual measures. Obviously, conspiracy theories are a collective phenomenon, depending on intra- and intergroup interactions. Yet, very little research focuses on such interactions.

## Conclusion

After a decade of research, social psychologists have highlighted the fact that conspiracy theories, despite often being presented as purely rational by their advocates, are related to a multiplicity of factors that impinge their endorsement. Hence, they appear to be only partly, if at all, rational. It is, however, important to note that in this regard, they are not different from many other types of beliefs. Conspiracy theories appear to be a particularly spectacular illustration of the fact that, most of the time, our beliefs about the world are more a reflection of a multi-biased information-seeking process than the logical conclusion of an objective investigation of reality.

## References

Abalakina-Paap, M., Stephan, W.G., Craig, T. and Gregory, W.L. (1999) 'Beliefs in conspiracies', *Political Psychology*, 20(3): 637–47.

Basham, L. (2017) 'Pathologizing open societies: a reply to the Le Monde social scientists, Lee Basham', *Social Epistemology Review and Reply Collective*, 6(2). Available at: http://wp.me/p1Bfg0-3sG. [Accessed 13 August 2019.]

Bronner, G. (2003) *L'empire des croyances*. Paris: PUF. Available at: http://journals.openedition.org/assr/2407. [Accessed 13 August 2019.]

Brotherton, R. and French, C.C. (2014) 'Belief in conspiracy theories and susceptibility to the conjunction fallacy', *Applied Cognitive Psychology*, 28(2): 238–48.

Brotherton, R., French, C.C. and Pickering, A.D. (2013) 'Measuring belief in conspiracy theories: the generic conspiracist beliefs scale', *Frontiers in Psychology*, 4: 279.

Bruder, M., Haffke, P., Neave, N., Nouripanah, N. and Imhoff, R. (2013) 'Measuring individual differences in generic beliefs in conspiracy theories across cultures: conspiracy mentality questionnaire', *Frontiers in Psychology*, 4: 225.

Cohen, J. (1988) *Statistical power analysis for the behavioural sciences*, Hillsdale, NJ: Erlbaum.

Crocker, J., Luhtanen, R., Broadnax, S. and Blaine, B.E. (1999) 'Belief in U.S. government conspiracies against Blacks among Black and White college students: powerlessness or system blame?' *Personality and Social Psychology Bulletin*, 25(8): 941–53.

Davis, J., Wetherell, G. and Henry, P.J. (2018) 'Social devaluation of African Americans and race-related conspiracy theories', *European Journal of Social Psychology*, 48(7): 999–1010.

Dieguez, S., Wagner-Egger, P. and Gauvrit, N. (2015) 'Nothing happens by accident, or does it? A low prior for randomness does not explain belief in conspiracy theories', *Psychological Science*, 26(11): 1762–70.

Douglas, K.M. and Sutton, R.M. (2008) 'The hidden impact of conspiracy theories: perceived and actual influence of theories surrounding the death of Princess Diana', *The Journal of Social Psychology*, 148(2): 210–21.

Douglas, K.M., Sutton, R.M., Callan, M.J., Dawtry, R.J. and Harvey, A.J. (2016) 'Someone is pulling the strings: hypersensitive agency detection and belief in conspiracy theories', *Thinking & Reasoning*, 22(1): 57–77.

Drinkwater, K., Dagnall, N. and Parker, A. (2012) 'Reality testing, conspiracy theories, and paranormal beliefs', *Journal of Parapsychology*, 76(1): 57–77.

Duarte, J.L., Crawford, J.T., Stern, C., Haidt, J., Jussim, L. and Tetlock, P.E. (2015) 'Political diversity will improve social psychological science', *Behavioral and Brain Sciences*, 38: e130.

Gilead, M., Sela, M. and Maril, A. (2018) 'That's my truth: evidence for involuntary opinion confirmation', *Social Psychological and Personality Science*, 10(3).

Goertzel, T. (1994) 'Belief in conspiracy theories', *Political Psychology*, 15(4): 731–42.

Golec de Zavala, A. and Federico, C.M. (2018) 'Collective narcissism and the growth of conspiracy thinking over the course of the 2016 United States presidential election: a longitudinal analysis', *European Journal of Social Psychology*, 48(7).

Goreis, A. and Voracek, M. (2019) 'A systematic review and meta-analysis of psychological research on conspiracy beliefs: field characteristics, measurement instruments, and associations with personality traits', *Frontiers in Psychology*, 10: 205.

Graumann, C.F. and Moscovici, S. (1987) *Changing conceptions of conspiracy*, New York: Springer.

Hagen, K. (2017) 'Conspiracy theorists and monological belief systems', *Argumenta*, 2: 1–24.

Henrich, J., Heine, S.J. and Norenzayan, A. (2010) 'Most people are not WEIRD', *Nature*, 466(29).

Husting, G. and Orr, M. (2007) 'Dangerous machinery: "conspiracy theorist" as a transpersonal strategy of exclusion', *Symbolic Interaction*, 30(2): 127–50.

Imhoff, R. and Lamberty, P. (2018) 'How paranoid are conspiracy believers? Toward a more fine-grained understanding of the connect and disconnect between paranoia and belief in conspiracy theories', *European Journal of Social Psychology*, 28(1).

Jolley, D. and Douglas, K.M. (2014a) 'The effects of anti-vaccine conspiracy theories on vaccination intentions', *PloS One*, 9(2): e89177.

Jolley, D. and Douglas, K.M. (2014b) 'The social consequences of conspiracism: exposure to conspiracy theories decreases intentions to engage in politics and to reduce one's carbon footprint', *British Journal of Psychology*, 105(1): 35–56.

Keeley, B.L. (1999) 'Of conspiracy theories', *Journal of Philosophy*, 96(3): 109–26.

Lantian, A., Muller, D., Nurra, C. and Douglas, K.M. (2016) 'Measuring belief in conspiracy theories: validation of a French and English single-item scale', *International Review of Social Psychology*, 29(1).

Lantian, A., Muller, D., Nurra, C. and Douglas, K.M. (2017) '"I know things they don't know!": the role of need for uniqueness in belief in conspiracy theories', *Social Psychology*, 48(3), 160–73.

Lantian, A., Muller, D., Nurra, C., Klein, O., Berjot, S. and Pantazi, M. (2018) 'Stigmatized beliefs: conspiracy theories, anticipated negative evaluation of the self, and fear of social exclusion', *European Journal of Social Psychology*, 48(7): 939–54.

Liddell, T.M. and Kruschke, J.K. (2018) 'Analyzing ordinal data with metric models: what could possibly go wrong?', *Journal of Experimental Social Psychology*, 79: 328–48.

Lord, C.G., Ross, L. and Lepper, M.R. (1979) 'Biased assimilation and attitude polarization: the effects of prior theories on subsequently considered evidence', *Journal of Personality and Social Psychology*, 37(11): 2098–109.

Marchlewska, M., Cichocka, A. and Kossowska, M. (2018) 'Addicted to answers: need for cognitive closure and the endorsement of conspiracy beliefs', *European Journal of Social Psychology*, 48(2): 109–17.

McCauley, C. and Jacques, S. (1979) 'The popularity of conspiracy theories of presidential assassination: a Bayesian analysis', *Journal of Personality and Social Psychology*, 37(5): 637–44.

Moscovici, S. (1987) 'The conspiracy mentality', in C.F. Graumann and S. Moscovici (eds.) *Changing conceptions of conspiracy*, New York, NY: Springer, pp. 151–69.

Nattrass, N. (2013) 'Understanding the origins and prevalence of AIDS conspiracy beliefs in the United States and South Africa', *Sociology of Health & Illness*, 35(1): 113–29.

Nickerson, R.S. (1998) 'Confirmation bias: a ubiquitous phenomenon in many guises', *Review of general psychology*, 2(2): 175–200.

Orosz, G., Krekó, P., Paskuj, B., Tóth-Király, I., Böthe, B. and Roland-Lévy, C. (2016) 'Changing conspiracy beliefs through rationality and ridiculing', *Frontiers in Psychology*, 7: 1525.

Perezgonzalez, J.D. (2015) 'Fisher, Neyman-Pearson or NHST? A tutorial for teaching data testing', *Frontiers in Psychology*, 6: 223.

Richard, F.D., Bond Jr., C.F. and Stokes-Zoota, J.J. (2003) 'One hundred years of social psychology quantitatively described', *Review of General Psychology*, 7(4): 331.

Silva, B.C., Vegetti, F. and Littvay, L. (2017) 'The elite is up to something: exploring the relation between populism and belief in conspiracy theories', *Swiss Political Science Review*, 23(4): 423–43.

Sutton, R.M. and Douglas, K.M. (2014) 'Examining the monological nature of conspiracy theories', in J.W. van Prooijen and P.A.M. van Lange (eds.) *Power, politics, and paranoia: why people are suspicious of their leaders*, Cambridge: Cambridge University Press, pp. 254–73.

Swami, V., Barron, D., Weis, L., Voracek, M., Stieger, S. and Furnham, A. (2017) 'An examination of the factorial and convergent validity of four measures of conspiracist ideation, with recommendations for researchers', *PloS One*, 12(2): e0172617.

Swami, V., Chamorro-Premuzic, T. and Furnham, A. (2010) 'Unanswered questions: a preliminary investigation of personality and individual difference predictors of 9/11 conspiracist beliefs', *Applied Cognitive Psychology*, 24(6): 749–61.

Świątkowski, W. and Dompnier, B. (2017) 'Replicability crisis in social psychology: looking at the past to find new pathways for the future', *International Review of Social Psychology*, 30(1): 111–24.

Van Elk, M. (2015) 'Perceptual biases in relation to paranormal and conspiracy beliefs', *PloS One*, 10(6): e0130422.

Van Prooijen, J.-W. (2017) 'Why education predicts decreased belief in conspiracy theories', *Applied Cognitive Psychology*, 31(1): 50–8.

Van Prooijen, J.-W. (2018) *The psychology of conspiracy theories*, Oxon: Routledge.

Van Prooijen, J.-W. and Douglas, K.M. (2017) 'Conspiracy theories as part of history: the role of societal crisis situations', *Memory Studies*, 10(3): 323–33.

Van Prooijen, J.-W. and Douglas, K.M. (2018) 'Belief in conspiracy theories: basic principles of an emerging research domain', *European Journal of Social Psychology*, 48(7): 897–908.

Van Prooijen, J.-W. and Jostmann, N.B. (2013) 'Belief in conspiracy theories: the influence of uncertainty and perceived morality', *European Journal of Social Psychology*, 43(1): 109–15.

Van Prooijen, J.-W., Krouwel, A.P. and Pollet, T.V. (2015) 'Political extremism predicts belief in conspiracy theories', *Social Psychological and Personality Science*, 6(5): 570–8.

Vitriol, J.A. and Marsh, J.K. (2018) 'The illusion of explanatory depth and endorsement of conspiracy beliefs', *European Journal of Social Psychology*, 48(7): 955–69.

Wagner-Egger, P. and Bangerter, A. (2007) 'La vérite est ailleurs: corrélats de l'adhésion aux théories du complot', *Revue Internationale de Psychologie Sociale*, 20(4): 31–61.

Wason, P.C. (1960) 'On the failure to eliminate hypotheses in a conceptual task', *Quarterly Journal of Experimental Psychology*, 12(3): 129–40.

Zonis, M. and Joseph, C.M. (1994) 'Conspiracy thinking in the Middle East', *Political Psychology*, 15(3): 443–59.

# 1.10
# SOCIAL NETWORK ANALYSIS, SOCIAL BIG DATA AND CONSPIRACY THEORIES

*Estrella Gualda Caballero*

## Introduction

In recent years, the use of social media has greatly increased. More than 8.5 billion devices are connected worldwide today (Fundación Telefónica 2018), outnumbering the world's inhabitants. In 2019, the main social networks, according to their active user accounts reported by We Are Social–Hootsuite (2019), were Facebook (2.3 billion), YouTube (1.9 billion) and WhatsApp (1.5 billion). This large concentration of users in specific platforms makes them susceptible to exposure to conspiracy theories and prone to their further dissemination on the Internet. This, in turn, has the potential to impact a society's perception of itself and of others, and how it conducts its politics. In addition, the increase in Internet users has become a structural phenomenon in societies, paving the way for the development and dissemination of different types of conspiracy theories in digital space. This high use of social network platforms, as well as the development and expansion of Web 2.0 as a collaborative website (Ackland 2013) allows social interaction and conversation between users on social networks, which in turn increases the number of users. However, it is not clear what the relationship is between the structural elements of social media and the seeming proliferation of conspiracy theories online: 'Has the internet increased the popularity of conspiracy theories or has it merely made them more visible?' (Butter, Knight 2016: 9).

The fact that many people are connected through social networking platforms (a reality that is unlikely to change any time soon) makes it necessary to understand how information dissemination and virality occur in social networks (Congosto Martínez 2016). This chapter provides a guide to research strategies in the areas of social network analysis and social big data mining. Both areas potentially will help us to study and understand the current development of conspiracy theories, especially when the Internet and social networks are used as key spaces through which data are generated.

## The use of social network analysis

Social network analysis can reveal patterns of relationships that are not obvious at first sight. This can include not only the hidden connections of actual conspiracies, but also the underlying connections of online producers and consumers and conspiracy theories. Social network analysis has thus proven useful, for example, in criminal investigations by institutions such as the F.B.I. The reasons for using social network analysis to understand criminal conspiracies (Davis 1981; Sparrow 1991) or illegal price fixing (Baker, Faulkner 1993) are also common to the study of conspiracy theories, and basic concepts from a broad spectrum of past social network analyses remain important today. However, the volume and speed with which data are produced and disseminated, through phenomena such as virality or contagion, create certain challenges in the use of social network analyses to understand conspiracy theories.

The field of social network analysis arose from different scientific traditions and academic disciplines: American sociology, graph theory, contributions from the Manchester School of Anthropology, Moreno's sociometry (1951), etc. (Scott 1996; Lin 1999). More recently, the analysis of large volumes of data has been made possible with the development of different software packages and analytical strategies (Bastian et al. 2009). Among the classic elements of social network analysis that can contribute to improving our understanding of the dissemination of conspiracy theories via the Internet is the possibility of measuring, in a quantitative way, aspects as diverse as:

- The existing relationships between actors who participate in a social network that disseminates conspiratorial content;
- The centrality of the actors, which can provide information about the leaders of the social networks and who is responsible for the dissemination of conspiracy theories;
- The ability of each actor to 'intermediate' and connect different actors and parts of the network, making it possible to identify which actors occupy a central position in terms of their betweenness or intermediation capacity. This capacity can be mobilised to manipulate the information that flows through the network;
- The structure of the network, which allows us to understand its density or cohesion and to be aware of the strengths or weaknesses of the network as a space through which these conspiracy theories can be disseminated;
- To predict which actors are likely to produce coalitions or alliances because they are more connected to each other;
- And the communities or groups in which the actors congregate.

As Lin (1999: 45) suggested, we are witnessing a revolutionary growth in social capital represented by social networks in cyberspace, as the emergence of the Internet has changed different patterns of daily life. Two decades after Lin's comment, what was seen as a promising field of research has already become vast, since the Internet has produced and promoted changes in many spheres: Business, entertainment, information, communication and so on. New technologies, together with social practices, have also opened up new fields of research, such as social big data. These developments have great potential for studying the conspiracy theories that are formed and disseminated through social media. The various possibilities of quantitative analysis, given the diverse information obtained from the Internet, can also be connected with more qualitative aspects, linking the actors with the discourses and narratives that they produce.

When social network analysis is applied within a big data scenario, that is, when the intention is to analyse millions of items of data that circulate through social networks, it opens up interesting new possibilities, such as the study of communication networks, whose potential to generate greater visibility, dissemination or contagion is based on the ability to reach others by sharing information with other actors or users. Sharing information through networks and from one platform to another is technically very easy today because the main social networking platforms (Twitter, Facebook, Instagram, Snapchat, WhatsApp, etc.) have enabled tools for this purpose. For example, in order to understand how the dissemination of information takes place on Twitter, retweet networks provide very valuable information on the development of the communication chain, its users and the information transmitted through the retweet (R.T.). We can know which users have been the most retweeted at a specific moment, thus indicating not only the impact or scope of their message but also its popularity and visibility. In this respect, classic measures of centrality typical for this technique, such as the degree, closeness or betweenness[1] prove useful (Hanneman, Riddle 2005). These types of mathematical indicators, together with the study of communities and links in the network, make it possible, for example, to clearly establish an image of the structure of a conspiracist network, through which conspiracy theories are disseminated, and to predict the communication patterns that structure it.

Likewise, a qualitative analysis based on a research logic that emphasises mixed methods and that focuses on the discourse in the most popular posts, messages and retweets could help us understand which basic messages are being conveyed by specific conspiracy theories, and assess the potential for harm of these messages (e.g. fake news, hate speech, etc.). It is also feasible, with a quantitative approach, to study the emotional profile of the most widespread messages. More specifically, a sentiment analysis approach is applied to identify aspects such as the degree of hate speech circulating through social networks (Burnap, Williams 2016; Ross et al. 2016; Schmidt, Wiegand 2017). To this end, novel approaches are being developed in the area of big data with a strong transdisciplinary potential that focus on the automatic detection and analysis of hate speech based on automatic and/or supervised machine learning (M.L.) strategies and natural language processing (N.L.P.) (Shu et al. 2017), which are useful in the study of social polarisation or extremism.

## Networks and dissemination through humans, bots and cyborgs

The dissemination of conspiracy theories online usually occurs as a result of certain groups manipulating others into endorsing a specific agenda or spreading propaganda, disinformation or fake news (Gualda, Rúas 2019). In recent years, some reasonably sophisticated technical strategies have employed social bots for these propaganda purposes. Bots enhance the contamination and manipulation of social networks through disinformation or fake news. In this scenario, it is key to understanding how information is propagated as networks evolve. Aggressive groups of bots and cyborgs that amplify their impact through the use of automated software have the potential to spread like wildfire on social media, influencing conversations and debates or online political processes on an unprecedented scale (see e.g. Alexander 2015; Mønsted et al. 2017; Allem, Ferrara 2018). Important recent cases include the 2016 E.U. referendum in the U.K., the 2017 referendum in Catalonia (Stella et al. 2018), the 2016 U.S. presidential election (Ferrara 2016) and the 2017 elections in France (Ferrara 2017).

The dissemination of conspiracy theories through social bots requires a previous deployment of strategies and actions that often include a conspiratorial component. Some specialised computer work is needed to launch any bot, and the types of tactics used are similar across social network platforms. In the report 'Far Right Networks of Deception', Avaaz (2019) revealed similar patterns that disinformation networks have used in several countries, many of which violate social media policies. Some of the disinformation tactics that Avaaz reports are:

- The use of false and duplicate accounts to amplify content, manage groups, hide real identities and publish extreme content;
- The abnormal coordination of websites and groups that publish fake content and disinformation, from places with no editorial reputation, through cyber-bullying tactics (clickbait);

- The so-called recycling of followers, when a website changes its name in order to deceive followers and provide harmful content that it did not publish before;
- The creation of clickbait websites, addressing innocuous topics; once the audience is built, other types of content, not obviously political, are promoted in a more extreme and sometimes coordinated manner. Avaaz (2019), for example, identified a group of Facebook pages spreading fake and hateful content that had almost three times more followers (5.9 million) than the pages of the main European extreme right and anti-E.U. parties combined, making it clear that the latter groups have weaponised social media on a large-scale.

Alexander (2015) studied the use of Russian bots in the service of the Kremlin and the way in which they were part of a broad strategy to generate disinformation and interfere in democratic processes. Although the Russian propaganda machine seems to have been key in some disinformation flows, it is not unique. To spread propaganda or disinformation, bots in social media often publish half-truths as if they were real news; some messages (tweets) are amplified regularly and automatically; and some websites that became the 'digital armies of the Kremlin' (Alexander 2015) fabricate stories and spread fake, exaggerated or biased news. This type of action can produce virality and exacerbate a crisis, creating social divisions. On social media platforms, there are both human users and bots or automated programs – activated by the action of people, groups or organisations – that are able to alter the diffusion of messages. In this way, bots and fraudulent accounts (that are, of course, ultimately controlled by human beings) exert political influence by spreading disinformation and supporting violent extremist groups.

The information disseminated via social media networks can be inaccurate and misleading, containing false statements even at the level of small nuances. As argued by the Atlantic Council's Digital Forensic Research Lab (2017: paragraph 19) regarding the campaign for Catalan independence: When the 'atmosphere [is] as heated as Catalonia's, nuance matters'. This assertion is equally true in other contexts. Although automatic bots are designed to look like real Twitter users, for example, there are technical means to identify them through social network analysis in conjunction with other techniques. It is possible to recognise key tactics used to achieve greater reach, as well as to detect manipulative actions, by bots or users hidden behind pseudonyms, when other signals are present, such as:

- Massively programmed and non-spontaneous harmful content (it is often possible to identify from which applications the messages have issued);
- Users without history on that platform (since they have only been created for that specific propaganda action);
- The creation of multiple profiles for individual users;
- Continually repeated or very similar messages;
- Bots that simulate real users (people, groups and organisations) but without personal information in their profiles (time zones, favourites, biographies etc.), that genuine users normally fill in when they open a social media account;
- And the sending of messages at regular times or with recognisable patterns in the ordering of the words in the posts.

## Virtual communities and conspiracy theories

Another classic aspect of social network analysis is the use of different measures of social distance to study how actors are grouped in particular structures and substructures. One of the standard ways to measure distance in networks is Euclidean distance, which is the shortest distance from one actor or node to another in a network (the shortest or geodesic path). The closer the connection between social media users, the faster the virality or contagion over the Internet is.

Groups can be defined differently. They are defined as cliques when, in a substructure or subgroup, all the members are connected by ties or direct links. More flexible ways of defining groups, not needing direct links, are n-cliques, n-clans, k-plexes, etc. (Hanneman, Riddle 2005: passim; Wasserman, Faust 2013). In an n-clique, an actor is a member of a clique if he or she is connected to all the members of the group at a distance greater than one (for example, at a distance equal to two when someone is a friend of a friend). The measurement of n-clan incorporates the idea that each subgroup is formed by actors who are connected through other members of the same clique or subgroup. In a k-plex, groups are formed by direct links with all but k members of the group, which allows us to study superimposed social circles. This means that an actor 'is a member of a clique of size n if it has direct ties to n-k members of that clique' (Hanneman, Riddle 2005). Compared to n-clique, k-plex analysis reveals overlaps and co-presence in groups (social circles), even when it is not necessary to have direct links with all the members of the group. One interesting feature of k-plex analysis is the possibility of discovering actors that play a 'bridging role among multiple slightly different social circles' (Hanneman, Riddle 2005; Wasserman, Faust 2013). Thus, the actors in a network, depending on the chosen subgroup definition, can be connected through direct or indirect ties. Although a communication network and transmission of messages would achieve greater efficiency by reducing the distance between the actors, the different forms of grouping in a network allow conspiratorial information to flow through indirect ties. However, depending on the type of grouping, the information can reach other members of the network in a faster or slower way.

In social networks on the Internet, the study of social distance is now of great interest and virtual communities are being studied, which is a basis for researching the conspiracy theories that can circulate in each community. The development of software to analyse the role of these communities in the development of conspiracy theories is proving productive. Some conspiracy theories disseminated on the Internet, especially those linked to the dissemination of hate, are expressed through polarised virtual communities. A substantial part of the polarisation that is found today on social media networks has to do with 'contaminating' political campaigns with fake news and hate speeches targeting specific people or groups (Muslims, Jews, women, etc.). People, groups or organisations who intend to produce polarisation often do so by deploying highly emotional content (Nicolaisen 2013; Barthel et al. 2016; Del Vicario et al. 2018).

Social network analysis of virtual communities (based on the relationships between users of social networks) allows the precise detection of how these extreme poles are formed and who creates them. The identification of actors assigned to communities that spread hatred or that generate behaviours associated with the dissemination of conspiratorial content (for example, in far-right populist discourse), also makes it possible to study the content disseminated in each community, deepening our understanding of extremism in all its forms.

Polarisation can be found between discourses (if we think about narratives), but also through the study of semantic networks (which allow us to identify, for example, the connections between the words that make up a conspiracy discourse). Polarisation can also be found among users or actors in a network. For instance, actors could be grouped into polarised communities depending on differences in sharing (or not) some type of relationship, retweeting (or not) the posts of the same leader or spreading (or not) the same webpages (Ackland 2013). It is common to find polarised communication networks on social media expressing situations of extremism, separation, rupture, etc. This means that the information is produced in a kind of closed system or echo chamber. Polarisation denotes the existence of groups or communities where interaction between similar users occurs, for example in the case of people who share the same points of view (Esteve del Valle, Borge 2017), meaning that the content that is most shared is that which reinforces the ideologies and information inside those communities. A detailed analysis of the dynamic of communities allows us to identify several behaviours on social media.

Knowledge of how social networks work in relation to homophily and heterophily is useful when considering the spread of conspiracy theories, because they are frequently supported by groups or communities that share ideas connected to the conspiracy theory. In social network analysis, homophily means that similar nodes (actors, users, etc.) are more likely to connect to each other than to dissimilar ones. Lazarsfeld and Merton (1954: 23) defined homophily as the 'tendency for friendships to form between those who are alike in some designated respect'. Heterophily addresses the existence of relationships based on dissimilarity. Polarisation in social networks connects with the idea of homophily because it refers to interactions between similar people – or those who share something, such as a retweet – in each community, who belong to the same party, share the same ideology, agree with the same idea, etc. The ideological effect of the echo chamber is based on both homophily (similarity) and heterophily (dissimilarity), if we think of the two extremes of a social structure (the complete community or a complete network). In this way, if ideological discourses or orientations are repeated inside each echo chamber (or subcommunity), the discourses – being ideologically similar – resonate, and the discourses are reproduced and reinforced within each online community, resulting in a non-dialogue between communities. This can lead to extremism, depending on the topics (see, for example, Mutz, Martin 2001; Boutyline, Willer 2017). Once a community built upon a shared ideology is detected, it is technically easy to inject harmful or fake content into it through social bots or other strategies, in order to promote division within society at large. This currently occurs in several spheres of social media through the spread of disinformation, fake news, videos or pictures with false information, and so on. Social network analysis applied to the identification of different communities is, therefore, useful for knowing which actors or users of a network are more likely to belong to one community or another according to the conversations and relationships that characterise them.

## Social big data and conspiracy theories

Web 2.0 distinguishes itself from its predecessor because it is collaborative. This means that it implements principles of user collaboration, dialogue and participation. A peculiarity of the development of the collaborative web, enhanced by social networks and I.C.T.s (Information and Communication Technologies), is that individuals, formerly consumers, are now also producers of information when they participate in social media. The term prosumer – which refers to the double dimension of a consumer and producer – captures this idea. A current feature of social reality is that many people around the world upload information to the Internet, contributing to the production of what is known as social big data, a term that includes the confluence of three elements: Social media, data analysis and big data (Bello-Orgaz et al. 2016).

Social media are social networking platforms such as Twitter, YouTube, Facebook, etc. Data analysis refers to the procedures associated with the analysis of these data that go beyond classical statistics and allow us to handle large amounts of data; usually these are the approaches of business intelligence, with repercussions for and applications of interest to the private sector in terms of competitiveness (Piccialli, Jung 2017; Jung 2017; Bartosik-Purgat, Ratajczak-Mrożek 2018). Programming languages such as Python or software such as R, among many others, contribute to this task. The specific area of big data refers to the most technical and infrastructural part of the necessary technologies for operations such as downloading, storing or handling these data. In order to produce a systematic study of large volumes of conspiracist information that is generated and disseminated through the Internet, it is necessary to have both the infrastructure and the strategies of data analysis for the processing and analysis of specific aspects of the data. One of the issues that creates more complexity in the study of conspiracy theories in a big data context is precisely the generation of large amounts of data.

Big data are thus conceptualised in terms of their large volume, their variety and the great speed with which they are produced, reaching previously unknown dimensions that hinder the different phases of research. It has been common to describe and summarise what big data are in terms of the so-called Vs: Volume, velocity, variety, veracity, variability, visualisation and value, described as 3-, 4-, 5- or 6Vs, by different authors (Beyer, Laney 2012; Hashema et al. 2015; Olshannikova et al. 2017). Other authors have incorporated other Vs into their descriptions of the characteristic features of big data. When the idea of 'social' is incorporated into 'big data', the focus is mainly on the data that occurs in social media, but the basic features are maintained. Among the features that characterise the social big data of conspiracy theories circulating online today are structural heterogeneity, the dynamism with which the data arise and change (for example, through streaming content), or their generation from different sources, as well as the importance of unstructured data (such as video).

There are many technical challenges that experts are working to address, drawing upon knowledge from diverse areas in order to improve the analysis of social networks. General features of social big data (such as the large volume, the speed of data generation or the fact that much data is unstructured and hence more complex to analyse) can be found in social networks promoting conspiracy theories. They can influence electoral processes and destabilise democracies, whether through influencing the results of referenda or, for example, disseminating anti-vaccination theories.

Other features, such as the injection of emotional components into the data circulating on the Internet in order to achieve greater virality and reach, are being addressed with specific techniques of sentiment analysis and machine learning strategies. It is not for nothing that this historical moment has been described by some authors as the 'post-truth era' (Keyes 2004), alluding to the incorporation of the emotional lies that are introduced in the processes of modelling public opinion, especially when the aim is to go viral in a disintermediated context, in which people use social media to become informed. Disintermediation involves the now widespread social practice of being informed without any filter, that is to say through direct contact with information circulated via mass or social media. With no intermediary – i.e. an authoritative source to validate the content – between consumer and producer of information, the risk of successfully disseminating fake news increases. In this context, emotions or radical content are used as powerful propaganda weapons.

The use of social big data for social research enables the analysis of documents published on the Internet on an unprecedented scale. Although the paradigm of big data seems to have been incorporated first into the 'hard sciences' and only subsequently into other fields (Burgess, Bruns 2012), with a strong impulse coming from business and marketing, the study of conspiracy theories can also benefit from advances in the area of social big data. One of the potential advantages of using the content generated and disseminated through the Internet for research is its relevance for the study of various social and communication processes that accompany the dissemination of conspiracy theories. The content highlights the importance of big data in relation to the fact that, for the first time in history, millions of people can be tracked whenever they express ideas, opinions or feelings. This tracking is enabled by access to their messages, videos or other images that they share, as well as through their interactions or conversations on social networks.

## Case study: Retweet networks in the 'Help Catalonia' campaign[2]

This case study describes a small sample taken from Twitter to illustrate the potential of social network analysis and social big data for understanding the spread of conspiracy theories through twenty-first-century social media. Communication networks can be observed through several channels, and retweet networks are an especially interesting channel for the study of virality and the most popular message distribution chains. This case study focused on the international 'Help Catalonia' campaign that was inserted in the Catalan Procés (the movement for Catalan independence) at the end of 2017. The campaign was supported by Carles Puigdemont, a former president of Catalonia; he was affiliated with the Catalan European Democratic Party (P.De.C.A.T.), one of the advocates of Catalan independence. This campaign had a strong propaganda element, exemplified by the release of the 'Help Cataluña' video. The term propaganda is understood here as the actions of spreading ideas, information, thoughts, opinions, etc. following an organised plan, with the goal of influencing people's opinions and behaviours. The campaign illustrates how the pro-independence organisation, Òmnium Cultural, contributed to the dissemination of a false news story in the international arena. It claimed that Catalonia, on 1 October 2017, was in a situation of political repression similar to that of Ukraine in 2014 (which resulted in an armed conflict between pro-independence supporters and the Ukrainian government). For different historic, socio-political, cultural and economic reasons, the two pro-independence movements are hardly comparable.

The Catalan Procés was kickstarted by the massive demonstration that took place in Barcelona on 11 September 2012, with the motto 'Catalunya, nou stat d'Europe' [Catalonia, New State of Europe] (Real Instituto Elcano 2017). The process involved a series of events that sought the independence of Catalonia from Spain. On 9 November 2014, the then premier of Catalonia, Arthur Mas, called a non-binding referendum on the political future of Catalonia, a precedent to the referendum of 1 October 2017, the self-determination referendum convened by the Government of Catalonia chaired by Carles Puigdemont. This referendum was suspended by the Constitutional Court on 7 September 2017 and deemed illegal for not complying with the requirements established in the Statute of Autonomy of Catalonia, as well as in the Spanish Constitution and legislation. Support for the referendum was accompanied by mobilisation in the streets and acts of violence carried out by both the security forces (who were ordered to stop the referendum) and citizens. On 10 October, the Catalan Parliament unilaterally proclaimed the independence of Catalonia, and suspended it a few seconds later. The next day the Spanish government began the procedure to activate Article 155 of the Spanish Constitution to suspend Catalan autonomy.

The data used here comes from a dataset of approximately 20 million tweets regarding the Catalan Procés from 1 October to 31 December 2017, extracted with the help of the *t-hoarder* tool (Congosto *et al.* 2017). From this dataset, we filtered 281,501 tweets about this campaign in three languages (Help Catalunya, Help Cataluña and Help Catalonia in Catalan, Spanish and English, respectively). From these tweets, we mapped out a network of retweets, taking into account the actors that posted the messages on Twitter with any of these tags or keywords: #helpCatalunya, #helpcatalonia #helpcatalonia; 'Help Catalunya', 'Help Cataluña', 'Help Catalonia'. The conversation about 'Help Catalonia' trended worldwide on Twitter. It reached tenth place on the world ranking on 17 October, keeping that position for almost ten hours and capturing international attention for much of the day (Trendinalia Worldwide 2017). In Spain, 'Help Catalonia' reached first position on the ranking on that day and trended for 18 hours, in a similar fashion in all the main Spanish cities. Most of the tweets with this content were published between 17 and 19 October 2017 (especially 17 October). This campaign took place a few days after the referendum, to promote the independence of Catalonia.

The international propaganda campaign launched on 17 October used the slogan 'Help Catalonia. Save Europe' in a video made by Òmnium Cultural, a representative entity of the Catalan independence movement, which generated great controversy and polarisation on social networks. With this campaign, the independence movement wanted to draw the attention of the international community. The video was widely disseminated, transmitting the idea that the Spanish state was repressive, while Catalans were peaceful. The video refers to European 'values under attack' in Catalonia, among other things.

The day the video was released, Jordi Sànchez and Jordi Cuixart, the presidents of the Catalan National Assembly (A.N.C.) and of Òmnium Cultural (O.C.), known as 'the Jordis', were accused of sedition as representatives of Catalan independence organisations, and imprisoned. This was accompanied by extensive participation on Twitter through diverse expressions of solidarity. On 17 October (and later), hashtags such as #LibertatJordis, #LlibertadJordis, #LlibertatPresosPolítics, #losjordis, #SanchezYCuixart, etc., spread on social networks. It was very common to find combinations of co-hashtags published in the same tweet that linked the campaign with the Jordis' incarceration:

#LaForcaDeLaGent #LlibertatJordis #helpcatalunya
#LlibertatJordis #SaveEurope #helpcatalonia

In the dataset of tweets we analysed, one of the patterns that stands out is that the label #helpcatalunya appears in conglomerates of co-hashtags that were strategically launched nationally and internationally by pro-independence Catalan groups committed to generating a narrative of repression by the Spanish state (especially in connection with #llibertatjordis or #saveeurope). The following are some of the most popular tweets, written in several languages:

RT @CataloniaHelp2: What happens in #Catalonia is not an internal, but a European affair. Share this video to #helpcatalunya https://t.co/... (1199 R.T.s)

RT @InigovanEyck: Increíble la repulsa desde el ayuntamiento de Bilbao al 155 de Rajoy #LaForcaDeLaGent #LlibertatJordis #helpcatalunya #Gol... (15,772 R.T.s)

RT @poloniatv3: Aquí podeu veure la nostra versió del vídeo #helpcatalunya d' @omnium #ForgetCatalonia #PolòniaTV3 #SaveEurope https://t.co... (1289 R.T.s)

RT @CataloniaHelp2: A masked Spanish unionist attack Catalan people in a bar tonight in #Barcelona Please #helpcatalunya https://t.co/X41ys... (2949 R.T.s)

RT @CasoAislado_Es: Así es el acoso de los independentistas a los ciudadanos catalanes que se sienten españoles #helpcatalunya https://t.co...(2314 R.T.s)

RT @324cat: El vídeo #helpcatalunya d'@omnium supera el milió de visites en 24 hores #SànchezCuixartTV3 https://t.co/ExyxCarGRR https://t.c... (2053 R.T.s)

The strong emotional component of the campaign is linked to the polarisation of online communities, which can be clearly identified from the retweet networks. Figure 1.10.1 represents the intense polarisation between the communities that supported the campaign and those that rejected it. This polarisation generates a type of conversation that has been theorised as a trait of echo chambers, in this case representing two opposed communities, where homophily is found inside each community and heterophily occurs through the communication between both communities. The communities associated with the Catalan independence movement are on the right in Figure 1.10.2), where some actors such as @gabrielrufian or mass media such as @poloniatv3 stand out by their greater InDegree or popularity by being highly retweeted, together with others identified as belonging to the independence movement, or even some anonymous ones such as @lekaconk, currently suspended from Twitter. Other actors not related to the independence movement are on the left, as is the case of @elmundo, one of the accounts with the highest InDegree in this series of data. Figure 1.10.2 shows the betweenness capacity

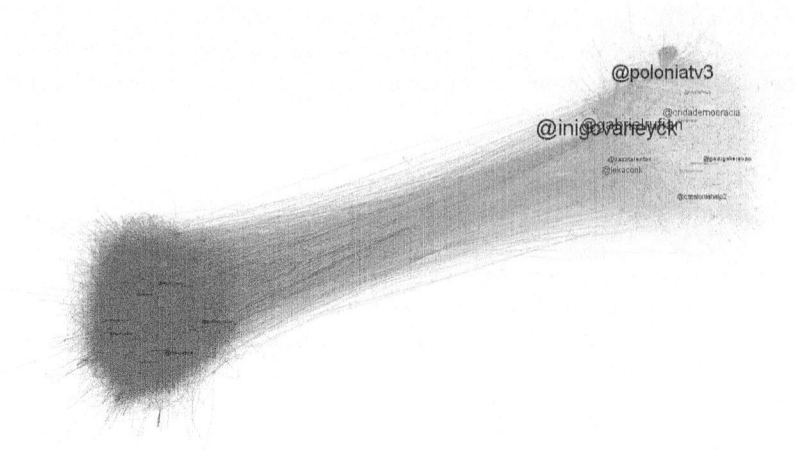

*Figure 1.10.1* Network of retweets about 'Help Catalonia' by InDegree.
Source: Author's elaboration.

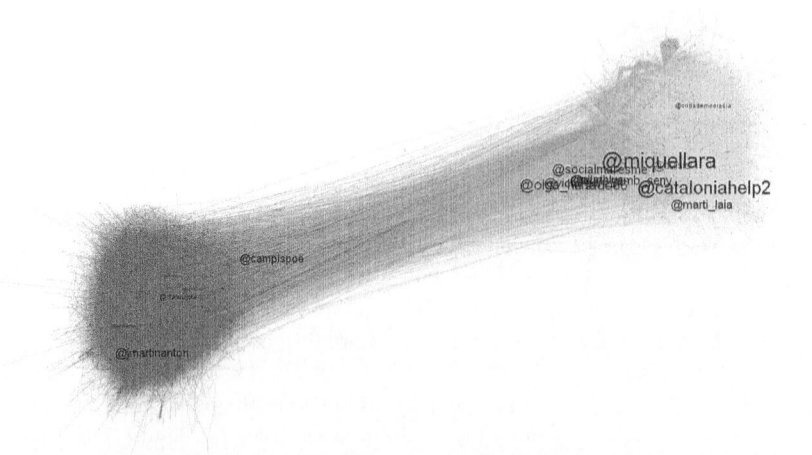

*Figure 1.10.2* Network of retweets about 'Help Catalonia' by Betweenness.
Source: Author's elaboration.

of each actor in the network (Hanneman, Riddle 2005; Wasserman, Faust 2013); that is, the ability to occupy a bridge position in a communication network through which many information flows circulate. Some of the most important relevant actors occupying this position are, on the independence side, @helpcatalonia2 (an account that has already been suspended and that played an important role in the dissemination of the campaign) and @cridademocracia.

The types of polarised reactions generated by this campaign, as well as its claim to internationalisation, are clearly understood when we connect Figures 1.10.1 and 1.10.2 with some popular tweets representative of the campaign. This provides an example of the fragmentation that underpins the polarisation between the communities of actors and that is reflected in the narratives.

## Conclusion

This chapter has developed the idea that conspiracy theories, which were earlier disseminated orally or in print, have in recent years become widespread in the collaborative space of the Internet. This has substantially altered their strategies and means of diffusion. However, although conspiracy theories can now achieve a greater reach through online social networks, some of their basic messages have remained unaltered. Social network analysis and social big data can shed light on one of the central questions in the study of conspiracy theories: Who is behind the creation and dissemination of a particular conspiracy theory? Classic social network analysis, enriched by newer techniques and tools, can contribute to revealing hidden patterns in these communication networks. It achieves this by revealing important aspects of the online operation of particular conspiracy theories or the groups that promote them, or by revealing which actors or communities are behind the spread of those theories. In doing so, it makes it possible to report and close users accounts, for example. In addition, the analytic potential of social network analysis has increased due to the technical advances in big data fields or as a result of improvements in storage and processing capacities. This knowledge can contribute to improving the ability to anticipate behaviour, which is useful both for security reasons and for promoting greater transparency or defending privacy in social networks.

In the face of the current risks of disinformation, fake news and propaganda disseminated through social media (Marwick, Lewis 2017; Shu et al. 2017; High-Level Expert Group on Fake news and Disinformation 2018), a deeper knowledge of the mechanisms that drive the dissemination and virality of conspiracy theories in social networks can also help protect democracies from those destabilising effects. This knowledge could also help us to ensure the reliability of disintermediated content, in a context in which ever more individuals access information on the Internet directly, without intermediaries or other types of filters. The use of these mixed analytical methods allows researchers to examine the interaction that occurs between actors and narratives when conspiracy theories are disseminated on the Internet. However, further research on how conspiracy theories are disseminated on the Internet is vital, given that online narratives are now being weaponised to exacerbate political and social divisions (Allenby 2017).

## Notes

1 Degree: Number of direct relationships with other actors in a symmetric network. InDegree: Direct links that an actor receives in asymmetric networks. OutDegree: Direct links that an actor emits in asymmetric networks. Closeness: Distance of an actor from the rest of the actors in the network. Betweenness: The frequency with which each actor is in the geodesic path of each pair of actors.
2 All the data mentioned in this section are taken from our project: 'Social fragmentation and polarization on Twitter: The Catalan 'Procés' as a case study' (2019).

# References

Ackland, R. (2013) *Web social science: concepts, data and tools for social scientists in the digital age*, London: Sage.

Alexander, L. (2015) 'Social network analysis reveals full scale of Kremlin's twitter bot campaign', *Global Voices*, 2 April. Available at: https://globalvoices.org/2015/04/02/analyzing-kremlin-twitter-bots/. [Accessed 20 July 2016.]

Allem, J. and Ferrara, E. (2018) 'Could social bots pose a threat to public health?' *American Journal of Public Health*, 108(8): 1005–6.

Allenby, B.R. (2017) 'The age of weaponized narrative, or, where have you gone, Walter Cronkite?', *Issues in Science and Technology*, 33(4).

Atlantic Council's Digital Forensic Research Lab (2017) '#ElectionWatch: Russia and referendums in Catalonia? Assessing claims of Russian propaganda in Spain', *Digital Forensic Research Lab*, 28 September. Available at: https://medium.com/dfrlab/electionwatch-russia-and-referendums-in-catalonia-192743 efcd76. [Accessed 29 September 2017.]

Avaaz (2019) 'Far right networks of deception', *Avaaz Report*, 22 May. Available at: https://secure.avaaz.org/avaaz_report_network_deception_20190522.pdf. [Accessed: 22 May 2019.]

Baker, W.E. and Faulkner, R.R. (1993) 'The social organization of conspiracy: illegal networks in the heavy electrical equipment industry', *American Sociological Review*, 58(6): 837–60.

Barthel, M., Mitchell, A. and Holcomb, J. (2016) 'Many Americans believe fake news is sowing confusion', *Pew Research Center*, 15 December. Available at: www.journalism.org/ 2016/ 12/15/many-americans-believe-fake-news-is-sowing-confusion/. [Accessed 27 January 2017.]

Bartosik-Purgat, M. and Ratajczak-Mrożek, M. (2018) 'Big data analysis as a source of companies' competitive advantage: a review', *Entrepreneurial Business and Economics Review*, 6(4): 197–215.

Bastian M., Heymann S. and Jacomy, M. (2009) 'Gephi: an open source software for exploring and manipulating networks', *International AAAI Conference on Weblogs and Social Media*. Available at: www.aaai.org/ocs/index.php/ICWSM/09/ paper/view/154. [Accessed 15 January 2015.]

Bello-Orgaz, G., Jung, J.J. and Camacho, D. (2016) 'Social big data: recent achievements and new challenges', *Information Fusion*, 28: 45–59.

Beyer, M.A. and Laney, D. (2012) *The importance of 'Big Data': a definition*, Stamford: Gartner.

Boutyline, A. and Willer, R. (2017) 'The social structure of political echo chambers: variation in ideological homophily in online networks', *Political Psychology*, 38(3): 551–69.

Burgess, J. and Bruns, A. (2012) 'Twitter archives and the challenges of "Big Social Data" for media and communication research', *M/C Journal*, 15(5).

Burnap, P. and Williams, M.L. (2016) 'Us and them: identifying cyber hate on Twitter across multiple protected characteristics', *EPJ Data Science*, 5(11).

Butter, M. and Knight, P. (2016) 'Bridging the great divide: conspiracy theory research for the 21st century', *Diogenes*, 1–13.

Congosto, M. (2016) *Caracterización de usuarios y propagación de mensajes en Twitter en el entorno de temas sociales*, thesis, University Carlos III de Madrid.

Congosto, M., Basanta-Val, P. and Sánchez-Fernández, L. (2017) 'T-Hoarder: a framework to process Twitter data streams', *Journal of Network and Computer Applications*, 83(1): 28–39.

Davis, R.H. (1981) 'Social network analysis: an aid in conspiracy investigations', *FBI Law Enforcement Bulletin*, 50(12): 11–9.

Del Vicario, M., Quattrociocchi, W., Scala, A. and Zollo, F. (2018) 'Polarization and fake news: early warning of potential misinformation targets', *ACM Transactions on the Web*, 13(2): 1–18.

Esteve del Valle, M. and Borge, R. (2017) 'Leaders or brokers? Potential influencers in online parliamentary networks', *Policy & Internet*, 10(1): 61–86.

Ferrara, E. (2016) 'How twitter bots affected the US presidential campaign', *ECN*, 8 November. Available at: http://theconversation.com/how-twitter-bots-affected-the-us-presidential-campaign-68406. [Accessed 15 January 2017.]

Ferrara, E. (2017) 'Disinformation and social bot operations in the run up to the 2017 French presidential election', *First Monday*, 22(6).

Fundación Telefónica (2018) 'Sociedad Digital en España 2017', *Fundación Telefónica*, 2 May. Available at: www.fundaciontelefonica.com/arte cultura/publicaciones-listado/pagina-item-publicaciones/item-publi/625/. [Accessed 15 January 2018.]

Gualda, E. and Rúas, J. (2019) 'Conspiracy theories, credibility and trust in information', *Communication & Society*, 32(1): 179–95.

Hanneman, R.A. and Riddle, M. (2005) *Introduction to social network methods*, Riverside, C.A: University of California.
Hashema, I.A.T, Yaqooba, I., Anuara, N.B., Mokhtara, S., Gania, A. and Khanb, S.U. (2015) 'The rise of big data on cloud computing: review and open research issues', *Information Systems*, 47: 98–115.
High-Level Expert Group on Fake news and Disinformation (2018) 'A multi-dimensional approach to disinformation: report of the independent High-Level Group on fake news and online disinformation', *European Commission, Directorate-General for Communication Networks, Content and Technology*, 30 April. Available at: https://publications.europa.eu/en/publication-detail/-/publication/6ef4df8b-4cea-11e8-be1d-01aa75ed71a1/language-en. [Accessed 15 May 2018.]
Jung, J.E. (2017) 'Discovering social bursts by using link analytics on large-scale social networks'. *Mobile Networks and Applications*, 22(4): 625–33.
Keyes, R. (2004) *The post-truth era: dishonesty and deception in contemporary life*, New York: St. Martin's Press.
Lazarsfeld P.F. and Merton R.K. (1954) 'Friendship as a social process: a substantive and methodological analysis', in M. Berger, T. Abel and C.H. Page (eds.) *Freedom and control in modern society*, New York: Van Nostrand, pp. 18–66.
Lin, N. (1999) 'Building a network theory of social capital', *Connections*, 22(1): 28–51.
Marwick, A. and Lewis, R. (2017) 'Media manipulation and disinformation online', *Data & Society Research Institute*, 15 May. Available at: https://datasociety.net/pubs/oh/DataAndSociety_MediaManipulation-AndDisinformationOnline.pdf. [Accessed 5 July 2017.]
Mønsted, B., Sapieżyński, P., Ferrara, E. and Lehmann, S. (2017) 'Evidence of complex contagion of information in social media: an experiment using twitter bots', *PLoS One*, 12(9): e0184148.
Moreno, J.L. (1951) *Sociometry, experimental method, and the science of society*, Ambler, PA: Beacon House.
Mutz, D.C. and Martin, P.S. (2001) 'Facilitating communication across lines of political difference: the role of mass media', *The American Political Science Review*, 95(1): 97–114.
Nicolaisen, J. (2013) 'Climbing mount dependable: how to detect misinformation on the internet', *International Conference on Internet Studies*, Hong Kong, China, 7–8 September. Available at: http://pure.iva.dk/files/35591543/CLIMBING_MOUNT.pdf. [Accessed 10 September 2019.]
Olshannikova, E., Olsson, T., Huhtamäki, J. and Kärkkäinen, H. (2017) 'Conceptualizing big social data', *Journal of Big Data*, 4(1): 1–19.
Piccialli, F. and Jung, J.E. (2017) 'Understanding customer experience diffusion on social networking services by big data analytics', *Mobile Networks and Applications*, 22(4): 605–12.
Real Instituto Elcano (2017) 'El conflicto catalán', *Real Instituto Elcano*, 23 October. Available at: www.realinstitutoelcano.org/wps/portal/rielcano_es/contenido?WCM_GLOBAL_CONTEXT=/elcano/elcano_es/zonas_es/cataluna-dossier-elcano-octubre-2017. [Accessed 9 September 2019.]
Ross, B., Rist, M., Carbonell, G., Cabrera, B., Kurowsky, N. and Wojatzki, M. (2016) 'Measuring the reliability of hate speech annotations: the case of the European refugee crisis', *NLP4CMC III: 3rd Workshop on Natural Language Processing for Computer-Mediated Communication*, Bochum, Germany, September. Available at: https://arxiv.org/abs/1701.08118. [Accessed 5 July 2018.]
Schmidt, A. and Wiegand, M. (2017) 'A survey on hate speech detection using natural language processing', *Proceedings of the Fifth International Workshop on Natural Language Processing for Social Media*, Valencia, Spain. Available at: www.aclweb.org/anthology/W17-1101. [Accessed 9 September 2019.]
Scott, J. (1996) *Social network analysis: a handbook*, London: Sage.
Shu, K., Sliva, A., Wang, S., Tang, J. and Liu, H. (2017), 'Fake News Detection on Social Media: A Data Mining Perspective', *ACM SIGKDD Explorations Newsletter*, 19(1): 22–36.
Sparrow, M.K. (1991) 'The application of network analysis to criminal intelligence: an assessment of the prospects', *Social Networks*, 13(3): 251–74.
Stella, M., Ferrara, E. and De Domenico, M. (2018) 'Bots increase exposure to negative and inflammatory content in online social systems', *Proceedings of the National Academy of Sciences of the United States of America*, 115(49): 12435–40.
Trendinalia Worldwide (2017). *Trendinalina Worldwide*, 17 October. Available at: www.trendinalia.com/twitter-trending-topics/globales/globales-171017.html. [Accessed 5 January 2019.]
Wasserman, S. and Faust, K. (2013) *Análisis de redes sociales: métodos y aplicaciones*, Madrid: Centro de Investigaciones Sociológicas.
We Are Social-Hootsuite (2019) *Digital 2019: global digital yearbook*. Available at: https://wearesocial.com/global-digital-report-2019. [Accessed 10 February 2019.]

# SECTION 2

# Psychological factors

# 2.0
# INTRODUCTION

*Jan-Willem van Prooijen, Karen M. Douglas,
Aleksandra Cichocka and Michał Bilewicz*

Why do some people believe many conspiracy theories, while other people disbelieve most of them? The question of what drives people's subjective beliefs about the world is the domain of psychology. Furthermore, given that most people who are susceptible to conspiracy theories are regular citizens who have no mental health problems, the study of what determines people's belief or disbelief in conspiracy theories is the domain of social psychology (see Chapter 1.9). Social psychology is defined as 'the branch of psychology dedicated to the study of how people think about, influence and relate to each other' (Sutton, Douglas 2013: 7). As such, social psychology is the study of how ordinary people think, feel and act in their everyday lives.

The founder of the academic field of social psychology was Kurt Lewin (1890–1947), who argued that both individual and environmental factors jointly contribute to human behaviour. Particularly well-known is the *Lewin equation*, which reads $B=f(P, E)$ (Lewin 1936). In this formula, 'B' stands for human behaviour, 'P' stands for the person and 'E' stands for the environment. Put differently, behaviour is a result of both the person and the environment. The Lewin equation implies that different people are likely to behave differently in the same situation. For example, a group of people may read exactly the same governmental conspiracy theory on the Internet, yet the extent to which different group members respond to the conspiracy theory may differ: Some people may believe the theory and subsequently join a populist party or protest movement, while others may not believe the theory and not act, or perhaps even ridicule it. These behavioural differences can be rooted in a range of factors that vary between people, including personality, demographic background, personal life history, education and so on.

Objectively the same situation hence elicits different responses among different people and, therefore, to understand behaviour one needs to take individual differences into account. Besides individual differences, however, the social environment also contributes significantly to behaviour. A person may not necessarily believe conspiracy theories about the pharmaceutical industry at one point in time yet become suspicious about the pharmaceutical industry following a disease epidemic. This environmental factor (an epidemic) may ultimately lead the person to join the anti-vaccine movement. Different situations elicit different behaviours from one and the same person; therefore, to understand behaviour, one also needs to take situational factors into account.

The Lewin equation reflects how social psychologists have approached the topic of conspiracy theories since the study of this topic gained momentum across the social sciences and humanities over the past decade. While the Lewin equation was originally about explaining behaviour, in a similar manner, the combination of individual and situational factors also explains people's perceptions of, and beliefs about, the world. Psychologists have therefore extensively investigated how a tendency to believe conspiracy theories is related to structural personality variables (e.g. openness to experience; agreeableness) and other demographic or individual difference variables (e.g. education level; narcissism; authoritarianism). Furthermore, psychologists have examined how situational circumstances (e.g. distressing societal events; conflict between groups; power differences) increase or decrease people's susceptibility to conspiracy theories. Finally, given that a core feature of the Lewin equation is that individual and environmental factors jointly determine people's perceptions, beliefs and behaviours, psychologists have investigated how situational experiences such as interpersonal rejection influence conspiracy beliefs differently depending on meaningful individual differences between people such as the fragility of one's self-worth (see Douglas et al. 2017; van Prooijen 2018).

This section is organised around the Lewin equation. Three chapters examine the role of the person in conspiracy beliefs. What specific differences between people, and what psychological processes that take place within people's own minds, influence the likelihood of believing or disbelieving conspiracy theories? The first chapter, by Lantian, Wood and Gjoneska (2.1), provides an overview of how a wide range of individual difference variables predict belief in conspiracy theories. The second chapter, by van Prooijen, Klein and Milošević Đorđević (2.2), illuminates how two complementary mental systems to process information contribute to belief in conspiracy theories. While the second chapter focuses on 'cold' cognition, the third chapter, by Douglas, Cichocka and Sutton (2.3), focuses on 'hot' motivation and emotion and addresses how various motivations and emotions that people have shape their belief in conspiracy theories.

The next three chapters of the section address the role of the situation: What specific factors in people's social environments increase or decrease the likelihood that they will believe in conspiracy theories? The fourth chapter, by Imhoff and Lamberty (2.4), examines the role of power differences and explains why people who lack power in social situations are more likely to believe conspiracy theories than people who have power. The fifth chapter, by Bangerter, Wagner-Egger and Delouvée (2.5), examines the spread of conspiracy theories: How do conspiracy theories transmit between people and within larger social or online networks? The sixth chapter, by Biddlestone, Cichocka, Žeželj and Bilewicz (2.6), examines the role of intergroup relations and conflict in conspiracy beliefs about social groups.

The final two chapters connect the psychology of conspiracy theories to societal issues. Lewin famously coined the maxim that, in social psychology, 'there is nothing as practical as a good theory' (Lewin 1943: 118). With this, Lewin meant that changing human perceptions or behaviours in society will be more successful if one does so by relying on psychological theories that are supported by evidence. The last two chapters therefore focus on the societal consequences of conspiracy theories, and possible interventions to reduce widespread belief in them, in particular when such beliefs pose some harm. The seventh chapter, by Jolley, Mari and Douglas (2.7), provides an overview of the behavioural and psychological consequences of conspiracy theories, illuminating the need for interventions in society. Finally, the eighth chapter, by Kreko (2.8), addresses the question if, and how, to debunk conspiracy theories. Together, these chapters provide an overview of the accumulating insights that social psychology has hitherto contributed to the study of conspiracy theories.

The social-psychological approach, as described in these chapters, has at least two features that give the field a unique place in the study of conspiracy theories. The first feature is that the majority of social-psychological knowledge is developed via quantitative hypothesis-testing, thereby complementing some of the more qualitative approaches to this topic. These quantitative methods enable researchers to examine what personal or environmental factors predict people's conspiracy beliefs above chance level. Usually, they rely on large (sometimes nationally representative) samples and multiple testing of the same hypothesis, which increases confidence in the findings. Furthermore, some of the research designs that social psychologists employ enable them to test causality, and hence empirically establish the causes and consequences of conspiracy beliefs.

While various other disciplines also study conspiracy theories using quantitative research methods, the second defining feature of the social psychological approach is that it studies conspiracy theories at micro- and meso-levels of analysis. This means that social psychologists try to understand how peoples' conspiracy beliefs are influenced by both individual differences and their direct social environment, as reflected in the Lewin equation. These micro- and meso-levels of analysis distinguishes psychology from other quantitative approaches such as sociology or political science, which typically endorse a more macro-level of analysis. This means that other quantitative disciplines place relatively more emphasis on examining conspiracy theories at a societal level, for instance by relating conspiracy beliefs to specific political or societal movements.

The study of conspiracy theories is a relatively new area of investigation in social psychology. Hence, there are many fruitful areas for future research in this domain. One limitation of the current state of affairs in social psychology is a strong reliance on survey-based questionnaires, in which participants indicate to what extent they agree or disagree with a range of statements. While such measures have the advantage that they provide direct information about how participants think and feel about certain topics, they are also sometimes restricted by, for instance, measurement errors (e.g. socially desirable responding) and limit the range of conclusions that a researcher can draw. Future research therefore needs to complement these measures with relatively 'hard' empirical data, which may include physiological measures, big data and real behaviours.

Physiological measures would be useful in the study of conspiracy theories because they provide information about processes that people cannot control. This complements research with rating scales in various ways, for instance by excluding the possibility that some findings are due to response bias. One example would be to study what happens in the brain while people think about conspiracy theories. Do conspiracy theories activate brain regions associated with analytic thinking (e.g. the dorsolateral prefrontal cortex), or brain regions associated with basic emotions (e.g. the anterior cingulate cortex) and threat experiences (e.g. the amygdala)? People can pretend to (not) be anxious in a questionnaire, but they cannot fake the physiological signature of such emotions. In a similar fashion, research may examine the relationship between conspiracy theories and stress, as for instance reflected in an activation of the sympathetic nervous system or the release of stress hormones (i.e. cortisol) in the body.

Modern technology provides ample opportunities to analyse big data, for instance in the form of Facebook or Twitter feeds. An emerging research approach in social psychology is to quantify (sometimes millions of) social media messages about a certain topic, and statistically relate them to, for instance, demographics (e.g. age or gender of the account holder) or political variables (e.g. how many liberal vs. conservative politicians does an account holder follow)? Such an approach has various advantages, including large sample sizes, the possibility to study social networks (e.g. do people mostly retweet conspiracy theories within their own ideological network, that is, is there an 'echo chamber' effect?), and the possibility to study people's spontaneous expressions of conspiracy beliefs (Del Vicario et al. 2016).

Finally, although research has extensively examined the consequences of conspiracy theories (see Chapter 2.7), most of these consequences have been behavioural *intentions*. This is problematic, because it is well-known that how people think they would behave often does not correspond to how people actually do behave in a given situation. Various other research domains within social psychology extensively focus on measures of actual behaviours (e.g. helping, aggression, cooperation and so on), and the psychology of conspiracy theories would benefit from also including such behavioural measures. For instance, do conspiracy theories influence people's aggressive behaviours, or their donations to charity? Do conspiracy beliefs about the government influence people's decisions about whether or not to cheat on their tax forms?

In sum, conspiracy theories are everywhere in society and large groups of citizens believe them. Social psychologists seek to understand conspiracy beliefs by examining the role of both individual and situational factors, and by examining the societal implications of conspiracy theories. Furthermore, although social psychologists have made significant steps in contributing to the study of conspiracy theories in recent years, there are fruitful opportunities for the field by incorporating physiological and behavioural measures, and by analysing big data. The chapters in this section reflect the current state of affairs in the psychology of conspiracy theories and are based on the principles laid out in this introduction. By combining the Lewin equation as a basic conceptual framework with a methodological toolbox that utilises quantitative hypothesis testing at micro- and meso-levels of analysis, social psychology has a unique place in the study of conspiracy theories.

## References

Del Vicario, M., Bessi, A., Zollo, F., Petroni, F., Scala, A., Caldarelli, G., Stanley, H.E. and Quattrociocchi, W. (2016) 'The spreading of misinformation online', *Proceedings of the National Academy of Sciences*, 113(3): 554–9.
Douglas, K.M., Sutton, R.M. and Cichocka, A. (2017) 'The psychology of conspiracy theories', *Current Directions in Psychological Science*, 26(6): 538–42.
Lewin, K. (1936) *Principles of topical psychology*, New York, NY: McGraw-Hill.
Lewin, K. (1943) 'Psychology and the process of group living', *Journal of Social Psychology*, 17: 113–31.
Sutton, R.M. and Douglas, K.M. (2013) *Social psychology*, Basingstoke, UK: Palgrave Macmillan.
Van Prooijen, J.-W. (2018) *The psychology of conspiracy theories*, Oxon, UK: Routledge.

# 2.1
# PERSONALITY TRAITS, COGNITIVE STYLES AND WORLDVIEWS ASSOCIATED WITH BELIEFS IN CONSPIRACY THEORIES

*Anthony Lantian, Mike Wood and Biljana Gjoneska*

## Introduction

Why do some people tend to believe conspiracy theories (i.e. describe events as clandestine plots by secret agents), while others do not? Psychologists have been asking this question since at least the 1960s, when Hamsher et al. (1968) examined why some people *accepted* conspiracy theories about the assassination of President Kennedy. Six years later, in the midst of another American political scandal, Wright and Arbuthnot (1974) investigated the same question, phrased differently: why do some people *dismiss* allegations of conspiracy – in this case, the idea that President Nixon might have been involved in the Watergate affair?

The central question of both investigations has dominated psychological research in this area since then. Why is it that, when two people are presented with the same information about the same situation, one sees coincidence or contingency, while the other sees evidence of conspiracy? We might see these people as having different levels of what psychologists call conspiratorial thinking, conspiracy mentality or conspiracist ideation – a relatively broad tendency to accept conspiratorial explanations for events. Empirical research supports the existence of such a mentality. Analyses of survey data show robust evidence that a single statistical factor predicts endorsement of different conspiracy theories, and several validated psychometric scales exist to measure it (Brotherton et al. 2013; Bruder et al. 2013; Lantian et al. 2016; Swami et al. 2017). Although the current evidence supports the view of conspiracy mentality as essentially one-dimensional, people differ on how they score on this dimension. This suggests that individual difference variables can play a deciding role in the tendency to explain world events through the lens of conspiracy theory. In addition, these individual factors can provide a more in-depth and fine-grained understanding of variation in conspiratorial thinking and are therefore pivotal for a better understanding of the subject at hand.

In this chapter, we will review some of the work on individual differences linked to conspiracy mentality, or to beliefs in specific conspiracy theories. We will touch on three distinct types of individual differences that may have an effect: personality ('can we predict someone's opinion on conspiracy theories from their personality traits?'), cognitive style ('how do habitual ways of thinking affect people's perception of conspiracy theories, and influence whether they will accept or reject them?') and worldviews ('how do broader views of society and humanity influence people's judgments of conspiracy?').

## The role of personality traits

Research on personality factors associated with conspiracy mentality has naturally targeted characteristics that are known to broadly influence religious, social and political beliefs (Swami, Furnham 2014). Namely, the general tendency to see the world as governed by conspiracies serves to provide alternative, simplistic explanations of events that are otherwise confusing, distressing, incomprehensible or uncontrollable, in the same manner as religious or ideological belief systems. This may seem an uncharitable view of conspiracy theories, but there is evidence to support such line of reasoning. Conspiracy theories, like many other human belief systems, are sometimes based on mutually contradicting propositions (Wood et al. 2012). Theories that are completely fabricated within the context of a psychological survey – like a variety of made-up claims about the Red Bull energy drink – can elicit enthusiastic endorsement from conspiracy-minded respondents (Swami, Coles et al. 2011). In addition, popular conspiracy theories often appear to be incoherent by conventional evidentiary criteria (Lewandowsky et al. 2018). Some authors have argued that people with a strong conspiracy mentality suffer from 'crippled epistemology' (Sunstein, Vermeule 2009; Brotherton, French 2014) since they support claims that are unjustified (relative to the available information in the wider society) or implausible (relative to other allegations of conspiracy). The overall inclination to accept or reject conclusions based on general predispositions, seems to suggest that personality indeed plays an important role in the tendency to (dis)believe in conspiracy theories.

According to some past research (Robins, Post 1997; Swami, Weis et al. 2016), conspiracist ideation is partly attributable to traits labelled as maladaptive for the individual since they are viewed as clinically latent anomalies in personality. However, such claims are subject to ethical scrutiny (against stigmatisation of people who are not diagnosed with a medical condition) and scientific criticism (Sunstein, Vermeule 2009). Here, we will delineate the inner worlds and elaborate on the worldviews of conspiracy theory believers through the perspective of both the adaptive personality traits and their so-called maladaptive variants.

As regards adaptive traits, we will focus on the Big Five model, which measures personality using five continuously-scaled dimensions: Extraversion, neuroticism, openness to experience, agreeableness and conscientiousness. The Big Five model enjoys broad empirical support and wide acceptance in personality psychology (McCrae, John 1992).

Specifically, several studies have reported negative correlations between conspiracist ideation and the agreeableness trait (i.e. willingness to be pleasant and compliant in social situations). In other words, conspiracy mentality may be higher among less agreeable people (Swami et al. 2010; Swami, Coles et al. 2011; Swami, Furnham 2012; Bruder et al. 2013; Galliford, Furnham 2017). However, other studies have failed to find such a correlation (Swami et al. 2012; Brotherton et al. 2013; Swami et al. 2013; Imhoff, Bruder 2014; Lobato et al. 2014; Orosz et al. 2016; Rose 2017; Imhoff, Lamberty 2018). Indeed, a recent meta-analysis including 13 studies on agreeableness and conspiracy theory beliefs (Goreis, Voracek 2019) failed to show a statistically significant link once the effect sizes were aggregated. If this relationship exists, it can be explained by the fact that people who are prone to trust conspiracy theories simultaneously tend to be distrustful of others, especially when they represent the system (Wagner-Egger, Bangerter 2007; Einstein, Glick 2015; Miller et al. 2016; Leiser et al. 2017; Imhoff, Lamberty 2018; Vitriol,

Marsh 2018; Goreis, Voracek 2019). Also, stronger believers in conspiracy theories tend to express higher interpersonal distrust, suspicion and antagonism (Hamsher *et al.* 1968; Goertzel 1994; Abalakina-Paap *et al.* 1999; Wagner-Egger, Bangerter 2007; Swami *et al.* 2010; Brotherton *et al.* 2013; Miller *et al.* 2016; Lantian *et al.* 2016; Rose 2017; Green, Douglas 2018; Imhoff, Lamberty 2018; Vitriol, Marsh 2018). This may be a bidirectional relationship: a vicious cycle in which distrust makes conspiracy theories seem more likely, and conspiracy theories in turn 'erode social capital and may frustrate people's needs to see themselves as valuable members of morally decent collectives' (Douglas *et al.* 2017: 540). Consistent with this idea, several studies investigated the broader aspects of social antagonism and found that conspiracy theory beliefs tend to correlate with anomie, disengagement from the system, discontent with or rejection of social norms and feelings of powerlessness, disaffection and hostility (e.g. Goertzel 1994; Abalakina-Paap *et al.* 1999; Brotherton *et al.* 2013).

Along with negative feelings toward the system and others in general, stronger believers in conspiracy theories tend to cultivate more negative feelings toward the self as well, expressed in the form of lower self-esteem (Abalakina-Paap *et al.* 1999; Swami, Coles *et al.* 2011; Swami, Furnham 2012; Stieger *et al.* 2013; van Prooijen 2016; Galliford, Furnham 2017). This might happen because people with low self-esteem would blame themselves or their ingroup for negative events, if it were not for conspiratorial explanations. Instead, conspiracy theories allow for a self-to-other shift in the blame game, thus preserving one's self-worth. In an analogous fashion, people with heightened anxiety tend to have a higher conspiracist mentality (Grzesiak-Feldman 2013; for a more extensive discussion of the role of anxiety and existential motives, see Chapter 2.3 in this volume). Here, too, conspiracy theories help to restore one's sense of agency by reinstating a sense of order, control and predictability (especially after a distressing external threat), thus regulating anxiety and negative emotions (Swami, Furnham *et al.* 2016). However, the negative association between conspiracy beliefs and self-esteem has proven to be somewhat inconsistent (i.e. not replicated) and conditional over the course of recent research (Crocker *et al.* 1999; Swami 2012; Cichocka *et al.* 2016; Radnitz, Underwood 2017; van Prooijen 2017). Namely, according to Cichocka *et al.* (2016), the link between conspiracy beliefs and self-esteem can be observed when the partial overlap between self-esteem and narcissism is taken into account. In fact, a string of studies directly confirms that people with higher conspiracist mentality score higher on the narcissistic trait (Cichocka *et al.* 2016), and a need for uniqueness as well (Imhoff, Lamberty 2017; Lantian *et al.* 2017; Imhoff, Lamberty 2018). Hence, recent developments suggest that believers in conspiracy theories cultivate a more ambivalent regard of the self, hinting that mechanisms for this relationship are more complex.

The thread from conspiracist mentality to negative affectivity could be extended to include various aspects of emotional instability (i.e. proneness toward psychological stress and susceptibility to unpleasant emotions, like anxiety and depression) and neuroticism (Swami, Furnham 2012; Swami *et al.* 2013; Lobato *et al.* 2014). The accentuated experience of negative emotions and attenuated engagement in analytical mental processes can be easily regarded as two sides of the same story. To put it simply, tuning in on our fears and anxieties could tune out our abilities for fact-checking and rational thinking. In fact, past research has demonstrated that stronger conspiracist thinkers tend to exhibit more uncritical receptiveness for unorthodox, unconventional or unusual ideas, main hallmarks of the Big Five personality trait of openness to experience (Swami *et al.* 2010; Swami, Coles *et al.* 2011; Swami *et al.* 2012, 2013). Some studies of conspiracy mentality, however, substitute the link with general open-mindedness with a more particular type of openness toward peculiarity, eccentricity and oddity (Darwin *et al.* 2011; Swami, Pietschnig *et al.* 2011; Swami *et al.* 2013).

That said, as with agreeableness, some caution is warranted regarding the correlation between conspiracy mentality and openness to experience. Namely, the findings have not been consistently replicated (see Brotherton *et al.* 2013; Bruder *et al.* 2013; Imhoff, Bruder 2014; Lobato *et al.* 2014; Orosz *et al.* 2016; Galliford, Furnham 2017; Leiser *et al.* 2017; Imhoff, Lamberty 2018; Goreis, Voracek 2019).

In line with the findings on eccentricity and conspiracy mentality, it has also been demonstrated that the odd beliefs of some conspiratorial thinkers encompass ideas of reference, magical thinking, paranormal beliefs and schizotypy (Swami, Pietschnig *et al.* 2011; Bruder *et al.* 2013; Swami *et al.* 2013; Barron *et al.* 2014; Lobato *et al.* 2014; Brotherton, Eser 2015; van der Tempel, Alcock 2015; Barron *et al.* 2018).

One possible explanation for such parallel findings is the observed concordance between the Big Five personality model and the matching five-domain model of maladaptive personality traits as referenced in the last version of the Diagnostic and Statistical Manual of Mental Disorders (American Psychiatric Association 2013). According to this analogy, the negative version of agreeableness would be social antagonism, neuroticism would align with negative affectivity, while an extremely negative variant of openness would be psychoticism (Gore, Widiger 2013; Krueger *et al.* 2011; Swami, Weis *et al.* 2016).

The link between conspiracist worldviews and maladaptive traits, however, is not exclusive in nature, since many people with no manifestation of psychopathology endorse conspiracy beliefs to some extent. This is especially true regarding the relationship between belief in conspiracy theories and paranoia, which are related to distinctively different constructs (Wilson, Rose 2014; Imhoff, Lamberty 2018).

In summary, conspiracist ideation cannot be described simply in terms of the Big Five dimensions or the maladaptive variants, thus some caution is warranted when regarding the inner worlds of conspiracy theory believers primarily in the context of their personality traits.

## The role of cognitive styles

Sense-making is a fundamentally cognitive process. When we try to make sense of what is happening in a particular situation – for instance, is this situation the result of a conspiracy or not? – we weigh evidence, consider sources of information and make a decision on what seems to be the best explanation. Our conclusions are affected, not just by the situation at hand, but also by our own psychological idiosyncrasies. We are subject to a tremendous number of biases, heuristics, attitudes, motives, other beliefs and overall patterns of thought. These factors change substantially from individual to individual, and can generally be grouped together under the broad label of *cognitive style*.

Cognitive styles are relatively stable, trait-like tendencies for people to acquire and process information in different ways, such as the tendency to jump to conclusions versus seek out more information before coming to a decision. Kozhevnikov (2007) argued that people develop these characteristic cognitive styles based on a complex interaction between their experiences and their abilities, as a general approach to dealing with the world in a flexible and accurate way. Cognitive styles are classified in a number of ways, but one of the most well-researched classifications of cognitive style, and probably the most relevant for conspiracy belief, is the tendency to think *analytically* (or *rationally*) versus *intuitively*. Analytic/rational thinking is relatively slow, explicit, effortful and detail-oriented, while intuition is relatively fast, implicit, effortless and concerned with broader, more general impressions (Norris, Epstein 2011; Dagnall *et al.* 2015). Many psychological processes work very differently when we are thinking in an effortful, analytical way versus an off-the-cuff, intuitive way, a fact that has given rise to many *dual-process models* across psychological subfields ranging from persuasion to health behaviour. We all use both of these styles of thinking, depending on the situation, but people vary in their tendency to default to one or the other. An individual's general analytic versus intuitive cognitive style, therefore, has profound consequences for how they are likely to react to a wide variety of different situations (Kahneman 2011; for a more extensive discussion on this topic, see Chapter 2.2 in this volume).

Psychological research has revealed that the tendency to think intuitively (rather than analytically) has a tremendous range of downstream effects on belief and behaviour. Intuitive versus analytic cognitive style predicts belief in a variety of unconventional topics, such as superstition, pseudoscience, the paranormal, pseudo-profound nonsense (Aarnio, Lindeman 2005; Pennycook et al. 2012; Pennycook et al. 2015) and conspiracy theories. Across one survey and three experiments, Swami et al. (2014) found that conspiracy belief is positively correlated with intuitive cognitive style, negatively correlated with analytic cognitive style and directly reduced by experimental manipulations that promote analytic thought. Van Prooijen (2017) likewise found a negative correlation between analytic thinking and conspiracy belief, and determined that this link partially explains why more educated people tend to take conspiracy theories less seriously: people with more years of education tend to think more analytically and therefore believe in conspiracies less (though this might depend on the conspiracy theory; for contrasting evidence regarding conspiracy theories about climate change and vaccination, see Zhou 2014; Hornsey et al. 2018).

So, the available research seems to show that analytic thinking largely suppresses conspiracy belief – as well as other types of unconventional belief – whereas intuitive thinking cultivates it. People who tend to rely on general impressions to make decisions about the world tend to believe more conspiracy theories, while people who tend to think carefully, explicitly and rationally tend to believe fewer. This extends to other anomalous beliefs as well, such as the paranormal. But why? One hypothesis concerns the nature of how we judge probability. Paranormal beliefs are correlated with probabilistic reasoning ability, apparently because people often infer paranormal causes for events that seem intuitively (but not always rationally) very unlikely to happen by natural means (Rogers et al. 2009). In a similar way, arguments in favour of conspiracy theories are often predicated on sinister interpretations of apparent coincidences. For instance, several airlines' stock prices dropped before the 9/11 attacks and this fact was used by promoters of 9/11 conspiracy theories to argue that someone was using foreknowledge of the attacks to carry out insider trading. Some psychological studies have shown that people with stronger conspiracy mentality are more likely to see patterns in random noise (van der Wal et al. 2018; van Prooijen et al. 2018), although others have not found such a correlation (Dieguez et al. 2015; Wagner-Egger et al. 2018). Moreover, conspiracy theories often require conjunctions of independently unlikely circumstances, such as everyone involved in a very large plot staying silent indefinitely (Grimes 2016). Therefore, many conspiracy theories might seem more plausible if the underlying probabilities are not examined closely, and therefore less plausible for people with the ability and inclination to assess these probabilities in detail.

Empirical research has supported this idea as an explanation for the correlation between conspiracy belief and cognitive style. Conspiracy belief is associated with usage of the *representativeness heuristic*, a biased shortcut in probabilistic reasoning that leads to various errors and fallacious judgements (Brotherton, French 2014; Moulding et al. 2016). In particular, people with a higher level of conspiracy belief are more likely to commit the *conjunction fallacy*, a specific case of the representativeness heuristic that involves misjudging the probability of two events occurring together (Dagnall *et al.* 2015). The conjunction fallacy occurs when people judge that the conjunction of two probabilities is more likely than either of those two probabilities on its own. This is a mathematical impossibility, but can seem subjectively true in particular circumstances.

Cognitive shortcuts of this kind are a signature feature of intuitive cognition, valuing quick shortcuts, rough estimates and general impressions at the cost of consistent, detailed accuracy (Tversky, Kahneman 1983; Kozhevnikov 2007). Indeed, the available research shows that analytic versus intuitive thinking is a strong determinant of the tendency to commit the conjunction fallacy.

Other psychological research falls into this general pattern, showing that conspiracy beliefs tend to co-occur with intuitive, heuristic and implicit styles of thought. People who believe more conspiracy theories are more likely to perceive patterns, deliberate action and agency in ambiguous stimuli (Brotherton, French 2015; Douglas *et al.* 2015; van der Tempel, Alcock 2015), to anthropomorphise inanimate objects (Douglas *et al.* 2015), to exhibit more general confusions about the ontological nature of objects in the world (for example, separating animate from inanimate; Lobato *et al.* 2014), to display impaired reality testing (Drinkwater *et al.* 2012), to jump to conclusions on the basis of limited evidence (Barron *et al.* 2018), to show a greater need for cognitive closure in the absence of official explanations for major events (Marchlewska *et al.* 2018) and to think that complex problems can generally be resolved with fairly simple solutions (van Prooijen *et al.* 2015; van Prooijen 2017). Some of these correlates also suggest plausible mechanisms for the correlation between conspiracy belief and cognitive style – for instance, the tendency to infer deliberate agency over random chance in interpreting a particular event has very clear relevance for inferences of conspiracy.

Intuitive cognitive style seems to predict conspiracy belief quite reliably, and conspiracy belief and cognitive style share many correlates. The analytic/intuitive cognitive style framework predicts many other psychological outcomes, though, and not all of these outcomes seem to correlate reliably with conspiracy belief. For example, a strong correlate of intuitive thought is a discomfort with uncertain, ambiguous situations, also known as intolerance for ambiguity (Ie *et al.* 2012). However, research to date has shown little or no evidence for a role of ambiguity tolerance in conspiracy mentality (Abalakina-Paap *et al.* 1999; Moulding *et al.* 2016). Similarly, despite the reliable correlation between analytic cognitive style and conspiracy belief, the evidence suggests a weak or non-existent correlation between conspiracy belief and *need for cognition*, a trait-like variable that describes someone's drive or motivation to think slowly, explicitly and effortfully in daily life (Abalakina-Paap *et al.* 1999; Lobato *et al.* 2014; Swami *et al.* 2014; Ståhl, van Prooijen 2018). However, given that a similar construct, need for closure, predicts conspiracy belief only under certain conditions (Marchlewska *et al.* 2018), need for cognition and ambiguity tolerance might indeed affect conspiracy belief in specific circumstances (e.g. high ambiguity or uncertainty).

Finally, it is important to note that most measures of rational/analytic cognitive style describe the inclination to engage in this kind of thought, but not necessarily the ability to do so very well. This naturally leads to the question of what effect cognitive *ability* (e.g. general intelligence), rather than cognitive *style*, might have on conspiracy beliefs. We have already reviewed some relevant evidence above: People who tend to reject conspiracy theories also tend to perform better on probabilistic reasoning tasks (e.g. Brotherton, French 2014; Moulding *et al.* 2016). More broadly, tests of mathematical and verbal reasoning ability show that conspiracy sceptics tend to score higher than conspiracy believers (Swami, Coles *et al.* 2011; Ståhl, van Prooijen 2018). This trend appears to extend to people's intellectual self-image as well: When asked to rate their own intelligence, people with stronger conspiracy beliefs tend to rate themselves as less intelligent (Swami, Coles *et al.* 2011; Swami, Furnham

2012). Not only do cognitive style and cognitive ability have independent effects on conspiracy belief, their effects depend on one another. In a recent investigation, Ståhl and van Prooijen (2018) found that higher cognitive ability is only associated with lower conspiracy belief when the person in question also finds rational thought to be important. Both the motive and the means must be present in order for rational/analytic thought to work against conspiracy belief.

In general, then, the cognitive factors underlying conspiracy belief fall under two broad categories: The tendency to take a careful, analytic and rational approach to thought (or not), and the ability to do it well. However, there are important limitations to these conclusions. Primarily, most of the available research in this tradition has been done on populations in Western, English-speaking nations. There is reason to believe that some of the effects of variations in cognitive style are culturally determined – for instance, Majima (2015) demonstrated that analytic and intuitive cognitive styles were both *positive* predictors of paranormal belief in a Japanese sample. Conspiracy theories are arguably even more culturally-bound than paranormal beliefs are, and how they are construed across different contexts is likely to profoundly alter how they relate to our underlying psychological dispositions.

## The role of worldviews

In the last part of this chapter, we will examine two specific worldviews associated with belief in conspiracy theories: Belief in the world as a dangerous place or as a competitive jungle. As already outlined by several researchers (Wilson, Rose 2014; Rose 2017), we will show to what extent the two worldviews are connected with personality traits and socio-political factors/generalised political attitudes shared by people who believe in conspiracy theories.

Belief in a dangerous world could be defined as the view that the social world is 'a dangerous and threatening place in which good, decent people's values and way of life are threatened by bad people' (Duckitt *et al.* 2002: 78). According to this worldview, people are by nature dangerous, hence they do not deserve to be trusted. There are many empirical results showing that people who believe more in conspiracy theories feel that they are living in a more dangerous social world (Wagner-Egger, Bangerter 2007; Moulding *et al.* 2016; Leiser *et al.* 2017; Leone *et al.* 2017; Rose 2017). Finally, according to some evidence, conspiracy believers consider not only that they live in a dangerous world, but also endorse a simplistic Manichean view. More explicitly, for them, politics is like a battlefield between the camps of absolute good and absolute evil (Oliver, Wood 2014; Green, Douglas 2018).

This worldview is a framework that nicely integrates several personality traits related to belief in conspiracy theories. For instance, belief in a dangerous world is consistent with the lack of interpersonal trust that conspiracy theorists express toward others (for cited literature please refer to earlier segment). Moreover, lower self-reported levels of agreeableness found occasionally amongst conspiracy theorists (e.g. Bruder *et al.* 2013) could be a defensive strategy for those who believe the world to be a dangerous and threatening place.

According to the dual-process motivational model developed by Duckitt *et al.* (2002), belief in a dangerous world is determined to some extent by personality traits, and in turn acts as a precursor to right-wing authoritarianism. Right-wing authoritarianism is a social attitude characterised by three facets: Authoritarian submission, authoritarian aggression and conventionalism (Altemeyer 2006; see Chapter 2.6 in this volume for a more extensive discussion about this topic). Given the connection between belief in a dangerous world and right-wing authoritarianism, it could be reasonable to predict a certain amount of shared variance between right-wing authoritarianism and belief in conspiracy theories. As reviewed by Grzesiak-Feldman (2015), these two variables indeed tend to be positively correlated (Abalakina-Paap et al. 1999; Grzesiak-Feldman, Irzycka 2009; Swami et al. 2012; Bruder et al. 2013; Wilson, Rose 2014; Rose 2017; Green, Douglas 2018; Federico et al. 2018; Imhoff, Lamberty 2018; Imhoff et al. 2018). Nonetheless, this association seems to be influenced by the type of conspiracy theories (e.g. right-wing authoritarianism being more correlated with pro- rather than anti-establishment conspiracy theories, Wood and Gray 2019) and the cultural background of the respondents, which could explain the conflicting results found occasionally (Swami, Coles et al. 2011; Swami 2012; Imhoff, Bruder 2014; Oliver, Wood 2014; Leiser et al. 2017; Wood, Gray 2019). In line with an authoritarian mindset, conspiracy belief is positively (though not strongly) correlated with support for governmental violations of human rights and restriction of civil liberties as part of the War on Terror (Swami et al. 2012).

People who endorse conspiracy theories tend to believe not only that the world is dangerous, but also that it is a competitive 'jungle' in which the strong dominate the weak (Wilson, Rose 2014; Rose 2017; however, this association is not significant in Leone et al. 2017). Belief in a competitive jungle is a worldview characterised by a brutal and amoral social environment in which people continuously struggle for resources, illustrated by the statement 'might is right' (Duckitt et al. 2002).

Several related personality traits can explain why stronger conspiracy believers tend to see the world as more of a competitive jungle. For instance, political cynicism and Machiavellianism both tend to increase with conspiracy mentality (Douglas, Sutton 2011; Swami, Coles et al. 2011; Swami, Furnham 2012; Swami 2012; Swami et al. 2012), forming an adaptive psychological stance tailored for a harsh social environment like the one depicted by the competitive-jungle worldview. However, there does not seem to be any correlation between conspiracy belief and free market ideology (Lewandowsky, Gignac et al. 2013; Lewandowsky, Oberauer et al. 2013), or a more broad support for the neoliberal economic view (Leiser et al. 2017; i.e. ideologies that emphasise the role of competition as a driving force behind the functioning of the economy). These findings suggest that the competitive jungle worldview, at least in terms of its association with conspiracy mentality, might be relatively domain-specific.

Beyond correlating with these personality traits and ideological views, the competitive-jungle worldview is also theorised as being a precursor to social dominance orientation (Duckitt et al. 2002). Social dominance orientation is a general social attitude characterised by a preference to hierarchical (rather than equal) relations between groups, as well as a willingness to see one's ingroup being dominant and superior to outgroups (Pratto et al. 1994). Consistent with the idea that the competitive jungle worldview is relevant to conspiracy mentality, social dominance orientation tends to show robust correlations with beliefs in conspiracy theories (Bruder et al. 2013; Wilson, Rose 2014; Rose 2017; Green, Douglas 2018; Imhoff et al. 2018; Wood, Gray 2019; see also Imhoff, Bruder 2014 for less stable correlations between conspiracy beliefs and social dominance orientation, and Swami 2012 for an unexpected negative correlation between these two variables). In short, in this section, we have seen that conspiracy beliefs are connected to the belief that the world is both dangerous and a competitive jungle, and that this connection brings together a wide variety of congruent personality traits and socio-political factors.

## A dynamic system of individual differences

In summary, research to date indicates that people with a stronger conspiracy mentality tend to have a relatively dark and pessimistic view of humanity. This includes higher general distrust and an increased willingness to exploit others for personal gain. Regarding Big Five personality factors, at the time of writing, we cannot conclude that they are reliably related to belief in conspiracy theories (Goreis, Voracek 2019). However, those with a weaker conspiracy mentality rely more on slow, explicit thought than fast, intuitive understanding. It should be acknowledged that there is not yet a comprehensive theoretical model that encompasses all individual differences known to be related to conspiracy beliefs. Moreover, most of the empirical work in this area is cross-sectional, meaning that we do not know how opinions of conspiracy theories change and develop over time. In addition, we cannot yet say which of these variables *cause* people to accept or reject conspiracy theories, and which ones are in turn affected by perceptions of the world as a place run by conspiracies. Some variables, such as interpersonal trust, likely have a reciprocal relationship with conspiracy theory belief; others, however, are relatively basic and stable characteristics of personality, and are therefore more likely to be purely antecedent to opinions of conspiracy theories. Future work may attempt to include the temporal dimension to help us to build a more detailed understanding of how worldviews, cognitive styles and personality traits dynamically interact with one another.

# References

Aarnio, K. and Lindeman, M. (2005) 'Paranormal beliefs, education, and thinking styles', *Personality and Individual Differences*, 39(7): 1227–36.
Abalakina-Paap, M., Stephan, W.G., Craig, T. and Gregory, W.L. (1999) 'Beliefs in conspiracies', *Political Psychology*, 20(3): 637–47.
Altemeyer, R.A. (2006) *The authoritarians*, Manitoba: University of Manitoba Press.
American Psychiatric Association (2013) *Diagnostic and statistical manual of mental disorders*, 5th edn, Washington, DC: American Psychiatric Association.
Barron, D., Furnham, A., Weis, L., Morgan, K.D., Towell, T. and Swami, V. (2018) 'The relationship between schizotypal facets and conspiracist beliefs via cognitive processes', *Psychiatry Research*, 259: 15–20.
Barron, D., Morgan, K., Towell, T., Altemeyer, B. and Swami, V. (2014) 'Associations between schizotypy and belief in conspiracist ideation', *Personality and Individual Differences*, 70: 156–9.
Brotherton, R. and Eser, S. (2015) 'Bored to fears: Boredom proneness, paranoia, and conspiracy theories', *Personality and Individual Differences*, 80: 1–5.
Brotherton, R. and French, C.C. (2014) 'Belief in conspiracy theories and susceptibility to the conjunction fallacy', *Applied Cognitive Psychology*, 28(2): 238–48.
Brotherton, R. and French, C.C. (2015) 'Intention seekers: conspiracist ideation and biased attributions of intentionality', *PLoS ONE*, 10(5).
Brotherton, R., French, C.C. and Pickering, A.D. (2013) 'Measuring belief in conspiracy theories: the generic conspiracist beliefs scale', *Frontiers in Psychology*, 4.
Bruder, M., Haffke, P., Neave, N., Nouripanah, N. and Imhoff, R. (2013) 'Measuring individual differences in generic beliefs in conspiracy theories across cultures: conspiracy mentality questionnaire', *Frontiers in Psychology*, 4(225).
Cichocka, A., Marchlewska, M. and de Zavala, A.G. (2016) 'Does self-love or self-hate predict conspiracy beliefs? Narcissism, self-esteem, and the endorsement of conspiracy theories', *Social Psychological and Personality Science*, 7(2): 157–66.
Crocker, J., Luhtanen, R., Broadnax, S. and Blaine, B.E. (1999) 'Belief in US government conspiracies against Blacks among Black and White college students: powerlessness or system blame?', *Personality and Social Psychology Bulletin*, 25(8): 941–53.
Dagnall, N., Drinkwater, K., Parker, A., Denovan, A. and Parton, M. (2015) 'Conspiracy theory and cognitive style: a worldview', *Frontiers in Psychology*, 6(206).
Darwin, H., Neave, N. and Holmes, J. (2011) 'Belief in conspiracy theories: the role of paranormal belief, paranoid ideation and schizotypy', *Personality and Individual Differences*, 50(8): 1289–93.
Dieguez, S., Wagner-Egger, P. and Gauvrit, N. (2015) 'Nothing happens by accident, or does it? A low prior for randomness does not explain belief in conspiracy theories,' *Psychological Science*, 26(11): 1762–70.
Douglas, K.M. and Sutton, R.M. (2011) 'Does it take one to know one? Endorsement of conspiracy theories is influenced by personal willingness to conspire', *British Journal of Social Psychology*, 50(3): 544–52.

Douglas, K.M., Sutton, R.M., Callan, M.J., Dawtry, R.J. and Harvey, A.J. (2015) 'Someone is pulling the strings: hypersensitive agency detection and belief in conspiracy theories', *Thinking & Reasoning*, 20(1): 57–77.

Douglas, K.M., Sutton, R.M. and Cichocka, A. (2017) 'The psychology of conspiracy theories', *Current Directions in Psychological Science*, 26(6): 538–42.

Drinkwater, K., Dagnall, N. and Parker, A. (2012) 'Reality testing, conspiracy theories and paranormal beliefs', *The Journal of Parapsychology*, 76(1): 57–77.

Duckitt, J., Wagner, C., Du Plessis, I. and Birum, I. (2002) 'The psychological bases of ideology and prejudice: testing a dual process model', *Journal of Personality and Social Psychology*, 83(1): 75–93.

Einstein, K.L. and Glick, D.M. (2015) 'Do I think BLS data are BS? The consequences of conspiracy theories', *Political Behavior*, 37(3): 679–701.

Federico, C.M., Williams, A.L. and Vitriol, J.A. (2018) 'The role of system identity threat in conspiracy theory endorsement', *European Journal of Social Psychology*, 48(7): 927–38.

Galliford, N. and Furnham, A. (2017) 'Individual difference factors and beliefs in medical and political conspiracy theories', *Scandinavian Journal of Psychology*, 58(5): 422–8.

Goertzel, T. (1994) 'Belief in conspiracy theories', *Political Psychology*, 15(4): 731–42.

Gore, W.L., Widiger, T.A. (2013) 'The DSM-5 dimensional trait model and five-factor models of general personality', *Journal of Abnormal Psychology* 122, 3, pp. 816–21.

Goreis, A. and Voracek, M. (2019) 'A systematic review and meta-analysis of psychological research on conspiracy beliefs: field characteristics, measurement instruments, and associations with personality traits', *Frontiers in Psychology*, 10(205).

Green, R. and Douglas, K.M. (2018) 'Anxious attachment and belief in conspiracy theories', *Personality and Individual Differences*, 125: 30–7.

Grimes, D.R. (2016) 'On the viability of conspiratorial beliefs', *PLoS ONE*, 11(3).

Grzesiak-Feldman, M. (2013) 'The effect of high-anxiety situations on conspiracy thinking', *Current Psychology*, 32(1): 100–18.

Grzesiak-Feldman, M. (2015) 'Are the high authoritarians more prone to adopt conspiracy theories? The role of right-wing authoritarianism in conspiratorial thinking', in M. Bilewicz, A. Cichocka and W. Soral (eds.) *The psychology of conspiracy*, 1st edn, New York: Routledge, pp. 99–121.

Grzesiak-Feldman, M. and Irzycka, M. (2009) 'Right-wing authoritarianism and conspiracy thinking in a Polish sample', *Psychological Reports*, 105(2): 389–93.

Hamsher, J.H., Geller, J.D. and Rotter, J.B. (1968) 'Interpersonal trust, internal-external control, and the Warren commission report', *Journal of Personality and Social Psychology*, 9(3): 210–5.

Hornsey, M.J., Harris, E.A. and Fielding, K.S. (2018) 'The psychological roots of anti-vaccination attitudes: a 24-nation investigation', *Health Psychology*, 37(4): 307–15.

Ie, A., Haller, C.S., Langer, E.J. and Courvoisier, D.S. (2012) 'Mindful multitasking: the relationship between mindful flexibility and media multitasking', *Computers in Human Behavior*, 28(4): 1526–32.

Imhoff, R. and Bruder, M. (2014) 'Speaking (un-)truth to power: conspiracy mentality as a generalised political attitude', *European Journal of Personality*, 28(1): 25–43.

Imhoff, R. and Lamberty, P.K. (2017) 'Too special to be duped: need for uniqueness motivates conspiracy beliefs', *European Journal of Social Psychology*, 47(6): 724–34.

Imhoff, R. and Lamberty, P. (2018) 'How paranoid are conspiracy believers? Toward a more fine-grained understanding of the connect and disconnect between paranoia and belief in conspiracy theories', *European Journal of Social Psychology*, 48(7): 909–26.

Imhoff, R., Lamberty, P. and Klein, O. (2018) 'Using power as a negative cue: how conspiracy mentality affects epistemic trust in sources of historical knowledge', *Personality and Social Psychology Bulletin*, 44(9): 1364–79.

Kahneman, D. (2011) *Thinking, fast and slow*. New York: Farrar, Straus and Giroux.

Kozhevnikov, M. (2007) 'Cognitive styles in the context of modern psychology: toward an integrated framework of cognitive style', *Psychological Bulletin*, 133(3): 464–81.

Krueger, R.F., Eaton, N.R., Clark, L.A., Watson, D., Markon, K.E., Derringer, J., Skodol, A. and Livesley, W.J. (2011) 'Deriving an empirical structure of personality pathology for DSM-5', *Journal of Personality Disorders*, 25(2): 170–91.

Lantian, A., Muller, D., Nurra, C. and Douglas, K.M. (2016) 'Measuring belief in conspiracy theories: validation of a French and English single-item scale', *International Review of Social Psychology*, 29: 1–14.

Lantian, A., Muller, D., Nurra, C. and Douglas, K.M. (2017) '"I know things they don't know!" The role of need for uniqueness in belief in conspiracy theories', *Social Psychology*, 48(3): 160–73.

Leiser, D., Duani, N. and Wagner-Egger, P. (2017) 'The conspiratorial style in lay economic thinking', *PloS ONE*, 12(3).

Leone, L., Giacomantonio, M. and Lauriola, M. (2017) 'Moral foundations, worldviews, moral absolutism and belief in conspiracy theories', *International Journal of Psychology*, 54(2): 197–204.

Lewandowsky, S., Cook, J. and Lloyd, E. (2018) 'The "Alice in wonderland" mechanics of the rejection of (climate) science: simulating coherence by Conspiracism', *Synthese*, 195(1): 175–96.

Lewandowsky, S., Gignac, G.E. and Oberauer, K. (2013) 'The role of conspiracist ideation and worldviews in predicting rejection of science', *PloS ONE*, 8(10).

Lewandowsky, S., Oberauer, K. and Gignac, G.E. (2013) 'NASA faked the moon landing—therefore, (climate) science is a hoax: An anatomy of the motivated rejection of science', *Psychological Science*, 24(5): 622–33.

Lobato, E., Mendoza, J., Sims, V. and Chin, M. (2014) 'Examining the relationship between conspiracy theories, paranormal beliefs, and pseudoscience acceptance among a university population', *Applied Cognitive Psychology*, 28(5): 617–25.

Majima, Y. (2015) 'Belief in pseudoscience, cognitive style and science literacy', *Applied Cognitive Psychology*, 29(4): 552–9.

Marchlewska, M., Cichocka, A. and Kossowska, M. (2018) 'Addicted to answers: need for cognitive closure and the endorsement of conspiracy beliefs', *European Journal of Social Psychology*, 48(2): 109–17.

McCrae, R.R. and John, O.P. (1992) 'An introduction to the five-factor model and its applications', *Journal of Personality*, 60(2): 175–215.

Miller, J.M., Saunders, K.L. and Farhart, C.E. (2016) 'Conspiracy endorsement as motivated reasoning: the moderating roles of political knowledge and trust', *American Journal of Political Science*, 60(4): 824–44.

Moulding, R., Nix-Carnell, S., Schnabel, A., Nedeljkovic, M., Burnside, E.E., Lentini, A.F. and Mehzabin, N. (2016) 'Better the devil you know than a world you don't? Intolerance of uncertainty and worldview explanations for belief in conspiracy theories', *Personality and Individual Differences*, 98: 345–54.

Norris, P. and Epstein, S. (2011) 'An experiential thinking style: its facets and relations with objective and subjective criterion measures', *Journal of Personality*, 79(5): 1043–80.

Oliver, J.E. and Wood, T.J. (2014) 'Conspiracy theories and the paranoid style(s) of mass opinion', *American Journal of Political Science*, 58(4): 952–66.

Orosz, G., Krekó, P., Paskuj, B., Tóth-Király, I., Bőthe, B. and Roland-Lévy, C. (2016) 'Changing conspiracy beliefs through rationality and ridiculing', *Frontiers in Psychology*, 7(279).

Pennycook, G., Cheyne, J.A., Barr, N., Koehler, D.J. and Fugelsang, J.A. (2015) 'On the reception and detection of pseudo-profound bullshit', *Judgment and Decision Making*, 10(6): 549–63.

Pennycook, G., Cheyne, J.A., Seli, P., Koehler, D.J. and Fugelsang, J.A. (2012) 'Analytic cognitive style predicts religious and paranormal belief', *Cognition*, 123(3): 335–46.

Pratto, F., Sidanius, J., Stallworth, L. and Malle, B. (1994) 'Social dominance orientation: a personality variable predicting social and political attitudes', *Journal of Personality and Social Psychology*, 67(4): 741–63.

Radnitz, S. and Underwood, P. (2017) 'Is belief in conspiracy theories pathological? A survey experiment on the cognitive roots of extreme suspicion', *British Journal of Political Science*, 47(1): 113–29.

Robins, R.S. and Post, J.M. (1997) *Political paranoia: the psychopolitics of hatred*, New Haven and London: Yale University Press.

Rogers, P., Davis, T. and Fisk, J. (2009) 'Paranormal belief and susceptibility to the conjunction fallacy', *Applied Cognitive Psychology*, 23(4): 524–42.

Rose, C. (2017) *The measurement and prediction of conspiracy beliefs*, thesis, Victoria University of Wellington. Available at: http://researcharchive.vuw.ac.nz/handle/10063/6420. [Accessed 20 June 2019.]

Ståhl, T. and van Prooijen, J.-W. (2018) 'Epistemic rationality: skepticism toward unfounded beliefs requires sufficient cognitive ability and motivation to be rational', *Personality and Individual Differences*, 122: 155–63.

Stieger, S., Gumhalter, N., Tran, U.S., Voracek, M. and Swami, V. (2013) 'Girl in the cellar: a repeated cross-sectional investigation of belief in conspiracy theories about the kidnapping of Natascha Kampusch', *Frontiers in Psychology*, 4(297).

Sunstein, C.R. and Vermeule, A. (2009) 'Conspiracy theories: causes and cures', *Journal of Political Philosophy*, 17(2): 202–27.

Swami, V. (2012) 'Social psychological origins of conspiracy theories: the case of the Jewish conspiracy theory in Malaysia', *Frontiers in Psychology*, 3(280).

Swami, V., Barron, D., Weis, L., Voracek, M., Stieger, S. and Furnham, A. (2017) 'An examination of the factorial and convergent validity of four measures of conspiracist ideation, with recommendations for researchers', *PloS ONE*, 12(2).

Swami, V., Chamorro-Premuzic, T. and Furnham, A. (2010) 'Unanswered questions: a preliminary investigation of personality and individual difference predictors of 9/11 conspiracist beliefs', *Applied Cognitive Psychology*, 24(6): 749–61.

Swami, V., Coles, R., Stieger, S., Pietschnig, J., Furnham, A., Rehim, S. and Voracek, M. (2011) 'Conspiracist ideation in Britain and Austria: evidence of a monological belief system and associations between individual psychological differences and real-world and fictitious conspiracy theories', *British Journal of Psychology*, 102(3): 443–63.

Swami, V. and Furnham, A. (2012) 'Examining conspiracist beliefs about the disappearance of Amelia Earhart', *The Journal of General Psychology*, 139(4): 244–59.

Swami, V. and Furnham, A. (2014) 'Political paranoia and conspiracy theories', in J. P. Prooijen, P. A. M. van Lange (eds.) *Power, politics, and paranoia: why people are suspicious of their leaders*, Cambridge: Cambridge University Press, pp. 218–36.

Swami, V., Furnham, A., Smyth, N., Weis, L., Lay, A. and Clow, A. (2016) 'Putting the stress on conspiracy theories: examining associations between psychological stress, anxiety, and belief in conspiracy theories', *Personality and Individual Differences*, 99: 72–6.

Swami, V., Nader, I.W., Pietschnig, J., Stieger, S., Tran, U.S. and Voracek, M. (2012) 'Personality and individual difference correlates of attitudes toward human rights and civil liberties', *Personality and Individual Differences*, 53(4): 443–7.

Swami, V., Pietschnig, J., Stieger, S. and Voracek, M. (2011) 'Alien psychology: associations between extraterrestrial beliefs and paranormal ideation, superstitious beliefs, schizotypy, and the big five personality factors', *Applied Cognitive Psychology*, 25(4): 647–53.

Swami, V., Pietschnig, J., Tran, U.S., Nader, I.W., Stieger, S. and Voracek, M. (2013) 'Lunar lies: the impact of informational framing and individual differences in shaping conspiracist beliefs about the moon landings', *Applied Cognitive Psychology*, 27(1): 71–80.

Swami, V., Voracek, M., Stieger, S., Tran, U.S. and Furnham, A. (2014) 'Analytic thinking reduces belief in conspiracy theories', *Cognition*, 133(3): 572–85.

Swami, V., Weis, L., Lay, A., Barron, D. and Furnham, A. (2016) 'Associations between belief in conspiracy theories and the maladaptive personality traits of the personality inventory for DSM-5', *Psychiatry Research*, 236: 86–90.

Tversky, A. and Kahneman, D. (1983) 'Extensional versus intuitive reasoning: the conjunction fallacy in probability judgment', *Psychological Review*, 90(4): 293–315.

Van der Tempel, J. and Alcock, J.E. (2015) 'Relationships between conspiracy mentality, hyperactive agency detection, and schizotypy: supernatural forces at work?', *Personality and Individual Differences*, 82: 136–41.

Van der Wal, R.C., Sutton, R.M., Lange, J. and Braga, J.P.N. (2018) 'Suspicious binds: conspiracy thinking and tenuous perceptions of causal connections between co-occurring and spuriously correlated events', European Journal of Social Psychology, 48(7): 970–889.

Van Prooijen, J.-W. (2016) 'Sometimes inclusion breeds suspicion: self-uncertainty and belongingness predict belief in conspiracy theories', *European Journal of Social Psychology*, 46: 267–79.

Van Prooijen, J.-W. (2017) 'Why education predicts decreased belief in conspiracy theories', *Applied Cognitive Psychology*, 31(1): 50–8.

Van Prooijen, J.-W., Douglas, K.M. and De Inocencio, C. (2018) 'Connecting the dots: illusory pattern perception predicts belief in conspiracies and the supernatural', *European Journal of Social Psychology*, 48: 320–35.

Van Prooijen, J.-W., Krouwel, A.P.M. and Pollet, T.V. (2015) 'Political extremism predicts belief in conspiracy theories', *Social Psychological and Personality Science*, 6(5): 570–8.

Vitriol, J.A. and Marsh, J.K. (2018) 'The illusion of explanatory depth and endorsement of conspiracy beliefs', *European Journal of Social Psychology*, 48(7): 955–69.

Wagner-Egger, P. and Bangerter, A. (2007) 'La vérité est ailleurs: corrélats de l'adhésion aux théories du complot', *Revue Internationale de Psychologie Sociale*, 20: 31–61.

Wagner-Egger, P., Delouvée, S., Gauvrit, N. and Dieguez, S. (2018) 'Creationism and conspiracism share a common teleological bias', *Current Biology*, 28(16): R867–R868.

Wilson, M.S. and Rose, C. (2014). 'The role of paranoia in a dual-process motivational model of conspiracy belief', in J.W. van Prooijen and P.A.M. van Lange (eds.) *Power, politics, and paranoia: why people are suspicious of their leaders*, Cambridge: Cambridge University Press, pp. 273–91.

Wood, M.J., Douglas, K.M. and Sutton, R.M. (2012) 'Dead and alive: beliefs in contradictory conspiracy theories', *Social Psychological and Personality Science*, 3: 767–73.
Wood, M.J. and Gray, D. (2019) 'Right-wing authoritarianism as a predictor of pro-establishment versus anti-establishment conspiracy theories', *Personality and Individual Differences*, 138: 163–6.
Wright, T.L. and Arbuthnot, J. (1974) 'Interpersonal trust, political preference, and perceptions of the Watergate affair', *Personality and Social Psychology Bulletin*, (1): 168–70.
Zhou, M. (2014) 'Public environmental skepticism: a cross-national and multilevel analysis', *International Sociology*, 30(1): 61–85.

# 2.2
# SOCIAL-COGNITIVE PROCESSES UNDERLYING BELIEF IN CONSPIRACY THEORIES

*Jan-Willem van Prooijen, Olivier Klein and Jasna Milošević Đorđević*

## Introduction

People differ in whether they perceive evidence for a conspiracy in similar stimuli. For instance, based on the same video footage, some people see irrefutable evidence that the moon landings were fake (e.g. the U.S. flag appears to be waving despite the lack of wind on the moon), while others do not see such evidence. This suggests a prominent role for psychology in the study of conspiracy theories, as this discipline examines what individual and social factors determine whether people believe or disbelieve conspiracy theories (van Prooijen 2018). In the current chapter, we specifically focus on the role of social cognition: How does the human mind process information about conspiracy theories, and what specific social-cognitive processes increase the likelihood that people believe these theories?

A central idea in the field of social cognition is that the human mind has two functional systems in place to process information about the physical and social environment (e.g. Kahneman 2011). These systems are complementary, as both are necessary to help human beings effectively navigate their world. According to these so-called 'dual-process models' (Evans 2008), one of these mental systems is fast, and evaluates information through intuitions, emotions and heuristics ('System 1'). For instance, through System 1 a perceiver may experience an immediate, gut-level suspicion that a new political candidate is not to be trusted. The other mental system is slow, and evaluates information through analytic thinking, rational deliberations and a thorough assessment of the available information ('System 2'). For instance, through System 2 a perceiver may extensively assess the history of corruption of a new political candidate, and eventually conclude that this candidate is not to be trusted. In these examples, the final judgment is the same (the politician should not be trusted), but the social-cognitive processes underlying this judgment is different. In the first case, the perceiver has drawn this conclusion based on a feeling that emerged quickly and, in the second case, the perceiver has drawn this conclusion after an extensive analysis.

One important insight in the field of social cognition is that most beliefs that people hold about the world originate from System 1 thinking. For instance, Gilbert, Tafarodi and Malone (1993) noted that people's first intuitive impulse after comprehending a proposition is to believe it, and they need to exert active mental effort (System 2) to *un*believe a proposition. They found that imposing time pressure on participants – disabling their capacity to use analytical System 2 processes – increased the influence of obviously false information on participants' ratings of how to punish a criminal. Apparently, people need some time and effort to recognise information as false, and to adjust their evaluations of the criminal accordingly. Pantazi, Klein and Kissine (2018) have found that, even in the absence of such time pressure, people may display such a 'truth bias', that is, a tendency to believe information regardless of whether it is true. The idea that not believing but *un*believing requires System 2 thinking corresponds to findings pertaining to the social-cognitive basis of specific belief systems. For instance, research reveals that analytic thinking mediates the relationship between religiosity and happiness (Ritter *et al.* 2014), and increases the likelihood that people disbelieve religious claims (Gervais, Norenzayan 2012). Furthermore, belief in paranormal phenomena is associated with increased intuitive thinking and decreased analytic thinking (Aarnio, Lindeman 2005).

It is not necessarily self-evident that these insights generalise to conspiracy beliefs, however. Some conspiracy theories have turned out to be true (e.g. in 1973 many people already suspected that President Nixon was personally involved in Watergate (Wright, Arbuthnot 1974)). Also, conspiracy theories that are unlikely to be true often involve a long list of articulate arguments (Wagner-Egger *et al.* 2019), however, suggesting a role for System 2 processes. Even an outlandish conspiracy theory such as the Flat Earth movement (the conspiracy theory that the Earth is flat, and that scientists have been deceiving the public for over 400 years) has a long list of arguments to support its theory. These arguments include accusations of deception by N.A.S.A. (which supposedly fabricates satellite pictures of a round Earth), rigged plane windows to create the perceptual illusion of a curving Earth and testimonies of plane pilots who claim to not see the Earth's curvature at high altitude. Even though these arguments are implausible, it is difficult to maintain that no deliberative thinking was involved in constructing such elaborate theories.

In sum, most beliefs that people have about the world are the result of System 1 thinking, but it is plausible to suspect a role for System 2 thinking in conspiracy beliefs as well. The present chapter seeks to resolve this discrepancy. We will argue that, like other forms of belief (e.g. Gilbert *et al.* 1993; Aarnio, Lindeman 2005; Gervais, Norenzayan 2012) conspiracy beliefs are primarily rooted in System 1 thinking. We will also argue that, after forming initial conspiracy suspicions, however, people subsequently use System 2 processes to justify and rationalise these suspicious sentiments. Through motivated reasoning, perceivers develop extensive and articulate conspiracy theories based on valid arguments, wild speculations or a combination of these. Most conspiracy theories hence *originate* from System 1 thinking, but people *justify and maintain* them through System 2 thinking.

## Cognitive roots: Intuitive versus analytic thinking

Here, we review the evidence for two indicators of System 1 versus System 2 thinking in conspiracy theories: (1) intuitive versus analytic thinking and (2) the intensity of feelings and emotions, most notably anxious uncertainty (i.e. uncertainty as an anxious emotional experience, which is distinct from cognitive uncertainty due to a lack of information), as a result of threatening experiences. If belief in conspiracy theories originates from System 1 thinking, it should be reliably and positively associated with intuitive thinking. In addition, it should be associated with a range of feelings and emotions reflecting anxious uncertainty. If belief in conspiracy theories originates from System 2 thinking, however, it should be reliably and positively associated with analytic thinking, and unrelated, or even negatively related, with feelings of anxious uncertainty.

As to the first indicator, despite the observation that many conspiracy theories are complex and articulate, evidence suggests that belief in such theories is rooted in intuitive thinking. In general, people's beliefs about many societal issues that are subject to conspiracy theories (e.g. climate change, vaccines, nuclear power, G.M.O.) depend strongly on their cultural values or political attitudes (Kahan *et al.* 2011). When these values or attitudes are inconsistent with scientific evidence, people often reject the evidence (Washburn, Skitka 2017). This suggests that people's beliefs about the world largely depend on what they intuitively feel is true.

One set of studies offered a straightforward test of the relationships between intuitive thinking, analytic thinking and conspiracy beliefs. Following experimental manipulations designed to stimulate analytic thinking, participants' belief in conspiracy theories decreased. Measures of intuitive thinking, instead, reliably predicted increased belief in conspiracy theories (Swami *et al.* 2014). Correlational studies support these conclusions. These studies found that analytic thinking is insufficient to promote scepticism towards conspiracy theories; also, the motivation to be rational and base conclusions on evidence is critical. Put differently, only people who combine the skill with the will to think analytically display decreased conspiracy belief (Ståhl, van Prooijen 2018). Furthermore, lower education predicts a slight increase in conspiracy belief, a finding that is mediated by decreased analytic thinking and an increased tendency to perceive simple solutions for the problems that society faces (van Prooijen 2017).

In addition, belief systems that rely heavily on intuitive thinking are associated with greater conspiracy beliefs. Empirical studies have found positive and consistent relationships between conspiracy beliefs and beliefs in the paranormal, pseudoscience, superstition, precognition, witchcraft and extraordinary life forms (Darwin *et al.* 2011; see also Barron *et al.* 2014; Lobato *et al.* 2014; Swami *et al.* 2014; van Prooijen *et al.* 2018). Furthermore, recent studies investigated the phenomenon of 'Bullshit receptivity', which is a tendency to perceive a deeper meaning in statements that are grammatically correct and appear profound, but actually are a randomly chosen string of buzzwords (e.g. 'Hidden meaning transforms unparalleled abstract beauty'). Findings revealed that bullshit receptivity is associated with reduced analytic thinking, increased faith in intuition and increased belief in conspiracy theories (Pennycook *et al.* 2015).

Complementary evidence suggests a role for heuristics and cognitive biases in conspiracy beliefs. Heuristics are mental shortcuts to evaluate complex information quickly and efficiently and are therefore part of System 1 thinking (Kahneman 2011). While heuristics are functional and often lead to correct conclusions with minimal mental effort, they often mislead perceivers into false judgments and bad decisions. One such heuristic is representativeness, which is the idea that the more strongly exemplars resemble a category prototype, the more strongly people assume that this exemplar possesses the salient attributes of this category (Kahneman, Tversky 1972). For instance, people widely regard a sparrow (an exemplar) as more representative for the category 'birds' than an ostrich; people are therefore more likely to assume that a sparrow instead of an ostrich can fly. In this example, the representativeness heuristic produces a correct conclusion (sparrows indeed can fly, and ostriches cannot). In various other instances, however, the representativeness heuristic contributes to cognitive biases.

One such cognitive bias is the conjunction fallacy, which is an error in probabilistic reasoning pertaining to the likelihood that two events co-occur (Tversky, Kahneman 1983). A well-known example of the conjunction fallacy is the 'Linda-problem' in which participants receive a description of a woman named Linda that is representative of the category 'feminists' (e.g. she is 31 years old, single, outspoken, majored in philosophy, and is deeply concerned with issues of discrimination and social injustice). Then, participants rated the likelihood of a range of options that included the following: (a) Linda is a bank teller; or (b) Linda is a bank teller and active in the feminist movement. Statistically, option (a) is always more likely than option (b): The probability of one of the constituents occurring (she is a bank teller) can never be lower than the probability of this constituent co-occurring with a different constituent (besides a bank teller she is also active in the feminist movement). Yet, a majority of participants rated option (b) as more likely than option (a) (Tversky, Kahneman 1983). Of interest for the present purposes, the more often research participants make this conjunction fallacy, the more strongly they believe conspiracy theories (Brotherton, French 2014). This suggest that heuristic thinking, and the biases that result from it, is associated with belief in conspiracy theories.

Another cognitive bias resulting from the representativeness heuristic is stereotyping, that is, (over-)generalised beliefs about groups of people. Various studies suggest that stereotyping is closely associated with belief in conspiracy theories. For instance, one study revealed that, in German samples, conspiracy beliefs are associated with anti-Americanism, and with stereotyping of high-power groups (e.g. managers; politicians: Imhoff, Bruder 2014). Likewise, antisemitism is closely associated with belief in Jewish conspiracy theories (e.g. Kofta, Sedek 2005). Also, individual difference variables that predispose people to stereotyping and prejudice are often associated with belief in specific conspiracy theories, notably authoritarianism (i.e. a tendency to value order and authority) and social dominance orientation (i.e. a tendency to accept or even prefer inequality between groups) (see Abalakina-Paap et al. 1999; Swami 2012).

What are the more specific automatic cognitive processes underlying conspiracy beliefs? Various authors have highlighted the role of at least two processes, namely pattern perception and agency detection (e.g. Shermer 2011; Douglas et al. 2016; van Prooijen, van Vugt 2018). Pattern perception refers to the mind's tendency to perceive causal connections between stimuli. This mental faculty is functional for human beings because many stimuli in fact *are* causally connected, and recognising these causal relationships is essential to survive and stay healthy (e.g. large predators can harm or kill humans; eating contaminated food causes illness). Quite often, however, people mistakenly perceive causal connections that do not exist, referred to as *illusory pattern perception*. For instance, illusory pattern perception is strong among habitual gamblers, who in casinos often perceive patterns in random outcomes (Wilke et al. 2014).

Conspiracy theories by definition contain patterns, that is, assumptions of causal relationships between events, people and objects. For instance, a celebrity can die of a drug overdose without a conspiracy being involved. Once people start seeing a causal link between such an event and a distrusted powerful group (e.g. a secret service agency), however, a conspiracy theory becomes more likely ('the celebrity did not overdose but was murdered'). One interesting hypothesis, therefore, is that people who tend to perceive patterns in random stimuli (i.e. illusory pattern perception) are particularly likely to believe conspiracy theories. Various studies support this hypothesis. Van Prooijen, Douglas and De Inocencio (2018) found that perceiving patterns in random strings of coin toss outcomes, or in the abstract paintings by Jackson Pollock, predicted belief in conspiracy theories. Furthermore, Van der Wal, Sutton, Lange and Braga (2018) presented participants with a range of existing but likely spurious correlations (e.g. chocolate consumption within a country predicts the number of Nobel Prize winners within that country). Results revealed that the more strongly participants believed that these relationships represented actual causal effects, the more strongly they believed conspiracy theories. These findings suggest that a tendency to (over)perceive patterns predicts conspiracy beliefs.

However, other scholars (Dieguez et al. 2015, Wagner-Egger et al. 2018) have failed to observe a link between pattern perception (in coin tosses) and endorsement of conspiracy theories. More research is needed to establish the robustness of the association between conspiracy belief and illusory pattern perception, and its boundary conditions. Furthermore, most findings establishing this link are correlational, and future research needs to establish the causal relationships between pattern perception and conspiracy belief.

The second cognitive process underlying conspiracy theories, agency detection, refers to the mind's tendency to perceive intentionality behind others' actions and events. This mental faculty is functional to regulate social relationships. For instance, recognising if actions were intentional improves accountability judgments, and helps perceivers establish the quality of their interpersonal relationships (e.g. if one gets hurt by a friend, it matters whether one believes that the friend did this on purpose or by accident). Like pattern perception, however, people also regularly detect agency where none exists. Does over-perceiving agency predict belief in conspiracy theories? By definition, conspiracy theories involve agency: Assuming that a group of actors collude in secret to commit harm implies that these actors have a purposeful goal, and hence are agentic. Studies indeed support the idea that over-recognising agency predicts increased belief in conspiracy theories. For instance, belief in conspiracy theories is related with anthropomorphism, that is, ascribing human intentions to non-human stimuli (e.g. assuming that the environment experiences emotions); moreover, it is related with ascribing agency to a series of moving geometric figures on a computer screen (Imhoff, Bruder 2014; Douglas et al. 2016; see also Wagner-Egger et al. 2018).

A cognitive process closely associated with agency detection is teleological thinking, or the tendency to ascribe function and a final cause to natural facts and events. An example would be to view a rainbow at the top of mountain as a 'reward' for a long hike. Teleological thinking often presumes that an entity was behind the observed factor or natural event. For example, the hiker may presume that God has intentionally placed the rainbow there. Nonetheless, Wagner-Egger et al. (2018) have measured the tendency towards teleological thinking in large Swiss and French samples and found that it was correlated with endorsement of conspiracy theories, independently of other forms of agency perception, such as animism (i.e. attribution of consciousness to non-living entities).

In sum, the first indicator of System 1 thinking, intuitive thinking, predicts belief in conspiracy theories. Conspiracy beliefs are related with intuitive belief systems (e.g. belief in the paranormal), heuristic thinking and the automatic cognitive processes of pattern perception and agency detection. Analytic thinking instead predicts *decreased* belief in conspiracy theories. These findings support the assertion that conspiracy theories originate from System 1 thinking.

## Cognitive roots: Threat and uncertainty

A second indicator of System 1 versus System 2 thinking is the intensity by which people have feelings and emotions that are associated with threatening experiences: System 1 thinking can be 'hot' and emotional, whereas System 2 thinking tends to be 'cold' and calculative (Kahneman 2011). One pertinent finding in conspiracy theory research is that particularly emotions or feelings reflecting uncertainty and fear increase belief in conspiracy theories. Conspiracy theories surge particularly following distressing and anxiety-provoking societal events, such as natural disasters, terrorist strikes, wars, economic crises and rapid societal change (e.g. Hofstadter 1966; Pipes 1997; van Prooijen, Douglas 2017, 2018). Studies indeed found that threatening and consequential societal events (e.g. a political leader dies) elicit stronger conspiracy beliefs than societal events that are less threatening or consequential, and therefore less likely to elicit feelings of anxious uncertainty (e.g. a political leader gets in a dangerous situation but survives; McCauley, Jacques 1979; van Prooijen, van Dijk 2014).

Both experimental and correlational studies have examined the role of feelings and emotions in conspiracy thinking more directly. For instance, in a range of experiments participants recalled a situation in which either they were in full control or lacked control. Lacking control is an experience closely associated with anxious uncertainty and, indeed, participants who recalled a situation where they lacked control subsequently reported stronger conspiracy beliefs than participants who recalled a situation where they had control (Whitson, Galinsky 2008; van Prooijen,

Acker 2015: Study 1). Likewise, subjective uncertainty (van Prooijen, Jostmann 2013) and threats to the societal status quo (Jolley *et al.* 2018) increase conspiracy thinking. Finally, attitudinal ambivalence – an unpleasant experience closely associated with feelings of anxious uncertainty, characterised by mixed (i.e. both positive and negative) evaluations of an attitude-object – increases belief in conspiracy theories (Van Harreveld *et al.* 2014). These findings suggest that feelings and emotions associated with threatening experiences causally influence belief in conspiracy theories.

Correlational findings are consistent with these observations. Numerous studies have found relationships of conspiracy beliefs with dispositional anxiety (Grzesiak-Feldman 2013), death-related anxiety (Newheiser *et al.* 2011), lack of control (van Prooijen, Acker 2015: Study 2), self-uncertainty (van Prooijen 2016), powerlessness (Abalakina-Paap *et al.* 1999) and system identity threat, that is, the perception that society's fundamental values are changing (Federico *et al.* 2018). While these correlations do not show that conspiracy theories originate from these feelings or emotions (and, indeed, the links between feelings, emotions and conspiracy beliefs are likely to be bidirectional; e.g. Douglas *et al.* 2017; van Prooijen, Douglas 2018), they are consistent with a model suggesting that System 1 thinking plays a prominent role in conspiracy beliefs.

The above evidence is limited by pertaining to negative feelings and emotions only. One study experimentally tested the causal influence of both emotional valence (i.e. positive versus negative) and emotional uncertainty, however (Whitson *et al.* 2015). Specifically, some negative emotions imply uncertainty about the world (e.g. worry and fear), but some positive emotions do so as well (e.g. surprise and hope). Likewise, some negative emotions imply certainty about the world (e.g. anger and disgust) as do some positive emotions (happiness and contentment). Interestingly, the results revealed that, not emotional balance, but emotional uncertainty increased conspiracy beliefs. These findings suggest that both positive and negative emotions may drive conspiracy beliefs, but only if they imply feelings of uncertainty about the world.

Trust is another crucial ingredient in conspiracy theories. When information comes from a trustworthy source, people are less likely to scrutinise it, which may result in accepting it using System 1 thinking. Conversely, distrust is likely to trigger the use of more reflection and critical appraisals of information. This implies that, when people feel disenfranchised, they may distrust official accounts and embrace conspiracy theories more easily. Conversely, trust in authorities may similarly foster a blind adhesion to official accounts (Miller *et al.* 2016).

Taken together, these findings suggest a prominent role for threatening experiences in conspiracy beliefs. Strong feelings and emotions that are closely coupled with anxious uncertainty drives belief in conspiracy theories. These findings complement the findings on intuition and heuristics, and further support the notion that conspiracy theories originate from fast (System 1) mental processes.

## Complex conspiracy theories

Does all of this imply that System 2 is not involved in conspiracy thinking? Assuming a lack of System 2 thinking is difficult to reconcile with the observation that many conspiracy theories are rather elaborate. Debating a committed 'conspiracy theorist' can be challenging (particularly if one enters the debate unprepared). For instance, the common conspiracy theory that the 9/11 terrorist strikes were an inside job by the U.S. government is based on extensive analyses of the temperatures at which steel melts, the maximum temperatures produced by burning kerosene, expert testimonies and analyses of video footage that seem to suggest hidden explosives in the Twin Towers.

Quite often, these deliberative analyses combine correct scientific facts with incorrect inferences, wild speculations and a selective assessment of the evidence. For instance, steel indeed melts at about 2750°F and burning kerosene only reaches a maximum of about 1500°F (a correct scientific fact). Raising this scientific fact as evidence for controlled demolition assumes, however, that it was necessary for the steel construction to melt in order for the building to collapse (an incorrect inference). In fact, the maximum temperatures reached by burning kerosene were more than enough to weaken the steel constructions of the Twin Towers up to the point that it could not carry the weight of the higher floors anymore, causing the buildings to collapse (for details, see Dunbar, Reagan 2011). Moreover, these conspiracy theories often include expert testimonies that support the theory (e.g. engineers who believe that the Twin Towers collapsed through controlled demolition) and ignore expert testimonies to the contrary (e.g. engineers who do not believe that the Twin Towers collapsed through controlled demolition).

These observations suggest that deliberative (System 2) thinking is involved when assessing these complex conspiracy theories. Such System 2 thinking appears to be motivated, however, by a desire to find evidence in support of the conspiracy theory. Put differently, while analytic thinking may lead some perceivers to *un*believe a conspiracy theory (Swami *et al.* 2014; see also Gilbert *et al.* 1993), it may help other perceivers to find evidence for a conspiracy that they started out assuming to exist. For example, Republicans who are motivated to believe that Democrats conspire are likely to find such evidence, and vice versa (Uscinski, Parent 2014; Miller *et al.* 2016).

These propositions are consistent with the basic notion that people are motivated to maintain a coherent worldview, in which beliefs and actions converge with their knowledge about the world (e.g. Festinger 1957). This implies a regular challenge to cope with information that is inconsistent with one's beliefs, however. For instance, people who believe that climate change is a hoax will inevitably come across – and may even actively pay attention to – news reports about melting icecaps in the Arctic, extreme weather in various parts of the worlds and reports of rising global temperatures. People can resolve such discrepancies in various ways, which sometimes may include adjusting their beliefs (e.g. people may accept the evidence that climate change is real). Alternatively, however, people might resolve such discrepancies through motivated reasoning strategies that enable them to uphold their beliefs. These strategies include invalidating the sources of the information (e.g. the news reports were produced by a conspiracy to persuade people of climate change) or embracing other explanations that preserve the worldview that they had prior to the discrepant information (e.g. climate change may be real but it was not caused by human activity; Kahan *et al.* 2011). Maintaining one's worldview may not only fulfil individual-level motives but also serve to maintain one's integration in important social groups, especially when these beliefs are central to the ideology of these groups. The need to achieve objective and accurate knowledge may be less crucial than to preserve one's social integration.

Such motivated reasoning is hence more complicated than the simple assertion that people believe whatever they want to believe. Instead, people's motivation to uphold a certain belief influences what information they consider, and how much value they place in each source of information. For instance, people often selectively embrace, or avoid, information to arrive at a certain conclusion (Sweeny *et al.* 2010). Perceivers might experience this information search as an objective epistemic analysis, yet it was likely to confirm the preferred conclusions. It is easy to find some support for almost any conspiracy theory (e.g. one empirical study about climate change that turned out fraudulent); likewise, it is easy to find some contradictory evidence for almost any scientific theory (e.g. a climate change model that failed to produce accurate predictions). It has been noted that people endorse lower evidentiary standards for preferred conclusions ('*Can* I believe this?') as opposed to un-preferred conclusions ('*Must* I believe this?'), resulting in a confirmation of one's initial beliefs (Epley, Gilovich, 2016). Put differently, when assessing conspiracy theories, people often do not act like independent scientists or judges, but as lawyers motivated to defend their case.

The idea that people intuitively make assumptions of conspiracies (based on System 1 thinking) and then selectively search for evidence to support their theory (which involves System 2 thinking) is consistent with broader models of human morality. These models are relevant for the current purposes, as arguably a conspiracy theory is a specific judgment of immoral behaviour (i.e. assumptions that actors develop evil schemes in secret and then carry them out). Notably, the social intuitionist model of morality (Haidt 2001) asserts that people form moral judgments intuitively, based on subjective feelings of right or wrong. People are then motivated to make sense of such feelings, however, and may occasionally be challenged to explain their moral judgments. To justify their moral sentiments, therefore, people search for rational reasons why they feel a certain way. Research offers evidence for this process, for instance by showing that people maintain their moral judgments even if they fail to find rational arguments – a phenomenon referred to as 'moral dumbfounding' (Haidt 2001).

In a famous study to illuminate these principles, Haidt (2001) first presented a text describing how a brother and sister end up having sexual intercourse together on their holiday, and then asked research participants whether it was morally right or wrong for them to do so. Participants largely felt that it was morally wrong for a brother and sister to have sex. Haidt then asked participants to explain *why* they felt this way, however. Interestingly, the text rebutted most of the standard arguments that people raise against incestuous brother-sister relationships. These arguments include the risk of inbreeding (they used two types of contraceptives); the risk of damaging their relationship (after the experience they felt closer than ever before); the risk of hurting their parents (they were abroad and kept the experience a special secret); the risk of abuse or pressure (the experience was fully consensual by two mature adults); and the risk of a slippery slope (they agreed to do it only once). After a while, many participants gave up trying to give rational reasons – but typically without altering their moral judgment. Apparently, a deep intuitive feeling of right and wrong shaped participants' moral judgments (i.e. incestuous brother-sister relationships are morally wrong), and they subsequently searched for rational reasons to support these sentiments.

A similar process is likely for conspiracy theories. When first confronted with a distressing societal event, perceivers may intuitively conclude that the event is suspect or that the facts do not add up (e.g. the death of Princess Diana cannot have been an accident). Perceivers want to make sense of these suspicious sentiments, however, and therefore try to find evidence for an initial suspicion that a conspiracy was responsible. Through motivated reasoning, perceivers selectively embrace evidence for a cover-up and dismiss evidence to the contrary. The result is an elaborate and sophisticated theory that appears well-grounded in reason and evidence. These processes rarely take place in isolation. People seek and evaluate evidence through communication with others, especially in-group members. The selective focus on evidence supporting one's beliefs can be amplified in 'echo chambers' in which such communication takes place (e.g. Internet; Klein *et al.* 2015).

In sum, we propose that the two basic modules of the human mind – System 1 and System 2 – are both involved in conspiracy theories. Through System 1 processes, people accept the basic premises of a conspiracy theory. System 2 processes, then, can have two distinct implications. Analytic thinking may lead some perceivers to *un*believe a conspiracy theory (Swami *et al.* 2014; see also Gilbert *et al.* 1993). For other perceivers, however (presumably those deeply invested in the idea that there must have been a conspiracy), analytic thinking may become part of a motivated reasoning process that reinforces the conspiracy theory into an elaborate and carefully crafted narrative.

## What about real conspiracies?

In this section, we address two remaining concerns. First, what do the cognitive processes described here imply for anti-corruption efforts that include uncovering actual conspiracies (e.g. the Iran-Contra Affair)? Second and relatedly, what do these insights imply for people who disbelieve conspiracy theories – do conspiracy sceptics accept non-conspiratorial narratives through similar cognitive processes, making them relatively oblivious to actual corruption?

As to the first concern, some scholars mistakenly propose that psychology as a discipline assumes that conspiracy beliefs are mostly irrational (e.g. Butter, Knight 2015). This, for instance, ignores the rich tradition within psychology to examine the causes of actual corruption and conspiracies (e.g. Weisel, Shalvi 2015; for overviews, see Köbis et al. 2016; van Prooijen, van Lange 2016), as well as the role of self-interest and dishonesty in human behaviour (e.g. Batson et al. 1997; Gino, Wiltermuth 2014). Psychological definitions of conspiracy theories do not assume them false per se, nor does the psychological approach imply a value judgment of believers or non-believers (van Prooijen 2018).

Instead, psychologists focus on individual or social factors that statistically predict *degrees* of conspiracy thinking. Some conspiracy theories are possible or even plausible (e.g. allegations that secret service agencies regularly violate privacy laws), while other conspiracy theories are unlikely in light of logic or scientific evidence (e.g. Chem-trail conspiracy theories). Citizens structurally differ in how many conspiracy theories they endorse, however, and how credible they find them (e.g. Goertzel 1994; Swami et al. 2011). Our arguments pertain to factors that predict people's susceptibility to unproven conspiracy narratives. Investigating such susceptibility does not make assumptions of how valid a specific conspiracy claim is. For instance, concluding that intuitive thinking statistically predicts an increased susceptibility to a range of conspiracy theories is quite different from assuming that Watergate did not happen. In fact, evolutionary psychology proposes that the human tendency to believe conspiracy theories evolved as an adaptive mechanism among ancestral humans to cope with the dangers of hostile coalitions, that is, truly existing conspiracies (van Prooijen, Van Vugt 2018).

What do the cognitive processes described in this chapter imply for legitimate suspicions of corruption? Would a police detective, who ends up uncovering a major conspiracy committing corporate fraud, also use System 1 and 2 processes in a similar fashion? We speculate here that quite often such a detective indeed might go through a similar mental sequence. Many corruption investigations start with an inconclusive piece of evidence that prompts an intuitive suspicion that 'something is fishy' (System 1), which subsequently warrants a more extensive investigation (System 2). This investigation, then, includes assessing eyewitness testimonies, collecting objective evidence such as payment transactions and consulting legal experts to establish if, and in what specific way, the suspected conspirators broke the law.

In fact, quite often the System 2 processes that are involved during such a police investigation may be comparable to the motivated reasoning account described in this chapter. Motivated reasoning is at the core of tunnel vision, which is common in legal investigations, and has led to many innocent convictions (Findley, Scott 2006). An important challenge, therefore – for both police detectives and concerned citizens – is to evaluate all the available evidence for actual conspiracies objectively, including pieces of evidence that are inconsistent with one's initial suspicions. To reduce the number of false-positives when trying to uncover existing conspiracies, people need to resist the temptation of acting like lawyers defending their case, but instead should behave like impartial judges or scientists (Epley, Gilovich 2016).

A second and related concern is what the propositions of the present chapter imply for citizens who *dis*believe most conspiracy theories. We speculate that the cognitive processes underlying such disbelief can take two distinct forms. One form is that people may disbelieve conspiracy theories through similar cognitive processes. In these cases, people intuitively believe in the nonexistence of a conspiracy, and then justify this intuition through motivated reasoning. This process may lead perceivers to ignore actual malpractice (e.g. Republicans who, as the Watergate scandal unfolded, firmly believed in Nixon's innocence until he resigned). Both belief and disbelief in conspiracy theories can be rooted in the cognitive processes described here.

A different form of disbelief, however, is the result of habitually processing information objectively and critically. We propose that the tendency to rely on impartial analytic thinking and value objective evidence is at the core of scepticism (Ståhl, van Prooijen 2018). Of importance, scepticism does *not* imply gullibly accepting any official statement of power holders, nor does it imply gullibly accepting any bizarre conspiracy theory. Instead, it implies a humble awareness that one's initial intuitions may be mistaken, along with a reliance on evidence, reason and logic to come to objective conclusions. The sceptic approach thus involves a critical analysis of policy proposals or official readings of distressing events, but, also, a critical analysis of conspiracy theories. Sceptics also may form initial impressions of societal events through System 1 processes, but, in contrast to non-sceptics, they subsequently are more likely to unbelieve these first impressions through System 2 processes untainted by motivated reasoning.

## Conclusion

> What is most opposed to the discovery of truth is not the false appearance that proceeds from things and leads to error or even directly a weakness of the intellect. On the contrary, it is the preconceived opinion, the prejudice, which, as a spurious a priori, is opposed to truth.
>
> *Schopenhauer, A. (1974 [1851]: 14)*

In the present chapter, we highlighted the cognitive processes underlying belief in conspiracy theories, and particularly challenged the notion that such beliefs are rooted only in System 1 thinking. The human mind is complex, and instead of being mutually exclusive, Systems 1 and 2 are complementary when people process information about the social world (Kahneman 2011). Specifying the role of both mental systems may integrate empirical findings suggesting a role of intuition (Swami *et al.* 2014) and emotion (Whitson *et al.* 2015) in conspiracy thinking, with the articulate nature of many conspiracy theories. We conclude that conspiracy beliefs largely originate through System 1 processes, yet people justify and sustain them through System 2 processes. Schopenhauer may have underestimated the role of reasoning in the quest for truth: Reason can greatly assist preconceived opinions in paving the road to conspiracy beliefs.

## References

Aarnio, K. and Lindeman, M. (2005) 'Paranormal beliefs, education, and thinking styles' *Personality and Individual Differences*, 39(7): 1227–36.

Abalakina-Paap, M., Stephan, W., Craig, T. and Gregory, W.L. (1999) 'Beliefs in conspiracies', *Political Psychology*, 20(7): 637–47.

Batson, C.D., Kobrynowicz, D., Dinnerstein, J.L., Kampf, H.C. and Wilson, A.D. (1997) 'In a very different voice: unmasking moral hypocrisy', *Journal of Personality and Social Psychology*, 72(6): 1335–48.
Barron, D., Morgan, K., Towell, T., Altemeyer, B. and Swami, V. (2014) 'Associations betweenschizotypy and belief in conspiracist ideation', *Personality and Individual Differences*, 70: 156–9.
Brotherton, R. and French, C.C. (2014) 'Belief in conspiracy theories and susceptibility to the conjunction fallacy', *Applied Cognitive Psychology*, 28(2): 238–48.
Butter, M. and Knight, P. (2015) 'Bridging the great divide: conspiracy theory research for the 21st century', *Diogenes*, 1(249–50): 21–39.
Darwin, H., Neave, N. and Holmes, J. (2011) 'Belief in conspiracy theories: the role of paranormal belief, paranoid ideation and schizotypy', *Personality and Individual Differences*, 50(8): 1289–93.
Dieguez, S., Wagner-Egger, P. and Gauvrit, N. (2015) 'Nothing happens by accident, or does it? A low prior for randomness does not explain belief in conspiracy theories', *Psychological science*, 26(11): 1762–70.
Douglas, K.M., Sutton, R.M., Callan, M.J., Dawtry, R.J. and Harvey, A.J. (2016) 'Someone is pulling the strings: hypersensitive agency detection and belief in conspiracy theories', *Thinking and Reasoning*, 22(1): 57–77.
Douglas, K.M., Sutton, R.M. and Cichocka, A. (2017) 'The psychology of conspiracy theories', *Current Directions in Psychological Science*, 26: 538–42.
Dunbar, D. and Reagan, B. (2011) *Debunking 9/11 myths: why conspiracy theories can't stand up to the facts*, New York, NY: Hearst Books.
Epley, N. and Gilovich, T. (2016) 'The mechanics of motivated reasoning', *Journal of Economic Perspectives*, 30(3): 133–40.
Evans, J.S. (2008) 'Dual-processing accounts of reasoning, judgment, and social cognition', *Annual Review of Psychology*, 59: 255–78.
Federico, C.M., Williams, A.L. and Vitriol, J.A. (2018) 'The role of system identity threaten conspiracy theory endorsement', *European Journal of Social Psychology*, 48(7): 927–38.
Festinger, F. (1957) *A theory of cognitive dissonance*, Stanford, CA: Stanford University Press.
Findley, K.A. and Scott, M.S. (2006) 'The multiple dimensions of tunnel vision in legal cases', *Wisconsin Law Review*, 2: 291–397.
Gervais, W.M. and Norenzayan, A. (2012) 'Analytic thinking promotes religious disbelief', *Science*, 336(6080): 493–6.
Gilbert, D.T., Tafarodi, R.W. and Malone, P.S. (1993) 'You can't not believe everything you read', *Journal of Personality and Social Psychology*, 65(2): 221–33.
Gino, F. and Wiltermuth, S. (2014) 'Evil genius? How dishonesty can lead to greater creativity', *Psychological Science*, 25(4): 973–81.
Goertzel, T. (1994) 'Belief in conspiracy theories', *Political Psychology*, 15(4): 733–44.
Grzesiak-Feldman, M. (2013) 'The effect of high-anxiety situations on conspiracy thinking', *Current Psychology*, 32(1): 100–18.
Haidt, J. (2001) 'The emotional dog and its rational tail: a social intuitionist approach to moral judgment', *Psychological Review*, 108(4): 814–34.
Hofstadter, R. (1966) 'The paranoid style in American politics', in R. Hofstadter, *The paranoid style in American politics and other essays*, New York, NY: Knopf, pp. 3–40.
Imhoff, R. and Bruder, M. (2014) 'Speaking (un-)truth to power: conspiracy mentality as a generalized political attitude', *European Journal of Personality*, 28(1): 25–43.
Jolley, D., Douglas, K.M. and Sutton, R.M. (2018) 'Blaming a few bad apples to save a threatened barrel: the system-justifying function of conspiracy theories', *Political Psychology*, 39(2): 465–78.
Kahan, D.M., Jenkins-Smith, H. and Braman, D. (2011) 'Cultural cognition of scientific Consensus', *Journal of Risk Research*, 14(2): 147–74.
Kahneman, D. (2011) *Thinking, fast and slow*, New York, NY: Farrar, Straus and Giroux.
Kahneman, D. and Tversky, A. (1972) 'Subjective probability: a judgment of representativeness', *Cognitive Psychology*, 3(3): 430–54.
Klein, O., Van der Linden, N., Pantazi, M. and Kissine, M. (2015) 'Behind the screen conspirators: paranoid social cognition in an online age', in M. Bilewicz, A. Cichocka and W. Soral (eds.) *The Psychology of Conspiracy*, London: Routledge, pp. 162–82.
Köbis, N., van Prooijen, J.-W., Righetti, F. and van Lange, P.A.M. (2016) 'Prospection in individual and interpersonal corruption dilemmas', *Review of General Psychology*, 20(1): 71–85.

Kofta, M. and Sedek, G. (2005) 'Conspiracy stereotypes of Jews during systemic transformation in Poland', *International Journal of Sociology*, 35(1): 40–64.

Lobato, E., Mendoza, J., Sims, V. and Chin, M. (2014) 'Examining the relationship between conspiracy theories, paranormal beliefs, and pseudoscience acceptance among a university population', *Applied Cognitive Psychology*, 28(5): 617–25.

McCauley, C. and Jacques, S. (1979) 'The popularity of conspiracy theories of presidential assassination: a Bayesian analysis', *Journal of Personality and Social Psychology*, 37(5): 637–44.

Miller, J.M., Saunders, K.L. and Farhart, C.E. (2016) 'Conspiracy endorsement as motivated reasoning: the moderating roles of political knowledge and trust', *American Journal of Political Science*, 60(4): 824–44.

Newheiser, A.-K., Farias, M. and Tausch, N. (2011) 'The functional nature of conspiracy beliefs: examining the underpinnings of belief in the *Da Vinci Code* conspiracy', *Personality and Individual Differences*, 51(8): 1007–11.

Pantazi, M., Klein, O. and Kissine, M. (2018) 'The power of the truth bias: false information affects memory and judgment even in the absence of distraction', *Social Cognition*, 36(2): 167–98.

Pennycook, G., Cheyne, J.A., Barr, N., Koehler, D. and Fugelsang, J.A. (2015) 'On the reception and detection of pseudo-profound bullshit', *Judgment and Decision Making*, 10(6): 549–63.

Pipes, D. (1997) *Conspiracy: how the paranoid style flourishes and where it comes from*, New York, NY: Simon & Schusters.

Ritter, R.S., Preston, J.L. and Hernandez, I. (2014) 'Happy tweets: Christians are happier, more socially connected, and less analytical than atheists on Twitter', *Social Psychological and Personality Science*, 5(2): 243–9.

Schopenhauer, A. (1974 [1851]) *Parerga and Paralipomena: Short Philosophical Essays*, vol. 2, E. F. J. Payne (ed.), Oxford: Clarendon Press.

Shermer, M. (2011) *The believing brain: from ghosts and gods to politics and conspiracies—how we construct beliefs and reinforce them as truths*, New York, NY: Henry Holt.

Ståhl, T. and van Prooijen, J.-W. (2018) 'Epistemic rationality: skepticism toward unfounded beliefs requires sufficient cognitive ability and motivation to be rational', *Personality and Individual Differences*, 122: 155–63.

Swami, V. (2012) 'Social psychological origins of conspiracy theories: the case of the Jewish conspiracy theory in Malaysia', *Frontiers in Psychology*, 3: 1–9.

Swami, V., Coles, R., Stieger, S., Pietschnig, J., Furnham, A., Rehim, S. and Voracek, M. (2011) 'Conspiracist ideation in Britain and Austria: evidence of a monological belief system and associations between individual psychological differences and real-world and fictitious conspiracy theories', *British Journal of Psychology*, 102(3): 443–63.

Swami, V., Voracek, M., Stieger, S. Tran, U.S. and Furnham, A. (2014) 'Analytic thinking reduces belief in conspiracy theories', *Cognition*, 133(3): 572–85.

Sweeny, K., Melnyk, D., Miller, W. and Shepperd, J.A. (2010) 'Information avoidance: who, what, when, and why', *Review of General Psychology*, 14(4): 340.

Tversky, A. and Kahneman, D. (1983) 'Extensional versus intuitive reasoning: the conjunction fallacy in probability judgement', *Psychological Review*, 90(4): 293–315.

Uscinski, J.E. and Parent, J.M. (2014) *American conspiracy theories*, New York, NY: Oxford University Press.

Van der Wal, R., Sutton, R.M., Lange, J. and Braga, J. (2018) 'Suspicious binds: conspiracy thinking and tenuous perceptions of causal connections between co-occurring and spuriously correlated events', *European Journal of Social Psychology*, 48(7): 970–89.

Van Harreveld, F., Rutjens, B.T., Schneider, I.K., Nohlen, H.U. and Keskinis, K (2014) 'In doubt and disorderly: ambivalence promotes compensatory perceptions of order', *Journal of Experimental Psychology: General*, 143(4): 1666–76.

Van Prooijen, J.-W. (2016) 'Sometimes inclusion breeds suspicion: self-uncertainty and belongingness predict belief in conspiracy theories', *European Journal of Social Psychology*, 46(3): 267–79.

Van Prooijen, J.-W. (2017) 'Why education predicts decreased belief in conspiracy theories', *Applied Cognitive Psychology*, 31(1): 50–8.

Van Prooijen, J.-W. (2018) *The psychology of conspiracy theories*, Oxon, UK: Routledge.

Van Prooijen, J.-W. and Acker, M. (2015) 'The influence of control on belief in conspiracy theories: conceptual and applied extensions', *Applied Cognitive Psychology*, 29(5): 753–61.

Van Prooijen, J.-W. and Douglas, K.M. (2017) 'Conspiracy theories as part of history: the role of societal crisis situations', *Memory Studies*, 10(3): 323–33.

Van Prooijen, J.-W. and Douglas, K.M. (2018) 'Belief in conspiracy theories: basic principles of an emerging research domain', *European Journal of Social Psychology*, 48(7): 897–908.

Van Prooijen, J.-W., Douglas, K.M. and De Inocencio, C. (2018) 'Connecting the dots: illusory pattern perception predicts beliefs in conspiracies and the supernatural', *European Journal of Social Psychology*, 48(3): 320–35.

Van Prooijen, J.-W. and Jostmann, N.B. (2013) 'Belief in conspiracy theories: the influence of uncertainty and perceived morality', *European Journal of Social Psychology*, 43(1): 109–15.

Van Prooijen, J.-W. and van Dijk, E. (2014) 'When consequence size predicts belief in conspiracy theories: the moderating role of perspective taking', *Journal of Experimental Social Psychology*, 55: 63–73.

Van Prooijen, J.-W. and van Vugt, M. (2018) 'Conspiracy theories: evolved functions and psychological mechanisms', *Perspectives on Psychological Science*, 13(6): 770–88.

Wagner-Egger, P., Bronner, G., Delouvée, S., Dieguez, S. and Gauvrit, N. (2019) 'Why 'healthy conspiracy theories' are (oxy)morons: statistical, epistemological, and psychological reasons in favor of the (ir)rational view', *Social Epistemology Review and Reply Collective*, 8(3): 50–67.

Wagner-Egger, P., Delouvée, S., Gauvrit, N. and Dieguez, S. (2018) 'Creationism and conspiracism share a common teleological bias', *Current Biology*, 28(16): R867–R868.

Washburn, A.N. and Skitka, L.J. (2017) 'Science denial across the political divide: liberals and conservatives are similarly motivated to deny attitude-inconsistent science', *Social Psychological and Personality Science*, 9(8): 972–80.

Weisel, O. and Shalvi, S. (2015) 'The collaborative roots of corruption', *Proceedings of the National Academy of Sciences*, 112(34): 10651–6.

Whitson, J.A. and Galinsky, A.D. (2008) 'Lacking control increases illusory pattern perception', *Science*, 322(5898): 115–7.

Whitson, J.A., Galinsky, A.D. and Kay, A. (2015) 'The emotional roots of conspiratorial perceptions, system justification, and belief in the paranormal', *Journal of Experimental Social Psychology*, 56: 89–95.

Wilke, A., Scheibehenne, B., Gaissmaier, W., McCanney, P. and Barrett, H.C. (2014) 'Illusory pattern detection in habitual gamblers', *Evolution and Human Behavior*, 35(4): 291–7.

Wright, T.L. and Arbuthnot, J. (1974) 'Interpersonal trust, political preference, and perceptions of the Watergate affair', *Personality and Social Psychology Bulletin*, 1(1): 168–70.

# 2.3
# MOTIVATIONS, EMOTIONS AND BELIEF IN CONSPIRACY THEORIES

*Karen M. Douglas, Aleksandra Cichocka and Robbie M. Sutton*

## Introduction

When we tell people that we study the psychology of conspiracy theories, they always ask: 'Why do people believe in them?' However, there is no easy answer to this question. There are many psychological reasons why conspiracy theories appeal to people, and much of this section of the handbook is dedicated to these explanations. This is also not to mention the other sections of this handbook that explore the social, historical, cultural and political foundations of conspiracy belief. Conspiracy theories are complicated, and the reasons people believe them are also complicated. However, in the past ten years or so, it has become somewhat easier to explain why conspiracy theories are so popular, since research on the psychological, social and political underpinnings of conspiracy belief has flourished during this time (Douglas, Sutton 2018; Douglas *et al.* 2019). In this chapter, we explore some of the psychological factors, specifically focusing on the motivational and emotional reasons why people adopt conspiracy theories. As we will see, more is known about the former than the latter, but this opens up many exciting opportunities for future research.

## Motivations

In reviewing the literature to date, Douglas, Sutton and Cichocka (2017) proposed a framework of the motives that people have for adopting conspiracy theories. Specifically, they argued that people are drawn to conspiracy theories when — compared with non-conspiracy explanations — they appear to satisfy three important social psychological motives. These motives are epistemic (e.g. the desire for understanding, accuracy and subjective certainty), existential (e.g. the desire for control and security) and social (e.g. the desire to maintain a positive image of the self or group; see also Jost *et al.* 2008). In other words, as a specific type of causal explanation, conspiracy theories allow people to understand the reasons underlying important events and circumstances in a way that addresses their broader motivational concerns to feel knowledgeable, safe and good about the self.

## Feeling knowledgeable: Epistemic motives

When something important happens or something worrying is happening in society, people naturally want answers. Finding causal explanations for events is an important part of building up a stable, accurate and internally consistent understanding of the world (Heider 1958). One of the most important psychological processes involved in this knowledge-seeking endeavour is the cognitive tendency to search for patterns and meaning. Social psychological research has shown that people are averse to the randomness of socio-political events and impose meaning on it cognitively by perceiving patterns in events, and making causal explanations, even when they do not exist (Zhao et al. 2014). Scholars have argued that beliefs in conspiracy theories are a response to this randomness (Wilman 1998; Spark 2000; Barkun 2003).

Social psychological research supports this argument. For example, van Prooijen, Douglas and de Inocencio (2018) measured belief in conspiracy theories alongside the tendency to see patterns in random stimuli (e.g. random coin tosses, abstract art paintings). They found that the tendency to see patterns where they did not exist – that is *illusory pattern perception* – was significantly associated with the tendency to believe in conspiracy theories. Further evidence supports the link between pattern perception and conspiracy beliefs. In events that are objectively structured, but between which no direct causal links exist (so called *spurious correlations* such as the relationship between national chocolate consumption and Nobel Prizes), van der Wal, Sutton, Lange and Braga (2018) found that beliefs that these events are directly causally connected were associated with belief in conspiracy theories. These findings provide evidence that seeing patterns and causal connections where they do not (or are very unlikely to) exist contributes to beliefs in conspiracy theories. Related findings have shown that conspiracy beliefs are associated with the tendency to overestimate the likelihood of co-occurring events (Brotherton, French 2014) and the tendency to detect agency and intentionality where it does not exist (Douglas et al. 2016), such as in the movement of random shapes on a screen or the intentional actions of inanimate objects. Attempting to satisfy the epistemic motive to gain meaning and knowledge may therefore sometimes lead people to look in the wrong places.

Other studies support the argument that conspiracy theories appeal to people for epistemic reasons. For example, beliefs in conspiracy theories appear stronger for people who routinely seek meaning and patterns in the environment, including believers in paranormal and other types of supernatural phenomena (e.g. Bruder et al. 2013; van Prooijen et al. 2018; but see Dieguez et al. 2015). Belief in conspiracy theories also appears to be stronger when events are especially large in scale such as when a president is killed, and people are therefore dissatisfied with mundane, small-scale explanations (Leman, Cinnirella 2013). This is related to the *proportionality bias* in which explanations for events must be on a similar scale to the event itself. So, when people are seeking an accurate explanation for an event, a small explanation does not seem satisfactory. Furthermore, Marchlewska, Cichocka and Kossowska (2017) found that the *need for cognitive closure* – is the motivation to seek out information that provides firm answers and avoids ambiguity (Kruglanski, Webster, 1996 – is associated with beliefs in salient conspiracy theories for events that lack clear official explanations. Finally, some research suggests that conspiracy belief is stronger when people experience distress as a result of feeling uncertain (van Prooijen, Jostmann 2013). As an aversive mental state, people attempt to reduce uncertainty and seek answers in conspiracy theories.

Research also suggests that people are attracted to conspiracy theories when they lack the ability or motivation to seek information elsewhere. For example, belief in conspiracy theories is correlated with lower levels of analytic thinking, meaning that people who do not adopt a methodical or step-by-step approach to thinking and problem-solving are more likely to succumb to conspiracy theories rather than seeking information from more credible sources (Swami et al. 2014). Furthermore, belief in conspiracy theories is consistently related to lower levels of education (Douglas et al. 2016), meaning that a lack of appropriate skills and tools to gather and filter information attracts people to less credible reports of events. People are also likely to believe in multiple conspiracy theories, even when they directly contradict each other (Wood et al. 2012). The motivation to seek meaning and order therefore may backfire for people who do not have the experiences that allow them to tell what information is reliable and what is not.

In summary, there is growing evidence that people are drawn to conspiracy theories to help them gain knowledge and accuracy. Whether or not these epistemic motives are met is a question that we return to later in this chapter.

## Feeling safe and secure: Existential motives

As well as their epistemic functions, causal explanations serve the need for people to feel safe and secure in their world and to exert control over their existence as autonomous individuals and as members of groups (Tetlock 2002). Scholars have suggested that people turn to conspiracy theories for compensatory satisfaction when these needs are threatened. For example, people who lack instrumental control may be able to find some compensatory sense of control by adopting conspiracy theories, because conspiracy theories offer people the opportunity to reject official narratives and feel that they possess some power by having an alternative perspective (Goertzel 1994).

Research supports this account of the motivation behind conspiracy belief. For example, studies have shown that people are likely to turn to conspiracy theories when they are anxious, such as when students are waiting to take an exam (Grzesiak-Feldman 2013). Other findings suggest that people who feel chronically powerless tend to believe in conspiracy theories more (Abalakina-Paap et al. 1999). Other research indicates that this might be even more important in the context of socio-political control. Specifically, Bruder and colleagues (2013) found that conspiracy belief is strongly related to lack of socio-political control or lack of psychological empowerment. Further supporting the idea that control is an important determinant of conspiracy belief, experimental studies have shown that, compared with baseline conditions, conspiracy belief is heightened when people feel unable to control outcomes and is reduced when their sense of control is affirmed (van Prooijen, Acker 2015). Finally, the experience of feeling that one's society is under threat (e.g. Jolley et al. 2017; Federico et al. 2018) is associated with belief in conspiracy theories.

Further support for the link between existential motives and conspiracy belief comes from research linking conspiracy beliefs with early child-caregiver experiences and relationships. Specifically, Green and Douglas (2018) measured beliefs in conspiracy theories alongside their attachment style (Bowlby 1982 [1969]). The primary goal of attachment behaviour is to alleviate feelings of anxiety and increase a sense of security. Attachment styles (avoidant, attachment and secure) result from early childhood experiences with primary caregivers and can persist throughout life, influencing how people experience their adult relationships. Green and Douglas (2018) found that anxious attachment style – which is characterised by a preoccupation with security and a tendency to exaggerate threats – significantly predicted conspiracy belief when the other two attachment styles did not. People may therefore adopt conspiracy theories in an attempt to cope with negative attachment experiences that stem from childhood and continue into adulthood.

In summary, there is evidence that people adopt conspiracy theories in an effort to restore their personal security and feelings of control. As is the case for epistemic motives, we will discuss later in the chapter whether conspiracy theories actually satisfy these motives.

## Feeling good about the self and groups: Social motives

Causal explanations in general are also informed by various social motivations, including the desire to belong and to maintain a positive image of the self and the groups to which we belong. Scholars have suggested that conspiracy theories also satisfy these types of motives. Specifically, it has been argued that conspiracy theories valorise the self and one's ingroups by allowing blame for negative outcomes to be attributed to others. Thus, they may help to uphold the image of the self and the ingroup as competent and moral but as sabotaged by powerful and corrupt others (Cichocka et al. 2016).

Research generally supports the social underpinnings of conspiracy beliefs. For example, experimental results suggest that experiences of ostracism cause people to believe in superstitions and conspiracy theories (Graeupner, Coman 2017). It is argued that this is the case because people are attempting to make sense of their negative experience. Furthermore, members of groups confronting objectively low (vs. high) status because of their ethnicity (Crocker et al. 1999) or income (Uscinski, Parent 2014) are more likely to endorse conspiracy theories. There is some evidence to suggest that people on the losing (vs. winning) side of political processes, such as supporters of opposition (vs. incumbent) parties, also appear more likely to believe conspiracy theories (Uscinski, Parent 2014). Conspiracy belief has also been linked to prejudice against powerful or elite groups (Imhoff, Bruder 2014) and those perceived as enemies of the ingroup (Kofta, Sedek 2005; Golec de Zavala, Cichocka 2012; Bilewicz et al. 2013; see also Chapter 2.6 in this volume).

These findings suggest that conspiracy theories may be adopted defensively, to relieve the self or ingroup from a sense of responsibility for their disadvantaged position. This idea is further supported by findings showing that conspiracy belief is associated with narcissism – an inflated view of oneself that requires external validation and is linked to paranoid ideation (Cichocka et al. 2016). Furthermore, conspiracy belief is also predicted by *collective narcissism* – a belief in the ingroup's greatness paired with a belief that other people do not appreciate or value this greatness enough (Cichocka, Olechowski et al. 2016; Marchlewska et al. 2019). Finally, groups who feel that they have been victimised – even when they have not – are more likely to endorse conspiracy theories about powerful outgroups (Bilewicz et al. 2013).

Another purely self-related motivation driving conspiracy belief appears to be the *need for uniqueness*. This construct is the need or desire to be different from other people (Lynn, Snyder 2002) and is associated with an interest in scarce or unique commodities that set the self apart from others (e.g. Snyder, Fromkin 1977). Lantian et al. (2017) measured the need for uniqueness and found it to be significantly associated with the endorsement of a range of conspiracy theories. Furthermore, manipulating the need for uniqueness increased conspiracy belief. In line with Billig's (1987) theorising on conspiracy theories, Lantian et al.'s results support the idea that the believer can feel they have become an 'expert', superior to others because they possess intelligence that others do not have. Arguably, therefore, believing in conspiracy theories affords people the opportunity to aggrandise the self in relation to others, satisfying the social need to feel good about the self because they know more than others and are therefore better compared to them.

Research evidence, therefore, supports the social motivations underpinning conspiracy beliefs. Whether these motives are met is another matter, which we will again return to later in the chapter. Now, we turn our attention to emotions.

## Emotions

Although the motivational underpinnings of conspiracy beliefs are becoming clearer, much less is known about their emotional foundations. Motivations and emotions are often closely related, but little is known about how emotions specifically – that is, complex mental feeling states that direct attention and guide behaviour (A.P.A., 2018) – are linked to belief in conspiracy theories.

Van Prooijen and Douglas (2018; see also Chapter 2.2 in this volume) proposed that conspiracy theories are likely to have emotional underpinnings since many of the cognitive processes that predict belief in conspiracy theories appear to be System 1 processes (Kahneman 2011). That is, fast, automatic and intuitive thinking – the type of thinking that is often driven by emotions – seems to be associated with higher levels of conspiracy belief. On the other hand, System 2 processes, which are slower, analytical and in which reason dominates, tend to be associated with lower levels of conspiracy beliefs (see the earlier section on epistemic motives for relevant research). Furthermore, because negative emotional experiences increase people's tendency to look for sense and meaning (Park 2010), they are also likely to attract people toward conspiracy theories. As we have noted earlier, conspiracy beliefs are associated with anxiety, uncertainty, threat and the feeling of lacking control (see the section on existential motives). These may be quick and intuitive 'knee-jerk' responses to problems and may also be associated with strong emotions.

One limitation of this theorising, however, is that some of the factors associated with conspiracy beliefs mentioned above (e.g. threat, uncertainty) are not emotions per se. Although they are likely to trigger emotional responses (e.g. threat might lead to fear), which may go on to trigger conspiracy beliefs, they are unlikely to be the root cause of conspiracy beliefs. What we know about the direct relationship between emotions and conspiracy thinking is very limited and there is little research that directly establishes relationships between the fundamental human emotions (i.e. fear, anger, sadness, happiness, surprise and disgust; Ekman 1992) and conspiracy beliefs.

Some research suggests that such relationships should exist. For example, Klein, Clutton and Dunn (2018) studied the posts of Reddit users and conducted a linguistic analysis of their posts using the L.I.W.C. tool (Linguistic Inquiry and Word Count; Pennebaker et al. 2001). They analysed a large set of posts and found that users who later went on to post on a conspiracy forum (r/conspiracy) tended to display more anger and negative emotion in their language compared to those who did not go on to participate in this forum. The conspiracy users and control group did not display different levels of sadness, however. This research suggests that anger, and negative affect generally, might lead people to join conspiracy communities. Perhaps people are drawn toward conspiracy theories in an effort to alleviate these emotions (see Franks et al. 2013), in much the same way as they are drawn to conspiracy theories to satisfy their psychological motives. Indeed, Sunstein and Vermeule (2009) theorised that people turn to conspiracy theories to help justify emotional states such as fear and outrage, and to help rationalise and relieve their negative emotional responses to troublesome events. Furthermore, Moscovici (1987) argued that belief in conspiracy theories constitutes a 'mentality' based on individuals' and groups' fears and antipathy against other groups. Again, however, we argue that it is important to know where the emotions such as fear come from in the first place to be able to understand why the conspiracy theories provide an attractive explanation to people.

Other research suggests that there could be direct emotional antecedents of conspiracy theories. Specifically, Whitson, Galinsky and Kay (2015) manipulated people's experience of emotions related to uncertainty about the world (e.g. worry, surprise and fear) vs. certainty (e.g. anger, happiness, disgust). They found that experiencing uncertain emotions increased belief in conspiracy theories compared to experiencing emotions associated with certainty. Finally, boredom proneness is associated with conspiracy belief, and boredom proneness has also been found to be associated with emotional distance from others, as well as depression, anxiety, hopelessness and aggression (Brotherton, Eser 2015). These findings suggest that conspiracy beliefs might therefore be associated with other negative emotions and experiences.

Nevertheless, we still know very little about the emotional underpinnings of conspiracy beliefs, but there are suggestions that these relationships do exist. However, they may also be explained by motivational factors (epistemic, existential, social). In the following section, we review the evidence that these motives are satisfied by adopting conspiracy theories and speculate about whether or not conspiracy theories might reduce negative emotions.

## Do conspiracy theories 'work'?

Overall, the limited research that exists to date suggests that, rather than satisfying important social psychological motives and making people feel better, conspiracy theories might further frustrate these motives and actually make people feel worse. That is, whilst conspiracy theories may appear attractive on the surface, they may not help people deal with the problems they face (Douglas et al. 2017; see also Chapter 2.7 in this volume).

To take epistemic motives first, there is some evidence to suggest that conspiracy theories frustrate rather than satisfy the need for knowledge and certainty. Specifically, Jolley and Douglas (2014a) presented people with persuasive conspiracy arguments about climate change and politics (vs. anti-conspiracy arguments or controls) and found that this material made people feel less (not more) certain about these issues. In another study, Jolley and Douglas (2014b) found a similar reduction in certainty after exposure to conspiracy theories about vaccination. Therefore, rather than satisfying people's epistemic need for knowledge and certainty, conspiracy theories might even worsen the situation. On the other hand, entrenched attitude positions are associated with conspiracy beliefs, suggesting that they may help people defend beliefs that are important to them from disconfirmation (Uscinski et al. 2016).

What about existential motives? Research conducted thus far does not indicate that conspiracy belief effectively satisfies these motives either. On the contrary, experimental exposure to conspiracy theories appears to immediately suppress people's sense of autonomy and control (Jolley, Douglas 2014a, 2014b; Douglas, Leite 2017). These same studies have also shown that exposure to conspiracy theories makes people less inclined to take actions that, in the long run, might enhance their autonomy and control. Specifically, they are less inclined to commit to their workplace and to engage in mainstream political processes such as voting and party politics. Recent research has also shown that exposure to conspiracy theories influences people's intentions to engage in everyday criminal actions (Jolley et al. 2019). Therefore, rather than leading people to disengage and become apathetic, conspiracy theories may sometimes lead to negative and potentially destructive behaviours. Furthermore, exposure to conspiracy theories may subtly undermine people's autonomy in another way. Specifically, Douglas and Sutton (2008) found that people were effectively persuaded by conspiracy-related material about the death of Princess Diana but were not aware that they had been persuaded. Instead, they falsely recalled that their pre-exposure beliefs were identical to their new beliefs. Therefore, rather than arming people with a new sense of power and control, belief in – and exposure to – conspiracy theories appears more likely to disempower people and decrease their sense of control further.

Finally, although people are clearly attracted to conspiracy theories when their social motivations are frustrated, it is not at all clear that adopting these theories fulfils their motivations. A feature of conspiracy theories is their distrustful representation of other people and outgroups. Thus, it is reasonable to suggest that they might not only be a symptom but also a cause of the feelings of alienation and anomie – a feeling of personal unrest and lack of understanding of the social world – with which they are associated (e.g. Abalakina-Paap et al. 1999). Indeed, experiments show that exposure to conspiracy theories decreases people's trust in governmental institutions, even if the conspiracy theories are completely unrelated to those institutions (Einstein, Glick 2015). Conspiracy theories increase disenchantment with, and distrust of, politicians, scientists and other knowledgeable sources (Jolley, Douglas 2014a; Imhoff et al. 2018). So far, therefore, research suggests that conspiracy theories serve to erode social capital and may, if anything, frustrate people's motives to feel good about themselves and their groups.

What about emotions? At present, we do not know if conspiracy theories help people cope with negative emotions, or if they make people feel better. Extrapolating from the literature on feelings of power, trust and control, and from our analysis of the impact of conspiracy theories on people's social psychological motivations, it seems unlikely. However, this remains an open area for future research. Also, more research needs to examine the role of conspiracy theories in fulfilling people's motives. We turn to these issues in the following section.

## Future research

Although research on the psychology of conspiracy theories has flourished in recent years, we still have a long way to go to understand their origins and impact. The literature to date suggests that, despite the appeal of conspiracy beliefs for people who have important epistemic, existential and social motives that they want to satisfy, conspiracy theories may ultimately frustrate those motives further and even lead to negative psychological consequences (Deci, Ryan 2000). Conspiracy theories, therefore, may be a defensive, ultimately self-defeating manifestation of motivated social cognition.

It is likely that further research will cohere with this analysis since, as we have discussed, conspiracy theories have some features that do not lend themselves to the fulfilment of these motives. For example, they are generally speculative, represent the public as ignorant and at the mercy of elites, and attribute antisocial and cynical motives to other individuals. However, since our analysis is based on little empirical evidence so far, much more research needs to be done to uncover the motivational consequences of conspiracy theories. We also need to begin to investigate their emotional consequences.

First, there are some grounds to expect future research to show that conspiracy theories fulfil the motives of some people but not others. The research we have based our analysis on thus far (e.g. Jolley, Douglas 2014a, 2014b; Douglas, Leite 2017) has sampled from populations such as undergraduate students and survey panellists (e.g. Mturk, Prolific) who are not typically disadvantaged or threatened. On the contrary, they are usually educated and from average to higher socio-economic status backgrounds. Furthermore, their belief in conspiracy theories tends to be quite low, and typically around midpoint on a seven-point or five-point scale measuring conspiracy beliefs (e.g. Douglas, Sutton 2011). These samples are not the same as those whom scholars have had in mind when they have argued that conspiracy theories may sometimes help people achieve their motivations and overcome their problems. Instead, these include groups and individuals who are already alienated from society and for whom conspiracy theories may offer some compensation. These include minority groups, groups from poorer backgrounds and socially isolated individuals who tend to live on the fringes of society. These groups may use conspiracy theories to subvert dominance hierarchies by formulating their own understanding of realities (Sapountzis, Condor 2013) and by encouraging solidarity and collective action

(Adams et al. 2006). In these communities, and also in online communities in which conspiracy theories represent normative positions (e.g. the 9/11 Truth Movement and anti-vaccine movement), belief in conspiracy theories may provide an important source of belonging and shared reality. Furthermore, history has repeatedly shown that political elites and other elite groups do indeed conspire against public interests.

To further investigate the impact of conspiracy theories on motivations and emotions, different types of research are therefore needed. Specifically, controlled longitudinal and experimental investigations of disadvantaged and threatened groups are needed. Future research also needs to examine individuals whose psychological needs are chronically or experimentally threatened and examine whether conspiracy belief moves them closer to or further away from the fulfilment of these needs. In one existing study that used such a design, Jolley et al. (2017) exposed people to threats to the legitimacy of their social system. Findings revealed that the harmful effects of these threats on satisfaction with the status quo were eliminated when participants were also exposed to conspiracy theories. Conspiracy theories – by allowing people to blame the ills of society on small groups of actions with malicious intentions – appeared to buffer people from the effects of threats to their social system. Future research using similar designs is needed to determine more clearly when conspiracy theories might help shield people from various types of problems.

More research is also needed to determine when conspiracy theories might be empowering rather than disempowering. Existing research suggests that they might be disempowering, leading people to disengage from important aspects of society such as voting, vaccination and climate change (Lewandowsky et al. 2013; Jolley, Douglas 2014a; Lewandowsky et al. 2015). However, others have shown that conspiracy theories might motivate collective action against elites (Imhoff, Bruder 2014). It is, therefore, important to understand when conspiracy theories promote action versus inaction, and this will tell us a lot about when and how conspiracy theories can fulfil people's social motivations. Emotions are likely to be important in this respect. For example, it is possible that some conspiracy theories make people sad or fearful, and both sadness and fear as more passive emotions may lead to an inactive response (e.g. disengagement from politics). On the other hand, some conspiracy theories may make people angry and promote action rather than inaction (e.g. collective action to challenge elites). We already know that conspiracy beliefs are associated with low-level criminal intentions (Jolley et al. 2019) and it possible that some conspiracy theories could increase feelings of moral outrage and disgust and trigger other more serious actions. Emotional responses to conspiracy theories are therefore likely to be an important determinant of the consequences of conspiracy theories, and therefore a determinant of whether conspiracy theories fulfil people's motives. Future research should examine this possibility. Future research might also investigate how conspiracy theories change people's emotions. For instance, an event may make people feel unhappy, but hearing that the event could have been the result of a conspiracy could transform that unhappiness into anger. How conspiracy theories might alter people's emotional experiences also remains an open question.

## Conclusion

In this review of the motivational and emotional factors that drive conspiracy belief, we conclude that conspiracy belief appears to stem to a large extent from epistemic, existential and social motives (see Douglas et al. 2017). Much less is known about the emotional underpinnings of conspiracy belief, but this provides many opportunities for future research. Furthermore, research has yet to fully demonstrate whether conspiracy theories effectively serve people's motivations and alleviate their negative emotions. Early indications suggest that they may not. It is possible, therefore, that conspiracy belief is a self-defeating form of motivated social cognition. However, our analysis is preliminary and many important questions remain open. More controlled and longitudinal research – especially on vulnerable and disadvantaged groups – is needed to fully understand how motivations and emotions contribute to, and are affected by, conspiracy theories.

# References

A.P.A. (2018) 'Emotion', *American Psychological Association*. Available at: https://dictionary.apa.org/emotion. [Accessed 7 August 2019.]

Abalakina-Paap, M., Stephan, W.G., Craig, T. and Gregory, L. (1999) 'Beliefs in conspiracies', *Political Psychology*, 20(3): 637–47.

Adams, G., O'Brien, L.T. and Nelson, J.C. (2006) 'Perceptions of racism in Hurricane Katrina: a liberation psychology analysis', *Analyses of Social Issues and Public Policy*, 6(1): 215–35.

Barkun, M. (2003) *A culture of conspiracy: apocalyptic visions in contemporary America*, Berkley, CA: University of California Press.

Bilewicz, M., Winiewski, M., Kofta, M. and Wójcik, A. (2013) 'Harmful ideas: the structure and consequences of anti-semitic beliefs in Poland', *Political Psychology*, 34(6): 821–39.

Billig, M. (1987) 'Anti-semitic themes and the British far left: some social-psychological observations on indirect aspects of the conspiracy tradition', in C.F. Graumann and S. Moscovici (eds.) *Changing conceptions of conspiracy*, New York, NY: Springer, pp. 115–36.

Bowlby, J. (1982) *Attachment and loss: Vol. 1 Attachment*, 2nd edn, New York: Basic Books. (Original work published 1969)

Brotherton, R. and Eser, S. (2015) 'Bored to fears: boredom proneness, paranoia, and conspiracy theories', *Personality and Individual Differences*, 80: 1–5.

Brotherton, R. and French, C.C. (2014) 'Belief in conspiracy theories and susceptibility to the conjunction fallacy', *Applied Cognitive Psychology*, 28(2): 238–48.

Bruder, M., Haffke, P., Neave, N., Nouripanah, N. and Imhoff, R. (2013) 'Measuring individual differences in generic beliefs in conspiracy theories across cultures: conspiracy mentality questionnaire', *Frontiers in Psychology*, 4.

Cichocka, A., Marchlewska, M. and Golec de Zavala, A. (2016) 'Does self-love or self-hate predict conspiracy beliefs? Narcissism, self-esteem, and the endorsement of conspiracy theories', *Social Psychological & Personality Science*, 7(2): 157–66.

Cichocka, A., Marchlewska, M., Golec de Zavala, A. and Olechowski, M. (2016) "'They will not control us': in-group positivity and belief in intergroup conspiracies', *British Journal of Psychology*, 107(3): 556–76.

Crocker, J., Luhtanen, R., Broadnax, S. and Blaine, B.E. (1999) 'Belief in U.S. government conspiracies against Blacks among Black and White college students: powerlessness or system blame?', *Personality and Social Psychology Bulletin*, 25(8): 941–53.

Deci, E.L. and Ryan, R.M. (2000) 'The 'what' and 'why' of goal pursuits: human needs and the self-determination of behavior', *Psychological Inquiry*, 11(4): 227–68.

Dieguez, S., Wagner-Egger, P. and Gauvrit, N. (2015) 'Nothing happens by accident, or does it? A low prior for randomness does not explain belief in conspiracy theories', *Psychological Science*, 26(11): 1762–70.

Douglas, K.M. and Leite, A.C. (2017) 'Suspicion in the workplace: organizational conspiracy theories and work-related outcomes', *British Journal of Psychology*, 108(3): 486–506.

Douglas, K.M. and Sutton, R.M. (2008) 'The hidden impact of conspiracy theories: perceived and actual impact of theories surrounding the death of Princess Diana', *Journal of Social Psychology*, 148(2): 210–21.

Douglas, K.M. and Sutton, R.M. (2011) 'Does it take one to know one? Endorsement of conspiracy theories is influenced by personal willingness to conspire', *British Journal of Social Psychology*, 50(3): 544–52.

Douglas, K.M. and Sutton, R.M. (2018) 'Why conspiracy theories matter: a social psychological analysis', *European Review of Social Psychology*, 29(1): 256–98.

Douglas, K.M., Sutton, R.M., Callan, M.J., Dawtry, R.J. and Harvey, A.J. (2016) 'Someone is pulling the strings: hypersensitive agency detection and belief in conspiracy theories', *Thinking & Reasoning*, 22(1): 57–77.

Douglas, K.M., Sutton, R.M. and Cichocka, A. (2017) 'The psychology of conspiracy theories', *Current Directions in Psychological Science*, 26(6): 538–42.

Douglas, K.M., Uscinski, J., Sutton, R.M., Cichocka, A., Nefes, T., Ang, J. and Deravi, F. (2019) 'Understanding conspiracy theories', *Advances in Political Psychology*, 40(S1): 3–35.

Einstein, K.L. and Glick, D.M. (2015) 'Do I think BLS data are BS? The consequences of conspiracy theories', *Political Behavior*, 37(3): 679–701.

Ekman, P. (1992) 'Are there basic emotions?', *Psychological review*, 99(3): 550–3.

Federico C.M., Williams, A.L. and Vitriol, J.A. (2018) 'The role of system identity threat in conspiracy theory endorsement', *European Journal of Social Psychology*, 48(7): 927–38.

Franks, B., Bangerter, A., and Bauer, M.W. (2013) 'Conspiracy theories as quasi-religious mentality: an integrated account from cognitive science, social representations theory, and frame theory', *Frontiers in Psychology*.

Goertzel, T. (1994) 'Belief in conspiracy theories', *Political Psychology*, 15(4): 731–42.

Golec de Zavala, A. and Cichocka, A. (2012) 'Collective narcissism and anti-semitism in Poland', *Group Processes and Intergroup Relations*, 15(2): 213–29.

Graeupner, D. and Coman, A. (2017) 'The dark side of meaning-making: How social exclusion leads to superstitious thinking', *Journal of Experimental Social Psychology*, 69, pp. 218–22.

Green, R. and Douglas, K.M. (2018) 'Anxious attachment and belief in conspiracy theories', *Personality and Individual Differences*, 125: 30–7.

Grzesiak-Feldman, M. (2013) 'The effect of high-anxiety situations on conspiracy thinking', *Current Psychology*, 32(1): 100–18.

Heider, F. (1958) *The psychology of interpersonal relations*, New York, NY: John Wiley.

Imhoff, R. and Bruder, M. (2014) 'Speaking (un-)truth to power: conspiracy mentality as a generalised political attitude', *European Journal of Personality*, 28(1): 25–43.

Imhoff, R., Lamberty, P. and Klein, O. (2018) 'Using power as a negative cue: how conspiracy mentality affects epistemic trust in sources of historical knowledge', *Personality and Social Psychology Bulletin*, 44(9): 1364–79.

Jolley, D. and Douglas, K.M. (2014a) 'The effects of anti-vaccine conspiracy theories on vaccination intentions', *PLOS ONE*, 9(2): e89177.

Jolley, D. and Douglas, K.M. (2014b) 'The social consequences of conspiracism: exposure to conspiracy theories decreases the intention to engage in politics and to reduce one's carbon footprint', *British Journal of Psychology*, 105(1): 35–56.

Jolley, D., Douglas, K.M., Leite, A. and Schrader, T. (2019) 'Belief in conspiracy theories and intentions to engage in everyday crime', *British Journal of Social Psychology*, 58(3): 534–49.

Jolley, D., Douglas, K.M. and Sutton, R.M. (2017) 'Blaming a few bad apples to save a threatened barrel: the system-justifying function of conspiracy theories', *Political Psychology*, 39(2): 465–78.

Jost, J.T., Ledgerwood, A. and Hardin, C.D. (2008) 'Shared reality, system justification, and the relational basis of ideological beliefs', *Social & Personality Psychology Compass*, 2(1): 171–86.

Kahneman, D. (2011) *Thinking, fast and slow*, New York, NY: Farrar, Straus and Giroux.

Klein, C., Clutton, P. and Dunn, A. (2018) 'Pathways to conspiracy: the social and linguistic precursors of involvement in Reddit's conspiracy theory forum', *PsyArXiv Preprints*, 18 January. Available at: https://doi.org/10.31234/osf.io/8vesf. [Accessed 7 August 2019.]

Kofta, M. and Sedek, G. (2005) 'Conspiracy stereotypes of Jews during systemic transformation in Poland', *International Journal of Sociology*, 35(1): 40–64.

Kruglanski, A.W. and Webster, D.M. (1996) 'Motivated closing of the kind: 'seizing' and 'freezing'', *Psychological Review*, 103(2): 263–83.

Lantian, A., Muller, D., Nurra, C. and Douglas, K.M. (2017) ''I know things they don't know!' The role of need for uniqueness in belief in conspiracy theories', *Social Psychology*, 48(3): 160–73.

Leman, P.J. and Cinnirella, M. (2013) 'Beliefs in conspiracy theories and the need for cognitive closure', *Frontiers in Psychology*, 4: 378.

Lewandowsky, S., Cook, J., Oberauer, K., Brophy, S., Lloyd, E.A. and Marriott, M. (2015) 'Recurrent fury: conspiratorial discourse in the blogosphere triggered by research on the role of conspiracist ideation in climate denial', *Journal of Social and Political Psychology*, 3(1): 142–78.

Lewandowsky, S., Oberauer, K. and Gignac, G.E. (2013) 'NASA faked the moon landing—Therefore, (climate) science is a hoax: an anatomy of the motivated rejection of science', *Psychological Science*, 24(5): 622–33.

Lynn, M. and Snyder, C.R. (2002) 'Uniqueness seeking', in C.R. Snyder and S.J. Lopez (eds.), *Handbook of positive psychology*, New York: Oxford University Press, pp. 395–419.

Marchlewska, M., Cichocka, A., Górska, P., Winiewski, M. and Łozowski, F. (2019) 'In search of an imaginary enemy: catholic collective narcissism and the endorsement of gender conspiracy beliefs', *Journal of Social Psychology*.

Marchlewska, M., Cichocka, A. and Kossowska, M. (2017) 'Addicted to answers: need for cognitive closure and the endorsement of conspiracy beliefs', *European Journal of Social Psychology*, 48(2): 109–17.

Moscovici, S. (1987) 'The conspiracy mentality', in C.F. Graumann and S. Moscovici (eds.) *Changing conceptions of conspiracy*, New York: Springer, pp. 151–69.

Park, C.L. (2010)' Making sense of the meaning literature: An integrative review of meaning making and its effects on adjustment to stressful life events', *Psychological Bulletin*, 136, 257–301.

Pennebaker, J.W., Francis, M.E. and Booth, R.J. (2001) *Linguistic inquiry and word count: LIWC 2001*, Mahwah NJ: Lawrence Erlbaum Associates.

Sapountzis, A. and Condor, S. (2013) 'Conspiracy accounts as intergroup theories: challenging dominant understandings of social power and political legitimacy', *Political Psychology*, 34(5): 731–52.

Snyder, C.R. and Fromkin, H.L. (1977) 'Abnormality as a positive characteristic: the development and validation of a scale measuring need for uniqueness', *Journal of Abnormal Psychology*, 86(5): 518–27.

Spark, A. (2000) 'Conjuring order: the new world order and conspiracy theories of globalization', *The Sociological Review*, 48(S2): 46–62.

Sunstein, C.R. and Vermeule, A. (2009) 'Conspiracy theories: causes and cures', *Journal of Political Philopsophy*, 17(2): 202–27.

Swami, V., Voracek, M., Stieger, S., Tran, U.S. and Furnham, A. (2014) 'Analytic thinking reduces belief in conspiracy theories', *Cognition*, 133(3): 572–85.

Tetlock, P.E. (2002) 'Social-functionalist frameworks for judgment and choice: the intuitive politician, theologian, and prosecutor', *Psychological Review*, 109(3): 451–72.

Uscinski, J.E., Klofstad, C. and Atkinson, M.D. (2016) 'What drives conspiratorial beliefs? The role of informational cues and predispositions', *Political Research Quarterly*, 69(1): 57–71.

Uscinski, J.E. and Parent, J.M. (2014) *American conspiracy theories*, New York, NY: Oxford University Press.

Van der Wal, R.C., Sutton, R.M., Lange, J. and Braga, J.P.N. (2018) 'Suspicious binds: conspiracy thinking and tenuous perceptions of causal connections between co-occurring and spuriously correlated events', *European Journal of Social Psychology*, 48(7): 970–89.

Van Prooijen, J.-W. and Acker, M. (2015) 'The influence of control on belief in conspiracy theories: conceptual and applied extensions', *Applied Cognitive Psychology*, 29(5): 753–61.

Van Prooijen, J-W. and Douglas, K.M. (2018) 'Belief in conspiracy theories: basic principles of an emerging research domain', *European Journal of Social Psychology*, 48(7): 897–908.

Van Prooijen J.-W., Douglas, K.M. and de Inocencio, C. (2018) 'Connecting the dots: illusory pattern perception predicts belief in conspiracies and the supernatural', *European Journal of Social Psychology*, 48(3): 320–35.

Van Prooijen, J.-W. and Jostmann, N.B. (2013) 'Belief in conspiracy theories: the influence of uncertainty and perceived morality', *European Journal of Social Psychology*, 43(1): 109–15.

Whitson, J.A., Galinsky, A.D. and Kay, A. (2015) 'The emotional roots of conspiratorial perceptions, system justification, and belief in the paranormal', *Journal of Experimental Social Psychology*, 56, 89–95.

Willman, S. (1998) 'Traversing the fantasies of the JFK assassination: conspiracy and contingency in Don DeLillo's 'Libra'', *Contemporary Literature*, 39(3): 405–33.

Wood, M., Douglas, K.M. and Sutton, R.M. (2012) 'Dead and alive: belief in contradictory conspiracy theories', *Social Psychological and Personality Science*, 3(6): 767–73.

Zhao, J., Hahn, U. and Osherson, D. (2014) 'Perception and identification of random events', *Journal of Experimental Psychology: Human Perception and Performance*, 40(4): 1358–71.

# 2.4
# CONSPIRACY BELIEFS AS PSYCHO-POLITICAL REACTIONS TO PERCEIVED POWER

*Roland Imhoff and Pia Lamberty*

### Some preliminary notes on questions of definitions

When discussing the relationship between conspiracy beliefs and power, it is a useful start to put out largely consensual definitions of both and analyse connections already at a basic semantic level. To do so, we will adopt a definition of conspiracy beliefs as a conviction that there is or was a 'secret plan on the part of some group to influence events by partly secret means' (Pigden 2015: 5). Missing from this approach is a certain magnitude or relevance of the above mentioned events. It seems reasonable that the suspicion of a secretly organised birthday party does not constitute a conspiracy theory. Past research has shown that conspiracy theories are more likely to relate to events that are perceived as collectively threatening (Kofta, Sedek 2005), and large and impactful (LeBoeuf, Norton 2011). This said, there needs to be a socially or politically relevant action harming others that few people have conjointly decided to make happen without making this fact of prior planning transparent (thus often implying additional steps to cover this fact, although this is not necessarily implied). By this definition, the notion that the Elders of Zion have met and decided how to secretly take over the world is a conspiracy theory, whereas the European Commission deciding to implement stricter limits of $C.O._2$ emissions for new cars is not (as it is clearly transparent). The idea again that the European Commission met with Chinese bike manufacturers to make this decision would be a conspiracy theory (when the role of Chinese bike manufacturers in the decision process is not made public). The (factually wrong) claim that vaccines cause autism is, in and of itself, not a conspiracy theory. Insinuating, however, that vaccine producers and/or health commissions know this fact is implying a conspiracy by omission, deciding not to remove something that is knowingly harmful.

Prototypical conspiracy theories go beyond the omission aspect by being enriched with explanations of why certain actors have an interest in having these specifically harmful substances on the market (e.g. for mind control, population control, to reach world domination). This leads to the very basic concept that a conspiracy belief is the belief that some people have conspired with the intent to harm other people (either as an ultimate goal or as an instrumental goal to gain profit on the costs of others). Importantly, we propose that actual veracity should not be a criterion here. Whether an allegation of a conspiracy turns out to be truthful should in our view not change its epistemic status of being a conspiracy theory, nor should its empirical refutation (Pigden 2015). Although the term conspiracy theory often bears the connotation of being a false belief, there are plenty of historical examples of a theory about a conspiracy being true. As maybe an extreme example, the conviction that the Nazi elite met in January 1942 at the Wannsee to make a determined decision and detailed plan to eliminate European Jewry was a conspiracy belief, as this was not – at that time – the officially announced purpose. Sadly enough, however, it was true. The fact that it was true does not, according to our definition, change its status of being a conspiracy theory, or a conviction that some people have secretly planned an action to harm others.

We are aware that such a definition of a conspiracy belief may provoke some contradiction. We would argue, however, that the often-included notion that a conspiracy theory must be factually wrong is neither epistemologically nor pragmatically useful. It introduces the danger of circular reasoning if one seeks explanations of conspiracy beliefs, as confounding conspiracy belief with merely wrong beliefs would make some connections in the literature seem trivial or even tautological. As an illustration, replace the term 'conspiracy belief' with the term 'wrong belief' in an overview of relevant findings: Analytical thinking reduces wrong beliefs (Swami et al. 2014). Wrong beliefs are more prevalent among those with lower education (van Prooijen 2016). People who hold wrong beliefs also believe 'bullshit' (Pennycook et al. 2015). People who (wrongfully) believe that objects have feelings also hold other wrong beliefs (Imhoff, Bruder 2014; Douglas et al. 2016). Epistemologically, it would be impossible to even decide whether any kind of utterance is a conspiracy belief unless we have firmly established ground truth. This is already next to impossible in the reductionist sciences, let alone in complex social happenings. If the qualification of the sentence 'The car lobby tries to suppress technological progress to keep oil prices up, as they benefit from this due to financial interest in this business segment' as a conspiracy belief is contingent on whether this sentence contains factual truth, it is unlikely that there will ever be a consensus. This would reduce the term to a polemical concept that might be used in disputes but there will never be an agreement of whether an allegation is a conspiracy theory. We would thus exclude any implication of veracity from the definition.

Another aspect that is missing in the above definition, but frequently present in others, is the notion of conspiracy theories as 'alternative explanations' for social events. While, for example, the U.S. government clearly names terrorism as the cause of the attack on the towers at the World Trade Center on 11 September 2001, the 'alternative explanation' is that the U.S. government itself blew up the towers and was thus responsible for the deaths of many people. Even if this approach may seem plausible at first glance, it conceals various problems. Conspiracy theories are not always the alternative explanation and conspiracy beliefs are not always a minority opinion. In different epochs and states, conspiracy theories were and are the mainstream opinion (for examples from Turkey, Russia or even U.S. history see Chapters 5.5, 5.7, and 5.10). In a recent survey covering eight European countries (plus the U.S.A.), only between 15 per cent (Hungary) and 48 per cent (Sweden) declared that, out of a number of items tapping into a conspiracy worldview (e.g. 'Regardless of who is officially in charge of governments and other organisations, there is a single group of people who secretly control events and rule the world together'), none was true (YouGov 2018). One half of U.S.-Americans believe in at least one conspiracy theory (Oliver, Wood 2014). In addition, the question arises to whom or what does conspiracy theory represent an alternative to? To the majority opinion? And what is exactly a majority opinion? When more than 50 per cent agree on one topic? Would that mean that if 46 per cent of the population believe that 9/11 is an inside job, it would be a conspiracy theory and if 55 per cent believe it, then not? Or is it about being an alternative to government narratives? That would also be problematic. Then the belief that the *Protocols of the Elders of Zion* are real would not be a conspiracy in the case of Nazi Germany (or the Palestinian territories under the reign of the Hamas), but it would be in post-war Germany.

Finally, a third aspect that we did not include in our definition is that of power. Many scholars have defined a conspiracy theory as the idea that a few *powerful* people have hatched plots in secret (Goertzel 1994). While we find this definition not as self-defeating as the previous, for the current purpose of exploring the association between conspiracy beliefs and power, this would introduce undesirable circularities. As we will argue below, even without incorporating the power of the agent into the very definition, it is still implied in the idea that the secret plot can at least potentially have a relevant impact. Thus, although we are convinced that conspiracy theories typically are beliefs about secret plans on the part of some *powerful* group to influence large-scale events by partly secret means, we propose to leave out this power aspect for the sake of an argument to be made after briefly reviewing what power refers to.

So, what is a psychological definition of power? A basic conceptualisation would be that someone has power to the extent that he or she can exert an influence on others, thus alter another person's condition or state of mind by either providing or withholding resources. One of the most widely accepted definitions of social power describes it as 'asymmetric control over valued resources in social relations' (Magee, Galinsky 2008: 361). These resources do not have to be necessarily material. Bosses have power over their employees not only via determining what income they will receive (although that plays a big role), but also via the power to grant or deny taking a day off, the power to give direct orders, etc. The police have power via the legal right to tell others what to do and what not to do, and the ability to withhold the resource of personal liberty in the case of non-compliance. The people, it might be argued, have power to the extent that they can influence governments and other rulers by providing or withholding support and obedience.

As is apparent from contrasting the latter two examples, power can be either formal or informal. Formal power here refers to the legitimacy to influence others granted by rules and structure (i.e. the police, the boss, the judge), whereas informal power connotes the factual power, not necessarily granted by a formalised code (as in the power of the people or the unions). Particularly such forms of informal power are easily confused with highly related aspects of strength, influence and control. Sometimes, the term power refers to strength or potential rather than asymmetric control over resources (as in Black Power or – for that matter – White Power). Likewise, it is not uncommon to confound it with the capacity to exert influence. A textbook example is that, allegedly, many constitutions give a lot of formal executive power to their president, but most presidents also have a great informal power, for instance because their voice has more weight in public discourse than those of a random other person. Clearly, the latter could be construed as asymmetric control over resources in the sense of airtime, but it also includes another element of stronger capacity to influence others. Such capacity to influence others has been included in older definitions of power (French, Raven 1959; Cartwright 1965), but explicitly refuted in more recent ones (Magee, Galinsky 2008). In our discussion of power – and it is important to note that we always refer to perceived or ascribed power, not 'objective' power –, we will incorporate the aspect of capacity to influence. One of the reasons is that some of our findings build on studies in which participants have rated the power of certain groups. In all likelihood, participants use both aspects, the asymmetric control over resources as well as the (resulting) ability to influence as indicators of power. Arguably, Jews are frequently rated as a powerful group (e.g. Imhoff, Bruder 2014) not only because people think they have greater control over resources (money, victimhood status), but also because they supposedly – thereby – have a greater ability to exert influence (on world politics or public opinion). Below, we will try to make it clear when we focus on influence rather than resource control.

Potentially most relevant for a discussion in relation to conspiracy beliefs is the connection between power and control. Lacking control is a frequently mentioned antecedent of endorsing conspiracy theories (Whitson, Galinsky 2008; Sullivan *et al.* 2010; van Prooijen, Acker 2015) and, throughout the literature, control deprivation and feelings of powerlessness have not always been clearly separated, both empirically and conceptually. We will thus briefly revisit the connection between the two. Personal control can be described as an individual's ability to gain predictability and influenceability of a certain kind of outcome (e.g. behaviour, thoughts, feelings; for an overview of the confusingly diverse proposal of definition, see Skinner 1996). Power, on the other hand, is typically conceptualised as a relational construct entailing influence over others and develops from an asymmetric control over valuable resources (Fast *et al.* 2009; Kay *et al.* 2009). Thus, although conceptually the two seem to be clearly separable, empirically they are intertwined to a certain extent (correlating between 0.29 and 0.47 in Cislak *et al.* 2018) and holding a position of power is associated with both greater personal control (i.e. autonomy) and influence over others (Lammers *et al.* 2016). Speaking to a bi-directional relation, exerting power over others also satisfied the need for personal control (Inesi *et al.* 2011).

## Who can pull off a conspiracy?

Now, finally to our question: what is the connection between power and conspiracy beliefs? The first is a logical aspect: many (us included) have argued that the very idea of a conspiracy necessitates an assumption of power on the side of the conspirators. This is particularly true for the large-scale conspiracies of world domination and population control, but even more modest conspiracies require the potency to not only pull off this conspiracy but to guarantee that it is kept in the dark. Clearly, it is in principle conceivable that a small group of people conspire to do X and hide this from the public eye, but – powerless as they are – fail at both and neither successfully reach X nor succeed in keeping their plans a secret. Formally, this might still be a conspiracy belief, and empirically most circulating conspiracy beliefs do not follow such a structure. Most conspiracy beliefs are not sad tales about failed and incompetent conspirators but are quite the opposite: vivid warnings against almost almighty but well-hidden enemies. Thus, presuming a (noteworthy) conspiracy almost necessarily implies great (informal) power of a group of people to reach their (sinister) goal (thus implying capacity to influence but also controlling the necessary resources to do so). Although many conspiracies involve agents with high formal power (e.g. governments, intelligence agencies, corporations), others do not (e.g. satanic cults). Importantly, however, even conspiracies about groups with low formal power typically imply tremendous informal power of potency (or capacity to influence). A Jewish world conspiracy or an Islamic plan to exchange the whole population of Europe for Muslims envision extremely powerful or potent conspirators. Describing a group as the source of a world-changing event ascribes tremendous informal power to them. Conspiracy beliefs are thus – almost necessarily – beliefs about the secret plans of groups perceived as powerful.

## Inferring threat from power

The connection between conspiracy beliefs and negative views of power, however, goes far beyond the more or less intuitive assertion that accusing someone of conducting a conspiracy implies a certain extent of power to realise this conspiracy. As maybe the most striking exemplification, endorsing a worldview that plots hatched in secret (*conspiracy mentality*) largely determine the fate of the world is systematically related to prejudice against groups perceived to possess a lot of power, even if no conspiracy is mentioned (Imhoff, Bruder 2014).

As an illustration of the principle, unlike other generalised political attitudes like *right-wing authoritarianism* (R.W.A.) and *social dominance orientation* (S.D.O.; for the relation of both R.W.A. and S.D.O. with prejudice against low-power groups see Duckitt and Sibley 2007), *conspiracy mentality* was systematically related to prejudice against groups perceived as powerful (Americans, bankers, Jews), but not against groups perceived as powerless (Muslims, Roma; Imhoff, Bruder 2014; surprisingly, however, exposure to antisemitic conspiracies increased prejudice against virtually any group; Jolley, Meleady et al. 2019). In a more systematic approach to the relation between perceived power of and prejudice against social groups, participants rated how powerful they saw each of 32 social groups (e.g. managers, gay men, asylum seekers, students and artists), how threatening they perceived each group to be and how likeable they thought each group was. Based on the 96 ratings, we calculated for each participant individually, whether their ratings of power were unrelated to their ratings of threat and likeability or whether they were positively or negatively related. Averaged across participants, impressions of power were completely unrelated to perceptions of likeability, $r=-0.02$, but more powerful groups were seen as more threatening, $r=0.38$. Importantly, these intra-individual correlations varied as a function of conspiracy mentality: The more people endorsed a conspiracy mentality, the stronger was their association of power with threat and the more they tended to see powerful groups as particularly less likeable (Imhoff, Bruder 2014).

What these data suggest is that conspiracy mentality is associated with seeing groups perceived as more powerful also as more threatening. What these data do not speak to is whether people high in conspiracy mentality see powerful groups as particularly threatening and dislikeable or whether they attribute greater power to groups that they perceive as threatening and dislikeable. This issue can be somewhat elucidated by means of a yoked design. As part of a larger project on relevant stereotype content dimensions (e.g. Koch et al. 2016; Imhoff, Koch 2017; Imhoff, Koch et al. 2018), 371 participants had rated all of the 41 social groups included in prior research on stereotype content (Fiske et al. 2002; Cuddy et al. 2007). Each participant rated each group only on one out of 17 possible dimensions and completed a measure of conspiracy mentality. This allowed us to re-analyse the correlation between consensual impressions of power (averaged across all raters) and individual ascriptions of warmth, as well as the opposite – the relation between consensual estimates of warmth and individual perceptions of power. These correlations could then again be related to individual differences in conspiracy mentality. What the results show is that the extent to which people attribute warmth to social groups consensually seen as high in power, depends significantly on their conspiracy mentality, $r=-0.39$, but the opposite is not true: The relation between consensual ratings of warmth and individual ascriptions of power does not significantly relate to conspiracy mentality, $r=-0.10$. Thus, people high in conspiracy mentality infer low warmth from high consensual power, but they do not infer high power from low consensual warmth.

Further evidence in support of the notion people endorsing a conspiracy worldview do not regard high power as a positive attribute comes from additional domains like epistemic trust in sources of knowledge or medical consumer decisions. Specifically, across a series of four studies, conspiracy mentality moderated the effect of source power on source credibility in the field of historical disputes (Imhoff, Lamberty et al. 2018). It is interesting to note, however, that the source bias was more on the side of the people rejecting conspiracy theories than those endorsing them. Whereas people low on conspiracy mentality employed a heuristic of finding the identical position more credible when it came from a high power source, people high on conspiracy mentality showed virtually no bias. Although – compared to people low on conspiracy mentality – they saw powerful sources as less and powerless sources as more credible, they saw both sources as equal in that regard.

A similar pattern could be observed in the domain of medical choices (e.g. Lamberty, Imhoff 2018). The belief in conspiracy theories attenuated preference for conventional over alternative medical approaches. People low in conspiracy mentality inferred medical effectiveness from the producing companies' high power, but people high in conspiracy mentality saw them as equally effective. These results at least suggest that conspiracy mentality is less characterised by an absolute negative perception of those in power, but rather by the absence of a *halo effect* for those in power. This may seem rational to the extent that such a halo effect of power is objectively irrational. Particularly in the fields of knowledge generation and medical treatments, however, it may seem functional, if not necessary to trust established institutions rather than judging no difference between the *New York Times* and a blog on medical science and alternative treatments.

## Feelings of powerlessness and conspiracy beliefs

So far, we have argued that conspiracy believers see power as a potential threat. Even at the level of objective power, arguably, power itself is thereby a relative construct: Once one person has more power, another person automatically has less power and influence – and vice versa. To be able to carry out conspiracies, people need a certain amount of influence. A homeless person is probably not able to commit electoral fraud, while political leaders are – at least potentially – capable of doing so. Therefore, the question naturally arises of how the connection between the belief in conspiracy theories and the power perceptions of the followers of this ideology is formed.

Perceived powerlessness has been described as the belief that one's actions do not affect outcomes. As is apparent here, powerlessness seems intimately connected to lack of personal control. Although having power may primarily relate to asymmetric control over valued resources in social relation rather than control over one's personal outcomes, these two are more tightly connected on the opposite side of the spectrum. Not having power does not only imply not having greater control over resources, but also that someone else has, which again reduces one's own ability to control one's outcomes. In the following paragraphs, we will thus not dissect 'powerlessness' (not having power) from lack of control, as – to a large extent – one follows from the other. Hofstadter (1964) has already suggested that beliefs in conspiracy theories can be traced to feelings of powerlessness. Past research has empirically confirmed this assumption: Conspiracy beliefs are more prevalent among people who feel powerless (e.g. Imhoff, Bruder 2014; Imhoff, Lamberty 2018). It has, for example, been shown that one's own life circumstances, when perceived as powerless, are also related to an increased belief in conspiracy theories. For example, when people are unemployed (thus not having control over valued resources and not having personal control), they tend to believe more strongly in conspiracy theories (Imhoff, Decker 2013; Imhoff 2015).

Although endorsement of conspiracies tends to correlate with perceived personal powerlessness (e.g. Abalakina-Paap *et al.* 1999; Imhoff, Bruder 2014), research tapping into different spheres of control deprivation (i.e. powerlessness) suggests that it is particularly the perception of low power to achieve socio-political goals (rather than personal or interpersonal goals) that show such a relation (e.g. Imhoff, Lamberty 2018). This view is also compatible with the frequent finding that people who endorse political beliefs on the fringes of the political spectrum (i.e. with politically 'extreme' views) tend to endorse more conspiracy beliefs (e.g. Imhoff, Decker 2013; van Prooijen *et al.* 2015). This curvilinear relation could just reflect that politically extreme ideologies are more conspiracy-laden (e.g. due to rather *Manichaean* worldviews), but it may also be that the constant experience of not being represented by the political rulers and the consequential deprivation of reaching one's political goals evokes conspiracy beliefs. A demonstration of this principle can be observed in two recent U.S. elections: after the election, supporters of the winning party showed less, supporters of the defeated party more, belief in election-related conspiracies (Edelson *et al.* 2017; Nyhan 2017).

Conspiracy beliefs are not only stronger in certain situations where people feel that they have less power: Research has established that conspiracy beliefs are more prevalent among social groups who have only little power in society – like migrants or social minorities (e.g. Goertzel 1994; Abalakina-Paap *et al.* 1999). Muslims in the Netherlands, for example, believed more strongly in conspiracy theories than non-Muslims (van Prooijen, Staman *et al.* 2018). Despite relatively robust evidence for stronger conspiracy beliefs among marginalised groups, there exists no consensus whether this is due to feelings of anomia (Goertzel 1994), feelings of deprivation (van Prooijen, Douglas *et al.* 2018) or system blaming (Crocker *et al.* 1999; see also Chapter 2.6 in this volume).

A power-inspired perspective also helps integrating some findings regarding the role of education, knowledge and power in conspiracy beliefs. A famous quip asserts that 'knowledge is power' (often ascribed to Francis Bacon) and, indeed, looking at the association between conspiracy beliefs and knowledge or education is another way to connect it to power. Not only because of the above-mentioned quip, but clearly information can easily be subsumed under the concept of a 'valued resource' (often distributed asymmetrically) in our original definition of power. Information and knowledge are typically acquired through education and education in general gives people the feeling that they are more strongly in control of their lives because they gain skills that give them the ability to influence their social environment (Mirowsky, Ross 1998). In line with the current argument that conspiracy beliefs are more prevalent among people with low power, it has been shown that education can also be a predictor for believing in conspiracy theories: People with less education are more likely to believe in conspiracy theories (e.g. Douglas *et al.* 2016; van Prooijen 2016), as are people with less knowledge (Miller *et al.* 2016). In addition to believing in simple solutions, two variables are particularly responsible for this connection, which are directly related to one's own power: feelings of powerlessness, and subjective social class (see van Prooijen 2016). Thus, less educated people endorse conspiracy theories to a greater extent, not because they are less intelligent, but because they feel powerless.

## Powerless and betrayed – what next?

After it has been consistently shown that the belief in conspiracy theories is associated with feelings of powerlessness, two questions naturally arise: first, the question of causality and – in line with this –, the question of the theoretical explanation for this effect. In principle, two theoretical directions are possible: Experiencing powerlessness may strengthen the belief in conspiracy theories or the belief in conspiracy theories leaves people feeling powerless.

The notion that powerlessness increases conspiracy beliefs is in line with the *compensatory hypothesis*: It has been described that power is an important source of a person's feeling of being in control and lacking control is one important predictor of why people believe in conspiracy theories (Whitson, Galinsky 2008). Individuals are more likely to endorse conspiracy beliefs in situations in which they feel powerless and the belief that negative events in one's own life are caused by external forces (e.g. Whitson, Galinsky 2008). They might help people to make sense of a world containing evil forces beyond the control of individuals and explain their difficulties by creating patterns – even if these patterns are just illusory (Hofstadter 1964; van Prooijen, Douglas *et al.* 2018). Another – and not contradictory – explanation why powerlessness might increase conspiracy beliefs could be that people who feel that they are powerless may find conspiracy theories appealing because they are so consistent with their own perception of themselves (*confirmation bias*). People might experience powerlessness and these feelings make those in power seem even more distant and different. People who believe in conspiracy theories might perceive managers as more distant or different from their own ingroup and therefore are more distrustful of them (Imhoff, Bruder 2014).

On the other hand, belief in conspiracy theories could also reinforce feelings of powerlessness (*reinforcement hypothesis*). If people assume that everything is controlled by a small elite, then it is also likely that they feel more powerless than if they assume that they can influence society as a member of a democratic community, for example. Jolley and Douglas (2014) were able to show that, when people are confronted with conspiracy theories about vaccination, they reported increased feelings of powerlessness. Of course, both ways are possible. This might trigger a downward spiral: Powerless people tend to believe in conspiracy theories, which in turn reinforce feelings of powerlessness. At this point, there are still too few experimental or even longitudinal studies devoted to this question. Further research would be necessary to clarify the question of causality.

## Levelling of power differences as a functional aspect of conspiracy beliefs?

So far, we have seen that conspiracy beliefs are to a certain extent intrinsically connected to the notion of powerful evil-doers and that endorsing conspiracy belief is associated with a negative view of power and a view of the self as powerless. Building on the reinforcement hypothesis, it could be that endorsing conspiracy beliefs exacerbates feelings of powerlessness, undermines perceptions of political efficacy and ultimately leads to political apathy and inaction. Logically, this would strengthen, if not intensify, power asymmetries, as being passive will not change the (objective) status quo. To the extent that powerlessness further increases the likelihood of perceiving and endorsing conspiracy beliefs (e.g. because they provide a desperately sought-after explanation for one's own lack of power as discussed in terms of *confirmation bias* above), this would allow the prediction of an escalation principle longitudinally. Powerlessness makes conspiracy theories more likely, which makes the self both objectively and subjectively more powerless, which in turn further biases the interpretation of the world. Such a cycle (see Figure 2.4.1, lower half) would be particularly destructive and the functional nature of adopting a conspiracy belief would be limited (at least in terms of power – it might still be that it fulfils other needs like creating a collective identity or feeling unique; Imhoff, Lamberty 2017).

There is, however, a perspective that may be seen as more functional and more in line with the general principle of homeostasis both for the individual and in its social effects. For the individual, seeing through the muddy waters of a conspiracy might actually increase feelings of agency and power. After all, not falling for the red herring to distract from the real conspiracy lays the very ground to expose and eventually stop it. To the extent that conspiracy beliefs fuel feelings of outrage and a resulting propensity to alter what is perceived as unjust, they might motivate rather than undermine political action. Indeed, conspiracy mentality has been connected to a greater willingness to engage in political action (Imhoff, Bruder 2014; Imhoff, Lamberty 2018), and non-normative forms of protest in particular. In two experimental studies, participants were asked to imagine living in a society that differed between experimental conditions in terms of whether it was aligned with a low, average or high conspiracy mentality (Imhoff, Dieterle et al., 2020). Afterwards, participants completed a 20-item scale of what kind of political engagement they would be willing to show in such a society. Ten items reflected normative, legal actions (e.g. voting, writing a blog, contacting local representatives), whereas ten items reflected non-normative, illegal, partially violent actions (e.g. tax refusal, vandalism, hacking). Across two pre-registered studies in two different cultural contexts (Germany and the U.S.A.), results showed less willingness to engage in normative action (likely as it seems futile if the political system is driven by self-interested and corrupt people in power) and more willingness to engage in non-normative actions (likely as it seems legitimate to break rules) for people who were assigned either an intermediate or strong conspiracy mentality (Figure 2.4.2).

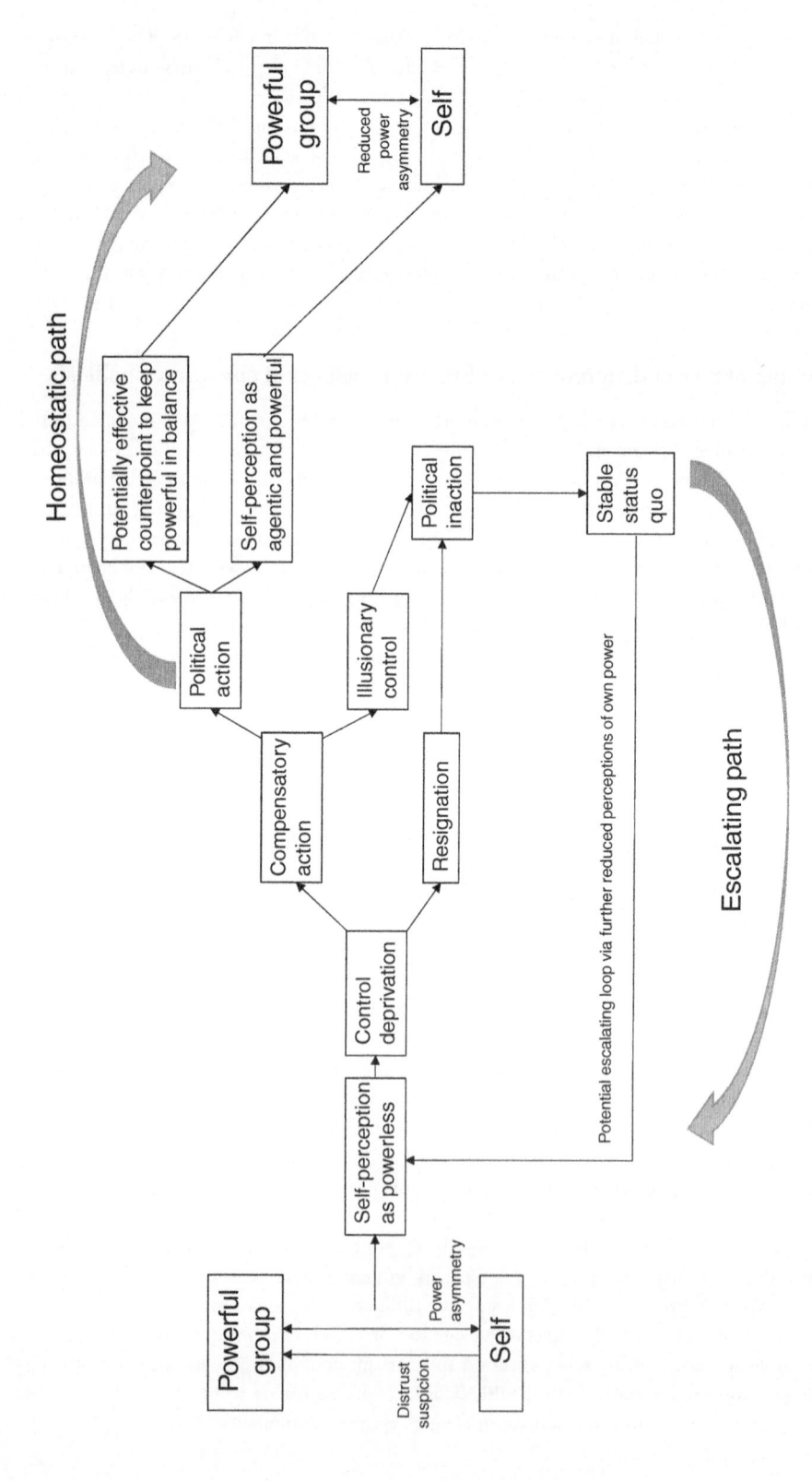

*Figure 2.4.1* Escalating (lower half) and homeostatic (upper half) models of conspiracy beliefs and political action. Figure available at https://osf.io/bg2tc/, under a CC–BY4.0 license.

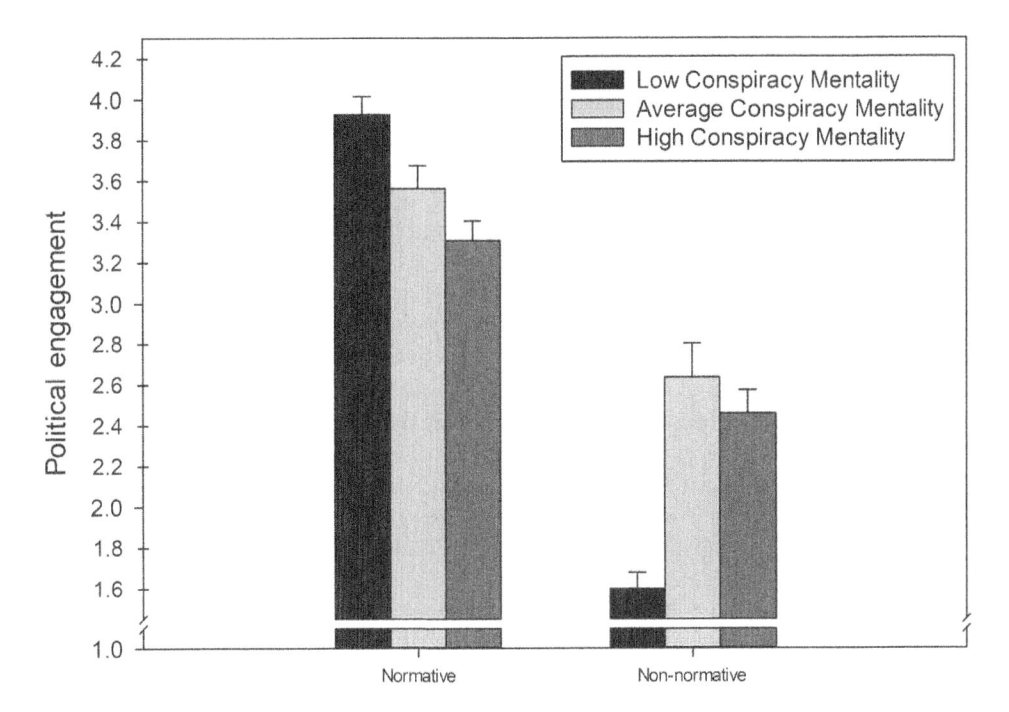

*Figure 2.4.2* Hypothetical willingness to engage in different forms of political engagement as a function of adopting a low, intermediate or high conspiracy mentality. Figure available at https://osf.io/bg2tc/, under a CC-BY4.0 license.

This greater propensity to engage in non-normative forms of protest for people who perceive their ability to achieve change as low is well-established in the literature on collective action (e.g. Ransford 1968; Wright et al. 1990; Tausch et al. 2011). Feeling a lack of control over events is positively correlated with willingness to engage in violence. Non-normative political action, then, is not only potent to change the self-perception as agentic and powerful, but also the objective reality (see Figure 2.4.1, upper half). Undermining the legitimacy of those in power might ultimately level power differences by pulling them down. This pattern of a homeostatic principle would ascribe a much greater extent of functionality of conspiracy beliefs – both for the individual, but also in the society's interest to regulate power asymmetries. Importantly, both paths (the homeostatic path via political action and the escalating path via political lethargy) are not mutually exclusive. It may very well be that either dispositional factors (e.g. self-efficacy beliefs, dispositional action orientation) or situational circumstances decide which path will be taken. At present, however, these are not well understood.

## The power paradox: integrating conspiracy research with power research

As discussed above, conspiracy beliefs are associated with a variety of outcomes that can legitimately be called non-normative: From support of terrorist or extremist groups (Bartlett, Miller 2010), illegal and violent forms of protests, to intentions to engage in everyday crime (Jolley, Douglas et al. 2019). If most aspects of our society are illegitimately influenced by a few powerful people, and the official rules and norms are just a means to uphold this scandalous situation, not complying with laws, rules and norms is not only legitimate but an almost necessary step toward autonomy and liberation. Conspiracy believers are thus, it seems, powerless, but more likely to be disobedient to social norms and inhibited by what others (the sleeping masses) think of their demeanour. This conception aligns very well with the association of feelings of powerlessness with non-normative protests and political violence, potentially following from the perception of having 'nothing to lose' (Saab et al. 2016).

This characterisation, however, creates some tension to a recurring theme in the social psychological literature on social power: here, having power reduces inhibitions and compliance with perceived norms, and liberates people to act on their impulses. Power reduces the impact of situational pressures (Galinsky et al. 2008) and general awareness of constraints (Lammers et al. 2008). This state of disinhibition has both positive (e.g. overcoming inertia to help others; DeCelles et al. 2012) and negative (e.g. unethical behaviour; Trautmann et al. 2013) outcomes (Hirsh et al. 2011). Both powerful men and women are more likely to engage in extramarital sex than their powerless counterparts (Lammers, Maner 2016). Men and women who reported to hold more power in the workplace not only admitted having greater interest in non-normative varieties of sexual behaviour (sexual masochism, sexual sadism), but did so disproportionately for the variant that was less frequent (and thus descriptively non-normative) for their gender role (men for masochism, women for sadism; Lammers, Imhoff 2016). Thus, a plethora of research is in line with the idea that power (not powerlessness) evokes a reduced reliance on social norms (and, by implication, powerlessness increases it).

Taking these two lines of thought together leaves a conundrum. Although a feeling of powerlessness should increase adherence to norms (according to the power literature), endorsing conspiracy theories is neither particularly normative, nor are other associates of conspiracy beliefs (e.g. crime intentions, non-normative protests). To our best knowledge, there is currently no authoritative solution to reconcile the psychological literature on a (comparatively) inhibiting and norm-compliant effect of low power, with the collective action literature making the opposite prediction of greater non-normative action in situations of powerlessness. One way to make sense of these findings might be to think about a curvilinear relation between power and norm compliance. Norm compliance could then be maximal for average levels of power and a deviation in either direction would reduce it. High levels of power would reduce norm compliance due to its general disinhibiting effect and because high power implies that one does not have to take others' reactions into one's consideration. Low levels of power would relate to reduced norm compliance because at some point one has 'nothing-to-lose' and therefore no reason to care about others' reactions. Future research is required to elucidate this relation in more detail (but see Cichocka et al. 2018).

## Conclusion

The above-mentioned power paradox is not the only avenue for future research, as many questions remain unanswered at this point. One of the most basic issues is the question of causality and empirical support for either the compensatory hypothesis or the reinforcement hypothesis, or both. With the help of prospective longitudinal studies, it would be possible to tease apart whether powerlessness increases the endorsement of conspiracy theories (as a way to deal with one's deprived sense of control) or whether endorsing such theories about almighty others will reduce one's sense of power (as these almighty others have all of it). The question might also be addressable with experimental manipulations of power, but only in their (relative) short-term effects of a single study.

A comparative perspective might shed more light into the intrinsic linkage between negative views of power and conspiracy beliefs. Most psychological studies so far have been conducted in context where conspiracy theories are heterodox knowledge, an outsider opinion, and the target frequently are the powerful. It is not pre-empirically clear whether we should expect the same in contexts where a conspiracy rhetoric is a strategy of those in power and the targets of the insinuations are marginalised minorities or outside groups. Comparisons between such contexts or even better across a large number of contexts differing in this regard may further elucidate how close this link is.

Seeing the world governed by a secret plan made behind closed curtains intimately evokes questions of power. We have argued that even if one does not include high power of the conspirators into the definition (and thus make the connection tautological), conspiracy beliefs are tightly connected to distrust of people, groups and institutions with power, both conceptually and empirically. Whether such theories in the long run empower individuals to either perceive themselves as more powerful or indeed achieve more agency and control over their surrounding (e.g. via political protests) is an exciting avenue for future research.

## References

Abalakina–Paap, M., Stephan, W.G., Craig, T. and Gregory, W.L. (1999) 'Beliefs in conspiracies', *Political Psychology*, 20(3): 637–47.

Bartlett, J. and Miller, C. (2010) *The power of unreason: conspiracy theories, extremism and counter-terrorism*, London, UK: Demos.

Cartwright, D. (1965) 'Influence, leadership, and control', in J. G. March (ed.) *Handbook of organizations*, Chicago, IL: Rand McNally, pp. 1–47.

Cichocka, A., Górska, P., Jost, J.T., Sutton, R.M. and Bilewicz, M. (2018) 'What inverted u can do for your country: a curvilinear relationship between confidence in the social system and political engagement', *Journal of Personality and Social Psychology*, 115(5): 883–902.

Cislak, A., Cichocka, A., Wojcik, A.D. and Frankowska, N. (2018) 'Power corrupts, but control does not: what stands behind the effects of holding high positions', *Personality and Social Psychology Bulletin*, 44(6): 944–57.

Crocker, J., Luhtanen, R., Broadnax, S. and Blaine, B.E. (1999) 'Belief in US government conspiracies against Blacks among Black and White college students: powerlessness or system blame?', *Personality and Social Psychology Bulletin*, 25(8): 941–53.

Cuddy, A.J., Fiske, S.T. and Glick, P. (2007) 'The BIAS map: behaviors from intergroup affect and stereotypes', *Journal of Personality and Social Psychology*, 92(4): 631–48.

DeCelles, K.A., DeRue, D.S., Margolis, J.D. and Ceranic, T.L. (2012) 'Does power corrupt or enable? when and why power facilitates self-interested behaviour', *Journal of Applied Psychology*, 97(3): 681–9.

Douglas, K.M., Sutton, R.M., Callan, M.J., Dawtry, R.J. and Harvey, A.J. (2016) 'Someone is pulling the strings: hypersensitive agency detection and belief in conspiracy theories', *Thinking and Reasoning*, 22: 57–77.

Duckitt, J. and Sibley, C.G. (2007) 'Right wing authoritarianism, social dominance orientation and the dimensions of generalized prejudice', *European Journal of Personality*, 21(2): 113–30.

Edelson, J., Alduncin, A., Krewson, C., Sieja, J.A. and Uscinski, J.E. (2017) 'The effect of conspiratorial thinking and motivated reasoning on belief in election fraud', *Political Research Quarterly*, 70(4): 933–46.

Fast, N.J., Gruenfeld, D.H., Sivanathan, N. and Galinsky, A.D. (2009) 'Illusory control: A generative force behind power's far-reaching effects', *Psychological Science*, 20, 502–8.

Fiske, S.T., Cuddy, A.J., Glick, P. and Xu, J. (2002) 'A model of (often mixed) stereotype content: competence and warmth respectively follow from perceived status and competition', *Journal of Personality and Social Psychology*, 82(6): 878–902.

French, J.R. and Raven, B. (1959) 'The bases of social power', *Classics of organization theory*, 7: 311–20.

Galinsky, A.D., Magee, J.C., Gruenfeld, D.H., Whitson, J.A. and Liljenquist, K.A. (2008) 'Power reduces the press of the situation: implications for creativity, conformity, and dissonance', *Journal of Personality and Social Psychology*, 95(6): 1450–66.

Goertzel, T. (1994) 'Belief in conspiracy theories', *Political Psychology*, 15(4): 731–42.

Hirsh, J.B., Galinsky, A.D. and Zhong, C.B. (2011) 'Drunk, powerful, and in the dark: how general processes of disinhibition produce both prosocial and antisocial behavior', *Perspectives on Psychological Science*, 6(5): 415–27.

Hofstadter, R. (1964) 'The paranoid style in American politics', *Harper's Magazine*, 229: 77–86.

Imhoff, R. (2015) 'Beyond (right-wing) authoritarianism: conspiracy mentality as an incremental predictor of prejudice', in M. Bilewicz, A. Cichocka and W. Soral (eds.) *The psychology of conspiracy*, London, UK: Routledge, pp. 122–41.

Imhoff, R. and Bruder, M. (2014) 'Speaking (un-)truth to power: conspiracy mentality as a generalized political attitude', *European Journal of Personality*, 28(1): 25–43.

Imhoff, R. and Decker, O. (2013) 'Verschwörungsmentalität als Weltbild [Conspiracy mentality as a worldview]', in O. Decker, J. Kiess and E. Brähler (eds.) *Rechtsextremismus der Mitte*, Wiesbaden, Germany: Psychosozial Verlag, pp. 130–45.

Imhoff, R. and Koch, A. (2017) 'How orthogonal are the Big Two of social perception? On the curvilinear relation between agency and communion', *Perspectives in Psychological Science*, 12(1): 122–37.

Imhoff, R. and Lamberty, P. (2017) 'Too special to be duped: need for uniqueness motivates conspiracy beliefs', *European Journal of Social Psychology*, 47(6): 724–34.

Imhoff, R. and Lamberty, P. (2018) 'How paranoid are conspiracy believers? Towards a more fine-grained understanding of the connect and disconnect between paranoia and belief in conspiracy theories', *European Journal of Social Psychology*, 48: 909–26.

Imhoff, R., Koch, A. and Flade, F. (2018) '(Pre)occupations: a data-driven map of job and its consequences for categorization and evaluation', *Journal of Experimental Social Psychology*, 77: 76–82.

Imhoff, R., Lamberty, P. and Klein, O. (2018) 'Using power as a negative cue: how conspiracy mentality affects epistemic trust in sources of historical knowledge', *Personality and Social Psychology Bulletin*, 44(9): 1364–79.

Inesi, M.E., Botti, S., Dubois, D., Rucker, D.D. and Galinsky, A.D. (2011) 'Power and choice: their dynamic interplay in quenching the thirst for personal control', *Psychological Science*, 22(8): 1042–8.

Jolley, D. and Douglas, K.M. (2014) 'The effects of anti-vaccine conspiracy theories on vaccination intentions', *PloS one*, 9: e89177.

Jolley, D., Douglas, K.M., Leite, A.C. and Schrader, T. (2019) 'Belief in conspiracy theories and intentions to engage in everyday crime', *British Journal of Social Psychology*.

Jolley, D., Meleady, R. and Douglas, K.M. (2019) 'Exposure to intergroup conspiracy theories promotes prejudice which spreads across groups', *British Journal of Social Psychology*.

Kay, A.C., Whitson, J.A., Gaucher, D. and Galinsky, A.D. (2009) 'Compensatory control: achieving order through the mind, our institutions, and the heavens', *Current Directions in Psychological Science*, 18(5): 264–8.

Koch, A., Imhoff, R., Dotsch, R., Unkelbach, C. and Alves, H. (2016) 'The ABC of stereotypes about groups: Agency/socio-economic success, conservative-progressive Beliefs, and Communion', *Journal of Personality and Social Psychology*, 110(5): 675–709.

Kofta, M. and Sedek, G. (2005) 'Conspiracy Stereotypes of Jews during Systemic Transformation in Poland', *International Journal of Sociology*, 35, 40–64.

Lamberty, P. and Imhoff, R. (2018) 'Powerful pharma and its marginalized alternatives: effect of individual differences in conspiracy mentality on attitudes towards medical approaches', *Social Psychology*, 49(5): 255–70.

Lammers, J., Galinsky, A.D., Gordijn, E.H. and Otten, S. (2008) 'Illegitimacy moderates the effects of power on approach', *Psychological Science*, 19(6): 558–64.

Lammers, J. and Imhoff, R. (2016) 'Power and sadomasochism: understanding the antecedents of a knotty relationship', *Social Psychological and Personality Science*, 7(2): 142–8.

Lammers, J. and Maner, J. (2016) 'Power and attraction to the counternormative aspects of infidelity', *The Journal of Sex Research*, 53(1): 54–63.

Lammers, J., Stoker, J.I., Rink, F. and Galinsky, A.D. (2016) 'To have control over or to be free from others? The desire for power reflects a need for autonomy', *Personality and Social Psychology Bulletin*, 42(4): 498–512.

LeBoeuf, R.A. and Norton, M.I. (2011) 'Consequence-cause matching: Looking to the consequences of events to infer their causes', *Journal of Consumer Research*, 39, 128–41.

Magee, J.C. and Galinsky, A.D. (2008) '8 social hierarchy: the self-reinforcing nature of power and status', *Academy of Management annals*, 2(1), 351–98.

Miller, J.M., Saunders, K.L. and Farhart, C.E. (2016) 'Conspiracy endorsement as motivated reasoning: the moderating roles of political knowledge and trust', *American Journal of Political Science*, 60(4): 824–44.

Mirowsky, J. and Ross, C.E. (1998) 'Education, personal control, lifestyle and health: a human capital hypothesis', *Research on aging*, 20(4): 415–49.

Nyhan, B. (2017) 'Why more democrats are now embracing conspiracy theories', *New York Times*, 15 February. Available at: www.nytimes.com/2017/02/15/upshot/why-more-democrats-are-now-embracing-conspiracy-theories.html. [Accessed 1 June 2019.]

Oliver, J.E. and Wood, T.J. (2014) 'Conspiracy theories and the paranoid style(s) of mass opinion', *American Journal of Political Science*, 58: 952–66.

Pennycook, G., Cheyne, J.A., Barr, N., Koehler, D.J. and Fugelsang, J.A. (2015) 'On the reception and detection of pseudo-profound bullshit', *Judgment and Decision Making*, 10(6): 549–63.

Pigden, C. (2015) *Conspiracy Theories and the Conventional Wisdom Revisited*, unpublished manuscript.

Ransford, H.E. (1968) 'Isolation, powerlessness, and violence: a study of attitudes and participation in the Watts riot', *American Journal of Sociology*, 73(5): 581–91.

Saab, R., Spears, R., Tausch, N. and Sasse, J. (2016) 'Predicting aggressive collective action based on the efficacy of peaceful and aggressive actions', *European Journal of Social Psychology*, 46(5): 529–43.

Skinner, E. (1996) 'A guide to constructs of control', *Journal of Personality and Social Psychology*, 71(3): 549–70.

Sullivan, D., Landau, M.J. and Rothschild, Z.K. (2010) 'An existential function of enemyship: evidence that people attribute influence to personal and political enemies to compensate for threats to control', *Journal of Personality and Social Psychology*, 98(3): 434–49.

Swami, V., Voracek, M., Stieger, S., Tran, U.S. and Furnham, A. (2014) 'Analytic thinking reduces belief in conspiracy theories', *Cognition*, 133, 572–85.

Tausch, N., Becker, J.C., Spears, R., Christ, O., Saab, R., Singh, P. and Siddiqui, R.N. (2011) 'Explaining radical group behavior: developing emotion and efficacy routes to normative and nonnormative collective action', *Journal of Personality and Social Psychology*, 101: 129–48.

Trautmann, S.T., van de Kuilen, G. and Zeckhauser, R.J. (2013) 'Social class and (un) ethical behavior: a framework, with evidence from a large population sample', *Perspectives on Psychological Science*, 8(5): 487–97.

Van Prooijen, J.-W. (2016) 'Sometimes inclusion breeds suspicion: self-uncertainty and belongingness predict belief in conspiracy theories', *European Journal of Social Psychology*, 46: 267–79.

Van Prooijen, J.-W. and Acker, M. (2015) 'The influence of control on belief in conspiracy theories: conceptual and applied extensions', *Applied Cognitive Psychology*, 29(5): 753–61.

Van Prooijen, J.-W., Douglas, K.M. and De Inocencio, C. (2018) 'Connecting the dots: illusory pattern perception predicts belief in conspiracies and the supernatural', *European Journal of Social Psychology*, 48(3): 320–35.

Van Prooijen, J.-W., Krouwel, A.P. and Pollet, T.V. (2015) 'Political extremism predicts belief in conspiracy theories', *Social Psychological and Personality Science*, 6(5): 570–8.

Van Prooijen, J.-W., Staman, J. and Krouwel, A.P. (2018) 'Increased conspiracy beliefs among ethnic and Muslim minorities', *Applied Cognitive Psychology*, 32: 661–7.

Whitson, J.A. and Galinsky, A.D. (2008) 'Lacking control increases illusory pattern perception', *Science*, 322(5898): 115–7.

Wright, S.C., Taylor, D.M. and Moghaddam, F.M. (1990) 'Responding to membership in a disadvantaged group: from acceptance to collective protest', *Journal of Personality and Social Psychology*, 58(6): 994–1003.

YouGov (2018) *YGC Conspiracy Theories (all countries)*. Available at: https://d25d2506sfb94s.cloudfront.net/cumulus_uploads/document/pk1qbgil4c/YGC%20Conspiracy%20Theories%20(all%20countries).pdf. [Accessed 28 August 2019.]

# 2.5
# HOW CONSPIRACY THEORIES SPREAD

*Adrian Bangerter, Pascal Wagner-Egger and Sylvain Delouvée*

## Introduction

Perhaps one of the most widespread and long-running conspiracy theories is about an alleged Jewish plot to undermine Christianity and dominate the world (Taguieff 2007). This recurring myth has appeared in various guises throughout history. In medieval Western Europe, the outbreak of the plague known as the Black Death led to the emergence of allegations that the deaths and suffering were caused by a Jewish plot to poison wells used by Christians. The original story featured lepers as the main villains, but, as it spread, Jews became associated with it. The popular wrath that was thus ignited led to pogroms that had the cumulative effect of eradicating much of the Jewish population of Western Europe (Kelly 2005). Eastern Europe and Russia were comparatively less affected by the Black Death. But that region had its own history of virulent Judeophobia, which originated in the Greek orthodox tradition, spreading from Byzantium with Christianity. It was in the court of Tsar Nicolas II that the *Protocols of the Elders of Zion* was first commissioned (Poliakov 1987). The document was widely translated and spread in many countries (notably, the American industrialist Henry Ford printed and distributed more than half a million copies of the Americanised version of the *Protocols*; Singerman 1981).

The longevity, spread and impact of the Jewish conspiracy theory is breathtaking. It has persisted over centuries and diffused in countless pages of text or hypertext, moved through innumerable brains and indirectly motivated the oppression and murder of millions of individuals. Nowadays, one might think that the Jewish conspiracy theory is an outlandish fairytale that has no place in the modern world. Nevertheless, it continues to resurface in many different forms and is actively used to motivate antisemitism around the world (Swami 2012). One example is the Rumour of Orléans, which, in 1969, accused Jewish merchants of the French town of Orléans of kidnapping young women (Morin *et al.* 2014). A more recent example is the Pittsburgh synagogue shooting on 27 October 2018, where the murderer believed migrant caravans moving towards the U.S.A. were part of a Jewish plot. The extreme malleability of the Jewish conspiracy theory, which explains its extraordinary longevity, is illustrated by the fact that it may be associated with ancient figures such as Satan (being members of the 'Satanic conspiracy', Taguieff 2007), but also with futuristic conspirators, such as extraterrestrial reptilians (and/or Illuminati).

The Jewish conspiracy theory illustrates an extreme point on three fundamental dimensions along which conspiracy theories can vary, namely *stick*, *spread* and *action* (Franks *et al.* 2013).

Stickiness refers to the potential of a representation for belief. The determinants of conspiracy theory belief have been amply researched, especially in terms of individual differences that predict belief (see Chapter 2.1). Action is the extent to which conspiracy theories motivate individual or collective behaviour (see Chapter 2.6 and 2.7). Spread refers to the transmission of conspiracy theories, and is the object of this chapter. It is arguably the least well understood dimension along which conspiracy theories vary.

Indeed, there are relatively few studies that directly investigate the transmission processes of conspiracy theories. However, there are many resources on which to draw from the study of transmission of other kinds of beliefs and representations in the social sciences. Insights from related phenomena like rumours, myths, gossip and folklore or urban legends can illuminate the transmission of conspiracy theories (see Chapter 4.1), as well as theoretical models like the epidemiology of representations approach (Sperber 1985) or the social representations approach (Sammut et al. 2015; Lo Monaco et al. 2016). In what follows, we first describe the process of transmission itself, before reviewing research on situational factors and features of conspiracy theory content that affect transmission. We emphasise individual-level processes or small-scale social interactions between individuals.

## The transmission process

We define transmission as the process of communicating about a conspiracy theory with other people. This process can take many forms. Conspiracy theories can be passed on in interactive conversations, where both tellers and their audience can interact with each other in real time. These can be face-to-face (in which case participants can engage a wide range of signals like language, gesture, facial expressions), or mediated (e.g. online chat forums), where text is the main channel of communication (but images can also be transmitted). Conspiracy theories can also be broadcast via mass media (as Henry Ford did when he printed and distributed the *Protocols* in the U.S.A.) or social media as when people debate the plausibility of conspiracy theories in online forums (Wood, Douglas 2013). Yablokov (2017) discussed the role of social networks in spreading conspiracy theories, where one can forward a link to one's followers by simply clicking on retweet.

As an important vehicle of information in modern societies, the Internet is perceived as a more democratic source, since it does not depend on a vertical process as in traditional media. It is supposed to give direct access to information and reveal the 'truth' (Aupers 2012). Several studies report a general decline in trust in traditional institutions and a very low level of vertical trust, particularly in new democracies (Mishler, Rose 1997; Dalton 2000; Macek, Markova 2004; Catterberg, Moreno 2006). The Internet is viewed as a space for criticism, making it possible to deconstruct official information and produce one's own theories (Aupers 2012). This makes it easier to believe in conspiracies, and more difficult to control their source and transmission (Stempel et al. 2007). Additionally, belief in such theories (Mulligan, Habel 2011; Swami et al. 2013; Jolley, Douglas 2014a, 2014b; Einstein, Glick 2015) can lead to decreased trust in government (Einstein, Glick 2015) and to a persistent cynicism about government, particularly towards political participation (Butler et al. 1995; Jolley, Douglas 2014b). Research has just begun to investigate the online propagation of conspiracy theories (Mocanu et al. 2015; Del Vicario et al. 2016, 2017), but simple Google or YouTube searches reveal many conspiratorial websites and videos (Bronner 2011).

Conspiracy theories are spread in two main communicative genres: storytelling and argumentation. Storytelling is the social activity (Norrick 2007; Bietti et al. 2019) by which groups of people tell stories, which are dramatised accounts of events that prominently feature the actions of protagonists (heroes, villains and the like; Propp 1987) and the goals they are trying to achieve. In essence, conspiracy theories are stories (e.g. the U.S. government manufactured A.I.D.S. to control the black population). Conspiracy theory narratives often feature similar plot elements: Conspirators, a plan, secrecy (Byford 2011), but also heroic depictions of the believers and their actions or attitudes (Franks *et al.* 2017). Argumentation is also a prominent conspiracy theory genre as when aficionados or sceptics debate the details that support or invalidate a particular version of events, e.g. that the flag in the alleged moon landing photos seems to flap in a – nonexistent – breeze as evidence for a hoax (Wood, Douglas 2013). Recent work in discourse analysis describes the argumentation strategies of conspiracy theory defenders. They often use source-related fallacies (*ad populum, ad verecundiam, ad hominem*), hasty generalisations, arguments from analogy and from ignorance, inductive and abductive arguments and shifts in the burden of proof. These arguments appear in refutational strategies directed against the official version rather than in defense of the conspiracy theory (Oswald 2016).

At the level of the individual, the transmission process can be defined as a dynamic interaction between five classes of variables: (1) related to individual differences, (2) related to the transmission situation or (3) related to the content of the conspiracy theory, all of which affect (4) belief and (5) the decision to communicate the conspiracy theory (Figure 2.5.1). The relations in Figure 2.5.1 have been simplified to convey the main points we emphasise (i.e. not all possible relations are depicted).

A key feature of the transmission process is the reciprocal relation between belief and transmission. On the one hand, belief affects transmission. Rumours believed to be true are more likely to be transmitted (Rosnow 1991; Guerin, Miyazaki 2006; Pezzo, Beckstead 2006), and the same holds for urban legends (Heath *et al.* 2001). But there are exceptions to the link between belief and transmission (Delouvée 2015). Members of online cancer discussion websites were not more likely to pass on cancer rumours they believed than rumours they did not believe (DiFonzo *et al.* 2012). Conversely, conspiracy theories (or other forms of belief) can get strategically transmitted by individuals who do not necessary believe them. For example, as Kapferer (1987) notes, rumours can be transmitted for many reasons: because they are new, because they convey information, because they may convince the listener to rally to the ideas of the narrator, because they are credible (Clément 2006), because they soothe certain tensions, because they allow the teller to be the centre of attention or because they are engaging (Allport, Lepkin 1943, 1945), and therefore not necessarily because they are believed. On the other hand,

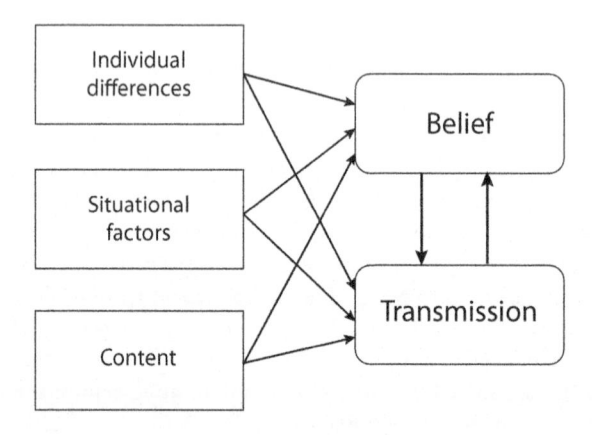

*Figure 2.5.1* The transmission process.

individuals may hesitate to share conspiracy theories they believe in because of a fear of being stigmatised (Lantian *et al.* 2018).

Transmission can also have consequences for belief. Over time, a conspiracy theory that is widely distributed may become strongly anchored in a culture via material artefacts (Boltanski 2012). For example, the J.F.K. conspiracy theory has been replayed in hundreds of television series, novels or movies. And the tenacity of the Zionist conspiracy theory in people's minds may also be related to its cultural prevalence. The widespread availability of these ideas increases the potential exposure of individuals to them, and thus their potential to be believed (Butler *et al.* 1995; Douglas, Sutton 2008; Nera *et al.* 2018).

The transmission variable in Figure 2.5.1 can be operationalised in multiple ways. First, the simplest way is to ask participants if they have transmitted a belief (rumour, urban legend or conspiracy theory) or have heard one circulating (DiFonzo, Bordia 2002) or use a proxy for transmission, namely the intention to transmit, e.g. asking participants how likely they are to pass on a conspiracy theory (Heath *et al.* 2001). Second, the cumulative effect of actual individual transmission on content can be studied by serial reproduction experiments (e.g. Bartlett 1932; Kirkpatrick 1932; Allport, Postman 1947). These experiments involve exposing participants to some textual or visual material and then getting them to recall and write down (or otherwise reproduce) what they recall. This recollection (e.g. a text) is then given to a next-generation participant who does the same. This creates a chain of successive recollections that typically feature systematic transformations of content. When using multiple parallel chains (Bangerter 2000), content-related trends can be averaged and compared across different experimental conditions. A third strategy for gauging the effects of transmission is to measure the distribution of conspiracy theories in various media at a point in time (i.e. analyse a cross-section of particular media). For example, sampling anti-vaccine websites reveals that they almost uniformly feature vaccine-related conspiracy theories, e.g. vaccines are a hoax propagated by pharmaceutical companies and medical professionals to maintain high levels of chronic disease and thus create a need for drugs (Davies *et al.* 2002; Kata 2010). Fourth, with the advent of social media, online transmission behaviour can be studied via the application programming interfaces (A.P.I.s) of social media like Facebook or Twitter, which allow researchers to download and analyse massive amounts of actual sharing or retweeting behaviour. A recent study of Facebook (Del Vicario *et al.* 2016) modelled 'cascades', or unbroken chains of reposted information with a common origin. The study found that conspiracy theories spread within 'echo chambers' (Bronner *et al.* 2018) of like-minded individuals and that – in contrast – science news spread within similarly homogenous, but distinct, networks. Bessi *et al.* (2015) also found that, on Facebook, information related to (1) mainstream scientific and (2) conspiracy news are consumed in communities polarised around distinct types of content. But regular consumers of conspiracy news were more self-contained and focused on their specific contents. This mirrors the experimental observation that conspiracy believers and nonbelievers are both prone to biased assimilation and attitude polarisation, but believers to a slightly higher degree (McHoskey 1995). Confirmation bias – the well-known tendency to confirm rather than disconfirm our beliefs (Nickerson 1998) – is thus reinforced in online search and transmission of information (Del Vicario *et al.* 2016, 2017; Bronner *et al.* 2018).

## Situational factors affecting transmission

In this section, we review research on the psychological features of particular social situations that make conspiracy theories and related forms of belief like rumours or urban legends more likely to spread. We suggested above that there is a dearth of research on conspiracy theory transmission. But it seems clear that many widespread (and thus widely transmitted) conspiracy theories propose alternative explanations to traumatic collective events, including terrorist attacks like 9/11 in the U.S.A. or the Charlie Hebdo attacks in France, disease outbreaks or the sudden death of celebrities like J.F.K. or Princess Diana. This, in turn, suggests that there is something about the psychological impact of such situations that generates a need for sharing conspiracy theories. However, conspiracy theories also get transmitted in the absence of a link to an obviously traumatic event (for example the conspiracy theories about the moon landings being a hoax) or even in the absence of any kind of event (for example conspiracy theories about a Zionist conspiracy). Thus, it is not the objective features of a situation that lead to conspiracy theory transmission, but rather its psychological characteristics (van Prooijen, Douglas 2017; Douglas et al. 2019).

Work from folklore studies further suggests that large-scale social change (i.e. concerning whole societies and lasting for years) generates feelings of alienation or anxiety that are conducive to the emergence and spread of rumours and urban legends. In Western societies, belief in conspiracy may be due to the ontological insecurity generated by the rationalised institutions (the state, the economy) that constitute modernity as well as the delegitimation of traditional sources of epistemic authority like religion or, more recently, science (Aupers 2012). One example from the U.S.A. in the 1970s involves the recurrent revival of urban legends around Halloween according to which children engaging in the traditional activity of trick or treat receive poisoned candy from sadists. The legend circulated in a context of 'intense social strain' (Best, Horiuchi 1985: 493) characterised by the unpopular Vietnam War and civil unrest (riots, student demonstrations, the spread of alternative lifestyles and drug use). A similar example was documented in Orléans, France in 1969 (Morin et al. 2014), where a rumour circulated for several months according to which Jewish merchants who owned fashionable clothing boutiques were drugging and kidnapping young female clients, who were then transported out of the country and sold into sexual slavery. Besides the obvious antisemitic overtones, the motifs of the rumour symbolise the dangers of modernity and the changing role of women (going out and being frivolous) rather than staying at home. These motifs resonated with contemporaneous themes of civil unrest in France like the events of May 1968 (see also Durkheim's famous [1899] analysis of how the Dreyfus affair was also facilitated by an acute outbreak of antisemitism brought on by social upheaval). A third example concerns rumours emerging in the 2000s in countries in Western Africa warning against the danger of shaking the hands of strangers (who can allegedly snatch men's penises away from them) or answering mobile phone calls from anonymous numbers (which can kill the answerer). They coincide with social change as well, as African society moves from a traditional, village-based structure to life in large cities where anonymous social relations and close contact with strangers are increasing (Bonhomme 2012).

More circumscribed, local events (i.e. concerning a geographical region or a particular group like an organisation) that take place over a shorter, more acute timescale can also foster belief transmission. Here, again, much of what we know comes from the study of rumours. One example concerns organisational changes, which create situations of uncertainty and anxiety, increasing in turn the transmission of rumours. In a study of change in a hospital (Bordia et al. 2006), individuals who felt more change-related stress reported more rumours. Insufficiently clear communication about the change may also encourage rumours, which may in turn increase perceptions of insecurity (Smet et al. 2016). Rumours also often emerge in situations like wartime (Allport, Postman 1947) or in the aftermath of natural disasters. Rumours about child trafficking surfaced in the aftermath of the 2004 tsunami that devastated many areas of Southeast Asia (Samuels 2015). These rumours now emerge regularly after natural disasters (Montgomery 2011). Likewise, Uscinski and Parent (2014) coded the presence of conspiracy theory narratives in letters to the editor from 1897 to 2010 in two prominent U.S. newspapers, alongside the characteristics of the villains depicted in the narratives. Villains were more right-wing and capitalist when a Republican president was in power and more left-wing and communist when a Democratic president was in power. Interestingly, when threat from external enemies was high, conspiracy theories focused more often on foreign villains than when threat was low. These effects suggest that spreading conspiracy theories is a way to manage threat, especially related to political defeat.

The field studies that link the content of rumours, urban legends or conspiracy theories to large-scale social change or to more local, acute events have a high ecological validity and are suggestive of the potential role of various psychological reactions that these situations might evoke and which might mediate their effects on the transmission of conspiracy theories. Possible reactions include an increase of anxiety (apprehension about potential negative outcomes), feeling threatened or feeling a lack of control. However, more controlled studies that manipulate causal variables are necessary to demonstrate specific effects of psychological variables like lack of control on the transmission of conspiracy theories.

Psychological processes may affect transmission via several paths. Change phenomena or perceptions of lack of control are basically violations of expectations. Even relatively small-scale expectation violations increase aversive arousal, which in turn motivates efforts to reduce that arousal (Proulx *et al.* 2012). Sensemaking processes in various forms, including storytelling (Bietti *et al.* 2019), help explain the inconsistency and, thus, reduce arousal. This possibility is supported by experiments where manipulating physiological arousal (via exposure to arousing emotional content) increases participants' propensity to transmit unrelated, emotionally neutral content (e.g. an online news article). The effect is independent of the emotional valence of the content, and neutral manipulations of arousal (getting participants to jog lightly in place for a minute) achieve similar effects (Berger 2011). The effect of change situations (be they diffuse or focused, large-scale or acute) on psychological outcomes like anxiety, threat or loss of control thus offer a plausible pathway to understand how these situations create aversively arousing states of expectancy violation. In turn, sharing conspiracy theories may serve sensemaking functions and thus reduce this arousal. While plausible, these processes require more research on actual transmission to be supported.

Increases in aversive arousal could also trigger emotions, as has been originally noted in rumour research. Many authors have observed that uncertainty, and the attendant anxiety, enhances rumour spreading (e.g. Allport, Postman 1947; Rosnow 1980). This fact is readily illustrated by the profusion of rumours that propagate during war. Anxiety also facilitates endorsement of conspiracy theories, be it personal anxiety in life (Grzesiak-Feldman 2007, 2013; Swami *et al.* 2016; Green, Douglas 2018), death anxiety (Newheiser *et al.* 2011) or situational anxiety (Grzesiak-Feldman 2013), as well as fear of social issues such as pollution, terrorism, globalisation (Wagner-Egger, Bangerter 2007); stressful life events (Swami *et al.* 2016) or feelings of social insecurity, as measured by the Belief in Dangerous World scale (Leiser *et al.* 2017; Hart, Graether 2018). While these findings document the link between anxiety and belief, the role of anxiety (and other emotions) in the spread of conspiracy theories needs urgent research attention.

## The reciprocal relations between content and transmission

According to Figure 2.5.1, the content of a conspiracy theory constitutes the third major class of variables affecting transmission. That is, do certain features of the content of a conspiracy theory make it more likely to be believed or to get spread? This link is perhaps one of the least well understood relations in research on conspiracy theories. Further, the inverse relationship, that is, how transmission affects content, is also poorly understood. Here again, much insight can be gained from research on rumours and other forms of belief.

From rumour research, we know that transmission will be favoured by the novelty of rumour content (Brooks *et al.* 2013), its credibility (Allport, Lepkin 1943, 1945; Rosnow *et al.* 1988), and the consistency of its content with the attitudes of the transmitters (Galam 2002). The spread will be also heightened when rumours relieve tensions (Rosnow 1980; Esposito, Rosnow 1984), or promote the ingroup (Bordia *et al.* 2005). The emotional content of a conspiracy theory may also affect transmission. In the domain of urban legends, Heath, Bell and Sternberg (2001) showed that stories rated as more disgusting were more often intended to be passed along by participants, and also distributed more widely on urban legend websites.

Some studies have investigated how the content of conspiracy theories affects belief. When interpreting events, people apparently rely on the 'proportion bias', or 'major event-major cause heuristic' (McCauley, Jacques 1979; Leman, Cinnirella 2007; van Prooijen, van Dijk 2014). For example, participants judging an event in which the president of a country has been shot during a parade perceive more conspiracies when the president was killed, rather than when he was only wounded (Leman, Cinnirella 2007). In a series of experiments, Kovic and Füchslin (2018) showed that conspiratorial thinking as an explanation for events increases as the probability of those events decreases. For example, one of their scenarios described an accomplished journalist who was critical of the government and who suddenly died in his apartment from a heart attack. The experimenters added probabilistic information about the medical risks, according to doctors, that someone like this journalist would die. The lower the probability, the more the death was interpreted as the result of a conspiracy, rather than of an accident. Because these studies concern cognitive biases for particular content, they may make conspiracy theories more plausible and thus facilitate belief. However, it remains to be seen whether these biases affect transmission as well.

A more social feature of the content of conspiracy theories is that they basically rely on an antagonistic representation of society (Moscovici 1987). For example, they play to distrust of elites (political, scientific and media, e.g. Wagner-Egger, Bangerter 2007; Wagner-Egger *et al.* 2011; Lewandowsky *et al.* 2013), and identify 'villains' and 'victims' in important social events, such as disease outbreaks (Wagner-Egger *et al.* 2011). Conspiracists see themselves as more clairvoyant than ordinary people, considered as a herd of sheep (Franks *et al.* 2017). This is also probably why research showed that conspiracy believers display a heightened need for uniqueness than non-believers (Lantian *et al.* 2017; Imhoff, Lamberty 2017).

Some authors draw on cognitive science of religion (e.g. Boyer 2001; Norenzayan *et al.* 2006) to propose hypotheses by analogy about the spread of conspiracy theories, suggesting that conspiracy theories may have a 'quasi-religious' function (Franks *et al.* 2013). First, conspiring agents in flourishing conspiracy theories are represented as minimally counter-intuitive, because they are most often humans (or sometimes human-like, like the extraterrestrials or reptilians), but they display extraordinary strategic omniscience and omnipotence, by controlling multitudes of people to take part to the conspiracy, and to keep the secret about it years after. This derives from religion studies where religious beliefs are 'minimally counter-intuitive': For example, a representation of a god is grounded on commonsense representations about people (e.g. people have agency, act according to beliefs and desires, have memories), but violates some physical and biological qualities of people (reincarnation, omniscience, etc.). Second, sharing conspiracy theories via communication rituals supports management of anxiety, by transforming unspecific anxieties into focused fears. In particular, intergroup conspiracy theories who accuse minorities have a scapegoat function, by pointing at the individuals or groups allegedly responsible for the anxiety-provoking events (Moscovici 1987). Third, conspiracy theory narratives framed as conflicts over sacred values may spread more successfully, as illustrated by the ancient and persistent 'satanic conspiracy' (involving, alternatively or jointly, Freemasons, Illuminati, Jews, Muslims and so on, pitted against Christianity; Taguieff 2007).

Many of the features above can be described as 'local' in the sense that they may appear in part of the text that constitutes a conspiracy narrative. But more 'global' properties of narrative organisation, like the overall plot structure (Byford 2011) or the concrete descriptions of important characters like the outgroup villain (Propp 1987; Raab et al. 2013; Franks et al. 2017), may also facilitate their transmission, by making the narrative easier to remember (an important precondition for transmission; Norenzayan et al. 2006) or more entertaining for audiences (Heath et al. 2001).

How does transmission affect content? As described above, the truth is not of primary importance for rumour-mongers (Rouquette 1990). The same holds for conspiracy theories, which circulate whether or not bearers consider them as true or false. They are not merely information transmitted by word of mouth, but are part of a privileged mode of expression of social thought (Rouquette 1973). Therefore, during interpersonal communication, rumours and conspiracy theories evolve and transform. Allport and Postman (1947) highlighted the distortions occurring in rumour spreading by means of the serial reproduction method. In their studies, after the seventh generation of retelling, the message took on its final shape, being sufficiently short to be easily remembered. Whereas no studies have been conducted on this issue, this process of reduction may be shorter for conspiracy theories, because they include core narrative elements (Keeley 1999; Byford 2011). Three mechanisms were described by Allport and Postman (1947), (1) reduction of information (only 20 per cent of the original information was left after seven generations), (2) accentuation (exaggeration of some details) and (3) assimilation (incorporation of the information to the pre-existing knowledge, beliefs, values and attitudes of individuals). In their framework, assimilation drives reduction and accentuation processes. While these mechanisms may serve as an initial guide for the study of how transmission affects content, they are based on the serial reproduction paradigm that necessarily leads to reduction through memory limitations. The online environments through which many conspiracy theories are spread nowadays allow much more potential for (multimodal) elaboration, and thus novel forms of how transmission affects content may be yet discovered.

## Discussion and outlook

Stick (belief) and spread (transmission) (Franks et al. 2013) are arguably two of the most important issues in the psychology of conspiracy theories. Much is known about how conspiracy theories stick, but little is known about how they spread. This is a significant imbalance, because understanding the spread of conspiracy theories is of the greatest theoretical and practical importance. Accordingly, based on the model in Figure 2.5.1, we identified three main factors susceptible to affect conspiracy theory transmission: Individual differences (see Chapter 2.1), situational factors and content of the conspiracy theory. We also discussed the relation between belief and transmission. While belief in conspiracy theories may predict their transmission, the relationship is complex. Often as not, conspiracy beliefs may not be transmitted, or conspiracy theories may be transmitted strategically, in the absence of belief. Thus, belief cannot be considered as a proxy variable for transmission, nor can the determinants of conspiracy theory belief be automatically assumed to affect transmission. These observations lead to three areas of research that require urgent attention.

The first area is the reciprocal relation between belief and transmission. Is it possible to know and spread, but not believe a conspiracy theory? Inversely, could some people know and believe a conspiracy theory but refrain from spreading it? Motivation may be at the interface between belief and transmission. Some individuals could be motivated to differ from others, and to feel superior to the 'herd of sheep' of nonbelievers by knowing, believing and spreading conspiracy theories (Franks et al. 2017), but others could refrain from spreading, to avoid being stigmatised by nonbelievers (Lantian et al. 2018). Social factors will also motivate believers to invest time, money and energy in order to spread the conspiracy theories (Bronner 2003, 2006). By means of 'social proof' (Cialdini 1984), the more believers one finds, the truer one's belief will seem. Conspiracy theory transmission could also create and reinforce social ties within groups (Franks et al. 2017), and even transmit ingroup norms and values (Baumeister et al. 2004). Thus, a refusal to transmit some conspiracy theories in a group of believers could lead to stigmatisation or even exclusion from the group.

The second area concerns the nature of the transmission process. We discussed two main modes, namely interpersonal transmission and transmission via mass media or social media on the Internet. The rise of social media is an important factor in explaining the current prevalence of conspiracy theories in our modern world, because it allows millions of people all around the world to share any content in a couple of hours (Del Vicario et al. 2016). We also identified two prominent communicative genres by which conspiracy theories may be transmitted: storytelling (Bietti et al. 2019) and argumentation (Oswald 2016). As with all communication processes, multimodality may play a role in transmission. Many conspiracy theories rely on iconic images (e.g. the all-seeing eye of the Illuminati) or video that may evoke strong arousal in audiences. Furthermore, the role of audience participation in amplifying transmission needs to be studied (e.g. transmission in interactive online chats versus broadcasting to many recipients simultaneously and unidirectionally).

The third area concerns the reciprocal relation between content and transmission. What aspects of content affect the likelihood of transmission, and how does transmission affect content? Here, insights can be gained from the study of rumours (Allport, Postman 1947). But the methodological arsenal of conspiracy theory research will need to be extended. Transmission can be modelled experimentally via the venerable serial reproduction paradigm (Bartlett 1932; Bangerter 2000), or transmission may be studied directly on social media (Del Vicario et al. 2016). The potential for capturing content automatically is, however, perhaps one of the most exciting and promising areas for development. The abundance of spontaneously produced digitised text on the Internet, as well as the existence of software packages to measure the presence of words in a text (e.g. L.I.W.C., Tausczik, Pennebaker 2010) or co-occurrences (A.L.C.E.S.T.E., Reinert 1990) make very fine-grained analyses possible. Beyond these packages, powerful A.I.-based approaches like natural language processing (Qazvinian et al. 2011) or sentiment analysis (Liu 2010) are becoming more and more accessible for social science researchers (Samory, Mitra 2018).

A fourth and final area requiring further attention derives from recent social and political phenomena. While conspiracy theories have traditionally been the purview of 'popular thought' or of laypersons (Moscovici 1987) or of the powerless (Uscinski, Parent 2014), with the recent rise of populism, many individuals and groups occupying positions of power, influence and leadership in society now routinely spread conspiracy theories. Much larger segments of the public than the marginalised, anomic or irrational individuals that have been identified as typical believers are now exposed to conspiracy theories spread from positions of authority, which will require a change in both theory and research focus.

Throughout this chapter, we have emphasised the dearth of research on conspiracy theory transmission. We mainly relied on neighbouring fields like rumour, urban legend, cognitive science of religion and social representations in order to map out domains requiring more attention and drawing plausible hypotheses about conspiracy theory spread, but, as a conclusion, we invite researchers to investigate this virtually unexplored but crucial field of research.

## References

Allport, F.H. and Lepkin, M. (1943) 'Building war morale with news-headlines', *Public Opinion Quarterly*, 7: 211–21.
Allport, F.H. and Lepkin, M. (1945) 'Wartime rumors of waste and special privilege: why some people believe them', *The Journal of Abnormal and Social Psychology*, 40(1): 3–36.
Allport, G.W. and Postman, L. (1947) *The psychology of rumor*, Oxford: Henry Holt.
Aupers, S. (2012) '"Trust no one": modernization, paranoia and conspiracy culture', *European Journal of Communication*, 27(1): 22–34.
Bangerter, A. (2000) 'Transformation between scientific and social representations of conception: the method of serial reproduction', *British Journal of Social Psychology*, 39(4): 521–35.
Bartlett, F.C. (1932) *Remembering: a study in experimental and social psychology*, Cambridge: Cambridge University Press.
Baumeister, R.F., Zhang, L. and Vohs, K.D. (2004) 'Gossip as cultural learning', *Review of general psychology*, 8(2): 111–21.
Berger, J. (2011) 'Arousal increases social transmission of information', *Psychological Science*, 22(7): 891–93.
Bessi A., Coletto, M., Davidescu, G.A., Scala, A., Caldarelli, G. and Quattrociocchi, W. (2015) 'Science vs conspiracy: collective narratives in the age of misinformation', *PLoS ONE*, 10(2): e0118093.
Best, J. and Horiuchi, G.T. (1985) 'The razor blade in the apple: the social construction of urban legends', *Social Problems*, 32(5): 488–99.
Bietti, L.M., Tilston, O. and Bangerter, A. (2019) 'Storytelling as adaptive collective sensemaking', *Topics in Cognitive Science*, 11: 710–32.
Boltanski, L. (2012) *Énigmes et complots: une enquête à propos d'enquêtes*, Paris: Gallimard.
Bonhomme, J. (2012) 'The dangers of anonymity: witchcraft, rumor, and modernity in Africa', *Hau: Journal of Ethnographic Theory*, 2(2): 205–33.
Bordia, P., DiFonzo, N., Haines, R. and Chaseling, E. (2005) 'Rumors denials as persuasive messages: effects of personal relevance, source, and message characteristics', *Journal of Applied Social Psychology*, 35(6): 1301–31.
Bordia, P., Jones, E., Gallois, C., Callan, V.J. and DiFonzo, N. (2006) 'Management are aliens! Rumors and stress during organizational change', *Group and Organization Management*, 31(5): 601–21.
Boyer, P. (2001) *Religion explained: the evolutionary origins of religious thought*, New York, NY: Basic Books.
Bronner, G. (2003) *L'empire des croyances*, Paris: PUF.
Bronner, G. (2006) *Vie et mort des croyances collectives*, Paris: Hermann.
Bronner, G. (2011) *The future of collective beliefs*, Oxford: The Bardwell Press.
Bronner, G., David, P. and Del Bueno, L. (2018) 'À la recherche de nouvelles traces sociales. L'exemple des conspirationnistes', *Revue Européenne des Sciences Sociales*, 56(1): 13–52.
Brooks, B.P., DiFonzo, N. and Ross, D.S. (2013) 'The GBN-dialogue model of outgroup-negative rumor transmission: group membership, belief, and novelty', *Nonlinear Dynamics, Psychology, and Life Sciences*, 17(2): 269–93.
Butler, L.D., Koopman, C. and Zimbardo, P.G. (1995) 'The psychological impact of viewing the film "JFK": Emotions, beliefs, and political behavioral intentions', *Political Psychology*, 16(2): 237–57.
Byford, J., (2011) *Conspiracy theories: a critical introduction*, Basingstoke: Palgrave Macmillan.
Catterberg, G. and Moreno, A. (2006) 'The individual bases of political trust: trends in new and established democracies', *International Journal of Public Opinion Research*, 1(1): 31–48.
Cialdini, R.B. (1984) *Influence: the psychology of persuasion*, New York: Harper Business.
Clément, F. (2006) *Les mécanismes de la crédulité*, Paris: Droz.
Dalton, R. (2000) *Democratic challenges, democratic choices: the erosion of political support in advanced industrial democracies*, Oxford: Oxford University Press.
Davies, P., Chapman, S. and Leask, J. (2002) 'Antivaccination activists on the world wide web', *Archives of Disease in Childhood*, 87(1): 22–5.
Del Vicario, M., Bessi, A., Zollo, F., Petroni, F., Scala, A., Caldarelli, G., Stanley, H.E. and Quattrociocchi, W. (2016) 'The spreading of misinformation online', *Proceedings of the National Academy of Sciences*, 113(3): 554–9.

Del Vicario, M., Scala, A., Caldarelli, G., Stanley, H.E. and Quattrociocchi, W. (2017) 'Modeling confirmation bias and polarization', *Scientific Reports*, 7: 40391.
Delouvée, S. (2015) 'Répéter n'est pas croire: sur la transmission des idées conspirationnistes', *Diogène*, 1–2(249–50): 88–98.
DiFonzo, N. and Bordia, P. (2002) 'Corporate rumor activity, belief and accuracy', *Public Relations Review*, 28(1): 1–19.
DiFonzo, N., Robinson, N.M., Suls, J.M. and Rini, C. (2012) 'Rumors about cancer: content, sources, coping, transmission, and belief', *Journal of Health Communication*, 17(9): 1099–115.
Douglas, K.M. and Sutton, R.M. (2008) 'The hidden impact of conspiracy theories: perceived and actual influence of theories surrounding the death of Princess Diana', *Journal of Social Psychology*, 148(2): 210–22.
Douglas, K.M., Uscinski, J.E., Sutton, R.M., Cichocka, A., Nefes, T., Ang, C.S. and Deravi, F. (2019) 'Understanding conspiracy theories', *Advances in Political Psychology*, 40(1): 3–35.
Durkheim, É. (1899) 'Antisémitisme et crise sociale', in H. Dagan (ed.) *Enquête sur l'antisémitisme*, Paris: Stock, pp. 59–63.
Einstein, K.L. and Glick, D.M. (2015) 'Do I think BLS data are BS? The consequences of conspiracy theories', *Political Behavior*, 37(3): 679–701.
Esposito, J.L. and Rosnow, R.L. (1984) Cognitive set and message processing: implications of prose memory research for rumor theory, *Language and Communication*, 4(4): 301–15.
Franks, B., Bangerter, A. and Bauer, M. (2013) 'Conspiracy theories as quasi-religious mentality: an integrated account from cognitive science, social representations theory, and frame theory', *Frontiers in Psychology*, 4(424): 1–12.
Franks, B., Bangerter, A., Bauer, M.W., Hall, M. and Noort, M.C. (2017) 'Beyond "monologicality"? Exploring conspiracist worldviews', *Frontiers in Psychology*, 8(861).
Galam, S. (2002) 'Minority opinion spreading in random geometry', *The European Physical Journal B-Condensed Matter and Complex Systems*, 25(4): 403–6.
Green, R. and Douglas, K.M. (2018) 'Anxious attachment and belief in conspiracy theories', *Personality and Individual Differences*, 125: 30–7.
Grzesiak-Feldman, M. (2007) 'Conspiracy thinking and state-trait anxiety in young Polish adults', *Psychological Reports*, 100(1): 199–202.
Grzesiak-Feldman, M. (2013) 'The effect of high-anxiety situations on conspiracy thinking', *Current Psychology*, 32(1): 100–18.
Guerin, B. and Miyazaki, Y. (2006) 'Analyzing rumors, gossip, and urban legends through their conversational properties', *The Psychological Record*, 56(1): 23–34.
Hart, J. and Graether, M. (2018) 'Something's going on here: psychological predictors of belief in conspiracy theories', *Journal of Individual Differences*, 39(4): 229–37.
Heath, C., Bell, C. and Sternberg, E. (2001) 'Emotional selection in memes: the case of urban legend', *Journal of Personality and Social Psychology*, 81(6): 1028–41.
Imhoff, R. and Lamberty, P.K. (2017) 'Too special to be duped: need for uniqueness motivates conspiracy beliefs', *European Journal of Social Psychology*, 47(6): 724–34.
Jolley, D. and Douglas, K.M. (2014a) 'The effects of anti-vaccine conspiracy theory on vaccination intentions', *PLoS ONE*, 9(2): e89177.
Jolley, D. and Douglas, K.M. (2014b) 'The social consequences of conspiracism: exposure to conspiracy theories decreases intentions to engage in politics and to reduce one's carbon footprint', *British Journal of Psychology*, 105(1): 35–56.
Kapferer, J.N. (1987) *Rumeurs: le plus vieux média du monde*, Paris: Le Seuil.
Kata, A. (2010) 'A postmodern Pandora's box: anti-vaccination misinformation on the internet', *Vaccine*, 28(7): 1709–16.
Keeley, B.L. (1999) 'Of conspiracy theories', *Journal of Philosophy*, 96(3): 18–28.
Kelly, J. (2005) *The great mortality: an intimate history of the black death, the most devastating plague of all time*, New York: Harper Collins.
Kirkpatrick, C. (1932) 'A tentative study in experimental social psychology', *American Journal of Sociology*, 38: 194–206.
Kovic, M. and Füchslin, T. (2018) 'Probability and conspiratorial thinking', *Applied Cognitive Psychology*, 32(3): 390–400.
Lantian, A., Muller, D., Nurra, C. and Douglas, K.M. (2017) '"I know things they don't know!": the role of need for uniqueness in belief in conspiracy theories', *Social Psychology*, 48(3): 160–73.

Lantian, A., Muller, D., Nurra, C., Klein, O., Berjot, S. and Pantazi, M. (2018) 'Stigmatized beliefs: conspiracy theories, anticipated negative evaluation of the self, and fear of social exclusion', *European Journal of Social Psychology*, 48(7): 939–54.

Leiser, D., Duani, N. and Wagner-Egger, P. (2017) 'The conspiratorial style in lay economic thinking', *PloS ONE*, 12(3): e0171238.

Leman, P.J. and Cinnirella, M. (2007) 'A major event has a major cause: evidence for the role of heuristics in reasoning about conspiracy theories', *Social Psychological Review*, 9(2): 18–28.

Lewandowsky, S., Gignac, G.E. and Oberauer, K. (2013) 'The role of conspiracist ideation and worldviews in predicting rejection of science', *PLoS ONE*, 8(10): e75637.

Liu, B. (2010) 'Sentiment analysis and subjectivity', *Handbook of Natural Language Processing*, 2: 627–66.

Lo Monaco, G., Delouvée, S. and Rateau, P. (eds.) (2016) *Les représentations sociales: théories, méthodes, applications*, Bruxelles: De Boeck.

Macek, P. and Markova, I. (2004) 'Trust and distrust in old and new democracies', in I. Markova (ed.) *Trust and democratic transition in post-communist Europe*, New York, NY: Oxford University Press, pp. 173–94.

McCauley, C. and Jacques, S. (1979) 'The popularity of conspiracy theories of presidential assassination: a Bayesian analysis', *Journal of Personality and Social Psychology*, 37(5): 637–44.

McHoskey, J.W. (1995) 'Case closed? On the John F. Kennedy assassination: biased assimilation of evidence and attitude polarization', *Basic and Applied Social Psychology*, 17(3): 395–409.

Mishler, W. and Rose, R. (1997) 'Trust, distrust, and skepticism: popular evaluations of civil and political institutions in post-communist societies', *Journal of Politics*, 59(2): 418–51.

Mocanu, D., Rossi, L., Zhang, Q., Karsai, M. and Quattrochiocchi, W. (2015) 'Collective attention in the age of (mis)information', *Computers in Human Behavior*, 51: 1198–204.

Montgomery, H. (2011) 'Rumours of child trafficking after natural disasters: fact, fiction or fantasy?', *Journal of Children and Media*, 5(4): 395–410.

Morin, E., Paillard, B., Burguière, É., Vérone, J. and de Lusignan, S. (2014) *La rumeur d'Orléans*, Paris: Le Seuil.

Moscovici, S. (1987) 'The conspiracy mentality', in C.F. Graumann and S. Moscovici (eds.), *Changing conceptions of conspiracy*, New York: Springer Verlag, pp. 151–69.

Mulligan, K. and Habel, P. (2011) 'An experimental test of the effects of fictional framing on attitudes', *Social Science Quarterly*, 92(1): 79–99.

Nera, K., Pantazi, M. and Klein, O. (2018) '"These are just stories, Mulder": exposure to conspiracist fiction does not produce narrative persuasion', *Frontiers in Psychology*, 9(684).

Newheiser, A.K., Farias, M. and Tausch, N. (2011), 'The functional nature of conspiracy beliefs: examining the underpinnings of belief in the Da Vinci Code conspiracy', *Personality and Individual Differences*, 51(8): 1007–11.

Nickerson, R.S. (1998) 'Confirmation bias: a ubiquitous phenomenon in many guises', *Review of General Psychology*, 2(2): 175–220.

Norenzayan, A., Atran, S., Faulkner, J. and Schaller, M. (2006) 'Memory and mystery: the cultural selection of minimally counterintuitive narratives', *Cognitive Science*, 30(3): 531–53.

Norrick, N.R. (2007) 'Conversational storytelling', in D. Herman (ed.) *The Cambridge Companion to Narrative*, Cambridge: Cambridge University Press, pp. 127–41.

Oswald, S. (2016) 'Conspiracy and bias: argumentative features and persuasiveness of conspiracy theories', *OSSA Conference Archive*, 168: 1–16.

Pezzo, M.V. and Beckstead, J.W. (2006) 'A multilevel analysis of rumor transmission: effects of anxiety and belief in two field experiments', *Basic and Applied Social Psychology*, 28(1): 91–100.

Poliakov, L. (1987) 'The topic of the Jewish conspiracy in Russia (1905–1920), and the international consequences', in C.F. Graumann and S. Moscovici (eds.) *Changing conceptions of conspiracy*, New York, NY: Springer, pp. 105–13.

Propp, V. (1968) *Morphology of the folktale*, 2nd edn, trans. Laurence Scott (1927), Austin: University of Texas Press.

Proulx, T., Inzlicht, M. and Harmon-Jones, E. (2012) 'Understanding all inconsistency compensation as a palliative response to violated expectations', *Trends in Cognitive Sciences*, 16(5): 285–91.

Qazvinian, V., Rosengren, E., Radev, D.R. and Mei, Q. (2011) 'Rumor has it: identifying misinformation in microblogs', in R. Barzilay and M. Johnson (eds.) *Proceedings of the 2011 Conference on Empirical Methods in Natural Language Processing*, Edinburgh: Association for Computational Linguistics, pp. 1589–99.

Raab, M.H., Ortlieb, S., Auer, N., Guthmann, K. and Carbon, C.C. (2013) 'Thirty shades of truth: conspiracy theories as stories of individuation, not of pathological delusion', *Frontiers in Psychology*, 4(406).

Reinert, M. (1990) 'Alceste une méthodologie d'analyse des données textuelles et une application: Aurelia De Gerard De Nerval', *Bulletin of Sociological Methodology/Bulletin de Méthodologie Sociologique*, 26(1): 24–54.

Rosnow, R.L. (1980) 'Psychology of rumor reconsidered', *Psychological Bulletin*, 87(3): 578–91.

Rosnow, R.L. (1991) 'Inside rumor: a personal journey', *American Psychologist*, 46(5): 484–96.

Rosnow, R.L., Esposito, J.L. and Gibney, L. (1988) 'Factors influencing rumor spreading: replication and extension', *Language and Communication*, 8(1): 29–42.

Rouquette, M.-L. (1973) 'La pensée sociale', in S. Moscovici (ed.) *Introduction à la psychologie sociale*, Paris: Larousse, pp. 299–327.

Rouquette, M.-L. (1990) 'Le syndrome de rumeur', *Communications*, 52(1): 119–24.

Sammut, G., Andreouli, E., Gaskell, G. and Valsiner, J. (eds.) (2015) *The Cambridge handbook of social representations*, Cambridge: Cambridge University Press.

Samory, M. and Mitra, T. (2018) 'The government spies using our webcams': the language of conspiracy theories in online discussions', *Proceedings of the ACM on Human-Computer Interaction*, 2(152).

Samuels, A. (2015) 'Narratives of uncertainty: the affective force of child-trafficking rumors in postdisaster Aceh, Indonesia', *American Anthropologist*, 117(2): 229–41.

Singerman, R. (1981) 'The American career of the "Protocols of the Elders of Zion"', *American Jewish History*, 71(1): 48–78.

Smet, K., Elst, T.V., Griep, Y. and De Witte, H. (2016) 'The explanatory role of rumours in the reciprocal relationship between organizational change communication and job insecurity: a within-person approach', *European Journal of Work and Organizational Psychology*, 25(5): 631–44.

Sperber, D. (1985) 'Anthropology and psychology: towards an epidemiology of representations', *Man*, 20(1): 73–89.

Stempel, C., Hargrove, T. and Stempel, G.H. III. (2007) 'Media use, social structure, and belief in 9/11 conspiracy theories', *Journalism & Mass Communication Quarterly*, 84(2): 353–72.

Swami, V. (2012) 'Social psychological origins of conspiracy theories: the case of the Jewish conspiracy theory in Malaysia', *Frontiers in Psychology*, 3(280): 1–9.

Swami, V., Furnham, A., Smyth, N., Weis, L., Lay, A. and Clow, A. (2016) 'Putting the stress on conspiracy theories: examining associations between psychological stress, anxiety, and belief in conspiracy theories', *Personality and Individual Differences*, 99: 72–6.

Swami, V., Pietschnig, J., Tran, U.S., Nader, I., Stieger, S. and Voracek, M. (2013) 'Lunar lies: the impact of informational framing and individual differences in shaping conspiracist beliefs about the moon landings', *Applied Cognitive Psychology*, 27(1): 71–80.

Taguieff, P.-A. (2007) *L'Imaginaire du complot mondial. Aspects d'un mythe moderne*, Paris: Mille et une nuits.

Tausczik, Y.R. and Pennebaker, J.W. (2010) 'The psychological meaning of words: LIWC and computerized text analysis methods', *Journal of Language and Social Psychology*, 29(1): 24–54.

Uscinski, J.E. and Parent, J.M. (2014) *American Conspiracy Theories*, New York, NY: Oxford University Press.

Van Prooijen, J.-W. and Douglas, K.M., (2017) 'Conspiracy theories as part of history: the role of societal crisis situations', *Memory Studies*, 10(3): 323–33.

Van Prooijen, J.-W. and van Dijk, E. (2014) 'When consequence size predicts belief in conspiracy theories: the moderating role of perspective taking', *Journal of Experimental Social Psychology*, 55: 63–73.

Wagner-Egger, P. and Bangerter, A. (2007) 'La vérite est ailleurs: corrélats de l'adhésion aux théories du complot', *Revue Internationale de Psychologie Sociale*, 20(4): 31–61.

Wagner-Egger, P., Bangerter, A., Gilles, I., Green, E., Rigaud, D., Krings, F., Staerklé, C. and Clémence, A. (2011) 'Lay perceptions of collectives at the outbreak of the H1N1 epidemic: heroes, villains and victims', *Public Understanding of Science*, 20(4): 461–76.

Wood, M.J. and Douglas, K.M. (2013) '"What about building 7?" A social psychological study of online discussion of 9/11 conspiracy theories', *Frontiers in Psychology*, 4(409): 1–9.

Yablokov, I. (2017) 'Social networks of death: conspiracy panics and professional journalistic ethics in the post-Soviet Russia', *Quaderni*, 94(3): 53–62.

# 2.6
# CONSPIRACY THEORIES AND INTERGROUP RELATIONS

*Mikey Biddlestone, Aleksandra Cichocka, Iris Žeželj and Michał Bilewicz*

## Introduction

Considering the prevalence of conspiracy beliefs, there is substantial consensus in the psychological literature that they are unlikely to be a function of pathology (Sunstein, Vermeule 2009; Oliver, Wood 2014). The implication that these beliefs could be held by almost anyone warrants careful consideration of this topic from a social psychological perspective. As aptly noted by van Prooijen and van Lange (2014: 238–9), 'most conspiracy beliefs can be framed in terms of beliefs about how a powerful and evil outgroup meets in secret, designing a plot that is harmful to one's in-group'. Understanding conspiracy beliefs, therefore, requires understanding of intergroup attitudes and behaviours (see Kramer and Messick 1998; Crocker *et al.* 1999). This chapter aims to illuminate the group processes involved in the development and endorsement of conspiracy beliefs. First, we review research on group perceptions and stereotyping, alongside its implications for conspiracy beliefs. Second, we discuss the motivational paths associated with beliefs in conspiring groups, focusing especially on the influences of fear, control and the need for recognition. Finally, we review the consequences of intergroup conspiracy beliefs.

### Conspiracy stereotypes and images of conspiring outgroups

In the first section, we discuss characteristics that might make outgroups especially likely to be accused of conspiring against the ingroup. We first illustrate the dimensions along which social groups are perceived, and then move on to address the unique aspects of conspiracy stereotypes.

People's perceptions of social groups are based on cognitive schemata, known as stereotypes (e.g. Phalet, Poppe 1997; Fiske *et al.* 2002). Kofta and Sedek (2005) have argued that conspiracy stereotypes (which usually refer to a whole group) are qualitatively different from other, trait-laden stereotypes (which usually refer to characteristics of individual group members). Although both can promote ingroup favouritism and involve ascribing collective outgroup goals, trait-laden stereotypes determine judgements about individuals belonging to a group, whereas conspiracy stereotypes may determine judgements about social groups as a whole.

One way we can illustrate differences between trait-laden and conspiracy stereotypes is the way they respond to a key mechanism of attitude change, namely intergroup contact. Having positive contact with stereotyped outgroup members (especially of the equal status) is an effective way to promote more favourable attitudes and decrease stereotyping of outgroup members (Pettigrew, Tropp 2006a, 2006b). However, attempts to use this paradigm in counteracting conspiracy stereotypes have been largely ineffective. A nationwide representative study in Poland found that intergroup contact, as well as intergroup friendships, were significant predictors of attitudes toward Jews, but they were not significantly related to belief in the Jewish conspiracy (Winiewski et al. 2015). To put it more simply, contact with Jewish people did not seem to reduce the 'Jewish conspiracy' myth. Similar findings were reported by Bilewicz (2007), who conducted an intervention bringing together Polish youth (with no prior contact with Jews) and Canadian and American Jewish peers. This intervention had many positive effects except for one: those who believed in the Jewish conspiracy did not change their opinion after the meeting.

This difference in effectiveness of intergroup contact illustrates the essential difference between trait-laden and conspiracy stereotypes. Trait-laden stereotypes are schemata and generalisations based on knowledge of specific exemplars of a given category. Contact provides such information that could be later generalised to the whole outgroup, and even to other, unrelated outgroups (Pettigrew 2009). Conspiracy stereotypes are based on essentialist thinking to a much greater extent than trait-laden stereotypes are. If someone believes that there is some biological basis for the intention of the outgroup to conspire, then any form of contact would not be effective, as individual experiences could not affect the general theory about the whole group.

In order to better understand the components of social stereotypes, Fiske et al. (2002) proposed the stereotype content model (S.C.M.), which assumes the attributes that comprise all social stereotypes can be grouped along two dimensions: warmth (i.e. sociability and morality) and competence (i.e. agency; but see Koch et al. 2016). The model aimed to provide an explanation for emotions felt towards outgroups based on their perceived level of warmth and competence. According to the S.C.M., feelings of pity are associated with perceptions of the outgroup as warm but incompetent, conceptualised as a paternalistic stereotype (e.g. of the elderly). Conversely, feelings of envy are associated with perceptions of the outgroup as cold but competent, conceptualised as an envious stereotype (e.g. of Asians). Envious perceptions of high-status competitive outgroups – induced by the perception of incompatible goals (see Fiske et al. 2002) – can justify ingroup resentment. These stereotypes have been linked to conspiracy beliefs: a group that is competent yet cold and unfriendly is most likely to be viewed as being able to plot against the ingroup (e.g. Winiewski et al. 2015; but see Fousiani and van Prooijen 2019 for a more nuanced view on competence).

Envious stereotyping has been implicated in such insidious views as hostile sexism (Glick et al. 1997) and antisemitic notions of economic Jewish conspiracies (Glick 2002). Due to their perceived high-status and competence, enviously stereotyped outgroups are likely to be the target of threat-detection. This threat detection encourages conspiracy beliefs about the enviously stereotyped outgroup. Consequently, Winiewski et al. (2015) argued that envious stereotyping can eventually lead to a belief system that views the outgroup as a scapegoat responsible for the ingroup's misfortunes. For example, Winiewski et al. (2015) demonstrated this process in Nazi caricatures depicting Jews as conspiring during the Second World War. Based on coding of hundreds of images that appeared in the notorious antisemitic magazine *Der Stuermer*, they found that the caricatures portraying Jews as conspiring also presented Jewish characters as highly competent, but simultaneously immoral and not sociable. When looking at this phenomenon from a chronological angle, one could see that the caricatures presenting Jews as conspiring were more frequent in the period of the Second World War (1939–1945), as compared the previous period of Nazi regime in Germany (1933–1939). This suggests that envious caricatures portraying certain enemy groups as conspiring can be used in propaganda to mobilise war efforts and to engage society in collective goals. Moreover, findings demonstrating that people show preferential attention to general envy-related stimuli (such as a successful protagonist; Zhong et al. 2013) may also reveal why this propaganda was so alarmingly effective.

The process of identifying enemies can also be facilitated by the tendency to personalise groups as collective agents (e.g. Morris 2000) – another important factor shaping conspiracy stereotypes. This tendency is associated with perceiving groups as entitative categories (that is being viewed as highly similar, and with common goals and fate; see Hogg et al. 2007; Lickel et al. 2000), which share a common essence (see Lickel et al. 2000; Rothbart and Taylor 1992). For example, Kofta and Sedek (2005) found that higher perceptions of entitativity of Jews predicted conspiracy stereotyping of this group (see also Wieckowska 2004). The grounding of these stereotypes in natural categories fosters perceptions oriented towards a prototypical symbol of the outgroup rather than a concrete, observable characteristic (see Rosch 1973, 1975). This focus on a prototypical symbol (rather than the more realistic perception of diversity within a group) makes it easier for ingroup members to project their own conspiracy stereotypes onto the outgroup (see Krueger 2000; Ames 2004).

We have thus far considered the group perceptions involved in conspiracy belief. This section aimed to illuminate the stereotype contents of groups, revealing that the stereotyping process is likely an evaluative system used to determine whether a group is threatening. If an outgroup's goals and intentions do not match the ingroup's, their perceived warmth and competence will likely determine whether they are a potential threat (however, for a detailed review on the complicated relationship between these dimensions, see Koch et al. 2016). Specifically, groups perceived as competent and agentic, but cold, are most likely to be viewed as threatening and conspiring. Because conspiracy stereotypes are based on essentialising perceptions of outgroups, they seem relatively resistant to change. Therefore, considering the antecedent motivations in conspiracy stereotyping and conspiracy beliefs more broadly may reveal the underlying mechanisms that lead ingroup members to endorse these beliefs.

## What motivates conspiring images of outgroups?

So far, we have discussed the perceived characteristics of outgroups that can increase their likelihood of being viewed as conspirators. Now, we will discuss the individual and group-level motives that can lead ingroup members to endorse conspiracy theories that target these outgroups. According to Krekó (2015), intergroup conspiracy theories serve to 1) explain significant and unexpected events, by managing the anxiety associated with them, 2) justify power strivings, and 3) help defend the image of the ingroup. Indeed, research indicates that conspiracy beliefs about outgroups can increase when people experience anxiety and fear, loss of power and control, or strive for recognition of their social groups. In the following section, we discuss each of these paths to embracing intergroup conspiracy theories (for a discussion of individual motives associated with conspiracy beliefs more broadly, see Douglas et al. 2017 and Chapter 2.3).

The first is the *fear* path. People can be motivated to view outgroups as conspiring against them when they experience fear and anxiety. Fear and anxiety generally lead to an overreliance on stereotype-consistent information (see Wilder and Simon 2001 for a review), making ingroup members evaluate ambiguous social information based on pre-existing beliefs about the outgroup (Kramer, Schaffer 2014). Further, given the connection between anxiety and threat detection (e.g. Yiend and Mathews 2001; Mathews, MacLeod 2002), it is unsurprising that people with high levels of anxiety tend to interpret ambiguous information as threatening (Mathews, MacLeod 2002). Thus, they might also be more susceptible to interpreting ambiguous intergroup behaviour as intentionally malevolent. This threat perception has been implicated in the endorsement of conspiracy theories as a way of preparing for collective self-defence from the outgroup (Kofta, Sedek 2005). A body of research has confirmed the link between anxiety and conspiracy beliefs. For example, Grzesiak-Feldman demonstrated that both trait (2007) and situationally induced (2013) anxiety are associated with endorsement of conspiracy stereotypes of Jews and also with more general conspiracy thinking. Thus, conspiracy theories may be adopted through a fear path, wherein anxious ingroup members tend to perceive higher levels of intergroup threat, leading them to adopt conspiracy theories to derogate the outgroup and protect the ingroup (see Kofta, Sedek 2005).

Conspiracy beliefs have also been linked to ideological predispositions that foster perceptions of threat. One such predisposition is right-wing authoritarianism (R.W.A.): A dispositional measure of adherence to authority (authoritarian submission), aggression towards outgroups (authoritarian aggression) and adherence to the social norms defined by the authority and society (conventionalism; Altemeyer 1996). Duckitt (2001) proposed a dual process model that outlines the personality, motivational and worldview antecedents of R.W.A. This model argues that individuals who believe their social environment is inherently dangerous and threatening are motivated to embrace ideological preferences that favour security and stability (Sibley et al. 2012). Consequently, Sibley and Duckitt (2013) demonstrated that the so-called dangerous worldview is associated with higher R.W.A. This is likely why R.W.A. has been shown to correlate with both generalised conspiracy thinking (e.g. Grzesiak-Feldman, Irzycka 2009) and belief in specific conspiracy theories (Abalakina-Paap et al. 1999). Also, Bilewicz et al. (2013) found R.W.A. to be weakly but significantly associated with the belief in the Jewish conspiracy in Poland (although this relationship was not observed in a different study of the same paper involving similar variables).

Some argue, however, that authoritarianism predicts different intergroup attitudes than a general conspiracy mentality (Imhoff, Bruder 2014). While authoritarianism predicts prejudice towards less powerful societal groups, conspiracy mentality can be seen as a distinct political attitude, with a stable ideological belief system that involves prejudicial attitudes towards more powerful groups. As previously discussed, in the process of scapegoating, outgroups are viewed as threatening when they are perceived as highly competent yet pursuing goals that are incompatible with the ingroup. Therefore, scapegoating usually fosters intergroup comparison with powerful outgroups (e.g. with high socio-economic agency; Koch et al. 2016). Conversely, R.W.A. can foster intergroup comparison with subordinate groups perceived as less powerful (see Imhoff, Bruder 2014). For example, an outgroup would be perceived as threatening if they were violating the perceived norms of the ingroup. Imhoff and Bruder (2014) argued that antisemitism was associated both with high levels of conspiracy mentality and R.W.A. Conspiracy mentality led to antisemitism through perceptions of Jews as more powerful, whereas R.W.A. led to antisemitism through perceptions of Jews as less powerful. Future research should examine in more detail the mutual associations between authoritarian tendencies and conspiracy beliefs.

The second path is the *loss of control* path. Rothschild et al. (2012) have argued that scapegoating an outgroup may also be a response to reduced feelings of personal control. People strive to feel in control over their life and environment – it is a fundamental human motivation (e.g. Deci, Ryan 1987, 2000). When people feel they do not have control over their fate, they tend to compensate by attributing control to other agents, be it God, government or powerful outgroups (Kay et al. 2008). In line with this reasoning, low personal control might increase a belief in powerful enemies conspiring against the ingroup. Indeed, Imhoff (2015) demonstrated that long-term lack of control was associated with general conspiracy beliefs (but see Bruder et al. 2013). Also, a high external locus of control (deferring responsibility for one's actions to external explanations) was associated with high levels of paranoia and conspiracy beliefs specifically (Hamsher et al. 1968; Mirowsky, Ross 1983). Finally, in a study by Sullivan et al. (2010), an experimental manipulation highlighting low personal control over external threat strengthened belief in the conspiratorial power of a political enemy (see also Whitson, Galinsky 2008).

Another factor that might show similar effects is uncertainty. In fact, personal control and uncertainty often elicit similar sense-making processes (Van Den Bos 2009; Park 2010). When feelings of uncertainty and reduced control are induced by crises, 'a conspiracy theory helps people to make sense of the world by specifying the causes of important events, which further helps them predict, and anticipate, the future' (van Prooijen, Douglas 2017: 327). Indeed, in an experiment by van Prooijen and Jostmann (2013), inducing uncertainty increased conspiracy beliefs about governments or big companies, especially when these entities were perceived as immoral. Also, a chronic intolerance for uncertainty has been found to be associated with blaming other national groups for dramatic social events (such as plane catastrophes), especially when these lacked a plausible official explanation (Marchlewska et al. 2018a).

The third path is the *lack of recognition* path. The two previous sections highlighted the role of threat and the frustration of basic needs in predicting conspiracy beliefs. These findings can at least partially explain why conspiracy beliefs are more prevalent among members of powerless and minority groups (Goertzel 1994; Abalakina-Paap et al. 1999; Stempel et al. 2007; Crocker et al. 1999; Imhoff, Bruder 2014), especially when they feel their disadvantage is not recognised. In fact, conspiracy beliefs seem to be stronger when group members experience relative deprivation: perceiving their group as being worse off and not given the same opportunities as other groups (e.g. Runciman 1966).

For example, van Prooijen et al. (2018) demonstrated that, for Muslims in the Netherlands, group-based deprivation significantly predicted both ethnic/national identity-relevant (e.g. 'I.S.I.S. was created by the U.S.A. and Israel') and identity-irrelevant conspiracy beliefs (e.g. 'The economic crisis of 2007 was created deliberately by bankers'). This suggests that the relative deprivation experienced by minority groups is associated with belief in general conspiracy theories, regardless of whether these theories are thought to target the ingroup directly. Van Prooijen et al. (2018) argued that this is due to the perception that the overarching societal system is rigged. Similarly, Bilewicz and Krzeminski (2010) found that economic deprivation in Poland was associated with antisemitic Jewish stereotypes. In both Poland and Ukraine, economic deprivation was associated with increased discriminatory intentions towards Jews, but the association with conspiracy stereotypes was only observed in Poland. This might be due to the fact that conspiracy-based antisemitism is prevalent in Poland (see Krzemiński 2004; Kofta, Sedek 2005), while groups other than Jews may have been focal objects of scapegoating in Ukraine (e.g. Caucasian ethnic groups). This difference led the authors to conclude that economic deprivation partially explains antisemitic scapegoating in those countries where previous ideologies point to the responsibility of Jews for economic situations.

When individuals feel powerless, the self-ascribed social identity of victim can lead to so called competitive victimhood (Suciu 2008; Reid 2010) – the motivation to establish that one's ingroup has endured more suffering and injustice than the outgroup (Noor et al. 2012). It is likely that competitive victimhood is a functional compensatory reaction to feelings of powerlessness due to a lack of control and feelings of intergroup threat (see Shnabel, Noor 2012). Competitive victimhood can result in a lack of intergroup trust and empathy (Bar-Tal, Antebi 1992; Noor et al. 2008), as well as searching for outgroups that can be blamed for the ingroup's misfortunes. This can lead ingroup members to endorse conspiracy theories that unite the ingroup against a common scapegoated enemy (see Reid 2010). For example, Mashuri and Zaduqisti (2014) demonstrated that strong Islamic identity was linked to competitive victimhood and subsequent belief in a Western conspiracy against Islam. This effect was especially prevalent when people felt a high degree of distrust towards the West. Also, Bilewicz and Krzeminski (2010) found a positive relationship between competitive victimhood and beliefs in a Jewish conspiracy in Poland. Overall, these studies suggest that long-term feelings of deprivation and victimhood can lead to the development of a form of collective conspiracy mentality – 'a more general collective mental state in which other nations are viewed as hostile and negatively intended toward one's own nation' (Soral et al. 2019: 373).

Such a mentality appears to lead to the perception that outgroups conspire against the ingroup, and would make conspiracy-driven explanations of political events more acceptable. Ultimately, it could create a societal rift between conspiracy-believers and conspiracy-nonbelievers. A study performed in Poland following the Smoleńsk air catastrophe shows that the tendency to interpret this event as caused by an anti-Polish Russian conspiracy was prevalent among people who focused their attention on the historical victimisation of their nation (Bilewicz et al. 2019). Those who believe in unique ingroup victimhood seem to treat their national history, as they see it, as a universal heuristic that allows them to understand current intergroup relations.

Feelings of the ingroup being relatively deprived and victimised are also associated with a broader defensive identification with one's social group, captured by the concept of collective narcissism (Golec de Zavala et al. 2009; Cichocka et al. 2016; Marchlewska et al. 2018b). Like competitive victimhood, collective narcissism involves the conviction that others do not sufficiently appreciate the uniqueness of one's group. However, collective narcissism also involves an inflated sense of ingroup greatness, contingent on external recognition, often leading to destructive intergroup attitudes (Golec de Zavala et al. 2009; Cichocka et al. 2016). The constant need for validation means that collective narcissists are especially sensitive to any signs of threat or disrespect coming from other groups. They also tend to be convinced that others seek to undermine the ingroup intentionally, which forms a fertile ground for conspiracy theorising (see also Kramer, Schaffer 2014).

Several lines of study have demonstrated that collective narcissism predicts belief in outgroup conspiracy theories. For example, Golec de Zavala and Cichocka (2012) found that Polish national collective narcissism predicted a belief in the Jewish conspiracy. In another set of surveys conducted in Poland by Cichocka et al. (2016), national collective narcissism was associated with the conviction that other nations are conspiring to undermine Polish achievements in fighting communism, and that Russians conspired to kill the former president (who died in the Smolensk plane crash in 2010). American collective narcissism also predicted a general conviction that other (although not one's own) governments are conspiring against the American people. The association between collective narcissism and conspiracy beliefs was driven by heightened perceptions of threat.

In all of these studies, ingroup identification without the narcissistic component was negatively associated with conspiracy beliefs, suggesting that only the defensive, narcissistic need for ingroup recognition, rather than ingroup positivity in general, drives conspiracy beliefs. In a different intergroup context, Marchlewska et al. (2019) found that collective narcissism in relation to Catholics as an ingroup was linked to a belief in a so called 'gender conspiracy' – a conviction that gender theory and gender studies are part of a conspiracy aimed at destroying traditional family values. Taken together, these studies suggest that conspiracy beliefs might stem from a conviction that any group misfortunes or failures are due to a conspiring enemy. Arguably, such a conviction might protect and restore feelings of ingroup superiority (see also Kofta, Sedek 2005).

In this section, we have outlined factors that can lead to outgroup conspiracy beliefs. For example, feelings of threat and low personal control can lead to a tendency to make sense of one's experience by seeing others as intentionally malevolent. Furthermore, viewing one's social group as disadvantaged and lacking recognition can foster the need to blame other groups for the ingroup's misfortunes. This can lead to conspiracy beliefs as a defensive reaction to protect the ingroup image. We next explore the potential consequences of intergroup conspiracy beliefs.

## What are the intergroup consequences of beliefs in intergroup conspiracy theories?

Although some researchers have argued that conspiracy theories can be utilised to confront social hierarchies and offer alternatives to the status quo (e.g. Sapountzis, Condor 2013; Imhoff, Bruder 2014), most empirical evidence suggests that they are likely to result in detrimental consequences more often than not. For example, conspiracy beliefs have been linked to undesirable health choices, political alienation and antisocial behaviours (e.g. for a review see Chapter 2.7; see also Jolley, Douglas 2014a, 2014b; Douglas, Leite 2017; Jolley et al. 2019). Here, we will consider the consequences of conspiracy beliefs for intergroup relations and perceptions of the overarching political system. Specifically, we will discuss implications for 1) prejudice and intergroup discrimination and 2) legitimisation of injustice.

The key outcomes that tend to be associated with intergroup conspiracy beliefs are *prejudice and intergroup discrimination*. Some researchers have argued that conspiracy stereotypes lead to 'high supportiveness for in-groupers combined with complete disregard for out-groupers' (Kofta, Sedek 2005: 42). As we highlighted before, conspiracy beliefs allow individuals to blame the outgroup for events that negatively affect the ingroup. In this way, they provide a 'moral justification for immoral actions' (Winiewski et al. 2015: 24), such as intergroup discrimination. Indeed, multiple studies have linked conspiracy beliefs to hostile intergroup attitudes. For example, Bilewicz et al. (2013) demonstrated that belief in Jewish conspiracies was the most prevalent predictor of antisemitic prejudice above all other forms of antisemitism (e.g. religiously grounded stereotypes). Beliefs in Jewish conspiracy theories were also linked to anti-Jewish social distance (being unwilling to accept the outgroup as their neighbours or co-workers; Bilewicz et al. 2013; Bilewicz, Sedek 2015), legal discrimination (support for laws that prevent the outgroup from establishing companies or buying land; Bilewicz, Krzeminski 2010), electoral discrimination (Bilewicz et al. 2013) and discriminatory decision making (e.g. in terms of fund allocation; Bilewicz et al. 2013). Furthermore, Jolley et al. (2019) recently showed that experimental exposure to antisemitic conspiracy theories increased prejudice and discrimination towards Jews.

This evidence shows that conspiracy stereotypes are strongly linked to different forms of discrimination of outgroup members who are accused of conspiring. The possible aim of such discrimination is to decrease ostensible control possessed by outgroup members, regardless of the perceived strength and power of such people. Interestingly, conspiracy stereotypes of certain outgroups (e.g. Jews) are strong predictors of discriminatory intentions toward other, unrelated outgroups (e.g. Germans; Kofta, Sedek 2005; Bilewicz, Sedek 2015; Jolley et al. 2019). This suggests that ascriptions of conspiracies to groups can cause more general discriminatory approaches to outgroup members, even if those outgroups are not perceived as directly involved in the conspiracy.

This shows similar results to the secondary transfer effects observed in the contact hypothesis research (Pettigrew 2009; Tausch et al. 2010): Having contact with members of a given outgroup improves attitudes toward unrelated outgroups. In the case of conspiracy beliefs, the reverse seems to be true: endorsing conspiracy theories about one outgroup can translate into more negative attitudes toward many unrelated groups. This supports the view that conspiracy stereotypes are elements of a general mindset, or conspiracy mentality (Imhoff, Bruder 2014). Furthermore, people believing in conspiracy theories tend to be more Machiavellian (Douglas, Sutton 2011), building their own conspiracies to defend against conspiring groups. Therefore, discrimination (depriving outgroups of their rights and resources) can be an observable strategy of such Machiavellian approaches to intergroup relations that are typical for conspiracy believers.

Kofta and Sedek (2005) suggested that the link between conspiracy beliefs and discrimination might depend on situational factors. For example, the motivation to detect and defend against any potential threats to the ingroup's power might be higher during political elections. As conspiracy theories might be especially useful in identifying threatening outgroups, they should predict prejudice more strongly in times of political uncertainty. Indeed, Kofta and Sedek (2005) demonstrated that conspiracy stereotypes about Jews in Poland were significant predictors of social distance towards Jews just before the election, but not a couple of weeks after. Similarly, in another analysis, the link between conspiracy stereotypes of Jews, and the social distance towards Jews and other outgroups (e.g. Germans), was strong in an election year, but became almost invisible in a year without elections (Bilewicz, Sedek 2015). The election circumstances may have temporarily heightened fears of what would happen in the event of a successful 'collective enemy'.

Intergroup conspiracy theories also have implications for *legitimisation of injustice*. Goertzel argued that 'a conspiracy theory gives believers someone tangible to blame for their perceived predicament, instead of blaming it on impersonal or abstract social forces' (2010: 494). Jolley et al. (2018) proposed that conspiracy theories may therefore function as a system justifying mechanism, deflecting the blame from the dysfunctional components of the system to a small group of malevolent people. Consequently, they found that conspiracy theories increased when the legitimacy of a social system was threatened. Conspiracy theories also bolstered satisfaction with the status quo, causing people to increasingly attribute societal issues to malevolent groups. This has particularly problematic implications for the situation of disadvantaged groups. For example, as relative deprivation (Bilewicz, Krzeminski 2010) and competitive victimhood (Bilewicz et al. 2013) are used to justify conspiracy beliefs, it is possible that disenfranchised groups will turn to conspiracy theories to explain their societal position, rather than focus on the more pervasive components of the societal structure that contribute to their disadvantaged position. Therefore, conspiracy beliefs might theoretically hinder social change for the groups that need it most.

## Conclusion

In this chapter, we sought to highlight the intergroup dimensions of conspiracy beliefs. We reviewed both chronic predispositions and situational factors that can strengthen people's endorsements of intergroup conspiracy beliefs. First, we explained that perceptions of outgroups as competent yet immoral are likely to breed conspiracy explanations for their actions. These perceptions are also likely to be motivated by individual perceptions of threat and lack of control, as well as by the general need for understanding the disadvantaged position of one's social groups. All of these factors can increase vigilance to potential threats stemming from other groups, as well as increasing the need to find explanations for one's misfortunes. Finally, we highlighted research that suggests that conspiracy beliefs can have undesirable consequences for intergroup relations, but at the same time these beliefs are difficult to change. Thus, in order to curtail the negative effects of intergroup conspiracy beliefs, interventions might need to target their varied psychological and societal antecedent.

# References

Abalakina-Paap, M., Stephan, W.G., Craig, T. and Gregory, W.L. (1999) 'Beliefs in conspiracies', *Political Psychology*, 20(3): 637–47.
Altemeyer, B. (1996) *The authoritarian specter*, Cambridge: Harvard University Press.
Ames, D.R. (2004) 'Inside the mind reader's tool kit: projection and stereotyping in mental state inference', *Journal of Personality and Social Psychology*, 87(3): 340–53.
Bar-Tal, D. and Antebi, D. (1992) 'Siege mentality in Israel', *International Journal of Intercultural Relations*, 16(3): 251–75.
Bilewicz, M. (2007) 'History as an obstacle: impact of temporal-based social categorizations on Polish-Jewish intergroup contact', *Group Processes & Intergroup Relations*, 10(4): 551–63.
Bilewicz, M. and Krzeminski, I. (2010) 'Anti-Semitism in Poland and Ukraine: the belief in Jewish control as a mechanism of scapegoating', *International Journal of Conflict and Violence (IJCV)*, 4(2): 234–43.
Bilewicz, M. and Sedek, G. (2015) 'Conspiracy stereotypes: their sociopsychological antecedents and consequences', in M. Bilewicz, A. Cichocka and W. Soral (eds.) *The Psychology of Conspiracy*, Abingdon, UK: Routledge, pp. 3–22.
Bilewicz, M., Winiewski, M., Kofta, M. and Wójcik, A. (2013) 'Harmful ideas, the structure and consequences of anti-Semitic beliefs in Poland', *Political Psychology*, 34(6): 821–39.
Bilewicz, M., Witkowska, M., Pantazi, M., Gkinopoulos, T. and Klein, O. (2019) 'Traumatic rift: how conspiracy beliefs undermine cohesion after societal trauma?', *Europe's Journal of Psychology*, 15(1): 82.–93.
Bruder, M., Haffke, P., Neave, N., Nouripanah, N. and Imhoff, R. (2013) 'Measuring individual differences in generic beliefs in conspiracy theories across cultures: conspiracy mentality questionnaire', *Frontiers in Psychology*, 4(255): 1–15.
Cichocka, A., Marchlewska, M., Golec de Zavala, A. and Olechowski, M. (2016) '"They will not control us": ingroup positivity and belief in intergroup conspiracies', *British Journal of Psychology*, 107(3): 556–76.
Crocker, J., Luhtanen, R., Broadnax, S. and Blaine, B.E. (1999) 'Belief in U.S. government conspiracies against blacks among black and white college students: powerlessness or system blame?', *Personality and Social Psychology Bulletin*, 25(8): 941–53.
Deci, E.L. and Ryan, R.M. (1987) 'The support of autonomy and the control of behavior', *Journal of Personality and Social Psychology*, 53(6): 1024–37.
Deci, E.L. and Ryan, R.M. (2000) 'The "what" and "why" of goal pursuits: human needs and the self-determination of behavior', *Psychological Inquiry*, 11(4): 37–41.
Douglas, K.M. and Leite, A.C. (2017) 'Suspicion in the workplace: organizational conspiracy theories and work-related outcomes', *British Journal of Psychology*, 108(3): 486–506.
Douglas, K.M. and Sutton, R.M. (2011) 'Does it take one to know one? Endorsement of conspiracy theories is influenced by personal willingness to conspire', *British Journal of Social Psychology*, 50(3): 544–52.
Douglas, K.M., Sutton, R.M. and Cichocka, A. (2017) 'The psychology of conspiracy theories', *Current Directions in Psychological Science*, 26(6): 538–42.
Duckitt, J. (2001) 'A dual-process cognitive-motivational theory of ideology and prejudice', *Advances in Experimental Social Psychology*, 33: 41–113.
Fiske, S.T., Cuddy, A.J.C., Glick, P. and Xu, J. (2002) 'A model of (often mixed) stereotype content: competence and warmth respectively follow from perceived status and competition', *Journal of Personality and Social Psychology*, 82(6): 878–902.
Fousiani, K. and van Prooijen, J.-W. (2019) 'Reactions to offenders: psychological differences between beliefs versus punishment', *British Journal of Social Psychology*.
Glick, P. (2002) 'Sacrificial lambs dressed in wolves' clothing: envious prejudice, ideology, and the scapegoating of Jews', in L. S. Newman, C. R. Browning and R. Erber (eds.) *Understanding genocide: the social psychology of the Holocaust*, Oxford Scholarship Online, pp. 113–42.
Glick, P., Diebold, J., Bailey-Werner, B. and Zhu, L. (1997) 'The two faces of Adam: ambivalent sexism and polarized attitudes toward women', *Personality and Social Psychology Bulletin*, 23(12): 1323–34.
Goertzel, T. (1994) 'Belief in conspiracy theories', *Political Psychology*, 15(4): 731–42.
Goertzel, T. (2010) 'Conspiracy theories in science', *EMBO Reports*, 11(7): 493–9.
Golec de Zavala, A. and Cichocka, A. (2012) 'Collective narcissism and anti-Semitism in Poland', *Group Processes and Intergroup Relations*, 15(2): 213–29.

Golec de Zavala, A., Cichocka, A., Eidelson, R. and Jayawickreme, N. (2009) 'Collective narcissism and its social consequences', *Journal of Personality and Social Psychology*, 97(6): 1074–96.

Grzesiak-Feldman, M. (2007) 'Conspiracy thinking and state-trait anxiety in young Polish adults', *Psychological Reports*, 100(1): 199–202.

Grzesiak-Feldman, M. (2013) 'The effect of high-anxiety situations on conspiracy thinking', *Current Psychology*, 32(1): 100–18.

Grzesiak-Feldman, M. and Irzycka, M. (2009) 'Right-wing authoritarianism and conspiracy thinking in a Polish sample', *Psychological Reports*, 105(2): 389–93.

Hamsher, J.H., Geller, D.J. and Rotter, B.J. (1968) 'Interpersonal trust, internal-external control, and the Warren commission report', *Journal of Personality and Social Psychology*, 9(3): 210–5.

Hogg, M.A., Sherman, D.K., Dierselhuis, J., Maitner, A.T. and Moffitt, G. (2007) 'Uncertainty, entitativity, and group identification', *Journal of Experimental Social Psychology*, 43(1): 135–42.

Imhoff, R. (2015) 'Beyond (right-wing) authoritarianism: conspiracy mentality as an incremental predictor of prejudice', *The Psychology of Conspiracy*, Abingdon-on-Thames, UK: Routledge, pp. 140–60.

Imhoff, R. and Bruder, M. (2014) 'Speaking (un-)truth to power: conspiracy mentality as a generalised political attitude', *European Journal of Personality*, 28(1): 25–43.

Jolley, D. and Douglas, K.M. (2014a) 'The social consequences of conspiracism: exposure to conspiracy theories decreases the intention to engage in politics and to reduce one's carbon footprint', *British Journal of Psychology*, 105(1): 35–56.

Jolley, D. and Douglas, K.M. (2014b) 'The effects of anti-vaccine conspiracy theories on vaccination intentions', *PLoS ONE*, 9(2): e89177.

Jolley, D., Douglas, K.M., Leite, A.C. and Schrader, T. (2019) 'Belief in conspiracy theories and intentions to engage in everyday crime', *British Journal of Social Psychology*, 58(3): 534–49.

Jolley, D., Douglas, K.M. and Sutton, R.M. (2018) 'Blaming a few bad apples to save a threatened barrel: the system-justifying function of conspiracy theories', *Political Psychology*, 39(2): 465–78.

Jolley, D., Meleady, R. and Douglas, K.M. (2019) 'Exposure to intergroup conspiracy theories promotes prejudice which spreads across groups', *British Journal of Psychology*.

Kay, A.C., Gaucher, D., Napier, J.L., Callan, M.J. and Laurin, K. (2008) 'God and the government: testing a compensatory control mechanism for the support of external systems', *Journal of Personality and Social Psychology*, 95(1): 18–35.

Koch, A., Imhoff, R., Dotsch, R., Unkelbach, C. and Alves, H. (2016) 'The ABC of stereotypes about groups: Agency/socioeconomic success, conservative–progressive Beliefs, and Communion', *Journal of Personality and Social Psychology*, 110(5): 675–709.

Kofta, M. and Sedek, G. (2005) 'Conspiracy stereotypes of Jews during systemic transformation in Poland', *International Journal of Sociology*, 35(1): 40–64.

Kramer, R.M. and Messick, D.M. (1998) 'Getting by with a little help from our enemies: collective paranoia and its role in intergroup relations', in C. Sedikides, J. Schopler, C. A. Insko and C. Insko (eds.) *Intergroup cognition and intergroup behavior*, Abingdon-on-Thames, UK: Routledge, pp. 233–56.

Kramer, R.M. and Schaffer, J. (2014) 'Misconnecting the dots: origins and dynamics of out-group paranoia', in J.-W. van Prooijen and P.A.M. van Lange (eds.) *Power, politics, and paranoia: why people are suspicious of their leaders*, New York: Cambridge University Press, pp. 199–217.

Krekó, P. (2015) 'Conspiracy theory as collective motivated cognition', in M. Bilewicz, A. Cichocka, and W. Soral (eds.) *The Psychology of Conspiracy*, Abingdon-on-Thames, UK: Routledge, pp. 63–78.

Krueger, J. (2000) 'Distributive judgments under uncertainty: Paccioli's game revisited', *Journal of Experimental Psychology*, 129(4): 546–58.

Krzemiński, I. (2004) *Antysemityzm w Polsce i na Ukrainie: Raport z badań*, Warsaw: Scholar.

Lickel, B., Hamilton, D.L., Wieczorkowska, G., Lewis, A., Sherman, S.J. and Uhles, A.N. (2000) 'Varieties of groups and the perception of group entitativity', *Journal of Personality and Social Psychology*, 78(2): 223–46.

Marchlewska, M., Cichocka, A. and Kossowska, M. (2018a) 'Addicted to answers: need for cognitive closure and the endorsement of conspiracy beliefs', *European Journal of Social Psychology*, 48(2): 109–17.

Marchlewska, M., Cichocka, A., Łozowski, F., Górska, P. and Winiewski, M. (2019) 'In search of an imaginary enemy: catholic collective narcissism and the endorsement of gender conspiracy beliefs', *Journal of Social Psychology*.

Marchlewska, M., Cichocka, A., Panayiotou, O., Castellanos, K. and Batayneh, J. (2018b) 'Populism as identity politics: perceived in-group disadvantage, collective narcissism, and support for populism', *Social Psychological and Personality Science*, 9(2): 151–62.

Mashuri, A. and Zaduqisti, E. (2014) 'We believe in your conspiracy if we distrust you: the role of intergroup distrust in structuring the effect of Islamic identification, competitive victimhood, and group incompatibility on belief in a conspiracy theory', *Journal of Tropical Psychology*, 4(e11): 1–14.

Mathews, A. and MacLeod, C. (2002) 'Induced processing biases have causal effects on anxiety', *Cognition and Emotion*, 16(3): 331–54.

Mirowsky, J. and Ross, C.E. (1983) 'Paranoia and the structure of powerlessness', *American Sociological Review*, 48(2): 228–39.

Morris, M. (2000) 'Lay theories of individual and collective agency', *Meeting of Society of Experimental Social Psychology*, Atlanta: Georgia State University, 19–21 October.

Noor, M., Brown, R.J. and Prentice, G. (2008) 'Precursors and mediators of intergroup reconciliation in Northern Ireland: a new model', *British Journal of Social Psychology*, 47(3): 481–95.

Noor, M., Shnabel, N., Halabi, S. and Nadler, A. (2012) 'When suffering begets suffering: the psychology of competitive victimhood between adversarial groups in violent conflicts', *Personality and Social Psychology Review*, 16(4): 351–74.

Oliver, J.E. and Wood, T. (2014) 'Medical conspiracy theories and health behaviors in the United States', *JAMA Internal Medicine*, 174(5): 817–8.

Park, C.L. (2010) 'Making sense of the meaning literature: an integrative review of meaning making and its effects on adjustment to stressful life events', *Psychological Bulletin*, 136(2): 257–301.

Pettigrew, T.F. (2009) 'Secondary transfer effect of contact: do intergroup contact effects spread to non-contacted outgroups?', *Social Psychology*, 40(2): 55–65.

Pettigrew, T.F. and Tropp, L.R. (2006a) 'A meta-analytic test of intergroup contact theory', *Journal of Personality and Social Psychology*, 90(5): 751–83.

Pettigrew, T.F. and Tropp, L.R. (2006b) 'Does intergroup contact reduce prejudice? Recent meta-analytic findings', in S. Oskamp (ed.) *The Claremont Symposium on Applied Social Psychology*, Mahwah, NJ: Lawrence Erlbaum Associates Publishers, pp. 93–114.

Phalet, K. and Poppe, E. (1997) 'Competence and morality dimensions of national and ethnic stereotypes: a study in six eastern-European countries', *European Journal of Social Psychology*, 27(6): 703–23.

Reid, A. (2010) 'Jewish-conspiracy theories in Southeast Asia: are chinese the target?', *Indonesia and the Malay World*, 38(112): 373–85.

Rosch, E. (1973) 'Natural categories', *Cognitive Psychology*, 4(3): 328–50.

Rosch, E. (1975) 'Cognitive reference points', *Cognitive Psychology*, 7(4): 532–47.

Rothbart, M. and Taylor, M. (1992) 'Category labels and social reality: do we view social categories as natural kinds?', in G.R. Semin and K. Fiedler (eds.) *Language interaction and social cognition*, Thousand Oaks, CA: Sage Publications, Inc., pp. 11–36.

Rothschild, Z.K., Landau, M.J., Sullivan, D. and Keefer, L.A. (2012) 'A dual-motive model of scapegoating: displacing blame to reduce guilt or increase control', *Journal of Personality and Social Psychology*, 102(6): 1148–63.

Runciman, W.G. (1966) *Relative deprivation and social justice*, London: Routledge.

Sapountzis, A. and Condor, S. (2013) 'Conspiracy accounts as intergroup theories: challenging dominant understandings of social power and political legitimacy', *Political Psychology*, 34(5): 731–52.

Shnabel, N. and Noor, M. (2012) 'Competitive victimhood among Jewish and Palestinian Israelis reflects differential threats to their identities: the perspective of the needs-based model', in K.J. Jonas and T. Morton (eds.) *Restoring civil societies: the psychology of intervention and engagement following crisis*, Hoboken, NJ: Wiley-Blackwell, pp. 192–207.

Sibley, C.G. and Duckitt, J. (2013) 'The dual process model of ideology and prejudice: a longitudinal test during a global recession', *Journal of Social Psychology*, 153(4): 448–66.

Sibley, C.G., Osborne, D. and Duckitt, J. (2012) 'Personality and political orientation: meta-analysis and test of a threat-constraint model', *Journal of Research in Personality*, 46(6): 664–77.

Soral, W., Cichocka, A., Bilewicz, M. and Marchlewska, M. (2019) 'The collective conspiracy mentality in Poland', in J.E. Uscinski (ed.) *Conspiracy theories and the people who believe them*, Oxford Scholarship Online, pp. 372–84.

Stempel, C., Hargrove, T. and Stempel, G.H. (2007) 'Media use, social structure, and belief in 9/11 theories', *Journalism and Mass Communication Quarterly*, 84(2): 353–72.

Suciu, M.E. (2008) *Signs of anti-semitism in Indonesia*, thesis, University of Sydney.

Sullivan, D., Landau, M.J. and Rothschild, Z.K. (2010) 'An existential function of enemyship: evidence that people attribute influence to personal and political enemies to compensate for threats to control', *Journal of Personality and Social Psychology*, 98(3): 434–49.

Sunstein, C.R. and Vermeule, A. (2009) 'Conspiracy theories: causes and cures', *Journal of Political Philosophy*, 17(2): 202–27.
Tausch, N., Hewstone, M., Kenworthy, J.B., Psaltis, C., Schmid, K., Popan, J.R. and Hughes, J. (2010) 'Secondary transfer effects of intergroup contact: alternative accounts and underlying processes', *Journal of Personality and Social Psychology*, 99(2): 282–302.
Van den Bos, K. (2009) 'Making sense of life: the existential self trying to deal with personal uncertainty', *Psychological Inquiry*, 20(4): 197–217.
Van Prooijen, J.-W. and Douglas, K.M. (2017) 'Conspiracy theories as part of history: the role of societal crisis situations', *Memory Studies*, 10(3): 323–33.
Van Prooijen, J.-W. and Jostmann, N.B. (2013) 'Belief in conspiracy theories: the influence of uncertainty and perceived morality', *European Journal of Social Psychology*, 43(1): 109–15.
Van Prooijen, J.-W., Staman, J. and Krouwel, A.P.M. (2018) 'Increased conspiracy beliefs among ethnic and Muslim minorities', *Applied Cognitive Psychology*, 32(5): 661–7.
Van Prooijen, J.-W. and van Lange, P. (2014) 'The social dimension of belief in conspiracy theories', in J.W. van Prooijen and P. van Lange (eds.) *Power, politics, and paranoia: why people are suspicious of their leaders*, Cambridge, UK: Cambridge University Press, pp. 237–52.
Whitson, J.A. and Galinsky, A.D. (2008) 'Lacking control increases illusory pattern perception', *Science*, 322(5898): 115–7.
Wieckowska, J. (2004) 'Perceptions of entitativity and essentialism of social categories as determinants of conspiracy stereotypes and prejudice', in M. Kofta (ed.) *Stereotyping and prejudice: their cognitive and affective mechanisms*, Warsaw: Polish Academy of Sciences, Institute of Psychology Press, pp. 79–94.
Wilder, D. and Simon, A.F. (2001) 'Affect as a cause of intergroup bias', in R.J. Brown and S.L. Gaertner (eds.) *Blackwell handbook of social psychology: intergroup processes*, Hoboken, NJ: Blackwell Publishers Ltd, pp. 153–72.
Winiewski, M., Soral, W. and Bilewicz, M. (2015) 'Conspiracy theories on the map of stereotype content: survey and historical evidence', in M. Bilewicz, A. Cichocka and W. Soral (eds.) *The Psychology of Conspiracy*, Abingdon, UK: Routledge, pp. 23–41.
Yiend, J. and Mathews, A. (2001) 'Anxiety and attention to threatening pictures', *Quarterly Journal of Experimental Psychology Section A: Human Experimental Psychology*, 54(3): 665–81.
Zhong, J., Liu, Y., Zhang, E., Luo, J. and Chen, J. (2013) 'Individuals' attentional bias toward an envied target's name: an event-related potential study', *Neuroscience Letters*, 550: 109–14.

# 2.7
# CONSEQUENCES OF CONSPIRACY THEORIES

*Daniel Jolley, Silvia Mari and Karen M. Douglas*

## Introduction

Conspiracy theories explain the ultimate causes of significant events and circumstances as the secret actions of malevolent groups who cover up information to suit their own interests (e.g. Douglas *et al.* 2017). Well-known conspiracy theories propose that climate change is a hoax orchestrated by the world's scientists to secure research funding, that Diana, Princess of Wales was murdered by members of the British government and that the harms of vaccines are being covered up so that pharmaceutical companies can continue to make huge profits. Conspiracy theories are popular, and some research suggests that around half of the U.S. population believes at least one (Oliver, Wood 2014). In recent years, psychologists have made significant progress in understanding why so many millions of people believe in conspiracy theories (see Douglas *et al.* 2017 for a review). However, much less is known about their consequences. In this chapter, we outline what is known to date, and review the psychological research on the positive and negative consequences of conspiracy theories. Overwhelmingly, this research suggests that conspiracy theories are harmful. We, therefore, argue that future research efforts should attempt to address the negative psychological and behavioural consequences of conspiracy theories.

## Belief in conspiracy theories

Conspiracy theories at first glance appear to satisfy important psychological needs (Douglas *et al.* 2017; see also Chapter 2.3 in this volume). For example, conspiracy theories may allow people to gain an accurate and consistent understanding of the world (epistemic need); for example, people who need concrete answers (Marchlewska *et al.* 2017) and those showing a tendency to overestimate the likelihood of co-occurring events (Brotherton, French 2014) are more likely to be drawn to conspiracy theories. Conspiracy theories may also allow people to meet the desire to be secure and in control (existential need); for example, people who are anxious (Grzesiak-Feldman 2013) and feel powerless (e.g. van Prooijen, Acker 2015) are likely to subscribe to conspiracy theories. Moreover, conspiracy theories may allow people to maintain a positive sense of the self and the social groups one belongs to (social need); for example, conspiracy theories appeal more to narcissists (Cichocka *et al.* 2016) and people who view themselves on the losing side of political processes (Uscinski, Parent 2014). Together, a growing body of literature on the psychology of conspiracy theories provides evidence that belief in conspiracy theories can be explained by everyday psychological needs and not simply the result of paranoia (cf. Hofstadter 1964).

## Consequences of conspiracy theories

Whilst psychologists now understand a great deal about the factors that draw people toward conspiracy theories (see Chapters 2.1, 2.3 and 2.4), less is known about their consequences. Scholars once suggested that conspiracy theories may be harmless fun and of little concern (Bratich 2008; Clarke 2002). Other than being perhaps foolish and illogical, it was therefore thought that conspiracy theories have little or no detrimental influence over society (e.g. Melley 2002; Willman 2002). Although this view is now less popular, whether conspiracy theories have more positive or negative consequences still remains open for debate. In the following sections, we review research on both the positive and negative outcomes of conspiracy theories.

## Positive consequences

Although there is little empirical evidence at present, some research suggests that there may be positive consequences of endorsing conspiracy theories. For example, believing in conspiracy theories might lead to a sense of shared community with others who endorse the same theories (Franks et al. 2017), thus satisfying a social need. As suggested by Miller (2002), conspiracy theories can provide individuals with the opportunity to question the credibility of governments, which in normal circumstances would likely be denied to them, and thus opens up possibilities for political debate.

In a similar vein, conspiracy theories may in certain contexts inspire collective action and social change attempts, especially in reaction to threatening events. Potentially, therefore, they have the capacity to satisfy existential needs. For example, Imhoff and Bruder (2014) found that Germans with higher levels of conspiracy belief were more likely to take political action, such as organising a protest, in response to the Fukushima nuclear disaster of 2011. In a different context, Mari et al. (2017) found that representations of the recent European economic crisis amongst Italian and Greek participants as a secret plot by powerful groups influenced different forms of political participation. Conspiracy beliefs triggered both classic positive forms of political responses such as legal activism (e.g. signing petitions) and other atypical forms, such as financial resistance (e.g. taking money abroad). Belief in conspiracy theories predicted political action beyond the effects of ideology and feelings of personal vulnerability.

Scholars have also suggested that conspiracy theories can reveal actual anomalies in mainstream explanations (e.g. Clarke 2002; Swami, Coles 2010). Indeed, some conspiracy theories have been proven to be true, such as the U.S. Department of Defence plans to orchestrate terrorism and blame it on Cuba, the Watergate scandal that involved a break-in at the Democratic National Committee headquarters where President Nixon's administration attempted to cover-up their involvement and the Tuskegee syphilis scandal, where treatment was withheld from 399 black men without their informed consent. Conspiracy theories may, therefore, allow people to question social hierarchies, which may encourage governments to be more transparent (see Swami, Coles 2010).

## Negative consequences

Whilst there may be some positive consequences of believing in conspiracy theories, empirical research examining these consequences is lacking. At present, the vast majority of research examining the consequences of conspiracy theories has focused on negative consequences, particularly in the domains of politics and health. These consequences can be broken down into different areas: Psychological, attitude polarisation, political, scientific and daily life. We now cover these each in turn.

## Psychological needs

As we have discussed, conspiracy beliefs are thought to satisfy important psychological needs (Douglas *et al.* 2017). However, emerging experimental research has demonstrated that conspiracy theories might thwart these needs more than they help people meet them. For example, exposure to conspiracy theories can directly increase feelings of powerlessness, disillusionment, uncertainty, mistrust and anomie rather than decrease them (Jolley, Douglas 2014a, 2014b; Jolley *et al.* 2019). That is, rather than helping alleviate negative psychological states, conspiracy theories might sometimes make them worse: As Douglas *et al.* (2017: 538) put it, '[conspiracy theories] may be more appealing than satisfying'.

Conspiracy theories may also be a source of social stigma (Harambam, Aupers 2015). Indeed, people subscribing to these beliefs may be aware of being the target of stigma. For instance, individuals advocating for alternative explanations through comments on news websites were reluctant to label and let others name their beliefs as 'conspiracy theories' (Wood, Douglas 2013). Lantian *et al.* (2018) experimentally tested whether people endorsing conspiracy theories experience social stigma. They found that French participants induced to endorse (vs. reject) conspiracy theories related to the Charlie Hebdo shooting event expected greater fear of social exclusion, via the mediation effect of anticipated negative evaluation of the self. A second study, where participants were asked to imagine the presence of an audience, replicated the results, thus underlying the importance of perceived social norms in such negative psychological consequences. Overall, therefore, research suggests that conspiracy theories may not help people meet important psychological needs and may make people feel as though they are outsiders.

## Polarisation and attitude change

Conspiracy theories may also change the way people think about events. Research more broadly exploring the influence of information has shown that external sources can play a critical role in shaping beliefs (cf. Swami *et al.* 2013). Based on this idea, Swami *et al.* (2013) argued that, as attitude formation is rarely based on a critical review of all the relevant issues, the nature of the information that an individual receives about a given phenomenon should have an impact on their attitudes. In testing this assertion empirically, Butler *et al.* (1995) found that people who had viewed the film *J.F.K.* – which highlights several prominent conspiracy theories surrounding the assassination of President John F. Kennedy – were more inclined to disbelieve official accounts than those who had not yet viewed the film. Similarly, Swami *et al.* (2013) exposed people to either information that argued N.A.S.A. faked the moon landing, a text critical of the moon landing conspiracy account or a control condition where no information was provided. Results demonstrated that those who were exposed to the moon landing conspiracy theory indicated a higher level of belief that the landing was faked, relative to the other conditions.

Further, Douglas and Sutton (2008) found that participants who read conspiracy information concerning the death of Princess Diana were more inclined to endorse conspiracy explanations, even though they perceived that their beliefs had not changed. Conspiracy explanations, therefore, are able to change people's attitudes, and this has wide-reaching implications when considering the ease of access to conspiracy theories within popular culture (e.g. Bessi *et al.* 2015).

Special attention has been devoted to online environments. The confirmation bias – the tendency to select the information that adheres to an individual's system of beliefs and to avoid contradictions – promotes the selective exposure to information relative to the specific narrative of interest while ignoring alternative viewpoints. Del Vicario et al. (2016a) showed that this is also true when considering conspiracy theories' online consumption and content diffusion. Moreover, online social media allow for the aggregation of individuals in communities with shared narratives and worldviews, acting as echo chambers, that reverberate and reinforce biased narratives. The main features of such communities, indeed, refer to the strong group homogeneity – the primary driver for the diffusion of content – and polarisation (Del Vicario et al. 2016a, 2016b).

Sunstein (2018) raised a concern about the perils of group polarisation when considering online misinformation – i.e. moving toward a more extreme attitude in the direction of the original inclination of the group's member. Fake news, unverified rumours and conspiracy theories cannot be easily filtered and suppressed by mainstream media or social pressure. Mocanu et al. (2015) found that conspiracy theories reverberate for as long as other types of information conveyed by online political activism, as well as mainstream media. Thus, such false information developed for minority audiences who may be already favourable towards conspiracy theories is particularly pervasive on social media, promoting collective credulity. Big data analyses of cascade dynamics of Facebook posts and interactions about conspiracy theories revealed that they were assimilated slowly but there was a positive relationship between the size of the cascade and lifetime (Del Vicario et al. 2016b). Moreover, Bessi et al. (2015) found that Italians believing in conspiracy theories and who were active online on Facebook concentrated their social media activities on four specific domains (diet, health, environment and geopolitics) and were actively engaged in posting comments on the same comments, contributing to the vitality of the conspiracy theories.

## Political consequences

Conspiracy theories propose that (perceived) powerful groups are involved in secret plots and schemes. Typically, the conspirator is seen to be the government but can also be other social groups, such as people who are Jewish (see Chapter 2.6; Golec de Zavala, Cichocka 2012). Subscribing to these conspiracy theories can lead to apathy and prejudice. For example, focusing on political behaviours, political scientists have found that conspiracy thinking is associated with behaviours such as not wanting to vote, donate to political parties or put up political yard signs (Uscinski, Parent 2014). To examine the impact of government conspiracy theories on political engagement experimentally, Jolley and Douglas (2014a) presented British participants with material arguing in favour of governments being involved in plots and schemes (e.g. 9/11), or arguing against government conspiracy theories. They found that participants who were exposed to conspiracy theories were less likely to engage in politics (e.g. voting) compared to those who had read arguments against government conspiracy theories. This effect was shown to be mediated by feelings of political powerlessness.

However, conspiracy theories can also be politically activating, such as organising a protest (Imhoff, Bruder 2014) or being involved in illegal political actions such as occupying buildings (Mari et al. 2017). As Jolley et al. (in press) discuss, depending on the context (such as feeling empowered by the [in]action), conspiracy theories may lead to inaction rather than action. For example, disengaging from voting might be empowering for people who believe the government is conspiring, but, at the same time, protesting against the government may be empowering for people who also believe sinister forces in the government ought to be challenged.

Alternatively, some conspiracy theories may breed a feeling of helplessness that promotes in inaction (such as feeling politically powerless, so not wanting to vote; Jolley, Douglas 2014a), whereas others may make people angry, leading to action (cf. Mari et al. 2017). Future research should explore these possibilities further.

Conspiracy theories are also associated with institutional distrust. Mari et al. (under review), using a cross-cultural dataset with almost 12 000 participants in 11 democracies, found that supporting general political conspiracy beliefs determined mistrust toward specific different institutions (the representative government; non-representative government bodies and security institutions) and the effect was generalised, with few exceptions, across the different countries. In an experimental study, Einstein and Glick (2015) revealed that exposure to a conspiracy claim reduced trust in the government and institutions not connected to the accusation. Conspiracy theories thus contribute to the diffusion of suspicion and the erosion of the necessary trust and confidence climate between citizens and central authorities, hence endangering the entire democratic system.

Conspiracy theories have also been shown to interfere with intergroup relations (see Chapter 2.6). For example, Swami (2012) has demonstrated that, among a Malaysian sample, belief in Jewish conspiracy theories – that propose Jewish people are involved in plots and schemes – was associated with greater racist attitudes towards Chinese citizens. Golec de Zavala and Cichocka (2012) also found that belief in conspiracy theories about Jewish domination of the world was associated with antisemitic attitudes. Moreover, research by Imhoff and Bruder (2014) has shown that conspiracy beliefs are a significant predictor of prejudice against a variety of high-power groups (e.g. Jews, Americans, capitalists). Similarly, in correlational data, Bilewicz et al. (2013) reported that conspiracy stereotypes of Jewish people – which refer to social schemas of groups that typically view group members with ill intentions – are a strong predictor of discrimination towards Jewish people (e.g. favouring policies that prevent Jewish people from buying Polish land, see also Bilewicz and Krzeminski 2010).

Building on this work, Jolley et al. (in press) found that British participants who were exposed to Jewish conspiracy theories displayed increased prejudice towards this group compared to a control group, which then translated into biased behavioural tendencies towards Jewish people. Specifically, participants who were exposed to Jewish conspiracy theories were less likely to vote for a Jewish political candidate in an election. Importantly, our work has extended previous work by demonstrating that exposure to Jewish conspiracy theories not only increased prejudice towards Jewish people, but also indirectly increased prejudice towards a range of other, uninvolved groups such as Americans, Asians and Arabs. This effect occurred via a process of attitude generalisation where prejudice towards secondary groups is increased *through* prejudice towards the group at the centre of the conspiracy theory (cf. Pettigrew 2009). Together, this research demonstrated that conspiracy theories can have a widespread negative impact on intergroup relations.

In addition to fuelling prejudice and discrimination, conspiracy theories have been shown to potentially fuel violence towards others. Bartlett and Miller (2010) analysed the content of writings and speeches of more than 50 extremist groups across the political ideology continuum. They discovered, whilst there was no difference in conspiracy thinking between violent and nonviolent extremist groups, conspiracy theories accelerated the process of radicalisation where conspiracy theories can change ingroup/outgroup dynamics and reinforce 'othering'. There has been anecdotal evidence that conspiracy theories were openly expressed by the perpetrator involved in the 2019 shootings at mosques in Christchurch, New Zealand (Davey 2019). Journalists have also suggested that the basis for aggression towards survivors in recent mass shootings in the U.S.A. appear to originate with conspiracy theorists, who believe that survivors are crisis actors employed by gun law reformists (Levin, Beckett 2017). For example, the survivors of a mass shooting at Marjory Stoneman Douglas High School in 2018 have been accused of being crisis actors by a variety of sources, including some mainstream media outlets (Pearce 2018). Whilst there is limited empirical research exploring this possibility, Uscinski and Parent (2014) have found that people high in conspiracy beliefs are twice as likely to oppose gun law reform and defend political violence.

## Science denialism

Conspiracy theories can also lead to inaction and disengagement in the scientific domain. For example, a popular conspiracy theory proposes that climate change scientists fake their data in order to receive research funding (Douglas, Sutton 2015). Polls indicate that upwards of 37 per cent of Americans believe that global warming is a hoax (Jensen 2013; also see Uscinski et al. 2017). This is potentially troublesome if people were to act on their beliefs and not wish to engage with climate science. Indeed, to explore the impact of climate change conspiracy theories on behavioural intentions, Jolley and Douglas (2014a) exposed British participants to materials arguing in favour of climate change conspiracy theories, or materials arguing against such theories. We also used a control condition where no arguments were provided. Results revealed that being exposed to climate change conspiracy theories reduced intentions to engage in climate-friendly behaviours such as using energy efficiency, in comparison to the other conditions. This effect was explained by feelings of powerlessness associated with climate change, uncertainty and disillusionment. Specifically, being exposed to the idea that climate change is a hoax directly increased the feeling of powerlessness and uncertainty towards tackling climate change, alongside feeling disillusioned with climate scientists, which led to lower intention to reduce one's carbon footprint. Similarly, Van der Linden (2015) found that participants who were exposed to a conspiracy video about global warming were less likely to sign a petition to help reduce global warming, in comparison to participants who watched an inspirational pro-climate video or a control group with no exposure.

Conspiracy theories have also been shown to impact important medical choices. For example, researchers have shown that endorsement of birth control and H.I.V./A.I.D.S. conspiracy theories, which propose that H.I.V./A.I.D.S. are a form of genocide against African Americans, are associated with increased negative attitudes towards contraceptive behaviours (e.g. the use of condoms; Bogart, Bird 2003; Bogart, Thorburn 2006). Indeed, negative attitudes towards condoms have been shown to partially explain the relationship between conspiracy beliefs and condom use (Bogart, Thorburn 2006). Similar results have been found in research conducted by Hoyt et al. (2012), where H.I.V. conspiracy beliefs were associated with increased risk relating to H.I.V. such as being more likely to avoid appropriate treatment behaviour.

Moreover, former South African President Mbeki publicly stated that H.I.V. is not the cause of A.I.D.S. and that antiretroviral (A.R.V.) drugs are not useful in controlling the H.I.V. infection (Chigwedere et al. 2008). The South African government, therefore, declined to accept donations of A.R.V. medication. It is plausible that such a public expression of conspiracy belief may have influenced the South African public's trust in biomedical claims (Rubincam 2017). It has since been estimated that over 330 000 South Africans died between the years 2000–2005, which could have been due, in part, to the actions of the South African government (Chigwedere et al. 2008).

In a similar vein, Oliver and Wood (2014) have shown using four nationally representative surveys sampled between 2006 and 2011 that over half of the U.S. population endorses at least one medical conspiracy theory, such as the link between vaccines and autism. When considering vaccinations, Jolley and Douglas (2014b) explored the link between anti-vaccine conspiracy theories and vaccination intentions. In the first study with British parents as the sample, Jolley and Douglas uncovered a correlation between belief in anti-vaccine conspiracy theories and intentions to have a fictitious child vaccinated against a made-up disease. In a second study, they employed an experimental design where British participants were exposed to anti-vaccine conspiracy theories (e.g. that vaccines harm more than help and that this fact is covered up), anti-conspiracy arguments or no arguments (control condition). The researchers found that exposure to anti-vaccine conspiracy theories reduced vaccination intentions, compared to the other two conditions. Jolley and Douglas (2014b) also included a number of mediators in order to explain this effect. It was found that the conspiracy theory account aroused suspicion concerning the perceived dangers of vaccinations, and made people feel powerless, disillusioned and mistrustful, leading to a lower intention to vaccinate the fictional child.

Moreover, Oliver and Wood (2014) found that people who endorse such conspiracy theories were less likely to use traditional vaccines such as flu shots and were more likely to indicate that they would trust medical advice from non-professionals such as friends and family. Similarly, Lamberty and Imhoff (2018) found that conspiracy beliefs were associated with more positive attitudes towards alternative and complementary medicine and more negative attitudes towards biomedical approaches. However, the consequences of conspiracy theories are not only constrained to the 'hard sciences' and medicine but have also been found to impact the humanities. Specifically, Imhoff *et al.* (2018) found that conspiracy theories lead to questioning of established narratives and facts, such as about history. Together, this provides empirical evidence that conspiracy beliefs can lead to disengagement with a range of established medical practice, but also with established narratives and fact.

## Daily life context

Conspiracy theories may not only influence people's medical decisions but also how they behave in their everyday work and social lives. For example, belief in organisational conspiracy theories – which is the belief that powerful groups act secretly to achieve objectives at the cost of employees – have been shown to have a detrimental impact in the workplace. Specifically, van Prooijen and de Vries (2016) discovered that organisational conspiracy beliefs predicted increased turnover intentions via decreased organisational commitment. Exploring this experimentally, Douglas and Leite (2017) exposed participants to organisational conspiracy theories, where participants were asked to read a workplace scenario in which a conspiracy had occurred (vs. control). Participants who were exposed to organisational conspiracy theories displayed a lower intention to remain in their workplace. This was mediated by organisational commitment and job satisfaction. Together, this work showcases the impact that conspiracy theories may have in organisational settings and that they should therefore not be dismissed as harmless gossip.

Conspiracy theories may also lead people to disengage from social norms, making them more likely to engage in counter-normative behaviour. Jolley *et al.* (in press) have explored this novel issue. Specifically, in a correlational study with British participants, they measured known predictors of everyday crimes – which are common offences that most people are likely to commit at some point in their lives, such as running red lights and paying with cash to avoid paying taxes (Karstedt, Farrall 2006), alongside belief in conspiracy theories. Results demonstrated that, along with other known personality predictors (e.g. Honesty-Humility), conspiracy theories (both general conspiracy beliefs and belief in well-known conspiracy theories in society) were found to uniquely predict an increased tendency towards everyday crime. A second study extended these findings in an experimental design. Participants were exposed to either conspiracy-related material that argued in favour of government conspiracy theories, anti-conspiracy material that argued against the theories or a control condition where no information was provided. It was found that participants who were exposed to conspiracy theories were more likely to engage in everyday crime in the future. This effect was mediated by anomie – or a general feeling of unrest and dissatisfaction (Abalakina-Paap et al. 1999). The researchers argued that feelings such as anomie can be exacerbated by conspiracy theories, which in turn change the perceptions about the particular ways in which social systems operate, leading to unethical behaviour. In other words, if others are perceived to be conspiring, then perhaps it is permissible to commit negative acts oneself. Together, this research provides evidence that endorsing the idea that *others* are involved in conspiracies may alter one's perceptions of social norms by signalling that unethical activities are permissible.

## Conclusion

Although there may be some positive consequences of holding conspiracy beliefs, and further research should explore how people's psychological needs might be met by conspiracy theories, the literature to date paints rather a pessimistic picture. Specifically, a growing body of research has shown that conspiracy theories can negatively impact people in a variety of areas, including their work life, medical choices and political engagement. Conspiracy theories appear to be a significant problem for modern society. It is, therefore, paramount that researchers explore avenues to address the detrimental consequences of conspiracy theories.

As further discussed in this volume (see Chapter 2.8), researchers are beginning to make progress in developing tools that can be used to combat the negative impact of conspiracy theories; however, there are challenges in ensuring that the interventions will work successfully in society. For example, Jolley and Douglas (2017) found that, once a conspiracy belief has become established, the consequences of conspiracy theories are difficult to correct. Counter-arguments that come before a conspiracy account may be promising as an intervention (e.g. in the case of anti-vaccine conspiracy theories), but often the conspiracy account is widespread before the official explanation is published. In these situations, conspiracy theories could be difficult to refute. Nonetheless, promising results were recently obtained in a series of studies by Bonetto et al. (2018), where priming resistance to persuasion reduced individual endorsement of conspiracy beliefs. Moreover, Mari et al. (under review) considered the differential impact of social media use on political conspiracy beliefs and institutional trust. They found that specific types of social media use (i.e. interactional, informational and political expressive) may soften the negative effect of conspiracy beliefs toward institutional trust. Interestingly, such types of social media use are precursors of political participation and can be utilised as a starting point in interventions of media literacy and consumption, to make people aware of the effects of social media use. Developing interventions is an important question for scholars in the future, where the emerging research is showcasing some early promising results.

Alongside focusing on developing interventions, scholars conducting future research must consider some methodological issues. For example, there is a scarcity of experimental and/or longitudinal designs used in the field. This is particularly troublesome as researchers are unaware whether the effects of conspiracy exposure on behavioural intentions last for a prolonged period of time. In a similar vein, there is a scarcity of real behavioural measurement – the literature to date is focused on intentions or fictional scenarios. It is unclear whether intentions translate into real behavioural engagement or disengagement. Moreover, the majority of the research literature has focused on participants who are relatively low in conspiracy beliefs. There is therefore limited research exploring the psychological make-up and consequences for the self of strong conspiracy beliefs. Future research could explore these important questions to enable a fuller understanding of the consequences of conspiracy theories.

In sum, the literature on the psychology of conspiracy theories has made some important strides in understanding conspiracy theories in contemporary society. Whilst scholars still have work to do, there is currently a dark picture of conspiracy theories emerging from the literature to date. Conspiracy theories have the power to seem appealing, but can go onto have a detrimental impact on the self and wider society.

## References

Abalakina-Paap, M., Stephan, W.G., Craig, T. and Gregory, L. (1999) 'Beliefs in conspiracies', *Political Psychology*, 20(3): 637–47.

Bartlett, J. and Miller, C. (2010) *The power of unreason: conspiracy theories, extremism and counter-terrorism*, London: Demos.

Bessi, A., Coletto, M., Davidescu, G.A., Scala, A., Caldarelli, G. and Quattrociocchi, W. (2015) 'Science vs conspiracy: collective narratives in the age of misinformation', *PLoS ONE*, 10(2).

Bilewicz, M. and Krzeminski, I. (2010) 'Anti-semitism in Poland and Ukraine: the belief in Jewish control as a mechanism of scapegoating', *International Journal of Conflict and Violence*, 4(2): 234–43.

Bilewicz, M., Winiewski, M., Kofta, M. and Wójcik, A. (2013) 'Harmful ideas: the structure and consequences of anti-semitic beliefs in Poland', *Political Psychology*, 34(6): 821–39.

Bogart, L.M. and Bird, S.T. (2003) 'Exploring the relationship of conspiracy beliefs about HIV/AIDS to sexual behaviors and attitudes among African-American adults', *Journal of the National Medical Association*, 95(11): 1057–65.

Bogart, L.M. and Thorburn, S. (2006) 'Relationship of African Americans' sociodemographic characteristics to belief in conspiracies about HIV/AIDS and birth control', *Journal of the National Medical Association*, 98(7): 1144–50.

Bonetto, E., Troïan, J., Varet, F., Lo Monaco, G. and Girandola, F. (2018) 'Priming resistance to persuasion decreases adherence to conspiracy theories', *Social Influence*, 13(3): 125–36.

Bratich, J.Z. (2008) *Conspiracy panics: political rationality and popular culture*, New York, NY: State University of New York Press.

Brotherton, R. and French, C.C. (2014) 'Belief in conspiracy theories and susceptibility to the conjunction fallacy', *Applied Cognitive Psychology*, 28(2): 238–48.

Butler, L.D., Koopman, C. and Zimbardo, P.G. (1995) 'The psychological impact of viewing the film "JFK": emotions, beliefs, and political behavioral intentions', *Political Psychology*, 16(2): 237–57.

Chigwedere, P., Seage, G.R. III., Gruskin, S., Lee, T.H. and Essex, M. (2008) 'Estimating the lost benefits of antiretroviral drug use in South Africa', *JAIDS Journal of Acquired Immune Deficiency Syndromes*, 49(4): 410–15.

Cichocka, A., Marchlewska, M. and de Zavala, A.G. (2016) 'Does self-love or self-hate predict conspiracy beliefs? Narcissism, self-esteem, and the endorsement of conspiracy theories', *Social Psychological and Personality Science*, 7(2): 157–66.

Clarke, S. (2002) 'Conspiracy theories and conspiracy theorizing', *Philosophy of the Social Sciences*, 32(2): 131–50.

Davey, J. (2019) 'The New Zealand atrocities prove that far-right terrorism is an organised, global threat', *Telegraph*, 15 March. Available at: www.telegraph.co.uk/news/2019/03/15/new-zealand-atrocities-prove-far-right-terrorism-organised-global/. [Accessed 12 August 2019.]

Del Vicario, M., Bessi, A., Zollo, F., Petroni, F., Scala, A., Caldarelli, G., Stanley, H.E. and Quattrociocchi, W. (2016a) 'The spreading of misinformation online', *Proceedings of the National Academy of Sciences*, 113(3): 554–9.

Del Vicario, M., Vivaldo, G., Bessi, A., Zollo, F., Scala, A., Caldarelli, G. and Quattrociocchi, W. (2016b) 'Echo chambers: emotional contagion and group polarization on Facebook', *Scientific Reports*, 6.

Douglas, K.M. and Leite, A.C. (2017) 'Suspicion in the workplace: organizational conspiracy theories and work-related outcomes', *British Journal of Psychology*, 108(3): 486–506.

Douglas, K.M. and Sutton, R.M. (2008) 'The hidden impact of conspiracy theories: perceived and actual influence of theories surrounding the death of Princess Diana', *The Journal of Social Psychology*, 148(2): 210–22.

Douglas, K.M. and Sutton, R.M. (2015) 'Climate change: why the conspiracy theories are dangerous', *Bulletin of the Atomic Scientists*, 71(2): 98–106.

Douglas, K.M., Sutton, R.M. and Cichocka, A. (2017) 'The psychology of conspiracy theories', *Current Directions in Psychological Science*, 26(6): 538–42.

Einstein, K.L. and Glick, D.M. (2015) 'Do I think BLS data are BS? The consequences of conspiracy theories', *Political Behavior*, 37(3): 679–701.

Franks, B., Bangerter, A., Bauer, M.W., Hall, M. and Noort, M.C. (2017) 'Beyond "monologicality"? Exploring conspiracist worldviews', *Frontiers in Psychology*, 8: 861.

Golec de Zavala, A. and Cichocka, A. (2012) 'Collective narcissism and anti-semitism in Poland', *Group Processes and Intergroup Relations*, 15(2): 213–29.

Grzesiak-Feldman, M. (2013) 'The effect of high-anxiety situations on conspiracy thinking', *Current Psychology*, 32(1): 100–18.

Harambam, J. and Aupers, S. (2015) 'Contesting epistemic authority: conspiracy theories on the boundaries of science', *Public Understanding of Science*, 24(4): 466–80.

Hofstadter, R. (1964) 'The paranoid style in American politics', *Harper's Magazine*, 229: 77–86.

Hoyt, M.A., Rubin, L.R., Nemeroff, C.J., Lee, J., Huebner, D.M. and Proeschold-Bell, R.J. (2012) 'HIV/AIDS-related institutional mistrust among multiethnic men who have sex with men: effects on HIV testing and risk behaviors', *Health Psychology*, 31(3): 269–77.

Imhoff, R. and Bruder, M. (2014) 'Speaking (un-)truth to power: conspiracy mentality as a generalised political attitude', *European Journal of Personality*, 28(1): 25–43.

Imhoff, R., Lamberty, P. and Klein, O. (2018) 'Using power as a negative cue: how conspiracy mentality affects epistemic trust in sources of historical knowledge', *Personality and Social Psychology Bulletin*, 44(9): 1364–79.

Jensen, T. (2013) 'Democrats and Republicans differ on conspiracy theory beliefs', *Public Policy Polling*, 2 April. Available at: www.publicpolicypolling.com/polls/democrats-and-republicans-differ-on-conspiracy-theory-beliefs. [Accessed 12 August 2019.]

Jolley, D. and Douglas, K.M. (2014a) 'The social consequences of conspiracism: exposure to conspiracy theories decreases intentions to engage in politics and to reduce one's carbon footprint', *British Journal of Psychology*, 105(1): 35–6.

Jolley, D. and Douglas, K.M. (2014b) 'The effects of anti-vaccine conspiracy theories on vaccination intentions', *PLoS ONE*, 9(2).

Jolley, D. and Douglas, K.M. (2017) 'Prevention is better than cure: addressing anti-vaccine conspiracy theories', *Journal of Applied Social Psychology*, 47(8): 459–69.

Jolley, D., Douglas, K., Leite, A. and Schrader, T. (2019) 'Belief in conspiracy theories and intentions to engage in everyday crime', *British Journal of Social Psychology*, 58: 534–49.

Jolley, D., Meleady, R. and Douglas, K.M. (2019) 'Exposure to intergroup conspiracy theories promotes prejudice which spreads across groups', *British Journal of Psychology*. In press [https://doi.org/10.1111/bjop.12385]. [Accessed 30 November 2019.]

Karstedt, S. and Farrall, S. (2006) 'The moral economy of everyday crime: markets, consumers and citizens', *British Journal of Criminology*, 46(6): 1011–36.

Lamberty, P. and Imhoff, R. (2018) 'Powerful pharma and its marginalized alternatives? Effects of individual differences in conspiracy mentality on attitudes toward medical approaches', *Social Psychology*, 49(5): 255–70.

Lantian, A., Muller, D., Nurra, C., Klein, O., Berjot, S. and Pantazi, M. (2018) 'Stigmatized beliefs: conspiracy theories, anticipated negative evaluation of the self, and fear of social exclusion', *European Journal of Social Psychology*, 48(7): 939–54.

Levin, S. and Beckett, L. (2017) 'US gun violence spawns a new epidemic: conspiracy theorists harassing victims', *Guardian*, 28 November. Available at: www.theguardian.com/us-news/2017/nov/28/us-guns-mass-shootings-hoax-conspiracy-theories. [Accessed 12 August 2019.]

Marchlewska, M., Cichocka, A. and Kossowska, M. (2017) 'Addicted to answers: need for cognitive closure and the endorsement of conspiracy beliefs', *European Journal of Social Psychology*, 27: 283–317.

Mari, S., Liu, J.H., Suerdem, A., Hanke, K., Brown, G., Gil de Zúñiga, H., Vilar, R, Boer, D. and Bilewicz, M. *Conspiracy theories and institutional trust: a cross-cultural study on the varied impact of active social media use*. Under review.

Mari, S., Volpato, C., Papastamou, S., Chryssochoou, X., Prodromitis, G. and Pavlopoulos, V. (2017) 'How political orientation and vulnerability shape representations of the economic crisis in Greece and Italy', *International Review of Social Psychology*, 30(1): 52–67.

Melley, T. (2002) 'Agency panic and the culture of conspiracy', in P. Knight (ed.) *Conspiracy nation: the politics of paranoia in postwar America*, 1st edn, New York: New York University Press, pp. 57–81.

Miller, S. (2002) 'Conspiracy theories: public arguments as coded social critiques: a rhetorical analysis of the TWA flight 800 conspiracy theories', *Argumentation and Advocacy*, 39(1): 40–56.

Mocanu, D., Rossi, L., Zhang, Q., Karsai, M. and Quattrociocchi, W. (2015) 'Collective attention in the age of (mis)information', *Computers in Human Behavior*, 51: 1198–204.

Oliver, J.E. and Wood, T.J. (2014) 'Medical conspiracy theories and health behaviors in the United States', *JAMA Internal Medicine*, 174(5): 817–8.

Pearce, M. (2018) 'Conspiracy theories about Florida school shooting survivors have gone mainstream', *Los Angeles Times*, 21 February. Available at: www.latimes.com/nation/la-na-conspiracy-theories-20180221-story.html. [Accessed 12 August 2019.]

Pettigrew, T.F. (2009) 'Secondary transfer effect of contact: do intergroup contact effects spread to non-contacted outgroups?', *Social Psychology*, 40(2): 55–65.

Rubincam, C. (2017) '"It's natural to look for a source": a qualitative examination of alternative beliefs about HIV and AIDS in Cape Town, South Africa', *Public Understanding of Science*, 26(3): 369–84.

Sunstein, C.R. (2018) *#Republic: divided democracy in the age of social media*, Princeton, NJ: Princeton University Press.

Swami, V. (2012) 'Social psychological origins of conspiracy theories: the case of the Jewish conspiracy theory in Malaysia', *Frontiers in Psychology*, 3: 280.

Swami, V. and Coles, R. (2010) 'The truth is out there: belief in conspiracy theories', *The Psychologist*, 23(7): 560–3.

Swami, V., Pietschnig, J., Tran, U.S., Nader, I. W., Stieger, S. and Voracek, M. (2013) 'Lunar lies: the impact of informational framing and individual differences in shaping conspiracist beliefs about the moon landings', *Applied Cognitive Psychology*, 27(1): 71–80.

Uscinski, J.E, Douglas, K. and Lewandowsky, S. (2017) 'Climate change conspiracy theories', in H. von Storch, *Oxford Research Encyclopedia of Climate Science*, New York: Oxford University Press.

Uscinski, J.E. and Parent, J.M. (2014) *American Conspiracy Theories*, Oxford: Oxford University Press.

Van der Linden, S. (2015) 'The conspiracy-effect: exposure to conspiracy theories (about global warming) decreases pro-social behavior and science acceptance', *Personality and Individual Differences*, 87: 171–3.

Van Prooijen, J.-W. and Acker, M. (2015) 'The influence of control on belief in conspiracy theories: conceptual and applied extensions', *Applied Cognitive Psychology*, 29(5): 753–61.

Van Prooijen, J.-W. and de Vries, R.E. (2016) 'Organizational conspiracy beliefs: implications for leadership styles and employee outcomes', *Journal of Business and Psychology*, 31(4): 479–91.

Willman, S. (2002) 'Spinning paranoia: the ideologies of conspiracy and contingency in postmodern culture', in P. Knight (ed.) *Conspiracy nation: the politics of paranoia in postwar America*, 1st edn, New York: New York University Press, pp. 21–39.

Wood, M.J. and Douglas, K.M. (2013) '"What about building 7?" A social psychological study of online discussion of 9/11 conspiracy theories', *Frontiers in Psychology*, 4: 409.

# 2.8
# COUNTERING CONSPIRACY THEORIES AND MISINFORMATION

*Péter Krekó*

## Introduction

There are many research studies on the functions and background motives underlying belief in conspiracy theories (Douglas *et al.* 2017) and also the negative consequences of conspiracy theories (Douglas *et al.* 2015; see also Chapter 2.7 in this volume). However, we so far only have a limited knowledge of the most practical implications of conspiracy theories: How they can be changed, debunked and modified. This chapter tries to systemically overview and summarise the most important research so far concerning the possibilities of changing conspiracy beliefs via targeted interventions.

I do not take it for granted that there is a consensus over the need for interventions. In the beginning of the chapter, we take a look at the epistemological, moral and democratic arguments on whether, and when, we need to use interventions to reduce conspiracy beliefs. Then we briefly overview some psychological obstacles in the way of interventions. In the next section, we propose a matrix as a theoretical framework for categorising the possible interventions and overview the available academic literature as well as some practical experiences concerning efficient ways of reducing conspiracy beliefs. In the final section, we identify a broader avenue for future research.

## To debunk or not to debunk? That is the question

The majority of the psychological research on conspiracy theories is based on the facts that most conspiracy theories are possibly harmful (van Prooijen, van Lange 2014; Douglas *et al.* 2015; van Prooijen 2018; see also Chapter 2.7 in this volume). However, before we jump into the practicalities of interventions and debunking, it is worth elaborating on the question of why and when interventions against conspiracy theories are needed and justified. We will consider three arguments why conspiracy theories may not always need interventions: the epistemic, the moral and the democratic argument. Then, based on these considerations, we identify the theories we think are the most important to get debunked.

1. *The epistemic argument.* As some philosophers argue, conspiracy theories can be, in some cases, accurate descriptions of events in the world since history is full of conspiracies and conspiratorial assumptions (e.g. Pigden 1995). Also, conspiracy theories can sometimes be the

official explanation of events, as in the case of the Iraq War, where the *casus belli* was the alleged existence of weapons of mass destruction in Iraq. It proved to be false – raising a new suspicion of conspiratorial intentions of political leaders who might have been aware of their non-existence, but manipulated the public to reach their political goals (Coady 2006). Therefore, a priori rebuttal of conspiracy theories can be problematic. Also, a lack of convincing evidence is not necessary proof for their non-existence. 'Whatever we might think about conspiracy theories generally, there is no prima facie case for a scepticism of conspiracy theories based purely on their use of evidence' (Dentith 2017: 1) Also, in some cases, we have some good reasons to question the knowledge that comes from traditional sources, especially when this 'knowledge' is still not rock-solid, and/or there is contradicting evidence on the field. As Uscinski (2018: 5) put it: 'Our knowledge generating institutions are not—nor should they be above suspicion or reproach'.

*2. The moral argument.* Some scholars who are more 'empathic' towards conspiracy theories argue that conspiracy theories are in fact beneficial, as they can foster more transparency via challenging the established social hierarchy as narratives of non-privileged groups (Fenster 1999; Clarke 2002). Also, sometimes believers of conspiracy theories can embrace democratic principles, as it was found among the supporters of the 9/11 conspiracy theories (Swami et al. 2010). Conspiracy theories, according to this line of argumentation, can serve as alarm bells and early warning systems (Uscinski 2018) and articulate the concerns of the 'losers' (Uscinski et al. 2011).

*3. Democratic argument: Freedom of speech and pluralism.* The third line of arguments is based on the notion that conspiracy theories are a legitimate part of the democratic discussion and deserve defence as a form of free speech as 'a crucial part of the marketplace of ideas' (Uscinski 2018: 6.). According to this perspective, debunking and regulation might be problematic as a form of political suppression.

Of course, while some of these arguments contain valid points, interventions against conspiracy theories are still important in most of the cases. At the same time, even without a general taxonomy, we can identify a sub-group of conspiracy theories that need to be challenged, based on the considerations above. The features of conspiracy theories that require urgent interventions share three characteristics: harmfulness, low plausibility and high popularity. However, not all of the three conditions should be fulfilled in order for an intervention to be justified. For example, in the case of ideological conspiracy theories of terrorist groups in the Western world, they are definitely not popular, but at the same time can be extremely harmful. Also, theories that are non-plausible but popular should be debunked (even if not prohibited) if they are not directly harmful.

*1. Plausibility.* While conspiracies sometimes occur, most conspiracy theories are not the most plausible explanations of events (e.g. Aaronovitch 2011). Not every conspiracy theory is necessarily false, but most of them contain logical pitfalls and weaknesses. While our capacity is limited when trying to separate the true conspiracy theories from the ones that are not true, several conspiracy theories fail to pass the most basic logical tests. There are logical tools to examine the veracity of conspiracy theories on an a priori basis or based on the available information (for an overview, see Coady 2006). Probably the most important logical fallacy behind conspiracy theories is that they assume that a massive conspiracy can take place and remain a secret at the same time. Grimes (2016) made an estimation of how many people would need to have been involved in the plot to make some conspiracies happen and found extremely high figures: U.S. moon landings were a hoax (411 000 people); climate change is a fraud (405 000 people); unsafe vaccinations are being covered up (22 000); the cure for cancer is being suppressed by the world's leading pharmaceutical firms (714 000 people).

*2. Impact.* Some conspiracy theories are harmless in themselves. For example, if one believes in lizard people, U.F.O.s, flat earth, the moon landing theory is fake – these beliefs (if not systemically connected to other conspiracy beliefs – which is often the case) are not necessarily causing any harm or manifesting in some problematic behaviour. At the same time, we can say that believing in these theories can dramatically erode trust in public institutions (lizard men, moon landing hoax) or spread distrust in scientists (flat earth), which can be an important reason to counterargue and debunk them (but not to prohibit them). However, many well-known and relevant conspiracy theories are directly harmful – not only for the individual but for broader society, as has been found in many studies (for a summary, see Douglas *et al.* 2015).

Political conspiracy theories can lead to alienation, cynicism and political disengagement (Butler *et al.* 1995). Exposure to conspiracy theories decreases trust in governmental institutions, even if the conspiracy theories are unrelated to those institutions (Einstein, Glick 2015). Conspiracy theories not only can cause disenchantment with politicians, but also with scientists and scientific institutions (Jolley, Douglas 2014a). Scientific findings such as vaccination, that can prevent diseases such as measles, are even questioned by some conspiracy theories, and exposure to these conspiracy theories can lead to lower vaccination intentions (Jolley, Douglas 2014a). More generally, medical conspiracy theories can lead to irrational health behaviour that shortens or terminates lives (Oliver, Wood 2014). Conspiracy theories about the H.I.V. virus (that it was created in governmental laboratories) can lead to reduced condom use as both are associated with the same belief of genocidal intentions against blacks by the U.S. government (Bogart, Thorburn 2005), therefore raising the chance of H.I.V. infection and unintended pregnancy. Also, conspiracy theories about climate change, such as that global warming is a hoax, can discourage steps to reduce one's carbon footprint (Jolley, Douglas 2014b; Van Der Linden *et al.* 2015). There may also be a more general 'conspiracy effect' such that exposure to conspiracy theories decreases pro-social behaviour and acceptance of scientific findings (Van Der Linden 2015). Conspiracy theories against Jews are the most important predictor of negative behavioural intentions towards them (Bilewicz *et al.* 2013). Conspiracy theories against outgroups can also serve as 'radicalization multipliers' (Bartlett, Miller 2010) and encouraging 'apocalyptic aggression' towards outgroups that seem to pose a danger (Berlet 2009).

While conspiracy theories are often stigmatised knowledge (Barkun 2003), in many cases this is justified. Popular conspiracy theorists such as Alex Jones provide very few arguments regarding when these theories should be defended, as they are epistemically wrong, morally malevolent and dangerous for democracies.

*3. Popularity.* Any countermeasures towards conspiracy theories should mainly target the popular theories that are shared by a significant portion of society, for two simple pragmatic reasons. First, popular theories are more likely to lead to negative consequences (see above). Second, refuting less well-known theories can have a countereffect: Making the previously unknown theories more known and popular. The popularity of conspiracy theories is sometimes the result of their political manufacturing. Conspiracy theories these days are not necessarily the 'theories of losers', but official or semi-official narratives of events that are spread by non-democratic actors. We can see current examples in Turkey, Russia and North Korea, but also Poland and Hungary. Conspiracy theories are spread by powerful actors such as Russia, using all the resources of the state (e.g. Yablokov 2015, 2018). Conspiracy theories exploiting a victim identity are disguised to be the tools of the weak and oppressed and are often dangerous tools in the hands of the strong and powerful. Solidarity with the powerless therefore should not translate to solidarity with conspiracy theorists.

Based on the summary above, when we talk about counterstrategies and debunking, we will mostly focus only on the theories that fit the three conditions set above: Non-plausible, harmful and popular at the same time. As we see from the list above, this is still a very broad category within conspiracy theories. Many conspiracy theories that are popular and not so plausible are harmful as well. For example, 'global warming is a hoax' theories that discourage efforts to save the environment as well as decreasing trust in science, are shared by 37 per cent of the U.S. electorate, and more than 60 per cent of the Republican voters in the U.S. (Jensen 2013).

## The difficulties of debunking conspiracy theories

It is easier to spread conspiracy theories than to refute them. Conspiracy theories have a strong functional basis: They can serve epistemic, existential, social motives at the same time (Douglas et al. 2017). Even if conspiracy theories are sometimes self-defeating forms of motivated cognition, their refutation is often extremely difficult. We can mention at least seven important psychological obstacles when we would like to debunk, or change, false beliefs, to take these factors into considerations when tailoring counterstrategies.

*1. The resistance of conspiracy theories to factual information.* Conspiracy theories are often non-falsifiable (Keeley 1999; Uscinski, Parent 2014), as they are referring to invisible, secret, dark dealings behind the curtain. Therefore, the lack of visibility of the conspiracy in a lot of cases is used as an argument for its success and its existence. Furthermore, refuting attempts are often incorporated in a 'metaconspiracy theory': The belief that people and institutions who try to debunk conspiracy theories may, themselves, be part of the conspiracy (Lewandowsky et al. 2015, 2013). Disconfirming evidence (e.g. scientific findings) can therefore be regarded as products of a conspiracy. Given that traditional knowledge-producing institutions are perceived as part of the 'establishment', their arguments are particularly easy targets in the eyes of conspiracy theorists. But this principle is not universal: the resistance of factual information is mainly an obstacle for changing the minds of the ones who already have very strong conspiracy beliefs: the 'true believers'.

*2. Lingering effect of misinformation: 'mud sticks'.* As Ecker et al. (2017) found, even after careful and repeated counter-argumentation, the original information still leaves traces on people's attitudes, as the cognitive representation does not disappear from memory. There is no such thing as perfectly refuted misinformation. This is a strong argument for interventions that aim to prevent exposure to a conspiracy theory.

*3. The sleeper effect.* As was found in early persuasion research and then confirmed by more recent metanalytic overviews (Kumkale, Albarracín 2004), if the information comes through with some discounting cue (e.g. the messenger is a highly unreliable source), it will still have an impact on the attitudes of the recipient. Furthermore, as time passes, the discounting cue, that is the 'tag' of lack of credibility, can gradually disappear from the original information. Therefore, the information prevails without the warning sign of non-credibility. It can be especially important in the case of fake news and conspiracy theories that mainly originate from highly unreliable sources. Even if the person is aware of the tainted nature of the source, the fake information can prevail in memory while the information of the source fades away. The cure for this problem could be to focus more on the content of the conspiracy theory than the source during the interventions, or to repeat the disconfirming information.

*4. Familiarity Backfire Effect.* In order to debunk a belief, one has to repeatedly mention it. However, this can have an unintended effect: The debunking effort itself can strengthen the belief by increasing its familiarity. Or, in the case that the belief was unknown, the debunking can spread the belief (Cook, Lewandowsky 2011). In the case of conspiracy theories, this question can be particularly relevant given that some conspiracy theories are rather unknown. To avoid the trap of unintentionally spreading conspiracy theories, we should therefore very carefully evaluate each conspiracy theory to determine if it deserves refutation or not. If a theory is not widespread (see popularity as a precondition above), or because of its weak presence in the public is therefore probably not highly accessible, debunking can do more harm than good.

5. *Reactance*. Individuals tend to reject persuasion efforts if they feel that the messenger wants to limit their personal freedom of opinion or limit their behavioural alternatives (Miron, Brehm 2006). The result can be an even stronger embrace of this particular belief to prove that the individual makes sovereign decisions. This danger is also particularly apparent when it comes to conspiracy theories, as it is difficult not to formulate the debunking message as 'lecturing' that comes from the position of a kind of intellectual authority. Too intense, propagandistic counter messaging can lead to stronger reactance.

6. *Identity and motivated reasoning*. It is difficult to refute group-based beliefs on the level of the individual. This is what Cook and Lewandowsky (2011) call the Worldview Backfire Effect. While most of the debunking and counter messaging efforts focus on refuting conspiracy theories as a form of 'crippled epistemology' and assume that providing adequate information is the cure, this 'information deficit model' is often totally insufficient, as conspiracy theories can be deeply rooted in group identities and a wider set of beliefs. Given that conspiracy theories are forms of 'motivated collective cognition' (Krekó 2015), they can serve important advantages for the ingroup, such as raising collective self-esteem, putting the blame on external actors and strengthening ingroup identity via self-victimisation. Also, more intense communication of a position can lead to a boomerang-effect via further polarising opinions about an issue, and just strengthening the beliefs of conspiracy theorists – as it was found in the case of climate change (Hart, Nisbet 2012).

7. *True believers and vulnerable groups*. Connected to the previous point, the conspiracy beliefs of 'true believers' (the ones for whom conspiracy beliefs constitute a strong, central part of their belief system) are more difficult to change. Generally, more central, extreme and polarised attitudes are resistant to change (Banas, Miller 2013). Also, conspiracy theories are frequently strongly connected to extreme political positions that are strong and stable (van Prooijen *et al.* 2015). Furthermore, some social groups are traditionally more receptive to conspiracy theories than others, notably low status groups, minority groups and groups with lower levels of education (for a summary, see Chapter 2.6). These groups can be logical targets of interventions, especially immunisation – but the problem is, they are more difficult to reach via institutions. The problem of 'true believers' and vulnerable groups can be especially acute when dealing with demand-side solutions (see below).

## The typology of counterstrategies

While there is abundant research on what induces conspiracy theories, the literature on how to reduce them is thinner. Given this limitation, in the section below I try to give a theoretical framework for the possible tools for debunking conspiracy theories, and also highlight some experiences beyond the strictly academic literature. According to this simple framework, every intervention aimed to counter conspiracy theories can be put on a two-dimensional matrix. The first dimension is temporal: does the intervention take place before the person meets with the conspiracy theory (prevention), or does it target a belief that the person has already encountered (harm reduction)? The second dimension deals with the target of the intervention: is it the messenger/source of the information (supply side) or the recipients of the intervention (demand side)?

This matrix gives us four possible options: (1) the intervention takes place before the spread of the message, and targets the supply side (pre-emptive strike); (2) it takes place before the dissemination, but targets the recipient (immunisation) (3); it takes place after the message was spread and targets the source, (striking back); or (4) it takes place after the dissemination but targets the recipient (healing).

In the remaining sections of this chapter, we go through these interventions one by one, evaluating them in the light of the academic literature and non-academic experiences so far.

Exposure to conspiracy theories is an important predictor behind such beliefs (Swami *et al.* 2010). Also, as discussed above, conspiracy theories are difficult to refute after the person was exposed to them. Furthermore, conspiracy theories have a hidden impact on the recipients' attitudes and behaviour (Douglas, Sutton 2008). That is, they can influence people without them even knowing that they have been influenced. For these reasons, preventative interventions, when possible, are better than focusing on harm reduction. Therefore, we start our discussion with the preventive strategies.

## Immunisation

'Theories of conspiracy represent a permanent temptation for us all' (Groh 1987: 2). Interventions focusing on immunisation aim to shield the audience with the necessary cognitive, emotional or motivational skills to resist this temptation. However, while it sounds like the 'magic wand' solution against conspiracy theories, it is not: People are often motivated to accept conspiracy theories and this is especially the case for some more vulnerable groups (see the 'difficulties we face when debunking conspiracy theories' above). Still, immunisation has been found to be successful in many cases. It can be general, aimed at reducing the general receptivity to conspiracy theories; or particular, focusing on specific beliefs.

Given that conspiracy thinking is often a result of a lack of logical thinking (e.g. Sunstein, Vermeule 2019), a general way of reducing the receptivity to conspiracy theories in advance can be the improvement of logical, analytic thinking. Swami *et al.* (2014) found that verbal fluency and cognitive fluency tasks eliciting analytic thinking reduced belief in conspiracy theories and conspiracist ideation.

Targeting the root causes of conspiracy theories can be another efficient approach for reducing conspiracy beliefs. While certain personality traits, social status or minority status are difficult or impossible to change, reducing feelings of uncertainty, mistrust, powerlessness and lack of control, that are found to be important factors that enhance conspiracy thinking, seems to be a possible way (Hamsher *et al.* 1968; Mirowsky, Ross 1983; Abalakina-Paap *et al.* 1999; Imhoff, Bruder 2014; Newheiser *et al.* 2011). While using interventions that reduce powerlessness and uncertainty on a social scale sound naïve and utopian, interventions in organisations might have a positive effect on trust and feelings of control that reduce conspiracy theorising (Kramer 1999; van Prooijen, de Vries 2016; Douglas, Leite 2017). To be more specific about the way of rebuilding feelings of control, we can think about reversing one important scientific finding. Specifically, many studies have found that it is easy to induce conspiracy thinking via recalling personal experiences where people failed to exercise control and therefore felt uncertain (Whitson, Galinsky 2008; Sullivan *et al.* 2010; van Prooijen, Acker 2015). Recalling experiences of successfully controlled events, on the other hand, might strengthen the feeling of self-efficacy and might contribute to reducing conspiracy ideation.

Also, a less self-evident specific way of immunisation against conspiracy theories can be the deliberate ignorance of false information to avoid its impact on our thinking (Hertwig, Engel 2016). It is a bit counterintuitive as our post-enlightenment ideals may suggest that knowing more is always better than knowing less. However, tactical avoidance of false information can protect the person from the inevitable impact of blatant lies, false information and conspiracy theories. The problem is, though, that this is very difficult to do, given that some popular conspiracy theories in politics (such as climate scepticism, Pizzagate, 9/11) surround people in the 'populist zeitgeist' (Mudde 2004) they live in and people can only avoid meeting them if they close their minds to political information in general.

Immunisation can also be specific, targeting particular conspiracy beliefs. Preliminary warning seems to be an efficient solution in raising awareness about the possible misleading nature of the information that the individual is going to encounter. As Cook and Lewandowsky (2011) propose, any mention of false information should be preceded by warnings to notify the audience that the upcoming information is not true. Similarly, inoculation strategies that present weak arguments of the conspiracy theory in advance, in order to raise the attitudinal immune system of the person against such threats in the future, have been found efficient in the case of misinformation on climate change (Cook *et al.* 2017). Jolley and Douglas (2017) found inoculation an effective tool against anti-vaccination theories, underlining that the counterargument is efficient only when presented *before* meeting with misinformation. Banas and Miller (2013) also found that inoculation strategies can be effective in creating resistance to conspiracy theory propaganda, with fact-based (vs. logic-based) treatment being the most effective. However, this latter study also revealed that inoculation is a double-edged sword that can be a dangerous weapon in the hands of conspiracy theorists as well. The positive effect of inoculation can be significantly diminished if it is used against the inoculated arguments, and therefore it can defend the original conspiracy theory (called meta-inoculation).

## Pre-emptive strike

Pre-emptive strikes against conspiracy theories aim to target the source of misinformation in order to reduce the chance that the target audience will encounter the undesirable piece of information. If this measure is successful, the piece of information will have no impact at all. The most obvious – but, at the same time, morally and technically most problematic – way of doing so is the removal of the harmful content or banning the source of misinformation from certain platforms. Especially after 2016 (the Brexit referendum and the U.S. presidential election campaign), social media companies came under increasing pressure to step up more harshly against disinformation, including conspiracy theories. Still, any specific strategy is controversial, and whilst some argue that social media companies are doing nothing, or not enough, against this challenge (e.g. Applebaum 2019), others argue that social media companies already poses an existential threat to freedom of speech (French 2019).

When it comes to the most popular social media platforms, Facebook's community standards (Facebook 2019) reserve the right to remove 'objectionable content': Hate speech, content that 'glorifies violence or celebrates the suffering or humiliation' or is 'cruel or insensitive'. Conspiracy theories that fall within these categories are often also targeted for removal. For example, in 2019, Facebook removed, among others, the profile of well-known conspiracy theorist Alex Jones, claiming that they remove sites that 'promote or engage in violence and hate, regardless of ideology' (Salinas 2018). Twitter made a similar decision, along with some other social media providers in 2016 (Salinas 2018).

Another typical reason for removal of sites that are spreading conspiracy theories can be malign foreign influence, and especially interference into elections. For example, in June 2019, Twitter announced that it banned almost 5000 accounts that it thought to be associated with foreign governments, claiming that Twitter has a responsibility to hamper 'attempts to manipulate TWITTER to influence elections and other civic conversations by foreign or domestic state-backed entities' (Roth 2019). Following a similar logic, Twitter banned the advertisements of Russian propaganda channels RT and Sputnik that are spreading conspiracy theories on an industrial scale (see for example Yablokov 2018), referring to the assessment of the U.S. intelligence agencies that they aimed to influence the result of the 2016 U.S. presidential elections (Twitter Public Policy 2017). This is also an important step, as no advertisement can substantially reduce the ability of these accounts to reach the target audience.

Facebook's new – and probably most fruitful – attempt is to 'bury' disinformation instead of 'banning' it – which means, significantly downplaying the chance of 'low quality' content appearing in one's News Feed or searches. This occurs through changing the algorithms. Pages that contain malicious or deceptive advertisements can be significantly downgraded (Facebook Business 2017). Facebook, at the same time, have a targeted policy against anti-vaccination sites that are often spreading conspiracy theories about the malicious impact of the vaccinations (Bickert 2019). Fight against anti-vaccine misinformation contains the following specific steps: Reduction of ranking of groups and pages that spread misinformation about vaccinations in news feeds and searches; rejecting advertisements that spread misinformation about the vaccines, removing related targeting options and disabling accounts that violate these policies. Of course, such interventions are the targets of intense political, moral and legal discussions (see, for example, Wood and Ravel 2017). Also, it is not only the social media companies that are exposed to such controversies: The French 'fake news law' was passed in 2018 (Young 2018) as a reaction to the wave of disinformation during the 2017 French presidential election campaign (Ferrara 2017).

A possible tool for journalists can be the ignorance of the source of disinformation and avoid covering disinformation pieces (see, for example, Hellman and Wagnsson 2017). This is what the French press did during the last phase of the French presidential election campaign in 2017. When President Macron's emails were leaked, the mainstream press refused to cover the content, and instead focused on the fact that hacking was used as a part of the influence operation, ignoring the content of the hacked material (Prier 2017, Lewandowsky 2019).

Based on the research above suggesting that conspiracy theories leave a trace on the psychological processes of the individual, these pre-emptive strike approaches, from a merely practical point of view, can be efficient. However, the broader assessment of impact of the measures aiming to ignore/exclude/tilt certain contents from the information environment are rather lacking. This is especially the case when it comes to conspiracy theories since the advocates of these theories can only feel assured that their theories about 'global censorship' of information are correct. Of course, most interventions do not focus on the 'true believers' but the general public, and less access to conspiracy theories can lead to less belief in them.

## Healing

If the target audience has already encountered conspiracy theories, one possibility is to try to minimise their negative impact. The most obvious form of this behaviour is debunking the arguments of the conspiracy theories in the hope that it will discredit them in the eye of the observer. Orosz et al. (2016) found in experimental research that rational and ridiculing arguments were effective in reducing conspiracy beliefs (with modest effect sizes), whereas empathising with the targets of conspiracy theories had no effect.[1] Individual differences played no role in the reduction of conspiracy beliefs, but the perceived intelligence and competence of the individual who conveyed the conspiracy belief-reduction information contributed to the success of reducing beliefs. Considering these results and previous studies focusing on the benevolent effects of analytic thinking (Swami et al. 2014), and fact-based inoculation (Banas, Miller 2013) in reducing conspiracy beliefs, it can be assumed that uncovering arguments regarding the logical and factual inconsistencies of conspiracy beliefs can be an effective way to discredit them. This statement goes against the mainstream of the communication literature and the notion of 'post-truth' in which emotions trump all other factors. One possible explanation why rationality might have a bigger impact on shaping (sometimes irrational) beliefs than previously expected might be that, in the current communication environment, people are overloaded with emotional messages coming from advertisements, and political and social campaigns, and therefore rational and factual arguments have more informational value.

According to Cook and Lewandowsky (2011), efficient debunking requires three major elements. First of all, refutation must focus on the facts instead of the myth or false belief to avoid the misinformation becoming more familiar. Second, mentions of the false information should be preceded by warnings to notify the audience of the falseness of the upcoming information. Third, refutation should include an alternative explanation. Finally, to avoid the 'overkill backfire effect', that the refutation fails to persuade the audience because of too many counterarguments, less but strong arguments are usually more efficient than more but weaker arguments. Conspiracy theory-related metacognition can also be an efficient tool in diminishing the impact of such beliefs. Conspiracy exposure increases conspiracy beliefs and reduces trust, but asking about the beliefs that the recipient just heard facilitates additional thinking about the conspiracy claims and can soften or even reverse the effect of exposure on the conspiracy beliefs and their impact on trust.

One other possible solution is 'cognitive infiltration' (Sunstein, Vermeule 2009), that, according to its proponents, can be an efficient tool for breaking up the closed epistemic universe of 'the hard core of extremists'. In this tool,

> government agents or their allies (acting either virtually or in real space, and either openly or anonymously) will undermine the crippled epistemology of believers by planting doubts about the theories and stylised facts that circulate within such groups, thereby introducing beneficial cognitive diversity).
>
> (Sunstein, Vermeule 2009: 95)

While sowing the seeds of doubt can in itself bring beneficial effects, this idea had mixed reception at best. The fact that a former media advisor to President Obama proposed that the state interferes into private discussions served as a proof for the worst nightmares of conspiracy theorists, and inspired books as well (Griffin 2011). Also, of course, diversity of views is not enough in itself: In order for any messenger to challenge the attitudes of a group, they should affirm other beliefs of that individual or group or the values or position of the group, to gain more sympathy for any attitude change (Sherman, Cohen 2006; Feygina et al. 2010; Sunstein 2014; Wolsko et al. 2016).

## Striking back

Interventions that target the source of information after the encounter with the message are rather rare, for the reason that this is not a particularly successful approach. Of course, measures of removing certain social media platforms because of their interference into the U.S. election are following this kind of 'retaliatory' logic, but we discussed them under the 'pre-emptive strike' solution because the real function of these measures is not to do harm for the source of the message after the damage is done, but to *prevent* further damage for other recipients. Discrediting the source of the information to do reputation damage fits in this logic, but according to the research on 'sleeper effects' (see above), it is not always highly efficient.

The logic of 'tagging' the information in an aim to undermine the credibility also follows the logic of 'striking back': The recipients become aware of the fact that this information was categorised as non-trustworthy by some players. Unfortunately, tagging items does not necessarily reduce their reach, and can rather trigger the opposite effect. Practical experience by Facebook that used this technique in cooperation with certified fact-checkers has shown that this tool can backfire and tagging certain articles as 'disputed' can only boost the interest towards them. As the author of misinformation told the *Guardian*: 'A bunch of conservative groups grabbed this and said, "Hey, they are trying to silence this blog – share, share," (...) With Facebook trying to throttle it and say, "Don't share it," it actually had the opposite effect.' (Levin 2017). At the same time, tagging is not always unsuccessful in raising scepticism towards the information provided. It was found, for example, that tagging messages as advertisements can decrease their persuasive impact. While consumers rarely notice the promotion on the tweets, tweets promoted by a political party increased recognition of the advertisement and thus reduced behavioural intention, increased scepticism and negatively affected the source and also the attitudes. This effect, however, was not present for corporate brands (Boerman, Kruikemeier 2016).

Fact-checking is an extensively used tool to undermine epistemologically flawed information – a tool that can be used against conspiracy theories as well. Existing sites such as snopes.com, euvdisinfo.eu, stopfake.org deal a lot with conspiracy theories. Fact-checking services can be used to filter and remove news that contains false information or to make consumers realise that what they have encountered is false. The efficiency of fact-checking sites is the subject of debates. Ecker *et al.* (2017) found that retractions (especially ones that explicitly repeated the misinformation) were efficient in reducing misinformation effects. At the same time, however, fact-checking efforts can have only an impact on the higher educated and the better informed, and trust in fact-checkers is not even on the political spectrum: Democrats tend to trust more in fact-checkers than Republicans (Nyhan, Reifler 2015). Also, not surprisingly, voters selectively share fact-checking messages that are beneficial for their own candidate and the opposing party's candidate (Shin, Thorston, 2017), which seriously limits the opportunities of objective fact-checking. The examination of Twitter networks spreading low credibility information found that moving from the periphery to the core of the network, fact-checking nearly disappears. Again, this highlights some limits of its efficiency (Shao *et al.* 2018).

A different approach that can be highly successful is cutting the financial resources of conspiracy websites via warning the social media advertisement companies not to channel advertisement to these sites. Konspiratori.sk first published a list of conspiracy websites spreading harmful content (Čižik 2017). Webpages spreading fake news often generate income by selling advertising space, thus konspiratori.sk tries to make advertisers aware and help them to prevent their advertisements appearing on such websites.

## Conclusion

This chapter provided an overview of the existing research and practical experiences of interventions against conspiracy theories. We found that theories that are popular, non-plausible and harmful are the ones that are obviously calling for some interventions. Intervention is difficult, and it has to overcome many obstacles.

The chapter proposed a matrix that, in our view, can be a useful but simple tool to categorise the possible ways of interventions using two dimensions: temporal (before or after the recipient met with the conspiracy theory), and the target (source – supply side vs. the recipient – demand side). It highlights four possible options: the intervention takes place before the spread of the message, and targets the supply side (pre-emptive strike), or it takes place before the dissemination, but targets the recipient (immunisation); it takes place after the message was spread and targets the source (striking back), or takes place after the dissemination but targets the recipient (healing). Most of the research suggests that prevention is more useful than harm reduction, as conspiracy theories that have already spread are already having an impact on the recipient that is often difficult to neutralise. Also, the research suggests that fact and logic-based interventions have found to be efficient in many cases.

There is good news and bad news from the research on interventions. The good news is that, especially as a result of the misinformation campaigns threatening the integrity of the elections in 2016 (the Brexit campaign and the U.S. presidential election), the discussion of the possible counterstrategies is on a much more advanced level both in academic discussions and in policy discussions than before. The bad news is that experiences and academic research results are, in many cases, contradictory (e.g. on the usefulness of fact-checking), and it is difficult to put together a holistic picture from the very small and sporadic mosaics of research. A multiannual research project, based on meta-analyses of the existing research, replications and filling the existing gaps using a coherent theoretical framework and research design would be needed to have a more solid knowledge. As we live in an era of information warfare, there would be a need for a similar grand project to know more on propaganda and how to resist it than the one that was implemented during the biggest traditional war of the twentieth century: the Yale-program was focusing on the possibilities for attitude change and the resistance to persuasion in the context of the World Wars (for an overview, see McGuire 1996).

## Note

1 Similarly, van Prooijen and van Dijk (2014) previously found that perspective taking can rather increase the receptivity to conspiracy theories.

## References

Aaronovitch, D. (2011) *Voodoo history: the role of conspiracy theory in shaping modern history*, New York: Riverhead Books.

Abalakina-Paap, M., Stephan, W.G., Craig, T. and Gregory W.L. (1999) 'Beliefs in conspiracies', *Political Psychology*, 20(3): 637–47.

Applebaum, A. (2019) 'Regulate social media now: democracy is at stake', *Washington Post*, 1 April. Available at: www.washingtonpost.com/opinions/global-opinions/regulate-social-media-now-the-future-of-democracy-is-at-stake/2019/02/01/781db48c-2636-11e9-90cd-dedb0c92dc17_story.html. [Accessed 21 August 2019.]

Banas, J.A. and Miller, G. (2013) 'Inducing resistance to conspiracy theory propaganda: testing inoculation and metainoculation strategies', *Human Communication Research*, 39(2): 184–207.

Barkun, M. (2003) *A Culture of Conspiracy: apocalyptic visions in contemporary America*, Berkeley: University of California Press.

Bartlett, J. and Miller, C. (2010) *The power of unreason: conspiracy theories, extremism and counter-terrorism*, London: Demos.

Berlet, C. (2009) *Toxic to democracy: conspiracy theories, demonization & scapegoating*, Massachusetts: Political Research Associates.

Bickert, M. (2019) 'Combatting vaccine misinformation', *Facebook Newsroom*, 7 March. Available at: https://newsroom.fb.com/news/2019/03/combatting-vaccine-misinformation/. [Accessed 29 August 2019.]

Bilewicz, M., Winiewski, M., Kofta, M. and Wójcik, A. (2013) 'Harmful ideas, the structure and consequences of anti-semitic beliefs in Poland', *Political Psychology*, 34(6): 821–39.

Boerman, S.C. and Kruikemeier, S. (2016) 'Consumer responses to promoted tweets sent by brands and political parties', *Computers in Human Behavior*, 65: 285–94.

Bogart, L.M. and Thorburn, S. (2005) 'Are HIV/AIDS conspiracy beliefs a barrier to HIV prevention among African Americans?', *JAIDS Journal of Acquired Immune Deficiency Syndromes*, 38(2): 213–8.

Butler, L.D., Koopman, C. and Zimbardo, P.G. (1995) 'The psychological impact of viewing the film "JFK": emotions, beliefs, and political behavioral intentions', *Political Psychology*, 16(2): 237–57.

Čižik, T. (2017) 'Russian information warfare in Central Europe', in T. Čižik (ed.) *Information warfare: new security challenge for Europe*, Bratislava: Centre for European and North Atlantic Affairs, pp. 8–31.

Clarke, S. (2002) 'Conspiracy theories and conspiracy theorizing', *Philosophy of the Social Sciences*, 32(2): 131–50.

Coady, D. (2006) 'Conspiracy theories as official stories', in D. Coady (ed.) *Conspiracy theory: the philosophical debate*, Hampshire: Ashgate, pp. 115–28.

Cook, J. and Lewandowsky, S. (2011) *The Debunking Handbook*, St. Lucia, Australia: University of Queensland.

Cook, J., Lewandowsky, S. and Ecker, U.K. (2017) 'Neutralizing misinformation through inoculation: exposing misleading argumentation techniques reduces their influence', *PloS One*, 12(5): e0175799.

Dentith, M.R. (2017) 'Conspiracy theories on the basis of the evidence', *Synthese*, 196(3): 1–19.

Douglas, K.M. and Leite, A.C. (2017) 'Suspicion in the workplace: organizational conspiracy theories and work-related outcomes', *British Journal of Psychology*, 108(3): 486–506.

Douglas, K.M. and Sutton, R.M. (2008) 'The hidden impact of conspiracy theories: perceived and actual influence of theories surrounding the death of princess Diana', *The Journal of Social Psychology*, 148(2): 210–21.

Douglas, K.M., Sutton, R.M. and Cichocka, A. (2017) 'The psychology of conspiracy theories', *Current Directions in Psychological Science*, 26(6): 538–42.

Douglas K.M., Sutton R.M., Jolley D. and Wood, M.J. (2015) 'The social, political, environmental and health-related consequences of conspiracy theories', in M. Bilewicz, A. Cichocka and W. Soral (eds.) *The psychology of conspiracy*, New York: Routledge, pp. 183–200.

Ecker, U.K., Hogan, J.L. and Lewandowsky, S. (2017) 'Reminders and repetition of misinformation: helping or hindering its retraction?', *Journal of Applied Research in Memory and Cognition*, 6(2): 185–92.

Einstein, K.L. and Glick, D.M. (2015) 'Do I think BLS data are BS? The consequences of conspiracy theories', *Political Behavior*, 37(3): 679–701.

Facebook (2019) 'Community standards, objectionable content', *Facebook*. Available at: www.facebook.com/communitystandards/objectionable_content. [Accessed 21 August 2019.]

Facebook Business (2017) 'Reducing links to low-quality web page experiences', *Facebook Business*, 10 May. Available at: www.facebook.com/business/news/reducing-links-to-low-quality-web-page-experiences. [Accessed 29 August 2019.]

Fenster, M. (1999) *Conspiracy theories: secrecy and power in American culture*, Minnesota: University of Minnesota Press.

Ferrara, E. (2017) 'Disinformation and social bot operations in the run up to the 2017 French presidential election', *First Monday*, 22(8).

Feygina, I., Jost, J.T. and Goldsmith, R.E. (2010) 'System justification, the denial of global warming, and the possibility of "system-sanctioned change"', *Personality and Social Psychology Bulletin*, 36(3): 326–38.

French, D. (2019) 'The social media censorship dumpster fire', *National Review*, 1 March. Available at: www.nationalreview.com/2019/03/the-social-media-censorship-dumpster-fire/. [Accessed 5 July 2019.]

Griffin, D.R. (2011) *Cognitive infiltration: an Obama appointee's plan to undermine the 9/11 conspiracy theory*, Massachusetts: Interlink Books.

Grimes, D.R. (2016) 'On the viability of conspiratorial beliefs', *PloS One*, 11(1): e0147905.

Groh, D. (1987) 'The temptation of conspiracy theory, or: why do bad things happen to good people? Part I: preliminary draft of a theory of conspiracy theories', in S. Moscovici and C.F. Graumann (eds.) *Changing conceptions of conspiracy*, New York: Springer, pp. 1–13.

Hamsher, J.H., Geller, J.D. and Rotter, J.B. (1968) 'Interpersonal trust, internal-external control, and the Warren commission report', *Journal of Personality and Social Psychology*, 9(3): 210–5.

Hart, P.S. and Nisbet, E.C. (2012) 'Boomerang effects in science communication: how motivated reasoning and identity cues amplify opinion polarization about climate mitigation policies', *Communication Research*, 39(6): 701–23.

Hellman, M. and Wagnsson, C. (2017) 'How can European states respond to Russian information warfare? An analytical framework', *European Security*, 26(2): 153–70.

Hertwig, R. and Engel, C. (2016) 'Homo ignorans: deliberately choosing not to know', *Perspectives on Psychological Science*, 11(3): 359–72.

Imhoff, R. and Bruder, M. (2014) 'Speaking (un-) truth to power: conspiracy mentality as a generalised political attitude', *European Journal of Personality*, 28(1): 25–43.

Jensen T. (2013) 'Democrats and Republicans differ on conspiracy theory beliefs', *Public Policy Polling*, 2 April. Available at: www.publicpolicypolling.com/polls/democrats-and-republicans-differ-on-conspiracy-theory-beliefs/. [Accessed 29 August 2019.]

Jolley, D. and Douglas, K.M. (2014a) 'The social consequences of conspiracism: exposure to conspiracy theories decreases intentions to engage in politics and to reduce one's carbon footprint', *British Journal of Psychology*, 105(1): 35–56.

Jolley, D. and Douglas, K.M. (2014b) 'The effects of anti-vaccine conspiracy theories on vaccination intentions', *PloS One*, 9(2): e89177.

Jolley, D. and Douglas, K.M. (2017) 'Prevention is better than cure: addressing anti-vaccine conspiracy theories', *Journal of Applied Social Psychology*, 47(8): 459–69.

Keeley, B.L. (1999) 'Of conspiracy theories', *The Journal of Philosophy*, 96(3): 109–26.

Kramer, R.M. (1999) 'Trust and distrust in organizations: emerging perspectives, enduring questions', *Annual review of psychology*, 50(1): 569–98.

Krekó, P. (2015) 'Conspiracy theory as collective motivated cognition', in M. Bilewicz, A. Cichocka and W. Soral (eds.) *The Psychology of Conspiracy*, London: Routledge, pp. 60–7.

Kumkale, G.T. and Albarracín, D. (2004) 'The sleeper effect in persuasion: a meta-analytic review', *Psychological Bulletin*, 130(1): 143–72.

Levin, S. (2017) 'Facebook promised to tackle fake news: but the evidence shows it's not working', *Guardian*, 16 May. Available at: www.theguardian.com/technology/2017/may/16/facebook-fake-news-tools-not-working. [Accessed 21 August 2019.]

Lewandowsky, S. (2019) *Wilful construction of ignorance: a tale of two ontologies*. In press.

Lewandowsky, S., Cook, J., Oberauer, K., Brophy, S., Lloyd, E.A. and Marriott, M. (2015) 'Recurrent fury: conspiratorial discourse in the blogosphere triggered by research on the role of conspiracist ideation in climate denial', *Journal of Social and Political Psychology*, 3(1): 142–78.

Lewandowsky, S., Oberauer, K. and Gignac, G.E. (2013) 'NASA faked the moon landing –therefore, (climate) science is a hoax: an anatomy of the motivated rejection of science', *Psychological Science*, 24(5): 622–33.

McGuire, W.J. (1996) 'The Yale communication and attitude-change program in the 1950s', in E.E. Dennis and E. Wartella (eds.) *LEA's communication series: American communication research – The remembered history*, Hillsdalfe, NJ: Lawrence Erlbaum Associates, pp. 39–59.

Miron, A.M. and Brehm, J. W. (2006) 'Reactance theory – 40 years later', *Zeitschrift für Sozialpsychologie*, 37(1): 9–18.

Mirowsky, J. and Ross, C.E. (1983) 'Paranoia and the structure of powerlessness', *American Sociological Review*, 48(2): 228–39.

Mudde, C. (2004) 'The populist zeitgeist', *Government and Opposition*, 39(4): 541–63.

Newheiser, A.K., Farias, M. and Tausch, N. (2011) 'The functional nature of conspiracy beliefs: examining the underpinnings of belief in the Da Vinci Code conspiracy', *Personality and Individual Differences*, 51(8): 1007–11.

Nyhan, B. and Reifler, J. (2015) 'Estimating fact-checking's effects', *American Press Institute*, 28 April. Available at: www.americanpressinstitute.org/wp-content/uploads/2015/04/Estimating-Fact-Checkings-Effect.pdf. [Accessed 21 August 2019.]

Oliver, J.E. and Wood, T. (2014) 'Medical conspiracy theories and health behaviors in the United States', *JAMA Internal Medicine*, 174(5): 817–8.

Orosz, G., Krekó, P., Paskuj, B., Tóth-Király, I., Böthe, B. and Roland-Lévy, C. (2016) 'Changing conspiracy beliefs through rationality and ridiculing', *Frontiers in Psychology*, 7(279): 1525.

Pigden, C. (1995) 'Popper revisited, or what is wrong with conspiracy theories?', *Philosophy of the Social Sciences*, 25(1): 3–34.

Prier, J. (2017) 'Commanding the trend: social media as information warfare', *Strategic Studies Quarterly*, 11(4): 50–85.

Roth, Y. (2019) 'Information operations on Twitter: principles, process, and disclosure', *Twitter Blog*, 13 June. Available at: https://blog.twitter.com/en_us/topics/company/2019/information-ops-on-twitter.html. [Accessed 29 August 2018.]

Salinas, S. (2018) 'Twitter permanently bans Alex Jones and Infowars accounts', *CNBC*, 6 September. Available at: www.cnbc.com/2018/09/06/twitter-permanently-bans-alex-jones-and-infowars-accounts.html. [Accessed 29 August 2018.]

Shao, C., Hui, P.M., Wang, L., Jiang, X., Flammini, A., Menczer, F. and Ciampaglia, G. L. (2018) 'Anatomy of an online misinformation network', *PloS One*, 13(4): e0196087.

Sherman, D.K. and Cohen, G.L. (2006) 'The psychology of self-defense: self-affirmation theory', in M.P. Zanna (ed.) *Vol. 38: advances in experimental social psychology*, San Diego, CA: Elsevier Academic Press, pp. 183–242.

Shin, J. and Thorson, K. (2017) 'Partisan selective sharing: the biased diffusion of fact-checking messages on social media', *Journal of Communication*, 67(2): 233–55.

Sullivan, D., Landau, M.J. and Rothschild, Z.K. (2010) 'An existential function of enemyship: evidence that people attribute influence to personal and political enemies to compensate for threats to control', *Journal of Personality and Social Psychology*, 98(3): 434–49.

Sunstein, C.R. (2014) *Conspiracy theories and other dangerous ideas*, New York: Simon and Schuster.

Sunstein, C.R. and Vermeule, A. (2009) 'Conspiracy theories: causes and cures', *Journal of Political Philosophy*, 17(2): 202–27.

Swami, V., Chamorro-Premuzic, T. and Furnham, A. (2010) 'Unanswered questions: a preliminary investigation of personality and individual difference predictors of 9/11 conspiracist beliefs', *Applied Cognitive Psychology*, 24(6): 749–61.

Swami, V., Voracek, M., Stieger, S., Tran, U. and Furnham, A. (2014) 'Analytic thinking reduces belief in conspiracy theories', *Cognition*, 133(3): 572–85.

Twitter Public Policy (2017) 'Announcement: RT and Sputnik Advertising', *Twitter Blog*, 26 October. Available at: https://blog.twitter.com/official/en_us/topics/company/2017/Announcement-RT-and-Sputnik-Advertising.html. [Accessed 29 August 2018.]

Uscinski, J.E. (2018) 'The study of conspiracy theories', *Argumenta*, 3(2): 233–45.

Uscinski, J.E. and Parent, J.M. (2014) *American Conspiracy Theories*, Oxford: Oxford University Press.

Uscinski, J. E., Parent, J. and Torres, B. (2011) 'Conspiracy theories are for losers', *APSA 2011 Annual Meeting Paper*. Available at: https://ssrn.com/abstract=1901755. [Accessed 20 June 2019.]

Van der Linden, S.L. (2015) 'The conspiracy-effect: exposure to conspiracy theories (about global warming) decreases pro-social behavior and science acceptance', *Personality and Individual Differences*, 87: 171–3.

Van der Linden, S.L., Leiserowitz, AA., Feinberg, G.D. and Maibach, E.W. (2015) 'The scientific consensus on climate change as a gateway belief: experimental evidence', *PloS One*, 10(2): e0118489.

Van Prooijen, J.-W. (2018) *The psychology of conspiracy theories*, Oxon, UK: Routledge.

Van Prooijen, J.-W. and Acker, M. (2015) 'The influence of control on belief in conspiracy theories: conceptual and applied extensions', *Applied Cognitive Psychology*, 29(5): 753–61.

Van Prooijen, J.-W. and de Vries, R.E. (2016) 'Organizational conspiracy beliefs: implications for leadership styles and employee outcomes', *Journal of Business and Psychology*, 31(4): 479–91.

Van Prooijen, J.-W., Krouwel, A. and Pollet, T. (2015) 'Political extremism predicts belief in conspiracy theories', *Social Psychological and Personality Science*, 6(5): 570–8.

Van Prooijen, J.-W. and van Dijk, E. (2014) 'When consequence size predicts belief in conspiracy theories: the moderating role of perspective taking', *Journal of Experimental Social Psychology*, 55: 63–73.

Van Prooijen, J.-W. and van Lange, P.A. (2014) *Power, politics, and paranoia: why people are suspicious of their leaders*, Cambridge, UK: Cambridge University Press.

Whitson, J.A. and Galinsky, A.D. (2008) 'Lacking control increases illusory pattern perception', *Science*, 322(5898): 115–7.

Wolsko, C., Ariceaga, H. and Seiden, J. (2016) 'Red, white, and blue enough to be green: effects of moral framing on climate change attitudes and conservation behaviors', *Journal of Experimental Social Psychology*, 65: 7–19.

Wood, A.K. and Ravel, A.M. (2017) 'Fool me once: regulating fake news and other online advertising', *Southern California Law Review*, 91(6):1223–78.

Yablokov, I. (2015) 'Conspiracy theories as a Russian public diplomacy tool: the case of Russia Today (RT)', *Politics*, 35(3–4): 301–15.

Yablokov, I. (2018) *Fortress Russia: conspiracy theories in the post-Soviet world*, Cambridge: Polity Books.

Young, Z. (2018) 'French parliament passes law against "fake news"', *Politico*, 7 April. Available at: www.politico.eu/article/french-parliament-passes-law-against-fake-news/. [Accessed 21 August 2019.]

# SECTION 3

# Society and politics

# 3.0
# INTRODUCTION

*Eiríkur Bergmann, Asbjørn Dyrendal, Jaron Harambam
and Hulda Thórisdóttir*

This section examines the impact of conspiracy theories in society and politics and, in turn, the impact of society and politics on the construction and dissemination of conspiracy theories. Conspiracy theories are an inherently social phenomenon as their meaning often derives from their specific social context. They are constructed and reconfigured in socio-historical circumstances, by both their creators and consumers. Dissemination of conspiracy theories is enabled and constrained by means of distribution, which in recent years has been facilitated by new powerful digital technologies.

Conspiracy theories can be highly political, and their framing often comes from ideas around power and authority. For instance, conspiracy theories may ascribe hidden socio-political power and ambition to an outgroup (e.g. Jews, Muslims or Freemasons), or they can be used to undermine the integrity of authorities. Similarly, they are often dismissed by those in positions of authority as offering distorted explanations of reality. In providing alternative knowledge, conspiracy theories can be seen as the product of taking political positions, and their description of the world is often constructed in an attempt to mobilise people in a specific political struggle.

The effect of conspiracy theories on society and politics has been widely discussed by both academics, politicians and journalists alike. As is illustrated in this section, they play multiple roles for a variety of actors. They can be propagated by those in power who seek to bolster their influence in society. And they can also be upheld by various underdogs who challenge precisely those practices and their active roles in shaping the world to their wishes (Harambam 2017). Regimes can spread conspiracy theories to sow distrust towards undesirable groups (e.g. Chapter 3.8). Citizens who feel powerless and marginalised may use them to justify their distrust, or even to find a sense of community with fellow conspiracy believers (Harambam, Aupers 2017).

While also drawing on examples from specific times and places, the emphasis in this section is on general questions and dynamics: Who believes in conspiracy theories, how conspiracy theories surface in different societies, who produces and consumes them, the role conspiracy theories play for different types of regimes, and how they are aligned with other belief systems.

Conspiracy theories are often seen as only being a discredited or stigmatised counter-knowledge, and, thus, not true. This can be misleading. Sometimes conspiracy theories are officially sanctioned explanations. The most notorious example here are the antisemitic conspiracy theories of Nazi Germany. In other types of regimes and at other times, they are counternarratives, as with the conspiracy theories of the 9/11 Truth Movement.

As counternarratives, conspiracy theories are usually rooted in distrust, defiance and even a desire to destabilise reigning powers. As such, they can be problematic when the reigning powers are democratically elected authorities whose policy agenda is obstructed or delayed due to conspiracy theories. An example would be President Obama, who had to spend significant amounts of time and public relations resources to quell the conspiracy theory that he was not born in the U.S.A., or that his health care reform would include 'death panels' in which people would be judged by the state whether worthy of receiving health care coverage or not.

As Uscinski and Parent (2014) have pointed out, there are also examples of conspiracy theories being a creative force for good in politics, the prime example being the foundation of the U.S.A. The founding fathers believed that the king of England at the time, George III, was scheming to ensnare the colonies under his rule and absolute authority. In response, they wrote the Declaration of Independence (Howe 1979: 80). The political struggle over slavery was exacerbated by conspiracy beliefs on both sides. 'Slave power' conspiracy theories were part of the motivation for the politics of the abolitionists, and anti-abolitionist conspiracy theories were important in driving the conflict into secession and the civil war that ultimately ended slavery (Butter 2014: 167–222).

Dealing with the interplay between conspiracy theories and society and politics requires an interdisciplinary approach. Different sources and research methods give us different forms of access to the complex questions raised. Quantitative studies (as in Chapter 3.1 and 3.4) give us more than just the numbers of how many believe in certain things. They can also tell us something about their backgrounds, their political stance, their other beliefs and worries, their social contexts and, sometimes, their other forms of interaction with society. However, quantitative studies are less good at giving deep understanding of the lived contexts of different types of people engaging with conspiracy theories.

Qualitative studies (as exemplified in Chapter 3.2) give us a chance at differentiating between different types conspiracy theorists and seeing which ideas and theories actually gain traction in lived lives. They can often tell us about the lifeworlds and worldviews of those engaging with conspiracy theories, how they negotiate and construct their identities, what epistemic strategies they deploy and how they resist the stigmatisation of conspiracy theories. Participant observation is one of the ways we may also learn more about the differences and similarities between 'leaders' and conspiracy theory consumers, between the conspiracy entrepreneurs and their audiences. When and to what extent are audiences mainly 'adherents', and when are they active participants, reconfiguring conspiracy theories and sharing those in new networks? Ethnographic studies can give us information that is often hard to get from historical sources, but detailed engagement with written sources, and not merely that which has seen print, remains vital to investigating conspiracy beliefs from different epochs. It allows us to trace networks of influence and transmission, and sometimes the contents and contexts of conspiracy lore.

The question of entrepreneurs, audience and consumption becomes particularly visible in the sphere of cultural production. As section 4 of this handbook makes clear, literature, film and other media are also important scenes for the imagination of society and politics, not least including the dark desires of conspiracy theory. Popular culture is a vital scene on which the social imaginary plays out and, as a scene which reaches large audiences, it gives us important information about the imaginations of society and their political consequences.

When studying the impact of conspiracy theories in society and politics, it is necessary to take into consideration both those who produce them and those that adhere to them. The relationship between the two is highly complex and researchers can easily be misled. Conspiracy theories about the politically powerful may work differently than those involving mostly ethnic or sexual minorities, activating different political identities and affiliations. Another way of inquiring

## Introduction

about participants is to analyse the nature of their entanglement, for instance by examining people's everyday liaison with conspiracy theories, be they explicit or implicit.

Such explorations will often have to take into account wide and varied relations between multiple positions, including the interplay between believers of a conspiracy theory and those sceptical of it. What positions do people take and why? What is at stake? Who is involved, with what outcomes and which dynamics of power are played out? These questions call for specific investigations, but some of the outcomes point to more general answers. In the first chapter of the section (3.1), Smallpage *et al.* look at and problematise what we think we know about who believes in conspiracy theories and how we know it. The chapter gathers data from multiple countries and regions, and addresses both their contents and shortcomings. This is complemented by Harambam's review of qualitative studies (3.2), which differentiates between the consumptive practices and social contexts of individual believers, the work of conspiracy entrepreneurs and the social activism of groups devoted to specific conspiracy beliefs. Some conspiracy believers are thus activists, but how does conspiracy belief more generally relate to political participation? This is the topic of the chapter by Thórisdóttir, Mari and Krouwel (3.4), who address whether and how conspiracy believers vote, and to what degree they are engaged in other political activities.

Conspiracy narratives involving gender roles have often been used to mobilise people to engage in collective action. These have often been of a conservative nature and may be intensely interested in 'correct' sexualities. Thiem (3.3) therefore discusses the connections between gender and sexuality. Drawing on historical data, she shows how a crisis of hegemonic masculinity is one of the key factors motivating conspiracy theories. She examines whether there is a distinction between men or women when it comes to belief in conspiracy theories. As shown by Borenstein (2019), conspiracy theories about sexuality and gender can also be part of regime-supportive or state sponsored propaganda. Giry and Gürpınar (3.5) take a broader look at the use of conspiracy theories as propaganda. They focus mostly on findings about authoritarian regimes, but they also have a broader outlook that includes the propaganda of populist politicians. Populist movements have been on the rise throughout the world for at least the last two decades, and conspiracy theories have played a role in this rise in many countries (Bergmann 2018). Bergmann and Butter (3.6) address the relationship between populism and conspiracy theory.

According to research done in social psychology (see section 2), extreme, anti-democratic political and religious positions correlate with conspiracy beliefs, and narratives of conspiracy often play a role in the internal culture of extreme movements. However, as Lee shows (3.7), the role of conspiracy theories in the processes of radicalisation is complex and necessitates taking into account their function in creating a shared identity among believers. Conspiracy theories tend to point out who the enemy behind the curtain is, and one of the more consistent answers to that question has been 'the Jews'. Simonsen (3.8) gives an overview of the development of antisemitism as a conspiracist tradition, from the high medieval period to the present. Jews are not the only minority that have been subject of conspiracy theories. Rounding out this section, Dyrendal (3.9) surveys some of the variety of relations between conspiracy theory and religion, looking through the lens of conspiracy theories *as, about,* and *in* religion.

There are of course many related issues to the interplay between conspiracy theories, society and politics that are not discussed in full detail here. Among them is the relation between race, ethnicity and conspiracy theory: the conspiracy beliefs *of* minorities, and the conspiracy beliefs *about* minorities, and how racial fears and fantasies play into that dynamic. Nor is there a specific focus on the complex, social use of conspiracy theory in political power games. Labelling something a 'conspiracy theory' can be a tool in policing epistemic boundaries, where one or both sides claim the mantle of rationality, attempting to expel the accused party from reasoned social dialogue (e.g. Bratich 2008; Harambam, Aupers 2015). Such power contests may tend to favour those already powerful.

Another power game involves strategically levelling specific conspiracy theories against different social actors on e.g. social media in a way that is designed to silence critical speech. Accusing opponents of being a part of the conspiracy you claim to unveil is a well-known gambit. Variations of Pizzagate or QAnon theories accuse opponents of being part of a (often satanic) cabal of pedophiles, and these theories can be put to devastating use on social media, something we also see with regard to survivors of massacres and relatives of the slain in mass murders deemed 'false flag' episodes in conspiracy culture (e.g. Debies-Carl 2017; Persily 2017). These topics also merit further study.

## References

Bergmann, E. (2018) *Conspiracy & populism: the politics of misinformation*, London: Palgrave Macmillan.
Borenstein, E. (2019) *Plots against Russia: conspiracy and fantasy after socialism*, Ithaca, NY: Cornell University Press.
Bratich, J.Z. (2008) *Conspiracy panics: political rationality and popular culture*, Albany, NY: State University of New York Press.
Butter, M. (2014) *Plots, designs, and schemes: American conspiracy theories from the Puritans to the present*, Berlin/Boston: de Gruyter.
Debies-Carl, J.S. (2017) 'Pizzagate and beyond: using social research to understand conspiracy legends', *Skeptical Inquirer*, 41(6).
Harambam, J. (2017) *'The truth is out there': conspiracy culture in an age of epistemic instability*, thesis, Rotterdam: Erasmus University.
Harambam, J. and Aupers, S. (2015) 'Contesting epistemic authority: conspiracy theories on the boundary of science', *Public Understanding of Science*, 24(4): 466–80.
Harambam, J. and Aupers, S. (2017) '"I am not a conspiracy theorist": relational identifications in the Dutch conspiracy milieu', *Cultural Sociology*, 11(1): 113–29.
Howe, D.W. (1979) *The political culture of the American Whigs*, Chicago, IL: University of Chicago Press.
Persily, N. (2017) 'The 2016 US election: can democracy survive the internet?', *Journal of Democracy*, 28(2): 63–76.
Uscinski, J.E. and Parent, J.M. (2014) *American conspiracy theories*, New York, NY: Oxford University Press.

# 3.1

# WHO ARE THE CONSPIRACY THEORISTS?

## Demographics and conspiracy theories

*Steven M. Smallpage, Hugo Drochon, Joseph E. Uscinski and Casey Klofstad*

### Introduction

Who are the conspiracy theorists? What do they look like and where do they live? Are they young or old, rich or poor, male or female, educated or not? What country are they from?

Unfortunately, the extent literature offers only hazy answers to these questions due to a lack of proper conceptualisation and measurement. For example, there is no clear definition of conspiracy theorist or any clear way to properly measure membership in that group. For now, the best way to address these questions is by defining important concepts. We first turn to the American context because of easy access to nationally-representative data; this case demonstrates how conspiracy theorising varies across within-context groups. In the next section, we broaden our scope to address conspiracy theorising across cultural contexts. We provide the only cross-nationally-representative data focusing on conspiracy theories currently available (Drochon 2018). We use this to show how cultural context conditions conspiracy theorising and as a consequence may frustrate attempts to study conspiracy theories cross-culturally. We conclude by offering both a summary and prospective avenues for further research.

### Definitions

Much analysis depends upon how concepts such as *conspiracy theory*, *conspiracy belief* and *conspiracy thinking* are defined. These definitions jointly determine how a particularly elusive term, *conspiracy theorist*, is defined. While this task might seem straightforward, these terms have long been items of contention (Walker 2018).

*Conspiracy theory* for our purposes is a proposed explanation of events or circumstances (past, present or future) which cites as the primary cause a conspiracy. Conspiracy theories could be either true or false, and, in most instances, contradict the proclamations of epistemological authorities (Levy 2007). This is a barebones definition, but even more detailed versions leave room to include or exclude theories arbitrarily. Importantly, there are an infinite number of conspiracy theories that researchers could study, meaning that the research will always be incomplete.

*Conspiracy beliefs* are individuals' acceptance of specific conspiracy theories as likely true. While beliefs are hard to measure directly, polling the public is the most practical way to measure beliefs and believers' demographic characteristics. Of course, polling leaves room for interpretation. First, how a survey item is worded can affect if the idea being asked about is a conspiracy theory or not. Note the difference between survey items that ask respondents to express agreement with: 'Vaccines cause autism' or with 'Pharmaceutical companies and governments are actively working to hide the dangerous effects of vaccines from the public'. The latter expresses a conspiracy theory, the former does not (Walker 2018). Second, what level of certainty qualifies as a belief? Consider a question asking respondents about the 'Chem-trail' conspiracy theory. One version of this question asked respondents to agree or disagree with the theory; 5 per cent agreed (Jenson 2013). Another version asked respondents to answer on a Likert scale from 'completely false' to 'completely true'. Researchers then asked 'unsure' respondents to make a best guess (Tingley, Wagner 2017). The result was that 40 per cent of the total sample indicated the theory was 'completely' or 'somewhat true'. The different ways of operationalising belief lead to estimates that varied by a factor of eight (Jenson 2013, Tingley, Wagner 2017). The 5 per cent and 40 per cent groups will likely vary greatly in terms of their demographic characteristics, and it is not clear which group is the 'right' one to consider as the conspiracy theorists. Third, it is important to note that people selectively believe in conspiracy theories. There are an infinite number of conspiracy theories, but surveys can only ask about one or a few. This means that some people who are certainly 'conspiracy theorists' (under some definition) will show no evidence of such on some surveys, and vice-versa.

The concept of *conspiracy thinking* provides equal trouble for researchers seeking to identify conspiracy theorists. Sometimes referred to as 'conspiracist ideation', conspiracy thinking is a stable predisposition that drives individuals to view events and circumstances as the product of conspiracies (Brotherton *et al.* 2013; Imhoff, Bruder 2013). All else equal, when a person with high levels of conspiracy thinking is presented with a conspiracy theory, they are more likely to believe it than a person with lower levels (Uscinski *et al.* 2016). Focusing on conspiracy thinking moves the inquiry away from the characteristics of specific conspiracy theories, to the characteristics of individuals that make them susceptible to conspiracy beliefs. We note that researchers use several different scales to measure this latent concept (Swami *et al.* 2017), and currently it is not clear how well these scales (or even the concept itself) travels across cultural contexts (Atari *et al.* 2019).

So, who, then, is a conspiracy theorist? It is with this term that definitions vary the most. *Conspiracy theorist* could refer to anyone who believes in any conspiracy theory. Presumably, most people are not conspiracy theorists. Yet, polls suggest that basically all Americans hold conspiracy beliefs. A poll by Fairleigh Dickenson University asked about belief in four conspiracy theories; 63 per cent believed at least one (Cassino, Jenkins 2013). Oliver and Wood (2014a) asked about belief in seven conspiracy theories, finding that 55 per cent believed at least one. A 2018 poll of Florida asked about belief in nine conspiracy theories, finding that 80 per cent believed at least one (Uscinski, Klofstad 2018). A poll of New Jersey residents asking about ten conspiracy theories found that 94 per cent believed in at least one (Goertzel 1994). The general trend is that, as more conspiracy theories are asked about, the number of people who believe one increases to approach 100 per cent. Therefore, using *conspiracy theorist* to refer to anyone who believes in any conspiracy theory is meaningless. If we use the term to refer to belief in a specific conspiracy theory, then the term has some limited meaning in that context: People who believe a particular conspiracy theory believe in that particular conspiracy theory.

*Conspiracy theorist* could refer to people who believe in several conspiracy theories, but it is not clear how many 'several' should be. If the number is set too low, then the term again becomes meaningless (everyone is a conspiracy theorist). If it refers to a person who believes in a certain number of conspiracy theories out of a finite set of conspiracy theories, then the term takes a more definitive shape, but it is still arbitrary.

We run into similar problems when we exchange conspiracy beliefs for conspiracy thinking. Because conspiracy thinking is a latent trait measured along a scale, there is no absolute high or low, and the median between surveys could refer to different absolute levels. Uscinski and Parent (2014) referred to the upper-third of respondents on their conspiracy thinking scale as conspiracy theorists, but the choice was due more to convenience than anything theoretically driven.

*Conspiracy theorist* could refer to people who invent, investigate or propagate conspiracy theories. This definition would cut the population of conspiracy theorists down significantly, making the belonging to that group dependent on action rather than beliefs. It would be cut down even further if we used the term to only refer to people who take part in such activities professionally (e.g. Alex Jones). Such a definition would again be useless, because it would refer to too few people.

We cannot here choose among these varying definitions. But our point is that scholars need to pay attention to the problem caused by settling on definitions: It leads to not being able to pinpoint who the conspiracy theorists are – even within contexts – that goes beyond any given study. This problem is further exacerbated when looking across cultural contexts. Before offering up a list of demographic characteristics and explaining how those might correlate with conspiracy beliefs and thinking in various studies, let us briefly address some of the important questions that scholars should address before considering relationships between demographics and conspiracy theories.

## Do we measure at all and what do we measure?

Many researchers skip the step of systematically measuring conspiracy beliefs or thinking, and instead rely on impressions. Take for example the *New York Times*, which in addition to suggesting that Americans are particularly prone to conspiracy theorising, has mentioned Mexicans, Arabs, Afghanis, Pakistanis, Bangladeshis, Iraqis, Africans, Egyptians, Russians, Bulgarians, Italians, Yemenis and the gay community as also being particularly prone (Orr, Husting 2018). Assertions like these have yet to be supported with systematic evidence. We suggest that, if one wants to make empirical claims about who engages in conspiracy theorising, they should begin by buttressing those claims with systematic comparisons.

Once a decision is made to measure some form of conspiracy theorising (conspiracy thinking or beliefs) to see if it is correlated to demographic measures, the question then becomes what exactly should be measured. Conspiracy thinking leads to specific conspiracy beliefs, but conspiracy thinking and conspiracy beliefs will be correlated with different demographics (Klofstad *et al.* 2019). The reason for this is that conspiracy beliefs are often determined by a combination of conspiracy thinking and one or a set of other predispositions that are themselves likely correlated with demographic characteristics (Enders *et al.* 2018). Conspiracy thinking is not spread perfectly even across demographic groups in the U.S.A., but it appears fairly random (with the exception of levels of education and income).

Conspiracy beliefs are partially dependent on demographic characteristics and group memberships because they cast one's own group as a victim of other groups. Conspiracy beliefs therefore vary widely across race, region, social class, age, gender, religion and party identification (Miller *et al.* 2016). Christians and Muslims are more likely than Jews to believe in Jewish conspiracy theories (Bilewicz, Krzeminski 2010; Nyhan, Zeitzoff 2018); people with New Age beliefs are more likely than Catholics to believe in DaVinci Code theories (Newheiser *et al.*

2011), and partisans are more likely to believe the opposing party, rather than their own, is conspiring against them. For example, polls show that 45 per cent of Democrats believed that President Bush was behind the 9/11 attacks but only 15 per cent of Republicans believed as much; about 40 per cent of Republicans believed that President Obama was born outside of the U.S.A. but only 15 per cent of Democrats believed as much (Nyhan 2009).

A final question addresses cross-cultural comparisons. Conspiracy theories, thinking and beliefs may translate well across similar regions – for example, it might not be too hard to make comparisons between the U.S.A. and U.K. But, comparing countries that have vastly different political cultures can present problems (Atari et al. 2019). As such, measurements of conspiracy thinking that have validity in Western democracies may not translate. Further, just because a conspiracy belief is popular in one country, does not mean that it would be popular in another. Cultural factors will drive the belief of specific conspiracy theories (Knight 2002).

## Demographics

In this section, we refer to a range of literature and surveys to demonstrate that demographic characteristics are established predictors of conspiracy thinking and others are more predictive of conspiracy beliefs across studies and operationalisations within countries. We follow this by looking cross-culturally as a starting point for future research.

One highly consistent finding across studies (and operationalisations) is that income and education are negatively correlated with conspiracy thinking in the U.S.A., meaning that those who make more money or have attained more education have lower levels of conspiracy thinking (Uscinski, Parent 2014). The connection between education and conspiracy thinking is a difficult puzzle to solve. On the one hand, most of the measurements used are simple 'level of education' ordinal variables ranging from 'less than high school' to 'postgraduate degree'. Given the general rise of education levels within the U.S.A. and other democracies, this is a necessarily clustered variable that makes inferences difficult. And, the relationship between education and conspiracy thinking is a function of the type of statistical analyses applied as well. Oliver and Wood (2014a), for example, find that education is negatively related to supernatural, paranormal, Manichean and end-times thinking, as well as with the belief that a secret cabal controls world events. However, in a more sophisticated statistical analysis, they find that education has only mixed effects. There is also the problem of understanding *why* education is negatively correlated with conspiracy thinking. Recent work (van Prooijen 2017; Dyer, Hall 2019) suggests that education makes individuals more analytical. However, it could be that institutions of higher education eschew conspiracy theorists (Smallpage 2018).

If conspiracy thinking is related to feelings of marginalisation, anomia and helplessness, then higher income levels should negatively predict belief in conspiracy theories. But, just like the case with education, the causal story is blurry: Having a low income could make one prone to conspiracy thinking, or institutions that offer lucrative salaries may not want to entrust the commensurate responsibilities to people who espouse conspiracy theories (Uscinski 2018).

While income and education appear to be significant negative predictors of conspiracy theorising across studies, they do not always predict specific conspiracy beliefs (e.g. Klofstad et al. 2019) and may have different effects across different groups (Miller et al. 2016). This highlights two issues, one particular to the American samples and one applicable regardless of context: First, conspiracy thinking in the U.S.A. is usually intertwined with partisanship and ideology – variables that capture an individual's worldview; second, more generally, there is a difference between believing *specific* conspiracy theories versus having higher levels of conspiracy thinking. The former is a product of demographic factors whereas the latter is less so (excepting education and income).

Beliefs in many prominent conspiracy theories in the U.S.A. can be attributed to partisan motivated reasoning (Enders *et al.* 2018). This does not mean that partisans will believe all conspiracy theories, or even that partisans are more likely to believe conspiracy theories than non-partisans (Smallpage *et al.* 2017). But, if we want to understand the engine behind American conspiracy theorising, we must begin with partisanship.

U.S. polling shows that conspiracy thinking is even between the two major parties and across political ideologies; independents and third parties tend to show higher levels of conspiracy thinking (Uscinski, Parent 2014). Particular conspiracy beliefs, however, vary greatly by party, with party identifiers tending to accuse opposing parties and their coalitions of conspiring (Miller, Saunders 2016). With this said, there is evidence that political extremists are more prone to conspiracy theorising than moderates (van Prooijen *et al.* 2015, Krouwel *et al.* 2017). As we outlined earlier, conceptual and measurement differences are likely driving some studies to find a U-shaped curve (van Prooijen *et al.* 2015) and others to find an upside-down U-shaped curve (Uscinski, Parent 2014).

Religion and its role in conspiracy theorising is beginning to be explored by scholars (Robertson, Dyrendal 2018). People's religious affiliation tends to drive their specific conspiracy beliefs, so that more devout members tend to think that other groups along with supernatural forces are conspiring (Oliver, Wood 2014a). But it is not clear yet if different religions foster higher levels of conspiracy thinking. It is well documented, however, that the style of thinking that allows for supernatural beliefs is closely related to conspiracy thinking (van Prooijen *et al.* 2018).

The typical caricature of an American conspiracy theorist is that of a white, middle-aged male. But, conspiracy thinking tends to be even between the sexes and races, and relatively flat across age groups (Uscinski, Parent 2014). With this said, more polling should be done on this matter because many polls lack sufficient samples for teasing out significant differences among subgroups. In terms of conspiracy beliefs, minorities often entertain conspiracy theories in which they are targeted by majorities (Farrakhan, Gates 1996); such beliefs are often the result of past mistreatment (Thomas, Quinn 1991). Older people appear more susceptible to conspiracy theories on the Internet, perhaps due to a lack of Internet literacy (Guess *et al.* 2019); but other studies suggest that young people are more susceptible to some conspiracy beliefs (Klofstad *et al.* 2019).

Perhaps the best demonstration of the staying power of conspiracy thinking in the U.S.A. is seen in the longitudinal public opinion polling data. Just the polling on the one belief – that Lee Harvey Oswald did not work alone in assassinating President Kennedy – shows that about 50 to 60 per cent of the American public believe at least one conspiracy theory (Enders, Smallpage 2018). Given that nearly 50 per cent of the U.S.A. believes in this one conspiracy theory, it would be difficult to find any systematic sociodemographic factors that would explain conspiracy thinking.

## Conspiracy theories across contexts

Now we turn to international data to make higher-order cross-cultural claims about conspiracy theories and demographics. While there has been a considerable amount of research on conspiracy thinking, much of it relies on U.S. samples. This makes generalisability into the global context difficult. However, in 2016, Drochon (2018) gathered representative survey data from seven countries (Argentina, Germany, Great Britain, Italy, Poland, Portugal and Sweden) through the polling house YouGov (for further details on data collection, see Drochon 2018). A number of questions were asked about respondents' commitments to democracy, their attitudes toward their government, as well as questions pertaining to their conspiracy thinking and their specific conspiracy beliefs. Drawing on these data, we now examine conspiracy theorising in a cross-cultural context.

One of the objections to conspiracy theory research is the claim that conspiracy theorising is often culturally dependent. Who counts as a conspiracy theorist in one country might not count as one in another. We suggest that there are large cultural and sociological factors that set the floor and ceiling for the number of 'conspiracy theorists' in a given country and that, even in mature democracies like Great Britain, nearly two-thirds of the population believe at least one of the conspiracy theories asked about in the short survey we presented.

One of the earliest explanations for conspiracy thinking was a 'macro' or sociological theory of political extremism and disengagement in which conspiracy thinking is a function of low self-esteem, feelings of powerlessness and low political efficacy and trust (Hofstadter 1964). Therefore, looking at a set of countries, we would expect that conspiracy thinking should be more prevalent where the citizens do not believe the country is truly democratic and, perhaps even stronger, where they believe the 'system is broken'.

Table 3.1.1 shows the extent to which individuals in various countries rated how democratic they thought their country was from 0 (completely undemocratic) to 10 (completely democratic). The top row of Table 3.1.1 shows the percentage of citizens that rated their country at or above 6 on that scale, which we take to show a more than minimal agreement that the country is democratic. The results confirm what many other scholars of comparative political culture have shown (Levitsky, Ziblatt 2018): Low levels of satisfaction in a country's commitment to democracy. Indeed, and perhaps most surprising, more 'mature' democracies like Sweden and Germany are barely above 50 per cent in agreement. This means that, if we take the larger sociological view of the origins of conspiracy thinking, we have good reason to think that the potential pool of 'conspiracy theorists' is quite high: Nearly half of a country's citizens may, through their dissatisfaction with the democracy in place, be prone to conspiracy theorising in some form, regardless of other factors.

To further focus on attitudinal explanations for conspiracy thinking, the second item of Table 3.1.1 shows the extent to which respondents agreed with the statement: 'The system is broken and it would take a total change of system to put things right.' The lowest level of agreement is Germany at 24 per cent, the average is 36 per cent and the highest is from Italy at 59 per cent. In short, if the belief that radical political interventions are needed is a component of conspiracy theorising, then a little over a third of the population are susceptible.

While the sociological factors help us frame our understanding, we should not overemphasise them. Dissatisfaction with the government may be linked to conspiracy theorising and, what we have investigated here shows us with the broadest brush, is that we have reason to think that the ceiling of conspiracy theorising – or the percentage of potential conspiracy theorists in a given country – is on average one-third, but varies across countries.

Moving down Table 3.1.1, respondents were asked the extent to which they agreed with statements that would indicate conspiracy thinking (items 3–5). Much like the broader sociological questions we analysed earlier, sometimes conspiracy theorising is less about any *particular* conspiracy theory and more about a general predisposition: These statements attempt to measure the latent trait that help conspiracy theorists 'connect the dots'.

The first (item 3) asks individuals the extent to which they agree that, 'Even though we live in what's called a democracy, a few people will always run things in this country anyway.' This matches with one of the more common, yet important, conspiracy psychology building blocks: A sense of powerlessness, alienation, that things are not what they seem and that there is an inevitable consolidation of political power, regardless of what is done or said. The notion of

Table 3.1.1 Agreement with conspiratorial statements, by country.

| Category | Statement | Argentina (%) | Germany (%) | Great Britain (%) | Italy (%) | Poland (%) | Portugal (%) | Sweden (%) | Item |
|---|---|---|---|---|---|---|---|---|---|
| Anti-democratic beliefs | Democratic country | 63 | 51 | 47 | 38 | 31 | 53 | 57 | 1 |
|  | Major changes needed | 28 | 24 | 26 | 59 | 38 | 47 | 31 | 2 |
| General conspiracy statements | Elite control | 68 | 51 | 51 | 60 | 49 | 71 | 33 | 3 |
|  | Global elites | 31 | 23 | 13 | 39 | 27 | 47 | 10 | 4 |
|  | Secret plots | 25 | 7 | 7 | 17 | 31 | 29 | 7 | 5 |
| Specific conspiracy theories | U.F.O. contact | 25 | 6 | 9 | 11 | 8 | 11 | 6 | 6 |
|  | A.I.D.S. created | 20 | 6 | 4 | 8 | 8 | 8 | 2 | 7 |
|  | Global warming hoax | 7 | 8 | 9 | 7 | 17 | 5 | 7 | 8 |
|  | Hiding immigrants | 20 | 42 | 41 | 29 | 20 | 16 | 31 | 9 |
|  | Holocaust denial | 4 | – | 2 | 4 | 7 | 3 | 1 | 10 |

elites coopting the democratic system is a hallmark of most conspiracy theories. There is generally overwhelming agreement, with the exception of Sweden (at only 33 per cent). Most countries have at least half of their population in agreement, which puts the ceiling of potential conspiracy theorists much higher than what we saw earlier. It also tempers the sociological findings somewhat, since belief that you are not in a democracy is different than a belief that democracy is itself a necessary sham.

Respondents were then asked if they agreed that, 'Regardless of who is officially in charge of governments and other organizations, there is a single group of people who secretly control events and rule the world together.' This question pushes their general conspiracy beliefs farther: Not only is democracy a sham, but perhaps even the idea of individual governments of any kind is too. Responses across countries are significantly varied, and range from ten to nearly 50 per cent. Like in many other instances, this belief may itself be a function of political and historical context that researchers have yet to capture (Atari et al. 2019). For example, perhaps some citizens of countries in the E.U. feel that this question matches their sentiment toward the E.U. quite well. Or, perhaps, the power dynamics in South America explain Argentina's agreement levels. Regardless, these levels of agreement represent the building blocks for many particular conspiracy beliefs.

Now we arrive at perhaps the most explicit question about general conspiracy thinking: 'Secret plots that harm the nation are more common in this country than in other countries.' While it does not ask about any particular conspiracy theory, it does solicit a general feeling for how frequently conspiracies and other secret plots happen in their country, relative to others. Again, we find wide variation across countries. On the high end are Poland and Portugal; at the low end are Germany, Great Britain and Sweden. It may be that more mature and better functioning democracies provide citizens with lower expectations of a conspiracy being perpetrated on them from within. However, more research is needed to tease apart these cultural differences.

Moving onto specific conspiracy beliefs (items 6–10), we preface by saying that there are a number of issues with surveying conspiracy beliefs across contexts, chief among these is selection, i.e. which conspiracy theories to measure or not. Conspiracy theories vary in popularity across contexts, so measuring the 'right' or representative ones (if such things exist) becomes very difficult. Nonetheless, we report levels of belief in five specific conspiracy theories. The first is that humans have made contact with aliens and that this is being hidden from the public. While this conspiracy theory is ubiquitous in popular culture, it is not popular in most of the countries surveyed. Nearly 25 per cent of Argentinians believe this, compared to around 9 per cent in the other counties. For comparison, surveys in the U.S.A. show that around 20 per cent of Americans believe this (Jensen 2013). In the U.S.A., alien-government conspiracy theories have been a trope in popular culture since the 1940s, but cultural research is needed to explain why they are popular in Argentina.

Next, respondents were asked the extent to which they agreed that 'the AIDS virus was created and spread around the world on purpose by a secret group or organization'. The rate of belief across countries is mostly low, again with the exception of Argentina, where one-in-five believe that there is a secret organisation that spread the A.I.D.S. virus. Coupled with their belief in alien cover-ups, there may be something about Argentina's political culture that drives them to believe these theories. In the U.S.A., 32 per cent have heard of, and 12 per cent agree with, a more specific theory that 'the CIA deliberately infected large numbers of African Americans with HIV under the guise of a hepatitis inoculation program' (Oliver, Wood 2014b). In South Africa, where elites have suggested that the A.I.D.S. epidemic is a hoax and that H.I.V. can be cured with vitamins and massage (Nattrass 2012), researchers asked adolescents to identify the origins of the H.I.V. virus; nearly one-third believed a conspiracy theory about the origins of H.I.V. (Hogg et al. 2017). This suggests, again, that cultural factors drive specific conspiracy beliefs.

As mentioned, one issue with using specific conspiracy theories to denote who the conspiracy theorists are is that those beliefs may be driven by a range of factors. In the American context, partisan motivated reasoning may drive people to believe conspiracy theories that they might not otherwise accept. One of these, which has been championed by the Republican Party and carbon-emitting industries, is that global warming is a hoax (Uscinski et al. 2017). While studies show that belief in climate change conspiracy theories is influenced by conspiracy thinking (Lewandowsky 2018), partisanship appears to be a much larger influence on these beliefs (Marietta, Barker 2018). As Table 3.1.1 shows, we find low levels of belief that, 'the idea of man-made global warming is a hoax that was invented to deceive people' with the exception of Poland. Climate change conspiracy theories have been much more prominent in the U.S.A., where partisan elites have used climate change as a wedge issue (Merkley, Stecula 2018).

Let us now turn to fears of government malfeasance in the area of immigration. Such conspiracy theories are timely and common in many of these countries (Gaston, Uscinski 2018), and also driven by conspiracy theories about outgroups and by partisan elites. Respondents were asked to agree with the statement that, 'The government is deliberately hiding the truth about how many immigrants live in this country.' The question, for example, was a primary contention of Brexit voters in the 2016 E.U. referendum (Swami et al. 2018). Indeed, even scepticism of water fluoridation has often been linked to an underlying euroscepticism (Griffin et al. 2008).

The immigration conspiracy theory garners higher levels of agreement. Indeed, in some countries – particularly those with considerable immigration or talks about immigration, like Germany and Great Britain – belief in this conspiracy theory rises to 40 per cent. Even 30 per cent of Swedes believe this. This provides evidence that, when even minimally mixed with a salient political issue, the ceiling for conspiracy belief is relatively high. When Americans are asked as similar question, if they believe that the government is hiding the true cost of immigration from taxpayers, 55 per cent agree (Gaston, Uscinski 2018).

Finally, unlike the other conspiracy theories discussed here, Holocaust denial theories are both politically charged and have a strong negative valence. Therefore, they are a conservative estimate of conspiracy theorising. The question (not asked in Germany) asks if respondents agree that 'The official account of the Nazi Holocaust is a lie and the number of Jews killed by the Nazis during World War II has been exaggerated on purpose.' There are considerably lower levels of agreement than with the other conspiracy theories – not a single country reaches double digits. However, there are two things to point out. On the one hand, that Poland is by far the most likely to believe in this conspiracy, there are bound to be long historical and structural reasons for this (Soral et al. 2018), i.e. when examining conspiracy beliefs, idiosyncratic findings may be due to some systematic, though omitted, variable. On the other hand, given that there is some level of agreement, albeit low, across all countries, we should like to think of this question as the *floor* of conspiracy thinking. Previously, we have discussed specific conspiracy theory beliefs as the ceiling of belief. Presumably, conspiracy theorists cannot outnumber those that actually believe conspiracy theories. However, given the presumed social desirability bias that pushes down response rates to this question about the Holocaust, we assume that this is the lower limit.

We should also note that specific conspiracy theories that reference Jews either explicitly or implicitly capture an aspect of conspiracy thinking directly related to antisemitism. For example, in places like Turkey and Poland, conspiracy beliefs are high when specific conspiracy theories referencing Jews are included (Bilewicz et al. 2013, Nefes 2013). Holocaust denialism is a prime example of the cultural differences between countries explaining conspiracy beliefs. Argentina's particular form of democratisation may play a role in its conspiracy theorising, and perhaps Poland's experience with Germany has produced a culture where Holocaust denial is more acceptable. And, less abstractly, the current debates about immigration happening across the world certainly influences the level of conspiracy beliefs at a given time.

## Conspiracy theories and ideology

One of the most important political predispositions is ideology in many Western countries. Here, we provide the ideological breakdown of those who agreed that there are secret plots. The correlation between ideology and this conspiratorial view is important to showing how left-right ideologies mediate the effect of historical and political contexts on conspiracy theorising. What is the relationship between left- and right-wing ideologies and general conspiracy thinking across countries?

For each country in Figure 3.1.1, there are three bars: the average agreement for 'left wing' and 'left of center' (Left), 'centre' (Centre) and the average agreement for 'right wing' and 'right of centre' (Right). There is mixed evidence for the relationship between ideology and belief in secret plots. Poland, Portugal, Argentina and Italy show a U-shape consistent with some studies (van Prooijen et al. 2015), Great Britain shows a flat distribution consistent with some studies (Uscinski, Parent 2014), and Sweden and Germany show that the right-wingers are more conspiracy-minded consistent with other studies (Berlet 2012). Nonetheless, these distributions raise further questions about political dynamics within countries.

Figure 3.1.2 shows the distribution of affirmative responses to the general and specific conspiracy statements (items 3–10). The way to read it is *at least one statement is true, at least three statements are true, and at least seven statements are true.* For example, in Argentina, nearly 93 per cent of the sample agreed with *at least* one statement, about 54 per cent with *at least* three statements and about 5 per cent with *at least* seven (out of eight) statements. The data tell an overwhelming story. Regardless if it is a specific conspiracy theory or a general one, and with exception of Sweden, nearly 80 to 90 per cent of each of our countries believe at least one statement to be true.

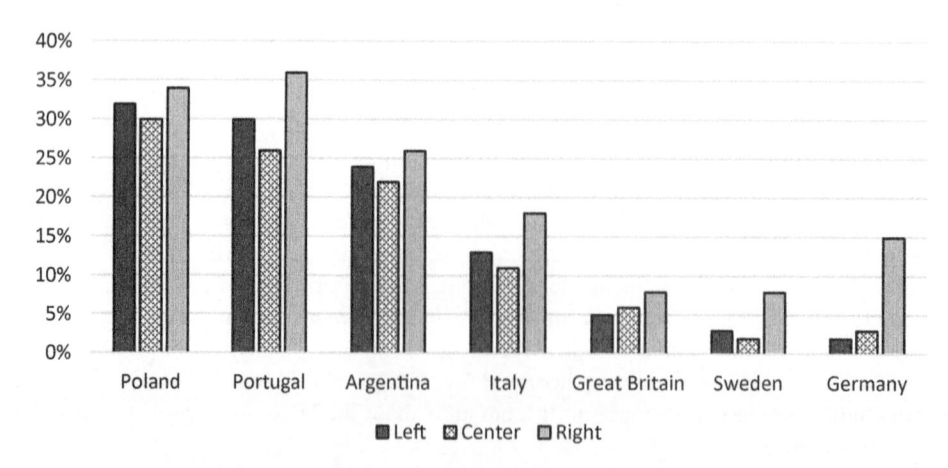

*Figure 3.1.1* Proportion of respondents who believe in secret plots by their self-identified ideology, by country. (Left = average of 'left wing' and 'left of centre'; Centre = 'centre'; Right = average of 'right of centre' and 'right wing'.

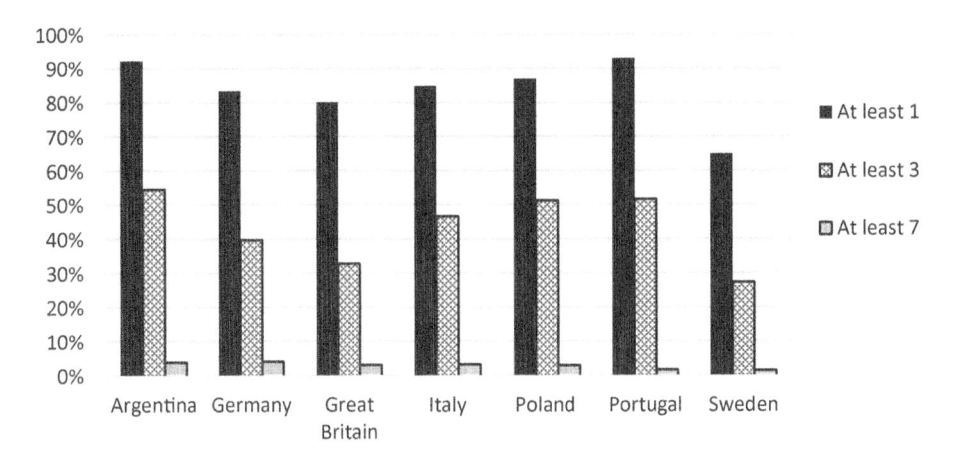

*Figure 3.1.2* Proportion of the respondents, by country, that believed in the eight conspiracy statements (*Germany's total is only out of 7 statements, since the Holocaust question was not asked).

In short, if we want to define a 'conspiracy theorist' as someone who believes at least one of the eight conspiratorial statements (three general conspiratorial statements, five specific conspiracy theories), then anywhere from 60 to 90 per cent of each country is a conspiracy theorist, depending on the country!

## Conspiracy theories outside of W.E.I.R.D. countries

So-called 'WEIRD' countries are those that are wealthy, educated, industrialised, rich and democratic (Henrich *et al.* 2010), and most people in the world are not 'WEIRD'. So, this may cast some doubt on the generalisability of our discussion above on who is or is not a conspiracy theorist. Reliable survey data is difficult to obtain outside of these countries. However, there are some studies that have obtained valuable data. For example, one study that focused on Chile, Uruguay, El Salvador, Mexico, South Africa, Spain and Portugal, the decline in trust – particularly in the legitimacy of the political system, a major component to general conspiracy ideation – is prevalent (Carlin, Love 2018). In Venezuela, researchers found nearly 54 per cent of the country believed in at least one conspiracy narrative (Carey 2017). But, we should note, that while there is mounting evidence globally that conspiracy thinking is prevalent, there may be some measurement biases for instruments that are developed largely in W.E.I.R.D. countries and applied elsewhere. In a study on a Turkish population, Atari *et al.* (2019) found that the three big general conspiracy thinking measures were only weakly related to the conspiracy beliefs in Turkey. This is not to say that they did not find a 'conspiracy dimension' – they did – it was just different from the scales validated by samples from W.E.I.R.D. countries. More research is needed to investigate the possibility of a *global* conspiracy dimension, so we can see who the conspiracy theorists are, accounting for cultural differences.

## Conclusion

Studying conspiracy theories is important for understanding contemporary political life. Much of the theorising of who counts as a conspiracy theorist has taken place in the U.S.A. and other English-speaking areas. This is not to diminish that research, but in fact to expand it to a global context. From what we have outlined above, we can cautiously answer the question who is a 'conspiracy theorist'. Conspiracy theorising is prevalent – most people believe at least one conspiracy theory, even in surveys that ask only about a few. Conspiracy thinking is more apparent in the marginalised – or those who think of themselves that way – populations. We do see a general correlation between conspiracy thinking and people who distrust their government. Conspiracy thinking is a worldview that often escapes any single socio-demographic categorisation, largely because it is so common even across cultural contexts.

One potential avenue of research would be to explain domestic conspiracy culture in light of international political dynamics. This is an avenue not readily available to American audiences, but absolutely integral for understanding conspiracy thinking in much more integrated, international areas – like the E.U. and South America. Additionally, how does (de)democratisation influence the conspiracy culture of a country? Is there an absolute level at which conspiracy thinking becomes so saturated that the larger political culture collapses? The mature democracies like Germany and Britain, which are constantly worried about the rise of populist, right-wing authoritarianism, have far lower levels of conspiracy thinking – even in the right-wing – than the moderates in other countries. Is the problem the relative difference between domestic partisans? Unlike in the U.S.A. where national surveys and polls that contain conspiracy questions are more frequent, outside of the U.S.A. there is no reliable longitudinal data to help us assess any potential increases or decreases in the level of conspiracy thinking. Future research should fill this gap by having repeated surveys with identical questions administered across many countries over a significant period of time.

A second potential area of research is to examine the peculiarities of Sweden a bit closer. For many, 'correcting' conspiracy beliefs is normatively important. And, considering that unlike all the other countries in our sample, Sweden's rate of disbelieving all of the conspiratorial statements in our sample is nearly 40 per cent of their public. Considering the next best is Great Britain at 20 per cent, we could look at the larger political culture and context to understand why conspiracy theories do not seemingly take root in Sweden. A further study of additional countries could tell us if Sweden is indeed an outlier.

Regardless of the precise next steps, the comparative analysis of conspiracy beliefs – which we hope to have contributed to with this paper – is itself the next leap for conspiracy theory research. But, before we can make that leap, we need to constantly remind ourselves that our definitions and operationalisations – even the key ones of 'conspiracy theory' and 'conspiracy theorist' – must be scrutinised. We should not focus too heavily on large sociological factors, like the simple dissatisfaction in democracy; nor should we go too far in the other direction and define conspiracy theories so narrowly that they are not helpful and almost trivial, nor should we define a conspiracy theorist as simply those that believe these overly-narrow conspiracy theories. Instead, as we have tried to show, as conspiracy research moves into unfamiliar terrain, we should be vigilant that we are adapting to our surroundings without losing sight of the larger global and scientific enterprise.

# References

Atari, M., Afhami, R. and Swami, V. (2019) 'Psychometric assessments of Persian translations of three measures of conspiracist beliefs', *Plos One*, 14(4): e0215202.

Berlet, C. (2012) 'Collectivists, communists, labor bosses, and treason: the Tea Parties as right-wing populist counter Subversion panic', *Critical Sociology*, 38(4): 565–87.

Bilewicz, M. and Krzeminski, I. (2010) 'Anti-semitism in Poland and Ukraine: the belief in Jewish control as a mechanism of scapegoating', *International Journal of Conflict and Violence*, 4(2): 234–43.

Bilewicz, M., Winiewski, M., Kofta, M. and Wójcik, A. (2013) 'Harmful ideas, the structure and consequences of anti-semitic beliefs in Poland', *Political Psychology*, 34(6): 821–39.

Brotherton, R., French, C.C. and Pickering, A.D. (2013) 'Measuring belief in conspiracy theories: the generic conspiracist beliefs scale', *Frontiers in Psychology*, 4: 279.
Carey, J.M. (2017) 'Who believes in conspiracy theories in Venezuela?', *Latin American Research Review*, 54(2): 444–57.
Carlin, R.E. and Love, G.J. (2018) 'Political competition, partisanship and interpersonal trust in electoral democracies', *British Journal of Political Science*, 48(1): 115–39.
Cassino, D. and Jenkins, K. (2013) 'Conspiracy theories prosper: 25% of Americans are "Truthers"', *Fairleigh Dickinson University's Public Mind Poll*, 17 January. Available at: http://publicmind.fdu.edu/2013/outthere. [Accessed 15 June 2019.]
Drochon, H. (2018) 'Who believes in conspiracy theories in Great Britain and Europe?', in J.E. Uscinski (ed.) *Conspiracy theories and the people who believe them*, New York: Oxford University Press.
Dyer, K.D. and Hall, R.E. (2019) 'Effect of critical thinking education on epistemically unwarranted beliefs in college students', *Research in Higher Education*, 60(4): 293–314.
Enders, A.M. and Smallpage, S.M. (2018) 'Polls, plots, and party politics: conspiracy theories in contemporary America', in J.E. Uscinski (ed.) *Conspiracy theories and the people who believe them*, New York: Oxford University Press.
Enders, A.M., Smallpage, S.M. and Lupton, R.N. (2018) 'Are all "Birthers" conspiracy theorists? On the relationship between conspiratorial thinking and political orientations', *British Journal of Political Science*, 1–18.
Farrakhan, L. and Gates, H.L., Jr. (1996) 'Farrakhan speaks: a conversation with Louis Farrakhan', *Transition*, 70: 140–67.
Gaston, S. and Uscinski, J.E. (2018) *Out of the shadows: conspiracy thinking on immigration*, London: The Henry Jackson Society. Available at: https://henryjacksonsociety.org/wp-content/uploads/2018/12/Out-of-the-Shadows-Conspiracy-thinking-on-immigration.pdf. [Accessed 30 August 2019.]
Goertzel, T. (1994) 'Belief in conspiracy theories', *Political Psychology*, 15(4): 733–44.
Griffin, M., Shickle, D. and Moran, N. (2008) 'European citizens' opinions on water fluoridation', *Community Dentistry and Oral Epidemiology*, 36(2): 95–102.
Guess, A., Nagler, J. and Tucker, J. (2019) 'Less than you think: prevalence and predictors of fake news dissemination on Facebook', *Science Advances*, 5(1): eaau4586.
Henrich, J., Heine, S.J. and Norenzayan, A. (2010) 'Most people are not WEIRD', *Nature*, 466(7302): 29.
Hofstadter, R. (1964) *The paranoid style in American politics, and other essays*, Cambridge: Harvard University Press.
Hogg, R., Nkala, B., Dietrich, J., Collins, A., Closson, K., Cui, Z., Kanters, S., Chia, J., Barhafuma, B., Palmer, A., Kaida, A., Gray, G. and Miller, C. (2017) 'Conspiracy beliefs and knowledge about HIV origins among adolescents in Soweto, South Africa', *Plos One*, 12(2): e0165087.
Imhoff, R. and Bruder, M. (2013) 'Speaking (un-)truth to power: conspiracy mentality as a generalised political attitude', *European Journal of Personality*, 28(1): 25–43.
Jensen, T. (2013) 'Democrats and republicans differ on conspiracy theory beliefs', *Public Policy Polling*, 2 April. Available at: www.publicpolicypolling.com/polls/democrats-and-republicans-differ-on-conspiracy-theory-beliefs. [Accessed 12 August 2019.]
Klofstad, C., Uscinski, J.E., Connolly, J. and West, J. (2019) 'What drives people to believe in Zika conspiracy theories?', *Palgrave Communications*, 5(36): 1–8.
Knight, P. (2002) 'Introduction: a nation of conspiracy theorists', in P. Knight (ed.) *Conspiracy nation: the politics of paranoia in postwar America*, New York: New York University Press, pp. 1–20.
Krouwel, A., Kutiyski, Y., van Prooijen, J.-W., Martinsson, J. and Markstedt, E. (2017) 'Does extreme political ideology predict conspiracy beliefs, economic evaluations and political trust?', *Evidence From Sweden. Journal of Social and Political Psychology*, 5(2): 435–62.
Levitsky, S. and Ziblatt, D. (2018) *How democracies die*, New York: Crown Publishing.
Levy, N. (2007) 'Radically socialized knowledge and conspiracy theories', *Episteme*, 4(2): 181–92.
Lewandowsky, S. (2018) 'In whose hands the future?', in J.E. Uscinski (ed.) *Conspiracy theories and the people who believe them*, New York: Oxford University Press.
Marietta, M. and Barker, D.C. (2018) 'Conspiratorial thinking and polarized fact perceptions', in J.E. Uscinski (ed.) *Conspiracy theories and the people who believe them*, New York: Oxford University Press.
Merkley, E. and Stecula, D.A. (2018) 'Party elites or manufactured doubt? The informational context of climate change polarization', *Science Communication*, 40(2): 258–74.
Miller, J.M. and Saunders, K.L. (2016) 'Conspiracy theories in the United States: more commonplace than extraordinary', *Critical Review*, 28(1): 127–36.

Miller, J.M., Saunders, K.L. and Farhart, C.E. (2016) 'Conspiracy endorsement as motivated reasoning: the moderating roles of political knowledge and trust', *American Journal of Political Science*, 60(4): 824–44.

Nattrass, N. (2012) 'How bad ideas gain social traction', *The Lancet*, 380(9839): 332–3.

Nefes, T.S. (2013) 'Political parties' perceptions and uses of anti-semitic conspiracy theories in Turkey', *The Sociological Review*, 61(2): 247–64.

Newheiser, A.-K., Farias, M. and Tausch, N. (2011) 'The functional nature of conspiracy beliefs: examining the underpinnings of belief in the Da Vinci Code conspiracy', *Personality and Individual Differences*, 51(8): 1007–11.

Nyhan, B. (2009) '9/11 and birther misperceptions compared', *Brendan-nyhan.com*, 10 August. Available at: www.brendan-nyhan.com/blog/2009/08/911-and-birther-misperceptions-compared.html. [Accessed 31 August 2019.]

Nyhan, B. and Zeitzoff, T. (2018) 'Conspiracy and misperception belief in the Middle East and North Africa', *The Journal of Politics*, 80(4): 1400–4.

Oliver, E. and Wood, T. (2014a) 'Conspiracy theories and the paranoid style(s) of mass opinion', *American Journal of Political Science*, 58(4): 952–66.

Oliver, E. and Wood, T. (2014b) 'Medical conspiracy theories and health behaviors in the United States', *JAMA Internal Medicine*, 174(5): 817–8.

Orr, M. and Husting, G. (2018) 'Media marginalization of racial minorities: "conspiracy theorists" in U.S. ghettos and on the "Arab Street"', in J.E. Uscinski (ed.) *Conspiracy theories and the people who believe them*, New York: Oxford University Press.

Robertson, D.G. and Dyrendal, A. (2018) 'Conspiracy theories and religion: superstition, seekership, and salvation', in J.E. Uscinski (ed.) *Conspiracy theories and the people who believe them*, New York: Oxford University Press.

Smallpage, S.M. (2018) 'Conspiracy thinking, tolerance, and democracy', in J.E. Uscinski (ed.) *Conspiracy theories and the people who believe them*, New York: Oxford University Press.

Smallpage, S.M., Enders, A.M. and Uscinski, J.E. (2017) 'The partisan contours of conspiracy theory beliefs', *Research & Politics*, 4(4): 2053168017746554.

Soral, W., Cichocka, A., Bilewicz, M. and Marchlewska, M. (2018) 'The collective conspiracy mentality in Poland', in J.E. Uscinski (ed.) *Conspiracy theories and the people who believe them*, New York: Oxford University Press.

Swami, V., Barron, D., Weis, L. and Furnham, A. (2018) 'To Brexit or not to Brexit: the roles of islamophobia, conspiracist beliefs, and integrated threat in voting intentions for the United Kingdom European Union membership referendum', *British Journal of Psychology*, 109(1): 156–79.

Swami, V., Barron, D., Weis, L., Voracek, M., Stieger, S. and Furnham, A. (2017) 'An examination of the factorial and convergent validity of four measures of conspiracist ideation, with recommendations for researchers', *Plos One*, 12: e0172617.

Thomas, S.B. and Quinn, S.C. (1991) 'The Tuskegee syphilis study, 1932 to 1972: implications for HIV education and AIDS risk education programs in the black community', *American Journal of Public Health*, 81(11): 1498–1505.

Tingley, D. and Wagner, G. (2017) 'Solar geoengineering and the chemtrails conspiracy on social media', *Palgrave Communications*, 3(12).

Uscinski, J.E. (2018) 'Down the rabbit hole we go!', in J.E. Uscinski (ed.) *Conspiracy theories and the people who believe them*, New York: Oxford University Press.

Uscinski, J.E., Douglas, K. and Lewandowsky, S. (2017) 'Climate change conspiracy theories', in H. von Storch (ed.) *Oxford Research Encyclopedia of Climate Science*. Available at: https://oxfordre.com/climatescience/view/10.1093/acrefore/9780190228620.001.0001/acrefore-9780190228620-e-328. [Accessed 31 August 2019.]

Uscinski, J.E. and Klofstad, C. (2018) 'Commentary: Florida believes in conspiracy theories too', *Orlando Sentinel*, 6 September. Available at: www.orlandosentinel.com/opinion/os-op-florida-conspiracy-theories-20180906-story.html. [Accessed 31 August 2019.] Not accessible in European countries at the moment.

Uscinski, J.E., Klofstad, C. and Atkinson, M. (2016) 'What drives conspiratorial beliefs? The role of informational cues and predispositions', *Political Research Quarterly*, 69(1): 57–71.

Uscinski, J.E. and Parent, J.M. (2014) *American Conspiracy Theories*, New York: Oxford University Press.

Van Prooijen, J.-W. (2017) 'Why education predicts decreased belief in conspiracy theories', *Applied Cognitive Psychology*, 31(1): 50–8.

Van Prooijen, J.-W., Douglas, K.M. and De Inocencio, C. (2018) 'Connecting the dots: illusory pattern perception predicts belief in conspiracies and the supernatural', *European Journal of Social Psychology*, 48(3): 320–35.

Van Prooijen, J.-W., Krouwel, A.P.M. and Pollet, T.V. (2015) 'Political extremism predicts belief in conspiracy theories', *Social Psychological and Personality Science*, 6(5): 570–8.

Walker, J. (2018) 'What we mean when we say "conspiracy theory"', in J.E. Uscinski (ed.) *Conspiracy theories and the people who believe them*, New York: Oxford University Press.

# 3.2
# CONSPIRACY THEORY ENTREPRENEURS, MOVEMENTS AND INDIVIDUALS

*Jaron Harambam*

### Introduction

Conspiracy theories – explanations of social phenomena involving the covert actions of certain people – are everywhere today. From narratives about alien invaders and government cover-ups in Hollywood productions to widespread popular suspicions about the hidden workings of mainstream societal institutions like science, media and politics, conspiracy theories have in recent decades become a massive and mainstream cultural phenomenon. They are for many people nowadays an increasingly normalised idiom to account for what *really* happens out there, whether we speak about natural disasters, terrorist attacks or financial crises. However, despite this apparent popularisation of conspiracy theories, academic research on *who* actually endorses these alternative readings of reality is inconclusive and puts forward contradictory findings.

On the one hand, we are confronted with many versions of the stereotypical depiction of the conspiracy theorist as an obsessive, militant and fundamental paranoid who sees fire at all instances of smoke, and who poses considerable dangers to society by inciting distrust and hatred towards certain groups (elites, outsiders, Jews, etc.) (e.g. Pipes 1997; Barkun 2006; Byford 2011). While conspiracy theories may have once been a legitimate and widespread response to historical events (e.g. Wood 1982; Butter 2014), various historians, social theorists and political scientists began to identify conspiracy theories since the mid-twentieth century as a problematic form of knowledge, and consequently stigmatise the people who held such ideas as pathological (see Bratich 2008; Fenster 2008; deHaven-Smith 2013; Thalmann 2019).

On the other hand, there is a growing academic recognition that this pathology frame is problematic for both theoretical and empirical reasons. Many scholars have, since the end of the 1990s, argued that conspiracy theories may not be that irrational in the complex globalised world of today, and that the framing of conspiracy theorists as paranoid loonies may actually be irrational in itself (e.g. Knight 2000; Birchall 2006; Coady 2006; Bratich 2008; Harambam 2017). Such scholars bring up the valid point that when so many people from so many different corners of society, even from 'science' itself, practice some form of conspiracy theorising, it is hard to maintain that conspiracy theorists are the lunatic fringe. Large quantitative studies similarly show that conspiracy theorists are found across various different demographic categories, such as age, gender, ideological conviction, religion, income, education and ethnicity (Oliver, Wood 2014; Uscinski, Parent 2014). But, as Smallpage *et al.* (see Chapter 3.1) show, there is fundamental disagreement about what constitutes a conspiracy theorist, and consequently much variety in the way scholars define and measure conspiracy theorists, leading to very different outcomes.

But, when everybody is a conspiracy theorist sometimes, can we still say something about the people engaging with them? Just as the common pathological stereotype obscures the wide variety of people following the alternative readings of reality generally called conspiracy theories, does not stating that there is a conspiracy theorist in all of us similarly prevent us from saying anything meaningful about these people? Or is there still something particular to say about conspiracy theorists and, if so, who gets to do that and how should that be done? Obviously, this points to the inherent power dynamics involved in describing some form of knowledge as conspiracy theory, and some sort of people as conspiracy theorists (cf. Husting, Orr 2007; Bratich 2008; Pelkmans, Machold 2011; Harambam, Aupers 2015). While I am sensitive to the politics and power of language, i.e. using these terms without any reflexivity simply reproduces the stigmatised connotations they have, I have nonetheless chosen to continue to use these terms in this chapter for reasons of clarity and aesthetics. This is not ideal, but nor are the alternatives. Perhaps the descriptive and non-pejorative usage of these terms neutralises or lessens the negative connotations they have.

Whereas Smallpage et al. (see Chapter 3.1) show what quantitative studies can say about conspiracy theorists, in this chapter I will review how qualitative studies, in all their disciplinary and historical variety, depict these people. Starting with a brief overview of the traditional, pathologicalising views on conspiracy theorists, I will work my way through the cultural studies from the 1990s onwards that de-pathologised conspiracy theorists but hardly engaged with them, to more contemporary examples of scholars who in their empirical work interact more directly with conspiracy theorists, in order to shed light on their ideas and practices. I will conclude with a short reflection on what a good qualitative study of conspiracy culture entails and yields.

## Academic work on conspiracy theorists

While conspiracy theories seem to emerge in all historical periods (e.g. Pipes 1997; Roisman 2006), widespread scholarly interest in the phenomenon is of a more recent nature. Most scholars locate the origins in the works of Sir Karl Popper (2013 [1945]), who actually coined the concept of 'conspiracy theory', and Richard Hofstadter (1996 [1964]), who popularised the theme in both academic and popular discourses. But there are good reasons to argue that several other scholars have contributed to academic knowledge on this subject matter since the 1930s onwards as well. Michael Butter and Peter Knight (2019) point, for example, to the works of Harold Lasswell and Theodor Adorno, who blamed the conspiratorial thought of authoritarian leaders for the rise of totalitarianism all over Europe, and to sociologists Leo Loewenthal and Norbert Guterman, who related conspiratorial thought to the complexities of modernisation processes. Mark Fenster (2008) situates the work of Hofstadter in a broader academic climate of consensus politics propagated by scholars such as Edward Shils, Seymour Martin Lipset and Earl Raab, who all saw conspiratorial thought as extremist threats to a well-functioning democracy. Lance deHaven-Smith describes in full detail the position and works of Leo Strauss and Karl Popper as major influences in discrediting conspiracy theories as legitimate explanations in the social sciences, and juxtaposes that with Charles A. Beard, a U.S. historian who actually entertained many such assumptions (2013: 76–105). With the exception of the latter, all of these scholars regarded conspiracy theories and their proponents to be highly irrational and dangerous aspects of modern societies, that played a large part in the twentieth-century surge of totalitarianism.

These seminal works greatly influenced subsequent research by making conspiracy theorists epistemologically, psychologically and morally suspect (e.g. Pipes 1997; Robins, Post 1997; Keeley 1999; Barkun 2006; Berlet 2009; Sunstein, Vermeule 2009; Byford 2011). Most of these scholars take a historical approach and study the books, articles, pamphlets, videos and Internet sites, and/or secondary sources about various kinds of people designated as conspiracy theorists. These include both mainstream authoritarian leaders (e.g. Joseph Stalin, Adolf Hitler, Pol Pot, Idi Amin, Ayatollah Khomeini, but also Senator Joseph McCarthy and President Richard Nixon) (Robins, Post 1997; Pipes 1997), and more fringe individuals, often writers or leaders of cults and sectarian movements, like Nesta Webster, Lady Queensborough, Pat Robertson, William Milton Cooper, Jim Keith and so on (Barkun 2006; Byford 2011). Very briefly put, such scholars make three interrelated points (see Harambam 2017: 11–22). Following Popper, conspiracy theorists are first depicted as 'bad scientists': They reduce complex phenomena to simple explanations, make flawed use of evidence, selectively look for confirmation instead of falsification, are resistant to contrary evidence and envision a universe governed by design instead of randomness. Following Hofstadter, they are second depicted as 'paranoids': Conspiracy theorists have systematised, delusional fears of conspiracy and deceit, and cast the world rather unproductively in apocalyptic battles between absolute good and absolute evil. Going against the political virtues of moderation, deliberation and consensus, conspiracy theorists are militant leaders with whom no compromise is possible. Because of these characteristics, such scholars warn against the lure of conspiracy theorists as they seriously threaten the health and functioning of democratic societies by promoting demonisation, scapegoating, cultural conflicts, political extremism, radicalisation, violence, terrorism and more. Based on a *pars pro toto* reasoning (the part is taken for the whole), they argue that because *some* disturbed extremists hold conspiracy theories dear, *all* conspiracy theorists must be disturbed and dangerously extremist as well. While such analyses may apply well to these very extreme figures, they actually say very little about the broader population of people adhering to conspiracy theories.

Not satisfied with such psychopathological understandings of conspiracy theorists, another line of scholars argued instead to take a more detached stance, and study why conspiracy theories have become such a broad societal phenomenon (Dean 1998; Fenster 1999; Knight 2000; Melley 2000; Birchall 2006). This requires, according to them, moving from condemning conspiracy theorists towards understanding them, and from debunking conspiracy theories towards exploring their meaning for those involved. Mostly coming from the field of cultural studies, such scholars dissect and analyse the many cultural forms in which the themes of paranoia and conspiracy theory surface in Western societies: From alien abduction stories to major Hollywood movies, and from rap music that discusses life in the *hood*, to highbrow tales of Kafkaesque bureaucratic entrapment in post-war literature. Deploying a discourse of conspiracy is, according to these scholars, a broad, cultural attempt to grapple with the complexities, anxieties and inequalities induced by large-scale social developments (globalisation, mediatisation, technocratisation, corporatisation) and the autonomous workings of opaque systems (bureaucracies, capitalist systems, mass-communication technologies). The idea of conspiracy offers an odd sort of comfort: It makes sense of unexplainable, complex events and opaque structures, and may therefore be actually quite reasonable, they argue. This rings especially true for those living in less laudable circumstances, and/or those that have endured systemic oppression, like African-American communities (Knight 2000: 143–67) and women more generally (see Chapter 3.3). But as conspiracy theories are all explained with a lingering functionalism of dealing with such complexities, these scholars similarly portray conspiracy theorists as a more or less homogenous group: The paranoid is all too easily exchanged for the anomic or the disenfranchised. Moreover, their sole reliance on conspiracy *texts* (books, films, social theory, music lyrics, newspapers, urban legends, television series, etc.) makes it difficult to hear conspiracy theorists, whoever that may be, themselves speak. What are *their* concerns, ideas, desires, doubts, fears, hopes, biographies, conflicts, practices, social lives and more, in all the variety that we expect from such a colourful group of people? These matters of identity appear elusive with such a methodological approach.

In recent years, there have been more and more studies by political scientists and psychologists who examine the demographic characteristics and personality traits of those endorsing conspiracy theories (see Chapter 3.1). These quantitative studies go some way in explaining the diversity of conspiracy theorists, but all construct their own analytical categories (e.g. education, race, party affiliation, personality scales, conspiracist ideation, etc.) into which conspiracy theorists should fit. While such quantitative analyses may be informative to some, it can be questioned whether these deductive characteristics of conspiracy theorists are the most relevant, but more importantly, they are most likely not the way these people would characterise themselves. In the remainder of the chapter, I will draw on several more ethnographically oriented scholars to show how their approach made it possible to speak about (the wide variety of) people that could be considered conspiracy theorists. Either by specifically focusing on people's own self-understandings, or by merely following them doing their everyday things, concrete conceptions of how they see themselves emerge. The effort here is to bring such studies into the limelight, and to show what is (analytically) gained by studying 'identity' as emerging out of ever present and continuous interactions with meaningful others in various (mental, social, institutional, discursive) contexts (Jenkins 2014). I start by reviewing works that write about conspiracy theory entrepreneurs, then discuss those studying conspiracy theory movements and end with the more dispersed conspiracy theorists out there, but, as can be expected, these categories are not always mutually exclusive. Social movements sometimes have leaders that become entrepreneurs, and a variety of dispersed individuals may come together and form social movements around a certain issue over time. The following categorisation is therefore ideal-typical and used mostly for analytical and organisational purposes.

## Conspiracy theory entrepreneurs

When thinking about contemporary conspiracy theorists, two main figures always come to mind: Alex Jones and David Icke. These two *men* are by far the most famous, popular, ferocious, outspoken and visible conspiracy theorists of today and the last 20 years, and they frequently come up in any newspaper article or academic work about conspiracy theories. It is no exaggeration to say that they are true conspiracy theory *celebrities*: well-known, admired and reviled. Alex Jones is from Texas, U.S.A., and is most famous for his popular daily radio talk show (*The Alex Jones Show*), website (*www.infowars.com*), and the more than 30 documentaries that he produced. Often described as a right-wing libertarian extremist, Jones promotes via all these media his ideas of a coming enslavement of people in a state-corporate surveillance prison world advanced by a shadowy world elite composed of bankers, military leaders, industrialists and politicians, also known as *New World Order* conspiracy theories (e.g. Zaitchik 2011). Of particular notoriety are his ideas that the so-called mass-shootings sadly occurring in the U.S.A. (e.g. Sandy Hook, Las Vegas and Orlando) are hoaxes deployed by that shadowy elite to restrict gun ownership and that they are carried out with the help of 'crisis actors' purporting to be victims. These accusations even led to a lawsuit against him in 2019, and he got banned from most mainstream social media in 2018 for repeatedly violating their user policies.

David Icke is British, and is no less controversial or popular. Having been in media, sports and (local) politics, Icke developed himself as a prolific writer (he has published more than 20 books, translated in 12 different languages) and public speaker. He now holds performances in large venues all over the world (e.g. London's Wembley Stadium), attracting crowds of thousands, and runs a popular website with many videos and interviews, which maintains an active discussion platform (www.davidicke.com). He is most famous (or notorious) for his reptilian thesis: the idea that a shape-shifting race of extra-terrestrial reptilians secretly rules the world. In his earlier days, Icke flirted more openly with antisemitic ideas, most notably those present in *The Protocols of the Elders of Zion*, which continues to be a complex issue for most commentators today (e.g. Robertson 2016: 149–53). Perhaps in contrast to Jones, Icke proclaims the idea that the enslavement of humankind has already happened long ago. Both, however, arouse supporters by emphasising how they are all part of a global mass 'awakening' of people rising up against their alleged oppressors. In their tying up of many different smaller conspiracy theories in one master narrative, Jones's and Icke's ideas are perfect exemplars of what Michael Barkun called 'super conspiracy theories' (2006: 6). And, last, they can be seen as conspiracy theory *entrepreneurs*: Not only have they made a living out of spreading their conspiracy theories in both the off- and online worlds, their websites also have shops that sell, besides their own videos and books, many different products, mostly in the realm of alternative healing and food supplements.

This crossover between apocalyptic conspiracy theories about a coming totalitarian New World Order and messianic visions of global awakenings into a New Age (including associated spiritualities and healing methods) may seem counter-intuitive and antithetical, but actually characterises much of today's conspiracy culture (e.g. Barkun 2006; Ward, Voas 2011; Robertson 2016). Alex Jones is, for example, widely popular in various extreme right U.S. patriot/militia movements with whom he shares much anti-government thought (e.g. Jackson 2017), yet at the same time publishes many articles on natural healing methods and sells food supplements that are popular in the alternative healing scene. David Icke is even more confluent: His more mundane assertions of intrigue and deceit by global power elites in the realms of finance, politics and media are effortlessly blended with New Age spiritualities detailing alternative histories, lost civilisations and extraterrestrial life. This seemingly odd combination of two opposing cultural streams, tapping from distinct social milieus with distinct ideologies, called 'conspirituality' by Ward and Voas (2011) (see Asprem and Dyrendal 2015, for a critique), is widely discussed in the works of Barkun (2006), Harambam (2017) and Robertson (2016), and forms, according to them, precisely the appeal of these conspiracy theory entrepreneurs. While none of these scholars actually managed to directly engage with or interview Jones nor Icke, both Robertson and Harambam attended Icke's nine hour performance (in London and Amsterdam, respectively) and interacted with his audience. What they show is that Icke is able to convince his audience of his extraordinary super conspiracy because he is able to draw on multiple epistemic strategies or sources of legitimation (e.g. science, tradition, experience, supernatural, sci-fi) (cf. Robertson 2016: 45–53; Harambam 2017: 107–40). It is therefore not just a hybridity of cultures, people and ideologies, but also of *epistemology* that characterises these conspiracy theory entrepreneurs.

Another unlikely crossover of different cultural worlds involving these conspiracy theory entrepreneurs is noted by Travis L. Gosa, who studied the production and circulation of conspiracy theories in hip hop counterculture (2011). He regards hip hop culture as an alternative knowledge system challenging mainstream ideas and institutions, and conspiracy theories are an important part of explaining both the structural racial disparities and the everyday discriminations African American's face. It is therefore interesting, Gosa notes, that different rappers and rap groups have made alliances with a person as right-wing and reactionary as Alex Jones. Gosa points to rapper KRS-One who was sharing New World Order and 9/11 conspiracy theories on the Alex Jones Show in 2009; rap group Public Enemy that encourage fans to watch an *InfoWars* documentary about Barack Obama; and Peruvian American rapper Immortal Technique who performed with Alex Jones on the fifth anniversary of the 9/11 attacks when Jones lectured and screened his 9/11 film (Gosa 2011: 195). The conclusion that Gosa and the aforementioned scholars all draw is that the 'cultic milieu' (a term Colin Campbell uses to describes the 'cultural underground of society' [2002 (1972): 14]) in which conspiracy theories thrive is flexible or heterodox enough to accommodate opposed factions and strange bedfellows as they are all united in their opposition to the dominant cultural orthodoxies. And, as Matthew Hayes' historical genealogical study of the case of Canadian U.F.O. researcher Wilbert Smith shows, conspiracy theories do not just 'travel' across communities and ideologies, but also across time with the help of influential conspiracy theory entrepreneurs that pick up on older works and connect them in new ways to other audiences (2017).

Besides these well-known conspiracy theory entrepreneurs that are documented by many commentators, other less visible and popular ones are (also) brought under attention by the more ethnographic work of Harambam (2017) and Rakopoulos (2018). Delving into the Dutch 'conspiracy milieu', Harambam speaks, for example, about Marcel Messing (writer, speaker, teacher, performer and visionary) as a prominent and influential person in that subcultural world and leader of the collaborative project *WeAreAwakening* (see below). In his work and thought, Messing similarly connects conspiracy theories with modern esotericism, religion, art, poetry and science, and strongly opposes the increasing technologisation of life which, according to Messing, will keep people docile and prevent them from achieving their true potential (Harambam 2017: 44–5). Rakopoulos presents Aris Dovlis, a central figure in the Greek alternative knowledge subcultural world, as a prolific writer, visionary and creator of the Greek nationalist *Epsilon* cosmology (2018: 380). This glorification of Hellenic history coupled with conspiracy theory fears of external invasion and destruction of Greece inspires many local extreme right groups, and even led some to carry out two bombings in the north of Greece in 2015 (no casualties) in order to 'liberate Greece from the New World Order' (Rakopoulos 2018: 379). Other, even lesser known conspiracy theory entrepreneurs are the several alternative bookstore owners Rakopoulos meets in Thessaloniki that all traffic in recent editions of the classic forged anti-Jewish conspiracy theory, *The Protocols of the Elders of Zion*. Some owners he describes as conservative, even elitist intellectuals, and others as more classic right-wing nationalists (Rakopoulos 2018: 382–6). Each national and/or regional context must have their own conspiracy theory entrepreneurs, some better able to reach larger audiences or make a greater fortune than others, but it is illuminating how ethnographic research brings such actors and economies into the limelight.

## Conspiracy theory movements

It is often argued that conspiracy theorists are lone individuals who lose themselves in imagining malicious schemes and intrigues from the dark corners of their messy basements or attics. Putting two conspiracy theorists together would inevitably lead to rifts and fights about the proper interpretation of events and evidence. And while that may be true in some instances, it is also true that they form alliances and group together to advance their cause. Perhaps the best known and well-organised one is the 9/11 Truth Movement (9/11 T.M.) that came into being in the years after the 9/11 2001 terrorist attacks in New York City. This group of more or less loosely affiliated people challenges the mainstream explanation that these attacks were the (sole and original) work of Islamic jihadists called Al-Qaeda and led by Osama Bin Laden, and that the crashes of the hijacked planes led to the collapse of the World Trade Center towers. Instead, they argue that this official explanation suffers from a number of gaps, inconsistencies and unexplained phenomena, which brings them to demand answers and clarifications, and advance their own theories of what happened instead. The most prominent alternative explanations are that it was an 'inside job', a 'false flag attack' and 'the new Pearl Harbor', meaning that the U.S. government either knowingly let the attacks happen or even made it happen (theories known as L.I.H.O.P. [Let It Happen On Purpose] and M.I.H.O.P. [Made It Happen On Purpose]) in order to garner support for the wars in Iraq and Afghanistan and to legitimise the restriction of civil rights and liberties under the guise of the 'War on Terror'. In the years after 9/11, many different people, including a wide variety of scholars, architects and engineers, gathered together in this social movement and they are still active 'to expose the official lies and cover-up ... to promote the best investigative reporting, scholarly research and public education ... to seek justice ... and to end the regime and illicit power structures responsible for 9/11' (www.911truth.org). While there has been quite some media attention to this movement over the years, and widespread support for their ideas among the general U.S. population according to several polls, there has been rather limited specific academic attention to 9/11 truth as a social movement. That is quite remarkable given their popularity and longevity, and their centrality in the wider conspiracy milieu. Byford argues that 'as well as attracting ideas, motifs and arguments from the conspiracy tradition, the 9/11 truth movement acts as a magnet for the wider conspiracist community' (2011: 109). For many different scientific reasons it thus makes good sense to focus on this movement. And, while Pelkmans and Machold are right that the academic study of 9/11 events itself 'is a precarious undertaking because of the potential to be seen as a conspiracy theorist unworthy of academic status' (2011: 66), researching the 9/11 T.M. instead should be less 'risky' (although that can also be questioned). The truth is that few academics ventured down this road.

Journalist Jonathan Kay is one of the exceptions and perhaps most known for his work on the 9/11 T.M. In *Among the Truthers*, Kay delves deep into what he sees as 'America's growing conspiracist underground' (2011). Like a real anthropologist, he 'immersed himself for two years in this dark subculture', as the front flap says, 'attending conventions of conspiracy theorists, surfing their discussion boards, reading their websites, joining their Facebook groups, and interviewing them in their homes and offices'. A first and very important observation he makes is that the people he met did not conform to the common stereotypes of conspiracy theorists as 'street corner paranoiacs' and 'freaks', but instead 'most were outwardly "normal", articulate people who kept up with the news and held down office jobs' and even 'looked and sounded a lot like [him]' (2011: 6–7). This observation and his wish to understand them notwithstanding, he ends up describing his 'correspondents' in rather denigrating and pathological ways, seeing their engagements with the movement as 'a symptom of a flight from reality [...] induced by any number of causes – midlife ennui, narcissism, profound psychic trauma, spiritual longing, or even experimental drug use' (2011: 150). He categorises the different people active in that movement as 'the midlife crisis case', 'the failed historian', 'the damaged survivor', 'the crank, the evangelical doomsayer' and so on, providing a far from neutral 'typology of the different varieties of conspiracists' (2011: 150). This raises the question of how the 9/11 Truthers that are depicted in these ways would identify with such descriptions. As both Ellefritz (2014), Harambam and Aupers (2017), and Jones (2010) show, people actively resist the conspiracy theorist label and associated pejorative connotations. To give a fitting example, Laura Jones shows in her ethnographic study of the 9/11 T.M. how its members reconfigure their derogative framing as being 'unpatriotic' in the highly polarised context of Bush's War on Terror ('you are either with us, or you are with the terrorists') by arguing how it is their 'patriotic duty' to participate in the 'active pursuit of truth and justice despite the ridicule and anger this may generate' (2010: 367).

This is not just rhetoric and self-legitimation, as Jones argues, members of the 9/11 T.M. go out on the streets to hand out flyers and encourage people to 'perform their patriotic right and constitutional duty to question the actions of their government' (2010: 367).

Kay (2011) eventually explains the appeal of the 9/11 T.M., and conspiracy theories more generally, in line with Popper as secularised, *ersatz* religion, providing people with similar psychological comforts. The 9/11 T.M. is, according to Kay, both symptom and cause of a larger societal and intellectual crisis that people would now call 'post-truth': Experts and institutions are no longer trusted, values or fantasies are prioritised over facts, and so-called 'rational intellectual criteria are treated as optional' (2011: XIX). Dreading this loss of a 'shared reality' and a 'collective sense of truth', Kay reverberates Hofstadter's desired consensus politics, and warns throughout the book for the societal consequences of this 'intellectual balkanization'. Whereas one could perhaps expect such a stance towards one's research population from a journalist, it is stranger to encounter that from an anthropologist. Steven Sampson, a U.S. anthropologist working in Sweden, did ethnographic research in the Copenhagen 9/11 Truth Movement, and studied their materials, as well as those of their (more prolific) U.S. originator. In an unpublished paper (2010), Sampson explains that he is interested in understanding the dynamics of the 9/11 T.M., and provides much information on it (its actors, ideologies, practices, schisms and media), but he is taking a clear epistemological and normative position towards his research subjects, which is unusual in the field of anthropology, as he acknowledges himself (2010: 22–3). According to Sampson, the 9/11 T.M. is fundamentally misguided and even dangerous to society, and he reiterates many of the aforementioned classical examples in the scholarly literature of the pathological ideas and practices of conspiracy theorists (false use of evidence, unwarranted conjectures, Manichean populism, excessive paranoia, etc.). This brings him to 'take a stand' against the 'obscurantism disguised as science' of the 9/11 T.M. (2010: 22–3). His questions are 'where do we anthropologists draw that relativist line?' (2010: 3), and 'how should responsible scholars deal with such groups?' (2010: 23). Unfortunately, he does not elaborate on this task, a challenge that has been tackled by various scholars in a special issue on this topic (Harambam, Drazkiewiecz 2019).

An important anthropological effort is to bring *context* into the study. Sampson does so by paying attention to the various sceptics and critics of the 9/11 T.M. as well. He writes about this loosely structured community of 9/11 'debunkers' as having their own media and materials that all focus on disproving the 9/11 T.M. (2010: 19–20). The 9/11 T.M. reacts in turn to their debunkers with refutations, giving rise to a seemingly infinite regress of debunking. Such a relational focus on the 9/11 T.M. and their critics is present in the PhD of Richard Ellefritz (2014), who focuses on their (discursive) interactions. Following his ethnographic study with the 9/11 T.M., Ellefritz highlights how their critics employ the label of 'conspiracy theory/ist' to stigmatise and discredit this movement. Following Husting and Orr (2007), he argues how attributing this derogatory label to someone functions as a 'transpersonal strategy of exclusion [...]' which allows 'one to go meta by sidestepping empirical claims in favor of the *ad hominem*' (Ellefritz 2014: 17–20). This critique – that opponents of conspiracy theorists hardly go into the evidence itself *because* they are framed as conspiracy theorists – is more widely shared in the conspiracy milieu (Harambam, Aupers 2017). Ellefritz argues that this practice is problematic, not just because it is unscientific, but also because it 'undermines respect for human subjects and social justice' (2014: 36). He eventually comes to the opposite position of most commentators on the subject by arguing that, unless people's claims can be proven *false*, scholars should refrain from using the 'conspiracy theory' label as it (un)wittingly discards popular claims of elite criminal activities and upholds 'existing ruling systems of authorities and their truth regimes' (2014: 266).

What is remarkable about Ellefritz's study is that he identifies himself as a 9/11 Truther (2014: 24), which brings many epistemological and ethical issues to the fore. As he himself argues, 'my reflexivity as an insider can be viewed as a sign of rigor and trustworthiness [...] or it can be viewed as a sign of inherent bias and unreliability' (2014: 26). This obviously depends on the degree of positivism to which a scholar subscribes, but even among ethnographically minded scholars there is much disagreement about the advantages and pitfalls of such auto-ethnographies (e.g. Denzin 2006). This is not the place to discuss these issues, but what can be said is that doing qualitative/ethnographic research with people who go about living their everyday lives *inevitably* draws the researcher into the picture, both while doing research and thereafter (e.g. Harambam 2017: 259–75). As Laura Jones explains in her ethnographic study of the 9/11 T.M. (2010), she too grapples with how to negotiate sameness and/or difference with one's research subjects. During her fieldwork, she 'had visibly associated herself with the group and their conspiratorial claims, despite [her] skepticism towards these claims and the regressive politics they may promote' (2010: 368). She emphasises the difficulties of 'wanting to connect with people and better understand their unique experiences', while being/staying an outsider as a researcher (2010: 368). While qualitative/ethnographic scholars often pay more explicit reflexive attention to their positionality as a scholar, and how that influences the research done, this is actually a quality *all* scholars from whatever discipline and methodological tradition should profess. To be sure: These are not mere academic questions and reflections. As Judy Wilyman and her PhD supervisor Brian Martin have experienced in the context of the heated (anti)vaccination debates, studying movements that challenge the status quo, or making a stance in favour of them, may result in being drawn into the battlefield. As a science and technology scholar, Martin has done much research and supervised many PhD projects on controversial (science) topics, but has never seen such sustained and abusive attacks on citizen critics of public policy as with the anti-vaccination movement (2018).

## Conspiracy theory individuals

While conspiracy theory entrepreneurs and movements may be most visible for the wider public, including academic scholars, arguably the largest group of people engaging with conspiracy theories are the ordinary individuals living among us. These people are hardly publicly recognisable as conspiracy theorists, often would not self-identify as such, and embody great diversity in age, class, education, race/ethnicity, worldview and so on. Yet, in their everyday lives, conspiracy theories (may) play a significant role, ranging from influencing the way these people eat, to the media they use to inform themselves or the health care services they make use of. But, as these everyday activities remain largely invisible to most scholarly and journalistic efforts, such people are often left out of academic analyses of conspiracy theorists. Women in particular seem to more often engage with conspiracy theories in their everyday lives, instead of publicly proclaiming their enthusiasm for such ideas. Moreover, these more dispersed conspiracy theory individuals empirically show how difficult it is to pinpoint conspiracy theorists: When do you actually count as such? Many people might have doubts about the way terrorists attacks are mediatised, distrust their governments and associated institutions, or hold multinationals responsible for various forms of serious corporate misbehavior, including tax evasion, corruption and cartel forming/collusion. But, does that make you a conspiracy theorist? It remains a tricky question. Quantitative studies, especially those based on large-N polling data (see Smallpage et al. Chapter 3.1 in this section), have made some progress in bringing these ordinary people to the surface, yet, by the nature of their methodology, it is hard to hear them speak about the role conspiracy theories play in their everyday lives. In what follows, I will draw on more ethnographic studies that have ventured into different cultural and social worlds in which conspiracy theories circulate in order to bring these ordinary conspiracy theory individuals and their thoughts, experiences and practices to the fore.

Although David Robertson focuses on three prominent figures (novelist and U.F.O. abductee Whitley Strieber, David Icke and channeller David Wilcock) in his study of 'millennial conspiracism' (the cross fertilisation between popular religious and conspiracist fields), he also studied the people that are in various ways interested in these figures (2016). Attending Strieber's 2012 fifth annual Dreamland festival in Nashville, Tennessee, Robertson speaks with many of the attendees (2016: 105–16). The festival was held at the Scarritt-Bennett Centre, 'a non-profit education, retreat and conference center' with 'a strong commitment to the eradication of racism, empowerment of women and spiritual formation' and featured talks (for example, by the well-known conspiracy theorist Jim Marrs), meditation sessions, spiritual workshops and more (2016: 105). After the opening presentation of Raven Dana, who described a 'family history of questioning authority, and how her grandmother would talk to the dead and that her grandfather had seen a UFO' and professed how a 'counter epistemic habitus' is intergenerational, Robertson engages with a variety of people, including Bill, a former U.S. army veteran who went into computer programming after retiring (2016: 106–7). He told Robertson how he was concerned about 'government secrecy', 'the removal of individual rights', 'security cameras everywhere', and 'the poor quality of food in the US and about the use of GM produce and hormone supplements in cattle' (2016: 107). After having visited David Icke's 2012 Wembley performance, Robertson ventures to the house of Belinda McKenzie in London's leafy and posh neighbourhood Highgate (106: 158–61). He finds there a variety of people: Besides Belinda, who had occupied herself mostly with child abuse cases and pedophilia networks in the U.K.'s power brokers, Robertson meets 'Tony Farrell, a former intelligence advisor for the Metropolitan police, [who] was allegedly fired after returning a report alleging that the UK government were responsible for the 7/7 London bomb attacks' (2016: 160). The next day, Robertson attended the 'David Icke Changed My Life' meeting held in an upstairs room of a pub in central London, after which he talks to attendees such as Steven, 'a fairly posh chap who described himself as a filmmaker' who talked about out-of-body Experiences (2016: 161). Based on these experiences, Robertson concludes that these

> were normal people. Male and female, working-class and wealthy, frequently highly educated and accomplished people. There was no sense of dysfunctionality […] no skinheads or people with right-wing or racist views, [merely people] motivated principally by concern; for crimes and abuses going unpunished, for the inequalities of the state etc.
>
> *(2016: 163)*

Although such statements are a bit dubious and partly reflect Robertson's own normative standpoints, they do show a great diversity of people, and highlight the fact that directly engaging with people who have nonmainstream ideas can make it more difficult to set them aside as mentally unstable.

While Robertson's display of ordinary conspiracy theory individuals is primarily descriptive and anecdotal, an ethnographic study by the present author and Stef Aupers into the Dutch conspiracy milieu offers a more systematic analysis of how ordinary people engaging with conspiracy theorists see themselves and others in that cultural world and beyond (Harambam, Aupers 2017). During my fieldwork, I conducted in-depth interviews with a wide variety of people whom I recruited from sources associated to a varying degree with conspiracy theory, ranging from particular Facebook groups to a public screening of a conspiracy theory documentary (Harambam 2017). Moving beyond common identity signifiers (age, class, education, political leaning, etc.), I let these variegated people speak about themselves in their own words, and analysed how they made distinctions between self and other. The first conclusion we draw is that 'people in the conspiracy milieu collectively distinguish themselves from the "mainstream" by arguing that they are "critical thinkers", they 'reclaim rationality' by arguing how the gullible mainstream, often called 'sheeple', are actually the irrational ones for simply believing what the authorities tell them (2017: 118). Being aware of the pejorative meaning of the 'conspiracy theorist' label, these people make no mistake in also distinguishing themselves from what they see as the 'real' conspiracy theorists who conform to that stereotypical image. Following such distinctions between self and other in the conspiracy milieu, we make three distinguishable groups apparent: What we call *activists*, *retreaters* and *mediators*. Activists are most visible and vocal as they actively make their conspiracy theory positions clear by demonstrating, openly protesting, confronting those in power and by rubbing against the grain. Their militancy is, however, not appreciated by all: The radical tone and practice of activists appears a divisive element in the conspiracy milieu (2017: 120). Retreaters have a more spiritual, New Age, worldview in which activism is rejected because it feeds from negative emotions like aggression and fear. Instead, they insist that one should focus on improving the self as societal change can only come when people change from within. Mediators argue that the way forward is to bring people with different ideas together, to build bridges instead of fighting for one's own truth. We show clear internal variety among conspiracy theorists and conclude therefore that it is hard to speak of them as one type of people, despite similarities in distrusting official narratives.

Even when not explicitly studying conspiracy theorists, ethnographic scholars may encounter people engaging with conspiracy theories. Elisa Sobo, for example, originally studied Waldorf (anthroposophical) education in California: 'how teachers leveraged [its] unique pedagogy to promote child health' and how aligned with parents' home health practices (2016: 344). Parents' vaccination practices turned out to play a central role, and in good anthropological fashion, she followed up on that in subsequent research. While it is more commonly known that vaccination rates are lower at such schools, it is less clear why parents do not follow official public health recommendations. As Sobo argues, such parents are 'traditionally lumped together as "refusers", yet great diversity exists within the lot' (2016: 344). She first points out that parents do not all refuse the same vaccines or doses, nor for all of their children, but also that parents have diverse reasons for refusing vaccinations. Some worry about side-effects or question their necessity and efficacy, whereas others distrust the medical-industrial complex promoting vaccinations. Many such motivations are often dismissed as conspiracy theory (Harambam 2017; Martin 2018), which is probably the reason why Sobo refrains from using that term. The important point she makes is that 'variation aside, parents' vaccine refusals were always highly social' (2016: 344): Sobo shows how local norms and expectations cultivate parent's decisions, how refusal can therefore be an 'affiliative act', letting people belong to a certain community, but also that it 'signals one's subversive opposition to the status quo' (2016: 345). Like the other scholars discussed in this chapter, Sobo makes it abundantly clear how conspiracy theory ideas and practices are complex, evolving and always embedded social environments. But, also, that qualitative, ethnographic research is perfectly suited to grasp and understand these dynamic webs of meaning.

## Conclusion

Conspiracy theories are everywhere, yet our understanding of their followers is still rather limited and inconclusive. This chapter has shown how qualitative studies, in all their disciplinary and historical variety, have written about conspiracy theorists. After briefly reviewing the traditional works that have mostly pathologised these people *and* the cultural studies scholars that highlighted the apparent rationality of conspiracy theorists instead, I have discussed the works of scholars that interacted more directly with conspiracy theorists in order to shed light on their ideas, practices and social contexts.

Distinguishing between conspiracy theory entrepreneurs, movements and individuals, this chapter has shown a wide variety of people engaging in one way or another with conspiracy theories. The very outspoken and publicly visible entrepreneurs embody how people can make a living out of spreading conspiracy theories in both the off- and online worlds. Particularly popular are those, like Alex Jones and David Icke, who fuse dark thoughts of a coming totalitarian New World Order with messianic visions of a global awakening into a New Age. The academic studies reviewed here show in much empirical detail how their conspiracy theories do not just 'travel' across communities and ideologies, but also across time when a new generation picks up on older works and connects them in new ways and to other audiences. While these entrepreneurs may represent prevalent stereotypes, the second section on movements makes that image harder to sustain. Taking the 9/11 Truth Movement as a case study, several scholars show how various kinds of conspiracy theorists come together to pursue common goals. Going against mainstream conceptions of reality, such movements can count on much criticism, both from academic scholars and the wider public. Some scholars include anti-conspiracy theory movements in their analyses as well, since they are part of the same interactional dynamic. The last section focused on ordinary people who in their everyday lives engage with conspiracy theories. While these people normally remain largely invisible, they arguably constitute the largest group, albeit a silent majority. Ranging from people attending New Age festivals to parents refusing vaccinations in Waldorf schools, the reviewed scholarly works show that there is not just great diversity in their ideas, motivations and practices, but also that identity and community formations play a central role in the cultivation and popularity of conspiracy theories.

While there is much diversity between qualitative scholars of conspiracy theories, this chapter has also highlighted what they share. A first and perhaps most important communality is the wish to make the world of those under study both intelligible and imaginable to a wider public. Especially among ethnographic scholars, there is a strong drive to empathise with interlocuters in order to be able to see *and* show the world from their perspective. This generally requires an agnostic (truth) stance towards people's ideas, but that does not mean endorsing those, merely that epistemological and/or normative judgements are suspended until further notice. This is often easier said than done: As this chapter has shown, doing ethnographic research seems to either blur or erect boundaries between self and other, both during and after doing research. But, as long as that is turned into an explicit reflexive practice, it may only add to the quality of the analysis. Focusing on what ordinary people think and do in their everyday lives highlights the enormous diversity of our worlds, but it inevitably brings *context* into the picture as well. People's lives do not stop at the (anticipated) conceptual borders of one's research project, but have meaningful relations with many different others that are hard to exclude. While counting people is important to get a broader picture of societal distributions, I hope to have shown in this chapter what a good qualitative study of conspiracy culture entails and yields.

# References

Asprem, E. and Dyrendal, A. (2015) 'Conspirituality reconsidered: how surprising and how new is the confluence of spirituality and conspiracy theory?', *Journal of Contemporary Religion*, 30(3): 367–82.

Barkun, M. (2006) *A culture of conspiracy: apocalyptic visions in contemporary America*, Berkeley, CA: University of California Press.
Berlet, C. (2009) *Toxic to democracy: conspiracy theories, demonization and scapegoating*, Somerville, MA: Political Research Associates.
Birchall, C. (2006) *Knowledge goes pop: from conspiracy theory to gossip*, New York: Berg.
Bratich, J.Z. (2008) *Conspiracy panics: political rationality and popular culture*, Albany, NY: State of New York University Press.
Butter, M. (2014) *Plots, designs, and schemes: American conspiracy theories from the Puritans to the present*, Berlin/Boston: de Gruyter.
Butter, M. and Knight, P. (2019) 'The history of conspiracy theory research: an overview and commentary', in J.E. Uscinski (ed.) *Conspiracy theories and the people who believe them*, Oxford University Press.
Byford, J. (2011) *Conspiracy theories: a critical introduction*, London: Palgrave Macmillan.
Campbell, C. (1972) 'The cult, the cultic milieu and secularization', in J. Kaplan and H. Lööw (eds.) *The cultic milieu: oppositional subcultures in an age of globalization*, reprint, Walnut Creek, CA: Altamira Press, 2002, pp. 12–25.
Coady, D. (ed.) (2006) *Conspiracy theories: the philosophical debate*, Aldershot, UK: Ashgate Publishing.
Dean, J. (1998) *Aliens in America: conspiracy cultures from outerspace to cyberspace*, Ithaca, NY: Cornell University Press.
DeHaven-Smith, L. (2013) *Conspiracy theory in America*, Austin, TX: University of Texas Press.
Denzin, N.K. (2006) 'Analytic autoethnography, or déjà vu all over again', *Journal of Contemporary Ethnography*, 35(4): 419–28.
Ellefritz, R.G. (2014) *Discourse among the truthers and deniers of 9/11: movement-countermovement dynamics and the discursive field of the 9/11 truth movement*, thesis, Oklahoma State University.
Fenster, M. (1999) *Conspiracy theories: secrecy and power in American culture*, Minneapolis, MN: University of Minnesota Press.
Fenster, M. (2008) *Conspiracy theories: secrecy and power in American culture*, rev. and upd. edn, Minneapolis, MN: University of Minnesota Press.
Gosa, T.L. (2011) 'Counterknowledge, racial paranoia, and the cultic milieu: decoding hip hop conspiracy theory', *Poetics*, 39(3): 187–204.
Harambam, J. (2017) *'The truth is out there': conspiracy culture in an age of epistemic instability*, Rotterdam: Erasmus University.
Harambam, J. and Aupers, S. (2015) 'Contesting epistemic authority: conspiracy theories on the boundary of science', *Public Understanding of Science*, 24(4): 466–80.
Harambam, J. and Aupers, S. (2017) '"I am not a conspiracy theorist": relational identifications in the Dutch conspiracy milieu', *Cultural Sociology*, 11(1): 113–29.
Harambam, J. and Drazkiewicz, E. (2019) 'What do we do about conspiracy theories? The role of social sciences and humanities in debunking conspiracy theories', *Cost Action 'Comparative Analysis of Conspiracy Theories' Conference*, Charles University and Vaclav Havel Library, Prague, 19–21 September. Unpublished.
Hayes, M. (2017) '"Then the saucers do exist?": UFOs, the practice of conspiracy, and the case of Wilbert Smith', *Journal of Canadian Studies*, 51(3): 665–96.
Hofstadter, R. (1996 [1964]) *The paranoid style in American politics and other essays*, reprint, New York: Knopf.
Husting, G. and Orr, M. (2007) 'Dangerous machinery: "conspiracy theorist" as a transpersonal strategy of exclusion', *Symbolic Interaction*, 30(2): 127–50.
Jackson, S. (2017) 'Conspiracy theories in the patriot/militia movement', *GW Program on Extremism*, May. Available at: https://extremism.gwu.edu/sites/g/files/zaxdzs2191/f/downloads/Jackson,%20Conspiracy%20Theories%20Final.pdf. [Accessed 26 August 2019.]
Jenkins, R. (2014) *Social identity*, London: Routledge.
Jones, L. (2010) '"How do the American people know …?": embodying post-9/11 conspiracy discourse', *GeoJournal*, 75(4): 359–71.
Kay, J. (2011) *Among the truthers: a journey through America's growing conspiracist underground*, New York: Harper Collins.
Keeley, B.L. (1999) 'Of conspiracy theories', *The Journal of Philosophy*, 96(3): 109–26.
Knight, P. (2000) *Conspiracy culture: from Kennedy to the X-Files*, London: Routledge.
Martin, B. (2018) *Vaccination panic in Australia*, Sparsnäs: Irene Publishing.
Melley, T. (2000) *Empire of conspiracy: the culture of paranoia in postwar America*, Ithaca, NY: Cornell University Press.

Oliver, J.E. and Wood T.J. (2014) 'Conspiracy theories and the paranoid style(s) of mass opinion', *American Journal of Political Science*, 58(4): 952–66.

Pelkmans, M. and Machold, R. (2011) 'Conspiracy theories and their truth trajectories', *Focaal*, 59: 66–80.

Pipes, D. (1997) *Conspiracy: how the paranoid style flourishes and where it comes from*, New York, NY: The Free Press.

Popper, K.R. (2013 [1945]) *The open society and its enemies*, reprint, Princeton, NJ: Princeton University Press.

Rakopoulos, T. (2018) 'Show me the money: conspiracy theories and distant wealth', *History and Anthropology*, 29(3): 376–91.

Robertson, D.G. (2016) *UFOs, conspiracy theories and the New Age: millennial conspiracism*, London: Bloomsbury Publishing.

Robins, R.S. and Post, J.M. (1997) *Political paranoia: the psychopolitics of hatred*, New Haven, CT: Yale University Press.

Roisman, J. (2006) *The rhetoric of conspiracy in ancient Athens*, Los Angeles, CA: University of California Press.

Sampson, S. (2010) 'Truthers: the 911 Truth Movement and the culture of conspiracy', paper presented at the *American Anthropological Association Conference*, New Orleans, LA, 16 November. Unpublished.

Sobo, E.J. (2016) 'Theorizing (vaccine) refusal: through the looking glass', *Cultural Anthropology*, 31(3): 342–50.

Sunstein, C.R. and Vermeule, A. (2009) 'Conspiracy theories: causes and cures', *Journal of Political Philosophy*, 17(2): 202–27.

Thalmann, K. (2019) *The stigmatization of conspiracy theory since the 1950s: 'A plot to make us look foolish'*, London: Routledge.

Uscinski, J.E. and Parent, J.M. (2014) *American conspiracy theories*, Oxford: Oxford University Press.

Ward, C. and Voas, D. (2011) 'The emergence of conspirituality', *Journal of Contemporary Religion*, 26(1): 103–21.

Wood, G.S. (1982) 'Conspiracy and the paranoid style: causality and deceit in the eighteenth century', *The William and Mary Quarterly: A Magazine of Early American History and Culture*, 39(3): 402–41.

Zaitchik, A. (2011) 'Meet Alex Jones', *Rolling Stone Magazine*, 2 March. Available at: www.rollingstone.com/culture/culture-news/meet-alex-jones-175845/. [Accessed 21 May 2019.]

# 3.3
# CONSPIRACY THEORIES AND GENDER AND SEXUALITY

*Annika Thiem*

## Introduction

The question of how gender and sexuality are connected to conspiracy theories comprises two different aspects. The first aspect concerns the question of how gender or sexuality influence conspiracy theory belief, i.e. who are the people believing in conspiracy theories and who are the people producing them? Are men more prone than women to believe in conspiracy theories or vice versa? The second aspect concerns the question of what importance gender and sexuality are to the content of specific conspiracy theories. In this chapter, I will first address how gender impacts belief in conspiracy theories (there are no studies that examine whether sexual orientation has any significant influence). Second, I will demonstrate by way of two case studies the centrality of gender and sexuality for the image of the alleged conspirators that many conspiracy theories paint and the issues around which they revolve. I will show that especially sexualities perceived as deviant play an important role in establishing the 'other' in conspiracy theory's typical us-versus-them narrative. In the nineteenth century, for example, many American Protestants believed that Catholic priests were sexually abusing innocent American girls and that this was part of a plot by the Pope and the Austrian emperor to conquer the U.S.A. A century later, fervent anti-communists thought that homosexual tendencies made otherwise ordinary Americans susceptible to communism. In contemporary Western societies, white supremacist and nationalist conspiracy theorists are particularly targeting members of the L.G.B.T.Q.+ and feminist movements because they perceive them as a danger towards traditional family values.

## The influence of gender and sexuality on conspiracy belief

The connection between conspiracy theories, on the one hand, and gender, on the other, is one of the most controversial issues in conspiracy theory research. Interestingly, quantitative and qualitative research arrive at very different, most often contradictory answers to the question whether gender influences belief in conspiracy theories. According to most quantitative studies, the stereotypical image of a conspiracy theorist as an 'unwashed, middle-aged white male' is wrong (Uscinski, Parent 2014: 73). Most studies in psychology and political science find no evidence that gender has any impact on belief in conspiracy theories, which directly contradicts this stereotypical image. Rob Brotherton summarises the psychological research on conspiracy theories and states that neither gender nor age nor education seem to have a significant effect on a person's belief in conspiracy theories (2015: 10). More specifically, Daniel Jolley and Karen Douglas, for example, found no significant correlation between the participants' gender and their belief in conspiracy theories (2014: 40). In accordance with these findings, Jan Willem van Prooijen and Michelle Acker detected no significant effect of gender in their study, which was concerned with the influences of control on conspiracy theory belief and for which they collected data from 1265 participants from all over the U.S.A. (2015: 756). Uscinski and Parent thus conclude that 'women are about as likely as men to be conspiracy theorists' (2014: 82). According to them, receptivity to conspiracy theories is mainly by feelings of powerlessness, which leads them to the conclusion that 'conspiracy theories are for losers' (2014: 131).

One must take into consideration, however, that gender was not the main concern in any of these studies, but merely a control variable such as age or education, which was cross-referenced with the other data. Moreover, there are also some quantitative studies that find that men are more likely to believe in conspiracy theories than women. A recent study on 'Catholic collective narcissism' and *'gender conspiracy beliefs'* in Poland shows that men are significantly more 'likely to believe in the *gender conspiracy*' than women (Marchlewska *et al.* 2019: 8 [italics in original]). The gender conspiracy theory the study refers to claims that feminism and the L.G.B.T.Q. movement, together with scientists and gender equality activists, form 'a group that strategically and purposefully seeks to deny the importance of the traditional differentiation of men and women ..., triggering conflict between sexes, promoting hostility to fatherhood and motherhood, finally leading to destruction of a family' (2019: 2). Since the study presented the alleged conspiracy as much as a threat to motherhood and femininity as to fatherhood and masculinity, one could expect that women might be equally concerned about it. However, the results show that men feel far more threatened by the idea that gender is a psychological and cultural construct than women. In fact, sex remained a significant variable throughout the study, indicating that men are significantly more likely to both believe in a gender conspiracy as well as to show hostility towards people perceived as undermining traditional Catholic values (2019: 8–9).

Similarly, the 2019 edition of the bi-annually published study by the Friedrich Ebert Foundation on political attitudes in Germany also found a gender difference in conspiracy mentality. According to the study, male participants are significantly more likely to believe in conspiracy theories (43.9 per cent) than female participants (33.9 per cent) (Rees, Lamberty 2019: 213). The study furthermore shows that this conspiracy mentality can be directly connected to sexism and the depreciation of transgender people, thus supporting the results of Marchlewska *et al.* (2019: 217–18).

Qualitative research in the humanities often also claims that men are more prone than women to believe in conspiracy theories. Frequently, these studies explain the gender difference by casting conspiracy theories as a reaction to a perceived crisis of masculinity. One example of such an approach is Kyle Cuordileone's study of American political language during the anticommunist scares of the 1950s (2005). The same applies to Timothy Melley and his research on the post-war era in the U.S.A. more generally. He develops the concept of 'agency panic', which he sees at the heart of the belief in and the production of conspiracy theories in the U.S.A. during the decades following the Second World War and the perceived threat to masculine notions of individuality and autonomy around which they revolve (2000: 14). He argues that, during this era, the long tradition of '[g]endered tales of socialization ... becomes coupled to a narrative of violated identity and agency-in-crisis' (2000: 32). Masculinity and heterosexuality become the normative model after which 'human agency and subjectivity' are conceptualised (2000: 33). Social forces that are perceived to take control over the individual and diminish their agency are – in this 'masculinist tradition' – portrayed as *'feminizing* forces' (2000: 33, 32 [italics in original]). Consequently, femininity as well as homosexuality are portrayed as both undermining and threatening traditional notions of hegemonic masculinity and male agency.[1]

Christ has built on Melley's argument and extended it to contemporary American culture at large: She argues that the question at stake for 'every white male U.S. conspiracy theorist since the 1960s' is about the meaning of masculinity and what it entails to be a man (Christ 2014: 311). While 'men externalize and employ their psychological problems as a public conspiracy ..., women at least suspect the perceived conspiratorial plot to be the result of their own psychological problems' (2014: 329). Men, then, she argues, are more prone to be seen in interaction with the public sphere and large political conspiracies, while women's fears – by themselves and others – tend to be pathologised and described as a symptom of female hysteria. Accordingly, for her, both believing in and producing conspiracy theories is closely connected to male identity and a perceived crisis of hegemonic masculinity. It is therefore no surprise that she concludes that American men are more likely to believe in conspiracy theories than women.

Moving beyond the U.S.A., Michael Butter has recently argued that belief in conspiracy theories is far more important for male than female identity – especially because the threat posed by social and political transformations is significantly higher to hegemonic masculinity than it is to different forms of femininity (Butter 2018: 120). According to him, white men have throughout history been more powerful than women or men of other ethnicities. Since the racial and gender hierarchies on which this position of power depends have been increasingly challenged since 1945, conspiracy theories offer an easy explanation for this shift in power structure. They cast this transformation not only as problematic but as part of malicious plots aimed at undermining society as a whole. Butter concludes that this is why men are more drawn to conspiracy theories than women (2018: 123).

However, there is hardly any ethnographic research and thus almost no empirical data to either confirm or refute the claim that conspiracy theorists are more likely to be men than women. Fieldwork studies of conspiracy theorists and their communities are rare and often do not live up to academic and ethical standards. This is because most of the fieldwork so far has been undertaken by journalists, whose methods are often highly problematic from an academic point of view. German author Tobias Ginsburg (2018), for example, went undercover in the German *Reichsbürger* movement, a conspiracy community that believes that the Federal Republic of Germany does not exist and that the country is a company controlled and exploited by other Western countries, most notably the U.S.A. Ginsburg assumed a secret identity to get access to this movement; he was not, as ethnographic standards demand, open about his intentions and did not seek the consent of the people he talked to. Moreover, his tone and style when writing about the community he investigated is by no means objective but, on the contrary, highly subjective and, at times, even polemic. Thus, even though his report offers illuminating insights into an otherwise closed-up community, it needs to be taken with a grain of salt. Still, most of the people he interacted with and who feature prominently in the book he wrote about his research were, in fact, men.

In similar fashion, Jonathan Kay, an American journalist who investigated the Truther Movement after 9/11, also found that there are far more men than women in this conspiracy theory community (2011). He furthermore identifies several different motivations for the belief in conspiracy theories, such as the midlife crisis, which can be described as a personal crisis of masculinity. He claims that, in order to 'understand these two men [two of the prominent Truthers he interviewed] is to understand the strangely sudden, strangely radicalizing effects that middle age can impose upon the male psyche' (2011). Becoming a truther, he argues, allowed these men to 'reinvent' themselves, escape from their lives and become somebody new who is not judged on the past but only on this 'newly created identity' (2011: 159). However, much like Ginsburg's, Kay's methods also do not live up to academic standards of research. Indeed, while Ginsburg does not even give the impression of trying to write objectively about the people he investigated, Kay claims to be objective, but turns out not to be. This is most obvious in the ways in which he categorises his interview partners. He identifies, for example, conspiracy theorists as 'The Midlife Crisis Case', 'The Failed Historian', 'The Damaged Survivor' or 'The Clinical Conspiracists', and even openly describes the last one as 'out-and-out insane' (2011: 151, 159, 170, 183). Following the tradition of Hofstadter (1964), Kay pathologises many of the truthers and treats them like patients in need of medical attention. Thus, he falls behind much of the work on conspiracy theories and the people who believe in them done in cultural studies and anthropology in the past two decades (see Chapters 1.2 and 1.6), because these disciplines have moved beyond Hofstadter and strongly oppose the pathologisation of conspiracy theorists.

One of the few existing academic ethnographies is a web-based study on *conspirituality* – a 'hybrid of conspiracy theory and alternative spirituality [that] has appeared on the internet' – by Charlotte Ward and David Voas (2011: 103). While New Age spiritual movements are dominated by women, the realm of conspiracy theory 'remains a largely male enclave of political and scientific foci', the authors suggest (2011: 106). However, according to them, New Age spiritualism shares with conspiracy theory the three main characteristics that Michael Barkun considers characteristic of conspiracy theorising: 'nothing happens by accident, nothing is as it seems, and everything is connected' (Ward, Voas 2011: 108). Recently, hybrid world views based on both New Age spiritualism as well as conspiracy theories have emerged and have gained increasing popularity. The idea of hybridity suggests that gender difference is not as significant anymore as it was in the separate categories of New Age spiritualism and conspiracy theory. However, when discussing the appeal of conspirituality, Ward and Voas do not refer to any data on gender.

In addition, Ward and Voas's assumption that 'conspirituality appears to be an internet-based movement' that has appeared online only in the mid-1990s has been contested by other scholars (2011: 104, 109). Egil Asprem and Asbjørn Dyrendal, for example, argue that the phenomenon Ward and Voas describe as 'conspirituality', can, in fact, be better understood as 'a result of structural elements in the cultic milieu, rising from its interest in stigmatized knowledge, promotion of mystical seekership, and suspicion of "Establishment" discourses' than a 'novel and surprising phenomenon' emerging out of New Age spiritualism and conspiracy theory (2015: 379, 367). What both studies ultimately suggest, then, is that conspiracy theorising proper is indeed more prominent among men, and that women only 'catch up' once spiritualism is added to the belief system.

However, this does not mean that women never conceive of politics or society in conspiracist terms. Popular feminist writers like Betty Friedan or Naomi Wolf, for example, have used rhetorical devices and arguments that draw on conspiracist language in order to write about the political system and the experiences of women within this system in the second half of the twentieth century. Their critique of patriarchy often treats it '*as if* it were a conspiracy, without ever fully cashing out the metaphor into literal fact' (Knight 2000: 124 [italics in original]). Even though they repeatedly insist that their arguments are not conspiracy theories, they nevertheless repeatedly use conspiracy as a metaphor to strengthen their claims (2000: 118). Naomi Wolf, for instance, states in the beginning of her analysis that '[t]his is not a conspiracy theory; it doesn't have to be' (2002: 17). Similarly, Betty Friedan concedes that the feminine mystique is '[o]f course, … not an economic conspiracy directed against women' but rather a 'byproduct of our general confusion' (1966: 198). Through these statements, even though they are careful to not make an explicit link, both authors nevertheless succeed in implicitly linking the idea of conspiracy to patriarchy. They never explicitly claim that a conspiracy exists, but use the language of conspiracist discourse in order to create a strong us-versus-them opposition.

Conspiracy, then, becomes a metaphor for larger structures at work. As is the case with Melley's concept of agency panic, conspiracy becomes a scapegoat, an enemy that can be blamed for structural problems and developments which are otherwise out of the individual's influence. The agency of the individuals – in this case the agency of women – is perceived to be threatened by societal structures. However, in order to address and discuss this issue, someone needs to be the scapegoat that can be blamed. For Friedan and Wolf, this someone is the patriarchal system itself. In fact, Melley's concept of *'postmodern transference'* can be fruitfully applied to their texts (2002: 63 [italics in original]). According to Melley, postmodern transference is one of the two key components of agency panic. When agency panic arises, vast organisations or systems are treated as if they were individuals, assigning to them individuality and motivation (2002: 63). Moreover, the individual's agency is transferred to the larger organisation or system, which can now act instead of them (Melley 2000: 41). This is exactly the case in these feminist texts: They treat patriarchy as a conspiracy to articulate their anger and frustration about the situation of women in society. In this way, the patriarchal system is imagined as maliciously acting against them and intentionally robbing them of their individual agency.

Obviously, this conspiracist language cannot adequately capture the real mechanisms of oppression, since societal structures and historical developments cannot be reduced to the actions of individual people. Peter Knight calls this the 'impossibility of naming the problem in an unproblematic way' because 'there is no language adequate to capture both the necessity of holding people responsible, and the knowledge that history is larger than the work of any group of individuals' (2000: 140). The metaphor of conspiracy has to fail because a system or societal structure cannot be treated as if it were a group of individuals.

However, the metaphor allows these feminist writers to analyse a structural problem as if there was somebody to hold personally responsible. The tropes of conspiracy enable them to address 'questions of blame, responsibility and agency, but also ... link the personal and the political in one transcoding metaphor around which a women's movement might coalesce' (Knight 2000: 118). The rhetoric of conspiracy, then, fulfils the important function of creating a group identity for those opposing patriarchal oppression. According to the familiar logic of 'us-versus-them' that underlies all conspiracy theories, it posits the women as the victims of a malignant plot, and the men as the conspirators and victimisers.

One important rhetorical strategy these accounts of patriarchy share with conspiracy theories is the insistence that there are no coincidences. In fact, the 'figuration of conspiracy articulates otherwise uncoordinated suspicions that daily life is controlled by larger, unseen forces which cannot be the result of mere coincidence' (Knight 2000: 117). Thus, just as conspiracy theorists point out connections unperceived or dismissed as mere coincidence by the official version to argue that events are secretly orchestrated by sinister groups, the feminists actively write against notions of coincidence and contingency and 'read coincidence as signs of conspiracy' (Knight 2000: 119). During her investigation of dissatisfaction in middle-class housewives, Friedan, for example, 'wondered if it *was* a coincidence' only to conclude that 'when [she] saw this same pattern repeated over and over again in similar suburbs, [she] knew it could hardly be a coincidence' (1966: 224, 226 [italics in original]).

Another example of the conspiracist rhetoric these texts employ is the motif of brainwashing, which featured prominently in many American conspiracy theories during the post-war period. The concept is used by Friedan in order to conjure up an image of 'women as innocent victims of a scientific process of mind manipulation by external forces' (Knight 2000: 120). Friedan evokes the image that women are brainwashed by professors, psychologists and the media into accepting their role as housewives rather than pursuing a career (1966: 120). The male conspirators, who all work in the media, educational institutions or as doctors, brainwash their female victims into accepting their 'right' place in society. Friedan uses the term 'brainwashing' to refer to this process, but she puts it in quotation marks. She argues that 'the feminine mystique ... "brainwashed" American women ... for more than fifteen years' (1966: 174). By putting the term 'brainwashed' in quotation marks, she achieves exactly the effect that Knight describes as treating patriarchy as a metaphorical conspiracy. She uses the terms and rhetoric conspiracy theorists would use, but she also distances herself from them at the same time through the quotation marks, implying that she is only using this language metaphorically.

More directly, Naomi Wolf claims that the 'rituals of the beauty backlash ... [are] *literally* drawing on traditional techniques of mystification and thought control, to alter women's minds' (2002: 88 [italics in original]). The images of 'mystification', 'thought control' and 'mind altering' are simply other terms for brainwashing. The beauty myth, which is her version of the feminine mystique, becomes personified. She ascribes direct agency to the beauty backlash in utilising techniques reminiscent of brainwashing in order to control and oppress the female population. She even explicitly states that this 'comparison should be no metaphor' (2002: 88). As a consequence, her analysis comes even closer to a conspiracy theory than Friedan's. Even though she still shies away from directly calling the beauty myth a conspiracy, she explicitly casts the oppression of women in terms historically associated with conspiracy theorising.

Nevertheless, overall the conspiracy in Wolf and Friedan remains a metaphorical one. But, there are of course many texts that are far more explicit and direct in their accusations of conspiracy. We may not know for sure yet if men are more prone to believe in conspiracy theories than women, even though much qualitative research and some quantitative studies suggest as much. But scholars agree that gender and sexuality are of central importance for many accusations of conspiracy across time and space, as I will demonstrate in the following section by way of two case studies.

## The importance of gender and (deviant) sexuality in conspiracy theory narratives

Gender and sexuality figure prominently in many conspiracy theories throughout the centuries. Many of them are fuelled by a crisis of hegemonic gender roles. In order to illustrate this, I will first examine the mid-nineteenth century anti-Catholic conspiracy theory in the U.S.A. by analysing a prominent example of a convent captivity narrative in which Catholic priests are portrayed as sexual predators preying on innocent Protestant girls. I will then move on to the second half of the twentieth century and the American anti-communist conspiracy theory in which the conspirators were predominantly portrayed as homosexuals, threatening not only the political system but again the very foundation of the patriarchal system in the individual's home as well as nationwide. Thus, I will show that gender and sexuality are indeed important aspects in conspiracy theory narratives over time and fulfil the important function of 'othering'. Anxieties about changing gender roles and norms regarding sexuality are often transferred to a different realm such as politics and, more often than not, are fuelled by a crisis of masculinity.

Anti-Catholic conspiracy theories in the antebellum U.S.A., for example, heavily relied on arguments about sexuality, painting an image of sexually abusive priests in Catholic convent schools preying on innocent American girls. Anti-Catholic sentiments in the U.S.A. date back to the seventeenth century, but during the Jacksonian era they developed into a conspiracy theory that claimed that the democracy and freedom of the American republic were threatened by Catholic immigrants who were only loyal to the Pope and the European monarchs. Between the 1830s and 1850s, a large number of Americans were convinced that Rome, together with the Austrian empire and other Catholic monarchies in Europe, were trying 'to subvert, through the instrumentality of the Catholic religion, the Democratic institutions of the country' (Morse 1855 [1835]: 12). One important step in this scheme was allegedly the establishment of educational institutions in the U.S.A. Samuel Morse, for example, points to the threat in observing that Catholic schools 'are establishing in all parts of the country, colleges, convents, and seminaries, by means of Austrian money in the hands of the Jesuits' (1855: 23). In the face of growing numbers of immigrants, the cultural work of these conspiracy theories was to promote national unity by clearly identifying the subverting other. As David Davis puts it in a seminal essay on the similarities of anti-Masonic, anti-Catholic and anti-Mormon conspiracy theories, the key function of these conspiracy theories was to promote unity and 'clarify national values' (1960: 215).

As Davis demonstrates, these three conspiracy theories are very similar in tone and tropes in that they cast the alleged conspirators as sexually deviant. In the case of the anti-Catholic conspiracy theory, the accusations could draw on a long history of suspicion that cast priests as sexual predators. According to Hofstadter, 'the anti-Catholics developed an immense lore about libertine priests, the confessional as an opportunity for seduction, licentious convents and monasteries, and the like' (1964: 21–2). He furthermore claims that '[a]nti-Catholicism has always been the pornography of the Puritan' (1964: 21). As Davis shows, priests were thought to have perfected their arts of seduction over centuries. They were believed to not recognise 'Protestant marriages as valid' and to be preying on the virtuous American housewives and daughters (1960: 218). Davis attributes this obsession with sex in these narratives to an 'increasing anxiety and uncertainty over sexual values and the proper role of woman', which were then projected into these conspiracy theories (1960: 219).

The genre of antebellum anti-Catholicism where the concerns about sexuality come to the fore most explicitly is the convent captivity narrative, a generic hybrid in which both the Puritan captivity narrative and the Gothic novel have left their traces. The reason for the popularity of this genre was the underlying recognition that the protagonist's experiences functioned as signifier for the republic as a whole (Butter 2014: 141). By threatening the integrity and morality of virtuous American Protestant girls, the republican virtue of the whole nation was threatened. These narratives typically consist of women's – allegedly true – accounts of time as captives in Catholic convents, where they were supposedly exposed to physical and psychological violence and moral corruption before they eventually managed to escape to tell their tales. These captivity narratives portray convents as locations of illicit sex and the Catholic priests as being sexually abusive, taking advantage of both the Catholic nuns and Protestant girls enrolled in the convent's school by their unsuspecting parents.

The most popular and influential narrative of this kind was Maria Monk's *Awful Disclosures of the Hotel Dieu Nunnery* (1837), 'which sold 20,000 copies within just a few weeks, and 300,000 copies by 1860, at home and abroad' (Schultz 1999: vii). Maria Monk was born in Canada about 1817 and, according to Schultz, it is uncertain whether she actually ever spent time at the Hotel Dieu Nunnery or whether she invented the whole story. Monk's mother claimed that she never went to the nunnery, but was, in fact, facing mental health problems that resulted from an early childhood accident (1999: xv–xvi). Nevertheless, Monk's narrative of the horrors she allegedly lived through in the convent was extremely influential and strengthened the image of the priests as villains and sexual predators. As Monk tells the story, she first entered the Congregational Nunnery in Montreal as a student before she decided to become a novice at the Black Nunnery and eventually even chose to enter the convent as a nun. She reveals that, after her taking the veil, 'one of [her] great duties was, to obey the priests in all things; and this [she] soon learnt, to [her] utter astonishment and horror, was to live in the practice of criminal intercourse with them' (1837: 47).

While this does not sound very conspiracist in itself, Monk's revelations have to be seen in connection with many other anti-Catholic texts that were circulating at the time and that her readers were undoubtedly familiar with. While the texts by male writers like Morse or Lyman Beecher exposed the larger picture of the Catholic plot, convent captivity narratives like Monk's provided the lurid details, 'exposing' how Protestant girls were corrupted in order to destroy the foundations of American democracy. Thus, by bringing into the open what was allegedly happening in nunneries and convent schools, Monk adds significantly to the national narrative of conspiracy in which Catholic immigrants are plotting the demise of the American republic.

The illicit sexual relationships between the priests and the nuns in their care furthermore illustrate that the central threat in these narratives is the removal of 'the control of female sexuality and reproduction from the Protestant patriarchy' to the convent, thereby granting 'access only to Catholics' (Schultz 1999: xxi). According to Butter, this loss of control threatened not only the women themselves but the very foundation of the American republic because women were believed to play a vital role in the republic by educating their sons and raising them to fulfil the republican value of 'civic virtue' (2014: 138). By removing virtuous American women from Protestant control and re-educating them in monasteries and boarding schools closed to the public, the very foundation of the republic was threatened.

Monk illustrates this threat most explicitly through her language which moves 'to a level of pseudo-pornography' in her revelations and warnings to the public (Schultz 1999: xxii). She justifies this almost pornographic language in the preface to her *Disclosures* by stating that 'it is a far greater offence against virtue and decency to conceal than to proclaim their crimes' (1837: 4). By this she refers to what were, for nineteenth-century standards, explicit and graphic descriptions of sexual abuse throughout the narrative. Monk claims that her words are supposed to be a 'warning' to the public (1837: 4). She is fulfilling her civic duties in publishing the horrific story because it will keep other girls from the dangers she herself was ignorant of (1837: 4). The scandalous language throughout the narrative – surely highly entertaining for a part of the audience – is justified by laying open the conspiracy through showing this sexual perversion and the resulting crimes inside the Catholic convent.

Indeed, the horror does not stop at sexual deviancy, but sexual deviancy directly results in murder and even infanticide since, as a consequence of sexual intercourse between the nuns and the priests, '[i]nfants were sometimes born in the convent: but they were always baptised and immediately strangled' (1837: 49). In Chapter 9, which marks the shift to a more horrific narrative, Monk describes the murder of one of the nuns, St Francis, who was ordered to be killed by the Bishop because she 'still wished to escape from the convent; and that she had firmly resolved to resist every attempt to compel her to the commission of crimes which she detested' (1837: 101). This episode does not only add to the list of sins the Catholic priests are guilty of and illustrate where this sexual deviancy leads to, but also shows the result of resistance to the Catholic authorities. In her determination to not let herself be morally corrupted, and even wanting to actively remove herself from these influences, St Francis has chosen her own death sentence.

The only reason why Monk herself is in the end able to escape the convent is her status as an expectant mother. Schultz observes that, at the close of her narrative, Maria Monk reveals being pregnant and 'asserts that she escaped from the convent to prevent the murder of the child she was carrying – whose father, she said, was a Catholic priest' (1999: xvi). In order to protect her child and thus fulfil her civic duty as an American woman and mother, Monk manages to escape the Catholic threat and return to Protestant patriarchal protection, where she and her unborn child are safe.

The sexual and gender politics conveyed in these convent captivity narratives, then, is a strong advocacy for Protestant notions of domesticity. Women who leave the domestic sphere, join a convent and consequently abdicate their role as mothers become victims of horrific crimes. The threat to American hegemonic femininity through sexual deviancy and moral corruption associated with the Catholic monasteries and boarding schools is thus a threat to the entire republic. The removal of the control over femininity from the patriarchy would mean the collapse of the latter since the whole system relied on the domestic role of women as educators. Thus, the convent captivity narratives, explicitly promoted as 'warnings', are supposed to keep parents from sending their daughters to Catholic schools and to keep Protestant girls from joining a convent by their own. According to Butter, these narratives 'projected domesticity not as the problem but as the solution to the perversions caused by convent life' (2014: 153). In domestic life and under strong patriarchal authority, the girls as well as the future of the republic as a whole are protected.

Similar to the anti-Catholic conspiracy theory in the nineteenth century, gender and sexuality perceived as deviant are central to the American anti-communist conspiracy theory during the 1950s. However, an important difference to the earlier conspiracy theory is that the causal connection between conspiracy and devious sexuality is now reversed. While the Catholic conspiracy in the nineteenth century manifested itself in devious sexuality – the abuse of Protestant women was a strategy to destroy the foundations of the American republic – sexuality in the Cold War U.S.A. allegedly led to conspiracy. Homosexuals, as well as women who did not fit into the ideal of hegemonic femininity, were considered the most likely candidates to become communist conspirators. The narratives of homosexual conspirators and American women subverting the U.S.A. from within illustrate the 'anxieties about sexuality, manhood, and the self [which] surfaced in cold war political rhetoric and intersected with anxieties about Communism and national security' – anxieties that were in no way new to national narratives (Cuordileone 2005: xx).

As already hinted at in the previous section, a crisis of masculinity fuelled the anti-communist and other conspiracy theories during the post-war period. It found expression in the twofold imagination of perceived threats by both homosexuals and women. While women were the victims in nineteenth century conspiracy narratives, they now became the perpetrators. As Melley highlights, F.B.I. Director J. Edgar Hoover, for example, claimed in *Masters of Deceit* that 'many high-ranking communist agents were "attractive," "smartly-dressed," apparently patriotic American women' (2008: 156). Femininity became the subverting 'other' in this conspiracy against which ideal masculinity was constructed. Cuordileone, for example, describes femininity during this crisis of masculinity at the height during the 1950s as the 'oppositional archetype against which a healthy autonomous male self could be measured, or as the purveyor of feminizing values and forces that emasculated the culture or crushed the male ego' (2005: 104). John Frankenheimer's *The Manchurian Candidate* (1962) is a prominent example which – from the perspective of the early 1960s when the wave of anti-communism had largely abided – reflects upon the central fears of the 1950s anti-communist scare and illustrates the two central motifs of 1950s anti-communist conspiracy narratives: Overbearing femininity and brainwashing.

*The Manchurian Candidate* combines two key motifs of 1950s conspiracist discourse, brainwashing and deviant sexuality, by establishing associations between 'hypnotic suggestion and female sexuality' (Melley 2008: 157). The threat of feminisation is most obviously represented by Senator Iselin's overbearing wife Eleanor, a communist spy, who embodies the movie's central threat to the U.S.A. She manipulates both her son and Raymond Shaw, the protagonist, in order to assassinate a presidential candidate. Her manipulation tool is thought control. As is revealed fairly early in the film, Raymond Shaw and his fellow soldiers have been brainwashed by Soviet and Chinese agents during the Korean War. Instead of remembering the brainwashing, however, the soldiers are led to remember an afternoon in a ladies' gardening club. This telling image explicitly links the idea of brainwashing to femininity. In addition, the trigger with which Eleanor Iselin can activate Shaw and turn him into a slave who does anything she orders is the deck card *Queen of Diamonds*, another obvious symbol of femininity. Male agency, as well as the whole patriarchal system, is thus depicted as threatened by the 'domestic female influence' (2008: 159). Therefore, Melley concludes, the movie's 'deepest worry is neither communism nor anticommunism but embattled human autonomy, specifically male autonomy' (2008: 157). Anti-communist conspiracy theories, thus, can be described as the battleground for negotiations of masculinity and male agency, which are threatened by changing gender roles.

In addition to overbearing femininity, homosexuality – especially among men – became a prime indicator for a communist conspiracy. One prominent event that inextricably linked the anti-communist cause to the perceived threat of homosexuality was, according to Cuordileone, the Alger Hiss case. When questioned by the House Un-American Activities Committee (H.U.A.C.), Whittaker Chambers, former *Time* magazine editor and accused communist, named Alger Hiss as a fellow communist offender. In his written statement to the F.B.I., Chambers claimed that his goal was to 'stop the Communist conspiracy', thus explicitly confirming the suspicions many harboured about large-scale infiltration and subversion (Chambers 1948: 151). In addition, he confessed in much detail to the F.B.I. about the 'promiscuous life he had secretly led as a "homosexual" and a married man, the parks and hotels he frequented, the compulsion with which he sought male sexual partners' (Cuordileone 2005: 42). His homosexuality soon became public knowledge and thus 'fed the imagination that linked communism and "sexual perversion" together' (2005: 44). Moreover, in the eyes of many conservatives, the case – and Hiss's undisputed guilt – 'proved both the legitimacy of the HUAC mission and the rumors of New Deal "treason" that had circulated for years' (2005: 41). In the following years, the hunt for communists in public office became closely intertwined with the cleansing of homosexuals from government positions.

However, the targeting of homosexuals and especially homosexual men in conspiracy theories is by no means limited to the 1950s or the U.S.A. In contemporary Russia, for instance, the anti-homosexual propaganda employs a very similar rhetoric. Homosexuality is closely linked to liberalism – the perverting and undermining 'other' in Russian society. Gender is one of the identity categories that, in recent years, has become an important part of liberal ideology and its efforts to promote tolerance. In ideologies that perceive liberalism as evil, as undermining national and Christian values, gender becomes the scapegoat to discuss issues of traditional family values. Homosexuals, as well as women who choose partners outside of their ethnicity, are seen as the subverting force working towards a complete destruction of those traditional family values (Borenstein 2019).

In addition, similar arguments about gender and sexuality can also be found in white supremacist conspiracy theories fuelling Islamophobia in contemporary Western societies. One such example would be the so-called 'Replacement Theory', which is based on the argument that 'white women are not having enough children and that falling birthrates will lead to white people around the world being replaced by nonwhite people' (Bowles 2019). The conspiracy theorists here claim that the feminist movement has indoctrinated white women to leave their place at home raising children in order to, for example, pursue a career. By following this ideology imposed by elites and gender equality activists to openly criticise gender imbalance and the patriarchal order, women actively contribute to the downfall of white people by weakening their position in contrast to other cultures in which this alleged feminist conspiracy does not have such strong influences. This new version of hegemonic femininity and the resulting removal of control over female reproduction from the patriarchal system – which is a narrative that can be seen as a direct continuation of the anti-Catholic conspiracy theory's narrative – is perceived as a threat to the national group and functions as an argument to denounce the other group, which is perceived as threatening.

These examples show that gender and sexuality are, in fact, central concerns for conspiracy rhetoric across time and cultures. Their function is to identify the deviant other, against which one's own (national) identity is constructed. Anxieties about gender and sexuality often become the battleground for conspiracist rhetoric in order to repudiate the political or religious other. The reason behind this is very often a crisis of hegemonic masculinity and a crisis of patriarchy. Just as Catholic priests were portrayed as taking control over female sexuality and thus reproductivity from Protestant men, homosexuality and female emancipation are perceived to threaten the hegemonic position of men as the protectors and leaders of modern society during the post-war era U.S.A. as well as in contemporary societies. Patriarchy is in both cases the institution threatened by the conspirators.

## Conclusion

Gender and sexuality are of great importance to conspiracy theories and their rhetoric. They play an essential part in the process of 'othering', as my discussion of different conspiracy theories has shown. Even though psychologists and political scientists mostly agree that gender has no or only little effect on the belief in conspiracy theory, most qualitative research suggests that masculinity plays a central part in both the production and dissemination of conspiracy theories. I identified the crisis of masculinity as one key factor fuelling conspiracy theories. In addition, sexuality and gender are of central importance to the content of many conspiracy theories since the enemy is often portrayed as the sexually deviant 'other'.

However, there is still very little research on these important aspects – especially concerning the first aspect of whether men or women are more prone to believe in conspiracy theories. The existing research suggests that there is far more work to be done. Concerning the question of who is more prone to believe in conspiracy theories, psychological studies need to focus directly on the question of whether or not gender has an influence on conspiracy belief. In addition, more ethnographic work needs to be done in order to support or dismiss the claims made by other disciplines. Concerning the importance of gender and sexuality for the content of conspiracy theories, it would be interesting to see if gender and sexuality are indeed central aspects in all kinds of conspiracy theories, or if they are particularly prominent in explicitly political conspiracy theories. In addition, most of the research so far has focused on masculinity and narratives produced by men. Additional work concerning femininity and conspiracy narratives by women should become a research focus across the disciplines.

## Note

1 However, Melley acknowledges that notions of gender are just as important in narratives by female writers who use this concept of 'agency panic to illuminate the violent effects of patriarchal social scripts' (2000: 33).

## References

Asprem, E. and Dyrendal, A. (2015) 'Conspirituality reconsidered: how surprising and how new is the confluence of spirituality and conspiracy theory?', *Journal of Contemporary Religion*, 30(3): 367–82.

Borenstein, E. (2019) *Plots against Russia: conspiracy and fantasy after socialism*, New York: Cornell UP.

Bowles, N. (2019) '"Replacement Theory", a racist, sexist doctrine, spreads in far-right circles', *New York Times*, 18 March. Available at: www.nytimes.com/2019/03/18/technology/replacement-theory.html?rref=collection%2Fspotlightcollection%2Fchristchurch-attack-new-zealand&action=click&contentCollection=world&region=stream&module=stream_unit&version=latest&contentPlacement=53&pgtype=collection. [Accessed 27 August 2019.]

Brotherton, R. (2015) *Suspicious minds: why we believe conspiracy theories*, London: Bloomsbury.

Butter, M. (2014) *Plots, designs, and schemes: American conspiracy theories from the Puritans to the present*, Berlin: de Gruyter.

Butter, M. (2018) *'Nichts ist wie es scheint': über Verschwörungstheorien*, Berlin: Suhrkamp.

Chambers, W. (1948) 'Statement to the FBI: December 3, 1948', in E. Schrecker (ed.) *The age of McCarthyism: a brief history with documents*, 2nd edn, reprint, New York: Bedford/St. Martin's, 2002, pp. 148–51.

Christ, B. (2014) '"What kind of man are you?": the gendered foundations of U.S. conspiracism and of recent conspiracy theory scholarship', in M. Butter and M. Reinkowski (eds.) *Conspiracy theories in the United States and the Middle East: a comparative approach*, Berlin/Boston: de Gruyter, pp. 311–32.

Cuordileone, K.A. (2005) *Manhood and American political culture in the Cold War*, London: Routledge.

Davis, D.B. (1960) 'Some themes of counter-subversion: an analysis of anti-Masonic, anti-Catholic, and anti-Mormon literature', *Journal of American History*, 47(2): 205–24.

Friedan, B. (1966) *The feminine mystique*, New York: Dell Publishing.

Ginsburg, T. (2018) *Die Reise ins Reich: unter Reichsbürgern*, Berlin: Das Neue Berlin.

Hofstadter, R. (1964) 'The paranoid style in American politics', *The paranoid style in American politics and other essays*, reprint, Cambridge: Harvard UP, 1996, pp. 3–40.

Jolley, D. and Douglas, K.M. (2014) 'The social consequences of conspiracism: exposure to conspiracy theories decreases intentions to engage in politics and to reduce one's carbon footprint', *British Journal of Psychology*, 105(1): 35–56.

Kay, J. (2011) *Among the truthers: a journey through America's growing conspiracist underground*, New York: HarperCollins.

Knight, P. (2000) *Conspiracy culture: from Kennedy to the X Files*, London: Routledge.

Marchlewska, M., Cichocka, A., Lozowski, F., Górska, P. and Winiewskim, M. (2019) 'In search of an imaginary enemy: Catholic collective narcissism and the endorsement of *gender conspiracy beliefs*', *The Journal of Social Psychology*, 159: 1–14.

Melley, T. (2000) *Empire of conspiracy: the culture of paranoia in postwar America*, London: Cornell UP.

Melley, T. (2002) 'Agency panic and the culture of conspiracy,' in P. Knight (ed.) *Conspiracy nation: the politics of paranoia in postwar America*, New York/London: New York UP, pp. 57–81.

Melley, T. (2008) 'Brainwashed! Conspiracy theory and ideology in the postwar United States', *New German Critique*, 103(35): 145–64.

Monk, M. (1837) *Awful disclosures of the Hotel Dieu Nunnery of Montreal*, 2nd rev. edn, London: James S. Hodson.

Morse, S.F.B. (1835) *Foreign conspiracy against the liberties of the United States*, 7th rev. edn, reprint, New York: American and Foreign Christian Union, 1855.

Rees, J.H. and Lamberty, P. (2019) 'Mitreißende Wahrheiten: Verschwörungsmythen als Gefahr für den gesellschaftlichen Zusammenhalt', in A. Zick, B. Küpper and W. Berghan (eds.) *Verlorene Mitte – feindselige Zustände: rechtsextreme Einstellungen in Deutschland 2018/19*, published for the Friedrich-Ebert-Stiftung by F. Schröter, Bonn: Dietz, pp. 203–22.

Schultz, N.L. (1999) *Veil of fear: nineteenth-century convent tales by Rebecca Reed and Maria Monk*, Madison: NotaBell Books.

Uscinski, J.E. and Parent, J.M. (2014) *American conspiracy theories*, New York: Oxford UP.

Van Prooijen, J.-W. and Acker, M. (2015) 'The influence of control on belief in conspiracy theories: conceptual and applied extensions', *Applied Cognitive Psychology*, 29(5): 753–61.

Ward, C. and Voas, D. (2011) 'The emergence of conspirituality', *Journal of Contemporary Religion*, 26(1): 103–21.

Wolf, N. (2002) *The beauty myth: how images of beauty are used against women*, New York: HarperCollins.

# 3.4
# CONSPIRACY THEORIES, POLITICAL IDEOLOGY AND POLITICAL BEHAVIOUR

*Hulda Thórisdóttir, Silvia Mari and André Krouwel*

## Introduction

It has been said that conspiracy theories are for outsiders (Uscinski, Parent 2014), referring to those who feel distant from authorities and other power holders. In this chapter, we explore the link between conspiracy theories, political beliefs and political engagement in order to answer the question of whether conspiracy theories can be viewed as a vehicle for the outsider to articulate their doubts about governments and ruling powers. In this context, we specifically examine whether belief in conspiracy theories is linked with a discernible profile of political engagement and participation. Do we see evidence for engagement or disengagement with conventional politics and actors, or does the conspiratorial mindset drive citizens towards anti-establishment and fringe political parties? What about non-conventional political participation?

After defining and clarifying our terms, we will start out by examining political attitudes and orientations in order to assess whether beliefs in conspiracy theories are more prevalent on the left or on the right, whether they are mostly found at the fringes of mainstream attitudes or if they are primarily a function of ideological content. After that, we will turn to research on conventional political participation like voting in elections. We demonstrate the strong relationship across Europe that conspiracy belief is linked with voting for a right-wing populist party. We also examine more generally if the likelihood of voting for an opposition party increases with belief in conspiracy theories. While evidence is scarcer than on voting behaviour, we then move on to political participation more widely, ranging from turnout at elections, political interest and other forms of civic engagement such as membership in civil society organisations.

In the chapter we distinguish between a *conspiracy belief* and *conspiracy mentality*. Conspiracy belief is when an individual assumes that a conspiracy theory provides an accurate explanation of particular events. Conspiracy mentality is a more general dispositional propensity to believe in conspiracies, which Imhoff and Bruder (2014) have argued functions as a generalised political attitude in itself.

Throughout the chapter, we will rely primarily on previously published studies but will supplement our coverage with recent data collected in 13 European countries – the European Voter Election Studies conducted by André Krouwel in 2019 – and data from a nationally representative survey conducted in Iceland.

## Conspiracy theories and politics

Conspiracy theories can be a constructive force in politics for several reasons. They may lead to pressure on authorities to disclose information and they can even unearth dishonest behaviour (Clarke 2002). Conspiracy theories can serve as a psychological tool for the political outsider to regain a sense of control and increase predictability because they offer an explanation for events that the official account attributes to coincidences, natural forces or a series or random events (Sullivan et al. 2010). Importantly, they also hold out the promise of control and even agency by opening up a channel for the conspiracy believer to potentially expose the fraudulent authorities and thereby undermine and even topple them. More often, however, conspiracy theories have negative political and societal consequences such as refusal to vaccinate, harassment of political actors or even victims of mass shootings (Douglas et al. 2019; see also Chapter 2.7).

Douglas et al. (2017) outlined three main reasons why people believe in conspiracy theories. The first reason is epistemic, that is, conspiracy theories help people to make sense of the world around them and to understand events they are struggling to comprehend. Second, conspiracy theories can offer security and predictability in uncertain and anxiety-provoking situations. Third, they claim that conspiracy theories can serve as a way to 'save-face' for those on the losing end of a situation, such as elections. Although people undoubtedly adopt conspiracy theories due to a mix of all three reasons, the primary causes and consequences of adopting them may differ between people. A person with a tenuous understanding and limited knowledge of complicated political events may reach out to a conspiracy theory for meaning-making whereas the seasoned and involved political observer may find solace in a conspiracy theory after a stinging defeat.

Although not the focus of this chapter, we note that it is not only citizens who engage with conspiracy theories; governments have used conspiracy theories to preserve the status quo against those they perceive as subversive or threatening to the regime. Conspiracy theories can thus be spread in order to squash unwelcome political movements, as happened in the U.S.A. during the McCarthy era with communist sympathisers (Uscinski, Parent 2014).

## Political trust and knowledge

Most research on the relationship between conspiracy beliefs and various indicators of people's relationship with the political system have been cross-sectional, making any causal claims debatable. Several well-established findings have emerged from the research. It is clear that belief in conspiracy theories is related both to low interpersonal trust (Hollander 2018) and to low political trust (Swami et al. 2010; Uscinski, Parent 2014; Miller et al. 2016). This is also confirmed in an 11-country cross-cultural study (Mari et al. under review) in which political conspiracy beliefs were linked to generalised mistrust toward specific institutions (the government, the non-representative state bodies and security institutions), with few exceptions, across the different countries. There is also some experimental evidence showing that exposing people to conspiracy theories reduces trust in government. Kim and Cao (2016) showed that exposure to a film portraying the moon landing as a governmental conspiracy resulted in less trust in government officials both immediately after exposure and two weeks later. Einstein and Glick (2015) found the negative effect of conspiracy theories on trust, but only if the conspiracy theory was not explicitly labelled as such. In their study, explicitly naming it a conspiracy theory seemed to 'inoculate' people against it. Accordingly, Douglas and Sutton (2008: 217) have discussed the 'hidden impact' of conspiracy theories on attitudes. Their study showed that, after people had been exposed to a conspiracy theory about the death of Princess Diana, they exhibited increased inclination to disbelieve official accounts. A study using data from the 2016 American National Election Study demonstrated that believing the government knew about 9/11 in advance was to a high degree related to scepticism that votes are counted fairly in elections (Norris et al. 2019).

The role of political knowledge is not as clear, although it seems to matter. Miller et al. (2016) found that political knowledge was positively related to belief in conspiracy theories, but only among those low on political trust. Oliver and Wood (2014) reported that lower political knowledge predicted support for ideologically consistent conspiracy theories (such as Republicans believing that Obama was not born in the U.S.A.), but that knowledge did not matter if the theories were further removed from party skirmishes. This goes against the idea that people with little knowledge are more likely to adopt conspiracy theories because they offer explanations for complicated events (Douglas et al. 2017). The findings by Oliver and Wood are in line with a study showing that greater factual knowledge about the news media predicted less belief in conspiracy theories (Craft et al. 2017), and that lack of interest in news and public affairs was much more prevalent among Americans categorised as high on conspiratorial disposition compared to other respondents (Uscinski, Parent 2014). This could be, as mentioned above, because different groups of people reach out for conspiracy theories under different circumstances. The less knowledgeable do so in order to understand complicated events, whereas the more involved and politically knowledgeable reach out to conspiracy theories in order to cope with defeat. Furthermore, it is well established that, across the board, belief in conspiracy theories is negatively related to education (van Prooijen 2017).

## Political ideology

Anyone who contemplates the relationship between conspiracy theories and politics will soon wonder if and how they are related to ideological leanings, in particular whether they are more prominent on the left or on the right. With some disciplinary differences, the literature also refers to political ideology as political orientation or ideological self-positioning (Knight 2006). Ideology is conceived of as a belief structure that people use as a lens through which they perceive and understand the world: The individual processes and systematises all the information of social and political relevance – including conspiracy theories – to orient themselves in the political realm and to reduce its complexity (Morgan, Wisneski 2017). Thus, political ideology provides meaning and may shape related cognitive, affective and behavioural reactions (Hatemi, McDermott 2016).

Most commonly, ideology is conceived of as a unidimensional construct that encompasses the left to right continuum (or, in the U.S.A., liberal-conservative) in which the left (or liberal) reflects preference for advocating social change and rejecting social and economic inequality. The right (or conservative) position, on the other hand, stands for resistance to change and acceptance of inequality (e.g. Jost et al. 2009).

As reviewed by Jost et al. (2018), meta-analyses have shown that, compared to liberals, conservatives tend to be more dogmatic and averse to ambiguity, exhibit more cognitive rigidity and need for cognitive closure, and demonstrate a stronger desire for order and structure (e.g. Jost et al. 2003). Additionally, people on the right tend to perceive the social environment as more threatening compared to those on the left; more generally, the occurrence of threatening events (e.g. the news of a terrorist attack) leads to the so-called 'conservative shift' in public opinion (Thórisdóttir, Jost 2011; Jost et al. 2017). According to this perspective, conservatism is a form of motivated cognition, where 'the rigidity of the right' represents a motivated reaction to insecurity and threat, satisfying epistemic needs. The perception of threat is a crucial element, also when considering why people embrace conspiracy theories. As reviewed by Douglas *et al.* (2017), conspiracy theories may be used for epistemic motives, as causal explanations to satisfy their need for safety and insecurity when feeling threatened. Conspiracy theories may restore a sense of control when this seems lost since conspiracy theories offer individuals the chance to reject the official – but threatening – explanation of the events by adopting an alternative – but reassuring – narrative (Goertzel 1994). Bost and Prunier (2013: 124) suggested that the conspiratorial beliefs are part of a 'cheater detector' mechanism, able to reveal dangerous situations and help to reduce or remove the perceived threat. The same idea was proposed by van Prooijen and van Vugt (2018) in an evolutionary explanation of conspiracy theories in which they describe them as a by-product of different psychological mechanisms, including threat management. Thus, in terms of motivation, conservatism and conspiracy theories seem to share the epistemic motive aimed at threat reduction. It is, therefore, reasonable to ask whether the left-right political continuum might be a determinant of conspiracy beliefs and whether there is a positive association between the right (conservatism) and endorsement of such beliefs.

The literature so far has found mixed results. On the one hand, some evidence supports this view: right-wing positions were found more predictive of political conspiracy beliefs (Galliford, Furnham 2017) measured with the Generic Conspiracist Beliefs Scale (Brotherton *et al.* 2013); similar results were also found in a representative sample from the 2012 American National Election Study (A.N.E.S.) dataset (Miller *et al.* 2016) and the Italian National Election Study dataset in Italy (Mancosu *et al.* 2017), in which specific conspiracy beliefs relevant to those countries were considered. On the other hand, some research did not find support for this relationship: Political ideology was not related to conspiratorial predispositions in an American sample (Uscinski, Parent 2014), nor did it determine support for specific anti-science conspiracy theories (Oliver, Wood 2014) or beliefs related to the economy in Greece and Italy (Mari *et al.* 2017).

The overall picture becomes even more complicated if we consider extremist ideological attitudes. People who adhere to extreme political ideologies manifest rigid self-convictions and rely on information about socio-political matters by other extremists, thus revealing a black-and-white style of processing (e.g. Fernbach *et al.* 2013). Such an epistemology leads to a pessimistic view about the functioning of society, independent of whether it is extremism on the right or on the left. Also, to cope with uncertainty and threat, extremists tend to construct a predictable understanding of the world. Evidence based on an Amazon Mechanical Turk U.S. sample and Dutch representative samples found that endorsement of conspiracy beliefs was stronger at the extremes of the political ideology continuum (van Prooijen *et al.* 2015). In particular, the authors revealed a 'slanted' U-shaped function: Individuals positioned at the far left and the far right of the continuum expressed stronger conspiracism compared to those in the middle, but conspiracy beliefs were even more prevalent among those on the far right. Moreover, these results were not attributable to general attitude extremity. Similar findings were described by Krouwel *et al.* (2017), who found support for the curvilinear relationship between the left/right continuum and conspiracism in Sweden. Interestingly, but conversely, the curve was steeper for participants on the left side of the continuum in Sweden, meaning that, in this case, leftists were more likely to subscribe to conspiracy beliefs.

Douglas *et al.* (2019), in their review, reflected on how to reconcile this variety of results on the political ideology-conspiracy theories link. A first explanation considers the dispositional factors: Even though people at both extremes of the continuum are likely to endorse various specific conspiracy beliefs, individuals positioned at the right side are even likelier because they are predisposed to do so. Indeed, their need to manage threat and uncertainty compels them to find explanations of the socio-political events (Jost *et al.* 2018), and conspiracy theories represent a way to manage the uncertainty. Such an explanation would not, however, account for Krouwel *et al.*'s (2017) findings from Sweden. Another explanation attributes the inconsistent results to the different methods, contexts and timing of data collection. For instance, talking specifically about extremism, Bartlett and Miller (2010) analysed the literature, ideology and propaganda of over 50 extremist groups from Europe and the U.S.A. that had been active over the last 30 years. They found that conspiracy theories were highly prevalent among those groups, although the specific content differed depending on the ideology of the extremist group. The authors hypothesised that, although conspiracy theories are not enough to cause radicalisation, they can serve as a 'radicalising multiplier' by increasing ingroup vs. outgroup distinction and by delegitimising dissenting voices by declaring them a part of the conspiracy. It is worth noting that research on the relationship between political ideology and conspiracy theories has almost exclusively focused on specific theories. Those are often highly partisan, and who supports them is dependent on political and cultural context. Future research should look into the role of ideology and a more general tendency to embrace conspiracy theories (Imhoff, Bruder 2014) more closely. An ongoing cross-cultural study conducted in 21 countries (Imhoff *et al.* 2019) has revealed a U-shape pattern in the whole sample, but with stronger prevalence of general conspiratorial thinking on the far-right side of the ideology continuum, thus resembling previous results that considered specific beliefs (van Prooijen *et al.* 2015).

Morgan and Wisneski (2017) advocate paying more attention to multi-dimensional conceptions of political ideology, such as the dual-process model of ideology. According to this model, individuals do not rely on the left-right (liberal/conservative) continuum but adopt broader social beliefs and values to orient themselves in the world and those beliefs drive their attitudes. More precisely, Duckitt's dual model includes right-wing authoritarianism (R.W.A.) and social dominance orientation (S.D.O.), dimensions that map onto social and economic attitudes, respectively. R.W.A. is a political attitude depicting an individual who tends to submit to the perceived established authorities and with a deeply rooted mentality following social conventions. S.D.O., in contrast, regards an individual's preference for hierarchy within society and dominance over lower status groups who are perceived as threatening to the advantaged group (see Duckitt 2001 for discussion of R.W.A. and S.D.O.).

Conspiracy beliefs, along with R.W.A. and S.D.O., work to protect and maintain the socio-political status quo (Goertzel 1994). Imhoff and Bruder (2014) suggested that people with high R.W.A. attitudes tend to embrace conspiracies that involve deviant high-power groups (e.g. antisemitic theories), whereas people with high S.D.O. attitudes tend to endorse beliefs involving the deviance of low-status and minority groups (e.g. anti-immigrant theories). Research exploring the relationships between these dimensions of political ideology and conspiracy theories has found that R.W.A. is a positive predictor of conspiracy mentality (Bruder *et al.* 2013; Imhoff, Bruder 2014), and specific conspiracy beliefs about the American presidents (Richey 2017) or groups in society (Grzesiak-Feldman, Irzycka 2009). However, this link is not always consistent: Berinsky (2012) did not find a relationship between R.W.A. and conspiracy beliefs. Only a few studies have found a positive association between S.D.O. and conspiracy beliefs (Swami 2012; see also Chapters 2.4 and 2.6 in this volume). Overall, it is clear that further research is needed to better understand and theoretically integrate the findings concerning political ideology and conspiracy theories. Research is needed that clearly accounts for different cultural contexts and whether the relationship is with specific conspiracy theories or a more general conspiracy mindset. In the next section, we turn to a proxy of political ideology, party affiliation.

## Party affiliation

To what extent is belief in conspiracies related to specific political parties and to which parties in particular? Some studies in the U.S.A. have found a relation between conspiracy thinking and political party affiliation, in particular with right-wing, conservative Republicans (Wright, Arbuthnot 1974) and preference for Trump during the 2016 presidential primaries (Oliver, Wood 2018). However, other work based on U.S. samples (Oliver, Wood 2014; Uscinski, Parent 2014) found no such link between political ideology or party affiliation and conspiracy belief. People are more likely to think that parties they did not vote for are involved in malevolent activities than representatives of the party they support (e.g. Claassen, Ensley 2016), yet this could also be attributed to dichotomous black and white thinking in systems in which two opposing parties dominate, the U.S. in particular. Another explanation for a lack of a clear pattern between party affiliation in the U.S. and belief in conspiracies could be attributed to the extremism effect discussed above (see also van Prooijen *et al.* 2015).

Yet, to what extent is conspiracy belief associated with party preference outside the U.S.A. in multi-party systems? One study (Krouwel *et al.* forthcoming) used the 2018 European Voter Election Survey (E.V.E.S.) dataset in which the relationship between vote propensities and conspiracy mentality in 13 European countries was analysed (Austria, Belgium, Germany, the Netherlands, Sweden, Italy, Spain, Portugal, Hungary, Denmark, Poland, Romania and France). In this study ($N = 88.488$), there was a strong negative correlation with belief in conspiracy theories and intent to vote for all of the progressive left, libertarian and centrist parties. In contrast, a clear pattern emerged of a strong positive correlation between vote propensity for populist anti-immigrant parties and conspiracy mentality. Among voters of the right-wing populist parties (Swedish Democrats, the P.V.V. in the Netherlands, Brothers of Italy, the A.f.D in Germany, the Danish People's Party in Denmark and Jobbik in Hungary), conspiracy mentalities were widespread. This suggests that extremist attitudes – in particular outgroup derogation (against immigrants) – is associated with conspiracy beliefs. This is in line with a previous finding showing that conspiracy beliefs were associated with support for populist politics (Castanho Silva *et al.* 2017).

Interestingly, the same positive relationship with conspiracy belief was also found for many radical left parties. In the Netherlands, for example, there is a strong correlation between a vote propensity for the Socialist Party (S.P.) and conspiracy belief, as is the case with Vänsterpartiet in Sweden, Alternativet and Enhedslisten in Denmark, and Die Linke in Germany. An explanation for this finding of conspiracy mentalities among voters at both ends of the political spectrum may be due to the relationship between conspiracy beliefs and anti-establishment attitudes, which are more widespread at the extremes (Schumacher, Rooduijn 2013; Mudde, Kaltwasser 2017).

In general, we find that likely voters for mainstream parties that often enter into governmental power are on the other end of the conspiracy-spectrum. In particular, voters for liberal, social democratic and Christian democratic parties are least prone to believe in conspiracies. This can be explained by the fact that political moderates have less need for epistemic clarity and are much more comfortable with the complexity of social problems and long-term policy commitments, rather than quick fixes by strong leaders (e.g. Hogg *et al.* 2010; van Prooijen, Krouwel 2019). Accordingly, Krouwel *et al.* (forthcoming) found that almost all establishment parties were immune to belief in conspiracies among their supporters. Exceptions from this overall pattern were found in Sweden, Portugal and, most prominently, in Austria. There, vote intention for the Freedom Party of Austria (a mainstream, conservative anti-immigrant party) was associated with conspiracy beliefs.

## Political participation

There is limited research on the relationship between belief in political conspiracy theories and political participation. Related research exists on the behavioural correlates of believing in science or health-related conspiracy theories. Among African Americans, believing that contraceptives are a plot to exterminate them leads to negative attitudes and less use of contraceptive methods (e.g. Bogart, Thorburn 2006). More generally, people who believe medical conspiracy theories are less likely to seek the help of medical professionals, and more likely to consult alternative sources instead (Oliver, Wood 2014). Causal evidence is scarcer, but Jolley and Douglas (2014a, 2014b) have shown that participants exposed to conspiracy narratives regarding vaccinations and climate change subsequently report lower intentions to vaccinate or to engage in climate-friendly behaviours.

Jolley and Douglas (2014a) argue that the influence of exposure to conspiracy theories may be a contributing factor to reduced levels of political engagement because people see no reason to partake in the political process if governments decide most things in shady deals anyway. Their own experimental studies supported this view. In a pair of experiments, they showed (with small effect sizes) that participants who were exposed to a text insinuating non-specified secretive plots by the government (Study 1) or that climate change is a hoax (Study 2) reported less intention to participate in politics in general and, in Study 2, to engage in climate-friendly behaviour in particular.

However, political participation takes on more forms than the conventional one. Lamberty and Leiser (2019) reported on four studies using diverse, but self-selected online samples, in which they examined how political action relates to both the conspiracy mindset and belief in specific conspiracy theories. In three studies with participants from the U.S.A. and Germany, they found that the conspiracy mindset and belief in specific conspiracy theories were related to lower intentions to take part in normative political action (e.g. voting) and increased willingness to engage with non-normative (e.g. unauthorised strike) and even violent action, both political and general. Their results stopped short of showing a causal relationship between conspiracy beliefs and non-normative or violent political behaviour. Similarly, Uscinski and Parent (2014) showed that around 16 per cent of survey respondents they categorised as high on conspiratorial predispositions deemed violence as an acceptable mode of expressing disagreement with the government. This is compared to around 8 per cent agreement by those with low or medium predisposition for conspiratorial thinking. Moreover, Mari et al. (2017) found that embracing economic conspiracy beliefs led to potential involvement in illegal political action (e.g. occupying buildings).

Studies have not uniformly demonstrated a relationship between adherence to conspiracy theories and lower intention to participate in conventional politics. Imhoff and Bruder (2014) found that, although conspiracy mentality positively predicted attribution of the Fukushima nuclear disaster to intentional misconduct, it interestingly also predicted a modest correlation with a desire to engage in both normative and non-normative anti-nuclear protests. Galliford and Furnham (2017) found no relationship between adherence to either medical or political conspiracy theories and intention to vote.

All the studies described above dealt with *intentions* to participate in politics. Even less is known about actual participation in various aspects of the political process. A survey among Americans published in Uscinski and Parent (2014) gives some of the best information we have. They divided respondents into three categories depending on their conspiracy predispositions. They found that 68 per cent in the high and 91 per cent in the low conspiracy predispositions categories reported to have voted in the 2012 presidential election. They also found people in the high category to be almost three times less likely to be registered voters compared to those in the low category. Their results also showed that people in the low conspiracy predisposition category were more likely than people in the other two groups to put up political signs, attend local meetings, work for a candidate, donate money or run for office. The difference in donations was stark, 37 per cent of those in the low categories had donated money but only 19 per cent and 16 per cent in the medium and high categories.

A more general view of the association between conspiracy beliefs and social engagement can be had from a study by Freeman and Bentall (2017). Using representative data from the U.S. population, they documented the correlation between endorsement of the item 'I am convinced there is a conspiracy behind many things in the world' and a plethora of factors tapping into physical, social and mental well-being. Their study demonstrated a remarkably robust relationship between endorsing the conspiracy item and virtually all measures of negative mental well-being, mental disorders, poor attachment and negative childhood family experiences, including the relative lack of friendships and closeness with their family. For the purposes of political engagement, the relative lack of friendship, closeness or engagement with relatives and families of those who endorsed the conspiracy item points to a lower societal and civic engagement overall.

## Supporting data

One of the authors (Thórisdóttir) of this chapter conducted a survey in the late spring of 2017 among a nationally representative sample of Icelanders ($N=651$) to examine the relationship between conspiracy beliefs and several indicators of social and political engagement. Many of the questions touched upon the topics discussed in the chapter above. First, the survey measured conspiracy beliefs by asking both about belief in specific theories but also by assessing a more general conspiracy mentality. Second, respondents were asked about their ideology, perceptions of threat, social engagement and voting intentions. Data was collected by the Social Sciences Research Institute (S.S.R.I.) at the University of Iceland.

Belief in conspiracy theories was measured in two ways: 1) *Conspiracy mentality questionnaire (C.M.Q.)* (Bruder *et al.* 2013), which has five statements rated on a scale from zero to 100 per cent (certainly not true to certain). For example, 'I think that many very important things happen in the world, which the public is never informed about'. 2) *Specific conspiracy theories*: Six conspiracy theories, four local and two global. For example, 'foreign creditors revealed damning information via the Panama papers in order to undermine the Icelandic Prime Minister at the time' and 'Islamists want to take over Europe and the USA and they have already sent infiltrators in order to make that happen'. Responses were from strongly disagree (one) to strongly agree (five). Statistical analysis showed that, despite some partisan differences, overall people were likely to either agree or disagree with all conspiracy theories, so they can be analysed together as one measure of specific conspiracy theories.

Other questions in the survey were the following: *Political orientation*: Measured as self-placement on the left-right scale from zero to ten (left – right). *Perceptions of societal danger*: Two questions on a scale from one to five: 'Do you agree or disagree that Icelandic language is under threat?' and 'Do you find it likely or unlikely that a terrorist attack will happen in Iceland in the next five years?'. *Civic efficacy*: Six questions measuring people's beliefs that ordinary citizens can influence society on a scale from one to five. For example, 'I can impact decisions made the government (local and general) if I want' and 'volunteering in society really has an effect'. *Close relationships*: Five questions on the quality and frequency of communications with one's family and friends, a question on the ability to approach them if needed and one question on loneliness. For example: 'Communication with my friends is good'. *Social engagement*: Six questions asking if people participate in the following: A political party, play sports with a club, are otherwise active with a sports club, other types of organised interest clubs, organised religion, boy scouts or similar, or other. *Intention to vote*: Three groups, a) those who stated a specific political party, b) those would not vote, or would turn in an invalid/blank vote, and c) those who did not know or declined to say.

Statistical analysis showed no relationship between political ideology and either the C.M.Q. or belief in specific conspiracy theories. Neither a linear nor a curvilinear relationship was found. Perceptions of impending terrorist attacks or that the Icelandic language is under threat were correlated with both measures of conspiracy beliefs, with a Pearson correlation coefficient ranging from about 0.10 to 0.40. Perhaps unsurprisingly, there was also a medium to strong correlation (around 0.40) between both conspiracy belief measures and civic efficacy. The more people endorse the conspiracy mentality or the specific six theories asked about in this survey, the less likely they are to believe ordinary citizens can influence authorities. There was also a small but significant relationship between the endorsement of conspiracy theories and poorer relationships with friends and family.

Turning to more direct measures of civic and political participation, the mean score on the conspiracy mentality questionnaire among people who reported participation in at least one volunteer organisation ($n=425$) was 0.37 points lower on the zero to ten scale than among those who did not participate in any organisation ($n=226$). For the specific conspiracy theories, the same pattern emerged. The mean endorsement was a little lower among people who participate compared to those who do not. In both cases, the difference between the means was significant using conventional statistical testing. Thus, people who participate in at least one volunteer organisation are to a slight extent less likely to endorse conspiracy theories compared to those who do not participate.

Finally, Table 3.4.1 shows the mean conspiracy endorsement of three different groups based on how they answered the question of what party they would vote for if the election were held tomorrow. The mean score on both the C.M.Q. and for specific conspiracy theories was significantly lower among those who mentioned a particular party or said they did not know, compared to the relatively small group of people who outright stated they would not vote or would turn in a blank vote.

To sum up, the data from the survey shows that the more people endorse conspiracy theories, the less they believe ordinary citizens are heard by or can influence authorities, the poorer their close interpersonal relationships, the stronger their perception of looming societal threat, the less likely they are to participate in volunteer organisations or to vote in elections. It is thus clear that all of the indicators available in the Icelandic data support the overall view that emerged from the literature review in the chapter so far: Belief in conspiracy theories is associated with less engagement, both interpersonally and politically, by those who endorse conspiracy theories compared to those who do not.

*Table 3.4.1* A comparison of conspiracy theory endorsement among different groups of Icelandic voters.

|  | Conspiracy mentality (1–10) | Conspiracy theories (1–5) |
| --- | --- | --- |
| Party mentioned ($n = 520$) | 6.86 (1.91) | 2.76 (0.85) |
| Don't know, will not tell ($n = 82$) | 6.87 (1.92) | 2.71 (0.72) |
| Will not vote, turn in blank ($n = 49$) | 7.62 (1.58) | 3.19 (0.65) |

## Conclusion

At the outset of this chapter, we posed the key question of whether conspiracy theories can legitimately be described as a vehicle for people to articulate their doubts about government and ruling powers. We further asked if belief in conspiracy theories is linked with a discernible profile of political engagement and participation, i.e. whether it promotes engagement or disengagement with politics, either conventional or non-conventional.

There is no doubt that conspiracy theories serve as a way to express distrust and discontent with authorities, and perhaps even distrust towards society more generally. As we reviewed above, several studies have demonstrated that conspiracy beliefs are linked with lack of political trust, especially when political knowledge is somewhat high. Conspiracy theories also seem to be linked with a discernible political profile, although this is much less clear for ideological leanings compared to political participation. Research on ideology has found mixed results for whether conspiracy beliefs are more pronounced on the left or on the right. It seems to depend on the national context, the way ideology is measured and whether conspiracy beliefs are measured as belief in specific conspiracy theories or as a general conspiracy mindset. The best generalisation we can make to date is that conspiracy beliefs are more common on the political extremes, and probably even more so on the right compared to the left. This was especially clear when we looked at new data from 13 European countries showing that, without exception, voters of right-wing populist parties scored relatively high on the conspiracy mindset. Voters of mainstream or extreme left-wing parties sometimes also scored relatively high, but this varied greatly between countries and probably depended on the current political climate within each country.

It is generally accepted that conspiracy theories form part of a monological belief system, that is, people tend to accept or reject most types of conspiracy theories and assimilate new information to fit under their current belief system. This makes conspiracy theories exceptionally difficult to repudiate (Goertzel 1994). The mechanism of motivated reasoning (e.g. Kunda 1990) may help illuminate what seems like contradictory results for the relationship between ideology and conspiracy beliefs. People who endorse different ideologies and worldviews may process the same information in different ways. They are motivated to interpret and adjust new information within their previous belief system. This is especially true when adopting conspiracy beliefs in line with party preference and political ideology (e.g. Uscinski, Parent 2014; Miller et al. 2016). For example, two individuals who are on the opposing ends of the political spectrum may share a general anti-establishment sentiment and thus both be high on the conspiracy mindset, but they may divide starkly along ideological lines when it comes to their endorsement of specific conspiracy theories.

The picture that emerges in the chapter from a review of the scant literature on political participation is fairly clear. The main theme is that belief in conspiracy theories is linked with less political and civic participation overall, with perhaps a slight uptick in proclivities for unconventional, even violent, participation. The literature also seems to support the idea that political outsiders use conspiracy theorising as a means to cope with threatening situations and environments. It has also been suggested that promotion of conspiracy theories may serve as a way to communicate with co-partisans and to promote collective action (Smallpage et al. 2017).

There are many potential avenues for future research on conspiracy theories and political functioning. Research on specific forms of participation is still scarce and, to date, the role of conspiracy beliefs or mindset in determining specific forms of civic engagement, such as membership in civil society organisations and unionisation, has received next to no attention. Likewise, it is unclear if, and when, conspiracy theories may promote political action. Relatedly, it may also help us better understand the function of conspiracy beliefs in the political arena if we study separately people high and low on political knowledge and interest. It is reasonable to assume that the people who follow politics may see conspiracy theories as a tool to voice dissatisfaction and may use them to propel like-minded citizens into action. Among people low on political interest, conspiracy theories may further solidify their distaste, lack of trust and alienation from the political process. Finally, as also suggested by Jolley et al. (see Chapter 2.7), it is possible that some conspiracies may lead to action because they generate anger, whereas others may generate a sense of greater vulnerability and powerlessness.

On a final note, researchers have just begun to study and debate the role of the Internet and social media in the development and diffusion of conspiracy theories (see e.g. Douglas *et al.* 2019). What is clear, however, is that online communities play a crucial role in the spread of conspiracy theories, and those communities tend to be both ideologically homogeneous and very polarised (Del Vicario *et al.* 2016). Future research on the effects of conspiracy beliefs on political participation needs to pay careful attention to if, and how, active engagement with conspiracy theories online translates to political participation, whether on- or off-line.

# References

Bartlett, J. and Miller, C. (2010) *The power of unreason: conspiracy theories, extremism and counter-terrorism*, London: Demos.
Berinsky, A.J. (2012) *'Rumors, truths, and reality: a study of political misinformation'*, Cambridge: Massachusetts Institute of Technology.
Bogart, L.M. and Thorburn, S. (2006) 'Relationship of African Americans' sociodemographic characteristics to belief in conspiracies about HIV/AIDS and birth control', *Journal of the National Medical Association*, 98(7): 1144–50.
Bost, P.R. and Prunier, S.G. (2013) 'Rationality in conspiracy beliefs: the role of perceived motive', *Psychological Reports*, 113(1): 118–28.
Brotherton, R., French, C.C. and Pickering, A.D. (2013) 'Measuring belief in conspiracy theories: the generic conspiracist beliefs scale', *Frontiers in Psychology*, 4: 279.
Bruder, M., Haffke, P., Neave, N., Nouripanah, N. and Imhoff, R. (2013) 'Measuring individual differences in generic beliefs in conspiracy theories across cultures: conspiracy mentality questionnaire', *Frontiers in Psychology*, 4: 225.
Castanho Silva, B., Vegetti, F. and Littvay, L. (2017) 'The elite is up to something: exploring the relation between populism and belief in conspiracy theories', *Schweizerische Zeitschrift für Politikwissenschaft*, 23(4): 423–43.
Claassen, R.L. and Ensley, M.J. (2016) 'Motivated reasoning and yard-sign-stealing partisans: mine is a likable rogue, yours is a degenerate criminal', *Political Behavior*, 38(2): 317–35.
Clarke, S. (2002) 'Conspiracy theories and conspiracy theorizing', *Philosophy of the Social Sciences*, 32(2): 131–50.
Craft, S., Ashley, S. and Maksl, A. (2017) 'News media literacy and conspiracy theory endorsement', *Communication and the Public*, 2(4): 388–401.
Del Vicario, M., Bessi, A., Zollo, F., Petroni, F., Scala, A., Caldarelli, G., Stanley, E. and Quattrociocchi, W. (2016) 'The spreading of misinformation online', *Proceedings of the National Academy of Sciences*, 113(3): 554–9.
Douglas, K.M. and Sutton, R.M. (2008) 'The hidden impact of conspiracy theories: perceived and actual influence of theories surrounding the death of Princess Diana', *The Journal of Social Psychology*, 148(2): 210–22.
Douglas, K.M., Sutton, R.M. and Cichocka, A. (2017) 'The psychology of conspiracy theories', *Current Directions in Psychological Science*, 26(6): 538–42.
Douglas, K.M., Uscinski, J.E., Sutton, R.M., Cichocka, A., Nefes, T., Siang Ang, C. and Deravi, F. (2019) 'Understanding conspiracy theories', *Advances in Political Psychology*, 40(1): 3–35.
Duckitt, J. (2001) 'A dual-process cognitive-motivational theory of ideology and prejudice', *Advances in Experimental Social Psychology*, 33: 41–113.

Einstein, K.L. and Glick, D.M. (2015) 'Do I think BLS data are BS? The consequences of conspiracy theories', *Political Behavior*, 37(3): 679–701.

Fernbach, P.M., Rogers, T., Fox, C.R. and Sloman, S.A. (2013) 'Political extremism is supported by an illusion of understanding', *Psychological Science*, 24: 939–46.

Freeman, D. and Bentall, R.P. (2017) 'The concomitants of conspiracy concerns', *Social Psychiatry and Psychiatric Epidemiology*, 52(5): 595–604.

Galliford, N. and Furnham, A. (2017) 'Individual difference factors and beliefs in medical and political conspiracy theories', *Scandinavian Journal of Psychology*, 58(5): 422–8.

Goertzel, T. (1994) 'Belief in conspiracy theories', *Political Psychology*, 15(4): 731–42.

Grzesiak-Feldman, M. and Irzycka, M. (2009) 'Right-wing authoritarianism and conspiracy thinking in a Polish sample', *Psychological Reports*, 105(2): 389–93.

Hatemi, P.K. and McDermott, R. (2016) 'Give me attitudes', *Annual Review of Political Science*, 19: 331–50.

Hogg, M.A., Meehan, C. and Farquharson, J. (2010) 'The solace of radicalism: self-uncertainty and group identification in the face of threat', *Journal of Experimental Social Psychology*, 46(6): 1061–6.

Hollander, B.A. (2018) 'Partisanship, individual differences, and news media exposure as predictors of conspiracy beliefs', *Journalism & Mass Communication Quarterly*, 95(3): 691–713.

Imhoff, R. and Bruder, M. (2014) 'Speaking (un-)truth to power: conspiracy mentality as a generalised political attitude', *European Journal of Personality*, 28: 25–43.

Imhoff, R., Zimmer, F., Klein, O., Babinska, M., Bangerter, A., Bilewicz, M., Blanuša, N., Bovan, K., Bužarovska, R., Cichocka, A., Delouvée, S., Douglas, K., Dyrendal, A., Gjoneska, B., Graf, S., Gualda, E., Kende, A., Krekó, P., Krouwel, A., Lamberty, P., Mari, S., Milošević Đorđević, J., Pantazi, M., Panasiti, M.S., Petkovski, L., Porciello G., Rabelo A., Schepisi, M., Radu, R., Sutton, R., Swami, V., Thórisdóttir, H., Turjačanin, V., Wagner-Egger, P., Zezel, I. and van Prooijen, J.-W. (2019) 'Conspiracy beliefs and political orientation across 21 countries: Data from the PICoM project'. Unpublished.

Jolley, D. and Douglas, K.M. (2014a) 'The social consequences of conspiracism: exposure to conspiracy theories decreases intentions to engage in politics and to reduce one's carbon footprint', *British Journal of Psychology*, 105(1): 35–6.

Jolley, D. and Douglas, K.M. (2014b) 'The effects of anti-vaccine conspiracy theories on vaccination intentions', *PLoS ONE*, 9(2): e89177.

Jost, J.T., Glaser, J., Kruglanski, A.W. and Sulloway, F.J. (2003) 'Political conservatism as motivated social cognition', *Psychological Bulletin*, 129(3), pp. 339–75.

Jost, J.T., Federico, C.M. and Napier, J.L. (2009) 'Political ideology: its structure, functions, and elective affinities', *Annual Review of Psychology*, 60: 307–37.

Jost, J.T., Stern, C., Rule, N.O. and Sterling, J. (2017) 'The politics of fear: is there an ideological asymmetry in existential motivation?', *Social Cognition*, 35(4): 324–53.

Jost, J.T., van der Linden, S., Panagopoulos, C. and Hardin, C.D. (2018) 'Ideological asymmetries in conformity, desire for shared reality, and the spread of misinformation', *Current Opinion in Psychology*, 23: 77–83.

Kim, M. and Cao, X. (2016) 'The impact of exposure to media messages promoting government conspiracy theories on distrust in the government: evidence from a two-stage randomized experiment', *International Journal of Communication*, 10(2016): 3808–27.

Knight, K. (2006) 'Transformations of the concept of ideology in the twentieth century', *American Political Science Review*, 100(4): 619–26.

Krouwel, A., Kutiyski, Y., van Prooijen, J.-W., Martinsson, J. and Markstedt, E. (2017) 'Does extreme political ideology predict conspiracy beliefs, economic evaluations and political trust? Evidence from Sweden', *Journal of Social and Political Psychology*, 5(2): 435–62.

Krouwel, A, Tremlett, L. and van Prooijen, J.-W. 'The partisan nature of conspiracy belief in Europe'. Forthcoming.

Kunda, Z. (1990) 'The case for motivated reasoning', *Psychological Bulletin*, 108(3): 480–98.

Lamberty, P. and Leiser, D. (2019) 'Sometimes you just have to go in: conspiracy beliefs lower democratic participation and lead to political violence'. Forthcoming.

Mancosu, M., Vassallo, S. and Vezzoni, C. (2017) 'Believing in conspiracy theories: evidence from an exploratory analysis of Italian survey data', *South European Society & Politics*, 22(3), pp. 327–44.

Mari, S., Liu, J.H., Suerdem A., Hanke, K., Brown, G., Gil de Zúñiga, H., Vilar, R, Boer, D. and Bilewicz, M. (2019) 'Conspiracy theories and institutional trust: a cross-cultural study on the varied impact of active social media use'. Under review.

Mari, S., Volpato, C., Papastamou, S., Chryssochoou, X., Prodromitis, G. and Pavlopoulos, V. (2017) 'How political orientation and vulnerability shape representations of the economic crisis in Greece and Italy', *International Review of Social Psychology*, 30(1): 52–67.

Miller, J.M., Saunders, K.L. and Farhart, C.E. (2016) 'Conspiracy endorsement as motivated reasoning: the moderating roles of political knowledge and trust', *American Journal of Political Science*, 60(4): 824–44.

Morgan, G.S. and Wisneski, D.C. (2017) 'The structure of political ideology varies between and within people: implications for theories about ideology's causes', *Social Cognition*, 35(4): 395–414.

Mudde, C. and Kaltwasser, C.R. (2017) *Populism: a very short introduction*, New York: Oxford University Press.

Norris, P., Garnett, H.A. and Grömping, M. (2019) 'The paranoid style of American elections: explaining perceptions of electoral integrity in an age of populism', *Journal of Elections, Public Opinion and Parties*, pp. 1–21.

Oliver, J.E. and Wood, T.J. (2014) 'Conspiracy theories and the paranoid style(s) of mass opinion', *American Journal of Political Science*, 58(4): 952–66.

Oliver, J.E. and Wood, T.J. (2018) *Enchanted America: how intuition and reason divide our politics*, Chicago: University of Chicago Press.

Richey, S. (2017) 'A birther and a truther: the influence of the authoritarian personality on conspiracy beliefs', *Politics & Policy*, 45(3): 465–85.

Schumacher, G. and Rooduijn, M. (2013) 'Sympathy for the "devil"? Voting for populists in the 2006 and 2010 Dutch General Elections', *Electoral Studies*, 32(1): 124–33.

Smallpage, S.M., Enders, A.M. and Uscinski, J.E. (2017) 'The partisan contours of conspiracy theory beliefs', *Research & Politics*, 4(4): 2053168017744655.

Sullivan, D., Landau, M.J. and Rothschild, Z.K. (2010) 'An existential function of enemyship: evidence that people attribute influence to personal and political enemies to compensate for threats to control', *Journal of Personality and Social Psychology*, 98(3): 434–49.

Swami, V. (2012) 'Social psychological origins of conspiracy theories: the case of the Jewish conspiracy theory in Malaysia', *Frontiers in Psychology*, 3: 280.

Swami, V., Chamorro-Premuzic, T. and Furnham, A. (2010) 'Unanswered questions: a preliminary investigation of personality and individual difference predictors of 9/11 conspiracist beliefs', *Applied Cognitive Psychology*, 24(6): 749–61.

Thórisdóttir, H. 'Social engagement and conspiracy beliefs'. Forthcoming.

Thórisdóttir, H. and Jost, J.T. (2011) 'Motivated closed-mindedness mediates the effect of threat on political conservatism', *Political Psychology*, 32(5): 785–811.

Uscinski, J.E. and Parent, J.M. (2014) *American conspiracy theories*, Oxford, UK: Oxford University Press.

Van Prooijen, J.-W. (2017) 'Why education predicts decreased belief in conspiracy theories', *Applied Cognitive Psychology*, 31(1): 50–8.

Van Prooijen, J.-W. and Krouwel, A.P.M. (2019) 'Psychological features of extreme political ideologies', *Current Directions in Psychological Science*, 28(2): 159–63.

Van Prooijen, J.-W., Krouwel, A.P.M. and Pollet, T.V. (2015) 'Political extremism predicts belief in conspiracy theories', *Social Psychological and Personality Science*, 6(5): 570–8.

Van Prooijen, J.-W. and van Vugt, M. (2018) 'Conspiracy theories: evolved functions and psychological mechanisms', *Perspectives on Psychological Science*, 13(6): 770–88.

Wright, T.L. and Arbuthnot, J. (1974) 'Interpersonal trust, political preference, and perceptions of the Watergate affair', *Proceedings of the Division of Personality and Society Psychology*, 1(1): 168–70.

# 3.5
# FUNCTIONS AND USES OF CONSPIRACY THEORIES IN AUTHORITARIAN REGIMES

*Julien Giry and Doğan Gürpınar*

### Introduction

Do conspiracy theorists believe in their theories? Are conspiracy theories the delusions of obsessed minds or are they sinisterly crafted by ambitious and manipulative actors, or something in between? This is an ongoing debate within the expanding field of conspiracy theory studies. This chapter will not argue that conspiracy theories are deliberate machinations, but will instead seek to demonstrate the underlying logic of conspiracy theories pervading non-democratic countries – deliberately or unknowingly – reinforcing the authoritarian character of the regimes.

The ideological formation and modes of legitimisation of authoritarian regimes are a major factor in the employment and pervasiveness of conspiracy theories. Authoritarian ideologies are characterised by an unshakeable belief in their righteousness and a tendency to provide comprehensive explanations for complex events, which renders them prone to conspiracy theories. Karl Popper (1945) famously defined conspiracism as an intrinsic component of Marxism. The relation between Marxism and conspiracism has been a stimulating theme amongst scholars – especially by ex-Marxist 'anti-totalitarians' (Christofferson 2004) – particularly with regard to Stalinism (Moscow trials), post-Second World War Eastern European 'witch-hunts' (foremost the Slansky trial) (Levy 2001; Appelbaum 2012) and Maoism.

Extreme nationalism is also conducive to conspiratorial culture, with Nazism as the climax. Fascism is described by many scholars as a negation simultaneously anti-Marxist, anti-liberal, anti-capitalist, anti-intellectual and even anti-conservative (Sternhell 1983; Payne 1995; Gentile 1996). In this regard, fascism obdurately needs (new) enemies to persevere – it would be pointless and indefinite in the absence of perpetual enemies. These enemies – whether real or imagined – need to be connected and amalgamated. For those reasons, conspiratorial thinking is a constitutive component of fascism, serving as ersatz ideology or semblance of ideology. Zionism and the 'Elders of Zion' plot becomes the super-conspiracy theory that binds, connects and envelops other accompanying conspiracy theories (Curtiss 1942; Bernstein 1971; Taguieff 1992).

Such necessity is equally true for populism (Hofstadter 1955, 1965; Bergmann 2018), both in democratic and authoritarian regimes. Different from ideologies of the modern age, contemporary populism (in the age of 'post-truth' in which improvisation outdoes the theoretical rigor of ideology) does not offer a robust theoretical base. Its raison d'état is its constitutive others. Authoritarian or non-democratic regimes and ideologies employ conspiracy theories as communicative and proactive propaganda tools to reinforce and legitimate their power, by emphasising 'foreign threats', 'deep state' activities or 'enemies within'. Using examples from several geographic areas such as the Middle East (see Chapter 5.8), Latin America (see Chapter 5.11) or post-Soviet space (see Chapter 5.5), this chapter will explore the uses and functions of conspiracy theories in authoritarian regimes, showing how conspiracy theories are used as propaganda, allowing regimes to identify and denounce perceived enemies and silence political opponents.

## Political functions of conspiracy theories

In authoritarian contexts, conspiratorial rhetoric used by the regimes is expedient for mobilising masses, reinforcing incumbent structures of power and authority, and assuring the loyalty of the people. This is particularly true during periods of social turmoil. This mobilisation is not necessarily physical, i.e. taken to the streets or digital space. It is instead a 'nudge' that stimulates hitherto indifferent, apolitical and apathetical individuals or groups towards a kind of political consciousness, one that is based on a Manichean dualism in which 'us'/'the self', i.e. the ordinary and innocent majority of 'good' people, are perceived to be threatened by an evil 'them'/'other' driven by a desire for absolute economic and political power (Groh 1987). In this dualistic vision, the conspirators are not only the enemies of the people or the regime; they are also genuine *outsiders*.

Conspiracy theories are used to reaffirm the dominant and established values of an ingroup while identifying and subsequently portraying outsiders in a negative light (Giry 2017). Conspiracy theories thrive only if they comply with the deep-rooted values of the dominant group and its social, historical or geographical background. The reception of the same conspiracy theory varies from one group to another because of differences in collective imaginary, collective memory, biases, stereotypes, etc. In other words, the plausibility of conspiracy theories, and their reception, is bound to communities' collective judgments (Fine 2007). What's more, people are more likely to believe in conspiracy theories when they seem to relate to them, when the conspiracy theories exonerate them or their group (Waters 1997; Frampton et al. 2016) and when they implicate their political opponents (Miller et al. 2016).

Operating like a political myth (Girardet 1986; Giry 2015), conspiracism is paradoxically reassuring – symbolically at least – because it purports to identify and unmask a hidden threat. Conspiracy theories express, then, a reductionism that serves and contributes to uphold, promote and reinforce conventional behaviours, while discrediting or delegitimising inappropriate or marginal ones. Conspiracy theories offer comfort, providing a refuge from complexity, uncertainties and qualms, and serving an 'ego-defensive' function (Katz 1960) that helps to build a positive self-image. The enemies or scapegoats portrayed as responsible for all society's ills are not anonymous; they have names and are identified, variously, as Americans, Zionists, Russians, Jews, Muslims or Freemasons, etc. They are often depicted as animals: rats, cockroaches, spiders, octopuses or snakes, etc. Such universally disparaged animals are employed to embody the 'conspiratorial other' and are often depicted crawling over or surrounding their enemy, as in a spider's web or octopus's tentacles (Giry 2015, 2017). Such enemies/scapegoats are identified as the single overwhelming cause behind the perceived threat, what Poliakov (1980) calls 'diabolic causality'.

Conspiracy theories centred on ethno-cultural or ethno-confessional prejudices and stereotypes powerfully contribute to the production and circulation of social hate and the exaltation of ingroup values, status and identities. Particularly endemic in periods of riots, violence or political destabilisation, their movements create the conditions under which ingroups 'become pitted against each other in fear and mutual hatred, constructing images of self and other' (Das, 1998: 109). Conspiracy theories and rumours of violence trigger actual violence, justifying, legitimating and reinforcing pre-existing stereotypes or prejudices (Festinger et al. 1948; Elias, Scotson 1965). Rumours of conspiracies in times of moral panic and disarray stimulate a tendency to take sides, contributing to segregation/ghettoisation, civil war and even genocide (Kalyvas 2006; Ternon 2009). These have been used and manipulated by authoritarian regimes that owe their rise, consolidation and perseverance to these propensities, with many authoritarian regimes establishing and legitimising themselves through civil wars and strife such as the Bolsheviks after the civil war, with its horrendous death toll; the Franco regime after the Spanish civil war, accusing Freemasons, Jews and communists for plotting; as well as the seventeenth-century English civil war, prompting anti-Popish frenzy and fear from Popish plots.

In the same way, revolution incorporates conspiratorial impulses. If revolutionary moments are, in fact, civil wars in which no legitimate authority can safely impose itself, then every revolution requires a counter revolution, conceived not as a web of resistance to the revolutionary effort but as a top-down scheme orchestrated by hidden plotters (Reaction with capital R). The French Revolution elicited a plethora of conspiracy theories for or against (Tackett 2000, 2003, 2004). Revolutionary fear had a real base:

> In any case, counterrevolution was real and tangible. It was not, in the main, a phantasm: an aristocratic or capitalist plot invented by Jacobin and Bolshevik zealots or strongmen to enliven their Manichaean ideology and rhetoric with a view to justifying and legitimating revolutionary terror. Besides, conspiracy mongering was common on both sides of the friend-enemy divide.
>
> *(Mayer 2000: 6)*

Yet, such abrupt ruptures inevitably unleash conspiratorial discourse: 'The Jacobin practice of conflating all resistances, without distinction, and tying them to an all-embracing conspiracy, gave the word-concept counterrevolution a distinct politico-ideological coloration.' (Mayer 2000: 47). The counter revolutionaries (Godechot 1984) also aspired to arrive at explanations for the French Revolution, which thereafter constituted the crux of all modern conspiracy theories, eventually evolving into *The Protocols of the Elders of Zion* in the early twentieth century (Oberhauser 2013). Denying any agency to the revolutionaries and any earnestness to their motivations, they perceived the French Revolution as devised by a cabal of evil-doers. Since then, a historical pattern based on this revolution-counterrevolution dualism has emerged. Whereas revolutionary regimes, whether republican, communist or Third-Worldist, replicated the revolutionary conspiratorial narrative, regimes built on counter-revolutionary scripts such as Cold War Latin American military dictatorships and European fascisms reproduced the counter-revolutionary account.

## Conspiracy theories as a tool of propaganda

In authoritarian regimes, the mobilisation function of conspiracy theories is used to reinforce and legitimate power by directing popular anger towards purported formidable and omnipresent enemies. In this respect, conspiracy theories are a propaganda tool in the hands of authoritarian regimes to justify their power, minimise their failures and silence/discredit their opponents. This way, the regimes also self-style themselves as indispensable, as only they can fight against, counter and defeat the ubiquitous and otherwise indomitable threat.

Not limited to authoritarian regimes (Bernays 1928; Tchakhotine 1940), propaganda can be roughly defined as mostly distorted information that political platforms or leaders publish, spread or broadcast in order to influence popular opinion and secure unconditional allegiance. In authoritarian regimes, given the restricted public sphere, propaganda is associated with unilateral censorship and state-controlled media (Yablokov 2015). Notwithstanding possible ideological affinities, authoritarian regimes use conspiracy theories to legitimise their transgressions, justify violence and discredit, defame or silence any dissent, alternative or opposition. To this end, all the enemies need to be amalgamated, interlinked and associated. Clearly, conspiracy theories are deliberate schemes for legitimacy and repression.

Conspiracy theories function to tame, intimidate and discredit political opponents. They implicate political adversaries as being in the payroll of treacherous enemies of the nation. This mechanism helps to delegitimise any dissenting view. Such a morally oppressive environment generated by mechanisms of repression and reinforced by conspiracy theories normalises self-censorship and moulds public opinion. The anti-communist witch hunts in the U.S.A. (1947–1957) are a historical example of the use of conspiracy theories as a political tool (Toinet 1999). While McCarthyism purported to identify the threat of communism, its implicit aim might have been to discredit liberals and democratic socialists alike (Bell 1955), accusing them of being covert communists (Schrecker 1998; Doherty 2005: 94). Although such accusations were absurd, they helped to mould public discourse and create a conservative-leaning Cold War consensus. Although McCarthyism was a craze or an epiphenomenon, it served to further a conservative agenda and the institutionalisation of the anti-communism of the 1950s (Gibson 1988).

South America is also generous in terms of its conspiratorial culture, as the Chavez-Maduro Bolivarian Venezuela regime well attests (Tarragoni 2012, 2018). Two centuries of U.S. economic, political and military predominance, and genuine conspiracies hatched and/or supported by the U.S.A. in the 1970s in Chile, made Latin Americans prone to anti-U.S. conspiracy theories. That the U.S.A. was responsible for repression, long before the onset of the Cold War, is the main source for this longstanding distrust of 'Yankees' (Brands 2012). Anti-imperialist ideologies in different forms, from anti-colonialist nationalisms and Third World socialisms of the 1960s to Islamism since the 1990s, are all imbued with conspiratorial culture. Imperialism is framed as the overarching conspiracy that explains and simplifies the otherwise tortuous, multi-faceted and intricate historical process. It is also a mechanism that exonerates guilt, responsibilities and inadequacies. The rhetoric of victimisation serves as an instrument to legitimise state terror, based on the presumption that anti-imperialist forces are exempt from undue violence, and thereby justifying ethnic cleansing, genocide and massacre as in the Young Turks' genocide of Armenians, Milošević's Serbia, Pol Pot's Cambodia, Mugabe's Zimbabwe and other Third Worldist regimes from the 1960s to 1990s.

While, in democratic regimes, the denunciation of pernicious plots and conspiracies orchestrated by foreign countries, deep state agents or enemies within emerges mainly in the rhetoric of fringe political opponents or cranks, in authoritarian contexts such denunciations usually originate from government sources and agents. Put another way, conspiracy theories in authoritarian regimes stand as official truths, they 'are not merely derivative but constitutive of political environments' (Ortmanna, Heathershaw 2012: 560) that complemented each other. For example, during the Second World War in Germany and France, antisemitic, anti-communist and anti-Masonic conspiracy theories helped to shape public policies. Foreign and domestic so-called conspiracies were seen as entwined, deriving from the same plot to destroy European civilisation.

In sum, in authoritarian regimes, top-down conspiracy theories play a decisive and essential role in legitimising and strengthening governments and the structures of power. They are constitutive tools of propaganda to mobilise the people on behalf of the state. They identify three main ideal-types of inherent enemies, which are often amalgamated: Foreign states, deep state forces and political opponents/enemies within.

## Historicisation

Authoritarian regimes offer a narrative of self-victimisation through conspiracy theories: Once mighty overlords commanding over vast territories, they are now in a miserable state. Every nation has a golden age: The glory of Byzantium for Greeks, the medieval kingdom of Dušan for Serbs, the Caliphate for Arabs (and Muslims in general), among many others. These golden ages are celebrated, not only to boost self-esteem, but also to monumentalise the threats and enemies both abroad and within. Belief in the historical greatness of Russia, China, India and the lost grandeur of Greece, Turkey (Gürpinar 2019) and Serbia continue to nurture conspiratorial scripts. The plotting of enemies within and without are shown as the main cause of these declines. The indisputable fact that past national empires had been ravaged by treachery and international collaboration reminds that the same threat is ever-present and equally relevant today. This rhetoric feeds a state of ontological insecurity, requiring constant vigilance and watchfulness against perceived nebulous threats. Thus, authoritarian regimes often rely on historical national greatness even when they are communist, such as in the cases of national communism of Romanian dictator Ceaușescu (Verdery 1991; Boia 2001) and Milošević's Yugoslavia, as well as many of the Third World socialist autocracies.

Historical legitimacy always serves as a trump card in the resolution of all immediate quandaries, contradictions and shortcomings. Identity politics also require a historical narrative that establishes absolute and irreconcilable nemeses that remain unchanged over time. The historical imagery couched in conspiracy theories suits such an agenda impeccably. The historicisation of conspiracy theories further trivialise the present, deeming it ephemeral and passing in the eternal grand theatre of history and struggles, and this historicisation also trivialises transient moral transgressions. As wars render morality a secondary concern that needs to be reassessed within the reality of war, while also justifying misdemeanours, the introduction of history as a theatre depicting a perpetual state of war also deems moral claims inconsequential and petty in the larger theatre of history. Conspiracy theories remain as an effective means of depoliticising public debate, imposing the politics of eternity and justifying temporary injustices in the name of rectifying historical injustices.

## The post-Soviet space and Russia as conspiracy state

Today, it is Russia that is most associated with conspiracy theories as state projects. Indeed, state-sponsored intellectuals and state-controlled media such as *Russia Today* and *Sputnik News* (Pomerantsev, Weiss 2014; François, Schmitt 2015; Yablokov 2015) are the main disseminators of conspiracy theories in 'Fortress Russia', which perpetuates the idea that, since the fall of the Soviet bloc, Russia is under constant threat from both foreign and domestic enemies. In this narrative, the West and domestic democratic forces are seen as plotting to weaken and destroy Russia (Ortmann, Heathershaw 2012; Yablokov 2018). In addition, Putin's 'troll army' spreads conspiracy theories on the Internet (Tüfekçi 2017). Both state-controlled traditional media and the Internet are manipulated to support Putin's 'virtual politics' (Wilson 2005), which includes denunciation of purported enemies, the creation of fake oppositional parties or rivals and 'scarecrow' opponents. The primary role of the mass media in Russia is to project these conspiratorial creations and falsify the entire political process. In order to do this, the Russian regime devised a quasi-ideology called 'sovereign democracy' to uphold and legitimise its autocracy. For this purpose, the regime employs what is known as 'political technology' (Wilson 2005) – a euphemism in the former Soviet states that refers to the highly developed industry of political manipulation and propaganda. This political technology was defined by Timothy Snyder (2018) in his analysis of Putin's strategies as the 'politics of eternity' (as opposed to *ordinary* politics) and he further observed that 'politics of doing' had been replaced by 'politics of being' (i.e. fixed – national, religious, cultural – identities). Putin's political technologists employ conspiracy theories as a means of effectively fortifying Putinism and delineating 'sovereign democracy'. Through this approach, all enmities are rendered moral, ontological and perpetual, ensuring the vanishing of the 'political'. This means that Putin and his aides selectively invent (new) domestic and foreign enemies, including homosexuals, feminists and liberals. Putin built on an inherited aversion to everything different, alien and indefinite in Russian nationalism and an enduring scepticism of the West. Putin's political technologies benefited from the ideational and emotive reservoir of Russian Orthodoxy, Russian nationalism and the syncretic Euro-Asianist fantasies of Aleksandr Dugin to devise conspiracy theories (Laruelle 2008, 2009; Clover 2016; Synder 2018).

This is also the function of cyberbullying on the part of the state, which prevents any dissent from being freely articulated and thus disseminated. Repudiating the optimism that had seen it as a liberating space, cyberspace came to be the perfect venue for the deliberate dissemination of conspiracy theories (Morozov 2012). Although most of the conspiracy theories articulated in cyberspace are fringe, they serve a purpose. Fuelling hatred sanitises cyberspace on behalf of authoritarian regimes. The conspiracy theories also silence cyberspace by nurturing a climate of hatred by targeting opponents. Once opponents were harassed and accused of conspiring with international cabals; now many are forced into silence both in cyberspace and real life (Tüfekçi 2017). Those trolls are not necessarily ordered by the authorities to slander critics of the regime, yet those volunteering partisans inadvertently serve their agendas.

In Russia, Putin and his aides routinely denounce secret manoeuvres for destabilisation orchestrated by the hidden hand of 'the West' (the U.S.A., the U.N., N.A.T.O., etc.) or a 'third force'. Since 1991, the idea that the fall of the Soviet Union resulted from a U.S. plot is central in the Russian conspiratorial imaginary and, since then, conspiracy theories, in everyday life, offer explanations for complex issues and traumatic experiences that the country and its former satellites have witnessed. As with the Arab Spring, conspiracy theories germinated to explicate the 'Colour revolutions' and subsequent turmoil in Russia and post-Soviet Central Asia. In such theories, not only does the West operate as an external foreign threat to the Russian regime, it also acts from within, through the support of subversive agents. This allows democratic uprisings or influential political opponents like Alexei Navalny to be accused of being agents of Western intrusion. In authoritarian regimes with very few media outlets, conspiracy theories are a means of discrediting any form of social or political discontent. Political opponents, especially those with a broad audience, are seen as enemies within, conspiring against the state and its interests for the benefit of the West, portrayed as traitors who seek to topple the regime and undermine Russia's status as a world power. Such narratives reappeared with great fanfare in the wake of mass protests against the election results of December 2011, and during the presidential campaign of early 2012. Laruelle (2009) observed that fears of foreign plots, domestic threats, as well as nefarious deep state activities, have long-standing roots in Russian nationalism and such affinity allowed them to be easily incorporated into Putin's conspiratorial reservoir. Consequently, conspiracy theories are not only discursive or rhetorical tools, but they also deliver political outcomes by legitimising or delegitimising particular political attitudes and supporting repressive policies. Conspiracy theories that revolve around threats from the West, its purported spies and the so-called Western-controlled opposition, are a powerful tool to disseminate Russian nationalism and legitimise the established regime as a bulwark against the decay of Russian civilisation.

In post-Soviet Central Asia, the themes of foreign threats and deep state machinations are equally paramount in the conspiratorial imaginary. The foreign threat, common in official conspiracy theories, is first and foremost embodied in the figure of the Russian elder brother, the historical hegemon of Eastern Europe and Central Asia. Ironically, 'when demonstrable examples of Russian hegemony are lacking, the conspiracy theory becomes one of the primary means by which such status is reproduced' (Heathershaw 2012: 611) in order to make sense of political turmoil. Russia's hidden hand is supposedly pulling the strings and pushing conspiracies. Hence, Russia is suspected of secretly controlling from afar to destabilise the entire region. Russia is also supposed to manipulate domestic political opposition, organise assassinations, upset geopolitical equilibrium and initiate wars or social movements to weaken governments, etc. Many of the usual suspects are also seen as potential foreign threats: U.S.A., U.N., N.A.T.O., Islamic groups, Israel, Jews/Zionists and Freemasons. As in Central and Eastern Europe, conspiracy theories that involve George Soros and his foundation are prevalent in Central Asia. The Hungarian-born billionaire is routinely accused of being a sort of puppet master who secretly masterminds global politics and the economy. All these narratives of foreign threats constitute practical expedients used by governments. In Ukraine and Georgia, for example, the hidden hand of Russia is supposed to be behind every social or political process. In these countries, conspiracy theories are disseminated by nationalist governments to explain away their economic failures and justify the authoritarian nature of their regimes as essential to resist the hegemonic ambitions of Russia and Western manipulations behind seemingly pro-democratic uprisings. This is particularly obvious in countries like Kazakhstan, Tajikistan and other ex-Soviet countries. Next to foreign threats, deep state conspiracy theories are also widespread in Central Asia. They usually relate to the inner workings of the state apparatus or the rulers's close circles and families/relatives (not unsurprisingly!).

## Populism and conspiracy theories: Populism in power and populism as manual for authoritarianism

Since the 2000s, Eastern Europe has seemed to be under the spell of conspiratorial visions. Victor Orban emerged as a pioneering populist and found a goldmine in the conspiracy theories revolving around George Soros, particularly those that incorporate *The Elders of Zion* narrative. Orban also accuses the E.U. of aiming to destroy Hungarian morals and culture. In his ascent to power, Orban relied on an inherent ideological, political and cultural milieu that was pervasive in post-communist Eastern Europe (Balint 2016; Lenvai 2018). The Soros narrative is widely used in Eastern Europe, in Romania or Slovakia for instance, by states as well as different political platforms across the left/right divide. It also builds on pre-existing antisemitic narratives. The post-communist milieu is also a factor, as it cultivates economic and social insecurity, disillusionment and general distrust. While communist Eastern Europe has also employed antisemitic vocabulary – as in Poland or Romania – the disorder and vulnerability in the post-Soviet space made people more prone to believing conspiratorial narratives as a way to explain the current miserable situation. Eurosceptic conspiracism is pervasive in both Western and Eastern Europe, although they show different traits. In Eastern Europe, it casts a shadow over historical and national contexts, with civil society seen as a disguise for this end. The abrupt rise and vocal display of L.G.B.T. and feminist communities, as seen in the Gay Pride and Women's Day parades, also unleashed a moral panic. Such displays of identity are associated with moral corruption as part of a global conspiracy to undermine traditional values and render nations and states vulnerable (Sperling 2014).

Contemporary varieties of populism differ from ideologies of the modern age for not offering an inflexible theoretical base. They designate enemies on purpose to serve their cause. Contemporary Western populism needs immigrants, Muslims, cultural Marxists, leftists, liberals and the liberal establishment to frame itself (Bergmann 2018; Müller 2018). The fear of the establishment of 'Eurabia' (Ye'Or 2005) and the 'Grand Replacement' (Camus 2011) of white Christian populations by non-white Muslims in Europe looms over this conspiratorial universe in Western Europe and elsewhere in the world (the U.S.A., Australia, New Zealand, etc.). Rather than simply singling out the Islamic threat, however, this form of conspiracism foregrounds the supposed 'complicity' of 'liberals' and 'cultural Marxists' for placating and espousing Islam in the guise of multiculturalism. Furthermore, their alleged complicity does not derive from their naivety, but from their innate hatred of Western civilisation's values that deem them willing collaborators of purported 'Islamofascism'. Different conspiracies needed to be inextricably related, amalgamated and coalesced. Hence, animosities towards marginal outsiders (powerless, but imagined to be omnipotent) and towards the 'establishment' (a nebulous term indicating excessive political and economic power combined) complement and reinforce each other. Conspiracy theories in this respect are communicative tools to reach out to targeted audiences. Although populism in Western Europe is a movement of the disgruntled, as with the case of Trump in the U.S.A., populist leaders may come to power and keep their base intact by leaning on conspiratorial rhetoric that demonstrates the commonality of these patterns and mechanisms, even in democratic countries. This has led scholars of comparative politics and historians of fascism to write jeremiads warning about how fascism comes to power, itself now a thriving genre (Snyder 2017; Ziblatt, Levitsky 2018).

Populists position themselves as the enemy of the establishment and global and national elites. Reference to the 'deep state' has emerged as a kind of shorthand, allowing populists to contrive an omnipresent, omnipotent force that conspires against the interests of the people. The term seamlessly connects a plethora of seemingly unrelated groups and renders them parts of the same overarching power network. Originating in Turkey (*derin devlet*) and coined in the mid-1990s to delineate a nebulous web of politicians, bureaucrats, military, mafia and businessmen, the term 'deep state' has been taken by populists as an expedient conspiratorial buzzword (Nefes 2018). Despite different interpretations of the concept (Blanuša 2018), deep state envisions the secret collusion of rogue and corrupted elements in the state apparatus (civil servants, army officers, secret service agents, etc.) with top-level financiers, business industrialists, mobsters and, eventually, terrorist groups. All together, they destroy governed consent, electoral processes and to foster their own agenda through legal and illegal means. As a state within the state, deep state elements supposedly operate independently of the political authority and are the effective policy makers unfettered from political clout. Such a scheme was first and most vocally crystallised in the notorious Italian P2 Freemasons' lodge, revealed after police raids in 1981 (Ginsborg 2003; Rayner 2005).

In the U.S.A., deep state became the catchphrase of far-right groups, pundits, tweeps and Internet forum and social media users. This was, however, not new ground for right-wing conspiracy theories, which had long incorporated the idea of a powerful underground liberal establishment in Washington D.C. and New York that maintained firm control of politics, academia and the arts. Many conspiracy theories surrounding the Kennedy assassination pointed to the presence of an imagined all-pervasive deep state. The idiom added a conspiratorial twist to pre-existing perspectives, as well as further fuelling right-wing libertarian qualms and mistrust of the federal state. Yet, in authoritarian states, the deep state as a concept was employed both as an excuse for their failures, as well as a pretext for more authoritarian grip. Deep state is a popular populist mantra that establishes the main dichotomy between the gullible people (as one overarching and indivisible metaphysical entity) and machinating establishment forces conspiring against the genuine interests of the people. Populists position themselves as siding with the people and speaking for them against a conspiring deep state and its agents and elements hidden from naked eyes.

## The Middle East and Islamic world

Throughout the Islamic world, conspiracy theories are a means to explain and come to terms with the mortifying downfall of the Islamic realm from its medieval glory. Conspiracy theories function to blame a real or hypothetical 'other' for this failure, whether at national or communal level. Keywords such as Crusades, Church or Freemasonry are freely employed to refer to the arch-enemies conspiring in close collaboration to achieve the historic mission to destroy Islam and are to be blamed for the present-day decay.

In the Middle East, conspiracy theories about foreign threats are widely disseminated. They stand for official statements spread through national media and a means for regimes to communicate with their people. Conspiracy theories usually focus on the U.S.A. and Israel, but they also identify banks, large corporations such as Coca Cola or Disney, and international institutions like the I.M.F. or the World Bank. They are shown to be passionately motivated to loot the Middle East and to destroy Islam. What is more, conspiracy theories centred on '"the Great Satan", "Zionism", "imperialism", and "Bolshevism", along with all their permutations, have been employed to explain many of the political, military, economic, and social defeats and setbacks suffered by the Arabs' (Zonis, Joseph 1994: 445). Since the colonial era and the emergence of Israel, Middle Eastern countries have grown suspicious of foreign motivations and intents. The Sykes–Picot Agreement, the Balfour Declaration or the Protocol of Sèvres have fostered conspiratorial views and helped to create a conspiratorial framework regarding the ominous intentions of the West towards the Middle East. Wars, too – such as the Six-Day War, the two Gulf Wars and the invasion of Afghanistan – and their aftermath are consistently explained in terms of a conspiracy led by the West and its allies – foremost Israel, and, depending on the geopolitical situation of the time, certain Arab countries like Egypt or Saudi Arabia – to destabilise the region. Conspiracy theories, Gray argues:

> Have the effect of strengthening popular nationalism, diverting opposition away from the state and its leadership, and reinforcing the state as a source of protection against a perceived enemy, and all are useful to states, such as those common in the Middle East, that lack structural legitimacy or whose policies are moving into a post-populist phase.
>
> *(2008: 169)*

The same fear is invoked by Islamic dissidents such as the Muslim Brothers, who see Baathist regimes as accomplices of the West to destroy Islam and use such theories as a mobilising platform. In addition to foreign threats, conspiracy theories in the Middle East also identify domestic menaces. Those purported agents of destabilisation are found among ethnocultural or ethnoreligious minorities such as Jews, Copts or Shias. They are accused, with the help of the state-controlled media, of constituting a fifth column and are shown to be responsible for governmental failures.

Gray relates the prevalence of conspiracy theories in the Middle East to the:

> Condition of ideological aimlessness and introspection, brought on by the failure of post-independence political and economic ideologies such as Arab Nationalism, Pan-Arabism, state-led economic development, and "Nasserism" … failing to widely or adequately fill the void left by the shortcomings of these earlier political and developmental strategies.
>
> *(2011: 110)*

For those reasons, he argues that in the Middle East states are a foremost source of conspiracy theories. Although he rejects the reductionist equivalence of state propaganda with conspiracy theories (2010: 130), Gray demonstrates that conspiracy theories are an effective tool in the hands of regimes. The existence of Israel is a boon for the Arab dictators who lavishly exploit the Israeli theme to garner obstinate loyalty from their populace. Hence, in 2001, Bashar al-Assad declared during the Pope's visit to Syria that 'we see [Israel] attacking sacred Christian and Muslim places in Palestine.... They try to kill the principle of religions in the same mentality in which they betrayed Jesus Christ and tried to kill the prophet Mohammed.' Conspiracy theories revolving around Zionism contribute to legitimise Baath dictatorships (De Poli 2014: 269–270). The *Protocols of the Elders of Zion* and Holocaust denial are indisputable historical facts in the Arab Middle East (Achcar 2010; Butter, Reinkowski 2014: 25).

In Iran, perhaps one of the most prolific countries in terms of conspiracism (Zonis, Joseph 1994), conspiracy theories are guides to understanding politics and history. Emphasising the (semi-)colonial legacy of Iran over the last two centuries, this conspiratorial narrative views the British as the puppet masters behind the entire course of world history. The British were accused of stealing Iran's oil, of corrupting Persian elites and of fomenting social turmoil – such as the coup against Mosaddegh in 1953. After the Islamic Revolution, the Soviet Union, the 'Lesser Satan' and the U.S.A., the 'Great Satan', played a major role in this conspiratorial imagery, with the U.S.A. as the heir to Great Britain as the global puppet master. Influenced by *The Testament of Peter the Great*, a forgery of 1795 by a Polish immigrant in Paris (Resis 1985), conspiracy theories about Russia were revived in the 1980s. According to the *Testament*, the Russians had two major secret goals: To subjugate Europe and to conquer Persia to obtain access to the Persian Gulf. Since then, Russophobia and memories of the Persian campaign of Peter the Great (1722–1723) are constantly harnessed by Islamic Revolutionary Guards and the Iranian regime. Conspiracy theories about the U.S.A, not surprisingly given U.S.–Iran relations after the Islamic Revolution, are also commonplace in contemporary Iran. According to these, political opposition, homosexuality, feminism or social movements, such as the widespread protests of 2009 following the re-election of Ahmadinejad, are stage-managed by the U.S.A. or their ally, Israel. More generally speaking, since the Islamic Revolution, the idea of a 'crusaders' conspiracy' against Islam is widely disseminated by the Iranian regime and its media outlets. Khomeini had articulated the grand conspiracy led by the Christian West to destroy Islam and its foremost nation, Shiite Iran:

> Since the Crusades, Western nations are supposed to have plotted to subjugate the Islamic world and to inhibit its prosperity and development, specifically to dissolve the Ottoman empire, foment conflict among Muslim communities, support Israel and world Zionism, and 'brainwash' the younger generation of Muslims In addition to those foreign threats, conspiracy theories in Iran also implicate domestic enemies.
>
> *(Ashraf 1992)*

Indeed, Iranian conspiracy theories accuse Freemasons, Illuminati or Zionist agents of acting secretly to overthrow the Islamic Republic. More specifically, the Bahais, a minority religious group, are also accused of constituting a fifth column, controlled by the U.S.A. or Israel and plotting to destroy the Islamic regime and Islam.

Islamic Republic also invokes Holocaust denial and conspiracies about Zionist world domination to legitimise governmental policies (Ashraf 1992). Mahmoud Ahmadinejad promoted conspiracy theories by openly articulating them, most notoriously in his Holocaust denial. This reached a climax in 2006, when he organised an international conference in Teheran on the Holocaust that gathered leading denialists and conspiracy theorists such as David Duke, Robert Faurisson, Roger Garaudy, David Irving and Fredrick Töben. Self-styled as a layman, outside of the Islamic clerical oligarchy, Ahmadinejad addressed his audience with a populist rhetoric matching the occasion, mixing Islamic and populist political conspiracy theories. Although the historical and cultural setting of the event facilitated this conspiratorial mind-set, the ideological agency of the authoritarian states should never be underestimated. Such tendencies are exploited by regimes for their own ends and agenda.

## References

Achcar, G. (2010) *The Arabs and the Holocaust*, New York: Picador.
Appelbaum, A. (2012) *Iron curtain: the crushing of eastern Europe, 1944–1956*, New York: Anchor.
Ashraf, A. (1992) 'Conspiracy theories', *Encyclopaedia Iranica*, 6(2): 138–47.
Balint, M. (2016) *The Mafia state: the case of Hungary*, Budapest: Central University Press.
Bell, D. (1955), *The new American right*, New York: Doubleday.
Bergmann, E. (2018) *Conspiracy and populism: the politics of misinformation*, New York: Springer International.
Bernays, E. (1928) *Propaganda*, London: Routledge.
Bernstein, H. (1971) *The truth about 'The Protocols Of Zion': a complete exposure*, New York: Covic Friede.
Blanuša, N. (2018) 'The deep state between the (un)warrant conspiracy theory and structural element of political regimes', *Critique and Humanism*, 49(1): 284–369.
Boia, L. (2001) *History and myth in romanian consciousness*, Budapest: Central European University Press.
Brands, H. (2012) *Latin America's Cold War*, Cambridge, MA: Harvard University Press, 2010.
Butter, M. and Reinkowski, M. (eds.) (2014) *Conspiracy theories in the United States and the Middle East: a comparative approach*, Berlin/Boston: de Gruyter.
Camus, R. (2011) *Le grand replacement*, Neuilly-Sur-Seine: David Reinharc.
Christofferson, M.S. (2004) *French intellectuals against the left: the antitotalitarian moment of the 1970s*, London: Berghahn Books.
Clover, C. (2016) *Black wind, white snow: the rise of Russia's new nationalism*, New Haven: Yale University Press.
Curtiss, J.S. (1942) *An appraisal of the protocols of Zion*, New York: Columbia Press University.
Das, V. (1998) 'Specificities: official narratives, rumor, and the social production of hate', *Journal for the Study of Race, Nation and Culture*, 4(1): 109–30.
De Poli, B. (2014) 'The Judeo-Masonic conspiracy: the path from the cemetery of Prague to Arab anti-Zionist propaganda', in M. Butter and M. Reinkowski (ed.) *Conspiracy theories in the United States and the Middle East A comparative approach*, Berlin/Boston: de Gruyter, pp. 251–71.
Doherty, T. (2005) *Cold War, cool medium: television, McCarthyism, and American culture*, New York: Columbia University Press.
Elias, N. and Scotson, J. (1965) *The established and the outsiders*, London: F. Cass.
Festinger, L., Cartwright, D., Barber, K., Fleischl, J., Gottsdanker, J., Keysen, A., and Leavitt, G. (1948) 'A study of rumor: its origin and spread', *Human Relations*, 1(4): 464–85.
Fine, G.A. (2007) 'Rumor, trust and civil society: collective memory and cultures of judgment', *Diogenes*, 54(1): 5–18.
Frampton, M., Goodhart, D. and Mamhood, K. (2016) *'Unsettled belonging: a survey of Britain's Muslim communities'*, London: Policy Exchange.
François, S. and Schmitt, O. (2015) 'Le conspirationnisme en Russie contemporaine', *Diogène*, 249–50: 120–9.

Gentile E. (1996) *The sacralization of politics in fascist Italy*, trans. K. Botsford, Cambridge: Harvard University Press.
Gibson, J.L. (1988) 'Political intolerance and political repression during the McCarthy Red Scare', *The American Political Science Review*, 82(2): 511–29.
Ginsborg, P. (2003) *Italy and its discontents*, London: Palgrave Macmillan.
Girardet, R. (1986) *Mythes et mythologies politiques*, Paris: Seuil.
Giry, J. (2015) 'Le conspirationnisme: archéologie et morphologie d'un mythe politique', *Diogène*, 249–50: 40–50.
Giry, J. (2017) 'A specific social function of rumors and conspiracy theories: strengthening community's ties in trouble times – a multilevel analysis', *Slovak Ethnology*, 65(2): 187–202.
Godechot, J. (1984) *La contre-révolution*, Paris: Presses Universitaires de France.
Gray, M. (2008) 'Explaining conspiracy theories in modern Arab middle eastern political discourse: some problem and limitations of the literature', *Critique: Critical Middle Eastern Studies*, 17(2): 155–74.
Gray, M. (2010) *Conspiracy theories in the Arab world: sources and politics*, London: Routledge.
Gray, M. (2011) 'Political culture, political dynamics, and conspiracism in the Arab Middle East', in A. Graf, F. Schirin and P. Ludwig (eds.) *Orientalism and conspiracy: politics and conspiracy theory in the Islamic world*, London: I.B. Tauris, pp. 105–25.
Groh, D. (1987) 'The temptation of conspiracy theory, or why do bad things happen to good people', in C.F. Graumann and S. Moscovoci (eds.) *Changing conception of conspiracy*, Berlin: Springer, pp. 1–13.
Gürpınar, D. (2019) *Conspiracy nation: conspiracy theories in Turkey*, London: Routledge.
Heathershaw, J. (2012) 'Of national fathers and Russian elder brothers: conspiracy theories and political ideas in Post-Soviet Central Asia', *The Russian Review*, 71: 610–29.
Hofstadter, R. (1955) *The age of reform*, New York: Vintage Book.
Hofstadter, R. (1965) *The paranoid style in American politics, and other essays*, New York: Knopf.
Kalyvas, S. (2006) *The logic of violence in Civil War*, Cambridge: Cambridge University Press.
Katz, D. (1960) 'The functional approach to the study of attitudes', *Public Opinion Quarterly*, 24(2): 163–204.
Laruelle, M. (2008) *Russian eurasianism: an ideology of empire*, Washington D.C.: Woodrow Wilson Press & Johns Hopkins University Press.
Laruelle, M. (ed.) (2009) *Russian nationalism and the national reassertion of Russia*, London: Routledge.
Lenvai, P. (2018) *Orban: Hungary's strongman*, Oxford: Oxford University Press.
Levy, R. (2001) *Ana Pauker: the rise and fall of a Jewish communist*, Berkeley: University of California Press.
Mayer, A.J. (2000) *The furies violence and terror in the French and Russian revolutions*, Princeton: Princeton University Press.
Miller, J.M., Saunders, K.L. and Farhart, C.E. (2016) 'Conspiracy endorsement as motivated reasoning: the moderating roles of political knowledge and trust', *American Journal of Political Science*, 60(4): 824–44.
Morozov, E. (2012) *The net delusion*, New York: Public Affairs.
Müller, J. (2016) *What is populism?*, Philadelphia: University of Pennsylvania Press.
Nefes, T.S. (2014) 'The function of secrecy in anti-semitic conspiracy theories: the case of Dönmes in Turkey', in M. Butter and M. Reinkowski (eds.) *Conspiracy theories in the United States and the Middle East: a comparative approach*, Berlin/Boston: de Gruyter, pp. 139–56.
Nefes, T.S. (2018) 'The conspiratorial style in Turkish politics: discussing the deep state in the parliament', in J. Uscinski (ed.) *Conspiracy theories and the people who believe them*, New York: Oxford University Press, pp. 385-395.
Oberhauser, C. (2013) *Die verschwörungstheoretische trias: Barruel – Robison – Starck*, Innsbruck: Studien Verlag.
Ortmann S. and Heathershaw J. (2012) 'Conspiracy theories in the post-Soviet space', *The Russian Review*, 71(4): 551–64.
Payne, S. (1980) *Fascism: comparison and definition*, Madison: University of Wisconsin Press.
Poliakov, L. (1980) *La causalité diabolique, t. 1: essai sur l'origine des persécutions*, Paris: Calmann-Lévy.
Pomerantsev, P. and Weiss, M. (2014) *The menace of unreality: how the Kremlin weaponizes information, culture and money*, New York: Institute of Modern Russia.
Popper, K. (1945) *The open society and its enemies vol. 2*, London: Routledge.
Rayner, H. (2005) *Les scandales politiques: l'opération "Mains propres" en Italie*, Paris: Essais.
Resis, A. (1985) 'Russophobia and the "testament" of Peter the Great, 1812–1980', *Slavic Review*, 44(4): 681–93.
Schrecker, E. (1998) *Many are the crimes: McCarthyism in America*, Little: Brown.

Snyder, T. (2017) *On tyranny*, New York: Tim Duggan Books.
Snyder, T. (2018) *The road to unfreedom*, New York: Tim Duggan Books.
Sperling, V. (2014) *Sex, politics & Putin*, New York: Oxford University Press.
Sternhell, Z. (1983) *Ni droite ni gauche: l'idéologie fasciste en France*, Paris: Gallimard.
Tackett, T. (2000) 'Conspiracy obsession in a time of revolution: French elites and the origins of the terror', *The American Historical Review*, 105(3): 691–713.
Tackett, T. (2003) 'Collective panics in the early French revolution, 1789–1791: a comparative perspective', *French History*, 17(2): 149–71.
Tackett, T. (2004) 'La grande peur et le complot aristocratique sous la révolution Française', *Annales historiques de la Révolution française*, 335: 1–17.
Taguieff, P.-A. (1992) *Les protocoles des sages de Sion. Faux et usages d'un faux*, Paris: Berg International.
Tarragoni, F. (2012) 'Conspirationnisme, anti-impérialisme et nouveau populisme: comment les 'théories du complot' politisent le social au Venezuela de Chávez', *Raison Publique*, 16: 77–91.
Tarragoni, F. (2018) *Le peuple et le caudillo: la question populiste en Amérique Latine contemporaine*, Rennes: PUR.
Tchakhotine, S. (1940) *The rape of the masses: the psychology of totalitarian political propaganda*, London: Labour Book Service.
Ternon, Y. (2009) 'Rwanda 1994: analyse d'un processus génocidaire', *Revue d'Histoire de la Shoah*, 190(1): 15–57.
Toinet, M.-F. (1995) *1947–1957: la chasse aux sorcières et le maccarthysme*, Bruxelles: Éditions Complexes.
Tüfekçi, Z. (2017) *Twitter and tear gas*, London/New Haven: Yale University Press.
Verdery, K. (1991) *National ideology under communism*, Berkeley: University of California Press.
Waters, A.M. (1997) 'Conspiracy theories as ethnosociologies: explanation and intention in African American political culture', *Journal of Black Studies*, 28(1): 112–25.
Wilson, A. (2005) *Virtual politics: faking democracy in the Post-Soviet World*, New Haven: Yale University Press.
Ye'Or, B. (2005) *Eurabia: the Euro-Arab axis*, New Jersey: Fairleigh Dickinson University Press.
Yablokov, I. (2015) 'Conspiracy theories as a Russian public diplomacy tool: the case of Russia Today (RT)', *Politics*, 35(3): 1–15.
Yablokov, I. (2018) *Fortress Russia: conspiracy theories in Post-Soviet Russia*, Cambridge: Polity Press.
Ziblatt, D. and Levitsky, S. (2018) *How democracies die?*, New York: Crown.
Zonis, M. and Joseph, C.M. (1994) 'Conspiracy thinking in the Middle East', *Political Psychology*, 15(3): 443–59.

# 3.6
# CONSPIRACY THEORY AND POPULISM

*Eiríkur Bergmann and Michael Butter*

## Introduction

In the last two decades, populist movements and parties have been on the rise all over the world. Politicians who have been labelled as populists currently govern the world's four largest democracies: Brazil, Indonesia, the U.S.A. and India. In Europe, too, populism is no longer restricted to the margins of politics and society. Populists are governing in Hungary, Poland, Italy, Switzerland and Norway, sometimes alone, sometimes as part of coalitions. Even where they are not (yet) officially in power, they have grown stronger and have shaped political agendas, as the Brexit campaign or discussions about the refugee 'crisis' in Germany and other countries show. Conspiracy theories have played a major role in these debates. Populist leaders – from Trump to Maduro, and from Orbán to Le Pen – often use conspiracist rhetoric, and many of their followers are receptive to it.

However, the relationship between populism and conspiracy theory remains understudied. As Hawkins and Rovira Kaltwasser put it, 'Despite the fact that various scholars have pointed out the link between populism and conspiratorial thinking …, there is a dearth of empirical research on this argument' (2017: 530). This article likewise cannot provide the much-needed comprehensive theory of the connections between conspiracy theories and populism, but it may help to pave the way for such an account. In the first part of the chapter, we first discuss the characteristics of populism and then the limited number of studies that address the relationship between the two phenomena. We provide a preliminary theorisation of our own that, however, requires further testing. In the second part of the article, we conduct two case studies – devoted to the anti-immigration discourse in Northern Europe and Donald Trump's 2016 presidential campaign – in order to demonstrate how conspiracy theories can merge with populist ideology and how populist leaders can employ them to achieve their goals.

## Defining populism

The word *populism* stems from the Latin word *populus*, simply meaning *the people*. The ancient population of Rome was, for instance, referred to as *populus Romanus*. The term corresponds to *Volk* in German, or *Folk* in Scandinavian languages. Unsurprisingly, all scholars of populism – and the field has exponentially grown in the last two decades – therefore agree that the category of the people is of central importance to populism. Apart from that, however, there is little agreement in populism research, with some scholars even questioning the usefulness of the concept as an umbrella for historically, regionally and politically diverse movements and parties. Defining who and what should be classified as populist is particularly challenging because the term carries – at least in popular usage – a derogatory meaning (Taguieff 1995). Populists are often accused of undue simplification and provocation, and therefore movements and parties do not embrace the label but rather reject it.

In recent years, populism has been conceptualised as a strategy that political leaders employ to establish a supposedly direct link to their followers (Weyland 2001; Barr 2009); as a political logic that considers society dominated by the antagonism between two groups that struggle for hegemony (Laclau 2005); as a specific discourse political leaders use to articulate their positions (de la Torre 2010; Hawkins 2010); as a style and thus as a specific performance of doing politics (Moffitt 2016); and even as 'unpolitics' because of its focus on popular sovereignty and disregard for all other aspects of democracy (Taggart 2019). The COST Action IS1308 has treated populism as a communication phenomenon and explored the interactions between political actors, the media and ordinary citizens (de Vreese et al. 2018). Most influentially, however, populism has been theorised as an ideology. According to this definition, populism is

> *a thin-centered ideology that considers society to be ultimately separated into two homogeneous and antagonistic camps, "the pure people" versus "the corrupt elite," and which argues that politics should be an expression of the* volonté générale *(general will) of the people.*
> (Mudde, Rovira Kaltwasser 2017: 6 [italics in the original])

Mudde and Rovira Kaltwasser conceive of populism as 'thin-centered' because it is not a fully developed ideology and therefore always occurs in combination with a thick ideology such as nationalism, socialism or fascism.

Importantly, these different approaches to populism are not mutually exclusive. Specifically, the 'discursive and stylistic turn in the study of populism' (Brubaker 2019: 29) does not challenge but rather complements approaches that conceptualise populism as a thin ideology and therefore as a limited set of ideas. As Woods convincingly argues, the distinction between ideology and discursive style is one of form and content, and both are 'integral to each other' (2014: 15). Following Stanley (2008), Woods also argues that the different approaches tend to converge in the identification of four core elements: (1) the existence of the two groups of the people and the elite; (2) their antagonism; (3) the celebration of popular sovereignty; and (4) the moral glorification of the people and the critique of the elites (2014: 11).

Despite their different nuances across time and regions, then, populist politicians unite in a Manichean worldview, in which societies are seen as divided between the elite and the people. According to this binary viewpoint, the pure people are unaware of the malignant parasitic forces exploiting not only their naivety but also their inherited goodness. They need the populist leaders to alert them to what is really going on and to channel their resistance into meaningful action. The loaded dichotomy between the elites and the people makes populism a particularly moralistic take on politics (Müller 2016) for which processes of othering are of central importance (Wodak 2015). For Hawkins (2003), populism is, then, about nothing less than the struggle between good and evil.

Beyond the core elements of populism identified by Woods, there are a number of secondary features (Taggart 2019) that appear in many populist movements, especially in right-wing ones. To begin with, contemporary populists usually accept democracy and parliamentarianism – they are anti-elite but not anti-system – yet reject the idea of liberal democracy. Since they consider the people one homogeneous group with a single will (the *volonté générale* mentioned above in the definition by Mudde and Rovira Kaltwasser), they cannot accept diverging opinions as legitimate. Rejecting diversity, individual rights and the separation of power, they favour an illiberal form of democracy. Accordingly, when in power, their goal is typically not to abolish democracy but rather to reshape it (Enyedi 2016; Seewann 2018).

Populist movements are usually organised around charismatic leader figures. They tend to be more leader-driven than based on clear party structures. One of their main appeals is positioning their leader as the saviour of the people, hence the leader is usually cast as 'a man of action rather than words, who is not afraid to take difficult and quick decisions' (Mudde, Rovira Kaltwasser 2017: 64). This leader always already intuitively knows what the people – the real people – want, and he articulates their concerns and fights for them. In fact, the leader is often seen to understand the true will of the people even more clearly than they might themselves (cf. Müller 2016: 34–5). Frederico Finchelstein consequently concludes that 'populism replaces representation with the transfer of authority to the leader' (2017: xvi).

The communication style of populist leaders is normally very specific. They tend to both dramatise and simplify the issues at stake in order to trigger an emotional response. They are deliberately provocative in order to draw attention and promote polarisation, for example, by manufacturing crises rhetorically (Moffitt 2015) or violating publicly accepted norms of political discourse. Such acts then usually trigger protest from the mainstream. In turn, the populists complain of ill treatment by the 'politically correct' mainstream, i.e. the interlinked established authority in politics and media. This dynamic can be structured into a four-step rhetorical formulation, by which populists come to dominate the political agenda (Wodak 2015). This strategy is well suited for the contemporary media environment where news channels are always on air and ever hungry for scandalous messages that promise a large audience (Wettstein *et al.* 2018). Moreover, populists are also very apt at using social media for their purposes. In fact, several scholars have argued that the new online platforms that have become so important to political and social communication over the past decade are particularly suited for populist communication (Groshek, Koc-Michalska 2017; Bobba, Roncarolo 2018). Not only does social media allow populists to speak directly to the 'ordinary' people without having their words twisted by what they consider corrupt bureaucrats or journalists serving the elite, social media – and Twitter even more than Facebook – also thrive on simplification and emotionality, exactly the aspects that set populists apart from other politicians (van Kessel, Castelein 2016).

However, as Ruth Wodak (2015) argues, right-wing populism is not only a form of rhetoric, it also contains specific and identifiable contents. Both style and substance are thus interlinked in populist politics. The fear that they instil is of a specific kind. It consists of several core aspects, one being the fear of losing jobs to immigrants and of migrants undermining the welfare state to the detriment of the unable and elderly amongst the native population. Furthermore, the rhetoric usually points to the increasing powerlessness of the nation-state in protecting the intranational public. It warns against the erosion of values and the demise of traditions and the native culture. Frequently, it detects conspiracies at the bottom of these negative developments.

## Populism and conspiracy theory

The existence of a connection between populism and conspiracy theory is already suggested by the fact that the rich bodies of scholarship on both phenomena often pose and discuss similar questions. Research has highlighted that both 'populism' and 'conspiracy theory' are problematic derogatory terms that are usually rejected by those thus described (Taguieff 1995; Knight 2000). Both are often seen as distorted and simplistic responses to pressing issues such as globalisation (Calance 2015; Brubaker 2019). Both are considered to thrive particularly well on the Internet with its echo chambers, alternative and social media, and counter-publics (del Vicario *et al.* 2015; van Kessel, Castelein 2016). Both are tied to questions of gender identity, although this issue remains understudied in both fields (Christ 2014; Abi-Hassan 2017). Both are frequently described as a danger to democracy and seen as closely tied to extremism (Akkerman 2017; van Prooijen 2018). Finally, both are sometimes cast as the opposite of politics proper (Hofstadter 1964; Abts, Rummens 2007). Taggart's labelling of populism as 'unpolitics' (2019) even echoes one of the earliest scholarly condemnations of conspiracy theories: Bunzel's dismissal of them as 'antipolitics' (1967).

However, despite these parallels, the relationship between populism and conspiracy theory has hardly been systematically explored within the scholarship on populism or that on conspiracy theories. Bergmann's study (2018) is the only monograph written on the topic so far. Apart from his book, the few studies from both fields that engage with the relationship at all fall into three categories. First, there is a small body of articles that highlights one or more of the characteristics that populism and conspiracy theory share. Hauwaert (2012) stresses that both share a Manichean worldview that postulates a conflict between good and evil, the people and the elite; with populism stressing the innocence of the people and conspiracy theories stressing their lack of knowledge about the secret plot. The quantitative analyses of Castanho Silva *et al.* (2017) and Oliver and Rahn (2016) identify the distrust of elites as the most important common factor. Moffitt (2016) argues that both engage in othering and deny the complexity of political reality.

Second, other studies discuss, albeit never in much detail, the possible function of conspiracy theories for populist discourse. Taggart (2000) argues that conspiracy theories are a tool of mobilisation and that they allow populist leaders to explain the problems their movements are facing. Gadinger (2019) explores in some detail the role of conspiracy allegations for the German Pegida Movement. Thalmann (2019) stresses that populist leaders can use conspiracy theories to fashion themselves as anti-establishment figures because both populism and conspiracy theory are stigmatised by the mainstream and the elites. In similar fashion, Ylä-Anttila (2018) argues that, in countries like Finland where conspiracy theories are considered illegitimate knowledge, populists use them to cast doubt on experts and challenge their claims to authority.

Finally, there are some attempts to theorise more specifically the relationship between populism and conspiracy theory. Priester (2012) identifies conspiracy theories as one of six defining features of right-wing populism. Wodak (2015) shares this position, while Stoica (2017) and Vassiliou (2017) even argue that there can be no populism without conspiracy theories. From the perspective of conspiracy theory studies, the relationship has been most thoroughly theorised by Fenster, who argues that all contemporary conspiracy theories are populist, but that not all populist movements rely on conspiracy theories. Accordingly, he considers conspiracy theories 'a non-necessary element of populist ideology' (2008: 84). Recently, Taggart, approaching the topic from the perspective of populism studies, has come to a similar conclusion. He considers 'a tendency towards conspiracy theory' as one of the secondary features that occur in many but not all populist movements (2019: 84).

From our perspective, the theorisations by Fenster and Taggart are the most convincing ones, but they require an amendment. As Butter has recently argued, there is empirical evidence that suggests that conspiracy theories are widely spread in many populist movements, but that not all followers actually believe them (2018: 174–5). For example, a poll conducted during the Republican primaries in 2016 showed that supporters of Donald Trump, the populist candidate, displayed a much higher tendency towards conspiracism than the supporters of the two establishment candidates, but there was no conspiracy theory that more than 40 per cent of Trump supporters believed in (Ehrenfreund 2016). This impression that conspiracy theorists usually constitute a significant minority within populist movements is also confirmed by the preliminary findings of an ethnographic study of conspiracy theories in the right-wing populist movements that have emerged in Germany in recent years (Hammel 2017).

Hence, rather than classifying a specific populist movement as conspiracist or not, it makes more sense to postulate that populist movements are obviously successful at integrating those who believe in conspiracy theories and those who do not. As Bobba and Roncarlo put it, 'The elites are generally accused of being incompetent and self-interested when not actually conspiring against the people and seeking to undermine democracy' (2018: 53). Conspiracy theories, then, offer a specific explanation as to why the elites act against the interests of the people. This explanation tends to co-exist within a populist movement or party with other explanations such as negligence or personal enrichment. In other words, conspiracy theories are a non-necessary element of populist discourse and ideology, and they are not necessarily believed by everybody in the populist movement or party in which they are circulating.

## Anti-immigrant conspiracy theories in the Nordic countries

Like elsewhere in Europe, conspiratorial populism has been on the rise throughout the Nordic nations (Bergmann 2017). In Denmark, the discourse on immigration drastically changed in the 1970s and 1980s when it went from emphasising openness, equal treatment and protecting human rights towards requirements of adhering to fundamental values of the native society. Karen Wren (2001) maintains that, paradoxically, the former liberal values were used to portray especially Muslims and refugees as a threat to Danish national identity. The change started with the emergence of the Progress Party in the early 1970s. Its leader, Mogens Glistrup, once compared Muslim immigrants to a 'drop of arsenic in a glass of clear water' (qtd. in Wren 2001: 155).

The Norwegian Progress Party (Fr.P) was established around the same time. In the 1987 election campaign, its then leader, Carl I. Hagen, quoted a letter he claimed to have received from a Muslim called Mustafa, effectively describing a conspiracy of Muslim immigrants planning to occupy Norway. This was quite remarkable as, still, Muslims accounted for only a fraction of the population. Later, the letter proved to be his own fabrication. Interestingly, after revelations that the entire story was a lie, Hagen's party only found increasing support.

A more fundamental shift occurred in Denmark, with the rise of the Danish People's Party (D.F.) in the mid-1990s. The party promoted homogeneity and ethno-cultural cohesion. Initially, it was widely and harshly criticised for flirting with racism. That, however, drastically changed after the terrorist attacks in the U.S.A. on 11 September 2001. For many, the terrifying event served as a validation of the D.F.'s criticism of Islam (Widfeldt 2015). The D.F. was instrumental in portraying Denmark as being overrun by migrants. Their representative in the E.U. Parliament, Mogens Camre, for example, described Islam as an 'ideology of evil' and suggested that Muslims should be 'driven out of Western civilization' (qtd. in Klein 2013: 111). He stated that the West had been 'infiltrated by Muslims', and that 'they are waiting to become numerous enough to get rid of us' (qtd. in Sommer, Aagaard 2003: 258).

Migration became the most salient political issue in Denmark and many mainstream parties started towing a similar line. The D.F. was highly successful in exploiting people's fear of mainly Muslim migrants. Against a backdrop depicting a veiled woman, the party, for example, ran on the following slogan: 'Your Denmark? A multi-ethnic society with gang rapes, repression of women and gang crimes. Do you want that?' (qtd. in Klein 2013: 111).

The Nordic nationalist right was highly successful in positioning immigrants as a threat to the welfare state. This can be labelled welfare chauvinism. The Norwegian Fr.P, for example, argued that the welfare system needed to be shielded from the infiltration of foreigners, who were sucking blood from it at the expense of native Norwegians, particularly the elderly, whom they vowed to protect (Jupskås 2015).

In Sweden, nationalist populists did not find significant support until the 2010 parliamentary election when the neo-racist Sweden Democrats (S.D.) passed the electoral threshold for the first time. Its leader, Jimmie Åkesson, positioned welfare and immigration as mutually exclusive and asked the electorate to choose between the two issues. This was, for example, illustrated in an S.D. advert in 2010: A native woman pensioner slowly moving with her wheeled walker is overtaken by a group of fast-moving Muslim women in burkas, who empty out the social security coffers before the Swedish woman finally arrives. Their slogan read: 'Pensions or immigration – the choice is yours' (qtd. in Klein 2013: 121).

The Nordic nationalist right was especially skilful in linking other political issues to immigration, such as welfare, economy and anti-elitism (Jupskås 2015). Immigration was also directly linked to gender issues. Often D.F. representatives argued that Islam was incompatible with the level of women's liberation in Denmark. On those grounds, the veiling of women in Islam, for example, became a central and symbolic issue.

While the Norwegian Fr.P refused to be associated with racism, their representatives positioned themselves as brave truth-tellers, defying the political correctness of the ruling class. In 2005, they, for example, published a poster depicting a juvenile of foreign descent pointing a gun at the viewer. The text stated that 'the perpetrator is of foreign origin'. When criticised for the xenophobic undertone, the party spokesmen said that it was simply necessary to 'call a spade a spade' (Jupskås 2015: 87).

Anders Hellstrom (2016) documents how the immigration issue gained salience in the Norwegian Fr.P's repertoire in the 1990s, when warning against the dangers of cultural heterogeneity. In that way, the immigration issue was transformed from an economic to also become a cultural issue. The anti-immigration rhetoric of the Fr.P gradually grew more distinctively anti-Muslim. Already in 1979, Carl I. Hagen described Islam as a 'misanthropic and extremely dangerous religion' (qtd. in Jupskås 2015: 84). In a report published by Fr.P parliamentarians in 2007, Muslim immigration was linked to terrorism, forced marriage and crime. Their rhetoric turned increasingly conspiratorial. The report, for instance, identified a need to fight against Sharia laws being implemented in Muslim areas in Norway.

Similarly, in their 1989 party programme, the Sweden Democrats promoted protecting Sweden as 'an ethnically and culturally homogeneous nation'. While surely moving to the mainstream, they still firmly and consistently flagged their anti-immigrant bias. This was, for example, well-illustrated in an open letter to the Finns Party in 2015, written by the leadership of the S.D.'s youth movement, warning their neighbour of repeating the same mistakes as had been made in Sweden. In the letter entitled 'Finland, you do not want the Swedish nightmare', they stated that, over the decades, Sweden had been 'destroyed' by immigration after 'undergoing an extreme transformation from a harmonious society to a shattered one'. They claimed that many Swedes totally opposed this system of 'mass immigration, extreme feminism, liberalism, political correctness and national self-denial' (qtd. in Bergmann 2017: 178).

A new master frame developed across many of the Nordics in which immigrants were presented as an economic burden and a cultural threat, rather than being biologically inferior. Widfeldt (2015) found that the D.F.'s anti-immigration rhetoric revolved around three main themes: First, that immigrants caused a threat to Danish culture and ethnic identity; second, that immigrants committed a disproportionate amount of crimes; and third, that they were a burden on the welfare state.

While avoiding being openly racist, the Danish People's Party clearly made a distinction between immigrants and ethnic Danes. This discursive distinction between *others* and *us* gradually became a shared understanding across the political spectrum (Boréus 2010). The identity-based rhetoric relied on a firm moral frame in which *others* were negatively represented as inferior to *us*. Jens Rydgren (2005) defined this as a neo-racist rhetoric, where national values were being framed as under threat by immigration. The D.F.'s 2009 manifesto stated that a multicultural society was one 'without inner context and cohesion' and 'burdened by lack of solidarity' and therefore 'prone to conflict' (qtd. in Widfeldt 2015: 141). The presence of ethnic minorities was, here, discursively problematised and presented as a threat to a fragile homogeneous Danish culture, which in Wren's description was 'perceived as a historically rooted set of traditions now under threat from globalization, the EU, and from "alien" cultures' (2001: 148).

The True Finns Party (P.S.) found electoral success in the 2011 election in Finland, first positioned against the Eurozone bailout. Their welfare chauvinism of first protecting native Finns but excluding others was also argued on ethno-nationalist grounds. On this platform, a more radical and outright xenophobic faction thrived within the party. Jussi Halla-aho, who became perhaps Finland's most forceful critic of immigration and multiculturalism, led the party's anti-immigrant faction. Later he became party leader. In a highly conspiratorial rhetoric, he, for example, referred to Islam as a 'totalitarian fascist ideology' and was, in 2008, accused of racial hatred, when for instance, writing this about immigration on his blog: 'Since rapes will increase in any case, the appropriate people should be raped: in other words, green-leftist do-gooders and their supporters' (qtd. in Bergmann 2017:86). He went on to write that the Prophet Muhammad was a paedophile and that Islam, as a religion, sanctified paedophilia.

In Sweden, the S.D. heavily criticised the lenient immigration policy of the mainstream parties, which they said had caused segregation, rootlessness, criminality, conflict and increased tension in society (Hellstrom 2016). Jimmie Åkesson (2009) implied a conspiracy in which the Social Democrats had effectively turned immigrant dominated areas into foreign-held territories, occupied by Muslims who were the country's greatest foreign threat and had even partially introduced Sharia laws on Swedish soil. One party representative, local council member, Martin Strid, went so far as indicating that Muslims were not fully human (Aftonbladet 2017).

Across the region, Nordic nationalist populist parties were able to place immigrants firmly on the political agenda. In the 2009 Norwegian parliamentary election debate, immigration was by far the most discussed issue by Fr.P candidates, mentioned twice as often as health care, the next most frequent topic of party members (Jupskås 2013). Party leader Siv Jensen warned against what she referred to as 'sneak Islamisation' of Norway, a term that was subsequently widely used in the political debate (qtd. in Jupskås 2015: 68). She maintained that demands of the Muslim community, such as halal meat being served in schools, the right to wear a hijab and of public celebration of Muslim holidays, were all examples of such 'sneak Islamisation'.

An interesting example of the conspiratorial nature of the rhetoric around Muslims in Norway is evident in the case of an alleged militant Pakistani milieu in Oslo. In 2005, the Fr.P spokesman on immigration, Per Sandberg, said that this secretive extremist Muslim network, which was 'fundamentalist, anti-democratic and potentially violent' had 30,000 members in Oslo (qtd. in Bangstad 2017: 241). Despite being utterly fabricated, this suspicion spread around Norway in many media reports whose authors did not check the claims.

In Denmark, the D.F. firmly kept up its anti-immigrant rhetoric. One example came in the wake of the Paris terrorist attack in late 2015, where Muslim jihadists, mainly from Belgium and France, killed 129 people. When responding to the terrible attack on television, D.F.'s foreign policy spokesman, Søren Espersen, said that Western military forces should now begin bombing civil targets in Syria, specifically also in areas where there were women and children (2015).

Many similar examples of promoting confrontation also exist in Finland. Olli Immonen, a well-known P.S. representative, posted on Facebook a photo of himself with members of the neo-Nazi extreme-right group, the Finnish Resistance Movement. Defending his actions, he wrote that he would give his life for the battle against multiculturalism. He said that these were the days 'that will forever leave a mark on our nation's future. I have strong belief in my fellow fighters. We will fight until the end for our homeland and one true Finnish nation. The victory will be ours' (qtd in Bergmann 2017: 87).

The aforementioned notion of sneak Islamisation alludes to a hidden process already in place. This worldview has led some within populist parties in Nordic countries to promote an active and sometimes forceful resistance against this alleged alteration of Nordic societies. It can be argued that Anders Behring Breivik was at least partially responding to this kind of rhetoric with his horrible actions on 22 July 2011, when killing 77 people, mainly young members of the Norwegian Labour party. Breivik was a believer in the *Eurabia* conspiracy theory and saw himself as a soldier fighting against Muslim invasion. In his 1500 page-long rambling document (2011), he argued that Europe was being ruined by the influx of Muslim immigrants, and that the continent was culturally under siege by foreign infiltrators. He went on to accuse mainly feminists and the social democratic elite of having betrayed the European public into the hands of their external enemies, presumably, he argued, in order to implement their malignant ideology of multiculturalism. With his act, Breivik wanted to prevent a cultural suicide of Europe, underway and orchestrated by those he described as cultural Marxists.

## Donald Trump's conspiracist populism

Almost from the moment he announced his campaign on 16 June 2015, Donald Trump was labelled a populist and a conspiracy theorist. This is hardly surprising given that Trump harked on populist rhetoric that day to fashion himself as a man of action who, unlike regular politicians, would return the country to its former glory: 'Well, you need somebody, because politicians are all talk, no action. Nothing's gonna get done. They will not bring us – believe me – to the promised land. They will not' (Trump 2015). He had also entered the realm of politics for the first time a few years earlier when he embraced the birther claim that Barack Obama was not born in the U.S.A., and therefore never should have been allowed to run for president.

However, Trump only turned into a populist on the campaign trail, and he used conspiracist rhetoric far more sparingly and strategically than is commonly assumed. In his announcement speech, Trump cast himself as an anti-establishment candidate, but not as a champion of the common people. In fact, the idea of the simple people suffering from the neglect or the malignance of the elites – an idea absolutely central to all definitions of populism – is strikingly absent from the speech, and it remained absent from his campaign for a considerable time. According to Friedman (2017), this only changed when Steve Bannon and Steven Miller gained more influence on the campaign during the summer of 2016. In his acceptance speech at the Republican National Convention in July, Friedman argues, Trump emerged for the first time as a full-blown populist, presenting himself as the protector of 'the forgotten men and women of our country' (Trump 2016a).

Trump reiterated this idea throughout the campaign against Hillary Clinton. His populist rhetoric culminated in his inaugural address in which he declared 'today we are not merely transferring power from one Administration to another, or from one party to another – but we are transferring power from Washington, D.C. and giving it back to you, the American People' (Trump 2017). Trump constructs here the established dichotomy between the political elite – represented by the metonymy 'Washington, D.C.' – and the people. At the same time, Trump excludes a considerable part of the electorate – everybody who voted for Obama, in fact – from the group of the people. As Jan-Werner Müller has highlighted, this is characteristic of populist discourse (2016: 21).

While Trump's actions as president – for example, tax cuts from which the rich and large companies benefit disproportionately – are rarely populist, he has continued to appeal rhetorically to the people. Especially on Twitter, which Trump uses very strategically to present himself as their unwavering advocate (Butter 2019), he constantly reinforces 'the concept of a homogeneous people and a homeland threatened by the dangerous other' (Kreis 2017: 607). As it is quite typical of right-wing populism, this 'other' comprises two groups: The corrupt elite inside the country and undeserving outsiders, that is, Democrats and liberals in general, on the one hand, and visitors from certain Muslim countries and (undocumented) immigrants from Mexico, on the other. While Trump focused on the external threat throughout 2017, over the course of 2018 he increasingly targeted Democrats because of their support for the Mueller investigation, the upcoming midterm elections and their allegedly obstructive role in the controversial confirmation process of Justice Brett Kavanaugh.

The tweets Trump posted as the Senate and the public discussed the Kavanaugh case indicate that Trump has not shed any of his campaign populism. On 4 October 2018, for example, he wrote: 'The harsh and unfair treatment of Judge Brett Kavanaugh is having an incredible upward impact on voters. The PEOPLE get it far better than the politicians' (Trump 2018a). A day later, he claimed that the people protesting against Kavanaugh were not really part of the people: '[L]ook at all of the professionally made identical signs. Paid for by Soros and others. These are not signs made in the basement from love! #Troublemakers', he wrote (Trump 2018b), insinuating that there was no popular protest against Kavanaugh and that the Democrats had to pay demonstrators to pretend there was.

In this tweet, Trump also articulates a conspiracy theory, in this case the implicitly antisemitic allegation that billionaire philanthropist George Soros is financing the resistance to Trump to promote the dark plans of an international financial elite. However, he does not develop this conspiracy theory and instead restricts himself to a single remark. This is characteristic of how Trump has been using conspiracist rhetoric both during the campaign and his time in office. With one notable exception, he has restricted himself to short allegations or conspiracy rumours rather than spreading fully developed conspiracy theories, which claim to reveal an alleged plan in detail and provide evidence for it. Frequently, he has also emphasised that he was only reporting what others had told him and that he was in no position to evaluate the accuracy of what he was passing on.

For example, when Supreme Court Justice Anthony Scalia died in February 2016, Trump immediately participated in conspiracy rumours that held that Justice Scalia had been murdered to allow Obama to send a more liberal judge to the court. During a live interview, he told talk-radio host Michael Savage:

> It's a horrible topic, but they say they found the pillow on his face, which is a pretty unusual place to find a pillow. I can't give you an answer … I literally just heard it a little while ago. It's just starting to come out now, as you know, Michael.
> 
> (qtd. in McCarthy 2016)

Trump never picked up on these rumours again but dropped the issue and moved on to the next topic.

The strategy behind Trump's constant but careful deployment of conspiracy theories is to appeal both to those who believe in the conspiracist allegations and to those who do not. By picking up and participating in the claims, Trump signals to those who believe in the conspiracy theories that he is one of them. By restricting himself to a few words or sentences and not providing any evidence or an outline of the alleged plan, he makes it easy for those who do not believe in the conspiracy theory to ignore his claims. Moreover, by often using the 'safety net' of hearsay, Trump ensures that he can always deny allegations that he is spreading conspiracy theories. This tactic was already evident in Trump's interview with Alex Jones in December 2015. Simply appearing on the show of America's conspiracy-theorist-in-chief was enough to send a strong message to conspiracy theorists; Trump did not need to openly embrace any conspiracy theory while on air. Thus, in order to appeal to those sceptical of conspiracy theories as well, Trump made sure Jones did not pin him down to any specific conspiracist claims.

Trump stuck to this strategy even after turning into a full-blown populist in the summer of 2016. He repeatedly contended that the election was 'rigged' but never elaborated on his claim (Trump 2016b). However, in mid-October when the race seemed definitely lost – he was still behind in the polls, the debates were over and the audiotape in which he discusses sexually assaulting women had been made public – Trump changed his approach. Most probably, he and his advisers understood that there was no way now for Trump to win over still undecided moderates. He could count on those supporters of the Republican Party who would always, albeit grudgingly, vote for the Republican nominee, and so they focused on mobilising those particularly receptive to his populist and conspiracist rhetoric. Accordingly, in a campaign speech in West Palm Beach, Florida, on 13 October – his first public appearance after the release of the tape – Trump merged populism and conspiracy theory by accusing Hillary Clinton of conspiring with the international financial elite against the American people.

Trump began the speech by constructing the familiar dichotomy between the people and the elite: 'Our movement is about replacing a failed and corrupt – now, when I say "corrupt," I'm talking about totally corrupt – political establishment, with a new government controlled by you, the American people' (Trump 2016c). Immediately afterwards, Trump finally crossed the threshold from 'mere' populism to conspiracist populism by explicitly claiming that there is a secret plot against the people and that Hillary Clinton is at its core:

> The Clinton machine is at the center of this power structure. We've seen this first hand in the Wikileaks documents, in which Hillary Clinton meets in secret with international banks to plot the destruction of U.S. sovereignty in order to enrich these global financial powers, her special interest friends and her donors.
> *(Trump 2016c)*

He then took the next 30 minutes to elaborate on this claim, and to fashion himself – in prototypical conspiracist fashion – as a renegade who can not only provide insider information, but also, because of his special knowledge, is in a privileged position to foil the conspiracy. He also claimed that the audio tape had been fabricated by the conspirators to silence him:

> In my former life, I was an insider as much as anybody else…. Now I'm being punished for leaving the special club and revealing to you the terrible things that are going on having to do with our country. Because I used to be part of the club, I'm the only one that can fix it.
> *(Trump 2016c)*

As everybody knows, Trump's strategy was successful and he narrowly won the election. Once this had been achieved, he immediately returned to his former mode of 'simultaneously affirming his belief in ... conspiracy theory and qualifying' it (Thalmann 2019: 199). For example, when asked about his earlier allegations of voter fraud in an A.B.C. interview a few days after the inauguration, he employed the same strategies that he had used throughout most of the campaign: 'You have a lot of stuff going on possibly. I say probably. But possibly' (A.B.C. 2017). It remains to be seen if and when Trump will become more explicitly conspiracist.

## Conclusion

Populism and conspiracy theory are clearly connected (Bergmann 2018), but how or to what extent exactly has not yet been adequately theorised. Our contention – that conspiracy theories are a non-necessary element of populist discourses, often cynically articulated by a movement's leaders but genuinely believed by a larger or smaller number of ordinary members – raises more questions than it answers: Is it possible to predict in which situations conspiracy theories are important for a specific populist movement? Within such movements, who is particularly receptive to conspiracy theories? Are conspiracy theories more frequently found in right-wing populism than in the left-wing variant, as some scholars have suggested (Priester 2012; Wodak 2015), or are they as prominent on the left as on the right, as others have argued (Thalmann 2019; Uscinski 2019)? To answer these and a plethora of related questions more research and, importantly, a shift in focus is needed. Future projects should study the significance of conspiracy theories for specific populist movements with regard to both leaders and ordinary members. So far, most research – including our two case studies – discusses how populist leaders employ conspiracist rhetoric. However, it is necessary to study how conspiracy theories circulate among the ordinary members of such movements and parties in order to arrive at a comprehensive understanding of the relationship between populism and conspiracy theory.

## References

A.B.C. (2017) 'Transcript: ABC news anchor David Muir interviews President Trump', *ABC News*, 25 January. Available at: https://abcnews.go.com/Politics/transcript-abc-news-anchor-david-muir-interviews-president/story?id=45047602. [Accessed 18 June 2019.]

Abi-Hassan, S. (2017) 'Populism and gender', in C. Rovira Kaltwasser, P. A. Taggart, P. Ochoa Espejo and P. Ostiguy (eds.) *The Oxford Handbook of Populism*, Oxford: Oxford University Press.

Abts, K. and Rummens, S. (2007) 'Populism versus democracy', *Political Studies*, 55(2): 405–24.

Aftonbladet (2017) 'Martin Strid lämnar SD efter muslimuttalande', *Aftonbladet*, 26 November. Available at: www.aftonbladet.se/senastenytt/ttnyheter/inrikes/a/L0eq1x/martin-strid-lamnar-sd-efter-muslimuttalande. [Accessed 18 June 2019.]

Åkesson, J. (2009) 'Muslimerna är vårt största utländska hot', *Aftonbladet*, 19 October. Available at: www.aftonbladet.se/debatt/a/VRx8zd/akesson-muslimerna-ar-vart-storsta-utlandska-hot. [Accessed 18 June 2019.]

Akkerman, T. (2017) 'Populist parties in power and their impact on liberal democracies in Western Europe', in R.C. Heinisch, C. Holtz-Bacha and O. Mazzoleni (eds.) *Political populism: a handbook*, Baden-Baden: Nomos, International studies on populism 3.

Bangstad, S. (2017) 'Norwegian right-wing discourses: extremism post-Utøya', in D. Pratt and R. Wodlock (eds.) *Fear of Muslims: international perspectives on islamophobia*, Basel: Springer, Boundaries of religious freedom: regulating religion in diverse societies 3.

Barr, R.R. (2009) 'Populists, outsiders and anti-establishment politics', *Party Politics*, 15(1): 29–48.

Bergmann, E. (2017) *Nordic nationalism and right-wing populist politics: imperial relationships and national sentiments*, London: Palgrave Macmillan.

Bergmann, E. (2018) *Conspiracy & populism: the politics of misinformation*, London: Palgrave Macmillan.

Bobba, G. and Roncarolo, F. (2018) 'The likeability of populism on social media in the 2018 Italian general election', *Italian Political Science*, 13(1): 51–62.

Boréus, K. (2010) 'Including or excluding immigrants? The impact of right-wing populism in Denmark and Sweden', in B. Bengtsson, P. Strömblad and A.H. Bay (eds.) *Diversity, inclusion and citizenship in Scandinavia*, Newcastle-upon-Tyne: Cambridge Scholars.

Breivik, A. (2011) *2083–A European Declaration of Independence*, London. Available at: https://fas.org/programs/tap/_docs/2083_-_A_European_Declaration_of_Independence.pdf. [Accessed 18 June 2019.]

Brubaker, R. (2019) 'Why Populism?', in G. Fitzi, J. Mackert and B.S. Turner (eds.) *Populism and the Crisis of Democracy*, vol. 1, London/New York: Routledge, Routledge advances in sociology.

Bunzel, J.H. (1967) *Anti-politics in America: reflections on the anti-political temper and its distortions of the democratic process*, New York: Knopf.

Butter, M. (2018) *»Nichts ist wie es scheint«: über Verschwörungstheorien*, Berlin: Suhrkamp.

Butter, M. (2019) 'Professional amateur: Trump and Twitter', in I. Klaiber, O. Scheiding and J. Stievermann (eds.) *Simplicity, brevity, and their complications in American literature and culture*, Trier: Wissenschaftlicher Verlag Trier.

Calance, M. (2015) 'Globalization and the conspiracy theory', *Procedia Economics and Finance*, 23: 677–81.

Castanho Silva, B., Vegetti, F. and Littvay, L. (2017) 'The elite is up to something: exploring the relation between populism and belief in conspiracy theories', *Swiss Political Science Review*, 23(4): 423–43.

Christ, B. (2014) '"What kind of man are you?" The gendered foundations of U.S. conspiracism and of recent conspiracy theory scholarship', in M. Butter and M. Reinkowski (eds.) *Conspiracy theories in the United States and the Middle East: a comparative approach*, Berlin/Boston: De Gruyter, Linguae & Litterae 29.

De la Torre, C. (2010) *Populist Seduction in Latin America*, 2nd edn, Athens, OH: Ohio University Press.

De Vreese, C.H., Esser, F., Aalberg, T., Reinemann, C. and Stanyer, J. (2018) 'Populism as an expression of political communication content and style: a new perspective', *The International Journal of Press/Politics*, 23(4): 423–38.

Del Vicario, M., Bessi, A., Zollo, F., Petroni, F., Scala, A., Caldarelli, G., Stanley, H.E. and Quattrociocchi, W. (2015) 'Echo chambers in the age of misinformation', *Computers and Society*, 5(43): 1–6.

Ehrenfreund, M. (2016) 'The outlandish conspiracy theories many of Donald Trump's supporters believe', *Washington Post*, 5 May. Available at: www.washingtonpost.com/news/wonk/wp/2016/05/05/the-outlandish-conspiracy-theories-many-of-donald-trumps-supporters-believe/?utm_term=.3696856boefc. [Accessed 18 June 2019.]

Enyedi, Z. (2016) 'Paternalist populism and illiberal elitism in Central Europe', *Journal of Political Ideologies*, 21(1): 9–25.

Espersen, S. (2015) 'DF om krigen mod IS: Vi bliver nødt til at bombe civile no – også kvinder og børn', *TV 2*, 15 November. Available at: http://nyheder.tv2.dk/2015-11-15-df-om-krigen-mod-is-vi-bliver-noedt-til-at-bombe-civile-nu-ogsaa-kvinder-og-boern. [Accessed 18 June 2019.]

Fenster, M. (2008) *Conspiracy theories: secrecy and power in American culture*, Minneapolis, MN: University of Minnesota Press.

Finchelstein, F. (2017) *From fascism to populism in history*, Berkeley, CA: University of California Press.

Friedman, U. (2017) 'What is a populist?', *The Atlantic*, 27 February. Available at: www.theatlantic.com/international/archive/2017/02/what-is-populist-trump/516525/. [Accessed 18 June 2019.]

Gadinger, F. (2019) 'Lügenpresse, gesunder Volkskörper, tatkräftiger Macher: Erzählformen des Populismus', in M. Müller and J. Precht (eds.) *Narrative des Populismus: Erzählmuster und -strukturen populistischer Politik*, Berlin: Springer.

Groshek, J. and Koc-Michalska, K. (2017) 'Helping populism win? Social media use, filter bubbles, and support for populist presidential candidates in the 2016 US election campaign', *Information, Communication & Society*, 20(9): 1389–407.

Hammel, L.L. (2017) 'Verschwörungsglaube, Populismus und Protest', *Politikum*, 3: 32–41.

Hauwaert, S.V. (2012) 'Shared dualisms: on populism and conspiracy theory', *Counterpoint*. Available at: counterpoint.uk.com/shared-dualisms-on-populism-and-conspiracy-theory/. [Accessed 18 June 2019.]

Hawkins, K. (2003) 'Populism in Venezuela: the rise of Chavismo', *Third World Quarterly*, 24(6): 1137–60.

Hawkins, K.A. (2010) *Venezuela's Chavismo and populism in comparative perspective*, Cambridge: Cambridge University Press.

Hawkins, K.A. and Rovira Kaltwasser, C. (2017) 'The ideational approach to populism', *Latin American Research Review*, 52(4): 513–28.

Hellstrom, A. (2016) *Trust us: reproducing the nation and the Scandinavian nationalist populist parties*, Oxford: Berghahn Books.

Hofstadter, R. (1964) *The paranoid style in American politics, and other essays*, Cambridge, MA: Harvard University Press.

Jupskås, A.R. (2013) 'The Progress Party: a fairly integrated part of the Norwegian party system', in K. Grabow and F. Hartleb (eds.) *Exposing the demagogues: right-wing and national populist parties in Europe*, Berlin: Konrad Adenauer Stiftung.

Jupskås, A.R. (2015) *The persistence of populism: the Norwegian progress party 1973–2009*, Faculty of Social Sciences, no. 527, Oslo: University of Oslo.

Klein, A. (2013) 'The end of solidarity? On the development of right-wing populist parties in Denmark and Sweden', in K. Garbow and F. Hartleb (eds.) *Exposing the demagogues: right-wing and national populist parties in Europe*, Berlin: Konrad Adenauer Stiftung.

Knight, P. (2000) *Conspiracy culture: from the Kennedy assassination to the X-Files*, Abingdon: Routledge.

Kreis, R. (2017) 'The "tweet politics" of President Trump', *Journal of Language and Politics*, 16(4): 607–18.

Laclau, E. (2005) *On populist reason*, Brooklyn, NY: Verso.

McCarthy, T. (2016) 'Trump sees "unusual" circumstances in Scalia's death amid conspiracy theories', *Guardian*, 16 February. Available at: www.theguardian.com/us-news/2016/feb/16/donald-trump-antonin-scalia-death-conspiracy-theories. [Accessed 18 June 2019.]

Moffitt, B. (2015) 'How to perform crisis: a model for understanding the key role of crisis in contemporary populism', *Government and Opposition*, 50(2): 189–217.

Moffitt, B. (2016) *The global rise of populism: performance, political style, and representation*, Palo Alto, CA: Stanford University Press.

Mudde, C. and Rovira Kaltwasser, C. (2017) *Populism: a very short introduction*, Oxford: Oxford University Press.

Müller, J.-W. (2016) *What is populism?*, Philadelphia, PA: University of Pennsylvania Press.

Oliver, E.J. and Rahn, W.M. (2016) 'Rise of the *Trumpenvolk*: populism in the 2016 election', *The ANNALS of the American academy of political and social science*, 667(1): 189–206.

Priester, K. (2012) *Rechter und linker Populismus: Annäherung an ein Chamäleon*, Frankfurt/Main: Campus.

Rydgren, J. (2005) 'Is extreme right-wing populism contagious? Explaining the emergence of a new party family', *European Journal of Political Research*, 44(3): 413–37.

Seewann, G. (2018) 'Hungary: history as a legitimizing precedent – "illiberal democracy"', *Zeitschrift für Ostmitteleuropa-Forschung*, 67(2): 239–49.

Sommer, N. and Aagaard, S. (2003) *Succes: historien om Pia Kjærsgaard*, Copenhagen: Lindhardt & Ringhof.

Stanley, B. (2008) 'The thin ideology of populism', *Journal of Political Ideologies*, 13(1): 95–110.

Stoica, M.S. (2017) 'Political myths of the populist discourse', *Journal for the Study of Religions and Ideologies*, 16(46): 63–76.

Taggart, P. (2000) *Populism*, London: Open University Press.

Taggart, P. (2019) 'Populism and "unpolitics"', in G. Fitzi, J. Mackert and B. S. Turner (eds.) *Populism and the Crisis of Democracy*, vol. 1, Abingdon: Routledge.

Taguieff, P. (1995) 'Political science confronts populism: from a conceptual mirage to a real problem', *Telos*, 103: 9–43.

Thalmann, K. (2019) *The Stigmatization of conspiracy theories since the 1950s: "A Plot to Make Us Look Foolish"*, Abingdon: Routledge.

Trump, D. (2015) 'Remarks announcing candidacy for President in New York City', *The American Presidency Project*, 16 June. Available at: www.presidency.ucsb.edu/documents/remarks-announcing-candidacy-for-president-new-york-city. [Accessed 18 June 2019.]

Trump, D. (2016a) 'Acceptance speech', *Republican National Convention*, 21 July. Available at: www.vox.com/2016/7/21/12253426/donald-trump-acceptance-speech-transcript-republican-nomination-transcript. [Accessed 18 June 2019.]

Trump, D. (2016b) 'This election is being rigged', *Twitter*, 15 October. Available at: https://twitter.com/realdonaldtrump/status/787258211283918848. [Accessed 18 June 2019.]

Trump, D. (2016c) 'Remarks at the South Florida Fair Expo Center in West Palm Beach, Florida', *The American Presidency Project*, 13 October. Available at: www.presidency.ucsb.edu/documents/remarks-the-south-florida-fair-expo-center-west-palm-beach-florida. [Accessed 18 June 2019.]

Trump, D. (2017) 'Inaugural address', *The American Presidency Project*, 20 January. Available at: www.presidency.ucsb.edu/documents/inaugural-address-14. [Accessed 18 June 2019.]

Trump, D. (2018a) 'The harsh and unfair treatment', *Twitter*, 4 October. Available at: https://twitter.com/realDonaldTrump/status/1047822816580722690. [Accessed 18 June 2019.]

Trump, D. (2018b) 'The very rude elevator screamers', *Twitter*, 5 October. Available at: https://twitter.com/realDonaldTrump/status/1048196883464818688. [Accessed 18 June 2019.]

Uscinski, J.E. (2019). 'Down the rabbit hole we go!', in J.E. Uscinski (ed.) *Conspiracy theories and the people who believe them*, Oxford: Oxford University Press.

Van Kessel, S. and Castelein, R. (2016) 'Shifting the blame: populist politicians' use of Twitter as a tool of opposition', *Journal of Contemporary European Research*, 12(2): 594–614.

Van Prooijen, J.-W. (2018) 'Populism as political mentality underlying conspiracy theories', in B. Rutjens and M. Brandt (eds.) *Belief systems and the perception of reality*, Oxon, UK: Routledge, pp. 79–96.

Vassiliou, P. (2017) 'Enemies of the people: Latin-American populism, political myth, and the psychodynamics of conspiracy thinking', *Επιστήμη και Κοινωνία: Επιθεώρηση Πολιτικής και Ηθικής Θεωρίας*, 35: 135–59.

Wettstein, M., Esser, F., Schulz, A., Wirz, D.S. and Wirth, W. (2018) 'News media as gatekeepers, critics, and initiators of populist communication: how journalists in ten countries deal with the populist challenge', *The International Journal of Press/Politics*, 23(4): 476–95.

Weyland, K. (2001) 'Clarifying a contested concept: populism in the study of Latin American politics', *Comparative Politics*, 34(1): 1–22.

Widfeldt, A. (2015) *Extreme right parties in Scandinavia*, Abingdon: Routledge.

Wodak, R. (2015) *The politics of fear: what right-wing populist discourses mean*, Thousand Oaks, CA: SAGE.

Woods, D. (2014) 'The many faces of populism: diverse but not disparate', in Woods and B. Wejnert (eds.) *The many faces of populism: current perspectives*, Bingley: Emerald, Research in Political Sociology 22.

Wren, K. (2001) 'Cultural racism: something rotten in the state of Denmark?', *Social and Cultural Geography*, 2(2): 141–62.

Ylä-Anttila, T. (2018) 'Populist knowledge: "post-truth" repertoires of contesting epistemic authorities', *European Journal of Cultural and Political Sociology*, 5(4): 356–88.

# 3.7
# RADICALISATION AND CONSPIRACY THEORIES[1]

*Benjamin Lee*

### Introduction

Radicalisation is an influential and yet contested concept. There have been hundreds of accounts of radicalisation processes that have attempted to explain why both individuals and groups adopt extreme beliefs and, in some instances, engage in violence. There is no single pathway to radicalisation and so it would be wrong to say conspiracy beliefs are an inherent component of radicalisation. While conspiracy beliefs are important for some of those engaged in extremism, they are likely to be a marginal factor for others and belief in conspiracy theories is also extensive even among non-extremist groups and individuals. There is little research that has explicitly considered the role of conspiracy theories in radicalisation, but, where this has emerged as a theme, researchers have tended to argue that conspiracy belief can be used to amplify and justify hostility towards opponents (Berger 2018) as well as the need for extraordinary actions against them (Bartlett, Miller 2010). Even where conspiracy theory and radicalisation are not linked directly, there are clear points of connection between the two literatures. (Extremism, however, is not the same as populism and there is a wider literature on conspiracy theories within populist politics; see Chapter 3.6.) This chapter sets out to highlight three broad roles that conspiracy theories can play in radicalisation:

1. Conspiracy theories can provide clear and unambiguous narratives, structuring the world into ingroups and outgroups, reinforcing the sense of specialness that comes from having access to insider knowledge, and overall enhancing the appeal of extremist narratives.
2. Belief in conspiracy theories and radicalisation may be linked, in part, by shared psychological factors.
3. Conspiracy theories can work to enhance in-group bonding and insulate adherents from outside influences.

Within this framework there are important limitations to be held in readers' minds. First, radicalisation and extremism are both contested terms (Berger 2018) and have been critiqued from a variety of perspectives. While the current interest in radicalisation and extremism stems largely from efforts made during the 'War on Terror', extremism and radicalisation have featured throughout history. Second, the focus in this chapter is on radicalisation processes, not extremism more generally. Throughout, this chapter concentrates on how conspiracy theories help to explain the processes that lead individuals to become attracted to extremist groups or ideas and potentially engage in violence in service of their cause. This approach will overlook some of the wider questions around conspiracy theories and extremism more generally. Third, this chapter is limited to a broadly social scientific perspective. Other approaches to radicalisation and conspiracy theories have drawn more heavily on other disciplines such as psychology. Although these approaches have informed this chapter tangentially, they are not the main focus of the work.

What follows sets out an overview of radicalisation as a concept, noting some of the main criticisms of the concept as well as how understandings of radicalisation have evolved over time. It then sets out the three main areas in which conspiracy theories can contribute to radicalisation: Narrative, psychological and social. The chapter concludes by emphasising the limited state of the existing literature on conspiracy theories and radicalisation, and the potential for conspiracy theories in explaining other aspects of extremist behaviour outside of radicalisation.

## On conspiracy theories and radicalisation

In this chapter, conspiracy theory is understood as 'the belief that powerful, hidden, evil forces control human destinies' (Barkun 2003: 2). However, other definitions are available (see Sunstein, Vermeule 2009). As with conspiracy theory research, one of the first challenges for any work dealing with radicalisation is definitional. There is no consensus definition of radicalisation, and no prospect of one emerging. At its most basic, radicalisation is essentially growing support for radical societal change that constitutes a threat to the 'existing order' (Dalgaard-Nielsen 2010: 798). This conceptualisation demonstrates fealty to language, but generally encompasses more than many researchers mean when they discuss radicalisation. History is full of radical movements seeking to change the status quo, many of which are today lionised as heroes, e.g. in the U.K. the suffragettes and in the U.S. the civil rights movement. To get around this problem, radicalisation is usually interpreted more practically as applying to a violent sub-set of those that have become radicalised, a process referred to as 'violent radicalization' (Dalgaard-Nielsen 2010), although even this definition tends to overlook some of the violent tendencies emerging from these movements. The distinction between cognitive radicalisation, meaning a belief in the need for radical change, and violent radicalisation, meaning the willingness to use violence to bring about change, is common in the literature on radicalisation and a potential source of confusion (Veldhuis, Staun 2009: 4). While those with a security agenda will likely be content to see radicalisation as linked only to violence, other policy agendas, for example those concerned with broader foreign policy or integration, are likely to also view non-violent radicalisation as an issue. Disagreement over the precise area of concern has, in some cases, left scholars and policy makers at cross-purposes (Sedgwick 2010).

The focus on the radical is also unfortunate for those who study the far right. Within the study of the far right, 'radical' is usually taken to mean at odds with mainstream politics, but still willing to work within democratic structures. Extremism, in contrast, is the label applied to groups and actors seeking to work outside of democratic norms (Mudde 2007; Ravndal, Bjørgo 2018). So, while radicalisation is clearly of concern to law and policy makers, radical groups and actors are potentially less of a concern than extremist groups with similar ideologies. This concern is even more pressing as a good deal of work on conspiracy theories draws on phenomena generally associated with the far right. In summary, like the concept of conspiracy theories itself, radicalisation has its problems. Although there is a general pragmatism in the literature that adopts a 'we know it when we see it' approach, it is important for researchers to take the time to clearly specify what they mean when they use the term radicalisation to avoid talking at cross-purposes.

## How radicalisation works

If scholars have been split in defining radicalisation, it should come as no surprise that accounts of radicalisation also differ in the explanations they offer. The key trend in the analysis of radicalisation has been the varying significance given to explanations based on individual factors, wider structural factors and contextual factors such as ideology and social relationships. The current position roughly centres on radicalisation as a complex set of processes in which different actors can take different pathways to extremism. Equally, however, a critical literature has grown up around radicalisation highlighting the difficulties arising from the concept, including the risks of pathologising and exoticising relatively common and normal experiences.

Although history is littered with both extreme and radical groups and individuals, the study of radicalisation as a phenomena took on a new impetus following the 9/11 attacks and the ensuing 'War on Terror'. Most accounts of radicalisation have focused specifically on violent Islamist extremism, using datasets composed of those engaging in global 'Jihad' (Sageman 2008; Bakker 2008; Borum 2011). Only a few have considered left-wing radicalisation (Tsintsadze-Maass, Maass 2014; Karpantschof 2015), or radicalisation on the extreme-right (Vertigans 2007; Koehler 2014). Explanations have also concentrated in different geographies, including Africa (Botha 2014), the U.S.A. (Vertigans 2007; Tsintsadze-Maass, Maass 2014) and in Europe (Bakker 2008; Karpantschof 2015). Efforts have come from varied academic perspectives, including sociology (Roy 2008; Dalgaard-Nielsen 2010), psychology (King, Taylor 2011) and terrorism studies (Sageman 2008; Horgan 2009).

Many of the conceptual models of radicalisation that have emerged are linear descriptions from the perspective of individuals (Borum 2011: 38–43). For example, the New York Police Department (N.Y.P.D.) model focuses on U.S.-based home-grown Islamist extremist terrorists. It suggests individuals engage in four stages of behaviour: Pre-radicalisation; self-identification, during which they explore and adopt ideological tenants; indoctrination, which is envisaged as an intensification of both belief and commitment; and, finally, 'Jihadization', which entails direct violent action (Borum 2011: 41). However, models have also begun to place individuals in a broader context and to consider external factors (Borum 2011). For example, a 2008 report from the U.S. Center for Strategic and International Studies (C.S.I.S.) highlighted three overlapping motivational elements in radicalisation that included narratives and sociological factors alongside psychological factors, whilst at the same time minimising the role of demographic and socio-economic factors (C.S.I.S. 2008). Other models, such as from the Joint Military Information Support Centre (J.M.I.S.C.) were more expansive, including elements such as 'socially-facilitated entry' to radical groups, emphasising the role of pre-existing social connections in gaining access to groups (Borum 2011: 45). Other approaches have likewise suggested that radicalisation may be linked to factors other than individual level processes (Veldhuis, Staun 2009). These have included attempts to suggest a greater role in radicalisation for wider society level factors (Roy 2008; Cesari 2008; Bakker 2008), ideology and group processes (Wiktorowicz 2005; Sageman 2008). Radicalisation is not likely an either/or explanation but is instead a product of the complex interplay of differing factors. It is a result of multiple causes, given that ideological justifications develop within a variety of individual and social contexts. Radicalisation is seldom uniform, and different pathways can lead to the same destination (Borum 2011: 57–8).

Radicalisation is also a concept that has attracted considerable criticism. The largest source of disquiet is that it conflates thought, rhetoric and action into a single concept. While each comes with its own potential harms, each relates very differently to wider society and the state. Security agencies, for example, tend to be primarily concerned with security issues, i.e. threats to life and property, and even then only in specific forms, e.g. terrorism over protest. In contrast, civil society campaigners may more readily intervene when rhetoric causes problems, while state agencies are constrained by the legal complexities surrounding the boundaries between freedom of speech, hate speech and incitement to violence. Other critics have identified further issues with the concept of radicalisation, for example that it has become needlessly exoticised. It should instead be considered mundane and a normal part of life. By focusing analysis of radicalisation on the moments when an individual may move from legality to criminality, they argue we are missing the potentially extensive collection of factors that may lead up to that moment. By taking a longer view of radicalisation, even the smallest of perceived slights can contribute to moving an individual towards alienation and mistrust (Bailey, Edwards 2017).

The greatest challenge facing the concept of radicalisation, however, has been to explain why so few individuals become radicalised when individual experiences and structural and contextual factors are common to so many. Jensen *et al.* (2018: 16) argue that approaches to radicalisation have been too linear in attempting to understand the phenomenon, and that it is a product of multiple complex interactions between individual psychology, community grievances, group biases and the promise of material reward. Schuurman and Taylor (2018: 4) seemingly go further, arguing that radicalisation has suffered as a concept as it has attributed too great a role to ideological belief in explaining violent action, while ignoring the fact that the vast majority of those with radical ideological beliefs remain non-violent. They go on to argue that radicalisation suffers from epistemological flaws, missing the fact that terrorists, once involved in groups, are conditioned to describe their actions in ideological ways that may overlook other causal factors unrelated to ideology.

The role of this chapter is not to fully explain violent radicalisation. The task here is to consider the points at which conspiracy theories may play a role in supporting radicalisation processes. There is little available research that directly considers conspiracy theories and radicalisation (one exception is Bartlett and Miller 2010). However, this chapter aims to suggest three broad areas where both phenomena potentially overlap. What follows considers the role of conspiracy theory in radicalisation from three perspectives: Radical narratives, psychological factors and group relationships.

## Conspiracy theories and extremist narratives

The clearest point of cross-over between radicalisation and conspiracy theory is in the creation and structuring of narrative accounts of the world. At their most basic, conspiracy theories represent explanations for malevolent events, attributing disasters real or imagined to a small group of secretive malign actors. In that respect, they have much in common with extremist narratives that seek to explain the world and the misfortunes besetting their cause, in unorthodox ways (Sunstein, Vermeule 2009). As a result, conspiracy theories are a common component within the narratives offered by extremist groups and may go some way to explaining their appeal (Bartlett, Miller 2010).

Probably the most familiar set of theories to a Western reader are those associated with the far right, foremost of which have been antisemitic conspiracy theories espoused in works such as *The Protocols of the Elders of Zion*, Henry Ford's *The International Jew* and A.K. Chesterton's *The New Unhappy Lords*. While the antisemitic basis of far-right conspiracy theories remains strong, it has been joined by influencers seeking to shift focus to the Islamic world such as Bat Y'eor's *Eurabia: The Euro-Arab Axis* and Fjordman's *Defeating Eurabia*. In addition, there are thousands of lesser conspiracy theories circulated in far-right circles, such as the anti-European conspiracy theory the Kalergi Plan. Writing on the U.K. National Front and breakaway formations in the 1970s, Michael Billig argues that the far right exhibited a tenacious 'conspiracy tradition' (Billig 1978: 185). An emerging trend is for conspiracy theories in the far right to be remixed to fit differing ideological perspectives, drawing in evidence from a range of sources to fit differing explanations for the state of the world. For example, the counter jihad movement has varied between espousing the secret 'Islamisation' of Europe as the result of a Faustian pact between European and Arab elites to counter American power, to a more straightforward 'Stealth Jihad' centred on the U.S.A. (Lee 2017).

Less often discussed has been the role of conspiracy theories in the narratives offered by various forms of Islamist extremism. Islamist ideologue Sayyid Qutb, for example, includes a warning in his seminal *Milestones* that some Westerners were part of a 'well-thought-out scheme, the object of which is first to shake the foundations of Islamic belief and then gradually demolish the structure of Muslim society' (Qutb 2002: 116; see also Sageman 2008: 78). This belief was well-represented in narratives of groups such as Al-Qaeda, who would frequently reference varying religious coalitions as working against Muslims (Bartlett, Miller 2010). There is also an enduring overlap between the apocalyptic narratives adopted by I.S.I.S. and a more generalised acceptance of antisemitic conspiracy theories that see the U.S.A. in particular as in the pocket of Israel (Stern, Berger 2015: 222). While we are often conditioned to think of far-right and Islamist groups as being opposed to one another, conspiracy narratives can overlap in unexpected ways. For example, the acceptance of the *Protocols* forgery amongst groups hostile to Israel, such as Hamas, seemingly points to some alignment with the far right (Bartlett, Miller 2010: 21). That conspiracy theories feature so heavily in the narratives of extremist groups is not surprising and they can potentially help to explain why extremist narratives resonate with potential supporters and therefore at least some elements of radicalisation.

Conspiracy theories are usually Manichean, referencing the polarisation of a world divided between dark and light or good and evil (Barkun 2003: 2). Although conspiracy theories can be massively convoluted and complex, they are often clear in identifying those seeking to cause harm (Raab et al. 2013). Writing on the 'war on Islam' concept present among some Islamist extremists, Sageman notes:

> This global conspiracy provides the dramatic background for the self-appointed role of the global Islamist terrorists. They view themselves as warriors willing to sacrifice themselves for the sake of building a better world, and this gives meaning to their lives. They are part of an elite avant-garde devoted to absolute principles regardless of personal cost. Their enemies, who pursue their self-interest and give into temptation, are symbolic of the decadence of the present world.
>
> *(Sageman 2008: 81)*

The explanatory power of conspiracy theories may be heightened when groups feel themselves to be threatened. When individuals and groups are stressed, for example through personal crisis (Schuurman, Taylor 2018), then conspiracy belief is likely to offer clear explanations for events and provide a clear opponent to fight. As a result, conspiracy theories are of value in extremist narratives as they clearly and unambiguously set out enemies to be opposed at every turn (Barkun 2003).

As well as their explanatory power, conspiracy theories further serve to enhance the appeal of extremist groups by casting adherents in a sometimes heroic – or at the very least knowledgeable – light, thereby enhancing individual agency. Uncertainty and lack of clarity are key factors that drive belief in conspiracy theories overall (Douglas *et al.* 2016: 59). Conspiracy theories are linked to wider crises of individuality through the idea of 'agency panic', where individuals feel their own autonomy is under threat, conspiracy theories are a way for them to affirm their own values (Raab *et al.* 2013: 2). Agency emerges over and over in accounts of conspiracy theories. Robertson's (2016) analysis of millenarian conspiracy notes that conspiracy theories stress the importance of individual agency. Similarly, discussions of conspiracy theory in the post-Soviet space also explore a lack of control as a possible explanation for the appeal of conspiracy theories (Ortmann, Heathershaw 2012: 556).

The appeal of conspiracy theories can be connected to wider societal trends linked to an 'age of uncertainty' brought about by advanced capitalism and globalisation, especially for those at the margins of societies (Parish 2001). In such a complex environment, older forms of explanation of cause and effect are clearly broken down and conspiracy theories then offer a 'compensatory fantasy' to their adherents (Knight 2001: 21). In a conspiracy-driven universe, nothing is accidental or coincidental and all events are capable of being read as meaningful and somehow tied to the wider conspiratorial narrative (Barkun 2003: 3; Douglas *et al.*: 2016). While conspiracy theories are frequently terrifying, they are also comforting in that they posit a universe in which patterns can be freely imposed on chaos (Barkun 2003: 4).

The baseline interpretation of conspiracy narratives as an attempt to bring order to an uncertain political and social picture resonates with understandings of radicalisation that link extreme ideas with wider societal factors, suggesting that conspiracy and radicalisation are born out of the same environment characterised by anxiety and uncertainty. Uncertainty brought about by changing economic practices and, in particular, the decline of manufacturing has been instrumental in driving radicalisation on the U.S. extreme right, despite the fact that many supporters have not been personally affected by economic changes (Vertigans 2007: 647). Similar factors were noted by Veldhuis and Staun (2009: 31) in their discussion of European Muslim integration in the context of Islamist radicalisation. They noted the lower socio-economic profiles of many European Muslims and further expanded this, arguing that Muslims were poorly integrated in the political domain, and noted that foreign policy in particular was often a source of grievance. In a study of limited open source data about 242 European jihadists, Bakker (2008) suggested that there was little evidence of jihadists being drawn from the upper classes, describing the majority of cases where information was available as being from middle or lower classes. In his conclusions on the data, Bakker noted the limited data available, but suggested that the broad trend was for violent Islamist extremist recruits in Europe to be drawn from lower social orders with a greater likelihood of having a criminal conviction (Bakker 2008: 43). However, these findings are often based on limited data about radicalised individuals (Bakker 2008) and cannot explain instances where highly educated and high-status individuals are seemingly radicalised. Economic uncertainty, then, may be one factor common to radicalisation, but the evidence suggests that those most at risk do not have a uniform socio-economic profile.

A more compelling explanation for radicalisation than immediate economic threats may be the extent to which economic and social change contributes to wider uncertainty around identity and status. Theories of the 'French sociology' school draw heavily on concepts such as identity and the search for meaning, including the experiences of the French Muslim population (Daalgard–Nielson 2010). These are not born from simple socio-economic or political causes, but instead derive, as the conspiracy theories above, from a wider backdrop of modernity in Western democracies, in particular increasing levels of uncertainty around values, morals and identity:

> The key contention of this group of sociologists is that violent radicalization arises out of the particular challenges faced by an increasingly Westernized generation of young

Muslims in Europe, who attempt to carve out an identity for themselves. The overall conditions of modernity and life in Western democracies – individualization and value relativism – prompt a search for identity, meaning, and community for a number of individuals.

(Dalgaard-Nielsen 2010: 800)

In a similar vein, radicalisation has been characterised as the result of a rupture between an individual and a society rather than as of any one socio-economic process (Roy 2008: 109). Those seeking to engage in the global jihad were uprooted, often lacking solid social integration and often seeking solutions to identity issues. In some cases this was caused by criminal involvement (Roy 2008: 112), and recruits often experience disconnection from family, environment, the state and moderate beliefs (Roy 2008: 109). Likewise, other researchers characterise radical recruits as being disembedded from society and social networks (Cesari 2008: 103).

Accounts of radicalisation and conspiracy theory both draw on wider societal developments as part of their explanations. For those concerned with conspiracy theories, the uncertainty of globalisation leads to an increase in the search for comfortingly simple explanations. Likewise, sociological accounts of radicalisation suggest the same uncertainty leads to the profound disconnect and rupture that opens up the possibility of engaging with groups and ideas that promise a radical alternative. To this overlap, we can also add the centrality of conspiracy narratives in many radical movements. This occurs most obviously in tropes about Jewish domination on the right wing, but is also a component of violent Islamism and other forms of extremism. That conspiracy theory and radicalisation both originate with global uncertainty and a quest for identity is the clearest point of overlap between the two literatures, and it is easy to see how the conspiratorial narratives adopted by extremist groups enhance their appeal to potential recruits.

## Psychological factors

As well as the crossover between radical narratives and conspiracy theories prompted in part by growing uncertainties, there is a strand of research on the psychological factors underpinning both radicalisation and conspiracy theories. This chapter is rooted in social science rather than psychology, however researchers of both conspiracy theories and radicalisation have speculated about the psychological factors that may contribute to the phenomena.

Accounts of radicalisation have often been sceptical about the role of psychological factors. Psychological profiling has been written off by some as a likely dead end that will never capture the evolving nature of terrorism (Horgan 2009). Horgan (2009) suggests that becoming involved in terrorist activity is a process and that psychological risk factors can only ever contribute to entry into a longer and more complex process such as those described above. Despite this, Horgan goes on to identify several risk factors for involvement in terrorism, which include temporary emotional states, dissatisfaction with current activities and 'permanent relevant individual factors' such as stress-seeking, that may prompt individuals to seek involvement in terrorism (2009: 11–12). A contrasting approach draws out the role of psychological factors in the critique of radicalisation, noting the prevalence of personal crises as being of interest in explaining different outcomes from similar patterns of extremist engagement. They go on to further emphasise the role of individual personality and behavioural factors in explaining violent action by suggesting abandoning the concept of radicalisation altogether in favour of fanaticism, as defined by a series of individual behavioural characteristics (Schuurman, Taylor 2018: 8–13).

Although there has been a trend away from viewing radicalisation as pathological, there is a similar argument within the literature on conspiracy theories that innate psychological characteristics make some individuals more likely to support conspiracy theories than others. An overview of psychological research into conspiracy theories suggests factors such as anomie, distrust in authority, political cynicism, powerlessness, Machiavellianism and schizotypy may be linked to conspiracy belief (Douglas *et al.* 2016: 58). The phenomenon of hypersensitive agency detection – a well-documented human tendency to overestimate the extent to which events are intentional – also helps to explain the appeal of conspiracy theories (Douglas *et al.* 2016: 59). However, the evidence provided describes personality characteristics associated with conspiracy belief, not causal mechanisms (Douglas *et al.* 2016: 59). In other words, the causal relationship between conspiracy belief and psychological factors is uncertain.

A further stand-out finding from psychological research on conspiracy theories has been that conspiracy beliefs are often mutually supportive. When individuals subscribe to one conspiracy theory, they are more likely to endorse others. This has led to claims that there is a specific conspiracy mindset in which conspiracy thinking becomes self-reinforcing (Goertzel 1994). Existing partisan pre-dispositions have also been found to play a role in individual acceptance of conspiracy theory (Uscinski *et al.* 2016: 57). One study of U.S. citizens concluded that exposure to conspiracy theory was only likely to increase belief for those already primed to accept the logic of conspiracy theories and for whom the conspiracy theory aligned with existing partisan belief (Uscinski *et al.* 2016: 67).

The argument that there is a psychological overlap between radicalisation and conspiracy belief is less developed than the case about shared narratives. However, both radicalisation research and conspiracy theory research have pointed, in some cases, to psychological factors that influence individual susceptibility to both phenomena. From a social science perspective, caution needs to be exercised here, as taking an overly reductive psychological approach risks drawing attention away from both wider societal level as well as group level approaches to both radicalisation and conspiracy theories. The major danger is that both radicalisation and conspiracy belief are reduced to pathologies unrelated to wider social trends. Despite this, if there is such a thing as a conspiratorial mindset, it could well overlap with the kinds of psychological risk factors identified by researchers working on radicalisation.

## Radicalisation and conspiracy theory as social context

As well as providing appealing narratives and the potential psychological overlap between conspiracy and radicalisation, conspiracy theories also work to reinforce the relationships within groups. While many people find extremist narratives laced with conspiracy theories such as those adopted by the extreme right or Islamist extremists appealing and may share a psychological disposition towards conspiracy theories and extremism, most do not participate in extremist groups. Social relationships are therefore an additional factor in explaining the appeal of extremist spaces and individual motivations to participate in them (King, Taylor 2011):

> It is certain that radicalisation does not play out in individual isolation. It is a social phenomenon: individuals learn from one another, on and off the Internet, and various radical movements compete vigorously with one another; arguments are exchanged, opponents are maligned, and every movement is convinced that it is in the right.
> *(Slootman, Tillie 2006: 5)*

Evidence of the importance of social bonds has mainly come from analysis of Jihadist terrorism. The breakdown of the central organisation within Al-Qaeda foreshadowed a transition to a strategy described as 'leaderless Jihad' (Sageman 2008). In this context, social relationships became more important for explaining participation. The majority of recruits had prior connections to one another and terror networks were largely home-grown conglomerations of friendship and kinship groups radicalised together (Sageman 2008: 141). Likewise, evidence from a study of 242 European-based Jihadi terrorists found that in 35 per cent of the sample there was evidence of social connections at the time of joining a group or network. This included 43 cases where friends joined together, and 50 cases of related individuals (Bakker 2008: 42). The importance of social relationships in radicalisation has also played out in the extensive debate around lone actor terrorism. An increasing consensus within terrorism studies has been that lone actors are generally not nearly as one as they seem and instead are connected to wider ideological communities (Berntzen, Sandberg 2014; Schuurman et al. 2017; Hofmann 2018). The generally accepted explanation has been that radicalisation also requires some form of social support structure. It is an 'inescapably social' process, reliant on both social connections and group-curated narratives (Conway 2012: 13).

As well as helping to explain participation in groups, social connections provide important interpretive frameworks for extremists. Within extremist groups, external events are not only interpreted by individuals but through the collective lens of a group:

> Social bonding within small peer groups can facilitate the adaptation of more extreme worldviews. They emphasize how the group provides individuals with a sense of belonging and community, with the feeling of being accepted and important, and even with a sense of superiority and mission. They also emphasize how social pressures apply to the members of the groups and how this increases group conformity over time.
>
> *(Dalgaard-Nielsen 2010: 803)*

The importance of social connections is not limited only to Jihadist groups but is also a feature of far-right groups. Research from the U.S.A. argues that ideas associated with white supremacy are embedded within U.S. society at a more mainstream level. However, by engaging with extremist groups, individuals are able to develop more extreme interpretations of events (Vertigans 2007: 647).

Social aspects are a significant point of overlap between conspiracy belief and radicalisation. Conspiracy theory belief contributes to a sense of group exceptionalism and outsider status, as well as improving resilience to external challenges. Conspiracy theories exist in the domain of 'stigmatised knowledge', sitting alongside other forms of knowledge such as esoteric teaching and 'political radicalism' (Barkun 2003: 12). As a result of their heterodoxy, those who subscribe to conspiracy theories have a shared outsider status. One analysis concludes by describing a 'theodicy of the dispossessed' in which adherents are located outside of time and with access to knowledge unavailable to those still bound by conventional modes of thought (Robertson 2016: 206). Those party to the conspiracy but not bound by it are 'an elect minority defined by exclusive knowledge' (Robertson 2016: 207).

Social relationships also contribute to the growth of conspiracy theories. In the context of extremist groups, information is often limited and often wrong, what one team of researchers termed 'crippled epistemologies' (Sunstein, Vermeule 2009). This kind of social context is primed for the growth of conspiracy theories as factually weak explanations gain traction within a social group and become the go-to explanation for events. For other activists, it is easier and simpler to go along with the established explanation rather than challenge it. As less-committed members of the group drop away, selection effects mean that explanations become ever more detached from reality and the median position shifts towards the extremes (Sunstein, Vermeule 2009).

Conspiracy theories also work for improving group resilience, providing groups members with an easy explanation for why a group is ostracised by the mainstream, or why events do not play out as scripted by group narratives. As 'monological' belief systems, i.e. reliant on a single immutable idea, conspiracy theories provide believers with a shield against new information that may threaten existing world views (Goertzel 1994). A good example is millenarian movements that lack a mass following and tend to use conspiracy theory to explain away their lack of popularity as well as the failure of the End Times to materialise: 'Surely the masses would believe if only they knew what the concealed malefactors were up to' (Barkun 2003: 3).

Conspiracy theories are valuable in maintaining solidarity against efforts to undermine group narratives. The acceptance of counter messaging as a component of policy in countering violent extremism has put a focus on the difficulties inherent in reaching those engaging with extremist spaces (Aistrope 2016; Braddock, Morrison 2018). Extensive interest in counternarrative and counter-messaging approaches to extremism from government and civil society are easier to combat when they can be interpreted as yet more evidence of both the righteousness of the cause and the malevolence of the forces acting against a group. Where conspiracy theories are a component of a narrative, they can dismiss any counternarrative as part of the wider plot and therefore unreliable evidence (Barkun 2003: 7). This feature is often described as limited falsifiability, suggesting that the theory put forward cannot be disproved. Although this has been a major criticism of conspiracy theories, some have argued that this feature is also present in more conventional explanations for political events (Räikkä 2009). There is also evidence from wider studies of decisions to accept and contest evidence that suggest that the limited falsifiability of conspiracy theories may not be that different from other situations (Leman, Cinnirella 2013).

There is a need to consider the direction of causality at work in this context. While the approach to conspiracy theories is generally utilitarian, arguing that they serve distinctive purposes in extremist spaces, the reality is likely to be more complex. For example, conspiracy theorising could easily be a by-product of engaging in extremist spaces as well as a cause. The isolation and hostility experienced by participants in extremist spaces could easily heighten the appeal of conspiracy belief. There is some evidence to suggest that, where groups are under pressure from unusual, unforeseen or traumatic events, dramatic new explanations for events become more attractive. For example, conspiratorial themes took on a heightened significance in the mainstream press in Serbia during the 1999 N.A.T.O.-led bombing campaign (Byford and Billig 2001), and similar explanations were offered for the interest in conspiracy theories developing after 9/11 in the U.S.A. (Barkun 2003: 2).

Both the literatures on radicalisation and conspiracy theory acknowledge a key role for social context. Radicalisation, for all the models and accounts focusing on push and pull factors towards participation in extremist groups, is at heart a social process, relying on established connections to access groups and, once inside extremist spaces, it involves interpreting the world in a way that preserves the group's vision. Likewise, the conspiracy theory literature highlights the social aspects of conspiracy theories, both in ostracising believers from wider society, granting them a shared outsider status, and in allowing groups to fend off external criticism and sustain their ideological commitment. Once inside an extremist space, conspiracy theories are powerful tools that create shared bonds and a sense of exceptionalism for extremist participants, especially against a hostile and often threatening mainstream.

## Conclusion

This chapter has focused on the intersection of conspiracy theory and radicalisation. As noted in the introduction, the focus here has been on conspiracy theories and the processes of engagement with extremist groups, i.e. radicalisation. Not discussed here, but of interest, is the extent to which conspiracy theories can appear to structure the behaviour of extremist groups. This is most clearly demonstrated in target selection. We know from the manifestos of far-right terrorists such as Anders Breivik and Brenton Tarrant that conspiracy narratives can be used to justify the targets of terrorism. Conspiracy theories often make claims that connections exist between seemingly disparate events and people. Although hidden from view, the hand of the conspiracy is everywhere. Barkun (2003: 4) describes conspiracy theorists as engaging in a constant process of 'linkage and correlation' between events. James (2001: 71), writing about Christian militias in the U.S.A., argues that the conspiratorial narrative of the Zionist Occupational Government (Z.O.G.) was a key component in bringing together the objects of delegitimisation for the movement. As racial enemies were reconfigured and viewed as having taken over the very state itself, groups once committed to the state and nationalism reframed their activism to focus both on racial minorities and the state (see also Sprinzak 1995; Kaplan 1995). Bartlett and Miller (2010: 24) contend that conspiracy theories act as 'radicalisation multipliers' within groups. Starting with the observation that extremist groups and actors share a common conception of ingroups and outgroups (see also Berger 2018), they argue that conspiracy narratives can lead groups towards violence by exaggerating the threat presented by outgroups, shutting down dissenting voices and legitimising the use of violence in order to awaken others. So, while it is plain that conspiracy theories play a key role in structuring and possibly motivating extremist behaviours, in particular violence, and it is equally clear that extremist narratives tend to be highly conspiratorial, the exact role of conspiracy theory in radicalisation remains an open question.

There is a frustrating lack of evidence for the role of conspiracy theories in underpinning radicalisation and it has been challenging to get the two literatures to address one another directly. However, if we squint, the connections between radicalisation and conspiracy theories are potentially manifold. This chapter has identified three possible points of overlap: First, that the presence of conspiracy theories in extremist narratives enhances the appeal of extremist narratives, thereby encouraging radicalisation. Conspiracy theories are powerful tools for making sense of an increasingly complex world and the appeal of clear and absolute narratives for those struggling to find identity and certainty cannot be overlooked. Second, and more tenuous, research has linked both conspiracy belief and radicalisation to psychological factors. In the context of radicalisation, this link has been questioned, not least because of the deep unease around separating radicalisation from its wider social context. The extent to which any conspiracy mindset and risk factors for radicalisation overlap remains an open question. Third, once inside an extremist space, be it a cell, party or wider network, conspiracy theories can work to improve solidarity and insulate believers from external challenges to their ideas. This is a case of conspiracy theories protecting believers and preventing de-radicalisation rather than supporting radicalisation.

Plainly, there is more work to be done in getting the radicalisation and conspiracy literatures to engage with one another. Further efforts to unpack the appeal of conspiracy theories for those seeking to involve themselves in extremist spaces would be welcome, as would analyses of conspiracy theories specifically in the contexts of political and religious extremisms. There also remains a question around the modes of distribution of conspiracy theories in extremist settings. While the growth of the Internet has generally been linked to growing belief in conspiracy theories and support for extremism, further research is needed to understand how these trends are interacting with one another.

## Note

1 This work was funded by the Centre for Research and Evidence on Security Threats (CREST). CREST is commissioned by the Economic and Social Research Council (ESRC Award: ES/N009614/1) with funding from the UK Intelligence Community.

## References

Aistrope, T. (2016) 'The Muslim paranoia narrative in counter-radicalisation policy', *Critical Studies on Terrorism*, 9(2): 182–204.
Bailey, G. and Edwards, P. (2017) 'Rethinking "radicalisation": microradicalisations and reciprocal radicalisation as an intertwined process', *Journal for Deradicalization*, 10: 255–81.
Bakker, E. (2008) 'Jihadi terrorists in Europe and the global Salafi Jihadis', in R. Coolsaet (ed.) *Jihadi Terrorism and the Radicalisation Challenge in Europe*, Ashgate: Aldershot, pp. 69–84.
Barkun, M. (2003) *A culture of conspiracy: apocalyptic visions in contemporary America*, Oakland: University of California Press.
Bartlett, J. and Miller, C. (2010) *The power of unreason*, London: Demos.
Berger, J.M. (2018) *Extremism*, London: MIT Press.
Berntzen, L.E. and Sandberg, S. (2014) 'The collective nature of lone wolf terrorism: Anders Behring Breivik and the anti-Islamic social movement', *Terrorism and Political Violence*, 26(5): 759–79.
Billig, M. (1978) *Fascists: a social psychological view of the National Front*, London: Harcourt Brace Jovanovich.
Borum, R. (2011) 'Radicalization into violent extremism II: a review of conceptual models and empirical research', *Journal of Strategic Security*, 4(4): 37–62.
Botha, A. (2014) 'Political socialization and terrorist radicalization among individuals who joined al-Shabaab in Kenya', *Studies in Conflict and Terrorism*, 37(11): 895–919.
Braddock, K. and Morrison, J.F. (2018) 'Cultivating trust and perceptions of source credibility in online counternarratives intended to reduce support for terrorism', *Studies in Conflict and Terrorism*, 1–25.
Byford, J. and Billig, M. (2001) 'The emergence of antisemitic conspiracy theories in Yugoslavia during the war with NATO', *Patterns of Prejudice*, 35(4): 50–63.
Cesari, J. (2008) 'Muslims in Europe and the risk of radicalism', in R. Coolsaet (ed.) *Jihadi terrorism and the radicalisation challenge in Europe*, Ashgate: Aldershot, pp. 97–109.
Conway, M. (2012) 'From al-Zarqawi to al-Awlaki: the emergence of the internet as a new form of violent radical milieu', *CTX: Combating Terrorism Exchange*, 2(4): 12–22.
CSIS (2018) 'Overcoming extremism: Protecting civilians from terrorist violence'. Available at: www.csis.org/analysis/overcoming-extremism-conference-report [accessed 14 February 2018.]
Dalgaard-Nielsen, A. (2010) 'Violent radicalization in Europe: what we know and what we do not know', *Studies in Conflict and Terrorism*, 33(9): 797–814.
Douglas, K.M., Sutton, R.M., Callan, M.J., Dawtry, R.J. and Harvey, A.J. (2016) 'Someone is pulling the strings: hypersensitive agency detection and belief in conspiracy theories', *Thinking and Reasoning*, 22(1): 57–77.
Goertzel, T. (1994) 'Belief in conspiracy theories', *Political Psychology*, 15(4): 731–42.
Hofmann, D.C. (2018) 'How "alone" are lone-actors? Exploring the ideological, signaling, and support networks of lone-actor terrorists', *Studies in Conflict and Terrorism*, 1–22.
Horgan, J. (2009) *Walking away from terrorism*, London: Routledge.
James, N. (2001) 'Militias, the patriot movement, and the internet: the ideology of conspiricism', in J. Parish and M. Parker (eds.) *The age of anxiety: conspiracy theory and the human sciences*, Blackwell: Oxford, pp. 63–92.
Jensen, M.A., Atwell Seate, A. and James, P.A. (2018) 'Radicalization to violence: a pathway approach to studying extremism', *Terrorism and Political Violence*, 1–24.
Kaplan, J. (1995) 'Right-wing violence in North America', in T. Bjørgo (ed.) *Terror from the extreme right*, London: Frank Cass, pp. 44–95.
Karpantschof, R. (2015) 'Violence that matters! Radicalization and de-radicalization of leftist, urban movements – Denmark 1981–2011', *Behavioral Sciences of Terrorism and Political Aggression*, 7(1): 35–52.
King, M. and Taylor, D.M. (2011) 'The radicalization of homegrown Jihadists: a review of theoretical models and social psychological evidence', *Terrorism and Political Violence*, 23(4): 602–22.
Knight, P. (2001) 'ILOVEYOU: viruses, paranoia, and the environment of risk', in J. Parish and M. Parker (eds.) *The age of anxiety: conspiracy theory and the human sciences*, Oxford: Blackwell, pp. 17–30.

Koehler, D. (2014) 'The radical online: individual radicalization processes and the role of the internet', *Journal for Deradicalization*, (1): 116–34.

Lee, B.J. (2017) '"It's not paranoia when they are really out to get you": the role of conspiracy theories in the context of heightened security', *Behavioral Sciences of Terrorism and Political Aggression*, 9(1): 4–20.

Leman, P.J. and Cinnirella, M. (2013) 'Beliefs in conspiracy theories and the need for cognitive closure', *Frontiers in Psychology*, 4: 378.

Mudde, C. (2007) *Populist radical right parties in Europe*, Cambridge: Cambridge University Press.

Ortmann, S. and Heathershaw, J. (2012) 'Conspiracy theories in the post-Soviet space', *The Russian Review*, 71(4): 551–64.

Parish, J. (2001) 'The age of anxiety', in J. Parish and M. Parker (eds.) *The age of anxiety: conspiracy theory and the human sciences*, Oxford: Blackwell, pp. 1–16.

Qutb, S. (2002) *Milestones*, New Delhi: Islamic Book Service.

Raab, M.H., Ortlieb, S.A., Auer, N., Guthmann, K. and Carbon, C.C. (2013) 'Thirty shades of truth: conspiracy theories as stories of individuation, not of pathological delusion', *Frontiers in Psychology*, 4: 406.

Räikkä, J. (2009) 'On political conspiracy theories', *Journal of Political Philosophy*, 17(2): 185–201.

Ravndal, J.A. and Bjørgo, T. (2018) 'Investigating terrorism from the extreme right: a review of past and present research', *Perspectives on Terrorism*, 12(6): 5–22.

Robertson, D. (2016) *UFOs, conspiracy theories and the New Age*, London: Bloomsbury.

Roy, O. (2008) 'Al-Qaeda: a true global movement', in R. Coolsaet (ed.) *Jihadi terrorism and the radicalisation challenge in Europe*, Ashgate: Aldershot, pp. 109–14.

Sageman, M. (2008) *Leaderless Jihad: terror networks in the twenty-first century*, Philadelphia: University of Pennsylvania Press.

Schuurman, B., Lindekilde, L., Malthaner, S., O'Connor, F., Gill, P. and Bouhana, N. (2017) 'End of the lone wolf: the typology that should not have been', *Studies in Conflict and Terrorism*, 42(8): 771–8.

Schuurman, B. and Taylor, M. (2018) 'Reconsidering radicalization: fanaticism and the link between ideas and violence', *Perspectives on Terrorism*, 12(1): 3–22.

Sedgwick, M. (2010) 'The concept of radicalization as a source of confusion', *Terrorism and Political Violence*, 22(4): 479–94.

Slootman, M. and Tillie, J. (2006) *Processes of radicalisation: why some Amsterdam Muslims become radicals*, Amsterdam: Institute for Migration and Ethnic Studies.

Sprinzak, E. (1995) 'Right-wing terrorism in comparative perspective: the case of split delegitimization', in T. Bjørgo (ed.) *Terror from the extreme right*, London: Frank Cass, pp. 17–43.

Stern, J. and Berger, J.M. (2015) *ISIS: the state of terror*, London: William Collins.

Sunstein, C.R. and Vermeule, A. (2009) 'Conspiracy theories: causes and cures', *Journal of Political Philosophy*, 17(2): 202–27.

Tsintsadze-Maass, E. and Maass, R.W. (2014) 'Groupthink and terrorist radicalization', *Terrorism and Political Violence*, 26(5): 735–58.

Uscinski, J.E., Klofstad, C. and Atkinson, M.D. (2016) 'What drives conspiratorial beliefs? The role of informational cues and predispositions', *Political Research Quarterly*, 69(1): 57–71.

Veldhuis, T. and Staun, J. (2009) *Islamist radicalisation: a root cause model*, Den Haag: Nederlands Instituut voor Internationale Betrekkingen 'Clingendael'.

Vertigans, S. (2007) 'Beyond the fringe? Radicalisation within the American far-right', *Totalitarian Movements and Political Religions*, 8(3): 641–59.

Wiktorowicz, Q. (2005) *Radical Islam rising: Muslim extremism in the west*, Lanham, MD: Rowman and Littlefield.

# 3.8
# ANTISEMITISM AND CONSPIRACISM

*Kjetil Braut Simonsen*

## Introduction

Conspiracy theories have been an important aspect of antisemitism through different historical phases. The representation of the Jew as an evil and disruptive figure, equipped with almost unlimited power, has been a recurrent feature of both premodern, religious anti-Judaism and modern nationalist and racist antisemitism. Although narratives of alleged Jewish conspiracies have been present in anti-Jewish sentiments from the high medieval period (1050–1300) until the present, the character and function of anti-Jewish thoughts and actions have changed considerably over time. Antisemitism is not an 'eternal hatred', evolving in a teleological manner from the Crusades to Auschwitz. Rather, anti-Jewish mobilisation in general – and anti-Jewish conspiracy theories in particular – have gained momentum under historical conditions marked by, for example, political polarisation, economic or social crises, or rapid social change. In this sense, the history of antisemitism is *conjunctural* rather than *linear*. In certain periods, the relationship between the majority and minority has been relatively calm and stable. In other historical periods, however, the demonisation of Jews has gained support, nourished religious and political mobilisation, and even escalated to mass violence.

## Premodern conspiracy narratives

During the medieval and early modern era, anti-Jewish representations were primarily rooted in a Christian worldview. Obviously, this does not mean that the causes of anti-Jewish actions were always religious in nature. Secular factors – such as political or economic interests – also played an important role. Indeed, factors such as economic motives were often given theological rationalisations (Eriksen *et al.* 2005: 8).

Negative representations of Jews were already present in the early history of Christianity as part of the process of separating the new religion from other belief systems, particularly from Judaism. The Jewish minority was represented as stubborn worshippers of an outdated religion and held responsible for the execution of Jesus by Christian theologians (Grözinger 1995: 57–66).

Still, from the high medieval period onwards, the demonisation of the Jews intensified. Several new accusations evolved, presenting the Jewish minority not only as a theological antithesis, but also as a deadly threat to the Christian population (Chazan 1997: 58–94). Such sharpened anti-Jewish demonology also developed in a context where the struggle against deviant groups, such as heretics and lepers, was intensified (see e.g. Chazan 1997: 78–94; Moore 2007). In many cases, anti-Jewish accusations were structured as conspiracy narratives. It was claimed that the Jews operated as a collective and evil unit, secretly plotting against Christianity and Christian society.

What was the content of the anti-Jewish conspiracy narratives of the medieval and early modern eras? On a general level, Jews were associated with the devil and the Antichrist (Eriksen 2005: 76–7); on demonisation, also see Trachtenberg 1943). In addition to these representations, three new accusations that developed in the twelfth, thirteenth and fourteenth centuries should be mentioned: The *ritual murder legend*, the *narrative of host desecration* and *the well-poisoning accusation*.

Accusations of ritual murder have been charged against different outgroups in various eras. During the medieval and early modern eras, real and imaginary enemies of the Church – such as heretics and witches – were accused of committing such cruelties (Cohn 1997). Still, the historical continuity of the anti-Jewish versions of the ritual murder libel have been particularly resilient (e.g. Erb 1995: 74–9). The first known example derives from Norwich, England in 1144. In the chronicle, *The Life and Passion of Saint William the Martyr of Norwich*, the monk Thomas of Monmouth states that a young apprentice named William was ritually crucified and murdered by the Jews in 1144 (see e.g. Langmuir 1990). During the decades that followed, similar accusations spread to other locations (Rose 2015: 127–85). The ritual murder libel was not embraced by the Church leadership. In fact, on 5 July 1247, Pope Innocent IV promulgated a papal bill devoted to the refutation of such accusations. Still, from the twelfth to the sixteenth century, ritual murder accusations continued to nourish violent persecutions in Western and Central Europe (Hsia 1988: 1–5). In Eastern Central Europe, this led to trials and executions as late as the eighteenth century (Guldon, Wihaczka 1997: 99–140). It should also be noted that the myth of Jewish ritual murder has been present even in the modern era. In fact, between 1891 and 1900, the Berlin section of *Verein Zur Abwehr des Antisemitismus* – an organisation combatting antisemitism – counted 79 instances of such charges in Austria-Hungary, Germany, Bulgaria, Serbia, Romania and the Russian Empire (Smith 2003: 123). In 1946, accusations of ritual murder even contributed to violent persecutions in Kielce, Poland (Gross 2006: 81–117).

The narrative of host desecration originated during the late thirteenth century and was closely related to the doctrine of transubstantiation, the notion that the bread and wine used in the Communion ritual were actually transformed into Christ's body and blood. This was officially recognised by the Church authorities at the Fourth Lateran Council of 1215. The host desecration narrative stemmed precisely from the notion that the host was a holy manifestation of the body of Christ. In brief, the narrative claimed that the Jews desecrated and tortured the host to mock the Christian religion. During the medieval era, accusations of host desecration led to violent persecutions. In 1298, a wave of anti-Jewish mass violence occurred in southern Germany, triggered by such rumours (Heil 2006: 242–72).

Anti-Jewish narratives such as host desecration accusations and ritual murder libels were used as 'evidence' for the truth of Christianity. The legend of Jewish ritual murder, for example, often followed a well-known narrative pattern. First, it described how the Jews murdered Christian children in an imitation of the execution of Jesus Christ, then the 'crime' of the Jews was disclosed through divine intervention (Heil 2012: 58). At the same time, they were often constructed as conspiracy narratives, in the sense that the Jews were claimed to be acting collectively and in secret to execute their evil plans. In his chronicle on William of Norwich, for example, Thomas Monmouth stated that Jewish leaders met annually in the city of Narbonne, planning the murder of Christian children (Heil 2012: 59). When host desecration accusations against Jews occurred, Johannes Heil claims, the Jewish community as a collective was represented as the enemy. Even when the alleged Jewish culprit was presented as an individual, or if the plot was primarily situated within a local framework, 'connections and the complicity of others were emphatically stressed' (Heil 2006: 247, my translation). The underlying premise was the image of the Jew as not only a timeless menace, but also a present threat to Christian society (Smith 2003: 92).

A third anti-Jewish conspiracy narrative, the accusation of well-poisoning, gained force in the fourteenth century. During the Black Death (1347–1352), the representation of the Jews as poisoners triggered huge waves of violent persecutions of Jews in the German-speaking areas and in Spain, France and the Low Countries (see Graus 1987). However, such narratives had actually already evolved decades before the plague. During the spring and summer of 1321, systematic persecutions of lepers occurred, mainly in south-western parts of France and the Kingdom of Aragon, on the basis of claims that lepers had organised a widespread plot to kill healthy Christians. A large number were executed (Barber 1981: 1–17; Barzilay 2017: 91–170). Later in the same year, similar accusations were then directed at the Jews (Barzilay 2017: 173–214; 240–1). According to some versions of the narrative, a Muslim ruler, the King of Granada, was also involved in the plot (Barzilay 2017: 213–9).

The question of continuity and breaks between premodern and modern conspiracy narratives has been interpreted in varying ways by scholars. Historian Johannes Heil, for example, concludes that medieval anti-Jewish conspiracy narratives shared important structural similarities with the antisemitism of later eras. The narrative of a Jewish conspiracy as presented in the fabrication *The Protocols of the Elders of Zion* is, he claims, in this sense neither unique nor exclusively modern (Heil 2012: 56). One common feature is the importance attributed to meetings and plans. A second is the notion that the Jews operate as a collective unit. A third shared element is the 'construction of a supralocal and supranational Jewish elite' (Heil 2012: 61). Further, a fourth commonality is the notion that the Jews pursue secret aims to the benefit of their own group and to the detriment of others (Heil 2012: 61–3). Still, Heil points out that an important change is that the medieval version of the conspiracy myth was rooted in the Christian world order. 'Even in their loyalty to the Antichrist', he states, 'the Jews would – as ultimate consequence – serve the Christians and contribute to the fulfillment of history' (Heil 2012: 66). In modern versions of the conspiracy beliefs, the Jews are no longer acting within the framework of such a divine plan.

## Modern antisemitism and conspiracism

During the eighteenth and nineteenth centuries, Europe underwent profound changes. In the 1700s, the new Enlightenment discourse challenged the hegemonic Christian and autocratic orthodoxy, culminating in the American (1765–1783) and French (1789–1799) revolutions. During the 1800s, the Industrial Revolution, the formation of new class constellations, rising urbanisation, the triumph of modern industrial and financial capitalism, and the development of new ideologies – such as liberalism, conservatism, socialism and anarchism – profoundly changed the political, social and intellectual landscape of the continent. An important aspect of the process of modernisation was also the emancipation of the Jews. In 1791, the French National Assembly decided that Jews and other religious minorities should be granted civil rights. In other parts of Europe, the process of emancipation evolved at a much slower pace. In Germany, for example, the emancipation of the Jews was first realised in all areas with the unification of 1871.

In the context of the changing political and social landscape of Europe during the 'long nineteenth century' of 1789 to 1914, antisemitism adopted new forms and shapes. Obviously, this did not mean that the old Christian images of the Jew as enemy disappeared overnight. Traditional Christian images of the Jew still served as a cultural precondition for modern forms of hostility (on the continuity and break between anti-Judaism and modern antisemitism, see e.g. Hoffmann 1994: 294–317). Nonetheless, some new developments should be noted.

During the eighteenth century, anti-Jewish argumentation based on Enlightenment forms of reasoning began to evolve. While the Church had accused the Jews of being the enemy of Christianity, Enlightenment philosophers such as Voltaire condemned the Jewish religion as barbaric and outdated, and as an obstruction to progress and reason (e.g. Sutcliffe 1998: 107–26). During the nineteenth century, a socialist antisemitism also developed, attacking what was described as 'Jewish financial power' (e.g. Green 1985: 347–99).

Still, antisemitism as a more or less coherent worldview first and foremost became a hallmark of the conservative and nationalist right. Three new features associated with this form of antisemitism should be noted. First, in the second half of the 1800s, antisemitism entered into modern mass politics. In Germany and Austria-Hungary, political parties and associations that claimed to struggle against an alleged 'Jewish influence' were founded (Pulzer 1988). In France, the Dreyfus affair activated political mobilisations against the Jewish minority (Wilson 1973: 789–806; Hyman 2005: 335–49). In Tsarist Russia, waves of anti-Jewish violence occurred between 1881–1884, in 1903 and again between 1905–1906 (de Klier, Lambroza 1992). Second, anti-Jewish agitation was increasingly formulated in nationalist and racist terms. Antisemitic ideologues in Germany and Austria, for example, often described the past and present as a 'racial' struggle between the Jews and 'the Germanic/Aryan' peoples (e.g. Pulzer 1988: 47–57). As a consequence, the Jews were claimed to be Jewish by blood: An identity they could not escape through conversion. Third, antisemitism was closely related to the fear of and attacks on modernity. In the worldview of German conservatives and anti-modernists, Jews and Judaism represented 'the perilous new that destroys the familiar structures of tradition' (Hoffmann 2001: 100; cf. Volkov 2006: 107–18). Similar tendencies can also be identified among antisemites in other European countries. In France, political Catholicism – fearing 'godless' atheism, the socialist movement and capitalism – was an important force in the rise of political antisemitism during the late 1800s (Caron 2009: 296, 300–1). In Russia, antisemitism was associated with the struggle for autocracy and religious orthodoxy against the forces of liberalisation and democratisation (Kellogg 2005: 30–46).

To what extent was the anti-Jewish hostility developing in the nineteenth century based on conspiracy narratives? The modern, political notion of a 'Jewish world conspiracy' can be traced back to the attacks against the French Revolution and the Enlightenment. In 1797, the French Jesuit priest Abbé Barruel published a four-volume book wherein he described the French Revolution as planned and initiated by a conspiracy consisting of the Philosophes, the Freemasons and the Illuminati (von Bieberstein 2008: 114–25). Nine years later, in 1806, Barruel received a letter from an army officer named Jean Baptist Simonini that stated that the Jews controlled the Illuminati and that they aimed to achieve a world government. This claim was not particularly original. In fact, since the 1770s, secret societies had been represented as puppets in the hands of the Jews (Byford 2011: 47).

It was particularly during the second half of the 1800s, when antisemitism rose as a modern political movement, that anti-Jewish conspiracy narratives were widely distributed. On a general level, antisemitic ideologues frequently represented the Jews as powerful, influential and threatening. During the 1870s, German antisemites also launched the term 'the Golden International' as a synonym for so-called 'Jewish capitalism' (Pulzer 1997: 199). This fear of international financial power – associated with the Jews – merged with the fear of 'Jewish' socialism and communism (see e.g. Friedländer 1997: 76).

In the latter half of the nineteenth and in the early twentieth centuries, several publications explicitly focusing on the alleged 'Jewish world conspiracy' emerged. One example is the document that, in antisemitic circles, was known as 'The Rabbi's Speech'. This script originated in a novel named *Biarritz* (1868), written by Hermann Goedsche, a former employee of the Prussian postal service. One of its chapters takes place at the Jewish cemetery in Prague, where the 'elders' of the 12 tribes of the Jews had gathered to plan the subversion of the political, economic and political order, with the aim of achieving world power (Cohn 1996: 38–41; Bronner 2000: 81–2). In 1872 and 1876, the document was published in St Petersburg and Moscow. By 1881, when it appeared in the French journal *Le Contemporain* under the name 'The Rabbi's Speech', the text was presented as authentic (Modras 1994: 90; Cohn 1996: 41–2). In 1887, 'The Rabbi's Speech' was republished in Theodor Fritsch's book entitled *Antisemiten-Katechismus* as well as in a French antisemitic anthology named *La Russe Juive* (Cohn 1996: 42). In 1903, the document seems to have been used to inflate pogroms in Bessarabia (Cohn 1996: 43).

The most widespread and well-known document within the genre of anti-Jewish conspiracy literature is the falsification known as *The Protocols of the Elders of Zion*. *The Protocols* were first published in Russia in 1903, in the *Znamia* magazine, edited by a far right-journalist named Pavel Krushevan (Langer 2007: 34–5, cf. Zipperstein 2018: 145–84). The version of the text that was translated and distributed worldwide after the First World War first occurred in 1905 as a part of Sergei Nilus' script *The Great and the Small: Antichrist as an Imminent Possibility*. Nilus, an orthodox Christian who was convinced of the second coming of Christ, interpreted *The Protocols* in accordance with a religious and apocalyptic worldview. According to these perceptions, 'Satanic forces' – represented by Jews and Freemasons – fought 'against the Divine forces of light, embodied in the Russian Orthodox Church' (Hagemeister 2012: 81).

Scholars still debate when and by whom *The Protocols of the Elders of Zion* was written (for two different interpretations, see Cohn 1996: 84–117 and Michelis 2004: 65). However, regardless of the origins of the text, the document is beyond doubt a fake, written by the antisemites themselves. Large parts of the text are actually plagiarised from the French book *A Dialogue in Hell: Conversations between Machiavelli and Montesquieu about Power and Right*, written by French lawyer Maurice Joly in 1864 as a polemic against the regime of Napoleon III (Cohn 1996: 80–3).

A main motif of *The Protocols* was obviously to influence politics in Tsarist Russia. For example, many newspapers associated with the far-right organisation known as *The Black Hundred*, founded in 1905, 'reprinted *The Protocols*, which they cited as proof of a worldwide Jewish conspiracy against the entire non-Jewish world' (Langer 2007: 35). In other words, the ideas promoted by the text have to be understood as a part of the reactionary worldview advocated within autocratic political circles in Tsarist Russia. Here, antisemitism was an integrated element (Bronner 2000: 76–7). *The Protocols* was published in a period when serious pogroms occurred in Russia, and it was only one of several anti-Jewish pamphlets and books published in this area during the same period (Bronner 2000: 93).

The ideological content of *The Protocols*, then, can best be summarised as a combination of antisemitism and anti-modernism. It offered a pseudo-explanation of the perils of modernity, as seen from the viewpoint of the ultraconservative and extreme right. As already pointed out, such a representation of modernity as a 'Jewish threat' was common within antisemitic circles during the second half of the nineteenth and the beginning of the twentieth centuries. Although the text is barely coherent and often self-contradictory, its main message is that a worldwide 'Jewish conspiracy' exists: That the Jews are working systematically and in secret, with the aim of achieving world power. Economic crises, revolutions, wars, capitalism, socialism, liberalism and democratic and anti-religious ideas are all claimed to be invented by the Jews as a part of this plot. In other words, *The Protocols* offers a simple and total model that claims to make sense of everything. Here, history and politics, and in fact the rise of modernity itself, is claimed to be orchestrated by a 'Jewish conspiracy'.

## World War, revolution and radicalisation

Although conspiracy theories were an integral part of modern, political antisemitism prior to 1914, during and after the First World War European antisemitism underwent radicalisation. The mass deaths of the war, and especially the Bolshevik Revolution of 1917, fuelled a 'pervasive apocalyptic mood that settled over Europe' (Friedländer 1997: 90). In this political context, anti-Jewish conspiracy theories were spread on a massive scale. Among those who feared a socialist revolution, Bolshevism and Marxism were frequently described as a 'Jewish phenomenon' (Blomqvist 2006: 49–60). During the civil wars following the Bolshevik Revolution, *The Protocols of the Elders of Zion*, as well as other antisemitic publications, were widely distributed among the counterrevolutionary 'White Forces' in the former Russian Empire (Bronner 2000: 107–8). In this area, the anti-Jewish conspiracy narratives also triggered mass violence. During the civil wars, Jews were attacked and murdered on a massive scale by counterrevolutionary forces, nationalists and rebellious peasants, particularly in Ukraine (Kenez 1992: 293–313).

During the first years after the First World War, *The Protocols* was translated into numerous languages and distributed widely throughout Europe, and even globally. A Swedish version came into print in 1919, and in 1920 the document was published in Germany, England, France, Norway, the U.S.A. and Poland. Emigrants from former Tsarist Russia played an important role in spreading the message. In Germany, for example, *The Protocols* seems to have been brought to the country by a Russian lieutenant and right-wing extremist named Pyotr Shabelskii-Bork (Kellogg 2005: 63). In other countries, such as the U.S.A., extreme rightists with a former Tsarist background were instrumental in introducing *The Protocols* (Singerman 1981: 48–78).

In the aftermath of the First World War, conspiracist antisemitism gained a particularly strong influence in Germany. Here, the political polarisation triggered by the Bolshevik seizure of power in 1917, and the Spartakist uprising in Germany itself in 1919, was reinforced by nationalist frustration born out of defeat (Friedländer 1997: 91). The extreme right claimed that the war was not lost on the battlefield, but that it was orchestrated by subversive enemies within: Social democrats, Freemasons, Communists and Jews (e.g. von Bieberstein 2008: 217–43). Within far-right circles, *The Protocols* was known from the beginning of 1919. Then, in January 1920, the text was published under the title *Die Geheimnisse der Weisen von Zion*. By the end of 1920, 120,000 copies had been printed (Zu Utrup 2003: 91–2). Moreover, other publications containing anti-Jewish conspiracy narratives were distributed in large numbers.

Although conspiracist antisemitism found an especially fertile ground in Germany, *The Protocols* was also distributed in large numbers – and discussed within mainstream circles – in other countries. In the U.S.A., the magazine *Dearborn Independent*, owned by industrial magnate Henry Ford, published a series of articles on the alleged 'Jewish world conspiracy'. The articles were later published as a book named *The International Jew*, of which half a million copies were printed in the U.S.A. and later translated into 16 different languages (Cohn 1996: 158, 162). In Britain, the prestigious newspaper *The Times* published an editorial on 8 May 1920, asking whether the message of *The Protocols* was authentic (Friedländer 1997: 95). One year later, however, an article by journalist Philip Graves determined that the text was indeed a forgery (Cohn 1996).

In Poland, the first version of *The Protocols* appeared in early 1920 and sold out within a year (Modras 1994: 92). At least nine editions were printed during the interwar period (Kosmala 2011: 133).

## Nazi antisemitism

The myth of the Jewish world conspiracy became a cornerstone of National Socialist ideology and propaganda. Although National Socialist *Weltanschauung* was interpreted in various ways by different fractions of the N.S.D.A.P., a racialist and social Darwinist outlook on the world was one of its core features. In short, within the National Socialist worldview, history and politics were perceived as a struggle between different 'races', particularly the 'Aryan/Germanic race' and the Jews (see e.g. Hitler quoted in Friedländer 1997: 97).

This racist interpretation of history was linked to the notion of a worldwide 'Jewish conspiracy' (Zu Utrup 2003: 100). During the formative years of the Nazi movement between 1920 and 1933, the N.S.D.A.P. presented itself as a community of struggle, fighting against an international 'Jewish conspiracy'. Leading Nazi party activists and ideologues actively embraced conspiracist antisemitism. Furthermore, the myth of a 'Jewish conspiracy' became a core element of daily propaganda. The N.S.D.A.P.-newspaper *Völkischer Beobachter*, for example, regularly claimed that the Jews pulled the strings behind international capitalism and communism and described the Weimar Republic as a 'Jewish system' or 'Jewish democracy'. In fact, according to Wolfram Zu Utrup, more than half of the articles published in *Völkischer Beobachter* that touched upon the so-called 'Jewish Question' from the beginning of 1925 to the end of 1932 contained motifs related to the concept of a 'Jewish conspiracy' (Zu Utrup 2003: 97, 102–20, 150–61, 185–92).

With the Nazi seizure of power in 1933, antisemitism became official policy in Germany. Between 1933 and 1939, the Jews were successively pushed out of German society: Socially, politically, legally and economically. The first wave of antisemitism, starting in March 1933, was closely related to the consolidation of the National Socialist regime. The second phase took place in 1935, resulting in the Nürnberg Laws. The last phase culminated in violent attacks on the Jews all over Germany during the night of 9–10 November 1938 (Longerich 2010: 30–130). After the outbreak of the Second World War, Nazi antisemitism was further radicalised. During the German invasion of the Soviet Union on 22 June 1941, the policy of persecution was radicalised to be a policy of mass murder. The German military forces advancing into Soviet territory were followed by killing squads, organising mass executions of Jewish civilians (Longerich 2010: 191–253). In the autumn of 1941 and the first half of 1942, the death camps were constructed and Jews from all parts of Nazi-occupied Europe were arrested and deported to these killing installations in the East.

The cumulative process of radicalisation, from persecution to extermination, can of course not be explained exclusively through ideological factors. Still, racist and conspiracist antisemitism was a necessary – although not sufficient – precondition for the genocide. In fact, between 1939 and 1945, the Nazis's anti-Jewish outlook was adapted to the war context, and even further radicalised. In his study of the anti-Jewish propaganda of the Nazi regime during the Second World War, historian Jeffrey Herf (2006) concludes that the most dangerous aspect of this antisemitism lay in the paranoid, political belief in an entity called 'International Jewry', allegedly striving to undermine Germany. Conspiracist antisemitism, he claims, served as a framework for interpreting historical and contemporary events, particularly the ongoing development of the war. The enemies of Nazi Germany – the U.K., the Soviet Union and the U.S.A. – were represented as puppets in the hands of a global Jewish cabal. As a result, both the Second World

War and the policy of extermination within Nazi circles were perceived as parts of the same struggle: A struggle of life and death between Germany and 'International Jewry' (Herf 2006: 1–16).

In this sense, the myth of a Jewish world conspiracy served both as an ideological motivation for the extermination policy and as a rationalisation of the atrocities. In short, the Nazis justified mass murder as a legitimate act of 'self-defence'. In this sense, they also advocated what Saul Friedländer has termed *redemptive* antisemitism (Friedländer 1997: 73–112). From when the N.S.D.A.P. was founded in 1920 until the fall of the Hitler regime in 1945, the Jews were described as the driving force behind all negative developments in the past and the present, and as the hidden hand pulling the strings behind all of National Socialism's political enemies. The struggle against this alleged conspiracy was perceived as a necessary prerequisite for national and 'racial' rebirth and salvation.

## Post-war developments

The defeat of the Hitler regime in 1945 marks a turning point in the history of European antisemitism. Due to the experiences with Nazism and Fascism, particularly the Holocaust, antisemitism in its open, ideological form was no longer accepted in the public sphere, at least in Northern, Western and parts of Central Europe (see e.g. Bachner 2003: 15). However, this does not mean that antisemitism as a cultural structure disappeared. While open antisemitism was to a large extent forced out of the public sphere, it continued to exist as attitudes and exclusionary social practices in the private sphere. Sociologists Rainer Erb and Werner Bergmann call this phenomenon *communicative latency* (Erb, Bergmann 1991: 275–9). It should also be pointed out that the taboo against antisemitism during the first decades after the Second World War was not established all over Europe. In fact, in Poland, the first years after the war were marked by waves of anti-Jewish violent outbursts. Probably 1500 to 2000 Jews were killed between 1944 and 1947 (Dahl, Lorenz 2005: 560).

Still, in large parts of Europe, the establishment of antifascist norms in general and the tabooing of political antisemitism in particular changed the conditions for anti-Jewish conspiracy thinking after 1945. The fact that outspoken antisemitism became taboo in mainstream public debates led to a development where *full-blown* anti-conspiracy narratives primarily became a trademark of political extremism. Several versions of conspiracy theories have developed in this regard, including the Z.O.G.-mythology of the far right (see below), antisemitism masked as anti-Zionism in the Stalinist tradition and Jihadist antisemitism.

However, it should also be mentioned that antisemitism in a more latent form also persists in broader parts of contemporary conspiracy culture. Social psychologist Jovan Byford claims that a clear example of discontinuity in this culture is the 'shift away from the emphasis on the Jewish conspiracy towards a new variant of secret society mythology' (Byford 2011: 97). A closer inspection nevertheless shows that antisemitism as a legacy still influences conspiracy literature, even when the writers seek to distance themselves from anti-Jewish sentiments. This tendency is expressed most clearly when believers in a conspiracy attempt to place their theories into a historical context. Because antisemitism was for a very long time a dominant conspiracy narrative, when contemporary authors seek to expose the historical roots of the alleged plot, they 'invariably come into contact with the antisemitic legacy of the conspiracy culture' (Byford 2011: 102).

## Far-right antisemitism

Among European and American neo-Nazis, the myth of a 'Jewish conspiracy' has often served as an explanation for the lack of support and acceptance within the mainstream sphere. Such ideas have circulated within far-right circles throughout the postwar period. According to historian Nicholas Goodrick-Clarke, 'despite their overriding concern with colored races, neo-Nazi ideology still identified the Jews as the demonic adversary of the white Aryan peoples' (Goodrick-Clarke 2002: 3).

One phrase that has functioned as a signal marker within the far-right conspiracist discourse during the last three to four decades is the abbreviation 'Z.O.G.', short for Zionist Occupied Government. The term itself originated within racist political circles in the U.S.A. during the 1970s and 1980s and then spread to the European racist-revolutionary milieu (Sprinzak 1995: 26). Although the term is new, the Z.O.G.-discourse is clearly a modern adaption of the old notion of a 'Jewish conspiracy'. The believers claim that the Jews pull the strings of global capitalism, multiculturalism and the mass media, and that political opponents are puppets of the same (Jewish) conspiracy. The emergence of the Z.O.G.-discourse is closely related to a process of radicalisation that occurred within the American racist right during the 1980s and 1990s. Increasingly, within far-right circles, the American political system as such was claimed to be conquered by the Jews and their puppets (Gardell 1998: 170–1). This belief in the myth of a 'Jewish conspiracy' is still present within neo-Nazi and racist-revolutionary circles, both in Europe and in the U.S.A.

A new element within post-war antisemitism, particularly on the far right, is Holocaust denial: The claim that the National Socialist genocide of the Jews is a 'myth' that never occurred. Holocaust denial evolved as a discourse within extreme right circles shortly after the Second World War. Already during the latter half of the 1940s and into the 1950s, writers such as French fascist Maurice Bardèche, American revisionist Austin J. App and the former concentration camp inmate Paul Rassinier published tracts rejecting that the murder of six million Jews actually took place (Lipstadt 1994: 49–64, 85–92).

Holocaust denial as a discourse is based on conspiracy theories. As a form of argumentation, it consists of four core elements. First, the deniers claim that the number of Jews killed by the Nazis was far less than six million. Second, they deny that the gas chambers were used for murdering humans. Third, they assume that neither Hitler nor the Nazi leadership systematically worked towards the extermination of European Jews. Fourth, the Holocaust is described as a myth, 'invented by Allied propaganda during the war and sustained since then by Jews who wished to use it to gain financial support for the state of Israel or for themselves' (Evans 2001: 110). In other words, deniers claim that the history of the Holocaust has been 'created' by a powerful conspiracy that controls academic institutions as well as the media.

As a discourse, Holocaust denial in Europe is prevalent on primarily the far right and was from the very beginning marked by a clear political-ideological tendency. From the 1970s onwards, however, the deniers have increasingly tried to present themselves as 'serious academics'. In 1979, they even founded their own 'institute', the *Institute for Historical Review* in the U.S.A.

## Stalinism and anti-Zionism

Post-war antisemitism has also been closely related to the Israel/Palestine debate. Although criticism of Israel's policy in itself is not by any means antisemitic, conspiracy narratives linking 'anti-Zionism' to notions of 'Jewish power' have emerged within certain political circles, the clearest of which can be seen in the history of Soviet anti-Zionism.

Although Lenin and the Bolshevik party emphasised the struggle against antisemitism, the party was also, from early on, highly critical towards Jewish nationalism and demands for national autonomy (Bachner 2003: 187). On the one hand, Lenin held up the progressive, assimilated Jew as an ideal. On the other hand, he and the Bolsheviks promoted a negative image of the 'bourgeois' and 'reactionary' Jew, which they associated with capitalism, traditions and the old society (Gjerde 2011: 16–55). During the Stalin era, antisemitism increasingly became an element of the totalitarian worldview and politics of the Soviet regime. In 1948, Stalin launched a political campaign against 'rootless cosmopolitanism' and 'bourgeois, Jewish Nationalism', leading to the persecution of members of the Jewish intelligentsia and the prohibition of Jewish cultural organisations. In 1951 and 1952, communist leaders of Jewish origin were tried and executed for treason in Czechoslovakia, and in 1953 a group of doctors, most of them Jews, were falsely accused of an attempted plot against the Soviet leadership. As a result of Stalin's death in March 1953, this campaign was eventually called off (Bachner 2003: 188–9).

Under and after Stalin, anti-Zionism within the Soviet Union and its satellite states also became more explicitly based on conspiracy theories. Stalin perceived Zionism as a fifth column of American and British imperialism (Wistrich 2015: 190). After the Arab-Israeli Six-Day War in 1967, this conspiracist outlook intensified. In 1968, for example, an anti-Jewish campaign was launched in Poland, barely coded as anti-Zionist. As a result of the campaign, approximately 15 000 Jews left the country (Stola 2006: 175–201; Kosmala 2011: 133–46). In fact, during the campaign, the party committee of The Polish United Workers Party in Łódź reprinted *The Protocols of the Elders of Zion* for distribution within the party (Kosmala 2011: 133–46).

As a discourse, Soviet anti-Zionism consisted of two main motifs. First, Zionism and Israel were associated with Nazism and fascism. Second, Zionism was represented as a tool for, or even as the core of, an international conspiracy; as a 'great invisible power whose influence extended into every nook and cranny of politics, finance, religion, and the communications media in the Western world' (Wistrich 2012: 433). Still, the character of Soviet anti-Zionism and antisemitism has been interpreted somewhat differently by scholars. Some historians have claimed that the word Zionism in Soviet propaganda simply worked as coded references to 'Jews' or 'Jewry', with *The Protocols* as a model (see e.g. Bachner 2003: 200). Others have claimed that the Soviet Union's anti-Zionist propagandists – in contrast to traditional antisemitic narratives – perceived the Zionist conspiracy 'as merely one part of a larger imperialist conspiracy against the Soviet Union' (Gjerde 2011: 115).

Scholars have disputed how far the mixture of antisemitism and anti-Zionism as it appears in the Soviet context has influenced Western anti-Zionism. In his study of Swedish post-war antisemitism, Bachner concludes that, while criticism of Israel has in most cases been free of anti-Jewish sentiment, the Israel/Palestine debate also became a forum where antisemitism could be legitimately expressed, 'since it was here where they could be packaged and rationalized as criticism of Zionism or Israeli policy' (2003: 474). Historian Brian Klug has criticised the claim that the anti-Zionist position is inherently antisemitic. Nonetheless, he agrees that attacks on Israel are at times coloured by anti-Jewish images (Klug 2003: 117–38). Byford claims that the conspiracist element of the 'new antisemitism' is most obvious in discussions regarding the Israel/Zionist/Jewish lobby (Byford 2011: 111).

## Antisemitism in the Middle East

Another new development in the post-war period is that conspiracy theories focused on the Jews and Zionism have been spread on a large scale in the Middle East.

Historically, modern antisemitism was to a large extent imported from Europe to the Arab world during the late 1800s and early 1900s (Krämer 2006: 243–76). The first Arabic translation of *The Protocols of the Elders of Zion* was even published by local Christians in Palestine and Syria during the mid-1920s (Webman 2011: 175–95).

However, during the postwar years – and especially after the establishment of the state of Israel in 1948 – anti-Jewish conspiracy literature has been distributed in large numbers in this region. At the time of the Six-Day War in 1967, at least nine Arabic translations of *The Protocols* had been published. In Egypt alone, 50 political books based on the text were issued between 1965 and 1967. *The Protocols* was adopted by nationalist, Islamist as well as leftist writers (Webman 2011: 171–95). The Islamist organisation Hamas even cited it in their 1988 Charter (Hamas 1988). After the terrorist attacks on the Pentagon and the World Trade Center, Osama Bin Laden sought to legitimise Al Qaeda's actions by using anti-Jewish conspiracy narratives. In his *Letter to America*, first published in Arabic, and then translated by British Islamists, he claimed that the Jews controlled American politics, the economy and the mass media (*Guardian* 2002).

Even Holocaust denial became widespread in the Middle East from the 1950s onwards (Litvak, Webman 2009: 156). In contrast to Western denialism, which has been located primarily on the far-right fringe, here it has been articulated within the political mainstream. In 1964, Egyptian president Nasser told the German *National-Zeitung* that 'no persons, not even the simplest one, takes seriously the lie of the six million Jews that were murdered' (Litvak, Webman 2009: 161). In 2011, the deputy chair of the Egyptian Wafd Party stated in an interview with the *Washington Times* that 'the Holocaust is a lie' (Birnbaum 2011).

In the last couple of years, anti-Jewish attitudes within Muslim communities in Europe have also received public attention. In an overview of surveys published in 2015, historian Günther Jikeli claims that, the level of anti-Semitic attitudes is significantly higher among Muslims than among non-Muslims, although many European Muslims do not share anti-Semitic beliefs" (2015: 19). One particularly aggressive form of antisemitism is the totalitarian and anti-Jewish worldview proclaimed by Islamist extremism. In 2015, Islamist extremists also committed fatal attacks against Jews in France and Denmark.

## Antisemitism as a tradition of conspiracism

The history of antisemitism, like all other historical phenomena, is marked by both continuity and change. In one sense, antisemitism has functioned as a flexible prejudice that has been rearticulated and reshaped in different historical, ideological and social circumstances.

Still, antisemitism as a long-time phenomenon also has some persistent traits. One recurrent feature is the representation of 'the Jew' as a threatening other: Powerful, well-organised and evil. During the medieval and early modern era, the Jews were accused of undermining the Christian order as well as the Christian majority. In the nineteenth and early twentieth centuries, they were represented as a national and 'racial' threat, and as the hidden force behind 'decadent modernity'. Within the Nazi worldview, the Second World War was represented as an apocalyptic battle between 'the Germanic peoples' and the alleged conspiratorial entity termed 'International Jewry'. After 1945, a 'Jewish conspiracy' has been accused of fabricating the history of the Holocaust. In this sense, the history of antisemitism proves how conspiracism works from a long-time historical perspective: How narratives of the threatening other survive changing historical conditions, and how they change over time.

# References

Bachner, H. (2003) *Återkomsten. Antisemitism i Sverige efter 1945*, Stockholm: Natur och kultur.
Barber, M. (1981) 'Lepers, Jews and Moslems: the plot to overthrow Christendom in 1321', *History*, 66(216): 1–17.
Barzilay, T. (2017) 'Well-poisoning accusations in medieval Europe: 1250–1500', Phd Thesis, New York, NY: Columbia University.
Birnbaum, B. (2011) 'Egypt party leader: Holocaust is a "lie"', *Washington Times*, 5 July. Available at: www.washingtontimes.com/news/2011/jul/5/egypt-party-leader-holocaust-is-a-lie/. [Accessed 6 September 2019.]
Blomqvist, H. (2006) 'Judebolsjevismen – en antikommunistisk världsbild', in M. Gerdin and K. Östberg (eds.) *Samtidshistoriska frågor 11: hur rysk är den svenska kommunismen? Fyra bidrag om kommunism, nationalism og etnicitet*, Huddinge: Södertörns högskola, pp. 49–60.
Bronner, S.E. (2000) *A rumor about the Jews: antisemitism, conspiracy and the protocols of Zion*, New York: St. Martin's Press.
Byford, J. (2011) *Conspiracy theories: a critical introduction*, New York: Palgrave Macmillan.
Caron, V. (2009) 'Catholic political mobilization and antisemitic violence in fin de siècle France: the case of the Union Nationale', *The Journal of Modern History*, 81(2): 294–346.
Chazan, R. (1997) *Medieval stereotypes and modern antisemitism*, Berkeley, CA: California University Press.
Cohn, N. (1996) *Warrant for genocide: the myth of the Jewish world conspiracy and the protocols of the elders of Zion*, London: Serif.
Cohn, N. (1997) *Europas indre demoner: demoniseringen av kristne i middelalderen*, Oslo: Humanist forlag.
Dahl, I.A. and Lorenz, E. (2005) 'Øst-Europa etter 1945', in T.B. Eriksen, H. Harket and E. Lorenz (eds.) *Jødehat: antisemittismens historie fra antikken til idag*, Oslo: Cappelen Damm, pp. 559–77.
De Klier, J. and S. Lambroza (eds.) (1992) *Pogroms: anti-Jewish violence in modern Russian history*, Cambridge: Cambridge University Press.
Erb, R. (1995) 'Der "Ritualmord"', in J. Schoeps and J. Schlör (eds.) *Antisemitismus: Vorurteile und Mythen*, München: Piper, pp. 74–9.
Erb, R. and Bergmann, W. (1991) *Antisemitismus in der Bundesrepublik: Ereignisse der empirischen Forschung von 1946–1989*, Opladen: Leske & Budrick.
Eriksen, T.B. (2005) 'Svartedauden: giftblandere og barnemordere', in T.B. Eriksen, H. Harket and E. Lorenz (eds.) *Jødehat: antisemittismens historie fra antikken til idag*, Oslo: Cappelen Damm, pp. 69–85.
Eriksen, T.B., Harket H. and Lorenz, E. (2005) 'Forord', in T.B. Eriksen, H. Harket and E. Lorenz (eds.) *Jødehat: antisemittismens historie fra antikken til idag*, Oslo: Cappelen Damm, pp. 7–11.
Evans, R. (2001) *Lying about Hitler: history, Holocaust and the David Irving trial*, New York: Basic books.
Friedländer, S. (1997) *Nazi Germany and the Jews: the years of persecution, 1933–1939*, London: Harper & Collins.
Gardell, M. (1998) *Rasrisk: rasister, separatister och amerikanska kulturkonflikter*, Stockholm: Federativs förlag.
Gjerde, Å.B. (2011) 'Reinterpreting Soviet "Anti-Zionism": an analysis of "Anti-Zionist" texts published in the Soviet Union, 1967–1972', MA thesis, Oslo: University of Oslo.
Goodrick-Clarke, N. (2002) *Black sun: Aryan cults, esoteric Nazism and the politics of identity*, New York, NY: New York University Press.
Graus, F. (1987) *Pest – Geißler – Judenmorde: das 14. Jahrhundert als Krisenzeit*, Göttingen: Vandenhoeck & Ruprecht.
Green, N.L. (1985) 'Socialist anti-Semitism: defense of a bourgeois Jew and discovery of the Jewish proletariat: changing attitudes of French socialists before 1914', *International Review of Social History*, 30(3): 374–99.
Gross, J.T. (2006) *Fear: Anti-Semitism in Poland after Auschwitz: an essay in historical interpretation*, New York: Random house.
Grözinger, K.E. (1995) 'Die "Gottesmörder"', in J.H. Schoeps and J. Schlör (eds.) *Antisemitismus: Vorurteile und Mythen*, München: Piper, pp. 57–66.
Guardian (2002) *Full text: bin Laden's 'letter to America'*, 24 November. Available at: www.theguardian.com/world/2002/nov/24/theobserver. [Accessed 6 September 2019.]
Guldon, Z. and Wihaczka, J. (1997) 'The accusation of ritual murder in Poland, 1500–1800', in G.D. Hundert (ed.) *Polin vol. 10: Jews in modern Poland*, Liverpool: Liverpool University Press, pp. 99–140.
Hagemeister, M. (2012) '"The Antichrist as an Imminent Political Possibility": Sergei Nilus and the apocalyptical reading of *The Protocols of the Elders of Zion*', in R. Landes and S.T. Katz (eds.) *The paranoid*

*apocalypse: a hundred-year retrospective on 'The Protocols of the Elders of Zion'*, New York: New York University Press, pp. 79–91.
Hamas Covenant (1988) 'The Covenant of the Islamic Resistance Movement', *Yale Law School Lillian Goldman Law Library*, 18 August. Available at: http://avalon.law.yale.edu/20th_century/hamas.asp. [Accessed 6 September 2019.]
Heil, J. (2006) *Gottesfeinde – Menschenfeinde: die Vorstellung von jüdischer Weltverschwörung (13.-16. Jahrhundert)*, Essen: Klartext.
Heil, J. (2012) 'Thomas Monmouth and the Protocols of the Sages of Narbonne', in R. Landes and S.T. Katz (eds.) *The paranoid apocalypse: a hundred-year retrospective on 'The Protocols of the Elders of Zion'*, New York: New York University Press, pp. 56–76.
Herf, J. (2006) *The Jewish enemy: Nazi propaganda during World War II and the Holocaust*, Cambridge, MA: The Belknap Press.
Hsia, R.P.-C. (1988) *The myth of ritual murder: Jews and magic in reformation Germany*, New Haven: Yale University Press.
Hoffmann, C. (1994) 'Christlicher Antijudaismus und moderner Antisemitismus: Zusammenhänge und Differenzen als Problem der historische Antisemitismusforschung', in L. Siegle-Wenschkewitz (ed.) *Christlicher Antijudaismus und kirchliche Programme Deutscher Christen*, Haag: Herschen Verlag, pp. 293–317.
Hoffmann, C. (2001) '"The New" as a (Jewish) threat: anti-modernism and antisemitism in Germany', in L.A. Ytrehus (ed.) *Forestillinger om 'den andre'*, Kristiansand: Høyskoleforlaget, pp. 99–114.
Hyman, P.E. (2005) 'New perspectives on the Dreyfus affair', *Historical Reflections/Réflexions Historiques*, 31(3): 335–49.
Jikeli, G. (2015) *Antisemitic attitudes among Muslims in Europe: a survey review*, New York: Instittute for the Study of Global Antisemitism and Policy.
Kellogg, M. (2005) *The Russian roots of Nazism: white émigres and the making of national socialism 1917–45*, Cambridge: Cambridge University Press.
Kenez, P. (1992) 'Pogroms and white ideology in the Russian civil war', in J. de Klier and S. Lambroza (eds.) *Pogroms: Anti-Jewish violence in modern Russian History*, Cambridge, New York: Cambridge University Press, pp. 293–313.
Klug, B. (2003) 'The collective Jew: Israel and the new antisemitism', *Patterns of Prejudice*, 37(2): 117–38.
Kosmala, B. (2011) 'The re-emergence of *The Protocols of the Elders of Zion* in Łódź, 1968', in E. Webman (ed.) *The global impact of 'The Protocols of the Elders of Zion': a century-old myth*, London: Routledge, pp. 133–46.
Krämer, G. (2006) 'Anti-Semitism in the Muslim World: a critical review', *Die Welt des Islams*, 46(3): 243–76.
Langer, J. (2007) 'Corruption and the counterrevolution: the rise and fall of the black hundred history dissertation', Phd Thesis, Durham, NC: Duke University.
Langmuir, G. (1990) 'Thomas of Monmouth: detector of ritual murder', in G. Langmuir (ed.) *Toward a definition of antisemitism*, Los Angeles: University of California, pp. 209–36.
Lipstadt, D. (1994) *Denying the Holocaust: the growing assault on truth and memory*, New York: Plume Book.
Litvak, M. and Webman E. (2009) *From empathy to denial: Arab responses to the Holocaust*, London: Hurst and Company.
Longerich, P. (2010) *Holocaust: the Nazi persecution and murder of the Jews*, Oxford: Oxford University Press.
Michelis, C.G.D. (2004) *The non-existent manuscript: a study of the Protocols of the Sages of Zion*, Jerusalem: The Vidal Sassoon International Center for the Study of Antisemitism.
Modras, R. (1994) *The Catholic church and antisemitism: Poland, 1933–1939*, New York: Routledge.
Moore, R.I. (2007) *The formation of a persecuting society: authority and deviance in western Europe 950–1250*, 2nd edn, Oxford: Blackwell.
Pulzer, P. (1988) *The rise of political antisemitism in Germany and Austria*, Cambridge, MA: Harvard University Press.
Pulzer, P. (1997) 'The return of old hatreds', in M. A. Meyer and M. Brenner (eds.) *German–Jewish History in Modern Times*, vol. 3, New York: Colombia Press, pp. 196–251.
Rose, E.M. (2015) *The murder of William of Norwich: the origins of the blood libel in medieval Europe*, Oxford: Oxford University Press.
Singerman, R. (1981) 'The American career of the Protocols of the Elders of Zion', *American Jewish History*, 71(1): 48–78.

Smith, H.W. (2003) *The butcher's tale: murder and anti-Semitism in a German town*, London: W.W. Norton & Company.

Sprinzak, E. (1995) 'Right-wing terrorism in a comparative perspective: the case of split legitimation', *Terrorism and Political Culture*, 7(1): 17–43.

Stola, D. (2006) 'The anti-Zionist Campaign in Poland, 1967–1968', *Journal of Israeli Politics, Society, Culture*, 25(1): 175–201.

Sutcliffe, A. (1998) 'Myth, origins, identity: Voltaire, the Jews and the Enlightenment notion of toleration', *The Eighteenth Century*, 39(2): 107–26.

Trachtenberg, J. (1943) *The devil and the Jews: the medieval conception of the Jew and its relation to modern anti-Semitism*, New Haven: Yale University Press.

Volkov, S. (2006) *Germans, Jews and Antisemites: trials in emancipation*, New York: Cambridge University Press.

Von Bieberstein, J.R. (2008) *Der Mythos von der Verschwörung: Philosophen, Freimaurer, Juden, Liberale und Sozialisten als Verschörer gegen die Sozialordnung*, Wiesbaden: Marixverlag.

Webman, E. (2011) 'Adoption of the protocols in the Arab discourse on the Arab-Israeli conflict, Zionism and the Jews', in E. Webman (ed.) *The global impact of the 'Protocols of the Elders of Zion': a century-old myth*, London: Routledge, pp. 175–95.

Wilson, S. (1973) 'The antisemitic riots of 1898 in France', *The Historical Journal*, 16(4): 789–806.

Wistrich, R. (2012) *From ambivalence to betrayal: the left, the Jews and Israel*, Lincoln/London: University of Nebraska Press.

Wistrich, R. (2015) 'The anti-Zionist mythology of the left', *Israel Journal of Foreign Affairs*, 9(2): 189–99.

Zipperstein, S.J. (2018) *Pogrom: Kishinev and the tilt of history*, London: W.W. Norton & Company.

Zu Utrup, W.M. (2003) *Kampf gegen die 'jüdische Weltverschwörung': Propaganda und Antisemitismus der Nationalsozialisten 1919 bis 1945*, Berlin: de Gruyter.

# 3.9
# CONSPIRACY THEORY AND RELIGION

*Asbjørn Dyrendal*

## Introduction

The relation between conspiracy beliefs and religion has often been treated as having three different components: Conspiracy theory *as* religion, conspiracy theories *about* religion and conspiracy theories *in* religion (e.g. Robertson et al. 2019). These draw on different sides of complex cultural dynamics. Conspiracy theory *as* religion centres on the philosophical and psychological underpinnings of ideation, while the other two deal with case studies of socio-political relevance. Conspiracy theory *about* religion typically focuses on ingroup/outgroup dynamics in complex socio-political situations. Conspiracy theories *in* religion deal with different sets of conspiracy beliefs ideologically attuned to the particular religious group and circumstance. This chapter will give a brief introduction to all these relations.

It will do so by paying some attention to the dimensionality of the terms and their associated behaviours. Both religion and conspiracy theory are complex cultural concepts; they are contested, second-order constructs whose meaning varies between social formations (Dyrendal et al. 2019). Both terms are loaded with vernacular meanings that inform academic perspectives. In academic treatments, their meaning is constructed by, often implicitly, calling upon lower-level building blocks that vary between academic disciplines. As shown in the first section of this handbook, the disciplines study conspiracy theories in different ways. For psychology, belief is an important dimension of both conspiracy theory and religion, and the cognitive and emotional underpinnings (see Chapters 2.2 and 2.3) are central building blocks in how both are constructed. Studies that relate the two constructs focus on surveys of individual beliefs and characteristics.

Other Western academics have classically also in good, Protestant tradition tended to focus their construct of religion on (supernatural) beliefs. Such a categorisation is, implicitly or explicitly, based on theories that religion *is* something specific, i.e. 'belief in supernatural beings'. These yield *substantive* definitions. *Functional* definitions focus on what behaviours we call religions *achieve*. They have been more important to approaches where the history of religions consists of histories where particular communities with various ideologies and amount of power interact with each other. Such approaches focus on the discourses, practices, communities and institutions we call religion. Belief is transformed to religious discourses, the ways they are authorised and how they again authorise practices, communities and institutions (cf. Lincoln

2006). Relations between e.g. discourse and community vary. Holding a religious identity (e.g. 'Catholic') does not necessarily mean holding religious beliefs, nor even partaking in related practices. It may be a mere marker of belonging to one community rather than another. Nor does holding certain supernatural beliefs mean agreeing with the discourse of the institution of one's ascribed community in these and other matters.

All of this is relevant for relations between conspiracy theories and religion in specific sociopolitical contexts. The collective organisation of identity can become central when religious identity becomes a marker of ingroup or outgroup. That 'religion' also carries connotations of being a unifying discourse (or coherent set of beliefs), organised in communities and controlled by institutions, can go some way towards legitimating fantasies of hidden, organised conspiracy. From another angle, 'religion' covers strategies for legitimising and delegitimising claims to authority, moral behaviour and ideas about what is the correct relation to other social groups, and may thus be used as a resource in both the promotion and the arrest of conspiracy beliefs. From the mainstream to the margins of society and politics, religious actors participate in the economy of conspiracism as targets, promotors, bystanders and, perhaps least recognised, as organised opposition. This chapter will give a short overview of these through the use of examples.

Conspiracy theory *as* religion will be illustrated briefly through the lenses of philosophy, psychology and esotericism studies. We shall look briefly at the argument that 'the conspiracy theory of history' is a substitute for or the continuation of religion by other means. This will lead us to consider the psychological building blocks of religion and conspiracy theory, before looking at the argument for conspiracy beliefs as 'esoteric knowledge'.

Conspiracy theories *about* religious groups, imagined or real, are numerous throughout history (see e.g. Chapters 5.4, 5.8 and 5.11). Here, we shall note some general, transferable tropes that imagining conspirators as organised religion make possible, and look briefly at conspiracy theories about Islam. Conspiracy theories *in* religion will be the central focus of this chapter, with examples from Nigeria, Russia and Norway. The cases will illustrate some of the variety of roles religion has played in relatively high profile cases of controversy over conspiracy theories. The stress is on context, social dynamics and relations to different kinds of power. Two examples deal with mainstream, majority religions. The Orthodox Church in Russia gives an example of a strong, hierarchical national institution with close relation to an authoritarian regime, and a religious (semi-)monoculture. Nigeria gives an example of a strong, local religious majority in a pluralist country, in a situation of contested power and multiple locations of identity. The final example, Norway, deals with a minority, ambiguous religious identity, where a small number of entrepreneurs had partial control of access to the marketplace of ideas. Together, these give some idea of the complexities involved when translating 'religion and conspiracy theory' into the realities of society and politics.

## Conspiracy theory as religion – or its substitute

Widely encompassing conspiracy beliefs, sometimes called conspiracism, have been seen as a continuation of religious modes of thinking. Among other things, both are seen to explain evil ('theodicy'), and promote narratives about hidden, intentional agency that control large-scale events. Conspiracy beliefs as 'mythical' narratives identify values and social actors in stark contrasts of good and evil, and may follow the lines of prophetic speech in revealing evil's hidden plans. Through the presentation of this (secret) knowledge, they make salvation from evil consequences possible. Both moreover present a worldview that is largely teleological, and they present parallel epistemologies that make claims 'unfalsifiable'. The two thus may be presented as sharing similar content, form and function (Franks *et al.* 2013), albeit with some difference (Wood, Douglas 2019).

Some of these ideas date back to the philosopher Karl Popper and his conceptualisation of 'the conspiracy theory of society' in *The Open Society and Its Enemies* (Popper 1963). He argued that such encompassing conspiracy beliefs were a result of secularisation, with superstitious, unfalsifiable beliefs in providence and evil forces replaced by all-knowing, powerful conspirators. His specific claims and the boundary work they perform have been criticised from both philosophy (e.g. Pigden 1995) and sociology (e.g. Aupers, Harambam 2019). In addition to the critical remarks that have been made, one could add that secularisation usually is thought to mean domain loss for religion, so that one would expect 'secularists' to be those taking to conspiracy beliefs to make up for the loss of the 'outdated' form of enchantment. Since recent quantitative studies suggest that we have, if anything, less conspiracy beliefs now than when religious adherence was more common, and since religion is usually not negatively correlated with conspiracy beliefs, the secularisation argument seems weak (Oliver, Wood 2018; Uscinski, Parent 2014).

The parallels in form and function seem better grounded. Some of the general predictors of conspiracy thinking are increased, including illusory agency detection (Douglas *et al.* 2016), teleological thinking (Wagner-Egger *et al.* 2018) and anthropomorphism. All these also relate to an increase in the proclivity to see intention as a cause of events (Brotherton, French 2015). Moreover, these also seem to correlate with increased holistic, intuitive, symbolic and magical thinking, which again correlate to an increase in the tendency towards seeing things as related in meaningful patterns (Oliver, Wood 2018; Wood, Douglas 2019). To the cognitive science of religion, these are all lower-level building blocks of religious ideation, thus conspiracism and religion share important, underlying cognitive factors.

They also share something in the affective domain. Both conspiracy beliefs and religion are related to anxiety and used in terror management (Vail *et al.* 2010; van Prooijen 2018a), and certain forms of religious *experience* seem to predict increased conspiracism (e.g. Dagnall *et al.* 2015). These may be related to experiential dimensions of schizotypy (van der Tempel, Alcock 2015).

Since there are vital, shared underlying mechanisms, and shared forms and functions, one might ask whether it makes more sense to consider conspiracy theory *as* religion in the sense that they overlap, rather than as a substitute. The answer is more complicated. While some of the general mechanisms behind conspiracy beliefs and religious beliefs are identical, the empirical relations vary. Simple questions about e.g. to what degree respondents consider themselves 'religious' or believe in 'God' correlate only very weakly or not at all with general proclivities for conspiracy thinking and for most specific conspiracy beliefs (Oliver, Wood 2014; Hart, Graether 2018). However, other religious beliefs are more clearly predictive of conspiracy beliefs. Culturally rejected beliefs like ufology and conspiracy theories are related, and entrepreneurs within the scene of believers present as an alternative epistemic elite (cf. Robertson 2016), a 'priesthood'.

There are thus two angles from which one may argue that it can be analytically helpful to look at conspiracy beliefs as a particular form of religion or 'esotericism': The social and the epistemic. They are partially intertwined in Kocku von Stuckrad's definition of esoteric discourse as a 'rhetoric of hidden truth, which can be unveiled in a specific way and established contrary to other interpretations of the universe and history – often that of the institutionalised majority' (von Stuckrad 2005: 10). Their epistemic status as counterknowledge is important here, but so are the particular ways these hidden truths are uncovered; they may follow common esoteric knowledge strategies (see Asprem, Dyrendal 2019). Furthermore, there can be an initiatory element to both belief and participation. Acceptance of this higher counterknowledge separates those on the inside from an unknowing outside, and the degree to which one is accepted as initiated in the knowledge can be 'organised' in levels. There are thus parallels between the sociology of conspiracy culture and esoteric societies. For both, the secret knowledge holds salvific potential, although in the case of conspiracy beliefs mostly on a collective and political level (see Dyrendal 2013).

## Conspiracy theories about religion(s)

Conspiracy beliefs often have an intergroup dimension, as narratives involved in how we construct, maintain and mobilise community. They can be part of how we manage group- and self-image by exaggerating differences between ingroup and outgroup, and present the outgroup as a cause of social ills and a threat to moral order. Conspiracy theories about religious groups have been employed in larger social conflicts, mostly in attempts to deflect responsibility for problems on scapegoats, thus attempting to unify and mobilise a conflicted ingroup (cf. Butter 2014). The historically most consequential examples of this involve antisemitic conspiracy theories (see Chapters 3.8 and 5.4).

The social imagination of religion and religious identity that assist the elaboration and justification of outgroup constructions can start at a very basic level. A conspiratorial 'they' involved in coordinated subversion of all that is good must be highly unified. In typical conspiracy stereotypes, outgroup members are nothing but subordinate executors of a collective will (Kofta, Sedek 2005). This coordination of a collective will can be imagined along folk models of religion: As religious identity, controlled by religious ideology and the authority of religious institutions. One example of this can be seen in nineteenth- and twentieth-century anti-Catholic conspiracy narratives, where the hierarchical nature of the Church, with one man, the Pope, as its head, has served as one way to make narratives of a unified conspiracy more plausible. In anti-Muslim conspiracy narratives, religion as identity and ideology does the same work: Muslims are united by 'Islam', and this (relatively unmediated) 'Islam' unites them all in a common plan for domination.

The combination of a folk model of religion and some practical knowledge can also combine to deliver other content. The ritual practice of confession became both an arena of crime, a control mechanism and a scene of intelligence gathering in anti-Catholic conspiracy narratives (e.g. Sobiech 2014). In conspiracy theories about esoteric, secret societies, the degree system with initiation into new levels with gradual revelations of knowledge serves as an argument that only the top levels *really* know what is going on, and that the lower levels are dupes in sinister plans hidden from them. This 'practical knowledge' is often a mixture of experienced-based stereotypes and flights of fancy. The latter ruled alone in anti-satanist conspiracy narratives, where the alleged ideology and practice of 'satanism' was a mere inversion of idealised Christianity. Since this made a 'Satan' that was pure evil, satanists were presented as worshippers of evil, and satanism as an ideology and practice of evil. This 'satanism' was used to explain the motivations for imaginary, but horrifying, crimes and the imagined crimes themselves were often presented as 'rituals' (e.g. Victor 1993).

We see examples of all these dynamics in current, and sometimes global, sets of conspiracy beliefs about Islam. 'Islam' may be configured mostly along the lines of a civilisation in a 'clash of civilisations', where it is typically represented as backwards, fanatic and violent. It is presented as always also being a totalitarian, political doctrine. These elements are combined in and are made to typify the religion, and they are usually tied to religious ideology through terminological references to a 'global jihad', waged against 'the house of war' to force indigenous people into 'submission' (e.g. Zuquete 2018: 172–4). Adherents are, as in antisemitic conspiracy stereotypes, mere executors of a religiously based, collective will. The references to a global jihad are made to mirror the discourse of radical jihadists, who with the worst regimes thus come to typify Islam. All Muslims are conflated with jihadists through an essentialising approach: Islam is presented as having a fanatical, fundamentalist nature and, in the end, every believer will be made to follow its radical version. Muslims who identify as anything but radical Islamists on a scale are often presented as wilfully disguising their true purpose. This alleged dishonesty is tied to religion by using the term 'taqiyya' (in a distorted manner) to mean lying to hide the religion's conspiratorial plans.

Religious identity also tends to be presented as immutable. The essentialised religion-as-culture is made to stand in for 'race'. Thus, jihad is conceptualised along some fairly similar lines throughout the world, as a demographic 'great replacement' by routes that mirror local concerns. In large parts of Europe, the populist and radical right present refugees as a Trojan horse in a demographic war, while 'birth jihad' in various versions seems a more global concern (cf. Frydenlund 2019: 294–7).

Islamophobic conspiracy theories tend to be invoked in reactionary, nativist politics and serve as a mobilising crisis narrative. The enemy invoked is not only that of Islam, but of what is seen as emasculating, passive and destructively cosmopolitan politics committed by political and cultural elites. While there are versions where these enemies within are merely weak and easily fooled, they are also presented as greedy and traitorous partners in paving the road for 'Eurabia' (e.g. Fekete 2012). Such conspiracy beliefs are tied to increased support for violence, and they form a vital background for the target selection of massacres such as the terrorist attacks on the Christchurch mosques in New Zealand in March 2019 and Utøya in Norway in July 2011.

## Conspiracy theory in religion: 'W.E.I.R.D.' people

Conspiracy beliefs about religions are legion. They can also be examples of conspiracy beliefs held *within* religions, as expressions of troubled interreligious relations. Are any types of religion more associated with conspiracy beliefs than others? What answers we have to that question are mostly related to Western, Educated, Industrialised, Rich and Democratic (W.E.I.R.D.) countries.

A first observation is that religious adherence does not necessarily predict specific conspiracy beliefs one way or the other. Nor does religious adherence typically predict direction of belief or disbelief in conspiracy theories in general. But some types of religion seem to have a higher, more general propensity towards conspiracy beliefs than others. One of these groups is the cluster of religious identities commonly dubbed 'Fundamentalists' in folk categorisations (cf. Oliver, Wood 2014). Conforming to the original description of the 'paranoid style' of politics (Hofstadter 1996 [1965]), these groups are more likely to hold a clearly dualist, 'Manichean' worldview. They are more likely to have apocalyptic expectations, and their political language is characterised by jeremiads listing woes as signs that the hour is drawing nigh. They are somewhat less likely to have had higher education, and measures of right-wing authoritarianism are 'highly related to religious fundamentalism' (Altemeyer 2003: 24). All these factors contribute on their own to conspiracy beliefs and, in combination with cultural pessimism and high symbolic thinking, evidence clearly indicates that this form of religion tends more towards conspiracism than others (Oliver, Wood 2018).

Individualised, alternative spirituality and some related forms of new religious movements may also be particularly prone to conspiracy thinking. In so far as they already include a lot of other 'stigmatized knowledge-claims' (Barkun 2003) – such as ufology, alternative medicine or alternative history – conspiracy beliefs indeed fit a pattern (Stone *et al.* 2018). Considering established individual difference predictors of conspiracy beliefs, this confluence is unsurprising, as the cognitive style of the spirituality-scene is characterised by holistic, intuitive, magic and symbolic thinking. Furthermore, the emic historiography of the scene is characterised by conspiratorial root narratives, and the related economic practices give ample opportunity to employ conspiracy theories in self-defence as collective, motivated rejection of science-related criticism (Asprem, Dyrendal 2019).

These different forms of religion may both be more prone to conspiracism, but that does not necessarily translate into holding the *same* conspiracy beliefs. Both groups may be inclined to believe badly about established authorities opposed to their own ideologies, but conspiracy stereotypes about other religious minorities seems more the province of fundamentalists (Dyrendal *et al.* 2017; cf. Oliver, Wood 2018). The latter will be more likely to hold conspiracy beliefs about outgroups and theories that attack enemies of those they deem legitimate authorities (cf. Imhoff, Bruder 2014; Wood, Gray 2019). We see that conspiracy beliefs in religion relate to power and authority, a complex field better understood by looking at some specific dynamics.

## Conspiracy theories in religion: State, Church and Pussy Riot

Religions are part of a larger social fabric. They are heterogenous, and often contested scenes that are related to a variety of mechanisms of power, and their interaction with a specific conspiracy theory often changes over the latter's public life cycle. One such example is the role of the Russian Orthodox Church in the controversy over the feminist punk band, Pussy Riot (Yablokov 2018).

The conflict started with a staged protest on the soleas of the Cathedral of Christ the Saviour in Moscow. Pussy Riot's target was two-fold: Putin's regime, and the Church leadership for supporting him. The criticism of Patriarch Kirill was already far-reaching. His support for Putin in the upcoming elections was just one element. Lawsuits had also shown that he owned suspiciously expensive items, including 'an expensive flat in the centre of Moscow' (Yablokov 2018: 100). This set the stage for a deliberate deployment of authority-supportive conspiracy theories with religion cast in the role of both supportive structure and violated victim. First, the band was merely accused of hooliganism, but in an ongoing campaign to make Orthodoxy 'the key element of Russian identity' (Yablokov 2018: 100), the protest was soon viewed as part of the West's supposed conspiracy against Russia. By attacking and undermining faith and Church, the argument went, the West and its Russian proxies were trying to deny Russia its true, messianic role in world history.

Representatives of the Church played important roles in the beginning of the affair. Patriarch Kirill stated that the Church 'had become the victim of an "information war"' (Yablokov 2018: 101). The Moscow Patriarchate decreed prayer services defending the relics of the Cathedral of Christ the Saviour, now redefined as having been 'desecrated' by the protest. Official, political narratives tied the band and its supporters to a conspiracy consisting of the internal opposition, the intelligence operations of the West, atheism, a 'Neo-Bolshevism' that might instigate new pogroms against the Church and sexual deviance. The Orthodox Church played a role as the injured party, as the sacred institution upholding the values threatened by the conspiracy and as entrepreneurs pressing the conspiracy claims. Later, all these faded into the background. As court proceedings followed a different discursive regime, the emphasis shifted to the alleged collusion between internal and external political conspirators, and the 'narrative of Orthodoxy under threat was replaced by attempts on the part of public intellectuals and politicians to justify the Kremlin's policy in relation to the opposition' (Yablokov 2018: 107).

The role of religion in the episode is complex. Its role as guardian of threatened, traditional values in the face of internal and external threats is a common conspiracy trope, and its role as violated victim of evil a common trope of the culture wars. However, Ilya Yablokov (2018) demonstrates that the conspiracy theories were instrumental, a tool for promoting the Church and state power while distracting the public from less palatable topics, such as corruption and political partisanship. Religious and nationalist sensibilities were wielded as a tool in the service of state power through the use of conspiracy theories, consolidating internal support. The interests of Church and state became intertwined, as was their external discourse. However, the state took the lead, with the Church playing a supporting role in the symbolic assertion of Russianness and nation.

## Conspiracy theory in religion: Islam and polio vaccine theories in Nigeria

An example from northern Nigeria shows more complex relations, when political power is contested and religion is brought in on both sides. Polio is endemic to the northern parts of Nigeria, thanks to its wild strains of the bacteria. Health care is often sparse and expensive, and vaccination numbers vacillate according to circumstance. In the early 2000s, the campaign to rid the region of its endemic polio was well under way. The Global Polio Eradication Initiative (G.P.E.I.) had reduced the incidence of polio from more than 350 000 cases in 1988 to just under 500 in 2001 (Ghinai *et al.* 2013). Then, conspiracy rumours about the oral vaccine took hold. It was a Western plot to sterilise girls, spread H.I.V. and cancer, the rumours said. Five states of the mostly Muslim north discontinued the vaccine (Ghinai *et al.* 2013), with new polio outbreaks inside and outside the region as a result (Jegede 2007; Yahya 2007).

The boycott seemed driven by religion, with Islamic regions at the heart of it. Muslim scholars and politicians spread the rumours, made decisions from their seats of political office and supported the decision from their role as legal and theological authorities. The rumours also functioned as part of Islamist responses to the American 'War on Terror', which was seen as a more general, worldwide attack on Islam (Robbins 2011).

Religion serves here as a regional and group identifier, where it is also explicitly identified with political power. The majority of religious identity in the region flows directly into the political arena, into legal and theological authority. But it is not merely local. The role of Islam as group identifier translates into identification with a global *ummah*. Religion as identifier on a global stage facilitates infusion of tropes and narratives from globalised, political discourses on religion and power, including conspiracy narratives.

The choice to use these global tropes were, of course, grounded in the situation of local actors. Contextualising the vaccine boycott, Ayodele Jegede (2007) ranges from geography of religion to colonial and recent political history. The older colonial histories resulted in primarily Muslim northern regions, and a Christianity-dominated south. More recently, power in Nigeria had passed from a military regime from the north to an elected regime dominated by the Christian south. The contested elections of 2003 gave the country a Christian, southern president.

The elections themselves may have driven partisanship, but they also took focus away from the vaccination drive, which was concentrated in the north. When the drive was resumed in the aftermath of elections, the political climate made it easy to draw on both international and more local conspiracy theories about vaccines. The head of the Supreme Council for Sharia in Nigeria (S.C.S.N.) may have gotten his conspiracy theories from then-current international sources (Yahya 2007: 188), but rumours that vaccines were tools for population control were not new to the region. They had been in popular circulation in both the north and the south following 1980s population control policies (Jegede 2007). The policies may have added to suspicion about vaccination, since it was a *free* element of health care that was made more easily available. A recent scandal with a medical trial going wrong ('the Trovan trial') added to suspicion, as likely did the fact that the treatment of victims and population in the aftermath was not seen as transparent and fair (cf. van Prooijen 2018b).

Many factors known to drive conspiracy rumours were thus in place: Ideological divisions, a recently lost election, long-standing distrust re-actualised and elite signals supporting a folk belief. Religion served as a collective identity that could be threatened by the conspiracy's alleged goals and mobilise collective action around a common goal. Religion also supplied the elites that legitimised the rumours and the ideological, religio-political context that made them make sense in a global perspective.

If religion could be employed as a resource to spread the conspiracy rumours, it would also be one of the resources drawn on to quell them. This is what both outsiders and regional opponents did. The World Health Organization appealed to, among others, the Organisation of the Islamic Conference (O.I.C.) and the Arab League. It got their support. Late in 2003, the O.I.C. 'adopted a resolution to pressure Islamic countries to make greater efforts to eradicate polio' (Yahya 2007: 191). The O.I.C.-associated, prestigious International Fiqh Council – a council of Islamic jurisprudence – spoke out against the vaccine boycott, with the prominent Sheikh Yusuf Al-Qaradawi stating that the views of international 'fellow scholars in the Muslim ummah' should take precedence over the local authorities (Yahya 2007).

Such appeals to stronger, international Islamic theological and legal authorities and their rulings constituted only one usage of religion as a resource in fighting the conspiracy theory and its consequences. Political authorities also tried to allay fears by getting the vaccine first *tested* by Muslim countries, then also had it *produced* there. Both at the time locally, and later, on the global scene, separate lines of juridical-theological arguments were employed to support the use of ingredients that might be religiously controversial, followed by a more concerted effort to make *halal*-certified vaccines (Ahmed et al. 2018).

The example above shows a situation that is easy to overlook in discussions of religion and conspiracy beliefs, because it can work both ways. Religion in context includes arguing about authority and content: Who speaks for religion, and what does religious content entail with regard to behaviour? Even when we define religion as a socially authoritative discourse, 'whose defining characteristic is its desire to speak of things eternal and transcendent with an authority equally transcendent and eternal' (Lincoln 1996: 225), desire does not translate into reality. Religious communities do not speak with one voice. There are always potential cleavages that can be made larger. The radical Islamists who called on a threat towards a global *ummah* of their own imagining (a threat by a Western conspiracy using vaccines to destroy them) were creating a local crisis narrative to recruit eligible ingroup members into radicalised positions (cf. Berger 2018). The local *authorities* were engaging in conspiracy speech in a way that, instrumentally intended or not, supported their own, local political power against national rivals. On the other side, religion as a source of moral authority was used to *combat* the conspiracy rumours, but not as full narratives to be debunked. These critics undermined select aspects of the rumours as a route to re-establish trust and vaccine-acceptance. Getting data about vaccine safety from Muslim populations and moving production to Muslim countries undermines the discourse about vaccines being un-Islamic and harmful. The theological arguments for vaccines being acceptable, and the later production of *halal*-certified vaccines, serve the same function: Adopting religious authority to bolster the argument for vaccination. The counter-discourse rejected the more explicit arguments against the conspiracy rumours and its anti-Western elements. It also resisted defining the ingroup in terms of behaviour related to the conspiracy rumours, and thus additional division. It did, however, very consciously draw on religious authority to oppose the crisis narrative the conspiracy theory presented.

## Conspiracy theory in religion: New Age and 'conspirituality'

Religion and religious elites, in their role of conservative power brokers for the social order, may often act to dampen crisis narratives that threaten disruption. This may, to some extent, be why the public find it so interesting when religious authorities *promote* false accusations of conspiracy. At other times, the same public may be more surprised when everyday *adherents* turn out to be conspiracy prone, such as in the case of 'conspiritual' New Ageism (Asprem, Dyrendal 2015).

In the autumn of 2011, the organisers of Norway's central 'New Age' venue disinvited noted conspiracy theorists from their fairs, and issued a general warning against the attractions of conspiracism. The general prohibition of conspiracist speakers came in the wake of Anders Behring Breivik's terrorist attacks on a government building and a political youth camp, attacks which left 77 people dead and many more wounded. The warning showed and addressed an internal discursive divide, which effectively made it stronger.

As noted above, in W.E.I.R.D. countries the religious expressions that are strongly tied to paranormal beliefs are also closely associated with conspiracy thinking. 'New Age' religion is one such arena. This can be seen as strange, as New Age practitioners tend to be white, middle class and well educated. If 'conspiracy theories are for losers' as, among others, Uscinski and Parent (2014) proclaim, New Age believers do not fit the typical profile. Nor are the beliefs typically associated with New Age what one would assume to be conducive to conspiracy beliefs. New Age is typically marketed as a world-affirming religion with a positive view of human nature, warning against attracting negative forces through focus on them. This would, arguably, make it seem paradoxical to find so much of conspiracy beliefs in the milieu (e.g. Ward, Voas 2011). Evangelical conspiracy theories about New Age religion have been legion (e.g. Saliba 1999), and being subject to conspiracy thinking has been used in warnings against harmful othering in conspiracist form.

However, esotericism is an important background for New Age. The polemical accusations of conspiracy between the religiously orthodox and those marginalised as heterodox have been reciprocal. These polemics have been partially embedded in esoteric identity discourse. This is part of what esoteric discourse shares with conspiracy theories, as a 'rhetoric of hidden truth … established contrary to other interpretations of the universe and history' (von Stuckrad 2005: 10). Conspiracy narratives flow, moreover, between different identities; there is a 'dark occulture' (Partridge 2005), which fundamentalists and New Agers both draw on. The narratives share in the 'grand polemical tradition' that created esotericism (Hanegraaff 2012), and which constitutes an ongoing dynamic in the production of identity.

A central part of the polemical tradition revolves around knowledge claims, with identity discourse including opposition to perceived orthodoxies. This is partly held together by a network-based circulation of 'rejected knowledge' that includes conspiracy lore. Conspiracy theories serve in identity protection as e.g. the language of motivated reasoning; they are part of the explanation why promised paradigm shifts in their own direction continue not to happen (see Asprem, Dyrendal 2019: 218–20). Tales of how a conspiracy tries to suppress the practices and evidence for their effect serve as identity-protection, mobilisation narrative and theodicy in one go. Conspiracy narratives explain failure and absolve guilt. For those who want to present as an alternative knowledge elite (Robertson 2016), this is important, as failure is exacerbated by the rudimentary, unstable organisation and market vulnerabilities of New Age practices. Uscinski and Parent note that: 'Sharing conspiracy theories provides a way for groups falling in the pecking order to revamp and recoup from losses, close ranks, staunch losses, overcome collective action problems, and sensitize minds to vulnerabilities' (2014: 132). Presenting criticism as part of an evil conspiracy is part of confronting it and serves to confer a stronger sense of ingroup identity, and thus to mobilise for collective action.

This brief excursion should make it clear that conspiracy narratives are a useful and natural component of New Age cultural production and heritage. This does not, however, mean that any belief goes equally well, nor that it does so in any climate – which returns us to our empirical example.

Considered as religion, New Age is not a prototypical case. Neither a set of organisations nor a common creed, it is an outsider term for networks of loosely overlapping practices and beliefs served up mostly to a market of individual consumers. There is little formal power outside therapy-client relations, and customers move on, consuming new commodities. This means that market access becomes vital. The Norwegian New Age scene has been held together and promoted through two central venues: A popular journal and alternative fairs. Both have been under the relative control of a very small set of entrepreneurs. With the advent of Internet 2.0, they also moved into the sphere of interactive online activity. While conspiracy theories of different stripes, mostly by way alternative history and alternative medicine, had been a recurrent topic in the journal and at fairs, the entrepreneurs had control and employed editorial discretion. After 2001, conspiracy beliefs grew in popularity within the milieu. The milieu leans left, and has been highly liberal, but even explicitly far-right radical conspiracy theories got more coverage. This increased interest in and sympathy for encompassing conspiracist ideation was even more pronounced in online venues (Dyrendal 2017). However, with increased interaction between hardline conspiracy believers came an increasingly clearly expressed unease among the more conventional New Age practitioners. Drawing on the world-affirming side of the discourse, their interests revolved more around spiritual self-development, their politics tended more towards liberal and green, and they found the conspiracist focus harmful and hateful. The silent majority became more vocal as the conspiracists established their own additional venues, but an internal, New Age ethos of tolerance for all 'alternative' discourse made it hard to censure discussion online. It was even more difficult in the public venues.

The rhetorical situation shifted with Breivik. The mass murder of Norwegian citizens by an extreme right-wing conspiracy theorist made public opinion rise against conspiracism in general. This facilitated more direct intervention from the owners and directors of the fair and journal. Suddenly, there was both an increased call for taking responsibility for others' utterances from their platform, and for controlling access. In practice, they made use of the dominant market position of their own venues to explicitly combat a segment of their public, including 'de-platforming' popular speakers and writers. While the idea of censorship had long been deemed problematic, and the conspiritual segment had established their own outlets, this cemented the situation. The conflict became open and hardened. This to some degree deprived the conspiracist segment of internal legitimacy. Conspiracist entrepreneurs had to look elsewhere for a platform and recruit customers through their own networks. Coalitions within the conspiracist segment were loosened. The constricted market for their lectures, goods and services added to internal strains (see Dyrendal 2017). While conspiracism obviously did not disappear within the 'alternative mainstream' of Norwegian New Age, the conflict pushed it into the background and marginalised those deemed too consumed by such concerns.

## Conclusion

The term religion covers not only a range of cognitions, it also covers very different private and social behaviours, forms of social organisation and power relations. As such, the relations between conspiracy theory and religion are diverse and complex. Each is at the same time a possible resource for understanding the world, for identity construction, for ordering social relations, and for gaining or disputing authority and power. Even secular conspiracy narratives often serve as templates for predicting future troubles – 'prophecy' – as well as stories of what has already gone wrong. When imbued with extra status from association with values and institutions people hold sacred, such roles can become even more important. But religion does not play a simple, unified role. Even in simple religious communities, there will always be struggles over authority. We should always ask questions about who speaks, in what context and for which interests, as well as about what authority they claim, and the effect on the audience they address.

The causes of and intentions behind the narration of conspiracy are complicated, with 'belief' being but one possible aspect involved. Religious elites and their dominant discourses may be more or less ideologically attuned to a conspiracy narrative. This will tend to be one of the factors that select tales for re-telling, combined with other elements of fitness to group or elite purposes in their current situation. Neither group nor elites being homogenous, the potential for disagreement on what religious authority or religious identity should mean for interaction with the conspiracist ideas is always there.

There are some important social differences. Church religions, those a local population are born into, and heterodox religion will typically be embedded differently in power structures. This will tend to involve different social dynamics of conspiracy theory. In psychological research, conspiracy mentality predicts beliefs about the powerful, whereas authoritarianism better predicts conspiracy beliefs that protect power (cf. Imhoff, Bruder 2014; Wood, Gray 2019). The marginal and marginalised tend to use conspiracy theory more as a language of opposition, while dominant religion will, as in the Russian and Nigerian cases above, use them more as a language of counter-subversion. In the nativist variety, this can make 'religions' the target of conspiracy theory, as in the classical antisemitic arguments about Jews acting as a hidden 'state within the state', or in the case of Buddhist 'counter-jihadism' in Myanmar and Sri Lanka (Frydenlund 2019).

With the increasing dominance of a market economy, including in the area of religion, the dynamics of power may change again. In an open information economy with increasingly diminishing costs to establishing an outlet, any conspiracy entrepreneur has cheap access to disseminating their ideas. Being heard is another matter. One way of finding an audience can be speaking from and appealing to an established spiritual market, using established tropes and narratives to interpret news. As we saw from the Norwegian example, those who dominate the market can to some extent regulate access and serve to delegitimise even what they have earlier legitimised. Religious belief, even in the sense of established Church religions with doctrine, is often less a coherent, doctrine-based phenomenon, and more a selective, context-related pattern of feeling and thinking. Religiously authorised values and narratives are chosen, consumed and applied according to social and individual circumstance. The specific narratives are not chosen randomly; socio-political context activates types of religion and religious 'beliefs' as much as they activate conspiracy suspicions and narratives.

## References

Ahmed, A., Lee, K.S., Bukhsh, A., Al-Worafi, Y.M., Sarker, M.R., Ming, L.C. and Khan, T.M. (2018) 'Outbreak of vaccine-preventable diseases in Muslim majority countries', *Journal of Infection and Public Health*, 11(2): 153–5.

Altemeyer, B. (2003) 'Why do religious fundamentalists tend to be prejudiced?', *International Journal for the Psychology of Religion*, 13(1): 17–28.

Asprem, E. and Dyrendal, A. (2015) 'Conspirituality reconsidered: how surprising and how new is the confluence of spirituality and conspiracy theory?', *Journal of Contemporary Religion*, 30(3): 367–82.

Asprem, E. and Dyrendal, A. (2019) 'Close companions? Esotericism and conspiracy theories', in A. Dyrendal, D.G. Robertson and E. Asprem (eds.) *Handbook of Conspiracy Theory and Contemporary Religion*, Leiden: Brill, pp. 207–33.

Aupers, S. and Harambam, J. (2019) 'Rational enchantments: conspiracy theory between secular scepticism and spiritual salvation', in A. Dyrendal, D. Robertson and E. Asprem (eds.) *Handbook of conspiracy theory and contemporary religion*, Leiden: Brill, pp. 48–69.

Barkun, M. (2003) *A culture of conspiracy: apocalyptic visions in contemporary America*, Berkeley, CA: University of California Press.

Berger, J.M. (2018) *Extremism*, Cambridge, MA: MIT Press.

Brotherton, R. and French, C.C. (2015) 'Intention seekers: conspiracist ideation and biased attributions of intentionality', *PLOS ONE*, 10(5): e0124125.

Butter, M. (2014) *Plots, designs, and schemes: American conspiracy theories from the Puritans to the present*, Berlin: de Gruyter.

Dagnall, N., Drinkwater, K., Parker, A. and Clough, P. (2015) 'Paranormal experience, belief in the paranormal, and anomalous beliefs', *Paranthropology*, 7(1): 4–14.

Douglas, K.M., Sutton, R.M., Callan, M.J., Dawtry, R.J. and Harvey, A.J. (2016) 'Someone is pulling the strings: hypersensitive agency detection and belief in conspiracy theories', *Thinking and Reasoning*, 22(1): 57–77.

Dyrendal, A. (2013) 'Hidden knowledge, hidden powers: esotericism and conspiracy culture', in E. Asprem and K. Granholm (eds.) *Contemporary Esotericism*, Sheffield: Equinox, pp. 200–25.

Dyrendal, A. (2017) 'New Age and Norwegian "conspirituality"', in I. Gilhus, Ingvild, S-E. Kraft and J.R. Lewis (eds.) *New Age in Norway*, Sheffield: Equinox, pp. 159–81.

Dyrendal, A., Asprem, E. and Robertson, D.G. (2019) 'Conspiracy theories and the study of religion(s): what we are talking about and why it is important', in A. Dyrendal, D.G. Robertson and E. Asprem (eds.) *Handbook of conspiracy theory and contemporary religion*, Leiden: Brill, pp. 21–47.

Dyrendal, A., Kennair, L.E.O. and Lewis, J.R. (2017) 'The role of conspiracy mentality and paranormal beliefs in predicting conspiracy beliefs among neopagans', *International Journal for the Study of New Religions*, 8(1): 73–97.

Fekete, L. (2012) 'The Muslim conspiracy theory and the Oslo massacre', *Race & Class*, 53(3): 30–47.

Franks, B., Bangerter, A. and Bauer, M.W. (2013) 'Conspiracy theories as quasi-religious mentality: an integrated account from cognitive science, social representations theory, and frame theory', *Frontiers in Psychology*, 4(424).

Frydenlund, I. (2019) 'Buddhist islamophobia: actors, tropes, contexts', in A. Dyrendal, D.G. Robertson and E. Asprem (eds.) *Handbook of conspiracy theory and contemporary religion*, Leiden: Brill, pp. 279–302.

Ghinai, I., Willott, C., Dadari, I. and Larson, H.J. (2013) 'Listening to the rumours: what the northern Nigeria polio vaccine boycott can tell us ten years on', *Global Public Health*, 8(10): 1138–50.

Hanegraaff, W. (2012) *Esotericism and the academy*, Cambridge: Cambridge University Press.

Hart, J. and Graether, M. (2018) 'Something's going on here: psychological predictors of belief in conspiracy theories', *Journal of Individual Differences*. Advance online publication.

Hofstadter, R. (1996 [1965]) *The paranoid style in American politics and other essays*, reprint, Cambridge: Harvard University Press.

Imhoff, R. and Bruder, M. (2014) 'Speaking (un-)truth to power: conspiracy mentality as a generalised political attitude', *European Journal of Personality*, 28: 25–43.

Jegede, A.S. (2007) 'What led to the Nigerian boycott of the polio vaccination campaign?', *PLoS Medicine*, 4(3): e73.

Kofta, M. and Sedek. G. (2005) 'Conspiracy stereotypes of Jews during systemic transformation in Poland', *International Journal of Sociology*, 35(1): 40–64.

Lincoln, B. (1996) 'Theses on method', *Method and Theory in the Study of Religion*, 8(3): 225–7.

Lincoln, B. (2006) *Holy terrors: thinking about religion after September 11*, Chicago, Ill: University of Chicago Press.

Oliver, J.E. and Wood, T.J. (2014) 'Conspiracy theories and the paranoid style(s) of mass opinion', *American Journal of Political Science*, 58(4): 952–66.

Oliver, J.E. and Wood, T.J. (2018) *Enchanted America: how intuition and reason divide our politics*, London: University of Chicago Press.

Partridge, C. (2005) *The re-enchantment of the West*, vol. 2, London: T&T Clark.

Pigden, C. (1995) 'Popper revisited, or what is wrong with conspiracy theories?', *Philosophy of the Social Sciences*, 25(1): 3–34.

Popper, K.M. (1963) *The open society and its enemies*, 4th rev. edn, Princeton: Princeton University Press, 2002.

Robbins, M. (2011) 'Vaccines, the CIA, and how the war on terror helped spread polio in Nigeria', *Guardian*, 15 July. Available at: www.theguardian.com/science/the-lay-scientist/2011/jul/15/1. [Accessed 16 October 2018.]

Robertson, D.G. (2016) *UFOs, conspiracy theories and the New Age*, London: Bloomsbury.

Robertson, D.G., Asprem, E. and Dyrendal, A. (2019) 'Introducing the field: conspiracy theory in, about, and as religion', in A. Dyrendal, D.G. Robertson and E. Asprem (eds.) *Handbook of conspiracy theory and contemporary religion*, Leiden: Brill, pp. 1–18.

Saliba, J.A. (1999) *Christian responses to the New Age: a critical assessment*, London: Geoffrey Chapman.

Sobiech, M.J. (2014) *The ethos of conspiracy argument: 'character' as persuader in conspiracy rhetoric*, thesis, Louisville, KY: University of Louisville.

Stone, A., McDermott, M.R., Abdi, A., Cornwell, B., Matyas, Z., Reed, R. and Watt, R. (2018) 'Development and validation of the multi-dimensional questionnaire of scientifically unsubstantiated beliefs', *Personality and Individual Differences*, 128: 146–56.

Uscinski, J.E. and Parent, J.M. (2014) *American conspiracy theories*, New York, NY: Oxford University Press.

Vail, K.E., Rothschild, Z.K., Weise, D.R., Solomon, S., Pyszczynski, T. and Greenberg, J. (2010) 'A terror management analysis of the psychological functions of religion', *Personality and Social Psychology Review*, 14(1): 84–94.

Van der Tempel, J. and Alcock, J.E. (2015) 'Relationships between conspiracy mentality, hyperactive agency detection, and schizotypy: supernatural forces at work?', *Personality and Individual Differences*, 82: 136–41.

Van Prooijen, J.-W. (2018a) *The psychology of conspiracy theories*, New York: Routledge.

Van Prooijen, J.-W. (2018b) 'Empowerment as a tool to reduce belief in conspiracy theories' in J.E. Uscinski (ed.), *Conspiracy theories and the people who believe them*, New York: Oxford University Press, pp. 432–42.

Victor, J.S. (1993) *Satanic panic*, Chicago, Ill.: Open Court.

Von Stuckrad, K. (2005) *Western esotericism*, London: Equinox.

Wagner-Egger, P., Delouvée, S., Gauvrit, N. and Dieguez, S. (2018) 'Creationism and conspiracism share a common teleological bias', *Current Biology*, 28(16): PR867–PR868.

Ward, C. and Voas, D. (2011) 'The emergence of conspirituality', *Journal of Contemporary Religion*, 26(1): 103–21.

Wood, M.J. and Douglas, K.M. (2019) 'Are conspiracy theories a surrogate for God?', in A. Dyrendal, D.G. Robertson and E. Asprem (eds.) *Handbook of conspiracy theory and contemporary religion*, Leiden: Brill, pp. 87–105.

Wood, M.J. and Gray, D. (2019) 'Right-wing authoritarianism as a predictor of pro-establishment versus antiestablishment conspiracy theories', *Personality and Individual Differences*, 138: 163–6.

Yablokov, I. (2018) *Fortress Russia: conspiracy theories in post-soviet Russia*, Cambridge: Polity Press.

Yahya, M. (2007) 'Polio vaccines: "No thank you!" Barriers to polio eradication in northern Nigeria', *African Affairs*, 106(423): 185–204.

Zuquete. J.P. (2018) *The identitarians: the movement against globalism and Islam in Europe*, Notre Dame, IN: University of Notre Dame Press.

# SECTION 4

# Media and transmission

# 4.0
# INTRODUCTION

*Stef Aupers, Dana Crăciun and Andreas Önnerfors*

Conspiracy theorists are highly suspicious of modern media. Was the moon landing in 1969 actually filmed in a Hollywood Studio by the famous director Stanley Kubrick? Do video clips of celebrities like Rihanna, Beyoncé or Justin Bieber contain hidden messages to sell the New World Order to an ignorant audience? Should we trust our perception of reality when, in fact, our senses are increasingly dependent on media images? Indeed, media is everywhere and, according to Couldry and Hepp (2017), media participation is no longer an individual choice: Particularly with the Internet, social media and interconnected smartphones, they argue, we are entering a new phase of 'deep mediatisation' that overarches every domain of life. In a similar vein, Mark Deuze comments, 'we do not live *with*, but *in* media' (2012: xiii). This immersion in our media environment motivates 'agency panic' – the core assumption underlying conspiracy theories that social systems are controlling our minds (Melley 2000). The popularity that the *Matrix* metaphor enjoys in the conspiracy milieu is then not surprising (Harambam 2017): The world is considered by conspiracy theorists to be staged, mediatised, manipulated and hyper-real to conceal the real truth. Are we, like Neo in the movie *The Matrix* (1999), already living in a virtual reality produced by evil alien powers? Conspiracy theorists suggest that we are.

And yet the relation between media and conspiracy theory is highly ambivalent. Conspiracy theories are not only formulated *about* and *against* media; they are themselves prominently featuring *in* media and are rapidly transmitted and transformed *through* media. This, then, is the underlying assumption of this section of the handbook: Conspiracy theories are deeply mediatised. Indeed, their advocates may be highly suspicious of mass media-effects but they, simultaneously, depend on media to formulate and communicate conspiracy theories to a larger audience. Conspiracy theories can be latent assumptions or unstable rumours. But, often, they are manifest ideologies, worldviews or narratives that are self-consciously written down in books, used to develop a dramatic detective novel or produce a film script for a paranoia thriller; posted as a message on Facebook or turned into a vlog on YouTube. Such media texts, in turn, provide valuable sources to empirically study conspiracy theories in academia. Particularly in disciplines like history, sociology, ethnology, anthropology, cultural studies, media studies, literary studies, media texts are used to analyse the nature and meanings of conspiracy culture in rich, empirical detail. Notwithstanding the relevance of such studies on text, they often disregard the influence of the medium on the message. Consequently, literature, film, games or social media are seldom analysed in terms of their media-specific traits and the way these shape the content, form and transmission of conspiracy theories.

This section taps into these two aspects of the mediatisation of conspiracy theories. The first question addressed in the contributions is: What genres, themes and types of conspiracy theories are featuring *in* media texts and how are they related to the time/culture in which they are produced? From this perspective, media texts featuring paranoia, secret plots and conspiracies are often studied as sources to understand the nature of conspiracy theories in a particular historical and social-cultural context. Media texts are models 'of' and 'for' society – they both reflect and shape the public imagination and are hence good material to study the (transformation of) conspiracy theories. Pivotal here is the work of Fredric Jameson arguing that contemporary conspiracy theories in literature and (science) fiction are, essentially, 'cognitive maps' to represent modern systems that have become too complex to represent, or even 'to think the impossible totality of the contemporary world system' (1991: 38). Whether such 'cognitive maps' are elaborated in written theories, film scripts or visual schemes on the Internet – they allegedly function to make sense of the (post)modern institutional environment (e.g. Knight 2000; Melley 2000). In this respect, sociologist Luc Boltanski (2014) discusses the birth of the 'spy novel' in the U.K., France and other Western countries in the nineteenth century and ties it in with the emergence of the modern state, industrialism, capitalism and the social sciences. The day-to-day confrontation of ordinary people with this complex institutional environment, he argues, generated ontological uncertainties about the 'reality of reality' and nagging questions such as 'Where does power really lie, and who really holds it?' (Boltanski 2014: xv–xvi). The spy novel, but more recently books, films or series like *The X-Files*, *Homeland* or *House of Cards*, exemplify these uncertainties. Notwithstanding their fictitious nature, such media texts are valuable sources for scholars to study the public imagination about conspiracies and its relationship with Western society, where institutions are increasingly powerful, yet structurally evasive; omnipresent but principally opaque and, essentially, impossible to represent or control for ordinary citizens.

The different chapters in this section, then, first of all study conspiracy theory *as/in* media text and assess their meaning in historical and social-cultural context. The chapter by Astapova (4.1) already demonstrates that verbalised conspiracy stories about the Other – varying from alien tribes, ethnic groups or nations conspiring against the ingroup – are continuously re-invented and adapted to a local context. In sermons, letters, pamphlets distributed in eighteenth-century France, religious conservatives and 'Enlightened' liberals were imagining conspiracies about one another, as McKenzie-McHargh and Oberhauser (4.2) demonstrate, while conspiracy fiction, popularised in nineteenth-century England, was primarily preoccupied with the invasion of the nation-state, as Carver shows (4.3). Whether through verbal stories, letters, literary fiction or television, media texts thus channel particular, local, time-confined anxieties about conspiracies of an alien Other. That such anxieties about a fixed Other are transforming over time is demonstrated by the contributions of Melley (4.4), Caumanns and Önnerfors (4.5) and Butter (4.6). Melley depicts the problem of agency and epistemic certainty in twentieth-century American fiction, Caumanns and Önnerfors point to the networked nature of visualised conspiracy theories in modern art, whereas Butter demonstrates the shift from a straightforward representation of conspiracy to self-reflexive negotiations of conspiracy theory in movies and television shows over the last 50 years.

The second theoretical assumption that informs the chapters in this section, implicitly or explicitly, is that text should not be studied in isolation from the medium. The medium itself or, rather, the media-specific traits of written texts, films, series or social media, fundamentally shape the content and meaning of the text. In medium-centred theories (Meyrowitz 1994), most notable the work of Walter Ong (1982) and Marshall McLuhan, this general argument is developed. 'The medium is the message', as McLuhan aptly summarised in *Understanding Media* (1964). New media technologies, he famously argued, both stimulate and amputate different human senses, and facilitate and limit particular repertoires of thinking, experiencing and acting. The shift from oral culture to 'the Gutenberg Galaxy' (McLuhan 1962) of print for a mass audience in the sixteenth century, he claimed, was as revolutionary as the visual 'electronic age' of television and film in the twentieth century. And we may wonder: What difference does the Internet make? The World Wide Web, as a medium of information and communication, structured a non-linear, hyper-textual, memetic, audio-visual, hyper-real environment (e.g. Deuze 2012; Shifman 2014; Couldry, Hepp 2017) and opened up a 'participatory culture' (Jenkins 2006) where all citizens are allegedly included in communication.

The second point is, then, that we should take such modes of transmission into account if we want to understand conspiracy theories. In addition to discussing the meaning of conspiracy theories *as/in* media texts, we thus focus on the transmission of conspiracy theories *through* different media forms. The second question addressed in the section is: What influence do different media forms have on the way we formulate, visualise, produce, transmit, consume and appropriate conspiracy theories? The question is approached from different disciplines – folklore studies, literary studies, media studies, cultural history, sociology, political sciences. The overarching set-up of the section is loosely historical, and the individual chapters highlight different modes of transmission. In summary, the section deals with the perennial word-to-mouth-dissemination of conspiracy theories (4.1), print culture in eighteenth-century France (4.2), the literary imagination of conspiracies in the nineteenth-century U.K. (4.3) and twentieth-century U.S.A. (4.4), visual culture and art (4.5), in television series and films (4.6), and on the Internet, as Aupers (4.7), Stano (4.8), Leal (4.9) and Avramov, Gatov and Yablokov (4.10) discuss.

In a Foucauldian sense, it is tempting to consider such historical modes of transmission as successive media 'regimes' motivating the formation of particular ways of speaking, acting and experiencing conspiracies in society. Indeed, there may be an elective affinity between modern print culture and linear, hierarchical schemes of causality representing conspiracies whereas the age of the Internet motivates the production of non-linear, hyper-textual conspiracy theories in which 'everything is connected' (Knight 2000: 208–12). And what influence does social media have on the form and content of conspiracy theories? Does its technological infrastructure turn conspiracy theories into concise Tweets of 280 signs maximum or un-reflexive chats in WhatsApp groups? Have they become open-ended memes that are transmitted on a global scale? Are such conspiracy memes constantly 'circulated, imitated, and/or transformed via the internet by many users' (Shifman 2014: 41)? In any case, we need to be careful when considering different modes of transmission as successfully replacing one another in a linear, evolutionist and deterministic way; nowadays, different media forms complement, overlap and converge with one another. It is striking, in this sense, that allegedly 'premodern' word-to-mouth dissemination of conspiracy theories is not abolished but, rather, re-located to the Internet.

But there is another reason to avoid the pitfall of overly structuralist or deterministic interpretations of the medium on the message. The chapters show that modern modes of transmission – from mass print to the Internet – afford more democratic involvement, freedom and agency in the production and consumption of conspiracy theories. Print culture – the production, availability and dissemination of books, newspapers and libraries – opened up the public sphere where theories, including those about hidden conspiracies, were openly exchanged between members of the cultural elite. This popularisation and normalisation of the discourse increased with conspiracy in fiction, literature and film for the masses. The Internet, finally, provides the possibility for the audience to become (inter)active co-producers of conspiracy theories. Its non-hierarchical structure provides 'amateurs' the possibility to actively 'decode' mass media messages and to publicly express alternative conspiracy theories that compete with the truth claims of official experts, politicians, journalists and scientists. On the Internet, then, there is ample space for citizens to post, share, modify and appropriate conspiracy theories via Facebook, Instagram, Twitter and other digital platforms.

In conclusion, in this section on media and transmission, we aim to give an overview and analysis of the academic literature on media and conspiracy theories. Guided by the main assumption that conspiracy theories are deeply mediatised, all chapters deal, in one way or another, with conspiracy theories *as/in* media texts and their historical and multi-modal transmission *through* media. Although the chapters are essentially discussing the literature in a particular domain, this field is still new and developing. This section is therefore not only displaying the state-of-the-art but is also setting the agenda for future research: If we want to better understand the nature, meaning, shape and dissemination of conspiracy theories in contemporary Western society, we need to study them as a mediatised phenomenon.

# References

Boltanski, L. (2014) *Mysteries & conspiracies: detective novels, spy stories and the making of modern societies*, Cambridge, UK: Polity Press.
Couldry, N. and Hepp, A. (2017) *The mediated construction of reality*, Cambridge, UK: Wiley Publishers.
Deuze, M. (2012) *Media life*, Cambridge, UK: Polity Press.
Harambam, J. (2017) *'The Truth Is Out There': conspiracy culture in an age of epistemic instability*, thesis, Erasmus University Rotterdam.
Jameson, F. (1991) *Postmodernism, or, the cultural logic of late capitalism*, London: Verso.
Jenkins, H. (2006) *Fans, bloggers and gamers: exploring participatory culture*, New York/London: New York University Press.
Knight, P. (2000) *Conspiracy culture: from Kennedy to 'The X-Files'*, New York, NY: Routledge.
McLuhan, M. (1962) *The Gutenberg Galaxy: the making of typographic man*, London: Routledge & Kegan Paul.
McLuhan, M. (1964) *Understanding media: the extensions of man*, New York, NY: Mentor.
Melley, T. (2000) *Empire of conspiracy: the culture of paranoia in postwar America*, Ithaca, NY: Cornell University Press.
Meyrowitz, J. (1994) 'Medium theory', in D. Crowley and D. Mitchell (eds.) *Communication theory today*, Stanford: Stanford University Press.
Ong, W.J. (1982) *Orality and literacy: the technologizing of the word*, London: Routledge.
Shifman, L. (2014) *Memes in digital culture*, Cambridge, MA: MIT Press.

# 4.1
# RUMOURS, URBAN LEGENDS AND THE VERBAL TRANSMISSION OF CONSPIRACY THEORIES

*Anastasiya Astapova*

### Introduction

Despite the growing number of conspiracy theories on the Internet, their verbal transmission remains significant and topical due to their similarly drastic impact, including violence. Exemplary are, for instance, the so-called 'organ theft legends' still circulating verbally and implying that certain villains plot to kidnap children or adults in order to harvest their organs for the transplantation industry. Many groups have been accused of such acts, and violence has often been the result. One such example is what happened in the Guatemalan village of San Cristobal Verapaz in 1994, when American tourist Diane June Weinstock innocently said hello to a group of local children. Weinstock's only fault was that she did not know about the rumour that circulated all over Guatemala and Central America and motivated the assault of many other Americans who found themselves travelling in the region at that time. According to the rumour, Americans and Israelis came to Guatemalan villages to kidnap Guatemalan children, kill them and harvest their organs for transplantation into wealthy North American children. Enraged by these verbally circulating stories, a mob of Guatemalans assaulted Weinstock, inflicting eight stab wounds, several broken limbs and a fractured skull (Samper 2002: 1–2).

Seemingly local, such a plot is global and centuries old. Most infamously, it manifests in the blood libel legend that has claimed that Jews kill Christian children to add their fresh blood into the ritual food (Dundes 1991). Long before the invention of the Internet and mass media, versions of the legend transmitted orally, resulting in killings of Jews and Roma accused of the presumed crimes. Folklorists still record blood libel stories in contemporary Eastern Europe where Jews used to live, such as Latgalia region in Latvia (Amosova 2013). The circulation of these stories is illustrative of how conspiracy theories often manifest in bits and pieces rather than a full-fledged narrative.

This chapter sets out to trace the evolution of research on the 'word of mouth' as a mode of transmission for conspiracy theories. A thorough understanding of this evolution is instrumental for reassessing the impact of orally spread conspiracist beliefs and for designing new interdisciplinary analytical tools.

# Manifestations of conspiracy theories in verbal communication: Terms and definitions

Traditionally, the fragmented conspiracy theories transmitted orally have been mostly studied by social psychologists, sociologists and folklorists, who have come up with their own specific terminology. Social psychologists and sociologists agreed on the term 'rumour' rather early and unreservedly, while folklorists could hardly concur on a single term, moving between tall tales (Baughman, Holaday 1944), modern tales (Beardsley, Hanke, 1943), modern folk tales (Hobbs 1966), folk legends, belief legends, belief narratives (Dégh 1971), urban belief tales (Cunningham 1979), exemplary stories, apocryphal anecdotes (Campion-Vincent 2018: 15), contemporary legends (Pettitt et al. 1995), urban legends (Brunvand, 2000), etc. Most widely, they used the terms 'urban legends', 'contemporary legends' or simply 'legends'. As a result, a significant amount of research addressed rumours and legends separately, which eventually forced scholars from various disciplines to distinguish between them.

While many scholars argue that the borders between rumour and legend are hazy (Kapferer 1990: 9; Turner 1993: 5; Goldstein 2004: 25; Fine, Ellis 2010: 4), others have come up with two key differences between the genres. One such difference is the complexity of the narrative: A rumour is a short narrative without a particular plot, while an urban legend is longer and has a plot, including introduction, main part and culmination. The other difference is that the definition of the genre depends on the featuring villains: While rumour targets particular protagonists or institutions, legend protagonists are usually anonymous (Smith 1984; Brunvand 2002: xxvii). However, in practice, classifications have not been so simple, as scholars still study what they call 'legends' even when they depict, for instance, particular protagonists or institutions as villains. Since the study of oral rumours or legends shows that the same texts mutate in form and motif from person to person and even from one telling to another within the repertoire of the same person (Smith 1984), scholars have proposed the term 'rumour legend' to avoid the need to distinguish between the phenomena (Cornwell, Hobbs 1992: 609). This, however, has not become widely used.

Despite the differences in understanding the terms, the similarities between them are, perhaps, stronger. What definitions of rumour, legend and conspiracy theory genres have in common is the negative connotation of misinformation, lie, paranoia and even pathology (see the critical overviews of such a tendency in Shibutani 1966: 56–8; 62; Harambam 2017: 10–22; Bergmann 2018: 6). In folklore studies alone, the bias towards the study of legends 'as stories that we know to be untrue, but which the naïve teller does not' runs deep and feeds the vernacular perception that 'legend' and 'false story' are synonyms (Lindahl 2012: 141). Although folklorists have acknowledged that a narrative does not have to be false to qualify as a legend, this formal recognition is not really implemented in practice since folklore studies gravitate to narratives that they almost invariably believe to be false (Oring 2008: 159).

Another aspect uniting the understanding of rumour, legend and other forms of conspiracy theories, is their fluidity and inconsistency. Scholars have long agreed that it is hard to define legends or rumours with the help of their formal features, as they lack them (Dégh 1971: 73). The lack of formal features is, in fact, seen as key to their definition (Smith 1997: 493). A related characteristic of legends and rumours is their complete disregard of consistency and facts, or, as the title of Jan Brunvand's book put it, 'the truth never stands in the way of a good story' (2000). An example could be the conspiracy theory documented by Sona Burstein during the Second World War, when she observed how an American soldier was explaining how Jews avoided recruitment (supposedly, via their connections with the highest politicians, also Jews). When facts and figures were put before him to prove him wrong, his answer was, in effect, 'Yes, and they're getting all the best jobs in the Army' (Burstein 1959: 367). This is one of many examples demonstrating how inconsistent elements contradicting each other may merge into a larger conspiracy theory, in this case, an anti-Jewish one. With every new narrator transmitting the conspiracy theories in multiplicity of their verbal manifestations, they acquire new contradicting details. These peculiarities of rumour transmission were probably the first reason why scholars turned to studying them.

## Transmission of rumours: Observations and experiments before the Second World War

One of the first researchers to turn to the psychology of rumour was Carl Gustav Jung, who observed how each new narrator cultivates rumour by adding the details dictated by his or her unconscious motivations. Jung based his analysis on the case of a 13-year-old girl who was telling malicious rumours about sexual abuse by her male teacher. The girl was retelling a sexual dream about the teacher to her classmates, and, by repetition and transmission, it grew into the larger conspiracy theory about the teacher committing and concealing improper acts. While every new story about the teacher Jung documented had the same fundamentals, various additions and amplifications demonstrated how the rumour grew by each successive narrator adding a bit of his or her unconscious (Jung 1910).

Influenced by Jung, a lot of research followed on the loss and transformation of information taking place during the transmission of rumour and related folk narratives. Folklorists and social psychologists turned to this topic simultaneously and often independently, making different arguments and reaching different conclusions depending on their professional background. In 1920, psychologist Frederic Bartlett published his first work about the transmission of folk narrative using two folktales: one African and one North American Indian. He deliberately chose these unfamiliar and complicated cases, offered them to British subjects and asked them to pass the tales orally in one-to-one communication. The experiment demonstrated how much of the original content is lost during communication, that memory is never accurate and vulnerable to distortion (Bartlett 1920). Later, Bartlett (1958) attributed his experiment to a suggestion given by Norbert Wiener to make use of a folk game he called 'Russian Scandal', also known as 'Chinese Whispers' or 'Broken Telephone' (Cornwell, Hobbs 1992: 610). In his book on political propaganda, Bartlett applied the results of this experiment when theorising about the natural circulation of rumour (Bartlett 1940).

Drawing on the pioneering work of Bartlett, folklorist Walter Anderson continued the experiments on the transmission of legends. He read a little-known legend to three students and asked them to write it down the next day just as they remembered it. Then he asked each one to read it to another student, who would again write it down the next day. This procedure was repeated 12 times. As a result, Anderson obtained three sets of 12 texts each, and the final texts in these series were all totally distorted and contained major discrepancies between them. After a number of such experiments confirmed the initial result, Anderson claimed that normative elements in the text stabilise while each listener synthesises the variants heard from different sources (Anderson 1951; Oriol 2015: 153). The 'multi-conduit hypothesis', formulated by rumour researchers much later, confirmed that the rumour gets transmitted via like-minded individuals that lean towards the conservation of its normative content. Another conclusion the authors of this hypothesis arrived at was that

> there is no way to follow the progress of oral transmission in society. Even those who have attempted to track the route of a single story, that before their very eyes became popular overnight, lost the entangled thread in a labyrinth.
>
> (Dégh, Vázsonyi 1975: 178)

The experiments on the folk narrative transmission and the distortion of communication inspired by Bartlett and Anderson are still repeated, and their modifications show, for instance, that people transmit rumours that produce the strongest emotions, such as disgust. For instance, in one experiment, the rumour about finding a rat in a soda can was more likely to be passed on than other rumours (Heath *et al.* 2001). Whether one calls this the unconscious (see Jung) or the emotional, certain components in rumour effectively motivate a better transmission or they completely change the original text in accordance with one's emotional needs.

While experiment-based research prevailed before the Second World War, after the war started, scholars did not need to design experiments on rumour anymore: Plenty of real-life field materials fostered by bloodshed and economic instability emerged soon enough.

## Rumours in the Second World War: The real-life experiment in the circulation of misinformation

Despite previous scholarly interest in rumours, their purposeful and systematic study was spurred by the Second World War and the preoccupation of politicians with the wide circulation of frenzied misinformation (Bordia, Difonzo 2017: 87). This preoccupation and the desire to control rumours resulted in the spate of rumour clinics instituted at colleges and universities across the U.S.A. The clinics were specialised groups of professors and students who researched the most popular rumours and reported back to the Office of Wartime Information. A seminal formula for rumour popularity was invented based on this real-life fieldwork: $R = I \times A$. According to this formula, the amount of rumour in circulation varies with the importance of the subject (I) and the ambiguity (A) of the evidence. The relation between importance and ambiguity is not additive but multiplicative: If either importance or ambiguity is zero, there is no rumour. Gordon W. Allport and Leo Postman, who came up with the formula, illustrate this relation by arguing that an American citizen, for instance, is not likely to spread rumours concerning the market price for camels in Afghanistan because the subject has no importance for him. Similarly, they say, if one has personally experienced an issue, for instance, breaking a leg, no matter how important the issue is, one will not foster the rumour (Allport, Postman 1947: 502–3). Later, Schachter and Burdick (1955) set up an experiment by which they proved that the same rumour spreads twice as fast in situations of ambiguity and uncertainty. Other experiments showed that rumours do not reduce uncertainty, but may even create it (Bordia, Difonzo 2017: 90).

Moreover, the analysis of thousands of wartime stories indicated that nearly all of them expressed either hostility, fear, hatred, economic bewilderment or a fusion of these (Knapp 1944). Paradigmatic is, for instance, the conspiracy theory of 'Eleanor Clubs', which synthesised numerous rumours in southern states of the U.S.A. in 1943. According to these stories, Eleanor Roosevelt started off a secret spiritual union of black women with the ultimate purpose of rebellion against the existing social order (Odum 1943). The conspiracy theory combined xenophobic sentiments, fear of the superior villain and poverty at the same time. These elements also merged in the conspiracy theories, hinting that U.S. allies were purposefully misusing the aid provided by the U.S.A. Some examples are the tales of Russians using Lend-lease butter to grease their guns, or the British using the aid to purchase nylon stockings and other scarce and luxurious articles in the U.S.A. (Allport, Postman 1947: 512).

The context of the Second World War in which the study of rumours emerged in the U.S.A. predetermined the thematic focus for the research on rumour for many decades. The legacy of the Second World War research was particularly useful for the study of rumours about other dramatic events, for instance, those surrounding the Chernobyl catastrophe (Fialkova 2001), the atomic bombings of Hiroshima and Nagasaki (Miller 1985), the outbreak of A.I.D.S. (Goldstein 2004) and the 9/11 attacks (Marks 2001). Based on the example of rumours about another war, that in Vietnam, scholars showed that ambiguity causing rumours could emerge not only from the lack of news, but also from its abundance. When different information sources in a society with a free and divided press contradict one another, this inevitably adds to the confusion and increases the feelings of anxiety and fear (Rosnow, Fine 1976: 116).

## Post-war research on rumour: Folklorists take over

After the Second World War, social psychologists and sociologists largely lost interest in rumours. Folklore studies, however, took over the research on the verbal transmission of rumours, which, as clarified above, they mostly called 'urban legends' or 'contemporary legends'. As early as the war years, folklorists started to record such stories on the university campuses where they worked (Beardsley, Hankey 1943; Dorson 1958). However, the inception of the systematic study of contemporary legends by folklorists owes to the informal school that developed at the Indiana University folklore department under the supervision of Linda Dégh, who brought together graduate students and scholars interested in the issue.

It was first and foremost the transmission of contemporary legends and the emergence of their multiple versions that continued to capture the attention of folklorists. By that point, the so-called historic-geographic method of folk narrative research had formed and become really influential in folklore studies. The method implied the collection of as many versions of any given narrative as possible, the aim being to observe how its versions differ in various cultural settings and to find the narratives' hypothetical archetype, geographical starting point and historical travelling routes. The method was initially applied to the study of fairy-tales: Folklorists were searching for their multiple versions from all over the world to reconstruct the supposed proto fairy-tale. In a similar vein, contemporary legends with their many versions provided the materials for the further development of the method. This also coincided with the development of scholarly interest in migration and interethnic relations.

The comparison of multiple versions of one legend allows researchers to see how different the meaning they acquire may be, as each new version may mean something new in the given circumstances. The search for an implicit meaning has become a major endeavour for folklorists: They have been deconstructing legends in order to find the moral or secondary message, which supposedly allows concealed sentiments to enter public discussion (Fine, Ellis 2010: 8). Perhaps most baldly, folklorist Alan Dundes searched for the psycho-analytical meaning of contemporary legends. For instance, in his analysis of the Hookman urban legend popular in the U.S.A. (about a killer with a hook for a hand attacking couples in parked cars), Dundes employed Freudian interpretation to claim that the hook embodies a phallic symbol and its amputation projects a symbolic castration. The legend, according to Dundes, epitomises the fears of the first sexual contact as well as the marginalisation of disability in society (Dundes 1971). Swedish folklorist Bengt af Klintberg (1986) added that the Hookman legend projected a conflict between people who follow the rules and norms of society and those who deviate and hence threaten the 'normal' group. Most recurrent, however, has been the discovery of xenophobia in the contemporary legends.

In her book *I Heard It Through the Grapevine: Rumor in African-American Culture* (1993), Patricia Turner examines legends that circulate among African Americans in the U.S.A. about white enmity toward blacks. She argues that there is a congruity between some of these factually false legends and certain more realistic concerns of African Americans based on the historical realities of racism. Following other folklorists, Turner offers a comparative discussion of how similar rumours circulate in both black and white communities, arguing that differences in perceptions on each side of the colour divide are based on differences in cultural and historical circumstances. For instance, The Kentucky Fried Rat legend, in which consumers discover that a piece of their chicken is in fact fried rat, reflects white American anxieties about abandoning traditional family food rituals and eating fast foods. In the African-American community, however, the legends about contaminated foods express anxieties about the owners of K.F.C. being members of the Ku Klux Klan and targeting blacks by putting substances into the chicken, causing sterility (Turner, 1993; Prahlad, 2003: 495).

'Even minor variations can reveal culture specific concerns', as folklorists say (Goldstein 2004: 36), and many more (oftentimes xenophobic) legends are illustrative of this. One example is the organ theft legend described at the beginning of this chapter and known internationally as 'The Kidney Heist'. It is not only in the Guatemalan case that the legend accuses a particular group (Americans and Israelis in the Latin American version) of plotting the organ harvesting. In a German version, this happens to an unfaithful German husband who goes to Istanbul and is seduced by a Turkish woman (Campion-Vincent 1997: 4); in addition to distributing anti-Turkish sentiments, the legend bears a moral condemning infidelity. In Italy, the stories about organ harvesting blame the Roma (Campion-Vincent 1997: 6). In a Spanish version I overheard in 2014 in Zaragoza, organ theft almost happened to a woman in one of the small local Chinese stores. She was looking around the Chinese store with her husband, who, tired of shopping, eventually went out of the store to wait for her outside. As the wife did not come out after a while, he returned to the store to fetch her. He could not find her in the store, and then noticed a ladder leading into the cellar. He found his wife down there, sitting on a chair with her hands tied: There was a Chinese man with a scalpel prepared to cut her kidney out. Along with the story, the narrator expressed his indignation with the expansion of Chinese businesses coinciding with the Spanish financial crisis and the falling incomes of Spanish households. As such, urban legends easily change details and protagonists in order to transmit xenophobic sentiments topical for various localities.

This last example also illustrates how multi-faceted contemporary legends may be, combining xenophobic implicit meanings and critique of the expansion of certain businesses. Some stories, known as mercantile legends, primarily target certain trademarks and inform about the harmful activities of corporations. Such is the legend that emerged in the 1980s, claiming that Procter & Gamble's trademark logo contained satanic symbolism and reflected the evil essence of the trademark. Research sponsored by the company found that the rumours were transmitted primarily through informal communication networks beyond the reach of lawsuits: In small town church newsletters and word-of-mouth conversation (Koenig 1985). The persistence of the Procter & Gamble satanist rumour stories demonstrated the power and pervasiveness of the religious traditionalist communication network (Victor 1990: 65–6).

As the previously cited manifestations of Eleanor Club, K.F.C./Ku Klux Klan and other narratives also demonstrate, many legends would combine mercantile and xenophobic implicit meanings. Certain businesses may be associated with a despised ethnic group. For instance, some versions of the previously mentioned Kentucky Fried Rat legend target the migrant minority owning an exotic (e.g. Chinese) restaurant and allegedly contaminating the food of the majority group on purpose (Campion-Vincent 2018: 21). Similarly, the legend about urine found in Corona beer blames Mexicans for peeing into the drinks designed for Americans (Brunvand 2002: 461–2). A Dutch version of urban legends internationally known as 'Masturbating into food' tells the story of Dutch friends who end up in a hospital after having a kebab in a Turkish restaurant. After examination, the doctor asks if they had oral sex that evening, since sperm of several different men is found in their stomachs. Very soon, according to the legend, the commodity inspection department closes the Turkish restaurant down, having discovered that the garlic sauce they serve contains the semen of seven different men (Meder 2009: 257). Legends of this kind may often serve as a reason for the incipient rejection of certain products and brands associated with particular ethnic groups (Turner 1993: 174–9; Donovan 2007: 67).

As such, contemporary legends are often conservative and chauvinistic: They may epitomise distrust, hostility and hatred towards foreigners, and justify anti-immigration sentiments (Campion-Vincent 2018: 31). The war period research already showed that a rumour not only vents the prejudice, but justifies it as well, 'rationalizes what it relieves' (Allport, Postman 1947: 37). Rumours and legends become a fertile ground for clichés, as people tend to reproduce stereotype-consistent rather than stereotype-inconsistent messages (Kashima 2000). As Timothy Tangherlini argues, the telling of legends is a deeply political act, as legends are deployed to sway others' actions, according to the narrator's own goal (2007: 7–8). The motivation the narrators have in creating and spreading the rumours should not be underestimated, as religious and political leaders have been using rumours and legends to shape people's moods, often based on ideological preconceptions people may already have (Victor 1990: 79).

The ubiquity of seemingly unbelievable legends of different kinds as documented by folklorists raises the question of what makes them so appealing and credible? To answer this question, scholars have paid a lot of attention to the rhetoric of belief in legends, or the way their performers establish their credibility. Elliott Oring (2008) summarised these studies in terms of Aristotle's categories of persuasion: Ethos, logos and pathos, illustrating how these tropes work in the performance of legend. For instance, when using the ethos tropes, narrators of a legend may appeal to the authority of the source, demonstrate how much they risk by uncovering the story, distance themselves from the presumed source of the narrative, perform demonstrative reluctance to believe the story, confess of ignorance of the facts, etc. In addition to the role of belief and credibility, scholars acknowledge the role of sceptics and their disbelief in the spreading and evolution of rumours, finding that far from being squelched by widespread debunking activity, rumour simply regroups and then re-emerges as if it had never been dispensed with (Morin 1970; Suczek 1972; Donovan 2007: 66).

A significant milestone in the explanation of why legends spread has been the discovery of ostension. Borrowed from semiotics and first used in folklore studies by Grider (1984), the idea of ostension was most famously described by Linda Dégh and Andrew Vázsonyi in their analysis of the American Halloween legends about poisoned candies and apples with razors allegedly discovered in the trick-or-treat sacks. Dégh and Vázsonyi showed that people may often perform the legend: Having heard the stories of the apples with razors, they can pretend to have received an apple with a razor and then perform the prank on their friends. As such, not only can facts be turned into narratives but narratives can also be turned into facts (Dégh, Vázsonyi 1983). In addition to the deliberate re-enactment of a legend as a hoax or a practical joke, ostension may manifest in a case when a narrator transforms a rumour into a personal experience story (an act known as proto-ostension), or when pre-existing legends lead to false readings of normal facts, a mistaken interpretation of ordinary events on the basis of narratives in our heads (known as quasi-ostension, or later – confirmation bias) (Dégh, Vázsonyi 1983; Meder 2009: 261–2).

The folklorists' interest in studying the transmission, implicit meaning and credibility of legends has culminated in the contemporary legend conference that was first held at Sheffield University in 1982 and is still held annually, in the newspaper *Foaftale News* (F.O.A.F. is an abbreviation for 'Friend of a friend', usually defining the rumours spread verbally) and in the *Contemporary Legend* journal. As a result, when the interest towards the study of rumour re-emerged in social sciences again in 1990s, folkloristics had a lot to offer. At that point, sociologists, social psychologists and folklorists started an intensive research collaboration on rumour, writing several comprehensive handbooks, monographs and collections of articles together (Fine, Turner 2001; Fine, Ellis 2010; Bordia, Difonzo 2017). This cooperation still continues, even though the scholars' interest has shifted away from the study of verbal rumour to the study of the Web-produced forms of conspiracy theories.

## Conclusion: Word-of-mouth research in the age of the Internet

The research on conspiracy theories transmitted orally first peaked in social psychology research during and immediately after the war. Although the interest in this discipline declined in the post-war period, the study of rumour (mostly called legend now) was taken over by folklorists and then interdisciplinary, by folklore, sociology and social psychology, towards the end of the century. Before the war, these disciplines engaged in research on rumour transmission. Grounded in the war situation, the study of rumour in social psychology often focused on ambiguity and anxiety as the key factors conditioning rumours. In the post-war years, folklorists searched for implicit meanings in what they called legends and often discovered these to be chauvinistic in nature. In addition, folklorists paid a lot of attention to the content and form of the genre, in particular the fluidity of legends and the belief factor defining their transmission. The discovery of ostension has allowed researchers to observe that legends can be transmitted by re-enacting, which bolsters new legendary narratives about such re-enactments.

The 2010s saw a resurgence of research on rumour similar to that of the Second World War, except that this is the analysis of rumours on the Internet, spurred by the phenomena of information warfare, fake news, populism and post-truth (see also Chapters 4.8, 4.9 and 4.10). As a result, the verbally transmitted conspiracy theories are now mostly overlooked by scholarly literature. The takeover by the Internet has shifted scholarly attention away from the fact that conspiracy theories still manifest far beyond the Internet, in text, speech and images, in fiction and non-fiction, in popular and official discourses, mass media and oral communication. Only the observation of conspiracy theories as the combination of these representations, replete with contradictions, inconsistencies and idiosyncrasies (Heathershaw 2012: 612), allows for their comprehensive analysis. Intuitively, scholars have lately noticed this when developing the idea of 'conspiracy talk', implying that this is the recorded public discourse, spoken, written or otherwise expressed, which seeks to discuss or spread conspiracy theories, and that conspiracy theories are not monolithic narratives, but something dynamic and open-ended (Uscinski *et al.* 2017). Interestingly, the direct meaning of the term 'conspiracy talk' also implies the primary verbal nature of conspiracy theories, which gives hope for the rediscovery of verbally transmitted narratives.

After all, for many conspiracy theories, word-of-mouth remains the compelling information source. Social networks (real rather than those on the Web) may sometimes be much more impactful for the transmission of conspiracy theories than the information transmitted via the Internet. Among many others, anti-vaccination conspiracy theories demonstrate how powerful the sway of local word-of-mouth communication remains, as anti-vaccination sentiments tend to group around certain neighbourhoods or schools (such as Waldorf schools or Silicon Valley in the U.S.A.) (Reich 2014). Similarly, different localities may be exemplary of other off-line clusters of rumours, such as those about satanic rituals allegedly practiced by local cult organisations; the stealing of body parts, or the rumours about H.I.V.-infected syringes purposefully left in certain places to spread the disease there (Victor 1990; Heller 2015). As such, the verbal transmission of conspiracy theories is essential for understanding their complexity and for responding to many unanswered questions on their contents, spread, implicit meaning and impact.

# References

Allport, G.W. and Postman, L. (1947) *The psychology of rumor*, New York: H. Holt & Co.
Amosova, S. (2013) '"Poimaiut, ubiut, krov vytiagnut I pribavliaiut eto v matsu": rasskazy o krovavom navete v Latgalii', in S. Amosova (ed.) *Utrachennoe sosedstvo: Evrei v kulturnoi pamiati zhitelei Latgalii: materialy ekspeditsii 2011–2012 gg.*, Moscow: Sefer, The Moscow Center for University Teaching of Jewish Civilization and Jews in Latvia Museum, pp. 191–217.
Anderson, W. (1951) *Ein volkskundliches Experiment*, Helsinki: Suomalainen Tiedeakatemia.
Bartlett, F.C. (1920) 'Some experiments on the reproduction of folk-stories', *Folklore*, 31(1): 30–47.
Bartlett, F.C. (1940) *Political propaganda*, Cambridge: Cambridge University Press.
Bartlett, F.C. (1958) *Thinking: an experimental and social study*, London: George Allen and Unwin.
Baughman, E.W. and Holaday, CA. (1944) 'Tall tales and "sells" from Indiana University students', *Hoosier Folklore Bulletin*, 3(4): 59–71.
Beardsley, R.K. and Hankey, R. (1943) 'A history of the vanishing hitchhiker', *California Folklore Quarterly*, 2(1): 13–25.
Bergmann, E. (2018) *Conspiracy and populism: the politics of misinformation*, Basingstoke/New York: Palgrave Macmillan.
Bordia, P. and Difonzo, N. (2017) 'Psychological motivations in rumor spread: the social impact of rumor and legend', in G.A. Fine, V. Campion-Vincent and C. Heath (eds.) *Rumor mills: the social impact of rumor and legend*, New York: Routledge, pp. 87–102.
Brunvand, J.H. (2000) *The truth never stands in the way of a good story*, Champaign: University of Illinois Press.
Brunvand, J.H. (2002) *Encyclopedia of urban legends*, Santa Barbara: W.W. Norton.
Burstein, S.R. (1959) 'Folklore, rumour and prejudice', *Folklore*, 70(2): 361–81.
Campion-Vincent, V. (1997) 'Organ theft narratives', *Western Folklore*, 56(1): 1–37.
Campion-Vincent, V. (2018) 'Exemplary stories', *Studia Ethnologica Pragensia*, 2: 15–32.
Cornwell, D. and Hobbs, S. (1992) 'Rumour and legend: irregular interactions between social psychology and folkloristics', *Canadian Psychology*, 33(3): 609–13.
Cunningham, K. (1979) 'Hot dog! Another urban belief tale', *Southwest Folklore*, 3: 27–8.
Dégh, L. (1971) 'The "belief legend" in modern society: form, function, and relationship to other genres', in W.D. Hand (ed.) *American folk legend: a symposium*, Los Angeles/London: University of California Press, pp. 55–68.
Dégh, L. and Vázsonyi, A. (1975) 'The hypothesis of multi-conduit transmission in folklore', in L. Dégh (ed.) *Narratives in society: a performance-centered study of narration*, Helsinki: Suomalainen Academia Scientiarum Fennica, pp. 173–212.
Dégh, L. and Vázsonyi, A. (1983) 'Does the word "dog" bite? Ostensive action as means of legend telling', *Journal of Folklore Research*, 20(1): 5–34.
Donovan, P. (2007) 'How idle is idle talk? One hundred years of rumor research', *Diogenes*, 54(1): 59–82.
Dorson, R.M. (1958) *American Folklore*, Chicago: University of Chicago Press.
Dundes, A. (1971) 'On the psychology of legend', in W.D. Hand (ed.) *American folk legend: a symposium*, Los Angeles/London: University of California Press, pp. 21–36.
Dundes, A. (1991) *The blood libel legend: a casebook in anti-semitic folklore*, Madison: University of Wisconsin Press.
Fialkova, L. (2001) 'Chornobyl's folklore: vernacular commentary on nuclear disaster', *Journal of Folklore Research*, 38(3): 181–204.
Fine, G.A. and Ellis, B. (2010) *The global grapevine: why rumors of terrorism, immigration, and trade matter*, Oxford: Oxford University Press.
Fine, G.A. and Turner, P. (2001) *Whispers on the color line: rumor and race in America*, Berkeley: University of California Press.
Goldstein, D.E. (2004) *Once upon a virus: AIDS legends and Vernacular risk perception*, Logan: Utah State University Press.
Grider, S. (1984) 'The Razor Blades in Apples Syndrome', in P. Smith (ed.), *Perspectives on contemporary legends*. Sheffield: Sheffield Academic Press, 128–49.
Harambam, J. (2017) 'The truth is out there': conspiracy culture in an age of epistemic instability, unpublished thesis, Erasmus University of Rotterdam.
Heath, C., Bell, C. and Sternberg, E. (2001) 'Emotional selection in memes: the case of urban legends', *Journal of Personality and Social Psychology*, 81(6): 1028–141.

Heathershaw, J. (2012) 'Of national fathers and Russian elder brothers: conspiracy theories and political ideas in post-Soviet Central Asia', *Russian Review*, 71(4): 610–29.

Heller, J. (2015) 'Rumors and realities: making sense of HIV/AIDS conspiracy narratives and contemporary legends', *American Journal of Public Health*, 105(1): 43–50.

Hobbs, S. (1966) 'The modern folk tales', *Chapbook*, 3(4): 9–11.

Jung, C.G. (1910) 'Ein Beitrag zur Psychologie des Gerichtes', *Zentralblatt für Psychoanalyse (Wiesbaden)*, 11(3): 81–90.

Kapferer, J.-N. (1990) *Rumors: uses, interpretations, and images*, New Brunswick: Transaction Publishers.

Kashima, Y. (2000) 'Maintaining cultural stereotypes in the serial reproduction of narratives', *Personality and Social Psychology Bulletin*, 26(5): 594–604.

Klintberg, B. (1986) *Råttan i pizzan: folksagner i i vår tid*, Stockholm: Norstedt.

Knapp, R.H. (1944) 'A psychology of rumor', *Public Opinion Quarterly*, 8: 22–37.

Koenig, F. (1985) *Rumor in the marketplace: the social psychology of commercial hearsay*, Dover, MA: Auburn House.

Lindahl, C. (2012) 'Legends of hurricane Katrina: the right to be wrong, Survivor-to-Survivor storytelling, and healing', *Journal of American Folklore*, 125(496): 139–76.

Marks, A. (2001) 'From survival tales to attack predictions, rumors fly', *The Christian Science Monitor*, 23 October. Available at: www.csmonitor.com/2001/1023/p2s2-ussc.html. [Accessed 12 August 2019.]

Meder, T. (2009) 'They are among us and they are against us: contemporary horror stories about Muslims and immigrants in the Netherlands', *Western Folklore*, 68(2/3): 257–74.

Miller, D.L. (1985) *Introduction to collective behavior*, Belmont, CA: Wadsworth.

Morin, E. (1970) *Rumor in Orléans*, London: Heinemann.

Odum, H.W. (1943) *Race and rumors of race: challenge to American crisis*, Chapel Hill: University of North Carolina Press.

Oring, E. (2008) 'Legendry and the rhetoric of truth', *Journal of American Folklore*, 121(480): 127–66.

Oriol, C. (2015) 'Walter Anderson's letters to Joan Amades: a study of the collaboration between two contemporary folklorists', *Folklore: Electronic Journal of Folklore*, 62: 139–74.

Pettitt, T., Smith, P. and Simpson, J. (1995) 'Contemporary legend: the debate continues', *Folklore*, 106(1–2): 96–100.

Prahlad, A. (2003) 'Whispers on the color line: rumor and race in America', *American Anthropologist*, 105(2): 411–2.

Reich, J.A. (2014) 'Neoliberal mothering and vaccine refusal: imagined gated communities and the privilege of choice', *Gender & Society*, 28(5): 679–704.

Rosnow, R.L. and Fine, G.A. (1976) *Rumor and gossip: the social psychology of Hearsay*, New York: Elsevier.

Samper, D. (2002) 'Cannibalizing kids: rumor and resistance in Latin America', *Journal of Folklore Research*, 39(1): 1–32.

Schachter, S. and Burdick, H. (1955) 'A field experiment on rumor transmission and distortion', *Journal of Abnormal and Social Psychology*, 50(3): 363–71.

Shibutani, T. (1966) *Improvised news: the sociological study of rumor*, Indianapolis: Bobbs-Merrill.

Smith, P. (1984) 'On the receiving end: when legend becomes rumor', in P. Smith (ed.) *Perspectives on contemporary legend: proceedings of the conference on contemporary legend, Sheffield, July, 1982*, Sheffield, UK: The Center of English Cultural Tradition and Language, pp. 197–215.

Smith, P. (1997) 'Legend, contemporary', in T.A. Green (ed.) *Folklore: an encyclopedia of beliefs, customs, tales, music and art*, Santa Barbara, CA: ABC-Clio, pp. 493–5.

Suczek, B. (1972) 'The curious case of the "death" of Paul McCartney', *Urban Life and Culture*, 1(1): 61–76.

Tangherlini, R.T. (2007) 'Rhetoric, truth, and performance: politics and the interpretation of legends', *Indian Folklore – A Quarterly Newsletter*, 25: 8–11.

Turner, P.A. (1993) *I heard it through the grapevine: rumor in African-American culture*, Los Angeles/London: University of California Press.

Uscinski, J.E., Douglas, K. and Lewandowsky, S. (2017) 'Climate change conspiracy theories', in H. von Storch (ed.) *Oxford Research Encyclopedia of Climate Science*. Available at: https://oxfordre.com/climatescience/view/10.1093/acrefore/9780190228620.001.0001/acrefore-9780190228620-e-328. [Accessed 19 June 2019.]

Victor, J. (1990) 'Satanic cult rumors as contemporary legend', *Western Folklore*, 49(1): 51–81.

# 4.2

# CONSPIRACY THEORISING AND THE HISTORY OF MEDIA IN THE EIGHTEENTH CENTURY

*Andrew McKenzie-McHarg and Claus Oberhauser*[1]

## Introduction

In the first years of the nineteenth century, Johann August Starck, a cleric serving at the ducal court in Darmstadt, anonymously published *Der Triumph der Philosophie im achtzehnten Jahrhunderte* ('The triumph of philosophy in the eighteenth century', 1803). The title of this two-volume work effectively gave expression to its claim to have located the fulcrum around which so many events of the previous century had turned. Yet readers expecting a celebratory account of philosophy's eighteenth-century achievements were quickly disabused of any such preconceptions upon opening the book. On its pages, Starck substituted the venerable term 'philosophy' with the distinctly derogatory 'philosophism'. Although this movement celebrated its triumph by 'bestowing on the eighteenth century the name of the enlightened, philosophical century' (Starck 1803: I, 21), Starck's sympathies lay with the traditional order secured by the prestige of religious and secular authorities. This prestige had been tragically and treacherously undermined by 'philosophism's' intellectual assaults.

If Starck was at pains to document the 'triumph of philosophy – or, rather, philosophism – 'in the eighteenth century', our present perspective reveals this century to have also been a witness to the triumph of conspiracy theory. Such a characterisation is justified not least by the fact that, in portraying 'philosophism' as a grand conspiracy, Starck was in fact elaborating upon an interpretation of the origins of the French Revolution already fleshed out in considerable detail some years earlier by French (ex-)Jesuit Auguste Barruel in his *Mémoires pour servir a l'histoire du Jacobinisme* (1797–1798) and by Scottish scientist John Robison in his *Proofs of a conspiracy* (1797) (see Chapter 5.3 in this volume). Their conspiracy theorising was, however, more than just a response to the French Revolution, not least because it drew upon tropes and expanded upon arguments that had emerged in earlier decades of the eighteenth century. In fact, a frequent claim prevalent in the scholarship identifies the eighteenth century as the century that gave birth to conspiracy theory, or conspiracism, in a form that is recognisable to us today (Wood 1982; Pipes 1997; Butter 2014).

The present chapter submits this claim to closer scrutiny. It feels compelled to do so not least because historians have by no means reached a consensus on whether the eighteenth century genuinely merits this dubious distinction as the birthplace or incubator of conspiracy theory. The point of departure for the following analysis is provided by a stimulating thesis developed by Clifford Siskin and William Warner, two American scholars of eighteenth-century English literature, in their jointly co-edited volume entitled *This is Enlightenment* (2010). The title suggests a reprise of the effort to answer a question that already in 1784 had engaged the mind of Prussian philosopher Immanuel Kant, namely: What is Enlightenment? If the quotation cited above from Starck alleged a (self-)description of the eighteenth century as the 'enlightened ... century', Kant, who curiously enough was a neighbour of Starck's during the latter's tenure at the University of Königsberg in the early 1770s, would have demurred; according to his famous essay, the eighteenth century was not an 'enlightened age' but rather an 'age of Enlightenment'. Siskin and Warner, for their part, advance another characterisation: Not a state of being, nor a process of becoming, but an event. More specifically: 'Enlightenment is an event in the history of mediation' (2010: 1).

The particular form of mediation that Siskin and Warner see as playing a decisive role in this story was made available by the printing press with moveable type. According to their argument, Enlightenment marks the moment when this invention of the fifteenth century finally assumed primacy in determining how European society communicated within itself and thereby reproduced itself; in other words, Enlightenment was the tipping point when the logic of print began to fully permeate and fundamentally restructure society. This view dovetails neatly with the manner in which historian Rudolf Schlögl (2008) has characterised the early modern period (as the period ending in the eighteenth century) as a transitional period in which European society endeavoured to maintain structures built upon face-to-face interaction. By the eighteenth century, print had ceased, however, to merely buttress face-to-face interaction as it played out between spatially proximate subjects and was channelled by convention, ceremony and ritual. Print 'turbo-charged' the possibilities of communication that integrates subjects absent from a specific place and time.

Can the emergence of conspiracy theory be regarded as a corollary of this event? In other words: Did conspiracy theory 'triumph' in the eighteenth century because print media triumphed then also? An affirmative answer would tend to characterise conspiracy theories as a 'media effect'. We are familiar with other kinds of media effects or at least the speculative inferences that link, for example, increased levels of distraction with the Internet, school shootings with violent video games and anorexia with unrealistic ideals of body size and shape disseminated by advertising. If we shift focus to more historical phenomena, we can ask about public opinion (or at least its invocation). Other societies might have had vague intimations of this idea, but, given that its emergence depended upon a notion of the public that in turn 'implied access to the printed word' (Baker 1990: 172), it would seem possible to describe it at least in part as a media effect. How does it look for conspiracy theory?

In this chapter, we wish to examine this question by surveying the different media in which conspiracy theories were generated and in which they circulated. The primary focus will fall on the eighteenth century, but episodes from other centuries will be referenced in order to examine its claim to an exalted status in the annals of conspiracy theory.

## The history of media(tion)

Systematic reflection upon the media and its effects holds a prominent place in much contemporary academic discourse in large part because of attempts to anticipate and assess the risks and rewards associated with the Internet and social media. This holds for the field of conspiracy theory studies, particularly because a popular view identifies digital media as a boon for conspiracy theorising. However, technologies predating the digital age stimulated much of the theorisation of media that continues to inform these discussions. In particular, the effects, both real and potential, of television and radio were operating in the background when the Canadian media theorist Marshall McLuhan framed his accounts of media in the 1960s in terms of transformations wrought by technological innovations (see McDowell 2010 for a concise and insightful account).

Even if McLuhan often eschews linearity in his presentation of this story, essentially it amounts to a stadial model of human history. The stages are marked by the way in which the historical continuum is punctuated by a series of revolutions that refashioned the infrastructure of communication and that, in doing so, fundamentally re-'wired' human consciousness and culture. Thus, McLuhan identified a literate revolution achieved first by the invention of the phonetic alphabet. This revolution induced tribal societies to abandon the traditional forms of organisation now that communication within them was no longer purely oral. McLuhan's sensitivity to the impact of this early revolution was sharpened by the electronic revolution that in his own time was in the process of (re-)valorising oral communication through the media of radio and television. This resurgence of oral and audio-visual communication was expected to return society to a state akin in many ways to tribal society, yet by nullifying the distancing effects of space, the new electronic media would achieve this return in the form of a 'global village' (McLuhan, Powers 1989). In between the literate and the electronic revolution came the printing press with moveable type – an invention that had ushered in the world of print denoted by McLuhan as *The Gutenberg Galaxy* (1962). The heightened awareness that the medium of communication is a historical factor in its own right has percolated down through the academy and merged, for example, with bibliographic studies to yield the 'history of the book', which no longer simply treats books as the material substratum bearing and preserving the imprint of history but, instead, acknowledges that they themselves have been 'a force in history' (Darnton 1979: 2).

A critical appraisal of the conventional conception of history formulated by media theorists might inquire into how deeply and abruptly the technological innovations of writing, printing and electronic transmission inscribe themselves into a culture. Their status as 'revolutions' is diluted when consideration is given to other innovations such as the early nineteenth-century invention of the automated, steam-powered press, which, by industrialising print production marks to some minds a more profound caesura in communicative culture than Gutenberg's craft-based precursor (Johns 1998). As another example, the replacement of parchment by paper in the late medieval period was also fundamentally important. By providing a much more plentiful supply of writing material and by drastically augmenting the amount of information in circulation or available for ready retrieval, this 'paper revolution' enabled princes and their advisors to indulge a penchant for 'data-driven' activities. The endless combinatorics of realities and potentialities took the form of attempts to strategise on the basis of ever-shifting alliances, envision future outcomes, and contemplate hypothetical alternatives. Historian Cornel Zwierlein (2013) has argued that the intersection of this development with the volatile political rivalries existing between late-medieval Italian city states created the conditions under which conspiracy theorising first emerged as a distinct and recognisable activity.

Another objection that can be levelled at the stadial model of media history is that its effort to structure history around successive media technologies tends to attenuate the significance of the simple fact that people did not stop speaking as soon as they started writing, nor did they stop engaging in purely written forms of communication once print media had become available. Of course, McLuhan was alert to this fact, as was his student, the literary scholar Walter J. Ong, who noted how 'in all the wonderful worlds that writing opens, the spoken word still resides and lives' (Ong 1991: 8). Presumably people who have mastered the skill of writing will come to talk differently from those for whom language remains a purely oral phenomenon, but even for the literate it is not clear whether orality is demoted to merely epiphenomenal status. When print is added to the mix, it would seem that layers of oral culture, scribal culture and print culture can become imbricated in myriad ways.

An example of a genre with affiliations to all three media is the sermon. Its potential to serve as a vehicle for the propagation of conspiracy theories is evident from the three sermons with which the New England clergyman Jedidiah Morse in 1798 and 1799 spread disquiet in New England about alleged Illuminati infiltration into the young American republic. Yet, in issuing these jeremiads about the threat to the republic, Morse was clearly reliant upon the print media that had disseminated Barruel's and Robison's conspiracy theories in a manner that not only crossed oceans but also penetrated into Alpine valleys, as is demonstrated by the sermons in which the Capuchin monk Albert Komploier, almost at the same time as Morse, railed against the forces of subversions from the pulpit in Tyrolian towns such as Brixen and Bolzano. Thus, a sermon entitled 'The renewed fall of the angel at the end of the eighteenth century' observed a standardised format: Beginning with a passage from Scripture (on this occasion extracted from the Book of Revelations), the sermon embarked on a tirade against anti-Christian forces that culminates in the denunciation of 'the black fraternity of malicious Jacobins, Illuminati and freethinkers' (Komploier 1802: 408).

These sermons were, like all spoken sermons, events in orality amplified in their impact by their subsequent conversion into print. Yet, print and scribal communication were spliced into their genesis and their reception in other ways. As Michael Warner has noted in his reflections upon the public sphere created by preaching in eighteenth-century America:

> [The] idea of the preacher as a lively speaker is entirely enabled by script. Sermonizing practice ... enfolds many layers of script mediation: it required clergy specially qualified by the learning needed to navigate scriptures, theological literature, note-books, manuscripts, and the self-inscription of memory.
>
> *(Warner 2010: 374)*

Such remarks serve as a reminder that oral, scribal and print culture do not inhabit parallel worlds that never intersect, but that rather their synchronic presence engenders numerous subtle forms of entanglement and hybridisation. This will become obvious by looking at conspiracy theories as they were sustained, first within a number of strands of pre-print culture (namely: rumour, anecdote, correspondence and manuscript) and then by considering the changes they experienced in the wake of print's ascendancy.

## Pre-print culture

(i) *Rumour*: Does a primacy of orality correspond to a media ecology amenable or even conducive to the production and circulation of conspiracy theories? Of course, historians are only in a position to answer such a question if these conspiracy theories, hypothetically disseminated by word of mouth, somehow left a trace in the written record. Early modern efforts at state surveillance, although clearly rudimentary when compared to the comprehensive systems of observation and control installed by later regimes, were, however, sufficient to register and record the rumours whose content was often conspiratorial and even conspiracist in nature.

Inquiries into the relationship between rumours and conspiracy theory have thus far largely been undertaken from perspectives grounded in psychology or political science. The status of rumours in terms of their media profile awaits fuller investigation, yet the current research would seem to justify the presumption of a primary affiliation to oral communication; according to social psychologist Nicholas DiFonzo, 'Conspiracy theories *are heard and told*', and this in turn underpins his assertion that 'conspiracy theories are really a type of rumor' (DiFonzo 2018: 257–8; see also Chapter 4.1 in this volume). The status of a rumour as an unverified and possibly unverifiable claim would seem to reflect properties of oral communication, whose content is by its very nature more evanescent and, as such, not amenable to the same standards of evidence as written communication. The fact that many forms of contemporary social media are characterised by a similar evanescence would help to explain why rumours figure so largely in the contemporary media environment.

Turning our attention to historical contexts, American historian Steven Kaplan has examined what he called the 'Famine plot persuasion in eighteenth-century France' (1982), namely the often rampant suspicion that shortages in flour were artificially and nefariously engineered. This suspicion, which in part was symptomatic of the transition from a subsistence economy to a market one, was generated within a culture in which '[e]veryone depended on rumors and hearsay' (Kaplan 1982: 66). Rumours also fuelled *la Grande Peur* ('The Great Fear') that seized many people throughout France in the summer of 1789. This panic, memorably described by George Lefebvre (1973) in a virtuoso exercise in social history, built upon a long-standing, deeply ingrained wariness of vagrants and brigands by imagining them now as agents of an aggrieved aristocracy seeking vengeance for the humiliations it had suffered in the Revolution. Lefebvre charted how the panic spread like a contagion from town to town, carried both by written missives and word-of-mouth and travelling at an average speed of four kilometres an hour (1973: 155). Even minor details convey a vivid sense of its highly contagious nature. Thus, in the small town of Charlieu, the intense hunger for news led to the demand that an itinerant jeweller by the name of Girolamo Nozeda be fetched from his room at the local inn and forced to give account of what he had heard on his travels:

> He *said* that he had come from Luzy by way of Toulon-sur-Arrous, Charolles and La Clayette; that all the people there were 'in arms'; that in Charolles they had arrested a brigand carrying seven hundred and forty louis, which was perfectly true; that he knew from *hearsay* that in Bourbon-Lancy eighty other brigands had come and forced the population to pay them money, which was false; 'that everywhere people *talk* of nothing but brigands'. At this point, everyone burst out *talking*.
> (Lefebvre 1973: 73 [our italics])

The rumour reverberated and was then amplified by its absorption into print media. As Lefebvre notes: 'In due course [it] would reach the ears of a journalist who would imbue it with new strength by putting it into print'. (Lefebvre 1973: 74).

Although printed media amplified the rumours feeding the Great Fear and intensified the anxieties, the basic dynamic would seem to not differ fundamentally from the dispersion of excited rumours about well-poisoning long before the eighteenth century. Cultural historian Carlo Ginzburg has examined the episode in which, in 1321, such a fear gripped the population of southwest France. According to one anonymous chronicler, it 'was rumoured that Jews were accomplices of the lepers in this crime' (Ginzburg 1991: 35), and on this basis a repression originally targeting lepers soon spilled over into mob violence against Jews. The league of malcontents was completed by references to the 'King of Granada' and the 'Sultan of Babylon'. These figures were assigned roles as masterminds of the plot, though here scribal communication made its presence dimly felt in the postulate of letters through which these representatives of Muslim hostility to Christendom were imagined to instruct the lepers and Jews about the implementation of the nefarious plan.

(ii) *Anecdote*: As a short mini-narrative of dubious veracity and uncertain verifiability, the anecdote has an undeniable proximity to the rumour. And yet the etymology alone hints at contact and contamination with scribal culture. The term originally referred to unpublished writings (and, in a manuscript culture, 'unpublished' meant text that had not been circulated or made available for copying). The example that both defined and spawned the genre had been left behind by Procopius, the sixth-century historian who had dutifully documented the military achievements and architectural splendours of the reign of Emperor Justinian I (527–565), while covertly working on another history, the *Anecdota*, whose lurid contents would inform posterity about the debauchery of the Byzantine court. In writing both the public and the secret history of Justinian's reign, Procopius rehearsed a division of historical accounts that would later assume cardinal significance for conspiracy theory, namely the division between the official version and the behind-the-scenes, unofficial counter-history. Admittedly, the effect of Procopius's dual representation was akin to a delayed detonation; the explosion came over a millennium later with the genre of 'secret histories'. The genre's resonance derived in large part from what might be called a *contrast effect*; the anecdote with its affinity to rumours and, by extension, to oral culture, is imbued with a suggestion of secrecy because of the contrast implied by the general accessibility of printed information. As literary historian Rebecca Bullard has written in her study of the 'secret history' genre in late seventeenth- and early eighteenth-century England:

> Against the clandestine world of backstairs and closet, secret history pits the populist medium of print. While secrets are created in private, passed on through whispers or manuscripts that can be destroyed at a moment's notice, secret historians expose secrets in a printed and therefore highly public form. The medium in which their texts appear is thus central to their iconoclastic political aims.
>
> (Bullard 2009: 6–7)

But do such anecdotes condense in the aggregate into conspiracy theories? The main obstacle would seem to lie in the tendency for anecdotes to remain fragmentary and episodic. With an eye for the telling detail and the colourful character, historian Robert Darnton has shed much light on this literature, which titillates with its claims to peek behind the scenes and thereby reveal politics as 'a scramble for power and a contest of personalities' (Darnton 1996: 154). This view of politics is, however, some way off from the co-ordinated and covert campaigns that a quarter of a century later Barruel, Robison and Starck imagine as animating the actions of the *philosophes* and secret societies. This sense of a planned operation bestows upon their works a narrative coherence that no collection of anecdotes comes close to achieving.

(iii) *Correspondence*: One of the vital functions of written correspondence lies in its ability to traverse distance and thereby convey news and instructions. Historian Andrew Pettegree has argued that human messengers were long preferred as a more trustworthy source of information: 'Our medieval ancestors had a profound suspicion of information that came to them in written form' (Pettegree 2014: 2). And yet such suspicions do not seem to have condensed into the more generalised mistrust characteristic of conspiracy theories. Likewise, the infrastructure that emerged in the early modern period for the long-distance, regular exchange of information and that was public in the sense that its use was no longer restricted to an exclusive elite (Behringer 2003) was also not a source of conspiracy theories – unless one counts Trystero, the shadowy postal system that was reputedly driven underground by the historical Thurn and Taxis system sometime in the eighteenth century, as imagined by Pynchon in *The Crying of Lot 49* (1966).

The post did, however, facilitate the creation of supra-regional networks. Such an epistolary network is imagined and parodied in the *Epistolæ Obscurorum Virorum* (1515–1519), or the

*Dunkelmännerbriefe* as they are known in German. As a satire penned by German humanists with the aim of ridiculing those Dominican clerics who zealously advocated the confiscation of Jewish religious texts, the work represented one episode in the conflict between humanism and scholasticism. The 'network' of 'obscure men' is, however, bound less by conspiratorial aims and more by uncouth ignorance and the crudities of their rude Latin.

Conspiracy did, however, bind the network of correspondents that figures in the grand narratives penned by Barruel and Starck. Moreover, just as the subject matter of anecdotes had taken on an aura of secrecy in a world of print, under certain circumstances a similar *contrast effect* between media could imbue written correspondence with a covert character: It was not that it was per se secret, but that it now appeared so in comparison to print. This effect endured even after the correspondence was subsequently published, as, for example, had occurred with the inclusion of Voltaire's correspondence in the edition of his works produced by Beaumarchais. Thus, Barruel assured his readers that 'proofs shall be drawn from what we may properly term the records of the conspiracy, I mean from their most intimate correspondence, long time *secret* ...' (Barruel 1797: I, 26 [our italics]), while Starck was adamant that 'the great culpability of the so-called philosophers cannot be denied by anyone who has looked into their writings and their *secret* correspondence' (Starck 1803: I, 88 [our italics]).

(iv) *Manuscript*: Even if Umberto Eco transformed the scriptorium of a medieval monastery into the setting for a well-known piece of fiction full of allusions to conspiracist themes and constructs (Eco 1984), it does not seem to have been a site of production for texts that might later be assimilated to the category of conspiracy theories. And yet Eco's novel in its allusions to the monastery's labyrinthine library as a place preserving a copy of an otherwise missing book of Aristotle's *Poetics* also underscores a subversive quality of written communication that could generate conspiracist scenarios even before the arrival of print: Written communication not only possessed the capacity to traverse distances extending far beyond the earshot to which oral communication is limited; it could do so because it had been 'transubstantiated' into a material form that enabled its preservation. Text thus memorialises knowledge and can even suspend it in a latent state, only to then reactivate it when it might no longer be entirely compatible with the prevailing ideologies and legitimations of the civil and religious authorities. This subversive potential was most famously fictionalised in Ray Bradbury's *Fahrenheit 451* (1953).

Long before Bradbury's dystopia novel, the threat posed by text (and not just printed text) had come to full expression in the *Comparatio philosophorum Aristotelis et Platonis* (1458), a manuscript that paints a picture of subversive infiltration in a manner that would justify its characterisation as a conspiracy theory. Its author, George of Trebizond, was born in Crete, yet received his sobriquet because his ancestors hailed from the Trapuzentine Empire (i.e. the Empire of Trebizond), which existed on coastal tracts of land around the Black Sea for a period stretching roughly from the sack of Constantinople by crusading knights in 1204 to the subsequent conquest of the city by the Ottomans in 1456. The westward flight of Greek scholars infused into Western European intellectual discourse a high dose of Platonic philosophy. The *Comparatio* represented an impassioned intervention in the Plato-Aristotle controversy in which fifteenth-century scholars argued about the relative value of these philosophers and the relative degrees to which their philosophies were amenable to Christian doctrine. Trebizond, who championed Aristotle, became convinced that Platonism was a source of pagan heresy, that it had been carried into the inner sanctum of Latin Christianity by the Byzantine neo-paganist George Gemistus Pletho, and that his student, Cardinal Bessarion, aided by a coterie of *Platonici*, were continuing the corrosive work from within (Monfasani 1976: 156–62).

As an example of a conspiracy theory existing only in manuscript form before its conversion into print in a single edition published in Venice in 1523, half a century after Trebizond's death, the *Comparatio* prompts us to ask about eighteenth-century equivalents: Did this century also produce conspiracy theories that only circulated in manuscript form? A positive answer of sorts might be adduced by pointing to a memoire written by Johann Georg Zimmermann and submitted to the Austrian Emperor, Leopold II. Zimmermann, a physician of Swiss origins, had formerly been a respected man of letters with ties to Enlightenment figures. However, his sentiments underwent a profound change in the 1780s so that, by the time news began to arrive of the turmoil engulfing France, Zimmermann could count as one of the most impassioned opponents of Enlightenment and the Revolution that he saw as its issue. His *Memoire* seeks to reveal this connection.

While a written document, the *Memoire* is clearly also an artefact from a society steeped in the effects of print culture. Zimmermann is indignant about the pro-Enlightenment journals and recommends the promotion of opposing journals whose proto-conservative agenda will offset the corrosive effects of the former and steer public opinion in a direction supportive of traditional authority. In fact, an instructive parallel can be drawn by considering the printed pamphlet *Ueber die Gefahr, die den Thronen, den Staaten und dem Christenthume den gänzlichen Verfall drohet, durch das falsche Sistem der heutigen Aufklärer, und die kecken Anmassungen sogenannter Philosophen* ('Concerning the danger that threatens the thrones, the states and Christendom with their complete demise as a result of the false system of today's enlighteners and the impudent presumptions of so-called philosophers', 1791). In this pamphlet, Bavarian theosophist Karl von Eckartshausen advocated a similar policy and, as a 'friend of the princes', adopted a similarly obsequious posture toward the authorities. And yet Eckarthausen published his hortatory petition to the 'dignitaries of the world'. Zimmermann's *Memoire* was, by contrast, not anonymous as Leopold II was informed about his authorship (and even rewarded him for his efforts with a jewelled tobacco case). Yet Zimmermann insisted that the *Memoire* not be published and instead remain as a confidential, hand-written manuscript discreetly reserved for the exclusive instruction and singular edification of the Emperor. The diverging, yet complementary, strategies pursued by Eckartshausen and Zimmermann – anonymity of the author corresponding to the anonymity of print-media readership in the one case; named authorship of a manuscript corresponding to the individual readership of a known patron in the other – are indicative of broader issues that we will return to in the final section devoted to the presence of conspiracy theories in eighteenth-century print culture.

## Print culture

If the written word has a spatial reach and a temporal permanence that sets it apart from the spoken word, the most salient feature of the printed word would seem to be its capacity for replication and, on this basis, broad dissemination. Yet the printing press was not limited to text in the exploitation of this capacity. Working in the wake of the 'visual turn', scholars have become far more attuned to the image as a medium of communication. This alertness to visual communication is evident in recent work that reflects on how conspiracy theories were disseminated via printed images. Thus, in his analysis of the discourse on plots and conspiracies in seventeenth-century England, historian André Krischer has drawn attention to the printed illustrations that often depict conspirators sitting around a table as they deliberate and methodically plan their subversion (Krischer 2012: 119–20). Although Machiavelli gave budding conspirators the advice to never write anything down, lest such material be used as evidence against them if the conspiracy fails (Machiavelli 2003: 409), the presence of paper and writing implements on the table suggests that the advice was not always heeded – and, more generally, hints at the connection to the 'paper revolution' whose importance for both conspiring and conspiracy theorising Zwierlein has emphasised. Historian Christiane Vogel has exhibited a similar sensibility to the visual record in her analysis of the publicity campaign directed against the Jesuit order and culminating in its suppression in 1773 as a pan-European 'media event' (or series of events). Her examination of the 'visualisation of conspiracy theorizing' – thus the heading of a subchapter in her book – details how visual motifs such as the mask suggesting Jesuit duplicity formed part of a recurring symbolic language (Vogel 2006: 191–8; see also Chapter 4.5 in this volume). Clearly, the propaganda effect aimed at by such images was premised on the mass replication and dissemination made possible by the medium of print.

Moving back to the printed text, a survey of different genres uncovers conspiracy theories lurking in surprising locations. Travel literature could accommodate them, as demonstrated by the accounts in which Berlin publicist Friedrich Nicolai between 1783 and 1796 described his journeys into the Catholic territories of the German-speaking lands and which stoked Protestant fears of Catholic, (ex-)Jesuit subversion. Likewise, the lemma of encyclopaedias might give conspiracist interpretations the imprimatur of semi-official, authorised knowledge, as the *Encyclopædia Britannica* effectively did by enriching the supplementary volumes (1802–1803) to the third edition with an entry on the Illuminati that drew substantially upon the works of Barruel and Robison.

In the final section of the article, attention will, however, be limited to three points prompted by a reading of Zimmermann's *Memoire*, a text which, although existing for a long time only as a manuscript, exemplifies in its own way the capacity of print to promote conspiracy theorising.

(i) *Fictionality*: In attempting to understand the secret societies and their corrosive effect upon the old order, Zimmermann seeks guidance from a 'spirited German novel rich in deeply founded truth' (Zimmermann 1995: 21). The talk is of the *Enthüllung des Systems der Weltbürger-Republik* (1786) by Ernst August Anton von Göchhausen, a councillor in Eisenach in the employ of the Duke of Saxe-Weimar. This novel consists of a series of letters, exchanged between members and associates of a military family, which unveil a highly contrived, even if ingenious scenario: The secret societies that devote themselves to propagating Enlightenment are themselves instruments that unknowingly and unwittingly serve the Jesuits in preparing to return Protestant Europe into the fold of the Catholic Church. Göchhausen is adamant in his preface that he is not interested in delivering anecdotes; instead, he wishes to 'lay down history' ('Gechichte werd' ich hinlegen', Göchhausen 1786: viii). And yet it is important to not lose sight of the fact that Göchhausen has chosen a work of fiction, namely an epistolary novel, as the vehicle with which to achieve his (pseudo-)historiographical aim.

Literary theorist Hayden White has noted that '[t]here are many histories that could pass for novels, and many novels that could pass for histories, considered in purely formal ... terms' (White 1978: 121–2). As provocative as White's position is in light of its relativist implications, his work has sensitised its readership to the elements of literary fiction informing and discreetly guiding historiographical prose. And yet attention should also be given to the traffic flowing in the opposite direction: Works of fiction can be 'true' not just in an aesthetic sense but also because they clearly contain factual observations and elements of historical truth. In praising Göchhausen's work for the 'deeply-founded truth' it allegedly contains, Zimmermann exemplifies a relationship to fiction in general and conspiracy fiction in particular that still holds true today. It is only necessary to consider how the popular novels of a contemporary writer such as Dan Brown are consumed by readers not as pure fantasy but rather as novels that tantalise with glimpses of truths about secret history, even if transmitted in the mode of fiction (Önnerfors 2017: 118–19).

Such observations suggest a need to problematise the relationship between conspiracy theory and conspiracy fiction (Zwierlein 2013). In its application to the eighteenth century, this approach would register, for example, how Barruel had rehearsed some of the conspiracist charges levelled at the philosophes in the context of an epistolary novel titled *Les Helviennes* (1781–1788). In these same years, Starck was also employing the form of an epistolary novel to describe the false leads and dead ends that awaited those who were lured into the smoke-and-mirrors world of eighteenth-century German Freemasonry. Although *Saint Nicaise* (1785), as it was titled, did not unfold a narrative of conspiracy, its exposé of the competing Masonic systems provoked heated responses, in large part because readers attributed to the novel the intention and the pretence to reveal bona fide truths about this world. When French Romantic novelist George Sand immersed herself in this world over a half a century later, her sense of purpose was impelled by the conviction that 'the history of these mysteries, I believe, can never be carried out except in the form of a novel' (quoted in Ziolkowski 2013: 105).

(ii) *Secrecy*: In a public sphere whose norms were primarily derived from the medium of print, a *contrast effect* arose that enveloped the communication taking place in other media in an aura of secrecy. This also applied to the conversations or correspondence, either between like-minded authors or between authors and publishers, that preceded and prepared the way for any particular publication. For Zimmermann, this 'invisible' inner side to the medium of print condensed into his fixation upon an alleged secret society called the 'Club de Propaganda'.

The name encapsulates a more general quality of media: While the launch of a new medium might generate an enthusiasm about what it makes accessible and visible, this enthusiasm gives way over the longer or shorter term to an awareness – and even a suspicion – of the invisible, inaccessible rules determining exactly what does become accessible or visible. Such apprehensions are familiar to us at our present juncture in the context of our relationship to the Internet and social media: The effusive talk of connectivity has come to be overshadowed by concerns about the unseen or impenetrable algorithms that prescribe in any specific situation what the next connection will be. The contrast between the visible outer side and the invisible inner side manifested itself in Zimmermann's time in (proto-)conservative anxieties about both the public sphere and the secret societies, which, of course, were conscious in their own way of the contrast effect and which then cultivated the mystique suggested by their secrecy. The strangely interlocked development of the public sphere and the secret societies runs like a leitmotif through the (proto-)conservative, conspiracist commentary of the late eighteenth century and even attains a historiographical dignity in the twentieth century with Koselleck's *Critique and crisis*, which submits its own variation upon this theme by asserting that 'Enlightenment and mystery emerged as historical twins' (Koselleck 1988: 62).

(iii) *Anonymity*: Print enables a dissociation between communication and communicator in a manner that can only be achieved with a considerable investment of effort and a cunning deployment of artifice in the context of oral and scribal culture. As a result, the denizens of eighteenth-century print culture were moved by diverse motivations and constrained by multiple norms in avowing or disavowing authorship. Clearly one of the most powerful incentives for anonymity among the partisans of Enlightenment was the wish to express criticism about state and religious authorities and yet avoid detection and punishment. When Zimmermann, in his *Memoire*, describes 'anonymity as the great shield of the Enlightenment', he alludes to its use as a protective measure. And yet the hope of penetrating the 'shield' and identifying the offender yields to an awareness in the next sentence that there are legions of offenders participating in a culture of anonymity: 'using anonymity, the whole German mob of reviewers perpetrates its premeditated murders publicly yet with equanimity' (Zimmermann 1995: 43). This suggests that the issue for Zimmermann revolved less around pamphlets pitting republican principles against monarchical traditions or confronting orthodox doctrines with heterodox alternatives. The bone of contention was to be found in the role of judge that the reviewers in literary journals were thought to have usurped. They had been emboldened to do so because the anonymity made available by print media opened up options both for honest criticism and for dishonest misrepresentation.

Anonymity, meanwhile, was a characteristic often imputed to public opinion as the hallmark of the critical public sphere that had begun to unfold throughout the eighteenth century. In a recent article, one of the authors of this chapter has illustrated how eighteenth-century discourse tended to imagine public opinion either on the basis of a juridical or a conspiracist model (McKenzie-McHarg 2019). Those subscribing to the juridical model imagined a 'court of public opinion' issuing its infallible judgments. In this situation, anonymity could be made to align with impartiality and impersonality. Yet anonymity also awoke associations with secrecy and the absence of accountability. Characterising anonymity in these terms induced a resort to the alternative, conspiracist model in which public opinion devolved into a product of covert manipulation. In the minds of figures like Barruel and Starck, public opinion had become the Archimedean point at which the conspirators lodged the lever of their new ideas and were thus able to topple the old order (for Barruel, see Hofman 1993). At the same time, their anti-revolutionary conspiracy theories were themselves clearly attempts to influence public opinion.

## Conclusion

The triumph of philosophy – or Enlightenment – that many discerned in the eighteenth century was, according to Starck, a triumph of 'philosophism' achieved by distinctly underhand means. His interpretation has induced us to ask to what degree the eighteenth century was witness also to a triumph of conspiracy theory. We have explored this question on the basis of considerations of media theory and media history: Was the triumph of conspiracy theorising linked to the 'triumph of print' that some scholars have located in this period?

It would have been gratifying to arrive at a finding that declares conspiracy theory in the true sense of the word to only emerge in the wake of print technology, but our survey of sources attests to some kind of presence of conspiracy theories in purely oral or scribal contexts. Of course, one might consider whether rumours insinuating some form of subversion are better treated separately as 'conspiracy rumours'; Katharina Thalmann (2019), for example, dissents from DiFonzo's posited equivalence of conspiracy theory and rumour on the grounds that the former are highly complex, presumably in a manner only feasible on a textual basis. Rather than luring us into the nominalist futilities about what is and what is not a conspiracy theory, such differences should encourage more nuanced descriptions. It is noteworthy that recent German scholarship (Krause *et al.* 2011) that examines the media profile of conspiracy theory resists the temptation of reducing conspiracy theory to a mere 'media effect' of print culture.

The result is that conspiracy theory often seems a peculiarly amorphous object of study. One could more specifically characterise the reason for this amorphousness in terms of *media promiscuity*; as this chapter has demonstrated, conspiracy theories can arise in diverse media. Furthermore, within any one such medium, conspiracy theory exhibits *genre promiscuity*; multiple genres can serve as the vehicle for its dissemination. The unease felt by researchers because of this amorphousness might be best assuaged by a detailed investigation of the difference between pre-print, print and digital conspiracy theories, as attempted recently by Seidler (2016).

This chapter has, however, identified a number of aspects of print culture that add potency to conspiracy theorising within this medial context. Reviewing them in the reverse order to which they were presented, print culture offers scope for anonymous communication. This anonymity has in turn a proximity to both public opinion (as the opinion not of a specific, identifiable person, but rather of a collective) and secrecy, and this melange can suggest an occult control over how and what is communicated in society and ultimately an occult control over society itself. If heightened scope for anonymity is a quality inherent to print, the *contrast effects* discussed in this chapter arise as a result of its difference to older media. Such differences can bestow upon both face-to-face, oral interaction and written correspondence elements of secrecy. Finally, given Zwierlein's characterisation of conspiracy theories as occupying a no-man's land between fact and fiction, a fuller exploration of how this distinction is modulated and modified within print culture could be expected to yield highly relevant insights.

One final point deserves acknowledgment. The early pages of Starck's *Triumph der Philosophie* (1803) reference the paper revolution, the printing press and the westward migration of ancient but forgotten learning, carried in the trunks of Byzantine scholars seeking refuge after the fall of Constantinople. Starck shows himself here to be an astute observer of media phenomena. More fundamentally, the acknowledgment of these phenomena betrays his awareness that the maligned conspiracy had historical preconditions; in other words, the conspirators did not operate outside of history and, in this manner, steer and guide its course. Although a committed conspiracy theorist, Starck does not simply equate all of history with the progressive implementation of a conspiratorial plan. Such an 'absolutist' conspiracy theory has an affinity to the technological determinism that befalls media theory when it imagines technology as a force operating from outside of history. Furthermore, technological determinism mirrors the economic determinism thought to blight Marxist accounts of the rise of capitalism. Critics have elaborated upon these objections by questioning any simplistic dichotomy of technology and culture. As they point out, technologies might influence culture, yet they do so without transcending it; in other words, the distinction between technology and culture is undercut by the way in which technology is itself a part of culture. Such re-assessments have informed recent dissent from Elizabeth Eisenstein's ground-breaking *The Printing Press as an Agent of Change* (1979), a work that discreetly took its cues from McLuhan (see, for example, Johns 1998). In conclusion, we simply note that, regardless of whether we are talking about conspiracy, capital or communication technology, no entity can claim the status of an externality that, by standing outside history and acting inwards, is capable of steering and directing it.

## Note

1 Claus Oberhauser's research was supported by the F.W.F.

## References

Baker, K.M. (1990) *Inventing the French Revolution: essays on French political culture in the eighteenth century*, Cambridge: Cambridge University Press.
Barruel, A. (1797–1798) *Memoirs illustrating the history of Jacobinism*, London: T. Burton and Co.
Behringer, W. (2003) *Im Zeichen des Merkur: Reichspost und Kommunikationsrevolution der Frühen Neuzeit*, Göttingen: Vandenhoeck & Ruprecht.
Bradbury, R. (1953) *Fahrenheit 451*, New York: Ballantine Books.
Bullard, R. (2009) *The politics of disclosure, 1674–1725*, London: Pickering & Chatto.
Butter, M. (2014) *Plots, designs, and schemes: American conspiracy theories from the Puritans to the present*, Berlin: de Gruyter.
Darnton, R. (1979) *The business of enlightenment: a publishing history of the Encyclopédie, 1775–1800*, Cambridge, MA: Harvard University Press.
Darnton, R. (1996) *The forbidden best-sellers of pre-revolutionary France*, New York: Norton.
DiFonzo, N. (2018) 'Conspiracy rumor psychology' in J. Uscinski (ed.) *Conspiracy theories and the people who believe in them*, New York: Oxford University Press, pp. 257–68.

Eckarthausen, C. (1791) *Ueber die Gefahr, die den Thronen, den Staaten und dem Christenthume den gänzlichen Verfall drohet, durch das falsche Sistem der heutigen Aufklärer, und die kecken Anmassungen sogenannter Philosophen*, München.
Eco, U. (1984) *The name of the rose*, Boston: G.K. Hall.
Eisenstein, E. (1979) *The printing press as an agent of change*, Cambridge: Cambridge University Press.
Ginzburg, C. (1991) *Ecstasies: Deciphering the witches' sabbath*, New York: Pantheon Books.
Göchhausen., E.A.A. (1786) *Enthüllung des Systems der Weltbürger-Republik. In Briefen aus der Verlassenschaft eines Freymaurers. Wahrscheinlich manchem Leser um zwanzig Jahre zu spät publizirt*, Rom: Göschen.
Hofman, A. (1993) 'Opinion, illusion, and the illusion of opinion: Barruel's theory of conspiracy', *Eighteenth-Century Studies*, 27(1): 27–60.
Johns, A. (1998) *The nature of the book: print and knowledge in the making*, Chicago: University of Chicago Press.
Kaplan, S. (1982) 'The famine plot persuasion in eighteenth-century France', *Transactions of the American Philosophical Society*, 72(3): 1–79.
Komploier, A. (1802) 'Der am Ende des achtzehnten Jahrhunderts erneuerte Engelsturz', in A. Komploier (ed.) *Des Verfassers der Rede über den Freyheitsbaum, Pater Alberts, Kapuziners [...] sämmtliche Gebeth-, Buß-, Dank-, Siegs- und Ermunterungsreden*, Augsburg: Ignaz Veith und Mich. Rieger, pp. 393–410.
Koselleck, R. (1988) *Critique and crisis: enlightenment and the pathogenesis of modern society*, Cambridge, MA: MIT Press.
Krause, M., Meteling, A. and Stauff, M. (eds.) (2011) *The parallax view: zur Mediologie der Verschwörung*, Munich: Wilhelm Fink.
Krischer, A. (2012) 'Verräter, Verschwörer, Terroristen', in K. Härter and B. de Graaf (eds.) *Vom Majestätsverbrechen zum Terrorismus*, Frankfurt am Main: Vittorio Klostermann, pp. 103–60.
Lefebvre, G. (1973) *The great fear of 1789, rural panic in revolutionary France*, London: NLB.
Machiavelli, N. (1517) *The discourses*, reprint, London: Penguin, 2003.
McDowell, P. (2010) 'Mediating media past and present: towards a genealogy of "print culture" and "oral tradition"', in C. Siskin and W. Warner (eds.) *This is enlightenment*, Chicago: University of Chicago Press, pp. 229–46.
McKenzie-McHarg, A. (2019) 'Anonymity and ideology: when defenders of church and state opt for anonymity', *Publications of the English Goethe Society*, 88(3): 162–183.
McLuhan, M. (1962) *The Gutenberg Galaxy: the making of typographic man*, London: Routledge & Kegan Paul.
McLuhan, M. and Powers, B. (1989) *The global village: transformations in world life and media in the 21st century*, New York: Oxford University Press.
Monfasani, J. (1976) *George of Trebizond: a biography and a study of his rhetoric and logic*, Leiden: Brill.
Ong, W.J. (1991) *Orality and literacy: the technologizing of the word*, London: Routledge.
Önnerfors, A. (2017) *Freemasonry – a very short introduction*, Oxford: Oxford University Press.
Pettegree, A. (2014) *The invention of news: how the world came to know about itself*, New Haven: Yale University Press.
Pipes, D. (1997) *Conspiracy: how the paranoid style flourishes and where it comes from*, New York: Free Press.
Pynchon, T. (1966) *The crying of lot 49*, Philadelphia: J.B. Lippincott & Co.
Robison, J. (1797) *Proofs of a conspiracy against all the religions and governments of Europe, carried on in the secret meetings of Freemasons, Illuminati and reading societies: collected from good authorities*, Edinburgh: W. Creech, T. Cadell and W. Davies.
Schlögl, R. (2008) 'Kommunikation und Vergesellschaftung unter Anwesenden: Formen des Sozialen und ihre Transformation in der Frühen Neuzeit', *Geschichte und Gesellschaft*, 34(2): 155–224.
Seidler, J.D. (2016) *Die Verschwörung der Massenmedien: eine Kulturgeschichte vom Buchhändler-Komplott bis zur Lügenpresse*, Bielefeld: transcript-Verlag.
Siskin, C. and Warner, W. (eds.) (2010) *This is enlightenment*, Chicago: University of Chicago Press.
Starck, J.A. (1803) *Der Triumph der Philosophie im 18. Jahrhunderte*, 2 vol., Germantown [i.e. Frankfurt am Main]: Rosenblatt [i.e. Hermann].
Thalmann, K. (2019) *The stigmatization of conspiracy theory since the 1950s: 'A Plot to Make us Look Foolish'*, London: Routledge.
Vogel, C. (2006) *Der Untergang der Gesellschaft Jesu als europäisches Medienereignis (1758–1773): publizistische Debatten im Spannungsfeld von Aufklärung und Gegenaufklärung*, Mainz: Von Zabern.
Warner, M. (2010) 'The preacher's footing', in C. Siskin and W. Warner (eds.) *This Is Enlightenment*, Chicago: University of Chicago Press, pp. 368–83.
White, H. (1978) *Tropics of discourse: essays in cultural criticism*, Baltimore: Johns Hopkins University Press.

Wood, G.S. (1982) 'Conspiracy and the paranoid style: causality and deceit in the eighteenth century', *The William and Mary Quarterly*, 39: 401–41.

Zimmermann, J.G. (1995) *Memoire an seine kaiserlichkönigliche Majestät Leopold den Zweiten über den Wahnwitz unsers Zeitalters und die Mordbrenner, welche Deutschland und ganz Europa aufklären wollen*, ed. C. Weiss, St. Ingbert: Röhrig.

Ziolkowski, T. (2013) *Lure of the arcane: the literature of cult and conspiracy*, Baltimore: Johns Hopkins University Press.

Zwierlein, C. (2013) 'Security politics and conspiracy theories in the emerging European state system (15th/16th c.)', in C. Zwierlein and B. de Graaf (eds.) *Security and Conspiracy in History*, a special issue of *Historical Social Research*, 38: 65–95.

# 4.3
# GENRES OF CONSPIRACY IN NINETEENTH-CENTURY BRITISH WRITING

*Ben Carver*

## Introduction

In Dan Brown's Robert Langdon series, the pretext of the narrative action (of detection and pursuit) is the existence of secret societies that have persisted through history along a timeline that connects the twenty-first century literature to the European Renaissance and begins much earlier. To understand the possibility of a novel of this kind, which engages a modern historian-detective to demystify ancient conspiracy, requires an explanation of the scientific, print and political culture of the nineteenth century, whose narrative formations enabled the transmission of stories that articulated infiltration, detection and anxiety.

Genres that remain familiar to us today were established in the Europe in the nineteenth century: Detective, espionage and invasion stories and novels. The national focus of this chapter is on British literature and how the threat of conspiracy, imagined in popular fiction, depended on an idea of nationhood that was opposed by plots that threatened it from beyond its borders or by enemies at home, who served other interests and political programmes. Likewise, while conspiracy fiction evolved in relation to genres of popular fiction with distinct narrative features, the allure of conspiracy as a literary formula lay also in its mobility – the fact that it might not be restricted to the generic conventions within whose bounds it acquired intelligible and marketable narrative form. The transmission of conspiracy narratives required a developed and orderly system of print publication, whose success depended on recognition of these narrative conventions in their niches of the popular press. Arthur Conan Doyle's Sherlock stories could be found in the *Strand Magazine* for instance; if the reader was interested in future-oriented romances of the technological imagination, she might turn to *Pearson's Weekly* (among others). Narratives of conspiracy needed, however, to suggest the possibility of infiltration into and out of these literary enclaves, between life and fiction. Conspiracy was a creeping danger that could permeate the political order at large just as it did this well regulated print environment. The conspiracist imagination involved engaging – even if in the modes of generic fiction – the frisson of social paranoia.

This necessarily brief overview identifies the tropes and generic conventions in nineteenth-century fiction that gave rise to what can now be glossed as 'conspiracy fiction' – a retrospective term. Several of the figures that have entered the lexicon of conspiracy culture depended on technological conditions and political ideas of their time, for instance the political anarchist armed with dynamite operating in newly built sewage tunnels. The emplotment of the figure of conspiracy in narrative form, however, established literary tropes that persisted in conspiracy fiction much later. Thomas Pynchon's *The Crying of Lot 49* (1966) was not the first narrative to conflate conspiracies with postal networks and enemies conspiring to invade. It inherited motifs from late nineteenth-century British invasion fiction. Ironic, self-aware conspiracy theories are not new either: About 200 years ago, Richard Whately claimed that Napoleon was an entirely fictitious character and that Moscow had never burned down.

To attempt a list of nineteenth-century conspiracy fiction would present impossible boundary problems. Studying the transmission of figures and theories of conspiracy in the genre fiction of the nineteenth century is nonetheless valuable, for it illustrates how historical contexts informed conspiracist interpretations of dangers, which then acquired narrative forms in the rapidly changing print media by which they were transmitted to an expanding reading public. I focus here on two generic clusters: Narratives of invasion (which prepared the ground for espionage fiction) and detective stories (which inherited material from sensation novels).

## Conspiracy and suspicion in the nineteenth century

The meaning of 'conspiracy' changed in the nineteenth century. Albert Pionke informs our understanding of the term's usage in his analysis of the use of conspiracy as a legally effective term that government institutions in the Victorian period could resort to in order to discredit and prosecute dissident political movements (2004). This understanding of conspiracy as a legal concept and instrument for the consolidation of political constituencies echoes the first wave of conspiracy studies, for instance Richard Hofstadter's essay on 'The Paranoid Style of American Politics' (1966 [1964]), which referred to the circulation of conspiracist beliefs in nineteenth-century American history, and David Brion Davis's thematic studies of political conspiracy theories (Hofstadter 1966; Davis 1969, 1972).

More recent examination of conspiracy in the nineteenth century has paid attention to its figuration in the fiction of the period. Theodore Ziolkowski surveys the persistence of secret society novels in the nineteenth century (2013). Alex J. Beringer studies the figure of conspiracy in American literature and is alert to its creative capacity to organise anxieties into narrative form. In the works he studies from the *fin de siècle*, 'the term "conspiracy" did not simply describe a crime but became a vehicle through which dark suspicions about modernization and industrialization were channelled into exhilarating sensations of romance and mystery' (2012: 37). Adrian Wisnicki narrows the focus in his monograph on *Conspiracy, Revolution, and Terrorism from Victorian Fiction to the Modern Novel* to 'the conspiracy theory narrative', which is to say narratives that feature conspiracy theorising, whether as an expression of an emergent 'desire to know' (operative in Dickens, for instance) or to satirise a type of social anxiety (in G.K. Chesterton's *The Man who was Thursday*). This desire appeared as a diagnosable illness in the emergent science of psychology and as the formalisation of anxieties about dangers from abroad (Wisnicki 2008).

Luc Boltanski notices the contemporaneity, in the late nineteenth century, of detective fiction with the first instances of 'paranoia' as a psychiatric condition defined by Emil Kraepelin in 1899 and observes that '[t]he investigator in a detective story thus acts like a person with paranoia, the difference being that he is healthy' (2014: 15). Much earlier and without this diagnostic terminology, Edgar Allan Poe wove into his 'little stalking narrative' (Rachman 1997: 656) a type of illness whose symptoms are nervousness and hyper-observation. The narrator of Poe's 'The Man of the Crowd' (1840) describes himself as recovering from illness, 'in one of those happy moods ..., when the film from the mental vision departs ... and the intellect, electrified, surpasses as greatly its everyday condition' (2008: 84). He becomes so compulsively fascinated by one man in particular that he follows him through the city for an entire night and day. The 'paranoid' narrator is both a proto-detective, and a proto-conspiracy theorist, in the way he fabulates various criminal lives of his subject before giving up and reflecting on the resistance of some mysteries to penetration. Eugene Sue also explored the criminal underground of Paris in the 1840s, in *Les Mystères de Paris* (1842–1843), in which detection is again a pretext for plots that involve the mysteries of social mobility in the modern, impenetrable city.

The earlier elements of the conspiracist imagination find their way into other genres in our own contemporary culture, which seems appropriate for a complex of ideas to which infiltration is such a crucial mode of transmission. In Simon Sellars's recent novel of academic failure and readerly derangement, the narrator 'Simon Sellars' is unravelling (in both senses) the psychopathologies that traverse the boundaries of his own and the world's mental health in a doomed doctoral thesis on J.G. Ballard:

> My mission was to track what I considered to be Ballard's transdisciplinary mutant word virus, a mysterious code that could not be readily distilled into biography or literary theory. I wanted to analyse how that virus absorbs other cultural forces and the way other cultural forces absorb it and, in so doing, to arrive at a preliminary understanding of the dark forces that shape our lives.
>
> *(2018: 289)*

Sellars's book is a case study in contemporary anxiety and provides a model for thinking about the transmission of conspiracy-mindedness across literary genres of the nineteenth century. 'Trans-disciplinary word virus' is an excellent description of how conspiracy, thought of as a narrative arrangement of material, moved in the nineteenth century (and still does) through and across media environments, dropping hints of insidious plots that might just be real and inviting a readership to adopt a suspicious perspective, tuned to alertness and a distrust of surface appearances.

Luc Boltanski argues for a connection between the modern academic disciplines and nineteenth-century genre fiction, and links detective and espionage fiction to how sociology 'challenges *apparent* reality and seeks to reach a reality that is more hidden, more profound and more *real*' (2014: 30). His is one of several arguments that the emergence of conspiracies corresponds to the rise of modern societies (see also Koselleck 1988). Rita Felski diagnoses literary and critical theory's determination to penetrate false appearances as the institutionalisation of suspicion in academic practices; of particular influence has been the engagement of literary critics (new historicists especially) with nineteenth-century literature, notably the realist novel, which is 'charged with fraudulence and fabrication, with masking social contradictions by pulling the wool over the reader's eyes' (2015: 95). In these various ways, the nineteenth century produced the modern, suspicious reader.

## The spectre of invasion

Narratives of invasion conspiracies in the late-century looked suspiciously across the channel to Britain's European neighbours and remembered the prospect of invasion from earlier in the century. Napoleon Bonaparte's military adventures in continental Europe were hardly secretive or conspiratorial, but the fact that his troops never landed on British soil meant that his presence in the public imagination was volatile and malleable into exaggerated narratives. As Linda Colley writes, Napoleon was a spectral figure to the British and provided 'a chance for fantasy and wishful thinking, an opportunity for drama' (1994: 308). The French *émigré* population in the southeast of England mounted a personalised print campaign against him, amplifying and inventing a litany of his monstrous crimes into what is referred to as the 'Black Legend' (Semmel 2000). Natalie Petiteau's summary of the character attributed to him is telling, for it prefigures Richard Hofstadter's characterisation of the arch-conspirator. Napoleon was said to be 'a deserter, superstitious without Christian faith, violent, cynical, ambitious, unprincipled, puerile, cruel, sadistic, coarse, a charlatan without spirit, jealous, ingrate, unstable, untrustworthy' (Petiteau 1999: 32, my translation); Hofstadter's notional enemy of the people was, similarly, thought of as 'a perfect model of malice, a kind of amoral superman: sinister, ubiquitous, powerful, cruel, sensual, luxury-loving' (Hofstadter 1966: 32). The Napoleonic danger was painted in much the same anti-monarchical brush-strokes that had been applied earlier to secret societies and are repeated today when a political group is to be smeared as morally degenerate (Önnerfors 2018). Infiltration was also thought to be already underway, with French agents placed to assist an attack and an English radical faction that would welcome the new political order. The coordination of these narrative elements of foreign military threat and domestic subversion were assembled later in the century into the popular format of future war or (invasion) fiction.

Invasion fiction flourished between very precise dates in the late nineteenth and early twentieth centuries. Despite a few precursors and a revival of the genre after the First World War, its major phase began in 1871 with George T. Chesney's story 'The Battle of Dorking' and came to an end when the outbreak of war in 1914 made its prophecies temporarily redundant. It would be a stretch to describe Chesney's story as a conspiracy theory; he was responding to the Prussian army's recent decisive victory over the French army and used the format (an account of successful invasion in the near future) to draw attention from this future perspective to bear on what he saw as Britain's military and cultural complacency: 'For us in England it came too late. And yet we have plenty of warnings, if we had only made use of them' (1871: 532). Even so, Chesney adopted the distinctive time-stamp of the conspiracy narrative, which Hofstadter summarises when he writes that the conspiracy theorist is always convinced that 'he lives at a turning point' (1966: 30). The conspiracy theory consistently calls for measures to be taken in the present to counteract forces that, while still latent, threaten the immediate future of the social order – or, in the case of invasion fiction, the nation-state.

The story provoked so much discussion that its formula was rapidly copied and taken up in following years (see Clarke 1992). The incorporation of the format into serial publication in the 'new journalism' of the period deserves particular attention. Here, its narratives were aligned with the serial rhythms of publications such as the *Daily Mail* and *Pearson's Weekly*, where the presentation of the invasion fiction copied the format of news reportage. Much like its contemporary utopian (and dystopian) fiction, this genre was news from the near-future and its formulaic qualities (Matin 2011: 804) only served to underscore the plausibility of the danger in readers' minds. One example was *The Invasion of 1910* (1906), a tale of German invasion published in the *Daily Mail*. Its author, William Le Queux, cultivated the belief that he did, in fact, have intelligence of German military plans, which by disseminating in the *guise* of a fictional narrative, he effectively pre-empted (Sladen 1938: 136). A similar conceit is presented in the preface of the better known novel by Erskine Childers, *The Riddle of the Sands* (1903), in which the trappings of entertaining fiction are said to be deployed in order to alert as wide a readership as possible to the real threat of German invasion (2009 [1903]: xiii–ix).[1] The conspiracist nature of invasion fiction lies not only in the existence of hostile plotters, but in the genre's implied or explicit claims to be a realistic description of an imminent, if still-latent, danger that the government could only struggle to rebut. How do you prove a negative, once it has taken hold and offers the allure of dissident belief? John Attridge says of espionage fiction that it 'titillates a hidden counterhistory of public events' (Attridge 2013: 132). The conspiracy theory, likewise, combines popular culture with historical revisionism.

An engineering project that prompted conspiracist thinking was the proposal in 1882 of a tunnel to be built under the channel, linking England and France. The project became the subject of a spate of invasion novels that took this vulnerability as their pretext, several of which imagined that many of the French *emigrés* living in southeast England (the enemy within) would collaborate with their compatriots. These anxieties were not restricted to popular fiction: James Knowles, editor of the *Nineteenth Century*, petitioned against the tunnel in 1882 citing security risks. Signatories to his letter included Robert Browning, Alfred Tennyson, T.H. Huxley, Cardinal Newman, Herbert Spencer, the Archbishop of Canterbury, several journal editors, five dukes, ten earls, 26 M.P.s, 17 admirals, 59 generals and many more (Clarke 1992: 96). There was no such panic in France, so these scenarios probably reflected then (as now) an island mentality to free movement of people, who were supposed to be in some kind of hostile collaboration against British interests.

The principal enemies of Britain in these narratives published between 1871 and 1914 were the Prussians, then France and Russia, then Germany, the Ottoman Turks and, in some cases, China. Some invasion fictions adopted a more global perspective and used the format to make claims about the security of the Empire as a whole. M.P. Shiel's unpleasant novel, *The Yellow Danger* (1898), was one such narrative, which imagined a malevolent Chinese plot to bring down the British Empire. Consistent with Victorian race characterisation, the Chinese strategy is underhand and manipulative, and more effective even than the British concerns of 'a conspiracy of the three great Continental Powers to oust England from predominance in the East' (Shiel 1898: 2). The destruction of the West is achieved by orchestrating the antagonism of the European powers: Ceding Chinese territories to France and offering control of the protectorate of the Yangtse River (traditionally a British power base) to Russia. China then strikes an economic blow by defaulting on its debts to England. In this complex, racist novel, the central villain who executes these plans is portrayed as a miscegenated cosmopolitan (despite Shiel's own creole identity) with 'a brown, and dark, and specially dirty shade in the yellow tan of his skin' (Shiel: 4). It is precisely his fluency in the ways of the West (after an education in Germany and professional experience in America) that makes him so dangerous. 'No European could be more familiar with the minutiae of Western civilization' (Shiel: 5). The consequences of globalisation generated the idea of a threat that Britain was insufficiently alert to, an anxiety that was in keeping with late-century concerns that world power would soon be ceded by the Anglo-Saxon powers (Bell 2011). In its imagination of foreign danger as a coordinated plan for racial replacement, the invasion fiction resembled conspiracy theories of the present day.

Yumna Siddiqi is one of the few literary critics to consider the imperial dimension of domestic crime fiction in Britain. She reads the (proto-)detective and espionage stories of Wilkie Collins, Arthur Conan Doyle and John Buchan as indicative of doubts regarding the security of the imperial project, pointing out for instance that around 12 of the Sherlock Holmes stories, while set in England, narrate the consequences of crimes or mysteries that have been committed 'in the extra-national space of Empire' (2008: 40). Detective fiction requires a pre-history; its invitation to the reader is to solve 'the problem of the omitted beginning' (Bloch 1996: 51). That beginning must be outside the narrative frame, and in an imperial framework may even be outside a national setting. Stephen Arata's study of *Fictions of Loss in the Victorian* Fin de Siècle (1996) was influential for its placement of apparently diverse genres – late gothic, detective, espionage – in the same late-imperial frame. Invasion fiction, like detective fiction, requires a pre-history, and one that is geographically, politically remote. Like the conspiracy theory, it reverses the chronology of the detective story in its anticipation of a crime not yet committed.

The print context of invasion fiction is underexamined and informs the transmission of the genre as well as its relation to the idea of conspiracy. Many of these stories were serialised in weekly and daily publications. Cyril Arthur Pearson and Alfred Harmsworth both successfully adopted and adapted the formula early in their careers, employing authors who were also journalists (for instance George Griffith, William Le Queux, M.P. Shiel, Louis Tracy). They presented the threat of invasion as a foreign conspiracy and made espionage crucial to their narrative elaboration, and also established journalists and editors *in* the stories as professionals who were ideally placed to detect invasion plots. This is particularly evident in *The Spies of the Wight* (1899), a novel by Francis Edward Grainger and published under the pen name Headon Hill in the weekly *Black and White* magazine. In the opening chapter, the journalist Monckton is summoned to receive his assignment (to surveil the treacherous Baron Von Holtzman). His editor, Wreford, is equipped through his web of connections across the worlds of international politics, finance and the criminal underworld to root out and expose Britain's enemies amid the sublime complexities of modern life. Monckton reflects:

> I never knew quite how he gained and retained touch with every social and international undercurrent; but whether it was the first whispering of a Continental imbroglio that had to be caught and sifted, or a new grouping of City financiers that had to be dissected, he somehow and somewhere managed to get his information. Numberless were the sensations which he served up to an expectant world.
>
> *(1899: 10–11)*

Some looked back at the First World War and attributed responsibility in part to the jingoistic journalism of the *fin de siècle*. Assessing the causes of the First World War in the 1930s, Caroline Playne identified the Harmsworth press in particular for the feverish inflation of the threat of other European powers and 'the creation and nurture of the mental folly and nervous fears which helped set the world on fire in 1914' (1928: 112). Holbrook Jackson referred to the pre-war period's 'strangely inorganic patriotism' in 1913 (1976: 54) – a phrase that catches equally well our contemporary anxieties that patriotism is instrumentalised in media as an affective foundation for conspiracy beliefs about infiltration from abroad. Comparable claims about the distorting power of journalism had been made before: Suggestions regarding the effects of overheated writing on suggestible audiences went back to at least the 1820s, for instance in Henry Stebbing's (unsigned) description of the modern press in the *Athenæum* as 'one of the most extensively mischievous engines that can be placed in the hands of the shallow thinker, the mercenary speculator, or the *false theorist*' (1828: 273, emphasis added).

The language describes current opinions of the Internet as a breeding ground for conspiracy beliefs. It is only a little surprising, then, to encounter a conspiracy theory from the early nineteenth century that is just as outlandish as contemporary claims that there has been a cover-up to conceal the facts that the Earth is flat or that Greenland does not exist. Richard Whately, a polymath and later Archbishop of Dublin, responded to the unreality of Napoleonic representation in the British press (and the extraordinary drama of his career) to argue in 1819 that he could only be an invention of British editors, dreamed up to sell newspapers. Like a denier of the moon landings, he itemises the many unrealities of his reported exploits (for instance, the absurdly dramatic story of his escape from Elba and whirlwind recapture of most of Europe in the 100 days prior to Waterloo), and blames general credulity on that fact that '[m]ost persons would refer to the *newspapers* as the authority from which their knowledge on the subject was derived' (1852: 15, original emphasis). He even reports a first-hand account of Moscow intact long after it was meant to have burned down.

Whately's argument is in fact ironic, intended both as a satire upon David Hume's argument against the historical truth of Jesus' miracles in *An Enquiry Concerning Human Understanding* (1748) and more pointedly against the excesses of British print media (Carver 2017). Its interest in historians of conspiracy culture is therefore in its deployment of humour in the presentation of a conspiracy theory, and as a counterexample to the historical claim that conspiracy narratives circulated first only among credulous readers/listeners, and only later acquired an ironic, playful dimension.

## Networks (of detection)

The modernisation of conspiracy narratives in the nineteenth century can be viewed in light of new technologies that facilitated new networks of association and communication, as well as the detective methods employed to identify them. The rapidity with which dynamite became a dramatic feature in popular fiction of anarchist plotting in the 1860s is a case in point (Wisnicki 2008: 143). To simply observe the rapid adoption of new technology into conspiracist plots is only to get half of the picture, however.

Two genres that introduced conspiracist elements into their narratives were sensation and detective fiction, both of which encouraged readers to recognise the susceptibility of modern communications networks for dissident and criminal activity. E.P. Thompson in *The Making of the English Working Class* draws a rich picture of the reliance of radical association on the anonymity of the postal service and the subterfuge employed in the interception and maintenance of this communications infrastructure (1980). The London Corresponding Society was founded in 1792 with the aim of disseminating progressive pamphlets and allowing dissident groups around Britain to be in contact with each other and the outside world. Thompson is especially sensitive to the attempts by government spies to infiltrate these networks, and the methods of forgery and provocation by which they hyperbolised the coherence and intent of these networks in their written reports.

However real these subversive activities were, the figure of conspiracy that was attached to them was nonetheless the result of writing and at least partly confected description (Thompson 1980: 529). This repeats the creative process by which the exaggerated conspiratorial activities of the Illuminati circulated in written descriptions even after the group had disbanded. (For a detailed discussion of the development of the Illuminati conspiracy theories, see Chapter 4.2.) These societies had demanding writing requirements as conditions of membership and advancement, for instance the extensive reports and confessions that were required of the brethren (Koselleck 1988: 78–9).

The infrastructure of communications was likewise put to use in the plots of narrative fiction, where the potential for uneven distribution of knowledge could be made use of in literature that was realist inasmuch as it was set in a world bearing significant resemblance to the reader's own. The conspiracist character of the plots of invasion, detective and sensation fiction was not *only* the reflection of pressing contemporary anxieties, transmitted through the print culture where the new genre fiction was so successfully published. Conspiracy also served as what Anna Kornbluh, in her discussion of realism and the *Psychic Economies in Victorian Form*, calls a 'structuring metaphor … of the sort uniquely afforded by literature' (2014: 11). Conspiracy articulated the figures of invasion and network and attached itself to contemporary practices of writing. In doing so, it incorporated the infrastructure of modern communications as the basis for establishing the asymmetries of information – secrets and lies – that were and are necessary conditions for the transposition of conspiracy into narrative form.

Letters were a system for conspiracist association that became a structural feature in the criminal plots of novels. The use of letters in sensation fiction, a genre whose distinguishing feature was 'the element of mystery' (Brantlinger 1982: 2), united the excitement of intrigue with epistolary networks. The function of letters in sensation fiction can be revelatory of characters' true intentions, inscribing the separation of surface appearance and hidden reality, the quality that Boltanski (2014) sees as common to detective fiction and sociology. In Wilkie Collins's novel *Armadale* (1864–1866), the criminal intentions of the principal villain (Lydia Gwilt) are only made plain to the reader in the first chapter ('Lurking Mischief') of Book 2, when private correspondence between the two plotters, Lydia Gwilt and Mrs Oldershaw, is 'leaked' to the reader (Collins 1995). As Laura Rotunno notes, letters regularly indicate guilt in sensation fiction, and also serve as exonerating evidence of the falsely accused (2013: 24). Handwriting can also constitute a clue for the detective, as with *Lady Audley's Secret* (1862), in which Robert Audley, a proto-detective, performs early graphological analysis on a letter written by the woman he suspects of criminality.

The effectiveness of Sherlock Holmes's analysis of written communication later in the century continues the apparent consistency of new, scientific methods of detection between criminal science and fiction. 'He is the reader perfectly suited to the late-century innovations. Holmes is an expert in reading the postmark, the length of the telegram, the syntax of the postcard, the weight of the stationery, and the slant of the handwriting' (Rotunno 2013: 121). Holmes's techniques were influential on the developing methods of criminology at the end of the century (Truzzi 1983: 198). Graphology was a science promoted beyond its level of competency, however, and one notorious instance of its application illustrates its role in falsely generating the 'evidence' of a conspiracy and thus enabling a secondary conspiracy of its own.[2] Alphonse Bertillon developed 'anthropometry', which was adopted by the French police prior to fingerprinting as a system for recording and cross-referencing the biometric details of criminals and suspects: Cranial dimensions, relative finger lengths, photographic templates. His apparent success in identifying repeat offenders even though they assumed false identities led to the institution of anthropometric laboratories in several countries in the 1890s and influenced Francis Galton's research into eugenics (Csiszar 2013: 446). His elevation in the Paris Prefecture de Police led to his appearance as an expert graphologist in 1894 and 1899 in the case against Alfred Dreyfus for conspiring to betray France. His evidence assisted the wrongful conviction of Dreyfus, which was overturned in 1906.

The framing of criminality in conspiracist terms in the later nineteenth century had a wider social range than the fear of the urban underclass outbreeding the middle classes (the conspiracist dimension of social Darwinism). The anarchists were dangerous and distinctive because of the social verticality of their organisations. Representations of anarchist conspiracy drew on two axes of mobility: Plots that circulated underground and invisibly in the city's infrastructure, and the enthusiastic commitment to social disorder from within the refined upper classes.

In H.G. Wells's story 'The Stolen Bacillus', published in the *Pall Mall Gazette* in 1894, an anarchist steals what he thinks is a sample of cholera from a bacteriologist, who indulges in a flight of fancy as he holds up the sample to the would-be poisoner of the city:

> Only break such a little tube as this into a supply of drinking-water, say to these minute particles of life that one must needs stain and examine with the highest powers of the microscope even to see, and that one can neither smell nor taste – say to them, 'Go forth, increase and multiply, and replenish the cisterns', and death – mysterious, untraceable death, death swift and terrible, death full of pain and indignity – would be released upon this city, and go hither and thither seeking his victims.
>
> *(1965 [1894]: 196)*

The passage recapitulates so many elements of the conspiracy narrative in this period. There is the anarchist, committed to the violent subversion of society by secretive means. The bacillus is his ideal weapon for it operates along the very same pathways as he does: Underground, through the infrastructure of the modern city, with the purposes of infection and breakdown rather than sanitation and order. Anarchists and Fenians were both making use of dynamite at this time, and of the tunnels beneath the city to undermine their target buildings – a risk that led to the swearing in of sewer workers as Special Constables (Hwang 2013: 168). The anarchist dismisses his fellow terrorists as 'fools, blind fools – to use bombs when this kind of thing is attainable' (Wells 1965: 197). The introduction of infection through the city's waterworks is, effectively, a hack of modern systems intended to optimise urban health, but which also exposes it to risk. The same is true of the anarchist's other methods: He has forged a letter of introduction to gain access to these deadly pathogens and believes himself to be 'a human vector' in the biopolitics of the city, making life an instrument of death (Fifield 2019: 36). With spoiler alerts and apologies, the narrative is cautionary, not catastrophic: The anarchist has stolen a harmless sample, whose only effect is to turn anyone who consumes it – the anarchist – blue.

Representation of terrorist plots in British nineteenth-century fiction involved socially indeterminate figures and association between members of classes normally kept apart. Take Hyacinth Robinson, the hapless protagonist in *The Princess Casamassima* (1885–1886), Henry James's novel of bohemian anarchism in London. Hyacinth is the son of mixed nationalities and reputation: His mother (French, disreputable, volatile) has murdered his supposed father (English, a Lord, also wayward) for breaking off their affair and dies in prison. Orphaned to a seamstress, Hyacinth grows up in poverty but with romantic ideas of his own social value inculcated by his foster parent. His involvement in the plotting begins with a friendship with a musician, through whose connections he enters his trade as a bookbinder, where he encounters French former communards, by whom he is introduced to an assistant chemist, who is an anarchist radical, and then via a retired army captain to the titular princess. The working classes he believes himself willing to sacrifice his life for 'excite his disgust' (James 1987: 160). The ideal anarchist crosses social worlds even if he or she cannot belong properly in any one of them.

In *The Secret Agent* (1907), by Joseph Conrad, the social range is again very broad, moving rapidly between a consulate, the chief of police and a pornographer in east London. Conrad's story from the previous year, 'The Informer' (1906), differs in that its master-conspirator is socially elevated enough to alarm the narrator by having excellent taste but no loyalty to the class for whom such taste is normally a distinction. 'He [...] had the manner of good society, wore a coat and hat like mine, and had pretty near the same taste in cooking. It was too frightful to think of' (Conrad 1974: 76). The authors of sensation novels also arrayed conspiratorial forces of disorder against the comforting stabilities of the class system. In both *Armadale* and *Lady Audley's Secret*, the threats take the form of that socially indeterminate figure of the governess who insinuates her way into relationships above her acknowledged or pretended social status.

Sensation fiction agitated the patrician critics, not least because it seemed a kind of literature that might train suggestible readers to perceive conspiracies all around them. Ignatius Donnelly, one critic argues, wrote *Caesar's Column* (1890) in order to train readers to do exactly this: Discover clues to conspiracies in the real world (Beringer 2012: 53). This paranoid sensitivity was the concern of one reviewer of *Lady Audley's Secret*, who was representative of the pearl-clutching alarm that the genre provoked in the reputable quarterlies:

> The man who shook our hand with a hearty English grasp half an hour ago – the woman whose beauty and grace were the charm of last night, and whose gentle words sent us home better pleased with the world and with ourselves – how exciting to think

that under these pleasing outsides may be concealed some demon in human shape, a Count Fosco or a Lady Audley! He may have assumed all that heartiness to conceal some dark plot against our life or honour, or against the life or honour of one yet dearer: she may have left that gay scene to muffle herself in a thick veil and steal to a midnight meeting with some villainous accomplice.

(Henry Longueville Mansel [unsigned] 1863: 489)

The conspiracy form thus mediated the experiences and perception of fiction and life, and the normalisation of this paranoia occurred in the literary culture of the late nineteenth century, in newly consolidated literary genres that engaged the reader's suspicions, and his or her willingness to become a suspicious reader of genre fiction and of the real world.

## Conclusion

One of the causes that Peter Knight suggests for the proliferation of conspiracy culture in the American 1960s is the recognition of an increasingly interconnected world (2001). The Cold War had divided the world into power blocs; modern telecommunications fed images from all corners of the world map to an ever-expanding audience; Rachel Carson's book, *Silent Spring* (1962), was indicative of an emergent insistence on the world as a single complex system and a mode of scientific discovery that pieced together information from different disciplines into a unified theory – in this way, too, comparable with the conspiracy theory. A recent review of her selected writings quotes her correspondence with a Connecticut doctor, in which she writes: 'Recently some of my thinking on all this has begun to fit together like the pieces of a jigsaw puzzle ... a great light is breaking in my mind' (Crist 2019: 3).

The similarities to a comparable recognition of the world's webbiness in the nineteenth century are striking. As noted above, detective and invasion fiction registered an awareness that imperial systems could enable dangerous and hostile flows back to the seat of empire. These stories were published in the popular press alongside articles that described the daily routines – and the stranger happenings – of foreign lands; local and imperial news passed back and forth by ship and then by telegraph, a communications network that brought its visible technology into the urban centres. Richard Menke refers to Londoners' bemusement at the cables that were 'strung across the rooftops like a tangle of crazy knitting', citing Dickens's observation of the telegraph in *All the Year Round*, that 'its working is secret and bewildering to the average mind' (2008: 163). Dickens's article was published in 1859, the same year as the publication of Darwin's *On the Origin of Species*, which would infer from the geological record and the evidence of existing species that all life was bound together by a network of invisible lines of descent (Carver 2018). Darwin's speculations of entanglement recall Carson's discoveries of human and animal co-dependence, as well as Robert Langdon's sleuthing through the archives of past history.

The idea of foreign conspiracies to invade, absorbed into popular fiction, accustomed readers to plots that traversed countries and continents. Narrative representations of conspiracy have been internationalist since at least the time of secret societies' supposed involvement in the French Revolution, and this habit is now hard-wired into the genre, as with the high-speed journeys between European heritage sites and puzzle-solving in *The Da Vinci Code* (2003). Extreme cases are the Bond and Bourne films, to which a high number of city-breaks is an essential narrative feature. Both franchises lean heavily on the figure of the conspiracy – Spectre and the rogue U.S. intelligence agency respectively. These modern conspiracy thrillers' inheritance of detective and invasion fiction is most apparent in their principal structural difference: Jason Bourne's training makes him the ideal detective of a crime (his own) that has been committed in the past, while James Bond is tireless in his defence of the Western world from an attack that is always about to take place.

The absorption of conspiracy theories into narrative genres in the late nineteenth century – even if a 'conspiracy fiction' genre was yet to come – relied on the infrastructure of this period. Anarchists could make use of scientific discoveries and turn these and the very machinery of the city against itself. Secret association adopted new technologies of communication, which became the fields of detective expertise, a competition between criminals and police in a specialised print environment that cultivated distinctive genres – for example, the *Strand Magazine*'s successful run of Sherlock Holmes stories. Invasion fiction, published alongside news, was able to address readers as if the conspiracy were real, especially when these fictions made use of the realia of reportage. Nineteenth-century representations of conspiracy coalesced into genres that persist today, and did so in the modes of transmission that became available in the infrastructure of the modern city; dreams of infiltration acquired form in the process of their transmission.

## Notes

1 The website of the same name, www.theriddleofthesands.com/, provides a wealth of resources on invasion and espionage fiction in the Victorian and Edwardian period.
2 This is the same ambiguity of conspiracy culture that Thompson identified in radical organisations and their infiltration much earlier.

## References

Arata, S. (1996) *Fictions of loss in the Victorian fin de siècle*, Cambridge: Cambridge University Press.
Attridge, J. (2013) 'Two types of secret agency: Conrad, causation, and popular spy fiction', *Texas Studies in Literature and Language*, 55(2): 125–58.
Bell, D. (2011) *The idea of greater Britain: empire and the future of world order*, Princeton University Press.
Beringer, A.J. (2012) '"Some unsuspected author": Ignatius Donnelly and the conspiracy novel', *Arizona Quarterly: A Journal of American Literature, Culture, and Theory*, 68(4): 35–60.
Bloch, E. (1996) 'A philosophical view of the detective novel', in E. Bloch (ed.) *The utopian function of art and literature: selected essays*, trans. J. Zipes and F. Mecklenburg, Cambridge, MA: MIT Press, pp. 245–64.
Boltanski, L. (2014) *Mysteries and conspiracies: detective stories, spy novels and the making of modern societies*, 1st edn, Cambridge, UK: Polity Press.
Brantlinger, P. (1982) 'What is "sensational" about the "sensation novel"?' *Nineteenth-Century Fiction*, 37(1): 1–28.
Carver, B. (2017) *Alternate histories and nineteenth-century literature: untimely meditations in Britain, France, and America*, 1st edn, New York: Palgrave Macmillan.
Carver, B. (2018) 'An entangled forest: evolution and speculative fiction', *Urbanomic*. Available at: www.urbanomic.com/document/entangled-forest/. [Accessed 19 August 2019.]
Chesney, G.T. (1871) 'The battle of Dorking: reminiscences of a volunteer', *Blackwood's Edinburgh Magazine*, 109(667): 539–72.
Childers, E. (2009) *The riddle of the sands*, London: Atlantic Books.
Clarke, I.F. (1992) *Voices prophesying war: future wars 1763–3749*, 2nd edn, Oxford: Oxford University Press.
Colley, L. (1994) *Britons: forging the nation, 1707–1837*, London: Pimlico.
Collins, W. (1995) *Armadale*, ed. J. Sutherland, London: Penguin.
Conrad, J. (1974) *A set of six*, London: J.M. Dent and Sons Ltd.
Crist, M. (2019) 'A strange blight', *London Review of Books*, 41(11): 3–7.
Csiszar, A. (2013) 'Bibliography as anthropometry: dreaming scientific order at the fin de siècle', *Library Trends*, 62(2): 442–55.
Davis, D.B. (1969) *The slave power conspiracy and the paranoid state*, Baton Rouge: Louisiana State University Press.

Davis, D.B. (1972) *The fear of conspiracy: images of un-American subversion from the revolution to the present*, London: Cornell University Press.
Felski, R. (2015) *The limits of critique*, Chicago: University of Chicago Press.
Fifield, P. (2019) 'On the invisible threat: bacteriologists in fiction and periodical advertisements, 1894–1913', *Journal of Victorian Culture*, 24(1): 33–52.
Hill, H. (pseud.) (1899) *The spies of the wight*, London: C.A. Pearson.
Hofstadter, R. (1966) 'The paranoid style in American politics', in R. Hofstadter (ed.) *The Paranoid Style in American Politics and Other Essays*, London: Jonathan Cape, pp. 3–40.
Hwang, H. (2013) *London's underground spaces: representing the Victorian city, 1840–1915*, Edinburgh: Edinburgh University Press.
Jackson, H. (1976) *The eighteen nineties: a review of art and ideas at the close of the nineteenth century*, new illustrated edn, Hassocks: Harvester Press.
James, H. (1987) *The princess Casamassima*, Harmondsworth: Penguin.
Knight, P. (2001) *Conspiracy culture: from the Kennedy assassination to the X-Files*, London: Routledge.
Kornbluh, A. (2014) *Realizing capital: financial and psychic economies in Victorian form*, 1st edn, New York: Fordham University Press.
Koselleck, R. (1988) *Critique and crisis: enlightenment and the pathogenesis of modern society*, Oxford: Berg.
Le Queux, W. (1906) *The invasion of 1910: with a full account of the siege of London*, London: Eveleigh Nash.
Longueville Mansel, H. (1863) 'Sensation novels', *Quarterly Review*, 113(226): 481–514.
Matin, A.M. (2011) 'The creativity of war planners: armed forces professionals and the pre-1914 British invasion-scare genre', *ELH*, 78(4): 801–31.
Menke, R. (2008) *Telegraphic realism: Victorian fiction and other information systems*, Stanford, CA: Stanford University Press.
Önnerfors, A. (2018) 'Manichaean manipulation: Europe between apocalypse and redemption in the imaginary of the radical right', *Centre for Analysis of the Radical Right*. Available at: www.radicalrightanalysis.com/2018/05/15/manichaean-manipulation-europe-between-apocalypse-and-redemption-in-the-imaginary-of-the-radical-right/. [Accessed 19 August 2019.]
Petiteau, N. (1999) *Napoléon, de la mythologie à l'histoire*, Paris: Seuil.
Pionke, A.D. (2004) *Plots of opportunity: representing conspiracy in Victorian England*, Columbus: Ohio State University Press.
Playne, C.E. (1928) *The pre-war mind in Britain: a historical review*, London: Allen & Unwin.
Poe, E A. (2008) *Selected Tales*, ed. D. van Leer, 2nd edn, Oxford: Oxford University Press.
Rachman, S. (1997) 'Reading cities: devotional seeing in the nineteenth century', *American Literary History*, 9(4): 653–75.
Rotunno, L. (2013) *Postal plots in British fiction, 1840–1898*, New York: Palgrave Macmillan.
Sellars, S. (2018) *Applied ballardianism: memoir from a parallel universe*, Falmouth: Urbanomic Media Ltd.
Semmel, S. (2000) 'British radicals and "legitimacy": Napoleon in the mirror of history', *Past & Present*, 167: 140–75.
Shiel, M.P. (1898) *The yellow danger*, London: Grant Richards. Available at: http://archive.org/details/yellowdanger00shierich. [Accessed 19 August 2019.]
Siddiqi, Y. (2008) *Anxieties of empire and the fiction of intrigue*, Chichester: Columbia University Press.
Sladen, N. St. Barbe (1938) *The real Le Queux: the official biography of William Le Queux*, London: Nicholson & Watson.
Stebbing, H. (1828) 'Unpublished lectures on periodical literature', in J. S. Buckingham (ed.) *Athenæum*, 18, London, UK: William Lewer, pp. 273–5.
Thompson, E.P. (1980) *The making of the English working class*, rev. edn, London: Penguin.
Truzzi, M. (1983) 'Sherlock Holmes: applied social psychologist' in U. Eco and T.A. Sebeok (eds.) *The sign of three: Dupin, Holmes, Peirce*, Bloomington: Indiana University Press, pp. 55–80.
Wells, H.G. (1965) *The complete short stories of H. G. Wells*, London: Ernest Benn Ltd.
Whately, R. (1852) *Historic doubts relative to Napoleon Buonaparte*, 11th edn, London: John W. Parker and Son.
Wisnicki, A.S. (2008) *Conspiracy, revolution, and terrorism from Victorian fiction to the modern novel*, London: Routledge.
Ziolkowski, T. (2013) *Lure of the arcane: the literature of cult and conspiracy*, Baltimore: Johns Hopkins University Press.

# 4.4
# CONSPIRACY IN AMERICAN NARRATIVE

*Timothy Melley*

## Introduction

Conspiracy has always loomed large in American culture. Not only was Colonial American rhetoric frequently animated by conspiratorial demonology, but, as numerous scholars have shown, conspiratorial suspicion was a normative feature of eighteenth- and nineteenth-century political thought. It should be no surprise, therefore, that so many durable American literary works explore suspicion, hidden plots and organised systems for social or political control. What is more striking, however, is the veritable explosion of literary and cultural interest in conspiracy that characterised the period beginning roughly in 1960 (see Fenster 1999; Melley 2000; Knight 2000; O'Donnell 2000). Not only did conspiracy become an explicit organising principle in the most celebrated fictions of the post-Kennedy era, but this literature frequently embraced self-conscious paranoia as a reasonable response to state and corporate power.

In this chapter, I sketch this development from the colonial period to the present, arguing that the post-war American 'culture of paranoia' reflected a serious crisis of public knowledge fomented by a mushrooming security state, corporate capitalism and mass-mediated society. In emphasising the period after 1960, I do not mean to suggest that conspiracy is not a significant theme of earlier periods but, rather, that the intense and self-reflexive post-war embrace of 'paranoid' subjectivity marks a major shift in the cultural meaning of conspiracy. The post-war culture of conspiracy was fuelled by a new journalistic emphasis on the excesses of the Cold War security state and the rise of a new scholarly discourse that defined and delegitimated what is now commonly called 'conspiracy theory' (see Thalmann 2019; McKenzie-McHarg 2019). It is no accident that cultural interest in conspiracy mushroomed at almost the same moment that Richard Hofstadter defined the 'paranoid style' in 1965 as an aberrant and politically dangerous form of political speech. Yet, the post-war literature of paranoia differed markedly from both the Cold War demonology of Hofstadter's 'paranoid style' and the ferment of what is now commonly dismissed as 'conspiracy theory'. As I will suggest below, the post-war literature of paranoia was suspicious even of its own suspicion, yet it embraced the apparent irrationalism of paranoia as a creative, workable stance against the mystifying power of large institutions, public relations schemes, state propaganda, disinformation, advertising and other forms of mass mediated deception and social influence.

## Plotting conspiracy

Conspiratorial ferment has long animated American thought. As early as 1693, Cotton Mather's *The Wonders of the Invisible World* described some female residents of Salem as a 'terrible Plague, of Evil Angels' engaged in 'An Horrible Plot' to 'Blow up, and pull down all the Churches in the Country'. This sort of paranoid 'demonology', as the political scientist Michael Rogin (1987) termed it, has repeatedly marked periods of crisis in American political history. Demonology is an essential form of Anglo-American identity formation that is rooted in the scapegoating of racialised populations and has resurged in response to the Indigenous peoples of North America, European immigrants of the late nineteenth century, Cold War communists and jihadists in the wake of the attacks of 11 September 2001.

In his landmark 1964 essay, 'The Paranoid Style in American Politics', Richard Hofstadter associated this sort of rhetorical ferment with the tendency to see 'a "vast" or "gigantic" conspiracy as *the motive force* in historical events' (25; 29). While he did not use the phrase 'conspiracy theory', his essay helped to establish the modern sense of that term and to delegitimate it as a pathological and dangerous form of mostly right-wing political speech (Hofstadter 1965). Yet, as Bernard Bailyn, Gordon Wood, Michael Butter and others have shown, the tendency to formulate theories of conspiracy was rather commonplace in the eighteenth- and nineteenth-century U.S.A. (see Bailyn 1967; Wood 1982; Butter 2014). Assertions of conspiracy were widespread, among both elites and commoners, and they were widely accepted as a reasonable way of thinking about power, politics and even social influence more generally. As the dean of early American letters, Ralph Waldo Emerson, put it in his definitive 1841 essay, 'Self-Reliance', 'Society everywhere is in conspiracy against the manhood of every one of its members' (1841: 261).

It should thus be no surprise that conspiracies figure significantly in American fiction and drama. The discovery of secret plots is in some ways a natural topic for fiction. While there is an important distinction between *literary plot* (the organisation of events in a narrative) and *complot* (the gathering of people to enact a secret plan), plotting is a primary activity of the fiction writer. The unearthing of a secret *complot*, moreover, has long been a standard literary plot, and there is no shortage of such plots in popular American writing. Melodrama, with its emphasis on the heroic rescue of wronged innocents, has been a particularly consistent source of conspiratorial complot. Overwrought stories about schemes to defraud, deflower or harm unwitting commoners have been popular throughout American history. Narratives in the demonological tradition, which constitute a particular type of melodrama, have regularly imagined complex plots against the nation or some portion of its citizenry by a range of distant institutions and groups: Satanists, the Catholic Church, the Masons, European bankers and so on.

However, not all American literary explorations of suspicion and conspiracy have taken melodramatic form. In the late nineteenth and early twentieth centuries, a number of writers described economic and social structures as if they were organised plots. In *The Octopus* (1903), for instance, Frank Norris attempted to represent monopoly capitalism and corporate power as a unified organism with a single locus of planning and control (Knight 2017).[1] Other notable American fiction explored the problem of suspicion by generating ambiguity about threatening events or possible plots. Charles Brockden Brown's *Arthur Mervyn* (1799), the tales of Nathaniel Hawthorne and Edgar Allan Poe, Herman Melville's 'Benito Cereno' (1855) and *The Confidence Man* (1857), Charlotte Perkins Gilman's 'Yellow Wallpaper' (1892) and Henry James's *The Turn of the Screw* (1898), to name only a few, foreground a type of 'paranoid' suspicion. Of course, the term 'paranoia' is anachronistic when applied to most of these texts, which predate modern psychoanalysis, and none of these authors explicitly invokes the notion of paranoid suspicion. Yet, all of these works are essentially about what Sigmund Freud (1911) saw as 'the mechanism of paranoia': The psychic projection of internal mental content (intentions, emotions and suppositions) onto the world during the process of interpretation.[2] The characters of Poe, Gilman and James repeatedly seem to perceive imaginary projections of their own guilt and desire as real events and objects. Yet, these authors often restrict themselves to a first-person perspective, refusing to confirm the insanity or sanity of their protagonists. Melville's 'Benito Cereno' taunts readers to detect the barely hidden signs of an ingenious slave rebellion masked by the placid but odd behaviour of everyone aboard a distressed slave trading ship. The novella's protagonist, an affable and kind-hearted, but thoroughly racist, ship captain who has come to the distressed vessel's aid, is anything but paranoid: His good-natured racism prevents him from recognising the signs of conspiracy all around him. But the novella's reader is thus challenged to adopt the requisite suspicion to recognise the complot before it explodes into violence at the end of the tale. Melville's *Confidence Man* similarly challenges its readers to recognise the hidden motives behind its protagonist's glib social deceptions. These texts ask readers to engage in something like paranoid suspicion: A recognition that significance lies just under the visible surface of the fictional world, that apparent coincidences are in fact the result of prior design. They do so, moreover, to reveal the power of social convention to normalise racism and mask social violence.

Literary plots that foreground psychic projection and interpretive social dilemmas thematise something already at work in all literary texts: The discernment of patterns that lie just below the surface of social life is akin to the discernment of literary significance beneath the 'surface' of the text. The literary, in other words, always invites a form of suspicious, or revelatory, reading. As critics including Eve Kosofsky Sedgwick (2003) and Rita Felski (2015) have explained (and critiqued), literary interpretation has long been understood as something akin to paranoid interpretation. It is rooted in the modern cultural logic that Paul Ricoeur (1970: 32) first described as the 'hermeneutics of suspicion', the tendency of the great modern systemic thinkers of the nineteenth and twentieth centuries to focus on reducing 'the illusions and lies of consciousness'. Indeed, as John Farrell persuasively argues, paranoia is the 'dominant concern in modern literature, and its peculiar constellation of symptoms – grandiosity, suspicion, unfounded hostility, delusions of persecution and conspiracy – are nearly obligatory psychological components of the modern hero' (2006: 5). In short, the paranoid quest for knowledge is central to the canon of Western literature from Don Quixote to Rousseau and beyond.

## A new paranoid style

If American literature has always been engaged in the study of suspicion, it came to the very centre of American letters in the post-Kennedy era (see Fenster 1999; Melley 2000; Knight 2000; O'Donnell 2000). Beginning in the 1960s, an extraordinary array of notable American writers made conspiracy and paranoia the central theme of their work – among them, Thomas Pynchon, Don DeLillo, Margaret Atwood, Joan Didion, Kathy Acker, Allan Ginsberg, Vladimir Nabokov, William S. Burroughs, William Gibson, Philip K. Dick, Ralph Ellison, Ken Kesey, Ishmael Reed, Joseph Heller, Diane Johnson, Norman Mailer, William Gaddis and Joseph McElroy. For these figures, conspiracy was not simply complot or a metaphor for interpretive suspicion, it was an explicit cultural logic for thinking about systems, networks and complex social structures. For Don DeLillo (1978), the period after President John F. Kennedy's assassination, was 'the age of conspiracy' and the time in which 'paranoia replaced history in American life'. Many notable writers of this era embraced what Thomas Pynchon (1973: 25, 638) called 'creative paranoia' and 'operational paranoia' as a reasonable form of social engagement in the post-war regime of Cold War state secrecy and consumerist public relations. Suspicion, even potentially paranoid suspicion, the imagination of connections and plots without solid proof, was increasingly seen as an enabling, even necessary, way of understanding a mass-mediated world. As William S. Burroughs (1977: 159), the high priest of post-war American paranoia, put it, 'A paranoid is a person in possession of all of the facts'. The 'best minds of [this new literary] generation', to borrow the phrase of the Beat Generation poet Allan Ginsberg (1956), mounted social critiques that they knew would be perceived as 'madness', 'paranoia' and radical claptrap. In so doing, they popularised confessions of 'paranoia' as a way of expressing suspicion about official narratives and corporate propaganda. Over the next 60 years, the stigma of mental illness fell away from the term 'paranoia', and Americans became increasingly comfortable labelling their own suspicions 'paranoid' without any sense of self-criticism or pathology. So powerful was this trend that it eventually led to what Peter Knight (2000: 75) terms 'the routinization of paranoia' – a postmodern normalisation of 'paranoid scepticism ... in which the conspiratorial netherworld has become hyper-visible, its secrets just one more commodity'.

Thomas Pynchon gave paranoia one of its most memorable definitions in 1973 when the narrator of *Gravity's Rainbow* called it 'the leading edge of the discovery that *everything is connected*' (1997: 703). Twenty-five years later, in his own magnum opus, *Underworld* (1997), Don DeLillo reaffirmed the status of Pynchon's phrase as the official slogan of post-war paranoia; in an increasingly networked society, his most suspicious character notes, 'Everything is connected. All human knowledge gathered and linked, hyperlinked'. If the tendency to see social connections was a hallmark of paranoid thinking, DeLillo suggests, then it had become literalised in the structure of the Internet and the lived experience of quotidian American life (1997: 827).

Notable American fiction began to register this idea beginning in the late 1950s in ways that exceeded the general Western literary investment in paranoid reason. This new literature of paranoia was marked by several major propositions: First, a sense that conspiracy is not merely complot but an essential way of theorising the power of institutions (such as corporations, cartels, state agencies, knowledge systems and social networks) to influence historical events, public perceptions and individual behaviour; second, that such institutions had radically depleted individual human agency through new techniques of mass communication and social control; third, that extreme suspicion or 'paranoia' might be well-suited to discerning the nature of this power structure and therefore should not be shunned as a pathological condition; and finally, that fiction had a major social role in the exploration of possible hidden plots, connections and systems of meaning. This final proposition entailed the creation of sophisticated narratives that simulated, for readers, the difficulty of discerning actual conspiracies and plots. This fiction was distinctly different from the form of narrative Hofstadter described as the 'paranoid style'. It was endlessly suggestive but often refused to assert definite plots, which often seemed to elude human comprehension, ultimately out of reach, difficult to see, know or prove.

Post-war paranoid literature was deeply interested in conspiracy as an organising principle and a theme, but it rarely conceived of conspiracy in the traditional sense of a small group of subversives or plotters who literally 'breathe together' (conspirare). Rather, like academic social theory, it tended to understand 'conspiracies' as the work of large organisations, technologies or systems – powerful and obscure agencies that in many senses are the very antithesis of the traditional conspiracy. This conception entailed the imagination of social systems as if they were superhuman agents – coherent, wilful actors with the capacity to execute vast plans with godlike efficiency. This view of conspiracy was rooted in a burgeoning sociological imagination, and it required the form of thinking that Karl Popper dismissed in 1945 as 'the conspiracy theory of society' – the view that major social and economic events are planned by the 'direct design ... of powerful individuals and groups'. The major problem with this form of interpretation, Popper argued, is that it misunderstands the complexity of social events (1971: 94-5).[3] Hofstadter's examples, moreover, rarely allege traditional conspiracies (e.g. the plot to kill Caesar or the plot of the 9/11 bombers) but rather point to a giant machinery of influence. This quality is particularly evident in Hofstadter's Cold War examples, which assert not secret plots but widespread ideological controls. Like Popper, Hofstadter notes that the paranoid style often attributes quasi-divine powers to the enemy and that it often fears that an entire 'apparatus of education, religion, the press, and the mass media is engaged in a common effort to paralyze the resistance of loyal Americans' (1965).

Such claims are rooted in an all-or-nothing form of thinking I call 'agency panic'– the anxious view that one has fallen under the influence of an external agency – that one has been 'programmed', 'brainwashed', or converted into an automaton by some organisation, system or mysterious agency. They also tend to imagine the erosion of their own self-control but also to project autonomy and personhood onto social systems. In moments of agency panic, individuals imagine that social systems possess the will and self-control that seems depleted from themselves. The system is personified as 'them'. It appears to 'think', to have motives, to act with ruthless precision.

It is important to recognise two things about this notion. First, it reaffirms the tenets of an Enlightenment liberal individualism – that individuals are autonomous agents in control of their own thoughts and action – but it imagines these capacities at the level of the social order rather than the human individual. Second, it is a reaction to the sense that Enlightenment individualism cannot adequately explain the power of social institutions on human behaviour, thinking or social efficacy. The idea that 'society' (or some large subset of it) is 'conspiring' to govern social events is, paradoxically, a defence of the idea that individuals should be independent agents, free from social regulation. When faced with evidence that they are in fact influenced by social structures, corporate messages or state regulations, the paranoid subject clings to an embattled individualism, shocked at the apparent depletion of individual agency. Rather than adopting a more compelling, structural theory of social control (such as one finds in Marxism or sociology more broadly), the conspiratorial model projects the ideal qualities of the individual – rationality, intentionality and self-control – onto the social order itself, eventually seeing it as a wilful and malevolent being: A 'them'. Ironically, then, it is the frantic desire to theorise social regulation that pushes the conspiracy theorist to defend a set of concepts that cannot account for social regulation – except as a form of total and magical control (Melley 2000).

Perhaps no post-war American writer evinced this way of thinking more than William S. Burroughs, whose 18 novels and many essays relentlessly explore paranoia as a method for understanding and resisting social controls. For Burroughs, 'nothing happens in this universe … unless some entity *wills* it to happen' (1985a: 101). Burroughs adopts what he calls 'the "so-called primitive" tendency' (102) to blame *all* apparent accidents on a malicious agent. In this view, there are no accidents, everything is connected and apparent coincidences are really the result of wilful activity that is simply hidden to consciousness. The savvy individual must thus be attuned to the hidden structural connections between events. One of the perverse results of this view is that even trivial social events take on the qualities of plot, and motive seems to reside everywhere. 'Take a walk around the block', Burroughs suggests:

> Come back and write down precisely what happened with particular attention to what you were thinking when you noticed a street sign, a passing car or stranger or whatever caught your attention. You will observe that what you were thinking just *before* you saw the sign relates to the sign. The sign may even complete a sentence in your mind. You are getting messages. Everything is talking to you.
> 
> *(1985a: 103–4)*

This paranoid logic reverses what Max Weber called the modern 'disenchantment of the world'. If a street sign can complete one's thoughts, then the agent who 'thinks' such thoughts is not a human being but a supra-human communication system that includes individuals and social structures. It is this view of eroded human agency that induces Burroughs's perpetual sense of paranoia and panic. Indeed, Burroughs suggests that anyone engaging in his little exercise will 'become paranoid' (104) in a defensive attempt to ward off external control.

Burroughs's alarm about external control derived partly from his lifelong struggle with heroin addiction and withdrawal, which was a major subject of his many novels, stories and essays. Burroughs's characters are addicted not only to drugs, but also to commodities, images, words, human contact, power and even control itself. Burroughs understood addiction as a form of spiritual and bodily possession. 'I live', he wrote, 'with the constant threat of possession, and a constant need to escape from possession, from Control' (1985b: xxii). Burroughs explicitly rejected the Freudian notion that fears of possession and suspicion of coincidence are a projection of internal psychic content onto the world. In place of this modern, psychoanalytic understanding of suspicion, coincidence and control, he embraced a premodern understanding of demonic possession:

> My concept of possession is closer to the medieval model than to modern psychological explanations, with their dogmatic insistence that such manifestations must come from within and never, never, never from without. (As if there were some clear-cut difference between inner and outer). I mean a definite possessing entity. And indeed, the psychological concept might well have been devised by the possessing entities, since nothing is more dangerous to a possessor than being seen as a separate invading creature by the host it has invaded.
>
> *(1985b: xix–xx)*

Burroughs here suggests first that the difference between the inside and outside of persons is not clear-cut, but also that he is possessed and controlled by external agents. The 'subject', as a doctor puts it in *The Soft Machine* (1961), 'is riddled with parasites' (85). For Burroughs, who once worked as an exterminator, the idea of parasitism induced panic in which any sign of diminished voluntariness seems to indicate a complete transfer of agency from self to social order. 'When it comes to bedbugs', he writes, the 'only thing is to fumigate' (1973: 6).

Burroughs was in fact so worried about external possession that even his own thinking came to seem suspect, potentially hacked and controlled by outside influences. In response, he began to use a 'cut-up technique' adapted from the work of the artist Brion Gysin. In his essay 'The Invisible Generation' (1967), Burroughs explains this strategy of arbitrarily chopping up and reassembling passages as a method of resistance to social controls. The cut-up technique reintroduces the accidental into texts or even thoughts that might be controlled by external influences, thereby short-circuiting the power of social messages. The cut-up illustrates the hyper-individualist impulse of paranoia. While the technique's dictum – 'everybody splice himself in with everybody else' – (212) generates a fragmented, postmodern subject, it does in order to defend the individual (and individualism itself) from social systems that even powerful humans have 'no control over'.

Burroughs's dread of external controls was extreme but hardly unique. Post-war American literature, observed Tony Tanner in 1971, was thick with 'dread that someone else is patterning your life, that there are all sorts of invisible plots afoot to rob you of your autonomy of thought and action'.[4] This view was expressed in both popular and sober scholarly forms. In 1950, the Yale sociologist David Riesman declared the formation of a new kind of 'other-directed'

American subject, increasingly susceptible to external influences. In 1956, Don Siegel's iconic film *Invasion of the Body Snatchers* literalised this notion and, over the next decades, American fiction began to depict all manner of 'programmed' and 'brainwashed' persons: Addicts, automatons and 'mass-produced' figures (Riesman et al. 1950). Many post-war narratives depict characters who feel they are acting out parts in a script written by someone else, or who believe that their most individuating traits have been somehow produced from without. Thomas Pynchon's Mucho Maas, of *The Crying of Lot 49* (1966: 104), becomes 'less himself and more generic ... a walking assembly of man', and *Gravity's Rainbow* is premised on the possibility that its protagonist's sexual desire has been conditioned as part of a state-corporate espionage programme. In numerous novels, Margaret Atwood's characters re-enact classically feminine behaviour, even though they know it is harmful and undesirable to them. In *Libra* (1988), Don DeLillo's historical novel about the assassination of President John F. Kennedy, Lee Harvey Oswald feels that his participation in Kennedy's murder has been scripted in advance by powerful forces beyond his control. An astonishing number of post-war novels concern figures who feel they must defend themselves against powerful and dangerous institutions – the corporatised military of Joseph Heller's *Catch-22*, the 'Atonist' culture industry of Ishmael Reed's *Mumbo Jumbo*, the 'combine' of Ken Kesey's *One Flew Over the Cuckoo's Nest*, the vast network of state-cartel networks ('Them') in Pynchon's *Gravity's Rainbow*, Margaret Atwood's 'men', and the 'priestly' C.I.A. of Don DeLillo and Norman Mailer (see Knight 2000; Melley 2000; O'Donnell 2000) .

If such novels imagined frightening forms of institutional influence, they did so self-consciously, making paranoia and conspiracy explicit themes and matters of epistemological uncertainty. Mailer and Pynchon were, in the words of literary critic Frank Lentricchia (1991), the 'shamans of the paranoid novel' (205). They organised their narratives around political suspicion that ambitiously limned the forms of collusion between corporate and state power. They also mapped the spectrum of political suspicion, from consumerist zombification on one end to radical suspicion on the other. 'Since the assassination of John F. Kennedy', Mailer noted in 1992, 'we have been marooned in one of two equally intolerable spiritual states, apathy or paranoia'. Pynchon relentlessly explored these rival 'spiritual states'. His paranoid masterpieces, *V.* (1960), *The Crying of Lot 49* (1963) and *Gravity's Rainbow* (1973), cantered on self-proclaimed paranoids (Herbert Stencil of *V.* and Edward Pointsman of *Gravity's Rainbow*), but also set their obsessive interpretive zeal into relief against the comic apathetic counterparts (*V*'s 'human yo-yo', Benny Profane, and Tyrone Slothrop of *Gravity's Rainbow*). Pynchon's work is most notable for its refusal to resolve the tension between these positions. His suspicious characters frequently believe they have stumbled upon a massive plot involving a vast social, communicative and economic network, but they are never able to confirm its existence. Still, they are willing to embrace paranoia as a way of apprehending a sublime array of social relations too complex to bring fully into view. Unlike the practitioners of the demonological 'paranoid style', then, Pynchon offered a form of suspicion at once grandiose and self-scrutinising. His 'paranoia' was a self-conscious approach to the problem of public knowledge in a regime of state secrecy and corporate capitalism (see Jameson 1990[5]).

Other sophisticated post-war novels also explored paranoia in a self-effacing way, emphasising interpretive uncertainty, the difficulty of confirming hidden connections. Margaret Atwood and others framed misogynist violence as a coordinated system of oppression rather than an endless series of unrelated attacks. In novels such as *Bodily Harm*, *The Edible Woman*, *Lady Oracle* and *Surfacing*, Atwood's protagonists feel they are being stalked by a man (possibly their lovers). Although they are ultimately unable to determine who their stalkers are or whether they exist, Atwood suggests that their fears of being watched or hunted are a reasonable response to normal, heterosexual relationships. Indeed, the figure of the anonymous stalker allows Atwood to solve a pressing theoretical problem: How to represent the immense system of institutions, discourses and practices that contribute to violence against women. Joan Didion, similarly, used her own experience as a register of larger social patterns and pressures. Her essay 'The White Album' (1979) recounts a personal breakdown she suffered amid growing anxiety in Vietnam-era Los Angeles. In the wake of grisly murders committed by Charles Manson and his gang, Los Angeles, she feels, has become a place where 'all connections were equally meaningful, and equally senseless'. Her struggle to understand and explain how social events are related induces panic attacks that land her in a hospital. Didion describes her illness as 'paranoia', but it is too self-effacing to fit the clinical criteria for that term. It is better seen as a crisis of interpretation; a frustrating inability to account for outbursts of social violence that seem too patterned and meaningful to be merely 'random'.

Along with Don DeLillo, Didion would become the most incisive literary diagnostician of the Cold War national security state. Her novels *A Book of Common Prayer* (1977), *Democracy* (1984) and *The Last Thing He Wanted* (1996) repeatedly returned to the problem of public knowledge in a regime of state secrecy. In each, a privileged American woman in a colonial setting is torn between relationships with a major public figure and a covert agent. Each novel is narrated by a savvy, cynical female journalist in the mould of Didion herself. As in 'The White Album', these narrators struggle to piece together the secret actions of the male clandestine agents in the novel, and thus they often narrate their own failure to tell the story they intended to tell. But, they also develop a form of cynical suspicion modelled on the thinking of clandestine agents. In *Democracy*, for example, the narrator describes the thinking of the novel's C.I.A. officer:

> To Jack Lovett, all behaviour was purposeful, and the purpose could be divined by whoever attracted the best information and read it most correctly. A Laotian village indicated on one map and omitted on another suggested not a reconnaissance oversight but a population annihilated.... A shipment of laser mirrors from Long Beach to a firm in Hong Kong that did no laser work suggested not a wrong invoice but a transshipment, reexport, the diversion of technology to unfriendly actors. All nations, to Jack Lovett, were 'actors', specifically 'state actors' ('nonstate actors' were the real wildcards here, but in Jack Lovett's extensive experience the average nonstate actor was less interested in the laser mirrors than in M-16s, AK-47s, FN-FALs ...).
> (Didion 1984: 35)

Interestingly, Didion's narrator shares this view. The apparent 'unpredictability of human behaviour', she declares, is an illusion. There is actually 'a higher predictability ..., a more complex pattern discernible only after the fact' (205). This view is a version of William Burroughs's proclamation that 'nothing happens in this universe ... unless some entity *wills* it to happen' (1985a). Here, however, critical suspicion, or paranoia, is specifically harnessed to the problem of the secret security state. Citizens who are prohibited from knowing about state secrets must attempt to discern their signs in public information. A view that casts suspicion onto apparent accidents and discrepancies in the public record seems increasingly reasonable in a world where the state deliberately conceals its defence of the realm from the citizens of the republic.

## Periodising post-war paranoia

The post-war American literature of paranoia marked a major shift in the cultural work of suspicion. Its flourishing in the late 1950s and early 1960s may seem to confirm Hofstadter's sense that an age-old form of demonological suspicion was in full resurgence (see Butter 2014[6]). But, it is essential to note how strikingly different the post-war literature of paranoia is from Hofstadter's 'paranoid style'. For Hofstadter, the paranoid style is marked by a sense of grievance and 'persecution' (1965: 4); a defensive resistance to disconfirmation (or 'falsifiability' as Karl Popper called it); a pedantic quality in which an 'elaborate concern with demonstration' and 'heroic strivings for "evidence"' (36) compensate for the conspiracy's power to hide its activities; and, finally, a faulty sense of historical causality. 'What distinguishes the paranoid style', says Hofstadter, is the absence of an 'intuitive sense of how things do *not* happen' (40).

But, there is a more important, unstated component of Hofstadter's paranoid style: It is fundamentally melodramatic. Melodrama is often misunderstood as a sentimental populist genre. But, as Linda Williams (2018) has persuasively argued, melodrama is the dominant narrative form of our age (see also Anker 2014). It is not a genre, it is a mode, like tragedy or comedy. It, in fact, replaced the fated structure of tragedy with a Manichean ethical framework that pits dastardly villains against innocent victims and selfless heroes. It revolves around a 'morally legible' sense of good and evil, stock villains, victims and heroes, a nostalgic sense of the past and a breathless pace that heightens the need for urgent heroic action.

It is critically important to distinguish the melodramatic demonology of Hofstadter's 'paranoid style' from what I have been calling the post-Kennedy-era 'literature of paranoia'. The latter body of work is notably unmelodramatic. In sharp contradistinction to the quasi-religious conviction of the Cold War 'paranoid style', the post-war 'literature of paranoia' is self-aware, tolerant of unknowing and morally complex. Unlike the wide-eyed true believers of the paranoid style, authors such as DeLillo, Didion, Mailer and Reed meditate on the problem of suspicion, frequently interrupting and questioning their own narratives. Didion repeatedly suggests that she lacks the strength or moral clarity to craft a narrative. Pynchon and Burroughs undermine not only the notion of the hero but of individuality itself. They treat cells, organs and physical objects as characters. The protagonist of Pynchon's *Gravity's Rainbow* literally and physically disintegrates across Europe. Sophisticated paranoid film thrillers like *The Conversation* and *The Parallax View* moved away from melodramatic conventions to a more sublime and terrifying sense of an institutional power that can never fully be grasped. The confident and terrifying conspiratorial allegations of the paranoid style can usefully be contrasted to Don DeLillo's decidedly unmelodramatic conception of a possible conspiracy against President Kennedy:

> If we are on the outside, we assume a conspiracy is the perfect working of a scheme.... A conspiracy is everything that ordinary life is not. It's the inside game, cold, sure, undistracted, forever closed off to us. We are the flawed ones, the innocents, trying to make some rough sense of the daily jostle. Conspirators have a logic and a daring beyond our reach. All conspiracies are the same taut story of men who find coherence in some criminal act.... But maybe not. Nicholas Branch thinks ... that the conspiracy against the president was a rambling affair that succeeded in the short term mainly due to chance.
>
> (DeLillo 1988: 440)

In *Libra*, DeLillo suggests that both a lone gunman and a small group of conspirators independently planned Kennedy's assassination, and that both sets of plans changed multiple times for a variety of reasons, including individual motives, accidents and human failings. DeLillo resists the melodramatic notion of a 'vast' and diabolical cabal executed by a monolithic organisation – the mafia, the K.G.B., the C.I.A. – but also resists the notion that we should accept the official state explanation – that Kennedy was killed solely by Lee Harvey Oswald and that suspicions to the contrary must be dismissed as mere conspiracy theories.

In emphasising these examples, I do not mean to suggest that popular melodrama, including demonological melodrama, disappeared in the years after 1960. On the contrary, it continued to be a remarkably salient aspect of contemporary culture. But, even the conspiracy melodrama changed markedly in the 1960s and 1970s. While the demonological tradition emphasised foreign plots, post-war U.S. conspiracy melodrama increasingly depicted malfeasance by the U.S. government and Western corporations. As James Fulcher (1983) notes, the 1970s saw the development of a 'formula' conspiracy novel in which events themselves:

> Are manipulated and staged by other characters deliberately to violate the protagonist's sense of the way things are. Indeed, what often causes the protagonist to lose trust is that the incidents are staged by members of the American government to conceal the way things are from the protagonist and, for that matter, the American public.
> 
> *(Fulcher 1983: 153–4)*

Examples of this popular form include Loren Singer, *The Parallax View* (1960); Joseph DiMona, *Last Man at Arlington* (1973); William Goldman, *The Marathon Man* (1974); Richard Condon, *Winter Kills* (1974); Robert Ludlum, *The Chancellor Manuscript* (1977); Jeff Millar, *Private Sector* (1979) and *The Delphi Betrayal* (1981). Many novels and films of note, including *The Parallax View* and *The Conversation*, suggested plots of vast complexity involving members of the U.S. intelligence community. Many left viewers with a sense of uncertainty about the power and scope of major U.S. institutions.

The rise of such narratives marked a major shift in both Cold War ideology and American conspiracy discourse. This shift occurred shortly after the 1963 assassination of John F. Kennedy. The Kennedy assassination not only marked the end of a heroic Camelot narrative about the young president but the birth of a substantial new body of conspiracy theories promulgated not by tin-foil-hat-wearing gadflies but by journalists and academics of some reputation and statue. Over the next 15 years, an astonishing outpouring of discourse critical of the excesses of the U.S. national security state and the handling of the official investigation into Kennedy's death raised troubling questions about a possible conspiracy to kill the president and/or to cover up state malfeasance. Soon, the assassination became a prominent public event that was routinely understood through rival 'lone gunman' and 'conspiracy theories'. The year of Hofstadter's 'Paranoid Style' and the Warren Commission Report into the assassination of John F. Kennedy, 1964, was also marked by the publication of mainstream journalistic critiques of the national security state, chief among them Thomas Wise and David Ross's *The Invisible Government* (1964). It was also the year in which Stanley Kubrick's *Dr Strangelove* savagely satirised the security state and the logic of Cold War demonology. It was, in short, a historical pivot point in culture of the Cold War, one in which American conspiracy discourse shifted away from the McCarthyite 'demonology' of international enemies and toward the critique of state and corporate power. One of the great ironies of Hofstadter's essay is that all of his major examples of the paranoid style concern external threats to the nation – the Masons, the Illuminati, communists – and yet, almost the moment the essay was published, the emphasis of American conspiracy theories shifted to internal enemies and plots. The most salient and durable American conspiracy theories since 1964 are about the assassination of John F. Kennedy, the Apollo moon landings, alleged U.F.O. cover-ups around Area 51 and the attacks of 9/11. All express suspicion about the deceptions and powers of the U.S. security state.

It is important to note that this fundamental change in the nature of American conspiracy discourse coincided precisely with the discursive 'invention' of conspiracy theory – that is, the claim that 'conspiracy theory' and 'the paranoid style' are a recognisable, aberrant and pathological form of political discourse. While the form of thinking we now call 'conspiracy theory' is quite old, the notion that it constitutes an identifiable cognitive error ('conspiracy theory') is relatively new, dating roughly to Popper's use of the term in 1945. It is particularly notable that Hofstadter delivered 'The Paranoid Style' as a lecture at Oxford literally on the eve of Kennedy's murder. As a Google N-Gram shows, the phrase 'conspiracy theory' came into *widespread* usage during the years between Popper's *Open Society* (1945) and 1972. Its use surged amid debate over the *Warren Commission Report on the Assassination of John F. Kennedy*, which was published in 1964, two months before 'The Paranoid Style' appeared in *Harper's Magazine* (see McKenzie-McHarg 2019[7]). In the ensuing decade, a vibrant cultural debate about Kennedy's murder would repeatedly frame the case as a contest between the 'lone gunman theory' and various 'conspiracy theories'.

In the decades leading up to Kennedy's murder, a number of other American sociologists and historians – including Daniel Bell, Seymour Lipset, Talcott Parsons and Edward Shils – preceded Hofstadter in expressing concern about Cold War-era conspiracy mongering. The stakes seemed high during the Cold War for maintaining an idealised account of the U.S. public sphere as a model of rationality, openness and transparency. Paradoxically, as Shils brilliantly observed in *The Torment of Secrecy* (1956: 77), it was this American ideal of transparency and openness that made Americans overreact to the 'threat of secret machinations'. The 'paranoid style' was one such overreaction. During the rise of Senator Joseph McCarthy and then, later, Senator Barry Goldwater, stamping out this form of demonological excess seemed a reasonable way of protecting democratic institutions.

But, beginning in the 1960s, the national security state *itself* began to seem an even larger overreaction. 1964 was the year in which two prominent investigative reporters, Thomas Wise and David Ross, published their prominent critique, *The Invisible Government*, warning that the U.S. had established a parallel secret state headed by an out-of-control C.I.A. committed to undemocratic political manipulation around the world. A wave of embarrassing public disclosures soon followed, suggesting that the C.I.A. and U.S. military planners were out of control, routinely lying to the American public, which learned in turn that the U.S. had planned a massive false flag operation at the Bay of Pigs in Cuba, that widespread suspicions and inconsistencies haunted the assassination of President Kennedy, that the U.S. military had produced a massive study (the 'Pentagon Papers') showing that the Vietnam War was strategically flawed and doomed to failure, that President Nixon had ordered C.I.A. operatives to steal campaign information from his rivals and so on. In short, the early 1960s marked an inflection point in Cold War history. A growing number of intellectuals, mainstream journalists and thought leaders began to question the notion of 'total cold war', raising concerns that state secrecy had gone too far, seriously undermining democratic rule. During this period, the public grew increasingly concerned about a massive and growing national security apparatus charged with the conduct of covert operations, propaganda and psychological operations around the world. What had begun as a small exception to democratic oversight in 1947, when the C.I.A. received its charter, would grow by 2010 to a vast clandestine apparatus: 17 intelligence agencies, 28 other federal agencies, 1271 sub-bureaus, costing $75 billion per year. A primary function of this apparatus was what might be called 'conspiracy theory': The security state was expected to suspect, describe and stop plots against the state. However, its growing capacity for official suspicion also stimulated public suspicion about its activities. Ironically, then, just as Hofstadter succeeded in delegitimising conspiratorial explanation, the American public began to grow anxious about an 'invisible government', the critique of which would require the form of suspicion cast into doubt by Hofstadter's critique of the paranoid style. It is no accident that U.S.

cultural narratives of suspicion changed character radically around the time Hofstadter published his essay. The dominant post-war American conspiracy theories express anxiety about the deceptions and powers of the U.S. security state.

## Conclusion

The post-war literature of paranoia addressed two crucial intellectual problems of the Cold War era. The first was an epistemological problem, a sense that it had become difficult to know what is real and true in the world. The other was a problem of agency, a sense that complex institutions and forces might manipulate and control individual action and thought. In facing both of these challenges, the literature of paranoia resisted the melodrama of the 'paranoid style'. It used paranoid suspicion not as a demonological tool but as a way of imagining individual resistance to corporate and collective pressures. Heller's 'paranoid' bombardier, Yossarian, stays alive in part because he believes that 'everyone' is trying to kill him, an overtly paranoid view that seems increasingly sound as *Catch-22* unfolds. The hackers of William Gibson's novels recognise forms of state and corporate disinformation and redeploy them for their own purposes. Ishmael Reed's satire of conspiracy theories, *Mumbo Jumbo*, reveals the systemic racism connecting what are often said to be shameful historical episodes.

The post-war literature of conspiracy and paranoia, in other words, was driven by a sense that knowledge and power are inextricably linked, and that to be 'paranoid' means rejecting the normalising ideology of the powerful. In this sort of regime, cynical reason flourishes. Everyone assumes that the game is rigged, that 'They', whoever 'They' are, are keeping something from us and there's little to be done. Is it any wonder that so many leading American literary figures made paranoia and conspiracy central to their work?

## Notes

1 See Knight (2017) for a compelling account of *The Octopus* in relation to conspiracy.
2 Projection, according to Freud, is 'the most striking characteristic of symptom-formation of paranoia' (1911: 66).
3 Popper also clearly felt that this sort of historical interpretation was resistant to 'falsifiability' – the criterion at the heart of Popper's programme for distinguishing science from pseudoscience.
4 Tanner observes that, 'since the Cold War, a large number of Americans have come to regard society as some kind of vast conspiracy' (1971: 427).
5 Jameson argues that conspiracy theory is a crude attempt to map the structure of late capitalism.
6 Butter notes that 'The Paranoid Style in American Politics' is 'the urtext of American conspiracy theory research' (2014: 4).
7 As McKenzie-McHarg (2019) shows, the term 'conspiracy theory' has a much older history, notably in nineteenth-century legal discourse. My claim is that the contemporary popular notion of 'conspiracy theory' as a categorical form of irrational thought was established after the Second World War.

## References

Anker, E.R. (2014) *Orgies of feeling: melodrama and the politics of freedom*, Durham: Duke.
Bailyn, B. (1967) *The ideological origins of the American Revolution*, reprint, Cambridge: Harvard University Press, 2017.
Burroughs, W. (1961) *The soft machine*, New York: Grove.
Burroughs, W. (1967) 'The invisible generation', in W. Burroughs (ed.) *The ticket that exploded*, rev. edn, New York: Grove, pp. 205–17.
Burroughs, W. (1973) *Exterminator!*, New York: Penguin.
Burroughs, W. (1977) *The algebra of need*, London: Calder.

Burroughs, W. (1985a) 'On coincidence', in W. Burroughs (ed.) *The adding machine: selected essays*, New York: Arcade, pp. 99–105.
Burroughs, W. (1985b) *Queer*, New York: Penguin.
Butter, M. (2014) *Plots, designs, and schemes: American conspiracy theories from the Puritans to the present*, Berlin/Boston: de Gruyter.
DeLillo, D. (1978) *Running dog*, New York: Knopf.
DeLillo, D. (1988) *Libra*, New York: Viking.
DeLillo, D. (1997) *Underworld*, New York: Viking.
Didion, J. (1977) *A book of common prayer*, New York: Simon and Schuster.
Didion, J. (1979) 'The white album', in J. Didion (ed.) *The white album*, New York: Pocket, pp. 11–47.
Didion, J. (1984) *Democracy*, New York: Simon and Schuster.
Didion, J. (1996) *The last thing he wanted*, New York: Knopf.
Emerson, R.W. (1841) 'Self-Reliance', in J. Porte (ed.) *Essays and lectures*, reprint, New York: Liberty of America, 1983, pp. 257–82.
Farrell, J. (2006) *Paranoia and modernity: Cervantes to Rousseau*, Ithaca, NY: Cornell University Press.
Felski, R. (2015) *The limits of critique*, Chicago: University of Chicago Press.
Fenster, M. (1999) *Conspiracy theories: secrecy and power in American culture*, Minneapolis, MN: University of Minnesota Press.
Freud, S. (1911) 'Psycho-analytic notes on an autobiographical account of a case of paranoia (dementia paranoides)', in J. Strachey (ed.) *The standard edition of the complete psychological works of Sigmund Freud*, vol. 12 (1953–1974), trans. J. Strachey, London: Hogarth, pp. 3–82.
Fulcher, J. (1983) 'American conspiracy: formula in popular fiction', *Midwest Quarterly: A Journal of Contemporary Thought*, 24(2): 152–64.
Ginsberg, A. (1956) 'Howl', in A. Ginsberg *Howl and other poems*, San Francisco: City Lights.
Hofstadter, R. (1965) 'The paranoid style in American politics', in R. Hofstadter *The paranoid style in American politics and other essays*, New York: Knopf, pp. 3–40.
Jameson, F. (1990) 'Cognitive mapping', in C. Neslon and L. Grossberg (eds.) *Marxism and the interpretation of culture*, Urbana, IL: Illinois University Press, pp. 347–60.
Knight, P. (2000) *Conspiracy culture: from Kennedy to the X-Files*, London: Routledge.
Knight, P. (2017) *Reading the market: genres of financial capitalism in gilded age America*, Baltimore: John Hopkins.
Lentricchia, F. (1991) 'Libra as postmodern critique', in F. Lentricchia (ed.) *Introducing Don DeLillo*, Durham: Duke University Press.
Mailer, N. (1992) 'Footfalls in the crypt', *Vanity Fair*, 55(2): p. 124.
Mather, C. (1862) *The wonders of the invisible world: being an account of the tryals of several witches lately executed in New-England, to which is added a further account of the tryals of the New-England witches*, London: John Russel Smith, 1693.
McKenzie-McHarg, A. (2019) 'Conspiracy theory: the nineteenth-century prehistory of a twentieth-century concept', in J. Uscinski (ed.) *Conspiracy theories and the people who believe them*, Oxford: Oxford University Press, pp. 62–81.
Melley, T. (2000) *Empire of conspiracy: the cultural of paranoia in post-war America*, Ithaca: Cornell University Press.
O'Donnell, P. (2000) *Latent destinies: cultural paranoia and contemporary US narrative*, Durham, NC: Duke University Press.
Popper, K. (1971 [1967]) *Open society and its enemies, vol. 2: the high tide of prophecy: Hegel, Marx, and the aftermath*, New Jersey: Princeton University Press.
Pynchon, T. (1966) *The crying of lot 49*, New York: Bantam.
Pynchon, T. (1973) *Gravity's rainbow*, New York: Viking.
Ricoeur, P. (1970) *Freud and philosophy: an essay on interpretation*, trans. D. Savage, New Haven: Yale University Press.
Riesman, D., Glazer, N. and Denny, R. (1950) *The lonely crowd: a study of the changing American character*, abridged edn, New York: Doubleday, 1956.
Rogin, M. (1987) *Ronald Reagan the movie: and other episodes in political demonology*, Berkley: University of California Press.
Sedgwick, E.K. (2003) 'Paranoid reading and reparative reading, or you're so paranoid, you probably think this essay is about you', in E.K. Sedgwick (ed.) *Touching feeling: affect, pedagogy, performativity*, Durham: Duke University Press.

Shils, E. (1956) *The torment of secrecy: the background and consequences of American security policies*, New York: Free Press.
Tanner, T. (1971) *City of words: American fiction 1950–1970*, London: Jonathan Cape.
Thalmann, K. (2019) *The stigmatization of conspiracy theory since the 1950s: 'A Plot to Make us Look Foolish'*, London, UK: Routledge.
Williams, L. (2018) *Melodrama unbound: across history, media, and national cultures*, New York: Columbia University Press.
Wise, D. and Ross, T.B. (1964) *The invisible government*, New York: Random House.
Wood, G.S. (1982) 'Conspiracy and the paranoid style: causality and deceit in the eighteenth century', *The William and Mary Quarterly*, 39(3): 401–41.

# 4.5
# CONSPIRACY THEORIES AND VISUAL CULTURE

*Ute Caumanns and Andreas Önnerfors*

## Introduction

The bulk of the material studied in connection with the transmission of conspiracy theories is comprised of written sources. Texts can be investigated with regards to their formal aspects such as narrative structures, rhetorical figures and strategies to produce coherence (Butter 2014: 7). Yet, images are powerful tools – perhaps even more than text – for the diffusion of ideas and mirror the desire to represent the un-representable in the visual culture of conspiracy theory. By turning the imagined conspiracy into an image instead of a text-based theory, the invisible is turned into visible 'evidence', for instance, in picturing 'pyramids' and 'networks'. The image thus assumes a completely new quality: Seeing is believing and provides immediate knowledge. Thus, images of conspiracy locate themselves at the border between the seen and unseen; they portray dense and condensed narratives of causal connections in a play between graphic image, reality and imagination.

In this chapter, we argue that visuality in conspiracy culture is an under-researched phenomenon that promises fruitful investigations, an argument also relevant for other research areas (Meyer 2015: 333–60). Until now, there have been few, if any, systematic attempts to approach the relationship between conspiracy theories and their visual representation, despite their intimate relationship (Knight 2007, 2016; Krause *et al.* 2011; Großhans 2014; Eklund, Alteveer 2018). Conspiracy theories not only recur in verbal images, but they also are expressed through a host of materialised graphic images, pursuing visual strategies with multiple narrative aims. Drawing upon van Prooijen (2018: 5–6), we can distinguish five features that can be translated into a specific iconographic programme producing (conspiracist) meaning and thus creating potent tools of transmission. In the examples discussed below, we will demonstrate how the visual culture of conspiracy theories recognises patterns, detects agency, maps coalitions, crafts enemy images and visualises secrecy in various interrelations of mediality (intermediality), essentially between verbal and visual media. For art historian William Mitchell, this relation is constitutive: 'all media are mixed media' (Mitchell 1994: 95). Following Irina Rajewsky, we can distinguish three intermedial practices, all of which need to be addressed in the study of conspiracy theory: Meaning is either created by 'medial transposition' (e.g. text into picture) or through 'media combination' of at least two medial forms of articulation (e.g. text and picture in one product), or constituted by 'intermedial references' (Rajewsky 2005: 51–3). In the latter case, a picture refers to another conventionally distinct medium, thematising, evoking or imitating elements or structures of, for example, a concrete prior text, speech or another graphic image. Visuality, we argue, is an essential aspect of intermediality, and hence part of cultural production. In the conspiracist world of facts and fiction, visual metaphors, as much as materialised graphic images, contribute to an effective style of narration, communication, mediatisation, recognisability and memorability of messages. Our aim is thus to unpack the repertoire and narrativity of visual tropes that constitute the colour palette of the conspiracist imagination and its development over time. Finally, we will discuss a number of iconic visual representations of conspiracy in history, politics and art, focusing on (historical) case studies bridging five centuries: The antisemitic 'ritual murder' narrative, 'Jewish Bolshevism', *The Protocols of the Elders of Zion* and the purported conspiracy of secret societies. In a final section, we investigate the (syn-)aesthetic of conspiracy theories in modern art.

## A seminal precursor of the conspiracist style

As Leone has argued, it is Rembrandt and his *The Conspiracy of the Batavians under Claudius Civilis* (1661–1662), shown in Figure 4.5.1, who 'offers one of the first modern instances of visual conspiracy theory' (Leone 2016: 11). Whereas there certainly are instances of visual representations of 'conspiracy' before the seventeenth century, it is worthwhile to consider the emergence of tropes of conspiracy in art in connection with the paradigmatic development of conspiracy theories during the early modern period. Zwierlein (2013) has made a similar case with regards to political theory. The narrative of conspiracy turned into one mode of analysing the current state of affairs based on projections of a 'pool of possible pasts' and futures (Zwierlein

*Figure 4.5.1* Rembrandt, The Conspiracy of the Batavians under Claudius Civilis (1661–1662). Donated in 1798 to The Royal Academy of Fine Arts in Sweden, by Mrs Anna Johanna Peill, born Grill, widow of Mr Henrik Wilhelm Peill in memory of her late husband.

2013: 78), further fuelled by the emergence of political writing and political news dissemination through books and pamphlets, many of them illustrated. Renaissance art developed the idea that there is a hidden story to be (de-)constructed by the viewer, and Rembrandt excelled in a particular socratic and ironic style through which he guided his viewers to explore their own answers (Müller 2015: 1–19). His massive painting brings together many elements of later visual representations of conspiracy, such as a 'treacherous conniving, held in secret, cemented by unknown, barbaric rituals' (Leone 2016: 12). Without going too deeply into the image and its highly compelling context, Rembrandt visualises covert assembly at a secret, concealed location, involving plotting against the current state of affairs. These plotters are gathered in a circle to illustrate their bond, taking an oath 'intoxicated by conspiracy' (following Leone 2016: 12) and raising their cups to the plot. With their swords (as tokens of fidelity – as opposed to the dagger, which symbolises treason) they are pointing at the central figure, the master plotter (who has just delivered an inflammatory speech in which the enemy has been scapegoated). The visual aura of esoteric secrecy is evoked and enhanced by a conscious oscillation between opacity and transparency, darkness and light, blurriness and sharpness (e.g. some of the figures are distinct, while others disappear into the shadows, are dressed in a cloak or are even painted from behind) and what Leone (2016: 11) has called the 'chromatic promise of blood' – ruddy tones of colour that saturate the image. These, together with other elements of Rembrandt's painting, seem to characterise the conspiracist mindset, not least the quest for pattern recognition, coalitions and secrecy, and the search for intentional agency where there is none.

## Conspiracy theories and visual narrativity

Conspiracy theories interpret the world by telling a story. There are many concrete manifestations of this story, with structural similarities: In the most basic versions, a societal ill, styled as an existential crisis, is monocausally ascribed to the evil plan and secret machinations of a designated outgroup, scapegoated and blamed for the real or pretended problem. A 'group', a 'plan' and 'secrecy' are constitutive features of conspiracist narratives. In addition, there is the act of disclosure, which assigns the role of the narrator to the conspiracy theorist or, in modern terminology, the 'whistleblower'. What distinguishes him is his need for communication, to reach out in the face of the overabundance of available media. Already, Simmel noted the psychology of revelation in his ground-breaking essay on the sociology of secrecy and of secret societies (1906: 465): 'Secrecy involves a tension which, at the moment of revelation, finds its release. This constitutes the climax in the development of the secret.' This 'joy of confession' or publication may contain 'a sense of power' (Simmel 1906: 466), which explains the communicative impact of the conspiracy theorist as a revelator and public educator. It falls short to call – in Hofstadter's (1964: 7786) pejorative formula – the representatives of such theories 'paranoid' in the context of a 'political pathology', because their approach is linked to a 'specific kind of irrationality associated with a stubborn, highly rational, and highly operational logic' (Groh 1987: 4), not least with regards to strategic communication and dissemination of information. The conspiracy theorist aims to influence and convince his readers, his audience. To that aim, facts are amalgamated with fictions into a most convincing and compelling story. This mode of narrative operation from the side of the conspiracy theorist can be compared to what Anton has called a 'grey zone' between fact and fiction (Anton 2011: 14) or Barkun the 'fact-fiction reversal' (Barkun 2003: 29).

When exploring conspiracy narratives and the role of visual culture, trans-medial narratology research offers a methodological advantage: A narratological approach to other than epic texts also includes non-verbal representations. Basically, all media operate as intermediaries of semiotic signs, enabling communication (Rippe, Etter 2013: 192). Moreover, as material facilitators of information, their materiality matters. Marie-Laure Ryan, therefore, criticises the perception of media as 'hollow conduits for the transmission of messages' (Ryan 2004: 1–2): 'you cannot tell the same type of story on the stage and in writing, during conversation and in a thousand-page novel, in a two-hour movie and in a TV serial that runs for many years' (Ryan 2004: 356). The approach of a trans-medial theory of narrativity is helpful as it distinguishes media-specific discourse modes (modes of transmission) from the culturally acquired cognitive frame narrative, which is media-independent (Ryan 1992: 371; Wolf 2002: 357). With reference to the visual arts, narratologist Werner Wolf argues that the 'real question is not whether the visual arts can be narrative or not but to what extent they can be narrative' (Wolf 2003: 192). Thus, narrativity is not perceived as an absolute and stable category, but Wolf's approach opens up to explore dynamic expressions of 'narrative potential' in various media (Wolf 2002: 428–30, 2003: 192). Similarly, Ryan differentiates between '[h]aving narrativity' and 'being a narrative' (Ryan 2004: 9). Insofar, both concepts perceive narrativity in visual media.

## Visual metaphors

The conspiracy theorist exercises himself, both orally and in writing, as a sovereign narrator by establishing connections to his reader or his audience. This happens with reference to traditional verbal images, which, beyond textual culture, can also be realised graphically. Some visual tropes belong to the basic repertoire of conspiratorial thinking. They can act as introductions to a larger narrative, which the viewer in a concrete historical context is familiar with. The use of animal metaphors is popular, linked to the long legacy of symbolical anthropomorphism, such as in fables or codified in the many emblem books of the early modern period. As a rule, an animal represented strictly coded qualities and the emblems were used as inter-medial messages since they united a motto with an image and an explanatory text. One of the major purposes of identifying conspirators with threatening or negatively coded animals is their dehumanisation, creating distance and eliminating empathy with the 'other'. But, the use of animal metaphors is more complex, since there also is an inbuilt reference to imaginations of their essential qualities, which potentially correspond with the basic structure of the conspiracist narrative.

Some animal metaphors are more prolific than others to represent the invisible conspirators. One of the most prominent is the octopus, known in Egyptian culture and Greek mythology. With its many slimy and flexible (sometimes sexualised) tentacles directed by one all-seeing head, it can simultaneously and dynamically reach out in different directions, attach to, grab and devour its prey. And it will not die, as it is able to rebuild its tentacles. The metaphor is thus able to evoke multiple connotations of danger: Of intelligence, concealment and secrecy, of multi-directional, far-reaching and, yet, coordinated action, and of deadly embrace. It is depicted as a sea-monster threatening sailors such as in Pierre Denys de Montfort's *Colossal Octopus* (1801), at the time a popular book illustration, or in Victor Hugo's poem, 'Toilers of the Sea', published in 1866 and often referred to since. But, the octopus has also been used as a motif on the cover of editions of *The Protocols of the Elders of Zion* or in cartoons about large corporations, with the malevolent creature controlling the nation-states (Knight 2016: 111; Hagemeister 2019, forthcoming).

A more apocalyptic connotation, corresponding with the eschatological scenario of many conspiracy theories, is evoked through the visual metaphor of the snake. In the Judaeo-Christian tradition it represents sin, ambiguity and falsehood, but also intelligence. The split tongue of the snake corresponds to the basic assumption of conspiracist thinking, according to which a distinction should be made between a misleading appearance and the (evil) hidden reality. The concept of the snake again can be found in various editions of *The Protocols*, for instance in the popular French edition, commissioned by Jesuit priest Ernest Jouin: *Le Péril judéo-maçonnique: les 'Protocols' des Sages de Sion* (1927; Caumanns 2019, forthcoming). Apart from in antisemitic imagery, the snake was also used in Stalinist iconography for depicting 'enemies of the people'. For instance, during the Great Purge show trials of the 1930s, the exiled Leon Trotsky appeared as the double-tongued snake, conspiring with Nazi Germany, as it is visually expressed on Sergej D. Igumnov's infamous propaganda poster *We Will Eradicate the Spies and Saboteurs, the Trotskyist-Bukharinist Agents of Fascism!* (Moscow/Leningrad 1937). Virtually a collage of visual metaphors is presented in Gerald Burton Winrod's book *The Hidden Hand, the Protocols and the Coming Superman* (1932), represented in Figure 4.5.2.

*People reach for gold, not knowing that behind the scenes there is evidently a Hidden Jewish Hand characterized as the Symbolic Snake, which has produced the present Chaos by controlling the finances of the world.*

*Figure 4.5.2* Illustration in Gerald B. Winrod (1932; 6th edn 1933) The Hidden Hand, the Protocols and the coming Superman, Wichita, KS: Defender Publisher, 33 (https://archive.org/details/GeraldB.WinrodTheHiddenHandProtocolsComingSuperman1934).

Winrod (1900–1957), an antisemitic writer and preacher, propagated Nazi propaganda material in the U.S.A. in the 1930s. Although the picture lacks artistic credentials, it is worth scrutiny, as it presents a veritable catalogue of the metaphorical repertoire of conspiracist iconography: Central is the motif of the wire-puller or puppet master, as the mastermind, holding the strings; he exercises control over money ('gold') as well as over other phenomena of chaos ('filth', 'atheism', 'poverty', 'immorality', 'modernism', 'communism' and 'depression'). His hands reach through the (half-open) curtain while the rest of the body is concealed behind the scenery (in secrecy); the symbolic snake is on the curtain, while the globe in the foreground signifies the trope of 'Jewish world domination'. Windrod's commentary reminds the reader of the 'symbolic snake' from *The Protocols* and the trope of the 'Hidden Jewish Hand', 'which has produced the present Chaos by controlling the finances of the world' (Winrod 1933: 33). Next to animal metaphors, 'the puppemaster' and his 'puppets', the half-open curtain and the 'hidden hand' have been, as illustrated in the section on modern art below, most popular in representing the idea of global conspiracies.

Another popular visual signifier of conspiracy is the dagger. A book entitled *Le Tombeau de Jacques Molai* (De Gassicourt 1797; first published in 1795 with the subtitle 'the secret of the conspirators') establishes the argument that the French Revolution was orchestrated by dark forces, above all the infamous Knights Templar, who sought revenge for the execution of their last Grand Master, Jacques de Molay, by the French king and the Pope in 1314. *Le Tombeau* has an emblematic frontispiece worth dwelling on. At the centre of the scenery lies a naked beheaded male body, stretched out in a scandalous pose. To the right of the beheaded body we see the figure of a blindfolded perpetrator of the crime dramatically displayed against the background of a rising or setting sun. He holds a dagger in his left hand and the head of his victim, by his hair, in the right. On the ground of the cave are a broken sceptre, a crown and mitre. A figure outside the cave, armed with a sword, overlooks/directs the scenery. Without suggesting immediate genealogy, a similar imagery was displayed 115 years later in a more dramatised version on the 1912 election poster of the Belgian Anti-Masonic League (Önnerfors 2017: 117). Under the title 'The work of freemasonry: Revolution, Anarchy', we see, against a dramatic red and black sky, a blond woman pictured from behind, dressed in blood-red, with wild Medusa-like hair, carrying a torch in her left hand and a dagger in her right. In her wake, she has set a village on fire, turned over a cross and the (figurative) Tables of the Law, and broken a pillar, which probably held the crown and sceptre now scattered on the ground, together with a broken sword and a standard. Having trampled underfoot religion, law and political order (just as in the frontispiece of *Le Tombeau*), her next target is the calm village on the horizon. The woman in red does not act on her own. To the left of her we see a sinister character, dressed in a hood and Masonic apron, holding the Jewish Star of David in his left hand and pointing out the imminent target to her. As in *Le Tombeau*, the evil assassin is directed by someone else, who is the mastermind behind the plot. But, in contrast to the monochrome frontispiece from 1797, the 1912 election poster is saturated with the 'chromatic promise of blood' (Leone 2016: 11) and potentially the colour of all-consuming and apocalyptic fire and flames. Within a century, the conspiracy theories of the post-revolutionary era had been blended with virulent antisemitism, not least through the publication of the infamous *Protocols*. Ever since, the idea of the 'Jewish-Masonic plot' has turned into a visual representation of its own. Comparing the two images diachronically, it appears as if certain visual tropes are reused and recombined in new contexts and that the development of conspiracy tropes only generates new expressions as varieties of larger and general frames. This indicates that there is a distinctive mode of visual representation of conspiracy and a recognisable intermediality that has its own traditions and meanings.

## Examples of mixed mediality

One striking element of the visual culture of conspiracy is the intricate relationship between image and text. Following the emblematic tradition, highly charged visual representations are frequently paired with textual references, not only as titles, commentaries or framings (as in newspapers or ads), but as parts of the picture itself. Each form of mediality has specific qualities attractive to creators as much as to communicators (multipliers) of conspiracy theories. While the spoken or written word relies in these cases on (quasi-/pseudo-) rational-argumentative logic, visual communication follows an associative logic and communicates immediately to its spectators. Text and image are not competing forms of expression, but refer to each other, and, in combination, reinforce meaning. This holds true for cartoons, charts and posters, not least in political campaigning, as seen in the Belgian election advert from 1912. Twenty-five years later, the conspiratorial narrative of 'Jewish Bolshevism' was popularised by Nazi institutions and organisations through a series of large-scale propaganda exhibitions. One of these, *Der Ewige Jude* ('The Eternal Jew'), opened in 1937 and was accompanied by a widely disseminated poster. The origins of the trope originate in the Russian October Revolution of 1917, when one of the central themes of Russian antisemitism (that of secret manipulation) morphed into the notion that the revolution itself was masterminded by 'the Jews'. This trope soon made its way to the West. In the Weimar Republic, 'Völkisch' and especially Nazi propagandists made 'Jewish Bolshevism' their political battle cry and the poster for *The Eternal Jew* exhibition featured many of its visual tropes. The central figure is a stereotype of the poor Eastern European Jew, dressed in black, scruffy, his closed eyes, escaping the direct view of the beholder. In his right hand he carries the gold coins of the traitor and in his left the whip of despotic rule. Tucked under his arm, the figure holds a three-dimensional model of the European part of the Soviet Union, marked with hammer and sickle. At that time, everyone in Nazi Germany was familiar with the message: 'The Eternal Jew' is the true ruler of Soviet Bolshevism. For Hanno Loewy, this picture incorporates many of the antisemitic motifs turned into the 'basic equipment of the collective fantasy' in the Third Reich (Loewy 2009: 542). Indeed, in the eyes of experts in Nazi media, the poster genre, for its suggestive emotional impact, was of utmost importance in their communication strategy: 'The Jew is always represented as a type. [...] The posters do not burden the viewer with the scientific problem of the influence of Judaism [...]. The pictorial contents are charged with *subjective assertion*.' (Medebach 1941: 36–7 [our italics]).

Graphically, the possibilities of the poster as pictorial genre are exploited here. The author, Hans Schlüter (sometimes the name is given as Stalüter), and the exhibition organisers relied on striking colours – red and yellow – and prominent pseudo-Hebrew typography (as in anti-Jewish medieval iconography) suggesting both alienation and orientalist exoticisation. The motif became the symbol of the campaign. We can find a 'medial transposition' type of intermediality here, as the motif also was communicated through other visual media, including postcards and book covers. Placed in central locations, it furthermore dominated the public space: At main train stations like Munich and Vienna, and – of monumental size and illuminated at night – on the roof of the Deutsches Museum in Munich (Caumanns *et al.* 2012: 73). *The Eternal Jew* signature poster, along with the textual and visual material of the exhibition – one of the largest in German history –, transmitted the conspiracy theory of 'Jewish Bolshevism' to an audience of millions. Text and image reinforced one another, visually preparing this audience for a war against the Soviet Union and the extinction of the racial other, the Jewish 'sub-human being'.

A second mixed-media example with an equally close text-image relationship is the chart. The example in question once more refers to the conspiracy theory of 'Jewish Bolshevism'. Figure 4.5.3 shows a chart of 1941 from the Nazi Party (N.S.D.A.P.) wall newspaper *Parole der*

*Woche* ('Slogan of the Week'), published as indoor posters for showcases, e.g. in offices, railway stations and restaurants.

The graphic, entitled *Das jüdische Komplott* ('The Jewish Conspiracy'), takes up about two-thirds of the 84 × 120 cm surface area, with explanatory text on the remaining third (Caumanns *et al.* 2012: 76). In the centre is a brutally stereotyped visual representation of (the head of) 'the Jew', with caricatured features. To the left and right, names are inserted into Stars of David, 'Baruch' and 'Mosessohn'. These are the alleged 'Jewish puppetmasters' of the plot: Baruch the alleged close friend of 'Jewish descendant and high-degree freemason' Roosevelt and leading circles of U.S.-society; Mosessohn with direct links to Stalin and the Russian nomenclature. The henchmen of the Jewish puppetmasters, the poster claims, are Roosevelt, Churchill and Stalin – interrelated by Jewish interbreeding and corrupting affinities (and, as it happens, also Nazi Germany's main enemies of war). This major visual narrative of interconnectedness is constructed by yellow arrows, lines and text boxes against a black background, suggesting causality through a collective racial genealogy of culprits. Thus, the image presents a vast network of East-West-European or global relations under Jewish control that, in the context of the year 1941 and an evolving anti-Hitler coalition, developed certain plausibility and credibility for the German viewer.

The power of the chart in conveying conspiracy narratives lies in its pseudo-informative impact. As a multimodal technique of displaying 'evidence', it is able to combine two medial forms of articulation (Rajewsky 2005: 52): Verbal (e.g. names) and visual elements, thereby organising complex causal relations and identifying alleged coherences. This corresponds to the basic conspiratorial assumption that 'everything is connected' (Barkun 2003: 1–14). However,

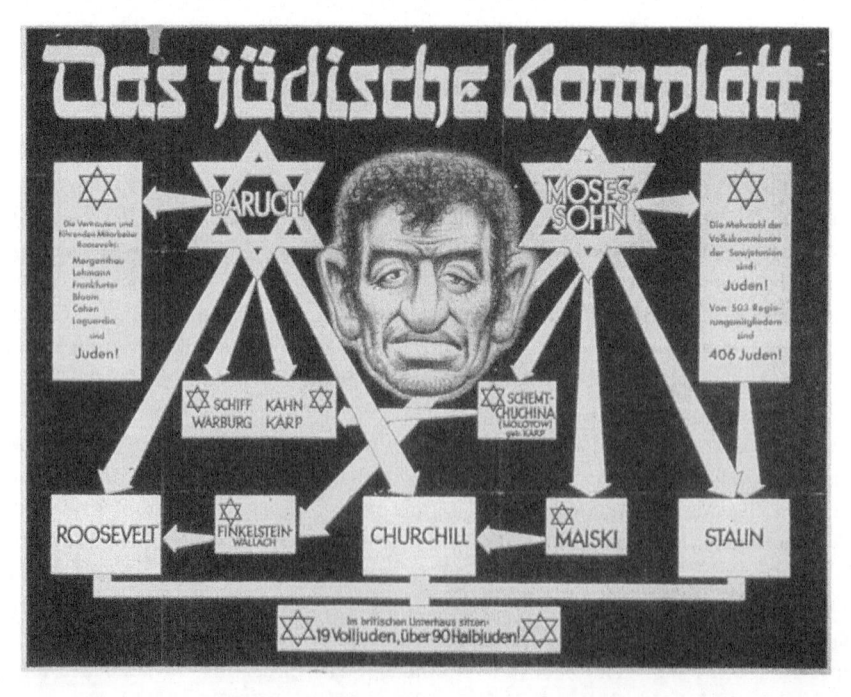

*Figure 4.5.3* „Das Jüdische Komplott" ('The Jewish Conspiracy') (1941) [fragment], colour lithography. Source: "Parole der Woche", edition A, no. 50, Reichspropagandaleitung der N.S.D.A.P. (ed), München: Eher Verlag. Reprinted with permission from the U.S. Holocaust Memorial Museum.

at the same time, the suggestive pictorial effect is relevant: Given the Stars of David and the stereotyped face at the centre of the visual axis, the viewer recognises at once that the Jewish mastermind in the 'conspiracy' is to be found on all sides. In a sense, the chart is a deconstruction and technical description of the octopus metaphor, a blueprint of its functionality.

## Performativity: Conspiracy as spectacle

Closely related to the mixed mediality of text and image is the performance of conspiracist narratives. By staging and re-enacting these narratives in front of a specific audience and involving a multitude of participants, it was possible to display and (rhetorically) demonstrate an example, immediately appealing to affects and emotions. Performativity transgresses textuality (and hence literacy) and visuality through its enactment of the 'Un-outspoken' (Gadamer 1986: 504) in time and space. This dynamic quality has the ability to develop explanatory power in multiple contexts, ranging from premodern times with widespread illiteracy to our contemporary state of hyper-mediality (Madisson 2016), where borders between text, image and performance once again are fluid. One example of the performativity of conspiracism discussed below is modelled on the powerful trope of 'Jewish ritual murder' and 'blood libel', the allegation of a Jewish conspiracy around Passover to abduct (Christian) children in order to mock the Passion of Christ, to ritually murder the children and consume their blood (Erb 1993: 9). This trope offers access to different transmissions in diverse historical contexts and was productive from at least the twelfth to twentieth centuries (and constant repercussions during the twenty-first) both on local or regional levels, but also as a general attribution to 'The Jew' worldwide. There are many representations of the trope of Jewish world dominance, but what concerns us here is the staging of 'conspiracy', 'ritual murder'-trials, enacted as a visual happening on the local level, targeted towards a local audience. Outside the theatre 'court room', the narrative was popularised by establishing a regional cult of martyrs who had suffered from alleged Jewish malevolence, such as Simon of Trent (1472–1475), who was celebrated as a beatified 'saint' in the Catholic Church until 1965. Simon was allegedly kidnapped and ritually killed by Jews (based on testimonies obtained under torture). His memory was glorified through iconic images of his violent martyrdom, highlighting the innocence of the Christian child and the monstrous barbarity of the Mosaic 'other'. The case of Anderl Oxner of Rinn (*c.*1459–1462) was modelled after the Simon of Trent story, his murder and memory immortalised in theatrical performances up to the 1950s.

However, the Order of Jesuits developed to perfection theatrical performance as a tool of strategic communication, not least during the Counter-Reformation of the seventeenth century. The didactic (and rhetorical) function of Jesuit theatre during this period cannot be overestimated. The order decided to stage the 'ritual murder' stories of both Simon and Anderl, turning them into spectacle. The first performance of the Anderl-drama took place in 1621 in the Austrian city of Hall, the first high-profile retelling of the legend (Tilg 2004: 624). It is only possible to reconstruct that performance to a very limited extent, based on an abstract ('Perioche') preserved from the 1621 staging. We know today that the story was simply invented by its author, the physician Hippolyt Guarinonius. Participation was the goal of religious theatre since the days of the medieval mystery plays; to this aim, new and impressive stage props were used. According to Szarota, the spectators went to these performances for stimulation (Szarota 1975: 140). This was achieved by the basic performative situation, in which actors demonstrated something through their actions (like a performed example in rhetoric), and the audience could identify with or reject specific characters. Not only saints and martyrs appeared, but also secular characters, such as the mother whose child was treacherously murdered (by Jews), as well as the murderers themselves. However shocking and cruel the story, the audience could expect a conciliatory ending: While Simon and Anderl, for example, were accepted into the circle of martyr saints, the 'Crudelitas' (personified 'cruelty' as a substitute for the Jews that had escaped) was banished from the stage and sent to hell, while angels snatched the perpetrators' cup and thus saved the martyr's blood.

Here, the spectators were made eyewitnesses to the 'blood libel' conspiracy, to the act of disclosing, as well as to the punishment of the crime, and had the opportunity to express sympathy or disapproval. The Jesuit 'ritual murder' drama was about listening, seeing and participating to become emotionally engaged, as well as about demonstrating something. The actors served through their actions as deterrents or as role models for what was right or wrong and thus – through the performance of conspiracist dualism – established solid ethical norms.

## Monophasic representation

If the ritual murder plays expressed dynamic performativity as the primary mode of transmission, the opposite can be said of static images, as they are displayed in 'monophasic representations', i.e. visual narratives along one particular string of narrative. The enemy images of conspiracy theories are not stable but fluctuate between a particular story and a general frame narrative known to contemporary audiences. In terms of composition, it is not enough to bring stereotypically drawn figures into a pictorial context: It is their context of action that resonates with the idea of conspiracy. In the case of graphic novels, in serial or multiphase pictures, the narrative quality is comparatively easy to identify, since they already through their form embody temporal progression of a story and thus the essential criterion of narrativity – time. Yet another example of the 'ritual murder' narrative in this context is represented by a thirty-part plate in the pilgrimage church of Judenstein (the purported geographical place of ritual murder turned into a place of religious devotion). The plate tells the story of Anderl of Rinn as a story of life, conspiracy, torture, murder and miracles in all their stations, similar to the Stations of the Cross. Underlining its didactic character, until the 1960s, the plate hung right next to the pulpit (Schroubek 1986: 3853). Monophasic pictures are more ambitious in terms of visual narrativity since they depict Jewish 'ritual murder' as one storyline. It is a moment that promises to open up the reflection of past and future. Wolf (2003: 190) has pointed out that this device, frequently a turning point in the story, or the ending, is a significant variety of potentially narrative visual works. This emerges also in another piece of art, represented in Figure 4.5.4, depicting the Anderl-motif, an eighteenth-century sculpture group from the workshop of Austrian woodcarver Franz Xaver Nißl (1731–1804).

The sculpture group is composed of five figures, four of whom would have been recognised at the time as Jews by their 'Oriental' clothing (which also evokes the Ottoman archenemy of the Habsburg empire) and by their facial features, and who surround a brightly dressed child. Originally, the group had been mounted on a large stone, the alleged martyr stone ('Judenstein') itself.

The context of action corresponds to the written and oral narrative and therefore is immediately accessible to the viewer: With the figures holding a knife to the throat of the half-sinking boy, strangling the child and collecting the blood, the act of desecration and ritual murder is anticipated. The action freezes the moral depravity of the antagonists at a gruesome moment.

Here, according to Wolf, we are dealing with a form of narrativity in which chronology, causality and teleology can be deduced. It is a representation of one phase where the temporal dimension is provided through 'frozen action' as a device within the composition. The viewer is able to 'evoke a story related to this action through external, inter-medial reference' to the

*Figure 4.5.4* Wooden sculpture group in the pilgrim church of Judenstein, Rinn, Austria, Franz Xaver Nißl, c. 1766 (coloured in the original). Photo: Heinrich Hoffmann, 1928. Source: German Historical Museum, Berlin. © Raumbildverlag Otto Schönstein / DHM.

ritual murder narrative as 'cultural script' (Wolf 2003: 193). Whereas the sculpture group of life-sized coloured figures, previously placed on top of the 'Judenstein', is inside and thus confined within the church – as a physical destiny for pilgrimages – other modes of transmission allowed regional, trans-regional, national and potentially global outreach through photographs and postcards. When these turned into a popular genre of media at the end of the nineteenth century, the ritual murder narrative was transformed into a modern means of dissemination for the purpose of memories, marketing and geographical branding.

## Conspiracy theories in modern art

The conspiracy narrative of 'ritual murder' migrated, as we have seen, over the centuries through various modes of transmission, from oral accounts to trials and finally beatification and reverence of local saints. Almost immediately, and in parallel with technical development of the printing press, the plot was depicted, performed, displayed and disseminated in different media. Already in the propaganda posters of Nazi antisemitism, modern graphic elements such as collage, arrows and text boxes were integrated into the visual narrative. In the twentieth century, conspiracy theories were communicated in the language of advertising or pseudo-scientific information campaigns. But, beyond intentional propaganda, a large number of post-1945 artists have attempted to engage with dimensions of socio-economic realities deliberately hidden from public record. Others have 'dived headlong into the fever dreams of the disaffected, creating fantastical works that nevertheless uncover uncomfortable truths in an age of information overload and weakened trust in institutions' as a recent exhibition at The Metropolitan Museum of Art (Met Breuer) in New York aimed to demonstrate (*Everything is Connected: Art and Conspiracy*, 2018). Both approaches aim to visualise what cannot be seen at first sight, to make the unseen seen, but with different purposes. The former is an artistic response to the increasing opacity of national and international politics (particularly in a U.S. context) and thus constitutes a clear political statement – a demand for transparency and an end to endemic lies as the primary mode of political communication. The latter is an expression of how art engages with conspiracy culture as a way to destabilise established knowledge-regimes, to illustrate the inbuilt irony of conspiracist imagination and meaning-making or the barely discernible differences between 'truth' and 'post-truth', 'news' and 'fake-news' of the modern and late modern ages (see Chapter 4.10).

How do these positions translate to art? First and foremost, both are replete with synaesthetics (merging different aesthetic expressions and sensations), since conspiracies, imagined or true, (etymologically) presuppose the 'breathing together' of their wicked puppetmasters, it is no surprise that the artistic response is to picture or craft toxic togetherness, outrageous overlaps and acid amalgamations. The ultimate representation of connections is the network. It combines our need for pattern recognition and to detect agency and it connects dots in order to visualise or imagine coalitions, hostile to us and operating in secrecy. In our age of global interconnectivity, the horizontal network has replaced the vertical pyramid as the primary depiction of conspiracy. Mark Lombardi's artwork explores such self-replicating network structures with independent cells and offshoots – not unlike self-growing metastases – spreading in the body politic: Unregulated transnational flows of black capital creating a mesh of interests and interrelations between legal and illegal enterprises across the globe. The revelation of political action beyond electoral control or insight appears to be a recurring feature of U.S. politics. But, modern artists also employ established motifs such as the puppetmaster, as illustrated by Emory Douglas's untitled artwork (1974) in which U.S. president Gerald Ford is depicted as a marionette controlled by a host of corporations.

The motifs of the octopus, or the mythological kraken, are reprised to depict the toxic entanglements of conspiracy. Peter Saul's *Government of California* (1969) is an ambiguous psychedelic example of tentacle-pornographic aesthetics in which Martin Luther King, Jr. is depicted as a black octopus with a halo, but yet completely and inseparably intertwined with the evil forces of economy, politics and drugs. Such zoomorphism has another sci-fi sub-category, alienisation. The *Martian Portraits* (1978) by Jim Shaw elaborate David Icke's conspiracy theories of a ruling class of shape-shifting alien lizards beneath human skin and belongs to the second category of artistic representations of conspiracy with no obvious political edge. Yet another strategy of bringing different aesthetics of conspiracy together is the collage, which, through its particular technology of assemblage establishes immediate interconnections between apparently unrelated images and events. Lutz Bacher's *The Lee Harvey Oswald Interview* (1976) is an elaborate imitation of the cognitive habitus of the conspiracy-theory believer, uniting several strategies of combining information and perspectives. Jim Shaw's cave *The Miracle of Compound Interest* (2006) offers a three-dimensional descent into a 1950s gas station covered by interwoven red spiderwebs. When entering the gas station, the visitor is immediately drawn into the conspiracy of three garden gnomes framed by two large crystalline formations and convening ritually around a fireplace and fluorescent material placed on a cushion. Approaching them resembles an initiation into an incomprehensible and primordial cult. Such epistemological fuzziness or blurring characterises the artwork of Gerhard Richter and Andy Warhol, who both had profound knowledge of advertising and political art. Locating both artists and their production within a shared ontology of the Cold War, John J. Curley (2013) points out that they also shared similar techniques to illustrate and uncover paranoid tensions of their time, such as blurred photography, cut-outs and collages. In the age of the Kennedy assassination, the Cuban Missile Crisis and the moon landing, pattern production and detection were at an all-time high in everything from grainy photographs, amateur movies and Jason Pollock's action painting (van Prooijen 2018: 44). As with *The Lee Harvey Oswald Interview*, it is possible to make the case here for the emergence of obsessive amateur reinterpretation of visual evidence (or what Aupers calls 'pop-semiotics', see Chapter 4.7 and 4.10). Due to the ready availability of media images, the conspiracy is now visible, 'hiding in plain sight', available to everyone (who also are provided with the 'right tools' of analysis, the conspiracist-revelatory gaze). The visual culture of conspiracy is no longer just an act of fictional imagination; it now entails actively deconstructing the true image in search of 'facts'. Whereas Rembrandt used his own irony to express ironic references to what is hidden in plain sight (*The Conspiracy of the Batavians* displays, for instance, a 'sword that nobody holds', Leone 2016: 15), the photography or moving image is now systematically searched for inconsistencies that can be used as evidence for the alleged conspiracy. The public readiness to accept grainy images as proof of ultimate evil developed considerable traction when a global audience was made to believe the existence of supposed Weapons of Mass Destruction on Iraqi soil (around 2002). In a reversed psychology, the narrative logic of conspiracist pattern detection could develop political persuasiveness but proved later to be fiction.

## Conclusion

In the age of hyper-medial meaning-making (Madisson 2016), it is challenging to delineate any limits to the visual expression of conspiracy theories. The amalgamation of aesthetic expression, temporality and spatiality through electronic media offers the potential for iconic representations of conspiracy, whether they are following traditional styles and expressions or are more performative in nature. Digital media provide even more tools to construct conspiracy theories through the abundance of raw material, easily assembled into a professional-looking form (see Chapter 4.7). A primary focus is on visual evidence, since it is instant and available. Nevertheless, we also witness a return to the use of visual shorthand, furthered by the need for quick communication and dissemination on social media through memes, pic-badges or GIFs. For instance, a search for 'Illuminati' and 'Conspiracy' GIFs on Facebook messenger, or the popular meme 'Illuminati confirmed' (as shorthand for evidence of a huge conspiracy), generates countless results displaying the all-seeing eye, a triangle shaped by two hands or the number '666'. Similarly, the badge 'QAnon' has within a year (2017–2018) established itself as a visual code of 'deep-state' conspiracy theories in the U.S.A., while coded imagery suggests that Europe is exposed to a conspiracy of inner and external enemies (Önnerfors 2019: 13–20).

As we have tried to illustrate through the above examples, the visual culture of conspiracy theory is an essential device for its transmission. Over the centuries, the visualisation of the unseen and the uncovering of the hidden real has occasioned the development of different tropes, employed in different situations and transmitted by different media. Particularly productive in this regard has been the complex of motifs attached to the racial 'other', amalgamated with powerful enemy images – as the diachronic variations of the themes 'Jewish ritual murder' and 'Jewish plot' forcefully demonstrate in different cultural contexts. Other tropes emerged parallel to these, such as that of secret societies in general or of Freemasonry in particular and were eventually merged into a similar visual message. Taken together, it has been possible to delineate a palette of visual narrativity in which particular symbols (such as the octopus, the puppetmaster or the dagger) are charged with meanings of conspiracy. What we also attempted to demonstrate is that – ranging from Rembrandt's *The Conspiracy of the Batavians* to Nazi propaganda charts – the visual culture of conspiracy is able to adapt to changing preconditions of mediality and of their inherent traits.

In this regard, antisemitic imagination over the last five centuries serves as a case in point. Whereas its tropes and their content remain, in principle, stable over time (and recur to an established canon of metaphors), their medialisation was adapted dynamically to shifting communicative aims and technologies (from woodcuts to charts), modes of expression, and audiences and their ability to decode the message. Thus, the Manichaean dualism of the 'ritual murder' narrative morphed slowly from representing a Christian enemy image to the vocabulary of the modern political conspiracy theory, aiming to uncover the vast interconnections of assumed causality in the complex state of affairs in global politics. A recent example of this is presented in the 8Chan manifesto of the April 2019 San Diego synagogue assassin, who – conceiving himself as the avenger of Simon of Trent – merged traditional religious anti-Judaism with the conspiracist world view of white supremacist racism. Moreover, when the image of conspiracy moved into the 'age of mechanical reproduction' (in Walter Benjamin's term), it also allowed for new forms of lay reinterpretations (or 'pop-semiotics') and particular styles of D.I.Y. pattern detection, reflecting the grassroots obsessive search for causal connections. In contemporary art, the revelation of conspiracy aims to reveal the hidden dimensions of political reality, whereas the art of conspiracy theory engages with the surreal imagining of malevolent manipulation behind the scenes. Finally, the hyper-mediality of the digital age appears to – once more – dissolve the borders between text, image, sound and performativity, and prepares the ground for visual as much as virtual dissemination.

# References

Anton, A. (2011) *Unwirkliche Wirklichkeiten: zur Wissenssoziologie von Verschwörungstheorien*, Berlin: Logos.
Bacher, L. (1976) *The Lee Harvey Oswald Interview* [Photocopies, typescript, tape, and ink], New York, NY: The Met. Available at: www.metmuseum.org/art/collection/search/283419. [Accessed 25 Septemer 2019].
Barkun, M. (2003) *A culture of conspiracy: apocalyptic visions in contemporary America*, Berkeley: University of California Press.
Butter, M. (2014) *Plots, designs, and schemes: American conspiracy theories from the Puritans to the present*, Berlin/Boston: de Gruyter.
Caumanns, U. (2019) 'Zeigbares: visuelle Narrativität in verschwörungstheoretischen Diskursen', in D. Römer and S. Stumpf (eds.) Verschwörungstheorien im Diskurs: interdisziplinäre Zugänge. Forthcoming.
Caumanns, U., Gronau, L., Lange, C. and Mörsch, T. (eds.) (2012) *Wer zog die Drähte?: Verschwörungstheorien im Bild*, Düsseldorf: Düsseldorf University Press.
Curley, J.J. (2013) *A conspiracy of images: Andy Warhol, Gerhard Richter and the art of the Cold War*, New Haven/London: Yale University Press.
Das jüdische Komplott [Nazi anti-Jewish propaganda poster entitled 'The Jewish Conspiracy'], Washington, D.C.: United States Holocaust Memorial Museum. Available at: https://collections.ushmm.org/search/catalog/pa1123132. [Accessed 25 September 2019.]
De Gassicourt, C.-L. (1797) *Le Tombeau de Jacques Molai*, Paris: Desenne.
De Montfort, P.D. (ed.) (1801) *Colossal Octopus* [pen and wash drawing], in *Histoire Naturelle Générale et Particulière des Mollusques*, Paris: L'Imprimerie de F. Dufart.
Douglas, E. (1974) *Illustrating how corporate interests controlled the president* [photograph], in the *Guardian* 'The revolutionary art of Emory Douglas, Black Panther', 27 October 2008. Available at: www.theguardian.com/artanddesign/gallery/2008/oct/28/emory-douglas-black-panther. [Accessed 25 September 2019.]
Eklund, D. and Alteveer, A. (eds.) (2018) *Everything is connected: art and conspiracy*, New Haven/London: The Metropolitan Museum of Art/Yale University Press.

Erb, R. (1993) 'Zur Erforschung der europäischen Ritualmordbeschuldigungen', in R. Erb (ed.) *Die Legende vom Ritualmord: zur Geschichte der Blutbeschuldigung gegen Juden*, Berlin: Metropol, pp. 9–16.
Gadamer, H.G. (1986) *Gesammelte Werke*, vol. 2, Tübingen: Mohr.
Großhans, S. (2014) 'Who watches the Watchm... – Verschwörungstheoretische Symbolhaftigkeit im Comic', in A. Anton, M. Schetsche and M. Walter (eds.) *Konspiration: Soziologie des Verschwörungsdenkens*, Wiesbaden: Springer, pp. 221–38.
Groh, D. (1987) 'The temptation of conspiracy theory, or: why do bad things happen to good people? Part I: preliminary draft of a theory of conspiracy theories', in C.F. Graumann and S. Moscovici (eds.) *Changing conceptions of conspiracy*, New York: Springer.
Hagemeister, M. (2019) 'Die "Weisen von Zion" als Agenten des Antichrist', in J. Kuber (ed.) *Verschwörungstheorien*, Stuttgart: Akademie der Diözese Rottenburg-Stuttgart, in press.
Hofstadter, R. (1964) *The paranoid style in American politics and other essays*, London: Anthony A. Knopf Inc.
Hugo, V. (1866) *Les Travailleurs de la mer*, Brussels: Verboeckhoven et Cie. https://en.wikipedia.org/w/index.php?title=Verboeckhoven_et_Cie&action=edit&redlink=1. [Accessed 26 November 2019.]
Igumnov, S. (1937) *We will Eradicate the Spies and Saboteurs, the Trotskyist-Bukharinist Agents of Fascism!* [Lithograph on paper], London: Tate Modern. Available at: www.tate.org.uk/art/artworks/igumnov-we-will-eradicate-the-spies-and-saboteurs-the-trotskyist-bukharinist-agents-of-p81656. [Accessed 25 September 2019.]
Jouin, E. (1920) *Le Péril judéo-maçonnique: les 'Protocols' des Sages de Sion*, 7th edn, Paris: Revue Intrnationale des Societes Secretes, 1927.
Knight, P. (2007) *The Kennedy assassination*, Edinburgh: Edinburgh University Press.
Knight, P. (2016) *Reading the market: genres of financial capitalism in Gilded Age America*, Baltimore: Johns Hopkins University Press.
Krause, M., Meteling, A. and Stauff, M. (eds.) (2011) *The Parallax View: zur Mediologie der Verschwörung*, München: Wilhelm Fink.
Leone, M. (2016) 'Preface', *Lexia. Revista de Semiotica*, 23–4: 11–6.
Loewy, H. (2009) '*Der ewige Jude*: zur Ikonografie antisemitischer Bildpropaganda im Nationalsozialismus', in G. Paul (ed.) *Das Jahrhundert der Bilder*, 1st edn, Göttingen: Vandenhoeck & Ruprecht, pp. 542–9.
Madisson, M.L. (2016) *The semiotic construction of identities in hypermedia environments: the analysis of online communication of the Estonian extreme right*, Tartu: Tartu University.
Medebach, F. (1941) *Das Kampfplakat: Aufgabe, Wesen und Gesetzmäßigkeit des politischen Plakates*, Frankfurt am Main: Diesterweg.
Met Breuer (2018) *Everything is connected: art and conspiracy*, exhibition. Catalogue available at: www.metmuseum.org/exhibitions/listings/2018/everything-is-connected-art-and-conspiracy. [Accessed 28 January 2019.]
Meyer, B. (2015) 'Picturing the invisible: visual culture and the study of religion', *Method and Theory in the Study of Religion*, 27: 333–60.
Mitchell, W.J.T. (1994) *Picture theory: essays on verbal and visual representation*, Chicago: University of Chicago Press.
Müller, J. (2015) *Der sokratische Künstler: Studien zu Rembrandts Nachtwache*, Amsterdam: Brill.
Nißl, F.X. (1766) Judenstein [photography of the wooden sculpture group in the pilgrim church of Judenstein], Rinn, Austria: Österreichische Nationalbibliothek. Available at: http://data.onb.ac.at/rec/baa9994142. [Accessed 21 May 2019.]
Önnerfors, A. (2017) *Freemasonry: a very short introduction*, Oxford: Oxford University Press.
Önnerfors, A. (2019) 'Manichaean manipulation: Europe between apocalypse and redemption in the imaginary of the new right', in A. Moberg (ed.) *European disintegration*, Gothenburg: CERGU, pp. 13–20.
Rajewsky, I.O. (2005) 'Intermediality, intertextuality, and remediation: a literary perspective on intermediality', *Intermédialités/Intermediality*, 6: 43–64.
Rembrandt (1661–1662) The Conspiracy of the Batavians under Claudius Civilis [Oil on Canvas], Stockholm, Sweden: National Museum Stockholm. Available at: http://emp-web-84.zetcom.ch/eMP/eMuseumPlus?service=ExternalInterface&module=collection&objectId=17581&viewType=detailView. [Accessed 25 September 2019.]
Rippe, G. and Etter, L. (2013) 'Intermediality, transmediality, and graphic narrative', in D. Stein and. J.N. Thon (eds.) *From comic strips to graphic novels: contributions to the theory and history of graphic narrative*, Berlin/Boston: de Gruyter, pp. 191–217.
Ryan, M.-L. (1992) 'The modes of narrativity and their visual metaphors', *Style* 26(3): 368–87.

Ryan, M.-L. (2004) 'Quest Games as PostNarrative Discourse' in M.-L. Ryan (ed.) *Narrative across media: the languages of storytelling*, Nebraska: University of Nebraska Press, pp. 361–76.

Saul, P. (1969) *Government of California* [Acrylic on Canvas], Frankfurt: Schirn Kunsthalle. Available at: www.schirn.de/en/exhibitions/2017/peter_saul/. [Accessed 25 September 2019.]

Schlüter, H. (1937) *Der Ewige Jude* [Poster of the propaganda exhibition 'The Eternal Jew'], Munich: Deutsches Museum. Available at: www.deutsches-museum.de/verlag/aus-der-forschung/abhandlungen-alt/museum-und-ns-zeit/der-ewige-jude/. [Accessed 25 September 2019.]

Schroubek, G.R. (1986) 'Zur Verehrungsgeschichte des Andreas von Rinn', *Das Fenster*, 20(39): 3845–55.

Shaw, J. (1978) *Martian Portraits* [Gelatin silver prints], New York, NY: The Met. Available at: www.metmuseum.org/art/collection/search/712545. [Accessed 25 September 2019.]

Shaw, J. (2006) *The Miracle of Compound Interest* [art installation], New York, NY: Metro Pictures. Available at: www.artsy.net/artwork/jim-shaw-miracle-of-compound-interest. [Accessed 25 September 2019.]

Simmel, G. (1906) 'The sociology of secrecy and of secret societies', *American Journal of Sociology*, 11(4): 441–98.

Szarota, E.M. (1975) 'Das Jesuitentheater als Vorläufer moderner Massenmedien', *Daphnis*, 4(2): 129–43.

Tilg, S. (2004) 'Die Popularisierung einer Ritualmordlegende im Anderl-von-Rinn-Drama der Haller Jesuiten (1621)', *Daphnis*, 33(3–4): 623–40.

Van Prooijen, J.-W. (2018) *The psychology of conspiracy theories*, London: Routledge.

Winrod, G.B. (1932) *The hidden hand, the protocols and the coming superma*, 6th edn, Wichita, KS: Defender Publishers.

Wolf, W. (2002) 'Das Problem der Narrativität in Literatur, bildender Kunst und Musik: ein Beitrag zu einer intermedialen Erzähltheorie', in W. Bernhardt (ed.) *Selected essays on intermediality by Werner Wolf (1992–2014)*, reprint, Leiden/Boston: Brill, 2018, pp. 349–438.

Wolf, W. (2003) 'Narrative and narrativity: a narratological reconceptualization and its applicability to the visual arts', *Word & Image*, 19(3): 180–97.

Zwierlein, C. (2013) 'Security politics and conspiracy theories in the emerging European state system (15th/16th c.)', *Historical Social Research*, 38(1): 65–95.

# 4.6
# CONSPIRACY THEORIES IN FILMS AND TELEVISION SHOWS

*Michael Butter*

## Introduction

'At the heart of conspiracy theory,' Mark Fenster observes, is 'a gripping, dramatic story' of the desperate efforts of a lone investigator or a small group of heroes to expose and foil the devious schemes of powerful enemies (2008: 119). Plots, that is, complots and intrigues, therefore make for exciting plots, that is, storylines in works of art. Hence conspiracy scenarios have been an important element in fiction of all kinds for many centuries, ranging at least from the intrigues of Shakespeare's villains via the cabals of secret societies in Schiller and his contemporaries to the plots of governments and powerful organisations in the novels of Robert Ludlum and Tom Clancy. After all, fictional representations of conspiracy hold at least two advantages over their – allegedly – factual counterparts. First, outside of fiction, conspiracy theorists can only ever postulate the existence of a conspiracy by offering what they consider conclusive evidence. Inside of fiction, by contrast, conspiracies can be real beyond any doubt, as readers and audiences witness the evildoings of the conspirators directly. Their suspicions are confirmed and become established facts within the diegetic world. Second, the function of allegedly factual conspiracist discourse is to expose the conspirators and move the audience to take action against them. Fictional texts, by contrast, often do not only dramatise the exposure of the conspiracy but also its defeat. The optimism that, despite its generally bleak outlook on the world, informs conspiracy theorising (Butter 2018: 110–11) comes to the fore here more explicitly than in conspiracist texts outside fiction.

This chapter discusses the representation of conspiracies and conspiracy theory in film and television. It focuses almost exclusively on American narratives because of the global dominance that the products of American culture still enjoy and the influence they exert on other national cinemas and television cultures. The first section discusses American fiction films from the 1950s to the present; focusing on the period from the 1990s onward, the second section addresses television shows. Throughout, I place the changing depictions of plots and intrigues in two different contexts: On the one hand, the stigmatisation that conspiracy theories underwent in the second half of the twentieth century, which did not make them unpopular but rendered them problematic; and, on the other hand, the shifting conventions and aesthetics of Hollywood film-making and serial television.

Most studies of American conspiracy theories claim that such suspicions have become more and more widespread and normal over the course of the twentieth century. As Peter Knight puts it, 'conspiracy theories have become far more prominent, no longer the favoured rhetoric of backwater scaremongers, but the lingua franca of ordinary Americans' (2000: 2). In the wake of the Kennedy assassination, revelations about the Vietnam War and the Watergate affair, this argument goes, widespread distrust of the government and its agencies such as the C.I.A. became reasonable and spread through the culture at large. As a result, conspiracy theories are 'no longer "on the fringe"', but have moved into the mainstream (Dean 1998: 10). However, as I have argued elsewhere, there is ample evidence that conspiracy theories were part of the mainstream from the colonial period until after the end of the Second World War. As orthodox knowledge, they were believed by ordinary people, articulated by the nation's most revered leaders such as George Washington and Abraham Lincoln, and thus significantly shaped culture and society (Butter 2014).

Recently, Katharina Thalmann (2019) has built on this argument and demonstrated that conspiracy theories have not become ever more influential since the 1960s but, on the contrary, have undergone a process of stigmatisation. They remain popular but, at least in their explicit form, have been largely excluded from mainstream discourse. As heterodox knowledge, they are derided and problematised by the media, but also constantly reported upon, which has created the impression that they have become more influential. But, what scholars and the mainstream media have mostly been concerned with in recent decades are no longer the potentially harmful effects of conspiracies, but rather the dangers of conspiracy theory. Even the 2016 election did not mark the return of conspiracy theories as legitimate knowledge. The alarmism with which the conspiracist allegations of Donald Trump were discussed in the media shows that they are still considered problematic and are not at all generally accepted (Thalmann 2019: 192; see also Chapter 5.10 of this volume).

## The conspiracy (theory) film

At first sight, it is surprising that larger political conspiracies only begin to feature prominently in American films in the early 1950s (Arnold 2008: 11). One could have expected that the conventions of classical Hollywood narratives would have made such scenarios a standard formula of films much earlier. As David Bordwell et al. (1985) have shown in their seminal study, Hollywood films in the first half of the twentieth century were extremely plot driven and invested into tightly-knit character-centred causality. Much like conspiracy theory, which operates on the assumption that 'nothing happens by accident' (Barkun 2013: 3), Hollywood films tried to exclude coincidence, confining it at most 'to the initial situation' of a film (Bordwell et al. 1985: 13). Moreover, the plot of classical Hollywood films is propelled forward by the combination of the goal that the protagonist wants to reach and the obstacles he faces along the way (Bordwell et al. 1985: 16). Accordingly, the foiling of a conspiracy that presents ever more obstacles to the protagonist would make for a classical plot par excellence.[1]

However, the rules that Hollywood imposed on itself prevented filmmakers until the end of the 1940s from picking up on suspicions of conspiracy circulating in American culture. Throughout the first half of the twentieth century, films were considered pure entertainment and not protected by the First Amendment, which guarantees freedom of speech. Censorship from outside was thus a threat looming large over the industry, and, in order to avoid it, film studios adopted the Production Code in 1934. It specified in much detail what could and could not be shown on screen, and, while it did not explicitly forbid the treatment of politics, filmmakers avoided controversial issues from that realm almost completely. Moreover, the Code explicitly stated that '[t]he history, institutions, prominent people and citizenry of other nations shall be represented fairly' (qtd. in Maltby 2003: 596). Since American conspiracy theories until 1960 tended to focus on foreign plots (see Chapter 5.10 of this volume), this guideline made it virtually impossible to represent conspiracies orchestrated from outside the country.

Accordingly, Hollywood only began to depict a political conspiracy when the vast majority of Americans agreed that such a plot was really underway, so that the filmmakers could claim that they were representing the matter 'fairly'. This was the case from the late 1940s onward when 'a broad anti-Communist consensus' had emerged and 'most liberals as well as conservatives, ... intellectuals as well as plain folks' were convinced that there was a Soviet plot to undermine all American institutions and destroy the country's way of life (Fried 1990: 34). Also fuelled by an investigation into communist subversion in Hollywood by the notorious House Committee on Un-American Activities (H.U.A.C.), the film industry, eager to demonstrate that it was not secretly controlled by communists, began to address the issue (May 1989). These efforts were greatly helped by a 1952 Supreme Court ruling that finally granted movies protection under the First Amendment. Within a few years, Hollywood produced a large number of films that cast the alleged communist conspiracy in the bleakest possible terms.

Films such as *Conspirator* (1949), *The Red Menace* (1949), *Walk East on Beacon* (1952) or *Big Jim McClain* (1952) either focus on ordinary Americans who realise that family members or close friends are secretly aligned with the communists, or on heroic government agents that fight communist intrigues invariably presented as parts of a larger plot. *Suddenly* (1954) combines these two plotlines to a certain degree. The film revolves around a small group of communist conspirators – their leader is played by Frank Sinatra – who want to assassinate the president from a family home, to which they have gained access under false pretence. When the town's sheriff and a secret service agent visit the house and detect their true intentions, the communists kill the agent and take the sheriff and the family members hostage, but they eventually manage to free themselves and kill the conspirators.

*Suddenly* is a typical example of the 'conspiracy film tradition' that began in the early 1950s. As Thalmann defines the genre, conspiracy films are 'narratives which dramatize a relatively small-scale, clearly delineated conspiracy and focus both on the machinations of and the fight against said conspiracy' (2017: 215). In these films, it is established early on that there is indeed a conspiracy. Thus, the story does not focus on the efforts of an investigator to find out what is going on and then to convince a sceptical public of his claims, but instead concentrates on the efforts to foil the plot. Reflecting the status of conspiracy theory as orthodox knowledge during the 1950s and, more specifically, the general belief in a communist plot, the genre peaked later in the decade. It comprises films such as Alfred Hitchcock's *North by Northwest* (1959) and science-fiction films such as *Invasion of the Body Snatchers* (1956), which dramatises the foreign plot against the U.S.A. metaphorically as an alien invasion, or *Them!* (1954), in which gigantic ants, another metaphor for communists, attempt to take-over the country.

The conspiracy film tradition continues throughout the following decades and into the present. Prominent examples include *Seven Days in May* (1964), in which the military tries to take-over the government because it objects to the president's goal to reach a disarmament treaty with the Soviet Union, *Executive Action* (1973), in which big businessmen and secret agencies plot the assassination of John F. Kennedy, *Three Days of the Condor* (1975), in which one part of the C.I.A. plots against some of its own agents to keep their plans for regime change in several countries a secret, *All the President's Men* (1976) about the Watergate scandal and *The Pelican Brief* (1993) about the plot of an oil company to drill in a protected area in the Louisiana marshlands; in the twenty-first century the tradition continues with films like *The International* (2009) or *Salt* (2010). Despite many parallels – for example, it is established beyond doubt that a conspiracy exists and this conspiracy is, with the exception of *Executive Action*, foiled in the end – these films also differ from their 1950s precursors in some respects. For once, the conspirators are no longer Soviet infiltrators or other foreign foes, but members of the administration, the military, the C.I.A. or powerful companies (Ryan, Kellner 1988: 95). Conspiracy films thus mirror the general shift in American conspiracy theorising that occurs during the 1960s: From plots directed against the state to plots by the state and its various institutions (Butter 2014: 59–60). They also reflect the increasing prominence of 'superconspiracies' that comprise different actors, groups and organisations (Barkun 2013: 6). The plots the films revolve around grow bigger and become more and more convoluted over time. Most importantly, the films also reflect the growing scepticism towards conspiracy theory by focusing more on the investigative process of the protagonist, his attempt – he is invariably male (see Chapter 3.3) – to find out what is going on and then convince others of the existence of the conspiracy.

This focus on the cognitive efforts of the protagonist is taken to extremes in conspiracy *theory* films, which emerge in the 1960s in reaction to the stigmatisation of conspiracy theories in the culture at large. Just as conspiracy theory narratives in literature, conspiracy theory films

> give extended attention to the complex, conspiracy-centred 'paranoia' of their protagonists. What matters in these narratives, what shapes and sustains the plot, is not the machinations of a genuine conspiracy per se. Rather, the narratives focus on the fear of their protagonist(s) that a conspiracy, often of immense proportions, might exist.
> (Wisnicki 2008: 2–3)

While this definition makes the films appear rather bleak, Thalmann also highlights that they also work to contain the depressing effects of the threat of paranoia that looms so large by 'constantly shifting from a serious mode of storytelling to an ironic, satiric, and playful mode' (2017: 216). In other words, in conspiracy theory films, the threat of conspiracy is simultaneously a serious *and* a facetious matter.

This filmic tradition begins with John Frankenheimer's *The Manchurian Candidate* (1962), which is based on Richard Condon's novel of the same title. Like the conspiracy films of the 1950s, *The Manchurian Candidate* is concerned with the fear of communist subversion. Unlike the earlier films, however, it both confirms and problematises this fear, thus effectively functioning as 'comment on and expression of common American ideas and ideologies at the height of the Cold War' (Jacobson, González 2006: 49). It is an 'expression' of 1950s ideas because the communist plot is absolutely real and only foiled at the very end; but it is also a 'comment' on such ideas because the film does not resolve right away whether or not the plot is real or if protagonist Major Marco is simply delusional. The brainwashing that Marco and his patrol of abducted soldiers underwent in Manchuria is only revealed gradually over the first half of the film. Moreover, since the narrative employs the device of character-centred flashbacks to disclose the communist plot, it remains also unclear for most of the film if the memories of Marco and another soldier are real or not. Thus, unlike the novel, where the reality of the plot is established from the outset, the film evokes the possibility that 'ungrounded paranoid suspicions' are at work (Dallmann 2007: 90).

Significantly, *The Manchurian Candidate* also breaks with some conventions of classical Hollywood cinema. Not only does it use flashbacks extensively, it also moves away from the goals-and-obstacles logic, featuring characters whose motivations remain unclear (and not because they are part of the conspiracy and keep their real agenda secret) and scenes that are only loosely connected to the overarching story. The most prominent example of this is the famous train scene during which Rosie, introduced in this scene, behaves so weirdly and says so many strange things to Marco that she left a large part of the audience puzzled, and film critic Roger Ebert suspecting that she was a conspirator talking in code (Jacobson, González 2006: 151). Thus, the beginning of the shift from conspiracy to conspiracy theory films is as much fuelled by the emerging discourse of stigmatisation as by the loosening of the conventions of classical Hollywood cinema.

It is therefore not surprising that the conspiracy theory film thrives during the late 1960s and 1970s, since this is both the time during which the stigmatisation of conspiracy theory, as Thalmann describes it, truly gains momentum and the period of New Hollywood. Each of the 'paranoia thrillers' of these years (Pratt 2001: 124) – for example, *Greetings* (1968), which features one character who is obsessed with the Kennedy assassination and clearly delusional, *The Parallax View* (1974), which revolves around a reporter's investigation into a secretive organisation, or *Winter Kills* (1979), a satirical engagement with Kennedy assassination theories – could be used to exemplify the poetics of New Hollywood:

> Disjunctive or associative editing ...; a privileging of mood and character over tightly plotted action; ... episodic, ambiguous, unresolved and/or temporally complex, non-linear narratives, sometimes combined with a flaunting (and hence questioning) of narrative agency itself; ... devices, which collectively heightened the self-consciousness and reflexivity of these films.
>
> *(Langford 2010: 134)*

*The Parallax View* employs these tropes to 'refuse its viewers the safe haven of omniscient knowledge' (Knight 2007: 153): It is never revealed who the conspirators are and what their goal is. In similar fashion, *Winter Kills* 'uses conspiracy as a causal explanation behind the president's death, but mocks and taunts both the protagonist's and the audience's conspiracy inklings' (Thalmann 2017: 252). The films thus problematise and simultaneously endorse conspiracy theorising.

The conspiracy theory film tradition ends in the late 1970s for two reasons. First, the process of stigmatisation that triggered the emergence of the genre in the first place has been completed by then, and films no longer need to perform the cultural work of negotiating this problematisation (Thalmann 2017: 255). As conspiracy theories are frowned upon in mainstream factual discourses, fiction – as a '"nonserious discourse"' where knowledge is 'invented, not found' (Melley 2012: 16) – becomes a space to playfully indulge in a way of making sense of the world that is disqualified as 'serious' discourse but remains nevertheless appealing. Consequently, more traditional films, received by audiences on a 'non-committed basis' (Knight 2000: 45) become more popular again. This shift back is, second, also motivated by the waning of New Hollywood at the end of the 1970s. Film narratives in general became more traditional, straightforward and goal-oriented again, and therefore neither producers nor audiences were much interested anymore in the playful, ironic and self-reflexive aesthetics of the conspiracy theory film. The career of Alan Pakula exemplifies this development, as he first made a prototypical conspiracy theory film with *The Parallax View* and then *All the President's Men* and *The Pelican Brief*, two typical conspiracy films. Another case in point is Jonathan Demme's remake of *The Manchurian Candidate* (2004), which sheds the self-reflexivity and irony of the original (Butter 2015).

However, post-New Hollywood films do not simply return to the straightforward conspiracy narratives of the studio era. Responding to the, by now, culturally dominant scepticism about conspiracy theorising as an adequate way of making sense of the world, the films often do not establish early on, but only later in the film, that a plot exists beyond doubt. Accordingly, these films focus much more on the process of investigating and providing evidence for the conspiracy than the films of the 1950s and 1960s did, which concentrated on the foiling of a plot that was early in the narrative established beyond any doubt. In fact, since the 1990s, the conspiracy film has undergone a development that could be described as a merging of the two traditions described here, resulting in what Mark Fenster has called the 'classical conspiracy narrative' (2008: 122). Fenster captures an interesting development, but the label he assigns it is misleading because 'classical' implies considerable longevity and stability, whereas the films thus categorised are a relatively recent phenomenon. Moreover, in the context of Hollywood film, the label evokes associations with the Hollywood of the studio era, which ended around 1960 and thus long before classical conspiracy narrative in cinema emerged.

Classical conspiracy narratives such as *JFK* (1991) or *Conspiracy Theory* (1997) are structured around 'narrative pivots', turning points in the narrative that occur when 'the protagonist gleans the single piece of information that enables him to realize the real nature of the forces that oppose him' (Fenster 2008: 135). More precisely, there are usually two major pivots in a classical conspiracy film: 'At the first one, the protagonist realizes that something is going on and starts to investigate; at the second one, s/he finally understands what is going on, as all the pieces of the puzzle fall into place' (Butter 2014: 25). Thus, although some classical conspiracy narratives, for example, *The Bourne Identity* (2002) or *The International* (2009), include many action scenes, their plots are not propelled forward by action but by the cognitive labour of the protagonist who tries to find out what is really going on. In addition, classical conspiracy narratives are characterised by a high degree of 'speed' – the narrative is fast-paced and 'a multiplicity of events [is depicted] in brief scenes' (Fenster 2008: 133) – and 'velocity', which refers to 'the geographic, geopolitical, and cognitive aspects of the conspiracy narrative's movement', which is 'both global and increasingly rapid as the narrative progresses' (Fenster 2008: 134). Finally, the films typically stage a 'restoration of agency'. The detection that something sinister is going on throws the usually male protagonist into a crisis, often one of masculinity, because nobody believes him and he begins to doubt himself. At the end, however, the protagonist overcomes this crisis because he manages to prove the existence of the conspiracy and often even 'arise[s] triumphant through [its] ultimate defeat' or at least its public exposure (Fenster 2008: 124).

The most prominent and definitely the most influential classical conspiracy narrative – used, in fact, by Fenster to define the genre – is Oliver Stone's *JFK*. Based on the story of New Orleans District Attorney Jim Garrison, the film suggests that Kennedy was killed by the military-industrial complex because he wanted to withdraw American troops from Vietnam. Indeed, Stone's version of events is, at first sight, extremely convincing because the film's rapid editing is designed to overwhelm the audience. In fact, for viewers it is virtually impossible to distinguish fact from fiction, as Stone 'blended original footage with archival footage ... and faux archival footage. Audiences were thus confronted with a stew of traditionally staged material, actual historical evidence, and fake historical evidence, all mixed together in a compelling story' (Arnold 2008: 138). Replacing logical with formal coherence, the film seeks to interpolate its viewers as conspiracy theorists.

This is nowhere as apparent as in the final courtroom scene. Talking to an assistant who is very sceptical that they will get a conviction for the one alleged conspirator they have managed to put on trial, Garrison implicitly breaks the forth wall:

> This war has two fronts – in the court of law, we hope, against the odds, to nail Clay Shaw on a conspiracy charge. In the court of public opinion, it could take another 25 or 30 years for the truth to come out, but at least we're going to strike the first blow.
> *(Stone 1991)*

Here, Garrison casts the film – released 28 years after the assassination – as another and maybe the decisive blow in the struggle for public opinion. Consequently, his revelations in court are not so much directed at the jurors, who dismiss them quickly, but at the audience for which they are made to appear far more convincing through clever use of editing and *mise-en-scène*. That Garrison is played by Kevin Costner, back then Hollywood's most authoritative voice of moral authority because of *Dances with Wolves*, makes his disclosures all the more powerful.

Since *JFK* so clearly aimed at leaving behind the safe space of fiction where conspiracist ideas can be indulged in with impunity, it is hardly surprising that the film was met with 'voluminous and vituperative criticism' for promoting a conspiracy theory (Fenster 2008: 118). Nevertheless, the film has been extremely influential, leading to a marked increase of those who believe that Lee Harvey Oswald was not a lone gunman (Carlson 2001). Furthermore, the film became a model for non-fictional online documentaries like *Loose Change* (2005–2009) and *Zeitgeist* (2007–2011) that came to dominate YouTube in the mid-2000s largely in response to 9/11. Like *JFK*, the various versions of *Loose Change* and the different versions of the *Zeitgeist* trilogy join very disparate material in rapidly edited sequences to visually overwhelm the audience and convince them of their conspiracist claims (Butter, Retterath 2010).

An interesting – and much less controversial – variation of the classical conspiracy narrative are the film versions of Dan Brown's mega sellers *The Da Vinci Code* (2006) and *Angels & Demons* (2009). Just as the novels, the films display all the characteristics of the classical conspiracy narrative. They focus on the cognitive labours of protagonist Robert Langdon, who restores his agency over the course of each narrative; they are characterised by a high degree of speed and velocity; and they are structured around narrative pivots. At the first pivot, which usually occurs about a third into each film, Langdon, who is very sceptical of conspiracy theories, accepts that there is a sinister plot going on. However, at the second narrative pivot, which occurs towards the end, Langdon does not finally understand what the plot is all about but comes to realise that there is no large-scale conspiracy. In *The Da Vinci Code*, everything has been planned by only one villain, Leigh Teabing, who has tricked two members of Opus Dei into supporting him. In similar fashion, in *Angels & Demons*, Langdon eventually finds out that there is no large Illuminati plot against the Vatican but that the dead Pope's chamberlain is orchestrating events with the help of an unwitting assassin to become the next Pope. In other words, the films are classical conspiracy narratives without conspiracies. As such, they reflect the status of conspiracy theory in the twenty-first century as an appealing but disqualified form of knowledge that can only be safely indulged in within the realm of fiction, where it makes for exciting narratives. Thus, it is no surprise that conspiracy scenarios have also become very popular in television shows in recent decades.

## Conspiracy (theory) in television shows

Since television became a mass medium in the U.S.A. during the Red Scare, it is hardly surprising that several series of the 1950s, for example, *Foreign Intrigue* (1951–1955), *I Led 3 Lives* (1953–1956) or *The Man Called X* (1956–1957), put the fight against communist subversion centrestage. The most successful of these shows was *I Led 3 Lives*, which was based on the memoir of the same title by former F.B.I. informant Herbert Philbrick. Since television shows until the 1980s were strictly episodic, each week's instalment revolved around the fight against a different group of communists trying to infiltrate yet another American institution or organisation. Over the years, the show thus painted 'an ever-expanding social canvas that ma[de] communism seem all the more pervasive and insidious' (Doherty 2003: 143), while also suggesting that as long as decisive action was taken, the threat could be contained within the 30 minutes of a single episode. In line with the general status of conspiracy theory at the time, the show did not aim for a playful 'as if'-reception, but presented the fight against communist subversion as an entirely serious matter. Accordingly, the show employed a variety of techniques to suggest that it was 'a documentary, rather than fictional, text' (Thalmann 2017: 111).

The spy shows that thrived on American television a decade later shared the basic narrative structure with *I Led 3 Lives* but were very different in tone. Clearly inspired by the tremendous success of the first James Bond movies, *The Man from U.N.C.L.E.* (1964–1968), the most successful of nearly a dozen similar shows of the 1960s no longer focuses on an undercover informer as *I Led 3 Lives* had done but focuses instead on the agents combatting the conspiracy. Much like the 1950s shows, though, *The Man from U.N.C.L.E.* revolves throughout around the conflict with one powerful enemy, with each weekly instalment offering a self-contained chapter in that fight. This enemy is now no longer one that also exists in real life like the communists, but a fictional organization, T.H.R.U.S.H., whose members and command structure remain vague but whose goal was clearly world domination. In fact, within the fictional world, T.H.R.U.S.H. is considered so dangerous that the U.S.A. and the Soviet Union join forces to fight it. Thus, the show clearly distances itself from reality and, reflecting the stigmatisation of conspiracy theories that was gaining momentum during the 1960s, invited a more playful reception from its audience than its 1950s predecessors. This is even more true for *Get Smart* (1965–1970), a show co-created by Mel Brooks that parodied shows like *The Man from U.N.C.L.E.* by taking the familiar ingredients of the genre finally over the top, thereby painting a 'portrait of reality ... in which secrets and fear and paranoia were harmless' (Arnold 2008: 78).

During the 1970s and 1980s, then, there were hardly any conspiracy-driven shows on American television and none with any larger cultural impact. The formula of the spy show had become too worn-out even for a medium that thrived on the formulaic. At the same time, the conventions of television did not allow for the highly self-reflexive and formally innovative treatment of the topic as in New Hollywood's cycle of conspiracy theory films. The conspiracy topic reappeared with a vengeance, however, in the early 1990s with *The X-Files* (1993–2002), the most famous and influential conspiracy-related show ever made. The plot revolves around two F.B.I. agents, Fox Mulder and Dana Scully, who not only solve mysterious and often supernatural cases on a daily basis but also slowly unveil a gigantic conspiracy that involves aliens and evil global elites. Often seen as indicative of the conspiracy culture of the 1990s (Knight 2000; Fenster 2008), the show 'brought the screen portrayal of conspiracy theory to a new level' (Arnold 2008: 145).

The narrative of *The X-Files* strikes a balance in two important ways. First, much like the 1970s films to which the show is 'overtly indebted' (Graham 1996: 59), *The X-Files* allows for both serious and ironic readings. In the terminology introduced in the previous section, then, *The X-Files* is both a classical conspiracy narrative and a conspiracy theory show. It can be read as entirely vindicating Mulder, who believes in a large-scale cover-up from the very beginning, and proving wrong Scully, who is very sceptical of Mulder and his suspicions for a long time. In fact, as the voice of reason who questions her partner's outlandish conspiracy theories, Scully embodies the scepticism towards conspiracism as a form of heterodox knowledge deeply ingrained in American culture at the time. That she eventually comes to believe Mulder can be read as a vindication of his suspicions within the diegetic world but not beyond. Unlike the anti-communist shows of the 1950s, '*The X-Files* operates in the key of "as if"' (Knight 2000: 48). However, the show constantly undermines even this certainty with regard to the fictional world. As Knight puts it, '*The X-Files* often deliberately and wittily exploits a self-ironizing aesthetic' that casts serious doubt on the findings of its two protagonists (2000: 50). Not only are there often 'different kinds of explanation' but no 'ultimate solution' for the strange and potentially sinister events the agents deal with each week (Knight 2000: 48); in addition, '[t]he sheer complexity of the conspiracy [and] the inclusion of so many competing references from popular culture … combine to stretch the limits of rationality' (Arnold 2008: 149). As a result, the show can also be read as a parody of the desire to give in to conspiracy theories.

Second, the show features both self-contained episodes, whose plotlines are resolved each week, and an overarching narrative of a global cabal that spans the whole show. In earlier shows like *I Led 3 Lives* or *The Man from U.N.C.L.E.*, the larger intrigues by communists or nefarious organisations constitute the background to each week's episode, but the protagonists hardly ever gain new information about their enemies and never come closer to defeating them. On *The X-Files*, the 'monster of the week' plot sometimes has nothing to do with the conspiracy, but just as often Mulder and Scully learn – or think they have learned – something new about the larger case they are pursuing: The mysterious connections between aliens, government agencies and global elites (Knight 2000: 217). As a consequence, the show featured a much larger recurring cast, as the villains, too, appeared repeatedly, and many of the episodes could no longer be fully appreciated when watched in random order or by somebody who tuned in only occasionally. The conspiracy plot of the show required a new viewing habit from a devoted audience.

In the larger history of television shows, *The X-Files* occupies an important place in the shift from series to serials that occurs during the 1990s and early 2000s and that had led to the emergence of what critics refer to as 'complex TV' (Mittell 2015). As Sarah Kozloff explains, 'Series refers to those shows whose characters and settings are recycled but the story concludes in each individual episode. By contrast, in a serial the story and discourse do not come to a conclusion during an episode' (1992: 92). Obviously, *The X-Files* are still considerably more episodic than many of the most celebrated shows in the 2010s whose tightly-knit narratives often focus on season-long arcs alone and hardly resolve anything at the end of an individual episode. Instead, the show employs its larger conspiracy narrative to balance the episodic and the larger arc. But conspiracy plots appear to be particularly suited for such a balancing. After all, one of the basic assumptions that drive conspiracy theorising is that 'everything is connected' (Barkun 2013: 3). Thus, the possibility that the monster of the week might be connected to the larger story always looms as a possibility for the knowing audience, and this suspicion is sometimes confirmed and sometimes not.

Arguably, shows with overarching conspiracy plots that balance the episodic and the serial are particularly well suited for 'what might be termed the "infinite model" of storytelling' on which much of American television still operates: 'programs generally keep running as long as they are generating decent ratings' (Mittell 2015: 33, 34). Strictly episodic shows like the spy series of the 1960s are best at satisfying this economic need, while shows that lean too heavily toward the serial pole of the series-serial continuum often progress too fast and get too convoluted too quickly or suffer in quality when one major plotline has been concluded and another one has to be thought up. The first two seasons of the German show *Dark* (2018–), whose time travel plot marries mystery and conspiracy in a manner reminiscent of *The X-Files*, are an example of the first problem. Unsurprisingly, the producers have already announced that the show, which explicitly uses the tagline 'Everything is connected', will end after season three. *House of Cards* (2013–2018) exemplifies the second problem. After the Underwoods' conspiracy to make Frank president succeeded at the end of season two, the producers did not know where to go with the plot, but the show's success demanded its continuation. By contrast, shows like *The X-Files* or a few years later *Lost* (2004–2010), which also revolves around a large and sinister conspiracy and develops a mythology much like that of *The X-Files*, reconcile the industry's needs and the desire of contemporary audiences for overarching plotlines, as they slowly but steadily add to the image of the conspiracy. Since conspiracy theory not only assumes that everything is connected but also operates under the assumption that '[t]here is *always* something more to know' (Fenster 2008: 94; original emphasis), the protagonists uncover more and more layers of the plot over the course of several seasons. This, in turn, makes the conspiracy more and more complicated and difficult to grasp.

Accordingly, what Mark Fenster describes as a problem with regard to *The X-Files* – a 'narrative tension between mystery and resolution [as] no single episode can resolve' the larger conspiracy plot (2008: 145–6) – is actually an asset of these shows and, in fact, their organising principle. However, Fenster has a point as these shows run the danger that their conspiracy arcs become so convoluted over time that parts of the audience become disaffected with it, as arguably happened to *The X-Files* in the later seasons (Mittell 2015: 19). Moreover, the complication of the conspiracy over several seasons can also turn into a liability when the shows eventually end, be it because they are no longer successful or because producers and cast want to move on to new projects. *Lost* is notorious for unsuccessfully resolving its conspiracy/mystery plot, whereas *The X-Files* did not even attempt this. In the final episode of season nine, teasingly entitled 'The Truth', which concluded the show's original run in 2002, Mulder and Scully appear to finally have found out everything there is to know about the conspiracy. However, they do not manage to defeat it, and the show ends with their vow to continue the fight. Unsurprisingly, the story then continued with a 2008 feature film – *The X-Files: I Want to Believe* – and two more seasons of the show (2016–2018), which capitalised on a different characteristic of conspiracy narratives – the sudden turnaround.

Another important assumption that all conspiracy theories share is that 'nothing is as it seems' (Barkun 2013: 3). The villains operate in secret, keeping their goals and actions hidden, and only the heroic investigator who has realised that something is going on can uncover their deeds and motives. During the investigative process, friends can turn out to be foes, and what, after much cognitive labour, seems to be the ultimate goal of the plotters can be revealed to be just another smokescreen to hide an even more horrible truth. Such realisations are a stock ingredient of conspiracy films and shows, but especially highly serialised shows employ them to take a plotline in a new direction or to reboot a show that appears to have reached a dead end. Thus, in seasons ten and 11 of *The X-Files*, which continue the story after a hiatus of almost a decade, Mulder has become convinced that everything he and Scully found out at the end of season nine is a sham and that not aliens but humans are the driving force behind the conspiracy he has been tracking for so long. This insight is clearly motivated by what the narrative necessitates of the story: The protagonists cannot simply fight the conspiracy but also need to keep investigating it. In even more extreme fashion, *Alias* (2001–2006), a far more serialised show than the original seasons of *The X-Files*, has repeatedly used shocking revelations to move the narrative into ever new directions. At the end of season four, for example, the protagonist, C.I.A. agent Sydney Bristow, learns that her fiancé, with whom she has been fighting several global crime organisations throughout the show, is not named Michael and does not work for the C.I.A., thus setting the scene for the fifth and final season. In *24* (2001–2010), which thrives just as much on the threat of conspiracy, similar turnarounds occur at least once in each season to move the plot into a new direction. Halfway through season three, for example, it transpires that the biological threat Jack Bauer and his colleagues have been fighting so far has only been staged by the real conspirators to get hold of the virus in question and use it against the American people.

In the twenty-first century, conspiracy theories have figured more prominently than ever in television shows. Currently, there are dozens of shows – *Stranger Things* (2016–), *Designated Survivor* (2016–) or *Bodyguard* (2018), to name just a few recent ones – that revolve to a large degree around conspiracies. What is markedly absent from these shows, however, is the postmodern self-reflexivity and often ironic negotiation of the promises and pitfalls of conspiracy theory that characterises both the films of the 1970s and a show like *The X-Files*. But there are of course exceptions. The first season of *Homeland* (2011–), for example, is as much a conspiracy theory narrative as it is a classical conspiracy narrative, because it is for a long time kept open whether Brody is really an Islamist sleeper or if Carrie, the C.I.A. agent investigating him, is paranoid. At the end, however, she is proven right, and subsequent seasons shed all self-reflexivity with regard to conspiracy theory. In similar fashion, the first season of *Berlin Station* (2016–2019) can be read as a dramatisation of why large-scale conspiracy theories fail to adequately grasp reality. In the show, the C.I.A. does not nearly work as smoothly as conspiracy theorists usually assume. As it turns out in the end, there is no large-scale Islamist plot, but the main suspect has been made to look like a terrorist by a branch of the C.I.A., who had planned to trap a mole inside the agency. However, another part of the agency has found this fiction so convincing that they have abducted and tortured the innocent man. As in the case of *Homeland*, though, in the following two seasons the plots are real, thus attuning the show to the dominant mode of representing conspiracies on television in the present.

## Conclusion

The ongoing popularity of conspiracy films and the sheer omnipresence of television shows that revolve completely or to a large degree around conspiracies have as much to do with the way in which conspiracy scenarios lend themselves to dramatisation in general and extended serialised narration in particular, as it has with American and, more generally, Western culture's fascination with conspiracy theory. Since all the shows mentioned here and virtually all conspiracy films of the past decade embrace the '"nonserious" discourse' of fiction (Melley 2012: 16), they should not be considered an indicator for an ever-continuing mainstreaming of conspiracism. Rather, they testify to and fuel in turn the long-standing appeal of conspiracy theories for those who believe in them and those who do not. For those who believe in them, the representation of plots and intrigues in film and television surely confirms the suspicions they harbour in real life. For those who do not believe in conspiracy theories, these representations are a way to indulge in a way of thinking that remains attractive but that they have learned not to apply to real life.

## Note

1 My argument in this section has been significantly shaped by the chapter on conspiracy (theory) films in Katharina Thalmann's doctoral dissertation (2017). Unfortunately, the chapter is not included in the version published later (Thalmann 2019).

## References

Arnold, G B. (2008) *Conspiracy theory in film, television, and politics*, Westport, CT: Praeger.
Barkun, M. (2013) *A culture of conspiracy: apocalyptic visions in contemporary America*, 2nd edn, Berkeley, CA: University of California.
Bordwell, D., Thompson, K. and Staiger, J. (1985) *The classical Hollywood cinema: film style and mode of production to 1960*, New York: Columbia University Press.
Butter, M. (2014) *Plots, designs, and schemes: American conspiracy theories from the puritans to the present*, Berlin: de Gruyter.
Butter, M. (2015) 'Exit gender, enter race: Jonathan Demme's "Update" of *The Manchurian Candidate*', in R. Heinze and L. Krämer (eds.) *Remakes and remaking: concepts – media – practices*, Bielefeld: Transcript, pp. 41–56.
Butter, M. (2018) *"Nichts ist, wie es scheint": Über Verschwörungstheorien*, Berlin: Suhrkamp.
Butter, M. and Retterath, L. (2010) 'From alerting the world to affirming its own community: the shifting cultural work of the Loose Change films', *Canadian Review of American Studies*, 40(1): 25–44.
Carlson, D.K. (2001) 'Most Americans believe Oswald conspired with others to kill JFK', *Gallup*, 11 April.

Available at: https://news.gallup.com/poll/1813/most-americans-believe-oswald-conspired-others-kill-jfk.aspx. [Accessed: 31 July 2019.]
Dallmann, A. (2007) 'Manchurian candidates: conspiracy fiction, visual representation, and masculinity in crisis', in A. Dallmann, R. Isensee and P. Kneis (eds.) *Picturing America: trauma, realism, politics and identity in American visual culture*, Bern: Lang, pp. 81–112.
Dean, J. (1998) *Aliens in America: conspiracy cultures from outerspace to cyberspace*, Ithaca, NY: Cornell University Press.
Doherty, T. (2003) *Cold War, cool medium: television, McCarthyism, and American culture*, New York: Columbia University Press.
Fenster, M. (2008) *Conspiracy theories: secrecy and power in American culture*, 2nd edn, Minneapolis: University of Minnesota Press.
Fried, R.M. (1990) *Nightmare in red: the McCarthy era in perspective*, New York: Oxford University Press.
Graham, A. (1996) '"Are You Now or Have You Ever Been?" Conspiracy Theory and *The X-Files*', in D. Lavery, A. Hague and M. Cartwright (eds.) *"Deny All Knowledge": reading* The X-Files, Syracuse, New York: Syracuse University Press, pp. 52–62.
Jacobson, M. and González, G. (2006) *What Have They Built You to Do?: The Manchurian Candidate and Cold War America*, Minneapolis: University of Minnesota Press.
*JFK* (1991) Directed by O. Stone [Film], Los Angeles, CA: Warner Bros Inc.
Knight, P. (2000) *Conspiracy culture: from the Kennedy assassination to The X-Files*, Abingdon: Routledge.
Knight, P. (2007) *The Kennedy assassination*, Edinburgh: Edinburgh University Press.
Kozloff, S. (1992) 'Narrative theory and television', in R.C. Allen (ed.) *Channels of discourse, reassembled: television and contemporary criticism*, London: Routledge, pp. 67–100.
Langford, B. (2010) *Post-classical Hollywood: film industry, style and ideology since 1945*, Edinburgh: Edinburgh University Press.
Maltby, R. (2003) *Hollywood cinema*, 2nd edn, Malden, MA: Blackwell Publishing.
May, L. (1989) 'Movie star politics: the Screen Actors' Guild, cultural conversion, and the Hollywood Red Scare', in L. May, *Recasting America: culture and politics in the age of Cold War*, Chicago, IL: University of Chicago Press, pp. 125–53.
Melley, T. (2012) *The covert sphere: secrecy, fiction, and the national security state*, Ithaca: Cornell University Press.
Mittell, J. (2015) *Complex TV: the poetics of contemporary television storytelling*, New York: NYU Press.
Pratt, R. (2001) *Projecting paranoia: conspiratorial visions in American film*, Lawrence, KS: University Press of Kansas.
Ryan, M. and Kellner, D. (1988) *Camera politica: the politics of ideology of contemporary Hollywood film*, Bloomington, IN: Indiana University Press.
Thalmann, K. (2017) *"A plot to make us look foolish": The marginalization of conspiracy theory since the 1950s*, unpublished thesis, University of Tübingen.
Thalmann, K. (2019) *The stigmatization of conspiracy theory since the 1950s: "A plot to make us look foolish"*, Abingdon: Routledge.
Wisnicki, A.S. (2008) *Conspiracy, revolution, and terrorism from Victorian fiction to the modern novel*, London: Routledge.

# 4.7
# DECODING MASS MEDIA/ ENCODING CONSPIRACY THEORY

*Stef Aupers*

## Introduction

Contemporary conspiracy theories are generally formulated about modern institutions such as the state, science, industries, capitalism and the 'power elite' (Melley 2000; Knight 2000; Aupers 2012; Boltanski 2014). Mass media play a particular role in this: From established newspapers to film, documentaries or news – mass media invoke distrust since they are powerful, omnipresent and highly influential in what we think, see and experience. Eva Horn argues in this respect: 'As media enable and inform our perception and our communication, as they surreptitiously intervene in almost every aspect of everyday life, they represent perfect tools of manipulation and thus ideal candidates for any kind of conspiratorial suspicion' (Horn 2008: 128).

Mass media *texts*, from the perspective of conspiracy theorists, are 'not what they seem' (Barkun 2006): They are generally considered staged (arte)facts and tools of manipulation to mislead the public and conceal the underlying conspiracy. From the reading of newspapers, official documents to the meticulous analysis of visual details in the Zapruder-film, the broadcasted moon landing in 1969 or the televised attacks of 11 September 2001 – media texts are both the object of suspicion and speculation. Notwithstanding the media distrust, conspiracy theories are themselves deeply mediatised since their developers depend on media in the formulation and communication of their ideas. This chapter therefore deals with the question of *how conspiracy theorists read and decode mass media texts*. This topic is understudied in the academic literature on conspiracy culture. One of the reasons may be that, generally, conspiracy theories are studied as texts in and of themselves. To study the 'worldviews' and 'beliefs' of conspiracy theorists, scholars often turn to text as a source – they analyse conspiracy narratives in fiction, literature and detective novels (see Chapters 4.2, 4.3 and 4.4), art and propaganda (see Chapter 4.5), or in film and television series (see Chapter 4.6). And, yet, this methodological focus on published texts blinkers the fact that conspiracy theories in everyday life are neither stable narratives nor full-fledged worldviews/beliefs. In fact, we might even question the label 'theory'. Rather, conspiracy 'theorists' are involved in interpretive practices – their 'theories' are unstable, open-ended and (often) non-conclusive interpretations about possible conspiracies (e.g. Dean 1998; Knight 2000; Fenster 2008). Conspiracy theorists are hence assembling information, collecting data, revising texts and are relentlessly involved in interpretive practices to make sense of events: 'Conspiracy theory's interpretive desire produces more than meaning. Conspiracy theorists' interpretive desire *moves* – back in time, around and through events, collecting details, surrounding the conspiracy and leaching it to a long and signifying chain' (Fenster 2008: 110).

Understanding conspiracy theory as an interpretive practice rather than a fully-fledged text, narrative or belief, this chapter focuses on how conspiracy theorists interpret mass media images. Theoretically, this question will be situated in the academic literature on audience reception (e.g. Hall 1980; Morley 1980; Fiske 1998) and participatory media culture (e.g. Jenkins 2006), to demonstrate the relevance of this field for the study of conspiracy theory. From the perspective of media studies and communication sciences, it will be demonstrated that conspiracy theorists are, essentially, (inter)active audiences involved in the decoding of mass media texts to, simultaneously, produce their theories. Empirically, I will use an illustrative case study of YouTubers decoding Illuminati signs and symbols in media texts and public performances of celebrities.

## Encoding/decoding mass media

How do audiences relate to mass media and, particularly, media content? We can make an analytical distinction between different intellectual traditions that were dominant in different historical phases. Halfway through the twentieth century, the majority of theories about mass communication and media effects were by and large informed by the 'mass culture approach' (Abercrombie, Longhurst 1998; e.g. Storey 2003). Audiences, in this approach, were unambiguously at the receiving end of information and communication. Most famously, Horkheimer and Adorno (2002 [1944]) wrote in this respect about the omnipotence of an emergent 'culture industry' – the complex of radio, film and advertising in modern society: Coming from a Marxist position and confronted with propaganda machinery in the Second World War, they warned against the ideological hegemony of media messages, its standardising workings on culture and alienating effect on individuals. The culture industry, they argued pessimistically, feeds on and consolidates the passivity of the audience: It can 'do as it chooses with the needs of consumers – producing, controlling, disciplining them' (Horkheimer, Adorno 2002: 115) since it infuses culture with 'sameness' and, ultimately, reduces 'the individual to a standardized commodity' (Horkheimer, Adorno 2002: 94).

Nowadays, such deterministic assumptions about the workings of media are generally problematised from a theoretical and empirical stance. During the 1970s and 1980s, fundamental critique was formulated on this mass media theory at the Centre of Contemporary Cultural Studies or the so-called Birmingham School. Various scholars (Hall 1980; Morley 1980; Radway 1987) argued that mass produced texts are not necessarily understood by the audience in conformity with the hegemonic ideology installed in them. Texts are fundamentally polysemic and the audience is not passive, but active, in its interpretive practices. In and through their readings of mass media texts, the consumers of novels, films or television create new cultural meanings. This approach represented a paradigm shift in studying the relation between media and audience (Abercrombie, Longhurst 1998). As scholar John Fiske formulated succinctly:

> Popular culture is made by the people, not produced by the culture industry. All the culture industries can do is produce a repertoire of texts or cultural resources for the various formations of the people to use or reject in the ongoing process of producing their popular culture.
>
> *(1998: 24)*

A theoretical model that was and still is highly influential was developed by Stuart Hall (1980). With his famous 'encoding/decoding model', Hall makes the argument that mass media texts with 'encoded' and (allegedly) hegemonic ideologies have different meanings for different people in different social-cultural contexts. Informed by the semiotics of Roland Barthes and others, he argues that 'already coded signs intersect with the deep semantic codes of a culture and take on additional, more active ideological dimensions' (1980: 168). In his work, he distinguishes three ideal-types of readings of texts by the audience: The 'preferred reading' that is passively reproducing the 'dominant-hegemonic position'; the negotiated reading in which consumers adapt the preferred meanings to their personal lives and identities and, finally, the oppositional reading. In the oppositional interpretation of a text, readers are actively resisting the encoded hegemonic ideology and, hence, reading becomes a political act: 'He/she detotalizes the message in the preferred code in order to retotalize the message within some alternative framework of reference' (Hall 1980: 172–3).

The key assumption in audience research as proposed by Stuart Hall is then that there is no inherent (ideological) meaning in a media text since consumers read, decode, reconstruct and, ultimately, produce meaning in different ways. Readings of people are polysemic and, particularly, oppositional readings 'exceed the norms of ideological control' (Fiske 2006: 114). This brings us to a first hypothesis related to conspiracy theories. As counter-narratives self-consciously formulated in opposition to the official interpretation of (mediatised) events, we can argue that *conspiracy theories are grounded in an oppositional reading of mass media texts*. In fact, conspiracy theories can be understood as oppositional readings par excellence. In their critical readings of newspapers, broadcasted news, film, policy dossiers, video clips or mediatised events in politics, sports, entertainment, conspiracy theorists actively resist (alleged) ideological control and, in the words of Hall, 'retotalize the message within some alternative framework of reference' (Hall 1980: 172–3). The adagio 'nothing is what it seems' (Barkun 2006) inspires an oppositional interpretation of the media text wherein it is assumed that ideology, power and manipulation are key. This 'deep' style of reading ideology shows similarities with what Paul Ricoeur called 'hermeneutics of suspicion' (e.g. Knight 2000: 73–5; Harambam 2017). Not unlike Marx, Freud and Nietzsche, conspiracy theorists detect deep structures underneath the surface of what is said, written or visualised in the text and, in a typical modernist way, reduce every empirical detail to the underlying theory. 'Signs and symbols', Harambam argues, 'are not fully understood by their manifest content, but are skeptically addressed for what they hide, repress or conceal' (2017: 248). Transparency can hence be decoded as a sign of concealment while every arbitrary number, letter, word, object or gesture, can have ultimate meaning. Reading the official report of the Warren committee about the cause of death of John F. Kennedy in 1963; watching the 26-second Zapruder film and meticulously analysing its 486 frames; observing the broadcasted moon landing in 1969 or screening the televised attacks of 11 September 2001 – the deep and intense readings of mass media texts bring conspiracy theorists to different (and substantially competing) interpretations about *what really happened*. Even seemingly non-political and aesthetically pleasing clips of pop stars like Rihanna, Madonna or Miley Cyrus, we will see, can be read as signifying a conspiracy to create a new world order. The practice of decoding mass media texts can, perhaps, be understood as key to making a contested conspiracy theory plausible and the invisible conspiracy visible to others. To prove, justify and legitimate their oppositional reading of mainstream media texts, conspiracy theorists actively search for textual/audiovisual evidence, signs and symbols.

The interpretive practices of conspiracy theorists can basically be understood as a form of *pop-semiotics*: Not unlike academic semioticians inspired by the works of Ferdinand de Saussure, Roland Barthes or Charles Sander Pierce, conspiracy theorists are self-consciously making distinctions between signs and what they *really* signify; between denotations and unconventional, *deep* ideological connotations to uncover the underlying conspiracy structuring the text. A rose shown in a video clip is never a rose; a dollar bill never a dollar bill; gestures, aesthetics or performances are never studied in isolation since they are ultimately embedded in a web of intertextual references to other events in history, narratives or forbidden texts. Ultimately, such deep symbolic readings of conspiracy theorists show an affinity with religious (sub)cultures where 'invisible power is made visible' through the use of pictures, aesthetics or other visual mediations (Morgan 2013; Meyer 2015). There is, however, a crucial difference: Conspiracy theorists are not trying to represent God, spirits or metaphysical elements in the natural world but, instead, opaque forces in the cultural world (Aupers, Harambam 2019).

Understanding conspiracy 'theories' as oppositional readings embedded in a practice of decoding of mass media texts, then, is crucial. And, yet, there's another important element in the encoding/decoding model of Stuart Hall and David Morley that is pivotal in *explaining the type of (conspirational) reading* of mass media texts. Interpretations of texts, they argue convincingly, are neither individual nor arbitrary since such readings are always embedded in a social context and related to the social-economic or cultural position of the audience – the (class) interest, education, cultural capital, gender, ethnicity or worldview of the group involved. Such sociological variables, after all, do not only structure *what* people consume but also *how* they evaluate and interpret the text, message or code of a cultural product (e.g. Bourdieu 1984). In the study of conspiracy theories, we can therefore hypothesise that the type of conspiracist reading people have of mass media texts is related to the particular audience – their socio-economic position, ideology or worldview. Quantitative research on conspiracy theories confirms in this respect that conspiracy theories flourish along the whole political spectrum (Oliver, Wood 2014), but that distinct political positions inform *the type* of conspiracy theory one believes in (van Prooijen, Krouwel 2015). Rightist-conservative citizens, for instance, affiliate more with conspiracy theories about climate change being a hoax and progressive-leftist citizens more with conspiracy theories about capitalism, multi-nationals or bankers. The same may be true if we apply other demographic variables such as age, gender, race, etc.

The encoding/decoding model gave rise to various empirical case-studies, varying from the way people from different classes are watching programmes, such as *Nationwide* in the U.K. (Morley 1980), soap series like *Dallas* (Ang 1982), or how women read novels (Radway 1987) and magazines (Hermes 1995). If we consider conspiracy theorists as an active audience, studies are called for that research how they read/decode mass media texts and if these readings can be understood from social context, ideology and worldview.

## 'Produsers'/'prosumers' on the Internet

The model of encoding/decoding, then, provides a valuable theory to empirically study the way conspiracy theorists read established media texts, decode encoded ideologies and formulate conspiracy theories that can be explained by social-economic position, ideology and worldview. Since the 1990s, audience studies were focused not only on the *reading* of *texts*, but, more fundamentally, it was considered that text, literature, film, television, video and music are used as *cultural resources* for young people to construct their personal and social identity (Fiske 2006, Willis 1990). Initially, this debate was launched in relation to the active appropriation of mass media material by, for instance, fans (Jenkins 1992; Hills 2002). This highly devoted audience actively produces narratives about pop stars, celebrities and idols by re-assembling material from songs, video-clips, television shows and news fragments. They are 'textual poachers' (Jenkins 1992) or 'textual performers' (Hills 2002: 41) since they 'produce and circulate among themselves texts which are often crafted with production values as high as any in the official culture' (Fiske 1992: 39).

Conspiracy culture, from this perspective, can be considered as the dark flip-side of fan-culture. Like fans, conspiracy theorists are *not just reading* mass media, they are also actively exploiting it as a cultural resource to build their worldview and construct their identity. Conspiracy theories are typically *bricoleurs*: They tap into various media sources, texts, images, fragments of news, scientific facts, literary fiction and audio-visual material (see Chapter 4.5). Instead of passive consumers, they are a highly productive audience since they use this material to build a coherent narrative and ground the plausibility of their conspiracy theory. A good example is David Icke who is most famous – or notorious – for his 'reptilian thesis': The idea that 'reptilian human-alien hybrids are in covert control of the planet' (Robertson 2013: 28), but also known for his assemblage and 'synthesis' of different sources (cf. Barkun 2006; Ward, Voas 2011) to claim epistemic authority (Harambam, Aupers 2015). Icke reads scientific reports, findings and theories about chemistry, quantum physics or evolution theory; he draws on science fiction texts like *The Matrix* (2000) and integrates these with conspirational readings of the Bible, esotericism, spiritual New Age literature and advertising. In fact, he is not just a consumer/reader of mass media texts, but uses media as a cultural resource to construct his own conspiracy narrative. Although David Icke is, of course, in no way representative for conspiracy theorists in general, his highly productive and eclectic stance vis-à-vis media texts exemplifies a broader trend in conspiracy culture where the distinction between encoding/decoding and production/consumption is eroding. This is not new but becomes more prevalent with the rise of the Internet in the 1990s and contemporary social media: The non-hierarchical structure and 'participatory culture' (Jenkins 1992) of this medium provides a platform for 'amateurs' to compete with 'professionals' in the production of knowledge. Academically trained scientists, professional journalists and politicians can now publicly be criticised with alternative knowledge claims. Andrew Keen (2008) writes in this respect (in a pejorative sense) about how the Internet cultivates a 'cult of the amateur' where the distinction between established (scientific) knowledge and alternative truth claims erodes. He argues:

> Can a social worker in Des Moines really be considered credible in arguing with a trained physicist over string theory? Can we trust a religious fundamentalist to know more about the origins of mankind than a PhD in evolutionary biology? Unfortunately, the Web 2.0 revolution helps to foster such absurdities.
>
> *(2008: 44)*

Pessimistic accounts such as these are, however, complemented with overly optimistic accounts about the end of the monopoly of mass media, the democratisation of knowledge and the rise of 'citizen journalism' (Bowman, Willis 2003) since lay-people are now actively and publicly 'collecting, reporting, analyzing and disseminating news and information' (Bowman, Willis 2003: 9; see also Önnerfors 2020).

Notwithstanding the overly moral underpinnings of this debate, it is pivotal for the empirical study of conspiracy theories to understand that, unlike with mass media, conspiracy theorists are not only 'decoding' established texts on the Internet (in the sense of Stuart Hall). Since the structure of the medium is principally democratic, they are essentially part of a global chain of communication where citizens are simultaneously 'decoding' and 'encoding', consuming and producing. There's yet another paradigm shift here from an *active audience* to an *interactive audience* that reads, negotiates and decodes texts, actively discusses worldviews on fora, uploads user generated content via blogs, vlogs or YouTube clips, and shares self-produced information with others on the Internet. This erosion of the typical modern distinction between encoding and decoding, production and consumption on and through the Internet is captured by concepts like the 'prosumer' (Ritzer, Jurgenson 2010) or 'produser' (Bruns 2008). The 'prosumer', it is agreed, adds to the value of the product – not only through interpretation – but by co-producing content and actively distributing and disseminating the information. If we apply this to contemporary conspiracy theorists on the Internet, we see that they are often decoding mass media messages and, based on that, encoding and producing their own texts. These vary from personal articles on websites, texts on Facebook, tweets on Twitter to audio-visual material on YouTube. Given the fact that these texts are, in turn, decoded by other 'prosumers', conspiracy theories on the Internet may potentially develop into global 'digital memes' (Shifman 2014): They are popular texts constantly 'circulated, imitated, and or/or transformed via the Internet by many users' (Shifman 2014: 41).

## Audio-visual readings on YouTube

The theories and concepts outlined above, then, are helpful to understand the way audiences (including critical audiences like conspiracy theorists) relate to texts on the Internet. They are no longer only decoding mass media by having particular interpretations (as Stuart Hall argued), but are often actively encoding, producing and 'publishing' their own texts based on mass media material. Of particular interest here is the video-sharing platform YouTube, founded in 2005, that exemplifies the participatory culture of the Internet (Burgess, Green 2018). Indeed, on YouTube, 'amateurs' can produce and broadcast their own videos on countless topics – varying from personal vlogs made on a smartphone to full-fledged documentaries.

Conspiracy theories are flowering on YouTube. They are broadcasted on channels like 'Conspiracy theories & Disclosures', 'Celebrity Conspiracy theories' and 'Government conspiracies', and vary from vlogs posted about media events like the 'Grammy Awards', the 'Super Bowl', 'State of the Union' to new, disastrous events like high-school shootings or terrorist acts. Such videos can be understood as audio-visual readings. A few formal elements are important here. In general, these videos are multi-media *assemblages* of textual, visual and audio fragments that are selected, edited and combined in a particular way by their producers to build a coherent and convincing narrative about a conspiracy. The reading, therefore, is already embedded in the personal arrangement of the mass media material: Selected fragments of interviews, public performances, visual cues, combined sometimes with inserted graphics, stats, animations, have the function to prove the conspiracy theory. The visual image is pivotal here: Guided by the modernist motto 'seeing is believing', audio visual readings rely on visual 'evidence' or, rather, 'virtual eyewitnessing' (McKenzie-McHarg 2019: 142). This reliance on visual information instead of text; visual rhetoric instead of argumentation, is not exclusive for YouTube videos of course, since it has a long tradition in propaganda and art (see Chapter 4.5), but is increasingly an important, yet undertheorised, element of modern conspiracy theories (McKenzie-McHarg 2019). In addition to the selection of visual fragments, the actual interpretation/reading/decoding or explanation of *what is really going on* is performed generally by a voice-over of the author. (S)he is taking the lead in the interpretation and showing that 'what we think we see' is actually 'not what it seems'. Do you think the broadcasted moon landing is real? Just look at the absence of stars and the direction of the shadows demonstrating the position of the cameras in the Hollywood studio! Do you really think the Twin Towers were attacked by Al Qaida instead of being an inside job? Just look at the (underlined) small explosions in the tower, just before it crumbles down! Do you think you are seeing an innocent video clip of a famous artist? Just learn to read the hidden signs and symbols in the media text to change your mind!

Selected visual evidence and voice-over operate in tandem and, in coalition, reinforce one another in the oppositional reading of mass media events. This constitutes the audio-visual reading on YouTube that differs from other media forms. Unlike elitist texts in books, literature or fiction, or professionally produced films, series or documentaries – YouTube provides the option for 'amateur' conspiracy theorists to visualise the invisible. Over 30 years ago, Sherry Turkle argued in psychoanalytical terms that 'the computer, like a Rorschach inkblot test is a powerful projective medium' (1984: 14). She considered the personal computer a 'mirror of the mind' (1984: 15) inviting people to project their individual concerns, personal ideas and private fantasies on the screen. In analogy, social media like YouTube provide open-ended platforms to express and share the *social imagery about the power elite* and the social systems they represent. The empirical question is, then, how are mass media messages reconstructed in the oppositional reading of a conspiracy theory? What style of decoding is used to make the invisible conspiracy visible? And, can we explain the different readings by looking at the social-economic position or ideology of the users? To explore these questions, an illustrative case study of YouTube videos will be discussed in the next section. It loosely covers a diverse cluster of conspiracy theories united by the well-known claim that a secret society of Illuminati is dominating the entertainment industry.

## Reading Illuminati in the culture industry

The ultimate question addressed in contemporary conspiracy theories is: What is the *real reality* behind the reality that is staged? And, more specific: Who, then, is *really* in control? (Boltanski 2014). The culture industry, in this respect, is a usual suspect: Halfway through the twentieth century, Horkheimer and Adorno (2002 [1994]) sketched a grim image of its omnipotence and radical influence on the minds, thoughts and experience of individuals in modern societies. Given the contemporary global, oligarchical and highly complex nature of major companies like Universal, Bertelsmann, Sony, Warner, Disney, Viacom, Corporation – the 'Magnificent seven' (Hesmondhalgh 2013: 195) – the culture industries have only become more powerful. Not surprisingly, they are hence a prime source for the conspiracist imagination. Since these companies are de facto producing the mass media messages that people see, watch, hear in everyday life, these messages are the object of oppositional readings and active forms of decoding: 'Nothing is what it seems'.

One of the most popular genres of conspiracy theories about the culture industry on YouTube is that organisations and companies operating in this field are not mainly interested in amusement for the people – let alone money-making. The goals of companies in the industry are political, since they are in fact ruled by the 'Illuminati' – a mysterious cultural and economic elite that allegedly strives for a new world order by using celebrities, implementing subliminal messages in songs, films, television shows and games and, in doing so, 'brainwash' the ignorant audience to complete their evil masterplan: The constitution of a new world order. Obviously, conspiracy theories about Illuminati have a long history in Western society. Secret societies varying from the Templars, Rosicrucians, Freemasonry to the 'Bilderberg group', have been a staple in conspiracy theory, at least, since the end of the 18th century (cf. Önnerfors 2017: 3, 114–5, 120). The 'Order of the Illuminati', founded in 1776 by Adam Weishaupt in Bavaria, was originally an organisation based on principles of the Enlightenment, with the goal to resist political corruption and reform society. Once banned ten years later, conspiracy theories about its persisting influence on historical events (i.e. the French Revolution) and world politics flowered in Europe and the U.S.A. (Önnerfors 2017). Such theories about 'Illuminati' have been a stable feature in the cultural margin ever since, but resurfaced over the past few years in various publications in the conspiracy milieu (Barkun 2006) and popular culture, varying from Umberto Eco's *Foucaults Pendulum* (1988), Dan Brown's *Angels and Demons* (2000, movie 2009), the film *Lara Croft: Tomb Raider* (2001) and recent video games such as *Deus Ex* or *The Secret World*. Countless theories flourish about Illuminati governing the complex global world of politics, the finance or science; in many prominent audio-visual readings on YouTube nowadays they even control the entertainment industry. Titles like 'The music industry exposed', 'Illuminati rebellion', 'Illuminati symbolism in video games', 'Illuminati control the world', 'Illuminati Idols: Who Really Controls the Pop stars?' or 'How the Illuminati runs Hollywood' illustrate that the culture industry is, ultimately, read as an exponent of the Illuminati.

A particular role in these conspiracy theories is played by celebrities who are in many ways representing the culture industry and – through their mediatised performances – allegedly indoctrinate the general public. As a 'power elite' (Mills 1956), they are literally the public faces of the culture industry and are incarnating its power. Hence, they are the pinnacle of conspiracist speculations on YouTube. The picture painted of celebrities in the context of Illuminati theories is extremely ambivalent: On the one hand, celebrities are considered 'puppets', 'programmed robots' or 'sex slaves' of the industry and the elite of the Illuminati. The standard narrative here is a Faustian one: Particularly female stars like Rihanna, Miley Cyrus, Britney Spears or Katy Perry sold their souls to the Illuminati to obtain fame and the stories point to a corrupted biography: 'good American girls', like Miley Cyrus, Ariana Grande or Britney Spears, raised and trained in the 'Disney factory', have 'gone bad' once they became famous. Rihanna, from this perspective, has been dubbed 'princess of the Illuminati' – a term that she playfully used in one of her clips, thereby fuelling the rumours about her alliance with the 'Illuminati'. On the other hand, celebrities are attributed with almost supernatural power. In their position carved out by their masters, they are capable of reaching a worldwide audience and, as programmed role-models, influencing the beliefs, identities and lifestyles of youngsters. Countless examples are used to prove the relations celebrities have with the Illuminati. 'Discovered' signs and symbols in clips (the all-seeing eye, pyramids, etc.), but also interviews, 'live' performances and song texts, allegedly demonstrate the alliance with the Illuminati. Indeed, in many theories, worldwide media performances, such as the Grammy Awards, the Super Bowl or the Oscars, are considered as 'ritual performances' in honour of the Illuminati.

In short, conspiracy theories about the Illuminati running the culture industry exemplify oppositional readings as described by Stuart Hall. The 'preferred reading' of the culture industry is self-consciously replaced by an alternative, critical or resistant reading. In fact, not unlike neo-Marxist academics, conspiracy theorists explicitly deconstruct the preferred reading of media texts as providing 'innocent' entertainment as a hegemonic ideology to install 'happy consciousness' in public consciousness to conceal the evil conspiracy of the Illuminati. In their paranoid readings, the culture industry is not about entertainment but worldwide domination; celebrities are not talented artists but slaves of the Illuminati; media is not a tool of representation but of manipulation.

## Decoding Illuminati symbolism

How, then, do conspiracy theorists on YouTube decode media texts produced by the entertainment industry? It is pivotal for the argument here that their claims about Illuminati are not just 'theories' but 'readings' since they are grounded in the practice of decoding mass media texts. A typical example is 'Does the Illuminati control the music industry?' (2014) – a professional-looking documentary in which the phenomenon is discussed in a quasi-journalistic style and open (yet highly suggestive) questions are formulated about the role of the Illuminati in the music industry. The video is an example of an audio-visual reading: Visual images are selected from mass media while written text and voice-overs reinforce one another to strengthen and communicate the oppositional reading.

The clip opens with a collection of visual fragments of celebrities making signs of a triangle with their fingers (allegedly signifying the Illuminati symbol of a pyramid), covering one eye with one hand (the 'all seeing eye') or showing other alleged 'Illuminati symbols'. The voice-over comments:

> The clues are everywhere. Symbolism can be found in almost all major music videos, concerts, merchandise and records. But what does it mean? Is all of this ... just a mere coincidence? Or is it in fact a secret message from our favorite popstars? Are Kanye, Lady Gaga, Drake, Jay-Z, all trying to tell us something – something that we shouldn't know about the darker side of the music industry?
>
> *(Uncovered 2014: 00–27 seconds)*

Then an image is shown of a meeting of European royalties, politicians and C.E.O.s and, after this, a picture of serious (business) men in suits before a large media screen. This is, in turn, followed by a close-up of the unfinished pyramid with the all-seeing eye pictured on top. A connection is then audio-visually established between what we see (signs and symbols) and the reading (the power of the Illuminati):

> Is it possible that Kanye West is referring to an elite organization thought to be manipulating the world's most powerful corporations? Or was Kanye perhaps referencing the secret and all-powering fraternity known as the Illuminati? And if so, what interest would this organization have in the music business?
>
> *(Uncovered 2014: 42–57 seconds)*

Particularly, more personal vlogs are dedicated to the decoding of signs and symbols to educate the general public. Self-proclaimed 'Illuminati watchers' analyse every detail of clips, films, texts or lyrics of songs in their videos. On the one hand, there are countless readings on YouTube of lyrics of songs of Rihanna and Jay-Z (*Umbrella*, 2008), Katy Perry (*Dark Horse*, 2013) or Taylor Swift (*Look what you made me do*, 2017), in which seemingly romantic sentences, words and meanings are decoded as metaphorical references to the Illuminati. Practices of decoding, however, are by no means restricted to words/texts and are more often focused on visual elements in media texts or public performances. In their audio-visual readings, conspiracy theorists commonly show celebrities like Jay-Z, Beyoncé or countless others making the 'ritual' gesture of the all-seeing eye; they explain the body movements of Rihanna that are similar to the iconic image of 'Baphomet' – the satanic, horned figure that allegedly was the God of the Templars; they decode the patterns of the dress of Lady Gaga conveying hidden references to the Jewish mystic current of Kaballah; they deconstruct the use of pyramids, triangles and occult symbols in performances; they refer to symbols of snakes, reptiles or reveal the shape-shifting behaviour of Beyoncé in an interview fragment; they detect the returning colours black and white in clips signifying the floors of Masonic lodges and speculate extensively about hidden Illuminati messages in films. Most notable are Walt Disney films like the *Little Mermaid* showing hidden phallus symbols in seaweed, the *Lion King*'s face hiding a nude woman and the ghost in *Aladdin* allegedly murmuring 'Young teenagers, take of your clothes'.

Indeed, given the assumption that 'the clues are everywhere', potentially everything can be/is decoded. Illuminati symbols can be detected in stage performances, choreography, gestures, body movements, close-up of eyes, pupils, clothing, props and so on. By analysing these signs, particularly in relation to one another, conspiracy theorists try to unveil the omnipresent ideology of the Illuminati and visualise what remains hidden to the general public. In addition to disentangling signs and signified, the authors often aim to strengthen their interpretation through intertextual references. The analysis of a text, in other words, is often embedded in a broader context of (pseudo)scientific references (i.e. theories about the 'unconsciousness', communication theories about 'subliminal messages', quotes of philosophers like Plato or Nietzsche), (pseudo)historical events or even (science) fiction. A good example of this intertextual form of meaning-making is the analysis of a performance of Katy Perry at the Grammy Awards in 2014 that was by many bloggers and vloggers understood as a ritual performance in order to honour the Illuminati. The performance of her new song *Dark Horse*, that had just been released, was analysed in detail and often embedded in a rich context of intertextual references: The 'Dark horse' with red, glowing eyes in the background, for instance, was considered a reference to the Apocalypse (one of the four horses described in the biblical chapter 'Revelation'), while the glowing red cross on Perry's dress was in many cases considered similar to the red cross of the Templars – ultimately indicating that she was, in fact, ritually re-enacting the murder of Jacques de Molay in 1314 who allegedly was the last grand master of the Templars. (As noted on Lara Atwood's (2014) blog: 'at the 2014 grammys, that event was symbolically relived to the cheers of a modern crowd'. The Templars, in turn, are then rhetorically connected to Freemasonry, the order of the Sith in the Hollywood movie *Star Wars* (white knights with red crosses) and, ultimately, the Illuminati in the contemporary music industry.

In short, by placing the Illuminati symbols spotted in contemporary media texts in a broader context of scientific, historical and fictional references, conspiracy theorists add to the meaning and urgency of their claim. After all, they communicate: The striving for a new world order is not new – it has always been the staple of secret societies and has been the driving force in history.

## Audiences and conspiracy theories

A final issue to deal with from the perspective of audience perception studies is: Who, then, is the audience? In the work of Hall, Morley and others, this question is not so much answered in psychological – or biographical – but rather sociological terms: If we want to understand the different readings of a media text, we have to relate it to the social-economic position, ideology or worldview of the audience.

If we apply this perspective to the producers of the videos on YouTube, we can, of course, first all conclude that such readings about Illuminati in the entertainment industry share a *habitus of distrust*. It is a mainstay in the literature on conspiracy theories that conspiracy theorists score high on distrust vis-à-vis the government, modern institutions and elitist groups (Oliver, Wood 2014). From this perspective, the culture industry is a usual suspect. Celebrities – representing the opaque system of the culture industry – are logically connected to this since they represent the culture industry and are, literally, the faces and incarnations of its power. Notwithstanding previous academic assumptions about celebrities being a 'powerless elite' with limited institutional power (Alberoni 2007), recent studies argued that they are the new status group par excellence. Like the traditional elite, Kurzman et al. (2007) state, celebrities enjoy interactional, normative, affectual and even legal privileges. According to Driessens (2013), 'celebrity capital' is a form of 'meta capital': Being a mediatised celebrity opens up access to social capital, economic capital and even political capital. There is, however, another important difference with the traditional cultural elite: Unlike stable, traditional status groups where status is inherited (Weber 2013 [1922]), celebrity thrives on the market and is 'status on speed' (Kurzman et al.

2007) – it exemplifies extremely rapid social mobility. In general, then, this perspective on celebrities being a new, global 'power elite' may explain the appeal of conspiracy theories about celebrities. They provide a subversive, yet clear, account about why some pop stars are suddenly very successful and explain to people the extraordinary status and influence of celebrities in contemporary society.

In general, the habitus of distrust vis-à-vis the opaque culture industry and elitist status of celebrities may, then, explain oppositional readings of the culture industry on YouTube. But, if we look at the 'authors' of the videos and the underlying ideology, we can detect differences as well. Within this resistant reading of the culture industry there are different audiences, with different biographies, motivations and ideologies. Although the reference to the 'Illuminati' is a *lingua franca* in conspiracy narratives about the culture industry, the term proves to be an 'umbrella category' (Barkun 2006: 52) – a common trope that refers to different groups with slightly different aims. Who the Illuminati 'really are' and what they 'really want' varies from text to text – seemingly in accordance with different, often radically contradicting, worldviews of the authors of YouTube clips. Typically, four variations on the theme can be distinguished:

- *Christian reading*. In this popular Christian scenario, generally brimming with biblical references, it is argued that Illuminati governing the culture industry are actually satanists. They are involved in a 'Luciferian scheme' to seduce (young) consumers to engage with occultism, esotericism, New Age and to use (hidden) symbols and sexualised messages to distract them from the Christian faith.
- *Antisemitic reading*. There is a widespread claim that the Illuminati are actually Jews (often connected to banker family Rothschild), controlling the companies for economic reasons and, ultimately, seeking world domination. This scenario converges with a long-standing tradition of antisemitic conspiracy theories (Pipes 1997) and, particularly, about Jews seeking world domination – a theory that flowered since the famous (fake) document *The Protocols of the Elders of Zion*, in which Jews conspired to take over the world, was fabricated in 1903, translated in different languages and circulated widely thereafter (see Chapter 3.8).
- *Neo-Marxist reading*. This leftist scenario is closely related to Horkheimer and Adorno's critical theory about the omnipresent 'culture industry' commodifying culture and indoctrinating a passive audience into 'false consciousness', 'sameness' and 'pseudo-individualism'. It exemplifies the fact that contemporary conspiracy theories often incorporate theories and assumptions from the social sciences and, as such, can be understood as a form of 'pop sociology' (Harambam, Aupers 2015).
- *Science fiction reading*. This scenario delves into various themes of science fiction, arguing that the Illuminati have a 'transhumanist' agenda, are aliens or (most notable) 'shape-shifting lizards' that have come to the Earth already thousands of years ago and have infiltrated humanity. Clips of celebrities like Rihanna or Beyoncé allegedly 'confirm' they have reptilian eyes, scales underneath their skin or are able to shape-shift. This scenario is rooted in works like that of Erich von Däniken and is particularly developed and popularised by David Icke – probably the most influential conspiracy theorist in the field today (cf. Barkun 2006).

These scenarios illustrate not only that there are different types of conspiracy theories about the culture industry being run by the Illuminati, but, more importantly, that different audiences adopt/create variations that are converging with their identities and ideologies. Christians have distinctly different readings of mass media texts than antisemitic groups, leftist neo-Marxist activists or sci-fi fans. Indeed: *mass media texts may be considered polysemic projection screens* that are, like Rorschach tests, open for various interpretations. However, the interpretations are neither individual nor arbitrary: They are embedded in and shaped by the worldviews of those who formulate them. The four ideal-typical groups formulated here are derived from the YouTube clips – several biographical references and explicit ideological statements made by the author – but the typology is more tentative than empirically grounded. A more systematic study of who the producers and audiences are and how their ideology relates to their interpretation/reading/decoding is called for.

## Conclusion

Conspiracy theories are often studied as stable media texts or narratives in literature, fiction, film or series. The goal of this chapter was to focus on how conspiracy theorists relate to mass media texts in everyday life. Given their ambivalent relation to media, the question was how they actively read, decode, use media texts in the formulation and communication of conspiracy theories. In the context of this concern, I discussed different theoretical perspectives in audience research and Internet studies and applied these to a specific case on conspiracy theories about Illuminati in the entertainment industry on YouTube. Conspiracy theorists on YouTube, it is suggested in this chapter, exemplify oppositional readings of mass media texts and performances and the paranoid style of decoding is characterised by a 'deep' reading of signs and symbols in seemingly trivial aesthetical details that, together, allegedly unveil the underlying ideology of the culture industry.

This reading/decoding/prosumption of media texts should be further studied if we want to better understand contemporary conspiracy culture. Conspiracy theorists are critical audiences and their different readings can be understood as a form of pop-semiotics: The academic discipline in cultural studies of analysing the deeper meanings embedded in texts, evidently, trickled down to the 'amateur' who is not just a passive audience. (S)he produces new, subversive texts and videos on the Internet that are shared and, in turn, interpreted and decoded by other users. Studying this phenomenon of pop-semiotics, particularly on the Internet, has its own epistemological and methodological complexities: On the one hand, conspiracy theorists are competing with the humanities in the interpretation of literature, films, series and video games. Trained scholars do not have the authority on the question: What do these texts *really* mean? One of the common academic reflexes of being involved in such an 'interpretive contest' (Melley 2000) is 'boundary work' (Harambam, Aupers 2015) – the making of a clear-cut distinction between good/rational (academic) and bad/irrational (amateuristic) interpretations of media texts to, ultimately, defend the superiority of science as a professional practice (Gieryn 1983). Rather, however, I suggest that we should face the complexity of 'double hermeneutics' (Giddens 1984) in analysing the interpretive practices of conspiracy theorists: As academics, we are now in the position to not only analyse, read and decode published texts, but to *read the readers* and *decode the decodings* of these readers on the Internet. Herein lies, I think, one of the challenges for future research of conspiracy culture.

## References

Abercrombie, N. and Longhurst, B. (1998) *Audiences: a sociological theory of performance and imagination*, London: Sage Publication.
Alberoni, F. (2007) 'The powerless "elite": theory and sociological research on the phenomenon of the star', in S. Redmond and S. Holmes (eds.) *Stardom and celebrity: a reader*, London: Sage Publication, pp. 65–84.

Ang, I. (1982) *Watching Dallas: soap opera and the melodramatic imagination*, London: Routledge.
Atwood, L. (2014) 'The symbolic burning of the Knights Templar at the 2014 Grammy Awards', *Sakro Sawel*, 22 September. Available at: https://sakrosawel.com/the-symbolic-burning-of-the-knights-templar-at-the-2014-grammy-awards. [Accessed 5 September 2019.]
Aupers, S. (2012) '"Trust No One": modernization, paranoia and conspiracy culture', *European Journal of Communication*, 26(4): 22–34.
Aupers, S. and Harambam, J. (2019) 'Rational enchantments: conspiracy theory between secular scepticism and spiritual salvation', in A. Dyrendal, D.G. Robertson and E. Asprem (eds.) *Handbook of conspiracy theory and contemporary religion*, Leiden: Brill Publishers, pp. 48–69.
Barkun, M. (2006) *A culture of conspiracy: apocalyptic visions in contemporary America*, Berkeley, CA: University of California Press.
Boltanski, L. (2014) *Mysteries & conspiracies: detective novels, spy stories and the making of modern societies*, Cambridge: Polity Press.
Bourdieu, P. (1984) *Distinction: a social critique of the judgement of taste*, London: Routledge and Kegan Paul.
Bowman, S. and Willis, C. (2003) *We media: how audiences are shaping the future of news and information*, Washington, DC: The Media Center at the American Press Institute.
Bruns, A. (2008) *Blogs, wikipedia, second life and beyond: from production to produsage*, New York: Peter Lang.
Burgess, J. and Green, J. (2018) *YouTube: online video and participatory culture*, Cambridge: Polity Press.
Dean, J. (1998) *Aliens in America: conspiracy cultures from outerspace to cyberspace*, Ithaca, NY: Cornell University Press.
Driessens, O. (2013) 'Celebrity capital: redefining celebrity using field theory', *Theory and Society*, 42(5): 543–60.
Fenster, M. (1999) *Conspiracy theories: secrecy and power in American culture*, 2nd edn, Minneapolis: University of Minnesota Press, 2008.
Fiske, J. (1998) *Understanding popular culture*, 2nd edn, London/New York: Routledge, 2006.
Fiske, J. (1992) 'The cultural economy of fandom', in L. Lewis (ed.) *The adoring audience: fan culture and popular media*, London: Routledge, pp. 30–49.
Giddens, A. (1984) *The constitution of society*, Cambridge: Polity Press.
Gieryn, T.F. (1983) 'Boundary-work and the demarcation of science from non-science: strains and interests in professional ideologies of scientists', *American Sociological Review*, 48(6): 781–95.
Hall, S. (1980) 'Encoding/decoding', in S. Hall, D. Hobson, A. Lowe and P. Willis (eds.) *Culture, media, language: working papers in cultural studies*, London: Hutchinson, pp. 1972–9.
Harambam, J. (2017) *'The truth is out there': conspiracy culture in an age of epistemic Instability*, unpublished thesis, Erasmus University Rotterdam.
Harambam, J. and Aupers, S. (2015) 'Contesting epistemic authority: conspiracy theories on the boundary of science', *Public Understanding of Science*, 24(4): 466–80.
Hermes, J. (1995) *Reading women's magazines*, Oxford: Blackwell.
Hesmondhalgh, D. (2013) *The cultural industries*, Washington, DC: Sage Publications.
Hills, M. (2002) *Fan cultures*, New York: Routledge.
Horkheimer, M. and Adorno, T. (2002 [1944]) *Dialectic of enlightenment: philosophical fragments*, reprint, Stanford: Stanford University Press.
Horn, E. (2008) 'Media of conspiracy: love and surveillance in Fritz Lang and Florian Henckel von Donnersmarck', *New German Critique*, 35(1103): 127–44.
Jenkins, H. (1992) *Textual poachers*, London: Routledge.
Jenkins, H. (2006) *Fans, bloggers and gamers: exploring participatory culture*, New York: New York University.
Keen, A. (2008) *The cult of the amateurs: how blogs, My Space, YouTube and the rest of today's user-generated content are killing our culture and economy*, London: NB Publishing.
Knight, P. (2000) *Conspiracy culture: from Kennedy to the X-Files*, New York: Routledge.
Kurzman, C., Anderson, C., Key, C., Lee, Y.O., Moloney, M., Silver, A. and Van Ryn, M.W. (2007) 'Celebrity status', *Sociological Theory*, 25(4): 347–67.
McKenzie-McHarg, A. (2019) 'Experts versus eyewitnesses: or, how did conspiracy theories come to rely on images?', *Word & Image*, 35(2): 141–58.
Melley, T. (2000) *Empire of conspiracy: the culture of paranoia in postwar America*, Ithaca, NY: Cornell University Press.

Meyer, B. (2015) 'Picturing the invisible: visual culture and the study of religion', *Method and Theory in the Study of Religion*, 27: 333–60.
Mills, C.W. (1956) *The power elite*, New York: Oxford University Press.
Morgan, D. (2013) 'Religion and media: a critical review of recent developments', *Critical Research on Religion*, 1(3): 347–56.
Morley, D. (1980) *The 'nationwide' audience*, London: British Film Institute.
Oliver, E. and Wood, T.J. (2014) 'Conspiracy theories and the paranoid style(s) of mass opinion', *American Journal of Political Science*, 58(4): 952–66.
Önnerfors, A. (2017) *Freemasonry: a very short introduction*, Oxford: Oxford University Press.
Önnerfors, A. (2020) 'Researching right-wing hypermedia environments: a case-study of the German online platform einprozent.de', in S. Asche, J. Busher, G. Macklin and A. Winter (eds.) *Researching the far right: theory, method and practice*, London: Routledge. Forthcoming.
Pipes, D. (1997) *Conspiracy: how the paranoid style flourishes and where it comes from*, New York: The Free Press.
Radway, J. (1987) *Reading the romance: women, patriarchy and popular literature*, London: Verso.
Robertson, D. (2013) 'David Icke's reptilian thesis and the development of New Age theodicy', *International Journal for the Study of New Religions*, 4(1): 27–47.
Ritzer, G. and Jurgenson, N. (2010) 'Production, consumption, prosumption: the nature of capitalism in the age of the digital "prosumer"', *Journal of Consumer Culture*, 10(1): 13–36.
Shifman, L. (2014) *Memes in digital culture*, Cambridge, MA: MIT Press.
Storey, J. (2003) *Inventing popular culture: from folklore to globalization*, New Jersey: Wiley-Blackwell.
Turkle, S. (1984) *The second self: computers and the human spirit*, New York: Simon and Schuster.
Uncovered (2014) 'Does the Illuminati control the music industry?' *YouTube*, 25 November. Available at: www.youtube.com/watch?v=ANlPZO12nQw. [Accessed on 27 August 2019.]
van Prooijen, J.-W. and Krouwel, A.P. (2015) 'Mutual suspicion at the political extremes: how ideology predicts conspiracy beliefs', in M. Bilewicz, A. Cichocka and W. Soral (eds.) *The psychology of conspiracy*, London: Routledge, pp. 79–99.
Ward C. and Voas, D. (2011) 'The emergence of conspirituality', *Journal of Contemporary Religion*, 26(1): 103–21.
Weber, M. (2013 [1922]) *Economy and Society*, Berkely, CA: University of California Press.
Willis, P. (1990) *Common culture: symbolic work at play in the everyday cultures of the young*, Maidenhead: Open University Press/McGraw-Hill Education.

# 4.8

# THE INTERNET AND THE SPREAD OF CONSPIRACY CONTENT[1]

*Simona Stano*

## Introduction: The mediatisation of conspiracy theories

Contemporary media represent a particularly fertile ground for conspiracy theories (Craft *et al.* 2017). While in the past it was difficult to disseminate alternative views of important events (Olmsted 2009), things have radically changed in today's communication environments, where advances in technology have made it relatively easy for people to disseminate a variety of narratives and points of view. This has resulted in a noticeable increase in media messages promoting conspiracy theories, with consequences on the public's belief in such theories (cf. Mulligan, Habel 2012; Swami *et al.* 2013; Jolley, Douglas 2014a, 2014b; Einstein, Glick 2015). Official news and information are now more frequently put side by side with alternative versions, including unverified data and fake news. In fact, according to German sociologist and philosopher Jürgen Habermas, the separation between fact and fiction is often abandoned altogether:

> News and reports and even editorial opinion are dressed up with all the accoutrements of entertainment literature.... What in this way only intimates itself in the daily press has progressed further in the newer media.... Under the common denominator of so-called human interest emerges the *mixtum compositum* of a pleasant and at the same time convenient subject for entertainment that, instead of doing justice to reality, has a tendency to present a substitute more palatable for consumption and more likely to give rise to an impersonal indulgence in stimulating relaxation than to a public use of reason.... With the arrival of the new media the form of communication as such has changed; they have had an impact, more penetrating (in the strict sense of the word) than was ever possible for the press.
>
> *(1991: 170)*

Furthermore, technological advances in communication have caused a profound societal change with regard to how information is handled: Mistrust in institutional authorities and official information has resulted:

> In the claim that everyone holds views of current events and of course also in the claim that these views are the only true ones.... Thus, conspiratorial interpreting in time has

become a part of the everyday self – evident handling of information for whose part it has gained popularity.

(Kimminich 2016: 36)

This does not necessarily mean that the Internet and new technologies are driving a new age of conspiracy theories (Uscinski, Parent 2014), but it is certainly relevant and indicates the need to deal with online communication to better understand conspiracy thinking in contemporary society. Therefore, this chapter aims precisely at analysing how conspiracy theories proliferate through contemporary online media – the so-called 'new media' – and with what effects. While a number of scholarly studies on conspiracy theories have focused on their manifestation in the mass media (e.g. literature, cinema, radio and television), in fact, only a few (see Erdmann 2016, Madisson 2016, Stano 2016, Thibault 2016 and, more generally, Leone 2016 for some case studies) have analysed them in digital media, providing interesting but limited results. The same applies to non-scholarly works (see, for instance, McMahon 2004). In order to fill this gap, the following paragraphs will make reference not only to research specifically addressing conspiracy theories, but also to relevant findings in communication studies, finally exploring a particularly relevant case study: Anti-vaccination conspiracy theories.

## The Web 2.0: Increasing participation or dis-/misinformation?

The expression 'Web 2.0' (or 'participatory' or 'social' Web) was introduced by Darcy DiNucci in 1999 in reference to websites promoting participatory culture, allowing their users to interact easily with each other through user-generated content in virtual communities. The first stage of the World Wide Web's evolution (the so-called 'Web 1.0') made access to online content mainly passive, because of the competences required to produce and distribute it. The Web 2.0, however, enhances users' activity and participation by providing them with simpler tools for the creation and diffusion of online information. Blogs, social networks, online forums and other digital media have made it easier to produce and share content online. They allow personalised and multidirectional communication (many-to-many) that exploits the bi-directional channel of the network to go beyond the broadcasting model (one-to-many) typical of mass communication. Social networks, for instance, not only allow users to easily create and propagate textual, visual or audio-visual posts, but also have specific functions to help users react to and comment on such posts, as well as to re-share them (e.g. Twitter's 'retweet' button, Pinterest's 'pin' function, Facebook's 'share' option or Tumblr's 'reblog' function).

While such a transition has resulted in evident advances in communication and information systems, enhancing the democratisation of information and making it easier for people to share ideas and knowledge, it has also fomented 'disinformation' and 'misinformation'. That is to say, it has resulted in the deliberate or unintentional spread of false or inaccurate information, allowing fake news and conspiracy theories to prosper. Information on social media, in fact, does not have to be investigated or confirmed in order to be shared, and this might lead to unsubstantiated and even false rumours spreading like wildfire. Some forms of control have been gradually introduced, precisely as a way to prevent, or at least try to reduce, misinformation, but as we discuss more in detail below, they have not proven to be particularly effective, and so deceptive and fake news still prosper on social media.

Evidently, such phenomena also existed before, but the speed and ubiquity of the Internet have provided an extremely fertile ground for alternative narratives, therefore resulting in their enlargement and rapid spread. Not only do people share and comment on official news and bulletins, but more frequently now, as facts occur, Internet users develop their own narratives through blogs and social networks even before such facts are covered by institutional media. As a result, the 'global village' postulated by Marshall McLuhan (1962; 1964) has rapidly taken the shape of an 'alternative media ecosystem' (Starbird 2017), namely a complex network of individuals and domains that, among other things, generate and promote conspiracy theories that undermine online readers' trust in official information.

## The propagation of conspiracy theories online

How do conspiracy theories propagate online? How do they manage to become at least as visible and shared as official and proven information? In order to answer these questions, the following paragraphs will briefly recall some models and theories developed to describe the spread of information on and through social media, to help us better understand how conspiracy theories circulate within contemporary mediascapes.

The metaphor of virality has been increasingly used to refer to online communication and, in particular, social networks (cf. Marino, Thibault 2016). The analogy with viruses suggests the idea of a sort of 'contagion' taking advantage of the permeability of culture to allow specific elements to penetrate, and therefore infect, its 'D.N.A.'. In accordance with microbiology, such a model conceptualises viral texts as small infectious agents existing in the form of independent particles, whose 'genetic code', which is protected by a capsule and other layers that make it impenetrable from the outside, is capable of infecting the D.N.A. of culture's 'cells', which have porous borders and are therefore open to external elements. In this view, viral particles evolve and reproduce by 'poisoning' (as the etymology of the word *virus* suggests) a host organism whose immune system is not able to impede – or at least limit – such a contagion.

Building on Richard Dawkins's description of meme as a 'unit of cultural transmission, or a unit of imitation' (1976), that is to say a sort of 'cultural gene' moving from one brain to another (exactly as genes do move from one body to another), both scholarly (see, for instance, Shifman 2013; Cannizzaro 2016) and common language have increasingly adopted the idea of 'Internet meme' to describe such mechanisms of contagion. More specifically, the idea of virality has been used to refer to viral content circulating on the Internet (McKenzie 1996), thus reinterpreting Dawkins' definition as a 'fitting metaphor for Internet culture, affording exact copies of digital artifacts, rapid person-to-person spread, and enormous storage capacity' (Marwick 2013: 12).

From such a perspective, the wide spread of conspiracy theories in contemporary mediascapes can be seen as an uncontrolled contagion that, thanks to both the permeability of culture and the agency of memes, has increasingly affected social discourses. Exactly as with other viral texts, conspiracy theories would have therefore progressively 'infected' the Internet, hence finding larger consent among its users.

However, this view is problematic, since it attributes to Web-users a passive role and represents them as infected objects of an external action (that of the viral content), rather than as active subjects. In other words, virality theories suggest the reductionist idea that messages are totally and unconditionally accepted by their receivers (as it was supported by some outmoded models of communication, such as the 'magic bullet' or 'hypodermic needle' theory). Conversely, research has shown that the media have selective influences on people and should be better described by step-flow models, which contrast the idea, claimed by the hypodermic needle theory, that people are directly influenced by mass media. According to the two-step flow model developed by Paul Lazarsfeld, Bernard Berelson and Hazel Gaudet (1948), for instance, ideas flow from mass media to opinion leaders, and from them to a wider population. Furthermore, as Henry Jenkins (cf. Jenkins *et al.* 2013) pointed out, memes do not have operational capacity in themselves, which means that they cannot propagate without the active intervention of users. The porosity of culture, in other words, is not to be confused with the passivity of those who belong to it, as Lotman (1984) effectively pointed out by insisting on ideas such as the semiosphere's resistance to change and the distinction between central and peripheral elements within it. Subjects inhabiting the cultural and communicative dimension cannot and should not be conceived as passive receptors, since they actively intervene on texts, making them become 'viral' precisely through an act of appropriation that refers not only to a specific intention but also to a particular knowledge (from the simple act of understanding such texts to their re-semantisation).

Consequently, if a contagion takes place, it seems to take the shape of a *contact*, as the etymology of the word suggests, rather than that of a *contamination*, as the common conception of virality assumes. In this respect, it is interesting to recall Giulia Ceriani's analysis (2004) of *contamination* and *fusion* as inter-object relationships. According to the Italian scholar, these two *modi operandi* relate to the semantic axis 'multiplicity' *vs.* 'unity' in opposite ways: Contamination favours multiplicity, by making the original objects that are combined together (i.e. 'contaminated') still recognisable in the resulting object; by contrast, fusion completely denies variety, by creating a new, unique object while annihilating the pre-existing ones. In online communication, neither the original content nor the acts generating viral texts are easily distinguishable; most commonly, a new object is generated and any trace of the pre-existing texts that gave origin to it is lost. If a contamination takes place, therefore, it merely represents the anticipation of a subsequent process of fusion, which tends to make the former invisible. Any 'fusioned' object, in other terms, seems to follow a 'rhizomatic development' (Deleuze, Guattari 1980): It has no roots, nor vertical connections, but spreads horizontally, opposing the organisational structure of the tree-system that charts causality along chronological lines and looks for the origins of things.

An alternative description of the processes through which online content is able to propagate and reach large amounts of people is provided by Henry Jenkins, Sam Ford and Joshua Green in their book *Spreadable Media: Creating Value and Meaning in a Networked Culture* (2013). Here they contrast the concept of 'stickiness' – aggregating attention in centralised places – with that of 'spreadability' – dispersing content widely through formal and informal networks. While theories on virality are mainly based on stickiness, the three scholars argue that online content is not replicated perfectly, but rather 'manipulated' by users, who play therefore a key active role in such a process. In this view, the Internet does not merely enhance the replicability of the texts that circulate within it, but rather fosters their personalisation and reinterpretation by means of mechanisms of manipulation that function as a hook to both users' engagement and agency (Marino 2015). In other words, each appropriation of an online text tends to restructure it, creating new forms and leading to its reinterpretation (Dusi, Spaziante 2006). Such mechanisms can be described primarily in terms of:

- *Sampling*: The adoption of a portion or 'sample' from a pre-existing text.
- *Remixing*: The structural modification of a text, including the insertion of new elements, which can be intentional but also unintentional.
- *Remaking*: The re-creation of a pre-existing text, which can more or less evidently alter such a text.

Regardless of the specific mechanism in action, it is important to notice that people tend not to simply share online content as it is, but rather to modify and incessantly reinterpret it (e.g. by adding comments, combining it with other texts, or de- and re-contextualising it). This evidently requires a specific effort from users, conferring upon them an active role, and thus undermining the simple idea of a passive infection generally associated with the metaphor of virality. In this view, online conspiracy theories are not understood as the passive repetition of the same 'infective' content across the Internet, but rather as the active reinterpretation and adaptation of such content by users, who thus confer different meanings on them.

Another crucial characteristic of contemporary communicative systems that can help us better understand conspiracy theories and their propagation in today's mediascapes is the so-called information overload: While the Internet has expanded the variety and amount of available information, creating a more diverse space for public debate, greater access to information has also made it more challenging for the user to evaluate the reliability of information. This has led scholars to denounce an excess of information, which has been described variously as 'infobesity' (Rogers et al. 2013), 'infoxication' (Chamorro-Premuzic 2014), 'information anxiety' (Wurman 2012), 'explosion' (Buckland 2017) or, most commonly, 'overload'. In other words – while indisputably enhancing pluralism – the abundance of sources, news and opinions available on social media produces an effect of confusion and uncertainty that makes it difficult for users to choose which information to trust and focus on.

Simultaneously, the Web has seen the emergence of so-called echo chambers, that is to say, situations in which individuals are exposed only to information from like-minded individuals:

> Selective exposure to content is the primary driver of content diffusion and generates the formation of homogeneous clusters, i.e., 'echo chambers.' Indeed, homogeneity appears to be the primary driver for the diffusion of contents and each echo chamber has its own cascade dynamics.
>
> *(Del Vicario et al. 2016: 554)*

Comparing Facebook pages reporting on scientific and conspiracy content, for instance, Quattrociocchi and Vicini (2016) showed that users who are deeply engaged in a community are more likely to become focused on particular topics, thus becoming 'isolated' from the neighbouring environment, i.e. other topics and views. Although there is no direct relation between such a phenomenon and the information overload, it is interesting to note the difference between the emotional effects deriving from them: Social media users are likely to find their opinions constantly 'echoed' back to them, which develops tunnel vision and reinforces individual belief systems over verified facts – the search for which is affected by the anxiety deriving from the unmanageable amount of information available on the Internet.

This configuration creates barriers to critical discourse on online media: It feeds propaganda and extremism and reduces democracy and critical debate (Sunstein 2017). In this respect, Cass Sunstein (2001) developed the idea of 'information cascade' – i.e. when Internet users pass on information they assume is true even though they cannot verify it – to claim that the Internet today creates 'cybercascades' of information that develop extremely rapidly and are therefore very difficult to control. Hence, fake news and conspiracy theories are more likely to prosper, generating large communities of supporters, as we will see in a specific case study below.

## The spread of anti-vax conspiracy theories: A case study

Opposition to vaccination dates back to the introduction of vaccines themselves (Wolfe, Sharp 2002). Figure 4.8.1, for instance, shows a print by Charles William published in the early nineteenth century as propaganda against the smallpox vaccination. Some opponents of the vaccination, such as Dr Benjamin Moseley (physician at the Royal Hospital Chelsea), are named on the

*Figure 4.8.1* 'A monster being fed baskets of infants and excreting them with horns, symbolising vaccination and its effects'. Etching by C. Williams, 1802(?). Wellcome Collection (https://wellcomecollection.org/works/vbux8st5). Creative Commons Attribution (CC BY 4.0)].

obelisk on the right; on the left the vaccinators, wearing bull's horns and a tail, feed babies to the 'Vaccination monster', which has the front legs of a lion and the hind legs of a cow – symbolising brutality and a literal reference to the animal from which vaccination originated.

This image reflects the huge opposition to the smallpox vaccine in England and the U.S.A. in the nineteenth century: While some objected that it was administered by piercing the skin, others disliked that the vaccine came from an animal. Moreover, a number of people had a general distrust of medicine and many opposed the vaccine because they believed it violated their personal liberty (see Fullerton Lemons 2016).

Controversies, then, also extended to other substances and acts, from the dispute on the efficacy and safety of the diphtheria, tetanus and pertussis immunisation to the still lively debate regarding the use of a mercury-containing preservative called thimerosal, aluminium compounds or other substances considered toxic in vaccines, etc. Among these cases, there is one more than any other that has resulted in a number of widespread 'anti-vax conspiracy theories': The measles, mumps and rubella (M.M.R.) vaccine controversy, which is directly related to the discredited British former gastroenterologist Andrew Wakefield.

In 1998, Wakefield (and other scientists who later retracted their names from the study) published an article in *The Lancet* – one of the world's oldest and most influential medical journals – suggesting a direct relationship between the M.M.R. vaccine and the development of autism and some chronic intestinal pathologies. In fact, the link was not explicitly stated in the paper, but research (Reeves 2005; Fahnestock 2009; Kolodziejski 2014, among others) has shown how the rhetorical and textual strategies adopted by Wakefield and his colleagues encouraged such an interpretation, while employing the same writing style of typical research papers.

Less than a month after publication, in fact, the journal published seven letters (Beale 1998; Bedford et al. 1998; Black et al. 1998; Lee et al. 1998; Lindley, Milla 1998; O'Brien et al. 1998; Payne, Maxon 1998) that raised concerns about the article, and interpreted it as claiming a link between the M.M.R. vaccine and autism. (A number of scientists, scholars and journalists have since reinforced such an interpretation; see, for instance, Woolcock and Hawkes 2006; Poland and Jacobsen 2011; Rope 2010; Ropeik 2011.) Later on, in 2004, journalist Brian Deer (2004: cf. Deer 2011a, 2011b, 2011c) published an investigative report denouncing a conflict of interest on Wakefield's part: While conducting the study, the then gastroenterologist received money from lawyers acting against M.M.R. manufacturers for parents of autistic children. Following Deer's report, *The Lancet* officially retracted the article and, in 2010, the General Medical Council declared Wakefield's research and conduct 'irresponsible' and 'dishonest' (G.M.C. report, quoted in Gorski 2010). As a result, Wakefield was struck off the U.K. medical register, and the *British Medical Journal* also declared his research 'fraudulent' in 2011.

Notwithstanding, this case seems to have caused a considerable drop in vaccination rates not only in the U.K., but also globally: By 2002, immunisation rates dropped below 85 per cent, and even 75 per cent in some areas, and fell under the minimum for maintaining 'herd immunity' (Fitzpatrick 2004; Mascarelli 2011). Despite scientific research disproving Wakefield's findings, anecdotal stories and personal experiences continue to keep the issue alive in the public sphere, specifically through new media, leading to the emergence of a new set of 'anti-vax conspiracy theories'. As a result, there have been reports in recent years of an upsurge in diseases previously under control by vaccination. For example, the latest data by the World Health Organization (W.H.O. 2019) reported a 30 per cent increase in measles cases globally, leading international bodies (such as the W.H.O. itself) to include 'vaccine hesitancy' on the list of the biggest global health threats today. In other words, not only is the M.M.R. case related to viruses from a medical point of view, but it has also become 'viral' in terms of communication, affecting current perceptions and behaviours in spite of all official rejection and legal action against its fraudulent promoter. How can this development be understood and, particularly, what is the role of the Internet in this?

A considerable part of scientific research does not gain much attention beyond a restricted community of interested scientists. However, Wakefield's article continues to garner attention on a global scale even 20 years after its publication, despite being repudiated by most of the authors involved in its publication and officially retracted by the journal that initially published it. Various factors should be considered to explain this.

First of all, it should be noted that 'much of the relevance of scientific articles is extratextual, not spelled out in the discourse but supplied by context' (Fahnestock 1986: 278). In this sense, a crucial role was played by the press conference held the day before the article's publication, in which Wakefield communicated his theory about M.M.R.-autism to the general public. Kolodziejski showed how, given the different interpretive practices employed in the public sphere, this communication created a sort of interpretative 'short circuit':

> Whereas a like-minded technical audience well versed in communicating uncertainty should understand the speculative nature of hedged claims and the need for additional research to substantiate them, a public audience less familiar with the discursive norms of scientific rhetoric may interpret such statements as established claims. This 'science by press conference' process causes concern because it creates opportunities for researchers to present information that extends beyond what the reviewers thought they were authorizing in approving a piece for publication.
> 
> *(2014: 180)*

It should also be remembered that Wakefield took part in a series of other speeches and public appearances, recommending single vaccines rather than the combined M.M.R. vaccine, thus evidently influencing the context of reception of his article. As a result, in the media, the link between the M.M.R. vaccine and autism immediately became predominant.[2]

What is more, Wakefield himself has continued defending his research and anti-vaccine theory through various media, including a book (*Callous Disregard: Autism and Vaccines – The Truth Behind a Tragedy*, 2010) and a movie (*Vaxxed: From Cover-Up to Catastrophe*, 2016). Such works not only insist on the relation between the M.M.R. vaccine and autism, but also re-contextualise the retraction of the 1998 paper and its consequences in the frame of a 'second level conspiracy theory'. This is manifest in their titles, which insist on ideas such as truth concealment, cruelty and tragedy (and even a real 'catastrophe'!), and finds particular expression in the trailer of the movie. Just after the sponsors' logos, in fact, the image zooms in on a 'warning' in white capital letters on a black background: 'THE FILM THEY DON'T WANT YOU TO SEE' (adopting the typical rhetorical style of conspiracy theories, with an undefined subject – 'they' – and a direct call to the addressee – 'you'). A provocative question therefore appears, while a toxic-looking blue substance invades the screen: 'ARE YOUR CHILDREN SAFE?' (with a reiterated call to the addressee). The following scenes then clarify the meaning of such notices: Not only does a link between vaccines and autism exist, as Wakefield's study revealed in 1998, but it has been covered up by the Centers for Disease Control and Prevention (C.D.C.), which allegedly manipulated and destroyed data about the effects of vaccines, as an insider revealed on a phone 'confession' to the environmental biologist Brian Hooker. Such arguments are supported by juxtaposing an audiovisual reconstruction of the phone call with short interviews with various 'experts' (from 'medical journalist' Del Bigtree to Doreen Granpeeshes, founder of the Center for Autism and Related Disorders, to 'Senior Research Scientist' Stephanie Steneff and Wakefield himself, presented as a 'gastroenterologist', without any mention of his expulsion from the medical register) and parents of children with autism, whose disorders are also insistently shown throughout the trailer.

The film recalls the textual strategies discussed for Wakefield's article, although with changes in style and tone, as required by this particular medium. These strategies resulted in the same interpretative processes as for the article. While first scheduled to premiere at New York's 2016 Tribeca Film Festival, the movie was withdrawn from the programme at a later stage, after doctors and health professionals denounced the screening and festival co-founder Robert De Niro reversed course, saying that the projection would not have contributed to a profitable discussion about medical and public health issues (see Goodman 2016; Ryzik 2016). Moreover, its description has been a matter of discussion, with Wakefield presenting it as a 'documentary', while critics (see, for instance, Kohn 2016; June 2016; Vonder Haar 2016) refer to it as a 'pseudoscience film'.

As illustrated above, the various media initiatives Wakefield organised around his article are essential to understand contemporary anti-vax conspiracy theories, from the claims concerning the correlation between the M.M.R. vaccine and autism to those denouncing the institutional and political interests in covering up scientific research. What is more, the media played a crucial role in making the M.M.R.-autism controversy stand up against the retraction of the paper: Wakefield used the media to provide alternative versions of what happened and for what reasons, while his arguments and ideas quickly moved from the mass to the new media, generating a widespread cybercascade. Since the publication of the *Lancet* article, in fact, an increasing number of autism advocacy groups and individuals have continued to support Wakefield's position on blogs, social networks (such as Facebook), comments to online articles about the retraction or on websites endorsed or founded by celebrities (e.g. Jenny McCarthy's *Generation Rescue*).

Such a phenomenon rapidly extended beyond Wakefield's case, making social networks key actors in the rise and spread of forms of anti-vaccine conspiracionism online (cf. Wong 2019). Facebook search results for groups and pages about vaccines, for instance, seem to be dominated by anti-vax propaganda, while YouTube's recommendation algorithm has been accused of driving users from fact-based medical information directly towards anti-vaccine misinformation. After criticism became manifest, both platforms started to address more efforts to control misinformation. However, their new policies have been primarily targeting fake news and hoaxes around politics (e.g. elections, immigration, racial discord, etc.), leaving anti-vaccination propaganda in the background. While both platforms have assured the public that they are exploring new options for addressing misinformation about vaccines and other health-related issues, as of writing, even a simple search for neutral words such as 'vaccine' or 'vaccination' steers users toward anti-vaccine groups. What is more, Facebook has been accepting advertising from anti-vax groups, such as *Vax Truther, Anti-Vaxxer, Vaccines Revealed, Stop Mandatory Vaccination* and others (Pilkington, Gleza 2019), thus further spreading misinformation. Such mechanisms evidently enhance an echo-chamber effect, since users are exposed only to anti-vax-oriented information, which reinforces tunnel vision. What is more, they function as a 'hook' for external users. People are redirected to the groups by search engines and algorithms, while the groups' posts tend to promote emotional involvement, leading their members not only to express their ideas by 'liking' or reacting to them, but also to share them on their personal profile or within their social circles (Chiou, Tucker 2018). As a result, a number of Internet memes against vaccines, such as ironic drawings denouncing the conflicts of interest behind vaccinations or accusing them of causing illness in perfectly healthy children, have widely spread through social networks. These memes both play to the viewer's emotion and employ sarcasm to create interest and involvement. In fact, humour and parody are among the factors that, according to Jenkins *et al.* (2013), make content spread, especially when they are used to criticise specific cultural patterns in contemporary societies. Despite their differences, both humour and parody foster spreadability because they represent 'a vehicle by which people articulate and validate their relationships with those with whom they share the joke' (Jenkins *et al.* 2013: 204). Furthermore, the visual aspect of these messages – with drawings, images, and captivating and easily readable fonts accompanying them – enhances their spreadibility.

Aware of such mechanisms, scientists and experts have also started to use social media to contrast anti-vaccinist propaganda, with ironic messages proving to be particularly effective. For instance, *Ah ma non è Lercio*, an Italian satirical website and Facebook page that features fictional news in order to make fun of contemporary sensational journalism, released in 2014 a provocative article entitled 'Anziano muore in un incidente stradale, la famiglia: 'L'ha ucciso il vaccino' ['Elderly man dies in a car accident; his family: "A vaccine killed him"']. This rapidly reached 1000 shares on Facebook and led to a number of ironic and also serious comments (for further details, see Stano 2016). Shares and interactions further increased as *Lercio* became more active on Facebook. Another nonsense satirical article entitled 'Troppi metalli nei vaccini: bambino arrugginisce dopo il bagnetto' ['Too many metals in vaccines: kid gets rusty after taking a bath'], released in 2017 and posted on *Lercio*'s Facebook page in February 2019, obtained more than 22 000 reactions, almost 1000 comments (with a number of reactions each) and more than 5500 shares.

However, in some cases, this type of communication turned out to have adverse effects. For instance, in 2013, the Photoshop Phriday forum on the humour website *Something Awful* launched a competition requiring applicants to create an ironic image on the correlation between vaccines and the physical or mental diseases generally asserted by anti-vaccinists. One of the examples related vaccines to heroin, ironically depicting a drug addict slumped in a corner with the text: 'Their first injection was a vaccination: protect your children from vaccinations', and slightly above, another satirical note: 'Vaccination leaves a lasting psychological belief that injecting is beneficial. Children who are vaccinated are 85% more likely to inject heroin than those who are not.' Although ironically intended, this image rapidly went viral on social networks and found its way on to Sunshine Coast Facebook pages, fomenting the idea that it illustrated a scarily real statistic linking heroin use to childhood vaccinations. The Sunshine Coast Local Medical Association president, Dr Minuskin, then publicly rejected the image, inviting everyone to stop sharing it:

> If anyone receives this image via social media I would recommend they swiftly assign it to the trash box where it belongs. Not only is the information outrageously incorrect, it is irresponsible to be creating unwarranted fear about such an important issue.
> *(in Mikkelson 2015)*

Nonetheless, users continued to comment on and to share the image. Ultimately, it also became appropriated by advocates of anti-vaccinists' propaganda, which accused vaccines of 'serv[ing] as a gateway drug to heroin' (Feminists Against Vaccination FB page, post left on 26 October 2015; the first post sharing the image appeared on 8 March 2015, as reported in Mikkelson 2015).

This example allows a series of interesting reflections. First of all, it is interesting to note that, unlike Charles William's vaccination monster, which has remained unaltered until now, Internet memes about vaccinations have evidently changed rapidly as a result of the interpretative and communicative acts performed by the people who received, appropriated and shared it. Here is where, as we have seen, the concept of 'spreadability' comes into play, emphasising the audiences' agency, since 'their choices, investments, agendas, and actions determine what gets valued' (Jenkins et al. 2013: 21).

Furthermore, this case evidently indicates the 'fusion processes' and the 'rhizomatic development' motivated by online content spreading: An explicitly ironic message was completely misunderstood (and therefore shared as real information) by various users and groups precisely because of the lack of roots indicating its origin and context. There is no identifiable author, nor context, since in most cases the original post was not included, and a new (sampled, and sometimes even remixed) object was generated. This further emphasises the users' crucial role in online content spreading, since they 'pluralize the meanings and pleasures mass culture offers, evade or resist its disciplinary efforts, fracture its homogeneity or coherence, raid or poach upon its terrain' (Fiske 1989: 28). The uncontrollable and unpredictable path of this Internet meme clearly shows how people produce culture precisely by integrating products and texts into their everyday lives, sometimes even implying forms of misunderstanding and aberrant decoding.

## Conclusion

The case of anti-vax conspiracy theories clearly shows how the Internet, and in particular social networks, have proved fundamental to the spread and development of such theories. Mass media played a crucial role in the reception and recognition of Wakefield's arguments and the conspiracy theories originating from them, also including his more recent claims re-interpreting its rejection as part of a broader conspiracy trying to hide the truth. Later, social media permitted anti-vax propaganda and conspiracy theories to reach as widely as they do today, in various cases even independently from the British former doctor's arguments. In fact, as we have seen, anti-vax conspiracy theories have developed in a horizontal fashion, lacking any hierarchical or causal structure that would allow us to easily trace their origin. On the contrary, they have been continuously sampled, remixed and even remade by online users, and, in the process, sometimes given new meanings. Such a rhizomatic development, in fact, is likely to cause misunderstanding and aberrant decoding, since it leaves no traces of the processes that led to it.

Nonetheless, this does not seem to acquire much importance within social media communications: Regardless of the truthfulness of posts and online content, people have not ceased sharing, reacting to and commenting on them, thus nurturing unpredictable and hardly stoppable cybercascades. In fact, the forms of 'online conviviality' (Varis, Blommaert 2014) brought about by the Web 2.0 have made 'social trust' emerge and become the base of a number of narratives whose verification transcends any reference to proven facts, and rather relies on other narratives (Perissinotto 2016; cf. Erdmann 2016; Madisson 2016).

From such a perspective, therefore, conspiracy theories can be conceived as a symptom of a larger problem embedded in the infrastructure of current communication systems, that is to say, the so-called 'post-truth' era: In contemporary rhetoric, the subjective and passionate component (i.e. appeals to emotion and personal belief) has become evidently more influential than the referential one, to the extent that personal beliefs have replaced verified facts (Lorusso 2018). The considered case study suggests that the Web 2.0, and especially social media, motivate today's post-truth society: The mechanism of followers and likes on which such media are based does not dismantle falsehoods, but rather reinforces them, making sharing and belonging prevail over reliability and truth. Thus, echoes resound louder and louder in the rooms of the Internet, where people, although creatively expressing their agency, are at risk of losing the crucial ability for effective communication and discerning reliable and accurate information from falsehood and fake news. In this sense, we would conclude, the rapid spread of conspiracy theories should not simply be dismissed as a symptom of a paranoid or unreasonable society, as it is sometimes claimed. It should rather be conceived and studied as a consequence of the limited access to factual truth and experiences characterising contemporary societies, as well as of the increased difficulty of verifying information brought about by the cybercascades of contemporary information systems.

## Notes

1 The theoretical part of this chapter is based on the first results of the research activities developed within the project COMFECTION, which has received funding from the E.U.'s Horizon 2020 research and innovation programme under the Marie Sklodowska-Curie grant agreement 795025. It reflects only the author's view and the European Research Executive Agency is not responsible for any use that may be made of the information it contains.
2 On 26 February 1998, for instance, the Royal Free Hospital School of Medicine distributed a press release entitled 'New research links autism and bowel disease', and, the day after, B.B.C. News included 'Child vaccine linked to autism' within its news.

## References

Beale, A.J. (1998) 'Autism, inflammatory bowel disease, and MMR vaccine', *The Lancet*, 351(9106): 906.
Bedford, H., Booy, R., Dunn, D., DiGuiseppi, C., Gibb, D., Gilbert, R., Logan, S., Peckham, C., Roberts, I. and Tookey, P. (1998) 'Autism, inflammatory bowel disease, and MMR vaccine', *The Lancet*, 351(9106): 907.
Black, D., Prempeh, H. and Baxter, T. (1998) 'Autism, inflammatory bowel disease, and MMR vaccine', *The Lancet*, 351(9106): 905–6.
Buckland, M. (2017) *Information and society*, Cambridge, MA: The MIT Press.
Cannizzaro, S. (2016) 'Internet memes as internet signs: a semiotic view of digital culture', *Sign Systems Studies*, 44(4): 562–86.

Ceriani, G. (2004) 'Contaminazione e fusione nella tendenza contemporanea: da modalità interoggettive a forme di vita', E|C. Available at: www.ec-aiss.it/index_d.php?recordID=100. [Accessed 1 March 2019.]

Chamorro-Premuzic, T. (2014) 'How the web distorts reality and impairs our judgement skills', *Guardian*, 13 May. Available at: www.theguardian.com/media-network/media-network-blog/2014/may/13/internet-confirmation-bias. [Accessed 1 March 2019.]

Chiou, L. and Tucker, C. (2018) 'Fake news and advertising on social media: a study of the anti-vaccination movement', *NBER Working paper series*, 25233.

Craft, S., Ashley, S. and Maksl, A. (2017) 'News media literacy and conspiracy theory endorsement', *Communication and the public*, 2(4): 388–401.

Dawkins, R. (1976) *The selfish gene*, Oxford: Oxford University Press.

Deer, B. (2004) 'Revealed: MMR research scandal', *The Times*, 22 February. Available at: www.thetimes.co.uk/tto/health/article1879347.ece. [Accessed 16 March 2019.]

Deer, B. (2011a) 'Secrets of the MMR scare: how the case against the MMR vaccine was fixed', *BMJ*, 342: 77–82.

Deer, B. (2011b) 'Secrets of the MMR scare: how the vaccine crisis was meant to make money', *BMJ*, 342: 136–42.

Deer, B. (2011c) 'Secrets of the MMR scare: the Lancet's two days to bury bad news', *BMJ*, 342: 200–4.

Del Vicario, M., Vivaldo, G., Bessi, A., Zollo, F., Scala, A., Caldarelli, G and Quattrociocchi, G. (2016) 'Echo chambers: emotional contagion and group polarization on Facebook', *Scientific Reports*, 6(37825).

Deleuze, G. and Guattari, F. (1980) *Mille plateaux*, Paris: Minuit.

DiNucci, D. (1999) 'Fragmented future', *Print*, 53(4): 221–2.

Dusi, N. and Spaziante, L. (eds.) (2006) *Remix–remake: pratiche di replicabilità*, Rome: Meltemi.

Einstein, K.L. and Glick, D.M. (2015) 'Do I think BLS data are BS? The consequences of conspiracy theories', *Political Behavior*, 37(3): 679–701.

Erdmann, J. (2016) 'Technological and semiotic code structures of conspiracist thinking online: PI news from a media-related point of view', *Lexia*, 23–4: 157–70.

Fahnestock, J. (1986) 'Accommodating science: the rhetorical life of scientific facts', *Written Communication*, 3(3): 275–96.

Fahnestock, J. (2009) 'The rhetoric of the natural sciences', in A.A. Lunsford, K.H. Wilson and R.A. Eberly (eds.) *The SAGE handbook of rhetorical studies*, Los Angeles: SAGE, pp. 175–95.

Fiske, J. (1989) *Understanding popular culture*, London: Routledge.

Fitzpatrick, M. (2004) *MMR and autism: what parents need to know*, London: Routledge.

Fullerton Lemons, J. (2016) 'Vaccine controversies', *CQ Researcher*, 26(8): 169–92.

Goodman, M. (2016) 'Robert De Niro pulls anti-vaccine documentary from Tribeca Film Festival', *New York Times*, 26 March. Available at: www.nytimes.com/2016/03/27/movies/robert-de-niro-pulls-anti-vaccine-documentary-from-tribeca-film-festival.html?module=inline. [Accessed 26 April 2019.]

Gorski, D. (2010) 'The general medical council to Andrew Wakefield: "The panel is satisfied that your conduct was irresponsible and dishonest"', *Science-Based Medicine*, 1 February. Available at: https://sciencebasedmedicine.org/andrew-wakefield-the-panel-is-satisfied-that-your-conduct-was-irresponsible-and-dishonest/. [Accessed 26 April 2019.]

Habermas, J. (1991) *The structural transformation of the public sphere: an inquiry into a category of bourgeois society*, trans. T. Burger and F. Lawrence, Cambridge, MA: The MIT Press.

Jenkins, H., Ford S. and Green, J. (2013) *Spreadable media: creating value and meaning in a networked culture*, London: New York University Press.

Jolley, D. and Douglas, K.M. (2014a) 'The effects of anti-vaccine conspiracy theory on vaccination intentions', *PLoS ONE*, 9(2), e89177.

Jolley, D. and Douglas, K.M. (2014b) 'The social consequences of conspiracism: exposure to conspiracy theories decreases intentions to engage in politics and to reduce one's carbon footprint', *British Journal of Psychology*, 105(1): 35–56.

June, L. (2016) 'Why is an anti-vaccine documentary by a proven quack being taken seriously?', *The Cut*, 22 March. Available at: https://web.archive.org/web/20160331042100/http://nymag.com/thecut/2016/03/tribeca-film-festival-anti-vaxx.html. [Accessed 24 April 2019.]

Kimminich, E. (2016) 'About grounding, courting and truthifying: conspiratorial fragments and patterns of social construction of reality in rhetoric, media and images', *Lexia*, 23–4: 35–53.

Kohn, E. (2016) '"Vaxxed: from cover-up to catastrophe" is designed to trick you (review)', *IndiWire*, 1 April. Available at: www.indiewire.com/2016/04/vaxxed-from-cover-up-to-catastrophe-is-designed-to-trick-you-review-21896/. [Accessed 20 April 2019.]

Kolodziejski, L. (2014) 'Harms of hedging in scientific discourse: Andrew Wakefield and the origins of the autism vaccine controversy', *Technical Communication Quarterly*, 23(3): 165–83.

Lazarsfeld, P., Berelson, B. and Gaudet H. (1948) *The people's choice: how the voter makes up his mind in a presidential campaign*, New York: Columbia University Press.

Lee, J.W., Melgaard, B., Clements, C.J., Kane, M., Mulholland, E.K. and Olivé, J.-M. (1998) 'Autism, inflammatory bowel disease, and MMR vaccine', *The Lancet*, 351: 905.

Leone, M. (ed.) (2016) 'Complotto/Conspiracy', monographic issue of *Lexia*, 25–6, Rome: Aracne.

Lindley, K.J. and Milla, P.J. (1998) 'Autism, inflammatory bowel disease, and MMR vaccine', *The Lancet*, 351(9106): 907–8.

Lorusso, A M. (2018) *Post-verità: fra reality tv, social media e storytelling*, Rome-Bari: Laterza.

Lotman, J M. (1984) 'Труды по знаковым системам', *Signs Systems Studies*, 17: 5–23.

Madisson, M.-L. (2016) 'NWO conspiracy theory: a key frame in online communication of the Estonian extreme right', *Lexia*, 23–4: 189–208.

Marino, G. (2015) 'Semiotics of spreadability: a systematic approach to internet memes and virality', *Punctum*, 1(1): 43–66.

Marino, G. and Thibault, M. (eds.) (2016) 'Viralità: per un'epidemiologia del senso', *Lexia*, 25–6, Rome: Aracne.

Marwick, A.E. (2013) 'Memes', *Contexts*, 12(4): 12–3.

Mascarelli, A. (2011) 'Doctors see chinks in vaccination armor', *Los Angeles Times*, 5 August. Available at: http://articles.latimes.com/2011/aug/05/health/la-he-vaccines-herd-immunity-20110801. [Accessed 13 March 2019.]

McKenzie, W. (1996) 'Nettime: is "meme" a bad meme?' *Nettime Archive*, 23 December. Available at: https://nettime.org/Lists-Archives/nettime-l-9612/msg00064.html. [Accessed 27 February 2019.]

McLuhan, M. (1962) *The Gutenberg galaxy: the making of typographic man*, Toronto: University of Toronto Press.

McLuhan, M. (1964) *Understanding media: the extensions of man*, New York: McGraw-Hill.

McMahon, D.M. (2004) 'Conspiracies so vast: conspiracy theory was born in the age of enlightenment and has metastasized in the age of the internet: why won't it go away?', *The Boston Globe*, 1 February. Available at: http://archive.boston.com/news/globe/ideas/articles/2004/02/01/conspiracies_so_vast/. [Accessed 27 April 2019.]

Mikkelson, D. (2015) 'Childhood vaccinations lead to heroin use?', *Snopes*, 23 March. Available at: www.snopes.com/fact-check/an-injection-addiction/. [Accessed 27 April 2019.]

Mulligan, K. and Habel, P. (2012) 'The implications of fictional media for political beliefs', *American Politics Research*, 41(1): 122–46.

O'Brien, S.J., Jones, I.G. and Christie, P. (1998) 'Autism, inflammatory bowel disease, and MMR vaccine', *The Lancet*, 351(9106): 906–7.

Olmsted, K.S. (2009) *Real enemies: conspiracy theories and American democracy, World War I to 9/11*, New York: Oxford University Press.

Payne, C. and Maxon, B. (1998) 'Autism, inflammatory bowel disease, and MMR vaccine', *The Lancet*, 351(9106): 907.

Perissinotto, A. (2016) 'Informazione vera, falsa e verosimile: giornalismo, bufale e le tre condizioni della menzogna virale', *Lexia*, 25–6: 155–72.

Pilkington, E. and Gleza, J. (2019) 'Facebook under pressure to halt rise of anti-vaccination groups', *Guardian*, 12 February. Available at: www.theguardian.com/technology/2019/feb/12/facebook-anti-vaxxer-vaccination-groups-pressure-misinformation. [Accessed 16 March 2019.]

Poland, G.A. and Jacobsen, R.M. (2011) 'Perspective: the age-old struggle against the antivaccinationists', *New England Journal of Medicine*, 364(2): 97–9.

Quattrociocchi, W. and Vicini, A. (2016) *Misinformation: guida alla società dell'informazione e della credulità*, Milan: Franco Angeli.

Reeves, C. (2005) '"I knew there was something wrong with that paper": scientific rhetorical styles and scientific misunderstandings', *Technical Communication Quarterly*, 14(3): 267–75.

Rogers, P., Puryear, R. and Root, J. (2013) 'Infobesity: the enemy of good decisions', *Bain & Company*, 11 June. Available at: www.bain.com/insights/infobesity-the-enemy-of-good-decisions. [Accessed 27 February 2019.]

Rope, K. (2010) 'The end of the autism /vaccine debate?', *CNN Parenting*, 10 September. Available at: http://edition.cnn.com/2010/HEALTH/09/07/p.autism.vaccine.debate/index.html. [Accessed 27 February 2019.]

Ropeik, D. (2011) 'Wakefield debunked, but vaccine fear lives', *The Huffington Post*, 25 May. Available at: www.huffingtonpost.com/david-ropeik/wakefield-debunked-but-va_b_805826.html. [Accessed 27 February 2019.]

Royal Free Hospital School of Medicine (1998) 'New research links autism and bowel disease', *Briandeer*. Available at: http://briandeer.com/mmr/royal-free-press-1998.pdf. [Accessed 27 February 2019.]

Ryzik, M. (2016) 'Pulled from festival, anti-vaccination film will run in theater', *New York Times*, 30 March. Available at: www.nytimes.com/2016/03/31/movies/pulled-from-tribeca-film-festival-vaccination-film-vaxxed-will-run-in-theater.html. [Accessed 26 April 2019.]

Shifman, L. (2013) *Memes in digital culture*, Cambridge: The MIT Press.

Stano, S. (2016) 'From hypochondria to hyperchondria: health communication in the web era', *Lexia*, 25–6: 211–29.

Starbird, K. (2017) 'Examining the alternative media ecosystem through the production of alternative narratives of mass shooting events on Twitter', *Association for the Advancement of Artificial Intelligence*. Available at: https://faculty.washington.edu/kstarbi/Alt_Narratives_ICWSM17-CameraReady.pdf. [Accessed 27 February 2019.]

Sunstein, C. (2001) *Republic.com*, Princeton: Princeton University Press.

Sunstein, C. (2017) *#Republic: divided democracy in the age of social media*, Princeton: Princeton University Press.

Swami, V., Pietschnig, J., Tran, S.J., Nader, I.W., Stieger, S. and Voracek, M. (2013) 'Lunar lies: the impact of informational framing and individual differences in shaping conspiracist beliefs about the moon landings', *Applied Cognitive Psychology*, 27(1): 71–80.

Thibault, M. (2016) 'Trolls, hackers, anons: conspiracy theories in the peripheries of the web', *Lexia*, 23–4: 387–408.

Uscinski, J.E. and Parent, J.M. (2014) *American conspiracy theories*, Oxford: Oxford University Press.

Varis, P. and Blommaert, J. (2014) 'Conviviality and collectives on social media: virality, memes and new social structures', *Tilburg Papers in Culture Studies*, 108.

Vonder Haar, P. (2016) 'Anti-vaccination doc vaxxed, booted from Tribeca, is a tragic fraud', *Houston Press*, 7 April. Available at: www.houstonpress.com/arts/anti-vaccination-doc-vaxxed-booted-from-tribeca-is-a-tragic-fraud-8302709. [Accessed 26 April 2019.]

Wakefield, A. (1998) 'Ileal-lymphoid-nodular hyperplasia, non-specific colitis, and pervasive developmental disorder in children', *The Lancet*, 351(9103): 637–41.

Wakefield, A. (2010) *Callous disregard: autism and vaccines: the truth behind a tragedy*, New York: Skyhorse Publishing.

W.H.O. (World Health Organization) (2019) 'Ten threats to global health in 2019', *World Health Organization*. Available at: www.who.int/emergencies/ten-threats-to-global-health-in-2019. [Accessed 12 March 2019.]

Wolfe, R.M. and Sharp, L.K. (2002) 'Anti-vaccinationists past and present', *BMJ*, 325(7361): 430–2.

Woolcock, N. and Hawkes, N. (2006) 'Decline in MMR uptake blamed for measles death', *The Times*, 3 April. Available at: www.thetimes.co.uk/tto/health/article1884070.ece. [Accessed 16 March 2019.]

Wong, J.C. (2019) 'How Facebook and YouTube help spread anti-vaxxer propaganda', *Guardian*, 1 February. Available at: www.theguardian.com/media/2019/feb/01/facebook-youtube-anti-vaccination-misinformation-social-media. [Accessed 16 March 2019.]

Wurman, R.S. (2012) 'Information anxiety: towards understanding', *Scenario*, 6. Available at: https://scenariojournal.com/article/richard-wurman/. [Accessed 16 February 2019.]

# 4.9
# NETWORKED DISINFORMATION AND THE LIFECYCLE OF ONLINE CONSPIRACY THEORIES

*Hugo Leal*

## Introduction

The World Wide Web is, presently, the centre stage for the dissemination of conspiracy theories. It is hardly surprising that a network with global reach has become such a fitting environment for the accelerated propagation, not only of news, fashions and fads, but also of rumours, falsehoods and conspiracy theories. As the technical infrastructure and the social relations of the Internet are governed by network principles, one could legitimately assume that, even in the absence of manipulation, facts and fakes encounter equally fertile ground to reproduce.

This chapter is an attempt to navigate through the form and function of online network topologies in the context of a rising tide of misinformation and disinformation campaigns. In particular, it tries to explain how network effects regulate the lifecycle of conspiracy theories. The chapter starts with a theoretical literature review to critically assess the ways in which scholars studied online network topologies to understand the dissemination of misinformation and conspiracy theories. It is argued here that the Internet, as a whole, is more than just a platform on which conspiracy theories can be studied since its networked structures fundamentally shape their form, dissemination and evolution. It is also claimed that these networked sociotechnical structures – namely the Internet, the Web and online social networks – should be taken as a meta-network whose topology and regulating processes favour both the concentration of network power and the dissemination of (mis)information. From this point of departure, the second part of this chapter focuses on the 'networked disinformation lifecycle' – a model that tracks the ideal-typical stages of a viral narrative, from the first time it surfaces until its eventual mainstreaming. The model promotes the idea that networked environments could be better understood with a research programme centred on network-based theories, methods and tools. In a succinct demonstration of how the research programme can be applied to study a concrete manifestation of the 'disinformation lifecycle' model, I analyse the lifecycle of a false rumour turned into a conspiracy theory, known as 'pizzagate'.

## Dwelling on the medium: Online network topologies

The E.U. membership referendum in the U.K. and the election of Donald Trump as the 45th president of the U.S.A., both in 2016, put the debates about the 'real-world' impact of

Web-mediated disinformation campaigns in the limelight. Although the phenomenon had already played an important role in the global rise of populism, from India (Sinha 2018) to the Philippines (Alba 2018) and Eastern Europe (Krekó, Enyedi 2018), it was the digitally-enabled disinformation surrounding the 2016 'Brexit' referendum and U.S. presidential election that grabbed the headlines and decisively caught our attention. As Figure 4.9.1 shows, some neologisms, such as 'fake news' (Allcott, Gentzkow 2017; Lazer et al. 2018) and 'post-truth' (Kucharski 2016; Lewandowsky et al. 2017), have debuted as trendy research topics after 2016 and, overall, the academic world responded to the public interest with a sudden increase of scholarly production (see Figure 4.9.1) on relevant misinformation-related matters (Pluviano et al. 2017; van der Linden et al. 2017).

However, academic research on disinformation is yet to fully address truly puzzling and worrying developments on the Web, like the propagation and mainstreaming of politically weaponised conspiracy theories. Considering that Donald Trump gained notoriety as a tweeting 'birther' – a conspiracy theory postulating that Barack Obama had been born in Kenya rather than in Hawaii and faked his birth certificate – it is surprising that academic researchers are giving relatively short shrift to the online diffusion of conspiracy theories and their use for disinformation purposes. Scholarship on conspiracism has generally gravitated around two poles: On the one hand, the thematic analysis of a given conspiracy theory, usually historically or regionally situated and, on the other hand, the attempt to explain the social determinants, mostly psychological, of conspiracy theorising. While the online sphere has been progressively integrated by scholars working on conspiracy theory studies, this situation has not changed. The Web often features as a socio-technical backdrop to collect data, observe and/or conduct experiments focusing either on the psychological dimension (Wood, Douglas 2013, 2015) or on single case studies, of which the vital public health research on anti-vaccine conspiracism and attitudes is a remarkable example (Nasir 2000; Kata 2010; Briones et al. 2012; Smith, Graham 2017; see also Chapter 4.8 in this volume).

Less common are medium-centred investigations that use the online network topologies themselves to gain better understanding of the propagation of misinformation and conspiracy theories (Anagnostopoulos et al. 2015; Bessi et al. 2015; Del Vicario et al. 2016). This type of

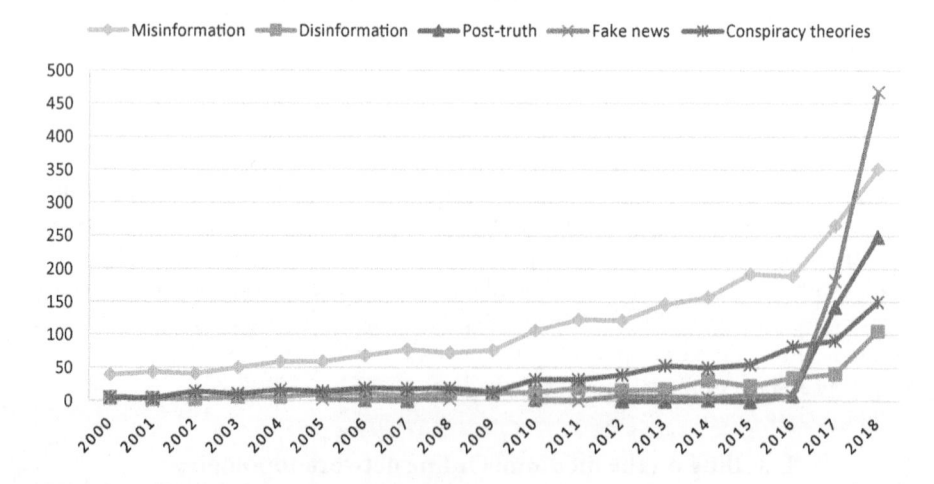

*Figure 4.9.1* Published articles on selected topics (2000–2018).
Source: Scopus. Pseudo search string.

digital research takes the influence of the medium as such into account by incorporating the underlying logic and overriding principles of online technical and social networks. Without taking the medium and its governing processes as an object of study, we cannot gauge the extent to which the Internet, the Web and its interconnected users are regulated by network dynamics. Focusing on the network characteristics and effects of the medium, the vast wealth of research on online rumour diffusion (Shah, Zaman 2011; Doerr *et al.* 2012; Starbird *et al.* 2014; Vosoughi *et al.* 2018) can, therefore, be used as an essential building block for studies on the spread and evolution of conspiracy theories. My proposed model and research programme of the lifecycle of disinformation-driven conspiracy theories is thus informed by the medium-specific nature of the Web and rests on online rumour propagation literature, well-established concepts of diffusion (Granovetter, Soong 1983; Rogers 1983; Berger, Milkman 2012; Goel *et al.* 2015) and network theory (Watts 2002; Newman *et al.* 2006; Cheng *et al.* 2014).

What are, then, the key characteristics of online social networks and what are their effects on (dis)information? Understanding the way networks operate and how they can be manipulated by actors with vested political or economic interests is key to this question. It potentially explains some recent trends, from the ascension of populism to the spreading of 'fake news' (Lazer *et al.* 2018) and the topic of this chapter: The mainstreaming of conspiracy theories. It's all connected. What we commonly call 'the Internet' is, in reality, a complex meta-network, a system of nested networks comprising interconnected machines (Internet), interconnected documents and resources (Web) and interconnected people (social networks). Within this meta-network, the circulation and access to information is the result of a trade-off between opportunities (such as scale and speed) and constraints (such as differential access, uneven distribution of positions and roles, and unregulated market activities). The opportunities and constraints for personal interconnections resulting from the technical characteristics of the medium, then, provide the infrastructure for a process that is largely fed by social, as in human, network structures. While the scale, speed and reach are generally conceived as providing equal opportunities for communication between people and the spread of narratives, the reality shows that this horizontality is illusory. Online networks are hierarchical and the power in their midst is unevenly distributed. In social networks, especially, it is not the equal distribution of interconnections, but the fact that some nodes are more well-connected than others that makes an idea or a virus circulate faster and more efficiently.

The topology of the online meta-network turns it into a fitting environment for the global spread of rumours, falsehoods and conspiracy theories. Online networks do not obey deterministic laws, but they do tend to follow regular patterns. Some network processes allow us to map and, to a certain degree, predict the creation and severance of links between people and, by extension, the diffusion of particular ideas and behaviours. The main point is that the circulation of information (and misinformation) is not driven by chance but regulated by network processes. Two of these processes illustrate the mode of operation of online networks: The 'Matthew effect' (related to centrality and power) and clustering (related to homophily and transitivity). The Matthew effect, the principle stating that 'the rich get richer' (Merton 1968) is a determinant of hierarchies in online social networks. The emergence of hubs, actors/nodes with many connections, is path dependent and favours those who are already central, powerful and influential. It is for this reason that public figures and users with older accounts have a higher probability of acquiring and maintaining an influencer status on social media platforms. Clustering, another well-studied social network process (Watts, Strogatz 1998), is also fundamental to understanding the formation and evolution of social network structures and their role in the diffusion of conspiracy theories. Essentially, it reveals our tendency to connect with people who are similar or close to us. It is associated with the concepts of homophily, the notion that 'similarity breeds connection' (McPherson et al. 2001: 415), and transitivity, the expectation that in social relations 'if A is related to B and B is related to C then there would be a relationship from A to C' (Borgatti et al. 2013: 179). This homogeny is a significant factor in our choices, from the city or neighbourhood we select (Bishop 2009) to the blogs we read (Adamic, Glance 2005). The flip-side and logical consequence of clustering is segregation. Political, religious, sexual and racial segregation is not only a defining characteristic of online communities, of course, but a general social proclivity. In the online sphere, dynamics of clustering are closely associated with the much debated processes of network fragmentation, polarisation and echo-chamber formation (Garrett 2009).

Together with the unequal distribution of network power and influence among people, we observe an unequal distribution of network power and influence among companies. Monopolistic digital corporations end up controlling the online information circuits. During the 1990s, the Web did little more than virtualising the pre-existing media ecosystem dominated by broadcasters and newspapers (Naughton 2014: 86), thus scaling up a model that relied on a limited number of prestigious media outlets producing and filtering information for the masses. With the growth of the Internet, the development of the Web and the consequent emergence of digitally native, globalised media platforms, the traditional media ecosystem was largely dismantled (Lanier 2011; Naughton 2014). During the 2000s, digital companies like Twitter and Facebook centralised the global circulation of information and decentralised its production, thereby creating the conditions for the wide dissemination of misinformation and disinformation. As the traditional information gatekeepers waned, the misinformation floodgates opened.

Against this background, it is only natural that different researchers have found the Internet to be a boon or a bane for conspiracy theorising (Wood 2013). In fact, while it has been argued that it 'slowed down the development of conspiracy theories' (Clarke 2007: 167), there is mounting evidence that online social network platforms speed up the spreading of misinformation (Doerr et al. 2012; Del Vicario et al. 2016; Vosoughi et al. 2018). This stresses the importance of understanding the specific mechanisms by which narratives generated in online culture cells spread and how they become defining features and mobilising factors for individuals and groups.

## Studying the online lifecycle of conspiracy theories

Having identified some of the characteristics and processes governing online networks, I aim to propose a model of the 'networked disinformation lifecycle'. It tries to unpack the online network dynamics of viral narratives, particularly when it assumes a conspiratorial form that lends itself to multiple forms of manipulation, for example for political or economic purposes. The model is presented alongside the description and analysis of 'pizzagate' – a weaponised conspiracy theory that emerged in the context of the 2016 U.S. presidential election and, from my perspective, a suitable proof of concept. The term 'pizzagate' refers to false claims linking the higher echelons of the U.S. Democratic Party to a child trafficking and prostitution ring, supposedly operating from the basement of the pizzeria 'Comet Ping Pong' in Washington D.C. The rumour dates back to October 2016 when two users of the microblogging platform Twitter claimed to possess reliable information from the New York Police Department about an investigation targeting Hillary Clinton due to her involvement in a 'paedophilia ring'. Allegedly, the incriminating evidence had been found on the laptop of Anthony Weiner, a former Democrat representative accused of sexual improprieties and ex-husband of Huma Abedin, by then one of Hillary Clinton's closest aides (Silverman 2016).

The rumour surfaced in the lead up to the 2016 U.S. presidential election and quickly evolved into a full-blown conspiracy theory, but it only generated significant public online engagement in the aftermath of the election. In particular, this happened as a consequence of a rare act of conspiracy theory verification. Indeed, coinciding with the escalating virality of the narrative within social networks close to the American alt-right, on 4 December 2016, a man armed with an assault rifle barged into the pizzeria with the intent of 'self-investigating' the crimes and rescuing the hostage children. The man fired several shots before being arrested by the police (Nashrulla, Dalrymple 2016). To his dismay, there were neither children in the restaurant's basement nor a basement in the restaurant. The conspiracy, at least in its #pizzagate incarnation, had been falsified by a true believer. As my model will show, this story is a good illustration of the lifecycle of conspiracy theories within the context of disinformation campaigns.

I introduce social network analysis (S.N.A.) as a way to empirically apply the proposed model and demonstrate that the online dynamics of networked disinformation could be better understood with a research programme centred on network-based theories, methods and tools.

As the model and analysis will show, conspiracy theories, such as 'pizzagate', are generated and thrive within certain clusters following traceable network processes, which can be explained by network theory and empirically examined through S.N.A. The empirical analysis of the 'pizzagate' conspiracy theory and disinformation campaign is based on data collected from the social media platform Twitter through the publicly available streaming A.P.I. During one week (1/12/2016–7/12/2016), all instances of the hashtag #pizzagate were collected and sliced into three windows of observation: Three days before the violent 'verification' event (T1: 1/12/2016), the date of the actual attack to the pizza parlour (T2: 4/12/2016) and three days after the occurrence (T3: 7/12/2016). Only relational data is taken into consideration. This includes mentions, retweets and replies, and excludes single tweets.

In Figure 4.9.2, we find the model of the networked disinformation lifecycle. A theoretical model is a necessary simplification of a much more complex reality. It is an artificial reduction of an intricate system to its elementary components and mechanisms, whose stated goal is to shed light on the whole process of how a viral narrative is born, develops, gets adopted, multiplies and, eventually, dies out. Central to the whole model description is the dynamics of online social networks, here represented as a set of distinct steps that will be discussed.

First of all, *events* occupy a central but not static position in the model (see Figure 4.9.2). They can simultaneously trigger, mediate and be the result of the circulation of misinformation. Considering the historical course of a conspiracy theory, the assassination of U.S. President John F. Kennedy, the moon landing and the 9/11 attacks in New York are all cases in which, regardless of the intentionality, conspiracy theorising was set off by one concrete event. In turn, our case study, 'pizzagate', can be seen as an event whose roots can be traced back to the specific conspiracy theory implicating senior members of the U.S. Democratic Party. More commonly, though, the sequence is not that linear. The massive killings that took place in Utoya island, Norway in 2011, in a Pittsburgh (U.S.) synagogue in 2018 and two mosques in Christchurch, New Zealand in 2019 were all violent episodes that can be inserted into broader chains of events whose historical sequence is intertwined with conspiracy theories targeting directly leftists, Jews and Muslims, or some combination of the above. This natural path dependence places the event in a mediating position. It is a justification for and justified by conspiracy theorising. Consequently, my model also merges different temporalities under the category of event. Events include discrete events (like the moon landing) and continuous events (like an electoral campaign or even a long period of economic crisis) that create historically situated opportunities for the

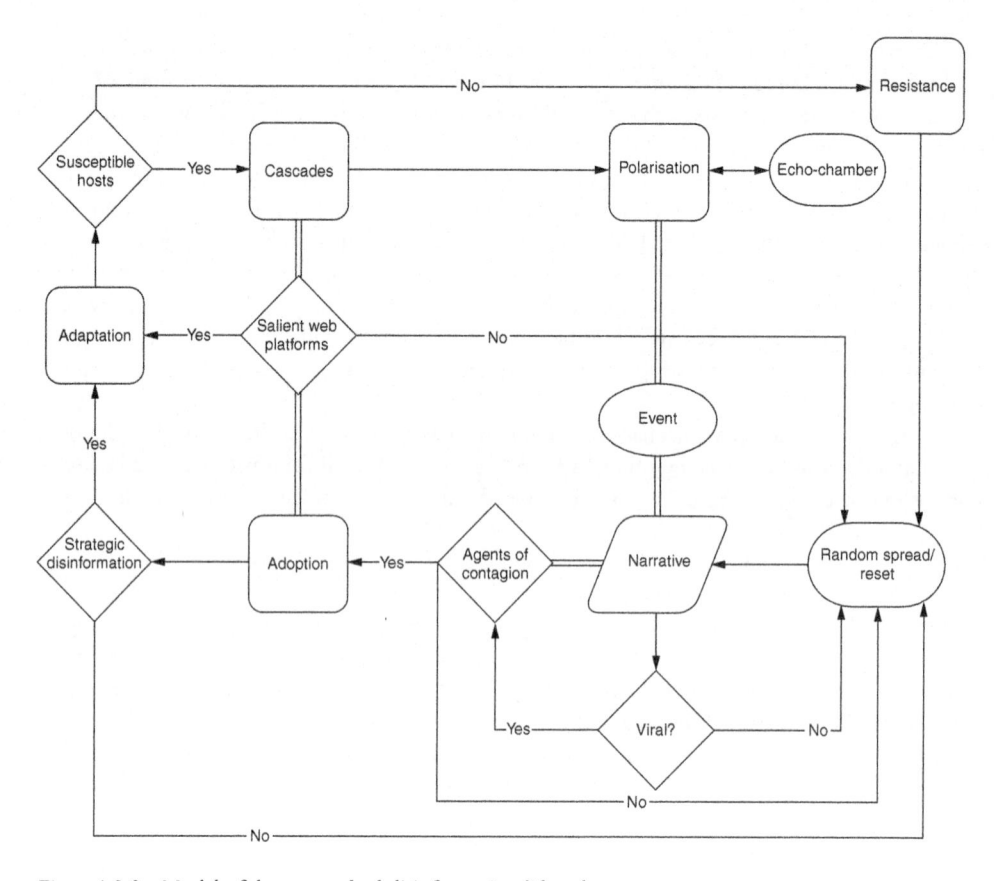

*Figure 4.9.2* Model of the networked disinformation lifecycle.

dissemination of misinformation and, more particularly, conspiracy theories. In that sense, events are placed in the model as a wildcard that assigns temporality and spatiality to an otherwise unbounded description of the process of information dissemination.

## Dynamics of diffusion

The injection of an intendedly viral narrative into the network is the first actual input of the model. While the unintended circulation of misinformation is worth studying, our focus is more on disinformation: The intentional dissemination of rumours, falsehoods and conspiracy theories with ulterior motives. Within this framework, *viral narratives* are specific claims about conspiracies embedded in more general ideas, ideologies or beliefs. For example, the 'pizzagate' conspiracy theory was part of a general disinformation campaign conducted by actors associated with the American alt-right and Republican Party aiming at discrediting the Democratic presidential candidate and her party. As it happens, violent outbursts fuelled by conspiratorial thinking, as the one that took place at the pizza parlour at the centre of #pizzagate, are still not the norm but the exception.

And, yet, the injection of an intendedly viral narrative alone does not guarantee dissemination. The successful diffusion of a narrative is related to *intent*, *content*, the *individual nodes' positions and roles* and the *whole network structure*. First up, intent speaks to the motivations of the initial agents of contagion – the individuals or groups who first inject and try to disseminate the viral narrative in the network, the active spreaders of the theory and those who, eventually, appropriate the narrative as part of a broader disinformation campaign. The initial spreaders of a conspiracy theory are aware they are formulating an explanation of an event or fact that is unknown to the public and contradicts an official version and/or the scientific consensus. The beliefs are accessory and subordinated to the genuine goal, which can range from egotistical self-promotion and individual gain to a more group-oriented commitment with the common good (Sunstein 2010). Upon the first transmissions and adoptions, the narrative will be adapted, further adopted or lay dormant. It is at this point that a simple rumour can evolve into a more elaborate viral narrative and further develop through the positive relation between the increasing number of hosts and the lifetime of conspiracy theories (Del Vicario *et al.* 2016: 556).

'Pizzagate' clearly illustrates this process. Starting off as a rumour tweeted by a white supremacist under a pseudonym (Silverman 2016), the narrative was adopted and adapted by alt-right Web outlets comprising message boards, blogs, partisan 'fake news' sites and some 'clickbait' webpages run from countries such as Georgia and the former Yugoslav Republic of Macedonia, whose only objective is to generate traffic and collect the dividends (Kristof 2016; Silverman, Alexander 2016). Across these networks, groups of self-identified 'Internet researchers', mostly users of online message boards linked to the alt-right movement, were instrumental in spreading the rumour and upgrading it to a conspiracy theory. They used the leaked emails of John Podesta, chairman of the 2016 Hillary Clinton presidential campaign, to prove the involvement of the Democratic Party in the child sex ring. Some Twitter users, members of the alt-right discussion boards on 4chan and individuals posting on the sub-reddit 'r/Donald_Trump', scraped Podesta's email dump and interpreted scattered mentions of Hillary Clinton, John Podesta, 'Comet Ping Pong' and 'pizza' as a ciphered code to order children for sexual practices (Aisch *et al.* 2016). The plot device in this story is the logical leap connecting pizza terms to paedophilia, which finds its basis in the use of the expression 'cheese pizza' as a code for child pornography on the message board 4chan (Aisch *et al.* 2016). The rumour was now a widespread conspiracy theory.

In addition to intent, this brings to the fore the importance of the narrative's *content*. It has been shown that 'emotion shapes virality … [and] … content that evokes high-arousal positive (awe) or negative (anger or anxiety) emotions is more viral' (Berger, Milkman 2012). This finding was replicated in studies of online social media platforms. For example, Stefan Stieglitz and Linh Dang-Xuan have demonstrated that 'emotionally charged Twitter messages tend to be retweeted more often and more quickly compared to neutral ones'. (Stieglitz, Dang-Xuan 2013: 217). Using data from the same social media platform, Vosoughi, Roy and Aral further showed that 'false political news travelled deeper and more broadly, reached more people, and was more viral than any other category of false information' (Vosoughi *et al.* 2018: 1148).

The logical corollary is that a political conspiracy theory designed to instigate psychological arousal will find more susceptible hosts and better environmental conditions to propagate. This was precisely one of the reasons for the virality of the 'pizzagate' narrative. Forged as an exposure of sexual exploitation of vulnerable children by liberal elites, the story was an explosive emotional cocktail with an explicit political content and context.

Intent and (emotional) content are thus important ingredients for the online diffusion of viral narratives. Even though epidemiological models provide suitable analogies and concepts, the dissemination of a conspiracy theory is more complex than the propagation of an infectious disease. In the most basic epidemic models, it is assumed that contagion happens naturally at the first contact of an infected node with a susceptible neighbour in the network (Ball *et al.* 1997).

However, as we learned from social influence studies (Zimbardo, Leippe 1991) and network theory (Watts 2002), simple exposure is a necessary but usually insufficient condition for the adoption of an idea or behaviour (see Chapter 4.8). Networked social influence is a *complex contagion* process by which an idea or behaviour, whose adoption is not free from social costs and risks, is espoused as the result of networked reinforcement from multiple nodes (Centola, Macy 2007: 703). A public declaration of belief in the 'pizzagate' conspiracy theory, in the form of a social media posting, is likely to be associated with the U.S. alt-right and support for Donald Trump. This affiliation is not without social costs. In the diffusion of controversial ideas, such as conspiracy theories, Duncan Watts postulated that 'each individual has a threshold for adoption ... When the fraction of a person's contacts who have themselves adopted the trend [idea] rises above this threshold, they adopt it also' (Newman et al. 2006: 423). For this to happen there must exist a modicum of individuals with very low adoption thresholds (Watts 2002) – people who will be persuaded when exposed to the narrative by a relatively small number of contacts. Online networks, especially, consisting of dense clusters of like-minded actors contribute to the wide circulation of these narratives because they lower the social costs of adoption and thus promote the mainstreaming of previously marginal narratives.

In the process of adopting a conspiracy theory, *cognitive biases* related to pre-existing individual beliefs and collective belongings are also a pivotal factor in the adoption of a conspiracy theory. Motivated reasoning, as one example of a cognitive bias, is 'a form of information processing that promotes individuals' interests in forming and maintaining beliefs that signify their loyalty to important affinity groups' (Kahan 2012: 407). Even the perception of expert consensus in science, like climate change or the efficacy of vaccines, can differ according to 'cultural predispositions' (Kahan et al. 2011: 150). A cognitive bias, in short, can be decisive in whether one adopts and spreads a viral (conspiracy) narrative or not.

The virality and eventual widespread adoption of rumours, falsehoods and conspiracy theories are of course further influenced by strategic disinformation through coordinated dissemination operations. When linked to disinformation campaigns, the circulation of conspiracy theories is used from this perspective to manipulate, recruit and mobilise the public and convert them into believers, voters and consumers. Within the spectrum of 'structural virality' (Goel et al. 2015) of online diffusion, typically, the content of a conspiracy theory does not gain 'its popularity through a single, large broadcast [but] grows through multiple generations with any one individual directly responsible for only a fraction of the total adoption' (Goel et al. 2015: 1). This was empirically verified with the diffusion dynamics of news on Twitter, where the 'spread of falsehood was aided by its virality, meaning that falsehood did not simply spread through broadcast dynamics but rather through peer-to-peer diffusion characterized by a viral branching' (Vosoughi et al. 2018: 1148). Faced with non-strategic, uncoordinated, random propagation and resistance to adoption, narratives will tend to linger in the periphery of social networks as marginal beliefs.

## Positions and roles in the network

Content and intent should then be considered as key elements in the successful dissemination and diffusion of a viral narrative. Equally important is the position that the first agents of contagion and the other spreaders occupy, as well as their role in the online networks. In this context, any thorough analysis of the lifecycle of a conspiracy theory should be able to identify 'conspiracy centrals', 'conspiracy brokers' and 'conspiracy amplifiers'.

*Conspiracy centrals* are actors at the centre of the network with a vested interest in the narrative and its implications. They craft the narrative and assure its propagation inside relatively dense clusters in which they are prestigious nodes. In our model, conspiracy centrals are instrumental for the process of strategic disinformation. *Conspiracy brokers* are actors situated in-between clusters. They act as connectors between relatively distant nodes or even different communities. On the one hand, they increase the size and reachability of the network. On the other hand, they are structural vulnerabilities because their removal potentially disconnects the network. Last, *conspiracy amplifiers* represent the biggest segment of the network, performing the crucial function of viral narrative transmitters. It is in this role that we will discern the action of human and/or automated agents decisively contributing to the reverberation of the conspiracy theory through the social network structures. The transmission can be an effect of the unwitting actions of vulnerable nodes, like digitally illiterate users, but, more often, results from premeditated activities. Conspiracy amplifiers can, for instance, be involved in 'clickbait' operations for economic gains (Subramanian 2017), they can use social bots that simulate real user profiles and replicate viral narratives (Shao et al. 2017), be involved in organised disinformation campaigns, for example by state actors and parties (Bradshaw, Howard 2018) or Internet trolling – 'a specific type of malicious online behaviour, intended to aggravate, annoy or otherwise disrupt online interactions and communication' (Coles, West 2016: 233). Obviously, conspiracy amplifiers can also be voluntary spreaders who enlist themselves either as true believers in the conspiracy theory or in the wider goals of a disinformation campaign.

A concise social network analysis of the 'pizzagate' conspiracy theory evidences a clear distribution of positions and roles within the whole network across the three sampled windows of observation. Indeed, the first time-window (T1) shows that, three days before the attack that made international headlines, the 'conspiracy centrals' (measured by eigenvector and in-degree centrality) in the Twitter #pizzagate network were an assortment of fringe far-right nativists led by Brittany Pettibone, a then self-described 'American Nationalist Proud Republican' who became a prominent figure in the Generation Identity movement. Others were the conspiracy theorist Alex Jones through his media franchise 'Infowars', the long-time Donald Trump advisor and strategist Roger Stone (tweeting with the handle @StoneColdTruth) and the video sharing platform YouTube, a regular facilitator of conspiracy theory broadcasters. At this point, a right-wing partisan website, which frequently spreads false news and conspiracy theories, was the most salient conspiracy broker, while a vast network of Republican and Donald Trump supporters, far-right activists, unwitting retweeters, clickbait operations and bots amplified the narrative. In doing so, they were rapidly spreading the theory and increasing the diameter of the network. The profile of the conspiracy brokers and amplifiers is largely maintained across the remaining two periods, with changes occurring, mostly, at the centre of the network. Indeed, the most significant transformation from the first to the second window of observation (T2), which coincides with the day 'Comet Ping Pong' was attacked, is the emergence of a small cluster of actors resisting and contradicting the narrative. As prestigious conspiracy theory rebutters, we can find a *Washington Post* journalist covering the Tea Party, bloggers familiar with the far-right spheres and Democratic Party supporters with large Twitter followings. Notwithstanding the new resisting pole, at T2, the individual attributes of the conspiracy centrals propagating 'pizzagate' are largely maintained with prominent far-right activists assuming the most prominent position. Among these were Jared Wyand, a white nationalist, Donald Trump supporter and founder of a fake news/conspiracy theory website (in which Pettibone also participated) and Mike Cernovich – a social media celebrity associated with the right-wing, conspiracy theories and anti-feminism. The final time slice (T3) shows some effects of the rare reality check event at the pizzeria on the 4 December, 2016. In structural terms, the conspiracy centrals of T1 retain their position and the small cluster of conspiracy rebutters dissipates. On this occasion, the short-term political intents of the conspiracy centrals seem to have failed. Within the 'tweetosphere', the 'pizzagate' conspiracy theory did not succeed in attracting a wide audience beyond an alt-right cluster, but it survived a conspicuous verification incident. This demonstrates a resilient capacity to perpetuate the publicly rebutted conspiracy theory: The storming of the pizzeria was recast as a cover-up and false-flag operation (Nashrulla, Dalrymple 2016). The video sharing platform YouTube re-emerges as a prestigious node that the spreaders use to reiterate the conspiracy theory and/or adapt it to the new environment.

## Whole-network structure and dynamics

The centrality of YouTube across the timeframe covered by my analysis confirms the overall importance of salient Web platforms for the dissemination of conspiracy theories. All major Web platforms are undisputed hegemons in their respective segments (Wu, 2012). As networking spaces in which an increasing volume of agents act within a growingly concentrated business environment, social media platforms, such as YouTube and Twitter, became the online backbone of strategic disinformation.

The importance for disinformation and conspiracy theorising also derives from the fact that social media platforms are imbued with arbitrarily stipulated community standards, opaque algorithms and filtering systems while the underlying business models rely on the monetisation of users' data and attention (Wu 2017). Social media platforms are, from this perspective, self-indulgent entities that reinforce the views of their users rather than challenge them, even at the cost of blurring the boundary between facts and fiction. Consequently, in addition to user-induced network effects, we have platform-induced user effects through the formation of 'filter-bubbles' – a term coined by Eli Pariser to qualify the online recommender systems that try to match the presented content with the users' preferences. It creates, Pariser (2011: 9) argues, 'a unique universe of information for each of us'. Even though a large-scale study on Facebook's News Feed conducted by Facebook researchers has shown that 'compared with algorithmic ranking, individuals' choices played a stronger role in limiting exposure to cross-cutting [news] content' (Bakshy et al. 2015: 1130), the fact remains that these choices should be considered as mutually reinforcing rather than mutually exclusive. It is the effect of automated filter-bubbles *and* individual decisions influenced by their networks that shields users from exposure to plurality, closing them down in ever expanding echo-chambers. For example, a Facebook user in 2016 who clicked on 'pizzagate'-related stories and had spreaders in his personal network could find himself immersed in unsolicited content about the conspiracy theory. Even several months after the violent event took place, both Google's autocomplete and YouTube's search algorithms still ranked 'pizzagate'-related content at the top when prompted with the word 'pizza'.

With such a favourable environment to reproduce conspiracy theories are bound to be adopted by mounting numbers of susceptible hosts that spread the viral narrative. At a certain percolation point, this generates the conditions for information cascades throughout the whole network. According to Duncan Watts' theory,

> once a sufficient number of people have adopted the trend it is virtually guaranteed that most of the rest will also, giving a kind of "avalanche" of adoption.... The trend will only propagate and cause a cascade if the density of these individuals is high enough that they form a percolating subgraph in the network.
> 
> *(Newman et al. 2006: 423)*

In the online transmission of viral narratives, we can speak of 'cybercascades', 'processes of information exchange in which a certain fact or point of view becomes widespread, simply because so many people seem to believe it' (Sunstein 2007: 44).

Social media networks reproduce and amplify this clannish pattern of information (Guerra *et al.* 2013) and specific platforms, such as Facebook or Twitter, end up showing a great deal of

*Disinformation and conspiracy theories*

fragmentation and polarisation (Bakshy *et al.* 2015; Conover *et al.* 2011). In a quantitative analysis of the circulation of scientific ideas and conspiracy theories on Facebook, Del Vicario *et al.* show that 'social homogeneity is the primary driver of content diffusion, and one frequent result is the formation of homogeneous, polarized clusters' (Del Vicario *et al.* 2016: 558). This online entrenchment shapes the formation of 'echo-chambers', a concept akin to that of 'information cocoons' (Sunstein 2007: 44). Echo-chambers are densely connected network clusters with few, if any, links to other groupings. They are bounded spaces marked by the internal reproduction of ideas rather than the external production of knowledge. In the online news environment, for example, it was found that people are more inclined to 'opinion reinforcement' than to 'opinion challenge' (Garrett 2009) – a preference that favours the echo-chamber effect. As clustered, tight-knit communities, echo-chambers forge particular beliefs and shield their members from outside influences. With little or no exchange of information with opposing or even different groupings, the adopted viral narratives will reverberate in feedback-loops leading to persistent worldviews and resistance to change. While this connective pattern can forestall adaptation and evolution, the strong ties that characterise it can also foster social bonding and sentiments of ingroup identification. As demonstrated by the most ambitious scientific experiment to date on the effects of online social influence, 'strong ties are instrumental for spreading both online and real-world behaviour in human social networks' (Bond *et al.* 2012: 295). This is one of the reasons why the vitality and survival of a social network is a function of the balance between strong and 'weak ties' (Granovetter 1973). If the former provide structural robustness, the latter assure the reproducibility of the network through exposure to new actors and information. Once a viral narrative is widely adopted, the echo-chamber will expand until it encounters constraints – such as the passage of time, a decrease of believers or, more rarely, a credible verification. By their very nature, conspiracy theories have great longevity since they are generally immune to falsification. It is the believers rather than the premises that make them theoretically irrefutable.

As my brief analysis of the dynamics of the 'pizzagate' social network demonstrates (see Figure 4.9.3), this rumour, which evolved into a conspiracy theory used in a broader disinformation

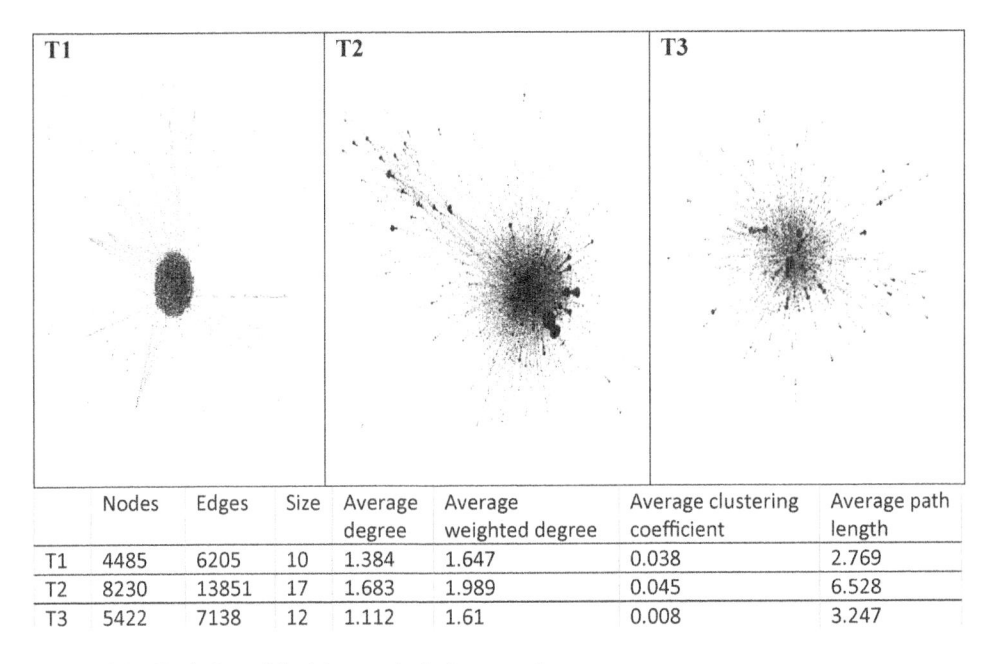

|    | Nodes | Edges | Size | Average degree | Average weighted degree | Average clustering coefficient | Average path length |
|----|-------|-------|------|----------------|-------------------------|--------------------------------|---------------------|
| T1 | 4485  | 6205  | 10   | 1.384          | 1.647                   | 0.038                          | 2.769               |
| T2 | 8230  | 13851 | 17   | 1.683          | 1.989                   | 0.045                          | 6.528               |
| T3 | 5422  | 7138  | 12   | 1.112          | 1.61                    | 0.008                          | 3.247               |

*Figure 4.9.3* Evolution of the 'pizzagate' whole-network structure.

campaign, is a good illustration of the proposed model. The whole-network dynamics are revealing and depict a stage of the lifecycle in which an echo-chamber is expanding through internal reverberation (T1). In just three days, the basic constitutive elements of the network – the active agents (nodes) and the connections established between them (edges) – almost duplicate their number (see Figure 4.9.3, T2). As the diameter of the network and the average path length grew (size), so did the probability of polarisation and fragmentation. Indeed, at T2 we see the emergence of a counter-group – a 'conspiracy rebuttal cluster' alongside the more centralised cluster of conspiracy centrals, brokers and amplifiers. The global increase of clustering (average clustering coefficient) indicates the fleeting consolidation of the polarised structures, which fades away again at T3. Rather than debunking the conspiracy theory, the falsification event, which is captured by the graph at T2, led to a retrenchment and a return to the echo-chamber dynamics.

## Conclusion

The perpetrator who stormed the pizza parlour where abominable acts were believed to take place acted on his beliefs in a conspiracy theory. This theory, I demonstrated, started as a viral narrative and has been produced and reproduced by conspiracy centrals linked to the far-right, alt-right, the Republican Party and Donald Trump. A host of willing converts, misinformed and disinformed users, clickbait operations and bots amplified the conspiracy theory, which, ultimately, motivated a violent event. 'Pizzagate' shows that extremism thrives in the shadows of an alternative reality nurtured by rumours, falsehoods and conspiracy theories. Powered by online technical and social structures, echo-chamber dynamics find far-reaching avenues of expression and new audiences to captivate – showing a capacity of adaptation that can go through phases of entrenchment, encroachment and retrenchment.

This is one of the reasons why mapping the network structure of the conspiratorial social space and studying the intent and content of the theory, the roles and positions of the different agents in the network and the dynamic of the whole-network is such an important matter. The networked disinformation lifecycle model provides a point of departure for such studies. Contrary to pre-Internet conspiracy theories – marked by isolation, exclusion and marginalisation – conspiracy theorists are now intruding in our public and private spaces. Although we have to specify the contexts and conditions, the more people are exposed to the unfiltered rumours and conspiracy theories on the Web, the more likely they will get contaminated. We live in a turbulent era of information cascades in which the traditional gatekeepers of the media ecosystem face extinction and disinformation reigns. 'Pizzagate' was a rare occasion to track the lifecycle of a conspiracy theory and a renewed opportunity to attest the importance of credible media validation. The conspiracy got out of hand and was forcefully verified through an act of violence. But, the lesson of 'pizzagate' is more about the easy path from conspiracism to populism and extremism than the difficulties facing rumour falsification. If the spread of a conspiracy theory fails, it does not necessarily expire. It goes back to the echo-chamber in search of future resonance. Conspiracy theories rarely die and the Internet does not forget. In our illustrative case study, the falsification forced the conspiracy theorists to adapt and, with time, 'pizzagate' morphed into other conspiracy theories, such as 'pedogate', a conspiracy theory about a world elite paedophilia ring, which used 'pizzagate' as a false flag to cover up their activities.

## References

Adamic, L.A. and Glance, N. (2005) 'The political blogosphere and the 2004 US election: divided they blog', *Proceedings of the 3rd international workshop on Link discovery*, New York: ACM, pp. 36–43.

Aisch, G., Huang, J, and Kang, C. (2016) 'Dissecting the #PizzaGate conspiracy theories', *New York Times*, 10 December. Available at: www.nytimes.com/interactive/2016/12/10/business/media/pizzagate.html. [Accessed 4 February 2017.]

Alba, D. (2018) 'Duterte's drug war and the human cost of Facebook's rise in the Philippines', *BuzzFeed News*, 4 September. Available at: www.buzzfeednews.com/article/daveyalba/facebook-philippines-dutertes-drug-war. [Accessed 8 July 2019.]

Allcott, H. and Gentzkow, M. (2017) 'Social media and fake news in the 2016 election', *Journal of economic perspectives*, 31(2): 211–36.

Anagnostopoulos, A., Bessi, A., Caldarelli, G., Del Vicario, M., Petroni, F., Scala, A., Zollo, F. and Quattrociocchi, W. (2015) 'Viral misinformation: the role of homophily and polarization', *WWW 2015 Companion*, Florence, Italy, 18–22 May. Available at: www2015.wwwconference.org/documents/proceedings/companion/p355.pdf. [Accessed 26 September 2019.]

Bakshy, E., Messing, S. and Adamic, L.A. (2015) 'Exposure to ideologically diverse news and opinion on Facebook', *Science*, 348(6239): 1130–2.

Ball, F., Mollison, D. and Scalia-Tomba, G. (1997) 'Epidemics with two levels of mixing', *The Annals of Applied Probability*, 7(1): 46–89.

Berger, J. and Milkman, K.L. (2012) 'What makes online content viral?', *Journal of Marketing Research*, 49(2): 192–205.

Bessi, A., Coletto, M., Davidescu, G.A., Scala, A., Caldarelli, G. and Quattrociocchi, W. (2015) 'Science vs conspiracy: collective narratives in the age of misinformation', *PloS one*, 10(2): e0118093.

Bishop, B. (2009) *The big sort: Why the clustering of like-minded American is tearing us apart*, 1st edn, New York: Mariner Books.

Bond, R.M., Fariss, C.J., Jones, J.J., Kramer, A. D.I., Marlow, C., Settle, J.E. and Fowler, J.H. (2012) 'A 61-million-person experiment in social influence and political mobilization', *Nature*, 489(7415): 295–8.

Borgatti, S.P., Everett, M.G. and Johnson, J.C. (2013) *Analyzing social networks*, London: Sage.

Bradshaw, S. and Howard, P.N. (2018) 'Challenging truth and trust: a global inventory of organized social media manipulation', *The Computational Propaganda Project*, Oxford: Oxford University Internet Institute. Available at: http://comprop.oii.ox.ac.uk/wp-content/uploads/sites/93/2018/07/ct2018.pdf. [Accessed 4 September 2019.]

Briones, R., Nan, X., Madden, K. and Waks, L. (2012) 'When vaccines go viral: an analysis of HPV vaccine coverage on YouTube', *Health communication*, 27(5): 478–85.

Centola, D. and Macy, M. (2007) 'Complex contagions and the weakness of long ties', *American Journal of Sociology*, 113(3): 702–34.

Cheng, J., Adamic, L., Dow, P.A., Kleinberg, J.M. and Leskovec, J. (2014) 'Can cascades be predicted?', *Proceedings of the 23rd International Conference on World Wide Web*, New York: ACM (WWW 2014), pp. 925–36.

Clarke, S. (2007) 'Conspiracy theories and the Internet: controlled demolition and arrested development', *Episteme*, 4(2): 167–80.

Coles, B.A. and West, M. (2016) 'Trolling the trolls: online forum users constructions of the nature and properties of trolling', *Computers in Human Behavior*, 60: 233–44.

Conover, M., Ratkiewicz, J., Francisco, M.R., Gonçalves, B., Menczer, F. and Flammini, A. (2011) 'Political polarization on Twitter', *ICWSM*, 133: 89–96.

Del Vicario, M., Bessi, A., Zollo, F., Petroni, F., Scala, A., Caldarelli, G., Stanley, H.E. and Quattrociocchi, W. (2016) 'The spreading of misinformation online', *Proceedings of the National Academy of Sciences*, 113(3): 554–9.

Doerr, B., Fouz, M. and Friedrich, T. (2012) 'Why rumors spread fast in social networks', *Communications of the ACM*, 55(6): 70–5.

Garrett, R.K. (2009) 'Echo chambers online? Politically motivated selective exposure among Internet news users', *Journal of Computer-Mediated Communication*, 14(2): 265–85.

Goel, S., Anderson, A., Hofman, J. and Watts, D.J. (2015) 'The structural virality of online diffusion', *Management Science*, 62(1): 180–96.

Granovetter, M.S. (1973) 'The strength of weak ties', *American Journal of Sociology*, 78(6): 1360–80.

Granovetter, M.S. and Soong, R. (1983) 'Threshold models of diffusion and collective behavior', *Journal of Mathematical sociology*, 9(3): 165–79.

Guerra, P.H.C., Meira Jr, W., Cardie, C. and Kleinberg, R. (2013) 'A measure of polarization on social media networks based on community boundaries', *The Seventh International AAAI Conference on Weblogs and Social Media*, Cambridge, MA: MIT Media Lab and Microsoft Cambridge, 8–11 July. Available at: http://comprop.oii.ox.ac.uk/wp-content/uploads/sites/93/2018/07/ct2018.pdf. [Accessed 26 September 2019.]

Kahan, D.M. (2012) 'Ideology, motivated reasoning, and cognitive reflection: an experimental study', *Judgment and Decision making*, 8(4): 407–24.

Kahan, D.M., Jenkins-Smith, H. and Braman, D. (2011) 'Cultural cognition of scientific consensus', *Journal of risk research*, 14(2): 147–74.

Kata, A. (2010) 'A postmodern Pandora's box: anti-vaccination misinformation on the Internet', *Vaccine*, 28(7): 1709–16.

Krekó, P. and Enyedi, Z. (2018) 'Orbán's laboratory of illiberalism', *Journal of Democracy*, 29(3): 39–51.

Kristof, N. (2016) 'Lies in the guise of news in the Trump era', *New York Times*. 12 November. Available at: www.nytimes.com/2016/11/13/opinion/sunday/lies-in-the-guise-of-news-in-the-trump-era.html. [Accessed 4 February 2017.]

Kucharski, A. (2016) 'Post-truth: study epidemiology of fake news', *Nature*, 540(7634): 525.

Lanier, J. (2011) *You are not a gadget: a manifesto*, London: Penguin.

Lazer, D.M., Baum, M.A., Benkler, Y., Berinsky, A.J., Greenhill, K.M., Menczer, F., Metzger, M.J., Nyhan, B., Pennycook, G. and Rothschild, D. (2018) 'The science of fake news', *Science*, 359(6380): 1094–6.

Lewandowsky, S., Ecker, U.K. and Cook, J. (2017) 'Beyond misinformation: understanding and coping with the "post-truth" era', *Journal of Applied Research in Memory and Cognition*, 6(4): 353–69.

McPherson, M., Smith-Lovin, L. and Cook, J.M. (2001) 'Birds of a feather: homophily in social networks', *Annual review of sociology*, 27(1): 415–44.

Merton, R.K. (1968) 'The Matthew effect in science: the reward and communication systems of science are considered', *Science*, 159(3810): 56–63.

Nashrulla, T. and Dalrymple, J. (2016) 'Here's what we know about the alleged "Pizzagate" gunman', *BuzzFeed*, 5 December. Available at: www.buzzfeed.com/tasneemnashrulla/heres-what-we-know-about-the-pizzagate-gunman. [Accessed 4 February 2017.]

Nasir, L. (2000) 'Reconnoitering the antivaccination web sites: news from the front', *Journal of Family Practice*, 49(8): 731–3.

Naughton, J. (2014) *From Gutenberg to Zuckerberg: disruptive innovation in the age of the Internet*, New York: Quercus.

Newman, M., Barabási, A.-L. and Watts, D.J. (2006) *The structure and dynamics of networks*, Princeton: Princeton University Press.

Pariser, E. (2011) *The filter bubble: what the Internet is hiding from you*, London: Penguin.

Pluviano, S., Watt, C. and Della Sala, S. (2017) 'Misinformation lingers in memory: failure of three pro-vaccination strategies', *PloS one*, 12(7): e0181640.

Rogers, E.M. (1983) *Diffusion of innovations*, New York: The Free Press.

Shah, D. and Zaman, T. (2011) 'Rumors in a network: who's the culprit?' *IEEE Transactions on information theory*, 57(8): 5163–81.

Shao, C., Ciampaglia, G.L., Varol, O., Flammini, A. and Menczer, F. (2017) 'The spread of fake news by social bots', *Nature Communications*, 9: 4787.

Silverman, C. (2016) 'How the bizarre conspiracy theory behind "Pizzagate" was spread', *BuzzFeed*, 5 December. Available at: www.buzzfeed.com/craigsilverman/fever-swamp-election. [Accessed 5 September 2019.]

Silverman, C. and Alexander, L. (2016) 'How teens in the Balkans are duping Trump supporters with fake news', *BuzzFeed*, 4 November. Available at: www.buzzfeed.com/craigsilverman/how-macedonia-became-a-global-hub-for-pro-trump-misinfo. [Accessed 4 February 2017.]

Sinha, S. (2018) 'Fragile hegemony: modi, social media and competitive electoral populism in India', *International Journal of Communication*, 11(2017): 4158–80.

Smith, N. and Graham, T. (2017) 'Mapping the anti-vaccination movement on Facebook', *Information, Communication & Society*, 22(9): 1–18.

Starbird, K., Maddock, J., Orand, M., Achterman, P. and Mason, R.M. (2014) 'Rumors, false flags, and digital vigilantes: misinformation on Twitter after the 2013 Boston marathon bombing', in M. Kindling and E. Greifeneder (eds.) *iConference 2014 Proceedings*, Illinois: iSchools, pp. 654–62.

Stieglitz, S. and Dang-Xuan, L. (2013) 'Emotions and information diffusion in social media: sentiment of microblogs and sharing behavior', *Journal of Management Information Systems*, 29(4): 217–48.

Subramanian, S. (2017) 'Meet the Macedonian teens who mastered fake news and corrupted the US election', *Wired*, 15 February. Available at: www.wired.com/2017/02/veles-macedonia-fake-news. [Accessed 5 September 2019.]

Sunstein, C.R. (2007) *Republic.com*, Princeton: Princeton University Press.
Sunstein, C.R. (2010) *On rumours: how falsehoods spread, why we believe them, what can be done*, London: Penguin.
Van der Linden, S., Leiserowitz, A., Rosenthal, S. and Maibach, E. (2017) 'Inoculating the public against misinformation about climate change', *Global Challenges*, 1(2).
Vosoughi, S., Roy, D. and Aral, S. (2018) 'The spread of true and false news online', *Science*, 359(6380): 1146–51.
Watts, D.J. (2002) 'A simple model of global cascades on random networks', *Proceedings of the National Academy of Sciences*, 99(9): 5766–71.
Watts, D.J. and Strogatz, S.H. (1998) 'Collective dynamics of "small-world" networks', *Nature*, 393(6684): 440–2.
Wood, M.J. (2013) 'Has the internet been good for conspiracy theorising', *PsyPAG Quarterly*, 88(3): 31–4.
Wood, M.J. and Douglas, K.M. (2013) '"What about building 7?" A social psychological study of online discussion of 9/11 conspiracy theories', *Frontiers in Psychology*, 4: 409.
Wood, M.J. and Douglas, K.M. (2015) 'Online communication as a window to conspiracist worldviews', *Frontiers in psychology*, 6: 836.
Wu, T. (2012) *The master switch: the rise and fall of information empires*, London: Atlantic Books.
Wu, T. (2017) *The attention merchants: the epic struggle to get inside our heads*. London: Atlantic Books.
Zimbardo, P.G. and Leippe, M.R. (1991) *The psychology of attitude change and social influence*, New York: Mcgraw-Hill Book Company.

# 4.10
# CONSPIRACY THEORIES AND FAKE NEWS

*Kiril Avramov, Vasily Gatov and Ilya Yablokov*

## Introduction

On 30 October 2016, nine days before the final vote in the U.S. presidential elections, Twitter user @DavidGoldbergNY posted a message – 'Rumors stirring in the NYPD that Huma's emails point to a paedophilia ring and @HillaryClinton is at the centre. #GoHillary #PodestaEmails23'. Seven days later, on the wake of election day, the hashtag #pizzagate emerged and, within hours, absolutely false rumour was disseminated all around conservative, pro-Trump sectors of social networks. When the shocking morning of Donald J. Trump's victory arrived, more than 6000 re-tweets attracted traditional media to the claim (Fisher *et al.* 2016). The tweet was the foundation of a news-related conspiracy theory that claimed an existence of a Democrat-run paedophile network tied in with the highest ranks of the party, if not Hillary Clinton herself. The theory was based on the interpretation of some cryptic emails found in the hacked account of John Podesta, Clinton's campaign chief, and allegations that similar cryptic texts show up in the investigated case of Anthony Weiner (unfaithful husband of Hillary Clinton's closest aide, who digitally flirted with underage teenagers).

As Kline deconstructed the case later (Kline 2017), he had found in #Pizzagate both very archetypal elements of conspiracy thinking and propagation and a very new and distinctive specificity of this modern 'urgent' conspiracy theory. Metaxas and Finn (2017) used the dedicated investigative service *Twittertrails* to detail this innovation: The #Pizzagate theory developed within an isolated, pro-Trump echo-chamber that took 'rumour' for reality and never challenged neither a source nor an idea of such wild accusations (see Chapter 4.1). Fuelled by partisanship, the conspiracy theory grew in the minds of Trump supporters who were ready to believe – and support through dissemination – every lie if it could harm the Democratic candidate, even after the elections were over. When, after a few days of isolated 'boiling', #Pizzagate broke out to a broader media distribution, the theory already had thousands of 'adepts' who amplified every text that referred to #Pizzagate regardless of its polarity to its main narrative claims (fact-checking and even official denials were amplified, with acid comments, as much as 'supporting' opinions – including false and even fictional, created by jokers and pranks). First of all, the whole story was a complete fake. Even wildest conspiracy theories address as a rule some existing problems (or facts or beliefs), while providing believers with a false plot narrative explaining the allegedly true 'nature of events' (Knight 2001). The #Pizzagate scandal took instead a complete fabrication as a starting point, offering a real narrative (candidate of Democratic party wanted to win the elections) as foundation of supposed vicious actions. As Cohn (1977) observed, conspiracy theories develop in societies at a moderate pace as they 'collect and process what the adepts assume an evidence to support the plot'. His observations on conspiracy theories (1960–1970s) indicate that 'established plots' usually develop two–three years after a certain 'trigger event' that ignites the original author or authors of a theory. On Twitter, the circumstances of massive linking to sources – real, fake, purposely falsified – contributed to the fact that the #Pizzagate theory took off in days.

Normally, conspiracy theories can be considered as *'slow streams'* flowing in a shadow zone of human communication, as developers and believers process and co-produce 'evidence' and recruit/cultivate those who come along conspiratorial scripture occasionally. But, one day, a 'slow stream' has the potential to turn into a flood when some mass media outlet unwittingly or intentionally propels the narrative, typically with political intentions. In #Pizzagate, the model worked upside down: Political intention to defeat the Democratic presidential candidate produced a fabricated news scandal that seemingly was intended as a watershed of partisan approval. Unlike the type of classic conspiracy theories, detailed development and actualisation of a conspiracy theory was happening along (not prior to, as normal for conspiracy theories) with its distribution and not for years before the actual watershed in opinion emerges. The fake story received a falsified development due to highly partisan sentiment and made it into mass media coverage particularly because it was spreading like wildfire on social media – a mutually reinforcing relationship between 'old' and 'new' media (Šlerka, Šisler 2018: 61–86; see also Chapter 4.9 of this volume). Because the initial audience of the conspiracy theory was critical, if not negative or even hostile, to mainstream media, the debunking and fact-checking of a wild claim worked contrary to expectation: The conservative, anti-Clinton base perceived any rebuttal as a cover-up, which in turn reinforced and intensified the transmission of the original conspiracy theory. But, #Pizzagate lived on and it consumed a whole year of efforts by media, fact-checkers, analysts and academic writers to exterminate the cause (it continues to flame irregularly but far from its original calibre at the wake of Trump's victory). Thus, the so-called #Pizzagate scandal provides us with a distinct example of interconnections between studies of long-known conspiracy theories and an emerging area of 'fake news' studies.

## The advent of 'fake news' as a communicative praxis

The concept of 'fake news', along with a more eloquent term describing the same subject ('post-truth'), emerged within the political and academic debate alongside the U.S. presidential campaign in 2016. The term 'fake news' itself had been occasionally used by academics and journalists years before, however, the modern version of 'fake news' became a complex subject of discussions and research after 2016. In general, it is rare that a new concept of academic analysis makes its way into popular culture and day-to-day language. Within just a couple of years (2016–2018), the usage of the term spiked. According to the Elsevier Scopus database (of scientific abstracts and citations), 'fake news' as a subject or keyword has been used in nine and ten articles indexed in 2015–2016; in 2017 the number of publications jumped to 239, in 2018 it peaked at 568 and in 2019 (as of July 2019) already there have been 313 mentions of the term. A similar pattern could be spotted on Google Trends: While search interest index in 'fake news' barely surfaced before October 2016, it then could be found among the Top-100 searches in January 2018. The modernity and complexity of the subject – along with political connotations – turn 'fake news' into a research topic in various disciplines: While most references are found in communication studies and political science, researchers from fields as diverse as military strategy, health studies or economics strive to comprehend a recent term and apply it to already known or newly discovered issues in their domains.

In this context, we argue that conspiracy thinking plays an important, if not a crucial, role in the advent and proliferation of the so-called 'fake news' phenomenon and vice versa regardless of what particular attribution we use. Zonis and Joseph (1994) suggest that conspiracy theories are 'commonly defined as explanatory beliefs of how multiple actors meet in secret agreement in order to achieve a hidden goal that is widely considered to be unlawful or malevolent'. 'Fake news', meanwhile, comes in many forms and attributions: As (1) intentionally deceptive communication practice by rogue actors who falsify, forge, distort or invent information for the public (see, for example, Peters et al. 2018: 3–12), as (2) a concept of adversarial (to politician, ideology or country/nation) mass media that 'lies' to the public or 'conceals truth' about a particular policy, politician, cause, country or any other entity (Kalb 2018).

At least in part, both facets of 'fake news' attribution commonly exploit all or partial features of the conspiracy theory logic: For attribution (1), conspiracy theories work as a fertile ground of deception and falsification; for attribution (2), the narrative mechanics of a conspiracy theory is applied to an invented vicious 'plot' against a public figure, idea or even country. Also, we argue that 'fake news' and conspiracy thinking create a loopback cycle as the former constantly provides an input to well-known conspiracy narratives by inventing and distributing lies (or any other form of deception and disinformation) that conspiracy theory peddlers immediately appropriate and include as a 'proof' to whatever they believe in and what they want others to believe.

## The mechanism of interaction between 'fake news' and conspiracy theories

'Fake news' surfaced as a research subject before 2016. Among other cases, it played a central role in regards to the information conflict and disinformation campaigns/influence operations preceding and during the actual annexation of Crimea by the Russian Federation and the occupation and insurgency in Eastern Ukraine. However, we intend to concentrate on 2016 and beyond, since it was then the term finally was formed and inquiries could be conceptualised. While the 2016 U.S. presidential campaign was the first where digital technology played a significant role (and contestants had dedicated teams for this purpose), it was the very first major political event in which digitally distributed information and narratives played an equal, if not a prime, role in the formation of public opinion (as compared to 'traditional' media) and, possibly, consequently also affected voting and electoral behaviour.

Obama's victories in 2008 and 2012 are often attributed to clever use of social networks by the candidate and his political team. For the 2012 campaign, social media was the tool that drove voters to traditional media and campaign events, assisted mobilisation and rectification of campaign messages (Richardson 2017), while, in 2016, social media became a central battlefield. Americans (and some malign foreign actors) turned to social networks like Facebook, Twitter and Instagram, as well as collective communication tools like Reddit, 4Chan and other similar instruments, in an attempt to determine the outcome of the presidential elections. Television and organised mass media (formerly known as newspapers, news agencies and magazines) could therefore not ignore the debate on social media. Abstaining from proper protocols and routines of source criticism and objectivity, or blindsided by partisanship, most influential mass media amplified false, malaise and even adversarial messaging that – at least in part – was targeting a core value of organised mass communication, public trust and reliability.

As 'fake news' became an instant sensation after Donald J. Trump's victory, academics started to look for approaches and to develop definitions for it. Philosopher Axel Gelfert (2018) addressed the problem of definition, suggesting that it is possible to frame the broader subject to 'deliberate presentation of (typically) false or misleading claims as news, where claims are misleading by design'. Earlier, communication and network scientist Ciampaglia (2018) suggested that 'fake news' is a central component in what he calls a 'disinformation pipeline' – a broader set of 'human actions, algorithm flaws and perception biases that deceit people and have a goal to avert (or at least influence) their rational behaviour'.

The difficulty in exploring 'fake news' academically derives from a vague list of connotations that had been applied to the phenomenon during the political discussions of recent years. The subset of meanings associated with 'fake news' depends on many factors, but political views and affiliations with a particular political party are dominant (Schulz et al. 2018). In the U.S.A., President Trump and his allies in media characterise unfavourable coverage of his term as 'fake news'. To the contrary, liberal media and politicians attribute the label of 'fake news' to false, manipulated and misleading information Trump himself uses extensively.

Yet, it seems possible to trace a close relationship between fake news and the application of conspiracy theories in modern politics. As we know from conspiracy theory research, both the design of such theories and dissemination routes of conspiracy theories have strident political shadows (Fenster 2008). Historically, many conspiracy theories are developed and disseminated as a component of propaganda and political warfare: It is a very useful and powerful way of highlighting the threat of the 'Other' to the community that shares the conspiratorial notion, besides of other versions discussed in literature (Knight 2003). To picture the connection between both phenomena and explain the interconnectedness, we should concentrate on specific features of 'fake news' and 'conspiracy theories', leaving aside the political interpretation of the later term. For this, we suggest understanding 'fake news' as Gelfert defined it and fully incorporated into a modern Internet communication method, from websites to social networks to messengers. It has to be specifically noted that both conspiracy theories and fake news emerged as a confluence of political warfare and features of selective exposure to communication, but they differ in many ways while constantly staying interconnected and mutually reinforcing. For most conspiracy theories, (what are considered as) 'facts' are important (and even 'sacred') as they construct an interpretational frame that conspiracy theories communicate to their believers in particular ways. The same assembly of selected (and purposely curated) facts may fully indoctrinate a believer or provide him with a mental/conceptual framework that allows further development of conspiracy theories. Sometimes conspiracy theories development requires fabrication of facts (either forgeries or creative yet biased retelling of something real – like 'the Dulles Plan' in Russia).

The 'Dulles Plan' is, in fact, a rant by a vicious character in a 1960s novel written by Anatoly Ivanov, fantasising how the U.S.A. is waging a secret war against the Soviet Union using tools of psychological, ethical, sexual and behavioural subversion. It merely resembles some – at the time – declassified or even public U.S. documents, like George Kennan's 'Long Telegram', N.S.C. Directive 10/2 (1947) and 162/2 (1954), which outlined a political analysis of the relationship between the U.S.A. and the Soviet Union. But, the so-called 'Dulles Plan' is fictional, wrapped into scary, cynical and offensive language adapted to the taste of the Soviet reading public at the time. A few years after its initial publication, many Soviet propagandists and conspiracy theory peddlers were referencing the 'Dulles Plan' as something real. Noticeably, the 'Dulles Plan' narrative has some 'facts' in the background (there were actual N.S.C. and Congress documents that suggested P.S.Y. warfare against the Soviets), while clearly the interpretation of these facts is more important together with all the other elements of 'creative forgery'. So, in logical terms, conspiracy theories necessarily collect a matrix of facts of different quality (from indisputable to fringe, from hard data to forgery) and then operate this matrix (or parts of the matrix) in order to construct a range of acceptable results that prove, suggest or at least hint on a real presence and threat of the conspiracy. The logical flaw here is not the theory itself but using it as both a predicate and conclusion; facts are collected and organised with an ontological valence of importance for the initial conspiracy theories (and all evidence to the contrary is ignored or discounted). In case of fake news, this flawed but (internally) logical process is excluded. For the creators of fake news, the goals are more important than a supportive matrix of facts (if necessary, a certain fake news producer will just invent an event, a person, circumstances or connections). As noted above, conspiracy theory is a much older issue in human communications and, possibly, a much older social and communications phenomenon. Belief in conspiracy is rooted in specifics of human nature, thinking and group dynamics. Conspiracy theories are narrative creations of the human mind, and their existence is rather natural as they are invented to explain societal events that otherwise are either too complex or too obscure. As research consistently demonstrates (Douglas et al. 2019), conspiracy theory uses a fact or an interpretation of a fact or both combined as a starting point (i.e. 'Jews are proportionally small ethnicity [fact] but they own a disproportionate share of national wealth [interpretation]'). Then, instead of providing a rational inquiry that could have presented an approval, denial or explanation for this hypothesis, conspiracy theory suggests that the [fact] may be explained with an existence of a covert plot [theory] to achieve and maintain perceived reality [interpretation]. Only after the [theory] is established ahead of rational inquiry, the creator(s) of a conspiracy theory begin their 'research' that discovers additional [facts] that support [interpretation] and therefore approve [theory]. Because this logical process resembles (or imitates) the natural method of deductive inquiry, it can captivate or impose an opinion to otherwise rational human consciousness without scrutinising its inherent epistemic insecurity. There are scores of distinctive details or narrative techniques that are commonly used in conspiracy theories while being in rare occurrence in other explanatory storytelling. Conspiratorial narratives normally rely on the receiver's capacity to contextualise [theory] and serve selected [facts] as they offer 'optics' providing the respective view. For conspiracy theories, factuality is an important feature. While some historical conspiracy theories in the past had a fabricated source of 'facts' (*The Protocols of the Elders of Zion* is the most common example), falsification is not a permanent feature: Storytellers in the conspiracy domain rely on power and explanatory attractiveness of their narrative, xenophobia or selective exposure much more than on forgeries or outright false sources. Characteristically, the conspiracy theory narrative is crafted (intentionally) – similar to a religion or cult – to attract followers over time, as it offers a lasting explanation of societal or historical 'facts' that bother people diachronically (economic or ethnicity-based inequality, suppression of or by a particular group, diseases-related continuity, etc.). 'Fake news' is, to the contrary, a short-lived eruption in communication (primarily, digital mass media communication). Unlike the case of conspiracy theories, outright deliberate fabrication is central to 'fake news', whether it happens in a form of lie (invention of non-existing event, fact or even person who is the source of information), manipulation with context or meaning or a substitution of a fact (that may or may not be real) with someone's opinion that claims this fact to be real. Neither [fact] nor [theory] are important for 'fake news' producers – because they intentionally discard and disregard factuality as they can 'sell' their production only to the consumers who already subscribed to one or the other partisan narrative theory. In 'fake news', [interpretation] is central, whether it comes in a form of plot, narrative or even opinion; all other elements could be just invented or falsified as they 'sell' the story to those interested because of the applicable (or politically comforting) [interpretation].

Using the same apparatus we applied to describe the narrative of conspiracy theories, we can broadly describe 'fake news' procedure as this: [A fabricated fact] put into [fact]-based news agenda with an [interpretation] serving political, economic or social interest of the narrator, sometimes serving as confirmation to a [theory] that may take a form of policy, or strengthen an existing biased narrative (including but not limited to [conspiracy theory]). So, the procedural difference of 'fake news' is its reliance on existing bias rather than – in the case of conspiracy theories – framing the bias itself; also, where conspiracy theory relies on contextualisation by their addressees, 'fake news' substitutes it with opinionated and manipulated context (usually, by connecting [a fabricated fact] with a current hot news agenda topic(s) using authority (either real or invented or appropriated).

Unlike conspiracy theories, 'fake news' are not crafted to sustain over time, although there are some 'fake news' narratives that tend to develop into more robust and sustainable conspiracy theories (#Pizzagate could serve a good example). They imitate the nature of the time-sensitive media cycle – a daily routine of mass media consumption, whether on traditional platforms or digital networks of distribution, and blend into this dynamic process as an integral part of their communication strategy. Both phenomena make use of each other: Developing conspiracy theories benefits from crafted 'fake news' items that fit their narrative, while 'fake news' fabricators commonly refer to known conspiracy theories as conceptual frames, as if they validate their interpretations, biases and false contextualisation.

## Synergy and distribution

Yet, we argue that one of the most important connections between conspiracy theories and 'fake news' lies in the field of distribution and transmission, not content or intent. As Burkhart explains (2017), in historical perspective, 'fake news' is a recurring phenomenon that complicates every technological shift since Gutenberg invented movable type and early newspapers and pamphlets arrived. In the 1800s, fabrication of news stories became a common tool in electoral politics, in the U.S.A. in particular – the whole 1828 campaign was flawed with outlandish claims and fabricated stories that both candidates, Andrew Jackson and John Quincy Adams, propelled against each other in media. It was reinforced by the anti-Masonic conspiratorial discourse of the so-called Morgan Affair (Önnerfors 2017: 18). Until the arrival of media ethics and legal regulation that insisted on impartiality of public information, falsification and other typical tools of the craft of 'fake news' were important to state actors, publishers and even broadcasters as amplification resources. Even if rebuked later, false and fabricated stories could greatly enhance copy sales or viewership.

Further development of media communications, especially after 2007, when social real-time networks assumed their role of 'mass self-communication' (a term coined by Manuel Castells), provided 'fake news' with a considerable and expanded playground. With millions and even billions of users, loose regulation and various psychological 'trust mechanisms' that compliment or substitute trust in media sources, networked communities are a fertile soil for deception and manipulation. For traditional media, brands and reputations with a developed audience is an asset. For 'fake news' producers, nothing of this kind counts – as the only aim is maximised distribution and audience exposure (regardless of whether it follows a political aim or just an economic or ideological one). Viral effects are also a goal within its own right (as people may seek other goals as futile as self-promotion or bare curiosity) – and in absence of regulation no one could effectively prevent social network users from producing falsified content and, thus, as 'prosumers', crossing the border between consumers and producers (see Chapter 4.8; Önnerfors 2019). In order to explore the development of the interaction between 'fake news' and conspiracy theory production, distribution and consumption, it should be noted that, prior to the spike of popular and scientific interest in the phenomenon of fake news, academia has coped with the challenges posed by disinformation and deception from multiple angles. This has included classic rumour theory, organisational psychology, narrative theory and folklore, among others (Allport, Postman 1947; Tamotsu 1966; Shibutani 1966; Mullen 1972; Rosnow 1980; DiFonzo et al. 1994; Bernardi et al. 2012; see also Chapter 4.1 in this volume). Thus, it is logical to gain valuable insights from these various interdisciplinary research approaches in studying rumours, urban legends, formation of political opinion and mass culture (Oliver, Wood 2014), as well as the spread of cyclical public panics and hysteria, in order to apply and combine them with new observations pertaining to the emerging field of 'fake news' analysis.

As noted above, the distribution mechanism of fake news relies heavily on the pre-existing individual or group biases on the part of the intended or targeted receivers and subsequent consumers of fake news and conspiracy theories. This mechanism closely resembles the well-researched mechanics of rumour transmission and proliferation (Campion-Vincent 2017). These employ so-called 'informational' and 'conformity cascades' that in turn rely on creating an initial 'critical mass' of consumers accepting the false or misleading information for fact due to the lack of direct access or understanding of issues discussed and subsequently conforming to the 'accepted wisdom' of crowds, once the viral 'snowball effect' has kicked in (Sunstein 2014: 176). When the outcomes of these cascades are coupled with the dynamics of group polarisation (Sunstein, Vermeule 2009), where 'members of deliberating group predictably move toward a more extreme point in the direction indicated by the members' pre-deliberation tendencies', the environment for 'cross-pollination' between 'fake news' and conspiracy theories is ripe for exploitation (Sunstein 2002: 176).

In such environments, producers and proliferators of 'fake news' and conspiracy theories, whether instinctively or deliberately, exploit their potential in regards to weaponised propaganda features within the existing 'echo chambers' in pursuit of multiple political, economic or psychological goals. These can range from political character assassinations and attempted market manipulations to wedge driving, outgrouping and self-serving ends motivated by psychological motives. Such motives include relationship maintenance, coping with uncertainty and self-enhancement, or 'copy cat behaviour' (Bordia, DiFonzo 2017: 87–102; Bauman 2017: 30). In pursuit of satisfaction of these motives, and in order to further their individual or group political, economic, social or cultural agenda, the proliferators of fake news, wittingly or not, exploit the propaganda potential of the dynamic interaction between disinformation and conspiracy theories.

It should be noted that this particular potential is key in the process of 'weaponization' of disinformation (Pynnöniemi, Rácz 2016) and is of specific interest in the domain of classic and contemporary information and psychological warfare, mass manipulation and propaganda studies (Ellul 1973; Snegovaya 2015; Linebarger 2015 [1948]; Woolley, Howard 2018). In line with their multiple earlier findings (Cialdini, Goldstein 2004), individual proliferators of 'fake news' and conspiracies, in similar fashion to their state-backed propaganda counterparts, in their pursuit of specific desired outcomes, when attempting to reach of maximum targeted audience exposure and catering to the above-mentioned own psychological motives, consciously or not, attempt to modify the perception, cognition and behaviour of their addressees (Mackay et al. 2011; Jowett, O'Donnell 2018). Such attempts are clearly detectable when scrutinising the key features and elements of #Pizzagate's 'urgent' conspiracy theory, one based on the 'explosive' example of 'fake news', where the intent was determined to be a modernised version of a classical reputation damage and political character assassination manoeuvre aided by the prowess of contemporary social media. In essence, the #Pizzagate scandal is a highly illustrative contemporary example of the chain reaction effects in the framework of dynamic interaction between 'fake news' and wider conspiracy theory utilisation in the pursuit of satisfying political partisan agenda. However, the inclusion of conspiracy theories supported by proliferation of 'fake news' and amplified by social media and subsequently weaponised against political opponents are not a recent novelty in Western (see, for example, Walker 2013) or non-Western political traditions (Yablokov 2018). Whether adversarial political opponents are engaged in continuous search of Barack Obama's 'original' birth certificate (Warner, Neville-Shepard 2014) in order to reveal his 'true' origin, or in a completely different context are tuned into a constant mode of exposing the purported 'agents of perestroika' (Yablokov 2018: 50–79) accelerating the pre-meditated Soviet collapse, the fusion between 'fake news' and complex conspiracy theories emerge as one of the favourite tools for fierce partisan political combat in West and East alike.

## Complementation and reinforcement

In our discussion regarding the mechanism of interaction between 'fake news' and conspiracy theories, we have described the difference between the two phenomena in regards to factuality, interpretation and framing. In differentiating between the different aspects of the respective phenomena, it was possible to determine that the major difference in mode of engagement of 'fake news' and conspiracy theories lies in reliance on existing biases, as opposed to the process of conceptually framing specific biases, as in the case of conspiracies. In other words, the production and proliferation of 'fake news' is not concerned with factuality and theory at all, as the centrality of their potency is grounded in the producers' and consumers' interpretation and subsequent intended perceptional, cognitive and behavioral changes. Despite the observed procedural differences of the respective discussed phenomena from the standpoint of communication theory, we argue that these interact together rather well, in terms of complementation and reinforcement. We refer to this dynamic in the context of political partisanship, as 'cross-pollination', where 'fake news' has the ability and potency to transmit conspiracy theories in a rather rapid fashion. The net effects of such transmission are greatly amplified by the low-barriers to entry and the speed of reproduction over multiple mediums located in the digital domain (Önnerfors 2019). Key drivers for this process of 'cross-pollination' are the deliberate search for exploitation of their potentials for amplification of existing ingroup polarisation (Schulz et al. 2018) and signalling for ideological supporters in on- and off-line mobilisation.

In addition to these, the dynamic interaction is exploited for purely utilitarian political purposes. Namely, as non-factual (invented or distorted) information in the form of text, sound or altered image carrying elements (so-called 'deep fakes') – providing cognitive cues or reinforcing well-established conspiracy theories that provide 'alternative' explanations of observable political facts. Events or adversarial political behavioral patterns can quickly be appropriated, as a 'rhetorical weapon' with a potent capacity for lasting destruction of public and private reputation. These drivers allow us to gain insights into the mechanics of what we have earlier referred to, as a 'loopback cycle', where the non-factual and/or distorted information is incorporated into existing or emerging conspiratorial narratives, as a form of a 'factual evidence' pointing to the veracity of the claims of the producers and distributers of disinformation. In sum, it could be argued that the process of 'cross-pollination' is beneficial to both kinds of disinformation entrepreneurs, as the complementation and reinforcement of 'fake news' and conspiracy narratives allows for advancement of the agenda of professional or amateur disinformation entrepreneurs and desired outcomes on the side of their intended (and often unintended) targeted audiences.

## Political but not strictly partisan?

Obviously, such instrumentation that is readily available for exploitation in the framework of political combat makes both 'fake news' and conspiracy narratives highly attractive commodities sought after by competitive political actors, formal and informal organisations and networks. However, it could also be argued that the nature of the substance of 'fake news' in their capacities as 'micro-stories' (mini-narratives) are not necessarily always related or could be readily incorporated into larger, purely political, conspiracy narratives (i.e. non-political 'fake news', such as formerly published in magazines such as *Weekly World News* 1979–2007, on the border between cunning satire and intended deception). Nonetheless, it could also be claimed that non-political 'fake news' almost always could be politicised and thus indirectly related to politics, but not necessarily in immediate 'hot' political contests. In addition to these observations, a number of findings point out that the different extremes of the political spectrum engage, interpret and endorse different types of conspiracy theories, however members belonging to both extremes are prone to accept conspiratorial beliefs (van Prooijen *et al.* 2015). Yet, certain types of conspiracy theories that interact and, in turn, are supported by proliferation of non-factual based information appeal to political moderates, extremist partisans of both sides of the spectrum, as well as independents, simultaneously.

An illustration of the aforesaid variation would be the multiple variety of conspiracy theory narratives concerning climate change (Uscinksi *et al.* 2017) and, specifically, the one concerned with so-called 'chemtrails', that is sometimes referred to as 'solar and geoengineering'. 'Chemtrails'-conspiracy represents the firm belief and preoccupation of certain social segments that certain government/s and subcontracted private corporations are engaged in massive covert climate control and weather modification via the so-called contrails left by passing aircraft in the sky that contain a mix of toxic chemicals or dangerous biological agents. The alleged motives for such covert governmental activity range from crude profit-making to an omnipotent and borderless global mind-control exercise, in other words a very real and massive plot that Daniel Pipes would consider a 'world conspiracy' (Pipes 1999).

The core of the conspiracy theory that is constantly supplied by freshly recruited civic activists and pseudo-scientific 'evidence' in forms of texts and images is centred on the idea that the spray of toxic chemicals and harmful biological agents by planes represents powerful covert control mechanisms over unsuspecting individuals worldwide. The adverse control effects over the clueless subjects is manifested via very direct and personal negative consequences that range from blood, respiratory sicknesses and psychological anomalies to food deprivation, famine and drought attributed to weather pattern alterations and the spread of harmful biological agents. In essence, the most commonly found 'chemtrails'-narratives, backed by stories and images supplied by networks of 'sky watchers', represent a sample of experienced cognitive dissonance on behalf of the 'awakened' believers regarding man-made climate change, as well as complications connected to loss of agency (Bakalaki 2016). This dissonance is dispersed across the political left-right spectrum and illustrates how difficult it is clearly to attribute the belief in the 'chemtrail'-conspiracy to a particular group of proponents. This ambiguity is accurately captured by Cairns, as she correctly observes that:

> On the one hand, the chemtrail discourse chimes with concerns sometimes characterized as more traditionally 'left-wing' (for example, concerns with social injustice, corporate power and the environment); on the other hand, anxieties about 'big government' expressed in belief in the New World Order, climate scepticism, fears about limits to individual freedoms etc. chime with more 'right-wing' subject positions.
>
> *(Cairns 2016: 80)*

In a similar fashion, in further search of clarity concerning this existing ambiguity in regards to political affiliation of the 'chemtrails believers' base, Tingley and Wagner find that:

> [...] per the CCES results, chemtrails conspirators are not confined to generally extreme political beliefs. Neither 'extreme' Democrats or Republicans are more likely to subscribe to the conspiracy theory than 'moderate' ones [...]. However, further detailed analysis of online behaviour reveals an affinity of those tweeting about geoengineering toward other topics that could be grouped into more partisan extremist causes.
>
> (Tingley, Wagner 2017: 4)

These, and other similar results, demonstrate that specific conspiratorial narratives with related features that are connected to disbelief and anxiety, such as so-called H.A.A.R.P. (i.e. High Frequency Active Auroral Research Program) or 5G related conspiracies, the anti-vaxxer movement (i.e. belief in the link between vaccination and autism, 'vaccine overload', exposure to toxic elements, etc.), that are also highly resistant against factual scientific evidence, possess the ability to appeal across the political spectrum. They also suggest that it could be speculated that 'fake news' production related to simultaneous complementarity and reinforcement of these narratives for multiple purposes may act as 'magnets' for the proliferators of suitable types of spurious or misleading claims, which are presented as news, observations or validation. It could be further hypothesised that such interaction between conspiratorial beliefs and false claims, presented as authentic news, would concentrate on 'complicated' themes and 'controversial' topics with complex causality in the eyes of public opinion. Thus, the more obscure and complex the correlations and causality links are, in combination with neglect and arrogance by the political, economic, cultural and scientific elites, the higher the attraction to the producers and distributors of 'fake news' and conspiracy theories to offer 'alternative' explanations and supporting 'evidence'. As this hypothesis might be valid in Western societies, where conspiracy theories gain traction mainly from 'bottom up' channelling suspicions towards their own government, it would be informative to test its validity in countries with illiberal and autocratic regimes of governance, as in the case of the Russian Federation under Putin, where we observe a reversed dynamic (Olmsted 2009). In other words, further research would be beneficial to explore the 'top-down' instrumentalisation of the conspiratorial discourse with a broad political appeal for the purpose of replacing the lack of coherent ideology, strengthening internal coherence, suppressing internal political dissent and reshaping national identity (Yablokov 2018: 192–3).

## Conclusion

This overview attempts to theorise connection and interaction between conspiracy theories (as media phenomenon) and fake news (as both media and political phenomenon). While both subjects still have no finalised theory and remain in the centre of academic and expert debate, we consider that the analysis above provides sufficient contribution to research. We contend that both phenomena share similar transmission models, while they systematically differ in the nature of content. Conspiracy theories are created and developed under a condition of 'fact-digging', though subjective and ontologically flawed; outright fabrication is a supplementary and secondary tool. When a 'factual base' of a conspiracy theory is established, it is used to strengthen a narrative that may (or may not) be a political tool or even a component of political warfare. 'Fake news' on the contrary, are tools – created and fabricated to be an instrumental part of political warfare or commercial scam that masquerades as political or pseudo-scientific or even entertainment media agenda. In this sense, 'fake news' represent a narrative 'conspiracy method' rather than a theory. Our research provides case studies, a theoretical discussion and an analysis that establish the foundation for an argument above open to further scholarly debate.

The suggested frame provides a non-contradictory distinction between the phenomena of conspiracy theories and fake news, and establishes connections, differences and synergies between the two. In this regard, we have argued that conspiracy theories have a vital role in the emergence and distribution of 'fake news' and vice versa, regardless of what particular attribution of the latter we use. In support of our argumentation, we applied the apparatus of description and classification of conspiracy theories to 'fake news', in order to distinguish and focus on the centrality of interpretation for this phenomenon and its further implications. Subsequent sections of our discussion concentrated on the mechanism of 'cross-pollination' between the two phenomena, as well as the implications of their synergy and distribution, as we argue that for the producers of 'fake news', distribution and outcomes in targeted audiences are of prime interest and importance. In the same line of thinking, we suggest that both phenomena interact rather well, as 'fake news' represent an almost ideal carrier of whole or partial conspiracies in certain cases, as they are instrumental in garnering political support, increasing polarisation and as they represent useful instruments for reputational damage. In conclusion, we discussed specific conspiracy theories with broad cross-sectional political and partisan appeal that attract non-factual and not necessarily strictly political disinformation, that subsequently is politicised. Our main suggestion is to apply the available conspiracy theory research apparatus (augmented by the insights gained from narrative theory, rumour and propaganda studies) towards a fuller scrutiny of the 'fake news' phenomenon. This approach enables further insights about its interaction with the conceptualisation of conspiracy beliefs in regards to specific topics and themes in different national, social and cultural contexts.

# References

Allport, G.W. and Postman, L. (1947) *The psychology of rumour*, New York: Henry Holt and Company.
Bakalaki, A. (2016) 'Chemtrails, crisis, and loss in an interconnected world', *Visual Anthropology Review*, 32(1): 12–23.
Bauman, Z. (2017) *Retrotopia*, London: Polity.
Bernardi, D.L., Cheong, P.H., Lundry, C. and Ruston, S.W. (2012) *Narrative landmines: rumors, islamist extremism, and the struggle for strategic influence*, New Brunswick, NJ: Rutgers University Press.
Bordia, P. and DiFonzo, N. (2017) 'Psychological motivations in rumour spread', in G. A. Fine, V. Campion-Vincent and C. Heath (eds.) *Rumor mills: the social impact of rumor and legend*, London: Routledge, pp. 87–102.
Burkhardt, J.M. (2017) 'Combating fake news in the digital age', *Library Technology Reports*, 53(8). Available at: https://journals.ala.org/index.php/ltr/issue/view/662. [Accessed 13 July 2019.]
Cairns, R. (2016) 'Climates of suspicion: "chemtrail" conspiracy narratives and the international politics of geoengineering', *The Geographical Journal*, 182(1): 70–84.
Campion-Vincent, V. (2017) *Rumor mills: The social impact of rumour and legend*, London: Routledge.
Cialdini, R.B. and Goldstein, N.J. (2004) 'Social influence: compliance and conformity', *Annual Review of Psychology*, 55: 591–621.
Ciampaglia, G.L. (2018) 'The digital misinformation pipeline', in O. Zlatkin-Troitschanskaia, G. Wittum and A. Dengel (eds.) *Positive learning in the age of information*, Wiesbaden: Springer, pp. 413–21.
Cohn, N. (1977) *Europe's inner demons: an enquiry inspired by the great witch-hunt*, New York, NY: New American Library.
DiFonzo, N., Bordia, P. and Rosnow, R.L. (1994) 'Reining in rumors', *Organizational Dynamics*, 23(1): 47–62.
Douglas, K.M., Uscinski, J.E., Sutton, R.M., Cichocka, A., Nefes, T., Ang, C.S. and Deravi, F. (2019) 'Understanding conspiracy theories', *Political Psychology* 40(S1): 3–35.

Ellul, J. (1973) *Propaganda: the formation of men's attitudes*, New York: Vintage.

Fenster, M. (2008) *Conspiracy theories: secrecy and power in American culture*, Minneapolis: University of Minnesota Press.

Fisher, M., Cox, J.W. and Hermann, P. (2016) 'Pizzagate: from rumour, to hashtag, to gunfire in D.C.', *Washington Post*, 6 December. Available at: www.washingtonpost.com/local/pizzagate-from-rumor-to-hashtag-to-gunfire-in-dc/2016/12/06/4c7def50-bbd4-11e6-94ac-3d324840106c_story.html?utm_term=.5546ff3afdb8. [Accessed 13 July 2019.]

Gelfert, A. (2018) 'Fake news: a definition', *Informal Logic*, 38 (1): 84–117.

Jowett, G.S. and O'Donnell, V. (2018) *Propaganda and persuasion*, London: Sage Publications.

Kalb, M. (2018) *Enemy of the people: Trump's war on the press, the new McCarthyism, and the threat to American democracy*, Washington, DC: Brookings Institution Press.

Kline, J. (2017) 'C. G. Jung and Norman Cohn explain Pizzagate: the archetypal dimension of a conspiracy theory', *Psychological Perspectives*, 60(2): 186–95.

Knight, P. (2001) *Conspiracy culture: from Kennedy to the X-Files*, London: Routledge.

Knight, P. (ed.) (2003) *Conspiracy theories in American history: an encyclopedia*, vol. 1, Santa Barbara, CA: ABC–Clio.

Linebarger, P.M. (1948) *Psychological warfare*, reprint, USA: Pickle Partners Publishing, 2015.

Mackay, A., Tatham, S. and Rowland, L. (2011) *Behavioural conflict: why understanding people and their motivations will prove decisive in future conflict*, Saffron Walden: Military Studies.

Metaxas, P. and Finn, S. (2017) 'The infamous #Pizzagate conspiracy theory: insight from a TwitterTrails investigation', *Faculty Research and Scholarship*, 188.

Mullen, P.B. (1972) 'Modern legend and rumour theory', *Journal of the Folklore Institute*, 9(2/3): 95–109.

Oliver, J.E. and Wood, T.J. (2014) 'Conspiracy theories and the paranoid style(s) of mass opinion', *American Journal of Political Science*, 58(4): 952–66.

Olmsted, K.S. (2009) *Real enemies: conspiracy theories and American democracy, World War I to 9/11*, Oxford: Oxford University Press.

Önnerfors, A. (2017) *Freemasonry: a very short introduction*, Oxford: Oxford University Press.

Önnerfors, A. (2019) 'Researching right-wing hypermedia environments: a case-study of the German online platform einprozent.de', in S. Asche, J. Busher, G. Macklin and A. Winter (eds.) *Researching the far right: theory, method and practice*, London: Routledge.

Peters, M.A., Rider, S., Hyvönen, M. and Besley, T. (eds.) (2018) *Post-truth, fake news: viral modernity & higher education*, Singapore: Springer.

Pipes, D. (1999) *Conspiracy: how the paranoid style flourishes and where it comes from*, New York: Simon and Schuster.

Pynnöniemi, K. and Rácz, A. (eds.) (2016) *Fog of falsehood: Russian strategy of deception and the conflict in Ukraine*, Helsinki: Ulkopoliittinen Instituutti.

Richardson, G. (ed.) (2017) *Social media and politics: a new way to participate in the political process*, Santa Barbara, CA: Praeger.

Rosnow, R.L. (1980) 'Psychology of rumour reconsidered', *Psychological Bulletin*, 87(3): 578–91.

Schulz, A., Wirth, W. and Müller, P. (2018) 'We are the people and you are fake news: a social identity approach to populist citizens' false consensus and hostile media perceptions', *Communication Research*, August.

Shibutani, T. (1966) *Improvised news: a sociological study of rumor*, Indianapolis, IN: Bobbs-Merrill Company.

Šlerka, J. and Šisler, V. (2018) 'Who is shaping your agenda? Social network analysis of anti-islam and anti-immigration movement audiences on Czech Facebook', in A. Önnerfors and K. Steiner (eds.) *Expressions of radicalization: global politics, processes and practices*, London: Palgrave, pp. 61–85.

Snegovaya, M. (2015) *Putin's information warfare in Ukraine: Soviet origins of Russia's hybrid warfare*, Washington, DC: The Institute of the Study of War.

Sunstein, C.R. (2002) 'The law of group polarization', *Journal of political philosophy*, 10(2): 175–95.

Sunstein, C.R. (2014) *On rumors: how falsehoods spread, why we believe them, and what can be done*, Princeton University Press.

Sunstein, C.R. and Vermeule, A. (2009) 'Conspiracy theories: causes and cures', *Journal of Political Philosophy*, 17(2): 202–27.

Tamotsu, S. (1966) *Improvised news: a sociological study of rumor*, Indianapolis, IN: Bobbs-Merrill Company.

Tingley, D. and Wagner, G. (2017) 'Solar geoengineering and the chemtrails conspiracy on social media', *Palgrave Communications*, 3(1).

Uscinski, J.E., Douglas, K. and Lewandowsky, S. (2017) 'Climate change conspiracy theories', in H. von Storch (ed.) *Oxford research encyclopedia of climate science*, New York: Oxford University Press. Available at: https://oxfordre.com/climatescience/view/10.1093/acrefore/9780190228620.001.0001/acrefore-9780190228620-e-328. [Accessed 13 July 2019.]

Van Prooijen, J.-W., Krouwel, A.P. and Pollet, T.V. (2015) 'Political extremism predicts belief in conspiracy theories', *Social Psychological and Personality Science*, 6(5): 570–8.

Walker, J. (2013) *The United States of paranoia: a conspiracy theory*, New York: Harper.

Warner, B.R. and Neville-Shepard, R. (2014) 'Echoes of a conspiracy: birthers, truthers, and the cultivation of extremism', *Communication Quarterly*, 62(1): 1–17.

Woolley, S.C. and Howard, P.N. (eds.) (2018) *Computational propaganda: political parties, politicians, and political manipulation on social media*, Oxford: Oxford University Press.

Yablokov, I. (2018) *Fortress Russia: conspiracy theories in the post-Soviet world*, Cambridge: Polity.

Zonis, M. and Joseph, C.M. (1994) 'Conspiracy thinking in the Middle East', *Political Psychology*, 15(3): 443–59.

# SECTION 5

# Histories and regions

# 5.0
# INTRODUCTION

*Ilya Yablokov, Pascal Girard, Nebojša Blanuša and Annika Rabo*

Conspiracy theories are often seen as a phenomenon whose origins lie in the era of the Enlightenment and the French Revolution (Popper 1962: 7; White 2002: 4), with the imagination of Masonic and Illuminati plots linked to both dramatic transformations in society and thought, and the appearance of actual secret societies. For conservative elites, the French Revolution was seen as the triumph of subversive conspirators, a milestone in the global conspiracy against humankind (see Chapter 5.3). Yet, if we look further back in the past, we see that conspiratorial thinking has been part and parcel of history for much longer. Indeed, rudimentary conspiracist narratives already existed during antiquity and the Middle Ages (see Chapters 5.1 and 5.2), and this fits with the claims of some anthropologists and social psychologists who consider that conspiracy theories are the product of a universal mental mechanism when confronted with the unknown (Groh 1987).

Yet, historians usually consider that a recognisably modern form of conspiracy theory appeared during the early modern period at the earliest, and was a result of changes in political, social and cultural conditions (see Chapters 5.2 and 5.3). During the nineteenth and twentieth centuries, conspiracy theories thrived and increasingly took the shape of world conspiracy theories, that in turn circulated transnationally. From this broad historical perspective, the rise and transformation of conspiracy theories can be seen as the result of the process of modernisation of European society.

The first cluster of chapters in this section thus develops a historical framework, analysing the change in the nature and popularity of conspiracy theories through time. It becomes clear that the current popularity of conspiracy theories, as well as the fragmentation of the public sphere and the increasingly blurred line between fiction and truth, is far from unprecedented. In other words, a detailed genealogy of conspiracy theory is liable to change our interpretation of conspiracist discourses in the present, which are the result not only of their immediate context but also the legacy of narratives that have over time spread, changed, faded away and been revived.

Indeed, a historical approach sheds light on the astonishing persistence of particular conspiracy theories. The most prominent example is antisemitism, the importance of which is acknowledged by several contributions to the other sections of this handbook (e.g. Chapters 2.5 and 3.8). Developing into an all-encompassing conspiracy theory in the nineteenth century (see Chapter 5.3) and contaminating public speech in Europe in the twentieth century (see Chapter

5.4), antisemitic conspiracy theories are still very much alive in the post-9/11 era and have become enmeshed with other superconspiracies (Barkun 2013).

Antisemitic conspiracy theories have long played a significant role in the politics of Western Europe, but in recent decades their influence is perhaps even greater in Eastern Europe (see Chapters 5.5, 5.6 and 5.7), the Middle East (5.8) and parts of Southeast Asia such as Indonesia (5.9). This underlines the importance of developing a comparative and transnational approach in order to shed light on the specific characteristics of conspiracy theories in different social and political contexts. Moreover, these national and regional case studies can also cause us to question some of the common assumptions about conspiracy theories, for example that they are necessarily a sign of a 'crippled epistemology' (Sunstein, Vermeule 2009: 219) or that they inevitably lead to political apathy (see e.g. Chapters 5.9 and 5.11 in this volume). And developing a geographical perspective can also provide detailed and nuanced evidence about how conspiracy theories work on the ground, causing us to rethink some of the more universalising conclusions produced in this field of inquiry.

Historical and comparative studies tend to take into account the political, economic, sociological, cultural and religious dimensions of each case study, and they necessarily provide multifactorial explanations. When focusing on political aspects, for example, these studies highlight how conspiracy theories operate across the political spectrum and are embraced both by those in power and those attempting to resist domination. Many of the chapters in this section also make clear that different dimensions of conspiracism are often intertwined, with, for example, religious differences often rooted in political oppositions (see, for example, Chapters 5.2, 5.8 and 5.9). More generally, the chapters in this section develop a multidisciplinary perspective that emphasises the local impact of particular economic, social and cultural problems, even when they are drawing on globally familiar conspiracy tropes. These chapters suggest that social and cultural change is a powerful driver for the surge of conspiracy theories in different historical moments and political regimes. There is a striking parallel, for example, between the transformations of the early modern period and the advent of the digital age (see Chapters 4.8 and 5.2).

The following chapters attempt to provide a more inclusive and critical account of how conspiracy theories emerged and developed across different historical periods and in various parts of the world. In her reading of historical documents from the Roman Empire, Victoria Pagán (5.1) demonstrates the existence of numerous conspiracist narratives within Roman politics. Cornel Zwierlein (5.2) outlines the continuity between antiquity and the Middle Ages, when conspiracy narratives began to circulate in the manuscripts of the literate elite. In this view, fully-fledged conspiracy theories only appeared in the early modern period and developed into their modern form in the eighteenth century, as the product of deep changes in politics (the rise of nation-states and the emergence of political debate), in religion (the establishment of homogenous confessional boundaries) and in society (the surge of anonymous print media and the development of a public sphere). This dramatic mutation is confirmed by Claus Oberhauser (5.3), whose contribution underlines the decisive role of the anti-Enlightenment authors and networks in the fabrication of conspiracy theories that spread across continents during the nineteenth century.

The golden age of conspiracy theories, however, seems to be the first half of the twentieth century. To explain their significance in this period, Pascal Girard (5.4) stresses the impact of wartime, nationalism, extremist political movements and totalitarian regimes, which led to the fabrication and use of various conspiracy theories as political tools.

After the Second World War, the situation diverged: Although conspiracy theories became less significant in Western Europe, they played a more prominent role in the Balkans. Nebojša

Blanuša (5.6) explains the particular attraction of conspiracy theories in the Balkans, and why they persisted – not least because of the residual communist political culture and the outbreak of war in the 1990s.

The evolution of conspiracy theories in the U.S.A. seems to match that of Western Europe. Michael Butter (5.10) challenges the idea that conspiracy theories are now more prevalent in U.S. culture compared to earlier centuries. While conspiracist thinking was a widespread and orthodox form of knowledge until the 1960s, it has since been delegitimised. Butter argues that the apparent current prominence in conspiracy theories does not prove their overwhelming power, but instead is due to the fragmentation of the American public sphere.

The evolution of conspiracy theories takes different forms in other parts of the world. Doğan Gürpınar and Türkay Salim Nefes (5.7) emphasise the fact that the current prominence of conspiracy in Turkey is a legacy of that country's particular history. After the collapse of the Ottoman empire, Kemalist nationalism promoted various conspiracy theories. Later, Turkish Islamism and the rule of the A.K.P. enforced them as part of a mainstream political discourse based on the threat of foreign and internal enemies. The case of Venezuela, studied by Rosanne Hooper (5.11), shows many similarities: The prominence of conspiracist speech has to do with turbulent political history, economic and social issues, and above all the propaganda of the Bolivarian leaders, using conspiracy theories as means of government.

Ilya Yablokov (5.5) demonstrates that the importance of New World Order conspiracy theories in post-Soviet Russia is the result of an authoritarian regime relying on propaganda; the revival of former conspiracy theories among far-right nationalists; the incredulity about the downfall of the Soviet Empire; and the integration of Russian society into the processes of globalisation. Discussing the Middle East, Matthew Gray (5.8) explains the remarkable importance of conspiracism in this region in terms of social and political factors, such as the propaganda of weak and authoritarian states, the fragmentation of societies and the repeated interference of foreign powers. The conclusions of Viren Swami *et al.* (5.9) about Southeast Asia likewise stress the impact of economic, social and ethnic divisions, the political use of conspiracy-mongering by governments and also by Islamist movements, leading to inter-group violence.

Taken together, these contributions underline that (except perhaps for the West), the influence of conspiracy theories is increasing, as they play into a wide variety of specific political, social and religious contexts. While well-established democracies seem to have, at least until recently, managed to confine conspiracism to the margins of politics, conspiracy theories spread in weakened or more recently established democracies, and authoritarian states in particular very often use them as a tool of government. Indeed, conspiracy theories have become driving forces for creating national and political identities, and help governments channel often quite legitimate political, economic and social dissatisfaction onto the supposedly dangerous conspiring 'other'. These chapters thus confirm that easily transmissible ideas about plots and schemes are not a part of an isolated national discourse. Indeed, the transnational dimension of conspiracy rhetoric and the importance of networks of transmission has been a key feature of the phenomenon since the early modern period.

Academic research on conspiracy theories developed primarily in the context of the U.S.A. and was then expanded to consider Western Europe. To date, research about countries or regions of the world such as Africa, China, India, Latin American or the Central Asian republics is scarcer. This does not necessarily mean that there are no significant conspiracy theories in these regions. In Africa, for example, the recurrence of the Fula people conspiracy theory in Guinea and its recent translation into Nigeria, or the pervasiveness of H.I.V./A.I.D.S. conspiracy theories in South African society (Nattrass 2012), suggest that there is much scope for research in these areas. The need for further research is particularly important concerning the period before the Enlightenment and the contact with the West, especially in the Middle East or Asia, and this research might well call into question the dominant accepted chronology of conspiracy theories developed in the study of the West.

The authors of this section acknowledge the shortcomings of the current state of research. It has been a conscious decision of the editors to begin to overcome the current Eurocentric focus in the study of conspiracy theories. While obviously not closing all the gaps, several chapters (5.5, 5.8, 5.9 and 5.11) try to point out the peculiarities of the non-Western manifestations of conspiracy theories and underline their similarities and stark differences with European and American conspiracy cultures.

It is also important to recognise that the historical and regional approach provides a perspective on cultures mainly based on the study of the most available sources: Statements of politicians, works of intellectuals and the mainstream media. This focus on the elites is certainly a flaw of most of the grand conspiracist narratives. But the focus on one kind of evidence can only scratch the surface of national cultures of conspiracies, and is in danger of overlooking what happens on the grassroot level. The next step would be to analyse how prevalent those elite discourses are among citizens through nationally representative surveys (Turjačanin et al. 2018), and more with qualitative, ethnographic research on groups particularly prone to conspiracism. This would be a first step in problematising conspiracy discourses across time and space, and we hope that the current volume will open the way for the further debates and studies in various national and regional contexts.

# References

Barkun, M. (2013) *A culture of conspiracy: apocalyptic visions in contemporary America*, 2nd edn, Berkeley: University of California Press.
Groh, D. (1987) 'The temptation of conspiracy theory, or: why do bad things happen to good people?', in C.F. Graumann and S. Moscovici (eds.) *Changing conceptions of conspiracy*, New York: Springer, pp. 1–37.
Nattrass, N. (2012) *The AIDS conspiracy: science fights back*, New York: Columbia University Press.
Popper, K.R. (1962) *Conjectures and refutations*, London: Basic Books.
Sunstein, C. and Vermeule, A. (2009) 'Conspiracy theories: causes and cures', *Journal of Political Philosophy*, 17(2): 202–27.
Turjačanin, V., Puhalo, S. and Šajn, D. (2018) *Conspiracy theories in Bosnia and Herzegovina*, Sarajevo: Friedrich-Ebert-Stiftung.
White, E. (2002) 'The value of conspiracy theory', *American Literary History*, 14(1): 1–31.

# 5.1
# CONSPIRACY THEORIES IN THE ROMAN EMPIRE

*Victoria Emma Pagán*

## Introduction

In his philosophical treatise, 'On Providence', the Neronian philosopher and statesman Seneca the Younger asks, 'Why do so many bad things happen to good people?' (*Dialogues* 1.2.1). This enduring question has two equally discomfiting answers. Either good people are subject to the fickle, capricious, unstable forces of fate, or they are victims of evil plots. Such is the irresistible 'temptation of conspiracy theory', in the seminal formulation of Dieter Groh (1987). Although there is no word for 'conspiracy theory' in the Latin language, the ancient Romans proposed explanations for historical events in which conspiracy played a significant causal role. Furthermore, sometimes proposed explanations conflicted with official explanations of the same historical events.

## Definition and method

Building on the pioneering work of Brian Keeley (1999), David Coady provides a three-part definition of conspiracy theory:

> A conspiracy theory is a proposed explanation of an historical event, in which conspiracy (i.e., agents acting secretly in concert) has a significant causal role. Furthermore, the conspiracy postulated by the proposed explanation must be a conspiracy to bring about the historical event which it purports to explain. Finally, the proposed explanation must conflict with an 'official' explanation of the same historical event.
> *(Coady 2006: 117)*

It is controversial, perhaps, to apply the term 'conspiracy theory', when no such word or phrase exists in extant Latin literature. Surely the historical conditions are far too different to make the juxtaposition of ancient and modern worthwhile. Patent objections are obvious: Contemporary conspiracy theory thrives in mass social media that did not exist in antiquity. The Internet encourages the distribution and sharing of information and provides a platform for the proliferation of powerful visual presentations like the documentary *Loose Change*, which questions the events surrounding the 9/11 attacks. Furthermore, contemporary conspiracy theory is understood to be a populist phenomenon, a frequent and dangerous cry and expression of rage from the fringes of society. 'Conspiracy theory is populist in its evocation of an unwitting and unwilling populace in thrall to secret machinations of power' (Fenster 2008: 83–84).

Moreover, as the study of classical antiquity is bound by sources that were produced and consumed by elite male audiences, so the study of conspiracy theory is further bound by the dilemma that any secretive events were never intended for public record in the first place. Consequently, the conspiracy theories that we can detect emanate from the centre of power as the prerogative of the ruling class and especially the emperor, who was subject and object of both conspiracies and conspiracy theories. Of course, ancient historians regularly used rumours to discredit the Roman populace and to portray them as an irrational crowd. However, Cyril Courrier demonstrates that, even though historians may invent or distort rumours, nevertheless they are a mechanism by which the common people could interpret or comment on political events. Rumours thus 'inform us about the collective action of expressed feelings', allowing us 'to identify definite links between political conversations and collective actions' (Courrier 2017: 154). Rumour is as close as we can come to understanding populist sentiment in antiquity (a fair amount of graffiti also survives, but not directly connected to conspiracies).

Thus, the methodological concerns presented by our sources are not unmanageable, and conspiracy theory is now recognised as a fruitful avenue of inquiry for understanding the promotion and reinforcement of values in the ancient Mediterranean world. Joseph Roisman (2006) was the first to analyse the rhetoric of conspiracy in ancient Athens. He mined the corpus of Attic orators for evidence of a conspiratorial mindset and examined how such a worldview contributed to the maintenance of the Athenian democracy in the late fifth and early fourth centuries. His book begins with the rhetoric of conspiracy as evidenced in cases of homicide and inheritance and in cases in which litigants attempted to entrap their opponents. He then moves to the rhetoric of conspiracy in the public sphere, with chapters devoted to the charges of conspiracy in speeches that deal with the internal politics of Athens, especially in the wake of the violent regime known as the Thirty Tyrants, a pro-Spartan oligarchy that ruled for eight months after the Athenians lost the Peloponnesian War. The last two chapters take up the rhetoric of conspiracy as it is employed in instances of foreign and international policy.

According to Roisman, the rhetoric of conspiracy is dynamic and fluid, a strategy useful in a wide variety of forensic and deliberative situations. Adapted by prosecutors and defendants, the rhetoric of conspiracy is deployed always to strengthen the litigant's case and to discredit his opponent. In disputes over inheritance, the rhetoric of conspiracy compensates for a weak argument (Roisman 2006: 35). When a litigant claims entrapment, the rhetoric of conspiracy reminds jurors of the opponent's attempt to divert them from their obligation to justice (Roisman 2006: 64). Speakers who claim that the democracy is the target of conspiracy sustain democratic ideology. By virtue of its 'elasticity' (Roisman 2006: 141), the rhetoric of conspiracy can also apply to foreign policy. The ubiquity of the rhetoric of conspiracy therefore points to the receptiveness of the audience to this kind of thinking. Its prevalence derives from its efficacy.

From the rhetoric of conspiracy, Roisman draws conclusions about a conspiratorial mindset in ancient Athens. Amply attested across the board, the rhetoric of conspiracy was produced and consumed by the masses as well as the elite, and it suggests an Athenian anxiety about conspiracy. With a suspicious worldview, the conspiracy 'spoiler' (Roisman 2006: 154) had the ability to police Athenian society; in this sense, the rhetoric of conspiracy reminded fellow Athenians of the fundamental value of accountability: Their behaviour was always under scrutiny and their attempts at conspiracy were detectable. Finally, Roisman collates the similarities between ancient and modern conspiracy theory. Both design for themselves a perfect logic born of fantastic tales that explain hidden agendas. Both are born of a state of crisis in which scapegoats are blamed for the misfortune of others.

In similar respects, the pages of Roman history are filled with conspiracy theories. From Cicero's prosecution of the corrupt governor of Sicily in 70 B.C.E. to the suspicious circumstances and secret assassinations surrounding the accession of Emperor Hadrian in the year 117 C.E. in Syria, Roman politics were driven by fear, suspicion and mistrust that easily mushroomed into conspiracy theory (Pagán 2012). Even so, the good fortune of the Roman people sometimes did prevail over threatening dangers. For example, historian Livy records that, in the year 419 B.C.E., slaves conspired to burn the city as a distraction from their attempt to take up arms and seize the capitol. 'Jupiter averted the unthinkable plans, and the guilty, arrested on the information of two, were executed' (Livy 4.45.2). The prominence in the narrative of the good fortune of the Roman people deflects attention from the facts that contributed to the outcome: Namely, the betrayal of two slaves. Luck overshadows disloyalty. Historian Tacitus also tells a story of a thwarted slave conspiracy: 'Luck checked the seeds of a slave revolt' (*Annals* 4.27), as, once again, fortune keeps a conspiracy from gaining ground. The best defence against conspiracies, it would seem from both Livy and Tacitus, is fortune, an irrefutable force impervious to contradiction. Yet, it is hollow comfort to concede that the powder keg of contingency is doused by something so intractable as luck. When our Roman sources are unable to claim a world free from conspiracies, such crafted apprehension is a cautionary tale that aims to govern the shadowy territory between the insecurity of a world vulnerable to absurdism and the reassurance of a world governed by the invisible and therefore undeniable (if unprovable) forces of conspiracy.

## The death of Germanicus

For example, in the year 17, Emperor Tiberius sent his adopted son and heir apparent, Germanicus, to the Roman province of Syria, with military command to settle affairs in that region of the empire. According to Tacitus, Tiberius did so on the pretence of distinction, when in fact he was determined to dislodge Germanicus from public life (*Annals* 2.42.1). Creticus Silanus, the father-in-law of Germanicus' eldest son, was governor of Syria, but Tiberius replaced him with Piso, a man with a violent temperament and innate defiance (*Annals* 2.43.2). When Piso arrived in Syria, he interfered with the troops. Germanicus, on the other hand, made a point of being friendly and even rescued Piso from a potential shipwreck. When Piso and Germanicus finally met in Armenia, they parted in open enmity (*Annals* 2.57.3). Germanicus returned to Syria to find his orders reversed and his troops in disarray. Piso departed Syria for Seleucia. Suddenly, Germanicus fell gravely ill. Elements of voodoo were found in the camp (remains of human bodies, spells and curses, and the name 'Germanicus' etched on lead tablets) and poison was suspected. Furthermore, Piso was said to have sent slaves back to Syria to bring him updates in Seleucia about the state of Germanicus' declining health (*Annals* 2.69.3). Germanicus' condition worsened. On his deathbed, he blamed Piso and his overweening wife, Plancina (*Annals* 2.71), but in private, to his own wife Agrippina the Elder, Germanicus said that he feared Tiberius was behind his death.

Once Germanicus was out of the way, Piso's friends urged him to grab Syria, on the grounds that he had the emperor's favour, even if unexpressed (*Annals* 2.77). Here was his chance to obtain power. But, Piso equivocated and was eventually convinced to return to Rome. Germanicus was cremated at Antioch and his widow, Agrippina the Elder, transported his ashes back to Rome to be interred in the mausoleum of Augustus with other members of the Julio-Claudian dynasty. When her ship encountered Piso's vessels on the coast of Anatolia, hostilities flared up but quickly subsided.

According to Tacitus, when Agrippina the Elder arrived in Rome with the ashes of Germanicus, the general populace knew and perceived Tiberius' guilt (*Annals* 3.2, 3.3). Meanwhile, Piso hoped to find an ally in Germanicus' adoptive brother Drusus, who, with Germanicus dead, advanced in the line of succession. Drusus let it be known publicly that, in spite of the rumours of poison and Piso's involvement, he preferred to believe that no one was to blame for the untimely death of his brother. Drusus attributed the death of Germanicus to fate; however, according to Tacitus, 'there was no doubt that the words had been prescribed for him by Tiberius' (*Annals* 3.8.2); such is the temptation of conspiracy theory, to posit an evil plot rather than accede to an absurdist explanation of the world. Thus, Tacitus insinuates that Tiberius was complicit in the death of Germanicus; that the general public was aware of his complicity; and that Tiberius therefore needed to control public perception. Indeed, throughout the trial against Piso for treason and murder, rumours against the emperor were rampant: 'At no other time did a more attentive people give itself greater permission for concealed utterances against the *princeps*' (*Annals* 3.11). According to Courrier, such rumours 'acted as an indicator of opinions, values, and attitudes. It was a kind of political speech in a public space, which revealed Tiberius' unpopularity as much as Germanicus' popularity' (Courrier 2017: 157).

The prosecution presented its case; Piso was found guilty of treason but the charge of murder was unprovable. Piso's wife Plancina, implicated in the crime, deserted her husband in pursuit of her own immunity from prosecution (*Annals* 3.15.1). The next day, Piso attempted to continue his defence but was publicly assailed by the senators and utterly rebuffed by Tiberius. That night he wrote a few words, handed them to his freedman and ordered his bedroom door closed. In the morning, he was found with his throat slit, a sword lying nearby. Tacitus remembers hearing from elder statesmen that Piso had often been seen with a letter from Tiberius with instructions to attack Germanicus. This suggests that Piso was murdered before he could implicate Tiberius; the suicide was staged to protect the emperor (*Annals* 3.16).

Tacitus leaves us with two bodies and no transparent explanations for their deaths. Tacitus hints but does not assert that Germanicus and Piso died under suspicious circumstances, to the advantage of Tiberius, who perhaps ordered their deaths. In the absence of certainty and factual evidence, explanations for these mysterious deaths gained ground. However, we are fortunate to be able to check Tacitus' narrative against an external source. Between 1987 and 1990, near Seville, clandestine searches using metal detectors revealed fragments of six copies of a decree of the Roman senate inscribed on bronze tablets. This 'Decree of the Senate concerning Gnaeus Piso the Father' (*senatus consultum de Gn. Pisone patre*, abbreviated S.C.P.P.), ratified on 10 December in the year 20 C.E., records the punishments imposed on Piso, his son and his accomplices. As a piece of contemporary evidence, the inscription represents an official version of events. This is not to say it records events more faithfully or with more factual basis than our historian; rather, it is evidence of a senatorial version of events. Obviously, the senate could not fabricate information that could be refuted by living witnesses any more than the historian, but it could mould and shape, not only its own account of events, but also public perception, in the interest of promoting an imperial ideology and political culture that protected their interests and especially the interests of the imperial family (Rowe 2002: 41–66). As Miriam Griffin points out, at the very least, 'the document establishes that Tacitus did not exaggerate the importance of the events surrounding the death of Germanicus, which clearly convulsed Rome ... evoking the possibility of civil war' (Griffin 2009: 178). Yet, we do well to remain sceptical of official versions, especially those published by totalitarian regimes (Griffin 2009: 180).

Germanicus was convinced he was poisoned by Piso, but our historian is ambiguous. Tacitus does not provide any details about the administering of poison, as he does elsewhere (for example, poison is explicitly mentioned in the death of Britannicus, *Annals* 13.15–6). Instead, he offers an obfuscated scene of gruesome magic (*Annals* 2.69.3). When the corpse was exposed to public view before cremation, only those looking for evidence of poison found any (*Annals* 2.73.4). In the 176-line inscription (one of the longest Latin inscriptions to survive), there is not one mention of poison. Instead, it records only that 'the dying Germanicus' declared Piso 'to have been the cause of his death' (*S.C.P.P.*, lines 27–8). In fact, the inscription records no interest in the cause of Germanicus' death. Instead, the senate focuses on Piso's insubordination. The inscription records thanks to the gods because Piso failed to stir up civil war, not because Germanicus' death, whatever the cause, was avenged. As for the death of Piso, the first clause of the inscription specifies suicide. Tiberius refers to the senate for deliberation 'whether he seemed to have taken his life with due cause' (*S.C.P.P.*, line 6). Officially, then, Piso committed suicide; anything else is speculative (for a comparison of Tacitus' account and the inscription, see Damon 1999).

In the story of the death of Germanicus, there are haunting parallels to one of the most notorious conspiracy theories of modern times. A young man of military experience, beloved by the populace and marked for political greatness, dies in a city far from the capitol. His grieving widow travels back with his remains. Business comes to a halt as the people grieve openly. The cause of his death is unclear; foul play is suspected. A murderer with motive is identified, but he dies soon after indictment under equally suspicious circumstances and before any verdict can be rendered. The senate produces an exceptionally lengthy version of events and orders it to be published, not only in Rome, but 'in the most frequented city of every province and in the most frequented place of that city' and in the winter quarters of every legion in the empire (*S.C.P.P.*, lines 170–2). Only Diocletian's edict fixing maximum prices in the year 301 is preserved in more copies and, while this may be an accident of circumstance, it also suggests a strong desire on the part of the Tiberian senate to control the narrative. And, yet, other versions of the story circulated; conjectures and rumours found their way into the historical record. In the end, doubt prevails. Think then of the assassination of President John F. Kennedy in Dallas; Jacqueline Kennedy accompanying the body back to Washington, D.C.; the national outpouring of grief; the arrest of Lee Harvey Oswald, who insisted he was just being used; Oswald's unexplained murder by Jack Ruby; the hefty Warren Commission Report; the endless scepticism.

Lest we get carried away, let us remember that Germanicus may have died of disease or illness, at the mercy of fate, not a victim of an orchestrated assassination or malicious plot. His death may have been due to contingencies beyond his or anyone's control. Yet, however misguided conspiratorial explanations for his death may be, still they offer 'the comfort of knowing that while tragic events occur, they at least occur for a reason' (Keeley 1999: 124). Conspiracy theories – whether ancient or modern – arise in part from the desire for a rational accounting that ascribes misfortunes to human control.

## The Great Fire of 64 C.E.

Natural disasters and catastrophic events beyond human control beg the question, why do bad things happen to good people, and thereby tempt conspiracy theory. The great fire that consumed most of the city of Rome in the year 64 was blamed on the tyrannical emperor, Nero, who then deflected guilt onto a newly formed religious sect known as Christians. Tacitus begins his account of the fire with the alternative between fate and a conspiracy theory: 'Next came a calamity, whether by accident or by the emperor's treachery is uncertain' (*Annals* 15.38.1; translations from Woodman 2005). When Tacitus gives two reasons for a statement, the second is usually meant to be considered more seriously than the first (Develin 1983: 85). Thus, from the start, Tacitus guides the reader towards a conspiracy theory.

On the night between 18 and 19 July in the year 64, a fire broke out amid the crowded shops near the Circus Maximus that blazed for five days. Tacitus adds another loaded alternative:

> Nor did anyone dare to fight back the fire, given the frequency of threats from the numbers who prevented quenching it, and because others openly threw torches and shouted that they had authorization—whether to conduct their looting more licentiously or by order.
>
> *(Annals 15.38.7)*

Since no agent for the order is specified, the reader is free to infer that Nero gave the orders, even though he was not in Rome and did not return until the fire approached his palace complex. Although he provided relief for the victims of the fire, the rumour still circulated that he fiddled while Rome burned (*Annals* 15.39.3). On the sixth day, when the fire was all but extinguished, it rekindled, thus worsening public opinion of Nero who was suspected of using the fire as an opportunity to acquire land for his 'Golden House', a vast megalomaniacal complex in the centre of the city. He was even rumoured to have burned Rome to make way for the founding of a new city named after himself. Once again, as Courrier shows, 'rumour serves to make sense of an unexplained event, at a time when not enough information is available' (2017: 149).

No matter how much Nero tried to help, he could not control the rumours:

> But despite the human help, despite the princeps's lavishments and the appeasements of the gods, there was no getting away from the infamous belief that the conflagration had been ordered.
>
> *(Annals 15.44.2)*

The rumour conveys a negative perception of Nero. Yet, because rumour is a form of discourse that serves as a 'collective laboratory in which opinion [is] cautiously shaped' (Courrier 2017: 154), the negative perception is also malleable. Thus, Nero is able to capitalise on fundamental fears in order to redirect popular hatred:

> Therefore, to dispel the rumour, Nero supplied defendants and inflicted the choicest punishments on those, resented for their outrages, whom the public called Chrestiani. (The source of the name was Christus, on whom, during the command of Tiberius, reprisal had been inflicted by the procurator Pontius Pilatus; and, though the baleful superstition had been stifled for the moment, there was now another outbreak, not only across Judaea, the origin of the malignancy, but also across the City, where everything frightful or shameful, of whatever provenance, converges and is celebrated.)
>
> *(Annals 15.44.2–3)*

This is the earliest mention of Christians in classical literature, and it has stirred a robust scholarly debate that demonstrates the accretion of conspiracy theory over time.

According to Richard Carrier, the sentence, 'The source of the name was Christus, on whom, during the command of Tiberius, reprisal had been inflicted by the procurator Pontius Pilatus', was added to the original manuscript of Tacitus by a late antique Christian copyist. No contemporary or classical evidence attests to the implication of the Christians in the fire. Given the enormity of the tragedy that Tacitus describes, it is unlikely that no one would have heard of, mentioned or used Christian involvement for his own rhetorical purposes (Carrier 2014).

For Brent Shaw, on the other hand, the passage is Tacitean, but with two telling anachronisms that undermine the credibility that the Christians were the cause of the fire. First, under the reign of Tiberius, the governor of Judaea was a 'prefect', not a 'procurator'; this is a distinction that Tacitus observes elsewhere. Second, the appellation 'Christians' was not a Neronian term. Peter and Paul were routinely referred to as 'Nazoreans', not 'Christians' (Shaw 2015: 87). According to Shaw, Tacitus was not deliberately mendacious; rather, he forged a link between the fire and the Christians that was plausible but not probable and in fact not even possible: Nero simply did not persecute Christians. The connection between the fire and the Christians developed later because Roman officials became aware that local communities were upset by Christian activity and because of the growing negative populist mythology about Nero.

In response, Christopher Jones defends Tacitus, arguing that there was in fact a group already identifiable as followers of Jesus in Rome as early as the Neronian period, and that Nero blamed them for the fire (Jones 2017). Jones's critique prompted Shaw to clarify his position: There is no evidence that, in the year 64, in the city of Rome, a group of individuals known as Christians was consciously targeted and deliberately persecuted for their identity as Christians. That is to say, yes, people were scapegoated for starting the fire, but whether they were actual Christians is not proven to Shaw's satisfaction (Shaw 2018).

Finally, independent of the Shaw–Jones debate, John Pollini argues that we ought to take Tacitus at his word (Pollini 2017: 232). Later writers do not mention persecution of Christians under Nero because it was not systematic. Any mention of such an ad hoc persecution would detract from the fact that later Christians *were* systematically punished specifically for identifying as Christians. Pollini goes so far as to suggest that later writers do not mention the Neronian persecution because the Christians may have actually started the fire; at least Christian involvement is not out of the question.

Whether regarded as spurious, anachronistic or accurate, the passage manifests the scapegoating of Christians over time and, regardless of its empirical status, the accusation of Christians for arson conveys habits of mind inconspicuously. So, rather than sort out genuine Tacitus from late antique interpolation, or the correct from the erroneous, it is more useful to see this episode as illustrative of the potency of conspiracy theory in Roman political discourse.

Tacitus is our only source for the persecution of Christians in 64, and therefore our only source for the earliest state persecution of Christians. Of course, he may have inserted into his narrative an ideological position that was consonant with the reigns of Trajan and Hadrian, under whom he was writing. Or, someone else altogether may have inserted into the narrative an ideological position that was consonant with the late antique times in which he was copying the text. Yet, this unresolvable textual impasse is actually a useful heuristic device, for the effectiveness of sentence *Annals* 15.44.3 lies squarely in the malleability of conspiracy theory that allows for the easy replacement of historical specificity with utilitarian generality. Conspiracy theory operates by replacement and substitution that can lift Christians from one historical context and drop them into another. Such historical relocation imparts a sense of alarming timelessness and also ubiquity, seen for example in the coordinating conjunction 'not only across Judaea, the origin of the malignancy, but also across the City, where everything frightful or shameful, of whatever provenance, converges and is celebrated' (*Annals* 15.44.3). Through evocations of the Christians, Tacitus can ground the morality of the case against Nero in a complex set of temporal reverberations: What happened in the past (the fire of 64) carries into his present (Rome in the time of Trajan), signalling a constellation of conspiratorial themes that link continually to other times and other places across the empire.

The substitution of general for specific contexts renders conspiracy a-temporal, omnipresent and all the more worrisome. Each changing context (Neronian, Trajanic, late antique), however, involves its own historical specificity and erodes any original sense of the conspiracy, including the questionable culpability of the Christians for the fire. The reference to the Christians in Tacitus is valuable for its potential to bury the traces of a particular situation (the fire of 64) under a self-evident and unquestionable verity (Christians were eventually persecuted). The result is an effortless slip into a timeless and believable, if unproven or unprovable, indictment of Christians as conspirators.

In the end, the Romans who were looking for an explanation for the devastation of the city, the loss of life and the damage to so much property were not interested in, or possibly not even capable of, evaluating the underlying socio-economic disparities that produced such a disaster: Crowded slums, a disregard for safety or building codes, a dysfunctional senate bound by fear. Conspiracy theory thus serves as a replacement for genuine political engagement.

According to Steve Clarke, the conspiracy theorist is a victim of cognitive failure who is unusually prone to committing what social psychologists call the 'fundamental attribution error' (Clarke 2002: 133–4). Humans systematically make the mistake of severely overestimating the importance of dispositional factors, while simultaneously underestimating the importance of situational factors (Clarke 2002: 144). Rome was crowded; it was a hot July; the wind was blowing. These situational factors explain why the fire was so devastating, but are perceived as insufficient. Furthermore, if Nero were really grabbing land for his Golden House, then why did he start the fire near the Circus Maximus? According to Pollini, the fire consumed much of what was already annexed (Pollini 2017: 241–2; for a step-by-step heat map of the progress of the fire, see Panella 2011). Instead, more importance is placed on Nero's profligacy, greed and extravagant building program as an explanation for the disaster. At first, it was just a rumour that Nero fiddled while Rome burned: 'a rumour had spread that at the very time of the City's blaze he had actually mounted his domestic stage and sung of the extirpation of Troy, assimilating present calamities to olden disasters' (*Annals* 15.39.3). But, eventually, the rumour became an etiology: 'there was no getting away from the infamous belief that the conflagration had been ordered' (*Annals* 15.44.2) And, even though the perpetrators of the fire deserved their grisly punishment, they aroused pity 'as though it were not in the public interest, but for one man's savagery' (*Annals* 15.44.5) that they perished. In spite of the copious supply of fuel, heat and oxygen necessary to ignite a fire, it was believable that Nero started it for his own purposes. Rather than admit a frightening truth, that Rome was vulnerable, it was easier to accept that Nero instigated the fire. It was easier to fear tyranny than contingency.

Into this narrative is inserted (whether by Tacitus or a later Christian copyist) a second layer of conspiracy theory, by which once again a dispositional explanation is favoured over a situational. The situation in Rome in 64 was as follows: Nero was tyrannising the senate. His murder of his mother, Agrippina the Younger, resulted in political upheaval. He had poisoned his stepbrother Britannicus, divorced and killed his wife, Octavia and married the sinister and scheming Poppaea. His advisor, Seneca the Younger (quoted at the beginning of this essay), had retired and the trusted praetorian prefect, Afranius Burrus, died under suspicious circumstances, replaced by the notoriously cruel and violent Tigellinus. Nero was spending money well beyond his means on costly leisure pursuits. He ransacked the provinces for works of art and squeezed every penny he could to cover the costs of warfare in the eastern part of the empire that had lasted from 54 to 63, during which time the Britons put up a fierce revolt that precipitated further army costs and interrupted revenue from the island. Yet, over these situational factors that ought to explain sufficiently why Nero would burn the city, or why, given the behaviour of the emperor, the gods would be so displeased as to abandon protection, a dispositional explanation gained ground.

Obviously, Nero had to deflect blame; but, I would argue that senators also gained from the deflection of blame onto the Christians, since did they not contribute to Nero's tyranny, with their self-serving sycophancy or at least with their blind eyes toward his crimes? Tacitus concludes his encomiastic biography of his father-in-law, Julius Agricola, with an indictment of his fellow senators for their behaviour under the tyrannical emperor, Domitian: 'Soon our hands dragged Helvidius to prison; we were afflicted by the sight of Mauricus and Rusticus, Senecio splattered us with his innocent blood' (*Agricola* 45.1, my translation). Similarly, many of the senators of Nero's day stood by idly – the outspoken Thrasea Paetus notwithstanding (Strunk 2017: 104–21). To accept Nero as arsonist meant accepting a degree of complicity in the construction and maintenance of a tyrannical regime (see Haynes 2012, especially pp. 299–300 on the 'politics of acquiescence', and Osgood 2017: 60–1 on the senators' eagerness to maintain ties with Nero, even after the murder of his mother, Agrippina the Younger). Therefore, it is understandable to overestimate the dispositional explanation that the Christians were responsible for the fire. The Romans of the time would have believed that either the Christians were guilty of arson or that they were indirectly responsible for the fire because of a lack of piety toward the gods, who let Rome burn. Their involvement was perceived not only as possible but probable. As blaming Nero was easier than admitting the vulnerability of contingency, so blaming the Christians was easier than admitting complicity in tyranny.

Finally, conspiracy theories have the virtue of attempting to preserve a rationale for disasters that can be understood in human terms. Otherwise, we are left with absurdism, a world in which absolutely nobody is in control (Keeley 1999: 124) – not even Nero. This observation returns us to Tacitus' opening statement, which offers either chaos or conspiracy theory: 'Next came a calamity, whether by accident or by the emperor's treachery is uncertain' (*Annals* 15.38.1). Conspiracy theory is thus an irresistible temptation for those who need to believe that the world is governed by perceivable causes and effects.

Whether Nero or the Christians, a conspiracy theory that explains the cause of the fire seduces because it is a radical counter-thesis to chance as an epistemic artefact of causality. It works because it explains (slightly) better than what Denis Feeney calls the 'portentous arithmetic' (Feeney 2007: 106) that Tacitus holds in disdain:

> There were those who noted that the start of this conflagration arose on the fourteenth day before the Kalends of Sextilis, on which the Senones too ignited and captured the City; others have gone to such trouble as to total the same number of years, months and days between each of these conflagrations.
>
> (*Annals* 15.41.2)

Note that Tacitus refers to the month of August by its Republican name, Sextilis, evidence of his careful observation of differences between past and present, between the Republican history he is narrating and the imperial present in which he is writing, a detail that lends some weight to the argument that 'procurator' is an interpolation. Between the infamous sack of Rome in 390 B.C.E. by the Senones and the fire of 64 C.E., there had passed 418 years, 418 months and 418 days. Such a metaphysical explanation appeals because it allows the Romans to project evil on the conspirators without direct interaction that would result in moral contamination. The seemingly objective mathematical facts confine the evil and prevent good citizens from being directly allied with the conspirators (on 'metaphysical' conspiracy theories, see Butter 2014: 55).

Mark Fenster describes the appeal of eschatology and millennialism, the theological belief in the end of human history and the return of Christ that inaugurates a glorious age lasting 1000 years (Fenster 2008: 197). Such a belief appeals because it is an accessible narrative frame that explains the past, present and future, and this kind of thinking is a form of historiography that articulates and circulates a method of historical interpretation, a general theory of historical agency and an underlying conceptual structure that makes human history intelligible. It is an actively resistant cultural practice that challenges explanations of historical actions, agents and forces. In such an interpretive system, even the most negligible detail can signify consequences of great import.

In much the same way, a numerological explanation for the great fire displaces the possibility for recognising and enacting affirmative social and political change for current and past problems in favour of an abiding belief in a metaphysical solution (Fenster 2008: 199, 230, 231). Yet, Tacitus is categorically dismissive of such vapid observations of the commoners, who are overly impressed with nothing more than luck. When one form of reasoning is dismissed, another rushes in. The conspiracy theory of the Christians is all the more potent because numerology is so easily rejected. Each sentence, each word of Tacitus conveys the ongoing struggle to represent and understand the past and to assert control over the forces of history.

In the end, the scapegoating of Christians in the narrative of Tacitus is so logically coherent with later hermeneutic patterns that it almost does not matter whether they started the fire or not: The core of the conspiracy theory resides in the collective ethos of its Roman producers and consumers across time. Conspiracy theory gains momentum and force in part by replacement, by means of an effortless slip from fact into fiction, from provable to unprovable. This is evident in Tacitus' *Annals*, in which the scapegoats who were blamed for starting the fire and who served to deflect blame from Nero are easily replaced with the Christians. The conspiracy theories surrounding the fire derive in part from the fundamental attribution error, which allowed Romans to create their own comforting realities: Easier to fear tyranny than contingency; easier to blame Christians than admit complicity in tyranny. The punishment of Christians for the fire obfuscated the suspicions held against Nero, but only after suspicions against Nero weakened the ever-resilient forces of contingency. Conspiracy theory is most virulent when it promises to dismantle the forces of chaos and pointlessness in the world, and in this we may have more in common with the ancient Romans than we may wish to acknowledge.

# References

Butter, M. (2014) *Plots, designs, and schemes: American conspiracy theories from the Puritans to the present*, Berlin/Boston: de Gruyter.
Carrier, R. (2014) 'The prospect of a Christian interpolation in Tacitus, Annals 15.44', *Vigiliae Christianae*, 68(3): 264–83.
Clarke, S. (2002) 'Conspiracy theories and conspiracy theorizing', *Philosophy of the Social Sciences*, 32(2): 131–50.
Coady, D. (2006) 'Conspiracy theories and official stories', in D. Coady (ed.) *Conspiracy theories: the philosophical debate*, Hampshire: Ashgate, pp. 115–27.
Courrier, C. (2017) 'The Roman plebs and rumour: social interactions and political communication in the early principate', in C. Rosillo-López (ed.) *Political communication in the Roman world*, Leiden: Brill, pp. 139–64.
Damon, C. (1999) 'The trial of Cn. Piso in Tacitus' *Annals* and the *Senatus Consultum de Cn. Pisone Patre*: new light on narrative technique', *American Journal of Philology* 120(1): 143–62.
Develin, R. (1983) 'Tacitus and techniques of insidious suggestion', *Antichthon*, 17: 64–95.
Feeney, D. (2007) *Caesar's calendar: ancient time and the beginnings of history*, Berkeley: University of California Press.
Fenster, M. (2008) *Conspiracy theories: secrecy and power in American culture*, Minneapolis: University of Minnesota Press.
Griffin, M. (2009) 'Tacitus as a historian', in A.J. Woodman (ed.) *The Cambridge companion to Tacitus*, Cambridge: Cambridge University Press, pp. 168–83.

Groh, D. (1987) 'The temptation of conspiracy theory, or: why do bad things happen to good people? Part I: Preliminary draft of a theory of conspiracy theories', in C.F. Graumann and S. Moscovici (eds.) *Changing conceptions of conspiracy*, New York: Springer-Verlag, pp. 15–37.

Haynes, H. (2012) 'Tacitus' history and mine', in V.E. Pagán (ed.) *Companion to Tacitus*, Malden: Wiley-Blackwell Press, pp. 282–304.

Jones, C.P. (2017) 'The historicity of the Neronian persecution: a response to Brent Shaw', *New Testament Studies*, 63(1): 146–52.

Keeley, B. (1999) 'Of conspiracy theories', *Journal of Philosophy*, 96(3): 109–26.

Osgood, J. (2017) 'Nero and the senate', in S. Bartsch, K. Freudenburg and C. Littlewood (eds.) *Cambridge companion to the age of Nero*, Cambridge: Cambridge University Press, pp. 34–47.

Pagán, V. (2012) *Conspiracy theory in Latin literature*, Austin: University of Texas Press.

Panella, C. (2011) 'Nerone e il grande incendio del 64 d.C.', in M.A. Tomei and R. Rea (eds.) *Nerone*, Milan, pp. 76–91.

Pollini, J. (2017) 'Burning Rome, burning Christians', in S. Bartsch, K. Freudenburg and C. Littlewood (eds.) *Cambridge companion to the age of Nero*, Cambridge: Cambridge University Press, pp. 212–36.

Roisman, J. (2006) *The rhetoric of conspiracy in ancient Athens*, Berkeley: University of California Press.

Rowe, G. (2002) *Princes and political cultures: the new Tiberian senatorial decrees*, Ann Arbor: University of Michigan Press.

Shaw, B. (2015) 'The myth of the Neronian persecution', *Journal of Roman Studies*, 105: 73–100.

Shaw, B. (2018) 'Response to Christopher Jones: the historicity of the Neronian persecution', *New Testament Studies*, 64(2): 231–42.

Strunk, T. (2017) *History after liberty: Tacitus on tyrants, sycophants, and republicans*, Ann Arbor: University of Michigan Press.

Woodman, A.J. (trans.) (2004) *Tacitus: The Annals*, Indianapolis: Hackett.

# 5.2
# CONSPIRACY THEORIES IN THE MIDDLE AGES AND THE EARLY MODERN PERIOD

*Cornel Zwierlein*

## Introduction

Though the *coniuratio* was one of the most essential patterns of European medieval constitutional realities, one might argue that there were no fully fleshed conspiracy *theories* until the Renaissance. Indeed, the *coniuratio*, the Latin term for the making of reciprocal oaths, was the founding act of communities and medieval cities by which a not yet formally integrated social group was forged into a legally constituted corporation; a city, basically, was nothing more than the *coniuratio* of its citizens (Oexle 1985; Bader, Dilcher 1999: 366–87). As *coniurare* – i.e. conjuring – was pointing to the socially binding power between people with common goals before any constituted commonwealth, *coniurationes* are found in many other medieval contexts and particularly within then constituted cities; people could even go back to that original form of establishing social binding as a means to oppose the constituted institutions. In fact, parts of the population could separate themselves from the rest or from the elite and even conjure against each other, forming conjurations in competition for power behind the same city walls. The *fazioni* and *congiure* of late medieval Italian city states were in the end nothing more than this reciprocal enactment of the founding principle of cities within and against the city itself (Guidi 1992; Villard 2008). The emergence of modern conspiracism was an urban phenomenon intrinsically linked, from the beginning, with germs of local forms of a public sphere (*fama, rumore*) and was certainly the medieval seedbed for the modern conception of conspiracy theory (Crouzet-Pavan 1997: 223–55). This double-bind semantics of *con-iuratio* was mirrored by the same positive and negative double semantics of the *con-spiratio*: in Ciceronian language, 'being of one mind or spirit' could imply the 'con-spiratio' between two or several philosophical friends.

However, in medieval times, *conspiratio* as a term was used far less than *coniuratio*. This is not of great importance as long as both words were used as vaguely synonymous, but it might be an indicator for what could be called the spiritualisation of the conjuratory practice and the emergence of conspiracy theories as a distinct phenomenon in early modern times. This later conception of conspiracy refers to:

> a narrative of a possible past and present, often also containing elements of future predictions, claiming to be the true representation of *the* past and present which is built from some commonly accepted elements ('facts', sequential and causal relationships)

and some elements that are not proven but possible and that bridge the gaps of knowledge and understanding concerning a certain event or a sequence of events. The possibility of the formative elements of the narrative depends on the character of the representation of reality in the given society and the form of distinction between fiction and factuality accessible in that time and that society. The not-proven elements of the conspiracy narrative are mostly adapted to the convictions of a given community of values. A conspiracy theory mostly has an explanatory, an appellative-affective and a denunciation function.

*(Zwierlein 2013: 72–3)*

As 'a narrative', I do not mean two lines in a letter or the rendering of a rumour that was orally communicated, but a longer and more or less carefully, consciously and purposefully crafted text that was circulating independently within a given communication context, such as decision-making circles of early modern governments or several public sphere(s). According to this perspective, medieval Europe was full of *coniurationes* in the above-defined sense, while conspiracy *theories* could be detected only very seldomly, and in embryonic form.

## Conspiracy theories during the Middle Ages

Yet, the current state of research on antisemitic, anti-'heretical', anti-sorcery and anti-Muslim beliefs, movements and violence like pogroms, massacres and other forms of persecution suggests, to some extent, the existence of structured conspiracy theories during the Iberian *convivencia* (Nirenberg 1996; Catlos 2004) with the persecution of Hussites (Šmahel 2002; Oberste 2003) or during the Crusades (Jaspert 2014). For instance, studies on the complex situation of *convivencia* between Jews, Muslims and Christians in the medieval Iberian Peninsula have drawn attention to many instances of domestic mass violence among those factions, mostly of Christians against Jews. Many studies have been done on the persecution of Jews throughout Europe, specifically preceding and during the crises of plague epidemics. Research on the anti-Jewish persecutions in France in 1320–1321 have understood them as exploiting pre-existing tensions in the service of a royal scheme to seize property (Brody 1974: 92–3; Ginzburg 1991: 49–50). Nirenberg has made the point that one should not understand these accusations as 'the panic of irrational masses, nor [as] a closely planned conspiracy coordinated by some unidentifiable elites, but [as] the formulation and widespread adoption of a rhetoric that momentarily "worked"' (Nirenberg 2015: 122). Nirenberg demonstrated that, in the kingdom of Aragon in this period, 'although the form and vocabulary of stereotypes about and accusations against minorities (poison, magic, sexuality, and so forth)' were also to be found there, there is no evidence of belief in large conspiracy 'theories' or plots; the outbreak of – partially conscious and organised – violence has to be understood as the enactment of 'doing and stimulating cruelty with words' (124). It was common to interpret the world through stereotypes that employed 'conspiracy' thoughts and practices. Many similar stereotypes and beliefs found in chronicles and homiletic works have been analysed by Heil as illustrative of an all-encompassing idea of a Jewish world conspiracy. In the late thirteenth century, Richer of Sens wrote in the *Gesta Senoniensis Ecclesiae* that 'in the whole world the Jews commit serious crimes', claiming that these plans were constantly elaborated and cultivated 'in their heart', aiming, ultimately, for the ruin of Christianity (Heil 2006, 209). However, those 'germs' of conspiracy theories rarely transcended the text that described them to a larger narrative.

Things seemed to change during the late-Middle Ages. By the end of the fifteenth century, larger narratives appeared, like the 'Vengeance of Our Savior' stories (Nirenberg 2015; Heil

2006). This evolution fits with the general assumption that fully-fledged conspiracy theories only emerged in tandem with the new print culture and modes of communication around 1500. The papacy in Avignon and the Great Schism of 1376 triggered a pluralisation and multiplication of manuscript communication and quick exchange and diffusion of ideas. One could see a conspiratorial character in the early example of the use of a historical argument against the papacy, which can be found in Marsilius' *Defensor pacis* (II: 25) (Marsilius 1958 [1324]: 846–83) in which the whole of ecclesiastical history after late antiquity was interpreted as a tyrannical usurpation of the Church by the papacy. The motive of the *papa haereticus* ('heretical pope'), already considered a problem by the canon lawyers and scholarly commentators (Tierney 1998), was turned here into a historical narrative with an explanatory power. However, the aim of Marsilius in writing his tract was to render a true historical account, albeit one which might have not been shared by his opponents. In the early modern period, there was no clear distinction between 'fiction' and 'factuality', and Marsilius' narrative was not conceived in a specific metaphysical framework governed by these terms (leaving aside the fact that every ecclesiastical historical narrative in Europe – at least before 1700 – was conceived 'metaphysically' within the framework of biblical time and Jewish–Christian teleology). In this regard, not every work of rhetoric, tendentious explanatory scheme or rendering of history should be categorised as a potential 'conspiracy narrative'. Research on conciliarism, for example, has never insisted on the existence of fully-fledged conspiracy theories as a major element of conciliarist communication in the context of the Councils of Constance or Basel.

Sorcery and magic in late medieval times, particularly in the fifteenth century, have also been analysed as forerunners of modern conspiracism. Behringer has shown how sorcery and witch stereotypes could be transferred from one 'minority' to the other, in his case to the Waldensian heterodox community (Behringer 2004). Political conspiracies that made use of sorcery stereotypes are part of the late medieval imaginary: The accusation or mere idea that there were plans to murder popes and kings by way of magic and forms of magical poison, spells or similar means are spread through the chronicles and epistolary sources of the Wars of the Roses. The use of 'image-magic' as part of real plots of murdering governing princes and kings was referred to during inquisition processes or secular trials of the *crimen laesae maiestatis* type; this adds a metaphysical element to the usual schemes of plotting and the rumours about them in late-medieval court societies. Despite this, the role of conspiracy theories as a means of explaining the larger plot was kept to a minimum (Jones 1972).

Crusader sermons and similar texts would only partially fit the above definition of conspiracy theories; there was indeed no need for a construction of such explanatory narratives as the theological positions about the heretical and enemy quality of the persecuted were settled (positively or negatively). And the most extensive recent studies on the late medieval Italian *congiure, lotte* and *fazioni* that reconstruct many real plots and conjuring events, murders, overthrow or transfer of power in the cities, and quote and relate 'rumors' that were spreading, hardly mention one central clear-cut conspiracy narrative that would have circulated and that would have had its own causal agency (Villard 2008; Bowd 2018).

## The notion of conspiracy in the early modern age

Machiavelli analysed the political conditions and functions of conspiracies in several works, including the biography of Castruccio Castracani and, most notably, in the famous chapter six of Book III in the *Discourses on Livy* ('On conspiracies'). But, he neither crafted a conspiracy theory himself nor analysed a consistent text, ideology or concept as major driving force or causal element, but instead examined the power relationship through the characters and deeds of the men involved. Though his method of political analysis was very new, with his use of *congiure* he still referred to the medieval realities, using it only in its negative meaning within already constituted commonwealths. His reasoning – referring obviously to Tacitus and Livy (on Piso and other Roman conspiracies) – was already informed by the Humanist revival of ancient Greek and Roman concepts. Explicitly referring to *congiure* against the 'fatherland [*patria*]' of a city-republic and a prince in his territory, he aligned the notion of conspiracy to political action – as preparations or enactments of regicides, tyrannicides or revolts – punished in legal terms as *crimen laesae maiestatis* (Machiavelli 1997 [1499–1512]; Fasano Guarini 1996).

Conspiracy/conjuration and its legal response as *crime de lèse majesté* evolved together in medieval and modern times. The respective laws of the *Codex Iustiniani* (Cod. IX; 8: 5, which was taken from Cod. Theod. IX, 14, 3) had always been known during the Middle Ages, and when the Digests from the eleventh century in Bologna (with the central *lex julia majestatis*, fragments of which are in Dig. 48, 4, 1, 1) were revisited, the academic legal commentary tradition also started to address the *crimen laesae maiestatis*. The Codex text was applied to the medieval Holy Roman Emperor by Charles IV and the collective of the electors as an amendment to the Golden Bull in the Metz laws of 25 December 1356. The electors were then included into the protection provided by the *lèse-majesté* laws that had been, in antiquity, the core of the ancient Roman emperor's *familia* and the members of his 'consilium et consistorium' (Fritz 1932: 80–2), even if the term 'conjuratio', though existing, was not prominent in Roman legal terminology. The reception of the Roman law and this adaptation to the present political realities by including the electors shows how crimes against superiors, attempts of assassination and conjuring evidently were perceived, again, to be an urgent threat and problem.

However, while the problem of conjurations against the life of reigning princes or the emperor were present from the normative point of view of prohibition and punishment, actual conspiracy theory narratives were not existing or have not survived. Proliferation and pluralisation of such forms, sometimes hard to distinguish from 'rebellion', 'revolt' and 'sedition', which would have had a different *sedes materiae* in legal terms, were taking place. Machiavelli questioned how to 'cope' with them in political, not legal terms – but the old notion of the *con-juratio* as the even positive founding moment of a community did not form part of this reasoning.

## The historical conditions for the emergence of real conspiracy theories

Real early modern conspiracy theories seemed to emerge only when three historical conditions – intrinsically connected – were in place: a) The establishment of a stable information public sphere of political news in anonymous form, independent from only one or the other ambassadorial networks. b) The change on the epistemic level of how politics was perceived and made: Quattrocento Italian men of politics in city-republics and princely courts were constantly relying on and became independent from the information feed as a representation of the political present state and as the starting point for secular forms of prognostics and calculations. c) The stabilisation and at the same time pluralisation of the post-Reformation confessional schisms, forming extremely consistent boundaries between we-groups and 'enemies' from the micro-levels of the villages to European state politics.

The reason why, after around 1560, we do find, even on a European scale, conspiracy theories with an 'autonomous actor status' as defined above is probably not to be found in the first instance in a new form of political *habitus*. In fact, medieval men of politics were probably as 'wicked', 'prudent' or even 'Machiavellian' as Richelieu and Mazarin, and this claim can be transferred to the micro-levels of society. The reason is not to be found mainly on the internal side of literary discourse, its genres and the development of contents (though both are co-evolving at the same time). The decisive difference – visible in every state archive from 1450 onwards in Italy and later in the other European countries – was on the side of the media, of news communication and the empowerment of individual anonymous authors as participants. Those could be princes like Lorenzo de' Medici, agents, ambassadors, secretaries like Machiavelli or his collaborator Biagio Buonaccorsi and hundreds of similar office holders, *familiari*, courtiers, clients of princes and cardinals and, finally, the writers of self-made newsletters (e.g. *avvisatori, menanti, novellanti* in Italy, which appeared decades later north of the Alps, mostly thanks to linking news communication to print). Producing as well as receiving the steady flow of political representation, they created a constantly changing sphere of the present, 'the contemporaneity' as a textual universe, which became independent from a single communicator, even from the princes themselves.

In comparison, despite the communication of a large quantity of manuscripts (codices), the late medieval 'public sphere' remained more local, even in conciliarist periods, eventually becoming multi-local and then connected (e.g. Avignon – Constance – Basel). It was also more oral, far more dependent on individual bilateral communication, and less triggered by the continuity and steady (weekly or higher) frequency of communication relying on postal networks. Far from being only the other side of an early modern, well-developed concept of authorship and a by-product of censorship, anonymity emerged far earlier due to the separation of universal and common news that should and could be available for all from the secret ones. It was this anonymous communication – in which sender and receiver were unimportant – that created 'the present reality'.

It is when the present state of affairs became somehow an anonymous 'unit' to which one could 'connect', that one could perceive, ask for or even buy on the *avvisi* market, that conspiracy theories could be a second-degree genre, a parasite medium linked to and emulating the already established form of political explanation and analysis, of future plans and projects. Print added to this a different medium, but historically the first steady news communication as described above emerged beyond print and even remained for centuries in Italy a manuscript form. In contrast, in Northern Europe, the media situation effectively 'jumped' from parchment to print before having really explored and exhausted all possibilities of mass manuscript communication as in Italy (Zwierlein 2006: 557–610, 2013).

That is why conspiracy theory texts were not necessarily communicated in print: We find texts of European-wide conspiracy theories in manuscript form in the archives of the smaller Catholic or Calvinist princes of Germany's territories as well as in London, France or the Netherlands, and later in Bohemia. They were mixed up with the letters, papers and newsletters (often in bundles of 'Newe Zeytungen' or 'Newes') that served the councillors and princes with information about movements of mercenary troops or events in foreign courts.

Evidently, there *were* also plots and attempts to kill princes, queens and kings, many of them in sixteenth- and seventeenth-century Europe. The list of attempts against the life of Elizabeth I is long; William of Orange was murdered in 1584, Henri III of France in 1589; Henri de Navarre, the leading Protestant prince of France and then first Bourbon king, Henri IV, escaped many attempts on his life before finally been killed in 1610.

However, the distinct element of early modern communication was that conspiracy theories had now become agents of their own account in actor-text relationships; transferring the concepts about actor-thing relationships to our context, those texts, once produced and in circulation, had a certain autonomy of agency and influence because of this newly emerged communication context. In other words, they emerged from real plot situations, they influenced these situations and eventually they produced the fear of plots. An example were the many stories about a large alliance of Catholic powers (mainly the French and the Spanish kings) that began in 1565 as a detailed fictitious narrative (Kluckhohn 1869; Boutier *et al.* 1984: 87–92;

Zwierlein 2006: 653–64, 2013: 82–8). This alliance, as far as we know today, never existed, at least not with any clear 'grand design'. Yet, many singular *discorsi/discours* and serious attempts to build trans-regional alliances were circulating and were evidently part of confessional politics: Conspiracy theories worked as the parasite of other narratives of possible present states explaining past events and reaching into the future.

## The impact of religion on the shaping of conspiracy theories

Law and legal thought and practice are a realm of quite slow development, but the difference between the medieval and early modern periods is visible within the doctrine of the *crimen laesae maiestatis*. The constant communication about plotting and its many forms – evidently with examples of real actions like troops, gatherings, fortifications and occupations of parts of France, like during the Biron conspiracy of 1601 – was becoming a problem. The traditional medieval understanding of the crime was that no one could be punished just for a mere idea ('Cogitationis poenam nemo patitur' ['Just for a thought, no one can be punished']). Though it was formulated for civil, not criminal law, medieval lawyers usually adopted this position for capital crimes. But, around 1600, lawyers started 'spiritualising' the crime, agreeing that not only such actions, but also a serious plan of revolt or regicide, clearly formulated and worked out, was enough to be punished, Dig. 48, 19, 18. Biron was executed for the crime of conjuring, though nothing real had happened – at least less than in the Essex affair or the Gunpowder plot in England shortly after. One can understand this as the reaction of the legal system to that new autonomous role of conspiracy theories and plotting practices as agents and elements of the political communication.

However, no conspiracy theories or narratives about another group that would aim for world hegemony in a secular sense emerged or, at least, were important or successful. Admittedly, the *monarchia universalis* that Charles V was perhaps really aiming for and that his son, Philip II, and his successors were still blamed and feared for was the subject of several Protestant anti-Spanish narratives.

In this confessional period of the sixteenth and seventeenth centuries, during which religion shaped thought and representation, a religious-metaphysical dimension was often added to the plot narrative. In Protestant Northern Europe, pamphlets and *Flugschriften* transmitted conspiracy theories about (half-real, half completely fictitious) pan-European Catholic alliances and plans to subjugate Protestantism. They contained images and frontispieces depicting the three-headed Antichrist, and the Antichrist narrative always served as a framework, sometimes just loosely alluded to with one word or a line, sometimes in a more elaborate form by blending the apocalyptical Biblical texts of Daniel and John with the present political actors. Jesuit Nicolas Sander reacted as early as 1571 to that Protestant conceptual framework by writing a whole folio volume against the different Protestant theological identifications of the Pope with the Antichrist and Rome as his seat.

This religious dimension explains the particular role of anti-Jesuitism. As the most active and newly found Counter-Reformation order (McCoog 1996, 2012), the Society of Jesus stood in every pamphlet as part of the Antichrist's rotten crowd (Lake, Questier 2002; Houliston 2007; Doran, Kewes 2014; Zwierlein 2018: 42). In this respect, among the most infamous is the *Monita privata Societatis Jesu*, published in Cracovia in 1614 and immediately put on the index of prohibited books. The text is an alleged code of conduct for Jesuits, describing how they should behave when they enter a new city, how they should gain the favour of Christian and Ottoman princes, how they should gain influence over the princes as their confessors, and how they should exercise power by indicating those to be nominated for state offices (Pavone 2000: 274). First translated into Italian and printed only in 1667–1671, the text would go on to have great success in the late seventeenth and eighteenth centuries, during the Jansenist and anti-Jesuitist struggles, and preparing the way for nineteenth-century forms of anti-Jesuitism (Cubitt 1993).

Although a sophisticated forgery, it was not as far from real secret Counter-Reformation plans as one might think. The reception of Giovanni Botero's *Reason of State* could have led to politico-confessional reasoning at the Curia about the opportunities and occasions for regaining ground against Protestantism, as well as against Islam and schismatic aberrations. *Discorsi* (i.e. plans, projects) communicated within the Roman Curia could have a similar 'reason-of-Church' form. To approach a member of a Protestant family with the goal of reconversion, to collect money in order to bribe Ottomans to provide a *berat* for a Catholic instead of a schismatic Patriarch and even to write, print and diffuse Arabic texts purporting to be by and for Muslims but introducing Catholic catechetical principles were all tactics considered and put into practice since at least the time of Gregory XIII (Zwierlein 2007). While Catholic theoreticians were still fighting 'Machiavellism' as political content, their political language and method of Counter-Reformation might owe a debt to common Renaissance roots that Machiavelli had perfected. The forged *Monita* used these narrative strategies as parasites of existing genres, remaining and *seeming possible* despite, eventually, not being absolutely real.

## The decline of conspiracy theories in the European state system

During the seventeenth century, conspiracism as well as plotting was on the wane, at least in some regions of Europe (Dekker 1996: 580). However, Britain and its empire remained a stronghold for ongoing religious conspiracism, commonly referred to in the sources as 'anti-popery' and 'anti-Puritanism' (Lake 1989, 2006). This could manifest itself in a wide range of beliefs, from the simple conviction that Catholics were the enemy to fully-fleshed narratives and inventions as defined above.

Around 1600, in the Tudor/Stuart succession crisis, government circles were continually suspicious about Jesuit and popish 'plotting'. A recent study summarised these pamphlets as 'the standard, Cecilian popish conspiracy theory, centred on the alliance between the pope and Spain' (Lake, Questier 2018: 23). Pamphlets like Oates's own *A True Narrative; The Discovery of the Popish Plot* (1679) and *A True Narrative of the Horrid Hellish Popish Plot* (1682) as well as Robert L'Estrange's and dozens of other pamphlets of the late 1670s and the early 1680s continued to repeat the alleged 'grand design' of continental Catholicism, adapting the 'highly malleable ideology' of anti-popery to every current situation in a very precise manner (Knights 1994, 2005; Hinds 2010; Morton 2016: 422, 427).

Anti-Jacobitism and anti-popery would remain major discursive forces throughout the eighteenth century (Donovan 1987; Haydon 1994). The perceptions of the Gordon Riots of 1780 were predominantly framed like this (Haydon 2004), even across the British Empire and the Atlantic world (Jones 2013), in which anti-Catholicism intersected with xenophobia (Rabin 2017; Wein 2018: 31–65). Arguably, in the British case, nineteenth-century anti-Catholic discourse across the 'second' British Empire had more in common with its early modern antecedents (Burstein 2017) than was the case between early modern and neo-confessionalised nineteenth-century antagonisms on the Continent, particularly in France (Cubitt 1993) and Germany. However, we must recall in seventeenth- and early eighteenth-century France the flourishing of anti-Jansenist conspiracy theories next to the anti-Jesuit ones since the *Lettre circulaire de Port-Royal* and the *Projet de Bourg-Fontaine* (Ceyssens 1975).

Those cases and traditions of conspiracist discourses put aside, it seems, that with the early eighteenth century, a period of low frequency and conjuncture of conspiracy communication was starting. The European state system in its pre- and post-1756 settlement was far less prone to the circulation and influence of conspiracy theories with a religious-metaphysical bias. Research has certainly reminded several 'real' conjurations, often of nobles such as the three 1674 conjurations against Louis XIV or the insurrection of Hungary's magnates of 1664–1671 (Bérenger 1996; O'Connor 1996), but these real projects of conspiracies were not necessarily part of the conspiracy communication. The political language of a Colbert (Soll 2009), a Maurepas (Zwierlein 2016: 51–72) or a Choiseul, a Kaunitz (Schilling 1994) or a Pombal (Maxwell 1995) – just to quote some important first ministers – was usually far from being dictated by conspiracism. This is in great contrast to the discourse of Philippe Duplessis-Mornay, of a Catholic prince like Carlo Emanuele of Savoy, of the Cardinal William Allen or of some of the popes themselves around 1600.

## Conspiracy theories during the Enlightenment

A major change was at work in the second part of the eighteenth century. Public and ideological discourse, but also the culture of enlightened sociability right up to the proliferation of secret societies, became more detached from the sphere of political decision-making, despite the continuity of evolving reciprocal referencing and (often somehow dialectical) relationships. Large parts of enlightened sociability were no forum for conspiracism. Visitors to Paris salons partially overlapped with the network of foreign politics and spies, but, as far as we know, the discussions in the salons themselves usually remained less concentrated on politics and confessional debates (Lilti 2005).

Only the smaller part of enlightened sociability, the secret societies or Freemasonry and its offsprings, might be related to conspiracism. Obviously, as for real noble revolts of the seventeenth century, the proliferation and spread of (the usually politically very innocent) Freemasonry and real secret societies (Beaurepaire 1998; Zaunstöck 1999; Cazzaniga 2006; Porset, Révauger 2013; Gerlach 2014; Péter 2016) must be distinguished from the conspiracist discourse interpreting them as purportedly important agents working covertly for some unknown dreadful purpose or revolution (Cazzaniga 2006: 22–7; 185–92; 312–30). Kant had noted that secret societies were the product of a state that had not yet given its citizens the liberty that they deserved by nature, and therefore those circles were embryonic niches of liberty. This has parallels with how the development towards bourgeois society is constructed: Freemasonry and other secret societies were usually only 'political' in transcending the borders between estates concerning membership, though the content of what was discussed in the meetings was usually moral philosophy or other non-political issues.

Weishaupt's Illuminati were an exception, as the manuscript plans found with him when he was imprisoned betray a philosophico-historical progressivist attempt to alter society – or rather, humankind, the *Menschengeschlecht* – into some form of egalitarian, non-monarchical eudaimonist commonwealth. His method was to peacefully install members of the order in all governments of the world (*Weltall*), who could then protect and recommend Illuminati for the next free position (van Dülmen 1975: 107–13, 212–13, 350–1; Agethen 1984: 187–224, 225–42).

The French Revolution and revolutionary wars made this project both obsolete and more suspect (as proved by the renewed Bavarian anti-Illuminati edict of 1791), and contributed to the myth of its continued, hidden existence (Gregory 2009: 393–411). More important is that, as with the evolution of Freemasonry during the late eighteenth century, the Illuminati's hierarchical revelation of secrets within the different provinces and lodges led to the content of the secret(s) becoming a matter of public discourse (McKenzie-McHarg 2016).

However, the suspicion that some hidden unknown superiors or *eminences grises* were manipulating society and politics predated late eighteenth-century Freemasonry; one such example can be found as early as 1710 within the discourse criticising party politics. Henry Sacheverell, Benjamin Hoadly and Simon Clement argued that behind the Tories, Court Tories, Whigs and Country Whigs, there were 'designing men' exploiting the dysfunctional powers of factionalism and opposition to paralyse civil libertarian society and to pursue selfish goals (Knights 2004: 160–8).

In the end, despite all forms of genuinely clandestine radical Enlightenment communication and exchange of thought, such as regarding forms of atheism (Cavaillé 2002; Mulsow 2018), the ascription of conspiratorial and seriously destructive power to 'philosophers' and secret societies happened mostly later in the century, combining those hidden forces with elements similar to the condemnation of factionalism and plotting behind visible party politics at the beginning of the century. That is why, in France, this could emerge only during the French Revolution, as before then there was no possibility for 'party' politics. Most famous for these developments are Barruel, Robinson and Starcke, who all published their major works in the 1790s (Schaeper-Wimmer 1985; Perronet 1990; Bianchini 1999; Reinalter 2004; Waterman 2005; Cazzaniga 2006, 312–30; Oberhauser 2013).

## Conspiracy theories as a tenet of revolutionary and counter-revolutionary thought

It would be too simple to characterise the conspiracy theories of the Enlightenment in contrast to those of the times of confessional antagonism as merely the secularisation of the latter, because there was still a religious dimension in Weishaupt's teleological concepts of the formation of a perfect society (Illuminati) or in French revolutionary conspiracism. Certainly, the secular form of conspiracy theories was, even in revolutionary times, to some extent a continuation of the steady repeated communication of the Renaissance and the emergence of the European state system. Revolutionary fears about a pan-European conspiracy, about the enemies outside of France, such as the Bourbon princes and nobles exiled to an allegedly mighty 'Coblentz' (Henke 2000), and about the enemies inside, such as the royalists in the Vendée, were fabricated as narratives, just as they had been 200 years before.

However, during the former confessional age, apocalyptical or similar confessionally antagonistic interpretations gave an overall framework to such narratives; this was replaced in revolutionary times, roughly speaking, with the vague philosophic-historical concept that each threat, each step, and all conspiracies were part of the larger struggle between the achievement of the new society and the Old Regime. The battleground was therefore an imagined humankind's timeline of destiny, achieving either to take the step forward toward a new *epoché* or to fall back into barbarism. According to Koselleck, this conception of history is part of a succession of competing teleological utopian social self-understandings that started in the late Enlightenment and went on until the Cold War (Koselleck 1959). For Furet, French revolutionary conspiracism was an unfolding of the binary thought of Rousseau, radicalised foremost by Robespierre (Furet 1981; Cubitt 1999; Leuwers 2016: 309–29). In all his major speeches, Robespierre employed a rhetoric of antagonism between liberty and tyranny: 'Without, all the tyrants encircle you; within, all the friends of tyranny conspire' (Robespierre 1967 [1793–1794]: 353–6). This antagonism also related to the confrontation between the friends of the revolution, and the enemies both internal and external, between the *gouvernement populaire* and the *gouvernement despotique*, between a normal state of society and a revolutionary state of emergency that even required terror as a legitimate instrument of bourgeois politics.

The self-understanding of the revolutionaries resulted in the quick succession of emerging antagonisms within and outside of the National Assembly and Convention from 1792 to 1794.

(Tackett 2000; Campbell *et al.* 2007) This antagonism was conceived through the prism of ancient patterns: Robespierre compared the 'conspirations contre la République' with the Catiline conspiracy (Robespierre 1967 [1793–1794]: 358). The abstract form of those antagonisms (Girondins against Montagnards, both competing for the control of the majority of the moderate so-called *plaine*) has indeed similarities with the old pattern of a city-republic suddenly eroding and being deconstructed into competing factions – this struggle somehow representing the drift of French revolutionary politics as a whole.

Conspiracy patterns were similarly shaped on the side of the counterrevolutionaries. For Edmund Burke, the royalists or Barruel, the Revolution itself threatened to drag humankind back into forms of barbarism (Pestel 2015). From this perspective, Englishmen could compare to the chaos in France their good, and allegedly peaceful, 'Glorious Revolution' of 1688 as the morally successful example of establishing a civilised commonwealth. In Europe, fears were of conspiracies that tacitly or consciously opposed the old European hierarchical society with a new yet-to-be-created egalitarian bourgeois society. But, outside of Europe, in the colonies, conspiracism and fear of revolts were usually framed within the divisions of the stratified society of colonisers and colonised. During the Saint-Domingue/Haiti Revolution, revolutionaries could be both pro-colonial and defend at the same time the execution of Louis XVI, while anti-revolutionary exiles could opt against slavery. As a consequence, although they may have started on common ground, discourses and fears of conspiracies could become very multifaceted (Knight 2000; Geggus 2000: 149–70; Girard 2005; Sharples 2015; Dillon, Drexler 2016; Pope 2017).

## Conclusion

Conspiracy theories in a narrower definition are an early modern 'invention' or a phenomenon only emerging after the Renaissance, during the confessional age. Two major types of conspiracy theories were evolving at this time: Those with a confessional, eventually apocalyptic framework from the 1560s to the eighteenth century that were based on anti-popery, anti-Puritanism, anti-Jansenism and so on; and those conspiracy theories informed by the new Enlightenment secret societies and social transformations that were first only imagined in utopian forms. These deep changes in society were then realised during the age of revolutions, with the reiteration and pluralisation of friend-enemy oppositions and antagonisms along the framing social and philosophic-historical divisions between an Old and a New Order. The older confessional and the new Enlightenment type of conspiracy theories merged with each other, using similar vocabulary and stereotypes. All those early modern conspiracy theories, finally, fed upon other factual types of future-oriented narratives – plans, projects and causal analysis of past events for reasons of taming the future (Bode, Dietrich 2013) – that had emerged with the evolution of modern anonymous news communication and the visibility of participants within the political public sphere.

## References

Agethen, M. (1984) *Geheimbund und Utopie: Illuminaten, Freimaurer und deutsche Spätaufklärung*, Munich: Oldenbourg.

Bader, K.S. and Dilcher G. (1999) *Deutsche Rechtsgeschichte: Land und Stadt – Bürger und Bauer im alten Europa*, Berlin: Springer.

Beaurepaire, P.Y. (1998) *L'autre et le frère: l'Etranger et la Franc-maçonnerie en France au XVIIIe siècle*, Paris: Champion.

Behringer, W. (2004) 'Detecting the ultimate conspiracy, or how Waldensians became witches', in B. Coward and J. Swann (eds.) *Conspiracies and conspiracy theory in early modern Europe: from the Waldensians to the French Revolution*, Aldershot: Ashgate, pp. 13–34.

Bérenger, J. (1996) 'La conjuration des Magnats hongrois (1664–1671)', in Y.-M. Bercé and E. Fasano Guarini (eds.) *Complots et conjuration dans l'Europe moderne*, Rome, Italy: Ecole Française de Rome, pp. 317–45.

Bianchini, L. (1999) 'Le annotazioni manoscritte di Augustin Barruel ai "Mémoires pour servir à l'histoire du jacobinisme"', *Annali della Fondazione Luigi Einaudi*, 33: 367–443.

Bode, C. and Dietrich, R. (2013) *Future narratives: theory, poetics, and media-historical moment*, Berlin: de Gruyter.

Boutier, J., Dewerpe, A. and Nordman D. (1984) *Un tour de France royal: le voyage de Charles IX (1564–1566)*, Paris: Aubier.

Bowd, S.D. (2018), *Renaissance Mass Murder: Civilians and Soldiers during the Italian Wars*, Oxford: Oxford University Press.

Brody, S. (1974) *The disease of the soul: leprosy in medieval literature*, Ithaca, NY: Cornell University Press.

Burstein, M.E. (2017) '*In ten years there is an increase of 450 priests of antichrist*: quantification, anti-Catholicism, and the *bulwark*', *Journal of British Studies*, 56: 580–604.

Campbell, P.R., Kaiser, T.E. and Linton, M. (eds.) (2007) *Conspiracy in the French Revolution*, Manchester: Manchester University Press.

Catlos, B.A. (2004) *The victors and the vanquished: Christians and Muslims of Catalonia and Aragon, 1050–1300*, Cambridge: Cambridge University Press.

Cavaillé, J-P. (2002) *Dis/simulations: Jules-César Vanini, François La Mothe Le Vayer, Gabriel Naudé, Louis Machon et Torquato Accetto: religion, morale et politique au XVII siècle*, Paris: Champion.

Cazzaniga, G.M. (ed.) (2006) *Storia d'Italia: la Massoneria*, Turin: Einaudi.

Ceyssens, L. (1975) 'Lettre circulaire de Port-Royal: un faux indestructible', *Jansenistica Minora*, 12: 361–96.

Crouzet-Pavan, E. (1997) *Venise: une invention de la ville (XIIIe-XVe siècle)*, Paris: Champ Vallon.

Cubitt, G. (1993) *The Jesuit myth: conspiracy theory and politics in nineteenth-century France*, Oxford: Clarendon.

Cubitt, G. (1999) 'Robespierre and conspiracy theories', in C. Haydon and W. Doyle (eds.) *Robespierre*, Cambridge: Cambridge University Press, pp. 75–91.

Dekker, R. (1996) 'Complots dans la République des Provinces-Unies au XVIIe siècle', in Y.-M. Bercé and E. Guarini (eds.) *Complots et conjuration dans l'Europe moderne*, Rome, Italy: Ecole Française de Rome, pp. 579–95.

Dillon, E.M. and Drexler, M.J. (2016) *The Haitian Revolution and the early United States: Histories, textualities, geographies*, Philadelphia: University of Pennsylvania Press.

Donovan, R.K. (1987) *No popery and radicalism: opposition to Roman Catholic relief in Scotland 1778–1782*, New York and London: Garland.

Doran, S. and Kewes, P. (eds.) (2014) *Doubtful and dangerous: the question of succession in late Elizabethan England*, Manchester: Manchester University Press.

Fasano Guarini, E.F. (1996) 'Congiure *contro alla patria* e congiure *contro ad un principe* nell'opera di Niccolò Machiavelli', Y.-M. Bercé and E. Fasano Guarini (eds.) *Complots et conjuration dans l'Europe moderne*, Rome, Italy: Ecole Française de Rome, pp. 9–53.

Fritz, W.D. (ed.) (1932) *Monumenta Germaniae Historica, Fontes iuris germanici antiqui, vol. XI: Bulla Aurea Karoli IV: imperatoris anno MCCCLVI promulgata*, Weimar: Böhlau.

Furet, F. (1981) *Interpreting the French Revolution*, Cambridge: Cambridge University Press.

Geggus, D. (2000) 'La cérémonie du Bois Caïman', in L. Hurbon (ed.) *L'insurrection des esclaves de Saint-Domingue*, Paris: Karthala: pp. 149–70.

Gerlach, K. (2014) *Die Freimaurer im Alten Preußen 1738–1806*, 2 vol., Innsbruck, Vienna and Bozen: Studienverlag.

Ginzburg, C. (1991) *Ecstasies: deciphering the witches' Sabbath*, New York: Pantheon Books.

Girard, P.R. (2005) 'Caribbean genocide: racial war in Haiti, 1802–4', *Patterns of Prejudice*, 39(2): 138–61.

Gregory, S. (2009) *Wissen und Geheimnis: das Experiment des Illuminatenordens*, Frankfurt/Basel: Nexus.

Guidi, G. (1992) *Lotte, pensiero e istituzioni politiche nella Repubblica fiorentina dal 1494 al 1512* vol. 3, Florence: Olschki.

Haydon, C. (1994) *Anti-Catholicism in eighteenth-century England, c.1714–80*, Manchester: Manchester University Press.

Haydon, C. (2004) '"Popery at St. James's": the conspiracy theses of William Payne, Thomas Hollis, and Lord George Gordon', in B. Coward and J. Swann (eds.) *Conspiracies and conspiracy theory in early modern Europe: from the Waldensians to the French Revolution*, Aldershot: Ashgate, pp. 173–96.

Heil, J. (2006) *'Gottesfeinde' – 'Menschenfeinde': die Vorstellung von jüdischer Weltverschwörung (13. bis 16. Jahrhundert)*, Essen: Klartext-Verlag.

Henke, C. (2000) *Coblentz: Symbol für die Gegenrevolution, die französische Emigration nach Koblenz und Kurtrier 1789–1792 und die politische Diskussion des revolutionären Frankreichs 1791–1794*, Stuttgart: Thorbecke.

Hinds, P. (2010) *The Horrid Popish Plot: Roger L'Estrange and the Circulation of Political Discourse in Late Seventeenth-Century London*, Oxford: Oxford University Press.

Houliston, V. (2007) *Catholic resistance in Elizabethan England: Robert Persons's jesuit polemic, 1580–1610*, Aldershot: Ashgate.

Jaspert, N. (2014) *Die Kreuzzüge*, 6th ed., Darmstadt: Die wissenschaftliche Buchgesellschaft.

Jones, B.A. (2013) '"In Favour of Popery": patriotism, protestantism, and the Gordon Riots in the revolutionary British atlantic', *Journal of British Studies*, 52: 79–102.

Jones, W.R. (1972) 'Political uses of sorcery in Medieval Europe', *The Historian*, 34(4): 670–87.

Kluckhohn, A. (1869) 'Zur Geschichte des angeblichen Bündnisses von Bayonne: nebst einem Originalbericht über die Ursachen des zweiten Religionskriegs in Frankreich', *Abhandlungen der Historischen Classe der Königlich Bayerischen Akademie der Wissenschaften*, 11(1): 150–99.

Knight, F.W. (2000) 'The Haitian Revolution', *American Historical Review*, 105(1): 103–15.

Knights, M. (1994) *Politics and Opinion in Crisis 1678–81*, Cambridge: Cambridge University Press.

Knights, M. (2004) 'Faults on both sides: the conspiracies of party politics under the later Stuarts', in B. Coward and J. Swann (eds.) *Conspiracies and conspiracy theory in early modern Europe: from the Waldensians to the French Revolution*, Aldershot: Ashgate, pp. 153–72.

Knights, M. (2005) *Representation and misrepresentation in later Stuart Britain: partisanship and political culture*, Oxford: Oxford University Press.

Koselleck, R. (1959) *Kritik und Krise*, Frankfurt/Munich: Suhrkamp.

Lake, P. (1989) 'Anti-Popery: the structure of a prejudice', in A. Hughes and R. Cust (eds.) *Conflict in early Stuart England*, London/New York: Longman, pp. 72–106.

Lake, P. (2006) 'Anti-Puritanism: the structure of a prejudice', in: K. Fincham and P. Lake (eds.) *Religious Politics in post-reformation England: essays in honour of Nicholas Tyacke*, Woodbridge: Boydell, pp. 80–97.

Lake, P. and Questier, M. (2002) *The Antichrist's lewd hat: protestants, papists and players in post-reformation England*, New Haven: Yale University Press.

Lake, P. and Questier, M. (2018) 'Thomas Digges, Robert Parsons, Sir Francis Hastings, and the politics of regime change in Elizabethan England', *The Historical Journal*, 61(1): 1–27.

Leuwers, H. (2016) *Robespierre*, Paris: Pluriel.

Lilti, A. (2005) *Le monde des salons: sociabilité et mondanité à Paris au XVIIIe siècle*, Paris: Fayard.

Machiavelli, N. (1499–1512) *I primi scritti politici*, ed. Corrado Vivanti, reprint, Turin: Einaudi, 1997.

Marsilius of Padua (1324) *Defensor pacis: der Verteidiger des Friedens*, trans. W. Kunzemann and H. Kunsch, 2 vol., reprint, Berlin, 1958.

Maxwell, K. (1995) *Pombal: paradox of the Enlightenment*, Cambridge: Cambridge University Press.

McCoog, T.M. (1996) *The Society of Jesus in Ireland, Scotland, and England 1541–1597 – 'Our Way of Proceeding?'*, Leiden: Brill.

McCoog, T.M. (2012) *The Society of Jesus in Ireland, Scotland, and England, 1589–1597: building the faith of Saint Peter upon the King of Spain's Monarchy*, Aldershot: Ashgate.

McKenzie-McHarg, A. (2016) '"Unknown Sciences" and Unknown superiors: the problem of non-knowledge in eighteenth-century secret societies', in C. Zwierlein (ed.) *The dark side of knowledge: histories of ignorance, 1400–1800*, Leiden: Brill, pp. 333–57.

Morton, A. (2016) 'Popery, politics, and play: visual culture in succession crisis England', *The Seventeenth Century*, 31(4): 411–49.

Mulsow, M. (2018) *Radikale Frühaufklärung in Deutschland 1680–1720* 2 vol., Göttingen: Wallstein.

Nirenberg, D. (2015) *Communities of violence: persecution of minorities in the Middle Ages*, upd. edn, Princeton: Princeton University Press.

Oberhauser, C. (2013) *Die verschwörungstheoretische Trias: Barruel – Robison – Starck*, Innsbruck/Vienna/Bozen: Studienverlag.

Oberste, J. (2003) *Der 'Kreuzzug' gegen die Albigenser: Ketzerei und Machtpolitik im Mittelalter*, Darmstadt: Die Wissenschaftliche Buchgesellschaft.

O'Connor, J. (1996) 'Une conspiration chimérique tramée par un *comte imaginaire*', in Y.-M. Bercé and E. Fasano Guarini (eds.) *Complots et conjuration dans l'Europe moderne*, Rome, Italy: Ecole Française de Rome, pp. 411–21.

Oexle, O.G. (1985) 'Conjuratio und Gilde im frühen Mittelalter: ein Beitrag zum sozialen Problem der sozialgeschichtlichen Kontinuität zwischen Antike und Mittelalter', in B. Schwineköper (ed.) *Gilden und Zünfte: kaufmännische und gewerbliche Genossenschaften im frühen und hohen Mittelalter*, Sigmaringen: Thorbecke, pp. 151–214.

Pavone, S. (2000) *Le astuzie dei Gesuiti: le false istruzioni segrete della compagnia di Gesù e la polemica antigesuita nei secoli XVII e XVIII*, Roma: Salerno.

Perronet, M. (1990) 'L'abbé Barruel, "inventeur du jacobinisme"', in E. Pii (ed.) *Idee e parole nel giacobinismo italiano*, Firenze: Olschki, pp. 153–79.

Pestel, F. (2015) *Kosmopoliten wider Willen: die "monarchiens" als Revolutionsmigranten*, Berlin/Boston: de Gruyter.

Péter, R. (ed.) (2016) *British Freemasonry, 1717–1813*, vol. 5, London/New York: Routledge.

Pope, J. (2017) 'Inventing an Indian Slave Conspiracy on Nantucket, 1738', *Early American Studies: An Interdisciplinary Journal*, 15(3): 505–38.

Porset, C. and Révauger, C. (eds.) (2013) *Le monde maçonnique des Lumières (Europe-Amériques & Colonies): dictionnaire prosopographique*, vol. 3, Paris: Champion.

Rabin, D. (2017) *The Gordon riots: politics, culture and insurrection*, Cambridge: Cambridge University Press.

Reinalter, H. (ed.) (2004) *Typologien des Verschwörungsdenkens*, Innsbruck, Vienna and Bozen: Studienverlag.

Robespierre, M. (1793–1794) *Œuvres, vol. 10: Discours (27 juillet 1793–27 juillet 1794)*, ed. and rev. M. Bouloiseau and A. Soboul, Paris: Presses Universitaires de France, 1967.

Sander, N. (1571) *De visibili Monarchia Ecclesiae, libri octo [...] Denique de Antichristo ipso & membris eius: deque vera Dei et adulterina Diaboli Ecclesia, copiose tractatur*, Louvain: Reynerus Velpius.

Schaeper-Wimmer, S. (1985) *Augustin Barruel (1741–1820): Studien zu Biographie und Werk*, Frankfurt am Main: Lang.

Schilling, L. (1994) *Kaunitz und das Renversement des alliances: Studien zur außenpolitischen Konzeption Wenzel Antons von Kaunitz*, Berlin: Duncker & Humblot.

Sharples, J.T. (2015) 'Discovering slave conspiracies: new fears of rebellion and old paradigms of plotting in seventeenth-century Barbados', *American Historical Review*, 120(3): 811–43.

Šmahel, F. (2002) *Die Hussitische Revolution*, 3 vol. Hannover: MGH.

Soll, J.C. (2009) *The information master: Jean-Baptiste Colbert's secret state intelligence system*, Ann Arbor: Michigan University Press.

Tackett, T. (2000) 'Conspiracy obsession in a time of revolution: French elites and the origins of the terror, 1789–1792', *American Historical Review*, 105: 691–713.

Tierney, B. (1998) *Foundations of conciliar theory*, Cambridge: Cambridge University Press.

Van Dülmen, R. (1975) *Der Geheimbund der Illuminaten: Darstellung Analyse Dokumentation*, Stuttgart: Frommann-Holzboog.

Villard, R. (2008) *Du bien commun au mal nécessaire: tyrannies, assassinats politiques et souveraineté en Italie*, Rome: Ecole française de Rome.

Waterman, B. (2005) 'The Bavarian Illuminati, the early American novel, and histories of the public sphere', *The William and Mary Quarterly*, 62(1): 9–30.

Wein, T. (2018) *Monstrous Fellowship: 'Pagan, Turk and Jew' in English popular culture, 1780–1845*, Frankfurt am Main: Lang.

Zaunstöck, H. (1999) *Sozietätslandschaft und Mitgliederstrukturen: die mitteldeutschen Aufklärungsgesellschaften im 18. Jahrhundert*, Tübingen: Niemeyer.

Zwierlein, C. (2006) *Discorso und Lex Dei: die Entstehung neuer Denkrahmen im 16. Jahrhundert und die Wahrnehmung der französischen Religionskriege in Italien und Deutschland*, Göttingen: Vandenhoeck & Ruprecht.

Zwierlein, C. (2007) 'Convertire tutta l'Alemagna – Fürstenkonversionen in den Strategiedenkrahmen der römischen Europapolitik um 1600: Zum Verhältnis von Machiavellismus und Konfessionalismus', in U. Lotz-Heumann, J.-F. Missfelder and M. Pohlig (eds.) *Konversion und Konfession in der Frühen Neuzeit*, Gütersloh: Gütersloher Verlagshaus, pp. 63–105.

Zwierlein, C. (2013) 'Security politics and conspiracy theories in the emerging European state system (15th/16th c.)', *Historical Social Research*, 38(1): 65–95.

Zwierlein, C. (2016) *Imperial unknowns: the French and British in the Mediterranean, 1650–1750*, Cambridge: Cambridge University Press.

Zwierlein, C. (2018) 'Tyrannenmord, Majestätsverbrechen und Herrscherwechsel bei Shakespeare: Resonanzen konfessioneller Polarisierung um 1600', *Shakespeare Jahrbuch*, 154: 31–58.

# 5.3

# FREEMASONS, ILLUMINATI AND JEWS

## Conspiracy theories and the French Revolution

*Claus Oberhauser*

### Introduction

When writing his famous *Reflections on the Revolution in France* (1790), Edmund Burke was in touch with French émigrés who had fled to Great Britain. One of these refugees was the Abbé Augustin Barruel. In his book, Burke drew upon many of the arguments already developed by French anti-philosophes prior to the revolution. Interpreting the revolution as a thorough break with the past, he attacked the arbitrary rejection of experience, tradition, historical developments, religion or natural hierarchy that came with it (McMahon 2003; Aston 2004). Warning of coming upheavals, he wrote: 'Many parts of Europe are in open disorder. In many others there is a hollow murmuring underground; a confused movement is felt, that threatens a general earthquake in the political world' (Burke 1790: 229). In a footnote to this passage, Burke referred to the correspondence of the Illuminati Order (1787), which had been published at the behest of the government of Palatinate-Bavaria.

While Burke was no mere conspiracy theorist, this footnote has been taken to establish a link between a conservative interpretation of the French Revolution and conspiratorial thinking (Freeman 1978; Armitage 2000). Although the debate on the causes of the French Revolution has cooled off noticeably, these conspiratorial explanations still form the ideological foundation of many contemporary conspiracy theories. Freemasonry and the Illuminati, in particular, are supposed to be hidden actors with revolutionary intentions who, in essence, plot a conspiracy against society as a whole.

This chapter will evaluate the impact of the ideas of the Enlightenment with regard to a conspiratorial interpretation of the French Revolution. Taking three major publications as examples, it will show how conspiratorial thinking emerged as a reaction to changes and developments of the eighteenth century, which culminated in the French Revolution. The three publications are contextualised and the networks behind the texts are shown. After the evaluation of real Masonic influence on the French Revolution, this chapter examines the conspiratorial interpretation of revolution as a travelling concept, particularly in New England. It concludes by showing how anti-philosophe, anti-Masonic and anti-Illuminati conspiracy theories combined with antisemitism in the nineteenth century to create an ideological hotbed that led to the publication of *The Protocols of the Elders of Zion*.

## The Enlightenment and the revolutions – a conspiratorial era

Gordon S. Wood (1982) has pointed out that, during the seventeenth and eighteenth centuries, in Britain and North America at least, conspiratorial thinking was a common way of lending meaning to particular events, conditions and developments. It was widely accepted that some men had the (secret) power to be the driving force behind any kind of observable change – a belief that was shared across all social classes. It was François Furet (1978) who drew attention to the fact that Rousseau's political ideas, such as his concept of the general will, an invisible power, led to conspiratorial thinking. Jakob Tanner (2008) has highlighted that the year 1776 saw not only the drafting of the Declaration of Independence in Philadelphia and the founding of the Illuminati Order in Ingolstadt – a well-known coincidence that is debated in various conspiracy theories today – but also the publication of Adam Smith's *Wealth of Nations*, whose metaphor of the 'invisible hand' could be (misleadingly) understood as the product of forces obscured from view. No wonder that the nexus between the great revolutions of the eighteenth century and Enlightenment ideas, as well as the emergence of secret societies, has been a contentious issue ever since.

It would be a mistake to believe that conspiracy theories only arose in conjunction with the French Revolution. Indeed, the early modern era is full of conspiracy theories (Coward, Swann 2004; Zwierlein, de Graaf 2013; see also Chapter 5.2 in this volume), but only the one focusing on the supposedly revolutionary aims of Freemasonry became a lasting element of Western conspiratorial thinking throughout the nineteenth and twentieth centuries. It prevailed over others, such as the famine plot (Kaplan 1982), the various conspiracy fears following the outbreak of the French Revolution known as the Great Fear (Lefèbvre 1932) or the alleged infiltration by an 'Austrian Committee' during the first phase of the revolution (Tackett 2000), all of which proved to be ephemeral by comparison.

But it should be emphasised that, during the French Revolution, much of the revolutionary discourse and the struggle for interpretive sovereignty were themselves highly conspiratorial. While Furet tried to explain this using Hegelian dialectics, Timothy Tackett (2000) provided empirical insights: He found that, during the first phase of the revolution (1789–1791), actual conspiracies were thwarted. It seems that these real plots and conspiracies that contaminated organised politics (Hunt 1984: 43), along with the radicalisation of the revolution, led to a widespread belief in numerous conspiracy theories. By late 1791, the fear of a 'Grand Conspiracy' had become a staple of revolutionary rhetoric.

Campbell *et al.* (2007) have also highlighted this connection between both real and imagined conspiracies and their unstable historical context. The outbreak of the French Revolution certainly opened up a communicative space that referred to new values such as publicity or the justification of national claims. Conspiracy theories were one, if not the only, answer to questions about justifications for various actions of revolutionaries, and noticeably the use of political violence. In addition to these legitimation discourses as political means, the practice of denunciation also developed. This became more and more apparent in various partial diffuse suspicions of conspiracy, expressed in the most important newspapers (Münch 2008).

## Anti-revolutionary conspiracist narratives: Barruel, Robison and Starck

The year 1797 came to be a culminating point for modern conspiracy thinking: Augustin Barruel published the first two volumes of his *Mémoires pour sérvir à l'histoire du Jacobinisme* and, almost simultaneously, John Robison, an Edinburgh professor of natural philosophy, accused the Illuminati of being the main perpetrators of the French Revolution in his equally famous *Proofs of a Conspiracy against all the religions and governments of Europe, carried on in the secret meetings* of *Freemasons, Illuminati and Reading Societies*. In his book, Barruel developed the conspiracy theory that the French Revolution was the end result of a conspiracy of Enlightenment philosophes (Voltaire, d'Alembert, Diderot and King Frederick II of Prussia), high-degree Freemasons and the Illuminati, all of whom preceded and inspired the Jacobins. Barruel traced the core ideas of the French Revolution back to the Manichaean concepts of 'equality' and 'freedom'. He regarded Mani as a paternal father of Freemasonry and the Knights Templar as their precursors. Barruel's conceptual acuteness of the Illuminati in his first two volumes was still very vague. Only through the mediation of Johann August Starck and his comrades-in-arms was his conspiracy theory specified in the third and fourth volume.

Robison was already convinced of the Illuminati conspiracy in 1797. His *Proofs of a conspiracy* have overshadowed his central importance for the Scottish Enlightenment. Robison wrote his book as a professor of natural philosophy and secretary of the Royal Society of Edinburgh. Delivering what appeared to be, at least at first glance, a factual political analysis, Robison also showed the reader that he was a Masonic insider. According to him, fanaticism had spread in the French lodges throughout Europe because of the influence of the Illuminati. He described this process in the following important passage:

> I have been able to trace these attempts, made, through a course of fifty years, under the specious pretext of enlightening the world by the torch of philosophy, and of dispelling the clouds of civil and religious superstition which keep the nations of Europe in darkness and slavery [...] till, at last, AN ASSOCIATION HAS BEEN FORMED for the express purpose of ROOTING OUT ALL THE RELIGIOUS ESTABLISHMENTS, AND OVERTURNING ALL THE EXISTING GOVERNMENTS OF EUROPE. I have seen this Association exerting itself zealously and systematically, till it has become almost irresistible. And I have seen the most active leaders in the French Revolution were members of this Association [...]. And, lastly, I have seen that this Association still exists, still works in secret, and that not only several appearances among ourselves show that its emissaries are endeavoring to propagate their detestable doctrines among us.
> (Robison 1798: 11–12)

In 1803, Johann August Starck anonymously published *Der Triumph der Philosophie im 18. Jahrhunderte*, two volumes in which he set out to correct the record and supersede Barruel and Robison. In addition to being a scholar trained in oriental languages and Enlightenment theology, Starck served as a Protestant court preacher, first in Königsberg and then in Darmstadt (Vesper 2012) and had also been an active Freemason. Because of disputes with the Illuminati and with German Enlightenment figures, he was well known in Germany in the second half of the eighteenth century, and a plethora of publications for and against him has been published. He is the author of Masonic books, academic disputations about the history of religion and, above all, of conspiracy theoretical writings. His *Triumph* is different from Barruel's and Robison's books, insomuch as Starck knew some of the alleged conspirators in person.

The *Triumph* is, as far as the first part is concerned, a history of ideas about the origin of the term 'philosophism'. For Starck, this term stood for the wrong notion that philosophy sought to destroy monarchies, to repress the influence of religious faith and to spread equality everywhere. For him, this kind of philosophy was nothing less than fanaticism. In his book, he attributed the spread of 'philosophism' to the rise of printing in the early modern period and accordingly wrote a history of a conspiracy. Starck was one of the key figures in the making of the Illuminati conspiracy theory and his writings, networks and biography should be given much more consideration in English and French publications (Luckert 1993).

## The crucial impact of networks

Barruel came to be supported by Johann August Starck and his network of like-minded men through an intermediary in Great Britain, the Swiss scientist Jean André Deluc. Robison remained outside the networks of Barruel and Starck due to a scientific dispute. Deluc was an old friend of the famous physician, popular philosopher and conspiracy theorist Johann Georg Zimmermann. After Zimmermann's death in 1795, Deluc remained in touch with his widow, Luise Margarethe, who also acted as an intermediary between Barruel and the German critics of the revolution (Oberhauser 2013). A letter by Deluc, dated 23 October 1797, was printed in the *Mémoires* of Barruel. Deluc warned that the book might be met with great resentment in the press and suggested that Barruel should send him a copy first and get in contact with other important people, above all Edmund Burke; Barruel had made the acquaintance of Burke upon his arrival in London, in 1792. He sent him the newly published first volume of the *Mémoires* and asked him for his opinion about it. Burke had this to say about them, in a letter to the author dated 1 May 1797:

> I cannot easily express to you how much I am instructed & delighted by the first Volume of your History of Jacobinism. The whole of the wonderful Narrative is supported by documents & Proofs with the most juridical regularity & exactness. [...] I long impatiently for the second Volume; but the great object of my Wishes is, that the Work should have a great circulation in France, if by any means it can be compassed; & for that end, I should be glad upon the scale of a poor Individual to become a liberal Subscriber.
>
> (Burke 1978: 38–9)

Barruel was very pleased by Burke's flattering words and promptly sent him the next instalment of the *Mémoires* and asked for permission to make use of the letter. Since Burke died soon thereafter, his thoughts about the second volume were never recorded. Barruel had always spoken positively about England in his writings. He did not interpret English Freemasonry as part of the conspiracy, nor did he mention Britain as an important branch of the Jacobins (Schilling 1950).

These networks clearly show that, with regard to these conspiracy theories, there has been a transnational transfer of ideas bound to different actors; the German networks in particular worked to send Barruel different materials and to change his perspective. It should be emphasised that it is research into these networks that helps to move beyond the mere interpretation of the various published works. In fact, many people participated in the making of these conspiracy-theoretical writings and, through their actions, shared responsibility for the dissemination of these ideas.

## A common ground: Counter-Enlightenment

Barruel, Robison and Starck had in common a reliance on earlier criticism of the Enlightenment and of Freemasonry (Oberhauser 2013). Darrin McMahon (2003) has rightly pointed out that focusing on the historical context of the rejection of the philosophy of Voltaire and the *Encyclopédie* means seeing the construction of Enlightenment discourse as a struggle against the opponents of Enlightenment movements. Therefore, the opponents helped sharpen the arguments of Enlightenment thinkers (Garrard 2006). Regarding Barruel's conspiracy theory, he built on strong discursive strands; the anti-philosophical discourse in particular played a major role in his work. Indeed, Barruel had already made a name for himself in this respect before the revolution when he tackled in a highly polemical manner the main ideas of the French Enlightenment in his pamphlet *Les Helviennes* (Hofman 1993; 1988). Barruel also contributed to the journal *L'Année littéraire*, the leading journal of French anti-philosophes. To some extent, his later conspiracy theory was coined before the outbreak of the revolution.

Nevertheless, concerning French anti-Masonry, it appears that several anonymously published writings formed the basis of Barruel's book (Lemaire 1985). One of the first and most important French conspiratorial authors quoted by Barruel is Abbé Lefranc (1791, 1792), who already blamed the outbreak of the revolution on the Freemasons. Barruel himself published in 1793 (as an emigrant) the study *Histoire du Clergé*, in which he interpreted various events of the first phase of the revolution in a conspiratorial way. Barruel also referred to books by Cadet de Gassicourt (1796), a former Mason, and Christophe Félix Louis Ventre de la Touloubre, called Galart de Montjoie (1795, 1796). However, Barruel initially wanted to write about the theosophical Illuminés around Saint-Martin and what has been called 'Super Enlightenment' (Edelstein 2010), but decided through the intervention of Starck and his colleagues to write about the German Illuminati. Although the French anti-philosophical context played a major role in Barruel's writings, the historically momentous link between the outbreak of the revolution and the Illuminati could only be construed on the basis of German materials and publications.

In fact, anti-Masonry was a Western European issue: Anti-Illuminati discourse was constructed in Germany, but adapted by the writings of Barruel, Robison and Starck. General works tend to highlight the impact of Barruel's and Robison's conspiracy theories, overlooking Starck's publications, but it was Starck and the publications in his corresponding circles that made *Mémoires* and *Proofs of a conspiracy* possible (Valjavec 1951; Epstein 1966; Rogalla von Bieberstein 1976; Klausnitzer 2007).

From this perspective, it should be noted that conspiracy theories about the Illuminati from this period are a specific product of mostly German Masonic debates on the origins of Freemasonry and what 'true' Freemasonry should be like. These debates culminated in the Masonic congress of Wilhelmsbad in 1782 (Reinalter *et al.* 2019).

## The religious and political dimension of anti-Masonry

The spreading of Freemasonry on the European continent in the eighteenth century went hand in hand with an increasingly powerful anti-Masonry ideology. The democratic potential of the Masonic lodges created a problem with the authorities in several European countries, especially in the second half of the eighteenth century. However, as early as 1698, a leaflet distributed in London warned of anti-Christian Masons (Knoop *et al.* 1978). Subsequently, English writings dealt with the moral reprehensibility of the secret society and the very idea of secrecy. In this early phase, the two great ideological guidelines of anti-Masonry emerged: First was the notion of secrecy itself, of the Freemasons holding information accessible only to the initiated, which was certainly guided by religious implications; second, were the debunking notes of former Freemasons.

The second phase is a mixture of English resentment with an aggressive French-Spanish discourse. Soon after the founding of the first lodges in France, religious writers such as José Torrubia or Abbé Larudan claimed that Freemasonry was intent on destroying religion, especially the Christian faith. In 1738, Pope Clement XII signed 'In Eminenti', the first bull directed against Freemasonry as an organisation; Freemasonry was referred to in the bull as a sect whose members protected themselves by an oath and had secrets and therefore could hide heretical ideas. Some (Mellor 1961) argue that the condemnation by the Pope had a political motivation as well: He probably wanted to protect the Catholic Stuarts from the Protestant lodges. These allegations were repeated by Benedict XIV in 1751 (Ferrer Benimeli 1976–1977).

In addition, the disputes about origins and future direction from within German Freemasonry itself contributed to the suspicion about the organisation, while the reappearance of the Knights Templar created a target from the Catholic side. Freemasonry was banned in a number of countries and cities: 1735 in Holland and Frisia, 1736 in Geneva, 1737 in Tuscany, 1738 in Hamburg and in Sweden, and 1794 in Russia under Empress Catherine II, and many Masons were imprisoned. Elsewhere, despite the assurances of the Masonic lodges that behind their closed doors nothing political or blasphemous was going on, Freemasonry was placed under state supervision: In 1785 by Emperor Joseph II in his dominions, in 1788 in Prussia, in 1799 in Great Britain. In 1795, the lodges were forced to close by Emperor Francis II (Oberhauser 2018).

## The real Illuminati

This repression underlines the fact that the late eighteenth century was obsessed with the idea of 'unknown superiors' in possession of powerful secrets. This was exacerbated by the development of various secret societies pretending to be in possession of knowledge. Among these, with regard to conspiracy theories, the Illuminati occupy the most prominent position. The Illuminati Order was founded in 1776 by Adam Weishaupt (1748–1830), a professor of canon law, in Ingolstadt, Bavaria. His aim was to establish a secret structure to train young men destined to obtain important administrative positions. Though not Masonic from the outset, the Illuminati system, as developed by Adolph von Knigge on the basis of Weishaupt's teachings, came to incorporate the degrees of Freemasonry. The Illuminati degrees were meant to divulge more and more secrets and insights as the candidate ascended through the ranks (Wäges, Markner 2015). In less than a decade, the Illuminati attracted about 2000 members, among whom were a few well-known German Enlightenment intellectuals as well as high-ranking Freemasons.

Knigge left the order in 1784, due to irreconcilable differences with Weishaupt, the order was banned a year later in Bavaria and the Illuminati went into decline. Burke refers in his work to the publication by the Bavarian government of the so-called *Originalschriften*, which contain correspondence, some degrees and other instructions, of the Illuminati. Around them, a conspiracy theory arose, based on real events and on imagined conspiracy mythemes that still exists today. The main one is that the leading Illuminati member Johann Joachim Christoph Bode, on a journey to Paris in 1787, met Masons of the 'Amis réunis' lodge to bring the Illuminati to France. The outbreak of the French Revolution was then attributed to this journey.

The principal proponents of the Illuminati conspiracy theory were based in Darmstadt, Hanover and Vienna, all connected with Johann August Starck. Opponents of the Illuminati, such as Leopold Alois Hoffmann, Ludwig Adolph Christian von Grolman, Heinrich Martin Gottfried Köster, Christian Girtanner and Heinrich August Ottokar Reichard, contributed to the journals *Wiener Zeitschrift* and *Eudämonia* and were the authors of very influential conspiracy theoretical books about the Illuminati and other secret societies (Weiß, Albrecht 1999). Hoffmann, for example, also worked as a spy to gather information about radical societies in Hungary (Silagi 1960). Von Grolmann, an Illuminati renegade possessing first-hand knowledge about the secret order, published anonymously the book *Die neuesten Arbeiten des Spartacus und Philo* (1793), which was heavily used by both Barruel and Robison. A few years later, this same group helped translate Barruel's *Mémoires* into German.

## Robison's 'good authorities'

Since Robison did not work with this network of correspondents, he depended on other people to provide him with sources and literature. For *Proofs of a conspiracy* he harvested the review *Neueste Religionsbegebenheiten* published by Köster. In addition, Robison presumably corresponded with anonymous experts, the 'good authorities' mentioned on the title page of his *Proofs*. Two Scottish monks of the Scots Monastery in Regensburg, Germany, have been identified as Robison's sources (Hammermayer 1966; Dilworth 2004). Maurus (Alexander) Horn, the monastery's librarian, a staunch adversary of the French Revolution who repeatedly mentioned the Illuminati in autobiographical documents, shared pertinent material with Robison (Beattie 1849: 116). The second monk, Gallus (James) Robertson came into contact with Robison. He told him in January 1798 that, ten years earlier, he had been in Ratisbon, when in Germany the exposure of the Illuminati was a much-discussed subject, and, travelling from Munich to Edinburgh, he had taken a copy of the *Originalschriften* with him. While he was assured that Scottish Freemasonry had nothing to do with the Illuminati, Robertson also told him that there was evidence of correspondence between Germany and Scotland (Oberhauser 2013).

In his *Proofs of a conspiracy*, Robison quoted several Illuminati letters from the *Originalschriften*, but in an unreliable fashion (for an example, see Robison [1798 (1797): 134] and Markner et al. [2005: 214–7]). In addition, there are sentences in Robison's version that cannot be found in the *Originalschriften*. Robison's false translations and compilations were often quoted in this form, despite the publicly available writings of the Illuminati (Oberhauser 2013).

## Secret societies and the French Revolution

Any discussion of the intellectual origins of the French Revolution will have to touch upon the role of Freemasonry (Mornet 1933). The problem of researching secret societies is that there is a vast number of pseudo-scientific books about alleged actions of those societies. Therefore, scholarly work has to focus, on the one hand, on the 'empirical' history of secret societies and, on the other hand, on the 'imagined' history. This latter aspect was analysed by John Morris Roberts in *The Mythology of Secret Societies* (1972), studying the mythological representations and assumptions about the clandestine work of secret societies. Albert Soboul (1974) pointed out at least three ways of conceiving the role of Freemasonry in bringing about the French Revolution. First, Freemasonry has been accused of being the main protagonist in the causes that led to the revolution, a revolution that was nothing but a conspiracy conceived in the lodges. This counter-revolutionary reading was called 'barruélisme' in reference to Augustin Barruel (Ligou 1982). The second extreme position considers Freemasonry as the culmination of Enlightenment ideas, which contributed to a large part to the outbreak of the French Revolution. The third position is more moderate: It concedes that Freemasonry played a role in the propagation of Enlightenment ideas, but was not the deciding factor. The lodges were divided among themselves, had no unique and homogeneous ideologies and philosophies, and certainly not all were politically interested. This means that Freemasonry in itself was not capable of leading a large conspiracy, as it is supposed by conservative thinkers.

François Furet (1978) believed that the French Revolution should be conceptually grasped in order to prevent being overwhelmed by the various interpretive approaches. He reintroduced the books and ideas of Augustin Cochin as his point of reference in the debates. Cochin was accused of being a follower of 'barruélisme', but to Furet he was a conceptual thinker. Cochin tried to avoid conspiratorial thinking by using sociological categories: He interpreted Freemasonry and other societies as a revolutionary 'machine' that led to the outbreak of the French

Revolution. Drawing upon Cochin's work, Furet regarded these philosophical clubs – *societés de pensée* – as a force that controlled public opinion and ultimately culminated in the Terror. Daniel Roche's investigations put these interpretations on an empirical foundation. He was able to show clearly that the number of Masonic lodges had increased dramatically since the 1750s. With regard to social composition, it can also be stated that Masonic lodges were distinguished from other societies by the fact that they were more socially diverse, with more members from the third estate, especially members working in trade and commerce. In contrast to other societies, these lodges seemed most to demonstrate the principles of liberty, equality and fraternity.

It should be noted that, although the Masonic lodges did not play a direct role in the events of 1789, some of its members were important to the course of the French Revolution (Ligou 1989). However, Masons can be found across the political spectrum in relation to the revolution, from avid supporters to staunch opponents (Roche 1989 [1978]). Beaurepaire has pointed out that some Masons even sympathised with anti-philosophical and conservative ideas (Beaurepaire 2013). It should be noted, therefore, that, in view of the short-term events that led to the outbreak of the French Revolution, there is no evidence that there was anything like a Masonic plot. However, it remains unclear what influence Freemasonry had in terms of long-term developments.

More recent research on the age of the Enlightenment and, in particular, research on radical Enlightenment currents, paints a differentiated picture of radical thinkers and discourses. Interpreting Freemasonry as a radical society is in any form controversial. Margaret Jacob, as one of the leading researchers in this field (1981, 2013), assumes that there was a connection between Masonic lodges and freethinkers in the Dutch Republic and England, and that clandestine literature led to the spreading of these radical ideas. This would mean that certain lodges served as a means of transporting materialistic, if not atheistic, thought. But, this position is not commonly shared by other researchers and has been strongly criticised (Israel, Mulsow 2014), as there were various strands of Freemasonry that emerged throughout Europe. The same can be said with regard to the interpretation of the Illuminati, whose founder is said to have radiated a 'diffuse radicalism' (Markner 2017), or the idea of the 'Deutsche Union'. In the end, the question remains about how radical these societies were.

## The transfer of the Illuminati conspiracy theory to New England

Illuminati-related conspiracy theories became a travelling concept in 1798 and 1799 when they reached New England (Stauffer 1918). Jedidiah Morse's sermon on National Fast Day on 8 May 1798, held in Connecticut, was the first to deal with the Illuminati in the U.S.A. Morse relied on *Proofs of a conspiracy* despite the fact that Robison himself had only vaguely hinted at the possible existence of several lodges of the Illuminati in the U.S.A. before 1786 (Robison 1798 [1797]: 202). In two further sermons, Morse tried to prove Robison's assumption about possible American Illuminati. In this he clearly failed, but his conspiracy theory spread quickly anyway and permeated the circles of conservative Federalists such as Theodore and Timothy Dwight, David Tappan and others, before reaching the newspapers. Even presidential candidate Thomas Jefferson was accused of being one of the Illuminati. After his election victory in 1800, however, interest in the matter waned and the scare was over. But, this example shows how the Illuminati conspiracy theory could be used in critical situations. The theory was constructed by Morse and others to show that evil people from abroad were in the country to undermine the principles of liberty and equality. It was also a weapon in the fight for a conservative Calvinist tradition, which was at stake at these times (Moss 1995).

In a similar vein, the Anti-Masonic Party was founded in New York in 1828 and found its strongest following in New England. Its supporters saw it as a democratic opposition (Butter

2018: 170–8) against populist President Andrew Jackson. Freemasonry was seen as an elite body directing American politics and aiming at the destruction of civil liberties. This party, whose voters mostly lived in the countryside and suburban areas, existed until about 1838, and later merged with the Whig Party (McCarthy 1902; Vaughn 1983). During the party's national convention in 1830, former Mason Moses Thatcher presented a history of anti-Masonry that drew upon Barruel and Robison (but not mentioning Starck). Another renegade Mason among the party's members, Henry Dana Ward, used Robison and Barruel as reference sources in his books and pamphlets (Oberhauser 2013).

## Conclusion: Freemasonry and antisemitic conspiracy theories

In the mid-1780s, Starck became a target of the Berlin Enlightenment around Johann Erich Biester, Friedrich Gedicke and Friedrich Nicolai, who were famous authors and editors of journals. He was accused of secretly furthering Catholic aims while overtly fulfilling his duties as a Protestant court preacher. Starck responded to these allegations with an unsuccessful lawsuit as well as several publications. In one of them, a scathing satire, he accused his detractors of being crypto-Jews, and Freemasonry of having Jewish roots and being subverted by Jews. This incident shows, among other things, that the relationship between Judaism and Freemasonry, although not a strongly discussed topic, was not friction-free (Katz 1970).

At the beginning of the nineteenth century, the founding of the Jewish Masonic Lodge 'Zur aufgehenden Morgenröthe' in Frankfurt by Sigmund Geisenheimer took place. Although the lodge wanted to accommodate both Jews and Gentiles, it almost always remained a purely Jewish affair. Johann Christian Ehrmann, himself a Freemason as well as a former member of the Illuminati Order, wrote the short pamphlet *Judenthum in the M[aurere]y 1816*. The author branded the Jews as a people who helped to bring about the atrocities of the French Revolution and Napoleon's triumph. In regard to the lodge, Ehrmann claimed that the Jews were infiltrating Freemasonry in order to fulfil their role as a chosen people and bring the world under their control. Ehrmann's short pamphlet would later be used in Nazi propaganda (Rosenberg 1920).

With regard to conspiracy thinking at that time, Jews played only a minor role in the works of Barruel, Robison and Starck. But, their role in these great conspiracy-theoretical syntheses about the interpretation of revolution was dramatically changed by a single document (Oberhauser 2015).

On 20 August 1806, Augustin Barruel received a letter written by one Jean-Baptiste Simonini in Florence. Simonini introduced himself as an avid reader of the *Mémoires*, and congratulated Barruel for having written them. But, he believed that Barruel should have covered the Jews as well, since they were in fact the 'unknown superiors' behind Freemasonry and the Illuminati. Realising that this might seem an exaggeration, Simonini tried to convince Barruel by sharing some autobiographical reminiscences with him. Simonini described how, as a young man growing up in Piedmont, he had become friends with Jews who, one day, wanted him to become part of their large conspiracy and so divulged their secrets to him. They had inaugurated him in Turin, disclosing their concealment tactics, plans and goals achieved. They claimed Mani and the Old Man of the Mountain were Jews; and Freemasonry and the Illuminati were founded by two Jews; that anti-Christian sects, which descended from Mani, had millions of followers in various positions throughout the world, with over 800 adherents within the Italian clergy and many members in Spain. They claimed that the Bourbons were the greatest enemies of the sect; and that Christians were led astray through false baptismal certificates. They described to Simonini how they planned to use money to take over governments and, since they now had the same rights, they would rob Christians by usury. In less than a century, they wanted to become the rulers of the world and enslave those of other faiths (Cohn 1967: 33–6; Taguieff 1992: 109–13).

Simonini's letter was first printed in 1878 in the Catholic journal *Le Contemporain* as part of the memoirs of Père Fidèle de Grivel, who had become a close friend of Barruel towards the end of his life (Taguieff 2013: 32). The letter, forwarded by Barruel to Grivel in 1817, was accompanied by comments in which Barruel explained that, when he had convinced himself that Simonini's letter was genuine, he had brought it to the attention of the chief of the Paris secret police, Pierre-Marie Desmarest, as well as Cardinal Fesch and Pope Pius VII, who all confirmed Simonini's credibility. Barruel then explored the matter further and found that many Jews had indeed ascended to the higher degrees of Freemasonry. In 1819, Barruel told Grivel that he had learned that the Grand Orient was run by the 'Très-Grand Orient' with its own Grand Master, a secret body without a fixed seat consisting of only 21 members, nine of them Jews. The communication, which was based on a system of constantly changing headquarters, seemed to have worked well, as the conspiracy was supposed to have reached the smallest villages.

Since Simonini's letter was only published in 1878 and no original has ever been found, some researchers have assumed it to be a forgery. It was even suggested that it had been fabricated by the French secret police under Fouché (Markner 2014: 256). However, archival findings demonstrate that Barruel pondered over this letter from 1806 to 1820. Meanwhile, at least three copies of it are still extant in Western European archives, all of which were commented upon by Barruel himself (Oberhauser 2013: 269). Little is known about Simonini, apart from the fact that he did exist and was not an offspring of Barruel's imagination. He had the rank of captain in the Sardinian army and was dispatched to the Aosta Valley in 1815 on behalf of the government in Turin (Markner 2014: 254–5).

Barruel refrained from publishing the letter himself because he feared that it might trigger a pogrom. Grivel received the letter in 1817 but chose not to publish it either. Fidèl de Grivel, initially a Sulpician who joined the Jesuits in 1803, became acquainted with the famous conservative thinker and conspiracy theorist Joseph de Maistre in Saint Petersburg. Recent archival research by Anastasia Glazanova has established that Simonini's letter circulated in Russian elite circles due to the popularity and influence of de Maistre. It is highly likely that de Maistre received his copy of the letter from Grivel.

In his memoirs, Grivel also reported that Barruel had burnt two unfinished book manuscripts two days before his death, one of them a refutation of Kant's philosophy. The other one was a history of ancient Jacobinism. Barruel had intended to prove that the revolutionary slogan 'liberté, egalité' had its origins in ancient Greece, from where it was passed on by the Manicheans to the Knights Templar, who in turn founded Freemasonry.

Four years after its first publication, Simonini's letter was reprinted in the Jesuit journal *La Civiltà Cattolica*. Strangely, there was no reference to Grivel, but instead the letter was presented as a hitherto unedited document, allegedly confirming that the 'Jewish race is the natural seat of high masonry'.

In the same year, the sixth edition of the conspiracy-theoretical work *Les Sociétés Secrètes* by Nicolas Deschamps was published with Simonini's letter in its third volume (a compilation of posthumous material that Claudio Jannet provided with annotations and documents). This work strongly recalled the ideas of Barruel as the anti-Masonic conspiracy theory was recounted and related to the subsequent revolutions of 1830 and 1848. Freemasonry itself was blamed in this book for social changes since 1789.

The influence of Masons under Jewish direction was emphasised by various other European authors in books, newspapers and journals throughout the nineteenth century. With regard to the history of the Judeo-Masonic conspiracy theory, the role of the Jews in these texts changed noticeably. Among these was the prominent title *Le juif, le judaisme et la judaisation des peuples chrétiens* by Gougenot des Mousseaux, published in 1869, which Alfred Rosenberg brought onto the market as a German translation in 1921. The work claimed that the Jews were not only the enemy of Christianity, but also of the whole world, with a world republic as their goal. Above all, it denounced the so-called 'kabbalistic Jews', allegedly connected with Freemasonry. The well-known occultist and anti-Semite, Édouard Drumont, regrouped the relationship: Freemasons were not the motor of Jewish emancipation, but the Jews were the secret superiors of Freemasonry. In his voluminous work *La France Juive* (1886), he sought to demonstrate that Freemasonry was controlled by Jews intent on destroying Christianity. Barruel, Deschamps and Jannet were also quoted in 1893 by the Jesuit Léon Meurin in his work *La Franc-Maçonnerie Synagogue de Satan*, which cited Simonini's letter in an attempt to prove the link between the Jews and the Manicheans.

Finally, Simonini's letter would again resurface in pamphlets interpreting the First World War as a conspiracy. Most importantly, Nesta H. Webster discussed it in her book *World Revolution* (1921) and became the first author to connect this letter and *The Protocols of the Elders of Zion*. Having read both Barruel and Robison, she used their conspiratorial approach in order to explain the nature of historical revolutions in general. In her widely read publications, the anti-Illuminati tropes were merged with antisemitic and anti-Bolshevist elements.

The legacy of Simonini's letter leads to Alfred Rosenberg, known to be one of the publishers of a German edition of *The Protocols of the Elders of Zion*. The Protocols, whose author is still unknown, were also based on a fabricated story about the plan of a Jewish elite group wanting to seize world domination through the infiltration and instrumentalisation of Freemasonry. But, far from being only an interpretation of history, this forgery proved to be a propaganda weapon with tragic consequences.[1]

## Note

1 The research for this contribution was made possible by the F.W.F.

## References

Armitage, D. (2000) 'Edmund Burke and reason of state', *Journal of the History of Ideas*, 61: 617–34.
Aston, N. (2004) 'Burke and the conspiratorial origins of the French Revolution: some Anglo-French resemblances', in B. Coward and J. Swann (eds.) *Conspiracies and conspiracy theory in early modern Europe: from the Waldensians to the French revolution*, London: Routledge, pp. 213–34.
Barruel, A. (1793) *Histoire du clergé pendant la Révolution française*, London: J. Debrett.
Barruel, A. (1797–1798) *Mémoires pour sérvir à l'histoire du Jacobinisme 4 vols*, London: Le Boussonier et Co.
Beattie, W. (ed.) (1849) *Life and letters of Thomas Campbell*, vol. 2, London: Edward Moxon.
Beaurepaire, P.-Y. (2013) *Franc-maçonnerie et sociabilité: les métamorphoses du lien social XVIIIème–XIXème siècle*, Paris: Edimaf.
Burke, E. (1790) *Reflections on the revolution in France, and on the proceedings in certain societies in London relative to that event. In a letter intended to have been sent to a gentleman in Paris*, London: Dodsley.
Burke, E. (1978) *The correspondence of Edmund Burke*, vol. X, Cambridge and Chicago, Ill.: Cambridge University Press/The University of Chicago Press.
Butter, M. (2018) *'Nichts ist, wie es scheint': über Verschwörungstheorien*, Berlin: Suhrkamp.
Cadet de Gassicourt, L.C. (1796) *Le Tombeau de Jacques de Molay, ou le Secret des Conspirateurs, à ceux qui veulent tout savoir*, Paris: Marchands de Nouveautés.
Campbell, P.R, Kaiser, T.E. and Linton, M. (eds.) (2007) *Conspiracy in the French Revolution*, Manchester: Manchester University Press.

Cohn, N. (1967) *Warrant for Genocide*, New York: Harper & Row.
Coward, B. and Swann, J. (eds.) (2004) *Conspiracies and conspiracy theory in early modern Europe: from the Waldensians to the French Revolution*, London: Routledge.
Deschamps, N. (1874–1876) *Les Sociétés secrètes et la société ou philosophie de l'histoire contemporaine*, vol. 3, Avignon: Seguin.
Dilworth, M. (2004) 'Horn, Alexander', in H.C.G. Matthew and B. Harrison (eds.) *Oxford dictionary of national biography*, vol. 28, Oxford: Oxford University Press, pp. 113–14.
Drumont, É. (1886) *La France Juive: essai d'histoire contemporaine 2 vols*, Paris: Marpon & Flammarion.
Edelstein, D. (ed.) (2010) *The super-enlightenment: daring to know too much*, Oxford: Voltaire Foundation.
Ehrmann, J.C. (1816) *Judenthum in der M–y, eine Warnung an alle deutschen [Logen]*, [Frankfurt am Main].
(1787) *Einige Originalschriften des Illuminatenordens, welche bey dem gewesenen Regierungsrath Zwack durch vorgenommene Hausvisitation zu Landshut den 11. und 12. Oktob. etc. 1786 vorgenommen worden*, Munich: Lentner.
Epstein, K. (1966) *The genesis of German conservatism*, Princeton, NJ: Princeton University Press.
Ferrer Benimeli, J.A. (1976–1977) *Masonería, Iglesia e Ilustración: un conflicto ideólogico-politico-religioso 4 vols*, Madrid: Fundación Universitaria Española.
Freeman, M. (1978) 'Edmund Burke and the theory of revolution', *Political Theory*, 6(3): 277–97.
Furet, F. (1978) *Penser la Révolution française*, Paris: Gallimard.
Galart de Montjoie (1795) *Histoire de la conjuration de Robespierre*, Paris: Marchands de Nouveautés.
Galart de Montjoie (1796) *Histoire de la conjuration de Louis Philippe Joseph d'Orléans*, Paris: Marchands de Nouveautés.
Garrard, G. (2006) *Counter-enlightenments: from the eighteenth-century to the present*, London/New York: Routledge.
Gougenot des Mousseaux, H.R. (1869) *Le Juif, le judaïsme et la judaïsation des peuples chrétiens*, Paris: H. Plon.
Hammermayer, L. (1966) 'Die europäischen Mächte und die Bewahrung von Abtei und Seminar der Schotten in Regensburg (1802/03)', *Verhandlungen des Historischen Vereins für Oberpfalz und Regensburg*, 106: 291–306.
Hofman, A. (1988) 'The origins of the theory of the philosophe conspiracy', *French History*, 2(2): 152–72.
Hofman, A. (1993) 'Opinion, illusion, and the illusion of opinion: Barruel's theory of conspiracy', *Eighteenth-Century Studies*, 27(1): 27–60.
Hunt, L. (1984) *Politics, culture, and class in the French Revolution*, Berkeley, Los Angeles/London: University of California Press.
Israel, J.I. and Mulsow, M. (eds.) (2014) *Radikalaufkärung*, Berlin: Suhrkamp.
Jacob, M.C. (1981) *The radical enlightenment: pantheists, freemasons and republicans*, London: Allen & Unwin.
Jacob, M.C. (2013) 'The radical enlightenment and Freemasonry: where we are now', *Philosophica*, 88: 13–29.
Kaplan, S. (1982) 'The famine plot persuasion in eighteenth-century France', *Transactions of the American Philosophical Society*, 72(3): 1–79.
Katz, J. (1970) *Jews and Freemasons in Europe, 1723–1939*, Cambridge, MA: Harvard University Press.
Klausnitzer, R. (2007) *Poesie und Konspiration: Beziehungssinn und Zeichenökonomie von Verschwörungsszenarien in Publizistik, Literatur und Wissenschaft 1750–1850*, Berlin/New York: de Gruyter.
Knoop, D., Jones, G.P. and Hamer, D. (1978) *Early masonic pamphlets*, London: Q.C. Correspondent Circle.
Köster, H.M.G. (ed.) (1778–1797) *Die neuesten Religionsbegebenheiten mit unpartheyischen Anmerkungen*, Gießen: Krieger.
Lefèbvre, G. (1932) *La Grande Peur de 1789*, Paris: Colin.
Lefranc, J.-F. (1791) *Le Voile levé pour les curieux, ou le Secret de la Révolution révélé, à l'aide de la Franc-Maçonnerie*, Paris: Lepetit et Guillemard.
Lefranc, J.-F. (1792) *Conjuration contre la religion catholique et les souverains, dont le projet, conçu en France, doit s'exécuter dans l'univers entier, ouvrage utile à tous les Français*, Paris: Lepetit.
Lemaire, J. (1985) *Les origines françaises de l'anti-maçonnisme (1744–1797)*, Brussels: Éd. de l'Université de Bruxelles.
Ligou, D. (1982) 'Albert Soboul et l'Histoire de la Franc-maçonnerie Française', *Annales historiques de la Révolution française*, 250: 554–6.
Ligou, D. (1989) *La Franc-maçonnerie et la révolution française, 1789–1799*, Paris: Chiron.

Luckert, S. (1993) *Jesuits, Freemasons, Illuminati, and Jacobins: conspiracy theories, secret societies, and politics in late eighteenth-century Germany*, thesis, Binghamton, NY: State Univiversity of New York.

Markner, R. (2014) 'Giovanni Battista Simonini: shards from the disputed life of an Italian anti-semite', in M. Ciccarini, N. Marcialis and G. Ziffer (eds.) *Kesarevo Kesarju: Scritti in onore di Cesare G. De Michelis*, Florence: Firenze University Press, pp. 311–19.

Markner, R. (2017) 'La radicalité diffuse d'Adam Weishaupt: une lecture des "degrés intermédiaires" jusqu'alors inédits des Illuminés de Bavière', *Politica Hermetica*, 31: 32–44.

Markner, R., Neugebauer-Wölk, M. and Schüttler, H. (eds.) (2005) *Die Korrespondenz des Illuminatenordens, vol. 1: 1776–1781*, Tübingen: Max Niemeyer.

McCarthy, C. (1902) 'The Antimasonic party: a study of political antimasonry in the United States, 1827–1840', *Annual Report of the American Historical Association*, 1: 365–574.

McMahon, D.M. (2003) *Enemies of the enlightenment: the French counter-enlightenment and the making of modernity*, Oxford: Oxford University Press.

Mellor, A. (1961) *Nos frères séparés: les francs-maçons*, Paris: Mame.

Meurin, L. (1893) *La franc-maçonnerie, synagogue de Satan*, Paris: Victor Retaux et Fils.

Mornet, D. (1933) *Les origines intellectuelles de la Révolution française 1715–1787*, Paris: Librairie Armand Colin.

Moss, R.J. (1995) *The life of Jedidiah Morse: a station of peculiar exposure*, Knoxville, TN: University of Tennessee Press.

Münch, P. (2008) *Le pouvoir de l'ombre: l'imaginaire du complot durant la Révolution française (1789–1801)*, thesis, Quebec City, QC: Université Laval.

Oberhauser, C. (2013) *Die verschwörungstheoretische Trias: Barruel-Robison-Starck*, Innsbruck and Vienna: Studienverlag.

Oberhauser, C. (2015) 'Die Konstruktion des jüdisch-freimaurerischen Verschwörungsmythos: Augustin Barruel, Simonis Brief und die Folgen', in C. Oberhauser (ed.) *Juden und Geheimnis: interdisziplinäre Annäherungen*, Innsbruck: Innsbruck University Press, pp. 103–22.

Oberhauser, C. (2018) 'Antimasonismus', in H. Reinalter (ed.) *Handbuch der Verschwörungstheorien*, Leipzig: Salier, pp. 39–46.

Reinalter, H., Markner, R., Oberhauser, C. and Volk, P. (eds.) (2019) *Aktenedition über den Wilhelmsbader Freimaurer-Konvent 1782*, vol. 1, Basel: Schwabe.

Roberts, J.M. (1972) *The mythology of the secret societies*, New York: Charles Scribner's Sons.

Robison, J. (1797) *Proofs of a conspiracy against all the religions and governments of Europe, carried on in the secret meetings of Freemasons, Illuminati and Reading Societies. Collected from Good Authorities*, 3rd edn, Edinburgh/London: T. Cadell, W. Davies and W. Creech, 1798.

Roche, D. (1978) *Le Siècle des Lumières en province: Académies et académiciens provinciaux, 1689–1789 2 vols*, reprint, Paris & Den Haag: Mouton, 1989.

Rogalla von Bieberstein, J. (1976) *Die These von der Verschwörung 1776–1945: Philosophen, Freimaurer, Juden, Liberale und Sozialisten als Verschwörer gegen die Sozialordnung*, Frankfurt am Main: Lang.

Rosenberg, A. (1920) *Die Spur des Juden im Wandel der Zeiten*, München: Deutscher Volks-Verlag.

Schilling, B.N. (1950) *Conservative England and the case against Voltaire*, New York: Columbia University Press.

Silagi, D. (1960) *Ungarn und der geheime Mitarbeiterkreis Kaiser Leopolds II*, thesis, München: University of Munich.

Soboul, A. (1974) 'La Franc-maçonnerie et la Révolution Française', *Annales historiques de la Révolution française*, 215: 76–88.

Starck, J.A. (1803) *Der Triumph der Philosophie im 18. Jahrhunderte*, 2 volumes, Germantown [i.e. Frankfurt am Main]: Rosenblatt [i.e. Hermann].

Stauffer, V. (1918) *New England and the Bavarian Illuminati*, New York: Columbia University Press.

Tackett, T. (2000) 'Conspiracy obsession in a time of revolution: French elites and the origins of the terror, 1789–1792', *The American Historical Review*, 105(3): 691–713.

Taguieff, P.-A. (1992) *Les Protocoles des Sages de Sion: faux et usages d'un faux*, upd. edn, Paris: Berg International, 2004.

Taguieff, P.-A. (2013) 'L'invention du complot "judéo-maçonnique": avatars d'un mythe apocalyptique moderne', *Revue d'histoire de la Shoah*, 198(1): 25–97.

Tanner, J. (2008) 'The conspiracy of the invisible hand: anonymous market mechanisms and dark powers', *New German Critique*, 103: 51–64.

Valjavec, F. (1951) *Die Entstehung der politischen Strömungen in Deutschland 1770–1815*, Munich: Oldenbourg.

Vaughn, W.P. (1983) *The Antimasonic party in the United States, 1826–1843*, Lexington: University Press of Kentucky.
Vesper, M. (2012) *Aufklärung, Esoterik, Reaktion: Johann August Starck (1741–1816): Geistlicher, Gelehrter und Geheimbündler zur Zeit der deutschen Spätaufklärung*, Darmstadt: Verlag der Hessischen Kirchengeschichtlichen Vereinigung.
Von Grolman, LA. C. (1793) *Die neuesten Arbeiten des Spartacus und Philo in dem Illuminaten-Orden jetzt zum erstenmal gedruckt, und zur Beherzigung bey gegenwärtigen Zeitläufen herausgegeben*, Frankfurt am Main: Hermann.
Wäges, J. and Markner, R. (eds.) (2015) *The secret school of wisdom: the authentic rituals and doctrines of the illuminati*, Addleston: Lewis Masonic.
Webster, N.H. (1921) *World revolution: the plot against civilization*, London: Constable.
Weiß, C. and Albrecht, W. (eds.) (1999) *Von 'Obscuranten' und 'Eudämonisten': gegenaufklärerische, konservative und antirevolutionäre Publizisten im späten 18. Jahrhundert*, St. Ingbert: Röhrig.
Wood, G.S. (1982) 'Conspiracy and the paranoid style: causality and deceit in the eighteenth century', *The William and Mary Quarterly*, 39(3): 401–41.
Zwierlein, C. and de Graaf, B. (eds.) (2013) 'Security and conspiracy in modern history', *Historical Social Research*, 38(1): 7–45.

# 5.4

# CONSPIRACY THEORIES IN EUROPE DURING THE TWENTIETH CENTURY

*Pascal Girard*

### Introduction

Through the lens of the Internet, it would seem that there are more conspiracy theories than ever before – and it might be true. But conspiracy theories are not a new phenomenon: To a certain extent, the twentieth century could be considered their real golden age. This has been acknowledged by scholars, sometimes retracing their genealogy back to the Middle Ages (Pipes 1997). But, as conspiracy theories were not thought of as a fully-fledged historical topic until relatively recently (Münch 2008: 27–31), the research often remains fragmented and incomplete, with its most important contributions mainly investigating American history (Knight 2003; Butter 2014; Uscinski, Parent 2014).

Given their significance in totalitarian ideologies, conspiracy theories have also been studied by historians of the Soviet and Nazi regimes but, depending on the country, conspiracy theories in other contexts have remained under the radar of history. Because of this, information should be gathered as isolated evidence within the broader framework of political or cultural history. As a consequence, this chapter will not give an exhaustive panorama but will instead summarise what we can learn from existing studies, from which we will draw some conclusions.

### The obsession with spies and traitors in the First World War

The early twentieth century continued with the conspiracy obsessions of the previous one. Because of the triumph of nationalism in Europe, fears of a Jewish or Masonic conspiracy, often linked to foreign powers, continued to thrive. Many documents denouncing the Jewish conspiracy circulated in Europe, but none have been as ubiquitous as *The Protocols of the Elders of Zion*. The origins and the propagation of this forgery are still discussed by specialists, but Norman Cohn's acclaimed work states that the text was fabricated in 1903 by Russian fanatic nationalists. Several publications circulated within the tsarist empire during the following years, but its popularity was at this time confined to the monarchist and nationalist Russian milieu. It is during the First World War and its aftermath that it was used as widespread propaganda, as well as a lethal political tool (Cohn 1967; Taguieff 2004).

The war increased the echo of conspiracy theories in the public opinion of the participating countries. The French population became gripped by the so-called *espionnite*, i.e. an obsession with German spies, and by alarmist rumours about their agencies. This paranoia, particularly intense at the beginning of the conflict, was understandable in the context of an invaded country. The French army mutinies of April 1917, provoked by a predictable crisis of morale among the soldiers, were interpreted by French High Command as the result of secret and subversive agencies of a nebulous pacifist organisation operating on behalf of Germany. This conviction, apparently widely accepted by the public, was strengthened by the Bolshevik Revolution, considered to be the result of a German conspiracy successfully weakening the Triple Entente. At the end of 1917, the struggle against traitors and defeatists became the watchword of the government, which led to investigations against of some politicians that were being accused of seeking a 'white peace' or organisations that were being suspected of fomenting a revolution (Monier 1998: 90–7).

In the U.K., hostility towards Germans and 'spy-fever' that were already existing before the war increased with the outbreak of the conflict. It developed into the myth of the 'hidden hand' of Germans (and sometime Jews) secretly operating in the U.K.; one conspiracy theory claimed German agencies caused the death of Kitchener in 1916 (Heathorn 2007). While it was first and mainly supported by radical-right organisations, this conspiracy theory gained in significance in the press and public speech throughout the war and was one reason for a strict policy of internment of German citizens. The success of this 'hidden hand' theory might have been the need for an explanation of the British decline as well as a means to federate the whole nation into the fight against Germany (Panayi 1988). Despite no concluding evidence of such a plot, in 1917, fighting the supposed pro-German subversion (at work behind the Bolshevik Revolution) became a priority of MI5 and the British government, with predictably disappointing results. In this particular context, the authorities' zeal was less bound to a strong belief than to the wish not to expose themselves to accusations of weakness against subversion (Andrew 2009: 102–3, 2018: 551–5)

## Conspiracy theories as an explanation for catastrophe

After the war, fears of the spread of the Russian Revolution, which was supposedly orchestrated by a Bolshevik conspiracy, increased throughout Europe. However, the significance of this new conspiracy theory varied widely depending on the respective country. In the victorious states of Western Europe, it was endorsed by conservative organisations and the press; and successive governments generally executed relatively erratic and inefficient repressive measures against communist organisations performing subversive agitation-propaganda work (Gerwarth, Horne 2012: 40–51). In 1924, a few days before the British general election, the *Daily Mail* published the Zinoviev Letter, the alleged directives from the head of the Comintern to the communists of the U.K. to provoke a civil war. Proven to be fake, it aimed to undermine the foreign politics of the Labour Party within the perspective of the elections, but its impact on the results was only limited (Bennett 2018: 46–77). In France, throughout the 1920s, many supporters of the right-wing warned against the danger of a communist conspiracy to launch an insurrection and establish a Bolshevik dictatorship (Monier 1995: 50–77, 245–348). This conspiracy theory was built on the occurrence of violent demonstrations, spying, anticolonial agencies and the outrageously antipatriotic propaganda of the French Communist Party. But it only led to recurrently unsuccessful trials that would sometimes enable conservatives to confederate with each other against the Red Menace (Monier 1998: 105–68; 187–230).

Stemming from a different ideological basis than in Western Europe, in Central Europe the belief in a Bolshevik conspiracy was stronger, and quickly mixed with pre-existing and deeply embedded strains of antisemitism, which resulted in a powerful programme of mobilisation and bloody repression. During the Russian Civil War, the belief in a Jewish-Bolshevik conspiracy became increasingly popular among White Russian Army leaders, and *The Protocols* and similarly fake reports were published and disseminated (Budnitskii 2012: 187–92). The Whites' propaganda claimed that the war, the fall of the tsar and the October Revolution were the result of a Jewish conspiracy, which led to mass slaughter and atrocities against the Jews (Gerwarth 2016: 88–9). In newly independent Poland, the denunciation of Jewish Bolshevism developed from ancient stereotypes about criminal Jews into the belief in a Jewish conspiracy to undermine the foundations of the Polish nation. In the face of a strong Soviet threat, the Bolshevik-Jew conspiracy theory was promoted by the Catholic Church and ethno-nationalists and ultimately resulted in collective violence against Polish Jews (Michlic 2008: 89–93).

## Conspiracy theories within Nazism

Although *The Times* revealed in 1921 that *The Protocols* were a forgery – a statement spectacularly confirmed in the Berne trial of 1935 (Hagemeister 2011) – they continued to spread throughout the rest of Europe, particularly in Germany. The endemic antisemitism, which inspired the ignominious Jewish census of 1916, was widely shared among military and völkisch nationalist movements flourishing during the Weimar Republic; some of their members combined the Jewish conspiracy theory with the myth of the 'stab in the back' that they disseminated.

The Nazis used the allegations of a communist conspiracy behind the Reichstag fire of 1933 as a justification for the suspension of civil liberties, which, along with violence and intimidation, was a decisive step towards the establishment of a single-party regime. But, according to Nazi ideology, this communist plot was part of a wider Jewish conspiracy. This could be related to the antisemitism embedded in Central Europe – beliefs in Jewish conspiracies were noticeable in Austria before the Anschluss (Pauley 1992: 269–70), but it was also influenced by *The Protocols*: Indeed, German theorists, such as Alfred Rosenberg, themselves influenced by White Russian émigrés (Kellogg 2005), had a deep impact on Hitler's thought and contributed to his endorsement of *The Protocols* as proof of a genuine conspiracy. Since his early speeches and writings, he claimed to have been inspired by *The Protocols* for his belief in a Jewish conspiracy of world domination, at work behind military defeat, economic issues and the threat of a Bolshevik Revolution aimed at destroying the German nation (Redles 2012: 118–20). This conspiracy theory later aggregated new events, such as the boycott on German goods initiated by Jewish organisations in 1933 that the Nazis claimed to be proof of the 'economic war' of the Jewish conspiracy (Reinharz, Shavit 2018: 47; 122).

Nazi propaganda spread the idea of a Jewish world conspiracy through publications such as the *Völkische Beobachter* or the *Stürmer*, headed by Julius Streicher; this newspaper published negative stereotypes and lies about Jews, among which were some explicitly based on *The Protocols*. But, despite the importance of the international Jewry conspiracy theory in mass propaganda, *The Protocols* themselves were only used with caution, seemingly because Nazi leaders were dubious about the text's authenticity (Bytwerk 2015).

The belief in a Jewish world conspiracy, so obsessively embedded in Nazi ideology, became through Nazi propaganda a means to legitimate anti-Jewish legislation and persecution, and to build an antisemitic consensus (Bytwerk 2001: 132–41, 171–81). For example, Kristallnacht in November 1938 was presented as a spectacular burst of popular violence in reaction to the Jewish plot, and shortly preceded the announcement of the war against Bolshevisation and Jewry threatening the world. However, the relentless antisemitism of Hitler and the Nazi leaders, and especially their concern about the Jewish world conspiracy, was not necessarily entirely shared by the German population (Kershaw 2008: 173–86).

## Conspiracy theories under the Soviet regime

Germany was not the only regime in Europe that used conspiracy theories as a legitimation of power, repression and mass killing. Belief in conspiracy was used by some Soviet leaders as one of the many justifications for the Red Terror during the Russian Civil War. After the war, the official discourse of the new-born Soviet Union spread the obsession with an internal enemy, forging the image of a nation besieged by counter-revolutionary forces (Raleigh 2002: 71–2). This resulted in the Petrograd conspiracy theory and spectacular trials of conspirators as early as 1921. The next year, a trial was held against a faked conspiracy of socialist revolutionaries; its purpose was to be the model for the trials that Lenin wanted to organise to intensify repression against political opponents (Jansen 1982: 27–8, 150).

In the 1930s, with Stalin now the undisputed leader, conspiracy theories became a central tenet of the regime rhetoric (Werth, Moullec 1994: 470–1) disseminating a culture of conspiracy not only within the party but also throughout the whole population of the Soviet Union (Rittersporn 1993: 99–115). These conspiracy theories had several goals. One was to put the Soviet regime into a defensive position legitimating the use of harsh state repression (Getty, Naumov 1999: 17–21). In particular, they enabled Stalin to eliminate all his actual, potential or hypothetical opponents through show trials. For instance, the trial of the Ukrainian nationalists of 1931 meant that Stalin could quickly get rid of some of his last opponents and of the spokesmen of the Ukrainian nation, and thereby thwart any attempt of resistance against his policy of collectivisation (Conquest 1986: 211–20).

The assassination of Sergei Kirov in 1934 and the vast investigation that followed brought to light a supposed huge anti-Soviet conspiracy; translated into several successive official conspiratorial narratives, it was then used as a pretext by Stalin to eliminate his rivals within the party – the Trotskyist Left and the right opposition – through the three dramatic and widely publicised Moscow show trials of 1936–1938 (Conquest 1989: 48–68; 77–103). The accusation of the Trotskyists plotting with hostile foreign powers also led to the brutal and secret purge of the head of the Red Army on the basis of fabricated evidence (Jansen, Petrov 2002: 69–70).

But these very famous show trials were only the tip of the iceberg of the Stalinist Great Purge, a mass repression that led to the arrests of millions of people and the deaths of hundreds of thousands. This 'wider purge' was brutal social engineering, a deep operation of prophylactic cleansing to eliminate actual and potential opponents to the establishment of the Soviet state and the implementation of collectivisation. This preventive operation was executed through secret operations of the N.K.V.D. and based on quotas of arrests and shootings, targeting parts of the territory alleged to host the biggest concentration of enemies. As a result, the struggle against the conspiracy expanded to many broad social categories (kulaks, priests and intellectuals) as well as ethnic minorities considered more likely to conspire with foreign powers (Werth 2003: 216–39; Khlevniuk 2004: 140–8).

The conspiracy theories and the repression that derived from them were also a means of political education and mobilisation. The purge of the party was a way to find scapegoats for its failures and abuses. In 1928, the Shakhty trial against the 'bourgeois experts', a group of engineers in the mining industry accused of sabotage (Shearer, Khaustov 2015: 59–67), was used to establish a new pro-worker policy in the recruitment of cadres (Fitzpatrick 1979: 379–83) and to put pressure on ineffective industry administrators. In the later context of Stakhanovism, workers as well as administrators were constantly under the threat of accusation of sabotage if they did not reach the quotas of production (Goldman 2007: 95–109, 225–36). Inside the party, it helped to promote new cadres with a better Soviet ethic; the vigilance and the capacity to detect political enemies became crucial qualities of the Bolsheviks (Getty 1985: 113).

Yet, the use of conspiracy theories to legitimate Soviet repression proved to be an uncontrolled and counterproductive political tool in the hands of Stalin. The zeal of local officials of the party during the Great Purge led to a destructive 'overfullfilment' of quotas of deportation and executions. Despite the incredulity of the population (Davies 1997: 118–23) and the passivity of the local communist cadres, the campaign against the Trotskyist conspiracy eventually descended in 1937 into a vortex of denunciations and arrests within the factories (Goldman 2007: 80–92, 204–47), which completely disorganised the production (Goldman 2011: 130–5). The elimination of the head of the Red Army on the basis of forged evidence was not only useless, but also dramatically weakened Soviet military capacity (Harris 2008: 34–6). This purge even dangerously affected the Comintern (McDermott, Agnew 1996: 151–6).

Historians are still debating the reasons why Stalin involved himself in a mass repression dramatically affecting Soviet economic and military capacity. If the traditional explanation were that Stalin wanted to secure his power over the party, the Army and the population, recent contributions suggest that the Great Purge might also have been the result of a genuine belief in conspiracy. The paranoia and siege mentality of the Soviet leader (Whitewood 2015: 201–86) and the deep feeling of insecurity and vulnerability founded on real anti-Soviet agencies (Harris 2016) create a misperception about how foreign enemies managed to infiltrate large fractions of the population.

## The intensification of conspiracy theories during wartime

The return of war in Europe in the 1930s saw an intensification in the obsession with clandestine enemy agencies. In Western Europe, the Spanish Civil War was significant in this regard, first, because the Spanish extreme right that carried out the military uprising of 1936 used the idea of a communist conspiracy to legitimate its actions (Southworth 2002). While being a classic tool to justify 'defensive violence' (in the shape of a putsch) (Seidman 2011: 38; 180), the myth of a communist-Masonic conspiracy seems to have been supported by the regime until the end, resulting in the relentless repression of Freemasonry (Ruiz 2005: 192–225, 2011).

Second, it was during the Spanish Civil War that the expression 'fifth column' originated, first used in Republican propaganda to name a clandestine group of infiltrated enemies spying and committing acts of sabotage or destabilisation (Carr 1984: 30), and providing explanation for Republican misfortunes (Kirschenbaum 2015: 105; 108; 139). This scare induced great vigilance and repression, especially from the Soviet-led communist troops (Payne 2004: 206, 227). As the Second World War began, this expression flourished within the propaganda of countries subject to spy-fever, which had been in many ways directly in contact with the Republican forces – France, the U.K. and also the Soviet Union.

The impact of the Second World War on totalitarian regimes provoked an increase in conspiracist propaganda and state repression. In the Soviet Union, war increased vigilance against saboteurs and spies, as well as repression against national minorities, including those of newly conquered territories, which increased the number of unredeemable enemies of the Soviet destined to spend the rest of their lives in the Gulags (Barnes 2011: 143–53).

In Nazi Germany, antisemitic discourse redoubled during the war, while the head of the party organised the Holocaust of the Jews from Eastern Europe. The conspiracist rhetoric prospered in multiple Nazi publications, as well as in speeches of the most prominent Nazi leaders, such as Goebbels, presenting the persecution of the Jews as a legitimate defensive reaction against a conspiracy of international Jewry seeking to ruin Germany. In this view, the war, the alliance between Bolshevism and Anglo-Saxon plutocracy, the defeats of the German Army, as well as the massacre of Katyn, were the result of an international Jewish plot (Gellately 2001:

145–50; Herf 2006). However, criticisms of the brutal methods (Kershaw 2008: 205) and the secrecy of the extermination of the Jews from Eastern Europe suggest that belief in the Jewish conspiracy threat was merely a smokescreen rather than a conviction, used to justify the abomination of the genocide (Brayard 2012).

Germany also used international propaganda – such as public exhibitions – to attempt to convince the allied and neutral nations that the fight against Bolshevism was linked to a Jewish world conspiracy threatening Europe (Waddington 2007: 190–5). Nazis could rely on former transnational fascist networks (Bauerkämper, Rossoliński-Liebe 2017: 2–7) and on common beliefs about Jewish conspiracy, shared by allied regimes such as Ustachis in Croatia and other Balkan regimes allied to the Nazis (see also Chapter 5.6 in this volume).

## A weapon in the ideological conflict of the Cold War

The Cold War is often seen as a Golden Age of conspiracy theories, especially the belief that domestic communist parties were a fifth column. This is partly due to the projection of U.S. McCarthyism onto the European context. But, while McCarthyism in the U.S.A. has long been explored, specific studies about the Red Scare in Europe are surprisingly few and sometimes politically driven, and this issue still waits to be thoroughly researched.

The two Western countries with the strongest communist parties were, by far, Italy and France. In both countries, there was a fear that the party would try to undermine the nation in order to seize power or facilitate a Soviet invasion, a view shared by right-wing and centre political movements and, to a lesser extent, social-democrat organisations. But this fear was just a part of the greater concern with the threat of the Soviet Union and came second after other political and social issues. This 'moderate Red Scare' appears to have been spurred by the outbreak of national violence (such as the 'insurrectional strikes' or riots of 1947–1950), public defeatist claims (Santamaria 2006: 81) and the deterioration of international relations (beginning with the Korean War in the summer of 1950). But, even so, it rarely led to public and explicit denunciation of a communist fifth column. In the 1950s, with the death of Stalin and the decline of internal communist activism, this concern clearly decreased in public opinion and politics (Girard 2012: 370–461, 555–697).

In the U.K., too, the fear of the communist enemy within, whether expressed through political discourse or film, was closely linked to the international confrontation with the Korean War (Guy 1993: 36). In this context, the propaganda of the Partisans of Peace could have been interpreted as part of a wider Soviet conspiracy aimed at weakening the West (Jenks 2003: 55).

At the same time, Soviet-originated conspiracy theories spread throughout the People's Democracies of Eastern Europe, following the establishment of repressive institutions. From 1950, and more intensively after the uprising of June 1953, the East German Ministry for State Security began to establish a broad network of surveillance and control that aimed at arresting enemies within, monitored by Western Germany (Bruce 2003). The geopolitical divorce between the Soviet Union and Yugoslavia became a witch hunt, which converted the Soviet purges into the newly born Soviet regimes. In Hungary, because of internal rivalry, communist minister László Rajk was accused of Titoist activities and was, after a show trial along with other members, executed in 1949.

After early signs of antisemitic repression (Rubenstein, Naumov 2001: 32–47), the 1949 anti-cosmopolitan campaign gave birth to a grand conspiracy theory including a strong anti-Zionist strain (Pinkus 1988: 145–61; Azadovskii, Egorov 2002). Some prominent Czechoslovakian communists – among which was Rudolf Slánský, and the majority of whom were Jews – were arrested in 1951 and condemned to death in 1952 for Trotskyism, Titoism and Zionism. Because of dissent within the Romanian Party, Ana Pauker was arrested, sentenced and jailed in 1953 for being an agent of Israel (Gellately 2013: 250–60). All these show trials revealed a clear antisemitic subtext (Wistrich 2010).

Notwithstanding the prompt stop of the arrests related to the so-called Doctors' Plot after Stalin's death in 1953 (with the unsolved question of the extent of the planned purge) (Brent 2004), the Zionist conspiracy theory survived de-Stalinisation and confirmed its antisemitic and repressive potential. In 1968, the head of the Polish Communist Party launched a violent anti-Zionist campaign that had strong antisemitic features, preventing any contestation and support for reforms within the party and the population (Stola 2005: 284–300). Throughout the following decades, this Zionist conspiracy became an obsession and a recurring explanation that sometimes obscured the understanding of the West by the Soviet leaders and their secret services (Andrew, Mitrokhin 1999: 19; 224–5, 473).

These Soviet-originated conspiracy theories were disseminated in the West, among the communist parties. After the Conference of Szklarska Poręba in September 1947, during which the Cominform was created, the Soviet Union turned to communist parties in the West, seeking to provoke greater conflict and a more dramatic and conspiracist view of their domestic political situation (Procacci *et al.* 1994). In Italy and France, the communist parties endorsed a conspiracy theory first targeting Trotskyists, corporate trusts and far-right organisations and that, after 1948, expanded to greater proportions and comprised all other political parties and the states of the Western bloc (including Yugoslavia). Thanks to their unrivalled propaganda machine, communists relentlessly promoted the idea of a 'governmental conspiracy', but the comparative political isolation of these parties meant that their ideas did not have significant impact (Girard 2012: 129–304).

The Soviet Union also tried to propagate some ad hoc conspiracy theories dedicated to weakening the Western bloc. The K.G.B. in particular performed 'active measures', i.e. disinformation campaigns aimed at spreading conspiracy theories around the world, notably about the Kennedy assassination (Andrew, Mitrokhin 1999: 225–30). Still discussed are the allegations, supported by the Soviet Union, about the use of biological weapons by the U.S.A. during the Korean War; this germ warfare suspicion continues to produce heavily contradictory works, fuelling the controversy and vivid accusations from North Korea to this day. Quite similar was the disinformation campaign launched in 1983 by the Soviets that claimed that the A.I.D.S. pandemic had been provoked by a U.S. biological weapons research programme (Romerstein 2001; Boghardt 2009; Jeppsson 2017); the impact of this campaign remains notable today (Nattrass 2012).

## The rise of anti-elite conspiracy theories in Western Europe

These Soviet-originated narratives did not have a significant impact on Western societies, and, by contrast with the Soviet bloc, state-sponsored conspiracy theories arguably had less impact on the public sphere in the West. After the 1950s, fewer political movements developed long-lasting or consistent conspiratorial speech; the détente of the Cold War and the progressive integration of communist parties into domestic politics reduced the importance of conspiracy theories in communist propaganda as well as the related fear of a communist conspiracy.

New kinds of anti-establishment conspiracy theories progressively emerged from the 1970s, often drawing on some unusual event, such as the suspicious death of a high-profile personality. In 1979, the body of a French minister, Robert Boulin, was found in a pond and, despite evidence of suicide, his family, as well as some journalists, began to spread the idea of a murder linked to the misappropriation of money by his political party in the 1980s. In the U.K., the

1984 assassination of the antinuclear activist Hilda Murrell led to conspiracy theories accusing the British Security Service, publicly supported by a Labour M.P. At the very end of the century, the death of Princess Diana in Paris in 1997 also resulted in numerous conspiracy theories claiming her death was not an accident and putting the blame on the British Royal Family.

The shooting of Olof Palme, prime minister of Sweden, took place in Stockholm in 1986, but, despite a trial, the uncertainty about the murderer and his motives became the source of various conspiracy theories, blaming figures and organisations as diverse as the Yugoslav security service to a South African spy. In 1987, in West Germany, the suspicious death of Uwe Barschel, a prominent Christian Democrat politician, gave rise to several conspiracy theories including, among others, the Mossad.

In Italy, the kidnapping and assassination of the prominent Christian Democrat and former Prime Minister, Aldo Moro, by the Red Brigades in 1978 gave birth to many and sometimes very elaborate conspiracy theories, which are still continuing today. An enduring theory involves the then leader of the Christian Democracy party manipulating the Red Brigades to kill Aldo Moro, who was working to establish ties with the Communist Party. The most dramatic event was the 'Ustica massacre', the crash of an Italian passenger plane off the coast of Sicily in 1980, which caused 81 deaths. Whether it was due to a terrorist bomb or missile shot is still debated, but this later hypothesis became the grounds of a conspiracy theory based on a N.A.T.O. Air Force incident that was covered up by the Italian authorities. Conspiracy theories even hit the Vatican through the Estermann case, a murder involving a Swiss Guard in 1998, which ever since has been the focus of various conspiracist publications.

In the end, these post-war conspiracy theories, rather than a social category or a defined political movement, targeted governments and the political elite, suspected to be the accomplices of covert organisations such as Freemasonry, as denounced by British investigative books and television documentaries (Önnerfors 2017: 5–6, 29–30). More often, these groups were supposed to be the domestic and foreign secret services, particularly – and inevitably – the C.I.A. This suspicion towards the secret service was sometimes even shared at the highest office. In 1977, British Labour Prime Minister Harold Wilson accused the security service of his own country of spying on him. Despite the support of a 1987 book by a former MI5 agent, there was in fact no real evidence of such a conspiracy.

## The renewal of world conspiracy theories in the pre-9/11 era

The military interventions of the U.S.A. during the 1990s renewed conspiracy theories related to covert U.S. action and international organisations such as the Bilderberg Group and the Trilateral Commission. Developed in the U.S.A., these conspiracy theories combined with the New World Order grand-conspiracy narratives of a coming one-world government. For example, *Poker Menteur*, a Marxist book published in Belgium in 1998, developed a conspiracy theory that the U.S. military intervention in Yugoslavia was the result of a capitalist plot enabled by the mainstream media spreading deceitful narratives. In Serbia, the U.S. military intervention has sometimes been interpreted as a conspiracy of Bilderberg and the Jews (Byford, Billig 2001).

These anti-Western global-elite conspiracy theories mix historical and contemporary elements, until they are becoming as heterogeneous as catch-all theories. In France, the roots of far-right conspiracy beliefs in an international technocracy including the Trilateral Commission and the Bilderberg Group can be retraced to the synarchy conspiracy theory of the 1940s (Dard 1998: 156–70), while Holocaust denier Robert Faurisson supported his claims by referring to the Zionist conspiracy, with reference to *The Protocols* in particular. Due to transnational networks and supports, this conspiracy theory spread all over the world and amalgamated into the melting pot of the New World Order conspiracy (Jamin 2009: 64–6; Taguieff 2013). The most extravagant conspiracy theory to date emerged in the U.K. in the 1990s, thanks to David Icke, which combined a large number of disparate elements, including old narratives such as the Illuminati and *The Protocols*, and a postmodern obsession with the New World Order and extraterrestrial (reptilian) entities.

But it should be noted that in the late twentieth century these conspiracy theories and the groups supporting them remained marginal, as they were unsupported by the firepower of global social networks. After 2001, many of the conspiracy theories related to the suspicious deaths of high-profile personalities saw a resurgence of interest due to publications and documentaries riding the wave of the post-9/11 era. This revival was also noticeable in Russia, where the Dyatlov Pass incident of 1959 received increasing public attention after the collapse of the Soviet Union.

Indeed, the denunciation of conspiracy in post-war Western Europe in the public sphere, and especially in public political debate, remained a self-disqualifying argument rather than a claim that might be taken seriously. An analysis of British parliamentary debates during the second half of the twentieth century shows a decline in already sporadic conspiracist statements and conspiracy discourse (McKenzie-McHarg, Fredheim 2017); an observation which has parallels in other Western democracies.

This observation is not applicable to Eastern Europe and Russia (Yablokov 2018), which have seen a renewal of antisemitic conspiracy theories (Patai 1996: 48; Wistrich 2010), and, to a lesser extent, Italy. A recent scientific survey reveals that conspiracy theories are particularly widespread in Italy (Mancosu, Vassallo et al. 2017) compared to neighbouring states; Italy could be considered 'a land of conspiracy', which has seen the acceptance of the popular neologism '*dietrologia*', i.e. the science of hidden facts (Fortichiari 2007). An examination of the press reveals that, during the 1980s and 1990s, even the most prominent newspapers repeatedly used the term 'conspiracy' (Danesi 2001), revealing the extent to which the conspiracist perspective infused political discourse; indeed, since the 1990s, a kind of 'secret history' has flourished, often involving conspiracy theories, by widely read authors such as Giorgio Galli or Sergio Flamini.

The significance of conspiracy theories in Italy could be explained by the historical and political Italian 'anomaly' of the past. Renzo di Felice sees the legacy of the fascist regime as the 'double State', meaning the parallel institutions controlled by the far right to influence and undermine the newly created Republic. This 'double State' was suspected to be the source of the deadliest wave of far-right terrorism that struck the country during the 1960s to 1980s. This violence, added to the attempted coup d'état of Valerio Borghese in 1970, the left-wing terrorism culminating with the assassination of Aldo Moro and the discovery of the seditious agencies of the P2 Masonic lodge in 1981, have contributed to narratives of the conspiratorial nature of the Italian Republic (Rayner 2008). The long-lasting interference of the C.I.A., the pervasive influence of the Catholic Church and the corruption of the mafia also give weight to the idea of a 'controlled democracy' in which decisions are made behind the scenes. In this context, the disclosure of the Gladio operation in 1990 (a modest Cold War stay-behind organisation) fuelled conspiracy theories in Italy, whereas it went by relatively unnoticed in most parts of Europe (Coco 2015).

## Conclusion

The significance of conspiracy theories in Europe during the twentieth century depends a lot on the political situation, broadly fitting with geography. The democratic countries of Western

Europe were not immune to beliefs in conspiracy, but conspiracy theories were endorsed by extremist organisations from both sides of the political spectrum, although generally more often by the minorities. It was in a context of war (interstate war, civil war or even the Cold War) with existing enemies that conspiracies were most credible and accepted by the public sphere, with outbreaks of spy-fever or scapegoating.

In Central and Eastern Europe, where authoritarian states, dictatorships and totalitarian regimes ruled for a large part of the century, conspiracy theories were very often top-down official discourses, spread within society through long-lasting and consistent propaganda. The case of Nazi and Soviet totalitarian states that shared 'theories of conspiracy, phobias of encirclement, the fear of "fifth columns"' (Geyer, Fitzpatrick 2009: 414) underlines the fact that conspiracy theories were a twofold phenomenon. They were a political belief thriving on state-sanctioned Manichean ideology and the pre-existing diegesis of 'imagined wars' against peoples, social categories and foreign powers. They were also used as a political tool, enabling totalitarian regimes to create a narrative of victimhood and assuming a defensive posture legitimating the exercise of violence against real or supposed enemies. From this perspective, the real state of war did not create but rather intensified the fear of conspiracies and the violence that it justified.

Beyond this broad divide between democracies and dictatorships that paralleled to a large extent the one between Western and Eastern Europe, the fate of diverse conspiracy theories diverged. One conspiracy theory appeared to be so strongly embedded into society and culture that it contaminated all other conspiratorial narratives, especially in Eastern Europe. Quite apart from Nazi ideology, the Jewish world conspiracy theory proved to be ubiquitous: Crucial in the political discourse of many nationalists, it also reappeared under the guise of a Zionist conspiracy in the post-war Soviet bloc, and survived not only de-Stalinisation, but also the end of the Soviet Union.

In Western democratic countries, conspiracy theories followed a trajectory similar to the conclusions drawn by Michael Butter (2014) about the U.S.A. Indeed, from the 1970s, a new form of anti-authoritarian conspiracy theories emerged, denouncing government agencies of the ruling elite of apparently peaceful democracies. First limited to explaining isolated events such as suspicious murders or accidents, those conspiracy theories progressively developed into superconspiracy theories (Barkun 2013) involving apparently outdated protagonists as well as post-war free-trade organisations and allied foreign states (in the first instance, the U.S.A.). The spread of the New World Order conspiracy theory during the 1990s was the result of transnational contacts and reciprocal influences between the U.S.A. and Europe.

This evolution has certainly contributed to the current conception of conspiracy theories in the West as the grass-roots discourse of innocuous, if not laughable, marginal groups or individuals fighting mainstream narratives and trying to find meaning in a disruptive and confusing world (Byford 2011: 129–33). But history reminds us that conspiracy theories were deeply rooted political beliefs – and evidence suggests that they still are (Uscinski et al. 2016). The past century also teaches us that conspiracy theories could be mainstream, official and normative narratives, established on a set of strong ideological dogmas and certainties and used to fuel victimhood – a weapon of mass crimes in the hands of ruthless and paranoid rulers.

## References

Andrew, C. (2009) *The defence of the realm: the authorized history of MI5*, London: Penguin Books.
Andrew, C. (2018) *The secret world: a history of intelligence 2018*, New Haven: Yale University Press.
Andrew, C. and Mitrokhin, V. (1999) *The sword and the shield: the Mitrokhin archive and the secret history of the KGB*, New York: Basic Books.

Azadovskii, K. and Egorov, B. (2002) 'From Anti-Westernism to Anti-Semitism', *Journal of Cold War Studies*, 4(1): 66–80.
Barkun, M. (2013) *A culture of conspiracy: apocalyptic visions in contemporary America*, 2nd edn, Berkeley, CA: University of California Press.
Barnes, S.A. (2011) *Death and redemption: the Gulag and the shaping of Soviet society*, Princeton: Princeton University Press.
Bauerkämper, A. and Rossoliński-Liebe, G. (eds.) (2017) *Fascism without borders*, New York: Berghahn Books.
Bennett, G. (2018) *The Zinoviev letter: the conspiracy that never dies*, Oxford: Oxford University Press.
Boghardt, T. (2009) 'Operation Infektion: Soviet Bloc intelligence and its AIDS disinformation campaign', *Studies in Intelligence*, 53(4): 1–24.
Brayard, F. (2012) *Auschwitz, enquête sur un complot nazi*, Paris: Le Seuil.
Brent, J. (2004) *Stalin's last crime: the plot against the Jewish doctors, 1948–1953*, New York: Harper.
Bruce, G.S. (2003) 'The prelude to nationwide surveillance in East Germany: Stasi operations and threat perceptions, 1945–1953', *Journal of Cold War Studies*, 5(2): 3–31.
Budnitskii, O. (2012) *Russian Jews between the reds and the whites, 1917–1920*, Philadelphia: University of Pennsylvania Press.
Butter, M. (2014) *Plots, designs, and schemes: American conspiracy theories from the Puritans to the present*, Berlin/Boston: de Gruyter.
Byford, J. (2011) *Conspiracy theories: a critical introduction*, London: Palgrave Macmillan.
Byford, J. and Billig, M. (2001) 'The emergence of antisemitic conspiracy theories in Yugoslavia during the war with NATO', *Patterns of Prejudice*, 35(4): 50–63.
Bytwerk, R.L. (2001) *Julius Streicher: Nazi editor of the notorious Anti-Semitic newspaper Der Stürmer*. New York: Cooper Square Press.
Bytwerk, R.L. (2015) 'Believing in "Inner Truth": the protocols of the elders of Zion in Nazi propaganda, 1933–1945', *Holocaust and Genocide Studies*, 29(2): 212–29.
Carr, E.H. (1984) *The Comintern and the Spanish Civil War*, Basingstoke: Palgrave Macmillan.
Coco, V. (2015) 'Conspiracy theories in republican Italy: the Pellegrino Report to the parliamentary commission on terrorism', *Journal of Modern Italian Studies*, 20(3): 361–76.
Cohn, N. (1967) *Warrant for Genocide*, New York: Harper & Row.
Conquest, R. (1986) *The Harvest of Sorrow*, New York: Oxford University Press.
Conquest, R. (1989) *Stalin and the murder of Kirov*, New York/Oxford: Oxford University Press.
Danesi, M. (2001) *Complotto, congiura, cospirazione: l'uso politico della teorie cospiratorie nei quotidiani italiani*, unpublished thesis, University of Sienna.
Dard, O. (1998) *La synarchie: le mythe du complot permanent*, Paris: Perrin.
Davies, S. (1997) *Popular opinion in Stalin's Russia*, Cambridge: Cambridge University Press.
Fitzpatrick, S. (1979) 'Stalin and the making of a new elite, 1928–1939', *Slavic Review*, 38(3): 377–402.
Fortichiari, A. (2007) 'Italia, terra di complotti', in J. McConnochie and R. Tudge (eds.) *Complotti e cospirazioni*, Milan: Antonio Vallardi Editore.
Gellately, R. (2001) *Backing Hitler: consent and coercion in Nazi Germany*, Oxford: Oxford University Press.
Gellately, R. (2013) *Stalin's Curse: battling for communism in war and Cold War*, Oxford: Oxford University Press.
Gerwarth, R. (2016) *The vanquished*, London: Penguin Books.
Gerwarth, R. and Horne, J. (2012) 'Bolshevism as fantasy: fear of revolution and counter-revolutionary violence, 1917–1923', in R. Gewarth and J. Horne (eds.) *War in peace: paramilitary violence in Europe after the Great War*, Oxford: Oxford University Press.
Getty, J.A. (1985) *Origins of the Great Purges*, Cambridge: Cambridge University Press.
Getty, J.A. and Naumov, O.V. (1999) *The road to terror*, New Haven: Yale University Press.
Geyer, M. and Fitzpatrick, S. (eds.) (2009) *Beyond totalitarianism: Stalinism and Nazism compared*, Cambridge: Cambridge University Press.
Girard, P. (2012) 'Les complots politiques en France et en Italie de la fin de la Seconde Guerre mondiale à la fin des années 1950', unpublished thesis, European University Institute, Florence.
Goldman, W.Z. (2007) *Terror and democracy in the age of Stalin*, Cambridge: Cambridge University Press.
Goldman, W.Z. (2011) *Inventing the enemy: denunciation and terror in Stalin's Russia*, Cambridge: Cambridge University Press.
Guy, S. (1993) '"High treason" (1951): Britain's Cold War fifth column', *Historical Journal of Film, Radio and Television*, 13(1): 35–47.

Hagemeister, M. (2011) 'The Protocols of the Elders of Zion in court: the Bern trials, 1933–1937' in E. Webman (ed.) *The global impact of 'The Protocols of the Elders of Zion'*, London/New York: Routledge, pp. 241–53.
Harris, J. (2008) *The split in Stalin's secretariat, 1939–1948*, Plymouth: Lexington Books.
Harris, J. (2016) *The great fear: Stalin's terror of the 1930s*, Oxford: Oxford University Press.
Heathorn, S. (2007) '"A Great Grey Dawn for the Empire": great war conspiracy theory, the British state and the "Kitchener Film" (1921–1926)', *War & Society*, 26(2): 51–71.
Herf, J. (2006) *The Jewish enemy: Nazi propaganda during World War II and the Holocaust*, Cambridge: Harvard University Press.
Jamin, J. (2009) *L'imaginaire du complot*, Amsterdam: Amsterdam University Press.
Jansen, M. (1982) *A show trial under Lenin: the trial of the Socialist revolutionaries, Moscow 1922*, The Hague: Martinus Nijhoff Publishers.
Jansen, M. and Petrov, N. (2002) *Stalin's loyal executioner: people's commissar Nikolai Ezhov, 1895–1940*, Stanford: Hoover Institution Press.
Jenks, J. (2003) 'Fight against peace? Britain and the Partisans of Peace, 1948–951', in M.F. Hopkins, M.D. Kandiah and G. Staerck (eds.) *Cold War Britain, 1945–1964: new perspectives*, London: Palgrave Macmillan.
Jeppsson, A. (2017) 'How East Germany fabricated the myth of HIV being man-made', *Journal of the International Association of Providers of AIDS Care*, 16(6): 519–22.
Kellogg, M. (2005) *The Russian roots of Nazism: white émigrés and the making of national Socialism, 1917–1945*, Cambridge: Cambridge University Press.
Kershaw, I. (2008) *Hitler, the Germans, and the final solution*, New Haven/London: Yale University Press.
Khlevniuk, O.V. (2004) *The History of the Gulag*, New Haven/London: Yale University Press.
Kirschenbaum, L.A. (2015) *International communism and the Spanish Civil War: solidarity and suspicion*, New York: Cambridge University Press.
Knight, P. (2003) *Conspiracy theories in American history: an encyclopedia*, Santa-Barbara: ABC-CLIO.
Mancosu, M., Vassallo, S. and Vezzoni, C. (2017) 'Believing in conspiracy theories: evidence from an exploratory analysis of Italian survey data', *South European Society and Politics*, August.
McDermott, K. and Agnew, J. (1996) *The Comintern: a history of international communism from Lenin to Stalin*, London: Palgrave Macmillan Press.
McKenzie-McHarg, A. and Fredheim, R. (2017) 'Cock-ups and slap-downs: a quantitative analysis of conspiracy rhetoric in the British Parliament 1916–2015', *Historical Methods: A Journal of Quantitative and Interdisciplinary History*, 50(3): 156–69.
Michlic, J.B. (2008) *Poland's threatening other: the image of the Jew from 1880 to the present*, Lincoln: University of Nebraska Press.
Monier, F. (1995) 'L'apparition du complot communiste en France (1920–1932)', unpublished thesis, Université Paris X Nanterre.
Monier, F. (1998) *Le complot dans la république*, Paris: La Découverte.
Münch, P. (2008) 'Le pouvoir de l'ombre: l'imaginaire du complot durant la Révolution Française 1789–1801', unpublished thesis, EHESS Paris.
Nattrass, N. (2012) *The AIDS conspiracy: science fights back*, New York: Columbia University Press.
Önnerfors, A. (2017) *Freemasonry: a very short introduction*, Oxford: Oxford University Press.
Panayi, P. (1988) '"The hidden hand": British myths about German control of Britain during the first world war', *Immigrants & Minorities: Historical Studies in Ethnicity, Migration and Diaspora*, 7(3): 253–72.
Patai, R. (1996) *The Jews of Hungary: history, culture, psychology*, Detroit: Wayne State University Press.
Pauley, B. (1992) *From prejudice to persecution: a history of Austrian Anti-Semitism*, Chapel Hill: University of North Carolina Press.
Payne, S.G. (2004) *The Spanish Civil War, the Soviet Union, and communism*, New Haven/London: Yale University Press.
Pinkus, B. (1988) *The Jews of the Soviet Union: the history of a national minority*, Cambridge: Cambridge University Press.
Pipes, D. (1997) *Conspiracy: how the paranoid style flourishes and where it comes from*, New York: Simon & Schuster.
Procacci, G., Adibekov, G. and di Biagio, A. (1994) *The Cominform minutes of the three conferences 1947/1948/1949*, Milano: Fondazione Giangiacomo Feltrinelli.
Raleigh, D.J. (2002) *Experiencing Russia's civil war: politics, society, and revolutionary culture in Saratov, 1917–1922*, Princeton/Oxford: Princeton University Press.

Rayner, H. (2008) 'Les théories du complot dans les interprétations du terrorisme en Italie: la prégnance du point de vue cryptologique', in G. Gargiulo and O. Seul (eds.) *Terrorismes: l'Italie et l'Allemagne à l'épreuve des 'années de plomb' (1970–1980): réalités et représentations du terrorisme*, Paris: Michel Houdiard Editeur.

Redles, D. (2012) 'The turning Point: the Protocols of the Elders of Zion and the eschatological war between Aryans and Jews', in R. Landes and S.E. Katz (eds.) *The paranoid apocalypse: a hundred-year retrospective on the Protocols of the Elders of Zion*, New York: New York University Press.

Reinharz, J. and Shavit, Y. (2018) *The road to September 1939: Polish Jews, Zionists, and the Yishuv on the eve of World War II*, Waltham: Brandeis University Press.

Rittersporn, G.T. (1993) 'The omnipresent conspiracy: on Soviet imagery of politics and social relations in the 1930s', in J.A. Getty and R.D. Manning (eds.) *Stalinist terror: new perspectives*, Cambridge: Cambridge University Press.

Romerstein, H. (2001) 'Disinformation as a KGB weapon in the Cold War', *Journal of Intelligence History*, 1(1): 54–67.

Rubenstein, J. and Naumov, V. (2001) *Stalin's secret pogrom: the postwar inquisition of the Jewish anti-fascist committee*, New Haven/London: Yale University Press.

Ruiz, J. (2005) *Franco's justice: repression in Madrid after the Spanish Civil War*, Oxford: Oxford University Press.

Ruiz, J. (2011) 'Fighting the international conspiracy: the Francoist Persecution of Freemasonry, 1936–1945', *Politics, Religion & Ideology*, 12(2): 179–96.

Santamaria, Y. (2006) *Le Parti de l'ennemi?*, Paris: Armand Colin.

Seidman, M. (2011) *The victorious counterrevolution*, Madison: Wisconsin University Press.

Shearer, D R. and Khaustov V. (2015) *Stalin and the Lubianka*, New Haven: Yale University Press.

Southworth, H.R. (2002) *Conspiracy and the Spanish Civil War*, London: Routledge.

Stola, D. (2005) 'Fighting against the shadow: the Anti-Zionist campaign of 1968', in R. Blobaum (ed.) *Antisemitism and its opponents in modern Poland*, Ithaca: Cornell University Press, pp. 284–300.

Taguieff, P.A. (2004) *Les Protocoles des Sages de Sion*, Paris: Berg International-Fayard.

Taguieff, P.A. (2013) *Court traité de complotologie*, Paris: Mille et une nuits.

Uscinski, J.E., Klofstad, C. and Atkinson, M.D. (2016) 'What drives conspiratorial beliefs? the role of informational cues and predispositions', *Political Research Quarterly*, 69(1):1–15.

Uscinski, J.E. and Parent, J.M. (2014) *American conspiracy theories*, New York: Oxford University Press.

Waddington, L. (2007) *Hitler's Crusade*, London: Tauris Academic Studies.

Werth, N. (2003) 'The mechanism of a mass crime: the great terror in the Soviet Union, 1937–1938', in R. Gellately and B. Kiernan (eds.) *The specter of genocide mass murder in historical perspective*, Cambridge: UK: Cambridge University Press.

Werth, N. and Moullec, G. (1994) *Rapports secrets soviétiques, 1921–1991: la société russe dans les documents confidentiels*, Paris: Gallimard.

Whitewood, P. (2015) *The Red Army and the Great Terror*, Lawrence: University Press of Kansas.

Wistrich, R. (2010) *A lethal obsession: Anti-Semitism from antiquity to the global Jihad*, New York: Random House.

Yablokov, I. (2018) *Fortress Russia: conspiracy theories in the Post-Soviet world*, Cambridge: Polity Press.

# 5.5
# CONSPIRACY THEORIES IN PUTIN'S RUSSIA
## The case of the 'New World Order'

*Ilya Yablokov*

## Introduction

On 17 January 1991, U.S. President George Bush gave a televised speech in which he announced the military operation in Iraq:

> We have before us the opportunity to forge for ourselves and for future generations a new world order – a world where the rule of law, not the law of the jungle, governs the conduct of nations. When we are successful – and we will be – we have a real chance at this new world order, an order in which a credible United Nations can use its peacekeeping role to fulfil the promise and vision of the UN's founders.
> *(Bush 1991)*

The speech was meant to symbolise the end of the Cold War and reflected the new state of global affairs in which the U.S.A., as sole superpower, should play a bigger role than it had done in the past. Yet Bush's messianic claim for the United Nations has been perceived by some Americans with great suspicion: In their view, for the first time in decades, their leader admitted his participation in a global conspiracy aimed at building a New World Order which would strip the U.S.A. of sovereignty and put it under U.N. control. These ideas, which had been brewing for some time amongst the American far right, seemed to receive confirmation after Bush's speech (Barkun 2006: 62).

In the Soviet Union, Mikhail Gorbachev's democratic changes had dramatically undermined the decaying political regime, and its collapse in 1991, just a few years later, opened the gates to a variety of conspiratorial ideas. Among these, the notion of the New World Order quickly found its supporters and spread through various communities within the Russian conspiracy milieu (see Bratich 2008). Within the post-Soviet Russian context, the notion of a global order, with one centre of power, echoed concerns over the incontestability of the leadership of the U.S.A. in the world and its challenge to Russia's place in international affairs. Since 1991, various concepts of the New World Order conspiracy have been developing across the Russian political spectrum and successfully conquering, on the one hand, so called patriotic, pro-Kremlin authors, and, on the other, far right antisemitic activists critical of Kremlin policies.

This chapter analyses the evolution of the New World Order conspiracy theory in post-Soviet Russia: It aims to provide a comparative analysis of the theory both in the U.S. context and in that of post-Soviet Russia, in order to highlight the peculiarities of the post-Soviet Russian conspiracy culture, and to consider its functions in Russian politics and society. I argue that the astonishing popularity of these ideas lies in the very nature of the New World Order conspiracy theory, which has turned out to be equally popular in the U.S.A. and in Russia in the aftermath of the Cold War.

As Barkun argues (2006: 64), the concept of the New World Order attained a particular popularity in the 1990s due to the convenience of bringing together diverse conspiracy theories into one metanarrative structure. The grand plan of the one world government is capable of including all events that are of interest to conspiracy theorists, and it allows for the shifting of focus from global politics to the domestic agenda. In the Russian context, this means that the New World Order conspiracy theory is able to explain the collapse of the regime in 1991 as an act carried out by a powerful external force, and to make sense of a new reality in which millions of people lost their jobs, savings and even lives.

Second, as Timothy Melley observes, conspiracy theories are a manifestation of agency panic: 'the intense anxiety about an apparent loss of autonomy and self-control, the conviction that one's actions are being controlled by someone else, that one has been "constructed" by powerful external agents' (2000: 12). The sense of losing agency in the Russian context overlapped with the collapse of statehood, national identity and existing social institutions, which affected millions of Russians. At the same time, politicians and intellectuals projected their anxieties about the loss of international influence and increasing dependence on Western financial help onto the sinister global power brokers (the so called *mirovaia zakulisa*, i.e. the global cabal).

The popularity of the concept can also be explained by the convenience it has provided for various political and social actors in Russia. The accusation of working for the New World Order is a powerful tool with which to strip the opponent, either on the left or the right of the political spectrum, of political legitimacy. The possibility that one was inadvertently working for foreign plotters fed the suspicion of subversion popular in the Cold War period, and so helped to perpetuate the rich conspiracy culture that already existed in the Soviet Union.

Intriguingly, opponents of the regime often used the same claim to delegitimise the Kremlin's actions and to mobilise supporters against its current policies. The claim that the president or the government were implicated in a plot against the people has provided a prevailing idea among the far-right with which to interpret the Kremlin's domestic activities.

## New World Order conspiracy: An overview

In 1991, the Reverend Pat Robertson, a businessman and a priest, published *The New World Order*. Robertson explained that several think tanks (such as the Trilateral Commission and the Council on Foreign Relations) and U.S. political leaders had brought the country under the control of a group of highly influential individuals. Behind that group, Robertson saw the shadow of the Illuminati – a secret society founded by Adam Weishaupt in the eighteenth century in Bavaria. The Illuminati were disbanded in 1784, but an imagined Illuminati order had supposedly outlived the founding organisation. Robertson claimed that the shadow of the Illuminati could be found behind all of the biggest political events since the eighteenth century: Revolutions, financial crises and wars (Porter 2005).

Robertson's take on the Illuminati was based on a premise that they were atheists, and that this was a clear sign of their work with the devil. The Christian fundamentalist ideology promoted by Robertson saw human history as a battle between God and Evil, in which the U.S.A.

would be the saviour of the world. This messianic role on the part of the U.S.A. in global history is one of the pillars of U.S. conspiracy culture. Throughout the nineteenth and twentieth centuries, U.S. exceptionalism encouraged individuals to look for some malign plot aimed at destroying the nation, and bred distrust in both the government for failing to realise its prophetic role, and in random actors who were supposedly intent on diverting the U.S. leadership from the path of Christianity and freedom (Goldberg 2001). For that reason, the active involvement of the U.S.A. in foreign affairs, and its membership in international organisations and trade deals, dealt a blow to American isolationism, led to further loss of independence, and opened the gates to the country's foes.

The twentieth century was the most crucial historical period in this respect: The U.S. promotion of global democracy and its standoff with the 'atheist' Soviet bloc provided a clear, dualistic view of the world that is a traditional feature of conspiracy theories. As Paul Boyer demonstrates, the narratives of the Cold War were successfully appropriated by the discourses of American Christian fundamentalists who perceived the Soviet Union as the Antichrist (Boyer 1992).

Since the beginning of the Cold War, the fear of being infiltrated by communists was key to the U.S. far right. The era of McCarthyism demonstrated how keen conspiracy theorists are on show trials. One can find a lot in common between General Prosecutor Andrei Vyshinskii's public accusations against Stalin's enemies and Joe McCarthy's ranting about the communists who infiltrated the State Department (for more on the Soviet campaign against 'people's enemies', see Harris 2016). In the time of the Cold War, these two cultures of conspiracy – American and Soviet – have officially been fed by the official ideological premises of fighting against the ideological rival. Robert Welch, the leader of the far-right John Birch Society, presented communist Russia as the embodiment of the global power of the Illuminati, 'a gigantic conspiracy to enslave mankind, an increasingly successful conspiracy controlled by determined, cunning, and utterly ruthless gangsters, willing to use any means to achieve its end' (Welch 2016). This plan included the Council on Foreign Relations, the Trilateral Commission, the Bilderbergers and the U.N. as steps towards the creation of a global government. These organisations were seen as promoters of socialism in the capitalist U.S.A., which were meant to destroy its foundations. The ultimate goal of the plotters was the creation of 'totalitarian socialism', which would achieve total control of the world population (Cooper 1995).

Political figures such as Henry Kissinger, as well as presidents from both parties, were presented as both promoters of the global plot against the U.S.A., and as ragdolls in the hands of faceless plotters, famous bankers such as the Rothschilds and the Rockefellers. Furthermore, the Federal Reserve system was supposedly in the hands of the plotters and so was helping to keep U.S. citizens in a state of financial slavery. By means of deflation and inflation, the plotters intended to destroy the 'God-given, inalienable, "self-evident" right to private property' (Epperson 1990). As Gary Allen (2013) described it, the international financial elite ('the Insiders') took control of the U.S. financial system, jeopardised U.S. isolationism by means of the country's involvement in the League of Nations and ensured that the Bolshevik government in the Soviet Union was a constant threaten to the U.S.A.

Ironically, the collapse of the Soviet Union in 1991 did not bring fears of a global conspiracy to an end. On the contrary, these fears reached an intergalactic level (Icke 1999). On a more mundane level, Bush's famous remark, which placed 'new world order' and the U.N. in the same paragraph, became the starting point in a hunt for more evidence of a developing conspiracy against the U.S.A. As Barkun notes (2006: 64), the New World Order conspiracy became a convenient umbrella concept when discussing U.S. domestic politics and the country's growing socio-economic problems. It was old enough to allow the claim of legitimacy in the public sphere, and yet vague enough to make possible a combination of critiques of financial elites, the globalisation of economy, international organisations, philanthropic foundations and active U.S. involvement in conflicts beyond its borders.

It was precisely the U.N. and its potentially bigger role in solving conflicts in the post-Cold War era that concerned many in the far-right U.S. milieu, since the proliferation of such big international organisations was a clear example of the stripping of the U.S.A. of its sovereignty and military power:

> Our nation is plunging headlong toward 'convergence' and the eventual 'merger'.... Our nation – along with the other nations of the world – is being steadily drawn into the tightening noose of 'interdependence'. Our political and economic systems are being intertwined and are increasingly being subjected to control by the United Nations and its adjunct international organizations. Unless this process can be stopped, it will culminate in the creation of the omnipotent global governance and the 'end to nationhood'.
>
> (Jasper 1992)

In the post-Cold War era, the New World Order theory has evolved into a sharp and aggressive criticism of the global political and financial elite that supposedly uses all means available to accomplish its plan to destroy ordinary people. Climate change and vaccines are presented as the next step towards the extermination of 80 per cent of the population and its replacement with robot technologies (Jones 2007). The populist criticism of modern capitalism made by conspiracy theorists combines moral criticism traditional to Christian fundamentalists with secular criticism of political and financial institutes. The rise of antisemitism both in Europe, the U.S.A. and Russia poses new challenges for the scholars to deal with this hatred on a global scale (see Judaken 2008; Taguieff 2004; Yablokov 2019). Terms such as 'diaboligarchy' provide the perfect context for the ultimate rejection of elites and opens the floor to all manner of speculations that would be accepted by various ideological communities (Kay 2011). Thanks to the rapid development of communication technologies, the spread of ideas from the U.S. conspiracy culture has allowed European and Russian conspiracy theorists to perceive, reconsider and reproduce these ideas, giving them a local twist.

## Post-Soviet Russian conspiracy culture: Enemies within and outside

The collapse of the Soviet Union in 1991 has brought incredible changes to the post-Soviet Russian culture of conspiracy theories. The abrupt end of the state came in December 1991, when then president of Russia Boris Yeltsin and his colleagues from Ukraine and Belarus signed the Belovezha accords (see Plokhy 2014). However, the trauma of the collapsed state became the foundation of the conspiracy culture that is centred on the notion of the lost state greatness and the assumption that the West (namely the U.S.A.) is behind the Soviet collapse.

At the beginning of the 1990s, the notion of the Soviet collapse and the alleged agents of the West became a useful populist tool of power relations (Fenster 2008) among the nationalist opposition and the ruling Kremlin elites. The Kremlin ruled by Yeltsin was seen as the agent of the U.S.A., whose goal was to destroy the population and abandon Russia's natural riches and military prowess to the U.S.A. The opposition successfully benefitted from the neoliberal economic reforms initiated by Yeltsin for Russia's economic recovery. The outcome of these reforms was mass poverty and the loss of jobs among millions of Russians who shared negative attitudes to Yeltsin's policies. Consequently, many of those who have been affected by the reforms became the support base of anti-Western conspiracy theories aimed at Yeltsin. The high point in this battle became the attempt to impeach Yeltsin in 1999 by accusing Yeltsin of destroying the Soviet Union and letting a small 'cabal' of 200 rich families loot the economy and destroy those remnants of the population that remembered prosperous life in the Soviet Union (Iliukhin 2017). The impeachment failed, but the attempt to use populist conspiracy theories in the parliament caused serious panic among the Kremlin elites (Yablokov 2018). As a result, in the 2000s, the notion of anti-Western conspiracy theories was turned into the key instrument of the governmental tool box to put the opposition under control.

Anti-Western conspiracy theories became part and parcel of Putin's authoritarian turn: Both domestic and external opponents from 2004 onwards started to be seen by the pro-Kremlin elites as plotters that aim at destroying Putin's regime. The wave of colour revolutions in the post-Soviet states in the mid-2000s have put into question the safe transition of power from Putin to his successor in 2008. As a result, the Kremlin initiated the campaign to search for internal enemies allegedly connected to the West. These 'enemies' included Russian liberal opposition and Russian nationalists – the two groups that were in power to question Kremlin's control of the state. After the 2008 transfer of power to Putin's successor, Dmitry Medvedev, the scale of political paranoia in the country went down slightly but became useful again when the Kremlin faced two major political challenges: The wave of street protests in 2011–2012 and the annexation of Crimea in 2014. The former required an aggressive response to suppress the opposition and the people who went to the streets expressing their dissatisfaction with the election's outcome have been branded 'puppets' in the hands of the West. The latter demanded popular mobilisation to support the Kremlin's fairly illegitimate actions abroad and hence all resources were used to achieve at least rhetorical unity within the nation. Anyone who opposed the annexation of Crimea has been automatically excluded from the community of 'true, patriotic Russians' and his/her loyalty to the state was put into question.

What is important is how the Kremlin supported and developed anti-Western conspiracy discourse in the 2000s. Across various platforms (television, book publishing, Internet), various speakers and authors emerged who constantly reproduced anti-Western conspiracy theories. No matter what their ideological background was, many speakers had enough chances to be incorporated into the Kremlin propaganda machine and spread their very own interpretation of the Western plot against Russia (Yablokov 2018).

## The 'Mondialists' come to Russia

Aleksandr Dugin, who is widely accepted as Russia's leading conspiracy theorist of the post-Soviet period, published an article in 1992 entitled 'The ideology of the world government'. He argued that Mondialism – the French synonym of the New World Order – is based on the Western capitalist view of the global economy, promotes multiculturalism and embraces the eschatological expectation of the messiah coming to this world (Dugin 1992a). Dugin's article was a development of a previous publication. One year before, he published 'The great war of the continents', a conspiratorial manifesto that described a Manichean division of the world between the forces of the land and the sea, which he claimed had been shaping global history for centuries (Dugin 1991). Curiously, he found the inspiration for these ideas abroad.

In 1990, he made a trip to France, which proved to be an important step towards exploring the European far right and enabled him to make useful contacts with philosophers and activists, from whom he learned much about foreign conspiracy cultures (Clover 2017: 175–205). Dugin's interest in the French far right most probably explains how he learned about the New World Order and also shows the limitations of his knowledge of the U.S. conspiracy scene. In his article 'The paradigms of conspiracy', he refers to the 'mondialist' conspiracy theories and mentions predominantly French authors who see the threat of global government behind the U.S.A.

> Americanism is the starting point of mondialism, because it is precisely the USA which became the strategic and ideological center of post-industrial neo-capitalism, and it is there that the ideological implications of capitalism reached their logical end from the cultural and economic point of view.
>
> (Dugin 1995)

For Dugin, the global financial elite that promotes globalisation and the creation of single state entities (like the E.U.) is related to pro-U.S. politicians who form the world in accordance with U.S. views of a liberal economy. At the same time, Dugin argues, due to the decrease in religious beliefs, Christian fundamentalist theories of the New World Order are 'rather rare'. That certainly is not the case with U.S. conspiracy culture, in which Christian fundamentalism is one of the two main strands of the New World Order conspiracy theories (see Boyer 1992; Barkun 2006).

In the context of the collapsing Soviet bloc, the conspiracy theories critical of the U.S.-led New World Order seemed the most appropriate to Dugin, because they reflect the growing dominance of the U.S.A. in global affairs. Perestroika and Gorbachev's reforms were interpreted by Dugin as the successful realisation of the malicious plan that turned life upside-down with radical liberal reforms. The ideological core of these reforms – individualism and the technocratic approach – are the basis of the changes that the New World Order plotters want to spread across the world (Dugin 2005).

The second issue of the magazine *Elementy* ('Elements'), published in 1992, was devoted to the crisis in Yugoslavia and interpreted it as a rebellion against the New World Order and politicians promoted by global plotters:

> Instead of the peaceful entrance of the Eastern bloc to the New World Order, especially when the USSR was led by shameless mondialists and other supporters of the global government ... nations woke up ... and rebelled against Utopia, against the new global seduction, against the End of History.
>
> (Dugin 1992b)

The role of the Balkans in defining Russia's great status in world politics was crucial after 1991 (Samokhvalov 2017). Thus, the U.S. participation in the conflict in the Balkans in the early 1990s that followed a unilateral decision to invade Kuwait has been framed by Dugin as the first step towards the occupation of Russia, and the destruction both of Russia's statehood and its great power status. Any further attempts on the part of the U.S.A. to challenge Russia's power in the post-Soviet space were read in a similar way by Dugin: The U.S.A. was building the New World Order to realise its global plot against Russia (Ganapolskii, Dugin 2008).

Dugin's efforts to transplant European conspiracy culture to Russian soil have in many ways been successful and have laid the foundation for further explorations of the concept by Russian conspiracy theorists. Yet, linguistic issues (his lack of English language proficiency) limited his ability to draw a more detailed picture of the globalist plans. He vigorously promoted globalist conspiracy theories in works that the Kremlin found useful in the late 2000s. Nevertheless, Dugin did not manage to monopolise the market, and Russia's conspiratorial scene was soon filling up with numerous authors who enriched Russian conspiracy culture with U.S. ideas of the New World Order, and at times used them against the ruling political and financial elite.

## In search of Khazaria: The antisemitic undertones of the concept

In the early 1990s, Russian conspiracy culture was a repository of many antisemitic concepts. The rapid economic reforms of the 1990s, which left many people poor and disillusioned, created a fruitful ground for conspiracy mythmaking. Many observers were concerned that Russia might become the site for new grand anti-Jewish attacks, and criticised politicians for their lack of policies against the far right (Gitelman 1991). Following U.S. Christian fundamentalists, who saw the Jews as being behind the New World Order, Russian conspiracy theorists perceived the ruling elite of Russia in the 1990s as a sort of the Zionist occupational government (Bartlett, Miller 2010). Many of the leading business tycoons in the 1990s were, indeed, of Jewish origin, and this provided an argument to support antisemitic conspiracy theories and helped frame the economic reforms as a malicious plan to destroy Russia (Gidwitz 1999). This conspiratorial rhetoric in many ways helped explain the social and economic crisis post-1991 and promote the populist division of the country between the people, on the one hand, and the foreign elite imposed on the nation by the world government on the other.

It is curious to see how quickly antisemitic conspiracy theories adopted the concept of a New World Order and turned it into a new Jewish plot against Russia. Certainly, the turning point in the plotters' success was the collapse of the Soviet Union in 1991. Russia's integration into Western financial and political networks, which followed the 1991 disaster, allegedly opened the gates to Jewish conspirators and put Russia under the power of the secret cabal of the Jerusalem temple. For example, Vladimir Putin's invitation to turn Moscow into a global financial centre was interpreted unambiguously as the end of Russia's sovereignty (Katasonov 2013).

According to Oleg Platonov, the leading propagator of these theories, the satanic nature of the New World Order destroys Christianity and the moral values of spiritual people. Platonov argues that the first attempt to extinguish religious morality was made by Adam Weishaupt and the Illuminati in the eighteenth century, and since that time the plotters – the Jewish financial moguls – have been working to create a single global government. In the twentieth century, nation-states and the Christian values of the Europeans were replaced by the Zionist principles of Talmud and the power centre has shifted to financial Jewish families such as the Rothschilds and the Rockefellers (Platonov 2014: 14). It is no surprise that Platonov discovers the power centre in the U.S.A. and, following Dugin, calls the New World Order 'mondialism'. Platonov warns of the electronic control of the population through biochips and personal tax numbers, which he interprets as evil signs. The U.S. political leadership, puppets in the hands of the plotters, supposedly promotes artificial intelligence and super powerful computer technologies to achieve global control over people.

Among the fiercest Russian conspiracy theorists are the Church representatives who infused traditional religious antisemitism into the concept of the New World Order. In the 1990s, Metropolitan Ioann Snychev accused Jews of now running the global government that they had supposedly been planning for 2000 years (Snychev 1996). The fact that Russia experienced socio-economic and political problems after 1991 was explained by the messianic role the Russian state and its Church had played in global history:

> Russia, which was historically formed as the repository of Christian values, today is the main obstacle [to the destruction of religions and nation-states]. Not a single religious denomination, aside Orthodox Christianity, has sufficient spiritual power for successful resistance ... [to the] architects of the "new world order".
>
> *(Snychev 1996)*

Traditional anti-Jewish conspiracy theories popular among Russian far-right nationalists have often been incorporated into the idea of the 'Jewish state of Khazariia' – an imagined country that symbolises the Jewish conspiracy against the Russians. The idea of Khazariia has been in a process of development for 200 years, since the nineteenth century; and in the post-Soviet period it has been successfully adopted by anti-Western conspiracy theorists. It was inspired by the medieval state of Khazariia, located in the south of present-day Russia; the elite of the state professed Judaism and had a certain influence on the state of Kievan Rus, the heyday of which was in the eleventh century. Khazariia disappeared more than 1000 years ago, but, in the minds of many Russian far-right nationalists, this 'invisible' Jewish state continues to wage war against the Russians and their religion (Shnirel'man 2012).

In her book *Invisible Khazariia* (2011), Tat'iana Gracheva skilfully merges antisemitic and anti-Western conspiracy theories, in many ways repeating the Soviet propaganda tricks that saw Zionist actions behind U.S. policies. She explains that the goal of the New World Order is to eliminate Russia's statehood and the moral principles of religion, traditional family and social equality that bind Russians together. These principles define Russia's sovereignty and the global political agency that helped the nation survive. In contrast, the plotters seek to introduce same sex marriage, non-religious life principles and the cult of money. Gracheva claims that Russia's ruling elite, as well as many ordinary citizens, are paralysed by the propaganda of the West.

A peculiar detail of Gracheva's assertions is that she turns the U.S. conspiracy tradition of the New World Order upside down. In the Cold War period, Christian fundamentalists in the U.S.A. described the Soviet Union as Gog, a biblical representation of the Devil, who was intent on waging war against Christianity. This demonisation of the country's ideological opponent served as a powerful tool to keep the Christian fundamentalists mobilised (Boyer 1992: 115–52). Yet, Gracheva suggests that those evangelists who compared the Soviet Union to Satan were themselves being used as tools by Jewish plotters who wished to destroy the Soviet Union by means of a nuclear attack (201). She argues that, in the Bible, Gog and Magog had no nationality, were cosmopolitans and also had no faith in God, but the people trusted them as they perceived them to represent the oldest of the nations on the planet (206). Behind this description can be seen a clear antisemitic stereotype of the Jews, while Israel is depicted as the locus of power that controls the U.S.A., which is Russia's main adversary.

The reason for Khazariia's war against Russia is supposedly to achieve revenge for the destruction of the old Khazar state by Christian Russian tribes. The global Khazar state spreads its control through transnational companies; its cosmopolitan citizens have no nationality, just like the biblical Gog and Magog. Russia, however, is a completely different type of state, one which cherishes its spiritual values, territory and sovereignty; moreover, its citizens respect the authorities and have patriotic feelings towards the motherland. According to this line of thought, the destruction of Russia's statehood is the only way in which the global Khazar state can complete its project and realise the New World Order. The Khazars have united all of the states of the West, which have become the sole global subject of international affairs: Capitalist, satanic and faithless.

A clearly antisemitic perception of the New World Order is shared by many more authors among the far-right nationalist groups in Russia. The ease with which antisemitic authors have appropriated the new ideas shows how swiftly Western concepts can be used to criticise the West itself. Yet, the most popular combination of anti-Western ideas can be found amongst pro-Kremlin intellectuals, who have also rapidly transformed the idea of the New World Order, which originated in the U.S.A., to criticise the U.S.A.

## Sovereignty in question

In the early 1990s, when Dugin published the issue of *Elements* that was concerned with the New World Order, he included an interview with Sergei Baburin, a nationalist politician and a long-time deputy in the Russian parliament. Baburin shared an idea that was popular at the time among the Russian far right:

> After the collapse of the bipolar world the USA strives to become the sole global dictator, the only superior judge in international affairs. Do other nations need that? I am not sure. Moreover, the planetary dictatorship will eventually destroy the USA.
> *(Sokolov 1992)*

Fifteen years later, these ideas have been repeated almost word by word by the top-ranking politician in Russia:

> The unipolar world that had been proposed after the Cold War did not take place either. The history of humanity certainly has gone through unipolar periods and seen aspirations to world supremacy…. However, what is a unipolar world? However one might embellish this term, at the end of the day it refers to one type of situation, namely one centre of authority, one centre of force, one centre of decision-making. It is a world in which there is one master, one sovereign. And at the end of the day this is pernicious not only for all those within this system, but also for the sovereign itself because it destroys itself from within.
> *(Putin 2007)*

Criticism of the unipolar leadership of the U.S.A. by Russia's political leader does not just stem from the trauma of Cold War defeat; it also points to the irritation felt by the Russian elites following U.S. involvement in the domestic politics of the post-Soviet countries (Ó Beacháin, Polese 2010). The range of regime changes in the states that the Kremlin considered to be its own sphere of influence put into question the stability of Russia's political regime. Consequently, the pro-Kremlin intellectuals invented the notion of Russia as a sovereign democracy that had to resist U.S. attempts to rule the world and make up its own rules for the game. Moreover, the West, and the U.S.A. in particular, have been depicted as states driven by the interests of various elite groups, some of which share pro-Russian attitudes while others are anti-Russian. The most important issue here is the ability to construct criticism of U.S. policies by focusing on particular groups of interests among the U.S. elite. In this context, the Kremlin has managed to legitimise conspiracy theories as a valid tool with which to understand U.S. policies towards Russia, and that has helped to infuse elements of the New World Order conspiracies into Russian political discourse. That, in turn, has helped many authors of conspiracy theories to tailor their views to the political mainstream and to use foreign ideas to reinforce the notion that Russia is encircled by enemies (Yablokov 2018: 79–111).

A comparison of two works about the Soviet collapse, both written by ex-K.G.B. officers, provides an instructive example. These are Viacheslav Shironin's *Agenty perestroiki* (1995, 'Agents of perestroika') and Igor Panarin's *Pervaia Informatsionnaia Voina* (2010, 'The first information war'). The former is based on classic Cold War ideas about the war between intelligence services. The latter, written 15 years later than Shironin's book, argues that the Committee of 300, the Trilateral Commission and the Council on Foreign Relations waged war against the Soviet Union by organising subversive campaigns.

A close inspection of these two works indicates the impact that U.S. conspiracy theories about the New World Order had on Russian conspiracy culture. Shironin's ideas are mainly concerned with subversive U.S. activities aimed at global domination. He portrays Russia as a key adversary of the U.S.A., with the latter attempting to undermine the former through a highly sophisticated combination of intelligence operations. Shironin's analysis is thus reminiscent of Soviet propaganda, and its main features can be traced back to the popular culture of the Cold War period. Panarin's work, in turn, is clearly influenced by foreign literature on conspiracy theories available in Russia at that time and could even be said to function as a Russian guide to Western conspiracy theories.

In the early 2000s, Russian publishers released two titles that have often been quoted in New World Order conspiracy theories. John Coleman's *The Conspirator's Hierarchy: the Committee of 300* (2000) and Daniel Estulin's *The True Story of the Bilderberg Club* (2009); both provide detailed descriptions of the global plot. The availability of these works in Russian helped to familiarise Russian readers with the Anglo-American paradigm of the New World Order conspiracy. For instance, Panarin identified American banker David Rockefeller as a key mastermind behind the Soviet collapse; he also referred to the Committee of 300, the Council on Foreign Relations and the Trilateral Commission as the main centres of anti-Russian conspiracy in the West (2010: 154–5). However, while these organisations do play major roles in the corpus of New World Order conspiracy theories, none of the works originally published in the U.S.A. about the New World Order specifically mention Russia.

John Coleman's concepts of the New World Order serve as a means to interpret the lack of economic development in post-Soviet Russia. Though Putin is often presented in the patriotic literature as the defender of Russia's national interests, he is also portrayed as part of the Western plot against Russia. Oleg Kotolupov (2017) writes in the far-right newspaper *Zavtra* ('Tomorrow') that the current ruling elites in Russia have promised the founder of the Russian state, Boris Yeltsin, that they will ensure that Russia remains under the influence of the West. The Kremlin's strategy of economic development is supposedly aimed at the destruction of the country's ability to prosper economically, and the West does not allow Russia to modernise its economy (Kotolupov 2017).

Russia's entry into the World Trade Organization (W.T.O.) has been read by many conspiracy theorists as an extremely damaging act that has jeopardised Russia's sovereignty and will eventually destroy the Russian economy. The question as to whether Russia should join the W.T.O. was debated for more than two decades and, when this eventually happened, it was interpreted as the country's downfall. A prolific pro-Kremlin conspiracy theorist, Nikolai Starikov, protested against the W.T.O. at an early stage in his career, thereby increasing his popularity:

> The WTO is the embodiment of the world's economic globalisation. The task of the globalisers is to bring all economies into this agreement. Without Russia's involvement it is impossible to consider the process accomplished.... Imagine that someone will decide where we shall plant tomatoes and potatoes. We are not going to decide it, but an abstract man in Brussels and Washington will.
>
> *(Starikov 2012)*

Starikov's argument is very populist and is similar to arguments put forward in the E.U. countries and the U.S.A. from far-right populist politicians (Bergmann 2018: 117–19). Indeed, integration always poses a threat to individual agency (Grewal 2016: 28). In the case of Russia, these fears are tied to the economic reforms of the 1990s, which put the country under pressure by foreign monetary organisations and caused the rapid impoverishment of millions of Russians. Starikov's followers similarly explain Russia's entry into the W.T.O. as the work of 'foreign agents' inside the Russian government. They aim to turn Russia into a colony of the West and exploit its resources under the cabal of the global government, which destroyed the Soviet Union and 'enslaved' Russia by means of foreign loans (Kolomitsyn 2011).

The high point of the New World Order conspiracy against Russia is the destruction of the Russian population. The methods of extermination are very similar to those put forward by the American authors of these theories. The Russians, like other nations in the world, will be exterminated through genetically modified food, the promotion of L.G.B.T. marriages that don't produce children and through epidemics that would kill 80 per cent of the global population (Martinis09 2013). Again, Russia's messianic role in the global battle against the plotters is to be the vanguard in resistance to the U.S.-led genetic modification of the world's foods, and protection of its birth ate through anti-L.G.B.T. legislation and the promotion of 'traditional family values' (Tsar'grad TV 2018).

Russia's sovereignty is highly dependent on high oil prices and the price of foreign currencies (first and foremost, the U.S. dollar) that also are subjects of conspiratorial mythmaking. Russia's inclusion into the global political and financial networks is perceived as a sort of colonisation of Russia for economic purposes: The theory goes that this will eventually mean that the country's sole function is to be a supplier of natural resources for the global financial oligarchy, and that it will completely lose the status of global superpower. As a result, Russia will be divided into several parts to enable the easiest extraction of natural resources: Oil, gas, timber and water (Subetto 2013). Starikov explains (2009a: 22–3) that global oil prices are set at small meetings of Anglo-American financial tycoons. Moreover, the internal cabal of liberal economists pushes Russia into the hands of the New World Order by keeping Russia's savings in foreign currencies in foreign banks. Like his counterparts in the U.S.A., Starikov sees the Federal Reserve system of the U.S.A. as the centre of power in the globalists' conspiracy (2009b).

Mikhail Khazin, a former adviser to Russia's Presidential administration, and a prolific author of works on the imagined Rothschild-Rockefeller conspiracy against Russia, supports the idea that Russia should not be engaged in global financial markets, and encourages the decrease of Russia's dependence on natural resources. He warns that the global plotters control Russia by oil prices, and through Russian members of financial elites that are highly integrated into the global financial elite and hence dependent on their decisions (Rychkova 2013). Other authors warn that Russia is being attacked by the New World Order by means of international agreements to protect the environment from global warming. Vladimir Pavlenko (2012) argues that these agreements allow foreign plotters access to the country's riches and enable them to strip Russia of sovereignty. He claims that the Club of Rome, the Trilateral Commission and the U.N. control Russia's oil and gas by means of the climate agreement. 'The ecological chain of "control over natural resources – control over climate – control of food – control of people and spaces" has come to geopolitics' and turned it into an instrument of the global oligarchic New World Order; 'gas and other energy sources, including rare metals, forests, water and biological sources, will become a reason for the US military invasion of Russia'.

The focus on natural resources as the target of the New World Order in Russia is explained by the huge role oil plays in global politics. High oil prices, which were the key to Russia's economic prosperity in the 2000s, and Russia's inability to control these prices, have led to various conspiratorial interpretations that identified the U.S.A. as the centre of decision making. As demonstrated elsewhere, Russia's superrich, all of whom are loyal to the Kremlin, as well as the Kremlin itself, find it hard to recognise that the financial source of their modern state is located in Siberia, is underdeveloped technologically, cannot compete with global economies and is also largely under the control of global markets that are hard to predict.

> [Russian elites'] insecure sentiments easily mix with the conspiratorial, defensive, and person-centred understanding of how global markets and financial institutions operate. In contrast to its supposed function as harbinger of rationality and sobriety, the Russian public sphere is saturated by isolationism, misinterpretations of the global economy, and glorification of authoritarian policies.
>
> *(Etkind, Yablokov 2017)*

## Conclusion

The notion of sovereignty as the way to protect the agency of the post-Soviet political elite has resulted in the perceived globalisation and technological domination of the U.S.A. being seen as a serious threat to the political survival of Russia's elite. In post-1991 Russia, suspicion of the global political elite, which drives fear of the New World Order, has become a useful way of channelling criticism of unipolarity in international relations and has legitimised the Kremlin's authoritarian policies. Yet, the heterogeneity of the concept and the active exchange of ideas have provided much leeway for authors to develop it in all possible ways. This can be used as a tool to back the isolationist policies of the Kremlin. However, at times that are critical for the regime, such as the 1990s, this theory can seriously tarnish the Kremlin's public image and empower the opposition forces critical of the Kremlin's actions. So far, the pro-Kremlin elites are extremely skilful in keeping control of the country. However, as a populist tool that helps redistribute power among all political actors, anti-Western conspiracy theories (including the New World Order conspiracy theories) could become an important factor in the future evolution of the political regime in Russia.

## References

Allen, G. (2013) *None dare call it conspiracy*, United States: Dauphin Publications.
Barkun, M. (2006) *A culture of conspiracy: apocalyptic visions in contemporary America*, Berkeley: University of California Press.
Bartlett, J. and Miller, C. (2010) *The power of unreason: conspiracy theories, extremism and counter terrorism*, London: Demos.
Bergmann, E. (2018) *Conspiracy and populism: the politics of misinformation*, London: Palgrave.
Boyer, P. (1992) *When time shall be no more: prophecy belief in modern American culture*, Cambridge: Belknap Press.
Bratich, J. (2008) *Conspiracy panics: political rationality and popular culture*, New York: State University of New York Press.
Bush, G.W. (1991) 'President Bush announcing war against Iraq', *The history place: great speeches collection*. Available at: www.historyplace.com/speeches/bush-war.htm. [Accessed 27 December 2018.]
Clover, C. (2017) *Black wind, white snow: the rise of Russia's new nationalism*, New Haven: Yale University Press.
Coleman, J. (2000) *The conspirator's hierarchy: the committee of 300*, Lexington, MA: Global Insights.
Cooper, M.W. (1995) *Behold! A pale horse*, Moreton-in-Marsh, UK.: Windrush Publishing Services.
Dugin, A. (1991) 'The great war of the continents: the fourth political theory', *4 Political Theory*. Available at: www.4pt.su/en/content/great-war-continents. [Accessed 28 December 2018.]
Dugin, A. (1992a) 'Po kom streliaiut pushki Bukovara', *Arctogeia*, 2. Available at: http://arcto.ru/article/411. [28 December 2018.]
Dugin, A. (1992b) 'Ideologiia mirovogo pravitelstva', *Elementy*, 2. Available at: http://arcto.ru/article/409. [Accessed 28 December 2018.]

Dugin, A. (1995) 'Ideologiia "Novogo Mirovogo Poriadka"', *Istoriia propagandy*. Available at: http://propagandahistory.ru/books/Aleksandr-Dugin_Konspirologiya/10. [Accessed 28 December 2018.]

Dugin, A. (2005) 'Mondialism and anti-mondialism', *Arcto*. Available at: http://arcto.ru/article/1326. [Accessed 28 December 2018.]

Epperson, R.A. (1990) *The New World Order*, L. Cranor, A. Rubin and M. Waldman (pub.): Publius.

Estulin, D. (2009) *The True Story of the Bildelberg Club*, Walterwille, OR: Trine Day.

Etkind, A. and Yablokov, I. (2017) 'Global crises as Western conspiracies: Russian theories on oil prices and the ruble exchange rate', *Journal of Soviet and Post-Soviet Politics and Society*, 3(2): 47–85.

Fenster, M. (2008) *Conspiracy theories: secrecy and power in American culture*, Minneapolis, MN: University of Minnesota Press.

Ganapolskii, M. and Dugin, A. (2008) 'Osoboe mnenie', *Radio Ëkho Moskvy*, 8 August. Available at: www.echo.msk.ru/programs/personalno/532383-echo/. [Accessed 28 December 2018.]

Gidwitz, B. (1999) 'The role of politics in contemporary Russian antisemitism', *Jerusalem Center for Public Affairs*, 15 September. Available at: http://research.policyarchive.org/18025.pdf. [Accessed 28 December 2018.]

Gitelman, Z. (1991) 'Glasnost, perestroika and antisemitism', *Foreign Affairs* 70(2): 141–59.

Goldberg, R.A. (2001) *Enemies within: the culture of conspiracy in modern America*, New Haven/London: Yale University Press.

Gracheva, T. (2011) *Nevidimaia Khazariia: algoritmy geopolitiki i srategii voin mirovoi zakulisy*, Moscow: Zerna-kniga.

Grewal, D.S. (2016) 'Conspiracy theories in a networked world', *Critical Review*, 28(1): 24–43.

Harris, J. (2016) *The great fear: Stalin's terror of the 1930s*, Oxford: Oxford University Press.

Icke, D. (1999) *The biggest secret: the book that will change the world*, United States: Bridge of Love Publications.

Iliukhin, V. (2017) 'Obviniaetsia El'tsin', ИЛЮХИН Виктор Иванович. Available at: www.viktor-iluhin.ru/node/328. [Accessed 26 November 2017.]

Jasper, W.F. (1992) *Global Tyranny…Step by Step*, Appleton: Western Islands.

Jones, A. (2007) 'Endgame: blueprint of the global enslavement', *YouTube (ChangeDaChannel)*, 13 November 2009. Available at: www.youtube.com/watch?v=x-CrNlilZho. [Accessed 28 December 2018.]

Judaken, J. (2008) 'So what's new? Rethinking the "new antisemitism" in a global age', *Patterns of Prejudice* 42(4–5): 531–60.

Katasonov, V. (2013) *Kapitalizm: Istoriia i ideologiia 'denezhnoi tsivilizatsii'*, Moscow: Institut Russkoi Tsivilizatsii.

Kay, J. (2011) *Among the truthers: a journey through America's growing conspiracist underground*, New York: HarperCollins.

Kolomitsyn, A. (2011) 'Rossiia i VTO', *Nikolai Starikov's Blog*, 23 November. Available at: https://nstarikov.ru/blog/13352. [Accessed 28 December 2018.]

Kotolupov, O. (2017) 'Zagovor Mirovogo Pravitel'stva Protiv Rossii', *Zavtra*, 23 May. Available at: http://zavtra.ru/blogs/zagovor_mirovogo_pravitel_stva_protiv_rossii. [Accessed 28 December 2018.]

Martinis09 (2013) 'Shokiruiushchie tsitaty mirovoy elity, govoriashchei ob unichtozhenii chelovechestva… Monsanto ikh instrument?', *Martinis09's Personal Blog*, 27 February. Available at: https://martinis09.livejournal.com/582309.html. [Accessed 28 December 2018.]

Melley T. (2000) *Empire of conspiracy: the culture of paranoia in postwar America*, Ithaca: Cornell University Press.

Ó Beacháin, D. and Polese, A. (2010) *The colour revolutions in the former soviet republics: successes and failures*, London: Routledge.

Panarin, I. (2010) *Pervaia informatsionnaia voina: razval SSSR*. Saint-Petersburg: Piter.

Pavlenko, V. (2012) '"Ustoichivoe razvitie" kak ideologiia "novogo mirovogo poriadka"', *Akademiia Geopoliticheskikh Problem*, 9 April. Available at: http://akademiagp.ru/ustojchivoe-razvitie-kak-ideologiya-novogo-mirovogo-poryadka/. [Accessed 28 December 2018.]

Platonov, O. (2014) *Tainoe Mirovoe Pravitel'stvo*, Moscow: Rodnaia Strana.

Plokhy, S. (2014) *The last empire: the final days of the Soviet Union*, New York: Basic Books.

Porter, L. (2005) *Who are the Illuminati?*, London: Collins & Brown.

Putin, V. (2007) 'Speech and the Following Discussion at the Munich Conference on Security Policy', *WikiSource*, last edited on 7 August 2018. Available at: https://en.wikisource.org/wiki/Speech_and_the_Following_Discussion_at_the_Munich_Conference_on_Security_Policy. [Accessed 28 December 2018].

Robertson, P. (1991) *The New World Order*, United States: W Pub Group.
Rychkova, E. (2013) 'Mikhail Khazin: Putin ob"iavil voinu "liberal'no-semeinomu klanu" v ramkakh global'noi bor'by finansovykh elit', *Nakanune.ru*, 1 October. Available at: www.nakanune.ru/service/print.php?articles=8160. [Accessed 28 December 2018.]
Samokhvalov, V. (2017) *Russian-European relations in the Balkans and black sea region*, London: Palgrave.
Shironin, V. (1995) *Agenty perestroika*, Moscow: Éksmo.
Shnirel'man, V. (2012) *Khazarskii mif: ideologiia politicheskogo radikalizma v Rossii i ee istoki*, Moscow: Mosty Kul'tury.
Snychev, I. (1996) 'Pastyr' dobryi: trudy mitropolita Ioanna', *Wco.ru*. Available at: www.wco.ru/biblio/books/ioannsp2/Main.htm. [Accessed 28 December 2018.]
Sokolov, A. (1992) 'Mondializm i taina Rossii', *Elementy*, 2. Available at: http://arcto.ru/article/416. [Accessed 28 December 2018.]
Starikov, N. (2009a) *Cherchez lia neft':Pochemu nash Stabilizatsionnyi fond nakhoditsia tam?*, Moscow: Piter.
Starikov, N. (2009b) *Krizis: ka keto delatesia*, Moscow: Piter.
Starikov, N. (2012) 'Nikolai Starikov: Dlia VTO Rossiia budet prosto "neftianoi vyshkoi" i svalkoi iadernykh otkhodov', *Argumenty i fakty*, 13 July. Available at: www.aif.ru/money/nikolay_starikov_dlya_vto_rossiya_budet_prosto_neftyanoy_vyshkoy_i_svalkoy_yadernyh_othodov. [Accessed 28 December 2018.]
Subetto, A.I. (2013) 'Vsemirnaia torgovaia organizatsiia v kontekste teorii global'nogo imperializma', *KPRF*. Available at: http://cprfspb.ru/8765.html. [Accessed 28 December 2018.]
Taguieff, P.-A. (2004) *Rising from the muck: the new antisemitism in Europe*, Chicago: Ivan D. Ree.
Tsar'grad TV (2018) 'Rossiia meshaet SShA ustanovit'global'nuiu GMO diktaturu', *Tsar'grad TV*, 6 March. Available at: https://tsargrad.tv/articles/rossija-meshaet-ssha-ustanovit-globalnuju-gmo-diktaturu_115785. [Accessed 28 December 2018.]
Welch, R. (2016) *The blue book of the John Birch society*, United States: Pickle Partners Publishing.
Yablokov, I. (2018) *Fortress Russia: conspiracy theories in the Post-Soviet World*, Cambridge: Polity.
Yablokov I (2019). Anti-Jewish Conspiracy Theories in Putin's Russia. *Antisemitism Studies*, 3 (2), pp. 291–316.

# 5.6
# CONSPIRACY THEORIES IN AND ABOUT THE BALKANS

*Nebojša Blanuša*

## Introduction

Dealing with conspiracy theories has its own historical and political underpinnings and only superficially neutral usage in public discourse, already studied as the 'pathologizing effect' in the name of so-called universal and rational subjectivity (Pigden 2007; Bratich 2008; Blanuša 2011a; Dentith 2014). By focusing on the Balkans as a specific region that has experienced a shared psychic and cultural normalisation, it is important not to amplify the same pathologising effect by studying the region through the prism of conspiracy theories. Such an 'order of knowledge' (Foucault 1980: 128), which belongs to a European rationalist and colonial tradition and tries to divide universal normality from insanity, described the Balkans as a geopolitical region that has produced in the last few centuries more history than it can bear and consume. It was usually perceived as Europe's inner 'Other', the bloodiest part of 'Restern' Europe, or an intermediate area, permeated by political instability, wars, changes of borders and 'spheres of influence' between imperial powers and emerging nation-states, with the climax in the dissolution of Yugoslavia and post-Yugoslav wars in 1990s. The rocky road of problematic political consolidation and accession to the E.U. was perceived as its normalisation, permeated by internal turmoils, conflicts and international frictions in the last two decades. Moreover, most of the Balkan countries are still troubled by their violent pasts from the Second World War, the post-war Socialist period and recent wars.

However, with the emergence of the E.U. crisis, seen most prominently in Greece, followed by waves of migrants and refugees from the Middle East, something unexpected happened. The Balkanian self-colonised sense of incompleteness, threats of fragmentation and tendency to civilisational 'regressions' – in the form of xenophobia, rabid nationalism, authoritarian populism and welfare chauvinism – became the spectre haunting the whole of Europe. Something that was constantly relegated to the edges of sanity suddenly became common reality. The normal pathology of the Balkans became the pathological normality of Europe. The ugly face ascribed to the Balkans suddenly became the face of Europe itself, latently present and repressed, as if the European identity has been played out before in the Balkans, which

> constitutes a *local projection* of forms of confrontation and conflict characteristic of all of Europe ... not a monstrosity grafted to its breast, a pathological "aftereffect" of underdevelopment or of communism, but rather an image and effect of its own history.
> 
> *(Balibar 2004: 5–6)*

All these processes in the Balkans were permeated thoroughly by conspiracy theories in various cultural and political discourses and praxes, which reflected fears and hopes, ideological underpinnings, antagonisms and larger structural cleavages during the last few centuries. In that sense, conspiratorial interpretations were not (only) a peculiarity of radical and extremist groups and forces from the margins of political life. As previous research shows (Blanuša 2010, 2011b, 2013; Turjačanin *et al.* 2018), conspiracy theories were also highly relevant for mainstream political discourse and actors. Therefore, it is possible to consider them as symptoms and indicators of wider societal troubles and turbulences, expressed in specific emotional and condensed form. Similar tendencies and processes are today present in the whole of Europe, carrying the same explosive potential.

The main goal of this chapter is to show the relevance of conspiracy theories in and about the Balkans from the late nineteenth century to the present, and analyse their role in various political contexts, movements, critical events and processes, mostly during the 'age of empire' and 'age of extremes' (Hobsbawm 1995), through to today. In order to differentiate between different varieties of conspiracy theories, I will start the analysis with conspiratorial discourses from the West, which still perceives the Balkans as the land of conspiracies. Then I will proceed with more universal, versatile conspiracy theories, the most poisonous of which is antisemitism in its various forms. The next is anti-imperialism, including its trajectory to anti-Western conspiracism and New World Order conspiracy theories. The idea is to explore the ways in which these worldwide conspiracy discourses were expressed in the Balkans, and what kind of political consequences they produced. By exploring them on the level of individual countries, I would like to show the whole variety of historico-ideological contexts, which made functional those conspiratorial discourses, and how they were differently accepted or disputed. Lastly, I will analyse local and politically relevant conspiracy theories related to the last 30 years of traumatic social changes.

## Western conspiratorial discourses in/about the Balkans

If we would adopt the Orientalist paradigm of the Eastern Question (Stamatopoulos 2018), our story of the Balkans would probably start in the following way: At the beginning of the twentieth century, most of the Balkans were still under the rule of the Austro-Hungarian and decaying Ottoman empires. Greece achieved its independence in 1830 after nine years of bloody war. At the Berlin Congress (1878), Montenegro, Romania and Serbia became independent states. Bulgaria lost Eastern Rumelia but regained it in 1885 and defeated Serbia in the same year. However, Bulgaria remained a vassal state under the Ottoman Empire until 1908, gaining full independence after the Young Turk Revolution. As they had no great-power sponsors, Macedonia and Albania remained under the Ottomans, engaging themselves in the politics of conspiracy and guerrilla warfare (Glenny 2012: 154), while Bosnia and Herzegovina was occupied by Austro-Hungary, not without rebelling against it, clandestinely supported with arms by the Ottomans. Due to their territorial aspirations and opportune political situation, the kingdoms of Serbia, Bulgaria, Montenegro and Greece formed the Balkan League and started the First Balkan War in 1912 against the Ottomans. However, after the League's victory, it fell apart due to overlapping territorial ambitions. The Second Balkan War broke out in 1913, unifying Serbia, Montenegro, Greece and Romania against Bulgaria, and finally defeating it. Encouraged by the weakness of Bulgaria, the Ottomans invaded it and regained some previously lost territories. The preparation and execution of war activities included unofficial agreements between involved states, support and numerous secret diplomatic actions of the then great powers, constantly concerned with their competing influence over this important geopolitical area. In such a context of inter-state alliances, the upcoming crisis between the Austro-Hungarian Empire and Serbia, provoked by the assassination of Franz Ferdinand in Sarajevo, led to the First World War.

One could say these were the usual imperial and nationalist politics of that time, and, yet, such an approach neglects the broader historical context, especially the influence of the French Revolution and the inspiration it provided for emerging national movements. Nevertheless, what is more interesting for this study is the conspiratorial overtone of such historiography, as well as the focus on processes that necessarily include secret plans and plotting against enemies, together with describing states as collective agents with unified will. Such historical interpretation condenses numerous uncontrollable and contingent events and processes into competing conspiracies, similar to a board game, but with the real-life consequences. This historiography led to the popular conspiratorial discourse often applied to the history of the Balkans. It significantly contributed to the perception of the Balkans as alienated from Western civilisation, an immature, ambivalent and unstable entity, imagined as the decomposing phantom limb of the 'Sick man of Europe'.

The Balkanist discourse, characteristic of journalistic and quasi-journalistic literary forms, adds even more conspiratorial flavour. Maria Todorova finds in Arthur D. Howden Smith's adventurous experiences in 1907 the exemplary description of the Balkans' mystical appeal of medieval knighthood, arms and plots:

> To those who have not visited them, the Balkans are a shadow-land of mystery; to those who know them, they become even more mysterious.... You become, in a sense, a part of the spell, and of the mystery and glamour of the whole. You contract the habit of crouching over your morning coffee in the café and, when you meet a man of your acquaintance, at least half of what you say is whispered, portentously. Intrigue, plotting, mystery, high courage, and daring deeds – the things that are the soul of true romance are to-day the soul of the Balkans.... Intrigue is in the air one breathes. The crowds in the Belgrade cafés have the manner of conspirators.
> (Howden Smith 1908, cited in Todorova 2009 [1997]: 14)

Furthermore, Todorova (2009 [1997]: 17) claims that a distinctive feature of this area are 'howling Balkan conspiracy theories and the propensity to blame one or the other or all great powers for their fate'. For her, that indicates not only a sense of victimisation but also a certain sense of autonomy, which constitutes the Balkans as a semi-colonial entity with transitionary character. The ideological articulation of such in-between-ness from the position of the European gaze is in the form of the lowermost case or an incomplete self (Todorova 2009 [1997]). Looking back to the history of the late nineteenth and twentieth centuries, together with responses to the current global crises, I seriously doubt if such self-beautification of the West (Bjelić, Savić 2002: 9) is sustainable, at least if we analyse the dynamics of conspiratorial discourses in the Balkans – not because the Balkan face is prettier, but because it is possible to find similar conspiratorial articulations related to collective fears, distrust and victimhood at least all around Europe, often in the more intensive form and with even more violent consequences in the twentieth century (see Chapter 5.4.). In that sense, conspiracy theories in the Balkans are not homogenous, because it is a region with multifarious historical experience, different cultural traditions and political affiliations. In that sense, my cognitive mapping of the Balkans will be pluralistic in terms of periods between and across traumatic events and changing borders.

## Worldwide travelling conspiratorial discourses in the Balkans: Antisemitism and anti-imperialism

Antisemitism in the Balkans was, until 1918, relatively weaker than in other parts of Eastern Europe (Déak 2010: 225). Due to ethnic and religious differences important in the symbolic formation of Balkan nations, it was often accompanied with anti-Islamism (Hoare 2017:166). This was especially prominent among newly established nations who were previously under the Ottoman rule, including pogroms, expulsions, discrimination or religious conversion of non-Christian inhabitants (Hoare 2017: 167). However, that was not the case in Croatia, whose nationalists were Islamophilic, considering Bosnian Muslims as the genetically purest Croats (Hoare 2017: 174). Antisemitism in Croatia was accompanied mostly with anti-Hungarianism and, to a lesser degree, with anti-Germanism, involving violent protests against Jews and claims for their expulsion in 1883 and 1903. Jews were depicted as representatives of 'foreign interests', profiteers of liberalism and swindlers, and portrayed as various types of animal (see Chapter 3.8, and Vulešica 2014: 120). Leading Croatian bishop Josip Juraj Strossmayer supported such attitudes, as did some political groups in Croatia at the turn of the twentieth century who praised the work of Huston Steward Chemberlain (Goldstein 2005: 147–8). Furthermore, journalist Milan Obradović translated *Biarritz* in Croatia in 1912, under the title 'Jews and their secret plans to enslave the whole world and all nations on Earth'. Antisemitic riots took place in 1918 and 1919, with violent attacks on Jewish property justified by the charge of 'responsibility for the war and the catastrophic postwar situation', which even had the approval of the new government (Goldstein 2005: 132). Early twentieth-century antisemitism in the Balkans was a religious, social and political phenomenon, and these elements were intertwined even before the arrival of the notorious *Protocols of the Elders of Zion*. The political dimension of antisemitism appeared after the 1848 revolution with the political emancipation of Jews, resulting in the anti-Jewish laws in Slovenia and Dalmatia in 1867 (Sekelj 1981: 181), and in the Romanian Constitution in 1866 (Silvestru, 2012: 113). During the 1870s, the book *The Jew, Judaism and the Judaization of the Christian*, written by Henri Gougenot des Mousseaux (1869), gained popularity in the Austro-Hungarian Empire and Romania, claiming that Jews conspire 'to dominate and destroy the world through … high finance, Freemasonry, the liberal press and Jewish self-defense organizations' (Leff 2005: 282). The Berlin Congress demands for equal civil rights for all religions and ethnic groups in the Balkan countries led to political antisemitism, intermixed with old racial, economic and religious prejudices, together with the new oncological metaphors of a 'social virus that spreads cancer in the midst of the nation' (Leff 2005: 121). Romania refused to introduce that element of the peace treaty and responded with 'unprecedented outbursts of antisemitism in public and political discourses', involving the idea that at the Berlin Congress Jews demanded 'the mastery of the world' (Leff 2005: 114, 118).

Critique of the Berlin Congress for its unfairness toward Balkan Christians in favour of Jews was also present in Serbia. Serbian nationalist Vasa Pelagić translated from German the pamphlet *The Mirror of Kike's Honesty* (1879), which depicted Jewish culture as vicious and perverted, pursuing the long-time goal of 'world government'. The pamphlet was a part of an emerging antisemitic campaign in the last decades of the nineteenth century in Serbia, whose legacy continues to haunt Serbia. Together with *The Protocols* and later local antisemitic texts, it can be found at several extreme right-wing Internet pages even today.

In 1880s Bulgaria, most of the religious antisemitic literature came from Russia, while at the end of the nineteenth and the beginning of twentieth century, antisemitism in Bulgaria acquired a more socio-economic flavour. It included accusations that Jews are trying 'to financially overpower all societies, peoples and countries and ultimately the whole world' (Kulenska 2012: 74).

The Bulgarian antisemitic press portrayed Jews as international leeches, wolves and parasites who 'settled down in the diseased organism in Turkey and ... to a great extent contributed to Turkish corruption', participating in the massacres of Armenians and supporting the Turks in the Russo-Turkish war (Kulenska 2012: 77–82).

In Greece, the economic and ethno-cultural antagonism between Orthodox Christians and Jews were for a long time related to blood libel conspiracy narratives and subsequent pogroms (Margaroni 2014: 180). Later on, it included accusations of collaboration and spying for the Ottoman Empire, especially during and after the struggle for independence (Margaroni 2014: 187).

Generally speaking, until the outbreak of the First World War, as in other parts of Europe, antisemitism became a multidimensional phenomenon. Jews were hated because of their religious beliefs, imagined racial features, economic and political power, 'and their assumed leadership or support of subversive political and social movements' (Brustein, King 2004a: 38). The real 'Black Hand' conspiracy and assassination of Archduke Franz Ferdinand was the spark that ignited the First World War. During the war, antisemitism took various forms in most of Europe, due to unfulfilled expectations of a quick victory, the involvement of the U.S.A. and especially after the October Revolution in 1917. Belief in a Judeo-Bolshevik conspiracy very soon gained support among right-wing groups throughout Europe (Bergmann, Wyrwa 2017: 11), including the Balkans.

After the war, a rise in nationalism, revolutions and counterrevolutions, accompanied by the spread of *The Protocols*, further radicalised antisemitism. Such antisemitism was especially prominent in Romania, where the first translation of *The Protocols* in the local language appeared in 1923 (Cohn 2005: 305). The book had appeared earlier in the Balkans in Russian, among refugees from the Soviet Union and published in Serbia in 1921, with the commentary of Grigorij Bostunič Vasilevič, who later immigrated to Germany and wrote for *Völkischer Beobachter* and *Der Stürmer*. From the late 1920s to the early 1940s, *The Protocols* were published in most of the Balkans: In Greece (1928, 1932, 1934, 1940), in the Kingdom of Serbs, Croats and Slovenes – renamed the Kingdom of Yugoslavia in 1929 – (1926, 1929, 1934, 1936, 1939), again in Romania in 1934, in Bulgaria (1925, 1943), in Serbia (1941), in the Independent State of Croatia (1942) and in Slovenia (1945). During the 1920s, antisemitic propaganda and attacks increased in the Kingdom of Serbs, Croats and Slovenes, accusing Jews of Zionist imperialism, lack of patriotism, sabotage of the state and the spread of cosmopolitanism, as well as of centralism and republicanism, while antisemitism almost disappeared after the proclamation of the dictatorship in 1929 (Goldstein 2002: 56). This period lasted only a few years – after the Nazis came to power in Germany in 1933, they began to finance pro-Nazi and antisemitic groups in Yugoslavia, spreading racist attitudes and accusations of international Jewry (Goldstein 2002: 57–8).

In the first years of the Second World War, Yugoslavia assumed a neutral position, but, pressured by Hitler, Yugoslavia signed the Tripartite Act in 1941, provoking the military *coup d'état*, German invasion, occupation and partition of its territories between Germany, Italy, Hungary and Bulgaria, and the establishment of the puppet state of the Independent State of Croatia, led by the local fascist organisation, Ustasha. A self-proclaimed Croatian liberation movement, its leadership demonised Serbs, Jews, Freemasons and communists. Claiming that antisemitism is a ridiculous phenomenon and no more than a delusion, the then very popular politician and leader of the Croatian Peasant Party, Vladko Maček, was accused by newspapers of plotting with the Jews, leading to his later imprisonment in the notorious Jasenovac concentration camp (Goldstein 2002: 60), known as 'the Auschwitz of the Balkans'.

In Serbia, which was 'judenfrei' already in May 1942, antisemitic literature flourished before and during the Second World War. The leader of the local fascist movement, Zbor, and collaborator of German Nazis, Dimitrije Ljotić wrote in 1940 a pamphlet *The Drama of Contemporary Humankind*, inspired by *The Protocols* (Kerenji 2005: 432). Beside the mass atrocities they committed during the Second World War, both Ustasha and Zbor organised antisemitic exhibitions in capitals of their countries as part of conspiratorial antisemitic propaganda.

Conspiratorial antisemitism in Romania rapidly increased in the first part of the twentieth century, backed up by *The Protocols* and other similar publications, mostly about the Jewish control of socialist and communist parties and movements, especially after the Bolshevik revolutions in Russia and Hungary (Brustein, King 2004b: 446–8). Prominent Romanian intellectuals played a significant role in disseminating conspiratorial antisemitism. Well-known scientist and politician Nikolae Paulescu (Brustein, King 2004b: 439) wrote about a Judeo-Masonic plot against the Romanian nation in 1913. His writings influenced Alexandru Cusa, minister of the state (1937–1938), who was an organiser of the Universal Antisemitic Alliance and author of the foreword to *The Protocols* in 1933, and Corneliu Codreanu, leader of the Iron Guard (Wedekind 2010: 52). Although Bulgaria is usually considered a country with a low level of antisemitism during the Second World War, antisemitism was constantly present and stimulated by refugees from the Soviet Union in the form of Judeo-Bolshevism, including the exhibition against it in 1933, as well as pursuing its own Kristalnacht in 1939 (Stefanov 2002: 7). Even though the deportation of Bulgarian Jews never occurred, many non-Bulgarian Jews were sent to labour camps, and the Bulgarian government 'delivered every single Jew in the Bulgarian-occupied parts of Greece and Yugoslavia to the Nazis' (Déak 2010: 231).

Antisemitism in Greece after the First World War became a part of Helleno-Christian ideology, blending the perception of Jews as simultaneously adversaries of Orthodox Christianity and enemies of the nation, expressed in pogroms and anti-Jewish riots, whose symbolic remnants are still present in the tourist 'attraction' of the Burning of Judas (Blümel 2017: 183–4). Political antisemitism in Greece increased in the form of a Jewish-Zionist conspiracy theory, especially after the Treaty of Laussanne (1923), spread by the monarchist and liberal press, and reinforced by the first Greek edition of *The Protocols* in 1928 (Psarras 2013, cited in Blümel 2017: 185). The peak of such antisemitism was in the 1931 pogrom in Salonika, led by the National Union of Greece, a proto-fascist organisation campaigning against 'foreign and communist Jews' as national traitors (Lewkovicz 1999: 83). Blümel (Lewkovicz 1999: 83) claims that antisemitic violence in Greece was the consequence of the failure to resurrect the Byzantine Empire after the First World War and was framed similarly as the German stab-in-the-back myth from the same period. Under Metaxas's totalitarian regime (1936–1941), the status of Jews significantly improved. During the Second World War, Jews fought together with Greeks against Axis powers and suffered mass deportations to Nazi Germany extermination camps, but also experienced the strong support and rescue organised by local Greeks and officials. Unfortunately, the previously developed Greek politico-religious pattern of demonising the Jews prevailed long after. It was nefariously institutionalised in state schools, the judiciary and the army, supported by further editions of *The Protocols* in 1971 and 1980, as well as by other local publications (Lewkovicz 1999: 188, 195).

After the Second World War, most countries in the Balkans became communist states. These regimes were prone to ignore the memory of the Holocaust, arguing that 'these old-regime crimes would not occur again', but in some of them, a Soviet-style anti-Zionism just replaced antisemitism (Déak 2010: 233). Nevertheless, anti-Zionism was often a part of anti-imperialist conspiratorial discourse, mostly against the U.S.A., but not in all Balkan countries. For example, Yugoslavian early support for the establishment of Israel was motivated by an anti-imperialist attitude (Abadi 1996: 288). Furthermore, the Soviet-led show-trial of Rudolf Slánský and 13 other leading Czechoslovakian communists in 1952 accused the Yugoslavian high-ranking communist of Jewish origin, Moša Pijade, of being part of a Trotskyite-Titoist-Zionist conspiracy (Thompson 1953). However, the pro-Israel attitude of socialist Yugoslavia changed during the formation of the Non-Aligned Movement and especially after the Six-Day War in 1967, when Yugoslavia broke diplomatic relations with Israel. Sekelj (2002: 93) distinguishes three phases of antisemitism in socialist Yugoslavia: 1945–1967 saw no antisemitism in public life; 1967–1988 saw a revival of antisemitism in the form of anti-Zionism; and 1988–1991 saw the advent of antisemitism that became a legitimate worldview afterwards. In the second and third period, anti-Zionist articles appeared in mainstream Serbian newspapers *Politika* and *Borba*, and *The Protocols* were even broadcast in 1971 on state television, *TV Beograd*, while in Slovenia, in 1988 and 1989, the student magazine *Tribuna* published first excerpts and, then, in 1990 the complete *Protocols* and *Mein Kampf* (Toš 2012: 203, 207). Several official reactions against this antisemitic literature, as well as criticism from intellectuals, did not stop it. The most prominent representative of this counter-discourse was acclaimed Yugoslavian writer Danilo Kiš, who wrote a fictional story 'The Book of Kings and Fools' (1983) as an alternative history of *The Protocols*, 'in order to dramatize the absurdity and danger of the Plot' (Boym 1999: 114). However, this was no match for the long list of conspiratorial antisemitic books published in Yugoslavia and post-Yugoslavian states. In 1983, the Catholic Church in Croatia published the book *Freemasonry among Croats: Freemasons and Yugoslavia*, written by Ivan Mužić. From then until 2005, the book was re-issued seven times. This 'history' of the local branch of Freemasonry describes, among other secret activities, the assassination of Franz Ferdinand in 1914 as their work (Mužić 2000: 58). In the context of post-Yugoslavian war and rabid nationalism, in 1993 and 1994, the mainstream Serbian weekly *Ilustrovana politika* published a series of supplements on Freemasons. Since 1991, *The Protocols* were published numerous times in Serbia, especially after the N.A.T.O. bombings in 1999, while in Croatia they were published in 1993, 1996, 1999 and 2003. Simultaneously in Croatia and Serbia, there were attempts to deny or trivialise antisemitism (Byford 2008; Blanuša 2011b).

A strong tradition of antisemitism in Romania prevailed after the Second World War, together with Soviet-style anti-Zionism. Nevertheless, this was the only Eastern European country preserving diplomatic relations with Israel after 1967. Romania under Ceausescu played the role of mediator in the Middle East, as well as 'selling' their Jewish citizens to Israel for cash or other forms of economic help (Abadi 1996: 306). Anti-Zionist show-trials and purges in Romania were the most intensive in the early 1950s, including even communist leader Ana Pauker (Gordon 1954: 300). Post-communist Romania witnessed the rehabilitation of Ion Antonescu, leader of the military government established in 1940, responsible for systematic persecutions, deportations and mass murders of Romanian Jews. Together with public denial of responsibility for the death of 400 000 Romanian Jews, antisemitism was, during the early 1990s, articulated among extreme right-wing parties. *The Protocols* were published in 1997, 1998, 2000 and 2012. However, some prominent publications, such as *Europa*, claimed that 'Romania had fallen victim to a Zionist world conspiracy and that Jewish agents wanted to turn the country into "Israel's colony"' (cited in Totok 2005: 620). Since 1989, even more extreme conspiratorial antisemitism was regularly featured in the magazine *România Mare* [Greater Romania], based on historical Judeo-Bolshevik and Judeo-Masonic conspiracy theories and recently epitomised in the figure of George Soros as a representative of a Jewish financial conspiracy (Colăcel, Pintilescu 2017: 35–6).

The majority of Bulgaria's 50 000 Jews immigrated to Israel after the Second World War, mostly influenced by the Zionist movement. According to Georgieff (2013), under communism, Bulgaria was compliant with Soviet international politics, while Jewish life inside the country rapidly declined from the 1950s to the 1980s, as Jews were stripped of their minority rights, abandoned synagogues were turned into sports halls, storage depots or left in ruins, and some Jewish cemeteries were destroyed. Diplomatic relations with Israel were severed in 1967 and re-established in 1990. In the last three decades, Bulgarian extreme right-wing groups and parties actively promoted antisemitism, including continuous attacks on Jewish properties, cemeteries and synagogues, and publishing old and new antisemitic books (Georgieff 2013). *The Protocols* were republished in 2003 and 2013 and can be found in mainstream bookstores together with other conspiratorial antisemitic literature, such as *The Power of Mamon* and *The Evil Boomerang*, written by Volen Siderov, leader of the ultranationalist anti-Turkish and antisemitic party *Ataka*. In the 2006 presidential elections, Siderov won 24 per cent of the popular votes in the second round. According to the A.D.L. Global 100 survey in 2015, Bulgaria and Greece were the most antisemitic countries in the Balkans, with 44 per cent of citizens in Bulgaria and 69 per cent in Greece believing antisemitic stereotypes are probably true, including the idea that Jews hold great power in business, international financial markets and control over global affairs. Although such attitudes in Greece were widely interpreted as the consequence of the recent government-debt crisis and the rise of the neo-Nazi political party Golden Dawn, antisemitism in Greece has historically been strongly supported by the Greek Orthodox Church, state institutions, the education system, the media and book publishers. *The Protocols* in Greece have a prominent status in conspiratorial culture, published in dozens of different versions (Rakopoulos 2018: 383), as is evidenced by the 2013 book by Dimitris Psarras, *The Best Seller of Hatred: The Protocols of the Elders of Zion in Greece, 1920–2013*.

Although, today, *The Protocols* mostly circulate among extremist right-wing groups in the Balkans, it appears that significant numbers of citizens in the Balkans accept some of their poisonous ideas. According to the same A.D.L. Global 100 survey, on average, 39 per cent of citizens in the Balkans believe antisemitic stereotypes as probably true (the detailed breakdown by country is: 27 per cent in Slovenia, 33 per cent in Croatia, 32 per cent in Bosnia and Herzegovina, 42 per cent in Serbia, 29 per cent in Montenegro, 35 per cent in Romania, 44 per cent in Bulgaria and 69 per cent in Greece). In the context of global resurgence of antisemitism (Rosenfeld 2013: 1), these results show that such ideas are not simply lingering prejudices from the past and call for serious concern. Compared to the rest of Europe in terms of historical trajectory and current expressions of antisemitism, the Balkans seems to play an integral part in pursuing its own abominable ideas and affairs.

According to Pipes (1997: 82), one of the broadest themes in conspiratorial discourse in the twentieth century was anti-imperialism. One strand was developed as part of the communist ideology, especially Leninism and Stalinism, that spread around Soviet satellite states, as we saw in previous examples of anti-Zionism. However, anti-imperialism also assumed a special form and prominent place in the Non-Aligned Movement. This still active global association of countries was established in 1961 as an alternative to the Cold War blocs of the U.S.A. and Soviet Union, mostly by so-called developing and Third World countries. Until the late 1980s, Yugoslavia was one of its leading countries, due to the prominent figure of President Josip Broz Tito. The Non-Aligned Movement was created as a reaction to the threats of the Cold War, nuclear arming and superpower interventions around the world, and was shaped by concerns of the then recently independent and decolonised states striving for modernisation. Its core values were anti-imperialism, anti-colonialism, anti-militarism and anti-apartheid, and respect for sovereignty and solidarity among small and less powerful states. These conditions and values made the Movement particularly prone to conspiratorial interpretations of superpowers' military actions and their attempts to weaken the Movement through some of their member countries.

However, conspiratorial interpretations that paved the way to the formation of the Movement appeared even before this. The inclination of socialist Yugoslavia toward the Movement was shaped by its unique position of having an authentic anti-fascist and national liberation movement during the Second World War, as well as by concerns about superpower intrusive politics, e.g. fears of a secret agreement between Churchill and Stalin to divide Yugoslavia into spheres of influence. Tito referred to this in his speeches immediately after the Second World War, but it continued to circulate in the mainstream press in Yugoslavia even into the 1980s (Blanuša, 2011b: 93–4). After the split between Tito and Stalin in 1948, the subsequent denouncement of treaties with Eastern European Soviet satellites included a series of official notes to Yugoslavia with open accusations about a plot 'engineered by the Soviet Government' including various conspiratorial activities, such as a planned invasion on Yugoslavian territory, spying, sabotage, fifth columnists in Cominform, etc. On the other side, Moscow radio personally attacked Tito, inter alia depicting his face as a 'mask, disguising the malicious, cunning, egoistic soul of a skillful sneak' (*Keesing's Contemporary Archives* Vol. 7 1949: 10135). Yugoslavia then geared its foreign policy to the West, gaining significant financial, military and food aid. From 1953, Yugoslavian rapprochement with the Soviet Union and its satellites slowly improved until the 1956 Soviet intervention in Hungary. Yugoslavia was then accused of acting as an imperialist agent, especially after it gave political asylum to Imre Nagy's group in the Yugoslavian Embassy in Budapest, while Nagy's later kidnapping, trial and execution was interpreted as 'another link in the chain of the new anti-Yugoslav campaign, being conducted by the USSR and other bloc countries' (Granville, 1998: 507). Another attack on Yugoslavia came primarily from China and the Soviet Union in 1958. They claimed that the 1948 Cominform resolution was basically correct, criticising Yugoslavia for being a part of an imperialist 'sabotage of the world Communist movement' or 'Trojan horse of Imperialism' (*Keesing's Contemporary Archives* Vol. 11 1958: 16229). Among similar attacks from other Communist countries, Albanian leader Enver Hoxha took his part in conspiratorial accusations, claiming that Yugoslavian leaders are 'traitors, incorrigible revisionists, enemies of the Soviet Union and Marxism, and hardened agents of American imperialism' (*Keesing's Contemporary Archives* Vol. 11 1958: 16395). In 1959, such rabid propaganda diminished, as well as economic cooperation with the Soviet bloc, turning Yugoslavia more to the West.

Tito's visits to India and Burma in 1954 were his first steps that led to the formation of the Non-Aligned Movement. Initiative for its establishment had begun in 1956 on Brijuni (today's Croatia), at the meeting of Josip Broz Tito, Gamal Abdel Nasser and Jawaharlal Nehru in the shadow of the Hungarian Revolution and Suez Crisis. The first conference, involving 25 countries, was held in 1961 in Belgrade in the context of a protracted international crisis. Tito's opening address adopted a dramatic tone and expressed concern. The implicit conspiratorial logic in his speech is prominent in the general descriptions of a divided Cold War world and the critique of blocs, considering their actions as having sinister intentions, dangerous for world peace. Contrary to that, he assumed a non-violent anti-bloc position:

> Actually, constant efforts are being exerted for the purpose of achieving superiority, in order to attain specific goals from a position of strength; ... to solve outstanding questions in one's own favor. In these efforts lie the greatest danger of an outbreak of armed conflict and of a new catastrophe for the entire world. The recent past has shown clearly that the grouping of states into blocs usually leads to a settling of accounts by the force of arms. The history of recent years has also demonstrated that there need not even be two blocs, but that it is sufficient to have only one bloc for war to break out ... [I]t is obvious that such a course was most unfortunate and has led to the present abnormal and perilous situation in the world.... The economic arrangements within bloc frameworks have a discriminatory character in regard to other countries.

Embargoes are imposed on various products with the aim of exercising pressure upon a given country or several countries. All this and many other characteristic features of blocs are in contradiction with the general interests and views of nonaligned countries and, above all, with the fact that these countries preclude the use of military forces for the solution of any dispute.

*(J.F.K. Presidential Library and Museum)*

Given the circumstances of nuclear-war threat, colonialism and neo-colonialism, as well as the economic and international status of nonaligned countries, such implicit conspiratorial logic with anti-conspiratorial intent was a form of prudent political thinking. Although some other members of the Non-Aligned Movement were more open in expressing conspiracism, such 'Titoist' anti-imperialist logic was constantly applied, at least in Yugoslavian foreign policy, promoting the *détente*. For example, Tito applied it during the Cuban Missile Crisis in 1962, which brought Yugoslavia closer to the Soviet Union, but without any major break with the West, even after the Yugoslavian condemnation of the U.S. policy in Vietnam in 1965 (Hasan 1981a: 117). Things changed with the Six-Day War in 1967. Tito and six other leaders of communist states (except Romania) signed a statement denouncing Israeli aggression as 'the result of the collusion of certain imperialist forces, and first of all the United States, against the Arab countries …[that] would be used for the restoration of the foreign colonial regime' (Keesing's Contemporary Archives Vol. 16 1967: 22105). Another phase of Yugoslavian foreign policy occurred with Soviet intervention in Czechoslovakia in 1968. Alongside public condemnation of intervention, Tito held a secret meeting with Ceausescu because of possible Soviet invasions on their countries. Moscow accused them both of giving 'active assistance to anti-Socialist forces in Czechoslovakia and of taking the same line as imperialist N.A.T.O. followers and the Maoist group in China' (Keesing's Contemporary Archives Vol. 16 1967: 22994). A direct consequence of the Czechoslovakian crisis was the Yugoslavian development of a total national defence and further improvement of economic cooperation with the West (Johnson, cited in Hasan 1981b: 67). However, relations between Yugoslavia and the Soviet bloc have improved in the following years, undisturbed even by the 1974 Belgrade trials of Cominformists, 'charged with the crime of conspiracy against the state' (Hasan 1981b: 74).

Similar trials and imprisonment of people accused of counter-revolutionary propaganda and endangerment of the state would continue even after Tito's death in 1980 (Blanuša 2011b), but that is another story that mostly belongs to internal affairs of Yugoslavia and other Balkan countries. However, alongside the proclaimed meaning and rhetoric of the Non-Aligned Movement, anti-imperial and similar anti-Soviet conspiratorial interpretations served an important ideological and political function in Yugoslavian international politics, as well as conflict-management inside this multinational country. Communist leaders used these conspiracy theories as an ideological 'glue' for the purpose of internal identity politics of 'brotherhood and unity' among constituent ethnic groups of Yugoslavia. The aim was not only to enforce the same perception of threat, but also to demonstrate that gathering so many countries in the world against common enemies expressed Yugoslavian inner strength. However, with enduring economic and political crises in Yugoslavia and other Balkan communist states, such conspiracy theories would lose their importance. With the downfall of communism and transition, anti-Western and New World Order conspiracy theories, imagined mostly from the nationalist worldview, took their place as the new form of ideological resistance to ruthless capitalism. Several empirical studies conducted in the Balkan countries already confirmed this hypothesis (Blanuša 2013; Colăcel, Pintilescu 2017; Turjačanin et al. 2018).

## Conspiracy theories about dissolution of Yugoslavia, wars and social change

The scholarly literature (e.g. Fink-Hafner 1995; Ramet 2007) describes several converging reasons for the violent breakup of Yugoslavia. First, economic deterioration and high unemployment led to widespread social discontent. Then, the growing political illegitimacy of the communist system led to ideological 'disillusionment' and requests for democracy. Another problem was a dysfunctional and rigid federal system, decentralised along ethnic lines. A further factor was the nationalistic leadership agency that leaned on authoritarian political culture. These leaders built mutually incompatible national grand narratives, imbued with the sense of being victimised by other constituent nations, heightened by the memory of past atrocities, mostly from periods of the Second World War and the rule of the Ottoman Empire. The most elaborate conspiracy theory of this kind was outlined in the Memorandum of the Serbian Academy of Sciences and Arts, which appeared in 1986 in the Serbian press, and in Croatia is usually considered a fundamental text of Serbian nationalists' project of Greater Serbia. Another aspect of human agency refers to the international community and its leaders, whose role was variously depicted along a wide range, from being victims of their own prejudices toward the Balkans to accusations of political manipulation and conspiracy. For example, Veljko Kadijević, minister of defence in the Yugoslavian government, claimed in 1991 'an insidious plan has been drawn up to destroy Yugoslavia. Stage one is civil war. Stage two is foreign intervention. Then puppet regimes will be set up throughout Yugoslavia.' (B.B.C. 1995) Slobodan Milošević also used the theory of international conspiracy against Yugoslavia in his defence at the International Criminal Tribunal for the former Yugoslavia: 'It existed through the joint forces of the secessionists, Germany and the Vatican, and also the rest of the countries of the European Community and the United States' (cited in Gordy 2013: 103). Conspiratorial interpretations in public discourse often accompanied scholarly explanations, giving them a more ominous tone. For example, the reasons for the economic deterioration of Yugoslavia were attributed to international financial institutions, N.A.T.O. and the U.S.A., as well as to neighbouring countries, blaming them for secret plans to secure the main routes of oil and/or to strengthen the N.A.T.O. influence, as part of a larger conspiracy to attain world leadership in the post-Cold War era. However, beliefs in conspiracies orchestrated by external and internal enemies did not stop with the establishment of post-Yugoslavian states. The content and sinister reasons behind the alleged conspiracies may have changed at least partially, but the sense of being the victim of conspiracies endured in each of these former Yugoslavian republics, contributing to their internal and external politics.

Wars waged between states usually lead to opposite interpretations about causes, responsibilities, leading actors, victims, perpetrators and consequences. These traumatic experiences produce conflictual narratives about a violent past and reproduce themselves for new generations. In the last three decades, coming to terms with the violent past in the former Yugoslavia was mostly unsuccessful and resisted by nationalistic mythology in the new states. Furthermore, all these societies were in the last three decades passing through the trauma of social change (Sztompka 2000: 155) toward pluralist societies, market economy, liberal democracy and a wider process of globalisation. In these processes, narratives expressing various enmities and collective concerns often took the form of conspiracy theories. In that sense, recent survey researches of local conspiracy theories in Bosnia and Herzegovina, Croatia, Macedonia and Serbia (Milošević Đorđević et al. 2018) have found a strong inclination to believe in contrasting conspiratorial explanations of the causes and key events of post-Yugoslavian wars by those ethnic groups that were a part of mutual conflict. For example, Croatian citizens for the most part do not believe that the Croatian government had a plan for ethnic cleansing of Serbs from Croatian territory in its military operations, and strongly believe that the Serbian intellectuals, politicians and Yugoslav Peoples' Army started the wars in Croatia and Bosnia with a goal of creating Greater Serbia. Serbian citizens in these matters have the completely opposite view. An even bigger contrast in these views exists between ethnic Serbs and Croats in Bosnia and Herzegovina, which shows even more homogenous beliefs in conspiracy theories in line with their ethnic grand narratives. Compared to them, Bosniaks (as the third party in the conflict) and Macedonian citizens (who were out of the conflict) do not show such stark differences in their beliefs in war-related conspiracy theories. Regarding conspiracy theories indicating the trauma of social change, i.e. troubles with privatisation, international financial institutions and the E.U., the pattern of such beliefs is much more similar in those countries (Bovan et al. 2018).

## Conclusion

All previously studied instances of conspiratorial discourses show their embeddedness in the historico-political context inherent to European collective experience since the late nineteenth century. Through the lenses of Orientalism and Balkanism, worldwide travelling conspiratorial discourses, and local conspiracy theories about the war and social change, Europe and the Balkans mutually constitute each other as opposites, and yet the process remains permanently unfinished. How similar or different the Balkans are from other parts of Europe in these terms is a matter of further research, and it is rather a question of degree, not of kind. However, by analysing these wild hermeneutics of suspicion, we can confirm that it is possible to:

> Write a [piece of] history of limits – of those obscure gestures … through which a culture rejects something which for it becomes the Exterior. [However,] interrogating a culture on its limit-experiences, is to question it within the confines of history, on a rupture which forms the very birth of its history.
> *(Foucault, 1961, cited in O'Farrell 2005: 91)*

## References

Abadi, J. (1996) 'Israel and the Balkan states', *Middle Eastern Studies*, 32(4): 296–320.
Balibar, É. (2004) *We, the people of Europe? Reflections on transnational citizenship*, Princeton/Oxford: Princeton University Press.
B.B.C. (1995) 'The Death of Yugoslavia'.
Bergmann, W. and Wyrwa, U. (2017) 'Antisemitism', in U. Daniel et al. (eds.) *1914–1918 online international encyclopedia of the First World War*, Berlin: Freie Universität Berlin.
Bjelić, D. and Savić, O. (2002) *Balkan as metaphor: between globalization and fragmentation*, Cambridge, London: The MIT Press.
Blanuša, N. (2010) 'The structure of conspiratorial beliefs in Croatia', *Anali Hrvatskog politološkog društva 2009*, 6(1): 113–43.
Blanuša, N. (2011a) 'Depathologized conspiracy theories and cynical reason: discursive positions and phantasmatic structures', *Politička misao*, 48(1): 94–107.
Blanuša, N. (2011b) *Teorije zavjera i Hrvatska politička zbilja 1980–2007*, Zagreb: Plejada.
Blanuša, N. (2013) 'Internal memory divided: conspiratorial thinking, ideological and historical cleavages in Croatia: lessons for Europe', *European Quarterly of Political Attitudes and Mentalities*, 2(4): 16–33.
Blümel, T. (2017) 'Antisemitism as political theology in Greece and its impact on Greek Jewry, 1967–1979', *Southeast European and Black Sea Studies*, 17(2): 181–202.
Bovan, K., Blanuša, N., Milošević Đorđević, J. and Vranić, A. (2018) 'Oh brother, where art thou? Common specters and antagonistic views on conspiratorial politics in B&H, Croatia and Serbia', *COST Conference: COMPACT*, Dubrovnik, Croatia, 20 October.
Boym, S. (1999) 'Conspiracy theories and literary ethics: Umberto Eco, Danilo Kiš and the protocols of Zion', *Comparative Literature*, 51(2): 97–122.

Bratich, J.Z. (2008) *Conspiracy panics: political rationality and popular culture*, Albany: State University of New York Press.
Brustein, W.I. and King, D.R. (2004a) 'Anti-Semitism in Europe before the Holocaust', *International Political Science Review*, 25(1): 35–53.
Brustein, W.I. and King, D.R. (2004b) 'Balkan Anti-Semitism: the cases of Bulgaria and Romania before the Holocaust', *East European Politics and Societies*, 18(3): 430–54.
Byford, J. (2008) *Denial and repression of Anti-Semitism: post-communist remembrance of the Serbian bishop Nikolaj Velimirovic*, Budapest: Central European University Press.
Cohn, N. (2005) *Warrant for genocide: thy myth of the Jewish world conspiracy and protocols of the Elders of Zion*, London: Serif.
Colăcel, O. and Pintilescu, C. (2017) 'From literary culture to post-Communist media: Romanian conspiracism', *Messages, Sages and Ages*, 4(2): 31–40.
Déak, I. (2010) 'Antisemitism in eastern Europe (excluding Russia and the Soviet Empire) since 1848', in R.S. Levy and A.S. Lindemann (eds.) *Antisemitism: a History*, New York: Oxford University Press, pp. 222–36.
Dentith, M. (2014) *The philosophy of conspiracy theories*, Basingstoke: Palgrave Macmillan.
Fink-Hafner, D. (1995) 'The Disintegration of Yugoslavia', *Canadian Slavonic Papers*, 37(3–4): 339–56.
Foucault, M. (1980) *Power/knowledge: selected interviews and other writings 1972–1977*, trans. C. Gordon et al., New York City: Pantheon Books.
Georgieff, A. (2013) 'Double faced Bulgaria', in F.S. Cecilia, B. Jerichow and A. Jerichow (eds.) *Civil society and the Holocaust: international perspectives on resistance and rescue*, Copenhagen: Humanity in Action.
Glenny, M. (2012) *The Balkans: nationalism, war, and the great powers, 1804–2012*, Toronto: House of Anansi Press.
Goldstein, I. (2002) 'The Jews of Yugoslavia 1918–1941: antisemitism and the struggle for equality', *Jewish Studies at the Central European University*, 2 (1999–2001): 51–64.
Goldstein, I. (2005) 'Croatia', in R.S. Levy (ed.) *Antisemitism: a historical encyclopedia of prejudice and persecution*, Santa Barbara/Denver/Oxford: ABC CLIO, pp. 147–8.
Gordon, J. (1954) 'Eastern Europe', *American Jewish Yearbook*, 55: 263–302.
Gordy, E. (2013) *Guilt, responsibility, and denial: the past at stake in post-Milošević Serbia*, Philadelphia: University of Pennsylvania Press.
Granville, J. (1998) 'Hungary, 1956: the Yugoslav connection', *Europe-Asia Studies*, 50(3): 493–517.
Hasan, S. (1981a) 'Yugoslavia's foreign policy under Tito (1945–80) – 1', *Pakistan Horizon*, 34(3): 82–120.
Hasan, S. (1981b) 'Yugoslavia's foreign policy under Tito (1945–80) – 2', *Pakistan Horizon*, 34(4): 62–103.
Hoare, M.A. (2017) 'Islamophobia and antisemitism in the Balkans', in J. Renton and B. Gidley (eds.) *Antisemitism and islamophobia in Europe: a shared story?*, London: Palgrave Macmillan, pp. 165–85.
Hobsbawm, E. (1995) *The age of extremes: 1914–1991*, London: an Abacus Book.
J.F.K. Presidential Library and Museum, 'Non-Aligned nations summit meeting, Belgrade, 1 September 1961'. Available at: www.jfklibrary.org/asset-viewer/archives/JFKPOF/104/JFKPOF-104-004. [Accessed 9 September 2019.]
*Keesing's Contemporary Archives*, vol. 7 (1949), Cambridge: Longman Group.
*Keesing's Contemporary Archives*, vol. 11 (1958), Cambridge: Longman Group.
*Keesing's Contemporary Archives*, vol. 16 (1967), Cambridge: Longman Group.
Kerenji, E. (2005) 'Ljotić, Dimitrije (1891–1945)', in R.S. Levy (ed.) *Antisemitism: a historical encyclopedia of prejudice and persecution*, Santa Barbara/Denver/Oxford: ABC CLIO, p. 431.
Kiš, D. (1983) *The encyclopedia of the dead*, reprint, Evanston: Northwestern University Press, 1997.
Kulenska, V. (2012) 'The antisemitic press in Bulgaria at the end of the 19th century', *Quest: Issues in Contemporary Jewish History – Journal of Fondazione CDEC*, 3: 72–85.
Leff, L.M. (2005) 'Gougenot des Mousseaux, Henri (1805–1876)', in R.S. Levy (ed.) *Antisemitism: a historical encyclopedia of prejudice and persecution*, Santa Barbara/Denver/Oxford: ABC CLIO, p. 282.
Lewkovicz, L. (1999) *The Jewish community of Thessaloniki: an exploration of memory and identity in a Mediterranean city*, thesis, London, UK: University of London.
Margaroni, M. (2014) 'The blood libel on Greek island sin the nineteenth century', in R. Nemes and D. Unkowski (eds.) *Sites of European antisemitism in the age of mass politics, 1880–1918*, Hannover/London: University Press of New England, pp. 178–96.

Milošević Đorđević, J., Žeželj, I., Turjačanin, V., Lukić, P., Gjoneska, B. and Krouwel, A. (2018) 'Conspiracy theories about the conflict: blaming the enemy or finding a joint culprit', *Conspiracy theories in/about the Balkans*, Zagreb, Croatia, 18 December.

Mužić, I. (2000) *Masonstvo u Hrvata: Masoni i Jugoslavija*, Split: Laus.

O'Farrell, C. (2005) *Michel Foucault*, London: Sage.

Pigden, C. (2007) 'Conspiracy theories and the conventional wisdom', *Episteme: A Journal of Social Epistemology*, (4)2: 219–32.

Pipes, D. (1997) *Conspiracy: how the paranoid style flourishes and where it comes from*, New York: Free Press.

Psarras, D. (2013) *The best seller of hatred: the protocols of the elders of Zion in Greece, 1920–2013*, Athens: Polis.

Rakopoulos, T. (2018) 'Show me the money: conspiracy theories and distant wealth', *History and Anthropology*, 29(3): 376–91.

Ramet, S.P. (2007) 'The dissolution of Yugoslavia: competing narratives of resentment and blame', *Südosteuropa: Zeitschrift für Politik und Gesellschaft*, 55(1): 26–69.

Rosenfeld, A.H. (eds.) (2013) *Resurgent antisemitism: global perspectives*, Bloomington: Indiana University Press.

Sekelj, L. (1981) 'Antisemitizam u Jugoslaviji (1918–1945)', *Revija za sociologiju*, XI(3–4): 179–89.

Sekelj, Laslo (2002) 'Antisemitizam u S(F)R Jugoslaviji (1945-1991-2000)', *Nova srpska politička misao*, Posebno izdanje br. 1: 93–115.

Silvestru, O. (2012) 'The Jewish question "resolved": the morphology and purpose of anti-semitic discourses in Romania after the congress of Berlin (1878–1879)', *Anuarul Institutului de Istorie 'George Barițiu' din Cluj-Napoca*, LI: 113–34.

Stamatopoulos, D. (2018) *The eastern question or Balkan nationalism(s): Balkan history reconsidered*, Vienna, Austria: V&R Unipress and Vienna University Press.

Stefanov, P. (2002) 'Bulgarians and Jews throughout history', *Occasional Papers on Religion in Eastern Europe*, 22(6): 1–11.

Sztompka, P. (2000) 'Cultural trauma: the other face of social change', *European Journal of Social Theory*, 3(4): 449–66.

Totok, W. (2005) 'Romania, Post-Soviet', in R.S. Levy (ed.) *Antisemitism: a historical encyclopedia of prejudice and persecution*, Santa Barbara/Denver/Oxford: ABC CLIO, pp. 419–20.

Thompson, E.M. (1953) *Communist anti-semitism: editorial research reports 1953 (Vol. I)*, Washington, DC: CQ Press.

Todorova, M. (1997) *Imagining the Balkans: updated edition*, reprint, Oxford: Oxford University Press, 2009.

Toš, M. (2012) *Zgodovinski spomin na prekmurske Jude*, Ljubljana: Založba ZRC.

Turjačanin, V., Puhalo, S. and Šajn, D. (2018) *Conspiracy theories in Bosnia and Herzegovina: a psychological study of conspiracy theory beliefs in a post-conflict society*, Sarajevo: Friedrich-Ebert-Stiftung.

Vulešica, M. (2014) 'An antisemitic aftertaste: Anti-Jewish violence in Habsburg Croatia' in R. Nemes and D. Unkowski (eds.) *Sites of European antisemitism in the age of mass politics, 1880–1918*, Hanover and London: University Press of New England, pp. 115–134.

Wedekind, M. (2010) 'The mathematization of the human being: anthropology and ethno-politics in Romania during the late 1930s and early 1940s', *New Zealand Slavonic Journal*, 44: 27–67.

# 5.7
# CONSPIRACY THEORIES IN TURKEY[1]

Doğan Gürpınar and Türkay Salim Nefes

## Introduction

The Turkish national metanarrative, already in place by the late nineteenth century, stemmed from the fear of imperial dismemberment provoked by threats from abroad and within. This apprehension and perceived vulnerability and exposure brought about not only a nationalist furor, but also a conspiratorial mindset that spotted enemies everywhere against whom one should be ever watchful. Although the metanarrative was first propounded by the state discourse of the declining late Ottoman Empire (especially the Hamidian state) and inherited by Young Turks and Kemalists, the Islamist metanarrative arose from the same context. The birth of conspiracy theories relating to Jews and Freemasons can be dated to the early twentieth century, exacerbated by Zionist demands to settle in the then Ottoman territory of Palestine, and by the existence of the community of *Dönme* (Jewish converts, also known as 'conversos'). The association – at times, even the identification – of Young Turks, and then Kemalists, with Freemasonry and Zionists, was at the root of Islamist conspiracy theories (Nefes 2012). Contemporary Turkish conspiracy theories are deeply rooted within a specific historical and discursive space. Their emergence, dissemination and proliferation are possible only if they comply with pre-existing ideas and sentiments. Examining the traumas revolving around the collapse of the Ottoman Empire, this chapter will explain the origins and fantasies of Turkish nationalism undergoing an imperial collapse (for studies of Turkish conspiracy theories, see Gürpınar 2011, 2013a, 2014; Özman, Dede 2012; Yeğen 2014; Nefes 2017, 2018a, 2018b).

## The demise of an empire: The Ottoman legacy

The late Ottoman/early Turkish nationalist metanarrative presumed that the Ottoman Empire had been partitioned as a result of the plots of international and domestic foes. The former were the great European powers, first and foremost arch-imperialist Britain. Domestically, the enemies of the nation were imagined to be non-Muslims, who were supposedly being steered and manipulated by their political and religious leaders, encouraged by ethnically Turkish rootless, liberal, cosmopolitan intellectuals who had fallen under the spell of Western propaganda, along with other subversives. All enemies were thus amalgamated, tightly associated, and rendered as extensions and accomplices of the overarching global plot. Denying them any political and ideological agency, domestic enemies were perceived as not only willing fifth columns, but also on the payroll of a mastermind.

The non-Muslims, as the usual suspects, were affirmed as the main enemies within the nation's borders, harbouring agendas, predispositions and interests that not only complied with, but also collectively contradicted, the interests of the Ottoman state. The non-Muslims grew rich throughout the nineteenth century, acting as middlemen between the incoming European merchants and the local peasantry (Kasaba 1988). Their complicity with encroaching European capitalism ensured their self-interests diverged from those of the Ottoman state. Their enrichment was evidence of their treachery in the eyes of those who considered the economy to be a zero-sum game, presuming that non-Muslims would have grabbed the wealth of the Muslims in the first instance (Kaiser 1997; Ihrig 2016: 74–9). The elusive 'cosmopolitans' (*kozmopolitler*) also had a share in the Ottoman retreat. By being ideologically depraved and unreliable, they were influential in the dissemination of perilous ideas with the potential to weaken and corrupt national awareness and vigilance.

Whereas nineteenth-century Ottoman reformism marked the liberal phase of Turkish modernisation, failures and disillusionment led the empire toward alternative policies in an effort to avoid the otherwise inevitable imperial fate. Sultan Abdülhamid II (who reigned 1876–1909) not only ruled the empire with an iron fist, but also introduced a pervasive culture of conspiracy. Suspecting subversion at every instance, he designed a surveillance state obsessed with collecting information from spies within the empire and by embassies abroad, further feeding his paranoia (Riedler 2011; Gürpınar 2013b). The Hamidian culture of conspiracy was inherited and appropriated by the Young Turks who had dethroned the sultan. The Young Turks in power drifted towards radical Turkist and authoritarian policies, despite their hitherto rhetoric of rights, liberties and freedom (Hanioğlu 2008: 62–111). For the Young Turks, non-Muslims were only exploiting the rhetoric of rights and liberties while deviously pursuing agendas that were in diametric opposition to the interests of the imperial centre and the gullible Turks (Kayalı 1997; Zürcher 2010).

In the age of high imperialism, Western powers aspired to grab territories for themselves, from Africa to Asia. For the Young Turks, the picture was crystal clear: European capital had always been fully integrated and freely exchanged across the Ottoman territories, running banks, railways and facilities, and buying cheap raw materials and selling industrial goods, killing local proto-industry and artisanship. According to this scenario, the Ottoman lands would eventually surrender to the clutches of imperialism unless countered by an effective military resolve. The 'cosmopolitan' intellectuals were also seen to be complicit, inadvertently serving the grand plot, and were caricatured as naïve ignoramuses with no grasp of actual politics, incapable of gauging the real intentions of the ominous European powers who had easily duped them.

Amidst such a geopolitical quagmire and legitimisation crisis in the Ottoman Empire, it did not take long for the Young Turks to come up with a scheme that amalgamated all of the 'enemies' that they should overwhelm. Their evolving ideology presumed a far-reaching showdown between 'us' and 'them', the two categories being inherent, impermeable and prevailing, fixed through the centuries. For them, war was not merely a military involvement pursued at the fronts, but a lifetime encounter that was fought in times of both war and peace on different fronts, and beginning with the rearing and training of pre-school children (Beşikçi 2012: 203–45; Ateş 2012; Grüßhaber 2018: 114–29). Conspiracy was ever-present, omnipresent and omnipotent, meaning that a patriot had to be constantly vigilant. The rise of nationalism, demanding rights and liberties as well as outright independence, appalled the empire, which failed to respond and accommodate. This brought the dissolution of the multi-ethnic and multi-confessional Ottoman Empire. Whereas a Turkish nation-state that Turkified the remaining territory offered the only viable political exit from this predicament, conspiracies were sought for the separationist movements refusing to accommodate the age of nationalism. The Sharif Hussein rebellion helped and partially organised by T.E. Lawrence during the First World War further boosted this scare and fostered a stab-in-the-back account of events, accusing Arabs of treason against the caliph. This narrative was also instrumental in the Kemalist rhetoric depicting Arabs as willing accomplices of imperialism who were zealously favoured and praised by Turkish conservatives for being Muslim brethren. This also demonstrated Turkish Islamists' ideological fixation and foolhardiness (Çiçek 2012). Armenian genocide was also justified on the grounds of Armenians being fifth columns stemming from the same ontological insecurity and fear of national annihilation (Ekmekçioğlu 2016: 7–8).

## The Sèvres Treaty vs. the Lausanne Treaty

The post-First World War invasion of Turkey and Istanbul following the Ottoman defeat was perceived as the darkest hour of Turkish history. This fright, however, resulted in the eternalisation, naturalisation and normalisation of the existential fear of national annihilation as the order of the day. The sentiment would later be dubbed 'Sèvres Syndrome' after the Treaty of Sèvres that was signed in 1920 between the victorious Allies and the defeated Ottoman Empire, requiring the Turks to dissolve most of its military and relinquish significant territory, including Turkish-majority areas.

Sèvres was overturned by Mustafa Kemal Atatürk, who reorganised and assumed the command of the rump Ottoman army and defeated the invading Greek army. Following his military victory, the treaty was rescinded and renegotiated, introducing favourable clauses to the Turks in the Treaty of Lausanne signed in 1923, which annulled the former Treaty of Sèvres. In Turkish political discourse since then, however, Sèvres and Lausanne imply so much more than two treaties. The term 'Sèvresphobia' was coined in the 1990s to describe the unyielding belief that Turkey was under imminent attack from the West, in a bid to overturn the Treaty of Lausanne (Kirişci, Winrow 1997: 184, 193; Piccoli et al. 2001: 115–18; Yılmaz 2006: 29–40; Guida 2008: 37–52; Göçek 2011; Nefes 2013, 2018a).

This ontological insecurity established a mutually exclusive dichotomy between the two treaties. While the Lausanne treaty epitomised the deliverance from the throes of imperialism that had been imposed upon the Ottoman Empire for at least a century, Sèvres, in contrast, was seen as the very quintessence of the mischievous ends sought and attained by the West, as a metaphysical entity. Sèvres implied subjugation to Western imperialist enemies not only in political, but also ideological, terms, smacking of empty imperial pageantry, sycophancy, a servile culture, the self-serving Ottoman *ancien régime* and cosmopolitan liberals. Lausanne, in contrast, denoted selfless zeal, commitment, masculinity, audaciousness and resolve, along with ideological self-righteousness. The Treaty of Lausanne was regarded as sacrosanct by secular nationalists, in that it resulted in the establishment of the secular republic and the liberation of Anatolia from European and Greek occupation (and imperialism); the two were inseparable, for them there could be no secular republic without Lausanne.

This dichotomy also offered 'history in a nutshell', making a definite and compact interpretation of the course of modern Turkish history. In brief, this narrative posited the Sèvres and Lausanne treaties as two antagonistic, decisive moments in modern Turkish history, and suggested that the Western powers had never renounced their claims or longing for the Sèvres treaty. According to this position, Westerners never forget, but only change the means by which they conspire, switching to subtler schemes that were more difficult to fathom unless the beholder was adequately equipped to spot such conspiracies. To these ends, they have, since then, supported and sponsored the subversive forces within Turkey, especially the Kurdish separatist and Islamic movements that aimed to weaken the Kemalist-republican ethos (Cevizoğlu 2007; Baytok 2007; Çekiç 2014).

The Manichean and conspiratorial iconography also served well in the dissemination and perpetuation of this fear. The Sèvres map became a household image that every Turkish student encountered in textbooks and in the media. This imagery clearly depicted the innate incompatibility of the two discursive universes: One being republican, idealist, patriotic and selfless, and the other selfish, unpatriotic and impervious to social woes. As we will see, this perceived dichotomy became all the more apparent in the post-1980 neoliberal and post-national order.

## Kemalism and Neo-Kemalism from the 1930s to 2000s

For the Turkish secular-nationalist conspiratorial universe, as proven impeccably by the Treaty of Lausanne, the national idea is robustly and inextricably ingrained within the very self of Atatürk. Any diversion from his principles is tantamount to national treason. Furthermore, it is unimaginable that anyone would ever willingly renounce and dismiss national belonging. Anyone who deviates from this ideal could only be construed as accomplices to the global master conspiracy, or commanded and readily manipulated by a puppet master, namely the U.S.A.

Kemalism conceived two irreconcilable camps: The camp of reaction versus the camp of progressivism. Kemalist progressivism was resolutely nationalist, firmly upholding national vigour and ethos and the project of national enlightenment. As an ideology, it blended nationalism and faith in modernity, perceiving modernisation as a transformative agent of the nation. This conviction was almost unequivocally endorsed by intellectuals, although the Kemalist-nationalist consensus gradually eroded as the new generation of intellectuals came to move towards the left. This necessitated adjustments and mutations to the Kemalist premise, although a more drastic appropriation came in the 1960s with the adaption of Third World left-nationalism. This new permutation was dubbed 'neo-Kemalism'. It challenged and repudiated the status-quo Kemalism that was strictly pro-U.S. and was called 'wardrobe Kemalism' (Selçuk 1966), to indicate it as nationalist only in appearance. The 1960s Cold War conjuncture was to be historicised and posited within a historical scheme nationalising the Marxist rendering of history and global order.

It is not difficult, however, to detect the Kemalist coating that survived intact under alternative disguises within this leftist/Marxist scheme, in which no difference between the West, Christendom and global capitalism is discernible. The elusive designation 'West' serves as an amorphous term that enables the ontologisation, essentialisation and eternalisation of the hostility. This narrative supplies the necessary flexibility to allow the nature and underlying motives behind this elusive West to be spotted. The ambiguity of the term renders its articulation interchangeable, whether referring to Christians, imperialists, capitalists or nation-states (British, French, etc.) against the Turks. In this respect, the conspiracy narrative can easily adapt to Islamist, nationalist (Kemalist) or socialist scripts. The pivot of this meta-account envisaged a sharp and irreconcilable dichotomy that exists between the 'West' and 'us'. This essentialised and eternalised antagonism is shared in leftist, rightist, Islamist or Kemalist conspiratorial minds.

The rising Third-Worldist and Maoist currents and Marxist imperialism scheme were built on and well suited to this inherited national framing. Whereas the 1970s witnessed a rise of socialism, especially among students and intellectuals, and, to a lesser degree, workers, the military coup of 1980 came down hard on the Turkish left, leading to the arrest of tens of thousands of leftist sympathisers and activists and the banning of leftist organisations (Zürcher 1998:

293–4). The 1980s heavily tarnished the public prominence and power of the left as a towering social force, leading, by the end of the decade, to the demise of global socialism as a feasible project with mass appeal. Many disillusioned Turkish socialists abandoned or moderated their leftist commitments and faith in the global revolution for the promise of a better, more progressive and peaceful world guided by Marxist theory; others sought refuge in reformist and democratic socialism. The new leftist focus gravitated toward anti-militarist, environmentalist, feminist and L.G.B.T. agendas, yet many other disillusioned leftists shunned and even disdained these refuges, claiming they were tantamount to the wrecking and undoing of socialism. For them, gay rights, the environment and identity politics were mere shallow fads, distracting from the socialist pledge to transform the world (Perinçek 2000).

Harbouring deep hostility to the new left agendas, these disillusioned socialists drifted overwhelmingly toward anti-imperialist Kemalism, keeping their anti-imperialism intact but abandoning their hitherto egalitarian agendas and utopias. In many ways, this was a homecoming and brought about a new ideological amalgamation known in Turkish as *ulusalcılık*. Although the phrase's direct translation into English would be nationalism per se, partially because it is a Turkish (Mongolian) word as opposed to the Arabic loanword *milliyetçilik* (the standard word standing for nationalism), it was tinged exclusively with left-leaning, hard-line and radically secularist connotations. From their Marxist anti-imperialism, they arrived at a republican nationalism (resembling French *souverainisme*) that represented the main dichotomy between the enlightened and national republic and its enemies in the age of globalisation and the demise of nation-states (Gürpınar 2011: 265–71). This new ideological amalgamation coalesced leftist, rightist and centrist features claiming to assemble 'patriots' against those traitors in thrall to the nation-statist ethos, including Islamists, Kurdish nationalists, liberals and socialists in the service of imperialism.

This xenophobic nationalism claimed to be the only true form of Kemalism, alleging a direct genealogy from Mustafa Kemal Atatürk and his political discourse right up to the 2000s. However, this appropriated form of Kemalism differed greatly from the mainstream Atatürkism that had prevailed from the 1950s onwards in its sharp intolerance of ethnic and cultural diversity, its xenophobic nationalism and its blatant authoritarianism, which was in stark contrast to the conditional and pragmatic peace of Kemalism with democracy. It was, nonetheless, staunchly built on Kemalist vocabulary and cultural affinities, and this predisposition was made possible thanks to the perpetuation of a mindset that had been produced under the distinctive circumstances of a given historical juncture, at a time of imperial retreat and the partitioning of the Ottoman Empire. Benefiting from a historical reservoir of more than a century, the neo-nationalist ideologues twisted the national narrative to suit their political agenda and rendered it the only legitimate and national programme. Arguably, this shift was a symptom of the crisis of nation-statist ideologies in the age of globalisation, as well as the rise of identity politics and pluralism. The hitherto consensual national narrative became conspiratorial in an effort to respond to and debunk perceived threats, as it failed to explain the new social, political and cultural realities.

A wealth of conspiracy theories allegedly exposing secret plots by the 'global elite' to partition Turkey came to circulate on the Internet, as well as in the popular press and on television, promoted by high-profile pundits whose books had a large readership. Many conspiratorial themes were exploited exhaustively including: Christian missionary activity in Turkey (Sabah 2005); the alleged Greek claims in the Eastern Black Sea (Pontus) (Sarınay et al. 1999; Bulut 2007; for an academic treatment of this fear, see Asan 2009); Israel's territorial claims in southeastern Turkey; the aspirations of the ecumenical Greek patriarchy in Istanbul (Yıldırım, M. 2004; Altındal 2004); and the intrigue in the Vatican regarding Turkey (Altındal 1993, 2005,

2006). Not surprisingly, the E.U. was accused of orchestrating these covert schemes, which were naively overlooked or consciously obscured by the liberal intelligentsia.

The themes, premises and assumptions of these conspiracy theories are concomitantly novel and age-old and are derived from the lexicon and grammar of the founding nationalist ideology of the secular Turkish republic. All of the circulating conspiracy theories were built on the preconceived historical setting and national episteme that perceived the course of the late Ottoman Empire and the Turkish War of Independence (1918–1922), not belonging to a distinctive historical context, but as recurring episodes in an enduring and eternal struggle between two unchanging and perpetually antagonistic parties (Özkan 2001; Yıldırım, U. 2004; Manisalı 2006; Coşkun 2008;).

## Islamist conspiratorial universe

Although Kemalist aversion to imperialism and liberalism was fraught with conspiracy theories, Islamism was even more profoundly infatuated with a conspiratorial outlook. Islamists and conservatives had long conceived of themselves as in a perpetual war with the Zionist-Freemasonic plot aiming to subjugate Turkey and Islam. Accordingly, only the Islamic and conservative bulwark posed the weighty pillar of resistance against this threat. For them, in fact, Westernisation itself was a conspiracy imposed by the West and carried out by local accomplices, including the Freemasons, Jews and *Dönmes* pulling the strings of the Westernised elite duped by Western ideological propaganda. This Westernisation sought to undermine traditional morals and values, to disassociate Islamists from the national past. This would render the Turkish people defenceless, feeble and misguided against Western transgression, and was a course that was implemented by no lesser accomplices than those who ruled the country, beginning with Mahmud II (reigned 1808–1839). The Tanzimat reforms were considered tantamount to an abandonment of the Islamic mores and culture that reigned over the moral landscape that secured the grandeur and splendour of the polity and the nation. The Tanzimat Westernisation was followed by the Young Turk and Kemalist regimes in the same vein, with the only diversion being the reign of Abdülhamid II, who seemingly was deposed by the Young Turks, but was, in reality, deposed by those behind them, i.e. the Jews, Freemasons and Western imperialists. The Islamists long believed that the Turkish establishment (which they were sure existed as an intact and commanding entity since the onset of Turkish Westernisation) had been under the influence of the Freemasons, Jews and *Dönmes* since then. The Bilderberg narrative that had become fashionable by the 1970s was also superimposed upon this narrative, according to which the global super elite and international Jewry were puppet-mastering their lackeys (Yesevizade 1979; Çetin 1997).

Antisemitism was also rife among Islamic and conservative circles (Nefes 2015a). *The Protocols of the Elders of Zion* had been the quintessential ur-text of this conspiratorial mindset, which had been slightly appropriated for the Islamist agenda since its earliest translations and dissemination throughout the Islamic world (Achcar 2010). During the Cold War, this mental framework was incorporated into the anti-communist frenzy amalgamating communism, Jewry and the West. The conservative and Islamic anti-communist strand perceived communism less as an economic doctrine than as a transgression of moral and social order and an ominous threat to the family and the nation. It was, in fact, perceived as a sinister plot run by the global order, not far from the visions of *The Protocols*, yet built upon local cultural references. Aversion to the encroachment of modernity was universal, replicating the same pattern.

Necip Fazıl Kısakürek (1904–1983) emerged as the most vocal Islamic public intellectual, having mastered and rebranded this narrative for consumption for the next generation by the late 1940s. Since then he became an iconic and unassailable authority among Islamic circles. His book on Abdülhamid II (1965) became essential reading, establishing a cult in which the sultan was portrayed as the saviour of Islamic lands and dignity. According to this narrative, Abdülhamid was deposed by the Young Turks in the service of the Zionists/Jews vexed with his (alleged) obstruction of their colonising Palestine and his pledge to reinvigorate the empire and keep it intact.

Realising that they would have little opportunity to colonise Palestine as long as the formidable sultan remained in power, Herzl and his cabal considered the possibility of a coup. The link was so obvious that 'whereas hitherto the constitutionalist movement was hazy, chaotic and obscure, it was transformed into a well-organized offensive subsequent to Herzl's dismissal by Abdülhamid' (Müftüoğlu 1985: 246). Tainted with secularist, libertinist and positivistic ideas, the Young Turks became easy prey, operating as willing accomplices in the Jewish conspiracy. Alienated from their authentic culture, and hence losing their morals and consciousness, they would serve as docile zombies, easily manipulated by their puppet masters:

> As Abdülhamid II was well-aware ... the Jews were well-disciplined and commanded power in different areas. They controlled international finance, trade and the European press. They first activated the European press and then galvanized the anti-Abdülhamid forces and instigated instability.

They also, according to this theory, spurred a campaign of slander, and it was the Jews who dubbed Abdülhamid II the 'Red Sultan' (*le sultan rogue*), a term coined allegedly in reference to his Armenian 'policies', but in fact attributed perniciously by the Jews (Mısıroğlu 1971: 360).

For one conservative author, the mischievous intentions of the Zionists 'had crashed the steel-clad stature of Abdülhamid II.' For him, Abdülhamid II's overwhelming preoccupation in his office was Zionism, in that he not only tracked the Zionist network and activities abroad closely via the Ottoman embassies, but also spied on the Zionist congresses (Çabuk 1990: 243).

The Treaty of Lausanne was a further example of servility to Westernism in the Islamic conspiratorial mind. Although the dichotomy drawn between Lausanne and Sèvres was a quintessentially Kemalist penchant, the Islamists were no less enthusiastic about interpreting the causes of the imperial demise and national decay in a Manichean framework. The Islamist version, however, blamed the Kemalists of subordination, arguing that Lausanne had been a testimony of betrayal and a succumbing to the British mandate, amounting not only to a surrender in material terms (loss of territory, economic concessions), but also, and more importantly, to an ideological capitulation and catastrophe. 'Lausanne as treachery' became a popular Islamist trope, first articulated by Kısakürek (1950). Rıza Nur's erratic autobiography (1967) provided evidences to those who wanted to debunk Lausanne to overturn the Kemalist narrative. Yet, the cult book that most vocally exposed the 'Lausanne treachery' was Kadir Mısıroğlu's 1971 book, aptly titled *Lausanne: Victory or Defeat?*

The *Dönme* community (or *conversos*) is a crypto-Jewish minority in Turkey that originated in the seventeenth century. Due to their secretive nature, there is little reliable information about this group, which is obviously a bonanza for conspiracy theorists who seek to expose what is deliberately concealed. It is estimated that there are 70 000–80 000 people of *Dönme* origin in Turkey, of which around 3000–4000 still follow the *Dönme* belief system (Sisman 2010: 16). The *Dönme* theme has been a salient one in the Islamist conspiratorial mindset. Since the early twentieth century, there have been accusations by Islamists of secret *Dönme* power in Turkish politics (Nefes 2012), with Sèvres syndrome seeming to play an important role in the prevalence of such conspiracy rhetoric in Turkey. In-depth interviews with the conspiracy theorists on this topic (Nefes 2015a) and their readers (Nefes 2015b) demonstrate that the conspiracy theories about the community are related to and triggered by the ontological insecurities deriving from imperial dismemberment and mistrust of non-Muslims.

## Deep state: Reality, discourse and conspiracy theory

The 'deep state', both as a reality and as a discourse, was an original contribution by Turkey to the global conspiracy theory community. The term, in fact, metamorphosed from the term 'Counter-Guerilla' (*Kontrgerilla*) that disseminated among leftist activists arrested during the period of martial law (1971–1973) to refer to the nefarious authority that ran the brutal crackdown and conducted interrogations. The C.I.A. was also accused of being behind the Counter-Guerilla, using torture as an effective counter-insurgency method (Kılıç 2009).

Bülent Ecevit, the incoming leftist prime minister following the period of martial law, first articulated the term. He had become aware of a private branch within the government, unaccountable to political authority, after being asked to approve of the channelling of discretionary funds but advised by the military generals not to inquire into their purpose. Ecevit fulminated against the state-within-state order, identifying it as Counter-Guerilla, and positing himself and his leftist stand in direct conflict with this security establishment. Since then, leftists in Turkey have used the term often to refer to structures outside the reach of political accountability and visibility, whose main role is to counter and repress leftist subversion through extra-legal and unaccountable means.

This was in fact the Turkish branch of a N.A.T.O.-wide stay-behind organisation, the clandestine connections of which were first revealed in Italy (Ganser 2004), although the Turkish case seems to have differed slightly (Söyler 2015). The body was well incorporated into the inherited authoritarian bureaucratic system, and became, inevitably, its constitutive part, persisting after the Cold War but with the new mission of 'defending' the state, not from the communist menace, but from other perceived subversive threats. Whereas the stay-behind schemes were silently eliminated in other NATO countries, the Turkish wing survived, but was directed towards other perceived threats.

The term 'Counter-Guerilla' gave way abruptly to the phrase 'deep state' in late 1996, after a mysterious car accident in the countryside exposed a matrix of power at the intersection of the state security establishment, the mafia and other shady connections. The phrase was first used in 1995 by Ertuğrul Özkök, the flamboyant editor-in-chief of mainstream Turkish newspaper *Hürriyet*, who later attributed the term to Mehmet Ağar – a police chief and *éminence grise* of the deep state who had murmured about the 'reflexes of deep state' to Özkök at a dinner.

Uğur Mumcu (1942–1993), a leftist journalist who was killed in 1993 in a mysterious car bombing, whose perpetrators and motivations still remain unknown, wrote consistently and succinctly about and sought after Çatlı and his connections back in the 1980s (Mumcu 1981; 1984). Mumcu's books and researches were impressive and daring, making him an icon and paragon of investigative journalism. He also introduced the Italian anti-communist establishment to a Turkish readership, exemplified in the notorious revelation of the P2 Masonic lodge, establishing the imagery in Turkey of deep state bureaucrats, politicians and mobsters colluding. Inspired by Mumcu's mastery of the art, in the 1990s, 'deep state revelations' became fashionable among mostly leftist journalists – some mediocre, others seasoned and breath-taking. The 'deep state' also became an attractive theme for professional conspiracy buffs who spotted unlikely liaisons, named names and connected ostensibly unrelated events based on simple reasoning, assumptions and guesswork. These revelations were in fact partially reverberations from the ongoing battles between factions in the 'deep state' (mainly left-wing and right-wing factions, but also organised thought networks and personalised connections and allegiances). The 'deep state' served also as a discourse, functioning as a ploy amid the power struggles in which many 'deep state exposers' were inadvertently manipulated.

Whereas the 'deep state revelation' genre was predominantly a leftist pursuit, by the 2000s Islamists had also taken up the endeavour. In the leftist deep state narrative, the nemesis of the deep state was inherently the left (and, by the 1990s, increasingly the Kurds, in parallel to the rise of the P.K.K.). The Islamist account twisted the narrative, depicting the archenemy of the deep state as Islam and its political outlets. Neither account was wrong, given the shift of the perceived threats after the end of the Cold War and the global rise of Islamism. In particular, the Gülen religious order became highly effective in disseminating the Islamist account, making it the most hegemonic.

It became crystal clear that the Gülenists themselves had infiltrated the state's security bodies as part of a deliberate strategy that had been launched already by the 1980s, backed by centre-right politicians seeking to engender a support base. By the 2000s, Gülenists had become preeminent not only within the police and judiciary, but also, and more troublingly, in the military, which had long been viewed as a secular bastion closed to any infiltration, as the self-assured Turkish military was known for obsessively monitoring the military schools and cadets (Şık 2014). The extent of the infiltration was such that the Gülenists dared to attempt a coup in 2016, that failed spectacularly. In short, by the 2010s, the Gülenists had themselves become 'the deep state' while feigning to oppose it, manipulating the leftist and liberal intellectuals who had heartily supported them against Kemalist authoritarianism. This was a 'conspiracy within a conspiracy'. What was branded as an elimination of the deep state turned out to be an incursion, and an attempt to take over the state, corroborating the claims of those who had argued that Islamists were creating their own deep state, and thus embarrassing liberal optimists.

Once the Gülenists clashed with the A.K.P. in a bid to retain their bureaucratic power and further increase their clout, they were eradicated by the A.K.P. after an atrocious showdown between the two. In the period that followed, Gülenism-bashing became a new source of conspiracy theories, and the Gülenist bureaucratic network came to be known as 'the parallel state' that operated independently of the 'official state'. The deep state was, and is, a fact, without question. Yet it has prompted a conspiratorial craze/industry in the hands of intellectual entrepreneurs. The 'deep state' concept was exported from Turkey to the international arena, both as a serious analytic concept and as a conspiratorial buzzword (Blanuša 2018).

## Conspiracy theories during A.K.P. rule

The conspiratorial rhetoric became more explicit with the consolidation of power of the ruling A.K.P. Although it came to power in 2002 as a reformist party, its enthusiasm for progress waned, and the party would become increasingly authoritarian, shifting to populist discourses melding populism with Islamism. The triumphalism subsequent to the elimination of military defiance rendered it more authoritarian than ever. Imposing its grip on power by 2010, it was able to forsake its erstwhile semi-liberal attitudes and, distancing itself from its liberal allies, the party fostered a home-grown Islamist intelligentsia as its need to employ liberal rhetoric diminished. This intelligentsia promoted a conspiratorial culture that blended inherited Islamist discourses with conspiracy theories imported from the West in the age of populism. Different from conventional Islamic conspiratorialism, the cult of Erdoğan lay at the centre of this metanarrative, in which Erdoğan is depicted as the target of a global conspiracy. In fact, Erdoğan himself deliberately voiced an array of conspiracy theories fulminating against enemies that allegedly co-conspire in secret. This discourse was obviously a reflection both of his Islamist background and a political strategy. Although the similarities with the Islamist mindset are obvious, several twists and diversions are also apparent. First, although political Islamism had existed as an ideology with inflexible preconceptions and dictums, the new conspiratorial universe of the A.K.P. is designed, somewhat haphazardly, around a single man: Erdoğan. A major motivation behind the boosting of these conspiracy theories by the pro-government media was, in fact, the establishment of the cult of Erdoğan.

Not just another political party competing for votes and seeking temporary political office via the ballot box, A.K.P projected itself as representing a timeless and metaphysical ideal. With no difference observed between the ideal, the party and the state, this presumption brought in a trivialisation of politics. The Islamist intelligentsia invented a new political lexicon to espouse the sacralisation of politics (Gentile 1996), ushering in a political vocabulary that sharply distinguished between what was referred to as 'old Turkey' vs. 'new Turkey' (Çağlar 2014). 'Old Turkey' (imagined as a power bloc consisting of businessmen, military and bureaucracy, but also intellectuals, N.G.O.s and 'White Turks', see below) was demonised as the nemesis conspiring with the global order and its proponents. Especially in the aftermath of the Arab Spring, domestic politics and foreign policy became inextricably intertwined in Turkey, and this shift birthed a new conspiratorial universe in which the domestic and the international could not be dissociated. Accordingly, all domestic opposition, including the leftists, Kemalists, P.K.K. and the Kurdish movement, was to be framed as in an alliance with Zionists, neocons, Baathists and other dark forces.

Enemies were legion, being both domestic and international, and apparent rival states were enemies, as in any other nationalist imagination. Although Turkey was not lacking in solid state-level enmities in the previous decades, globalisation and the erosion of state power brought more treacherous and elusive enemies into view, some of which were super-state, and some sub-state. In this conspiratorial universe, the 'enemy' was not an agent one could easily identify, but rather a diffuse, amorphous, obscure and omnipresent one. Furthermore, these singular enemies were depicted as derivations, puppets or agents of a mastermind. Although they may enjoy their own autonomy and own reasons and motivations, there prevails over all one omnipotent enemy, an imagery that is best captured in the visions of *The Protocols of the Elders of Zion*. The 'West', as discussed above, is an abstraction that cannot be said to refer to an identifiable material reality. The 'West' has been construed as the ultimate and irreconcilable enemy of 'us', whether this 'us' referred to 'Turks', 'Muslims' or any amalgamation of these two partially overlapping, partially contesting identities. Yet, the demonisation of this elusive 'West' was carried to new heights by the A.K.P. According to A.K.P. intellectuals, the enemies within are not only legion, but also constantly changing appearance, while remaining the same behind their façades. Another accompanying demonised categorisation were the 'White Turks' who were allegedly dominant in 'Old Turkey'. This was a label employed to stigmatise the secular and well-off upper-middle class, who were implicated as not rooted within society – not sufficiently Turkish – hence 'white', meaning more European looking than the average Turk, and living in their urban secluded habitats, separated from the cultural and moral norms of society (Bali 2002: 324–77; Gürpınar 2011: 170–9). This discourse was further exacerbated with the Gezi protests that broke out in 2013 (Albayrak 2008; Kutlu 2014a, 2014b).

The Gezi protests became the *bête noir* of the Islamist intelligentsia and their conspiratorial universe. Demonstrators had gathered initially to protest the planned building of a shopping mall on the site of Gezi Park at the very centre of the city's bohemian quarter, yet what started out as a small-scale protest turned into a massive anti-governmental demonstration after the brutal police crackdown (Özkırımlı 2014; Öğütle, Göker 2014; Gürpınar 2016: 199–326; Nefes

2017). Failing to attain the moral upper hand against the popular sympathy shown to the protestors, it was the task of the A.K.P. intelligentsia to frame the course of events in such a way that they would secure moral superiority and claims of legitimacy, against all odds. The most direct approach was to shift the debate from the Gezi protests and police brutality to the 'big picture' that lay behind, implicating the Gezi protestors as unknowing or deliberate pawns in the service of global powers aiming to topple Erdoğan and to destabilise Turkey (Ertem, Esayan 2013; Güngör 2013a, 2013b; Aktay 2013). Denying the protestors agency, the pro-government media lost no time in depicting them as on the payroll of foreign intelligence services. George Soros was one of several household names who was blamed. Previously a favourite in Kemalist conspiracy theories, being seen as working on behalf of neoliberalism and imperialism, he became a hate figure. 'Civil society' (and the 'open society' of Soros) was thus seen in some circles as a smokescreen concealing subversive activities in the name of rights, liberties and democracy. Any opposition to the Islamist government could, and was, inevitably conceived as being in the service of this overarching global plot.

The historicisation of conspiracy theories further trivialised 'today', deeming it a nuisance in the eternal grand theatre of history and struggles, and this historisation also trivialised transient moral transgressions. As war renders morality a secondary concern that needs to be reassessed within the reality of war, while also justifying misdemeanours, the introduction of history as a theatre depicting a perpetual state of war also deems moral claims inconsequential and petty in the larger theatre of history. Conspiracy theories remain an effective means of depoliticising public debate and imposing the politics of eternity, having served these ends succinctly in Turkey. Several television series produced by the state boosted such historical conspiratorialism and depicted late Ottoman history accordingly.

The A.K.P. also used the Internet and social media to disseminate conspiracy theories to discredit its foes and sharpen the rift between the two seemingly irreconcilable camps in order to consolidate its base. This strategy had become much more brazen by the mid-2010s, epitomised most blatantly by a network known somewhat ominously as the 'Pelicans'. The curious name came from an anonymous manifesto posted on Wordpress on May 2016 entitled the 'Pelican files' (for no sensible reason), which accused the then-prime minister Ahmet Davutoğlu of conspiring against Erdoğan behind the scenes, prompting his resignation in just three days (on the 'Pelican files', see Oğur 2016; Sözeri 2016). The unit that came to be known as 'Pelicans' since then operated as intellectual thugs, with the main mission being to discredit and defame A.K.P. and Islamist heavyweights with the potential to threaten Erdoğan's grip on power. Funded generously by shady money channelled from state funds, the unit ran a sizeable social media operation for the effective dissemination of conspiracy theories. These social media accounts, as well as journalists, academics and public figures affiliated with the network, promoted conspiracy theories to defame opposition of all kinds, while also making pre-emptive strikes against potential threats. A constellation of journalists, academics, twitter opinion leaders and trolls made up this notorious network, contributing by acting, tweeting and retweeting, and the Pelicans remain notorious for their shameless defaming and disseminating of conspiracy theories to this end. State-funded or state-sponsored trolls devised conspiracy theories effectively to slander alternative views and groups through invention, promotion and dissemination through Internet memes and infographics. Pro-government media also served the same purpose. The independent media has been gradually destroyed, its owners forced to sell their newspapers and television channels to businessmen allied with the government by means of credit supplied by state banks and public tenders. The government-designed media served as propaganda, revealing new alleged conspiracies spearheaded by an array of enemies masterminded by the New International Order (de Medeiros 2018).

Authoritarian regimes need enemies to legitimise their existence. Furthermore, as ideologies wane, they seek unidentified, elusive and metaphysical enemies, such as demonised alternate ideologies and political movements. To secure subservience, the ruling A.K.P. also needs enemies whose hostilities are not mundane, nor grounded on a conjectural realpolitik or national interests, but rather on an ontological grounding as a political strategy (Snyder 2018: 33–40).

## Conclusion

Although the preeminent ideologies reigning in Turkey, such as Kemalism, Islamism and nationalism displayed different and even antithetical ideological tendencies, they shared similarities, although couched in different terms. This is because they inculcated in the same historical milieu. They rose on deep mistrust against not only imperialist foreign powers but also unreliables within. Conspiracy is omnipresent and omnipotent. Such an intellectual climate fostered an environment in which conspiracy theories flourish. This clearly shows that Turkey is not an outlier, but another geography in which national euphoria and populist urges search for conspiracy theories to render their narratives impeccable and moral.

## Note

1 Parts of this chapter have previously been published in Doğan Gürpınar's book *Conspiracy Theories in Turkey* (Routledge, 2019). We thank Routledge for the permission for reuse. We also express our gratitude to Alp Yenen for his comments and suggestions.

## References

Achcar, G. (2010) *The Arabs and the Holocaust*, New York, NY: Metropolitan Books.
Aktay, Y. (2013) 'Gezi'deki komplo ve sosyoloji', *Yeni Şafak*, 22 June. Available at: www.yenisafak.com/yazarlar/yasinaktay/gezideki-komplo-ve-sosyoloji-38264. [Accessed 16 September 2019.]
Albayrak, Ö. (2008) 'Şehit ve beyaz Türk'ün kaynama noktası', *Yeni Şafak*, 11 October. Available at: www.yenisafak.com/yazarlar/ozlemalbayrak/ehit-ve-beyaz-turkun-kaynama-noktasi-13233. [Accessed 16 September 2019.]
Altındal, A. (1993) *Üç İsa*, Istanbul: Anahtar Kitaplar.
Altındal, A. (2004) *Gül ve Haç Kardeşliği: Avrupa Birliği'nin Gizli Masonik Kimliği*, Ankara: Alfa.
Altındal, A. (2005) *Vatikan ve Tapınak Şövalyeleri*, Istanbul: Alfa Yayınları.
Altındal, A. (2006) *Papa XVI: Benedikt Gizli Türkiye Gündemi*, Istanbul: Destek Yayınları.
Asan, Ö. (2009) 'Trabzon Rumcası ve Pontos Etnofobisi', in G. Bakırezer and Y. Demirer (ed.) *Trabzon'u Anlamak*, Istanbul: İletişim Yayınları.
Ateş, S.Y. (2012) *Asker Evlatlar Yetiştirmek: II. Meşrutiyet Döneminde Beden Terbiyesi, Askeri Talim ve Paramiliter Gençlik Örgütleri*, Istanbul: İletişim Yayınları.
Bali, R. (2002) *Tarz-ı Hayat'tan Life Style'a*, Istanbul: İletişim Yayınları.
Baytok, T. (2007) *İngiliz Belgeleriyle Sevr'den Lozan'a*, Istanbul: Doğan Kitap.
Beşikçi, M. (2012) *The ottoman mobilization of manpower in the first World War*, Leiden: Brill.
Blanuša, N. (2018) 'The deep state between the (un)warranted conspiracy theory and structural element of political regimes?', *Critique and Humanism*, 48(2): 63–82.
Bulut, A. (2007) *Çift Başlı Yılan: Karadeniz'de yüzyılın ikinci Rumlaştırma operasyonu*, Istanbul: Bilge Oğuz.
Çabuk, V. (1990) *Osmanlı Siyasi Tarihinde Sultan II. Abdülhamid han*, Istanbul: Emre Yayınları.
Çağlar, I. (2014) 'Yeni Türkiye'den Eski Medyaya Bakmak', *SETA*, 6 September. Available at: www.setav.org/yeni-turkiyeden-eski-medyaya-bakmak/. [Accessed 13 September 2019.]
Çekiç O. (2014) *Mondros'tan İstanbul'a: İmparatorluk'tan Cumhuriyet'e*, Istanbul: Kaynak Yayınları.
Çetin, M. (1997) *Boğaz'daki Aşiret*, Istanbul: Edille.
Cevizoğlu, H. (2007) *1919'un Şifresi*, Istanbul: Ceviz Kabuğu Yayınları.
Çiçek, M.T. (2012) 'The impact of the Sharif Hussein's revolt on the nation-building processes of Turks and Arabs', *Journal of Academic Approaches*, 3(2): 98–111.

Coşkun, A. (2008) *Yeni Mandacılar*, Istanbul: Cumhuriyet Kitapları.
De Medeiros, J. (2018) *Conspiracy theory in Turkey*, London: I.B.Tauris.
Ekmekçioğlu, L. (2016) *Recovering Armenia: the limits of belonging in post-genocide Turkey*, Stanford: Stanford University Press.
Ertem, C. and Esayan, M. (2013) *Dünyayı Durduran 60 Gün*, Istanbul: Etkileşim Yayınları.
Ganser, D. (2004) *NATO's secret armies: operation Gladio and terrorism in Western Europe*, London: Routledge.
Gentile, E. (1996) *The sacralization of politics in Italy*, Cambridge; MA: Harvard University Press.
Göçek, F.M. (2011) 'Why is there still a Sèvres syndrome? An analysis of Turkey's uneasy association with the West', in F.M. Göçek (ed.) *The transformation of Turkey: redefining state and society from the Ottoman Empire to the Modern Era*, London: I.B. Tauris, pp. 98–184.
Grüßhaber, G. (2018) *The 'German Spirit' in the Ottoman and Turkish Army, 1908–1938*, Oldenburg: de Gruyter.
Guida, M. (2008) 'The Sévres syndrome and "komplo" theories in the Islamist and secular press', *Turkish Studies*, 9(1): 37–52.
Güngör, N. (2013a) 'On maddede Gezi saldırısı', *Star*, 17 June. Available at: www.star.com.tr/yazar/on-maddede-gezi-saldirisi-yazi-763151/. [Accessed 16 September 2019.]
Güngör, N. (2013b) 'Yeni Türkiye'yi anlatmak', *Gazeteoku*, 12 September. Available at: www.gazeteoku.com/yazar/nasuhi-gungor/yeni-turkiyeyi-anlatmak/63921. [Accessed 16 September 2019.]
Gürpınar, D. (2011) *Ulusalcılık: İdeolojik Önderlik ve Takipçileri*, Istanbul: Kitap Yayınevi.
Gürpınar, D. (2013a) 'Historical revisionism vs. conspiracy theories: transformations of Turkish historical scholarship and conspiracy theories as a constitutive element in transforming Turkish nationalism', *Journal of Balkan and Near Eastern Studies*, 15(4): 1–22.
Gürpınar, D. (2013b) *Ottoman imperial diplomacy*, London: I.B.Tauris.
Gürpınar, D. (2014) *Komplolar Kitabı*, Istanbul: Doğan Kitap.
Gürpınar, D. (2016) *Kültür Savaşları*, Istanbul: Liber Plus Yayinlari.
Gürpınar, D. (2019) *Conspiracy Theories in Turkey*, London: Routledge.
Hanioğlu, M.Ş. (2008) 'The second constitutional period, 1908–1918', in R. Kasaba (ed.) *The Cambridge history of Turkey*, New York, NY: Cambridge University Press.
Ihrig, S. (2016) *Justifying genocide*, Cambridge MA: Harvard University Press.
Kaiser, H. (1997) *Imperialism, racism, and development theories: the construction of a dominant paradigm on Ottoman Armenians*, London: Gomidas Institute.
Kasaba, R. (1988) *The Ottoman empire and the world economy: the nineteenth century*, Albany: State University of New York Press.
Kayalı, R. (1997) *Arabs and young Turks: Ottomanism, Arabism, and Islamism in the Ottoman empire, 1908–1918*, Berkeley: University of California Press.
Kılıç, E. (2009) *Özel Harp Dairesi*, Istanbul: Turkuvaz Kitap.
Kirişci, K. and Winrow, G. (1997) *The Kurdish question and Turkey*, London/Portland: Frank Cass.
Kısakürek, N.F. (1950) 'Dedektif X bir, "İsmet Paşa ve (Lozan)ın İç Yüzü"', *Büyük Doğu*, 29: 10–1.
Kısakürek, N.F. (1965) *Ulu Hakan*, Istanbul: Ötüken Neşriyat.
Kutlu, A.N. (2014a) 'Beyaz Türklere mektup', *Yeni Şafak*, 23 April. Available at: www.yenisafak.com/yazarlar/alinurkutlu/beyaz-turklere-mektup-51448. [Accessed 13 September 2019.]
Kutlu, A.N. (2014b) 'Merkez kim, çevre neresi? Anadolu insanı mı, beyaz Türkler mi?' *Yeni Şafak*, 16 April. Available at: www.yenisafak.com/yazarlar/alinurkutlu/merkez-kim-cevre-neresi-anadolu-insani-mi-beyaz-turkler-mi-51336. [Accessed 13 September 2019.]
Manisalı, E. (2006) *AB Süreci mi? Sevr Süreci mi?*, Istanbul: Derin.
Mısıroğlu, K. (1971) *Lozan: Zafer mi? Hezimet mi?*, Istanbul: Sebil Yayınları.
Müftüoğlu, M. (1985) *Her Yönüyle Sultan İkinci Abdülhamid*, Istanbul: Çile Yayınları.
Mumcu, U. (1981) *Silah Kaçakçılığı ve Terör*, Istanbul: Tekin Yayınevi.
Mumcu, U. (1984) *Papa-Mafya-Ağca*, Istanbul: Tekin Yayınevi.
Nefes, T.S. (2012) 'The history of the social constructions of Dönmes (converts)', *Journal of Historical Sociology*, 25(3): 413–39.
Nefes, T.S. (2013) 'Ziya Gökalp's adaptation of Emile Durkheim's sociology in his formulation of the modern Turkish nation', *International Sociology*, 28(3): 335–50.
Nefes, T.S. (2015a) *Online anti-Semitism in Turkey*, New York: Palgrave Macmillan.
Nefes, T.S. (2015b) 'Understanding the anti-Semitic rhetoric in Turkey through the Sevres syndrome', *Turkish Studies*, 16(4): 572–87.

Nefes, T.S. (2017) 'The impacts of the Turkish government's conspiratorial framing about the Gezi Park Protests', *Social Movement Studies*, 16(5): 610–22.
Nefes, T.S. (2018a) 'Political roots of religious exclusion in Turkey', *Parliamentary Affairs*, 71(4): 804–19.
Nefes, T.S. (2018b) 'Framing of a popular conspiracy theory', in E. Asprem, A. Dyrendal and D. Robertson (eds.) *Brill handbook of conspiracy theory and contemporary religion*, Leiden: Brill.
Nur, R. (1967) *Hayat ve Hatıratım*, Istanbul: Altındağ Yayınları.
Oğur, Y. (2016) 'Pelikan'ın inine doğru', *Türkiye*, 13 May. Available at: www.turkiyegazetesi.com.tr/yazarlar/yildiray-ogur/591435.aspx [Accessed 16 September 2019.]
Öğütle, V.S. and Göker E. (2014) *Gezi ve Sosyoloji: Nesneyle Yüzleşmek, Nesneyi Kurmak*, Istanbul: Ayrinti Yayinlari.
Özkan, I.R. (2001) *Yeni Mandacılık*, Istanbul: Ümit Yayıncılık.
Özkırımlı, U. (2014) *the making of a protest movement in Turkey*, Basingstoke: Palgrave.
Özman, A. and Dede, K. (2012) 'Türk sağı ve masonluğun söylemsel inşası: iktidar, bilinmezlik, komplo', in I. Kerestecioğlu and G.G. Öztan (eds.) *Türk Sağı: Mitler, Fetişler, Düşman İmgeleri*, Istanbul: İletişim Yayınları.
Perinçek, D. (2000) *Eşcinsellik ve Yabancılaşma*, Istanbul: Kaynak Yayınları.
Piccoli, G., Ahmad, R. and Ives, B. (2001) 'Web-based virtual learning environments: a research framework and a preliminary assessment of effectiveness in basic IT skills training' *MIS Quarterly*, 25(4): 401–26.
Riedler, F. (2011) *Opposition and legitimacy in the Ottoman empire: conspiracies and political cultures*, London: Routledge.
Sabah (2005) 'AB'ye gireceğiz diye dinimiz elden gidiyor', *Sabah*, 3 January. Available at: http://arsiv.sabah.com.tr/2005/01/03/siy105.html. [Accessed 13 September 2019.]
Sarınay, Y., Pehlivanlı, H. and Saydam, A. (1999) *Pontus Meselesi ve Yunanistan'ın Politikası*, Ankara: Atatürk Araştırma Merkezi.
Selçuk, I. (1966) 'Gardrop Atatürkçülüğü', *Yön*, 9 September.
Şık, A. (2014) *Paralel Yürüdük Biz Bu Yollarda*, Istanbul: Postacı Yayınevi.
Sisman, C. (2010) 'Cortijo de Sevi: kültür mirası Sabetay Sevi'nin evi'nin geçmisi, bugünü ve Geleceği', *Toplumsal Tarih*, 196: 14–25.
Snyder, T. (2018) *The road to unfreedom*, New York: Tim Duggan Books.
Söyler, M. (2015) *The Turkish deep state*, London/New York: Routledge.
Sözeri, E.K. (2016) 'Pelikan Derneği: Berat Albayrak, Ahmet Davutoğlu'nu neden devirdi?', *Medium*, November 3. Available at: https://medium.com/@efekerem/ pelikan-derne%C4%9Fi-berat-albayrak-ahmet-davuto%C4%9Flunu-neden-devirdi-5fabad6dc7de#.3q4vkwf4v. [Accessed 16 September 2019.]
Yeğen, M. (2014) '"Yahudi-Kürtler" ya da Türklüğün Yeni Hudutları', *Doğu-Batı*, 29: 159–78.
Yesevizade (1979) *Bilderberg group*, Istanbul: Kayıhan Yayınları.
Yıldırım, M. (2004) *Sivil Örümceğin Ağında*, Istanbul: Toplumsal Dönüşüm Yayınları.
Yıldırım, U. (2004) *Dünden Bugüne Patrikhane*, Istanbul: Kaynak Yayınları.
Yılmaz, A. (2006) 'Two pillars of nationalist Euro-skepticism in Turkey: the Tanzimat and Sévres syndromes', in I. Karlsson and A.S. Melin (eds.) *Turkey, Sweden and the European Union: experiences and expectations*, Stockholm: Swedish Institute for European Policy Studies.
Zürcher, E.J. (1998) *Turkey: a modern history*, London: I.B. Tauris.
Zürcher, E.J. (2010) *The young Turk legacy and nation building*, London: I.B. Tauris.

# 5.8
# CONSPIRACY THEORIES IN THE MIDDLE EAST

*Matthew Gray*

**Introduction**

Conspiracy theories are a routine – some would say ubiquitous – feature of Middle Eastern social and political discourse. The U.S. planned the 9/11 attacks as an excuse to conquer the Middle East – or, according to others, Israel's intelligence service, the Mossad, did. British intelligence assassinated Princess Diana and Dodi Al-Fayed. Various Middle Eastern leaders are spies for the U.S. Or for Israel. Or others. The U.S. orchestrated the 2011 Arab uprisings – and the rise of the so-called Islamic State in 2014, too. One of a legion of even stranger ones in 2007 saw some southern Iraqis claim that the British military had bred and released killer monsters, bears, or some such creature; it turned out to probably be an aggressive group of local honey badgers (Farrell 2007). Even Israel, while very culturally and politically different to its neighbours, is not immune from such language: From the 1995 assassination of Prime Minister Yitzhak Rabin (Abramovich 2018) to, more recently, claims in 2018 that Prime Minister Binyamin Netanyahu was trying to plant a conspiracy theory in the Israeli media to counter a legal indictment against him (Verter 2018).

The examples are legion and are not only grievances of the socially marginalised and economically peripheral, but occur among more educated people and sometimes in the language of the state. They may focus on rulers, minorities, foreign powers or (more recently) on a murky 'deep state' (*al-dawla al-'amīqa*), a secretive, powerful clique of military intelligence, organised crime and (corrupt) state elites (Filiu 2015: 1). Yet, there has been only limited scholarly attention paid to them: A few book-length works (Pipes 1996; Gray 2010a; Graf *et al.* 2011; Butter, Reinkowski 2014; de Medeiros 2018), and a smattering of journal articles. There is a little more discussion among other observers, but often these contain little in the way of explanatory frameworks. To some such observers, for example, conspiracy theories are condemned as a simple but dangerous manifestation of ignorance; at best, they are seen as intellectually lazy, but sometimes it is argued that they feed political extremism and undermine the region's stability and development (Pipes 1996: 1–2, 8–9). Since the focus of conspiracy theorists' blame is often on foreign actors, some observers argue that this not only fosters ignorance but, crucially, also allows people to 'avoid the shame of having to admit that [an] event was their own societies' fault' (Field 1994: 167–8), to which some add claims of a culture of fatalism (Frydenborg 2018). It is not only outside observers who make these claims: Local commentators do, too, often frustrated by the prominence of conspiracy theories or concerned that they are a mass self-delusion (Al Shaali 2015; AlMuhaini 2017).

There is often merit to these arguments, but conspiracy theories come from a far wider range of sources, and their development, transmission and use are more complicated than such explanations typically allow. This chapter lays out some of these sources and dynamics, arguing that conspiracy theories are a multifaceted socio-political dynamic, but with important insights into, and implications for, the region's politics, development and social relations. It begins by examining the main sources of conspiracy theories, and then examines their transmission and impacts. While conspiracy theories are certainly not unique to the Middle East, their origins, uses and impacts include many dynamics specific to the region's socio-political structures and political cultures.

## Analytical points of departure

Not all conspiracy theories in the Middle East need to derive from complicated sources. In occasional cases they may simply be a manifestation of psychological problems or a sign of social isolation in the narrator. This is indeed the origins of U.S. research on conspiracy theories, which began in psychoanalysis and psychology (Melley 2000: 23–5) before being examined in socio-political contexts by Hofstadter (1965) and others in the 1950s and 1960s (Fenster 1999: 3–21).

Much more commonly, and true in any culture, they are sometimes simply a source of entertainment or amusement. They feature prominently in the plots of films, books, television series, plays and other popular entertainment (Gray 2010a: 27–9). In such contexts, they are rarely intended to be believed. They may have political ramifications if, for example, their cumulative effect is to undermine people's trust in the state or in other figures or institutions, and arguably this indeed has occurred to some extent since they are a relatively politically-safe means by which to criticise an authoritarian state or to otherwise question authority. Some plays and films in the Middle East have had such goals (Gray 2010a: 28), but the overwhelming majority have been more innocuous, serving only as amusement.

That noted, just as works that see Middle Eastern conspiracy theories as simple manifestations of ignorance, paranoia or extremism are inadequate in their explanatory utility, so too are others that claim that these theories are genuine and rational attempts to understand social reality. While the occasional conspiracy ultimately proves to be correct, for the most part such 'cultural perspective' arguments (Nefes 2017: 610) are weak. In trying to be both simplistic and comprehensive, they typically identify monolithic, omnipresent villains and offer homogeneous answers (Bale 2007: 47–50, 53–5), using data selectively and lacking falsifiability (Gray 2010a: 5–6). Even if some are attempts at 'naïve deconstructive history' (Rudmin 2003), meaning an accidental or inexpert attempt to deconstruct and explicate events, Rudmin's claim that conspiracy theorists focus on people rather than 'impersonal forces like geo-politics, market economics, globalization' (Rudmin 2003) is not generally true in the Middle Eastern case. Moreover, conspiracy theories are not something to be encouraged given their flaws in method and logic, however valid and laudable the attempts at agency that they represent. Instead, most Middle Eastern conspiracy theories find their origins and sustenance in more complex dynamics than entertainment or paranoia, and are grounded in a broad range of historical, political, economic, social, cultural and other dynamics and grievances.

## State, society and conspiracy theories

Arguably the most important political source of conspiracy theories in the Middle East is the distance between states and societies (Gray 2010a: 88–117). This covers a range of political dynamics: Weak states; authoritarian politics; fragmented societies; and personalised politics and social and economic interactions. One of the historical legacies of external intervention and regional weakness was the creation of states that are, in many senses, artificial. Many states' borders do not reflect historical boundaries, and are the product of Ottoman rule, European rivalries, manoeuvring by local elites and other factors beyond the control of most local people at the time. Some states, such as Jordan, Syria, Iraq, Egypt and others, have unusually-shaped or artificial-looking borders with at least some of their neighbours; others such as Israel lack full and final borders; and some, such as the Arab monarchies of the Gulf, are extremely small entities (Bahrain, Kuwait, Qatar) or a federation of micro-sheikhdoms (the United Arab Emirates, or U.A.E.), reflecting the dominance of certain families under British domination. As a result, border disputes have been common and the Israeli-Palestinian conflict, and wider Arab-Israeli one, is also at its core a territorial conflict; a dispute between two peoples over the same land.

Artificial borders also meant that states often inherited populations that were diverse and divided, contributing in part to societal fragmentation in many places. Some have sharp ethnic or sectarian divisions, most famously Lebanon, Iraq and Syria. Others have minority regimes: The ruling al-Asad family in Syria is from the minority Alawi community, while the majority of Syrians are Sunni, and, in Bahrain, the Sunni Al Khalifa dynasty rules over a society that is 70 per cent or more Shia. Even where rulers come from a majority social or religious group, conflict or tension with minorities is often a feature of politics and social relations. Some, like Lebanon, are a conglomeration of different groups: The overwhelming majority are Arabs, but no religious sect constitutes a majority, and the Lebanese constitution recognises 18 different religious sects and groups. Elsewhere, a majority group may exist but alongside large minorities, as in Iran – where the majority are Persian, but at least one-quarter are Azeri, Kurds, Baluchis, Arabs and others – and Israel, where Arabs are about 20 per cent of the citizenry and there are divisions among the Jewish population. Iraq, Syria, Turkey and others also have large minority ethnic or sectarian populations. Sometimes, communal relations are quite harmonious, but many of these societies have suffered unrest and even civil war in modern times: Lebanon was torn apart by civil war over 1975–1990; Iraq likewise fell into chaos after the removal of Saddam Hussein in 2003; and Syria since 2012 has been torn apart by a number of disputes in which ethnicity or sect have played a role.

The region's history, borders, weak state institutions and social divisions all combine to create weak political systems (Bill, Springborg 1990: 31–85, 230–99). In the Arab republics, leaders often are the successors of military officers who seized power in the decades after independence. After a series of failed state-led policies, these regimes often lack legitimacy and maintain power through a combination of (increasingly unsustainable) welfarist cooptation and authoritarianism repression (Brynen et al. 2012: 17–91; Kamrava 2014: 17–45). Leaders often maintain their position through patron-client networks (de Elvira et al. 2019), making politics seem opaque and unfair. The weakness of state institutions means that in the bureaucracy, and in business too, strong hierarchies and informal personal connections deliver a similar result, privileging those who have good *wasta*, or connections through intermediaries (Cammett et al. 2015: 324–6), making processes unclear and often unfair, and undermining people's confidence in the system. Corruption derives from some of these dynamics, too, and is poisonous to the state-society relationship (Milton-Edwards 2006: 77–8, 87).

Individuals and social forces witness all these dynamics and may have trouble dissecting them. At the same time, unless they are one of the lucky few beneficiaries of the system, they resent these dynamics, or at least feel that they are unfair. This fuels conspiracy theories by making society feel as though the state is distant and uninterested in ordinary people, and by creating a perception (or reality) that the system is discriminatory or unfair (Gray 2010a: 102–9). In the absence of clear political and decision-making processes, it is easy for conspiracy theories to claim that the political elite are acting against society at large, sometimes in cahoots with foreign powers. Similarly, it is routine for conspiracy theories to credit the state and regime with enormous power and reach into society. If a small regime can control the country and maintain power, such reasoning goes, then surely they must be incredibly effective.

Of course, regimes and states typically are not this powerful. They control society primarily through a balance of cooptation and repression, and provided that these two tactics are reasonably balanced, and opposition suppressed quickly and sufficiently, ruling elites have the benefit of incumbency and can draw on the state's resources and capacity. However, they are also hampered by the difficulty in mobilising popular support for the existing order, since past policies, and then more recent economic reforms, have proven either ineffective or unpopular. State-led policies brought some benefits and opportunities to society, but also created the monolithic bureaucracies that today drain state coffers and hamper new initiatives and undermine transparency. More recent market-based reforms have not been popular either, often viewed as a risk to ordinary people's livelihoods, or even as a threat to the country's economic independence (Tripp 2013: 163–6, 173–5). Political Islamism attracts some people, but not usually a majority – and, even when people lean towards it, there is little agreement on what Islamisation ought to constitute in practice (Hamid, McCants 2017).

This ideological inchoateness also helps conspiracy theories flourish and spread (Gray 2010a: 102–11). Current leaders or conditions are often compared unfavourably to past ones, with an assumption that, if their policies lack popular support, then they must be maintaining power through more nefarious means. Such conspiracy theories arguably are a response to people feeling isolated from the political systems under which they live, but also stem from a lack of ideological cohesion and the absence of detailed, transparent information about how politics works (Pipes 1996: 363–4; Gray 2010a: 102–5). Where a leader comes from a minority group, or where a minority feels unfairly treated by the state, this too will spur conspiracy theories, either targeting a social group or alleging collusion between it and the political elite (Gray 2010a: 108). Not surprisingly, Islamists in secular systems and secularists in Islamist or Islamising ones also sometimes try to explain their situation, especially what they typically claim is their relative weakness, by alleging some sort of conspiracy, whether within the state or society or involving external forces (Gray 2010a: 110). Conditions of conflict, such as Iraq after 2003 and Syria after 2012, further amplify societal conspiracy explanations or add to their appeal (Gray 2010a: 107–9; Qiu 2017; B.B.C. 2018).

More recently, state-society dynamics were central as a source of the 2011 'Arab Spring', the uprisings that removed leaders in Tunisia, Egypt, Libya and Yemen, and sparked the 2012-civil war in Syria – but they also allowed many leaders to outmanoeuvre the protestors, minimise change or undermine new leaderships. There are a plethora of conspiracy theories that emerged from the uprisings, 'built on an assumption that an all-powerful Deep State was striking back and avenging itself on the post-dictatorial regimes' (Filiu 2015: 1) and then, more recently, blaming the failure of democratic transitions on the same deep state (Hanieh 2013: 161–6, 168–73; Filiu 2015: 200–5, 210–11, 249–53). State-society dynamics therefore also account for many conspiracy theories about the uprisings. The opacity of politics (along with seemingly-powerful external actors) has led people in the region to see the uprisings as the product of a Western plot to sow sectarian division and impose weak leaders towards the ultimate aim of (re-)gaining control of the region (M.R. 2013; Hasan 2014). As threatened regimes fought back against popular protests in 2011 and 2012, they were typically repressive. Where change did not occur, but the political environment now is as repressive as before 2011 (or even more so), people are tempted to explain the failure of the will of the people in conspiracy terms: 'the Arab Spring represents ... [for] Arab subjects ... "terrorism", economic collapse and an uncertain future' (Cherif 2017) given how little substantive change has thus far occurred.

## Real conspiracies and conspiracy theories

Beyond the political dynamics of the Middle East, conspiracy theories are supported by the fact that real conspiracies do occur (Gray 2010a: 49). This is the case elsewhere too, of course, but arguably is especially important in the Middle East because of the degree to which the region has been penetrated and shaped by external powers in modern times, from the Ottoman era through European colonialism and on to the Cold War (and post-Cold War) era, fuelling a propensity in the region to see structures and events as shaped by this history. Sometimes a conspiracy is widely accepted to have occurred, as with the 1956 Protocol of Sèvres and its role in the 1956 Suez War. It was agreed at a secret Anglo-French-Israeli meeting where the three parties agreed to regain control of the Suez Canal, which Egypt had recently nationalised, including through starting a military conflict (Shlaim 1997: 509). At the time, there was an assumption in the region that the U.K., France and Israel had conspired on the conflict, even though the details were not known (Heikal 1986: 179). There are other examples, such as various 'false flag' activities by Israel in Egypt in the 1950s (Gray 2010a: 66), and the Anglo-American collusion to overthrow Iranian Prime Minister Muhammed Mossadeq in 1953 (Gasiorowski 1991: 57–84; Kinzer 2003). Other events such as the 2003 U.S.-led Iraq War show signs of a conspiracy, too, and are widely viewed that way both in the region and in the U.S.A. (Cramer, Duggan 2012: 201–43; Hagen 2018: 32–5).

Such historical events have two main effects in promoting conspiracy discourse. First, and perhaps most obviously, they create genuine grievances that undermine trust in the alleged conspirator or other actors. Historical memories feed directly into contemporary political perspectives, especially when there is some continuity to events or where people perceive an immediate threat based on the past. At least one observer has argued that the idea of the 'paranoid style' is unsustainable because conspiracy theorists may be pointing to a genuine or real threat (Sivan 1985: 15, cited in Pipes 1996: 325). This points to the second, and very common, impact of historical memory: The potential for a real conspiracy to serve as a basis to legitimise other – often less plausible, or even clearly false – conspiracy theories. Real past conspiracies allow a conspiracy theorist to base their claims in initial agreement over a past conspiracy that is not in contention, and then to use this to build the plausibility and acceptability of their (usually less credible or unprovable) conspiracy theory (Gray 2010a: 49). In this way, the U.S. role in the 1953 Iranian coup may help support a conspiracy theory about the current U.S. role in Iran or the region; past Israeli efforts to deceive the region can be used, similarly, to mount all sorts of claims about present-day Israeli plotting. Historical events that now seem quite distant to people beyond the region are still recalled by conspiracy theorists (and many others) across the region: A prominent example is the Crusades, which are often used to explain contemporary Western interventions in the Middle East, with Americans or Europeans regularly and critically tagged as 'Crusaders' (*al-ṣalībīyūn*) by politicians, intellectuals and Islamists (Gray 2010a: 51–2).

## External influences and conspiracy theories

Beyond these dynamics, there are also externalities that can provoke or promote conspiracy theories. Some of these are generic to or very common in conspiracy theories elsewhere in the world, such as the fear that local cultures, religious values or economic conditions will be undermined by the forces of globalisation. Globalisation is also an opaque force, with economic, social, cultural and other impacts and influences, while at the same time also one with symbols such as corporate logos and globally-recognisable brands. In the Middle East, there is also a strong sense that globalisation is a homogenising and Americanising force; whatever the accuracy of this view, it is commonly-enough held that it has an impact on local opinion and ultimately on politics (Gray 2010a: 33–4).

Globalisation also matters because of the tools, and the cultures around them, that it has introduced. Satellite television, Internet and instant messaging have all made the transmission of conspiracy theories easier and faster, and have expanded the potential network through which they can travel. There has been an expansion of online Islamic space, where a range of people from traditional scholars to self-declared experts with no recognised training in religion compete for attention with a large, even confusing, array of views. At the same time, websites and other online spaces increasingly form part of people's identities (Bunt 2009: 7–54).

Globalising technology therefore reduces the importance of place and local authority figures to people. Arguably, a conspiracy theorist has a much easier time finding an audience, even a small or selective one, online, when compared with trying to challenge orthodox explanations for events made by traditional family, religious, tribal or community figures. Traditional figures were more likely to impose their authority, and more able to do so in the absence of the range of counter-narratives now available online. Instead, the Internet and other online systems have a broadening effect, allowing individuals to claim knowledge or authority on a topic and to spread their views easily. The impacts of this vary: When successful, such individuals may be able to undermine traditional authority figures and spread their opinions and analyses. Such theories often are successful, moreover, especially given problems such as the social divisions and state-society gaps noted earlier. Even if a conspiracy theorist does not succeed in building a large audience, the rise of so many online voices has the effect at times of crowding out more rational ones, or simply undermining clear debate on a topic because there are so many competing explanations for people to choose from.

The rise of satellite television news channels has been important in challenging many official state narratives, but also in propagating conspiracy theories. Hezbollah's Al-Manar has been most prominent in this role, but most others have played some role, too (Gray 2010a: 144–51). Beyond this, satellite news channels have also themselves been at the centre of conspiracy theories, as Al-Jazeera was when its Kabul office was struck by a U.S. missile in November 2001, and then in Baghdad in April 2003, when one of its staff was killed in a U.S. strike. In both cases, a range of conspiracy theories emerged, claiming that the U.S. strikes were deliberate. Some also point to a supposed memo of an April 2004 meeting between then U.S. President George W. Bush and U.K. Prime Minister Tony Blair in which the former supposedly suggested that the U.S. or its allies should bomb Al-Jazeera headquarters (Cowell 2005). Whatever the truth of it, this so-called 'Al-Jazeera bombing memo' is a reminder of how easily conspiracy theories can emerge and linger, especially when there is some factual detail on which it can be founded.

Often there is also an external or international link to a domestic dynamic, a recent example being the dramatic rise of the so-called 'Islamic State', or I.S.I.S., in early-mid-2014. While it derived from a range of factors, many of them political and social ones home-grown in the region, it was often claimed that I.S.I.S. was a creation of the U.S.A. (B.B.C. 2014), or Israel (Hasan 2014) – despite the fact that, in *Dabiq*, its main English-language publication, I.S.I.S. was highly critical of conspiracy theories as something that risked confusing potential members and steering them away from the group (Colas 2017: 180). Still, the rumours of I.S.I.S. as a U.S. plot were so widespread that, at one point in August 2014, the U.S. government took the unusual step of making a public statement denying the claims (Huffington Post 2014). This tapped into the broad sense in the region of U.S. power and reach into the region; the U.S.A. displaced the U.K. as the main target of such language as Israel's power increased in the 1960s, especially after the 1967 Six Day War and then after the U.S.A. rushed support to Israel during the 1973 Yom Kippur/October War (Brown 1984: 201–12, 268–77; Bill, Springborg 1990: 360–8).

## The state and political leadership as conspiracy theorists

A particular, but not unique, feature of Middle Eastern conspiracy theories is the prominent role that states and political elites often play in originating, spreading and encouraging conspiracy explanations. All governments seek to shape public perception and opinion, of course, and at times many prominent political actors have mouthed a conspiracy theory, but in the Middle East conspiracy narratives by such figures are more routine than what is typically found in more democratic or competitive political settings. Some leaders and elites are renowned for framing a situation and their decision-making in conspiracy terms. Former Iraqi leader Saddam Hussein did this in numerous statements (Gray 2010b). Just before his 1990 invasion of Kuwait, he alleged a 'grand conspiracy' between the Arab Gulf states and Western powers to maintain low oil prices at Iraq's expense (Long 2004: 20). During the subsequent January–February 1991 war over Kuwait, he also used conspiracy language when talking to Iraqis, saying for example

> ... some Arabs and ... many foreigners ... could not remember what Zionism and US imperialism have done against Iraq, beginning with the ... Iran-Contra scandal in 1986 until the first months of 1990, when the plot against Iraq reached its dangerous phases.
>
> *(Hussein 1991: 233)*

In Syria, both the state and state-controlled media have long used conspiracy theories to explain events or justify actions (Kedar 2005; Rabo 2014: 212–27). The post-revolutionary regime in Iran has done so even more prominently, often with especially colourful language, heavily peppered with conspiracy terms and claims (Beeman 2005: 49–67; Ashraf 2011). Other groups, such as Lebanese Hezbollah, while not technically ruling a state, nonetheless have some political authority and in that role have also done similar (Gray 2010a: 129).

State-narrated conspiracy theories come through three main channels in the Middle East: Directly in the speeches of a political leader; through articles and opinion pieces in state-owned or state-manipulated mass media; and through the speeches, statements and remarks of other members of a regime such as ministers of state, party officials, state capitalists and other well-connected figures (Gray 2010a: 122). But, why do leaders and other figures speak in conspiracy terms? Do they really expect their audience to believe them? In some cases, they do. Just as societal actors may genuinely believe a conspiracy theory, and base this in part on a past conspiracy that genuinely did occur, so some leaders do the same thing. Political leaders face conspiracies as a normal part of politics, attuning them to the likelihood that there are various actors and forces seeking to undermine and remove them. The distance between states and societies, and the fact that many regimes are dominated by minorities, as already discussed, along with the paucity of legitimacy that hobble many regimes, make this all the more likely. The same dynamic is a feature of international relations and diplomacy, where states are operating in an anarchic international environment and, at times, will seek to undermine or remove the leaderships of rival states. That noted, the evidence is usually scant as to whether a conspiracy theory is genuinely believed or not.

More commonly, however, there are political incentives lurking beyond state-narrated conspiracy theories. These are not inconsistent with them also believing what they say, although it is often assumed that they are cynically using such language for political gain or advantage. Perhaps most obviously, conspiracy theories can serve as a distraction or a diversionary tactic. In this sense, they are similar to lies or to opaque political language, but not typically of the same nature as propaganda, which in many cases is an expression of state authority and not something that necessarily has to be believed. A conspiracy theory used as a diversion, however, represents a tactic of debate and argument with society. It might seek to plant false or inaccurate thoughts in the minds of the audience, making them see the state in a more positive light, or to solidify societal views on events that are opaque or for which there exists multiple claims competing against the state's. Conspiracy claims may also serve nation-building and nationalism goals (Xu 2001: 155), by drawing people together (under the state and regime, of course) against a commonly-perceived external threat, although the risk is that this will prove a short-term benefit for the regime but at the longer-term risk of eroding trust in the state if a conspiracy theory is exposed as false. Finally, conspiracy explanations may make the state's control over society easier to maintain and manage (Gray 2010a: 131–2). People may be more likely to discount opposition claims if, stoked by conspiracy theories, the loyalties or intentions of the opposition have been called into doubt. Elements of society and businesspeople may also accept greater state intrusion into their lives and the economy if they have concerns about their safety or the stability of the political system. Claims against groups that are framed as primarily a threat to society rather than the state will often be an indicator of such a tactic. For these reasons, states not only articulate their own conspiracy theories, but are often tolerant of societal ones that suit the state's agenda and pose no threat to it.

There are more complex arguments about the state's motivations in articulating conspiracy theories. One of these is an extension of the argument, using the case of Egypt, that political language is not only about making claims to an audience, but also about asserting the authority, even domination, of a leader or a political system over that audience (Kassem 2004: 170). In authoritarian settings, the state may use conspiracy language to clarify for society what sort of topics are acceptable or not for discussion, or may claim that an opposition figure is part of a wider conspiracy in order to discredit them, but also to show that the person or group has crossed a particular 'red line'. Another idea, drawn from Syria, is that state narratives and language may seek to monopolise public discourse, confuse people and, by leaving out key facts or adding false ones, leave society unclear about the exact details of an event or unable to construct a clear, consistent counter-narrative to the state's (Wedeen 1999: 42, 44–5).

Propaganda is often used towards such ends. Conspiracy theories and propaganda share other features. They may be repeated and shared by people confused or misinformed by them, of course. Furthermore, when they are consistently articulated by an authoritarian state, and their propagation encouraged, people may decide to spread them more widely or repeat them, even if they know they are false or misleading, as a way of demonstrating their allegiance with the state or regime, or at least to send a message that they are not interested in challenging the system. This generates a veneer of deference to the state and unspoken acquiescence to the political order, and thus can be useful as a form of political control even in cases where the conspiracy theory is believed by neither the leader and state elite nor by the people in society who are repeating and spreading it (Gray 2010a: 134).

Similarly, conspiracy theories can also serve as counterfactual or counter-relevant political language; for example, to build a cult around a leader or send a message to society that they should pretend as though change is occurring when it is not, or is not occurring when it is. Society, and even members of the regime, therefore act 'as if', as Wedeen (1999: 81–3) argued, demonstrating obedience and being drawn into complicity with the regime. The Middle East is not alone in many of these dynamics – similar features are evident in China, the Soviet Union/Russia, some African states and elsewhere – but they are especially prominent in many Middle Eastern settings and in the region's politics.

## Transmission, evolution and impacts

Conspiracy theories don't just matter because of their multiple and complex sources and what they say about political systems, but also because of how they are transmitted and for the risks they pose for political systems, societies and individuals. As discussed, sometimes a conspiracy theory turns out to be the correct interpretation; a theory *correctly* explaining a conspiracy, in other words. Far more often, however, this is not the case.

The actors and groups that transmit conspiracy theories are often the same ones who originate them. A political leader will not just state a conspiracy theory and leave the subject alone: If its spread is in the leader's interest, then it will be reinforced by other elites, in the mass media and elsewhere, and perhaps repeated by members of the ruler's or ruling party's supporter base. Someone opposed to a regime, likewise, will usually not state a conspiracy theory only once or twice, but rather will repeat it regularly to different social circles, or perhaps join an online group, or spread it through other networks.

This noted, there are a couple of specific reasons why conspiracy theories may be adopted and spread. One is the political environment: It is safer for individuals, social groups and businesses to frame comments or criticism on politics in indirect ways. There is arguably an incentive in authoritarian contexts, therefore, to use conspiracy theories more often than might be typical in more liberal systems. At its simplest, criticism of a leader or system may be framed as a hypothetical observation. Other discursive tactics are important too. Just as joke-telling and humour can be an effective method for people to express opinions or assert some autonomy from the state (Kishtainy 1985: 128), conspiracy theories can be used in the same way. Both jokes and conspiracy theories offer an outlet that is politically safer for the narrator and more acceptable to a regime than would be direct political argument, due to their more conjectural style or non-specific framing. They also offer a degree of deniability; if a conspiracy theory is taken seriously or causes offence, its narrator can claim that they have been misunderstood or were only being facetious. Yet, if well framed and relevant, a conspiracy theory can be almost as clear and effective as direct politically-confrontational language (Gray 2010a: 103–4).

Second, conspiracy theories may also travel quickly and effectively, and in unique ways, because they often blend very effectively both a serious underlying message and an entertaining framework and style. Conspiracy theories can be engaging, even enjoyable, which probably reduces their social viscosity; they are also somewhat like rumour, in that in their articulation they are group-oriented and exclusivist (Hörner 2011: 99–100). At the same time, whether they are pointing to both real or constructed issues and grievances, the fact that conspiracy theories usually appear to be plausible – or at least are not falsifiable – and are relevant to people's experiences or biases, is an incentive to spread them further and usually gives them a long life.

Given all this, is the Middle East particularly prone to engaging with and spreading conspiracy theories? In other words, are conspiracy theories more common there than in other parts of the world? Some observers argue so: 'Unlike the West, where conspiracy theories are today the preserve of the alienated and the fringe, in the Middle East they enjoy large, mainstream audiences.' (Pipes 1996: 2). Other observers, including those in the region, have made similar claims:

> The difference between conspiratorial beliefs in the U.S. and in the Arab world is a matter of degree rather than kind. In the U.S., such thinking is marginal and limited to small circles. In the Arab world, unfortunately, such conspiratorial explanations are far more dominant and widespread, even among the educated.
>
> (Al-Ghwell 2018: n.p.)

While valid in some respects, it must also be noted that certain conspiracy theories in the West also are mainstream. Perhaps most famous are those surrounding the 1963 assassination of U.S. President John F. Kennedy – a 2013 Gallup poll found 'that 61 percent of Americans still believed that others besides Oswald were involved' (Baker, Shane 2017: n.p.) – and the 11 September 2001 terrorist attacks provoked a range of conspiracy theories, too, for example with a 2004 *New York Times/CBS News* poll finding that only 24 per cent of Americans believed the Bush Administration was 'telling the truth' about the attacks, while 16 per cent thought it was 'mostly lying' (*New York Times* 2004: 28).

If conspiracy theories are more common in the Middle East than the U.S.A. and other Western societies, it is most likely due to the region's political and social environments. This chapter argues that political and social explanations, with some relationship to economic issues as well, are of paramount explanatory utility. There is less evidence for culture or religion being key factors in and of themselves, although 'Occidentalism' – the 'dehumanizing picture of the West painted by its enemies' (Buruma, Margalit 2004: 5) – may sometimes provide a cultural source for conspiracy theories, in turn linking to religion as (sometimes) another expression of culture. The common association of Western culture with the Enlightenment, secularism and, more recently, trivial or materialistic popular culture (Buruma, Margalit 2004: 6–10) could lead religious people in other cultures, especially ones undergoing rapid modernisation or transformation, to interpret the West as a threat and to adopt Occidentalist explanations, including conspiracist ones, in either a genuine or manipulative attempt to convince others of such a threat. However, such arguments ultimately are founded on a political explanation.

Islamic groups routinely use conspiracy theories, too, but there is far less evidence that the nature of the religion itself promotes such language. As with the rise and fall of I.S.I.S., conspiracy theories routinely surround extremist groups such as al-Qaeda, including, perhaps most prominently, around its origins and events impacting its leadership. The 2011 U.S. raid that killed its then-figurehead Osama bin Laden is one such example, fed by a refusal – for various reasons – to believe that he had been killed, or because of how the raid was conducted, or simply from a more general mistrust of the U.S.A. in the Middle East and South Asia (Gray 2011).

However, when conspiracy theories come from Muslim figures or are framed in religious language, on closer inspection this, too, is typically the product of politics or societal tensions; see as examples the explanations for such language laid out in Gray (2010a: 107–11, 154–60), Pipes (1996: 206–12) and Schmid (2014: 157–76). Events specific to the region have been important, too, of course. The effects of the 9/11 terrorist attacks and the U.S.-led 2003 Iraq war arguably had unique impacts on the region, especially by lowering 'the thresholds for [both] aggressive anti-Western propaganda and Islamophobia' (Hörner 2011: 102). Supporting this is some quantitative evidence that strong anti-Western and anti-Jewish attitudes in the region help contribute to conspiracy theorising (Nyhan, Zeitzoff 2018: 1400–4); but, again, these attitudes have obvious political sources, as argued here and elsewhere (Gray 2010b: 28–46; Schmid 2014: 157–76; Nefes 2017: 610–22; Frydenborg 2018; among others). Anti-Western propaganda and a rise in Western Islamophobia may have increased the occurrence or transmission of conspiracy theories, but are only two factors in a large array of sources and explanations for them.

## Conclusion

Both the prevalence and the sources of conspiracy theories in the Middle East point to why they matter to observers of the region. They are sufficiently routine that they suggest the region has a sizeable population that is dissatisfied with the political system, economic conditions or other features of the region. There is a perception that the region is heavily penetrated and exploited by external powers, and has been for some centuries now as a result of the relative decline in its global prominence as Europe and, later, the U.S.A. rose to positions of global dominance. The anti-Westernism and anti-Israeli sentiments that are so common in the region are best seen in this light; as symbols of the anger and fear created by foreign intervention and by the endurance of the seemingly-insoluble Israeli-Palestinian issue. The conspiracy theories that see the state as a threat likewise point to the sense of powerlessness among so many people in the Middle East, and the widespread view that the political and commercial systems are rigged against ordinary people; against all but the best-connected or most corrupt. This provides fertile ground for conspiracy explanations. That the state, too, articulates conspiracy theories shows that the politics of such language goes further still, being embedded in authoritarian political structures and of use for elite consolidation, popular legitimisation and, ultimately, regime maintenance and the stability of the state.

The Middle East overall suffers from a range of formidable economic, social and political problems. The struggles of most regional states to deliver economic development has been a notable issue in recent decades, with the economy undermined by factors such as a high population growth, the reliance in many states on oil and gas revenue, and the challenge of competing economically at the global level in other sectors. Meanwhile, Islam is going through a period of turmoil, as many key figures and movements within the religion contest the long-term question of who should speak for Islam and on what tenets they should do so. Societies are both constrained by traditional hierarchies and traditions, while in many ways liberated by new communications technologies and other transformative products of globalisation. Conspiracy theories are important because they signify failings and disappointments among actors and forces across all these dynamics. At the same time, where they mislead or confuse or undermine faith in institutions, they are also adding new complexities to regional politics, undermining and complicating efforts at stabilising the region, hampering the development of the state-society relationship, and hobbling economic processes and outcomes. Conspiracy theories are thus an important component – if only one of many – in the formula that will determine the future of the region.

## References

Abramovich, A. (2018) 'Villain in a bottle: Rabin assassination conspiracy theories', *ynetnews*, 11 April. Available at: www.ynetnews.com/articles/0,7340,L-5388793,00.html. [Accessed 10 September 2019.]

Al-Ghwell, H. (2018) 'How conspiracy theories hold the Arab world back', *Arab News*, 23 June. Available at: www.arabnews.com/node/1326736. [Accessed 10 September 2019.]

AlMuhaini, M. (2017) 'Three conspiracy theories which have controlled Arab minds', *Al Arabiya*, 9 August. Available at: https://english.alarabiya.net/en/views/news/middle-east/2017/08/09/The-three-conspiracies-which-have-controlled-Arab-minds-.html. [Accessed 10 September 2019.]

Al Shaali, K.R. (2015) 'Arabs and conspiracy theories', *Gulf News*, 6 June. Available at: https://gulfnews.com/opinion/op-eds/arabs-and-conspiracy-theories-1.1530679. [Accessed 10 September 2019.]

Ashraf, A. (2011) 'Conspiracy theories', *Encyclopædia Iranica*, 28 October. Available at: www.iranicaonline.org/articles/conspiracy-theories. [Accessed 10 September 2019.]

Baker, P. and Shane, S. (2017) 'A half-century later, documents may shed sight on J.F.K. assassination', *The New York Times*, 25 October. Available at: www.nytimes.com/2017/10/25/us/politics/jfk-files-assassination.html. [Accessed 10 September 2019.]

Bale, J.M. (2007) 'Political paranoia vs. political realism: on distinguishing between bogus conspiracy theories and genuine conspiracy theories', *Patterns of Prejudice*, 41(1): 45–60.
B.B.C. (2014) 'The US, IS and the conspiracy theory sweeping Lebanon', *BBC News*, 12 August. Available at: www.bbc.com/news/world-middle-east-28745990. [Accessed 10 September 2019.]
B.B.C. (2018) 'Syria war: the online activists pushing conspiracy theories', *BBC Trending*, 19 April. Available at: www.bbc.com/news/blogs-trending-43745629. [Accessed 10 September 2019.]
Beeman, W.O. (2005) *The 'Great Satan' vs. the 'Mad Mullahs': how the United States and Iran demonize each other*, Westport CT: Praeger.
Bill, J.A. and Springborg, R. (1990) *Politics in the Middle East*, 3rd edn, Glenview, IL: Scott, Foresman/Little, Brown.
Brown, L.C. (1984) *International politics and the Middle East: old rules, dangerous game*, Princeton: Princeton University Press.
Brynen, R., Moore, P.W., Salloukh, B.F. and Zahar, M. (eds.) (2012) *Beyond authoritarianism: the Arab Spring & democratization in the Arab World*, Boulder, CO: Lynne Rienner.
Bunt, G.R. (2009) *iMuslims: rewiring the house of Islam*, London: Hurst.
Buruma, I. and Margalit, A. (2004) *Occidentalism: the West in the eyes of its enemies*, New York: Penguin.
Butter, M. and Reinkowski, M. (eds.) (2014) *Conspiracy theories in the United States and the Middle East: a comparative approach*, Berlin: de Gruyter.
Cammett, M., Diwan, I., Richards, A. and Waterbury, J. (eds.) (2015) *A political economy of the Middle East*, 4th edn, Boulder, CO: Westview Press.
Cherif, Y. (2017) 'Will the 2010s be the "wasted decade" of Arab hopes?', *Al Jazeera*, 18 December. Available at: www.aljazeera.com/amp/indepth/opinion/2010s-useless-decade-arab-hopes-171218072522055.html. [Accessed 10 September 2019.]
Colas, B. (2017) 'What does *Dabiq* do? ISIS hermeneutics and organizational fractures within *Dabiq* magazine', *Studies in Conflict & Terrorism*, 40(3): 173–90.
Cowell, A. (2005) 'Bush spoke of attacking Arab news channel, British tabloid says', *The New York Times*, 23 November. Available at: www.nytimes.com/2005/11/23/world/europe/bush-spoke-of-attacking-arab-news-channel-british-tabloid-says.html. [Accessed on 10 September 2019.]
Cramer, J.K. and Duggan, E.C. (2012) 'In pursuit of primacy: why the United States invaded Iraq', in J.K. Cramer and A.T. Thrall (eds.) *Why Did the United States Invade Iraq?*, London: Routledge, pp. 201–43.
De Elvira, L.R., Schwarz, C.H. and Weipert-Fenner, I. (eds.) (2019) *Clientelism and patronage in the Middle East and north Africa*, New York: Routledge.
De Medeiros, J. (2018) *Conspiracy theory in Turkey: politics and protest in the age of 'post-truth'*, London: I. B. Tauris.
Farrell, S. (2007) 'The latest Iraqi conspiracy theory: killer British badgers', *The New York Times*, 30 July. Available at: www.nytimes.com/2007/07/30/world/africa/30iht-badger.4.6902836.html. [Accessed 10 September 2019.]
Fenster, M. (1999) *Conspiracy theories: secrecy and power in American culture*, Minneapolis, MN: University of Minnesota Press.
Field, M. (1994) *Inside the Arab world*, London: John Murray.
Filiu, J. (2015) *From deep state to Islamic state: the Arab counter-revolution and its Jihadi legacy*, London: Hurst.
Frydenborg, B.E. (2018) 'On Arabs and conspiracy theories', *Small Wars Journal*, 31 August. Available at: https://smallwarsjournal.com/jrnl/art/arabs-and-conspiracy-theories. [Accessed 10 September 2019.]
Gasiorowski, M.J. (1991) *U.S. foreign policy and the Shah*, London: Cornell University Press.
Graf, A., Fathi, S. and Paul, L. (eds.) (2011) *Orientalism and conspiracy: politics and conspiracy theory in the Islamic world: essays in honour of Sadik J. Al-Azm*, London: I. B. Tauris.
Gray, M. (2010a) *Conspiracy theories in the Arab world: sources and politics*, London: Routledge.
Gray, M. (2010b) 'Revisiting Saddam Hussein's political language: the sources and roles of conspiracy theories', *Arab Studies Quarterly*, 32(1): 28–46.
Gray, M. (2011) 'The Bin Laden conspiracy theories: why falsehoods flourish in the Muslim world', *Foreign Affairs*, 4 May. Available at: www.foreignaffairs.com/articles/pakistan/2011-05-04/bin-laden-conspiracy-theories. [Accessed 10 September 2019.]
Hagen, K. (2018) 'Conspiracy theories and the paranoid style: do conspiracy theories posit implausibly vast and evil conspiracies?', *Social Epistemology*, 32(1): 24–40.
Hamid, S. and McCants, W. (2017) 'How likely is it that an Islamist group will govern in the Middle East before 2020?', *The Brookings Institution Markaz blog*, 2 August. Available at: www.brookings.edu/blog/

markaz/2017/08/02/how-likely-is-it-that-an-islamist-group-will-govern-in-the-middle-east-at-some-point-before-2020. [Accessed 10 September 2019.]

Hanieh, A. (2013) *Lineages of revolt: issues of contemporary capitalism in the Middle East*, Chicago: Haymarket Books.

Hasan, M. (2014) 'Inside jobs and Israeli stooges: why is the Muslim world in thrall to conspiracy theories?', *New Statesman*, 5 September. Available at: www.newstatesman.com/politics/2014/09/inside-jobs-and-israeli-stooges-why-muslim-world-thrall-conspiracy-theories. [Accessed 10 September 2019.]

Heikal, M.H. (1986) *Cutting the lion's tail: Suez through Egyptian eyes*, London: André Deutsch.

Hofstadter, R. (1965) *The paranoid style in American politics and other essays*, New York: Knopf.

Hörner, K. (2011) 'A cultural sense of conspiracies? The concept of rumor as propaedeutics to conspiracism', in A. Graf, S. Fathi and L. Paul (eds.) *Orientalism and conspiracy: politics and conspiracy theory in the Islamic world: essays in Honour of Sadik J. Al-Azm*, London: I. B. Tauris, pp. 87–104.

Huffington Post (2014) '"Password 360" conspiracy theories linking CIA to Isis actually bring a serious US denial', *The Huffington Post (UK)*, 14 August. Available at: www.huffingtonpost.co.uk/2014/08/14/cia-israel-isis-conspiracy-theories-hilary-clinton_n_5677687.html. [Accessed 10 September 2019.]

Hussein, S. (1991) 'Speech on Baghdad radio, February 21', reprinted in I. Bickerton, M. Pearson, G. Wilesmith, J. Holmes, M. McKinley and P. Krien (eds.) (1991) *43 Days: The Gulf War*, Melbourne: Text Publishing.

Kamrava, M. (ed.) (2014) *Beyond the Arab Spring: the evolving ruling bargain in the Middle East*, London: Hurst.

Kassem, M. (2004) *Egyptian politics: the dynamics of authoritarian rule*, Boulder CO: Lynne Rienner.

Kedar, M. (2005) *Asad in search of legitimacy: message and rhetoric in the Syrian press under Ḥāfiẓ and Bashār*, Brighton: Sussex Academic Press.

Kinzer, S. (2003) *All the Shah's men: an American coup and the roots of Middle East terror*, Hoboken, NJ: John Wiley & Sons.

Kishtainy, K. (1985) *Arab political humour*, London: Quartet Books.

Long, J.M. (2004) *Saddam's war of words: politics, religion, and the Iraqi invasion of Kuwait*, Austin, TX: University of Texas Press.

Melley, T. (2000) *Empire of conspiracy: the culture of paranoia in postwar America*, Ithaca, NY: Cornell University Press.

Milton-Edwards, B. (2006) *Contemporary politics in the Middle East*, 2nd edn, London: Polity.

M.R. (nom de plume) (2013) 'A Western plot to dish the Arabs', *The Economist: Pomegranate Blog*, 12 November. Available at: https://amp.economist.com/pomegranate/2013/11/12/a-western-plot-to-dish-the-arabs. [Accessed 10 September 2019.]

Nefes, T.S. (2017) 'The impacts of the Turkish government's conspiratorial framing of the Gezi Park protests', *Social Movement Studies*, 16(5): 610–22.

New York Times (2004) 'New York Times/CBS news poll: April 23–27, 2004', *New York Times*, 29 April. Available at: www.nytimes.com/packages/html/politics/20040429_poll/20040429_poll_results.pdf. [Accessed 10 September 2019.]

Nyhan, B. and Zeitzoff, T. (2018) 'Conspiracy and misperception belief in the Middle East and north Africa', *The Journal of Politics*, 80(4): 1400–4.

Pipes, D. (1996) *The hidden hand: Middle East fears of conspiracy*, Basingstoke: Macmillan.

Qiu, L. (2017) 'Syria conspiracy theories flourish, at both ends of the spectrum', *New York Times*, 10 April. Available at: www.nytimes.com/2017/04/10/us/politics/factcheck-syria-strike-conspiracy-theories.html. [Accessed 10 September 2019.]

Rabo, A. (2014) '"It Has All Been Planned": talking about *Us* and powerful others in contemporary Syria', in M. Butter and M. Reinkowski (eds.) *Conspiracy Theories in the United States and the Middle East: A Comparative Approach*, Berlin: de Gruyter, pp. 212–27.

Rudmin, F. (2003) 'Conspiracy theory as naive deconstructive history', *newdemocracyworld.org.*, April. Available at: www.newdemocracyworld.org/old/conspiracy.htm. [Accessed 10 September 2019.]

Schmid, S. (2014) 'Hizbullah between pan-Islamic ideology and domestic politics: conspiracy theories as medium for political mobilization and integration', in M. Butter and M. Reinkowski (eds.) *Conspiracy Theories in the United States and the Middle East: A Comparative Approach*, Berlin: de Gruyter, pp. 157–76.

Shlaim, A. (1997) 'The protocol of Sèvres, 1956: anatomy of a war plot', *International Affairs*, 73(3): 509–30.

Sivan, E. (1985) *Radical Islam: medieval theology and modern politics*, New Haven, CT: Yale University Press.
Tripp, C. (2013) *The power and the people: paths of resistance in the Middle East*, Cambridge: Cambridge University Press.
Verter, Y. (2018) 'Netanyahu's new Conspiracy theory borders on psychosis', *Haaretz*, 25 October. Available at: www.haaretz.com/israel-news/.premium-netanyahu-s-new-conspiracy-theory-borders-on-psychosis-1.6592353. [Accessed 10 September 2019.]
Wedeen, L. (1999) *Ambiguities of domination: politics, rhetoric, and symbols in contemporary Syria*, Chicago: The University of Chicago Press.
Xu, G. (2001) 'Anti-Western nationalism in China, 1989–99', *World Affairs*, 163(4): 151–62.

# 5.9
# CONSPIRACY THEORIES IN SOUTHEAST ASIA

*Viren Swami, Hanoor Syahirah Zahari and David Barron*

## Introduction

As an extraordinary event, there was bound to be differing explanations for the disappearance of Malaysia Airlines Flight 370 (MH370), which vanished on 8 March 2014 while flying from Kuala Lumpur to Beijing. However, within a remarkably short time after the flight's disappearance, an abundance of conspiracy theories emerged – in Malaysia and beyond – offering counter-narratives of the event and purporting to explain the role of heretofore unknown or hidden actors. One of the earliest conspiracy theories proposed that MH370 had been carrying 'sensitive' cargo and that the flight was 'remotely controlled' and flown to a secret location. Other conspiracy theories emerged almost as quickly. Some – such as the claim that the flight was lost in a 'second Bermuda triangle' in the Indian Ocean or that aliens transported the plane to the moon – appeared to be based on fantasy; other claims – such as the suggestion that the flight was inadvertently shot down in a military exercise, that the C.I.A. are intentionally withholding information about the flight's disappearance (a claim repeated by the then former Malaysian prime minister) or that secret military research had caused the plane to crash (see Frizell 2014) – seem to be based on kernels of (mis-) information that are extrapolated into broader conclusions.

The examples above suggest that conspiracy theories, while not unique to Southeast Asia, are a salient feature of social and political discourse in the region. While data do not exist to objectively and empirically assess changes in conspiracy theorising in Southeast Asia over time, that such conspiracist narratives are now ubiquitous in the region is beyond question. As such, conspiracy theorising is an important component when seeking to understand social and political life in Southeast Asia, even if it remains less studied than conspiracy theories in Europe and North America. In this chapter, we aim to consolidate available knowledge by introducing a number of Southeast Asian conspiracy theories that have been subjected to scholarly scrutiny. In doing so, it is important for us to acknowledge that our review is not exhaustive; that is, we have not sought to review every conspiracy theory that has emerged in the region. Rather, we have focused on several conspiracy theories in the Southeast Asian context that have received at least some empirical or analytic consideration and that point to broader similarities in conspiracy theorising across the region.

An implicit aim of this chapter is to challenge the reductionist – and often Orientalist – view that the ubiquity of conspiracy theories in Southeast Asia is a result of the supposed psychopathology of the region's populace or failed modernisation in these nation-states (see Graf *et al.*

2011). In this view, regional conspiracy theories are said to be the outcome of delusional beliefs produced by an irrational paranoia unique or exclusive to an undifferentiated populace of Southeast Asia or, alternatively, the result of supposed under-developed mindsets (Choiruzzad 2013). In contrast, our aim here is to provide an analysis of the sources and structures of conspiracy theories as they are shaped by the social and political dynamics of Southeast Asia. The salience of conspiracy theories in both popular and state discourses in Southeast Asia should be seen, in our view, as deriving from a complex confluence of sources that includes the nation-state elites and state institutions, groups and subgroups within society, and the political, socioeconomic and historical conditions at both national and regional levels. In short, the purpose of this chapter is to highlight a number of Southeast Asian conspiracy theories that have been subjected to academic research and to identify and explain the multiple sources of conspiracy theorising and the functions they serve in contemporary Southeast Asia.

## Anti-West conspiracy theories

In October 2002, three bombs were detonated in the tourist district of Kuta on the Indonesian island of Bali, killing 202 people and injuring a further 209 individuals. The militant Islamist group, Jemaah Islamiyah, were widely suspected as having perpetrated the terrorist attacks in retaliation for Indonesia's support of the global War on Terror and Australia's role in the liberation of East Timor. A number of Jemaah Islamiyah's members were later tried, sentenced to death and executed for committing the attacks, yet there remains widespread distrust of the legal proceedings against the perpetrators and, more broadly, the official narrative of events. Indeed, various scholars have highlighted the pervasiveness of conspiracy theories surrounding the 2002 Bali bombings, as well as other terrorist attacks in Indonesia (e.g. Fealy 2003; Kipp 2004; Smith 2005). In broad outline, these conspiracy theories suggest that, rather than having been perpetrated by homegrown extremists, terrorist attacks on Indonesian soil were instead perpetrated by foreign agents, most notably from the U.S. Central Intelligence Agency and Israel's Mossad (Fealy 2003).

When seeking to understand the popularity of such conspiracy theories, it is first important to appreciate that the impact of foreign (i.e. Western) powers in the region has not been benign, particularly in terms of the legacy of colonialism and, more recently, in shaping the region's economic environment. Important, therefore, is not simply a sense of socioeconomic decline in the region but also a fear of penetration, unjust influence and neo-colonialism by foreign powers. In the face of such fears, the state and its elite emerge as key narrators of conspiracism, either encouraging and nurturing conspiracy theories about Western influence or actively constructing narratives of the West seeking to intentionally undermine economic progress in Southeast Asia. For example, the 1999–2000 economic crisis in Southeast Asia produced a multitude of state-generated conspiracy theories that sought to shift blame away from regional economic mismanagement and onto a deliberate policy by the West of arresting the economic rise of Southeast Asia and bringing down authoritarian regimes, such as the Suharto regime in Indonesia (Wrage 1999; Soh 2000; Phongphaichit, Baker 2004; Rüland 2018).

For Southeast Asian political elites, nurturing this anti-Western conspiracy theory serves multiple functions. First, this 'survival discourse' serves a functional role in deflecting attention away from home-made political and economic failings: By narrating regional and national crises as primarily – if not wholly – externally caused, political elites are able to draw on historical accounts of victimisation by the West and to blame continuing Western interference as the cause of the region's decline. Second, conspiracy theorising about the nefarious Western influence in the region assists in rallying citizenry to defend the *status quo*: The rhetoric of vulnerability in the international area provides a useful plank on which to demand patriotism and loyalty to the establishment. Finally, and somewhat ironically perhaps, in employing this conspiracist narrative, Southeast Asian regimes also find a useful means of silencing local opposition. By accusing challengers to the *status quo* of 'conspiring' with foreign agents, the established elite are able to justify an expansion of authoritarian rule and the suppression of dissent – as has occurred in Thailand (Askew 2007; Johnson 2013), Indonesia (Yunanto 2003) and, more recently, Cambodia (Croissant 2018) and the Philippines (Cook 2018).

In Indonesia and Malaysia – the two predominantly Muslim states in Southeast Asia – a variant of the anti-Western conspiracy theory employed by political and religious leaders purports that foreign agents are specifically targeting Muslims and that globalisation is a concerted attempt to undermine Islamic identity, both at the level of the nation-state and the *umma* (i.e. the collective community of Muslims) (Barton 2002a, 2002b; Moten 2005; see also Chapter 5.8 in this volume). As before, this variant of the conspiracy theory plays multiple roles for elites, but further assists in helping to mobilise Muslim citizenry – who make up the majority of the population in Malaysia and Indonesia – in service of the nation-state, while contesting ground occupied by more extreme Islamic opposition. It is within this landscape that conspiracy theories about terrorist attacks find a natural home: Here, it is claimed that Western powers not only perpetrate terrorist attacks in Muslim countries like Indonesia, but also on their own soil (e.g. the 11 September 2001 terrorist attacks in the U.S.A.), in order to undermine Muslim unity and Islamic advancement (van Bruinessen 2003; Hassan, Salleh 2010).

In both Indonesia and Malaysia, this variant of the anti-West conspiracy theory has become a staple among Islamic militant groups (Choiruzzad 2013), who view it as a means of attacking their respective regimes (e.g. for complicity with foreign agents in allowing the terrorist attacks to occur) and as a public defence against claims that the same militant groups are responsible for the attacks. The wider appeal of the conspiracist narrative, however, has deeper roots. For example, some scholars have noted how the historical context in Indonesia breeds a level of distrust in relation to official narratives (e.g. Choiruzzad 2013), with the notion of 'extremism' (both of the left and right variety) historically being used to silence political opposition (Yunanto 2003). More recently, high-profile mis-arrests, extra-judicial killings and a lax attitude toward counter-terrorism generally have all fuelled conspiracy theorising. Choiruzzad (2013), for example, highlights a number of recent cases of false or manipulated testimonies obtained from suspected Islamic militants, as well as extra-judicial killings of suspected militants. He goes on to suggest that such mis-steps undermine official narratives of counter-terrorism and lead to a climate in which 'official' and 'alternative' narratives are equally contested. In short, mis-steps by those in positions of power have heightened community hostility and distrust toward the police, counter-terrorism agencies and the Indonesian regime in general, and fuels accounts of foreign actors committing acts of terrorism in Indonesia.

These explanations are consistent with the broader literature suggesting that conspiracy theories are more likely to gain acceptance when mainstream or 'official' explanations of events contain erroneous information, discrepancies or ambiguities (Miller 2002; Sunstein, Vermeule 2009; Swami, Furnham 2014). That is, in scenarios where there is little reliable information or when details of events are open to interpretation, contested and ambiguous, conspiracy theories gain acceptance because they purport to offer a coherent and comprehensive narrative. Among individuals who lack agency or who feel powerless, in particular, conspiracy theories – even if seemingly perplexing in relation to the knowledge held by wider society – offer a useful means of dealing with uncertainty sparked by complex economic, social or political phenomena. In other words, in a national context marked by competing narratives, and particularly where mainstream narratives are highly contested (Choiruzzad 2013), believing in conspiracy theories that terrorist attacks in Indonesia are being perpetrated by foreign agents seems intuitive.

A handful of studies have attempted to provide empirical support for these theoretical accounts and commentaries based on a social identities perspective. According to social identity theory (Tajfel, Turner 1986), individuals tend to achieve positive social identity through social comparisons between one's ingroup and relevant outgroups. In addition, individuals are expected to exhibit more negative attitudes and behaviours towards social outgroups to the extent that those outgroups are perceived as realistic threats (i.e. threats to a group's political or economic power, resources and general well-being) and symbolic threats (i.e. threats to a group's values, belief systems, morality, philosophy of life or identity) (Stephan, Renfro 2002; Stephan et al. 2009). Based on this broad theory, Mashuri and Zaduqisti (2015) tested the extent to which intergroup threat and social identity as a Muslim influenced belief in the conspiracy theory that Western powers are responsible for terrorist attacks in Indonesia.

Using a quasi-experimental design, Mashuri and Zaduqisti (2015) randomly assigned a sample of Muslim university students ($N = 139$) to one of four combined conditions, namely high or low intergroup threat (manipulated using a fictitious newspaper article predicting rising or decreasing political and cultural threat from Western powers toward Muslims) and high or low social identity salience (manipulated by asking participants to write a brief essay describing their Muslim identities or daily activities). In addition, participants were asked to rate their agreement with four statements that Western powers were conspiring to commit acts of terrorism in Indonesia. Their results showed that participants in the high intergroup threat condition were significantly more likely to believe in the conspiracy theory than those in the low threat condition, but only when Muslim social identity salience was also high. Cross-sectional studies with Muslim students in Indonesia have also supported these broad findings (Mashuri, Zaduqisti 2014a, 2014b; Mashuri, Akhrani et al. 2016; Mashuri et al. 2016).

In explanation, Mashuri and Zaduqisti (2014a, 2014b, 2015) suggested that participants experiencing threat and who strongly identified as Muslim were more likely to blame a derogated outgroup (i.e. Western powers) as a means of reasserting feelings of control. That is, by reducing and simplifying complex phenomena (i.e. terrorist attacks in Indonesia) and by tying together a series of events in relation to its purported causes and effects (i.e. attacks that are committed by Western powers in an attempt to weaken Muslims), conspiracy theories about Western machinations seemingly offer coherent explanations that may not otherwise be forthcoming. In this sense, the conspiracy theory helps individuals to identify a clear cause of a perceived injustice or tragedy and thereby helps individuals to make sense of the world. Moreover, believing in the conspiracy theory may also play a role in victim blaming, such as toward Muslim minority groups who are believed to be conspiring with Western agents (Putra et al. 2015).

Anti-West conspiracist narratives have also been documented in Timor-Leste in the form of 'cargo cults' that offer visions of radical transformation of society through hidden wealth (e.g. from gold and oil resources) accompanied by concerns of foreign (mainly Australian and U.S.) intervention (Bovensiepen 2016). Although the label of 'cargo cults' has largely been discredited because of its connotations of regional irrationality and for exaggerating differences between Timor-Leste and the West (Hermann 2004; Jebens 2004), Bovensiepen (2016) suggests that Timorese notions of future prosperity are often accompanied by fears that foreign powers are conspiring to rob the country of its natural resources, whether through sinister plots, foreign exploitation or war. For Bovensiepen, 'visions of prosperity and visions of conspiracy are two sides of the same coin' (2016: 76), in that both are an attempt to map the trajectories of regional and nation-state power. In one sense, these visions of conspiracy contain a kernel of truth, insofar as foreign powers have enriched themselves at the expense of Timor-Leste (Neves 2006), but they also highlight the way in which anti-West conspiracist narratives help to counter marginalisation and challenge political inequalities. In short, anti-West conspiracist narratives in

Timor-Leste have a 'sense-making' element, helping Timorese to understand unequal distributions of wealth and regional power.

## Conspiratorial Jews in a region without Jews

Closely related to anti-West conspiracy theories is the Jewish conspiracy theory, which borrows from early European antisemitism to posit the view that Jews are conspiring toward world domination (Johnson 1987). This particular conspiracy theory is a popular trope in Southeast Asia, particularly in Indonesia and Malaysia (Reid 2010). At the level of the state, for example, the spectre of Jewish world domination has frequently been raised as an argument for Muslim unity, particularly in the face of the economic crisis of the late 1990s (Malaysian Prime Minister Mahathir Mohamad claimed that the crisis had been orchestrated by 'Jewish financiers' in order to obstruct Southeast Asian development and industrialisation; cf. Bello 1998; Maswood 2002; Pieterse 2000) and Western intervention in the Middle East. At the level of popular culture, Holocaust denial is widespread even in academic circles, works and translations of works espousing Nazism and antisemitism are sold without restriction, and Nazi symbols are openly displayed (Hadler 2004; Suciu 2008; Reid 2010). Burhanuddin (2007), for example, notes that Indonesian translations of *The Protocols of the Elders of Zion* are widely available, with many Indonesians accepting it as a true account of the world economic order. Similarly, some scholars have noted the popularity of conspiracy theories suggesting that the augmented reality game Pokémon GO contained a hidden agenda glorifying Jews and derogating Islam (Umam et al. 2018).

Such antisemitism at the levels of the state and popular culture may seem puzzling when one learns that neither Malaysia nor Indonesia have sizeable Jewish populations. How, then, to explain the popularity of the Jewish conspiracy theory in these countries, where 'orthodox' factors that contribute to antisemitism (see Billig 1978, 1989; Copsey 2004) are unlikely to be a major influence? One argument distinguishes between the 'real Jew' living in Israel or in the diaspora and the 'perceived Jew', which is largely an imagined presence (Schulze 2006; Burhanuddin 2007). The distinction is important because the imagined presence of Jews allows Muslims in Indonesia and Malaysia to project their fears towards real or imagined threats from alien and impersonal actors. For example, Pieterse and Parekh (1995) discussed how rapid social change and economic turmoil left many Indonesians confused by their deteriorated situation, which they then blamed on an imagined or 'perceived Jew' controlling the world economy. In this sense, the imagined Jew as an invisible threat serves as a self-presentation function: While the 'real Jew' oppresses Muslims in Palestine, the 'perceived Jew' performs a similar role in Indonesia.

Other scholars have highlighted particular domestic factors that draw on the notion of the 'perceived Jew' in giving rise to popular antisemitism (Burhanuddin 2007; Reid 2010). These scholars variously discuss the Chinese minority or the emerging middle class in Indonesia as the real targets of Indonesian antisemitism. In this sense, the Jewish conspiracy theory affords Muslims in the region a means of implicitly scapegoating ethnic minorities or a broader range of perceived enemies (e.g. secularism, cosmopolitanism, Americanism and capitalism) by constructing an imagined enemy. Likewise, for Muslim leaders and politicians, the Jewish conspiracy theory also serves to unify Muslims around a political argument about threats to the nation-state and the *umma*. State- and elite-directed misinformation and conspiracy theorising, then, facilitates the denigration of real ethnic minorities, strengthens popular nationalism and deflects attention away from the elite's political and economic failings. In turn, conspiracy theorising about the 'perceived Jew' serves to reinforce the *status quo* state as a source of protection against perceived threats (Reid 2010). In short, the Jewish conspiracy theory should be read as a narrative that fulfils contextualised needs both at the level of state and popular culture in Indonesia and Malaysia.

There is some empirical evidence to support these ideas. For example, in a sample of Malaysian Malay-Muslims ($N = 368$), Swami (2012) reported that belief in the Jewish conspiracy theory was only weakly associated with belief in other conspiracy theories and indices of anomie, such as self-esteem and political alienation. In contrast, belief in the Jewish conspiracy theory was more strongly associated with both anti-Israeli attitudes and prejudice toward the Chinese minority ($N = 314$) in Malaysia (Swami 2012). Swami goes on to suggest that, among politically conservative Malay-Muslims, belief in the Jewish conspiracy theory may reflect perceptions of Muslim victimhood, motivated in part by the question of Palestine, as well as providing a means of implicitly attacking the Chinese minority in Malaysia. In terms of the latter, because explicitly attacking the Chinese is both illegal and politically unwise, the Jewish conspiracy theory may offer a means of voicing anti-Chinese polemic that would otherwise be difficult to articulate. In short, the Jewish conspiracy theory serves a performative role in allowing for the expression of victimhood, both internationally (vis-à-vis Palestine) and locally (vis-à-vis Chinese commerce and business interests).

Beyond purely academic reasons, studying the Jewish conspiracy theory in Indonesia and Malaysia remains important because it feeds a radical Islamist discourse that seeks to explain contemporary world affairs. This discourse constructs an essentialist image of an aggressive and evil West controlled by Jews and engaged in an ongoing and unprovoked 'crusade' to crush supposedly peaceful Muslims (Woodward 2006, 2010). This narrative both borrows and builds on antisemitic discourse and the Jewish conspiracy theory, which in turn influences wider, popular discourse of international relations. Indeed, the available evidence, reviewed above (Mashuri, Zaduqisti 2014a, 2014b, 2015; Mashuri et al. 2016), suggests that the portrayal of social conflict in terms of grand struggles between Muslims and Christians/Jews may serve as a convenient explanation for difficult-to-understand social and political processes, but may also serve a radicalisation function that promotes inter-ethnic violence when it bleeds into mainstream culture (Tambiah 1996; Woodward 2010; Muslimin 2011).

## Conspiracy theories and inter-group conflict

The theme of inter-group conflict and communal violence should come as no surprise in a region that is ethnically heterogeneous and, indeed, feeds a number of other regional conspiracy theories, particularly during periods of social and economic upheaval. In the Indonesian context, for example, Fanselow (2015) has discussed how the dynamics of inter-ethnic conflict fed various explanatory narratives among those involved, some of which were conspiratorial in nature. Specifically, they focused on outbreaks of ethnic violence between 1997 and 1999 in Kalimantan between Dayaks (an umbrella term used to refer to a multitude of ethnic groups indigenous to Borneo) and Madurese migrants to Kalimantan. While initial media reports attempted to frame the communal violence as a case of religious conflict between Muslims and Christians, these narratives were rejected by Dayak and Madurese leaders, who described it as a conspiracy theory propagated by the 'deep state' in order to provide support for the necessity of a powerful government that could avert the disintegration of the nation-state.

Moreover, Dayak and Madurese leaders accused security forces of intentionally creating disorder in order to create a climate of instability that would allow for a re-establishment of order. That is, by allowing violence to deliberately spin out of control, the security forces could create an impression of central government ineffectiveness and the need for security forces to assume a greater political role in maintaining national security. In addition, both the Dayak and Madurese constructed conspiracist narratives of the security forces siding with the other by, for example, forewarning of attacks, supplying weapons, allowing for safe passage or willingly allowing violence to continue. For Fanselow (2015), such conspiracist narratives should be viewed within the context of rapid socio-political change in Indonesia, with various national and provincial forces vying for political power. Such a climate created the conditions in which actors were able to use conspiracist narratives to exploit ethnic antagonisms to their own advantage.

In examining the same inter-ethnic conflict, Bouvier and Smith (2006) further highlighted how both the Dayak and Madurese constructed conspiracist narratives based on a piecing together of selective facts. For example, the fact that security forces profited from the evacuation of Madurese was used to support the Madurese conspiracist narrative that security forces were involved in creating a climate of violence. Conversely, the Dayak used an explosion at a factory as proof that the Madurese were stockpiling bombs for a terror campaign. In both examples, observations were made to fit conspiracist theories that the other side was working to a sinister, premeditated set of plans. As Bouvier and Smith put it, 'by interlocking coincidental or unusual events in a wider, more sinister, puzzle, conspiracy theories provide satisfaction and justifications to those who "understand"' (2006: 483).

This point about conspiracy theories emerging in periods of rapid change generally and in a climate where foundational information is either absent or contested is also reinforced in Butt's examination of the 'lipstick girl' conspiracy (2005; see also Butt et al. 2002). This particular conspiracy theory was held by some indigenous Papuans and purported that H.I.V./A.I.D.S. was intentionally introduced into Papua as part of an Indonesian programme of ethnic cleansing in the resource-rich region. More specifically, the conspiracy theory suggested that migrant Indonesian 'lipstick girls' (i.e. sex workers) infected with H.I.V./A.I.D.S. were being sent to military-controlled brothels in Papua, with the explicit intention of killing Papuans. Belief in this conspiracy theory went in tandem with the spread of rumours among Papuans and symbolic beliefs about Papuan men being overpowered by spiked drinks, magic dust on cigarettes and poisoned food.

Butt's (2005) analysis highlights both regional and local conditions that contributed to the spread of the lipstick girl conspiracy. At the macro level, Butt highlighted the rapid social and political change in Indonesia generally and the political conditions of disempowerment among Papuans specifically that allowed for the spread of rumours and conspiracy theories. In this sense, conspiracy theories afforded Papuans a means of concretely describing the threat of political disempowerment and violence, while simultaneously expressing their concerns about it. That is, in these situations, the contested nature of power, stark inequalities in wealth and the distribution of wealth, and the rapidly changing social landscape as a result of modernisation, steered disempowered individuals to explain their circumstances through rumour and conspiracy theories. Looked at from the obverse point-of-view, conspiracy theories about lipstick girls shine a light on the inconsistencies of Indonesian rule in Papua and the way in which power is managed by the nation-state to maintain hegemony.

At the micro level, Butt (2005) highlighted the way in which first-hand experience of aggression and abuse by non-Papuan military personnel and high-ranking Indonesian officers fuelled genocidal conspiracy theories. Contradictions in the healthcare system provided further fuel for conspiracy theories: The fact that Papuans were fined if they tested positive for a sexually-transmitted disease and that sex workers were regularly tested as part of a national campaign (despite sex work being illegal) provided 'evidence' that the Indonesian government sought to intentionally infect Papuans with H.I.V./A.I.D.S. while ensuring that sex workers themselves remained disease-free. In short, Butt discussed the way that the lipstick girl conspiracy theory helps to tie together seemingly disparate events and experiences into a coherent narrative, which builds on authoritarian and militarised forms of governance in Papua. Butt's (2005) analysis is important as it highlights the myriad ways in which macro- and micro-level factors overlap to provide fertile ground for the spread of conspiracy theories.

## Conclusion and future directions

At the outset of this chapter, we suggested that our aim was to counter the reductionist view that conspiracy theories in Southeast Asia are a result of collective psychopathology or failed modernisation. Instead, through the examples of conspiracy theories we have reviewed in this chapter, we have attempted to highlight the ways in which Southeast Asian conspiracist narratives are shaped by the socio-political and economic dynamics of the region. In some cases, conspiracy theories are utilised by political elites to maintain the *status quo* or to provide a justification for attacks on perceived political enemies. In other cases, conspiracy theories gain traction as a means of derogating outgroups and maintaining a sense of ingroup positivity, particularly during periods of rapid socio-political transformation. In yet other cases, conspiracist narratives emerge as a means of understanding and explaining trajectories of nation-state, regional or localised power asymmetries. In all such cases, however, it would be misleading to simply dismiss Southeast Asian conspiracy theories as the outcome of psychopathology or under-development; rather, these conspiracist narratives frequently have historical roots and reflect political, social and economic conditions at both national and regional levels.

Despite this, there remains much work to be done to better understand the pervasiveness and spread of conspiracy theories in Southeast Asia. For one thing, the majority of studies to date have focused on Indonesian samples and narratives, and empirical work in other Southeast Asian countries remain piecemeal or – in some cases – non-existent. Likewise, little attempt has been made to understand conspiracy theories that traverse nation-state boundaries, particularly those that may have broad regional appeal (e.g. anti-Western conspiracy theories but see Changsong *et al.* 2017). In addition, there is a marked disjuncture between studies that have approached the issue of conspiracy theories from a psychological perspective (primarily focused on social identity theory) and those that have approached it from a sociological or anthropological perspective (primarily focused on historical trajectories and power asymmetries). Bridging this gap may provide a fuller account of the ways in which conspiracy theories emerge, are disseminated and influence decision-making at both the levels of the nation-state and in popular culture.

## References

Askew, M. (2007) *Conspiracy, politics, and a disorderly border: the struggle to comprehend insurgency in Thailand's deep south*, Washington, DC: East-West Centre.
Barton, G. (2002a) 'Islam and politics in new Indonesia', in C. Rubenstein (ed.) *Islam in Asia: changing political realities*, Abingdon: Routledge, pp. 1–90.
Barton, G. (2002b) 'Islam, society, politics, and change in Malaysia', in C. Rubenstein (ed.) *Islam in Asia: changing political realities*, Abingdon: Routledge, pp. 91–164.
Bello, W. (1998) 'The end of a "miracle": speculation, foreign capital dependence, and the collapse of the Southeast Asian economies', *Multinational Monitor*, 19(1–2): 10–6.
Billig, M. (1978) *Fascists: a social psychological view of the National Front*, London: Harcourt Brace.
Billig, M. (1989) 'The extreme right: continuities in anti-Semitic conspiracy theory in post-war Europe', in R. Eatwell and N. O'Sullivan (eds.) *The nature of the right: European and American Politics and political thought since 1789*, London: Pinter, pp. 146–66.
Bouvier, H. and Smith, G. (2006) 'Of spontaneity and conspiracy theories: explaining violence in central Kalimantan', *Asian Journal of Social Sciences*, 34(3): 475–91.
Bovensiepen, J. (2016) 'Visions of prosperity and conspiracy in Timor-Leste', *Focaal: Journal of Global and Historical Anthropology*, 75: 75–88.

Burhanuddin, A. (2007) 'The conspiracy of Jews: the quest for anti-Semitism in media dakwah', *Graduate Journal of Asia Pacific Studies*, 5(2): 53–76.
Butt, L. (2005) '"Lipstick girls" and "fallen women": AIDS and conspiratorial thinking in Papua. Indonesia', *Cultural Anthropology*, 20(3): 412–42.
Butt, L., Numbery, G. and Morin, J. (2002) *Final report: the Papuan sexuality study*, Jakarta: Family Health International.
Changsong, W., Yiming, C. and Haji Ahmad, J. (2017) 'A comparative study of social media users' perception on the Malaysia Airlines Flight MH370 incident in mainland China and Malaysia', *International Journal of Culture and History*, 3: 142–7.
Choiruzzad, S.A. (2013) 'Within a thick mist: conspiracy theories and counter terrorism in Indonesia', *International Journal of Social Inquiry*, 6(2): 96–116.
Cook, M. (2018) 'The Philippines in 2017: turbulent consolidation', in M. Cook and D. Singh (eds.) *Southeast Asian Affairs 2018*, Singapore: ISEAS – Yusof Ishak Institute, pp. 267–83.
Copsey, N. (2004) *Contemporary British fascism: the British National Party and the quest for legitimacy*, Basingstoke: Palgrave Macmillan.
Croissant, A. (2018) 'Cambodia in 2017: Descending into dictatorship?', *Asian Survey*, 58: 194–200.
Fanselow, F. (2015) 'Indigenous and anthropological theories of ethnic conflict in Kalimantan', *ZINBUN*, 34: 131–47.
Fealy, G. (2003) 'Hating Americans: Jemaah Islamiyah and the Bali bombings', *Inside Indonesia*, 74(April-June): 6–8.
Frizell, S. (2014) 'The missing Malaysian plane: 5 Conspiracy Theories', *Time*, 12 March. Available at: www.time.com/20351/missing-plane-flight-mh370-5-conspiracy-theories. [Accessed 8 September 2019.]
Graf, A., Fathi, A. and Paul, L. (eds.) (2011) *Orientalism and conspiracy: politics and conspiracy theory in the Islamic world*, London: I.B. Tauris and Co.
Hadler, J. (2004) 'Translations of anti-Semitism: Jews, the Chinese, and violence in colonial and post-colonial Indonesia', *Indonesia and the Malay World*, 32: 185–313.
Hassan, M.H. and Salleh, M.R. (2010) '9/11 conspiracy theories: the absent perspectives', *RSIS Commentaries*, 46: 1–3.
Hermann, E. (2004) 'Dissolving the self-other dichotomy in Western "cargo cult" constructions', in H. Jebens (ed.) *Cargo, cult, and culture critique*, Honolulu, HI: University of Hawai'i Press, pp. 38–56.
Jebens, J. (ed.) (2004) *Cargo, cult, and culture critique*, Honolulu, HI: University of Hawai'i Press.
Johnson, A.A. (2013) 'Moral knowledge and its enemies: conspiracy and kingship in Thailand', *Anthropology Quarterly*, 86(4): 1059–86.
Johnson, P. (1987) *A history of the Jews*, New York, NY: Harper and Row.
Kipp, R.S. (2004) 'Indonesia in 2003: Terror's aftermath', *Asian Survey*, 44(1): 62–9.
Mashuri, A., Akhrani, L.A. and Zaduqisti, E. (2016) 'You are the real terrorist and we are just your puppet: using individual and group factors to explain Indonesian Muslims' attributions of causes of terrorism', *Europe's Journal of Psychology*, 12(1): 68.
Mashuri, A. and Zaduqisti, E. (2014a) 'The role of social identification, intergroup threat, and out-group derogation in explaining belief in conspiracy theory about terrorism in Indonesia', *International Journal of Research Studies in Psychology*, 3: 35–50.
Mashuri, A. and Zaduqisti, E. (2014b) 'We believe in your conspiracy if we distrust you: the role of intergroup distrust in structuring the effect of Islamic identification, competitive victimhood, and group incompatibility on belief in a conspiracy theory', *Journal of Tropical Psychology*, e11.
Mashuri, A. and Zaduqisti, E. (2015) 'The effect of intergroup threat and social identity salience on the belief in conspiracy theories over terrorism in Indonesia: collective angst as a mediator', *International Journal of Psychological Research*, 8(1): 24–35.
Mashuri, A., Zaduqisti, E., Sukmawati, F., Sakdiah, H. and Suharini, N. (2016) 'The role of identity subversion in structuring the effects of intergroup threats and negative emotions on belief in anti-West conspiracy theories in Indonesia', *Psychology and Developing Societies*, 28: 1–28.
Maswood, S.J. (2002) 'Developmental states in crisis', in M. Beeson (ed.) *Reconfiguring East Asia: regional institutions and organisations after the crisis*, London: RoutledgeCurzon, pp. 31–48.
Miller, S. (2002) 'Conspiracy theories: public arguments as coded social critiques', *Argumentation and Advocacy*, 39(1): 40–56.
Moten, A.R. (2005) 'Modernisation and the process of globalization', in K. Nathan and M.H. Kamali (eds.) *Islam in Southeast Asia: political, social, and strategic challenges for the 21st century*, Singapore: Institute of Southeast Asian Studies, pp. 231–52.

Muslimin, J.M. (2011) 'Polemics on "orientalism" and "conspiracy" in Indonesia: a survey of public discourse on the case of JIL vs. DDII (2001–2005)', in A. Graf, S. Fathi and L. Paul (eds.) *Orientalism and conspiracy*, London: I.B. Tauris, pp. 129–40.

Neves, G.N.S. (2006) 'The paradox of aid in Timor-Leste', *Cooperação Internacional e a Construção do Estado no Timor-Leste*, University of Brasilia, Brazil, 25–28 July.

Phongphaichit, P. and Baker, C. (2004) *Thaksin: The business of politics in Thailand*, Chiang Mai: Silkworm Books.

Pieterse, J.N. (2000) 'Globalization north and south: representations of uneven development and the interaction of modernities', *Theory, Culture, and Society*, 17(1): 129–37.

Pieterse, J.N. and Parekh, B. (1995) 'Shifting imaginaries: decolonization, internal decolonization, postcoloniality', in J.N. Pieterse and B. Parekh (eds.) *The decolonization of imagination*, London: Zen Books, pp. 1–19.

Putra, I.E., Mashuri, A. and Zaduqisti, E. (2015) 'Demonising the victim: seeking the answer for how a group as the violent victim is blamed', *Psychology and Developing Societies*, 27(1): 31–57.

Reid, A. (2010) 'Jewish-conspiracy theories in Southeast Asia: are Chinese the target?', *Indonesia and the Malay World*, 38(112): 373–85.

Rüland, J. (2018) 'Coping with crisis: Southeast Asian regionalism and the ideational constraints of reform', *Asia Europe Journal*, 16(4): 155–68.

Schulze, F. (2006) 'Antisemitismus in Indonesian', *Orientierungen*, 2: 123–45.

Smith, A.L. (2005) 'The politics of negotiating the terrorist problem in Indonesia', *Studies in Conflict and Terrorism*, 28(1): 33–44.

Soh, B. (2000) 'Mahathir's anti-Western world view: an intellectual origin of Malaysian reactions to the economic crisis in the late 1990s', *International Area Studies Review*, 3: 3–15.

Stephan, W.G. and Renfro, C.L. (2002) 'The role of threats in intergroup relations', in U. Wagner, L.R. Tropp, G. Finchilescu and C. Tredoux (eds.) *Improving intergroup relations: Building on the legacy of Thomas F. Pettigrew*, Oxford: Blackwell, pp. 55–72.

Stephan, W.G., Ybarra, O. and Rios Morrison, K. (2009) 'Intergroup threat theory', in T.D. Nelson (ed.) *Handbook of prejudice, stereotyping, and discrimination*, 2nd ed., New York, NY: Taylor and Francis, pp. 23–56.

Suciu, E.M. (2008) 'Signs of anti-Semitism in Indonesia', thesis, Syndey, Australia: The University of Sydney.

Sunstein, C.R. and Vermeule, A. (2009) 'Conspiracy theories: causes and cures', *Journal of Political Philosophy*, 17(2): 202–27.

Swami, V. (2012) 'Social psychological origins of conspiracy theories: the case of the Jewish conspiracy theory in Malaysia', *Frontiers in Psychology*, 3: 280.

Swami, V. and Furnham, A. (2014) 'Political paranoia and conspiracy theories', in J.-P. Prooijen and P.A.M. van Lange (eds.) *Power politics, and paranoia: why people are suspicious of their leaders*, Cambridge: Cambridge University Press, pp. 218–36.

Tajfel, H. and Turner, J.C. (1986) 'The social identity theory of intergroup behavior', in S. Worschel and W.G. Austin (eds.) *Psychology of intergroup relations*, 2nd ed., Chicago, IL: Nelson-Hall, pp. 7–24.

Tambiah, S.J. (1996) *Leveling crowds: ethnonationalist conflicts and collective violence in South Asia*, Berkeley: University of California Press.

Umam, A.N., Muluk, H. and Milla, M.N. (2018) 'The need for cognitive closure and belief in conspiracy theories: an exploration of the role of religious fundamentalism in cognition', in A. Amarina, H. Muluk, P. Newcombe, F.P. Piercy, E.K. Poerwandari and S.H.R. Suradijono (eds.) *Diversity in unity: perspectives from psychology and behavioral sciences*, London: Routledge.

Van Bruinessen, M. (2003) 'Post-Suharto Moslems' engagements with civil society and democracy', *Third International Conference and Workshop Indonesia in Transition*, Jakarta, Inonesia: Universitas Indonesia, 24–8 August.

Woodward, M. (2006) 'Religious conflict and the globalization of knowledge: Indonesia 1978–2004', in L. Cady and S. Sheldon (eds.) *Religion and conflict in South and Southeast Asia: disrupting violence*, London: Routledge, pp. 85–109.

Woodward, M. (2010) 'Tropes of the crusades in Indonesian Muslim discourse', *Contemporary Islam*, 4(3): 311–30.

Wrage, S.D. (1999) 'Examining the "authoritarian advantage" in Southeast Asian development in the wake of Asian economic failures', *Studies in Conflict and Terrorism*, 22: 21–31.

Yunanto, S. (ed.) (2003) *Militant Islamic movements in Indonesia and South-East Asia*, Jakarta: RIDEP Institute and Friedrich Ebert Stiftung.

# 5.10
# CONSPIRACY THEORIES IN AMERICAN HISTORY

*Michael Butter*

## Introduction

Unlike the history of many other regions and cultures, the history of American conspiracy theories has already been well researched (see, among others, Goldberg 2001; Olmsted 2009; Barkun 2013). This article can therefore draw on a comparatively rich body of previous research, without, however, sharing their assumptions and conclusions. More specifically, the narrative I will relate here differs significantly from the most well-known account of U.S. conspiracy theories provided by Richard Hofstadter in his seminal essay 'The Paranoid Style in American Politics'. Hofstadter acknowledged that conspiracy theories had a long history in the U.S.A. but argued that they had always 'been the preferred style only of *minority* movements' (1964: 7 [italics in the original]). Many scholars have drawn on this argument and have suggested that, ironically, exactly at the time when Hofstadter was making this claim, conspiracy theories were beginning to move from the margins to the mainstream of American culture. Focusing on the contemporary period, these studies argue that conspiracy theories have become more widely spread and influential than ever (Knight 2000; Melley 2000; Barkun 2013). This argument sounds very convincing at first, considering the attention that has been paid to conspiracy theories in recent years. With a president prone to use conspiracist rhetoric currently in the White House, it is not surprising that some very recent studies suggest that, due to political polarisation and the echo chambers of the Internet, conspiracy theories are now more popular than ever (Merlan 2019; Muirhead, Rosenblum 2019).

However, drawing on an approach from the sociology of knowledge (Anton *et al.* 2014), I will argue that the opposite is the case. Conspiracy theories have not increased, but decreased, in popularity and importance over time in American culture. They have moved from the mainstream to the margins, not the other way around. They were once orthodox, that is, officially accepted and legitimate knowledge, and became heterodox, that is, stigmatised and illegitimate knowledge after the Second World War. It is true that conspiracy theories have become more important again in recent years and are now more visible and influential than 30 years ago, but they are still far less widely spread and influential than 100 or 200 years ago.

This chapter therefore relates the history of American conspiracy theories in three steps. The first part focuses on the time from the seventeenth to the middle of the twentieth century. During that period, conspiracy theories change significantly in focus and rhetoric, but they are always considered legitimate knowledge. They are believed and articulated by elites and accordingly exert a significant influence on culture and society, shaping many important events. The second part addresses the period from the late 1950s to the turn of the millennium. Rather than rehearsing the well-known conspiracy theories of that period, such as the Kennedy assassination or the moon landing, it discusses the stigmatisation of conspiracy theories and its effects on their visibility and popularity. As heterodox knowledge they are increasingly perceived as a problem and a potential danger to democracy, a feeling powerfully articulated in Hofstadter's seminal essay, and they exert much less influence than before. The final part, then, suggests that conspiracy theories have become more popular and influential again in recent years. They remain stigmatised in the public at large but, mostly due to the Internet, counter-publics have emerged in which conspiracy theories are again considered legitimate knowledge. Since these counter-publics make savvy use of social media and have created their own news outlets and experts, they can circumvent the traditional gatekeepers who still consider conspiracy theories wrong and problematic. Thus, conspiracy theories remain illegitimate knowledge, but, unlike in previous decades, they are highly visible and therefore significantly influence public debates.

## From the colonial period to the Cold War: Conspiracy theories as influential orthodox knowledge

In recent years, there has been growing scholarly consensus that conspiracy theories are neither an anthropological given, as scholarship in the 1980s frequently claimed (Groh 1987), nor do they only emerge with the Enlightenment, as Karl Popper (1945) famously suggested. Scholars now identify the early modern period, more specifically the religious wars of the late sixteenth century, as the time when conspiracy theories emerged for the first time (Coward, Swann 2004; Zwierlein 2013). These conspiracy theories differ from most of the prominent modern ones in that they do not focus exclusively on human actors, but include supernatural ones as well. In fact, the struggle that these 'metaphysical conspiracy theories' (Butter 2014: 55) are concerned with is ultimately the apocalyptic confrontation between God and the devil.

European colonists brought their conspiracist suspicions with them when they settled in the Americas in the sixteenth and seventeenth centuries. Conspiracy theories were particularly prominent among the Puritans in New England, because these religious dissenters from the Church of England thought of themselves as a chosen people and confidently modelled themselves after the Israelites of the Old Testament. They saw themselves at the forefront of the cosmic struggle between God and the devil. They believed that all their enemies were secretly allied and that the devil orchestrated their attacks. The devil, they thought, considered them an important target because they had ventured deep into his territory: 'The New-Englanders are a People of God settled in those, which were once the *Devil's* Territories', Puritan minister Cotton Mather wrote in *Wonders of the Invisible World*, thus articulating the common conviction that the devil had fled to the New World when Christianity spread throughout Europe (1862 [1692]: 13). Finding a wilderness devoid of churches but full of easily seduced heathens, the devil 'had reign'd without any controul for many Ages' over the country, and, 'Irritated' by the Puritans' arrival, 'immediately try'd all sorts of Methods to overturn [their] poor Plantation' (Mather 1862 [1692]: 74, 13). He tempted individual souls, and he conjured up 'powerful "external" enemies – both human and non-human – dedicated to destroying the polity: storms, earthquakes, epidemics, pirates, foreign enemies, heretics, witches, imperial bureaucrats, Amerindians, and African slaves' (Cañizares-Esguerra 2006: 17). Interpreting each environmental disaster and conflict with any enemy as yet another episode in the battle against the forces of evil, the Puritans developed a veritable 'siege mentality' (Cañizares-Esguerra 2006: 29).

The conspiracy theory stabilised the Puritan community because it located the conspirators – except for the occasional witch or heretic – firmly on the outside. However, with the Salem witchcraft crisis of 1692–1693, it temporarily evolved into a socially destructive variant that shook the community to its core. Hundreds of people were accused, and among those accused – and even among those sentenced and executed – were many who were highly regarded or even in full communion with their churches. As we know today from the excellent studies by Paul Boyer and Stephen Nissenbaum (1974) and Mary Beth Norton (2002), the crisis was fuelled by trauma and disaffection connected to an ongoing war with Native Americans, as well as an economic conflict within Salem Village. These issues, however, could not be addressed openly at the time but were articulated as accusations of witchcraft. To the Puritans, it thus appeared as if the boundary between inside and outside had collapsed completely. 'An Army of *Devils* is horribly broke in upon the place' and '*The Walls of the whole World are broken down!*', wrote Cotton Mather in *Wonders*, his account of the crisis (1862 [1692]: 14; 79 [italics in the original]). The spiral of accusations and convictions could only be stopped when the colony's new governor dissolved the Court of Oyer and Terminer (to Hear and to Determine) responsible for the case, but 20 people were already dead. One man, Giles Corey, had been pressed to death because he refused to acknowledge the court that was trying him, and 19 convicted 'witches' – 14 women and five men – had been hanged.

The resolution of the witchcraft crisis did not mean that conspiracy theories became less influential in what was to become the U.S.A. While the period between 1700 and 1750 has not yet been researched in that regard, Bernhard Bailyn has demonstrated that, from the 1750s onward, conspiracy theories were a decisive factor in bringing about the War of Independence.

> [T]he fear of a comprehensive conspiracy against liberty throughout the English-speaking world – a conspiracy believed to have been nourished in corruption, and of which, it was felt, oppression in America was only the most immediately visible part – lay at the heart of the Revolutionary movement,

Bailyn writes in the 'Foreword' to *Pamphlets of the American Revolution 1750–1776* (1965a: x), a collection of primary sources that complements his seminal study *The Ideological Origins of the American Revolution* (1967). Over the course of the 1760s and 1770s, the colonists became increasingly convinced of the existence of what George Washington described as 'a regular, systematic plan ... to make us tame and abject slaves' (1971 [1774]: 34). This plot, the colonists claimed, was carried out by the king, his ministers, parliament, the Church of England and the crown's representatives in the colonies. What is more, the colonists believed that the conspirators wanted to abolish liberty everywhere. As Bailyn suggests, this perception was of 'the utmost importance to the colonists' because 'it transformed [their demands] from constitutional arguments to expressions of a world regenerative creed' (1965b: 82). As one pamphleteer put it, the cause of America 'is the cause of *self-defense*, of *public faith*, and of the *liberties of mankind*' (qtd in Bailyn 1965b: 83). In light of such a comprehensive conspiracy, the colonists felt that their revolt was justified. Their conspiracy theory thus fuelled and legitimised the revolution.

Bailyn's analysis indicates that Richard Hofstadter could not have been more wrong with his claims about the status and influence of conspiracy theory in American history. During both the seventeenth and the eighteenth centuries, conspiracy theories constituted a legitimate form of knowledge and significantly shaped the course of the country. They were sincerely believed and voiced by some of the nation's most revered leaders, among others by 'Founding Fathers' George Washington and John Dams, that is, figures who could not be further removed from the fringes of society to which, according to Hofstadter, belief in conspiracy theories was restricted at that time. As Gordon Wood (1982) has convincingly demonstrated, this propensity to perceive the world in conspiracist fashion was fuelled by a specific epistemology of cause and effect that maintained that the moral quality of an action was identical with the intention behind the action.

Wood also claims that conspiracy theories lost their status as legitimate knowledge in American culture at the end of the eighteenth century. He considers the French Revolution the turning point:

> Although … conspiratorial interpretations of the Revolution were everywhere … the best minds … now knew that the jumble of events that made up the Revolution were so complex and overwhelming that they could no longer be explained simply as the products of personal intentions.
>
> *(1982: 432)*

However, while Wood draws on a plethora of sources for his observations about the Revolutionary Period, he offers no evidence at all for this claim, implicitly admitting that the majority of people in the U.S.A. and Europe continued to think on the basis of the old paradigm and that only some thinkers moved on to a different one. Thus, as Geoffrey Cubitt pointedly puts it in his analysis of anti-Catholic conspiracy theories in nineteenth-century France, 'Quite simply, this recession [that Wood postulates] shows very little signs of having happened during the nineteenth and early twentieth centuries' on either side of the Atlantic (1989: 18). The specific logic of cause and effect described by Wood survived into the nineteenth century. Additionally, as I have argued elsewhere (Butter 2014: 37–54), in the nineteenth as much as in the eighteenth century, conspiracist thinking in the U.S.A. was further fuelled by two other sources: The influential republican ideology that saw republics in perpetual danger of being overthrown by conspiracies and the heritage of Puritanism with its belief in the U.S.A.'s mission in a Manichean struggle of cosmic dimensions between the forces of good and evil.

As a consequence, the status of conspiracy theories did not change throughout the nineteenth century.[1] Elites as well as ordinary people remained convinced that smaller or larger groups of conspirators could and did shape the course of events for years or even decades. These suspicions tended to focus on minorities and immigrants (Rogin 1987; Mottram 1989), but they also ran along partisan lines. Almost invariably, the alleged conspirators were cast as a threat to the American way of life, as a danger to the rights of the people won with the Revolution. In 1790, the Federalists around Washington and Adams accused Thomas Jefferson's Democratic Republicans of being in league with the European Illuminati, who, according to Jedidiah Morse and others, had already caused the French Revolution (Stauffer 1918; McKenzie-McHarg 2014). The Democratic Republicans in turn alleged that the Federalists were colluding with Britain in order to re-establish the monarchy. A little later, Andrew Jackson tried to capitalise on fears about the undue influence of bankers – the so-called money power. However, these conspiracy theories never became as prominent as suspicions about Masons, Mormons and Catholics during the antebellum period (Davis 1960). Fuelled by a steady influx of Irish immigrants, the Catholic conspiracy theory gained particular traction between the 1830s and 1850s (Butter 2014: 113–66). It claimed that the monarchs of Europe were conspiring with the Pope to destroy American democracy because it was setting a dangerous example to the oppressed masses of Europe. Many accounts identified Archduke Metternich as the mastermind behind the plot (Beecher 1835: 53; Morse 1835: 44–6). Founded in 1850, the anti-Catholic Know Nothing Party won about 25 per cent of the popular vote in the presidential election of 1856, which illustrates how widely spread and influential this conspiracy theory was for a while.

Unsurprisingly, the most influential conspiracy theories of the antebellum period revolved around the issue of slavery. During the 1830s, the supporters of slavery began to perceive abolitionism as a British plot to weaken the American economy and, as with the Catholic conspiracy theory, to disqualify the democratic example the U.S.A. was setting to the world. In the 1850s, then, the pro-slavery faction increasingly cast the members of the Republican Party as the masterminds behind this plot, constantly referring to them as 'Black Republicans' in order to suggest that they were abolitionists in disguise who wanted to outlaw slavery everywhere. Over the course of the decade, their indictments became more and more alarmist in tone, until, after Lincoln's election, they argued that the administration had now been captured by the conspiracy. However, for the other side in this conflict, conspiracy theories were arguably even more important. Founded in 1854, the Republican Party fought not against slavery as such but against what its members called the 'Slave Power', that is, the influence of the most powerful slaveholders over national politics. As Larry Gara explains, Republicans 'feared the effect of continued national rule by slaveholding interests on northern rights, on civil liberties, on desired economic measures and on the future of free white labor itself' (1969: 6).

The notion of the Slave Power conspiracy explains how resistance to slavery could eventually emerge as a majority position in the North. The abolitionists, who opposed slavery on moral grounds, always remained a minority and lacked the political influence to effect any significant change. But, from the 1840s onward, more and more northerners who had no moral problem with slavery (because they were often racists themselves) began to articulate concerns about the seemingly unstoppable expansion of slavery to new states. The notion of the Slave Power conspiracy, 'a symbol for all the fears and hostilities harboured by northerners toward slavery and the South' (Foner 1995: 91), united diverse groups such as abolitionists, conscience Whigs and renegade Democrats. As Leonard Richards puts it, 'Men and women could differ on scores of issues, hate blacks or like them, denounce slavery as a sin or guarantee its protection in the Deep South, and still lambast the "slaveocracy"' (2000: 3). During the 1840s, the opponents of the slaveholding interests came together in the Free Soil Party; a decade later, the Republican Party became their home. As the founding ideology of the Republican Party, the Slave Power conspiracy theory was an important cause of the Civil War.

The most famous conspiracist indictment of the Slave Power occurs in Abraham Lincoln's 1858 'House Divided' speech in which he suggests that Senator Stephen Douglas, Chief Justice Roger B. Taney and Presidents Franklin Pierce and James Buchanan have orchestrated all major events of the recent past to further the goals of the Slave Power. Lincoln uses the metaphor of the house – a trope he employs earlier to famously argue that 'this government cannot endure, permanently half *slave* and half *free*' (1858: 461 [italics in the original]) – to insinuate that these four have been acting according to a secret plan:

> But when we see a lot of framed timbers, different portions of which we know have gotten out at different times and places and by different workmen – Stephen, Franklin, Roger, and James, for instance – and when we see these timbers joined together, and see they exactly make the frame of a house or a mill ... – in such a case we find it impossible not to *believe* that Stephen and Franklin, and Roger and James all understood one another from the beginning, and all worked upon a common *plan*.
> (1858: 465–6 [italics in the original])

This idea that the conspiracy has brought the government completely under its control sets the Slave Power conspiracy theory apart from all other conspiracy theories of the eighteenth and nineteenth centuries. The capture of the state and its institutions is also presented as a *fait accompli* in anti-abolitionist texts written after 1860s, and earlier the election successes of both the Federalists and the Jacksonians had been cast by their opponents as the result of conspiracies. But, in these cases, the conspiracy theorists always assumed that the domestic plotters – the abolitionists, the Federalists and the Jacksonians – were puppets of foreign foes such as the French or the British. And in none of these conspiracy theories is the take-over of the government as comprehensive as in the Slave Power conspiracy theory, where Lincoln and others claim that the conspirators' plot has brought all three branches of government under their control.

The tendency of eighteenth- and nineteenth-century conspiracy theories to focus on plots against the government is a logical consequence of conspiracy theory's status as orthodox knowledge at the time. As long as conspiracy theories were believed and articulated by elites, they tended to target alleged plotters threatening their status, that is, enemies from inside and outside the country supposedly bent on taking power away from them. And, since conspiracy theory's status did not change in the second half of the nineteenth or the first half of the twentieth century, the most prominent accusations of these decades followed the familiar pattern. Between the 1890s and 1920s, both Catholic and Jewish immigrants were cast as conspirators and imagined to be in league with American Catholics or bankers respectively. With the rise of National Socialism in Germany, the focus shifted to the alleged activities of Nazi spies in league with German Americans. After the end of the Second World War, then, suspicions quickly centred on the Soviet Union and communism.

The 1950s are the last decade in which conspiracy theories constitute officially accepted knowledge. In popular memory, the Red Scare is nowadays often reduced to the rants of Senator Joseph McCarthy, but, as scholars agree, 'there was far more to the "McCarthy era" than Senator Joseph R. McCarthy'. Anti-communism was not a minority phenomenon, and 'there existed in Cold War America a broad anti-Communist consensus shared and seldom questioned by most liberals as well as conservatives, by intellectuals as well as plain folks' (Fried 1990: vii; 34). Throughout most of the 1950s, it was accepted as a given that there was a large-scale communist infiltration of schools, colleges, government agencies and society at large. The Truman and Eisenhower administrations and their respective Congresses took a variety of measures that ranged from initiating loyalty and security programmes, to infringing on the civil rights of suspects and passing legislation that virtually outlawed the Communist Party. This conviction was only shaken at the end of the decade, when conspiracy theories in general began to lose the status of orthodox knowledge.

## From the 1960s to 9/11: Conspiracy theories as stigmatised heterodox knowledge

The fate of the Red Scare conspiracy theory effectively exemplifies the shift in status that conspiracy theories underwent in American culture around 1960. Quite suddenly, it was no longer senators and congressmen who believed in this conspiracy theory, but people like Robert Welch, a candy manufacturer from Massachusetts, who founded the John Birch Society in 1958 in order to fight the communist conspiracy. The John Birch Society, named after an army captain killed by Chinese communists, was not exactly a minority movement – by 1967 it had 80,000 members (Bennett 1988: 319) – but, compared to the mass appeal that warnings of communist subversion had had a few years earlier, it was marginal. Whereas the anti-communists of the 1950s voiced their suspicions in official government publications, through the national media or in books that became bestsellers, Welch's publications, such as *The Blue Book of the John Birch Society* (1961) or *The Politician* (1975) (in which he accused President Eisenhower of being a communist conspirator), were privately printed and distributed. David Bennett takes this idea further and convincingly suggests that the John Birch Society appealed initially to at least some people not because of, but despite, Welch's accusations of conspiracy. Moreover, 'Welch's conspiratorial fantasies turned away many of these people by the late 1960s' (1988: 323). The society survived until the mid-1980s, but its few remaining members had no political influence and were largely ignored, if not forgotten, by the mainstream of society.

The shift from orthodox to heterodox knowledge constitutes the most important caesura in the history of American conspiracy theories. It is far more important than the Kennedy assassination, whose impact other scholars have highlighted. Peter Knight, for example, has argued that 'Following the assassination …, conspiracy theories have become a regular feature of everyday political and cultural life' (2000: 2), when, in fact, the opposite is true. The Kennedy assassination was the first event in American history that triggered large-scale conspiracy theories that were problematised immediately and on a completely new level. Whereas discussions in earlier decades and centuries had revolved around the question of whether a particular conspiracy theory was true, political elites and the media now began to question the foundations of this mode of thinking and they expressed concerns about its possible effects. Put briefly, where earlier ages had once worried about the effects of conspiracies, the public was now becoming concerned with the effects of conspiracy theories. Thus, conspiracy theories were much talked about but no longer believed.

The reasons for this shift have been thoroughly investigated by Katharina Thalmann (2019). The problematisation of conspiracy theories began within the social sciences and spread from there through the whole culture. More specifically, Thalmann argues that the stigmatisation of conspiracy theories occurred in three waves (2019: 29). During the first wave, which peaked in the years after the Second World War, social scientists began to challenge conspiracist knowledge in two different ways. On the one hand, writing under the impression of the war in Europe and the Holocaust, émigrés from the Frankfurt School – Adorno et al. in *The Authoritarian Personality* (1950) and Leo Lowenthal and Norbert Guterman in *Prophets of Deceit: A Study of the Techniques of the American Agitator* (1949) – stressed the potential dangers of conspiracy theories for peace and democracy. On the other hand, scholars like Karl Popper – in *The Open Society and Its Enemies* (1956) – criticised the epistemology of conspiracy theories, arguing that they overestimated intentional action and underestimated systemic conditions and structural effects.

These studies did initially not have much impact outside of the ivory tower, but their ideas were picked up a few years later by a younger generation of scholars. No longer concerned with Europe, but with the effects of the Red Scare in the U.S.A., scholars like Seymour Martin Lipset – in 'The Sources of the Radical Right' (1955) – or Edward Shils – in *The Torment of Secrecy* (1956) – sought to counter the widespread allegations that liberal scientists and intellectuals were puppets in a Soviet plot. They labelled such accusations either 'pseudoconservatism', following the path of the Frankfurt School, or 'pseudoscience', following the path of Popper. Unlike the earlier scholarship, the studies by Lipset and Shils received a much broader reception because they made efforts to write in ways accessible to larger audiences. Moreover, many liberal journalists, who also worried about the effects of the Red Scare, picked up on their ideas and popularised them. This popularisation was accelerated by an 'unprecedented growth in audiences who were receptive to and interested in scientific ideas' due to the 'G.I. Bill' (Thalmann 2019: 30), which paved the way to tertiary education for 2.8 million veterans (Luey 2010: 36).

As a consequence, conspiracy theories lost their status as orthodox knowledge and moved to the margins of society. This, in turn, motivated a third generation of scholars to investigate the links between conspiracy theory and extremism. Consensus historians like John Bunzel – in *Anti-Politics in America: Reflections on the Anti-Political Temper and Its Distortions of the Democratic*

*Process* (1967) – denounced belief in conspiracy theories as irrational and the very opposite of politics proper. The most important text of this wave, however, is Hofstadter's essay on 'The Paranoid Style in American Politics' in which he pathologises conspiracism as a form of paranoia. Hofstadter published the first version of the essay in *Harper's*, a widely read magazine. This shows what 'broad impact ... his, and others', dismissal of conspiracy theory as paranoia could develop at the time' (Thalmann 2019: 30). Accordingly, by the 1970s, conspiracy theorising had been so utterly stigmatised that the term 'conspiracy theory' itself had become an insult. As Peter Knight puts it, 'Calling something a conspiracy theory is not infrequently enough to end discussion' (2000: 11).

The stigmatisation did not mean, however, that conspiracy theories became unpopular. They never lost their commonsensical appeal, and it is safe to assume that belief in them remained widely spread. While some conspiracy theorists struggled to find a larger audience, for example, Harold Weisberg, who self-published *Whitewash* (1965), his critique of the Warren Commission Report, because he did not find a publisher, other conspiracist indictments, for example, Oliver Stone's film *JFK* (1991) were commercially very successful and reached a large audience. However, as Stone and many other conspiracy theorists experienced, their convictions could no longer be articulated with impunity in public, and they were rejected and sanctioned by the media, academics and other gatekeepers. Thus, explicit conspiracy theorising – not to be confused with an often alarmist discourse on conspiracy theories – largely disappeared from the public sphere and moved into subcultures. As they were now predominantly articulated by figures on the margins of society trying to come to terms with their own marginalisation, the nature of conspiracist accusations changed. Whereas earlier conspiracy theories had almost always focused on external enemies or plots from 'below', 'The 1960s ... witnessed a broad shift ... to conspiracy theories proposed by the people about abuses of power by those in authority' (Knight 2000: 58). In other words, ever since the 1960s, most American conspiracy theories have revolved, not around alleged plots *against* the state, but *by* the state.[2]

Not only did the focus of American conspiracy theories change because of their stigmatisation, their rhetoric shifted as well. As Thalmann highlights, their now precarious position within the culture left conspiracy theorists with two options that still organise conspiracist discourse to this day. Conspiracy theorists can either try to still appeal to the mainstream by rejecting the language of plots and schemes and by pretending to be just asking questions, or they can embrace their marginalisation and give up on appealing to a mainstream audience by openly adopting the language of conspiracy theory. The earliest conspiracist accounts of the Kennedy assassination, for example, firmly fell into the first category. Texts like Edward Epstein's *Inquest* (1966), Mark Lane's *Rush to Judgment* (1966) and Sylvia Meagher's *Accessories after the Fact* (1967) hardly used 'terms like "conspiracy" and "plot" and mostly pointed at inconsistencies in or raised questions about the *Warren Report*' (Thalmann 2019: 130). Forty years later, the first version of the immensely successful *Loose Change* films, 'the first Internet blockbuster' according to *Vanity Fair* (Sales 2006), employed the same strategy to cast doubt on the official version of the 9/11 attacks. In fact, the slogan of the Truth Movement – 'Ask questions. Demand answers' – can be seen as the self-conscious attempt to downplay its own conspiracy theorising and still appeal to the mainstream.

In general, though, the other option has become more important over time because the stigmatisation of conspiracy theory further increased during the 1970s and 1980s. Accordingly, later accounts of the Kennedy assassination such as New Orleans state attorney Jim Garrison's *On the Trail of the Assassins* (1988) or Oliver Stones's film *JFK* (1991) are far more explicit in their accusations and develop much grander visions of conspiracy. Following the Watergate affair, such explicit large-scale conspiracy theories were in the majority from the outset, and the latter versions of the *Loose Change* series: *Final Cut* and *An American Coup* also shed the restraints of the earlier versions and explicitly blamed the Bush administration for orchestrating the attacks (Butter, Retterath 2010). Thalmann convincingly links this development to 'conspiracy theorists increasingly abandon[ing] mainstream markets' and constructing their identities more and more in sharp opposition to those who ridiculed such worldviews (Thalmann 2019: 131).

Another characteristic of explicit conspiracy theorising since the late 1960s is the tendency to develop what Michael Barkun has called 'superconspiracy [theories]', conspiracy theories, that is, that do not merely revolve around one specific event – the Kennedy assassination or 9/11 – or a specific group of alleged conspirators – the Slave Power, the communists or the government – but merge several of these scenarios. Such conspiracy theories were first developed by Nesta Helen Webster in England in the 1920s. In the U.S.A., they were first picked up by Robert Welch, who linked the alleged communist conspiracy of the 1950s and 1960s to the working of the Illuminati in the eighteenth century. On a larger scale, however, they only gained traction about a decade later. Jim Garrison's 'ever-evolving and large-scale conspiracy theories [already] point toward the kind of superconspiracy theories that were increasingly promoted by conspiracy theorists in counter-cultural publications in the 1970s' (Thalmann 2019: 143). By the 1990s, superconspiracy theories had become the dominant type of conspiracy theories circulating in the U.S.A. Anxieties about the evildoing of a New World Order, articulated by Alex Jones, Pat Robertson and others, fall into this category, and so does the final version of the *Loose Change* films, *An American Coup*, which no longer focuses on 9/11 exclusively but instead presents that event as just another episode in a decade-long plot against the American people.

## Conclusion: Conspiracy theories as heterodox and orthodox knowledge in the fragmented public sphere the early 21st century

The rise of the Internet has, without doubt, had a tremendous impact on conspiracy theorising in the U.S.A. and elsewhere. Often, the dawn of the digital age is perceived as yet another step in the mainstreaming of conspiracy theory since the 1960s (for example, Barkun 2013). By contrast, in my narrative, which has focused on the marginalisation of conspiracy theory in the second half of the twentieth century, the Internet would appear as a factor moving conspiracy theories closer to the mainstream *again*. However, the story is more complicated. As any casual glance at the alarmism shows with which the conspiracist allegations of Donald Trump have been discussed in most American media (Thomas, Lerer 2016; Uscinski 2016), conspiracy theories have not (yet) returned to the position at the heart of mainstream and elite discourses that they occupied from the seventeenth century to the 1950s in American culture. The Internet has not simply removed their stigma and turned them into orthodox knowledge once more.

However, the Internet has clearly made conspiracy theories more popular and influential again. From the 1970s to 1990s, conspiracy theorists increasingly embraced their own marginalisation. They shunned the mainstream, and the mainstream shunned them, reporting on them critically at times and denying them access to its media channels and markets. Thus, conspiracy theorists had problems circulating their ideas beyond the subcultures in which they moved. If their ideas made it into the general public, then always already framed negatively by the mainstream media and its acknowledged experts. The Internet has changed this completely. Conspiracy theorists do not need the traditional media anymore to reach a large audience; they can set up their own websites and use social media platforms. Thus, their ideas are now far more visible and available than in previous decades. This surely means that their counter-narratives appeal to more people again and, therefore, it is safe to assume that there have been more convinced conspiracy theorists in the U.S.A. in recent years than in the decades before (Butter 2018: 182–90). A recent quantitative study found that every second American believes in at least one conspiracy theory (Oliver, Wood 2014). This is certainly an impressive number and surely higher than a comparable study would have found in, say, 1984. But, the number is almost certainly much lower than it would have been in 1914 or 1814, when conspiracy theories were still a widely accepted form of knowledge. As Uscinski and Parent conclude in their diachronic empirical study on the role of conspiracy theories in American public life, 'The data suggest one telling fact: we do not live in an age of conspiracy theories and have not for some time' (2014: 110–1).

Importantly, the Internet has facilitated the emergence of counter-publics with their own media outlets and experts. The fragmentation of the American public sphere began, of course, much earlier (Lütjen 2016), but the advent of the Internet has accelerated and intensified it. In the 1990s, a conspiracy theorist like Alex Jones still needed radio stations to reach a national audience; the Internet has made him independent and allows him to reach people from all over the world. Likewise, a news outlet like breitbart.com would have been impossible without the Internet. Accordingly, there are by now parts of the public sphere in which conspiracy theories are considered orthodox knowledge again, and where the denial of large-scale plots is considered the real problem. In fact, much of the alarmism that characterises current debates about conspiracies and conspiracy theories can be explained by the fact that there are by now at least two publics that debate the same topics, but on very different epistemological grounds. One is concerned about conspiracies, the other about conspiracy theories, and what happens in the one public has repercussions in the other. For the time being, then, conspiracy theories still remain stigmatised, but, as Thalmann puts it, 'that might not matter anymore' (2019: 192), because they exert their influence nevertheless.

## Notes

1 Davis (1971) provides an excellent overview of the various conspiracy theories discussed in this section and assembles key passages from the major sources that articulated them.
2 Olmsted also observes this shift, but dates it too early. She suggests that it occurred during the First World War as the expansion of the federal government turned this institution into a far more likely conspirator than it had been before: 'Sinister forces in charge of the government could do a lot more damage in 1918 than they could have done a few years earlier; in fact, in the view of some conspiracists, the state *was* the sinister force' (2009: 4; emphasis in the original).

## References

Adorno, T.W., Frenkel-Brunswik, E., Levinson, D.J. and Nevitt Sanford, R. (1950) *The Authoritarian Personality*, New York: Harper. Studies in Prejudice.
Anton, A., Schetsche, M. and Walter, M.K. (eds.) (2014) *Konspiration: Soziologie des Verschwörungsdenkens*, Springer VS.
Bailyn, B. (1965a) 'Foreword', in *Pamphlets of the American Revolution 1750–1776*, vol. 1, Cambridge, MA: Belknap, pp. vii–xii.
Bailyn, B. (1965b) 'General Introduction', in *Pamphlets of the American Revolution 1750–1776*, vol. 1, Cambridge, MA: Belknap, pp. 1–202.
Bailyn, B. (1967) *The Ideological Origins of the American Revolution*, Cambridge, MA: Belknap.
Barkun, M. (2013) *A Culture of Conspiracy. Apocalyptic Visions in Contemporary America*, 2nd edn, Berkeley, CA: University of California Press.
Beecher, L. (1835) *A Plea for the West*, New York: Leavitt, Lord & Co.
Bennett, D. (1988) *The Party of Fear: From the Nativist Movement to the New Right in American History*, Chapel Hill, NC: University of North Carolina Press.

Boyer, P. and Nissenbaum, S. (1974) *Salem Possessed: The Social Origins of Witchcraft*, Cambridge, MA: Harvard University Press.

Bunzel, J.H. (1967) *Anti-Politics in America: Reflections on the Anti-Political Temper and Its Distortions of the Democratic Process*, New York: Knopf.

Butter, M. (2014) *Plots, Designs, and Schemes: American Conspiracy Theories from the Puritans to the Present*, Berlin: de Gruyter.

Butter, M. (2018) *'Nichts ist, wie es scheint': Über Verschwörungstheorien*, Berlin: Suhrkamp.

Butter, M. and Retterath, L. (2010) 'From Alerting the World to Stabilizing Its Own Community: The Shifting Cultural Work of the *Loose Change* Films', *Canadian Review of American Studies*, 40(1): 25–44.

Cañizares-Esguerra, J. (2006) *Puritan Conquistadors: Iberianizing the Atlantic*, Stanford, CA: Stanford University Press.

Coward, B. and Swann, J. (eds.) (2004) *Conspiracies and Conspiracy Theory in Early Modern Europe: From the Waldensians to the French Revolution*, Aldershot: Ashgate.

Cubitt, G. (1989) 'Conspiracy myths and conspiracy theories', *Journal of the Anthropological Society of Oxford*, (20)1: 12–26.

Davis, D.B. (1960) 'Some Themes of Counter-Subversion: An Analysis of Anti-Masonic, Anti-Catholic, and Anti-Mormon Literature', *The Mississippi Valley Historical Review*, 47(2): 205–24.

Davis, D.B. (ed.) (1971) *The Fear of Conspiracy: Images of Un-American Subversion from the Revolution to the Present*, Ithaca, NY: Cornell University Press.

Epstein, E.J. (1966) *Inquest: The Warren Commission and the Establishment of Truth*, New York: Viking Press.

Foner, E. (1995) *Free Soil, Free Labor, Free Men: The Ideology of the Republican Party Before the Civil War*, New York: Oxford University Press.

Fried, R.M. (1990) *Nightmare in Red: The McCarthy Era in Perspective*, New York: Oxford University Press.

Gara, L. (1969) 'Slavery and the Slave Power: A Crucial Distinction', *Civil War History*, 15(1): 5–18.

Garrison, J. (1988) *On the Trail of the Assassins: My Investigation and Prosecution of the Murder of President Kennedy*, New York: Sheridan Square Press.

Goldberg, R.A. (2001) *Enemies Within: The Culture of Conspiracy in Modern America*, New Haven, CT: Yale University Press.

Groh, D. (1987) 'The Temptation of Conspiracy Theory, or: Why Do Bad Things Happen to Good People? Part I: Preliminary Draft of a Theory of Conspiracy Theory', in S. Moscovici and C.F. Graumann (eds.) *Changing Conceptions of Conspiracy*, New York: Springer, pp. 1–13.

Hofstadter, R. (1996) 'The paranoid style in American politics', in *The Paranoid Style in American Politics and Other Essays*, paperback edn, reprint, Cambridge, MA: Harvard University Press, 1964, pp. 3–40.

Knight, P. (2000) *Conspiracy Culture: From Kennedy to* The X-Files, London: Routledge.

Lane, M. (1966) *Rush to Judgment: A Critique of the Warren Commission's Inquiry into the Murders of President John F. Kennedy, Officer J. D. Tippit and Lee Harvey Oswald*, London: Bodley Head.

Lincoln, A. (1858) 'A House Divided', in R.P. Basler (ed.) *The Collected Works of Abraham Lincoln*, vol. 2, New Brunswick, NJ: Rutgers University Press, 1953, pp. 461–9.

Lipset, S.M. (1955) 'The Sources of the Radical Right', in D. Bell (ed.) *The New American Right*, New York: Criterion, pp. 166–234.

Lowenthal, L. and Guterman, N. (1949) *Prophets of Deceit: A Study of the Techniques of the American Agitator*, New York: Harper. Studies in Prejudice.

Luey, B. (2010) *Expanding the American Mind: Books and the Popularization of Knowledge*, Amherst, MA: University of Massachusetts Press.

Lütjen, T. (2016) *Die Politik der Echokammer: Wisconsin und die ideologische Polarisierung der USA*, Bielefeld: Transcript.

Mather, C. (1862) 'The Wonders of the Invisible World: Being an Account of the Tryals of Several Witches Lately Executed in New-England', *The Wonders of the Invisible World: Being an Account of the Tryals of Several Witches Lately Executed in New-England. By Cotton Mather, D. D. To Which Is Added a Farther Account of the Tryals of the New-England Witches by Increase Mather*, reprint, D. D. London: John Russell Smith, 1692, pp. 1–191.

McKenzie-McHarg, A. (2014) 'The Transfer of Anti-Illuminati Conspiracy Theories to the United States in the Late Eighteenth Century', in M. Butter and M. Reinkowski (eds.) *Conspiracy Theories in the United States and the Middle East: A Comparative Approach*, De Gruyter. Linguae & litterae 29.

Meagher, S. (1967) *Accessories after the Fact: The Warren Commission, the Authorities and the Report on the JFK Assassination*, New York: Vintage; reprint, New York: Skyhorse, 2013.

Melley, T. (2000) *Empire of Conspiracy: The Culture of Paranoia in Postwar America*, Ithaca, NY: Cornell University Press.

Merlan, A. (2019) *Republic of Lies: American Conspiracy Theorists and Their Surprising Rise to Power*, Metropolitan Books.

Morse, S. (1835) *Foreign Conspiracy against the Liberties of the United States*, New York: Leavitt, Lord, & Co; reprint, New York: Arno, 1977.

Mottram, E. (1989) *Blood on the Nash Ambassador: Investigations in American Culture*, Radius.

Muirhead, R. and Rosenblum, N.L. (2019) *A Lot of People Are Saying: The New Conspiracism and the Assault on Democracy*, Princeton, NJ: Princeton University Press.

Norton, M.B. (2002) *In the Devil's Snare: The Salem Witchcraft Crisis of 1692*, New York: Alfred A. Knopf.

Oliver, E.J. and Wood, T.J. (2014) 'Conspiracy Theories and the Paranoid Style(s) of Mass Opinion', *American Journal of Political Science*, 58(4), 952–66.

Olmsted, K.S. (2009) *Real Enemies: Conspiracy Theories and American Democracy, World War I to 9/11*, Oxford: Oxford University Press.

Popper, K.R. (1962 [1945]) *The High Tide of Prophecy: Hegel, Marx, and the Aftermath*, Vol. 2 of *The Open Society and Its Enemies*, 4th and revised edn, London: Routledge.

Popper, K.R. (1956) *The Open Society and Its Enemies*, 2nd edn, Princeton, NJ: Princeton University Press.

Richards, L.L. (2000) *The Slave Power: The Free North and Southern Domination, 1780–1860*, Baton Rouge, LA: Louisiana State University Press.

Rogin, M.P. (1987) *Ronald Reagan, the Movie and Other Episodes in Political Demonology*, Berkeley, CA: University of California Press.

Sales, N.J. (2006) 'Click Here For Conspiracy', *Vanity Fair*, 10 October. Available at: www.vanityfair.com/news/2006/08/loosechange200608. [Accessed 18 June 2019.]

Shils, E. (1956) *The Torment of Secrecy: The Background and Consequences of American Security Politics*, Glencoe, IL: The Free Press; Arcturus Books, 1974.

Stauffer, V. (1918) *New England and the Bavarian Illuminati*, New York: Columbia University Press.

Thalmann, K. (2019) *The Stigmatization of Conspiracy Theories since the 1950s: 'A Plot to Make Us Look Foolish'*, Routledge.

Thomas, K. and Lerer, L. (2016) 'Welcome to the Trump-Clinton Conspiracy Election', *AP News*, 25 August. Available at: www.apnews.com/a691bdb3ed24421ebc17a26641db294b. [Accessed 1 September 2018.]

Uscinski, J.E. (2016) 'Welcome to the Conspiracy Theory Election', *Newsweek*, 7 May. www.newsweek.com/welcome-conspiracy-theory-election-456654. [Accessed 1 September 2018.]

Uscinski, J.E. and Parent, J.M. (2014) *American Conspiracy Theories*, Oxford: Oxford University Press.

Washington, G. (1971) 'There Has Been A Regular, Systematic Plan', in D.B. Davis (ed.) *The Fear of Conspiracy: Images of Un-American Subversion from the Revolution to the Present*, Ithaca, NY: Cornell University Press, 1774, pp. 33–4.

Weisberg, H. (1965) *Whitewash: The Report on the Warren Report*, Hyattstown, MD: Weisberg.

Welch, R. (1961) *The Blue Book of the John Birch Society*, Belmont, MA: Welch.

Welch, R. (1963) *The Politician*, Belmont, MA: Welch.

Wood, G.S. (1982) 'Conspiracy and the Paranoid Style: Causality and Deceit in the Eighteenth Century', *The William and Mary Quarterly*, 39(3): 402–41.

Zwierlein, C. (2013) 'Security Politics and Conspiracy Theories in the Emerging European State System (15th/16th c.)', *Historical Social Research*, 38(1): 65–95.

# 5.11
# POPULISM AND CONSPIRACY THEORY IN LATIN AMERICA
## A case study of Venezuela

*Rosanne Hooper*

### Introduction

Despite the expansion within the field of conspiracy theory research, Latin America remains largely overlooked. However, the region has a complex culture of conspiracy theory, because of its postcolonial status, centuries-long struggle against the spectre of U.S. hegemony and the legacy of military intervention in politics. In Argentina, the death of Alberto Nisman – chief investigator into the 1994 bombing of a Jewish community centre – provided fertile ground for numerous conspiracy theories that tell of government-ordered assassinations, cover-ups and rogue intelligence officers (Rodriguez, Smallman 2016). In Chile, ex-president Salvador Allende's body was exhumed in 2011 to lay to rest the conspiracy theory that he was actually assassinated during the 1973 military coup (*Guardian* 2011). In Mexico, the death of one of ex-President Felipe Calderón's interior ministers in a helicopter crash equally engendered a wide range of conspiracy theories that he had been murdered – by the military on the order of the President, a drug lord or by the Partido Revolucionario Insitucional (Herrera 2018). The list goes on. Yet, there is no denying that conspiracy theories have captured the Venezuelan imagination perhaps more than any other Latin American nation.

Due to the myriad conspiracy theories that flourished under Hugo Chávez's presidency from 1999 to 2013, this chapter will use Venezuela as a case study to examine the role of conspiracy theories in Latin American political discourse. From indicting the U.S.A. for developing cancer as a biological weapon to assassinate leftist Latin American leaders, expelling the Drugs Enforcement Agency (D.E.A.) for spying on his government, exhuming Simón Bolívar's body to prove that he was assassinated and alleging 52 attempts on his own life, conspiracy theories undoubtedly played an integral role in Chávez's rhetoric (Hoy 2005; Padgett 2010; Ultimas Noticias 2011; Fernández 2013). Although the use of conspiracy theories as a rhetorical device has also been deployed by Chávez's successor, Nicolás Maduro, and the Venezuelan opposition, this chapter will focus on Chávez as the originator of this trend in modern Venezuelan politics.

The pernicious effects of conspiracy theories on Venezuelan politics have already been dealt with in detail by journalists and academics alike (Hernáiz 2008). Indeed, they are impossible to ignore. Not only have conspiracy theories been used to distract the public from ongoing problems related to security, hyperinflation, and the scarcity of essential goods, but they have also served to justify authoritarian acts, including the silencing of political opposition and the concentration of power in the executive (Hernáiz 2008). Yet, as important as this recognition and analysis is, it fails to fully engage with the complex role that conspiracy theories play in Latin American politics and overlooks the fact that they can have both a positive and negative impact within the same political ideology (Knight 2000: 21). Consequently, there is a lack of understanding as to why conspiracy theories have held such widespread appeal in Venezuela. This chapter therefore focuses primarily on the mobilising capacity of conspiracy theories within political discourse, and, in particular, how Chávez used them to unify 'the people' and coalesce a collective identity, in addition to providing believers with a sense of personal and collective agency. This is by no means intended to be a comprehensive analysis of the role of conspiracy theories in Latin American political discourse (and, indeed, one chapter could not do that justice). However, it is intended that the issues raised and discussed further our understanding of the popularity of conspiracy theories within Latin America and pave the way for further research.

The very terminology used to discuss conspiracy theories is undeniably problematic. Jack Bratich contends that a 'conspiracy theory' is merely a discourse that has been labelled as such by mainstream society in an attempt to marginalise and dismiss it (Bratich 2008: 3–5). Although Bratich's viewpoint is crucial in highlighting the role that nomenclature plays in the delegitimisation of dissent, using his framework makes it almost impossible to discuss a very real and active phenomenon. Therefore, this chapter follows Peter Knight's explanation that the term 'conspiracy theory' can be applied to anything from 'fully elaborated theories to passing suspicions about hidden forces' (Knight 2000: 11). This broader understanding of the term is particularly important in relation to historical episodes of conspiracism in Venezuela, where frequently a more generalised fear of conspiracy was expressed. 'Conspiracism' is defined here as 'the act of using conspiracy theories', whether in politics or for any other purpose (Gray 2010: 6).

This chapter will first examine the use of political demonology in the dictatorial governments prior to 1958 to assert that the 'conspiratorial nature of military politics' embedded conspiracism into the heart of the Venezuelan political tradition (Coronil 1997: 208). The second part will then examine the complex interrelationship between populism, *chavismo* and conspiracy theories, arguing that the appeal of populism in Latin America potentially lends conspiracy theories, with their populist underpinnings, greater legitimacy. This chapter uses Ernesto Laclau's definition of 'populism' as a *political logic*, rather than a movement attached to a specific political ideology or social base (Laclau 2005: 5). According to this definition, there are two preconditions of populism: (1) An 'antagonistic frontier' between 'the people' and the 'power bloc'; and (2) an articulation of social demands (which have been unfulfilled by the power bloc) into an equivalential chain, which allows for the emergence of 'the people' as a collective (Laclau 2005: 74). An 'empty signifier', according to Laclau, is a name or concept that 'both expresses and constitutes an equivalential chain' (Laclau 2005: 129, 217). In other words, it is 'empty' because it loses its own specific meaning when it functions as a substitute for the multiple demands that constitute the equivalential chain (Beasley-Murray 2006).

Finally, it will consider the limits of conspiracy theories as a meaningful method of dissent and political thought. While their function in Venezuela under Chávez as a means of constructing an identity for the previously marginalised is positive in some ways, there is no escaping their negative impact, as highlighted above. This precarious balance between conspiracy theory's varied mobilising capabilities is reflected in the tenuous space that Chávez's particular brand of populism occupies between a participatory democracy and authoritarianism and is a tension that runs through the chapter.

## Political demonology

Hugo Chávez's penchant for conspiracy theories has been portrayed as an aberration on the Venezuelan political landscape, or a perpetuation of a post-Second World War culture that is inherently suspicious of the U.S.A. (see e.g. Pipes 1997; Hernáiz 2008) There is no denying that U.S. intervention has left an indelible stain on the region and its inhabitants – one that lends a degree of legitimacy in Venezuela (and Latin America more generally) to conspiracy theories involving the U.S.A. that they might not achieve elsewhere. However, while foreign intervention in Latin America sets an important precedent upon which many contemporary conspiracy theories have been constructed, the reasons for the recent deluge in Venezuela are far more complex.

Like much of Latin America during the twentieth century, Venezuelan politics was blighted by a combination of military dictatorships, civilian and military coups between 1899 and 1958. This type of political system, in which coups are a quasi-acceptable form of political dissent, naturally cultivates an atmosphere of intense suspicion, primarily because coups occur through real conspiracy against a government, and second because, when power is taken by force, fears instinctively emerge that another group of plotters will try to take that power. Fears of conspiracy are frequently articulated through conspiracy theories, i.e. 'I fear that they *might* conspire to overthrow me' morphs into 'they *are* conspiring to overthrow me'. When expressed by the executive branch of government, these fears and theories can often result in a greater concentration of power in the executive and the repression of political opposition. In turn, this only animates or forces that opposition to genuinely conspire against those in power. This is what is referred to as the 'conspiratorial nature of military politics' in this chapter. For example, Judith Ewell notes that Cipriano Castro's regime was marked by 'paranoia', particularly when it came to his second-in-command, Juan Vicente Gómez. Although he could not prove it until it was a fait accompli, Castro was convinced that Gómez was secretly plotting to usurp power. When Gómez finally did seize power while Castro was in Europe (through the articulation and propagation of his own conspiracy theory that Castro was plotting his assassination), he was able to successfully prevent Castro from returning both to power and Venezuela (Ewell 1984: 46–7). Journalist María Teresa Romero compares the 'paranoid' outlook of Hugo Chávez with that of Cipriano Castro, lamenting that '[having paranoid rulers] has been one of our biggest political tragedies' (Romero 2007). Although Romero is correct in her observation of a connection between the outlook of Castro and Chávez, it is not the political pathology that she deems it to be. Indeed, the notion that conspiracy theories are indicative of clinical paranoia is an approach that the academic community now largely dismisses because it tends to pathologise and marginalise views that deviate from those of establishment liberals and conservatives (Fenster 2008: 34; Bratich 2008: 31). Moreover, since conspiracy theories emerge in such a wide variety of social, political, economic and historical contexts and are utilised by myriad actors within government and the general populace, it seems tenuous to diagnose such vast swathes of people with a particular psychological disorder.

Alleged conspiracies and attempted coups during Juan Vicente Gómez's 27-year rule culminated in a distinct form of conspiracism that Michael Rogin calls 'political demonology' (Ewell 1984: 54–5; Rogin 1987: xiii, xiv; Gray 2010: 6). In political demonology, those at the political centre attribute their opposition with nigh-on otherworldly powers that will (in the eyes of the demonologist) enable them to subvert the centre. In order to combat these subversive powers, the demonologist then mirrors these characteristics in the name of countersubversion (Rogin 1987: 284–5). However, while this demonology might be rooted in genuine fears, it is also unequivocally used as a vehicle of repression. For example, Gómez's appropriation of

U.S. fears about communist infiltration that arose during the first Red Scare of the 1920s led to the designation of most of his opposition as communists (Ewell 1996: 125). Naturally, fears of a communist conspiracy were rooted in ideas about protecting national security and interests with regard to oil, but they were also part of a more calculated campaign to whip up popular panics about labourers and unions, and to neutralise the threat of anti-*gomecistas*. However, in his battle with the 'Communist conspiracy' that was allegedly taking place in Venezuela, Gómez began to mirror the subversive characteristics he had attributed to his opposition, creating a covert network of spies at home and abroad to monitor, imprison and torture his opponent (Rangel 1974: 227; Ewell 1996: 55). This political demonology and countersubversive tradition did not terminate with Gómez, either. Eleazar López Contreras, Gómez's successor, also pursued the ideology of anti-communism; 47 pro-labour leaders and politicians were imprisoned and exiled for 'Communist activities' in 1937 alone (Ewell 1984: 76, 82). Coinciding with the apex of U.S. anti-communism and the increased reach of U.S. intelligence agencies, Pérez Jiménez's dictatorship (1948–1958) marked a heightened point of political demonology. Pérez Jiménez allowed agents from the F.B.I. and C.I.A. to record the fingerprints of oil workers and carry out other surveillance techniques in order to keep track of any potential subversives and communists (Rabe 1982: 120–1). In the name of national security and anti-communism, Pérez Jiménez's secret police force, the *Seguridad Nacional*, hunted down and tortured those considered a threat to the nation – coincidentally, members of the opposition (Galván 2013: 64–5).

The virulent anti-communism that marked the regimes of Gómez, Contreras and Pérez Jiménez, while being used to manipulate and repress the opposition, also expressed anxiety over national security and the spread of this little-understood ideology within the Western hemisphere. While Rogin attributes the countersubversive tradition in the U.S.A. to the concepts of rugged individualism (i.e. that anyone can succeed if they work hard enough), Western expansion and the construction of American identity in opposition to 'aliens' (whether racial, ethnic, class or gendered), its history in Venezuela, and Latin America more broadly, comes from a markedly different perspective (Rogin 1987: xiv). It is rooted in the conspiratorial nature of military politics that has shaped the country's political imagination since the early twentieth century, fears over the permeable nature of geographic and metaphorical borders (as a result of, for example, colonisation and U.S. interference) and the search for an inclusive national identity in a region where the Manichaean dichotomy of civilisation and barbarism continues to produce identity anxiety.

Since independence, the dichotomy of civilisation and barbarism has burdened the Latin American articulation of identity, and Venezuela is no exception. As the economic situation in Venezuela deteriorated at the end of the 1980s and throughout the 1990s, the image of unity and modernity began to shatter, exposing a deep-rooted crisis of identity. International oil prices dropped and the poor blamed the elite for being self-serving and failing to diversify the economy sufficiently, while the middle and upper classes scapegoated the poor (Ellner 2003: 19). Indeed, as social polarisation worsened and the myth of unity and progress started to fracture, so too did the myth of racial harmony as elite discourse during the 1983 devaluation of the Bolívar and the 1989 *caracazo* (a series of violent protests in Caracas) became increasingly racialised, with invectives such as 'mixed breeds' and 'Indians' being cast on the protestors and looters (Herrera Salas 2005: 72). It became evident that the *pueblo* had never truly been part of the official narrative of identity and modernity (Emerson 2011). The social, political and economic cleavages of the 1980s and 1990s thus unveiled a crisis of identity that had been corroding beneath the mask of 'civilisation' and unity since independence. Knight explains that conspiracy theories frequently thrive among marginalised sectors of society because they are a means of explaining the complex forces that perpetuate these communities' poverty and disenfranchisement (Knight 2000: 145–6). This is unequivocally true in Venezuela as well. The violence instigated against the working classes during the *caracazo* in 1989, the underlying racism within society that stemmed from the colonial era and their marginalisation as the 'barbarous masses' suddenly seemed to make more sense when Hugo Chávez voiced ideas of an elite conspiracy to subjugate the *pueblo* (Chávez 2003).

## Populism and conspiracy theories in Hugo Chávez's discourse

Throughout his 14-year presidency, Hugo Chávez alleged that there were 52 attempts on his life (Fernández 2013). This seems excessive in itself, yet it barely scratches the surface of the conspiracy theories that flourished during Chávez's presidency. As indicated above, Chávez has undoubtedly inherited a political legacy inclined towards demonology of political opponents, and yet these attributes also thrived under him in an unprecedented manner. The aim of this section is therefore to analyse the function and style of conspiracy theories within Chávez's discourse. In particular, the complex interrelationship between populism, *chavismo* and conspiracy theories.

A matter of contention within the definition of populism is the role of conspiracy theories. Kirk A. Hawkins contends that conspiracy theories are an intrinsic characteristic of populism because he understands the 'Us' versus 'Them' mentality as a cosmic battle between the good 'unified will of the people' and an evil '*conspiring* minority' (emphasis added) – otherwise known as Manicheanism (Hawkins 2010: 29). However, the concept of the 'power bloc' is largely an abstract concept and empty signifier that can be adapted and interpreted as required (at least in Laclau's work) but is not by definition conspiratorial, though it may be interpreted as such by individual populist movements. In the same vein, although many populist leaders use conspiracy theories as a means of soliciting support for their movement, as Chávez did, it is not a necessary component of populist discourse (Fenster 2008: 84). Therefore – and while this is undoubtedly an area for future research – although conspiracy theories often have populist foundations in which the power external to the people is definitively conspiratorial, this is not always the case within populism alone. As such, the presence of conspiracy theories is arguably not one of the preconditions to populism (Fenster 2008: 11, 84).

Indeed, those studying both populism and conspiracy theories frequently miss the nuanced relationship between the two. Fenster argues that some of the key theoretical frameworks often used to analyse conspiracy theories in the U.S.A. (namely, the symbolist and realist schools of thought) are characterised by an aversion to populism, which leads them to disregard conspiracy theories as a dangerous political phenomenon that requires 'surveillance' and 'discipline' (Fenster 2008: 83). However, populism and its reception – and therefore the populist foundations of conspiracy theories – manifest in a markedly different way in Latin America to the U.S.A. Rather than a form of political pathology or extremism, Beasley-Murray explains that populism holds a particular appeal in Latin America because of its promise (whether founded or not) to resolve the complex issue of identity (Beasley-Murray 2003: 29). This is because of the simple division of the nation into two opposing camps: The people and the power bloc, which is an articulation of antagonism that is easy to activate in Latin American societies due to existing structural conditions such as social, economic and political polarisation. Therefore, you are either with the people or against them (Beasley-Murray 2003: 29). That is not to say that academics, such as Kenneth Roberts, have not still disparaged populism as being a threat to democratic institutions within Latin America, but they also recognise that it is frequently a legitimate response to popular demands for an inclusion in politics and to be part of the national community (Roberts 2000: 1–32). Therefore – although it would need further ethnographic research – there is an argument that conspiracy theories achieve greater legitimacy within Latin America because their populist underpinnings are not automatically considered a danger to political rationality. As such, it may be that the reception of populism in different regions directly affects the reception of conspiracy theories and is an area of study that should be considered further.

It is not only through populism that Chávez's discourse attempted to resolve the complex issue of identity, however, but also conspiracy theories. As Matthew Gray and Peter Knight highlight, conspiracy theories work as potent group 'identifiers, mobilisers, and signifiers' by imagining that the group is at risk (Gray 2010: 31; Knight 2014: 361). By adding the conspiratorial element to the populist division of 'Us' versus 'Them' and insisting that 'the people' are under threat from the conspiring 'power bloc', conspiracy theories strengthen the collective identity of 'the people' by giving them a clear and malevolent enemy against which to mobilise. In addition, conspiracies (especially the 'imperialist conspiracy') as a broader concept also functioned as an 'empty signifier' in Chávez's discourse. While the conspiracies espoused by Chávez do not fully lose their literal meaning, they have functioned as an empty signifier in the sense that they are so open to multiple interpretations, yet they simultaneously assist the concretion of identity of 'the people'. This is why it is not especially important for Chávez's supporters to believe in their literal meaning, because they function as a conduit for expressing multiple anxieties and demands. For example, allegations that Chávez's political opposition, in collusion with U.S. agencies, have tried to assassinate him could be taken very literally, or it might be interpreted as symbolic of the historic mistreatment of poor, Afro-indigenous bodies by the Venezuelan political, social and economic elite. The point is that it could be appropriated differently by and hold different meanings for any number of groups and individuals within society.

In Venezuela, Chávez was thus able to strengthen group identity and unity through repeated references to conspiracies allegedly conducted by the domestic opposition and U.S. government (frequently referred to as '*la conspiración imperialista*'). This idea is particularly well represented in a quote from an episode of Chávez's television show, *Aló, Presidente*, in 2005:

> Their [the U.S.] attempts at blackmail will not be able to isolate Venezuela from our brother countries [in Latin America] … they [the U.S. and domestic opposition] have failed in their coup d'état, they have failed in their economic sabotage, because they know that the Bolivarian project moves forward victoriously in social issues.
>
> *(Chávez 2005)*

This quote demonstrates a number of charges that Chávez held against the enemy (domestic opposition and the U.S.A.), namely, the coup, blackmail and economic sabotage. Importantly, despite these purported attempts to subvert Chávez's government, the emphasis is on how the Bolivarian movement (i.e. the anti-imperialist political and social movement started by Chávez and designed to build 'twenty-first-century socialism') thwarted these efforts and thrived in addressing social issues. It emphasises that, despite these malicious conspiracies designed to weaken the movement, it became stronger than ever. Thus, by presenting the Bolivarian movement as under threat from powerful enemies yet managing to survive, Chávez cleverly projected an empowering image of unity and strength of the collective. Moreover, Chávez complemented this rhetoric with initiatives like the *misiones*, which aimed to achieve progress in inclusive social development, education and healthcare (Buxton 2014). Whilst the *misiones* suffered from many internal problems, at least partially stemming from neglect during Chávez's third term, they were a physical representation of the positive steps the Bolivarian movement was taking to address social inequalities and bring previously marginalised sectors of society into the Venezuelan social imaginary.

Although some commentators believe that Chávez created social polarisation through his 'Us' versus 'Them' mentality, in reality he embraced a 'repoliticisation of social inequalities' that already existed (Roberts 2003: 71). In the process, he inverted the civilisation and barbarism paradigm, proclaiming that 'They [the colonisers] were the barbarians. Civilisation existed here, they brought barbarism' (Chávez 2003). Memory historian Aleida Assman theorises that, in every society, whichever group is in power will 'canonise' certain memories and identities, whilst 'archiving' others (Assman 2011: 337). In Latin America, the typically lighter-skinned elite have largely regulated the canon, which, Chávez lamented, led to the exclusion of the indigenous peoples (and Afro-Venezuelans) and an attempt 'to erase us from collective memory' (Chávez 2003). Nonetheless, Assman also asserts that what is archive can become canon, and this is exactly what Chávez tried to achieve by targeting the elite and championing the rights of the historically downtrodden members of Venezuelan society, and challenging the previous perversion of the 'official historiography' (Zúquete 2008: 102). If, as Jeffrey Olick and Joyce Robbins suggest, identities are constructed and sustained through memory sites and practices, then Chávez also used conspiracy theories as one such type of mnemonic practice that served to reinforce the *chavista* identity, as will be seen in the following section (Olick, Robbins 1998: 124).

Perhaps one of the most potent empty signifiers used to coalesce and redefine Venezuelan identity in Chávez's discourse was that of Simón Bolívar (Cannon 2009: 68; Hawkins 2010: 57; Zúquete 2008: 101). 'Bolívar' has in many ways lost its specific meaning as it has become attached to nearly the whole gamut of the *Bolivarian* Revolution. From changing Venezuela's official name to the Bolivarian Republic of Venezuela, adding a 'Bolivarian' star to the flag and naming community groups the 'Bolivarian' Circles, 'Bolívar' has come to depict everything pertaining to *chavismo* (Zúquete 2008: 111). Moreover, Chávez combined Bolívar and conspiracy theories to convey a deep-rooted historical contiguity between himself and Bolívar in order to locate the present struggle against a conspiring power bloc as part of an on-going cosmic battle (Chumaceiro Arreaza 2003: 32). This is evident in a speech he gave in 2001 via V.T.V., the state television channel, in which he declared that:

> Bolívar was betrayed in life by the predatory oligarchy ... this same oligarchy that now threatens the revolutionary government in a ridiculous way, this is the same oligarchy that betrayed Bolívar, expelled him from Venezuela to God-knows-where in 1828–1830 and was sent to (and almost did) kill him.
> 
> *(quoted in Chumaceiro Arreaza 2003: 32)*

The parallels between the conspiring elite of Bolívar's time and Chávez's also reached their peak in the allegations that their ultimate motive was to assassinate the leaders. For example, during the airing of *Aló, Presidente* on 20 February 2005, Chávez candidly told his listeners that 'If I were to be assassinated, then there is a major culprit on this planet that is the President of the United States, George Bush' and that he was certain that 'Washington is planning my death' (Chávez 2005). In 2010, Chávez announced that a team of experts would exhume Simón Bolívar's body to discover the real reasons behind his death. Not convinced by the 'official' story that Bolívar died of tuberculosis, and spurred on by recent research by Dr Paul Auwaerter that suggested the Latin American hero might have died from arsenic poisoning, Chávez expressed his belief that 'they [the elite] assassinated him' (quoted in Padgett 2010; Primera 2010). The mirroring of assassination attempts between the two leaders further establishes the historical contiguity that is designed to mobilise supporters against this conspiring elite that has purportedly been attempting to subvert the Bolivarian dream since the days of Bolívar himself. It is through this reinterpretation of the past, particularly the past relating to Bolívar, that Chávez transformed these conspiracy theories into a mnemonic practice that reinforced his new interpretation of Venezuelan identity and mobilised support.

There is a distinctly moralistic and quasi-religious undertone to much of Chávez's discourse that was designed to illustrate that the Bolivarian Revolution was (and still is) irrefutably on the side of good, and that they must continue in their endeavours to thwart attempts at subversion. As he claimed during his 1998 presidential campaign, 'We're in Apocalyptic times, there's no middle ground. Either you are with God or you are with the Devil and we are with God' (quoted in Roberts 2003: 70). Since the 2002 coup and the U.S.A.'s believed involvement in orchestrating it, Chávez's frequent references to former U.S. President George W. Bush as 'the Devil', 'immoral', and 'psychologically ill', and the domestic opposition as 'los lacayos del imperialismo', clearly illustrate whom Chávez saw as being on the side of 'evil' (BF26A4F468341A4F 2006; Baronderothchild 2006). Zúquete and Hawkins assert that this strong moralistic tone to Chávez's discourse locates the Venezuelan 'mission' in a cosmic battle that reaches far beyond the present, or indeed just Venezuela (Zúquete 2008: 106; Hawkins 2010: 55). While this is certainly true, Zúquete and Hawkins both overlook the connection between this Manicheanism and Chávez's belief in conspiracy theories. It is now widely accepted among scholars that there are no intrinsic markers of a conspiracy theory as they can manifest in countless shapes and forms (Knight 2000: 11; Bratich 2008: 3–6). However, that is not to say that the characteristics outlined by Richard Hofstadter are not still relevant because the Manicheanism and apocalypticism that he identified *are* visible in Chávez's discourse, which is laced with conspiracy theories (Hofstadter 1964: 30–1). Hofstadter explains that the apocalyptic element within conspiracy theories inspires personal and collective agency because of the idea that, if we engage in this battle against evil now, then a 'doomsday' event can still be avoided (Hofstadter 1964: 30). Furthermore, he highlights that, since this is a battle between absolute good and evil, total victory is constantly postponed because (as he sees it) these demands are unrealistic (Hofstadter 1964: 31). However, in Chávez's case, this postponed victory over the opposition and the U.S.A. and the articulation of continued conspiracies against the movement functions to continually foster agency and mobilisation. Moreover, the vocalisation of victories (however small) towards achieving this triumph over 'evil' reminds followers that this is not a hopeless cause. For example, in Chávez's closing campaign speech in 2006, he proclaimed:

> Just as we defeated them [the enemy] in 2003 during the economic and oil sabotage, and how we defeated them in 2004 during the great and affirming referendum in 2004, and in 2005 in the government, most of the municipal and the National Assembly elections.
>
> *(Chávez 2006)*

If Chávez's supporters really believed that it was a hopeless cause, then they would not have voted him back into office with a staggering 62.8 per cent of the votes during this 2006 election (Consejo Nacional Electoral 2006).

Conspiracy theories, therefore, helped reconstruct Venezuelan national identity at a time when it was in crisis. They also inspired personal and collective empowerment and agency through their apocalyptic Manicheanism. This heightened sense of agency unquestionably contributed to higher levels of political participation, thus evidencing conspiracy theories' mobilising capacities. For example, between 1998 and 2006, the participation of voters in presidential elections rose from 65.5 to 74.6 per cent (Wilpert 2011). Moreover, this sense of agency manifested itself in greater pushes toward economic, political and social independence from the U.S.A. on behalf of the Chávez government. For example, in 2004, Chávez's belief that the U.S.A. orchestrated the 2004 recall referendum (a vote to remove Chávez from office) through their control of the Venezuelan media and funding of Súmate (the organisation that led the petition drive), confirmed in his eyes that the U.S.A. was looking for an excuse 'to call for international intervention in Venezuela' (Chávez 2004a). This conviction nurtured Chávez's desire to neutralise U.S. power and influence in Venezuela and Latin America and resulted in taking steps towards creating a 'multi-polar' world (McCarthy-Jones, Turner 2011: 557). The same year that Chávez accused the U.S.A. of trying to sabotage his government through Súmate and the recall referendum, he formally launched the Alternativa Bolivariana para las Américas (A.L.B.A.) designed to create greater regional solidarity of Latin American nations, particularly with regards to trade and development. A.L.B.A. has its own currency, the sucre, to maintain independence from the U.S. dollar. In 2005, A.L.B.A. also set up PetroCaribe, which supplies cheap oil to its members, particularly those in the Caribbean (McCarthy-Jones, Turner 2011: 558; Embassy of the Bolivarian Republic of Venezuela to the U.K. and Ireland). Additionally, Chávez initiated the revitalisation of O.P.E.C. (Organisation of the Petroleum Exporting Countries) in an effort to regain control over Venezuela's own oil industry (Kozloff 2007: 26). Not all of these initiatives were wholly successful; for example, A.L.B.A. is particularly dependent on Venezuelan oil money, which is subject to international price peaks and troughs (Hart-Landsberg 2009). However, they made important steps towards encouraging Latin American nations to rely on and help one another. For Chávez, Latin America spent too long as subordinate to foreign countries. As the late president articulated in his closing campaign speech in 2006, 'we were a colony of Spain for 300 odd years, and we have been a North American colony for the past 200 years' (Chávez 2006). Therefore, if conspiracy theories about economic sabotage, media brainwashing and covert funding of 'subversive' groups like Súmate motivated Chávez to pursue policies like A.L.B.A. that encourage greater independence and challenge the status quo of U.S. hegemony, then they had a clear mobilising impact – contrary to Fenster's assertion that conspiracy theories fail to foment any meaningful engagement with politics (Chávez 2005; Chávez 2006).

Nevertheless, as Hernáiz points out, conspiracy theories have also had undeniably negative consequences in Venezuela (2008: 1177). They have been used, amongst other things, to distract from very real socioeconomic problems and to displace blame onto external forces. For example, Chávez was heavily criticised when he unearthed the bones of Simón Bolívar for attempting to deflect public attention from the rising rates of inflation, corruption among government officials, increased crime and an accusation by Colombia that Venezuela was harbouring members of the F.A.R.C. (Fuerzas Armadas Revolucionarias de Colombia) (Primera 2010). Similarly, Maduro's entire presidency seems to have consisted of him blaming the Venezuelan opposition/U.S.A. for the spiralling socioeconomic and political problems that have brought the once prosperous nation to its knees (B.B.C. News 2019a; Guaido 2019).

Moreover, and perhaps more dangerously, they have been used to justify certain authoritarian attitudes. Fenster and Gray hypothesise that conspiracy theories are more likely to emerge within a state framework under an authoritarian regime, where the clear-cut boundary between the 'people' and the 'enemy' is likely to serve as a vehicle of repression against political dissent (Fenster 2008: 41; Gray 2010: 41). Supporting this assertion is Chávez's complex and antagonistic relationship with the oppositional Venezuelan media. The suspicion of an on-going conspiracy conducted against him and his government by the media was used to justify acts of authoritarianism. In 2004, Chávez passed the Law on Social Responsibility in Radio and Television, which invoked the right to suspend or revoke the radio or television licences of stations that 'promote, justify or incite war ... public disorder ... or crime; that are discriminatory; that promote religious intolerance; [or] that threaten the security of the Nation' (Asamblea Nacional de la República Bolivariana de Venezuela 2005). Some analysts believe, however, that the imprecise wording in this law justified arbitrary interference on behalf of government and engenders self-censorship among journalists (Human Rights Watch 2008: 66).

However, perhaps the most controversial attempt during Chávez's presidency to repress oppositional voices was his decision in 2007 not to renew R.C.T.V.'s broadcasting licence. As one of the main opposition television channels, international organisations like the Human Rights Watch jumped on this restriction of freedom of expression while the domestic opposition decried the increasing pressure to self-censor within the print and visual media (Human Rights Watch 2008: 67). However, since the opposition media, particularly main television stations like R.C.T.V. and Venevisión, participated in a media blackout during the 2002 coup, Chávez became convinced that the opposition were 'trying to sabotage the democratic process via the media' (Hellinger 2003: 50; Chávez 2004b). Despite these attempts to mute the opposition, however, Julia Buxton emphasises that Chávez's overthrow of the *ancien régime* went a long way towards creating a participatory democracy (Buxton 2011: xv–vi). Deborah Norden similarly suggests that Chávez's presidency actually occupied a tenuous space between a participatory democracy and authoritarianism (Norden 2003: 110). Therefore, the fact that Chávez toed a fine line between democracy and authoritarianism, and that conspiracy theories were not only used to further authoritarian attitudes during Chávez's presidency, demonstrates that the emergence and proliferation of conspiracy theories is not simply confined to authoritarian regimes. In fact, Knight pertinently questions whether conspiracy theories might ironically thrive more under democratic governments where 'the political reality fails to live up to an unrealistic utopian faith in egalitarianism' (Knight 2014: 362). Indeed, as numerous conspiracy theory scholars such as Kathryn Olmsted, Michael Rogin and Jack Bratich have documented, conspiracy theories have also played an integral role in U.S. state discourse, such as with anti-communism during the Cold War (Rogin 1987: xiii; Bratich 2008: 165; Olmsted 2009: 209). As such, there is clear evidence both in Venezuela and the U.S.A. that state discourses do not merge with conspiracy theories under authoritarian leaders alone.

In scholarly discussions of conspiracy theories, there has been a growing interest in a more utopian approach to the phenomenon, in which conspiracy theories are deemed a positive challenge to democracy. However, both Bratich and Fiske's understanding of conspiracy narratives, while important in recognising the healthy protest within democracy that they can provide, simultaneously suggest that *all* conspiracy theories are a worthwhile form of dissent (Fiske 1996: 192; Bratich 2008: 10). The danger with these treatments of conspiracy theory is that, by focusing too much on how conspiracy theories can be useful as a social critique and as a challenge to the status quo, they forget the ways in which they can concomitantly be tied to harmful projects and ideologies. Fenster's discussion of this tension is particularly adept; he suggests that conspiracy theories are neither necessarily harmful nor progressive, but their positive impact is determined by the political project to which they contribute. Some conspiracy theories undoubtedly provide a challenge to the status quo of hegemonic power relations, yet they can also lead to violence and repression (Fenster 2008: 279–89). Nonetheless, Fenster ultimately undermines this nuanced argument in his afterword when he concludes that, when it comes down to it, all conspiracy theories are 'wrong' because they preclude any 'real' engagement in politics (Fenster 2008: 289). Moreover, he does not seem to take into account the possibility that conspiracy theories might yield both positive and negative results within the *same* political project. For example, for Chávez, there were undoubtedly benefits to the use of conspiracy theories in his discourse, like their ability to help construct and maintain a strong national identity and provide a source of empowerment and agency when used alongside real social projects that aimed to improve access to healthcare, education, housing and social security, as well as independence from the U.S.A. (Buxton 2011). Yet, we have also seen how they have diverted attention from issues of security, inflation and shortages, as well as being used to justify repression of dissent. In this sense, the precarious balance between conspiracy theories as harmful and mobilising is reflected in Chávez's own struggle between democracy and authoritarianism.

## Conclusion

The current predilection for conspiracy theories in Venezuela is grounded in far more than an inherent suspicion of the U.S.A. and its intervention in the region. It is also rooted in the conspiratorial nature of military politics that has shaped the country political tradition since the early twentieth century. This is a tradition that is by no means limited to Venezuela – the military has played a leading role in politics across Latin America (see, for example, Castelo Branco in Brazil, Augusto Pinochet in Chile, Jorge Rafael Videla in Argentina, Anastasio Somoza Debayle in Nicaragua, Alfredo Stroessner in Paraguay), as has populism (see, for example, Juan Perón in Argentina, Alberto Fujimori in Peru, Rafael Correa in Ecuador, Daniel Ortega in Nicaragua). As such, and while it would require further research, it is suggested that the conspiratorial nature of military politics has ingrained conspiracy theories into the Latin American political tradition and that the appeal of populism in Latin America (including its promise to resolve the complex issue of identity) lends conspiracy theories, with their populist underpinnings, greater legitimacy.

Chávez undoubtedly inherited a political legacy prone to conspiracism, but also demonstrated the mobilising capacities of conspiracy theories on an unprecedented scale – from the positive to the negative. The lines between conspiracy theories being attached to a positive or harmful dogma are not clear-cut and this is particularly evident within Chávez's discourse. On the one hand, Chávez used conspiracy theories to help strengthen Venezuelan identity at a time when it was in crisis by constructing a clear enemy against which to mobilise (the Venezuelan elite and the U.S.A.). This enemy was then located within a historic and moral battle between good and evil designed to evoke a sense of duty towards the ultimate triumph of good. By imagining this new identity to be in danger of manipulation and interference by external forces, Chávez simultaneously used conspiracy theories to create a sense of agency among those who had historically been disenfranchised and marginalised within Venezuela.

On the other hand, it is impossible to ignore the negative side effects borne of conspiracism in Venezuela. Not only have conspiracy theories been used at points to distract the public from ongoing problems related to security, inflation and the scarcity of essential goods, but they have also served to justify authoritarian acts, like the silencing of opposition. While the latter undoubtedly started under Chávez (as highlighted above), the repression of dissent and the violation of human rights have become particularly fervent under Maduro. According to the Penal Forum, approximately 14 085 Venezuelan citizens have been arbitrarily arrested since January 2014 as a result of participating in anti-government protests and, as of 31 January 2019, 918 of those remain imprisoned (Foro Penal 2019). The reasons for such repression are numerous and complex. However, there is no denying that Maduro frequently justifies the use of force with allegations of a right-wing/U.S./Colombian coup conspiracy. Anyone either involved or supportive of these 'coup tactics' are subsequently detained, imprisoned, tortured and/or killed, thus fomenting a culture of fear and distrust (Phillips 2019). Not only do conspiracy theories thus exacerbate these problems of repression through fear of a conspiracy, but they also undermine the attempts of international arbiters to address these issues: As demonstrated by Maduro's recent rejection of U.S. humanitarian aid, which he alleged was part of a plot to justify U.S. military intervention in Venezuela (B.B.C. News 2019b).

The question then becomes: Is it possible to inhibit the adverse effects of conspiracy theories? (Carey 2017; Foro Penal 2017).[1] How and by whom would such a limit even be imposed?

Carey suggests that improving education levels, stabilising the economy and reducing political partisanship could help break the cycle of conspiracism in Venezuela (2019: 454). Yet, this ignores the fact that conspiracy theories also thrive in largely stable economies such as the U.S.A. (though they may surge in times of turmoil) and, arguably, if we really are moving towards a 'post-truth world' in which analysing objective evidence and facts is less important, it is questionable whether improving education levels would have any effect.

This chapter has shown that conspiracy theories are by no means restricted to the U.S.A., and that they are a complex phenomenon that offers considerable insight into the fears and anxieties that govern contemporary Latin American society. As such, it is hoped that the issues raised and discussed here will spark further research into the role and popularity of conspiracy theories in this fascinating region, and why the spectre of conspiracy continues to haunt Latin American politics.

## Note

1 According to data collected by the Venezuelan human rights organisation, Foro Penal, in its first three years and ten months, Maduro's government imprisoned 56 political opponents on conspiracy charges (as well as another 48, mostly on protest-related charges), sentencing 21 of them as of February 2017 (Amaro Chacón, Carey 2017; Foro Penal 2017).

## References

Amaro Chacón, G. and Carey, J. (2017) 'Counting political prisoners in Venezuela', *Global Americans*, 23 March. Available at: https://latinamericagoesglobal.org/2017/03/political-imprisonment-venezuela/#.WNOwIYXVKwo.twitter. [Accessed 23 September 2019.]

Asamblea Nacional de la República Bolivariana de Venezuela (2005) *Ley de Responsabilidad Social en Radio y Televisión*, 12 December. Available at: www.palermo.edu/cele/pdf/Regulaciones/Venezuela LegislacionLeydeResponsabilidadSocialenRadioyTelevision(2005).pdf. [Accessed 23 September 2019.]

Assman, A. (2011) 'Canon and Archive', in J.K. Olick, V. Vinitzky-Seroussi and D. Levy (eds.) *The Collective Memory Reader*, Oxford: Oxford University Press, pp. 334–7.

Baronderothchild (2006) 'Chávez "Bush You Are a Donkey"', *YouTube*, 11 August. Available at: www.youtube.com/watch?v=NYYQT21p7l8. [Accessed 23 September 2019.]

B.B.C. News (2019a) 'Venezuela's Maduro thanks military for defeating "coup"', *BBC News*, 10 March. Available at: www.bbc.com/news/world-latin-america-47512386. [Accessed 23 September 2019.]

B.B.C. News (2019b) 'Venezuela crisis: US planes carrying aid arrive in Colombia', *BBC News*, 17 February. Available at: www.bbc.com/news/world-latin-america-47268039. [Accessed 23 September 2019.]

Beasley-Murray, J. (2003) *Posthegemony: political theory and Latin America*, London: University of Minnesota Press.

Beasley-Murray, J. (2006) 'Review of Ernesto Laclau, on populist reason, and Francio Panizza, populism and the mirror of democracy', *Contemporary Political Theory*, 5: 362–7.

BF26A4F468341A4F (2006) 'El Show de Chávez: "Bush es El Diablo"', *YouTube*, 21 September. Available at: www.youtube.com/watch?v=eCHrEBY-fyY?. [Accessed 23 September 2019.]

Bratich, J.Z. (2008) *Conspiracy panics: political rationality and popular culture*, Albany, NY: State University of New York Press.

Buxton, J. (2011) 'Venezuela's Bolivarian Democracy', in D. Smilde and D. Hellinger (eds.) *Venezuela's Bolivarian democracy: participation, politics, and culture under Chávez*, London: Duke University Press, pp. ix–xxii.

Buxton, J. (2014) 'Social policy in Venezuela, bucking neoliberalism or unsustainable clientelism', *UNRISD project: towards universal social security in emerging economies: process, institutions and actors*, Geneva, Switzerland: UNRISD. Available at: www.unrisd.org/80256B3C005BCCF9/(httpAuxPages)/1D4EF25E12 C57738C1257D9E00562542/%24file/Buxton.pdf. [Accessed 23 September 2019.]

Cannon, B. (2009) *Hugo Chávez and the Bolivarian revolution: populism and democracy in a globalised age*, Manchester: Manchester University Press.

Carey, J.M. (2019) 'Who believes in conspiracy theories in Venezuela?', *Latin American Research Review*, 54(2): 444–57.
Chávez, H. (2003) *Aló, Presidente* (no. 159), Venezolana de Televisión 10 August.
Chávez, H. (host) (2004a) *Aló, Presidente* (no. 182), Venezolana de Televisión, 15 February.
Chávez, H. (2004b) *Aló, Presidente* (no. 205), Venezolana de Televisión, 26 September.
Chávez, H. (host) (2005) *Aló, Presidente* (no. 213), Venezolana de Televisión, 20 February.
Chávez, H. (2006) 'Discurso de cierre de campaña del candidato a la reelección', *Aporrea*, 26 November. Available at: www.aporrea.org/oposicion/a27627.html. [Accessed 23 September 2019.]
Chumaceiro Arreaza, I.C. (2003) 'El discurso de Hugo Chávez: Bolívar como estrategia para dividir a los venezolanos', *Boletín de Lingüística*, 20: 22–42.
Consejo Nacional Electoral (2006) 'Elección Presidencial', *Consejo Nacional Electoral*, 3 December. Available at: www.cne.gob.ve/divulgacionPresidencial/resultado_nacional.php. [Accessed 23 September 2019.]
Coronil, F. (1997) *The magical state: nature, money, and modernity in Venezuela*, London: The University of Chicago Press.
Ellner, S. (2003) 'The search for explanations', in S. Ellner and D. Hellinger (eds.) *Venezuelan politics in the Chávez Era: class, polarization, and conflict*, London: Lynne Rienner, pp. 7–26.
Embassy of the Bolivarian Republic of Venezuela to the U.K. and Ireland A.L.B.A. (n.d.) 'Bolivarian Alliance for the People of Our America Fact Sheet', http://embavenez.co.uk/sites/embavenez.co.uk/files/factsheets/factsheetalba.pdf. [Accessed 22 October 2013.]
Emerson, R.G. (2011) 'A Bolivarian People: Identity Politics in Hugo Chávez's Venezuela', Humanities Research, 17(1). Available at: http://press.anu.edu.au/apps/bookworm/view/Humanities+Research+Vol+XVII.+No.+1.+2011./5401/ch06.xhtml. [Accessed 2 February 2014.]
Ewell, J. (1984) *Venezuela: a century of change*, London: C. Hurst & Company.
Ewell, J. (1996) *Venezuela and the United States: from Monroe's Hemisphere to Petroleum's empire*, London: University of Georgia Press.
Fenster, M. (2008) *Conspiracy theories: secrecy and power in American culture*, 2nd edn, London: University of Minnesota Press.
Fernández, A. (2013) 'Infografía: en 14 años van 63 denuncias de magnicidio', *Ultimas Noticias*, 2 September. Available at: www.ultimasnoticias.com.ve/noticias/actualidad/investigacion/infografia--en-14-anos-van-63-denuncias-de-magnic.aspx. [Accessed 23 September 2019.]
Fiske, J. (1996) *Media matters: race and gender in U.S. politics*, London: University of Minnesota Press.
Foro Penal (2017) 'Presos políticos', *Foro Penal*, 9 August. Available at: https://foropenal.com/presos-politicos/. [Accessed 26 September 2019.]
Foro Penal (2019) 'Reporte sobre la repression en venezuela, agosto 2019', *Foro Penal*, 15 September. Available at: https://foropenal.com/reporte-sobre-la-represion-en-venezuela-agosto-2019/. [Accessed 23 September 2019.]
Galván, J.A. (2013) *Latin American dictators of the twentieth century: the lives and regimes of 15 rulers*, Jefferson, NC: McFarland & Company.
Gray, M. (2010) *Conspiracy theories in the Arab World: sources and politics*, London: Routledge.
Guaido, J. (2019) 'Nicolas Maduro blames Venezuela blackouts on U.S. weapons', *Global News*, 9 March. Available at: https://globalnews.ca/video/5039591/nicolas-maduro-blames-venezuela-blackouts-on-u-s-weapons. [Accessed 23 September 2019.]
Guardian (2011) 'Chile exhumes Salvador Allende's body for new probe into how president died', *The Guardian*, 23 May. Available at: www.theguardian.com/world/2011/may/23/chile-president-salvador-allende-remains-exhumed. [Accessed 23 September 2019.]
Hart-Landsberg, M. (2009) 'Learning from ALBA and the bank of the south: challenges and possibilities', *Monthly Review*, 61(4).
Hawkins, K.A. (2010) *Venezuela's chavismo and populism in comparative perspective*, Cambridge: Cambridge University Press.
Hellinger, D. (2003) 'Political overview: the breakdown of puntofijismo and the rise of chavismo', in S. Ellner and D. Hellinger (eds.) *Venezuelan politics in the Chávez Era: class, polarization, and conflict*, Boulder: Lynne Rienner, pp. 27–53.
Hernáiz, H.P. (2008) 'The uses of conspiracy theories for the construction of a political religion in Venezuela', *International Journal of Humanities and Social Sciences*, 2(8): 1167–78.
Herrera, E. (2018) '¿Quién mató a Blake Mora? Calderón recuerda a exsecretario a 7 años de su deceso', *La Neta Noticias*, 11 November. Available at: www.lanetanoticias.com/politica/337511/quien-mato-a-blake-mora-calderon-recuerda-a-exsecretario-a-7-anos-de-su-deceso. [Accessed 23 September 2019.]

Herrera Salas, J.M. (2005) 'Ethnicity and revolution: the political economy of racism in Venezuela', *Latin American Perspectives*, 32(2): 72–91.
Hofstadter, R. (1964) 'The Paranoid Style in American Politics', in R. Hofstadter (ed.) *The paranoid style in american politics and other essays*, London: Alfred A. Knopf, Inc.
Hoy (2005) 'Chávez: EU me espiaba a través de', *Hoy*, 8 August. Available at: https://hoy.com.do/chavez-eu-me-espiaba-a-traves-de-dea/. [Accessed 23 September 2019.]
Human Rights Watch (2008) *A decade under Chávez: political intolerance and lost opportunities for advancing human rights in Venezuela*, London: Human Rights Watch.
Knight, P. (2000) *Conspiracy culture: from Kennedy to 'The X Files'*, Oxon: Routledge.
Knight, P. (2014) 'Plotting future directions in conspiracy theory research', in M. Butter and M. Reinkowski (eds.) *Conspiracy theories in the Middle East and the United States: a comparative approach*, Berlin: de Gruyter, pp. 346–70.
Kozloff, N. (2007) *Hugo Chávez: oil, politics, and the challenge to the U.S.*, Hampshire, England: Palgrave Macmillan.
Laclau, E. (2005) *On populist reason*, London: Verso.
McCarthy-Jones, A. and Turner, M. (2011) 'Explaining radical policy change: the case of Venezuelan foreign policy', *Policy Studies*, 32(5): 549–67.
Norden, D.L. (2003) 'Democracy in uniform: Chávez and the Venezuelan armed forces', in S. Ellner and D. Hellinger (eds.) *Venezuelan politics in the Chávez Era: class, polarization, and conflict*, Boulder: Lynne Rienner, pp. 93–112.
Olick, J.K. and Robbins, J. (1998) 'Social memory studies: from "Collective Memory" to the historical sociology of mnemonic practices', *Annual Review of Sociology*, 24: 105–40.
Olmsted, K.S. (2009) *Real enemies: conspiracy theories and American democracy, World War I to 9/11*, Oxford: Oxford University Press.
Padgett, T. (2010) 'Why Venezuela's Chavez dug up Bolivar's bones', *Time*, 17 July. Available at: http://content.time.com/time/world/article/0,8599,2004526,00.html. [Accessed 23 September 2019.]
Phillips, T. (2019) '"They are murderers": special forces unit strikes fear in Venezuelans', *The Guardian*, 6 February. Available at: www.theguardian.com/world/2019/feb/06/venezuela-faes-special-forces-nicolas-maduro-barrios. [Accessed 23 September 2019.]
Pipes, D. (1997) *Conspiracy: how the paranoid style flourishes and where it comes from*, London: The Free Press.
Primera, M. (2010) 'Chavez "resucita" a Bolívar para salvarse', *El País*, 16 July. Available at: http://internacional.elpais.com/internacional/2010/07/16/actualidad/1279231207_850215.html. [Accessed 23 September 2019.]
Rabe, S.G. (1982) *The road to OPEC: United States relations with Venezuela, 1919–1976*, Austin: University of Texas Press.
Rangel, D.A. (1974) *Capital y desarrollo: la Venezuela agrarian*, Caracas: Universidad Central de Venezuela.
Roberts, K. (2000) 'Populism and democracy in Latin America', *Challenges to Democracy in the Americas*, Carter Center, Atlanta, 16–8 October. Available at: https://is.muni.cz/el/1423/podzim2016/POL333/um/Dr__Kenneth_Roberts_POPULISM_AND_DEMOCRACY_IN_LAT.pdf. [Accessed 26 September 2019.]
Roberts, K. (2003) 'Social polarization and the populist resurgence in Venezuela', in S. Ellner and D. Hellinger (eds.) *Venezuelan politics in the Chávez Era: class, polarization, and conflict*, Boulder: Lynne Rienner, pp. 55–72.
Rodriguez, L. and Smallman, S. (2016) 'Political polarization and Nisman's death: competing conspiracy theories in Argentina', *Journal of International and Global Studies*, 8(1): 20–39.
Rogin, M.P. (1987) *Ronald Reagan, the movie: and other episodes in political demonology*, London: University of California Press.
Romero, M.T. (2007) 'The touchy faultfinder and foreign critics', *El Universal*, 3 August. Available at www.eluniversal.com/2007/08/03/en_ing_art_the-touchy-faultfind_03A910233. [Accessed 23 September 2019.]
Ultimas Noticias (2011) 'Chávez se pregunta si cáncer de mandatarios es culpa de EEUU', *YouTube*, 28 December. Available at: www.youtube.com/watch?v=g3AllgyRy-E. [Accessed 23 September 2019.]
Wilpert, G. (2011) 'An assessment of Venezuela's Bolivarian revolution at twelve years', *Venezuela Analysis*, 2 February. Available at: http://venezuelanalysis.com/analysis/5971. [Accessed 29 September 2019.]
Zúquete, J.P. (2008) 'The missionary politics of Hugo Chávez', *Latin American Politics & Society*, 50(1): 91–121.

# INDEX

9/11 Truth Movement 6, 283–6, 289

Abdülhamid II 611, 615, 616
Adorno, T. 29, 71–2, 279, 470, 475, 479
agency 160, 348–9
agency detection 160, 171–2, 182, 351
agency panic 293, 296, 349, 431–3, 583
aggression 70–1, 154
agreeableness 156–7
Agrippina the Elder 533–4
Agrippina the Younger 538–9
A.K.P. (Justice and Development Party) 618–21
alternative medicine 78, 196–7, 375, 380
American exceptionalism 34, 39
American Revolutionary War 650–1
analytic thinking 158–9, 160–1, 168–77
Anderl Oxner of Rinn 449–50
Anderson, W. 393–4
anecdote 406
anthropomorphism 160
anti-Americanism 320
anti-Catholicism 291–2, 297–302, 548–9, 651
anti-communism 293, 297, 300–1, 320, 459–61, 463–4, 653–4, 663, 669
anti-establishment conspiracy theories 162; *see also* populism
anti-immigration discourse 272, 330, 334–6, 397, 651
anti-imperialism 601–5
anti-Jesuitism 547–8, 650
Anti-Masonic Party 517, 562–3
antisemitism 320, 357–67, 563–5, 571–3, 615; and anti-Judaism 357, 360, 543–4; and anti-modernism 361; and antizionism 364–5, 574–6, 602–3, 604; and Islamism 367, 501, 642–3; and 'Jewish Bolshevism' 447, 571, 600–2; and Jewish conspiracy theory 195, 196, 206, 209–19, 405, 447–9, 479, 569–74, 599–603, 615–16, 642–3; modern forms of 320, 323, 365, 367; and the 'Perceived Jew' 642; and racism 363, 365; and secret societies 360, 364, 601, 602
anti-vaccination conspiracy theories 132, 209, 487–92
anxiety 183, 185, 186, 210
anxious uncertainty 169, 172–3, 210, 223
'Arab spring' 627
Armenian genocide 612
Atatürk, M.K. 612, 613, 614
Athenian democracy 532
attachment 183
Attic orators 532
attitude change 233–4, 245–6
Atwood, M. 429, 433–4
audience reception 469–80
Audley, R. 422, 423
authoritarianism 661, 668–70; right-wing 161–2, 195, 222
Avery, D. 1, 3, 6

Baburin, S. 590
Bailyn, B. 29–30, 650
Bali bombings (2002) 639
Balkanism 596–8
Balkans, the 596–607
Barruel, A. 23, 29, 550, 551, 555, 556–9, 563–4
Bartlett, F. 393–4
'beauty myth' 297
Behrend, H. 88
belief systems 81–91, 155
Berlin Congress 597, 599
*Biarritz* (novel) 599
Big Five personality model 152, 156–8, 162–3
Bin Laden, O. 1, 283–4, 367

674

## Index

Birchall, C. 13, 33
'birther' conspiracy theory 498, 519
Bolívar, S. 660, 663, 666, 668
Bolshevik conspiracy theory 570–3
boomerang effect 246
bots 137–8, 140
Bratich, J. 17, 18, 33, 669
Breivik, A. 337, 379, 380
Brexit 498
Brown, D. 50, 409, 415, 463, 475
Broz Tito, J. 603–5
Buonaccorsi, B. 546
Burke, E. 551, 555, 558, 560
Burroughs, W.S. 36, 38, 430, 431–2, 434, 435
Bush, G. 284, 582, 584, 629, 633, 656, 666, 667
Butter, M. 12, 18, 31, 34, 37, 261, 279, 294, 299, 300, 333, 388, 428, 529, 578

cargo cults 641
Castro, C. 662
Catholic Church 84, 88
Central Asia 322–3
Centre of Contemporary Cultural Studies 470
Cernovich, M. 505
Chambers, W. 301
Chávez, H. 2, 660, 661, 662, 664–70
Chemtrails 176, 520–1
Christ, B. 13, 294
Christians, conspiracy theories about 535–9
CIA 433–5, 437–8
civic engagement 124, 199, 201
Clinton, H. 75, 337, 339, 500, 503, 512, 513
Coady, D. 57, 64–5, 531
cognitive: approaches 128, 130; diversity, infiltration 250; styles 155, 158–61
cognitive bias 504
cognitive closure, need for 182
Cold War 427, 429–38, 574–5
Collins, W. 419, 422–3, 423
colonialism 81, 86
colour revolutions (post-Soviet states) 585–6
Cominform plot 604
communication 483–93, 543–7
communication networks 136, 139, 142, 145, 497–508
communicative latency 364
Communist party 570, 574–6
community 284–5, 288–9
Conan Doyle, A. 415, 419
*congiure* 542–5
*coniuratio* 542–3
conjunction fallacy 159–60, 170–1
Conrad, J. 423
conservatism 306–7
conspiracies, real 4, 176–7, 193, 232, 242–3, 628
Conspiración imperialista, la 665
conspiracism 2, 372–3, 375–6, 379, 380, 661, 670
conspiracy belief 151, 155–67, 168–77, 181–8, 192–203, 206–15, 231–2, 263–71, 469, 648, 656–7
conspiracy belief scales 129–30, 132, 155
conspiracy culture 469–80
conspiracy ideation *see* conspiracy mentality
conspiracy mentality 155, 162, 195–6, 199
conspiracy mindset 351, 354
conspiracy theories: in Africa 210; in American history 393–8, 404, 517, 648–57; in American literature 427–38; and anthropology 81–92; and antisemitism 357–67, 374, 381; in authoritarian regimes 317–27; in British literature 415–25; and conceptual history 16–26; consequences of 152, 207, 225–6, 231–9, 243, 305; complex 169, 173–4; as counterknowledge 2–3, 193, 210, 373, 471, 480, 483; and crime 237–8; definition of 1–4, 56, 57, 63, 113–15, 121, 124, 192–4, 263–5, 416–17, 469, 661; and demographics 6, 152, 263–74; in the early modern period 442–3, 542–51, 649; about elites 3, 212, 475–8, 503, 655; and emotions 152, 157, 184–6, 211; and everyday life 151, 281–2, 286, 289, 469; epistemology of 61–3, 247–51; ethics of 61–3; in Europe 193, 206, 210; and external enemies 211, 415, 417–20, 624, 629, 639–42, 650; and fake news 137, 139–41, 452; and fantasy 67, 71, 73–7; and fear 221–2; and folklore studies 395–8; and the French Revolution 22–3, 401, 405, 549–51, 555–65, 651; and gender and sexuality 6, 292–302; in historical, literary and cultural studies 4, 28–39; and intergroup relations 195–6, 212, 219–26, 235, 627, 643–5, 665; and internal enemies 211, 415, 412–14, 629, 650; as interpretive practice 469–80; knowledge status of 2–3, 648–57; in Latin America 320, 660–71; lifecycle of 497–508; and mass media 387–90; mediatisation of 387–90, 404, 447–9; in the Middle East 325–7, 366–7, 624–34; and misinformation 242–52; as occult cosmology 83, 86–7, 92; online 213, 472–80, 483–93, 497–508, 512–2; and personality traits 151–2, 155–8, 161–2; and philosophy 5, 56–64; and political behaviour 234–6, 304–14; and political science and political theory 4, 108–16; and populism 2, 317, 323–5, 330–40, 660–71; and psychoanalysis 67–78, 625; and radicalisation 344–54; as reactions to power 192–203; and religion 212, 265, 267, 371–81, 472; in the Roman empire 531–40; and rumour 6, 207, 208–9, 210–11, 212, 213, 279, 282, 284, 287, 391–8, 404–5, 497, 499, 503, 512–18, 632; in Russia 206, 582–93; and social-cognitive processes 168–77; social psychology of 4, 5–6, 121–32, 151–4, 392–3; and social network analysis 135–45; and sociology and social theory 5, 70–2, 94–105; in Southeast Asia 638–45; stigmatization of 2–3, 233, 392, 458, 648, 649,

675

conspiracy theories *continued*
  654–5; as strategic claims 631; transmission of 6, 152, 206–15, 388–9, 391–8, 453–4, 483–93, 497–508, 632–3; in Turkey 193, 321, 324, 610–21; as viral narratives 485, 497–508; in the United States 193, 199, 427–38, 457–67, 512–3; and urban legends 211, 391–8; and visual culture 408–9, 441–54
conspiracy theory: concept of 2, 3, 661; conceptual history of 16–26, 654–5
conspiracy theory entrepreneurs 278–89
conspiracy theory movements 278–89
conspirituality 18, 26, 295, 379
control 172–3, 183, 185, 186, 194–5, 197–8, 222–3, 631
Convivencia, La 543
correlation 126–8, 131, 172–3; spurious 171, 182
correspondence 406–7
corruption 176–7
counter-Enlightenment 558–9
covert sphere 437–8
*crimen laesae maiestatis* 544–5, 547
critical theory 67–78
Cuixart, J. 143
cultural studies 4, 31–5
culture industry 470, 475–8
Cusa, A. 601

Davis, D. 30, 108, 298, 416, 657
Dayak 643–4
debunking 152, 242–52, 280, 285
deep state 320–5, 617–18, 627
DeLillo, D. 34, 36, 50, 429, 430, 433, 434, 435–6
Deluc, J.A. 558
democratisation 22–3
demonology 427–8, 435–8, 450–1, 661–4
Denmark 334–6, 367
desire 67, 71–8
detective fiction 415–17, 419–20, 421–2
Didion, J. 429, 434, 435
Dimock, M.E. 25–6
disinformation 137–8, 140, 145, 497–508
disintermediation 141
dissemination of conspiracy theories *see* conspiracy theories, transmission of
diversity 280–1, 286–9, 626
Dönme 610, 615–16
doubt 83, 85, 91–2
dual process models 159, 161, 168–77
Dugin, A. 322, 586–7, 588, 590

Eastern Europe 317, 323
Ecevit, B. 617
echo chambers 139–40, 143, 487, 507–8, 648
Eco, U. 37, 43, 46, 47, 50, 407, 475
economic crisis in Southeast Asia (1999–2000) 639, 642
education 159, 183, 265–6

Ellefritz, R. 284, 285–6
emotion 211
encoding/decoding 470–2
entitativity 221
epistemic authority 5, 210
epistemic strategies 282, 287
epistemic trust 61, 196
Erdoğan, R.T. 618–19, 620
escalating path 200–1
esotericism 372–4, 379
ethnography 283–8
Euclidean distance 138
Eurabia conspiracy theory 116, 301, 324, 337, 375
Evans-Pritchard, E.E. 83–4, 85–6, 91
extreme-right *see* far-right
extremism 2, 201, 344–54, 487, 624, 633

fan culture 473
far-right 2, 308, 324, 344–54, 364–5, 380, 501, 505, 575–7
Favret-Saada, J. 84, 91, 92
'feminine mystique' 295–7
Fenster, M. 11, 13, 31, 35, 36, 37, 46, 49, 74–5, 113, 279, 333, 457, 462, 466, 539–40, 664, 668, 669
fiction 467, 483; conspiracy scenarios in 409–10, 427–38, 457–67
fictionality 409, 443–4
fieldwork 286–7
fifth column 573–4, 578
film; and conspiracy 433, 435, 436, 458–63
Finland 330, 335–6
Fire of Rome 64 C.E. 535–40
First World War 418–20, 569–70
Foucault, M. 19–20, 68, 607
Frankenheimer, J. 300–1, 460
Franz, F. 598, 600, 602
Freemasonry 549, 555–65, 573, 575
French Revolution *see* conspiracy theories and the French Revolution
Freud, S. 37, 38, 70, 71–2, 74, 86, 395, 428–9, 432, 438, 471
Friedan, B. 295–7
fundamentalism 375–6, 379
Furet, F. 550, 556, 561–2

G.I. Bill 654
Gassicourt, C.L.C. de 446, 559
gender 82, 88–9, 210, 265
genre 404–8, 409, 411, 415–25, 475
Germanicus 533–5
Germany 199
Geschiere, P. 83, 85–7, 89
Gieryn, T. 12, 14
Ginsburg, T. 294–5
globalisation 87, 100, 102, 629
Göchhausen, E.A.A. von 409
Goedsche, H. 361

Goertzel, T. 123, 226
Gómez, J.V. 662–3
Google 506
Gosa, T.L. 104, 282–3
Gracheva, T. 589
Great Purge 572–5
'Great Replacement' conspiracy theory 2, 116, 195, 301, 324, 337, 375
Griesinger, W. 69
Groh, D. 17, 18, 531
Gulf War 628
Gunpowder plot 547

Haidt, J. 175
Hall, S. 114, 470–1, 472, 473, 474, 476, 478
Harambam, J. 82, 90–1, 97, 98, 99, 116, 261, 282, 283, 284, 471
'Help Catalonia' campaign 142, 144
Henry III, king of France 546
Henry IV, king of France 546
hermeneutics of suspicion 35, 46, 52, 417, 429, 471
hermetic semiosis 46
heterophily 140, 144
hip hop counterculture 282
Hiss, A. 301
Hitler, A. 103, 280, 364, 365, 571, 600
HIV/AIDS 236, 243, 270, 398, 644
Hofstadter, R. 17, 29–30, 103, 104–5, 108–9, 110, 197, 279, 280, 285, 295, 298, 416, 418, 427, 428, 430–1, 434–5, 436–8, 443, 625, 648–9, 650–1, 655, 667
Hollywood 458–63, 476; classical Hollywood cinema 458–61; New Hollywood 461; see also film
Holocaust 364; denial 271–2, 326–7, 365, 367, 642
homeostatic path 200–1
homophily 140, 143
Horn, A. 561
host desecration, accusations of 259
Howden Smith, A.D. 598
Hungary 129, 193, 244, 330, 560, 574
Hussein, S. 612, 626, 630
hypermedia 453

Icke, D. 281–2, 287, 289, 473, 452, 473, 479, 577
identity 199, 281, 288, 349–50, 354; construction 44, 45, 50–1, 53
ideology 6, 222, 304–14, 472, 627
Illuminati 206, 404, 409, 475–80, 549–50, 555–65
immunisation see inoculation
India 330, 498
Indonesia 639–44
information cascade 487
information overload 487
inoculation 247–8
Inquisition 544

Instagram 390, 514
intergroup contact 219–20, 225
intergroup relations 152, 219–21
intermediality 441–2
internet 6, 207, 389, 398, 420, 463, 472–4, 483–93, 497–508, 648, 649, 656–7; see also social media; Web 2.0
interpersonal relations 89
interventions 152, 226, 252–62
intuitive thinking 159–60, 168–77
invasion 417–20
invisible government 436–8
Iran 326–7
Iran-Contra affair 176
Islam 7, 223–4, 326–7, 348, 372, 374–5, 377–8, 640–3
Islamism 320, 350, 367, 615–21, 627, 639, 643
Islamophobia 375, 501

James, H. 423, 428
Jameson, F. 32, 38, 72–3, 95, 388, 438
JFK (film) 462–3, 655
jihad 346, 348–52, 374–5
Jiménez, P. 663
John Birch Society 653
Jolley, D. and Douglas, K.M. 124–6, 128, 186, 199, 234, 236–7, 238, 248, 310
Jones, A. 2, 111, 244, 248, 265, 281–3, 284, 289, 339, 505, 656, 657
journalism 23
Jung, C.G. 393–4

Kalergi plan 348
Kant, I. 402, 549, 564
Kay, J. 284–5, 294–5
Keeley, B. 531
Kemalism 613–14
Kennedy assassination 155, 209, 267, 433, 435–7, 633, 654
Kennedy, J.F. 111, 115, 123, 155, 233, 267, 324–5, 429, 433, 436–7, 453, 458, 459, 461, 462, 471, 501, 535, 575, 633, 649, 654, 655, 656
Khazars, the 588–9
Khazin, M. 592
Kiš, D. 602
Kısakürek, N.F. 615–16
Knigge, A. von 560
Knight, P. 11, 12, 13, 37, 113, 279, 296, 297, 424, 430, 457–8, 464–5, 654, 655, 661, 663, 665, 669
Kraepelin, E. 69–70, 416

La Fontaine, J. 84–5, 86, 89
Lacan, J. 67, 73, 74, 75–7, 78
Laclau, E. 661, 664
Lasswell, H. 70–1, 279
Latin America 318–20

Lausanne treaty 612
Leone, M. 13, 44, 46–7, 442, 453, 484
Lepselter, S. 89
Lewin equation 151–2
Lewin, K. 151–4
Lincoln, A. 458, 652–3
linear regression 128
linguistic turn 18–20
'lipstick girl' conspiracy theory 644
Ljotić, D. 601
Lombardi, M. 452
lone actors 352
longitudinal studies 128
*Loose Change* 1, 2, 3, 5, 6, 7, 531, 656
Lotman, J.M. 45–6, 47–8, 49, 53, 486

Maček, V. 600
Machiavelli, N. 22, 108, 162, 226, 351, 408–9, 544–6, 548
Madisson, M.-L. 47–8
Madurese 2, 643–4
Malaysia 638, 640, 642–3
Malaysia Airlines Flight 370 (MH370) 638
Malinowski, B. 81
*Manchurian Candidate, The* 460–1
Manicheanism 348, 651, 664, 667
Marsilius of Padua 544
Mashuri, A. and Zaduqisti, E. 223–4, 641
Masonic conspiracy theory 446, 601, 602, 615; *see also* Freemasons
mass media 469–80
Mather, C. 428, 649, 650
Mazarin, J. de 545
McCarthy, J. 67–8, 280, 305, 320, 338, 436, 437, 574, 584, 653
McLuhan, M. 388–9, 403, 412, 485
mediation *see* conspiracy theories, mediatisation of
Medici, L. de 546
Medvedev, D. 586
Melley, T. 11, 13, 31, 32, 36, 37, 293, 294, 296, 300–1, 302, 388, 583
melodrama 428–9, 435–8
Melville, H. 37, 428, 429
memes 485–6
Middle East 325–7, 366–7
misfortune 83–4, 87–92
misinformation 242–52, 497–508
mobilisation 333
modern art 451–3
modernity 86–7, 94, 101, 104, 210, 416–17, 421–4, 469
mondialism 586–8
Monk, M. 298–300
monological belief systems 123
moon landing conspiracy theories 168, 208
Morse, J. 299, 404, 562, 651
Moscovici, S. 123, 185
motivated reasoning 169, 174–6

motivation 152, 181–4, 221–5
motivational approaches 122
Mumcu, U. 617–18

Napoleon, B. 361, 416, 417–18, 563
narcissism 184; collective 184, 224–5
narrative 207–8, 212–13, 392, 415–25, 427–38, 457–67, 469, 512–17; classical conspiracy 462–3; discursive vs dramatising 35–6, 207–8, 457; serial 418–19, 463–37; visual 443–54, 457–67
Nazism 571–4, 363–4; antisemitism and 220, 447–9
Nero 535–40
networks 497–508; *see also* communication networks
Neumann, F. 71, 72
New Age 379–80
New World Order 281–3, 289, 576–8, 582–93
newspapers 23
Nietzsche, F. 16, 37, 471, 478
Nigeria 372, 377, 381
Nißl, F.X. 450–1
Non-Aligned Movement 602–5
Northern Europe 330
Norway 330, 334–6, 372, 375, 379, 501
numerology 540

Obradović, M. 599
occult cosmologies 83, 86–7, 92
octopus, image in conspiracist discourse 444, 452
Oliver, J.E. and Wood, T.J. 111, 236–7, 264, 266, 306
opacity 88, 91
orality 391–8, 404–6
orientalism 597–8, 638–9
Ottoman empire 610–12

Pakula, A. 461
Panarin, I. 590–1
Papua 644
paranoia 3, 67, 69–71, 76–7, 158, 392, 427–38, 625; culture of 429–38; 'insecure paranoia' 33; 'racial paranoia' 32
paranoid reading 37–8, 429
paranoid style 28–34, 429–38, 648, 650, 655
paranormal belief 158, 159, 161, 182
participant observation 81–2, 93
participatory culture 469–80, 484
pathologisation 67–70, 74, 78, 392
pattern perception 159, 171–2, 182
Paulescu, N. 601
Pavlenko, V. 592
Pelagić, V. 599
Pentecostalism 86
perestroika 587, 590–2
Pérez Jiménez, M. 663
Perry, K. 476–8

performativity 449–50
Pettibone, B. 505
philosophes 559
Piso, G.L. 533–5, 545
'pizzagate' 500–4, 512–13, 517
Plancina, M. 534, 553
Platonov, O. 588
plot, literary 415–25, 427–38, 457
Poe, E.A. 416–17, 428–9
pogroms 361
Poland 220, 222–6, 244, 267–72, 293, 309, 330, 358, 362–6, 569
polarisation 209, 233–4, 648, 665–6
polio 377–8
political engagement 243, 304–14
political trust 207, 243, 305–6, 313–14, 625
political violence 2, 235–6, 571, 573–4, 576
Popper, K. 29, 56, 95, 101, 373, 430–1, 435, 437, 438, 649, 654
popular culture 469–80; *see also* mass media
populism 2, 317, 323–5, 330–40, 498, 618; *see also* conspiracy theories and populism
positionality 283
possession 432
post-Soviet space 318, 321–3
post-truth 285, 452, 493
power 152, 194, 279, 282, 284, 287
powerlessness 183, 197–200, 223, 233
prejudice 184, 195–6, 222, 235
print culture 6, 401–12, 415
Procopius 406
'produser/prosumer' 389, 472–4, 486–7
propaganda 137–8, 141–3, 145, 318–22, 326, 487, 515, 518, 631
proportion bias 123, 128, 212
prosumer 140
*Protocols of the Elders of Zion* 192, 193, 206, 207, 347–8, 359, 361–3, 366–7, 445–6, 555, 565, 599–603, 615, 619, 642
psychoanalysis 67–78, 393, 428–9
psychology 121–32, 345–7, 350
public sphere 404, 411, 542–3, 545–6, 649, 657
Puritanism 649–50, 651
Pussy Riot 376
Putin, V. 321–2, 376, 521, 586, 588, 590, 591
Pynchon, T. 1–2, 36, 37, 38, 406, 416, 429, 430, 433, 435

qualitative approaches 122, 152–3, 279, 286, 288–9

*Rabbi's Speech, The* 361
race 265, 394, 395–7
racism 363, 365, 394, 397
radicalisation 344–54
Rakopoulos, T. 283
readings; audio-visual 472–4; negotiated 471; oppositional 471; preferred 471

realist vs symbolist approaches (Rogin) 31, 67–8
recognition, lack of 223
reflexivity 279, 286
regression 126, 128
relative deprivation 223–4
religion 212, 265, 267
Rembrandt van Rijn 442–4, 453, 454
representativeness heuristic 159–60
reptoid conspiracy theory 206, 473
republicanism 651
'Republican jeremiad' 36
resilience 352–3
Richelieu, A.-J. du Plessis 545
Rihanna 387, 471, 476–7, 479
ritual murder libels 358, 391, 449–54
Robertson, D. 282, 287, 349
Robertson, P. 280, 583–4
Robespierre, M. de 550–1
Robison, J. 23, 29, 401, 404, 406, 409, 556–9, 560–1, 562–3
Rogin, M. 31–2, 67–8, 662, 663, 669
Roisman, J. 532–3
Roosevelt, E. 394, 448
Rosenberg, A. 565, 571
Rumour of Orléans 206
rumours *see* conspiracy theory and rumour
Russia 320–3, 326, 372, 376–7, 381
Russophobia 326

Salem witchcraft crisis 649–50
Sampson, S. 285
Sànchez, J. 143
satanic conspiracy theories 206, 213
Satanism 84–6, 89, 374
*Sattelzeit* 22
scapegoating 222–3, 537, 540
science denialism 236–7
scientisation 22–3
Second World War 320, 392, 394–5, 398, 573–4, 648
secrecy 410, 443
Sedgwick, E.K. 37, 38, 429
self-esteem 157
self-reflexivity 31, 35, 37, 39, 430–8, 460–1
self-understandings 281
Sellar, S. 417
semiotics 5, 43–53, 470–2
Seneca the Younger 531, 538
sentiment analysis 137, 141
sermon 404
Sèvres treaty 612–13, 628
sexuality 89
Shaw, J. 452–3
Shiel, M.P. 419–20
Shironin, V. 590–1
Siderov, V. 603
Siegel, D. 433
signs 43–6, 49–51

679

Simon of Trent 449, 454
Simonini, J.-B. 563–5
Simonini's Letter 563–5
Slave Power 652–3
slavery 652–3
Snowden, E. 59
Snychev, I. 588
Sobo, E. 288
social big data 135–45, 153
social dominance orientation 162, 195
social intuitionist model 175
social media 135–45, 248, 484–5, 497–508, 512–22, 649, 656–67
social network analysis 135–45, 483–93, 497–508
social networks 135–45, 207, 483–93, 497–508
social power 201
social science 24–6
sorcery 82–3, 87–92
Soros, G. 323, 338, 602, 620
sovereign democracy 590–3
Soviet Union 572–8
Stalin, J. 280, 317, 364, 366, 572–3, 574–5, 578, 584, 603, 604
Starck, J.A. 23, 29, 401–2, 406, 407, 410, 411, 550, 412, 557–9, 560, 563
Starikov, N. 591–2
stereotypes 196, 219–21, 279, 288
Stone, O. 462–3, 655–6
Stone, R. 505
Suez War 628
superconspiracy theories 2, 460, 578, 656
suspicion 416–17, 429–30
Sweden 193, 267–74, 307, 335–6, 576
Switzerland 330
symbolic order 75–7
symbols 476–8

Tacitus 533–40
technology 483, 629
teleological thinking 172
television 463–7
terrorism 346–7, 350–3, 354, 423–4
theoretical modelling 124–5
Thomas of Monmouth 358
Thompson, E.P. 421, 425
Thorne, G. 73–4
threat, foreign 318, 321–3, 325–6
Tiberius 533–5, 536–7
Timor-Leste 87, 641–2
Tito, J.B. 603, 604–5
totalitarianism 4, 573, 578
transparency 87, 471
Trebizond, G. of 407–8
Trump, D. 2, 43, 309, 324, 330, 333–4, 337–40, 458, 497–8, 503–5, 508, 512, 513, 514–15, 656
trust 58–63, 207, 483, 625

Turkey 321, 324
Twitter 136–8, 140, 142–5, 153, 209, 248–9, 332, 338, 390, 484, 500, 503, 505, 506, 512–14
tyranny 544–5, 550

U.S.A. 330, 334, 337, 339; *see also* conspiracy theories and American history
uncanny, the 86, 89, 91
unconscious, the 68, 70–1, 73, 77–8
unemployment 45, 112, 197, 606
uniqueness, need for 157, 184, 212
urban legends 207, 391–8

vaccination 286, 288, 487–92
Vasilevič, G.B. 600
Venezuela 320, 660–71
victimhood 223–4, 244, 578
violence 235–6, 344–5, 347, 354
virtual communities 138–9
visual metaphors 441–54
voting behaviour 304–14

Wakefield, A. 488–91, 492–3
Ward, C. and Voas, D. 282, 295
Watergate 155
Web 2.0, 140, 484–5, 497–508; *see also* internet; social media
Weinstock, D.J. 391
Weishaupt, A. 475, 549, 550, 560, 583, 588
Welch, R. 584, 653–4, 656
well-poisoning accusations 358–9
Wells, H.G. 422–3
Whately, R. 416, 420
William, C. 487–8, 492
Williams, R. 18–19
Winrod, G.B. 445–6
witchcraft 82–92, 649–50
Wolf, N. 295–7
Wood, G. 30, 428, 556, 651
workplace 237
worldviews 155, 161–3
Wyand, J. 505

*X-Files, The* 34, 464–6

Yeltsin, B. 585–6
Young Turks 610, 611, 615–16
YouTube 207, 474–8, 491, 505–6
Yugoslavia 596, 600, 601, 602, 603–7

Zimmermann, J.G. 408–11
Zionism 616
Zionist Occupational/Occupied Government (Z.O.G.) 354, 364–5
Žižek, S. 67, 77, 78